BEST RESTAURANTS IN BRITAIN 1995

ABBEY WELL®
British Natural Mineral Water

Best Restaurants in Britain 1995

Produced by AA Publishing

Maps prepared by the Cartographic Department of The Automobile Association

Maps © The Automobile Association 1994

Restaurant assessments and rosette awards are based on reports of visits carried out anonymously by the AA's Hotel and Restaurant Inspectors.

Restaurant descriptions have been contributed by the following team of writers: Julia Hynard, Philip Bryant, Denise Laing, Daphne Jolley, Joy Nelson, Anne O'Rorke, Clare Hacking, Antonia Hebbert, Guidelines and Richard Mallinson. The feature *On Course for Cooking* was written by Julia Hynard.

Design and artwork by PPD, Basingstoke

Cover design by The Paul Hampson Partnership, Southampton

Illustrations by Sarah Kensington

Typeset by Anton Graphics Ltd

Printed and bound in Great Britain by Unwin Brothers Ltd, Old Woking, Surrey

The contents of this book are believed correct at the time of going to printing. Nevertheless, the Publisher cannot be held responsible for any errors or omissions or for changes in the details given in this guide or for the consequences of any reliance on the information provided in the same. Assessments of AA inspected establishments are based on the experience of the Hotel and Restaurant Inspectors on the occasion of their visit(s) and therefore descriptions given in this guide necessarily contain an element of subjective opinion which may not reflect or dictate a reader's own opinion on another occasion. We have tried to ensure accuracy in this guide but things do change and we would be grateful if readers would advise us of any inaccuracies they may encounter.

© The Automobile Association 1994

All rights reserved. No part of this publication may be reproduced, stored in a retrieval system, or transmitted in any form or by any means - electronic, mechanical, photocopying, recording, or otherwise - unless the written permission of the publisher has been given beforehand. This book may not be lent, resold, hired out or otherwise disposed of by way of trade in any form of binding or cover other than that in which it is published, without the prior consent of the publisher.

A CIP catalogue record for this book is available from the British Library

Published by AA Publishing, which is a trading name of Automobile Association Developments Limited whose registered office is Norfolk House, Priestley Road, Basingstoke, Hampshire RG24 9NY, Registered number 1878835.

ISBN 0 7495 0904 X

Published in the USA by Hunter Publishing Inc, 300 Raritan Center, Parkway, Edison NJ 08818

USA ISBN 1-55650-663-5

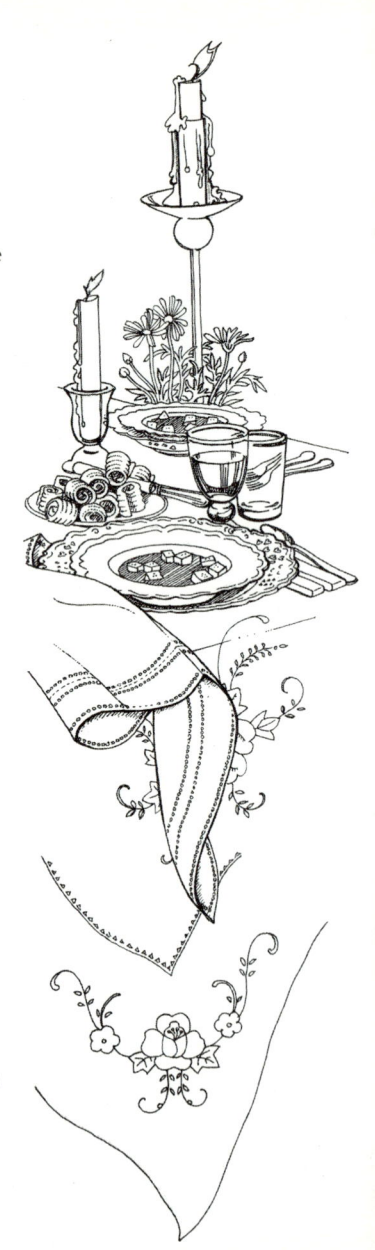

Best Restaurants in Britain 1995

CONTENTS

Phoneday 4

How to Use this Guide 5

The Top Ten Per Cent 7

On Course for Cooking 10
Chefs at AA-rosetted restaurants talk about their popular master-classes to Julia Hynard

Maps of Central and Greater London 14

Abbey Well Natural Mineral Water 17
Water on the Brain – Tony Robson, the man behind the brand
Still Waters – Terence Laybourne shares some trade secrets
A Splash of Colour – Nicholas Usherwood talks to artist Peter Blake

Restaurants
London 25

England 140

Channel Islands 473

Isle of Man 481

Northern Ireland 482

Scotland 484

Wales 546

Index of Restaurants 573

Maps 582

Readers' Recommendations 599

IMPORTANT
National Phone Codes Change - 16 April 1995

Increasing use of telecommunications services has meant an increase in the demand for numbers. In the current telephone numbering system only a few codes remain unused. To satisfy demand and create a more flexible structure for the future a new code system is being introduced.

LOCAL CODES

All local codes (usually 2 or 3 figures) will be changed to the national code number. This has already happened in many parts of the country.

When you use the national code for a local call, you will still only be charged the local rate.

REMEMBER If your call is to another number with the same code, there is no need to dial the code – just the number.

AREA CODES

From 16 April 1995 all area codes starting with 0 (with five exceptions – see below) will be changed to start with 01, for example:

York	0904	will be	01904
Basingstoke	0256	will be	01256
London	071	will be	0171

BRISTOL, LEEDS, LEICESTER, NOTTINGHAM AND SHEFFIELD

These five cities will have a completely new national code and one extra digit will be added to the individual subscribers number, for example:

Leeds	0532	will be	0113	2 + *old subscriber number*
Sheffield	0742	will be	0114	2 + *old subscriber number*
Nottingham	0602	will be	0115	9 + *old subscriber number*
Leicester	0533	will be	0116	2 + *old subscriber number*
Bristol	0272	will be	0117	9 + *old subscriber number*

The new '01' codes will be available on the BT and Mercury systems from August 1994 but callers will be able to go on using the existing '0' codes as well until 16 April 1995. After this date, all the old '0' codes will be changed to '01'

INTERNATIONAL CODES

On 16 April 1995 the code to dial abroad from the UK will also change from 010 to 00. This is part of a move to provide a single code for all European countries to access the international network.

Changes to phone codes will not affect:
- Individual subscribers numbers or local calls except in Bristol, Leeds, Leicester, Nottingham and Sheffield (see above)
- FreeFone or reduced rate services - eg 0800 or 0345 numbers
- Information and entertainment lines - eg 0891 or 0898 numbers
- Mobile phone numbers

For further information call Freefone 0800 01 01 01

HOW TO USE THIS GUIDE

How restaurants have been selected
Every restaurant in this guide, and a great many more, has had a meal visit from at least one anonymous inspector. Many, especially at the higher award levels, have been visited more than once by different inspectors at different times. Every item of the meal has been assessed – from the quality of the bread and butter and wine list to the strength and freshness of the coffee – not forgetting the service, the surroundings and the overall atmosphere. AA visits are anonymous; no favours are accepted; no charge is made for entries in this guide.

All assessment is subjective
Although our inspectors are highly-trained and very experienced professional men and women, it must be stressed that the opinions expressed are only opinions, based on the experience of one or more particular occasions. Assessments are therefore to some extent necessarily subjective. AA inspectors are experienced enough to make a balanced judgement, but they are not omniscient. We do ask our readers to bear this in mind.

Omissions
If a restaurant is not featured in this edition it does not necessarily mean that the AA has decided against a rosette award. It may be that there was no time to make a visit before the editorial deadline, or that our information network had failed us, and in that case we should be extremely grateful to our readers for their views.

Rosette Awards
Every restaurant included has been awarded one or more rosettes for the quality of the food, up to a maximum of five. The rosette symbol or symbols are printed immediately after the restaurant name. What they indicate is defined as follows:

❀ Enjoyable food, carefully prepared, that reflects a high level of culinary skills

❀❀ A high standard of food that demonstrates a serious, dedicated approach to cooking

❀❀❀ Very fine food prepared with considerable flair, imagination and originality

❀❀❀❀ Excellent standards of cuisine, service and wine consistently achieved

❀❀❀❀❀ Outstanding cuisine, service and wine reaching the highest international standards

Restaurants at the one, two, or three rosette level may on occasion rise to impressive heights of flair, imagination and originality in some dishes, but what sets the higher levels apart is consistency of achievement and finesse of presentation and service.

Locations
London has so many good restaurants that we feel it qualifies for a section on its own. Restaurants in London are listed alphabetically by name. (Throughout the book those with Le, La or Les as part of their name have been listed alphabetically under L). In the rest of Britain, establishments are listed alphabetically under county, then town or village location, and within that town or village alphabetically by name.

In the London section, each restaurant has a map reference number to help locate its approximate position on the Central or Greater London maps on pages 14-16. In the remainder of the guide, the map references refer to the 16 pages of maps of Britain at the back of the book.

Summary line
Every restaurant description begins with a short summary of its style of cuisine and atmosphere to help readers to see at a glance if it might suit their needs.

☺ At the beginning of each entry where we are confident you can obtain a good meal for under £25 a head we have inserted a smiley face.

Information column
Most of the statistical information about each restaurant is supplied in the narrow column. For the one-rosette entries, a slightly different format has been used and some information is located under their brief description. Although we try to keep our database as up-to-date and full as possible, occasionally restaurants do not supply us with new information and up-to-date costs or are awarded a rosette just before going to press. Where information is omitted this is because we have been unable to confirm our data.

Telephone numbers
During the currency of this guide all telephone numbers in Britain are due to change. We have given the new numbers in our listing but the details on page 4 will provide extra information.

Cost
Where applicable, we have calculated the average cost of an *à la carte (alc)* meal, for one person, of three courses including coffee and service but not wine. Fixed-price lunch and/or dinner menus come next. If these meals do not permit any choice at each course we have indicated this. This is followed by the cost of the house wine or one of the cheaper wines on the list. Prices quoted are a guide only, and are subject to change without notice.

♀ For restaurants where a good choice of wines can be purchased by the glass we have inserted a wine glass symbol.

Credit cards
For brevity, credit cards are indicated by number

1 - Access/Eurocard/ Mastercard

2 - American Express

3 - Barclaycard/Visa

4 - Diners Club

5 - Any other, including Switch

If no credit card details are given, please check with the restaurant whether or not they take credit cards before booking.

Times
Where possible we have given the *latest time* at which a meal may be ordered. Not all restaurants are open for both lunch and dinner all week. Remember that opening times are liable to change without notice.

Chefs and Proprietors
These names are as accurate and as up-to-date as we could make them at the time of going to press, but changes in personnel may occur, and may affect both the style and the quality of the restaurant.

Seats and Additional Information
Information about smoking regulations and special needs have been carefully checked, but if these are important to you, please telephone for confirmation before booking.

✪ Where a vegetarian choice is always offered on a menu we have used the standard ✪ symbol. Almost all the restaurants featured in the guide will prepare a vegetarian dish if given prior notice.

THE TOP TEN PER CENT

Five Rosettes
✿✿✿✿✿

England
LONDON
La Tante Claire
Le Gavroche
Nico at Ninety
The Restaurant

BERKSHIRE
Bray - Waterside Inn
Shinfield - L'Ortolan

OXFORDSHIRE
Great Milton - Le Manoir Aux Quat' Saisons

Four Rosettes
✿✿✿✿

England

LONDON
Aubergine
Bibendum
Four Seasons
Les Saveurs
L'Escargot
Pied à Terre

LANCASHIRE
Longridge - Heathcotes

LEICESTERSHIRE
Oakham - Hambleton Hall

WEST SUSSEX
Storrington – Manleys

SOMERSET
Taunton – Castle

Scotland

HIGHLAND
Ullapool - Altnaharrie Inn

Three Rosettes
✿✿✿

England

LONDON
Alastair Little
Auberge de Provence
Bentley's
Brown's
The Canteen
Capital
Chinon
Clarke's
Connaught
Daphne's
The Dorchester, Grill Room
Downstairs at 190 Queensgate
Fulham Road
The Greenhouse
Harvey's
Hilaire
Hotel Inter-Continental
The Ivy
The Lanesborough
Le Caprice
Leith's
Le Meridien Piccadilly
Mirabelle
Neal Street
Nico Central
Quaglino's
Regent
Ritz
River Café
The Savoy
Savoy Grill
Simply Nico
The Square
Stephen Bull
Turners

AVON
Bath – The Royal Crescent
Bristol – Harveys
Bristol – Restaurant Lettonie
Hunstrete – Hunstrete House

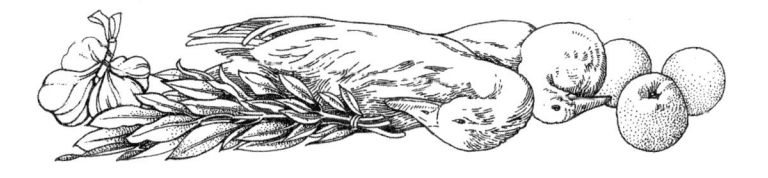

BEDFORDSHIRE
Flitwick – Flitwick Manor

BERKSHIRE
Maidenhead – Fredrick's
Yattenden – Royal Oak

BUCKINGHAMSHIRE
Taplow – Cliveden

CAMBRIDGESHIRE
Cambridge – Midsummer House

CHESHIRE
Chester – The Chester Grosvenor
Sandiway – Nunsmere Hall

CORNWALL & ISLES OF SCILLY
Liskeard – Well House
Padstow – The Seafood Restaurant

CUMBRIA
Cartmel – Uplands
Grasmere – Michael's Nook
Howtown – Sharrow Bay

DERBYSHIRE
Baslow – Fischer's
Ridgeway – The Old Vicarage

DEVON
Dartmouth – Carved Angel
Gulworthy – The Horn of Plenty
Plymouth – Chez Nous
Torquay – The Table
South Molton – Whitechapel Manor

DORSET
Evershott – Summer Lodge
Gillingham – Stock Hill

EAST SUSSEX
Hastings & St Leonards – Röser's
Uckfield – Horsted Place

GLOUCESTERSHIRE
Buckland – Buckland Manor
Cheltenham – Greenway
Cheltenham – Le Champignon Sauvage
Lower Slaughter – Lower Slaughter Manor
Stow-on-the-Wold – Wyck Hill House
Stroud – Oakes
Upper Slaughter – Lords of the Manor

GREATER MANCHESTER
Bury – Normandie

HAMPSHIRE
Brockenhurst – Le Poussin
Emsworth – 36 On The Quay
Old Burghclere – The Dew Pond
Lymington – Gordleton Mill
New Milton – Chewton Glen
Romsey – Old Manor House

HEREFORD & WORCESTER
Brimfield – Poppies

HERTFORDSHIRE
Ware – Hanbury Manor

Presentation Plates

Albert Hampson, Manager of AA Hotel Services, is obviously delighted with the special presentation plates designed by Villeroy and Boch Tableware Ltd, specialist suppliers for the hotel industry.

Villeroy and Boch have, for the last four years, very generously donated these plates to all establishments achieving three, four or five rosettes.

Fewer than 150 of the 1350 hotels and restaurants awarded rosettes by the Automobile Association will receive one of these sought after presentation plates.

Best Restaurants in Britain 1995

HUMBERSIDE
Winteringham – Winteringham Fields

KENT
Ashford – Eastwell Manor
Faversham – Read's
Royal Tunbridge Wells –
Thackeray's House

NORFOLK
Coltishall – Norfolk Place
Norwich – Adlard's

NORTH YORKSHIRE
Harrogate – Millers, The Bistro

OXFORDSHIRE
Minster Lovell – Lovells at Windrush Farm
Moulsford – Beetle & Wedge
Stonor – Stonor Arms

SHROPSHIRE
Worfield – Old Vicarage

SOMERSET
Ston Easton – Ston Easton Park
Williton – White House

STAFFORDSHIRE
Waterhouses – Old Beams Restaurant

SUFFOLK
Earl Stonham – Mr Underhills
Fressingfield – Fox & Goose
Hintlesham – Hintlesham Hall

SURREY
Bagshot – Pennyhill Park
Haslemere – Morels
Ripley – Michels

TYNE & WEAR
Boldon – Forsters
Newcastle-upon-Tyne – 21 Queen Street

WARWICKSHIRE
Stratford-upon-Avon – Billesley Manor
Royal Leamington Spa – Mallory Court

WEST MIDLANDS
Birmingham – Swallow
Hockley Heath – Nuthurst Grange

WEST SUSSEX
Climping – Bailiffscourt
East Grinstead – Graveyte Manor

WEST YORKSHIRE
Bradford – Restaurant Nineteen

WILTSHIRE
Bradford-on-Avon – Woolley Grange
Colerne – Lucknam Park

Channel Islands

JERSEY
St Saviour – Longueville Manor

Northern Ireland

Belfast – Roscoff

Scotland

CENTRAL
Aberfoyle – Braeval Mill

DUMFRIES & GALLOWAY
Auchencairn – Collin House
Portpatrick – Knockinaam Lodge

FIFE
Anstruther – Cellar
Cupar – Ostlers Close
Peat Inn – The Peat Inn

HIGHLAND
Kingussie – The Cross
Fort William – Inverlochy Castle

LOTHIAN
Edinburgh – Atrium
Edinburgh – Martins
Gullane – La Potinière
Linlithgow – Champany Inn

STRATHCLYDE
Port Appin – Airds

TAYSIDE
Dunkeld – Kinnaird

Wales

GWENT
Llanddewi-Skyrrid – Walnut Tree Inn

GWYNEDD
Llandudno – St Tudno
Pwllheli – Plas Bodegroes
Talsarnau – Maes y Neuadd

POWYS
Llyswen – Llangoed Hall

On Course for Cooking

A growing interest in good food is reflected in the number of master classes being held by top chefs. Several AA rosetted establishments now offer cookery demonstrations and courses, and Julia Hynard has been talking to some of the chefs and their pupils.

I could watch a painter paint, or a plasterer plaster come to think of it, and thrill to see a skilled exponent of the art. But cooking is different, because all of us who aspire beyond transferring a pre-packaged product from freezer to microwave must cook – or find someone else who will. Of course there are cook books, glossy and glorious, magazines with careful step-by-step instructions, and Mr Grossman and his Masterchefs, not to mention a whole pedigree of cooking clerics, galloping gourmets and kitchen-friendly TV personalities, for here we are talking art, craft and the stuff of life, and we're all intrigued. But to learn at the feet of the master – still more to dine with him/her and have a poke around his/her kitchen – is an opportunity available to a growing number of ordinary, amateur and enthusiastic cooks. And it is a privilege offered at a surprisingly modest cost at some of the best restaurants in Britain.

Cookery demonstrations vary greatly in scope. Renowned Soho restaurateur and media chef Alastair Little has put together a fabulous week-long Italian cookery course at La Cacciata, an estate overlooking the ancient city of Orvieto in unspoilt Umbria. Essentially, the guests watch their meals being prepared under the guidance of Mr Little himself, with plenty of time off for sightseeing and relaxation. At the other end of the scale, chef proprietor Richard Hughes, at Number Twenty Four in Wymondham, runs a monthly 90-minute session covering buying pointers, costings, preparation and cooking, followed by a meal with house wine and coffee for a very reasonable £15 – the evening regularly attracts a full house of 30 customers.

Getting a taste for it

There is also quite some variation in approach. In the context of a five-night residential cookery course at Le Manoir aux Quat'Saisons, Raymond Blanc's establishment at Great Milton, Clive Fretwell emphasises that he is not teaching recipes. He puts together a collection of dishes to be worked through, but each one is designed to illustrate a specific technique. This is a 'hands on' approach, where each participant makes every dish. Taste is the crucial issue – techniques can be applied to any number of ingredients, but educating the palate to discriminate between flavours and develop critical judgement – perhaps the hardest thing to teach – is given priority. Chef Fretwell might spend half an hour building a sauce with his group, making subtle alterations by lifting first one flavour then another. He hopes that by the end of the week his pupils may be criticising his cooking, and enjoying a heightened appreciation of good food.

Taste, again, is all at the Beetle & Wedge, Moulsford-on-Thames, where chef proprietor Richard Smith also starts from first principles. He believes that the single thing the home cook can do to best improve his/her food is to season correctly, and he teaches this through tasting a sauce before and after the addition of a simple sprinkling of salt. In the space of a day's tuition (£50) with his groups – preferably friends with a similar level of ability – he will discuss the areas they want to explore. He sees stocks and sauces as fundamental to most dishes, and that is where he likes to begin. He has found the most useful approach is to get people to analyse the end result and ask themselves 'what do I want to achieve? how do I do that? and do I have the necessary skills?' This simple device of working backwards to attain a desired goal has transformed peoples' cooking, being applied to anything from mashed potato to hollandaise sauce.

Horses for courses
The opportunity to learn from a professional is available all over Britain in a variety of formats. Many courses follow a theme and it is among these that one finds the most tempting titles, such as 'Heavenly Delights' from the engaging Andrew Wood of Lake Vyrnwy Hotel, Llanwddyn, a one-day course on the delights of chocolate and patisserie, with lunch, wine, afternoon tea and a chance to sample the goodies (£65). Norma and Keith Allan Makepeace, the mother and son team at Soar Mill Cove Hotel, Salcombe, list 'Posh Puds', 'Sauces for Courses', and the particularly illuminating 'Dinner Party Flare' (on do-it-yourself flambés), for which, incidentally, no charge is made to hotel guests.

The Balmoral Hotel, Harrogate, holds a one-day event on Christmas entertaining, demonstrating a meal and some ideas for Christmas decorations, along with a tasting of celebration wines and drinks, for £45, including lunch and refreshments. Or for a more dramatic break, Seymour House Hotel & Restaurant, Chipping Campden, combines a visit to the Royal Shakespeare Theatre one night with a cookery demonstration and gourmet dinner on the following evening (around £138 with accommodation).

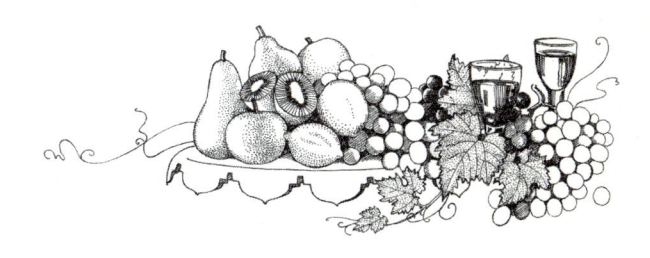

Getting right out of their restaurants, Enam Ali of Le Raj, Epsom (a recent Indian Chef of the Year), holds an evening class at a local college, while Hugh Rankin of Rankin's, Sissinghurst, gives lessons in people's own homes. He charges £50 per hour and suggests that groups of friends get together to spread the cost. They choose the subject and he throws in a bottle of wine and brings his wife to do the washing up for groups of six or more.

Some establishments favour the serial approach; Nick Nairn of Braeval Mill, Aberfoyle, for example, runs six sessions (one per month) beginning with stocks and sauces, covering all the component parts of a meal, finishing with puddings (£45 per day including lunch, or £250 the lot). Similarly, Janet Schuckardt at the Well View Hotel, Moffatt offers four progressive classes from starters to desserts at £14 per class (including a light lunch) or £52 for the four. Other chefs hold more occasional events, such as Colin White at Woolley Grange, Bradford-on-Avon, who will demonstrate a three-course menu and sit down with his guests to eat it (£28).

Home economics
In their demonstrations at Hanbury Manor, Ware, (including the recent Radio Times Master Class) chefs Albert Roux and Rory Kennedy concentrate on recipes that might be replicated at home with effective results using ingredients available in the high street. Monsieur Roux feels strongly that host cooks must be able to sit down and enjoy the meal with their guests. Lady Macdonald at Kinloch Lodge, Isle Ornsay, Isle of Skye, also takes a pragmatic approach. She combines short spring and winter breaks with cookery and gardening

demonstrations, or Christmas cookery and decorations (around £290 for three nights), and she is happy to advise on preparations and dishes to freeze ahead for the busy festive season, acknowledging that cooking for a family is a different matter from cooking professionally for a hotel or restaurant.

Sharing the secrets

One hardly needs to ask the chefs why they run the courses – their enthusiasm, and that of the students, is palpable. There are practical considerations of course: demonstrations can fill hotel bedrooms in off season months and restaurants on quiet days of the week. They also help to build a loyal clientele – many participants eat at the establishment anyway, and some courses are only advertised to customers, on menus or newsletters to regulars. But when talking to the chefs, it is clear that they very much enjoy the performance. Some actually have a teaching background, but their delight in sharing their skills, their recipes and in some cases their kitchens, is nothing short of generous. Even signature dishes, such as Andrew Woods' boozy lime and green Chartreuse jelly, infused with herbs of Provence, are up for grabs; these chefs have no secrets, no mystique, no insecurities. Nick Nairn has an interesting view on this – he feels that the professionals have much to contribute in raising the standards of cooking in the country generally and to enhance the public's appreciation of food, which in the long run can only benefit the restaurateur. Rory Kennedy welcomes the opportunity to 'meet the critics', not usually possible in a large hotel situation. As Richard Smith commented, one gets compliments and one gets criticisms, but rarely the chance to explain why one does things in a certain way.

Courting disaster

Of course things don't always go to plan – under demonstration conditions preparing several dishes at once while engaging an audience with recipes, anecdotes and repartée, means something will inevitably burn, split or separate. (Here I plead guilty to causing damage to at least one saucepanful during the course of my interviews!) There is, however, a divergence of opinion on disasters; some chefs feel that if they can't get it right then how can their pupils be expected to, while others, no doubt expediently, feel that their fallibility gives their pupils more confidence (anyone can make a mistake). One chef felt that at least one 'mistake' should be built in to each lesson to give one the chance to demonstrate remedial methods! In practice, most of the disasters are caused by the students who have a tendency to eat the exhibits and bin vital ingredients!

A passion for food

Who goes to cookery demonstrations? All the establishments I spoke to claim to attract a complete cross section of participants, though women and the over forties predominate, especially women who entertain a lot for business or pleasure purposes. Clearly price is a barrier to many, but there are those who will save hard to join a particular course. Other chefs, restaurateurs and cooking professionals crop up; retired men with a fairly academic interest, widowers who may well be beginners, and work hard/play hard professionals doing well in their lives for whom cooking is a more attractive leisure pursuit than, say, golf.

The unifying element is enthusiasm for food, described in turn as 'a great love of my life' and 'a great passion'. The former from Mrs Jess Vivers, a home economics teacher, who attended the Well View Hotel course and was greatly impressed by Janet Schuckardt, describing her as an artist, both creative and dextrous, with probably the cleanest kitchen in Moffat. The latter from Jenny Thornton, a woman with 130 cookbooks who claims never to eat 'an ordinary meal'. Her demonstration at Lake

Vyrnwy was a Christmas present from her husband. She had a wonderful time and couldn't believe the scope and variety of dishes Andrew Wood packed into the time. Dentist Alistair Kesson got a cookery course for Christmas too, at Braeval Mill. He was amazed at how exciting it was to see Nick Nairn in action doing a hundred things at once and pacing it brilliantly. Alistair is a keen cook, and according to Nick a star pupil, but he's experienced enough of the heat and pressure of the kitchen to know that he wouldn't take it up professionally.

A chef of one's own
Every participant I spoke to was keen to return for further demonstrations, so what is it they get out of the experience? All of them felt enthused and inspired, and several that their cooking had been kick-started out of a rut. Some of the courses have a club-like atmosphere, with regulars who grow into cohesive social groups. One couple, Mr and Mrs Dale have between them attended every one of Richard Hughes' demonstrations, and Mr Dale, who is semi-retired, has tried out most of the dishes at home. This loyalty was fittingly rewarded last year when they won 'a chef for Christmas' in the restaurant's Christmas raffle. Young chef Nigel Crane, apparently having no other plans for the day, volunteered his services. According to Mrs Dale, he arrived at their home with chilled champagne, cooked a marvellous meal, washed up and left the place immaculate – a real treasure!

Safe for singles
Londoner Kathy Owen had recently returned from a week at La Cacciata, Alastair Little's place in Umbria, when I spoke to her. She's a real foodie, but her husband – who 'can't boil an egg' – had enjoyed an equally good and relaxing holiday, and although he was not involved with the cookery he certainly enjoyed the marvellous food that resulted. Sarah Robson, manager of La Cacciata, also commented that this is a good holiday for the single person, where guests can socialise as much or as little as they wish. This is a point echoed by Lady Macdonald residents on her cookery courses may comprise groups of friends, couples and single people, but she has never yet seen anyone dine alone.

Most importantly, all the participants had a wonderful time, and the entertainment value of the courses noted was highly rated. The meals, an integral part of most demonstrations, are very sociable affairs, often shared with the chef, giving a further opportunity for an informal exchange of information. At the end of a course they leave laden with notes and recipes and in some cases clutching goody bags. These might include meringues, hand-made chocolates, an apron, or a brace of pheasants and a cookbook.

A gift of an idea
So for any enthusiastic amateur who longs to break out of the kitchen routine, a day, evening or even a holiday with your culinary hero is a real possibility. A cookery course could also make a gift with a difference for the chef de cuisine in your life – not without dividends for the donor – and some establishments actually produce gift vouchers. Le Manoir's course may be a bit beyond your budget at £1,095, though it is one of the cheapest ways of staying at this exclusive hotel and experiencing five days of exquisite food – particularly as partners of participants stay free of charge (except for meals and drinks). The week at La Cacciata isn't cheap either at £750 for seven nights accommodation with full board (not including flights), but as one satisfied customer pointed out, it compares favourably with hotel prices without the cookery tuition, and the quality of the food is guaranteed.

Programmes and prices for 1995 available direct from the establishments listed (telephone numbers in each Guide entry), except for La Cacciata 0171 243 8042

Central London

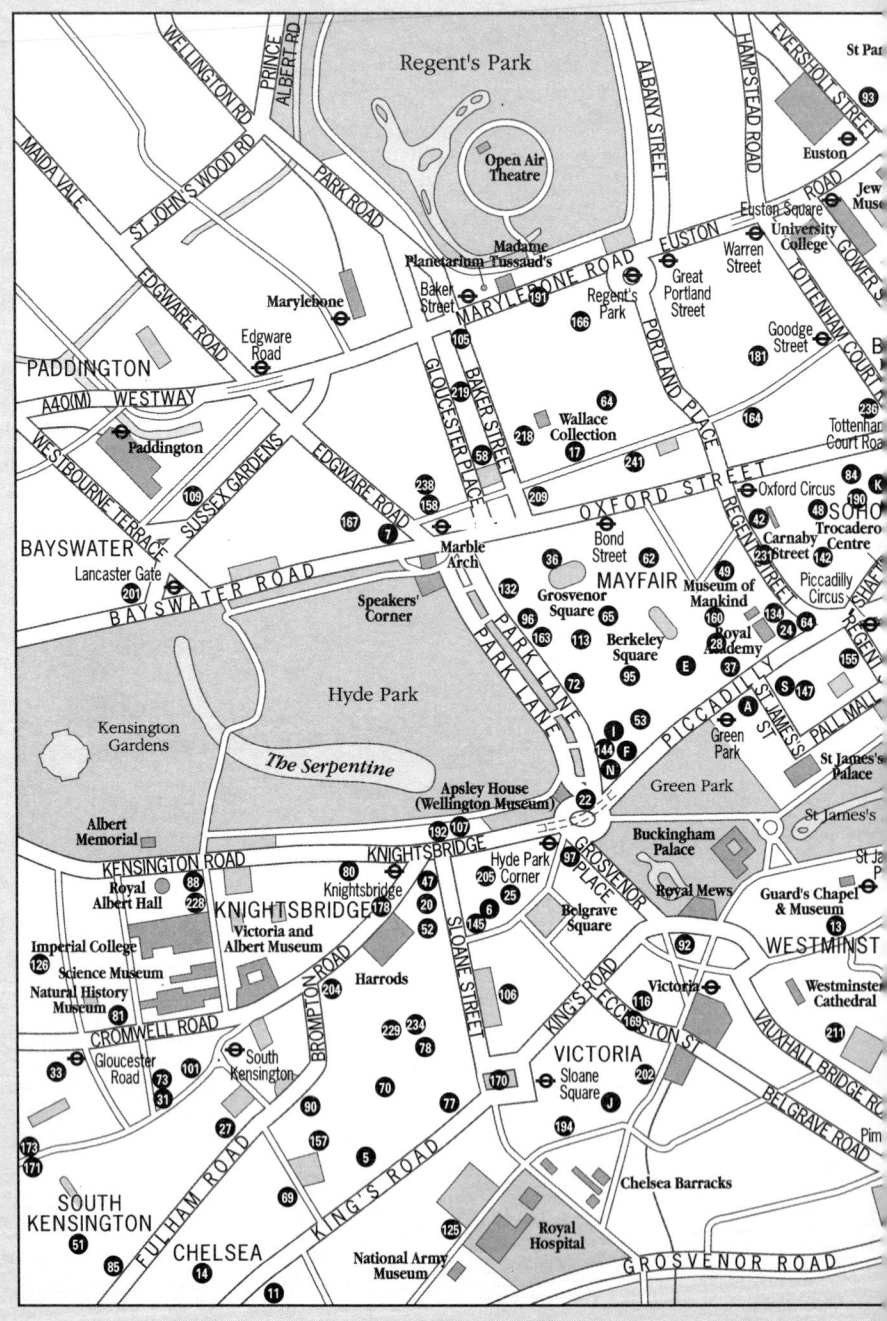

KEY TO RESTAURANT LOCATIONS

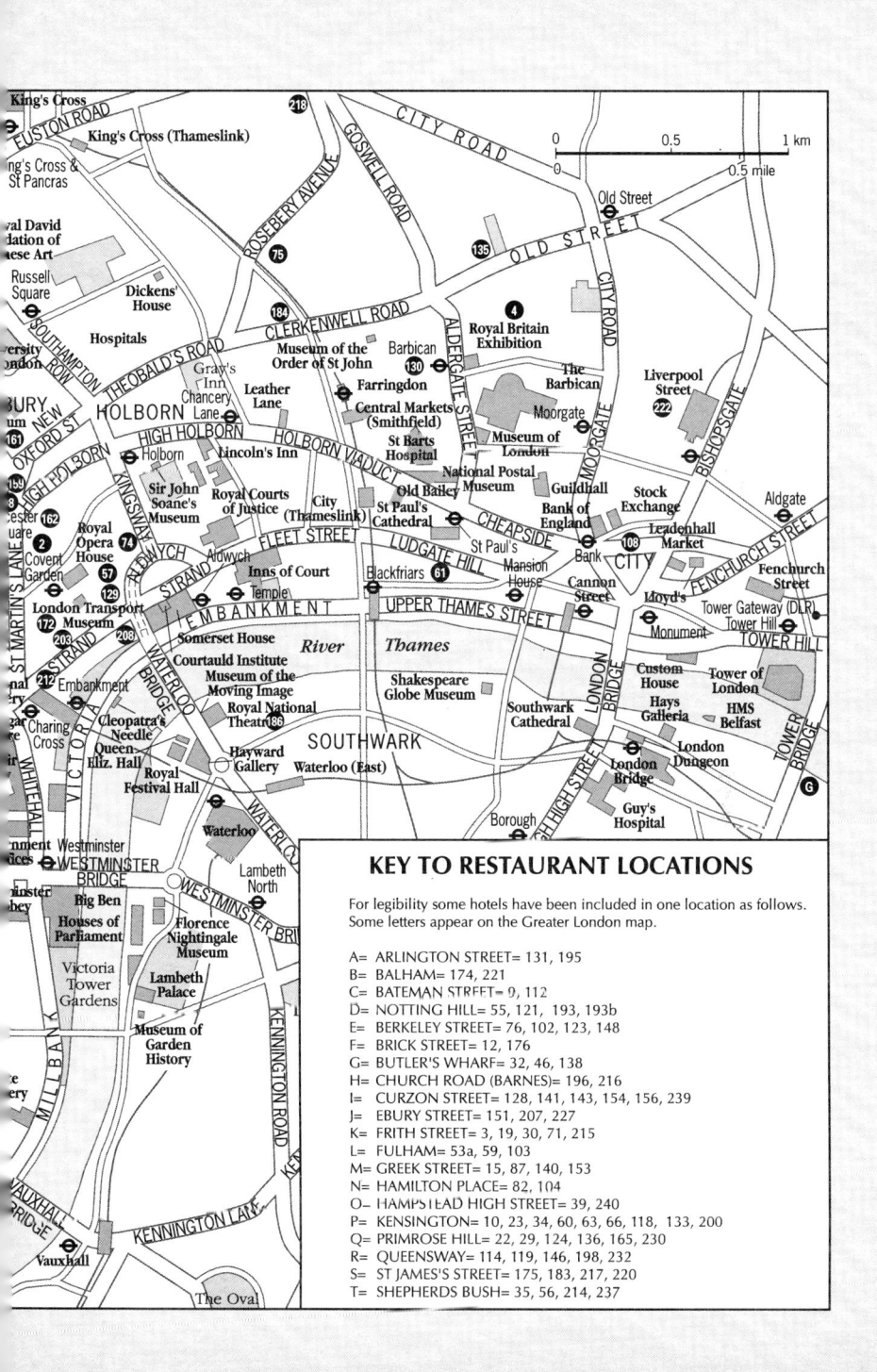

For legibility some hotels have been included in one location as follows. Some letters appear on the Greater London map.

A= ARLINGTON STREET= 131, 195
B= BALHAM= 174, 221
C= BATEMAN STREET= 9, 112
D= NOTTING HILL= 55, 121, 193, 193b
E= BERKELEY STREET= 76, 102, 123, 148
F= BRICK STREET= 12, 176
G= BUTLER'S WHARF= 32, 46, 138
H= CHURCH ROAD (BARNES)= 196, 216
I= CURZON STREET= 128, 141, 143, 154, 156, 239
J= EBURY STREET= 151, 207, 227
K= FRITH STREET= 3, 19, 30, 71, 215
L= FULHAM= 53a, 59, 103
M= GREEK STREET= 15, 87, 140, 153
N= HAMILTON PLACE= 82, 104
O= HAMPSTEAD HIGH STREET= 39, 240
P= KENSINGTON= 10, 23, 34, 60, 63, 66, 118, 133, 200
Q= PRIMROSE HILL= 22, 29, 124, 136, 165, 230
R= QUEENSWAY= 114, 119, 146, 198, 232
S= ST JAMES'S STREET= 175, 183, 217, 220
T= SHEPHERDS BUSH= 35, 56, 214, 237

Greater London

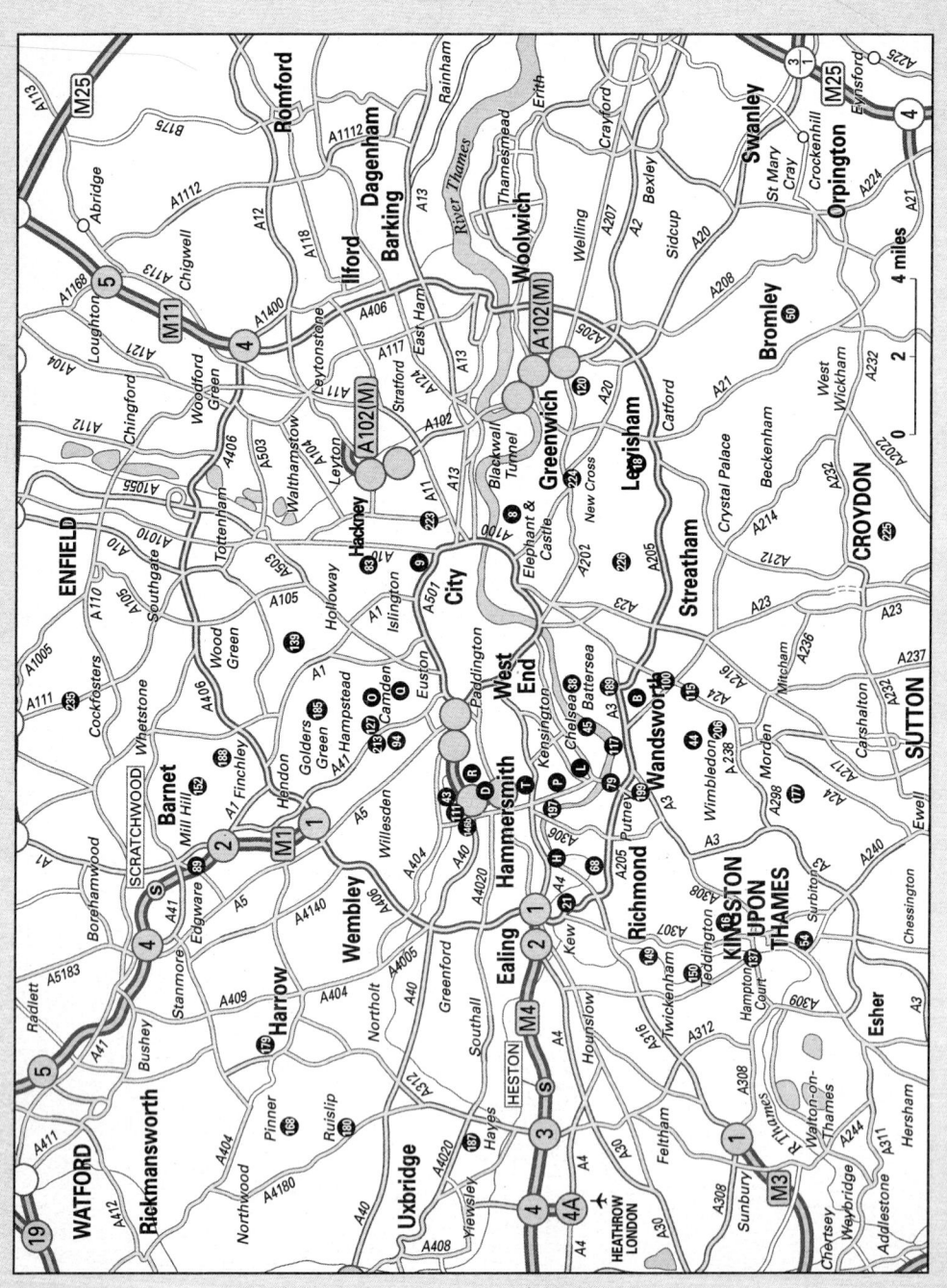

WELL
Matched

No population, no industry — therefore, no pollution

WATER ON THE BRAIN

Susan Gilchrist of The Times Business Section talks to Tony Robson, the man behind Abbey Well natural mineral water

'I'M AN ABBEY WELL BORE,' says Tony Robson, 51, its managing director. 'I try to convert everyone that I meet to the brand.' The efforts of this extrovert and dynamic Geordie have clearly not been in vain. Under his leadership Abbey Well has emerged in the past twelve years as one of Britain's leading premium natural mineral waters. It may only start life as rain falling on a Northumberland hillside but thanks to Robson's drive and vision it ends up on the tables of some of the country's best restaurants.

While Abbey Well has made a splash in the last decade, its history in fact goes back to the beginning of the century. Waters & Robson, the parent company, was founded in 1910 by Thomas Robson, Tony Robson's grandfather. He sunk his first well in Morpeth, Northumberland, using the water to make soft drinks which he sold to the local pubs and working men's clubs.

The company was passed down the generations and eventually inherited by Tony Robson in the early 1970's. By the time he took the helm he was already steeped in the business, having worked there since leaving school at the age of 18. 'I did everything from bottle-washing to driving HGV trucks,' he says. But his real *metier* was, and still is, selling. 'We didn't have any salesmen when I joined. So when I finished work I would still go out knocking on doors and selling to working men's clubs all over the north east.' There's no doubt Robson is a natural salesman. While his fast-talking and amusing patter may leave many of those around him gasping for breath, he is not an exponent of the 'hard sell'. He is simply passionate about his product.

The real turning point for Robson and the company came in 1982 when it first started to sell Abbey Well bottled mineral water. Although mineral water had been *de rigueur* in continental Europe for years, it was still largely an anathema to the British public. Yet Robson saw the potential and realised that, with more and more people holidaying abroad, it would only be a matter of time before the thirst for mineral water crossed the channel.

ABBEY WELL®
Natural Mineral Water

The chance to prove his theory came during the water workers' strike at the beginning of 1983. 'I thought - right, let's start bottling Abbey Well,' says Robson. 'We were up and running the fourth night of the strike. The opportunity was there and we just grabbed it.' Production of Abbey Well mineral water started in earnest and it has never stopped since.

The huge successes of the brand is all the more remarkable given that it has had to compete in a market dominated by the huge multi-national players such as Danone Groupe (formerly BSN) and Nestlé. Yet like David against Goliath, Abbey Well has managed to fight off its bigger rivals by playing to its own strengths. Robson decided early on that there was little point in trying to sell the brand through the grocery trade. Being a small player, it lacked clout with the supermarkets and the deep pockets needed to fund multi-million pound advertising campaigns. But the decision was also a personal one for Robson. 'I remember going to a supermarket in the north-east years ago, and they basically wanted what we had for nothing. It was hopeless. I just couldn't develop a relationship with them. I have always felt more comfortable dealing with pubs and restaurants.' But what some may see as a weakness, Robson and his team have converted into a strength. Their strict policy of not supplying the major grocery multiples has been warmly welcomed by the on-trade who enjoy doing business with a company dedicated to them. Robson believes that this was a crucial factor in helping the company break into the important London market. 'The question was how could we get Abbey Well accepted in the capital. Because we could sell to wholesalers on the basis of exclusivity and could give them a good deal, as we were not selling to supermarkets, the business very quickly took off.'

"Because we could sell to wholesalers on the basis of exclusivity and could give them a good deal, the business very quickly took off."

Although Abbey Well flourished on the back of the designer water boom of the 1980s, it has avoided getting tarnished with the yuppie image which so cruelly rebounded on some of its competitors in the austere 1990s. Robson says the company was anxious to establish a contemporary image but was careful not to get carried away on the yuppie bandwagon. Its label, which bears a portrait of David Hockney by Peter Blake, one of Britain's leading contemporary artists, is evidence of that says Robson. While it was designed to position Abbey Well in a modern urban environment, it was never going to appeal to the brasher elements of Thatcher's children.

Company turnover has rocketed to more than £10 million in the past 12 years. But Robson is not content with that. He believes the mineral water market is still in its infancy in this country with British consumers drinking only 9 litres per head a year. This compares with 120 litres in Italy, 105 litres in France and 89 litres in Germany. 'I can see us getting up to about 20 litres per head in about five years' says Robson. And he is determined that Abbey Well will be in the forefront of that growth.

STILL WATERS

Guardian food editor Matthew Fort visits 21 Queen Street, Newcastle upon Tyne, and meets Terence Laybourne, its chef proprietor

TERENCE LAYBOURNE is not the easiest man in the world to interview. It's not that he is shy or moody or that he has nothing to say, it's just he is incorrigibly modest about his own achievements.

How would you describe your food?
'I don't know. I don't have a philosophy or anything like that. I just cook the stuff.'
Do you see yourself as one of the leaders of the new wave of British chefs?
'No way. I'm just a competent cook.'
Why do you think 21 Queen Street has been such a success?
'We provide more than just a plate of food.'

So you begin to talk around the subject of food and cooking, and his deep and abiding passions keep peeping out from behind his dismissive, ironic humour. He had no thought of being a chef to start with. 'I was going to play centre forward for Newcastle United or become a guitar hero.' Then he heard about cooking from a school mate, and started cooking on a day release scheme while still at school. 'I must have been a nightmare to teach. I was always saying "Show me", "Why this?", "Why that?", "Why do you do it this way?" I always wanted to know how things worked. I still do. I read books. I get ideas from other people but I've always got to think it through for myself. Take that foie gras, for example.' I had taken it, as one course of five, for lunch, and marvelled at its profoundly velvety texture and unusually direct flavour.

'It wasn't cooked, you know. It was just marinated in salt. Now I first got the idea from a restaurant in Lyon, but it took me two years before I was happy with the result. I was trying to make a simple process too complicated. In fact, it was Paul Heathcote (of Heathcote's Restaurant, Longridge, Lancs) who came up with the answer.'

Unlike some of his peers, he is not afraid to acknowledge his debt to other chefs. In fact he thinks it absolutely essential to eat out as much as possible. There are few restaurants of note, in this country and France, that he hasn't slipped in and out of, unobtrusively.

For him, eating out is about pleasure, about having a good time. It would be wrong to get food out of perspective. He sees it as only one component in the whole experience of going to a restaurant. It's important, yes, but only one ingredient in the mix.

His cooking has evolved around local ingredients, his own background and the understanding that gives him of his customers' likes and dislikes. Although he now says that he doesn't have to please everyone, it is the customer who provides the impetus for the development of his cooking.

He runs a restaurant which manages to combine great professionalism with notable friendliness. There is one large table seating sixteen Japanese ladies. Their complicated order and multiple changes of mind and misunderstandings are handled by the staff with smooth control and good humour. Customers are still arriving for lunch at 2 o'clock. Some leave finally at 5pm. Terence Laybourne seems to know most of them, and is on cheerful terms with them all.

Relaxed manner and puckish humour notwithstanding, you get the strong impression that he is very much in charge. You cannot run a top class restaurant without a strong sense of discipline and an even stronger will. The greater the smoothness and charm of the front of house, the more delicious the food, the greater the investment of time and energy by those who run it.

He is a Geordie born and bred, although he left the city early to learn his craft in the Channel Islands, Germany, Switzerland and France. And then he came back. 'Actually, I came home for a couple of weeks holiday. That was eleven years ago. It wasn't much fun to start with.' And now?

He becomes self-deprecating again. 'I'm in it for the job satisfaction. I mean,' he adds jokingly, 'this is all I've got to show for 20 years slaving over a hot stove. You can't go into this business to get rich.'

In spite of the awards and critical praise he has been picking up by the hatful over the last few years, he regards himself as a craftsman chef, not as a creator. Yet a dish of turbot roasted with cracked white pepper in a bouillon is unexpected and startlingly effective. The pepper not only provides crunch and, well, pepperiness, but it also brings out the latent meatiness and sweetness of the fish. The bouillon is made with sweet white wine infused with lemon grass. The combination has a fragrance, balance and punch. Then there was a visually startling combination of raw salmon sliced as thin as lace, lifted by finely diced raw shallot and boulders of sea salt, and scattered with herb flowers, chopped nasturtium, marigold and rose petals. It was staggeringly beautiful dish to look at, and almost on the same scale to eat.

But all these pyrotechnics don't mean that Terence Laybourne's food is without humour. What about terrine of ham and foie gras with pease pudding? It's a dish that is very much like the man himself, a deeply satisfying combination of the romantic and the earthy. He'll probably wince at that, too.

ABBEY WELL®
Natural Mineral Water

"Customers are still arriving for lunch at 2pm. Some leave finally at 5pm. Terence Laybourne seems to know most of them."

A SPLASH OF COLOUR

Peter Blake, whose picture 'David Hockney in a Spanish Interior' appears on the label of Abbey Well natural mineral water, is widely regarded as the leader of the British pop art movement. Leading art critic Nicholas Usherwood caught up with him over lunch

FOR ALL ITS APPARENT Bohemian glamour, being an artist is an unfairly lonely and insecure way of earning your living. After hours spent with only yourself for company the need to go AWOL - regularly - becomes vital to creative sanity.

That's the real reason for the cafes and bars of Paris's Left Bank, from the Impressionists to the Existentialists, always being so full of wild and gesticulating artists - that heady combination of seminar and orgy functioning as emotional safety-valve. Victorian and Edwardian London had a similar idea with the Cafe Royal of Whistler and Augustus John and, post-war, the Soho restaurants and all-night drinking clubs haunted by Francis Bacon and his circle, most famously Wheelers and the Colony Room, serving much the same purpose.

Peter Blake, who first came to London in the mid-1950s to study at the Royal College of Art, remembers the Colony Room in particular when it was at the height of its notoriety. For him and most of his generation of artists though, food rather than drink was always of more immediate interest. His first experience of real eating, as opposed to a Lyons Cornerhouse or British Restaurant, came through visits to the Hong Kong restaurant on Shaftesbury Avenue in the company of his close friend, the painter Richard Smith. Smith had done his National Service in the Far East and knew his way around a Chinese menu, and Blake recalls with real pride the moment his work was beginning to sell well enough for him to graduate to the giddy heights of king prawns. From there Blake and his friends soon moved on to an altogether more upmarket restaurant, Mr Chow's in Knightsbridge, then run by Michael Chow, an owner who liked and collected contemporary art. A definite element of barter helped to make such places affordable (as it still does for artists today).

Peter Blake also used to take his students from the Royal College of Art to Mr Chow's for at least one tutorial a year. Informally christened the John Minton Memorial Lunch in honour of a great and eccentric tutor of Blake's whose tutorials would start in a London pub and end up the next day on Brighton beach, these meals not only loosened the students up socially but also encouraged their own taste in the pleasures of eating.

In the 70s a move to the country and a young family put a curb on Peter Blake's eating out that only really began again on his return to London in the 80s. Living on the busy Chiswick High Road in West London, everyday tastes - particularly those of his young daughter Rose - are well catered for by the local Tootsies and Pizza Express, and a delightful new restaurant, the Thai Bistro.

He has never lost his love of haute cuisine and high style however and eats out, with his wife Chrissie and friends, at least once a week at one or other of his two favourite West End restaurants - The Caprice and The Ivy. Both of them are run by Chris Corbin and Jeremy King, restaurateurs with a well-developed "feel" for contemporary art, an astonishing range of which finds its way on to the walls of their restaurants. At The Ivy, where we were eating, there was a Howard Hodgkin behind us and a Blake and a Paolozzi in front of us.

Blake now rarely eats anywhere else but these two places - 'Why, when they are the best?' he asks with undeniable logic. He does admit to occasional, six-monthly visits to Orso's in Covent Garden to which he always goes on his own and always on a Saturday when it is comparatively empty - just to remind himself of his long-gone bachelor days. This happens less now Rose is older as she too enjoys visits to The Ivy, particularly as the comfortable banquettes allow that certain freedom of lateral movement necessary to young children. Peter Blake, meanwhile, is just starting a two-year stint as Associate Artist at the National Gallery, his studio there lying en route to one of its restaurants. One wonders whether he will be tempted by these bright and well-used eateries when he feels that famous need for bustling society.

ABBEY WELL®
Natural Mineral Water

WELL SERVED

ABBEY WELL®

THE BRITISH
NATURAL MINERAL WATER
Sparkling and Still – 250ml, 330ml, 500ml, one litre

DEDICATED TO THE NEEDS
OF THE CATERING TRADE
Telephone: 01670 513113

LONDON

Each entry has a map number by which it can be located on the London maps on pages 14-16. For legibility some hotels have been included within one location and have been given a letter. The key is on the Central London map.

The Academy ❀❀

☺ *An elegant Georgian hotel with genuinely friendly staff and award-winning European cooking*

An attractive walled garden and summer terrace make a pleasant setting for a meal on clement days, while indoors the smart GHQ restaurant provides a mellow ambience all year round. A mostly Danish team offers a warm welcome and very approachable service, while the cooking of award-winning chef John O'Riordan is uncomplicated and most enjoyable. A short and selective carte and fixed-price menus offer seasonal dishes, including the restaurant's specialities of fresh fish, game and vegetarian dishes. For our inspector a recent meal was highlighted by a smooth and creamy duck parfait served with a warm home-made brioche, and this was followed by fillet of red mullet with a tasty red wine sauce and crisp, fresh vegetables. Puddings might include chocolate marquise and mango parfait, and the crème brûlée was well-made and richly flavoured, with a thick crunchy caramel topping. Other dishes on the set menu could be wild boar sausages with parsnip purée and red wine jus, or fillet of salmon with Chinese greens and beurre blanc, with perhaps a vegetarian choice such as pancakes with spinach, mushrooms and Mozzarella.

Directions: On the corner of Store Street/Gower Street, off Tottenham Court Road. Nearest Tube – Goodge Street

Map no: 1
17-21 Gower Street WC1
Tel: 0171-636 7612

Cost: Alc £19, Plat du jour £10, fixed-price lunch £14.95, fixed-price dinner £17.95. Wine £9.95 ♀ Service 12.5%
Credit cards: 1 2 3 4 5

Menus: A la carte, plat du jour, fixed-price lunch and dinner, pre-theatre, bar menu

Times: Last L 3pm, Last D 11.15pm

Chef: John O'Riordan
Proprietor: Miss Mette Doessing

Seats: 45. Air conditioned

Additional: Children welcome; children's portions. ❂ menu; Vegan/other diets on request

Ajimura ❀

☺ *In this Japanese restaurant, first opened in 1972 and run by Susmu and Harumi Okada, the cooking is authentic and skilfully prepared by chef Tora Tanizawa. Special foods are served on festive days. Nigiri and temaki sushi, deep-fried bean curd and sticky rice with pickles are recommended.*

Cost: Alc £20, fixed-price L £8/D £19.50, £35. H/wine £7.70. Service exc. **Credit cards:** 1 2 3 4. **Additional:** Children welcome; ❂ menu; Vegan/other diets on request
Directions: 100yds north of the Royal Opera House, crossing Endell Street. Nearest Tubes – Covent Garden, Holborn

Map no: 2
51-53 Shelton Street WC2
Tel: 0171-240 0178
Chef: Tora Tanizawa
Proprietor: Harumi Okada
Seats: 58. No-smoking area; no pipes or cigars. Air conditioned
Times: Last L 3pm/D 11pm. Closed Sat L, Sun, BHs

Alastair Little ●●●

Vibrant, international dishes in a simple Soho restaurant, where the atmosphere is casual and the food serious

The blue shop-fronted restaurant in the heart of Soho, bearing its proprietor's name, might easily be missed. The simply decorated dining room is at street level and there is a bar downstairs. Casually dressed staff greet customers warmly and offer a basic service. Yet this genial informality belies both the quality and price of the food. It has been observed that there is little relation between the prices charged and the service provided, but how much more would one have to pay for food of this standard *and* deluxe service? However, note has been taken of the criticism and while service remains much the same, there are now some good value set lunch menus, including 'Lunch for a Tenner'.
  It is the freshness of the produce and the honesty of its preparation that has established Alastair Little and his team over the last eight years. The food is vibrant in colour and ingredients, and the inspiration for the dishes is international, with a leaning towards Italy in view of the profusion of pasta. Our inspector began his meal, selected from the *carte*, with a dish that appears on the cover of Mr Little's recent book – papperdelle with field and wild mushrooms bound with a creamy, stock-based sauce – almost a meal in itself. His main course was a simple choice, fillets of firm Dover sole with freshly shaved Parmesan and the most delightful leaf spinach. This was accompanied by a correct and tasty Gratin Savoyarde served in an oven dish that had seen better days. Vegetarian dishes are more likely to appear as starters than main courses, but special menus can be arranged. Puddings feature favourites and variations on favourites, and the crème brûlée was as good as they come.
  The selection of about 50 wines is interesting and carefully chosen. The prices are also well-balanced.

Directions: Halfway up Frith Street from Shaftesbury Ave on the left. Nearest Tubes – Tottenham Court Rd and Leicester Square

Map no: K3

49 Frith Street W1
Tel: 0171-734 5183

Cost: *A/c* £35, fixed-price lunch £25. Wine £12 ♀ Service exc
Credit cards: 1 2 3

Menus: *A la carte*, fixed-price lunch, bar lunch

Times: Midday–Last L 3pm, 6pm- Last D 11.30pm. Closed Sat L, Sun, Xmas & BHs

Chef: Alastair Little
Proprietors: Alastair Little, Mercedes Andre Vega, Kirsten Pederson

Seats: 40. Air conditioned
Additional: Children welcome, children's portions; Vegetarian dishes; other diets on request

Alba ●●

Nothing too startling, just honest Northern Italian cooking and a genuine desire to please

The street got its name from the white cross that once stood outside a medieval priory, but both are long gone. Even the former bottom half of the street was obliterated in the Blitz and lies buried under The Barbican. One can reflect on this in a setting that owes much to Piedmont. Fresh flowers and fruitbowls near the entrance indicate a caring streak, happily extending to the kitchen where the chef is content to focus on seasonal ingredients, without succumbing to any new wave flourishes. Familiar ingredients pepper the menu – artichoke hearts, sage, Parma ham, tongue (poached) and aubergine among the antipasti, for instance. Pasta is represented by a few soundly-prepared dishes, such as spinach gnocchi with tomato

Map no: 4

107 Whitecross Street EC1
Tel: 0171-588 1798

Cost: *A/c* £28. Service charge 12.5%
Credit cards: 1 2 3 4

Menus: *A la carte*

Times: L from 12.15, 6pm-Last D 11pm (Mon-Fri)

Chef: Armando Liboi
Proprietor: Rudi Venerandi
Additional: Children welcome

and basil, enjoyable for their simplicity. Main courses (fish and meat) usually come with a sauce, such as the generous slice of veal breast, wrapped around a spinach and pancetta stuffing served with some of the stewing juices, sampled by our inspector. Quite a few of the desserts feature chocolate. The wine list is an all-Italian affair. Always busy at lunch, dinner might be quieter.

Directions: North of Barbican centre

Albero and Grana ❀❀

A Spanish restaurant and tapas bar with Mediterranean-influenced dishes in a distinctive setting

A strikingly decorated restaurant in the corner of an exclusive apartment block behind the Michelin building, Albero and Grana combines a busy tapas bar, open until 1am, and a raised area serving more serious Spanish and Mediterranean-style food. Chef Angel Garcia, formerly of the acclaimed Madrid restaurant 'Luculo', offers a *carte* written in Spanish with English translations. The tapas selection includes olives, Spanish omelette, mixed griddled vegetables, a selection of cured sausages and ham, baby squids in their ink, meatballs in tomato sauce, garlic chicken, and a choice of fish dishes. The menu lists half a dozen starters, such as cold escabeche of duck liver, or lasagna of black pudding with green pepper sauce, and a wider choice of fish or meat main courses (though vegetarians can be catered for). Examples might be scallops with ratatouille, or marinated pork fillet with roasted stuffed apples. To finish, the short dessert selection includes filled pastries and ice creams. The revised wine list presents a representative selection of Spanish wines, plus more available by the glass.

Directions: At crossroads of Fulham Road/Sloane Avenue/Brompton Road/Pelham Street, turn down Sloane Avenue

Map no: 5

Chelsea Cloisters
89 Sloane Avenue SE3
Tel: 0171-225 1048

Cost: *Alc* £27.50. H/wine £10

Menu: *A la carte*

Al Bustan ❀

A colourful, modern Middle Eastern restaurant serving typical Lebanese dishes in a warm and friendly atmosphere. Recommended choices include 'lahem mashwi' - tender chargrilled cubes of lamb, onions and tomatoes, and 'farrouji mousakhan' - a house chicken speciality.

Directions: Off Sloane Street, behind Carlton Tower Hotel. Nearest Tubes – Knightsbridge, Hyde Park Corner

Map no: 6
Motcomb Street, Belgravia SW1
Tel: 0171-235 8277
Chef: Tna'am Atalla
Proprietor: Riyad Atalla

Cost: *Alc* £24. H/wine £11. Service exc. Cover charge
Credit cards: 1 2 3 4 5

Al San Vincenzo ❀❀

A homely Italian restaurant offering authentic cooking and pleasant service from an involved husband and wife team

A warm and friendly atmosphere is always assured at this small, bright and homely Italian restaurant, where chef/patron

Map no: 7

30 Connaught Street W2
Tel: 0171-262 9623

Cost: *Alc* £26. H/wine £10. Service exc

Vincenzo Borgonzolo's cooking remains as reliable as ever. Good fresh ingredients are handled with great care to produce well-flavoured dishes, and the short carte offers an interesting choice: starters might be 'cozze al limone', mussels cooked in their juices with lemon, white wine and parsley, or 'carpaccio di tonno', thin slices of raw tuna with an olive oil, lemon and chilli dressing, while main dishes might be 'caniglio al fermo con patate', oven-baked rabbit with potatoes and herbs, and 'la lingua con fagioli', hot tongue with cannellini beans. Our inspector sampled a tasty and filling 'fusilli san Vincenza', pasta cooked in cream of tomato sauce with Mozzarella, Italian sausage and Parmesan, followed by 'ceslate di vitello con prosciutto', veal chop with parma ham and morels baked in a paper bag. Recommended desserts include paneltone bread and butter pudding, and hot compote of dried fruits with spices, and there's a short selection of well-priced Italian wines with a few half bottles. Service is friendly and attentive.

Directions: From Marble Arch end of Edgeware Rd take the second left into Connaught St. Nearest Tube – five minutes Marble Arch or Paddington

Credit cards: 1 3

Menu: A la carte

Times: Last L 2.15pm, Last D 10.15pm. Closed Sun, Sat Lunch, 2 weeks at Xmas

Chef: Vincenzo Borgonzolo
Proprietors: Vincenzo and Elaine Borgonzolo

Seats: 22. No cigars or pipes
Additional: Children permitted

Angel ❀

☺ *A delightful riverside pub restaurant overlooking Tower Bridge. The keen young chef combines good food with style, producing freshly prepared dishes with skill and dedication. Carte menus of modern British cuisine might include brandied hare terrine, rack of English lamb and caramel apple tart.*

Credit cards: 1 2 3 4 5. **Additional:** Children permitted; ◐ dishes
Directions: From the south side of Tower Bridge follow Jamaica Road towards Rotherhithe Tunnel. Cathay Street is the last turning before the tunnel, the Angel is straight ahead

Map no: 8
101 Bermondsey Wall East SE16
Tel: 0171-237 3608
Chef: Graham Barlow
Proprietors: Forte. Manageress: Joanne Grimwood
Seats: 50
Times: Last L 1.45pm/D 9.45pm. Closed Sun eve and BHs
Cost: Alc £20, fixed-price D £15.50. Wine £8.25. Service exc

Anna's Place ❀❀

A surprising taste and feel of Sweden in this warmly welcoming small restaurant

The blue of the Swedish flag is repeated in the decor of this pleasantly unpretentious small restaurant just off Newington Green. The restaurant has a wooden floor, Swedish pictures and vinyl-clothed small tables while in summer a vine-covered courtyard provides an inviting annexe. Homely service is friendly and informal . The seasonally changing menu changes little in format and offers the same items at lunch and dinner (when it is essential to book). Regular items include Sill Tallrik – two types of marinated herrings, gravad lax, Biff Strindberg – diced fillet of beef, marinated in Swedish mustard and served with a cucumber salad and waffles with blueberry compote and cream. A most enjoyable summer lunch featured good spicy Gazpacho with tasty fennel-flavoured warm rolls. A generous portion of moist salmon trout with an avocado and coriander mayonnaise, spinach and new potatoes (all very summery) and

Map no: 9

90 Mildmay Park N1
Tel: 0171-249 9379

Cost: Alc £22.50. H/wine £7. Service exc
Credit cards: None taken

Menu: A la carte

Times: 12.15-Last L 2.15pm, 7.15pm-Last D 10.45pm. Closed Sun, Mon, 2 weeks Xmas, 2 weeks Easter, Aug

Chefs: Beth Diadone, Richard Wells
Proprietor: Anna Hegarty

to finish a dense but moist chocolate cake with fresh fruit and whipped cream. The short wine list is supplemented by ice cold schnapps and Swedish beer.

Directions: Turn left off Balls Pond Road into Mildmay Park, Annas is on the corner of Newington Green. Bus – 73, 171, 141 to Newington Green

Seats: 45. Air conditioned
Additional: Children welcome, children's portions; ✪ dishes; Vegan ordered in advance

Arcadia ✿✿

☺ *An updated and improved reincarnation of a popular Kensington restaurant where reliability counts*

Map no: P10

Kensington Court, 35
Kensington Street W8
Tel: 0171-937 4294

Presumably they didn't want to spell it Arkadia, but they could have done so as a more obvious link with its predecessor, The Ark. Today, in smarter, more up-to-date surroundings, the focus of the restaurant is on Modern British cooking, a genre popular with Kensington's business community at lunchtime and social diners in the evening. Starters may be taken as main courses for a few pounds extra so, for example, a salad of marinated, grilled duck breast with spiced pecans and papayas will cost either £5.25 or £8.

The net is cast pretty widely for dishes involving fish – clams, wild salmon, cod, blue-fin tuna, huss and sea-bass all feature in one way or another, while chicken, quail, lamb and Angus sirloin steak, for example, form the backbone of the meat dishes. on the menus. There's nothing too fancy or complicated – just simple, honest cooking backed by a wine list which wisely remains in the same league. It is probably best to book, but Arcadia is the sort of place which will try hard to find a table at short notice.

Cost: A/c £19, fixed-price lunch £13.50 (2 courses), £16. H/wine £9.75 ¶ Service exc
Credit cards: 1 2 3 5

Menus: *A la carte*, fixed-price lunch

Times: Last L 2.30pm, Last D 11.15pm. Lunch not served Sat, Sun. Closed 3 days Xmas

Chef: Nicky Barraclough.
Proprietor: Nicky Barraclough

Seats: 78. No-smoking area. No pipes or cigars
Additional: Children welcome; children's portions. ✪ dishes; Vegan/other diets on request

Directions: From High Street Kensington Tube turn right and take the third turning on the right. A signed footpath leads to Kensington Court

The Argyll ✿✿

☺ *Friendly service and enthusiastically-prepared dishes reflecting the chef's quest for the best from the market*

Map no: 11

316 Kings Road SW3
Tel: 0171 352 0025

Once George III's favourite route to Kew, the King's Road is now Chelsea'a main artery, unlikely to be a favourite route to anywhere but its own shops and restaurants, such as The Argyll. On sunny days the open patio doors allow the breezes to waft through the spacious dining area.

An early morning call to his suppliers sets the day's menus for ex-Le Caprice chef, Tony Carey, revelling in his new role here. There is a short, three-course set lunch and a continually evolving carte for both lunch and dinner. His insistence on novel ingredients produced a feast of fresh mushrooms at a recent meal. A delicate variety, philottie, garnished a starter of too-mild smoked chicken terrine and a risotto Milanese had several other varieties, but whether they contributed much by way of flavour is debatable. Other lunch choices might be gazpacho or Caesar salad, followed by smoked salmon with

Cost: A/c £20, fixed-price lunch £12 (2 courses), £15. H/wine £10. Service exc
Credit cards: 1 2 3 4

Menus: *A la carte*, fixed-price lunch

Times: Midday-Last L 2.30pm, 7pm-Last D11.15pm (midnight Fri and Sat). Closed Sun, Mon lunch, BHs, Xmas

Chef: Tony Carey
Proprietor: Christian Arden

wild asparagus, or cold roast beef with salsa verde. A smooth, but not over-tangy, lemon tart indicated great competence in the pastry department. The succinct wine list shows bottles by grape variety which helps matching with the food.

Directions: From Sloane Square Tube, cross Old Church Street/King's Road. The Argyll is opposite the MGM cinema

Seats: 55. No pipes. Air conditioned
Additional: Children welcome; ✿ dishes; other diets on request

Athenaeum

As we went to print, this excellent Piccadilly hotel was undergoing a multi-million pound re-fit. The restaurant was being redesigned to reflect a lighter, brasserie style, and we look forward to reporting in next year's guide the fruits of David Marshall's new menus.

Map no: F12

116 Piccadilly W1
Tel: 0171-499 3464

Auberge de Provence ✿✿✿

Provençal style restaurant with famous associations, serving interesting food in a smart setting

Renowned for its in association with the Provençal village of Les Baux and its award-winning L'Oustau de Baumanière restaurant, this is one of three eating places in the large Victorian hotel complex of St James Court. A Provençal theme is displayed in the tiled floor, archways and rough textured white walls, and the cooking of chef Bernard Briqué relies heavily on that region of France, though the results are sometimes disappointing.

 In addition to the interesting, extensive *carte*, a Menu Surprise can be designed around individual tastes – at a price. Our inspector chose crab meat ravioli poached in a light saffron fish soup for starters from the fixed-price menu, but found the pasta to be rubbery and the soup flavour less than exciting. Fillet of sole soufflé came with a poor black olive gravy, but magret of duck breast with Marsala and rhubarb was beautifully cooked and served, although the meat was chewy and the sauce starchy. Popular desserts from a well-stocked sweet trolly included Paris-Brest, fruit salad and floating island, and the chosen chocolate mousse with crème anglaise feathered with raspberry purée was very tasty. Service was correct and efficient.

Directions: Nearer the Victoria Street end of Buckingham Gate, attached to St James Court Hotel. Nearest Tube – St James's Park. Evening valet parking

Map no: 13

St James Court Hotel
Buckingham Gate SW1
Tel: 0171-821 1899

Cost: *Alc* £30, fixed-price lunch £23.50, fixed-price dinner £30. H/wine £11.50 ♀ Service exc
Credit cards: 1 2 3 4

Menus: *A la carte*, fixed-price lunch and dinner

Times: Last L 2.30pm, Last D 11pm. Lunch not served Sat. Closed Sun, 1 week Jan, 2 weeks Aug

Chef: Bernard Briqué
Proprietor: Taj Group of Hotels. Manager: Christian Berger

Seats: 70. No-smoking area. Air conditioned
Additional: Children welcome; children's portions/menu; ✿ dishes

Aubergine ✿✿✿✿

Very smart Chelsea restaurant with a talented chef steadily developing an individual style

Tucked away in the lower reaches of Chelsea, Gordon Ramsay's restaurant has a summery decor and well-spaced tables set out behind a small foyer bar. A special lunchtime

Map no: 14

11 Park Walk SW10
Tel: 0171-352 3449

Cost: Fixed-price lunch £18, fixed-price dinner £28 (3 courses), £36. H/wine £23.

menu is excellent value for money, although choice is limited. The full *carte*, also fixed-price, offers around eight choices at each stage, and plenty to interest the diner. In the evenings there is also a six-course menu.

Starters at recent inspection meals showed Gordon Ramsay's potential to reach the heights – but were not always faultless. An elaborate tian of leeks and scallops, beautifully structured with slices of scallop topped with caviar on a bed of leek and salmon mousse set on a milky champagne sauce was ambitious and enjoyable, but the caviar triumphed over the scallops and the sauce was a touch over-salted. A generously sliced gelée of roasted langoustines and salmon with ratatouille, garnished with tapénade and gazpacho sauce, however, was a jewel-like delight to the eye, and exciting to the palate, while a warm soup of white haricots with truffle oil was a perfect blend of flavours. Fish dishes as main courses offered exciting and unusual combinations: red mullet inserted with slices of aubergine with beignets of sage served on a bed of aubergine caviar showed clear, strong flavours; sea-bass with a vanilla sauce was superbly successful. Game also proved a good choice, with an interesting guinea fowl en cocotte, served with a thyme jus and a tagliatelle of leeks; pigeon with wild mushroom ravioli and clear, intense Madeira jus was tender, full of flavour and accurately cooked.

An assiette of the tempting desserts (for two people) gives a chance to sample them all in miniature. An extremely rich chocolate pavé and a delicate orange tart were outstanding among an enjoyably varied selection. Efficient service, under the accomplished direction of Jean-Claude Breton, is delivered with charm.

Well chosen and sensibly priced, the wine list is neither exotic not overpowering. It concentrates on France, with a reasonable scattering of New World bottles.

Directions: From South Kensington Tube take the Fulham Road to the MGM cinema, then take the second road on left. Park Walk is near the pub

Service exc
Credit cards: 1 2 3 4 5

Menus: Fixed-price lunch and dinner

Times: Last L 2.30pm, Last D 11pm. Lunch not served Sat. Closed Sun, BHs, Easter, 2 weeks Aug, 1 week Xmas

Chef: Gordon Ramsay
Proprietor: Gordon Ramsay

Seats: 45. Air conditioned
Additional: Children welcome; children's portions. ◑ dishes on request

Au Jardin des Gourmets ❀❀

Classic French cooking at a long-established and well-loved venue with a relaxed atmosphere and attentive service

There may be new owners at this, one of Soho's oldest French restaurants, but some things never change: the superb, good value wine list featuring many half bottles; the agreeable upstairs rooms (there is also a Brasserie on the ground floor); and the style of cooking, which remains firmly French traditional. Given the restaurant's reputation as a haunt of show business glitterati, this latter may seem surprising, but many of the dishes, such as our inspector's main course of boeuf bordelaise, have featured on the menu for most of the Jardin's 64 years of operation. Its very longevity is a testament to this restaurant's integrity, cooking and formal, courteous service.

Chef Denis Lobry offers a *carte* featuring such classic dishes such as 'Cassolet d'escargots, Marchand de Vins' (a dozen snails with shallots and red wine sauce) or roast rack of lamb and poached salmon. Our inspector's meal was marked by its

Map no: M15

5 Greek Street, Soho Square W1
Tel: 0171-437 1816

Cost: A/c £27, fixed-price lunch and dinner £17.50 (2 courses), £21.50. H/wine from £8.75. Service 15%. Cover charge £1.50 for a/c
Credit cards: 1 2 3 4 5

Menus: A la carte, fixed-price lunch and dinner, pre/post theatre

Times: Last L 2.30pm, Last D 11.15pm. Closed Sat lunch, Sun, Xmas, Easter

simple, authentic, no-frills preparation from the first course of full-flavoured fish soup, through the good quality fillet steak (cooked as ordered) to the creamy crème brûlée pudding.

Additional: Children welcome; children's portions/menu. Pianist on ground floor
Directions: Near Soho Square and Oxford Street. Nearest Tube – Tottenham Court Road

Chef: Denis Lobry
Proprietor: Novoport Group.
Manager: Franco Zoia
Seats: 130-150. No-smoking room; no pipes or cigars. Air conditioned

Ayudhya ✿

☺ *A Thai restaurant with warm wood decor, the Ayudhya has spread to three floors, reflecting its growing popularity. The menu offers a huge choice of dishes, including a vegetarian section, though our inspector found an alarming homogeneity to the sauces of the different meat dishes he sampled.*

Cost: Alc £18, fixed-price D £15.30, £18.50. Wine £6.95. No service charge. **Credit cards:** 1 2 3 4 5. **Additional:** Children welcome; children's menu; ♥ menu; Vegan/other diets on request
Directions: On the A38 at the bottom of Kingston Hill in a parade of shops, a quarter of a mile from the town centre

Map no: 16
14 Kingston Hill, Kingston upon Thames
Tel: 0181-549 5984
Chef: Somjai Thanpho
Proprietor: Somjai Thanpho.
Manager: Panya Muenkum
Seats: 80
Times: Last L 2.30pm/D 11pm. Closed 25 Dec, 1 Jan, Easter Sun

Baboon ✿✿

☺ *The candlelit atmosphere and good modern cooking combine to make a comfortable dining experience.*

Its all change at this attractive basement restaurant, now under different mangement, and renamed Baboon, so that you won't forget it! Whilst the facilities remain unaltered, decoration and fittings are now slightly different, there is a comfortable bar lounge, and several smaller more intimate dining rooms for private parties.
   Our inspector sampled the delightful mousse of goat's cheese and red pepper on a tapénade blini. This was followed by an equally flavoursome poached fish and shellfish, with squid ink pasta and tarragon, beautifully flavoured with star anise, and part vegetable, part fish stock creamed sauce. The dessert of apple and pear tatin was slightly overcooked, but overall the kitchen was showing a very good innovative and modern approach.
   The wine list has also been thoughtfully put together, listing 22 interesting young vintage wines, including some good Domaine, and New World wine, by the glass. Service is attentive and friendly, creating a good atmosphere.

Directions: Off Wigmore Street. Nearest Tube – Bond Street

Map no: 17

Off Wigmore Street W1
Tel: 0171 224 2992

Cost: Alc £20; fixed-price lunch and dinner £10, £12.50. Wine £9.50 ♀ Service exc
Credit cards: 1 2 3 4 5

Menus: *A la carte,* fixed-price lunch and dinner, Sunday brunch, pre-theatre, bar menu (seafood), party menus

Times: MiddayLast L 2.30pm, Last D 10.30pm. Closed Sat lunch, Sun eve, BHs

Chef: Winston Hansle
Proprietor: Tony Kitous

Seats: 80. No pipes. Air conditioned
Additional: Children permitted; ♥ dishes; Vegan/other diets on request. Live entertainment

Babur Brasserie ☻☻

☺ *An Indian restaurant in south-east London needs to stand out from the crowd to succeed – this one does.*

Frequent visitors to Indian restaurants come to expect the same old dishes so it makes a welcome change to find some new ones, especially in Forest Hill, gateway to the erratic South Circular. The Rahman brothers specialise in Moghul cooking such as the delicious starter called patra - avari leaves layered with a spicy chick pea paste, steamed, sliced and then deep fried. Of the many unusual main courses, our inspector chose 'Babur-e-bhojan', a delicious selection of four different lamb and chicken dishes, all using fresh spices and herbs. Fish lovers may try 'Patrani machli', spiced fillets of sole flavoured with saffron, wrapped and steamed in a banana leaf. In addition, the wide selection of vegetable dishes deserves consideration.

Twice a year the Rahmans offer a festival of the British Raj with a menu based on Victorian records and interesting cocktails like Bengal Lancers Punch or Sargodha Club Tennis Cup. Once a year a chef comes over from Bombay to offer Parsee cooking for a month. This is an Indian restaurant that tries really hard – and succeeds.

Directions: Brockley Rise is off the South Circular/Stansted Road

Map no: 18

119 Brockley Rise, Forest Hill
SE23
Tel: 0181-291 2400

Cost: A/c from £11.95, Sunday lunch £7.50. Wine £6.95.
Service inc
Credit cards: 1 2 3 4

Menus: A/c, Sunday lunch buffet

Times: Midday–Last L2.15pm, 6pm–Last D 11.15pm. Closed Xmas

Chef: Enam Rahman
Proprietor: Barbur Ltd

Seats: 54. No-smoking area. Air conditioned
Additional: Children welcome; ❷ menu; Vegan/other diets on request

Bahn Thai ☻☻

☺ *Not cheap, but an excellent starting point for those new to Thai food with its carefully explained menu*

Last year, the ground floor of Philip Harris's renowned restaurant was refurbished to become a Thai 'tapas' bar, however, it is due to change back to a restaurant. We feel sure that diners will appreciate being back at this level with the bamboo weave wall covering and plain polished tables. For novices of Thai cuisine this is the ideal place to start, the menu is highly informative, giving advice on what and how to eat; dishes are freshly prepared, authentic and fragrant - three elements that are often missing.

Appetisers include succulent chargrilled tiger prawns with a sharp tamarind sauce or khanom jeep dumplings with a soya garlic sauce. Soups are eaten with the main meal and the classic hot and sour soup is good with or without coconut milk . The Somtam Poo Khem - a fiery, shredded papaya salad - is flavoured with salt crab and in the jungle curry there are both Thai and pea aubergines. If you've visited the Far East you will remember the awful smell of durian fruit but here it is found combined with coconut in a delicious ice cream. The 12.5% suggested gratuity can make a meal here rather pricy.

Directions: On the right hand side of Frith Street when approaching from Shaftesbury Avenue. Nearest Tube – Tottenham Court Road

Map no: K19

21a Frith Street W1
Tel: 0171-437 8504

Cost: A/c £20. H/wine £7.95 ♀
Service 12.5% (optional)
Credit cards: 1 2 3 4 5

Menus: A la carte, pre-theatre

Times: Last L 2.45pm, Last D 11.15pm. Closed Xmas, Easter, BHs

Chef: Mrs Penn Squires
Proprietor: Philip Harris

Seats: 120. Air conditioned
Additional: Children welcome; ❷ dishes; Vegan/other diets on request

Basil Street ❀

☺ *This fine understated Edwardian hotel has a gracious candle-lit dining room. Recent recommendations from the fixed-price carte include cassoulette of veal and sweetbreads, grilled fillet of salmon with saffron sauce and enjoyable home-made desserts. There is a good list of '83 vintage wines.*

Cost: Fixed-price lunch £12.95 (2 courses), £14.95, fixed-price dinner £15.95 (2 courses), £19.95. H/wine £9.95. Service exc
Credit cards: 1 2 3 4
Additional: Children welcome; children's portions/menu. ❂ dishes, Vegan/other diets on request. Pianist in evenings
Directions: Knightsbridge, off Sloane Street, behind Harrods

Map no: 20
Basil Street, Knightsbridge SW3
Tel: 0171-581 3311
Chef: James Peake
Manager: Stephen Korans
Seats: 70. No pipes or cigars in dining room
Times: Last L 2.30pm/D 10.15pm. Closed Sat Lunch

The Bedlington Café ❀

☺ *Frying by day and Thai by night, with its tightly packed formica tables, tourist posters, large cups of jasmine tea, there are no frills here. Cooking has been modified with fewer chillies, but amongst dishes well worth trying are the phad Thai-fried noodles with peanut, shrimps and bean sprouts.*

Seats: 30
Additional: Children welcome; ❂ dishes; Vegan on request
Directions: Off Sutton Court Road

Map no: 21
24 Fauconberg Road, Chiswick W4
Tel: 0181-994 1965
Cost: Alc £13. Service exc. Corkage charge
Credit cards: None taken
Menu: A la carte
Times: Last L 2.30pm, Last D 9.45pm. Closed Xmas Day
Proprietor: P Priyanu

Belgo ❀❀

A unique Belgian restaurant with a curious monastic setting and some very good value food

The atmosphere at this curious Belgian restaurant is truly unique: where else would you find waiters dressed as Trappist monks, and bawdy Rabelaisian comments inscribed on concrete walls? A clue to this crude monastic setting comes from the excellent range of beers served here, many of them brewed behind the closed walls of Belgiums's five Trappist monasteries, as well as the Belgo specials on tap. The food is remarkable too: lunch for a fiver includes one course and chips plus a beer or, for slightly more, all the mussels you can eat plus chips. Various set menus offer great value at dinner, such as the Menu Bruxellois for £10, and the Belgo Complet with its salad Liègeoise, a pot of mussels cooked in one of two different ways with chips, and a Hoegaarden white beer all for the same price. The *carte* includes dishes such as lobster cooked with garlic butter and herbs, langoustine with basil or a huge pot of mussels served with one of ten different sauces. Or try a Belgian speciality like smoked wild boar sausages with mash, and braised beef in beer with apples, plums and croquettes.

Directions: Towards Camden, about 100 yards from Chalk Farm Tube

Map no: Q22
72 Chalk Farm Road NW1
Tel: 0171-267 0718

Cost: Alc £25, fixed-price lunch £5, Belgo Complet £10. H/wine £8.75 ♀ Service inc
Credit cards: 1 2 3 4 5

Menus: A la carte, speciality and fixed-price Belgo Complet; fixed-price lunch Mon-Sat

Times: Midday-Last L 3pm, 6pm-Last D 11.30pm (Mon-Fri); Midday-Last D 11.30pm (Sat); Midday-Last D 10.30pm (Sun). Closed Xmas and 1 Jan

Chef: Philippe Blais
Proprietors: Andre Plisnier, Denis Blais

Seats: 120. No cigars or pipes
Additional: Children welcome; ❂ dishes; Vegan on request

Belvedere ❀❀

A restaurant in an oasis of green in the middle of London offering French and Mediterraneanan style food

Holland House is a splendid Regency house in the middle of the park overlooking formal English rose gardens. The restaurant, on two floors, is patronised by many celebrities and is a good setting for a romantic candlelit dinner
　A new chef, Duncan Wallace from the Capital Hotel, has recently taken over and we are pleased to confirm that he has continued with the same style of modern cooking, combining French and Mediterranean influences. We were impressed with chef's chicken and bacon terrine, layered with onions and basil, and served with a delightful turmeric riata textured with diced apples, from the winter *carte* (it changes every season). This was followed by the crab cake, which was well made but spoilt by the powerful flavour of the capers. The hot Soufflé of the Day is well worth the wait, but the espresso coffee lacked real flavour on this occasion. Service is amiable and well supervised. Wines complement the food, and the house Vin de Table at £10.50 is well worth a try. Good car parking is available by the restaurant.

Directions: Inside Holland Park at the Abbotsbury Road entrance. Nearest Tube – Holland Park

Map no: P23

Holland House
off Abbotsbury Road
Holland Park W8
Tel: 0171-602 1238

Cost: *Alc* £22; H/wine £10.50.
Service exc
Credit cards: 1 2 3 4 5

Menus: *A la carte*, Sunday lunch

Times: 12.30–Last L 3pm, 7pm-Last D 11pm (11.30pm summer). Closed Sun eve, 25 Dec, 1 Jan

Chef: Duncan Wallace
Proprietor: John Gold. Manager: Ian MacRae
Seats: 150. Air conditioned
Additional: Children welcome; children's portions; ❖ dish; Vegan on request

Bentley's ❀❀❀

A long established fish restaurant and oyster bar with a style reminiscent of a gentleman's club

The Swallow Street branch of Bentley's, London's renowned fish restaurant, has seen another change of staff in the kitchen, with Keith Stanley taking over after four years at the Ritz. The upstairs restaurant has the atmosphere of a gentleman's club, especially at lunchtime when it attracts many of the local business people, and the walls are adorned with Spy cartoons. Staff are well supervised and at times over attentive, perhaps because at the time of our visit the restaurant was not very busy. On the ground floor there is the less formal Oyster Bar, although the menus are similar, with simple dishes based on fresh produce. At lunchtime there is a short two or three-course fixed-price menu in addition to the *carte*. The latter includes a couple of meat dishes, perhaps fillet of lamb on vegetable cake with tarragon sauce, and sirloin of beef with ceps and baby leeks. Vegetarians can also be catered for on request, although no dishes are listed.
　Starters include oysters, lobster in a salad or risotto, and our inspector's choice, crisply fried crab croquette accompanied by a sauce of red peppers and finely chopped fennel, a delightful combination of flavours and textures. This was followed by smoked fillet of cod served between crisp sesame wafers on a light grain mustard butter sauce. A potato cake with spinach and a few crisply cooked mange-touts were also part of the dish. The fillet of red mullet on herb noodles with roast shallots and salmon jus looked appetising. The pudding was disappointing: a

Map no: 24

11-15 Swallow Street W1
Tel: 0171-734 4756

Cost: *Alc* £37.50, fixed-price lunch and dinner £16.50 (2 courses), £19.50. Wine £11.50 ♀
Credit cards: 1 2 3 4

Menus: *A la carte*, fixed-price lunch and dinner, Oyster bar

Times: Midday-Last L 2.30pm, 5.30pm-Last D 11pm. Closed Sun, BHs

Chef: Keith Stanley
Proprietor: Boddingtons. Manager: Michael Hoy
Seats: 75. Air conditioned
Additional: Children permitted; ❖ dishes; other diets on request

well flavoured tiramisù served with a delicious oat and syrup biscuit but with a heavy sponge base and a rather dry cream topping.

The largest section in the two page wine list is devoted to white burgundies. There are also some good Sauvignons and Chardonnays from the New World.

Directions: From Piccadilly Circus Tube take Piccadilly north exit, walk along Piccadilly and take the second left into Swallow Street

The Berkeley ✿✿

☺ *The stylish place to eat Italian at lunchtime, in the evening and after the theatre. Live music adds to the atmosphere*

Only a tiara's throw from elegant Knightsbridge, The Berkeley offers a choice of two restaurants. The main Restaurant (with a capital R) serves high standard French cuisine against a backdrop of English oak panelling and reproductions of Holbein's portraits from the Queen's Collection. The Perroquet in contrast provides contemporary Italian food with a splendid lunchtime buffet and a fixed-price dinner menu. All the food is home-made, freshly prepared, and professionally presented. Our inspector was impressed by a ravioli starter filled with Ricotta cheese and chopped walnuts with herbs, blended with Parmesan cheese and extra virgin olive oil. His 'Fegato alla Veneziana', calfs' liver served with triangles of pan-fried polenta and onions, came with a delectable Madeira sauce, gently flavoured with sage. The dessert trolley also earned praise, particularly for the pasteria made with chopped pine kernels, candied fruits and Ricotta cheese. Old and New World wines are abundant but the Italian selection is noticeably weak. Service is discreet and formal in these well-managed hotel restaurants.

Directions: The Berkeley is 200yds from Hyde Park Corner, on the corner of Knightsbridge and Wilton Place. Nearest Tube – Hyde Park Corner

Map no: 25

Wilton Place, Knightsbridge
SW1
Tel: 0171-235 6000

Cost: A/c from £35, fixed-price lunch £19.50, fixed-price dinner £21. H/wine £11.50 (carafe). Service inc. Cover charge £1
Credit cards: 1 2 3 4

Menus: *A la carte*, fixed-price lunch and dinner

Times: 12.30–Last L 2.30pm (Sun 12.45–2.15pm), 6.30pm–Last D 10.45pm (Sun 7pm–10.15pm). Closed Sat

Chef: John Williams
Proprietor: The Savoy Group.
Dir/Gen Man: Stefano Sebastiani

Seats: 70. Air conditioned
Additional: Children permitted;
♿ on request

The Berkshire ✿

☺ *Expect rich traditional British cooking here: the aim of the Berkshire is to recreate the style and tastes of the Edwardian era. A typical dish could be roasted pheasant with prunes, dried apricots and an intense, sticky dark sauce; desserts are for pudding lovers – such as diplomat pudding and treacle tart.*

Cost: A/c £33, fixed-price L £17.50 (2 courses), £23.40/D £17.50 (2 courses) £23.40. Wine £13.75. Service inc
Credit cards: 1 2 3 4
Additional: Children welcome; children's portions; ♿ menu; Vegan/other diets on request
Directions: From Bond Street Tube cross Oxford Street. The hotel is next to Debenhams, entrance in Marylebone Lane

Map no: 26
Oxford Street W1
Tel: 0171-629 7474
Chef: James Chapman
Proprietor: Radisson Edwardian.
Manager: Steven Hobden
Seats: 50. Air conditioned
Times: Last L 2.30pm/D 10.30pm. Closed L Sat, Sun and BH

Bibendum ❀❀❀❀

Pioneer of the modern bistro style of cooking, but the Hopkinson flair applied to essentially simple dishes lifts Bibendum to the top of its class

Flagship of Sir Terence Conran's restaurants, Bibendum, housed on the first floor of the splendid Art Deco Michelin building, continues to 'pack 'em in', in the words of our inspector. About a week's notice should secure a lunchtime booking, but for dinner you may need at least two to three week's forward planning. Representative of the clientele that keeps the place humming are media people, smart South-Kensingtonites and Americans. Even the ground-floor café/oyster bar seems always to have a queue.

At lunch, there is a daily-changing, fixed-price menu, with seven or eight choices at each stage, and in the evenings an extensive *carte*. Simon Hopkinson is renowned for his straightforward bistro style and dishes are reliably enjoyable and often brilliantly executed. French, Italian and British influences may still predominate, but the highlight of an inspector's lunch in summer was Spanish-style hake cooked with clams, peas and parsley, served in a lively broth that combined top-class ingredients in happy harmony. Her meal had begun with a terrine of pig's trotter, served in wafer-thin slices with a wonderfully gutsy mustard dressing with chopped egg, parsley and capers. An almond tart, simply served with thick Jersey cream, followed by good espresso and first-class chocolate truffles, rounded off a thoroughly satisfying meal. Service is competent and courteous, but scarcely justifies the hefty 15 per cent additional charge.

The fact that there are Gewürztraminers from Alsace and 27 Montrachet gives a good idea of the extent of the wine list. It concentrates on France, region by region and is strong in Burgundy and Bordeaux and the range from all the Italian regions is outstanding.

Directions: In the Michelin building at the Brompton Road end of the Fulham Road. Nearest Tube – South Kensington

Map no: 27

Michelin House, 81 Fulham Road SW3
Tel: 0171-581 5817

Cost: A/c £32, fixed-price lunch £25. H/wine £15 ♀ Service charge 15%
Credit cards: 1 2 3

Menus: A la carte, fixed-price lunch, Sunday lunch, Oyster Bar

Times: 12.30-Last L 2.30pm (3pm Sun), 7pm-Last D 11.30pm. Closed Easter Mon and 24-27 Dec

Chef: Simon Hopkinson
Proprietor: Graham Williams (Manager)

Seats: 72. Air conditioned
Additional: Children welcome; children's portions; ❂ dishes.

Bice ❀❀

A popular Italian restaurant in the heart of Mayfair with high quality cooking and charming service

This smart, year-old basement restaurant in Mayfair has older sisters in Paris, Tokyo and the United States, as well as in Italy itself. If this does not set Bice apart, then the high quality of its cooking and attentive, charming service should help to convince you. Skill and care are obvious in the preparation of the mainly northern Italian dishes on its frequently changing menu. Our inspector ordered a starter of 'Carpaccio tiepido di paesce spada al pepe verde', warm swordfish with green peppercorns, which he found good. Grilled calfs' liver with polenta, potatoes and leaf spinach followed and a tiramisu which was a good example of this traditional pudding. Vegetarians will enjoy the range of pasta and salads.

Map no: 28

13 Albemarle Street W1
Tel: 0171-409 1011

Cost: A/c £35, fixed-price lunch £20, fixed-price dinner £30. H/wine £15 ♀ Service exc
Credit cards: 1 2 3 4 5

Menus: A la carte, fixed-price lunch and dinner

Times: Last L 2.45pm, Last D 11pm. Closed Sat lunch and Sun

Chef: Vladimir Scanu

The long wine list features over 100 labels, representing almost every Italian region from Alto-Adige to Sicily, and there are thirteen varieties of grappa too. Although Bice is popular with Italians, dining in Mayfair means your companions will also include business executives, local residents and tourists.

Directions: From Green Park Tube walk towards Piccadilly, Albemarle Street is on the left

Proprietors: S Frittella and R Ruggeri

Seats: 105. No pipes. Air conditioned
Additional: Children welcome; ♥ dishes; Vegan/other diets on request

Big Night Out ❀❀

A smart, trendy place to eat but still friendly - a return visit would be on the cards

Apparently, customers speculate on how the restaurant got its name. Why worry, when the food is good, the service charming, one is away from the hubbub and it's a much better name than Boring Evening In! Owner Hugh O'Boyle greets and serves in a cheery, laid-back manner, while partner Richard Coates creates interesting dishes for the good value set menu and *carte*. The place is bright and informal with white-washed walls and polished floors and tables. Upstairs is the more intimate eating area with big, bold paintings by Richard's girlfriend, Susie, and where dining by candlelight can be requested when booking. At a recent lunch visit, the parfait of foie gras with brioche was good – smooth and full of flavour; confit of duck with a creamy tomato dressing was also a winner. Earning a similar accolade were calf's liver with mash in sage and onion gravy and fillet of red bream with a creamy basil sauce, served with sugar snap peas. Desserts not to be missed include caramel soufflé and the sticky toffee pudding, which came with a wickedly enjoyable, thick sauce. The wine list offers some excellent wines.

Directions: Near to Primrose Hill, just across the bridge from Chalk Farm Tube

Map no: Q29

148 Regents Park NW1
Tel: 0171-586 5768

Cost: *Alc* £28.50, fixed-price £18.50. Service exc
Credit cards: 1 2 3 5

Menus: *A la carte*, fixed-price, Sunday lunch

Times: Midday-Last L 3pm, 7.30pm-Midnight. D not served Sun, L not served Mon

Chef: Richard Coates
Proprietor: Hugh O'Boyle

Additional: N -smoking area. Children welcome; children's portions; ♥ dishes

Bistrot Bruno ❀❀

Very special French country cooking, strong on flavour and earthiness, prepared to perfection

Situated in the heart of London's gastronomic quarter, this lively and popular restaurant is part-owned by talented chef Bruno Loubet, ably aided in the kitchen by head chef Jason Hornbuchle and his small, enthusiastic team. Intimate in tone, it offers a relaxing atmosphere in which to savour the robust, rustic French cooking on the monthly-changing menu. A well-balanced and vibrant selection of dishes includes, typically, starters such as grilled squid with red pepper mousse, sardine and aubergine terrine and brain fritters. Varied main courses may feature wood pigeon with garlic sauce and guinea fowl and mushroom risotto, infused with rosemary. Expertly combined flavours are intense and portions generous – this is not food for the faint-hearted but if you enjoy 'cuisine terroir' with all its glorious earthiness, this is definitely a restaurant to visit: the

Map no: K30

63 Frith Street W1
Tel: 0171-734 4545

Cost: *Alc* £30. Wine £8.75 ♀ Service exc
Credit cards: 1 2 3 4

Menus: *A la carte*

Times: Last L 2.30pm, Last D 11.30pm. Closed Sat lunch, all day Sun, Xmas-New Year

Chef: Bruno Loubet
Proprietors: Kathleen and Pierre Condou

meal will be memorable. To complement the high standard of cooking, service is friendly and easy, provided by charming staff well-supervised by co-owner Pierre Condou. The interesting, accessible wine list completes a successful eating experience.

Directions: Between Shaftesbury Avenue and Soho Square. Nearest Tube – Tottenham Court Road

Seats: 40. No cigars or pipes.
Air conditioned
Additional: Children welcome

Bistrot 190 ✹✹

Noisy and popular, this modern bistro offers plenty of choice on its daily-changing carte

The high-ceilinged front room of the Gore Hotel provides the setting for this noisy and very popular modern bistro, open from 7am until after midnight. Kentia palms and closely-spaced wooden tables stand on bare floorboards, while walls adorned with sprays of dried flowers as well as dozens of pictures complete the bistro image. An eclectic, daily-changing *carte* offers plenty of choice - 16 or so reasonably priced starters and main courses – and the bread basket, communal tub of Echire butter, olives and tapénade, although 'extras', are certainly well worth having. Dishes often feature trios of ingredients such as chargrilled lamb steak with gingered barley and deep-fried basil, or bruschetta of grilled peppers, Mozzarella and plum tomatoes. Helpings are generous and flavours distinct; a robust dish of oxtail braised with roasted root vegetables might be followed by a tangy lemon tart with enough zest to cut through its creamy richness. Service is casual, but staff are eager to please, and a frequently changing short wine list offers small pitchers as an alternative to some whole bottles.

Directions: At the Hyde Park end of Queen's Gate, just round the corner from the Royal Albert Hall. Nearest Tube – High Street Kensington

Map no: 31

190 Queen's Gate SW7
Tel: 0171-581 5666

Cost: Alc £22, Sunday lunch £12.50. H/wine from £8.50.
Service exc
Credit cards: 1 2 3 4

Menus: *A la carte,* Sunday lunch

Times: Last D 12.30am. Closed 3 days at Xmas

Chef: Antony Worrall Thompson
Managers: Ian McKerracher (General), Paul McElhinney (Bistrot)

Seats: 55
Additional: Children welcome; children's portions; ❷ dishes; other diets on request

Blueprint Café ✹✹

Superb views over the Thames and a beautifully balanced menu, in a buzzing atmosphere

Another of Sir Terence Conran's hugely successful restaurants – this one is located on Butlers Wharf with glorious views of the Thames and Tower Bridge. In fine weather you can dine on the balcony, al fresco, but these tables are very popular so bookings are essential. Chef, Lucy Crabb and her talented team cook using a real awareness of the importance of balancing flavours. The menu offers a wide and exciting choice and the quality of ingredients and the freshness of the produce is allowed to shine through in the dishes which are prepared with skill and care. A most enjoyable meal began with a tasty leek and cheese terrine, followed by a succulent breast of chicken with a grain mustard and tarragon sauce – simply delicious, as was the calfs' liver with the pesto sauce. However the highlight of this particular meal was the most excellent hazelnut and poppy-seed parfait

Map no: G32

Design Museum
Butlers Wharf SE1
Tel: 0171-378 7031

Cost: Alc £28.30; H/wine £9.50
♀ Service inc
Credit cards: 1 2 3

Menu: *A la carte*

Times: Midday-Last L 3pm (3.30pm Sun), 6pm–Last D 11pm. Closed Sun eve and Xmas

Chef: Lucy Crabb
Proprietors: Sir Terence Conran,

with a white chocolate sauce... in a word, Heaven! There is a well thoughtout and good quality wine list. Service is very well paced and staff have a nice attitude to the guests. The restaurant is always busy, buzzing and fun.

Directions: In the Design Museum by Tower Bridge. Parking at the end of Curlew Street. Nearest Tube – Tower Hill

Joel Kissin
Seats: 85
Additional: Children permitted; ◊ dishes; other diets on request

Bombay Brasserie ❀❀

Popular Indian restaurant offering dishes from many different cuisines throughout the sub-continent

Specialities from all over India are brought together at this cosmopolitan restaurant to provide a unique culinary experience. Tandoori dishes from the North-West Frontier share the menu with dishes from Goa on the west coast, wholesome Punjabi fare, and the sumptuous cuisine of the Moghul emperors, and not surprisingly this remains one of the most popular restaurants in London. The strength of the cooking lies in the delicate saucing, and the results are well-balanced and full of flavour. A recent inspection meal began with 'jhinga pattice', a spicy dish of shallow-fried potato cake stuffed with minced shrimps and served with a medley of chutneys, and 'samosa chaat', a Maharashtrian roadside fare of vegetable samosas with chickpeas. Speciality dishes included lamb 'pasanda', escalopes of lamb stuffed with cottage cheese and nuts and cooked in a mild cashew sauce; lamb 'roganjosh', meat in masala with yoghurt; and prawn masala from Goa. The food is pricey, but the atmosphere is pukka, and staff are most helpful. The wine list is adequate and fruit juices are recommended with some dishes.

Directions: Opposite Gloucester Road Tube

Map no: 33

Courtfield Close
Courtfield Road SW7
Tel: 0171-370 4040

Cost: *A/c* £25, buffet lunch £14.95. H/wine £9.75. Service exc
Credit cards: 1 3 4

Menus: Fixed-price buffet lunch, *a la carte* dinner

Times: 12.30-Last L 3pm, 7.30pm-Last D midnight

Chef: Udit Sarkhel
Proprietor: Taj International.
Gen Manager: Adi Modi

Seats: 175. No-smoking area. Air conditioned
Additional: Children welcome; ◊ dishes; Vegan/other diets on request

Boyd's ❀❀

Boasting a firm reputaion for uncomplicated modern British cooking in a split-level restaurant

Chef/patron Boyd Gilmour has built up a solid reputation for his straightforward and uncomplicated modern style of British cooking. The split-level dining area now has more space in the front part but the well-appointed tables are a little close together in the glass domed rear conservatory section. The colour-coordinated interior has varnished flooring and illuminated heads of Greek goddesses adorning the walls. Our inspector started off with the charred scallops with mange tout, and a red pepper and chive butter sauce, garnished with tomato concasse. Very enjoyable with fresh good quality ingredients but the butter sauce was beginning to separate slightly. This was followed by the grilled calfs' liver, sweetbreads and kidneys, with an excellent foie gras sauce, set on fresh spinach topped with butter glazed sliced potatoes, enhanced by the excellent glace de viande. The strawberry brûlée for dessert was one of

Map no: P34

35 Kensington Church Street
W8
Tel: 0171-727 5452

Cost: *A/c* £35, fixed-price lunch £14. H/wine from £10. Service exc
Credit cards: 1 2 3 4

Menus: *A la carte*, fixed-price lunch

Times: 12.30-Last L 2.30pm, 7pm-Last D 11pm. Closed Sun, BHs and 2 weeks at Xmas

Chef: Boyd Gilmour
Proprietor: Boyd Gilmour

the best this year, full of rich flavour. Home-made chocolate cream truffles completed the meal. There is an excellent selection of vintage house wines all available by the glass or bottle.

Directions: Entrances on both Albemarle and Dover Streets. Best approach from Piccadilly. Nearest Tube – Green Park

Seats: 40. Air conditioned
Additional: Children welcome; ❂ dishes

The Brackenbury ✹✹

☺ *Interesting, assured cooking at basic prices in simple, busy surroundings*

Map no: T35

129 Brackenbury Road W6
Tel: 0181-748 0107

Situated in central Shepherd's Bush, this unpretentious café-style venue may be off the beaten track but is always packed, mainly with young locals attracted by the honest, robust cooking and the extremely good value for money it represents. Chef/patron Adam Robinson's imaginative *carte* features such varied first courses as leek and Gruyère tart, jellied terrine of salt beef and, our inspector's choice, marinated salt cod. Main courses include a vegetarian dish (typically a risotto) and a (usually grilled or steamed) fish dish, while pigeon breast, boiled leg of lamb and braised veal tendrons have all featured recently. The poached ox tongue, served on a tender breast of capon, was very enjoyable apart from the excessive liquid in which the dish was swimming.

Lack of attention to presentation and detail is perhaps the result of demands on both kitchen and staff, as The Brackenbury becomes a victim of its own popularity. But the informal service is attentive and the overall experience very agreeable. All but a handful of the inclusions on the wine list are available by the glass. Booking is advisable.

Cost: Alc £17.50. Wine £8.50 ♀
Service exc
Credit cards: 1 2 3 4 5

Menus: *A la carte*, Sunday lunch

Times: 12.30-Last L 2.45pm, Last D 10.45pm. Closed Mon & Sat lunch, Sun eve, BHs & 10 days at Xmas

Chef: Adam Robinson
Proprietors: Adam and Katie Robinson

Seats: 55. No cigars or pipes
Additional: Children permitted; children's portions. ❂ dishes; Vegan/other diets if notice given

Directions: From Goldhawk Road (to Chiswick), left into Brackenbury Road. Restaurant at end on left. Nearest Tube – Goldhawk Road

Britannia Inter-Continental ✹

Modern continental cooking by new chef, Neil Gray, created to a highly capable standard. The food is presented with great charm and confidence in the rosetted Adams restaurant of this busy Mayfair hotel.

Map no: 36
Grosvenor Square W1
Tel: 0171-629 9400
Chef: Neil Gray
Proprietors: Inter-Continental.
Manager: John H Acton
Seats: 40. No pipes. Air conditioned
Times: 12.30-Last L 2.30pm, 6.30pm-Last D 9.30pm. Closed Sat, Sun, all BHs except 25 Dec

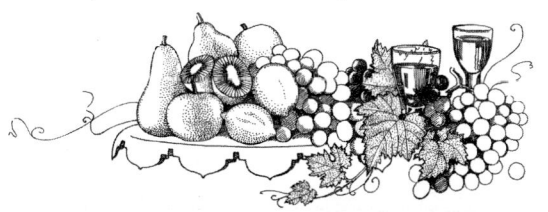

Cost: Alc £25, fixed price L £19.50 (2 courses), £22; fixed-price D £24. H/wine ♀ Service exc
Credit cards: 1 2 3 4. **Additional:** Children permitted (over 12); ❂ menu; Vegan/other diets on request. Pianist at dinner
Directions: Five minutes walk from Oxford Street and Bond Street, facing American Embassy. Nearest Tubes – Bond Street, Green Park

Brown's ❀❀❀

A venerable London hotel where a new chef has brought a breath of inspiration to classic English cooking

One of Forte's exclusive hotels of the world, Brown's has an illustrious history dating from 1837 when it began as a small town house hotel. Though it has grown considerably since then, stretching from Dover Street to Albemarle Street with an entrance in each, it has managed to retain its unique, intimate ambience. The dining room remains much the same, with warm panelling and rich fabrics, fine damask linen and polished silver - an oasis of peace in central London. However, there has been a revolution in the kitchen with the arrival of chef Aidan McCormack (formerly at Hartwell House, Buckinghamshire). The menus retain their classic English style but the simple descriptions belie the skill and complexity of the cooking. 'Scallop baked in its shell with lemon' gave little clue to the sumptuous creation that appeared at the table: soft scallop and roe in a pastry edged shell on a beurre blanc sauce with lemon and chives, garnished with crisp shredded vegetables. At another meal, 'tian of crab' comprised white crab meat mixed with mayonnaise, lemon juice and a little too much shallot, wrapped in cucumber, topped with tomato jelly and garnished with cucumber, tomato and avocado in a light lemon dressing. A continental influence, bringing a lightness of touch to traditional dishes, was evident in the roast loin of lamb served pink on a precisely diced ratatouille and lamb jus. The *carte* is extensive but the short daily menu is better value. Vegetarian dishes are not listed but are available on request. Desserts are from a trolley and seem pedestrian by comparison. Our inspectors have sampled fruit mille-feuille, and a cold pear tart with frangipane and good crème anglaise.

Map no: 37

Albemarle and Dover Streets
W1
Tel: 0171-493 6020

Cost: *Alc* £36, fixed-price £22.50
Credit cards: 1 2 3 4

Menus: *A la carte*, fixed-price

Times: 12.15-Last L 2.30pm, 6pm-Last D 10pm (Sun 6.30pm-Last D 9.30pm)

Chef: Aidan McCormack
Proprietors: Forte

Directions: Main entrance in Albemarle Street, off Piccadilly. Nearest Tubes – Piccadilly Circus, Green Park

Buchan's ❀

☺ *A popular restaurant with an informal atmosphere, it offers a wide choice of food from a café-bar menu or a formal menu. Examples from the latter include venison pâté served with oatcakes, and as a main course Scottish sirloin steak, peppered, grilled or flambéed in whisky*

Cost: *Alc* £16, Sunday L £8.50 (2 Courses), £10.50; fixed-price D £5.95 (2 courses, Sun and Mon only). H/wine £8.95 ♀ Service exc
Credit cards: 1 2 3 4 5. **Additional:** Children welcome; children's portions; ❷ dishes; Vegan/other diets on request
Directions: On Battersea Bridge Road, 300 yards south of Battersea Bridge.

Map no: 38
62-64 Battersea Bridge Road
SW11
Tel: 0171-228 0888
Chef: Alain Jeannon
Proprietors: Jeremy Bolam
Seats: 70. Air conditioned
Times: Last L 2.45pm/D10.45pm. Closed Xmas

Café des Arts ❀

In a listed building, Café des Arts has become more like a bistro recently. The menu style remains the same with Mediterranean influences cooked by Sally James. Good, wholesome dishes include panfried baby squid or chargrilled lamb gigot with shallots and mushrooms.

Map no: 39
82 Hampstead High Street NW3
Tel: 0171-435 3608
Chef: Sally James
Proprietor: Brian Stein
Seats: 65

Directions: Middle of Hampstead High Street, next door to the Post Office. Nearest Tube – Hampstead

Café Fish ❀

A bustling, convivial and very French atmosphere in this bistro-style fish restaurant, where an honest cooking style is complemented by good, fresh produce. A pianist and pleasant staff all contribute to an enjoyable experience. Usually busy so booking recommended.

Map no: 40
39 Panton Street Haymarket SW1
Tel: 0171-930 3999
Chef: Andrew Magson
Proprietor: Groupe Chez Gerard. Manager: Marie Jeanne Collins
Seats: 94. No-smoking area; no cigars or pipes
Times: Last L 3pm/D 11.30pm. Closed Sun, Xmas

Cost: A/c £21. H/wine £8.25 ♀ Service inc. Cover charge £1.25
Credit cards: 1 2 3 4. **Additional:** Children welcome; ✿ dishes.
Pianist in evenings
Directions: Just of the Haymarket. Nearest Tubes – Leicester Square, Piccadilly Circus

Café Royal Grill Room ❀❀

Interesting if expensive dishes prepared in the French classical style, traditionally served in splendid surroundings

Herbert Berger has risen to the challenge of executive chef of all the restaurants within the Café Royal, but in the principal restaurant, the famous Grill Room, chef Paul Lyndon (ex Mirabelle and Claridge's) is in charge. The rococo surroundings are appealing enough on their own account, and the cloche guéridon service is on traditional lines, with experienced staff showing off their skills at the table and flambé lamp. However, one or two lapses were noted at a test meal – the vegetables had only a passing resemblance to those described on ordering, and a different vintage of wine to that advertised was without comment. But on with the food, beginning with an good appetiser of peeled prawns in a provençale tomato sauce, followed by an open ravioli of langoustines with a light tarragon butter sauce. The pasta and sauce were good, but the langoustines slightly soft and pappy. The main course was better, crown of lamb fillet with provençale vegetables, pesto and balsamic vinegar sauce. The highlight of the meal, though, was the almond and apple pithivier served with blackberry coulis and vanilla ice.

Directions: At the Piccadilly Circus end of Regent Street. Nearest Tubes – Piccadilly Circus, Oxford Circus

Map no: 42
68 Regent Street W1
Tel: 0171-437 9090

Cost: A/c £46, fixed-price lunch £22.50, fixed-price dinner £36. Wine £15.50
Credit cards: 1 2 3 4

Menu: *A la carte*, fixed-price lunch and dinner

Times: Midday-Last L 2.30pm, 6pm-Last D 11pm. Lunch not served Sat. Closed Sun

Chefs: Herbert Berger, Paul Lyndon
Proprietors: Forte. Manager: David Arcusi

Seats: 45. No pipes. Air conditioned
Additional: Children welcome; ✿ dishes

Canal Brasserie ☯☯

☺ *Uncomplicated and freshly cooked modern British food with more than a hint of the Mediterranean*

A former chocolate factory converted into a modern complex, houses this unusual and spacious restaurant. The individual style and approach of chef John Goodall is clearly expressed in the *carte*, with dishes like Chinese roast duck pancakes with cucumber and sweet soy, and rib eye steak with chunky chips and salad. A recent inspection meal began with couscous jumbalaya – a riot of thick slices of smoked bacon, spicy Chorizo sausages, semolina pasta couscous, chopped spring onion, yellow peppers and coriander. Another interesting dish was coconut and smoked chilli chicken curry in a delightful, light, garam masala sauce. The dessert of white chocolate cheese cake with a coffee/chocolate custard sauce also came in for praise. The food is wonderful value for money, and service is both quick and flamboyant even at the busiest times. The food is not recommended on some evenings when the restaurant is franchised out, so phone to check who is in charge before booking. Wines complement the food well, and there are New and Old World, young vintages and some halves.

Directions: Top end of Ladbroke Grove, in Kensal Road, Camelot Studios. Nearest Tube – Kensal Green

Map no: 43

222 Kensal Road W10
Tel: 0181-960 2732

Cost: Alc £15; H/wine £8.95 ♀
Service charge 12.5%
Credit cards: 1 3 5

Menus: *A la carte*, bar menu

Times: Last L 3pm, Last D 10.30pm. Closed 1 week Xmas

Chef: John Goodall
Proprietor: Antony G Harris

Seats: 60
Additional: Children welcome; children's portions. ❖ dishes; Vegan on request

Cannizaro House ☯

Classic country house cooking – salmon and chive mousse, breast of duck with black pudding, tea blancmange - is attentively served in gracious, candle-lit surroundings. A slice of rural living on the capital's fringes.

Cost: Alc £33, Sunday L £16.95; fixed-price L Mon-Fri £16.95 (2 courses), £21.55; fixed-price D Mon-Thu £21.55, Fri-Sun £25.75. Wine £16.50. Service exc
Credit cards: 1 2 3 4. **Additional:** Children over 8 permitted at lunch only; ❖ menu; other diets on request
Directions: From Wimbledon Park Side turn right into Cannizaro Road, then right into West Side. Cannizaro House is 50yds on the left

Map no: 44
West Side, Wimbledon Common SW19
Tel: 0181-879 1464
Chef: Stephen Wilson
Proprietor: Mount Charlotte Thistle. Manager: Ray Slade
Seats: 50. No-smoking area; no cigars or pipes
Times: Last L 2pm/D 10.30pm

The Canteen ☯☯☯

An eclectic range of dishes in a bright new harbourside restaurant offering great value for accomplished cooking

1993 saw the brilliant Marco Pierre White join forces with Forte Hotels to create a new culinary shrine at the Hyde Park (see entry for The Restaurant), and the same year brought another successful liaison, this time with Michael Caine, and a highly publicised new restaurant. The Canteen is quite unlike most second string restaurants. Its name does its food and service little justice, although it does conjure up its sense of fun. Where The Restaurant is a flagship, exclusive and elitist, The Canteen

Map no: 45

Harbour Yard
Chelsea Harbour SW10
Tel: 0171-351 7330

Cost: Alc £23. H/wine £9.50.
Cover charge £1
Credit cards: 1 2 3 4

Menu: *A la carte*
Times: Midday-Last L 3pm, 6.30pm-Last D midnight

is a breadwinner, popular, accessible and fabulously good value. The smart, vibrant harbourside location is reflected in the imaginative interior design.
 The menu is seasonally correct and runs to around 11 starters and main dishes. The range covers vichyssoise and smoked haddock with poached egg to spaghetti of langoustines with basil and guinea fowl en cocotte, but vegetarian dishes are not included. Desserts incline towards the French though most of the descriptions are in plain English. The cooking can be brilliant, as in a stunning parfait of chicken livers and foie gras, but most of it is plain enjoyable - a sumptuous risotto of squid ink, a satisfying confit of duck, and a silky smooth crème vanille. Inevitably, given the turn around of diners, some of the cooking just misses the mark: rubbery calamari with the aforementioned risotto, slightly overcooked cod and wishy-washy espresso have all been encountered.
 The £1 cover charge seems unnecessary, but to enjoy this quality of cooking for £25 per head is a remarkable opportunity, grab it while you can!
 The compact list of some 60 wines is representative of good growers and estates around the world. You may also ask to see a reserve list of fine wines.

Directions: From Lotts Road park in the 2nd (green) car park in Chelsea Harbour. Take the lift to the upper ground level, the restaurant is in a corner

Chefs: Tim Payne, Peter Ressell
Proprietors: Marco Pierre White, Michael Caine, Claudio Pulze

Seats: about 100
Additional: Children welcome Sat and Sun

Cantina del Ponte ❀

The café, part of Conran's riverside gastrodome, serves earthy style Italian peasant food. The frequently changing menu is enjoyable, if not the price. Parmesan and semolina gnocchi with tomato sauce, baked rump of lamb with garlic, rosemary and chick peas were all tasty at our inspection meal.

Cost: Alc £30. H/wine £8.95 ♀ Service inc. **Credit cards:** 1 2 3 4.
Additional: Children welcome; ◐ dishes
Directions: On the river front, south-east of Tower Bridge

Map no: G46
The Butlers Wharf Building
36c Shad Thames SE1
Tel: 0171-4035 403
Chef: Louis Loizia
Proprietors: Sir Terrance Conran, Joel Kissin, David Burke
Seats: 90
Times: Last L 3pm/D 11pm. Closed Sun eve, Good Fri, 4 days at Xmas

Capital ❀❀❀

A creative interpretation of classical European cuisine served in the refurbished restaurant of a charming small hotel

It is a pity, in one respect, that this hotel is so small as more people deserve to experience its charms. Not least of these is the excellent service provided by professional staff led by owner David Levin. At the time of our visit the restaurant was due to be completely re-designed, with structural alterations in addition to a change of decor and furnishings. However, space is limited, and although the restaurant feels in no way cramped, it is vital to book well in advance.
 Chef Philip Britten has been here since 1988 (he was formerly head chef at Chez Nico) and his cooking has matured. He offers classic European dishes with more than a touch of creativity. The two fixed-price three-course lunch menus have about three

Map no: 47
Basil Street, Knightsbridge SW3
Tel: 0171-589 5171

Cost: Alc £40; fixed-price L £22, fixed-price D £40. H/wine £10.50 ♀ Service inc
Credit cards: 1 2 3 4

Menus: A la carte, fixed-price lunch and dinner, bar menu

Times: Midday-Last L 2.30pm, /pm-Last D 11.15pm. Closed 25 Dec dinner
Chef: Philip Britten

items at each stage, a more extensive *carte* with a fish course (and a minimum charge), and a six-course fish menu. Vegetarians can be catered for although no suitable main courses generally appear on the menus.

At recent test meals our inspectors have sampled starters of tomato, olive oil and basil soup, which had a splendid spicy flavour, and thinly sliced seared scallops with a heady mix of aubergine, courgette and pimento with ginger and coriander. One inspector was intrigued by the sauce served with a rich confit of duck – its colour and sweetness achieved by the addition of blackberries. Full flavoured jointed French pigeon was served on a bed of spinach with caramelised shallots, a brunoise of vegetables and a highly scented cinnamon jus. A puff pastry version of tarte tatin proved a lovely light dessert, well caramelised and served with sauce anglaise, others might be bitter orange parfait with a confit of cooked kumquat, or a trilogy of chocolate desserts. The mainly French wine list is notable for a marvellous selection of good claret vintages, many in magnums and half bottles.

Directions: Between Harrods and Sloane Street. Nearest Tube – Knightsbridge

Proprietor: David Levin

Seats: 35. No cigars or pipes in restaurant. Air conditioned
Additional: Children welcome (not babies); ✪ dishes; Vegan/other diets by arrangement

Cecconi's ✹✹

A pricey but high quality, authentic Italian restaurant with a lively atmosphere

Italian cooking at its best can be savoured at this smart restaurant where the high prices do not seem to put off customers and tables are keenly sought after. The smartly dressed, attentive Italian waiters help to create a lively atmosphere in which to enjoy the skilful cooking of the eponymous chef, Signor Cecconi. Sauces are one of his strengths, and although these may lack some of the finesse of their classical counterparts, they are full of authentic flavour. A recent inspection meal began with cannelloni Cecconi, a well-made dish of light pasta and a tasty filling of finely minced meat with a cheese, cream and tomato sauce. Tender pieces of lightly cooked meat formed the basis of scallopine of veal capricciosa, a full-flavoured dish made with another creamy sauce, this time with tomatoes, mushrooms and red peppers. Fresh green spinach and evenly cooked sautée potatoes were served with the main course. That ever-popular Italian dessert, tiramisù, was light and moist, and filter coffee came with home-made petit fours. There's a good list of Italian wines, some of them a little overpriced.

Directions: Visible at end of Burlington Arcade. Nearest Tubes – Green Park, Piccadilly Circus

Map no: 49

5a Burlington Gardens W1
Tel: 0171-434 1509

Cost: *Alc* £40. Service charge 15%. Cover charge £2.50
Credit cards: 1 2 3 4

Menus: *A la carte*

Times: 12.30pm-Last L 2.30pm, 7.30pm-Last D 11.30pm. Closed Sat Lunch, all day Sun, BHs

Chef: E Cecconi
Proprietor: E Cecconi

Seats: 120. No-smoking area. No pipes. Air conditioned
Additional: Children welcome; ✪ dishes; other diets by prior arrangement

Chandni Restaurant ☉

☺ *A new chef has recently taken over in this smartly decorated restaurant and will retain the current menu which features familiar tandoori and Biryani favourites and specialities. Try Jheenga Chaat, spicy shrimps tossed with onions, tomatoes, lemon juice and mint sauce*

Additional: Children welcome; ❂ dishes
Directions: 5 minutes from Bromley South Station

Map no: 50
123-125 Masons Hill, Bromley
Tel: 0181-290 4447
Chef: Abdul Karim
Proprietor: Mr A K S Choudhury
Seats: 75
Times: Last L 3pm/D 11pm
Cost: Alc £19. No service charge
Credit cards: 1 2 3 4.

Chapter 11 ☉☉

☺ *A lively, modern restaurant off the Fulham Road serving an internatinal array of dishes at very fair prices*

Bright and vibrant colour greet diners at this lively modern restaurant just off the Fulham Road. In fine weather an attractive garden comes into its own and meals can be enjoyed al fresco; otherwise there's a choice of bar area for casual eating and a more formal dining section where large windows let in plenty of light. The cooking of chef Christopher Daynes is essentially modern English with an international flavour, and his *carte* offers an interesting choice of good-value dishes, with the price of the main course including a pudding. For starters the choice might include a nest of quails' eggs and mushroom duxelle with hollandaise sauce, goats' cheese soufflé with chargrilled radicchio, or fettucine with parsley, garlic and cream. Main dishes offer some interesting combinations, such as pan-fried baby squid stuffed with wild mushrooms and served with a honey and ginger sauce, grilled calf's liver with bacon, and grilled turbot with beurre blanc, roast hassleback potatoes and spinach. A wine list of over 50 reasonably-priced bottles has a few halves and covers the produce of several countries.

Directions: Hollywood Road is off the Fulham Road, opposite the hospital. Nearest Tube – West Brompton

Map no: 51
47 Hollywood Road SW10
Tel: 0171-351 1683

Cost: Alc £13.50. H/wine £8
Credit cards: 1 2 3

Menu: A la carte

Times: 7pm-Last D11.30pm.
Closed Sun, BHs

Chef: Christopher Daynes
Proprietor: John Brinkley

Seats: 60
Additional: Children permitted; ❂ dishes

Chelsea Hotel ☉

☺ *Home-made breads and herb risotto, bouillabaisse and blackened brill feature on the interesting Mediterranean menu of the brasserie-style restaurant. Dramatic modern decor, stylish ambiance and good value cooking all serve to make this an attractive venue*

Cost: Alc £20, fixed-price D £25. H/wine £9.95 ♀ Service exc
Credit cards: 1 2 3 4 5. **Additional:** Children welcome; ❂ dishes; Vegan/other diets on request
Directions: Two minutes from Knightsbridge Tube

Map no: 52
17-25 Sloane Street,
Knightsbridge SW1
Tel: 0171-235 4377
Chef: Thierry Aubugeau
Manager: Edwin Theobald
Seats: 90. No-smoking area. Air conditioned
Times: Last L 2.30pm/D 10.30pm

Chesterfield Hotel ❀❀

New and exciting modern cooking, with a continental flavour, is on the innovative menu of this pleasant Mayfair restaurant

Chef David Needes has introduced a new seasonal *carte*, and a new and exciting style of modern cooking, with a strong Mediterranean influence. Innovative combinations of flavour and texture result in a very enjoyable and exciting meal experience. Our inspector singled out for special praise the home-made spinach fettucine tossed with pancetta, olives and tomatoes. Followed by a very tender and pink calf's liver with red onions, horseradish mash and a very tasty marsala gravy. The traditional cod and chips with mushy peas shouldn't be overlooked either. As well as sticky toffee pudding with vanilla ice cream, the gratin of seasonal fruit glazed with a Kirsch sabayon was delightful. The service remains very attentive and helpful and a new wine list was being selected as we went to press. The Conservatory Buffet fixed-price lunch at £5.00 is very good value and available Monday to Friday.

Directions: Charles Street is situated at the bottom of Berkeley Square. Nearest Tube – Green Park

Map no: 53

35 Charles Street W1
Tel: 0171-491 2622

Chef: David Needes
Proprietor: Peter Wood

Seats: 60. No-smoking area. Air conditioned
Times: Last L 2pm/D 10pm (9.30pm Sat). Closed for L Sat & BH

Cost: *Alc* £25, fixed-price L £10.50. H/wine £12.95 ♀ No service charge
Credit cards: 1 2 3 4.

Additional: Children welcome; children's portions; ❂ dishes; Vegan/other diets on request

Chez Max ❀❀

Classical French cooking and confident service from a professional husband and wife team

Just a blur for many Waterloo-bound commuters, Surbiton is worth a closer look. Chez Max is as good a reason as any for lingering longer in this suburb trying hard to retain its Surrey leafiness. For thirteen years Vahé-Max Markarian and his wife have provided their customers with the classical cuisine of France, pepped up with some careful modern touches. Front-of-house arrangements are efficiently controlled by Margaret Markarian and carried out by charming French assistants. There are fixed-price menus for lunch (a choice of five starters and main courses) and dinner (four of each, plus desserts); the dinner *carte* is about twice as long. Pigeon salad with lardons, and spicy duck in filo pastry with apricot sauce are two typical starters while whole American sea-bass, baked with fennel and butter or roast rack of lamb, shallots, mint and white wine sauce could make ideal main courses. A trolley, groaning under a wealth of home-made desserts, included sorbets and ice creams, plus selected fresh French cheeses. The 80 or so French wines, with a fair sprinkling of respectable clarets and Burgundies, are reasonably priced.

Directions: From Surbiton station, along St James' Road, turn right into Maple Road, on opposite side of road

Map no: 54

85 Maple Road, Surbiton, Surrey
Tel: 0181-399 2365

Cost: *Alc* £21.20, fixed-price lunch £15.95, fixed-price dinner £11.95 (Tue-Fri), £14.95 (Sat). H/wine £12.50. Service exc
Credit cards: 1 2 3 4

Menus: *A la carte*, fixed-price lunch and dinner

Times: 12.30-Last L 2pm, 7.30pm-Last D 10pm. Lunch not served Sat. Closed Sun, Mon, 24-30 Dec

Chef: Max Markarian
Proprietors: Margaret and Max Makarian

Seats: 40. No cigars or pipes. Air conditioned
Additional: Children over 4 permitted; children's portions; ❂ dishes; other diets on request

Chez Max ❀❀

Friendly, helpful service enhance talented and imaginative cooking in a residential area

Partners Marc and Max Renzland and Graham Thomson have brought to this residential backwater, yet another sought after 'in place' to enjoy the experiences of talented and imaginative cooking. Formerly the La Croisette, the only part of which remains is the the tricky spiral staircase to the dining-room below. Service is attentive and the menu is personally explained by the amiable French waiters. Chef Bruce Poole, from The Square and Bibendum, has been delighting the customers with such highly successful dishes as the beautifully constructed terrine of a central foie gras, surrounded with an intensely flavoured and larded herb and chicken liver pâté, served with a slightly overcooked onion marmalade. Our inspector followed this with crusted, roast wild salmon on fresh spinach cooked in wine, with a plum tomato concasse. Desserts include an excellent example of the classic crème brûlée and all the patisserie is produced by the kitchen and includes some very tasty olive oil and 'fleur de sel' breads. The wine list includes some good domaine and estate wines from around the world.

Directions: Turn off the Fulham Road into Ifield Road, the restaurant is 500yds on the left

Map no: 54

168 Ifield Road, SW10
Tel: 0171-835 0874

Cost: Fixed-price dinner £23.50. H/wine £11.50. Corkage £3.50 min. Service exc
Credit cards: None taken

Menu: Fixed-price dinner

Times: 12.30pm-Last L 2.30pm, 7pm-Last D 11pm. Lunch not served Sat and Mon. Closed Sun, Easter, Xmas, BHs

Chef: Bruce Poole
Proprietors: Marc and Max Renzland, Graham Thomson

Additional: Children over 12 permitted. ✆ dishes on request

Chez Moi ❀❀

A loyal clientele appreciate fine cooking in this formal, long established restaurant

Having enjoyed the same ownership since 1967, it's not surprising that this restaurant continues to attract a long and very loyal list of international devotees. Run by partners, chef Richard Walton and Colin Smith, the restaurant has continued to improve over the years.

Chef Walton has introduced an oriental flair whilst retaining the long established popular dishes such as 'Oursins' Chez Moi, scampi, prawn and scallop 'urchins' rolled in angel hair noodles and deep fried, then served with 'Mostarda de Fruita', and four ways with lamb, minted, mustard, grilled or flattened. Our inspector thoroughly enjoyed an unusual 'Velluto Nero' with a sauce Parmesan boletus, squid ink cappelletti pastaf illed with fresh crab, and served on a cheese and very tasty wild mushroom sauce. He followed this with delightful small fresh and smoked salmon dumplings with an enjoyable creamy lobster sauce. The purée of carrot made with shredded ginger and honey was delightful . Desserts range from Moroccan filo pastries to hot pancakes. Service is rather formal, but very attentive. •

Directions: North side of Holland Park Avenue, opposite Kensington Hilton. Nearest Tube – Holland Park

Map no: D55

1 Addison Avenue W11
Tel: 0171 603 8267

Cost: *Alc* £25, fixed-price lunch £14. H/wine £8. Service exc
Credit cards: 1 2 3 4

Menus: *A la carte*, fixed-price lunch

Times: Midday-Last L 2pm, 7pm Last D 11pm. Closed Sat lunch, Sun, BHs

Chef: Richard Walton
Proprietors: Richard Walton, Colin Smith

Seats: 45. No pipes. Air conditioned
Additional: Children welcome; children's portions; ✆ dishes. Vegan/other diets on request

Chinon ✿✿✿

Modern French cuisine with a Mediterranean flavour served in the stylish surroundings of this friendly restaurant

Located in a residential area running parallel to Shepherds Bush Road, this establishment has a loyal clientele and attracts diners from the nearby BBC and the business community, local residents and those who simply enjoy good food - and that is guaranteed here.

Chef Jonathan Hayes cooks with real flair and understanding of his ingredients, which are of excellent quality and freshness. His modern menus include a handwritten *carte* and a good-value set menu popular at lunchtime. These offer a good choice of French dishes, many with a Mediterranean theme. On one occasion a filo pastry parcel of goats' cheese was brightly presented with a coleslaw-style garnish of apple and celeriac plus slivers of sun-dried tomato - full of wonderfully fresh and honest flavours. This was followed by venison, served in two thick slices in the shape of a tournedos with an excellent sauce and a selection of vegetables chosen by Jonathan to complement the dish. Cabbage leaves wrapped into a parcel with a tasty lardon filling were particularly enjoyable. Vegetarian main courses are not featured but can be provided by arrangement. The dessert, pear tart, was also good with deliciously light and evenly cooked pastry and thinly sliced glazed pears, accompanied by vanilla ice cream.

Service is provided by partner Barbara Deane, who has a charming manner and takes great care of her guests. The restaurant has a happy and relaxed atmosphere, and the walls are adorned with pictures, some the work of a talented local artist. At the time of our visit there were plans afoot to convert the downstairs area, formerly a dining room, into a lounge for pre- and after dinner drinks.

Directions: Richmond Way is off Rockley Road at Shepherds Bush. Nearest Tubes – Olympia or Shepherds Bush

Map no: T56

25 Richmond Way W14
Tel: 0171-602 5968

Cost: Alc £25. Wine £9.50 ♀
Service 12.5%
Credit cards: 1 2 3

Menus: A la carte

Times: 12.30pm-Last L 2pm, 6pm-Last D 10.30pm
Closed most BHs

Chef: J Jonathan Hayes
Proprietors: J J Hayes and Barbara Deane

Seats: 50. Air conditioned
Additional: Children over 10 permitted

Christopher's ✿✿

US grill-style food, including hamburgers, steaks and fries, from a range of menus in rather grand surroundings

A former Victorian casino, with a sweeping stone staircase and fresco-style stencilled walls, provides an incongruously grand setting for some typical American grill fare at Christopher's. Shellfish and seafood is flown in from Maine and fish from Florida. Smaller lobsters come from Scotland and the menu evolves around market availability. The home-made hamburgers are also worthy of note. Chef Adrian Searing previously worked in New York and has brought his experience to bear on this popular setting. There is a range of menus: Sunday brunch, lunch, theatre and dinner, plus a selection of simpler items from sandwiches to steaks in the downstairs café/bar. Vegetarians can also be accommodated. This year our inspector sampled crab cakes with red pepper mayo and rocket, followed by a favourite lunch dish of seared calf's liver with

Map no: 57

18 Wellington Street WC2
Tel: 0171-240 4222
Cost: Alc £28.50. Sunday brunch £12 (2 courses), £15.50. H/wine £12. Service exc
Credit Cards: 1 2 3 4 5

Menus: A la carte, fixed-price Sunday brunch, pre-theatre

Times: Midday-Last L 2.30pm, 6pm-Last D 11.45pm. Closed Sun eve, BHs, Xmas

Chef: Adrian Searing
Proprietors: Christopher Gilmour, Fernanda Mayne

sage and prosciutto. Home-made lemon tart completed the meal, with slightly undercooked pastry but a good lemon and lime filling. Wines have been carefully chosen and include vintage New and Old World, Christopher's Choice and a good selection from the USA.

Directions: Christopher's is situated on the right-hand side of Wellington Street, 100 yards from the Royal Opera House. Nearest Tube – Covent Garden

Seats: 120. No pipes or cigars
Additional: Children permitted; ❷ dishes; other diets on request

Churchill Inter-Continental ❀

☺ *Clementine's, the Churchill Inter-Continental's newly fashioned restaurant, is fairly informal in style offering inventive cuisine with a touch of the Mediterranean. Chef Idris Caldora makes good use of fresh seasonal ingredients, simply prepared and attractively presented*

Cost: Alc £18. H/wine £10 ♀ Service exc. **Credit cards:** 1 2 3 4 5
Additional: Children welcome; children's portions; ❷ dishes; Vegan/other diets on request
Directions: Situated at corner of Portman Square/Seymour Street within The Churchill Inter-Continental. Nearest Tube – Marble Arch

Map no: 58
30 Portman Square W1
Tel: 0171-486 5800
Chef: Idris Caldora
Proprietor: Inter-Continental.
Manager: Luciano Paris
Seats. 91. No smoking area Air conditioned
Times: Last L 3pm/D 11pm.
Closed Sat L

Chutney Mary ❀❀

'Forgotten foods' from the sub-continent in what is claimed to be the world's first Anglo-Indian restaurant

Wherever there were British in India, there were Chutney Marys – Indian women who adopted British style, upsetting their more conservative sisters. Today, the name applies to a popular, colonial-style Chelsea restaurant whose unusual menu reflects how cuisines fused during the Raj. Starters include 'Moong bhel puri', a version of Bombay's famous street food made with sprouted beans, freshly made chutneys and yoghurt dressing, salmon samosas and noodles Mandalay, with shredded chicken in a spiced coconut soup. One of the Anglo-Indian specialities is roast shank of lamb cooked with spices and ground sesame seeds, served with masala roast potatoes. Another is the tasty 'Country Captain' selected by our inspector – suprême of chicken braised with red chillis, almonds, raisins and spices and served with lemon rice. There are Goan curries such as green chicken and Mangalore prawn as well as more familiar Indian dishes. Desserts include spicy baked apple and sweet crispy samosas. The wine list is reasonably priced and coffee, Indian teas or infusions are also available.

Directions: On Kings Road, just after juction with Lots Road. Nos 22 or 11 bus. Nearest Tube – Fulham Broadway

Map no: L59
535 King's Road
Chelsea SW10
Tel: 0171-351 3113

Cost: Alc £21.50, buffet Sunday lunch £13.95, fixed-price dinner after 10pm Sun-Fri £10, £12.95. H/wine £8.95 ♀ Service 12.5%. Cover charge £1.50
Credit cards: 1 2 3 4 5

Menus: *A la carte* lunch and dinner, fixed-price Sunday buffet lunch, bar menu

Times: 12.30–Last L 2.30pm (3pm Sun), 7pm–Last D 11.30pm (10pm Sun)

Chef: Hardev Singh Bhatty
Proprietor: Chelsea Plaza
Manager: Joe Mirrelson

Seats: 110. No-smoking area; no cigars or pipes in restaurant. Air conditioned
Additional: Children welcome; ❷ dishes; other diets on request

Cibo ❋❋

A friendly and relaxed Italian restaurant serving robust dishes in pleasant surroundings

A bustling, friendly and relaxed atmosphere immediately betrays this restaurant as Italian, although the menu is different from the expected style, and significantly shorter. The cooking by new chef Ivan Pontel – recently arrived from Italy – is competent if perhaps a little unpolished, and seasoning is sometimes over-enthusiastic.

At a recent meal our inspector sampled a starter of 'spinaci in padella con salsiccia di cinghiale e funghi' – sautéed fresh spinach with small pieces of wild boar and wild mushrooms which had an unusually enjoyable flavour. A selection of grilled fish and shellfish came under the title of 'la nostra grigliata mista', including some tasty white fish, lobster and crayfish, served with earthy boiled potatoes and slightly soggy spinach. There was an excellent flavour to the tiramisù, a light and moist version of the popular Italian trifle, and freshly made filter coffee came with home-made petit fours. Service from staff in long white aprons is very attentive and efficient, and proprietor Gino Taddei is often to be found greeting guests in his cheerful manner and settling them at their tables.

Directions: Russell Gardens is a residential area off Holland Road. Nearest Tubes – Kensington (Olympia); Shepherds Bush

Map no: P60

3 Russell Gardens W14
Tel: 0171-371 6271

Cost: Alc £27.50, fixed-price lunch £12.50. H/wine £8.90. Service exc
Credit cards: 1 2 3 4

Menus: *A la carte*, fixed-price lunch

Times: Last L 2.30pm, Last D 11pm. Closed Sun eve, Easter, Xmas

Chef: Ivan Pontel
Proprietor: Gino Taddei

Seats: 55. Air conditioned
Additional: Children welcome; children's portions; ❂ dishes

City Miyama ❋

Stylish and businesslike, this popular Japanese restaurant features a Sushi bar and Teppan-yaki counter on the ground floor, while downstairs the dining room carte offers the usual range of Zensai, Sashimi, Suimono, fish and meat dishes. It's well worth asking the chef for recommendations

Cost: Alc from £20, fixed-price lunch from £17, fixed-price dinner from £25. H/wine £10. Service inc **Credit cards:** 1 2 3 4 5
Additional: Children welcome; children's menu/portions. ❂ menu; Vegan/other diets on request
Directions: From the Tourist Information Centre by the dome of St Paul's walk down the hill for 50yds, turn right under the arch. The restaurant is on the right. Nearest Tube – St Pauls, Blackfriars

Map no: 61

17 Godliman Street EC4
Tel: 0171-489 1937
Chef: Isao Ebina
Proprietor: Foray. Manager: Kikuo Furuya
Seats: 80. Air conditioned
Menus: *A la carte*, fixed-price lunch and dinner, pre-theatre
Times: Last L 2.30pm, Last D 10pm. Closed Sun, Xmas–New Year

Claridge's ❋❋

This famous Mayfair hotel's two restaurants offer stylish cooking in surroundings to match

Claridge's, 'Resort of Kings and Princes' (queens and princesses too, no doubt?), still provides hotel-keeping of the highest standard. It may not suit everyone's taste or pocket, of course, with its fully-liveried footmen and general opulence. Relatively informal dining is possible, though, in The Causerie restaurant, with its celebrated lunchtime smörgåsbord buffet, featuring 32 cold and two hot dishes. There is also a pre-

Map no: 62

Brook Street W1
Tel: 0171-629 8860

Cost: Alc £45. Fixed-price lunch from £21 (2 courses), fixed-price dinner from £35. Wine £15 ♀ Service inc
Credit cards: 1 2 3 4 5

Menus: *A la carte*; Sunday

theatre/supper menu, or you can eat from the *carte*. For dinner, you might prefer the Art-Deco main Restaurant, beginning, as our inspector did, with a prawn, scallop and crab-filled pasta parcel, or baked goat's cheese with pimento chutney, or maybe artichoke and lobster salad. On that occasion, he was happy with his saddle of hare, leaf spinach and plain potatoes, but a poor crème brûlée undid some of the earlier good work. The cheapest main course, at £17.50, is aiguillettes of wild duck with onions, mushrooms and red wine sauce and the dearest, at £28.00, is lobster fricassée with cardamom and couscous. Vegetables are extra. But Claridge's never was intended for bargain-hunters.

Directions: Two minutes from Bond Street Tube. From exit, turn into Davies Street

lunch, fixed-price lunch and dinner, pre-theatre
Times: 12.30–Last L 3pm, 7pm–Last D 11.15pm. Closed Sat lunch

Chef: Marjan Lesnik
Proprietor: The Savoy Group. Manager: Ronald F Jones
Seats: 140. No-smoking area; no pipes. Air conditioned
Additional: Children welcome; children's portions/menu; ◐ dishes; Vegan/other diets on request

Clarke's ❀❀❀

A long established restaurant with a reputation built on quality, offering a short lunch menu and a set dinner

Sally Clarke has been here for many years and her restaurant is very popular. She has created an individual style which has always been at the forefront of London cuisine. The ambience is informal but civilised and correct, and service is provided by knowledgeable and smartly groomed staff. The restaurant comprises a small but light ground floor room and an airy lower ground floor dining room with an open plan kitchen. There is a short menu at lunchtime, priced for two or three courses, and a set, no choice, four-course dinner. Guests can check the menu before booking, and Sally is happy to discuss dietary variations in advance, including vegetarian dishes. Eating here is a healthy experience, the portions are not intimidating and the principal cooking technique remains char-grilling, but most importantly the ingredients are superb. Quality is such a critical factor that the menu may be changed at the last minute if the produce is not up to scratch.

The style of cuisine has often been categorised as 'Californian', meaning perhaps that the excitement comes from the harmonious blending of the elements and the raw materials, sourced from around the world, are left to speak for themselves and not overwhelmed by their sauces. Our inspector sampled a warm tartlet of sliced leeks, spinach and salmon, pungently marinated with dill - fragrant and delicious. This was followed by succulent plump pigeon breasts with spring vegetables and pecans, and a rich, sharp- flavoured warm lemon soufflé. The breads are legendary (our inspector tasted mixed nut wholemeal and Parmesan), and are available for sale in the Clarke's shop next door. There is a strong selection of Californian wines on the reasonably priced wine list, several of which are available by the glass.

Directions: Situated at the Notting Hill end of Kensington Church Street. Nearest Tube – Notting Hill Gate

Map no: P63

124 Kensington Church Street
W8
Tel: 0171-221 9225

Cost: Fixed-price Lunch £22 (2 courses), £26; fixed-price dinner £37. H/wine £8 ♀ Service inc
Credit cards: 1 3

Menus: Fixed price lunch, no-choice four-course dinner

Times: 12.30–Last L 2pm, 7pm–Last D 10pm. Closed Sat, Sun, 4 days Easter, 2 weeks Summer and 10 days Xmas

Chef: Sally Clarke
Proprietor: Sally Clarke

Seats: 90. No-smoking area; no pipes or cigars. Air conditioned
Additional: Well-behaved children only. ◐ dishes; Vegan/other diets on request

Clifton-Ford Hotel ❀

Fresh and subtle flavours characterise the modern British cooking at the informal brasserie of this pleasant, centrally-sited hotel, where quality produce is used to great effect. A variety of home-made breads and well made pastry complements the dishes.

Cost: Alc £21.50 ⚲ Service exc
Credit cards: 1 2 3. **Additional:** Children welcome; ❂ dishes; Vegan/other diets on request
Directions: From New Cavendish Street follow the sign to Marble Arch, turn to Welbeck Street then turn first on the right. Nearest Tube – Marble Arch

Map no: 64
47 Welbeck Street W1
Tel: 0171-486 6600
Chef: Mark Dancer
Proprietors Doyle's. Restaurant Manager: Fabio Mattioli
Seats: 106. Air conditioned
Times: Last L 2.30pm/D 10pm. Closed Sat and Sun L; Xmas

The Connaught ❀❀❀

Classic French and British cooking impeccably served in the opulent surroundings of a fine hotel

Small but perfectly formed, the Connaught is the *pied-à-terre* in London of some of the world's most discerning travellers. It is a bastion of traditional hotel-keeping, managed by Paolo Zago for over 21 years, with caring and unobtrusive service provided by a myriad of staff. Richly polished mahogany is a feature of the main stairwell and also the restaurant, where attentive staff buzz about with apparent calm, serving the much acclaimed cuisine of chef Michel Bourdin. Many of the dishes are permanent fixtures of the daily menu, though some fine adjustments to the popular and classical dishes are not unknown. During the game season guests eat at the Connaught for little else, such is the quality and consistency of the cooking. There is also a grill room serving exactly the same food but in a more intimate environment, and a new fixed price menu, specialising in British-style food.

  Our inspector dined on Valentine's night, amid many doting couples, and sampled the 'Prelude Gourmande Valentin et Valentine', an artistic creation set on aspic jelly embedded with little hearts and a centrepiece of quail's egg with caviar in a light pastry case, along with a lobster and prawn mousse, smoked salmon roulade with salmon mousse, game terrine with pistachios and a pâté de foie gras - a great chance to experience a number of specialities. This was followed by 'Rendez-vous Amoureux en Surprise, sauce légère aux truffes du Perigord' - assorted fish including salmon, scallop, lobster, prawn and brill, in a bisque-like stock covered with golden pastry. The trifle and excellent bread and butter pudding should not be missed, the latter fully living up to expectations on this occasion.

Directions: On corner of Mount Street and Carlos Place, between Oxford Street and Hyde Park Lane. Nearest Tubes – Bond Street, Hyde Park Corner

Map no: 65
Carlos Place W1
Tel: 0171-499 7070

Cost: Alc £80, fixed-price £25
Credit cards: 1 2 3 4

Menus: *A la carte*, fixed-price

Chef: Michel Bourdin
Proprietor: P Zago

Seats: 75 (Restaurant), 35 (Grill Room). No smoking. Air conditioned
Additional: Some vegetarian dishes

The Copthorne Tara ❀

In a quiet Kensington cul-de-sac, but the Tara is lively and popular with business travellers and tourists. Cuisine in the smart Jerome K. Jerome restaurant is international with a strong English accent - medallions of lamb fillet, roast Gressingham duck and Dover sole are examples.

Cost: A/c from £28. H/wine £10.20. Service exc
Credit cards: 1 2 3 4 5. **Additional:** Children over 10 welcome; ❂ dishes
Directions: Situated on the ground floor of The Copthorne Tara Hotel. Two minutes from nearest Tube – High St Kensington

Map no: P66
Scarsdale Place, (off Wrights Lane) W8
Tel: 0171-937 7211
Chef: Klaus Hohenauer
Proprietor: Copthorne.
Manager: Desmond Kent
Seats: 40. No-smoking area. Air conditioned
Times: Last D 11.30pm. Closed Sun, BHs

The Criterion ❀❀

☺ *Beautifully stylish West End restaurant offering simple, carefully cooked Mediterranean food*

Piccadilly Circus provides a perfect backdrop for this famous restaurant which serves food throughout the day, including tea in the afternoon. The effect on entering is stunning, with marble walls and magnificent ceiling mosaics by Thomas Verity creating a stylish, spacious feel.

The food is pretty impressive too, and the varied and interesting menu shows off the quality ingredients and imaginative flair of chef Brian Baker to the full. Typical carefully-cooked dishes might include penne and mussels in fennel cream, and beef carpaccio with anchovy and olive salad for starters, and grilled tuna and mushroom chutney, or a vegetarian broccoli, mushroom and Parmesan tart as a main course. The *carte* doubles as a set menu, with a very good value two course option. Our inspector relished a simple Caesar salad and a very tasty thin crust pizza, followed by loin of lamb with cold green bean salad and a richly-made jus. Seasonal vegetables were full of freshness and flavour, and a generous sticky toffee pudding left the diner fully sated. Service is relaxed but attentive and polite, and the whole atmosphere makes this place a pleasure to visit.

Directions: South side of Piccadilly Circus next to Lilywhites and Criterion Theatre. Nearest Tube – Piccadilly Circus

Map no. 67
224 Piccadilly W1
Tel: 0171-925 0909

Cost: A/c £19, fixed-price L/D £10 ♀ Service exc
Credit cards: 1 2 3 4 5.

Chef: Brian Baker
Proprietor: Forte. Manageress: Jane Lunniss

Times: Last D 11.30pm. Closed Sun eve, Xmas

Chef: Brian Baker
Proprietor: Forte. Manageress: Jane Lunniss

Seats: 200. No pipes or cigars
Additional: Children permitted; ❂ dishes; other diets on request. Harpist on Sunday

Crowthers ❀❀

Good food and good value in a family-run restaurant offering French and Modern British cooking

It is unusual to see rösti on a menu in Britain although the Swiss are rather fond of fried shredded potato and serve it in many ways. As a partner for Crowthers' rib-eye steak and glazed shallots, it is ideal. Rösti apart, this warm, friendly restaurant goes in for French and Modern British cooking, menus changing periodically. The six starters included baked

Map no: 68

481 Upper Richmond Road West, East Sheen SW14
Tel: 0181-876 6372

Cost: Fixed-price lunch £14.75 (2 courses), £17.50; fixed-price dinner £15.85, £20.50. H/wine £8.50 ♀ Service exc
Credit cards: 1 3

fresh goat's cheese in toasted sesame seeds with tapénade croûtes and, as our inspector discovered, excellent smoked mackerel and spring onion fishcakes with hollandaise sauce. From the six main courses he chose pink, moist and tender best end of lamb with a Provençal herb crust in a redcurrant and rosemary sauce. Two other possibilities could be grilled monkfish with mixed peppers and herbs, and ragoût of sweetbreads and kidneys with a grain mustard sauce. Six desserts completed the picture, including sticky toffee pudding with hot butterscotch sauce and vanilla ice cream, three-chocolate parfait with raspberry purée, or grilled fruit gratin with Calvados sabayon. The wine list is short but adequate and reasonably priced. Expect a warm welcome and attentive service.

Directions: On South Circular between Sheen Lane and Clifford Avenue. Rail to Mortlake or 317 bus

Menus: Fixed-price lunch and dinner

Times: Midday–Last L 2pm, 7pm–Last D 10.30pm. Closed 1 week Xmas, 2 weeks Aug

Chefs: Philip Crowther, Justin Gellatly
Proprietor: Philip Crowther

Seats: 32. Smokers requested to consider other diners. Air conditioned
Additional: Children welcome; children's portions; ✿ dishes; other diets on request

Dan's ✿

An attractive wooden-floored Chelsea restaurant with an attentive staff offering a short, discerning menu and wine list. Recent dishes in the Anglo/French tradition include salpicon of salmon, guinea fowl with ginger and honey and iced nougat parfait; good value set-price meals, too.

Cost: Alc £24.50, fixed-price L/D £14 (2 courses), £16.50. H/wine £9.50 ♀ Service inc
Credit cards: 1 2 3
Directions: At the Kings Road end of Sydney Street. Nearest Tube – South Kensington

Map no: 69
119 Sydney Street SW3
Tel: 0171-352 2718
Chef: Thierry Rousseau
Proprietor: Dan Whitehead
Seats: 50
Times: Last L 2.30pm/D 10.30pm. Closed Sat L, Sun D, Xmas week, BHs

Daphne's ✿✿✿

A popular, recently extended Italian restaurant with a good atmosphere and an attractive menu

Mogens Tholstrup, the handsome young Danish owner, is clearly popular with the well-heeled ladies who patronise this exciting Italian restaurant in large numbers at lunchtime. In the evening it is even harder to get a table, so attractive is the cooking of head chef Edward Baines and his team. Despite uneven service, bordering on the off-hand and disorganised at times, there is a real buzz to eating at Daphne's, especially now it has been extended to include a room at the rear with plants and a glass-top ceiling.
  The *cartes* at both lunch and dinner are mostly Italian inspired, the evening menu being an extension of the lunchtime version. At dinner there are around 10 starters, including delightful deep-fried soft shell crab, oysters, and hot foie gras with polenta, lentils and balsamic blackberry sauce. Half-a-dozen salads are also offered, such as spinach, avocado and crispy bacon, or grilled goats' cheese with aubergine, peppers and radicchio. One or two items from the pasta and risotto section might tempt vegetarians, and this is followed by a small choice of fish or meat main courses. Our inspector described a

Map: 70

110-112 Draycott Avenue, SW3
Tel: 0171-584 6883

Cost: Alc lunch £22, Alc dinner £30

Menus: A la carte lunch and dinner

Chef: Edward Baines
Proprietor: Mogens Tholstrup

simple dish of spaghetti with fresh plum tomatoes and basil as probably the best he'd tasted in this country, and a main course of lamb shank with mashed potato also received acclaim. Naturally, occasional lapses occur, with under-seasoned vegetables and a chocolate pot that had failed to set, marring an otherwise excellent meal.

Side orders range from chips to zucchini fritters, and artichoke mash to grilled vegetables, and among the pudding choices, almond and plum tart with hot Amaretto cream, tiramisù, and crostata with apples are featured.

The wine list comprises two pages of reasonably price wine, with an excellent selection from Italy very much to the fore.

Directions: From South Kensington Tube turn left down Pelham Street, cross over Fulham Road, turn left then immediately right into Walton Street. After 100 yds continue ahead into Draycott Avenue. Daphne's is on the left

Dell'Ugo ✻✻

☺ *Light Mediterranean and earthier Tuscan coooking in a delicious balance at this lively Soho venue*

Map no: K71

56 Frith Street W1
Tel: 0171-734 8300

Situated in central Soho, this lively venue has a café-bar at street level, a bistro on the first floor and a restaurant above. The bistro and restaurant share a menu and the latter, despite its popularity, has a relaxing atmosphere, in contrast to the faster pace downstairs. The *carte*, plus daily-changing specials, embraces both light Mediterranean/Californian cooking and the robust dishes of Tuscany. A cream of garlic soup of smooth, even texture and mild but distinctive flavour was the highlight of a recent meal. In the following main course, a generous serving of roast potatoes and garlic cloves formed a not entirely appropriate base for pan fried bream with ginger and lime butter, though in contrast lamb shank with flageolet beans was perfectly balanced and well-presented. Appealing puddings have included ginger brûlée tart and a Tuscan cheesecake with baked tamarillos, which imparted a sharpness that blended well with the cheesy topping. All three floors are buzzing; service is capable with no sense of urgency and though one is encouraged to choose between two dinner sittings, this seems flexible.

Cost: A/c £18.50, fixed-price lunch/dinner £8.50, £10. H/wine £8.45. Service exc
Credit cards: 1 2 3 4

Menus: *A la carte*, fixed-price lunch and dinner

Times: Last L 3pm, Last D 12.15am. Ground floor open all day. Closed Sun, BHs

Chef: Mark Emberton
Proprietors: Simpsons of Cornhill Ltd. Anthony Worrall Thompson, Francesca Hazard

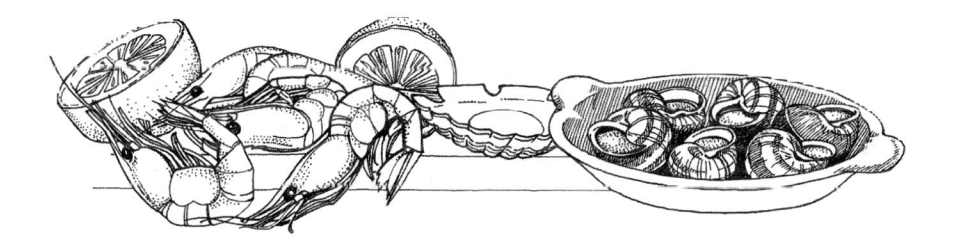

Seats: 200. No pipes or cigars. Air conditioned
Additional: Children welcome, children's portions; ❻ dishes; other diets on request

Directions: Nearest Tube – Leicester Square, Piccadilly. From Piccadilly go up Shaftesbury Avenue, turn into Wardour Street, right into Old Compton Street, left into Frith Street

The Dorchester, The Grill Room ❀❀❀

The Grill Room, with its Spanish decor and traditional English cooking, is now the Dorchester's premier restaurant

Undoubtedly one of the world's great hotels, and the chosen venue of many celebrities, royals and wealthy travellers, the Dorchester has a glow of opulence, from the foyer and Promenade, where afternoon tea can be taken, to the luxuriously appointed bedrooms. The Dorchester Bar is a popular meeting place with live jazz most evenings and excellent Italian food attracting a regular clientele. Opposite is the Grill Room, which remains much as it was when the hotel opened in 1931, richly decorated in the style of a Spanish palace. This is now their premier restaurant as their renowned Terrace has been set aside for private dining and Friday and Saturday night dinner dances, reviving a popular pursuit from former days.

In the Grill Room, chef Willi Elsener offers traditional English cooking based on mostly British ingredients. The *carte* is supplemented by a four-course fixed-price 'menu of the day', and a fixed-price three-course lunch. Starters include scrambled egg with smoked eel, black pudding with warm potato and bacon salad, and a lovely terrine of lamb, dense but with delicate flavours, studded with apricots and flavoured with rosemary. There is a choice of soups - brown onion soup with Guinness among them – followed by a fish and shell fish selection, which might feature grilled lobster with cardamom, herb and pepper butter. Vegetarian, low fat and other diets can be accommodated on request, although the dishes listed will be such as shepherd's pie or braised oxtail with vegetables. Breast of corn-fed chicken proved a bit of a disappointment on one occasion, the chicken being rather dry and the sauce over-reduced. To finish, a selection of perfectly kept cheese is offered, or a choice of pudding from the attractive trolley.

Directions: Two-thirds of the way down Park Lane, fronting a small island garden. Nearest Tube – Hyde Park

Map no: 72

Park Lane W1
Tel: 0171-629 8888

Cost: *Alc* £34.90, fixed-price lunch £23.50, fixed-price dinner £28. H/wine £16 ♀ Service exc
Credit cards: 1 2 3 4 5

Menus: *A la carte*, fixed-price lunch and dinner, Sunday lunch

Times: 12.30-Last L 2.30pm, 6pm-Last D 10.30pm

Chef: Willi Elsener
Proprietor: The Dorchester Hotel Ltd

Seats: 81. Air conditioned
Additional: Children welcome. ❖ menu; Vegan/other diets on request

The Dorchester, The Oriental ❀❀

Carefully cooked and rather expensive Chinese food for Western tastes, professionally served in elegant surroundings

The Oriental restaurant, another eating option at the Dorchester Hotel, must offer the most refined surroundings and service in London for the enjoyment of carefully cooked Cantonese dishes. Needless to say it is also very expensive. The restaurant is on two levels; three private dining rooms are on the ground floor with the main area directly above. This is an elegant room with silk hangings and porcelain. Much of the clientele is Western, so the menu features many of the usual combinations such as pork with cashew nuts and bamboo shoots. For the more adventurous, there is shark's fin and abalone imported directly from Hong Kong, and from among chef Simon Yung's recommendations there may be crisp, moist, roasted pigeon, with sweet pickled vegetable, directly from

Map no: 72

Park Lane W1
Tel: 0171-629 8888

Cost: Dim sum lunch £20, fixed-price lunch £22, fixed-price dinner £28. Wine £17.50 ♀ Service exc
Credit cards: 1 2 3 4 5

Menus: *A la carte*, Dim sum lunch, fixed-price lunch and dinner

Times: Midday-Last L 2.30pm, 7pm-Last D 11pm. Closed Sat lunch, Sun, Aug

among chef Simon Yung's recommendations there may be crisp, moist, roasted pigeon, with sweet pickled vegetable, lightly battered soft shell crab and eel with cinnamon blossom sauce. Interesting desserts include fried egg sponge doughnut, deep-fried water chestnut rolls, or a wobbly pudding of fresh mango. The Dorchester restaurants share the same wine list, outstanding in quality and choice with excellent vintages as far back as a 1929 Château Latour.

Directions: See Dorchester Grill Room

Chef: Simon Yung
Proprietor: The Dorchester Hotel Ltd
Seats: 71. No pipes. Air conditioned
Additional: ◊ menu

Downstairs at 190 Queensgate ◉◉◉

A lively and convivial place to eat, this mainly seafood restaurant offers accomplished cooking at reasonable prices

Another of Antony Worrall Thompson's restaurants, 'Downstairs ...' is popular and frequently busy, making it a necessity to book. He has a reputation for creating fun restaurants, and this is no exception. The menu offers a tempting variety of dishes with the emphasis on seafood. Prices are reasonable, cooking accomplished, and the results simply delicious. Worrall Thompson and head chef Harry Greenhalgh cook with great respect for the raw product and here the quality is first class.

The *carte* offers a choice of traditional appetisers, including rustic fish soup with crostini, rouille and Gruyère, and alternative appetisers, such as our inspector's roasted squash, onion and garlic soup with garlic and Brie toast – verdict excellent. Then there is a section of steamed shellfish dishes, eg marinière, or mussels/clams with chilli, coconut cream, lemon grass and lime leaves; and a selection of fishcakes, perhaps salmon on leaf spinach and sorrel sauce, or Thai oriental with spicy cucumber salad. The daily fish selection is served as traditional fish and chips, with beer batter, mushy peas and tartare sauce, or from the char-grill or steamer with a choice of accompaniments - perhaps hollandaise sauce, new potatoes and leaf spinach, or spicy lentils and Thai cabbage with wasabi butter sauce.

A few meat dishes are available, maybe peppered rump steak or chargrilled chicken, and a couple of vegetarian dishes, including tarte tatin of chicory with red chicory salad. There is a list of snacks - crostini, tapénade, tempura, and deep fried seafood, and a small dessert menu including lemon and lime tart, and chocolate delice with Drambuie ice cream.

Just about every country, including Moldavia, is represented on the reasonably priced wine list. The house wines are interesting and start at an amazing £8.50.

Directions: At the Hyde Park end of Queen's Gate, near the Royal Albert Hall. Nearest Tubes – High Street Kensington, South Kensington and Gloucester Road

Map: 73
190 Queen's Gate SW7
Tel: 0171-581 5666

Cost: Alc £24. H/wines from £8.50. Service exc
Credit cards: 1 2 3 4

Menu: A la carte

Times: 7pm-Last D midnight. Closed Sun, 3 days Xmas, BHs

Chef: Antony Worrall Thompson
Manager: Ian McKerracher

Seats: 70. Air conditioned
Additional: Children permitted.
◊ dishes; other diets on request

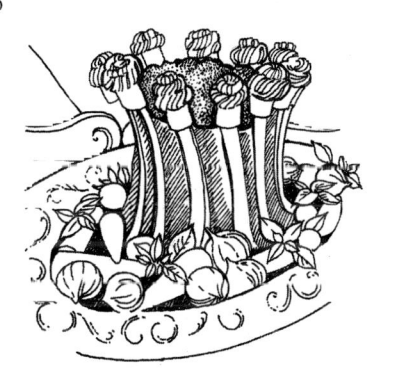

Drury Lane Moat House ✿

☺ *Well placed for theatreland and Covent Garden, this hotel offers smart public rooms including a comfortable bar and Maudie's restaurant. Despite the much shortened and simplified menus, Charles Cooper's food is interesting enough to fill the tables, with theatre-goers in particular.*

Cost: A/c £28, fixed-price lunch and dinner £13.45 (2 courses), £15.45. H/wine £11. Service exc. **Credit cards:** 1 2 3 4
Directions: On the corner of High Holborn and Drury Lane. Nearest Tubes – Holborn, Covent Garden

Map no: 74
10 Drury Lane WC2
Tel: 0171-836 6666
Chef: Charles Cooper
Proprietor: Queens Moat Houses. Manager: Oliver Sweeny
Seats: 75. No-smoking area. Air conditioned
Times: Last L 2.30pm/D 10.30pm. Closed for L Sat, Sun and BHs

The Eagle ✿

An atmospheric restaurant that can get somewhat smoky when it is busy as most dishes are chargrilled on the range in the bar – however this all adds to its charm. The blackboard menu changes daily and offers Mediterranean food including swordfish with salmariglio.

Cost: H/wine £7.90 ♀ **Credit cards:** None taken
Additional: Children welcome; children's portions; ❂ menu; other diets on request
Directions: On Farringdon Road, close to the junction with Roseberry Avenue (Mount Pleasant)

Map no: 75
159 Farringdon Road EC1
Tel: 0171-837 1353
Chef: David Eyre
Proprietors: Michael Belben, David Eyre
Seats: 50
Times: Last L 2.30pm/D 10.30pm. Closed Sat, Sun, 2/3 weeks at Xmas

Empress Garden ✿✿

Chinese food made from quality ingredients served in handsome surroundings

The opulence of these surroundings and some inflated prices lead to expectations about the food which are not always fulfilled. In typical Chinese style the number of dishes on the *carte* reaches well into the hundreds. There are several set menus ranging from expensive to much, much more, although two business lunches are well priced. In spite of the undoubted quality of the ingredients at a recent meal, however, the food was slightly disappointing, and some dishes lacked correct seasoning. Steamed fresh scallops got our inspector off to a good start, and turbot with preserved vegetables was still firm and white, with an unusual ginger and soy sauce. Aromatic crispy duck was meaty but not crisp, while broccoli with spicy salt arrived in a soggy state. The final tasted dish of stir-fried fillet of beef with fresh garlic and pine nuts was the highlight of the meal, and Chinese tea was above average. In spite of the problems there is plenty of choice here, including fresh fish like shark's fin, sea-bass and abalone, and vegetarians are well catered for. A good, mostly European, wine list with some very fine vintages.

Directions: Off Berkeley Square, opposite the Mayfair Hotel. Tube to Green Park or no 8 bus

Map no: E76
15-16 Berkeley Street W1
Tel: 0171-493 1381

Cost: A/c £31.50, fixed-price lunch £15, fixed-price dinner £30-£70. H/wine £12. Service charge 15%. Cover charge £1
Credit cards: 1 2 3 4 5

Menus: *A la carte*, fixed-price lunch and dinner

Times: Midday-Last L 2.30pm, 6.30pm-Last D 11.30pm. Closed Good Friday & Xmas

Chef: David Tam
Proprietors: Porchshire Ltd. Manager: Philip Wong

Seats: 150. Air conditioned
Additional: Children permitted; ❂ dishes; Vegan on request

English Garden ❀❀

English cooking prepared to a high standard and served in some of Chelsea's most stylish surroundings

Many restaurants could claim to be at the more fashionable end of the King's Road, near Sloane Square. Not all have flourished for seventeen years, though, as English Garden has. The two rooms – the extravagantly-draped Marble, and the Conservatory, with its splendid dried flowers – share the daily-changing *carte* and fixed-price lunch menu featuring mainly English dishes, some enhanced by judicious use of herbs and spices. A lunch starter could be warm monkfish mousse with smoked salmon sauce or goat's cheese salad with roasted pepper and spicy breadcrumbs. Main courses have included steamed sea-bass with fennel, and curry of lamb fillets with wild rice and tomato chutney. A recent meal confirmed that chef Brian Turner's standards remain high, judging by a crab mousse with ginger scallops and coriander starter and braised pheasant stuffed with duck's liver in a red wine sauce. There's a good selection of puddings, such as strawberry roly poly and rhubarb crumble with orange custard. France rules in the wine cellar but a few racks house German, Italian and Californian.

Directions: From Sloane Square turn right off the King's Road. At far end of Lincoln Street. Nearest Tube – Sloane Square

Map no: 77

10 Lincoln Street SW3
Tel: 0171-584 7272

Cost: A/c £28, fixed price lunch £14.75. Wine £9.50. ♀ Service exc

Credit cards: 1 2 3 4 5

Menus: *A la carte*, fixed-price lunch

Times: 12.30-Last L 2.30pm (Sun 2pm), 7.30pm-Last D 11.30pm (Sun & BHs 7pm-10pm). Closed Xmas

Chef: Brian Turner
Proprietor: Roger Wren

Seats: 85. Air conditioned
Additional: Children welcome; children's portions; ❶ dishes; Vegan/other diets on request

The English House ❀❀

Original and traditional English cooking in a friendly, intimate setting

As the name implies, the cooking at this intimate restaurant is solidly English, and the new chef, Australian Ian Waltisbuhl, is maintaining the highest standards. His own special style of cooking has brought many innovations to the cuisine, and the result is a seasonal *carte* offering interesting traditional and original dishes. Typical starters are warm chicken and Stilton mousse, and crab and smoked salmon parcels with whisky cream sauce, while main courses might include roast pigeon served on a celeriac and ginger pancake, or grilled fillet of beef stuffed with pickled walnut. Our inspector praised a rich duck and goose pâté with spiced plum chutney, followed by superbly cooked roast rack of new season's lamb with well-made pesto and a light and tasty brown sauce. Chocolate sponge with hot chocolate sauce was a delicious dessert. Vegetarian dishes like whole globe artichoke glazed with mustard hollandaise, and grilled red vegetables on a bed of rice with toasted spring onion, also appear on the menu. Meticulous service comes from smartly dressed, friendly waiters, and the blackcurrant-patterned background provides a fresh and colourful setting.

Directions: On Milner Street at the intersection with Harker Street and Rawlings Street. Nearest Tube – South Kensington

Map no: 78

3 Milner Street SW3
Tel: 0171-584 3002

Cost: A/c £28, fixed-price lunch £14.75, fixed-price Sun dinner £19.75. H/wine £9.50. Service exc

Credit cards: 1 2 3 4 5

Menus: *A la carte* (Mon-Sat), fixed-price lunch, fixed-price Sun dinner

Times: 12.30-Last L 2.30pm (2pm Sun & BHs), 7.30pm-Last D 11.30pm (10pm Sun & BHs). Closed 26 Dec

Chef: Ian Waltisbuhl
Proprietor: Roger Wren

Seats: 28, 26. No-smoking area
Additional: Children permitted; ❶ dishes

Enoteca ❀❀

Good southern Italian cooking in a warm, friendly atmosphere

Ugly office blocks loom over Putney High Street, dwarfing the parish church. Inside Enoteca, however, you can forget about architecture and concentrate on good southern Italian cooking in unpretentious surroundings. Owner Giuseppe Turi changes his menu every four weeks and there are also blackboard specials and vegetarian dishes. A starter might be 'Cotecchino con lenticchie', Italian sausage served hot on a bed of lentils with a touch of chilli and garlic, or 'Bresaola con ricotta alla griglia', cured northern beef served with grilled Ricotta, rocket and Tuscan olive oil. Then, perhaps, a main course of fillet of salmon with a crust of herbs, a touch of chilli (again) and served with leeks and potatoes, or 'Coniglio in salmi con verdura caramellata', rabbit marinated in red wine, cooked in its own juices and served with caramelised vegetables. The menu suggests a specific wine for each dish, but there are nearly fifty to choose from. Weight-watchers *could* pass on the desserts, but they'd miss a treat, especially the 'Torta di riso', a moist cake of rice, toasted almonds, pine nuts and dried fruit, served with orange sauce.

Directions: Tube to Putney Bridge or buses 74, 220 and 22

Map no: 79

Putney High Street SW15
Tel: 0181-785 4449

Cost: *A/c* £23, fixed-price lunch £6.50, £9.50. Wine £8. Service exc
Credit cards: 1 2 3 4

Menus: *A la carte*, fixed-price lunch

Times: 12.30–Last L 3pm, 7pm–Last D 11.30pm. Closed Sat lunch, Sun and 1 week at Xmas

Chef: P Pezzolesi
Proprietor: G Turi

Seats: 40 (45 in function room). No pipes or cigars
Additional: Children welcome. ❂ dishes; other diets on request

Fifth Floor at Harvey Nichols ❀❀

A stylish in-store restaurant where it is as trendy to be seen as it is to eat

When *Absolutely Fabulous*'s Patsy seeks refuge in Harvey Nic's she is likely to prefer the bar and its clientele to the restaurant. Here, in its hangar-like void, decor and lighting compete for minimalist effect, accentuating the near-palpable vibrancy as aproned waiting staff dash around. When not dashing they hover, while the smart and wealthy from Belgravia and South Ken. animatedly discuss whether to start with shredded duck confit, langoustine frittata or radicchio and red wine risotto. Should they follow with braised faggots or steamed dorade with ginger, or choose from the vegetarian menu?

Regrettably, none of our inspector's dishes worked perfectly. His salt cod fritters were tasty, crisp and smooth but the bland aubergine cream added nothing. The texture and colour of the pan-fried calfs' liver suggested it was not the best quality and, while the five varieties of wild mushroom were fine, they were spoilt by very poor puy lentils. The fig roulade was pretty but somehow it had lost its fig flavour. The Big wine list includes all the wines available in the shop and the price-ordered Little offers most by the glass.

Directions: On the Knightsbridge corner of Sloane Street. Nearest Tube – Knightsbridge

Map no: 80

Knightsbridge SW1
Tel: 0171-235 5250

Cost: *A/c* dinner £25.50, fixed-price lunch and dinner £17.50 (2 courses), £21.50. Wine £9.50 ♀ Service charge 12.5%
Credit cards: 1 2 3 4 5

Menus: *A la carte*, fixed-price lunch and dinner, pre-theatre, bar menu

Times: Midday–Last L 3pm (Sat 3.30pm), 6.30pm–Last D 11.30pm. Closed Sun, Xmas

Chef: Henry Harris
Proprietors: Harvey Nichols. Manager: Edward Hyde

Seats: 110. No pipes. Air conditioned
Additional: Children welcome; children's portions; ❂ menu; other diets on request

Forum ❀

☺ *The formal Ashburn restaurant on the first floor of this 27-storey hotel (the tallest in London) adds a Mediterranean flavour to essentially Modern British cooking with good flavour and fresh texture. On Sundays the hotel has a Jazz Brunch day.*

Cost: Alc £21.25, fixed-price D £22.50, £31.50 (with 3 wines). Wine £13 ♀ Service inc. **Credit cards:** 1 2 3 4 5. **Additional:** No children under 5; children's portions. ❂ dishes; Vegan/other diets on request

Map no: 81
97 Cromwell Road SW7
Tel: 0171-370 5757
Chef: Roy Thompson
Proprietor: Inter-Continental Hotels
Seats: 42. No-smoking area. Air conditioned
Times: 6pm-Last D 10.30pm.
Closed Sun, Mon, Easter, Aug, 1 Jan

Four Seasons ❀❀❀❀

Inspired cooking, drawing excitingly on a French birthright for dishes that are sometimes touched with genius

The exterior of the Four Seasons hotel is not memorable, but within, all is refined luxury, culminating in the Four Seasons Restaurant which is on such a different plane from the hotel's alternative, Lanes, that comparison would be absurd. Jean-Christophe Novelli is the latest talent to join the Park Lane drain, following Nico Ladenis and Marco Pierre White. Although he may draw his inspiration from his native France - he comes from Arras - his is a genuinely creative imagination. When he uses 'à ma façon' to describe a dish, your palate should tingle with anticipation. His 'blanquette de crustaces aux pointes de vanille "à ma façon"' was a sublime marriage of textures and tastes, combining baby squid tentacles, mouth-melting scallops and full-flavoured langoustines in an ambrosial vanilla-infused sauce. Even more distinctive flavours and textures met and enhanced one another in a dish of sea-bass stuffed with fresh-tasting scallop mousse set on a robust tapénade from which radiated finest mange-touts. As if this were not enough, at the other end of the plate, a baby aubergine topped with intense tomato paste and set out with asparagus tips added yet another dimension to a daring and successful creation.

For another inspector, an escabeche of prawns and tiny sweet vegetables in an audacious beetroot oil could not have been improved, and an Assiette du boucher showed just what a skilled artist can do with heartily stuffed calf's trotter, braised oxtail and calves' tails served with creamed celeriac and a rich but not over-reduced sauce. Slices of calves' tongue and poached brains came in a separate bowl in a strong broth. Not a dish for those of feeble appetite. Desserts have not been above criticism, however, in our inspectors' experience of a rather too eggy clafoutis and an over-caramelised tarte tatin with undercooked pastry.

The long and impressive wine list starts with a dozen or so carefully selected house wines from £14 to £30. The list is particularly strong on France; five vintages of Château Latour, including 1961, are offered.

Directions: At the west end of Piccadilly on Hyde Park Corner, which is the nearest Tube

Map no: N82

Hamilton Place, Park Lane W1
Tel: 0171-499 0888

Cost: Alc £44, fixed-price lunch £25-£28, Dinner Surprise £45. H/wine from £14 ♀ Service inc
Credit cards: 1 2 3 4 5

Menus: A la carte, Sunday lunch, Dinner Surprise

Times: 12.30-Last L 3pm, 7pm-Last D 10.30pm

Chef: Jean-Christophe Novelli
Proprietors: Four Seasons/Regent Hotels & Resorts

Seats: 50-55 No pipes. Air conditioned
Additional: Children welcome; ❂ dishes; Vegan/other diets on request. Alternative cuisine: low calorie, low cholesterol, low sodium

The Fox Reformed ✵

☺ *A very popular wine bar and restaurant with a blackboard menu changed according to market availability. There is a range of good value dishes, including Bresaola, thin slices of Italian beef served with sweet peppers in virgin olive oil and poached salmon with a creamed white wine sauce.*

Costs: Alc £14.50. H/wine £7.35. No service charge. **Credit cards:** 1 3
Additional: Children welcome; childen's portions; ❍ dishes
Directions: Opposite the junction with Woodlea Road

Map no: 83
176 Stoke Newington Church Street N16
Tel: 0171-254 5975
Chef: Paul Harper
Proprietors: Robbie and Carol Richards
Seats: 40
Times: Last L 2pm/D 10.30pm. Closed Xmas

French House Dining Room ✵

☺ *A very popular pub with a regularly changing carte. Despite the name, neither the chef, the staff nor the menu are French. In fact, the menu is modern English with slight Continental influences. Good food, including vegetarian dishes, at very reasonable prices for this area*

Cost: Alc £16. Wine £8.95
Directions: Turn into Dean Street, off Shaftesbury Avenue, restaurant is on the right

Map no: 84
49 Dean Street W1
Tel: 0171-437 2477
Chef: Fergus Henderson
Proprietors: Margot Clayton, Fergus Henderson, Jon Spiteri
Times: L and D served Mon to Sat. Closed Sun

Fulham Road Restaurant ✵✵✵

A fashionable new restaurant serving an original range of modern British/Irish cooking

Stephen Bull has installed Richard Corrigan as head chef in this his third and latest London restaurant and, to judge by its popularity (open seven days a week to include a good-value Sunday lunch), it is likely to prove his most successful. The restaurant comprises two adjoining rooms – light and modern, with a predominantly pale yellow theme setting off black and white banquettes and black and white prints. The soothing effect this creates is enhanced by first class service. The smart clientele are attracted primarily by Richard Corrigan's cooking, served at rather exclusive prices. Some Italian and Asian influences are evident, but his style can best be described as modern British/Irish.

At lunchtime there is a short, well-priced menu , although the *carte* gives more reign to Corrigan's ideas and originality. Not all his creations succeed, notably a too garlicky sauce accompanying some delicious roast scallops with creamed noodles. Desserts, too, have yet to match the standard of the rest of the meal. Bread and coffee are good though, and starters first class. These might include a tartare of veal, lemon and garlic, a fine twice-baked Cheddar soufflé with pousse and rocket, or a ravioli of suckling pig with wild mushroom consommé – the variety of choice is considerable. Fish figures strongly among the main courses and the originality extends to lamb as rump steak burgers, stuffed rabbit leg wrapped in cured ham, and faggots of pig's head with black pudding and red cabbage. Vegetarian dishes are not featured but can be provided on request. To finish there might be 'drunken brioche

Map no: 85
257-259 Fulham Road SW3
Tel: 0171 351 7823

Cost: Alc £27, fixed-price lunch £14.50 (2 courses), £17.50. H/wine £10.50 ♀ Service exc
Credit cards: 1 2 3 5

Menus: *A la carte*, fixed-price lunch, Sunday lunch

Times: Midday-Last L 2.30pm, Last D 11pm. Closed 1 week Xmas, BHs

Chef: Richard Corrigan
Proprietor: Stephen Bull

Seats: 80. No pipes or cigars. Air conditioned
Additional: Children welcome; children's portions. ❍ dishes; Vegan/other diets on request

and butter' pudding, ices and sorbets, or a selection of farmhouse cheeses.

Most of the best regions in the world are well represented by the 90-odd wines on the list. Most are priced at under £40.

Directions: From Michelin Building continue south-west along Fulham Road for 0.75 miles. Situated on the left near the Royal Marsen Hospital

Fung Shing ✿✿

☺ *Welcoming, homely Chinese restaurant serving interesting combinations of ingredients with subtle flavours*

Fish features fairly heavily on the extended *carte* at this friendly Chinese restaurant, but all of the dishes served here have the same hallmark of clear, subtle flavours and interesting combinations. There is evident good use of fresh ingredients, especially herbs, and the results are tantalising on the palate and satisfying on the stomach. Our inspector began a recent meal with a a very small portion of subtly flavoured crispy aromatic duck, followed by three main courses and some nicely seasoned boiled rice: beef with black bean and chilli was tender with an excellent flavour and a strong sauce, while eel with coriander was a tasty stir-fried dish with garlic, ginger and bamboo shoots resting on shredded prawn crackers. There was a good texture but only a light flavour to freshly steamed sea-bass. Seasonal vegetables included garlicky spinach, and fresh orange pieces were served at intervals. A choice of chef's specials on the *carte* include double-boiled fluffy shark's fin and crispy fried intestine. Smart, friendly staff offer a vigilant service, and there's a homely, family atmosphere.

Map no: 86
15 Lisle Street WC2
Tel: 0171-437 1539

Cost: *Alc* £18, fixed-price lunch and dinner from £11. H/wine £8.50. Service exc
Credit cards: 1 2 3 4

Menus: *A la carte*; fixed-price lunch and dinner

Times: Midday-Last D 11.30pm. Closed 24-26 Dec

Chef: Kwun Fu
Proprietor: Yan Fook Jim

Seats: 85. Air conditioned
Additional: Children welcome. ❷ dishes; Vegan on request

Directions: Between Leicester Square Tube and the Swiss Centre

Gay Hussar ✿

One of the most reliable London restaurants. Chef Lazlo Holecz's fixed-price menu at lunch and excellent value carte offers as a starter Disznó Sajt, pressed boar's head, and as a main course Hortobagyi Palacsinta, pancake stuffed with goulash and served with creamed spinach.

Cost: *Alc* £25, fixed-price L £16. H.wine £9.40. Service inc
Credit cards: 1 2 3 4 5. **Additional:** Children welcome; children's portions. ❷ dishes
Directions: Off Soho Square. Nearest Tube – Tottenham Court Road

Map no: M87
2 Greek Street W1
Tel: 0171-437 0973
Chef: Lazlo Holecz
Proprietor: Bela Molnar
Seats: 70. Air conditioned
Times: Last L 2.30pm/D 10.45

Gilbert's ✿✿

☺ *Simple, well-prepared British cooking in a small, friendly restaurant in museumland*

Proceeds from The Great Exhibition of 1851 were used to buy land south of the Hyde Park site. Exhibition Road, with its

Map no: 88
2 Exhibition Road SW7
Tel: 0171-589 8947

Cost: Fixed-price lunch £9.50 (2 courses), £13.50/dinner £14.50

museums, colleges and cultural institutes, was part of the subsequent development. Today, after traipsing round the V & A, one can revive at Gilbert's, courtesy of owner/chef Julia Chalkley and her straightforward yet creative British cooking. She offers a two-course, fixed-price menu with starters like Moroccan carrot salad or Roquefort-filled crêpe (£2.00 supplement) and main courses of spinach and saffron tart, and sauté of veal with Seville orange and cream. Our inspector chose succulent mussels served without shells in a cheese and cream sauce, and brochette of lightly-grilled sirloin with small butter mushrooms in a mustardy sauce. The monthly-changing menu has a rising price scale for lunch, pre-theatre (between 6 and 7 pm) and dinner, inclusive of olives, home-made bread, vegetables or salad in each case. Desserts include a selection of unpasteurised British cheeses. Descriptions of the well-chosen wines are simple but informative. There's complimentary home-made fudge too.

(2 courses), £18.50. H/wine £8.90 ♀ Service exc

Menu: fixed-price lunch and dinner, pre-theatre

Times: 12.30pm-Last L 2pm, 6pm-Last D 10.15pm. Closed Sat, Sun

Chef: Julia Chalkley
Proprietors: Julia Chalkley

Seats: 32. No pipes or cigars. Air conditioned
Additional: Children permitted; ◐ dishes

Directions: Near to Victoria & Albert Museum and Science and Natural History Museums. Nearest Tube – South Kensington

Good Earth Restaurant ✺

☺ *A bright modern Chinese restaurant with helpful and efficient service. The menu covers a number of regions, but the majority of dishes are Pekinese and Cantonese. Look for Cantonese roast duck and beef in oyster sauce. Sauces were noted as being particularly flavoursome*

Map no: 89
143-145 Broadway
Mill Hill NW7
Tel: 0181-959 7011
Chef: Ah Chiu
Proprietor: Joe Chan
Seats: 100. Air conditioned
Times: Last L 2.30pm. Last D 11.30pm Closed 24-27 Dec

Cost: Alc £15, fixed-price L £7.90 (1 course), £9.95; fixed-price D £17. H/wine £7.50 ♀ Service charge 15%
Credit cards: 1 2 3 4 5. **Additional:** Children welcome. ◐ menu
Directions: On Mill Hill Circus

Good Earth Restaurant ✺

☺ *A good choice of familiar dishes from various Chinese regions is available at this bright restaurant in the busy Brompton Road. Recommended choices include beef in oyster sauce, fish in lemon cream sauce, and the popular crispy duck. Smartly dressed staff are attentive and efficient.*

Map no: 90
233 Brompton Road SW3
Tel: 0171-584 3658
Chef: Ah Tak
Proprietors: Chris Tan, Stephen Ko
Seats: 160. Air conditioned
Times: Midday–Last D 11.30pm. Closed 24-28 Dec

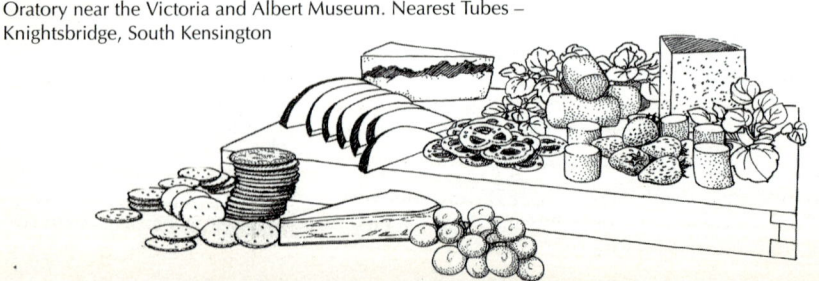

Cost: Alc £15, fixed-price L £7.95, £9.95/D £17. H/wine £7.50 ♀ Service charge 15%. **Credit Cards:** 1 2 3 4 5. **Additional:** Children welcome; ◐ menu
Directions: Five minutes from Harrods, opposite the Brompton Oratory near the Victoria and Albert Museum. Nearest Tubes – Knightsbridge, South Kensington

Gopal's ❋

☺ One of the 'Khaas baat', or specialities of the house, is 'Mutton Xacutti', lamb cooked with coconut, vinegar and rare spices, from Goa. Or there are 'Samundar ki godh se', dishes from the sea shore, as well as lamb dishes, poultry dishes and vegetarian dishes. A bright, attractive place.

Cost: Alc £17. Service exc. Cover charge £1. **Credit cards:** 1 2 3
Additional: Children welcome. ◐ dishes
Directions: Soho. Nearest Tubes – Leicester Square, Tottenham Court Road, Piccadilly Circus

Map no: C91
12 Bateman Street W1
Tel: 0171-434 0840
Chef: Mr N P Pittal
Proprietor: Mr N P Pittal
Seats: 50. Air conditioned
Times: Last L 2.45pm/D 11.15pm. Closed Xmas

Goring ❋❋

A fine traditional hotel with caring, friendly staff and imaginative classical European cooking

A traditional hotel which has been run by the same family for over 80 years, Goring offers a consistency which makes it attractive to regular guests and newcomers alike. Another reason for a visit is to sample the fine food of chef John Elliott, whose cooking follows the same ethos as the hotel and offers traditional dishes with modern touches. In the elegant dining room guests are invited by charming staff to peruse the fixed-price menus which include daily specials and a few recommended wines to complement the food.

There was an imaginative approach to the dishes sampled by our inspector, like salad of warm peppered monkfish with a surprisingly chilled sweet pepper sauce, and chicken and mushrooms in puff pastry - a delicious main dish of fine moist chicken breast with strongly-flavoured wild mushrooms and a faultless aromatic Madeira sauce. Apple tart with caramel ice cream was a chunky dessert with lots of syrup that tasted much better than it looked. Braised oxtail, saddle of hare or skate wing with capers have also been offered, and vegetarians are catered for with main dishes like vegetable curry with basmati rice.

Directions: Beeston Place is off Grosvenor Gardens, two minutes' walk from Victoria Station

Map no: 92

Beeston Place, Grosvenor Gardens SW1
Tel: 0171-396 9000

Cost: Fixed-price lunch £16.50 (2 courses), £19.50, fixed-price dinner £25. H/wine £14 ♀
Service exc
Credit cards: 1 2 3 4

Menus: Sunday lunch, fixed-price lunch and dinner, pre-theatre, bar menu

Times: Last L 2.30pm, Last D 10pm
Chef: John Elliott
Proprietor: George E Goring
Manager: William A Cowpe

Seats: 70. No pipes in restaurant
Additional: Children welcome; children's portions; ◐ dishes; Vegan/other diets on request.

Great Nepalese Restaurant ❋

☺ The menu does not change in this small but comfortable restaurant specialising in Nepalese cooking. Typical dishes are 'Masco-Bara', black lentil pancakes freshly cooked, well spiced and served with a light curry sauce, and 'Dumba curry' a moist tender lamb in a hottish sauce.

Cost: Alc £11. Fixed-price L £5.50/D £10.50. H/wine £6.25 (carafe). Service inc. **Credit cards:** 1 2 3 4 **Additional:** Children welcome; children's portions; ◐ menu
Directions: East side of Euston Station. Nearest Tube – Euston

Map no: 93
48 Eversholt Street NW1
Tel: 0171-388 6737
Chef: Masuk
Proprietor: G Manandhar.
Managers: Raju and Kiran Manandhar
Seats: 48
Times: Last L 2.45pm/D 11.45pm. Closed Xmas

Greek Valley ❀❀

☺ *A Greek-Cypriot restaurant that believes firmly in high standards of cooking and service*

Even back street tavernas in Piraeus or Nicosia can outclass some of London's rather dull Greek-Cypriot restaurants. But the Greek Valley successfully manages to invigorate the more predictable dishes such as houmus, tabouleh and beef stifado, as well as offer greater variety and more authenticity than many of its metropolitan competitors. 'Melitzanosalata' is a creamy aubergine dip and 'Loukanika', also a starter, are spicy pork sausages - a little chewy when our inspector visited – marinated in red wine and flavoured with coriander. Two people or more may begin with a 'meze' of cold starters and grilled dishes served with Greek salad and rice. There's good old 'Kleftiko', of course, but another lamb dish is 'Souvlaki apo arni', skewered with onions, peppers and mushrooms; there is also a chicken equivalent. Fish dishes include fried squid and 'Gharithes yiouvetsi', Mediterranean prawns baked in a special tomato sauce with feta cheese and served with rice. Vegetarians have a reasonable choice. Our inspector thought his baklava a good example of this typical Greco-Turkish dessert. All the wines are Greek or Cypriot.

Directions: Off Finchley Road, near Abbey Road. Nearest Tube – Swiss Cottage

Map no: 94

130 Boundary Road
St. John's Wood NW8
Tel: 0171-624 3217

Cost: *A/c* £11.75, fixed-price dinner £7.95 (3 courses), £10. Wine £6.50. Service exc
Credit cards: 1 3

Menus: *A la carte*, fixed-price dinner, pre-theatre

Times: 6pm-Last D midnight. Closed L

Chef: Peter Bosnic
Proprietors: Peter and Effie Bosnic

Seats: 62-75. Partially air conditioned
Additional: Children welcome; some children's portions. ❷ dishes; Vegan dishes on request

The Greenhouse ❀❀❀

Traditional British dishes with a modern interpretation served in a lively atmosphere at reasonable prices

A friendly, exuberant and incredibly busy restaurant, The Greenhouse is a tiny oasis of greenery amongst many stone buildings in a maze of narrow Mayfair streets, where, incidentally, it is very difficult to park. Its attractive courtyard of plants and trees leads to the semi-basement room. The bustling staff, closely packed tables and lively atmosphere are reminiscent of a school dining room, and the menus tap into the same nostalgic vein with salmon fishcakes, fillet of cod, braised oxtail, grilled calfs' liver, and onion and parsley tart. Gary Rhodes has long been an exponent of British dishes, imaginatively modernised, often by combining them with interesting European flavours. The cod is served with Italian Pecorino cheese-flavoured mashed potato, and skate with potato and red pepper salad with French Bayonne ham. Vegetarian dishes are also always available.

The menus offer a fixed-price lunch, a set dinner, a six-course fish dinner, and a *carte* with a minimum charge and dishes with varying supplementary charges. The cost is an important factor in the restaurant's success - much less than one would expect to pay for comparable quality elsewhere.

Our inspector ordered at the table, where he was offered an aperitif and bread. His meal began with 'mushroom and cep pancake', an understated title for a superb dish comprising five paper thin pancakes with much thicker layers of mushroom

Map no: 95

27a Hay's Mews W1
Tel: 0171-589 5171

Cost: *A/c* £30 (min charge per head), fixed-price lunch £22, £25, fixed-price dinner £40. Service inc
Credit cards: 1 2 3 4

Menus: *A la carte*, fixed-price lunch and dinner, bar menu

Times: Midday–Last L 2.30pm, 7.30pm–Last D 11.15pm

Chef: Gary Rhodes
Proprietor: Capital Hotels.
Manager: David Levin

Seats: 100. No cigars or pipes in restaurant. Air conditioned
Additional: Children welcome. ❷ dishes.

duxelle – rich and spirited – served in a wedge shaped portion. Grilled calfs' liver followed, with mashed potato, a rasher of smoked bacon, and a well reduced red wine sauce with lots of onions. For pudding, he chose crispy apple fritters with a good vanilla ice cream and apricot sauce.

Directions: Between the back of The Dorchester and Berkeley Square. Nearest Tube – Knightsbridge

Grosvenor House, Pavilion ❀❀

☺ *A relaxedModern English cooking at one of London's most exclusive addresses, plus an good Italian alternative*

A high profile hotel with an impressive Lutyens-designed facade, the Grosvenor is built on the largest possible scale, with 454 bedrooms and a staggering range of banqueting and function suites, plus its own shops and leisure club. The main restaurant is the Pavilion, where Sean Davies has developed an easy-going brasserie-style menu which changes little between lunch and dinner. A winter meal began with duck rillettes, without the promised onion marmalade, followed by boneless braised oxtail, nicely cooked, wrapped in Parma ham and served in a satisfyingly rich sauce. Vegetables included forked mashed potatoes with plenty of flavour (but quite a few lumps) and good leaf spinach. The meal concluded with crème brûlée and espresso coffee, the coffee being especially recommended. Vegetarian dishes may not appear on the menu but can be provided on request. The snappy, good-value wine list is a notable feature, with lots of decent wines by the glass.

The hotel's second restaurant, Pasta Vino, is styled after an Italian trattoria, serving fresh pasta and other traditional dishes with a good choice of Italian wines.

Directions: Just inside Parkland entrance of Grosvenor House. Nearest Tube – Marble Arch

Map no: 96

Park Lane W1
Tel: 0171-499 6363

Cost: A/c £15, fixed-price lunch £13.50. Wine £8.50 ♀ Service exc
Credit cards: 1 2 3 4 5

Menus: A la carte, Sunday lunch, fixed-price lunch, pre-theatre, bar menu

Times: 12.30–Last L 2.30pm, 6.30pm–Last D 10.30pm

Chef: Sean Davies
Proprietor: Forte. Manager: Ian Jenner

Seats: 130. No-smoking area. No pipes or cigars. Air conditioned
Additional: Children welcome; children's portions; Vegan/other diets on request

The Halkin ❀❀

Armani-suited waiters provide the service in elegant surroundings in a quiet Belgravia street

Discreetly tucked away near Hyde Park Corner is a strikingly contemporary luxury hotel with an intimate bar and a marble-floored, Italianate restaurant. Here, chef Stefano Cavallini offers classic regional dishes from his fixed-price menus, and from the *carte*. Recent recommendations include 'Sfogliata ai funghi porcini e sogliole', a feuillette of cep mushrooms and poached sole, served with a refined jus. The 'Ravioli d'anatra con verza e fegato grasso', pasta parcels filled with duck mousse on a bed of savoy cabbage with sautéed fois gras, was very good, but the highlight of one meal was a thinly sliced, intensely flavoured saddle of hare with grapes and a fine reduction of its blood blended with wine from the Veneto. Pumpkin purée with Amaretto and spinach, sultanas and pine kernels accompanied

Map no: 97

Halkin Street, Belgravia SW1
Tel: 0171-333 1234

Cost: A/c dinner £35, fixed-price lunch £19.50 (2 courses), £26. Wine £16 ♀ (dessert). Service inc
Credit cards: 1 2 3 4 5

Menus: A la carte, fixed-price lunch, bar menu

Times: 12.30pm-Last L 2.30pm, 7pm-Last D 11pm (10pm Sun). Closed Sat & Sun lunch

it well. Do leave room and time for desserts, though, especially if you want poppy-seed soufflé with a Kirsch sauce, since it takes half an hour to prepare. Or try stuffed dates with white chocolate mousse and satsuma salad. Wines from most of Italy north of Naples and a stunning French selection are available.

Directions: 300 yards from Hyde Park Corner between Grosvenor Place and Belgrave Square. Nearest Tube – Knightsbridge

Chef: Stefano Cavallini
Manager: Nicholas Rettie

Seats: 45/50. No cigars or pipes in dining room. Air conditioned
Additional: Children welcome; ✪ dishes; Vegan on request

The Hampshire ✿✿

The Hampshire has a comfortable and formal dining room. The menu covers plain grills, British favourites (casserole of pheasant) and international ideas (red mullet with Cajun spices). The cooking shows deft touches and sound technique and meals finish well with an appetising trolley of desserts.

Cost: Alc £35, fixed-price L £19.50/D £27.50. H/wine £13.50. Service inc. **Credit cards:** 1 2 3 4 5. **Additional:** Children welcome, children's portions. ✪ dishes; Vegan/other diets on request

Map no: 98
Leicester Square WC2
Tel: 0171-839 9399

Chef: Colin Button
Proprietor: Radisson Edwardian.
Manager: G Wafflart
Seats: 60. No-smoking area. Air conditioned
Times: Last L 2.30pm, Last D 11pm

Harbour City ✿

☺ *A busy and exciting restaurant in the heart of China Town. The choice on the menu is overwhelming with 88 varieties of Dim Sum. The chef's speciality menu includes braised aubergine in garlic sauce but – vegetarians beware – it contained diced pork.*

Cost: Alc £20, fixed-price D £10.50. H/wine £7.50. Service exc
Credit Cards: 1 2 3 4
Additional: Children welcome; ✪ dishes
Directions: At the Newport Place end of Gerrard Street. Nearest Tubes – Leicester Square, Piccadilly

Map no: 99
46 Gerrard Street W1
Tel: 0171-439 7859
Chef: Hing Lee
Proprietors: Mrs Kitty Lee
Seats: 160. Air conditioned
Times: Midday-Last D 11.15pm. Closed 24/25 Dec

Harvey's ✿✿✿

An eclectic range of dishes in the modern style served in a sunny restaurant overlooking the common

Harvey's, formerly Marco Pierre White's establishment, is a sunny, shop-fronted restaurant overlooking the common where one can eat and watch the world go by. The interior is crisp and white, with smart and efficient service in the French manner - the atmosphere of the place completely unaffected by its previous illustrious incumbent. Chef Mark Williamson's cooking is evolving, and he plans to incorporate more recipes from the Orient into his well established and essentially modern British repertoire.

The menu, priced for two courses plus optional dessert, is sensibly sized and straightforward, allowing the kitchen to produce the best of fresh food. A cosmopolitan range of starters includes sautéed gambas, noodle rösti and melted Mozzarella; sushi roll, vegetable tempura and sashimi with soy sauce; and crab pakora with julienne of vegetables. Our

Map no: 100

2 Bellevue Road Wandsworth Common SW17

Tel: 0181-672 0114

Cost: Fixed-price lunch from £13.50; dinner from £17.50. H/wine £8.50. Service exc
Credit cards: 1 2 3 4 5

Menus: Fixed-price lunch and dinner

Times: Midday-Last L 2pm, 7pm-Last D 10.30pm. Lunch not served Sat. Closed Sun, 2 weeks Aug/Sep
Chef: Mark Williamson

inspector chose seared baby scallops served with a black bean, ginger, garlic, grain mustard and home-made soy sauce. This was followed by rump of lamb, fresh, pink and full of flavour, with a veal stock and cooking jus reduction, served with baked aubergine and diced vegetables cooked together in virgin olive oil. Other options could be sesame-coated halibut with curried couscous and pimento sauce, and rabbit casserole with confit of peppers, olives and grilled polenta. Vegetarian dishes are always available but notice is preferred. To finish there is a choice of desserts, cheeses, or a savoury such as four cheese Welsh rarebit. Our inspector opted for apple tart layered with caramelised sliced apples, and crème fraîche flavoured with a cider reduction and topped with pistachio nuts.

The wine list is compact and easy to read, with a good choice of bottles available at under £25.

Proprietor: Tracey Evans

Seats: 55. Air conditioned
Additional: Children welcome; children's portions; ◐ dishes

Directions: Bellevue Road joins Trinity Road and Nightingale Lane

Hilaire ❀❀❀

A popular restaurant where good value modern European cooking is offered from a range of menus

A restaurant so full on a Monday night must have something to commend it, and our inspector certainly enjoyed his dinner. On finishing, he introduced himself to the ever attentive manager Bernard Esseul and was surprised to learn that chef-proprietor Bryan Webb was away and that assistant chef Denise Dunn was responsible for the cooking. The kitchen had certainly been left in capable hands, with standards carefully maintained.

The restaurant, on two floors in busy Old Brompton Road, has undergone a major extension and refurbishment during the summer of 1994, to provide a larger seating area and a fresh country appearance. The style of cooking is modern European with some Mediterranean flavours, such as sun-dried tomatoes, and Mascarpone, but Welsh influences are also evident and laverbread and Welsh lamb are equally popular. The *carte* offers a wide price range, and there is a modestly priced two-course lunch menu. A good-value fixed-price dinner menu is also available, and a two-course supper menu after 9.30pm.

Our inspector's meal began with a dish of interesting appetisers, a tiny sausage of Caerphilly cheese and herbs, a strong herb and garlic meatball and strips of deep-fried seaweed. He chose calfs' liver, bacon and foie gras pâté as a starter. A dense, well balanced terrine, low in fat, served with dressed lamb's lettuce and a smooth chutney. Lightly cooked, sliced duck breast followed, set on a heap of green lentils garnished with diced apple and served with a sauce of well reduced cider and duck stock. The dessert – orange caramel cream – had a good strong orange flavour and our inspector relished every morsel. There is an attractive selection of house wines available by the glass. Other wines are grouped according to their style and there are lots of half bottles.

Map no: 101

68 Old Brompton Road SW7
Tel: 0171-584 8993

Cost: A/c £28, fixed-price lunch £12.50, fixed-price dinner £16 (2 courses), £25. H/wine £10 ♀ Service exc
Credit cards: 1 2 3 4 5

Menus: *A la carte*, fixed-price lunch and dinner

Times: 12.30-Last L 2.30pm, 6.30pm-Last D 11.30pm. Lunch not served Sat. Closed Sun, BHs

Chef: Bryan Webb
Proprietors: Bryan Webb, Dick Pyle

Seats: 50. No pipes or cigars. Air conditioned
Additional: Children welcome; children's portions/menu; ◐ dishes; Vegan/other diets on request.

Directions: On the north side of Old Brompton Road, 300 yds west of South Kensington Tube

Holiday Inn Mayfair ❁

Between Piccadilly and Berkeley Square, this elegant and intimate hotel restaurant offers a choice of ambitious menus. Ingredients are good quality and successful combinations have included artichoke and rocket soup and fillet of hake with spinach and sweet pepper sauce.

Cost: Alc £36, fixed-price £21.75
Additional: ◊ dish
Directions: Between Piccadilly and Berkeley Square

Map no: E102
3 Berkeley Street W1
Tel: 0171-493 8282
Chef: Barry Brewington
Proprietors: Holiday Inn
Times: Last L 2.30pm/D 11pm. Closed Sat L

Hotel Conrad ❁❁

Classy food in an upmarket riverside hotel restaurant with a rags-to-riches tale to tell

Once upon a time, there was a run-down area of old docks, railway sidings and scrapyards. Then developers saw the site's potential and today Chelsea Harbour is one of London's most stylish developments and prestigious addresses. It's a long time since a humble coal barge entered what is now the marina, filled these days with sleeker-hulled craft. This is the view diners get in the Brasserie Restaurant where Chef Peter Brennan offers a short, but imaginative *carte* and a limited-choice, fixed-price menu. Our inspector was more than content with a shellfish linguine and Thai sweet and sour sauce, followed by warmed smoked salmon on savoy cabbage with lentils and then by poached fillet of beef with ginger and horseradish sauce, spinach pyramid and rösti. Finally, a warm soup of fruits with a spicy sabayon (the French version of zabaglione) and crisp palmier cake - a good mix of textures and tastes. Staff are smart, plentiful and generally cheerful. Don't forget that this is a hotel restaurant, so it is best to book to secure a table among an international collection of fellow-diners.

Directions: Chelsea Harbour, overlooking marina

Map no: L103

Chelsea Harbour SW10
Tel: 0171-823 3000

Cost: Alc £30, fixed-price £22. Service exc
Credit cards: 1 2 3 4

Menus: *A la carte*, fixed-price

Times: Open daily

Chef: Peter Brennan
Proprietors: Hilton

Additional: Children welcome; ◊ on request

Hotel Inter-Continental, Le Soufflé ❁❁❁

Traditional French cuisine in a smart modern hotel, where the house speciality is, of course, soufflés

On Hyde Park Corner, overlooking the park, Le Soufflé is an integral part of the modern five-star Hotel Inter-Continental. The restaurant is spacious and elegant, and the service impeccable. Chef Peter Kromberg presents an impressively long *carte* of traditional, mainly French cuisine, written in French with English descriptions. There is also 'Le Choix du Chef', a set menu priced for four or seven courses, and a daily fixed-price three-course lunch. As one might expect, soufflés are something of a house speciality. Among the starters, the *carte* offers lobster soufflé, baked in its shell and served on a

Map no: 104

1 Hamilton Place, Hyde Park Corner W1
Tel: 0171-409 3131

Cost: Fixed-price lunch £27.50, fixed-price dinner £37.50 (4 courses), £43. H/wine £14.50 ♀ Service exc
Credit cards: 1 2 3 4 5

Menus: *A la carte*, Sunday lunch, fixed-price lunch and dinner, bar menu

bed of lobster with Americaine sauce, and a spinach and Tête de Moine cheese soufflé with a softly boiled quail's egg in the middle. Four of the eight desserts are sweet soufflés, including the specially light, seasonal 'Soufflé du Chef'.

The *carte* provides several vegetarian starters and a main course comprising a puff pastry and walnut case filled with seasonal vegetables and a light cep mushroom and herb sauce. There is also a 'healthy heart' symbol denoting dishes that are low in fat and calories but high in fibre.

At a test dinner, following an appetiser of oxtail terrine, our inspector opted for 'Arlequin de Pâtes Fraîches aux Morilles', a selection of coloured pasta with wild mushrooms and a beautifully flavoured sauce of the same. The main course dish, succulent medallions of lamb, was cooked pink and served with a jus that, slightly overpowered by garlic, lost its promised fresh ginger flavour. The hot 'Soufflé à la Poire Williams', served with Williams Pear ice cream and wild cranberries, had only the mildest pear flavour.

The mainly French wine list is clear and straightforward, starting with several wines at around £15 a bottle. There are some excellent Burgundies and some rare vintages of claret.

Directions: On Hyde Park Corner. Nearest Tube – Hyde Park Corner

Times: 12.30-Last L 3.30pm (Sun midday/4pm), 7.30pm–Last D 10.30pm (Sat 11.15pm). Closed Sat lunch, Sun dinner, Aug

Chef: Peter Kromberg
Proprietors: Inter-Continental.
Manager: Josef Lanser

Seats: 80. No-smoking area. No pipes. Air conditioned
Additional: Children permitted; ❤ dishes; Vegan/other diets by arrangement

Hudsons ❀

A very English restaurant, which has recently changed its name and is now decorated with a Sherlock Holmes motif. The menu offers simple cuisine, including old favourites such as bubble and squeak and main courses like Professor Moriarty's Chicken also follow this Victorian theme.

Map no: 105
239 Baker Street NW1
Tel: 0171-935 3130
Chefs: Andrew Bailey, Mark Stapley

Directions: 200 hundred metres north of Baker Street Tube

Hyatt Carlton Tower ❀❀

Accomplished French cooking in relaxed, well-run surroundings

Situated in the heart of Knightsbridge, this busy international hotel offers splendid views of Cadogan Gardens and south London from its upper storeys. Within, three venues serve a variety of eating options to the mainly business clientele: light meals and refreshments in the Chinoiserie lounge, straightforward prime cuts of meat, poultry and fish in the Rib Room – which also features a very popular cocktail bar – and, in the Chelsea Room, serious French cooking of a more flamboyant character. Here, chef Bernard Gaume continues to cook with top class ingredients and finds some success.

An enjoyable inspection visit began with a tasty seafood terrine (though the choice of bread rolls was uncharacteristically disappointing), followed by good crab sausages, although the astringent lime dressing added a jarring note. As a main course, two succulent fillet steaks were served with shallot sauce to one side and bordelaise to the other; though both these were very successful, the raw shallot garnish

Map no: 106
Cadogan Place SW1
Tel: 0171-235 1234

Cost: *A/c* £28, fixed-price lunch £22.50, fixed-price dinner £29.50. Wine £14.50 ♀ Service inc
Credit cards: 1 2 3 4

Menus: *A la carte*, Sunday lunch, fixed-price lunch and dinner, bar menu

Times: 12.30-Last L 2.45pm, 6.30pm-Last D 11.15pm. Closed 1-3 Jan

Chef: Bernard Gaume
Managers: Michael Davidson, John Healy, Patricia Smerdon

was less so. After a crème brûlée from the trolley the meal ended on a high note with good espresso coffee and impressive petit fours.

Directions: On Cadogan Place adjacent to Sloane Street. Nearest Tube – Piccadilly

Seats: 96. Air conditioned
Additional: Children permitted before 7.30pm; children's portions; Vegan/other diets on request. Pianist in evenings

The Hyde Park, The Park Room ✤✤

A choice of Italian influenced menus offered in the elegant restaurant of Forte's premier British hotel

This splendid Edwardian hotel, the Forte British flagship, is in a fine location just where Knightsbride meets Hyde Park, offering some splendid views. Stylish public areas include the high ceilinged lobby and the Ferrari Lounge, which has the relaxed air of a genteel country house. There are two contrasting restaurants: The Restaurant (see separate, entry), featuring the outstanding cuisine of Marco Pierre White, a five-rosette establishment, and the elegant Park Room, now with Guiseppe Sistito at the helm.

The food in the latter is still Italian influenced, but no less so than in the past, and is offered from a lunch menu priced from one to four courses, and a four-course fixed-price dinner menu in addition to the *carte*. The style of cooking is light and the results pleasing. At a test meal this year our inspector sampled a good spinach and guinea fowl risotto, then chicken stuffed with wild mushrooms and served with a little jus, followed by a choice from the appealing desert trolley. Vegetarian and other special diets can also be accommodated on request. A short wine list, strong on Italian wines, is available.

Directions: Nearest Tube – Knightsbridge

Map no: 107

Knightsbridge SW1
Tel: 0171-235 2000

Cost: *A/c* £40, fixed-price lunch £14.50 (1 course), £19, £21.50, £25; fixed-price dinner £29.50. H/wine £16.50. Service exc
Credit cards: 1 2 3 4 5

Menus: *A la carte*, fixed-price lunch/dinner, pre-theatre, bar

Times: 12.30-Last L 2.30pm, 7.30pm-Last D 11pm (10pm Sun)

Chef: Giuseppe Sistito
Proprietor: Forte

Seats: 80. No-smoking area; no pipes. Air conditioned
Additional: Children welcome;· children's portions; ❶ dishes; Vegan/other diets on request

Imperial City ✤

☺ *Ken Hom advises this Chinese restaurant in a converted wine cellar undeneath the Royal Exchange. A limited menu, but flavoursome regional dishes from Shanghai, Peking and Szechuan, offering relief from the area's ubiquitous sandwich bars. Freindly service from traditionally-dressed waitresses.*

Cost: Fixed-price L/D £13.90 (3 courses), £18.90, £24.80. Wine £8.50 ♀ Service exc
Credit cards: 1 2 3 4 5. **Additional:** Children welcome; ❶ dishes
Directions: Royal Exchange is off Cornhill. Nearest Tube – Bank

Map no: 108
Royal Exchange, Cornhill EC3
Tel: 0171-626-3437
Chef: K L Tan
Proprietor: Thai Restaurants Ltd.
Manager: Nick Lee
Seats: 180. Air conditioned
Times: 11.30am–Last D 8.30pm. Closed Sat, Sun, Xmas, 1 Jan & BHs

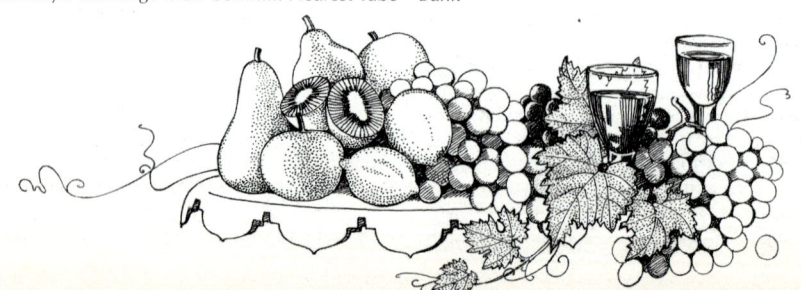

Indian Connoisseurs ☻

☺ *An unchanged menu of North Indian cuisine is presented at this small but cosy restaurant. This includes tandoori and biryani dishes, and sections of regional cuisine, seafood, and even game in season, such as tandoori pheasant and venison bhoona. Meat and vegetarian thalis (set meals) are listed*

Cost: Fixed-price L £6.50, fixed-price D £10.50. H/wine £5.95
Credit cards: 1 2 3 4. **Additional:** Children permitted; ◐ dishes; Vegan/other diets on request
Directions: From Paddington Station, go along Praed Street towards St Mary's Hospital. Opposite the main gate is Norfolk Place

Map no: 109
8 Norfolk Place W2
Tel: 0171-402 3299
Chef: Kabir Miah
Proprietor: Azizur Rahman
Seats: 40. no-smoking area. No pipes or cigars. Air conditioned
Times: Last L 2.20pm/D 11.50pm. Closed Xmas

The Ivy ☻☻☻

A theatreland restaurant with a lively atmosphere, serving a varied menu of international brasserie-style food

The Ivy is a thriving restaurant conveniently placed for theatreland and consequently popular for pre- and after theatre dining, the business community dominating at lunch. It occupies a corner site opposite the Ambassador Theatre, and has lattice windows with coloured glass, an inviting interior of wood panelling and good table appointments. The atmosphere is comfortably lively, and the attentive service is supervised by friendly maître d'hôtel 'Fernando'.

Executive chef Mark Hix and head chef Des McDonald present a varied menu of international brasserie-style food with modern European and traditional English influences. The menu allows for great flexibility with many dishes available as starters or main courses under the headings Seafood, Hors d'oeuvre, Soups, Eggs & Pasta, Fish, Roasts & Grills, Entrées, and Savouries & Desserts. Vegetarian dishes are always available, mostly in the Egg & Pasta category.

A recent visit proved enjoyable, with starters of intensely flavoured wild mushroom risotto, and basil gnocchi with shaved Parmesan and olive oil (both available in main course portions). The main courses chosen were braised knuckle of lamb, enhanced by a good herb cooking sauce and the contrasting texture of a delicate couscous, and pan-fried fillet of skate with black butter, lemon and capers. One inspector particularly enjoyed the tender fresh young vegetables, having forgotten just how good they can taste, but the highlight of his meal was the rich chocolate pudding soufflé, with a sponge base, soufflé topping and delicious top quality melted chocolate inside. The compact wine list is carefully chosen, and shows a good balance of European and New World wines. As London prices go, our inspectors considered this an overall good value meal.

Directions: West Street runs betweeen Monmouth Street and Shaftesbury Avenue. Nearest Tube – Leicester Square

Map no: 110
1 West Street
Covent Garden WC2
Tel: 0171-836 4751

Cost: A/c £22, fixed-price lunch £12.50 (Sat and Sun only). H/wine from £8.50 ♀ Service exc. Cover charge
Credit cards: 1 2 3 4 5

Menus: *A la carte*, fixed-price lunch Sat and Sun

Times: Midday–Last L 3pm, Last D midnight. Closed from dinner 24-26 Dec, August BH and BH lunches

Chefs: Mark Hix, Des McDonald
Proprietors: Jeremy King, Christopher Corbin

Seats: 110. Air conditioned
Additional: Children welcome.
◐ dishes; other diets on request

Jimmy Beez ❀❀

☺ *Simple, unfussy and honest food in a relaxed, friendly restaurant with weekend music*

An interesting young crowd frequents this lively restaurant during the week, making way for mainly local families at weekends, while the quality of the food stands out at any time. The cooking is refreshingly uncomplicated, with chef Simon Smith producing an interesting array of eclectic dishes from fresh ingredients. Food is served all day from separate lunch and dinner *cartes*, with a brunch menu proving popular at weekends. Our inspector enjoyed the relaxed and chatty atmosphere as well as a recent meal: wholemeal and white baguette served warm with delicious tapénade and olives to start, with goat's cheese tarte tatin topped with potato and a vivid splash of red peppers making an unusual full-flavoured dish. Calfs' liver was carefully cooked and served with prize-winning crispy spinach, lightly fried with a topping of sesame seeds. Sticky toffee pudding with lots of toffee sauce and caramel flavour was an acclaimed dessert, and good cappuccino and espresso coffee are just two of the hot drinks available. New York club steak, chargrilled chicken and baked rack of lamb are some of the other choices available.

Directions: From Notting Hill Gate Tube turn into Portobello Rd. Restaurant 1 mile down on left between Oxford and Cambridge Gardens

Map no: 111

303 Portobello Road W10
Tel: 0181-964 9100

Cost: *Alc* £18. Wine £7.75.
Service exc
Credit cards: 1 2 3

Menus: *A la carte*,
Saturday/Sunday Brunch

Times: Last L 5.30pm, Last D 11pm. Closed 1 week Xmas

Chef: Simon Smith
Proprietor: James Breslaw

Seats: 48. No pipes or cigars.
Partially air conditioned
Additional: Children welcome; children's portions; ❍ dishes; Vegan/other diets on request

Jin ❀

☺ *At Jin, much of the attraction is the do-it-yourself barbecues set within each table. The cuisine is South Korean, and sesame is the dominant flavour. Diners can enjoy a good Bulgogi, a Korean speciality, slices of beef marinated in soy sauce, sugar, garlic, ginger and pear*

Directions: Few minutes away from Soho Square and Shaftesbury Avenue in Piccadilly. Nearest Tube - Tottenham Court Road

Map no: C112
6 Bateman Street W1
Tel: 0171-734 0908
Seats: 80. Air conditioned
Times: Last L 2.30pm/D 11pm.
Closed Sat L,Sun, BHs
Cost: *Alc* £16. Service 12.5%
Credit cards: 1 2 3 4.
Additional: Children welcome

Kai Mayfair ❀❀

An elegantly expensive Chinese restaurant serving whimsically named dishes in an exclusive location

Smilingly hospitable staff greet guests at this rather expensive Chinese restaurant, located among the smart shops behind Park Lane. Service is formal, as befits the elegant surroundings and high prices. The lengthy menu offers exotic and interesting dishes, such as the Whims and Fancies of the Empress, the Bones of the Mayfair Dragon and Buddha jumps over the Wall (without any further explanation!). The 'Foods of China' menu is divided into sections: hot starters, cold starters, sharks' fin, duck, abalone and so on, and includes the more standard items sampled by our inspector - crispy aromatic duck, shredded beef with chilli, and chicken with cashew nuts. These all proved to be

Map no: 113

65 South Audley Street W1
Tel: 0171-493 8988

Cost: *Alc* £30. Wine £13.
Service charge (optional) 15%.
Cover charge £2
Credit cards: 1 2 3 4 5

Menu: *A la carte*

Times: Last L 2.30pm (3pm Sat/Sun), Last D 11.30pm (10.30pm Sun). Closed 25 Dec, 1 Jan

good examples of Westernised Chinese food, attractively presented and with sound flavours. Vegetarians can also be catered for - beancurd and vegetable dishes are featured on the carte. The wine list is also extensive, and has mostly European wines with lots of champagne but no sake or Chinese wine. A harpist plays at dinner creating a pleasant and relaxing atmosphere.

Directions: At the Curzon Street end of South Audley Street, behind Park Lane. Nearest Tube – Hyde Park Corner

Chef: Mr Na
Proprietor: Mr Dan Tan

Seats: 100. Air conditioned
Additional: Children welcome.
◐ menu; other diets on request

Kalamara's ❀

☺ *Very little changes at this popular Greek restaurant. The menu offers a varied selection of starters including dips, salads, vegetarian and dairy items as well as seafood and meat. There are many familiar main course dishes (none vegetarian), and a short list of desserts and Greek wines.*

Cost: Alc £16, fixed-price D £15.50. H/wine £8. Service inc
Credit Cards: 1 2 3 4 5. **Additional:** Children welcome; children's menu/portions. ◐ menu; Vegan/other diets on request
Directions: Opposite Bayswater Tube. Three minutes from Queensway Tube

Map no: R114
76-78 Inverness Mews W2
Tel: 0171-727 9122
Chef: Stellios Platonos
Proprietor: Stellios Platonos
Seats: 88. No pipes or cigars. Air conditioned
Times: Last D Midnight. Closed Sun and BHs

Kastoori ❀

☺ *Run by the friendly Thanki family, this bright vegetarian restaurant presents a good value carte menu of mainly southern Indian cooking with some recipes developed during the family's time in Africa, such as 'matoki', a green banana curry. There are also plenty of clearly marked vegan dishes.*

Cost: Alc £10. Wine £6.95. Service exc. **Credit cards:** 1 3
Additional: Children welcome; children' portions. ◐ menu; Vegan on request
Directions: Midway between Tooting Bec Tube and Tooting Broadway Tube

Map no: 115
188 Upper Tooting Road SW17
Tel: 0181-767 7027
Chef: Manoj Thanki
Proprietor: Dinesh Thanki
Seats: 82. Air conditioned
Times: Last L 2.30pm/D 10.30pm. Closed Xmas, 1 week mid Jan

Ken Lo's Memories of China ❀❀

Authentic Chinese cooking under the watchful control of a renowned master

If, having established a cookery school, you have the confidence to name it after yourself, you should know a good chef when you see one. Just like Ken Lo did when he brought Kam Po But over from Hong Kong. With the kitchen under his supervision, Memories has become one of the leading Chinese restaurants in the UK, with a reputation built upon consistently high standards and authentic cooking. The menu does not vary but even regulars can easily ring the changes. Our inspector began with crispy mixed vegetable spring rolls, served with a medium chilli dip. Honey-roasted 'Cha siu pork' is one chef's specials – tender slices of pork with water chestnuts and snow peas,

Map no: 116
67-69 Ebury Street SW1
Tel: 0171-730 7734

Cost: Alc £22.50, fixed-price lunch £15 (3 courses), £21; fixed-price dinner £26.50 (4 courses), £29.50. H/wine £10. Service exc. Cover charge
Credit cards: 1 2 3 4

Menus: *A la carte*, fixed-price lunch and dinner

served with a slightly sweet chilli sauce. 'Sichuan Yu-Hsiang monkfish' is another special in which lightly battered, succulent fish is served with vegetables and a tasty sauce. Set menus include the 'Gastronomic Tour of China' and 'The Lobster Feast'. Desserts are few, but include the popular toffee apple. A predominantly French wine list includes some rice wines from China and Japan. Service is attentive if, at times, a bit rushed.

Directions: At the junction of Ebury Street and Eccleston Street. Nearest Tubes – Sloane Square & Victoria

Times: Midday-Last L 2.30pm, 7pm-Last D 11.15pm. Closed BHs

Chef: Kam Po But
Proprietor: Franco Zanellato

Seats: 100. Air conditioned
Additional: Children welcome. ❂ dishes; Vegan on request

Ken Lo's Memories of China ❂❂

Superb oriental cooking prepared with talent and dedication in a pleasant, modern harbourside setting

Chef Tim Tang's Chinese cooking is arguably the best in London, his dishes superbly and lightly prepared, accompanied by confident and accomplished sauces. The *carte* at this contemporary restaurant set on Chelsea Harbour features over 70 dishes embracing Peking, Szechuan and Cantonese cooking plus 'Mongolian barbecue of lamb', our inspector's choice on a recent visit. Tim Tang's talent combined with top quality ingredients resulted in tender shredded meat, nicely flavoured and moist, its texture well-balanced by a crispy iceberg salad. The dish was completed by a delicious plum sauce. The quality of sauces was again outstanding in both the quick fried beef in oyster sauce and the hot black bean sauce accompanying succulent quick fried prawns. At lunchtime an alternative bar snack menu is offered, many of the dishes being drawn from the *carte*, but at lower prices. The smartly-dressed staff are attentive and professional and the whole atmosphere is welcoming.

Directions: Chelsea Harbour is off Lots Road. Approach via Kings Road or Cheyne Walk. Nearest Tube – Fulham Broadway

Map no: 117

Chelsea Harbour Yard, Chelsea Harbour SW10
Tel: 0171-352 4953

Cost: *Alc* £26, fixed-price lunch 315, fixed-price dinner £26, £29. H/wine £9 ♀ Service exc
Credit cards: 1 2 3 4

Menus: *A la carte*, fixed-price lunch and dinner

Times: Last L 2.30pm, Last D 11.45pm. Closed Sat lunch

Chef: Tim Tang
Proprietor: Ken Lo

Seats: 160. Air conditioned
Additional: Children welcome; ❂ menu; vegan/other diets on request

Kensington Place ❂❂

☺ *Buzzing with life at both lunch and dinner. Interesting, well-cooked food and polite, friendly service*

When a restaurant is always described as buzzing or frenetic it is pretty certain that no other words will do. Forget any hope of a quiet, intimate meal here, or of turning up without booking – this is where you find out what makes a restaurant popular. Clearly the ambience has something to do with it, but is the food good? Yes it is – on the whole excellent, but slightly marred by a cool main course and a poor crème brûlée dessert. Among the interesting starters are scarole, Roquefort and Jerusalem artichoke salad, griddled scallops with pea purée and mint vinaigrette, and pigeon crostini with truffle paste and rocket. Regular fish main courses include cod, roast sea bream or sole fillets, with sea-bass with shrimp and truffle sauce as an occasional special. Salt duck with potatoes and onions

Map no: 118

201/205 Kensington Church Street W8
Tel: 0171-727 3184

Cost: *Alc* £20, fixed-price lunch £13.50 (Mon-Fri). H/wine £9.75 ♀ Service exc
Credit cards: 1 3

Menus: *A la carte*, fixed-price lunch

Times: Midday-Last L3pm (3.30pm Sat & Sun), Last D11.45pm (10.15pm Sun). Closed 24-26 Dec, 1 Jan

couscous with rabbit, merguez sausages and harissa sauce, or rump steak with balsamic vinegar sound tempting too. If the crème brûlée doesn't appeal, try rhubarb fool or baked tamarillos with ice cream. The wine list should meet all tastes. Staff are knowledgeable and friendly, despite the pace.

Directions: At the Notting Hill end of Kensington Church Street. From Notting Hill about 50 yards on the right. Nearest Tube – Notting Hill Gate

Chef: Rowley Leigh
Proprietors: Nick Smallwood, Simon Slater

Seats: 140. Air conditioned
Additional: Children welcome/portions; ◐ dishes; Vegan/other diets on request

L'Accento ❀

A lively, popular Italian restaurant offering reasonably priced set menus and a short, imaginative carte. Basil tagliolini with lobster, tomato and fresh herbs was tasty, with good home-made pasta. Dishes range from shellfish to rabbit stuffed with spicy Italian sausage with a mushroom sauce.

Cost: Alc £30, fixed-price L/D £10.50. H/wine £7.95. Service 12.5%
Credit cards: 1 3 **Additional:** Children welcome; children's portions. ◐ dishes.
Directions: Off Westbourne Grove. Nearest Tube – Bayswater

Map no: R119
6 Garway Road W2
Tel: 0171-243 2201
Chef: Andrea Beltrami
Proprietors: Giovanni Tomaselli and Andrea Beltrami
Seats: 75. No pipes. Air conditioned
Times: Last L 2.30pm/D 11.30pm. Closed BHs

Laicram Thai ❀❀

A rare Thai restaurant offering authentically spiced and freshly-produced food that is faithful to its origins

Named after the pretty blue and white china on which the food is served, this well-established neighbourhood Thai restaurant continues to offer authentically spiced and freshly prepared versions of all the favourite dishes. Enjoyed at a recent meal were: Khanom jeeb - delicate steamed dumplings with minced prawns and pork; tasty marinated and charcoal grilled beef satay with peanut sauce and a sweet cucumber, carrot and red onion relish; Phat Thai – thin, flat rice noodles cooked with egg, peanut, spring onion, prawns and salted turnips; an excellent mixed seafood Tom yam - a classic Thai hot and sour soup with mussels, crab claw, white fish and prawns; green chicken curry which had perfectly balanced flavours; and stir-fried beef with red chillies and plenty of oriental basil and soy sauce. Some of the food served is quite hot, and our inspector discovered that the fragrant steamed Thai rice is more effective in cooling the mouth than the excellent well-chilled Singha beers. A vegetarian section has been added to the menu, offering soups, starters and several main dishes. Service is very polite.

Directions: Off the main shopping street, in a side road near the Post Office. Opposite the station

Map no: 120

1 Blackheath Grove, Blackheath SE3
Tel: 0181-852 4710

Cost: H/wine £7.50
Credit cards: 1 2 3

Menus: A la carte

Times: Midday-Last L 2.30pm, 6pm-Last D 11.30pm. Closed BHs

Chef: Amnury Suttwat
Proprietor: Somchitt Dhirabutra

Seats: 50
Additional: Children welcome. ◐ menu; Vegan/other diets on request

L'Altro ●●

Thoroughly enjoyable regional Italian cooking popular with the locals

Don't be misled by the address. This is not wealthy South Ken nor dowdy West Ken. This is North Ken, which prefers to be known as Ladbroke Grove, one of London's more effervescent districts. The owners have created here an unusual Italian restaurant style, with *trompe-l'oeil* frescoes, bare tables and what could either be stylishly-distressed chinaware or simply the result of clumsiness in the sink. The table layout is cramped but, if a jostle by a passing waiter or carelessly-flung diner's arm causes no offence, why worry? A modern Italian style is applied to food from the northern, central and southern regions, including a confident and pleasing array of fish dishes. From the perfectly prepared giant focaccia-style loaf, liberally moistened with olive oil, to the freshly-baked petits fours served with coffee, there is little to disappoint. The daily-changing dinner menu has four sections – antipasti, four home-made pasta dishes, main course and dessert; lunch consists of antipasti, plus one of four specials. The wine list is, frankly, meagre but, at the time of our visit, was about to be changed.

Directions: Northern end of Kensington Park Road. Nearest Tube – Ladbroke Grove

Map no: DP121

210 Kensington Park Road W11
Tel: 0171-792 1066

Cost: *Alc* £36. No service charge
Credit cards: 1 2 3 4

Menus: *A la carte,* fixed-price lunch

Times: Midday-Last L 3pm, 7pm-Last D 11pm. Dinner not served Sun

Chefs: Ottavio Rizzi, Maximo Bianchi
Proprietor: Gino Taddei

Seats: 42
Additional: children welcome; ❷ dishes

The Lanesborough ●●●

A wide range of modern dishes including a good vegetarian choice in the Conservatory restaurant of this luxury hotel

The Lanesborough Hotel, the extensively re-developed St George's Hospital with its period façade and luxurious interior, enjoys an exceptional location overlooking Hyde Park and nearby Buckingham Palace. The high-ceiled, marble-clad public areas include the flamboyant Conservatory restaurant with running water and an oriental mood to the decor. Here dedicated chef Paul Gayler offers dishes from around the world with imaginative combinations of flavours and ingredients.
  Breakfast, lunch, Sunday brunch, afternoon tea and dinner menus are available, with 'light and healthy' and good vegetarian options featured, such as basil stracchi with spring vegetables and watercress butter. Nibbles in the bar might include root vegetable 'crisps', smoked salmon canapés and tasty potted shrimps and quails' eggs, and at the table focaccia is a favourite bread. Our inspectors have sampled starters of chargrilled venison, and an excellent layered terrine of foie gras and chicory, served with dressed leaves and toasted brioche. Main courses have included good flaky cod, interestingly paired with lentils, crisp pancetta and a red wine jus; spring lamb, pink and full of flavour; and a carefully cooked fillet of turbot set on a bed of green mash and steamed baby leeks with a creamy muscat sauce and three poached oysters.
  A good range of sweets has included tangy lemon parfait, banana and passion fruit ravioli with spicy pineapple compôte, or a prune and Armagnac soufflé with caramel ice cream (20

Map no: 122

Hyde Park Corner SW1
Tel: 0171-259 5599

Cost: Fixed-price lunch £22.50; fixed-price dinner £28.50. Wine £3 ♀ Service inc

Menus: *A la carte,* fixed-price lunch and dinner, Sunday brunch, bar menu

Times: 7am-Last L 2.30pm, Last D midnight

Chef: Paul Gayler
Proprietor: Goodwill Nominees

Seats: 106. No-smoking area. Air conditioned
Additional: Children welcome; children's portions/menu; ❷ menu; Vegan/other diets on request. Live entertainment

minutes cooking time) which on his visit our inspector found a little overcooked. A comprehensive and solid wine list dominated by the classic areas of France also contains some good wines from Italy and Australia.

Directions: On Hyde Park Corner. Nearest Tube – Hyde Park Corner

Langan's Brasserie ❀❀

See and be seen in cult eating place where food quality is generally good and the buzz is intoxicating

People eat here because it's Langan's, not necessarily for the food which, on one recent inspection visit, was definitely under par. On a more positive note, even the heart of a staunch Eurosceptic would swell from reading the *carte*, with English staples like black pudding, kidneys and bacon, and baked knuckle of gammon. Even so, there are still many dishes whose culinary home country would have signed the Treaty of Maastricht – in fact, there are nearly 150 entries, including wines, on the handwritten menu. A second inspection visit was much better. No disappointment with a smooth duck liver terrine, or with the main course of grilled loin of venison in a red wine sauce and a generous portion of mixed fresh vegetables. There are desserts aplenty including dear old rice pudding. Friends meeting in their office lunch break will like the cheaper wine prices and even the company accountant won't object to the dearer ones. Some people eat in the large ground floor dining room hoping to be seen by passing friends or perhaps snapped by a lurking paparazzo! The upstairs Venetian Room is quieter.

Directions: Stratton Street is about half-way along Piccadilly. Nearest Tube – Green Park

Map no: E123
Stratton Street W1
Tel: 0171-491 8822

Cost: A/c £23. H/wine £8.25. Service charge 12.5%. Cover charge £1
Credit Cards: 1 2 3 4
Menu: A la carte
Times: 12.30-Last L 2.30pm, 7pm-Last D 11.45pm. Lunch not served Sat. Closed Sun, BHs, Easter and Xmas
Chefs: Ron Smith, Dennis Mynnot
Proprietors: Richard Shepherd and Michael Caine
Seats: 200. No restriction on smoking. Air conditioned
Additional: Children welcome; ❂ dishes

The Lansdowne ❀

☺ *A convivial, Bohemian pub with bare floors, stripped tables and vases of fresh flowers. The laid-back atmosphere attracts children, dogs and Sunday papers, and the food is rustically simple and very enjoyable.*

Cost: A/c £12.50; H/wine £8. No service charge **Credit cards:** None taken **Additional:** Vegetarian dish
Directions: From Chalk Farm Tube cross the footbridge to Regents Park Road and turn left.

Map no: Q124
90 Gloucester Avenue NW1
Tel: 0171-483 0409
Chef: Amanda Pritchett
Proprietor: Amanda Pritchett
Seats: 70
Times: Last L 2.30pm/D 10pm. Closed Mon lunch, Xmas

La Tante Claire ❀❀❀❀❀

French cooking in a league of its own, created by a dedicated chef in a very popular, busy restaurant

Pierre Koffmann's roots are very firmly planted in his native Gascony. He was born in Tarbe and inspiration from that south-west region is clearly to be seen in many of his dishes. He has a very distinctive and individualistic style of cooking but his

Map no: 125

68 Royal Hospital Road SW3
Tel: 0171-352 6045

Cost: Minimum charge at dinner £45. Fixed-price lunch £25. H/wine £13. Service inc
Credit cards: 1 2 3 4

is a sure hand. When it comes to the marriage of flavours and textures, he is a perfectionist indeed and well deserves this year's recognition of a fifth rosette. Signature dishes have been widely acclaimed and often copied, most famously, his 'Pied de cochon aux morilles', a pig's trotter stuffed with morille mushrooms, once again the highlight of an inspection lunch.

The meal began with a selection of his excellent home-baked breads, and although the 'risotto de grenouille aux épices' had a slightly crunchy texture, its delicately spiced sauce perfumed with coriander did much to rescue it. Then came the pig's trotter, served in a sauce of admirable depth and richness of flavour. The delicious taste of a fluffy light pistachio soufflé, for dessert, was enhanced by an accompanying pistachio ice cream.

Other signature dishes, for example, venison, with its perfect match of contrasting flavours, bitter chocolate and raspberry vinegar sauce, and scallops with black ink sauce, have also provided inspectors with memorable experiences. The fixed-price, daily-changing lunch menus – one fish, one meat – are excellent value and have helped to make the restaurant very busy, so booking will normally be a must. The *carte*, of course, gives best expression to Pierre Koffmann's abilities, and among his favourite combinations are meat and shellfish – 'hure (brawn) de langue de boeuf et langoustines et caviar', or, , 'râble de lapereau (saddle of rabbit) aux langoustines'.

The entirely French wine list includes some first-class vintages and some excellent regional wines from Gascony and beyond.

Directions: Between the National Army Museum and Chelsea Physic Garden, near Cheyne Walk. Nearest Tube – Sloane Square

Menus: *A la carte*, fixed-price lunch

Times: Last L 2pm, Last D 11pm. closed Sat, Sun

Chef: Pierre Koffmann
Proprietors: Pierre Koffmann, Bruno Bellemere

Seats: 45. Air conditioned
Additional: children permitted at lunch; children's portions; ◐ dishes

Launceston Place ✿✿

'New British cuisine' here means the best of English with Italian/French influences. More traditional on Sundays

Royalty eat here, possibly attracted by the English country-house style as well as the good, value-for-money food. The chef, Cathy Gradwell, previously worked at sister restaurant Kensington Place. There is a daily set menu for lunch and early evening and the *carte* changes every six weeks. The chicken liver pâté induced a flow of superlatives in our inspector's report and she rated the sourdough, topped with peppers, goat's cheese and courgettes, as highly for taste as for appearance. Baked fillet of cod with a creamy sauce of ceps, leeks and Parmesan, and roast wood pigeon with fresh herb risottto, both looked tempting, as did the special of roasted hake with chanterelles. Desserts not to be missed are the steamed vanilla pudding with a delicate, geranium-scented sauce and the traditional Bakewell tart. A late-supper menu includes lightish dishes such as smoked salmon with scrambled eggs and brioche. An interesting and varied wine list reflects regular purchases at auction. After a herbal tea or espresso you will leave feeling well fed and well cared for by the relaxed and friendly management and staff.

Directions: Just south of Kensington Palace. Between Gloucester Road and High Street Kensington Tubes.

Map no: 126

1A Launceston Place W8
Tel: 0171-937 6912

Cost: *Alc* £25, fixed-price lunch/dinner (7pm-8pm) £13.50 (2 courses), £16.50. H/wine from £8.50. Service exc
Credit cards: 1 2 3

Menus: *A la carte*, fixed-price lunch & early evening menu, post-theatre
Times: Last L 2.30pm (3pm Sun),Last D 11.30pm. Closed Sat lunch & Sun evening

Chef: Cathy Gradwell
Proprietors: Nick Smallwood, Simon Slater. Manager: David Watson

Seats: 85. No pipes. Air conditioned
Additional: Children permitted. ◐ dishes; Vegan on request

Laurent ❀❀

☺ *Here is where to find the best couscous in town! A busy lively restaurant with a long-standing reputation*

Laurent Farrugia's restaurant is famous for his couscous and the friendliness and warmth of welcome received here. He has been running the place for the last 11 years, and cooking in London for the past 37 years. In that time has made many, many friends, all of whom return frequently to his simple and cheery restaurant, which on a busy evening really buzzes with activity. The menu rarely alters, although main course dishes have recently been extended with the addition of two further types of couscous, one being chicken, which is delicious, corn fed, very plump and full of flavour, and the other a fish couscous – Laurent only uses halibut. For starter there is the very simple but exceptionally tasty brique à l'oeuf, a fried egg in a filo pastry parcel, and desserts include an enjoyable crème brûlée, but these are secondary to the main course, for those that eat here do so because of the couscous. Undoubtedly this meal was the best couscous our inspector has eaten for many years and certainly she plans to return very soon! The service is from Laurent, or his assistant in the kitchen, and is charming and attentive.

Directions: At the junction with Cricklewood Lane. Nearest Tube – Golders Green

Map no: 127

428 Finchley Road NW2
Tel: 0171-794 3603

Chef: Laurent Farrugia
Proprietor: Laurent Farrugia

Seats: 36. No cigars or pipes

Times: Last L 2pm/D 11pm

Cost: A/c £15. H/wine £8.
Service exc
Credit Cards: 1 2 3

Additional: Children welcome; children's portions. ❂ dishes

Le Boudin Blanc ❀❀

☺ *Good French fare in a no-nonsense, value-for-money bistro with a lively atmosphere*

Shepherd (no 's' please) Market is the 'village centre' of Mayfair. The May Fair itself was held here until building development by Edward Shepherd in about 1735 proved the most effective way of stopping this increasingly Saturnalian bash. Even today, the little warren of narrow streets has a slightly raffish reputation.

A good place, then, for this simply-furnished, cramped but popular bistro where, maybe not too surprisingly, at busy times finesse and attention to detail are not strong points. But the main reason for success here is a value-for-money commitment that at lunchtime, for example, extends to a two-course meal for either £4.95 or £6.95. The *carte* is more extensive and varied, but can promise more than it delivers. An inspector's boudin noir, black sausage from France, was tasty enough but failed to excite and his vegetables were rather dry. Nevertheless, the kitchen's use of basic ingredients is first-class and flavours are usually clean and well-defined. Add a sensibly chosen wine list (nothing over £30) and brisk service by mostly French staff, and Le Boudin's popularity is self-evident.

Directions: From Curzon Street turn into Trebeck Street. Restaurant is on the left

Map no: I128

5 Trebeck Street W1
Tel: 0171-499 3292

Cost: A/c £18, fixed-price £4.95, £6.95. H/wine £6.95.
Service charge 12.5%
Credit cards: 1 2 3 4 5

Menus: *A la carte*, fixed-price, Sunday lunch

Times: Midday-2pm, limited menu 3pm-6pm, 6pm-Last D 11pm

Chef: Phillip Suplet
Proprietor: Corret Holdings.
Manager: Sergio

Additional: Children welcome; ❂ dishes

Le Café du Jardin ✱

☺ *This bright Italian-style restaurant offers a mixed menu of French, Italian and modern European cuisine. The cooking is sound and well flavoured with unusual dishes such as Omelette japonaise, filled with smoked duck, shitake mushrooms, shallots and seaweed.*

Additional: Children permitted.; ❂ dishes
Directions: On the corner of Wellngton Street and Tavistock Street. Nearest Tube – Covent Garden

Map no: 129
28 Wellington Street WC2
Tel: 0171 836 8769
Chef: Tony Howarth
Proprietors: Tony Howarth, Robert Seigler
Cost: Alc £22, pre-theatre D £9.75. H/wine £8.95. Service inc.
Credit cards: 1 2 3 4

Le Café du Marché ✱✱

A French brasserie-style restaurant with a lunchtime grill room alternative

In a converted warehouse, once part of St Bartholomew's Hospital, this hearty replica of a French brasserie is situated in a cobbled mews leading off Charterhouse Square. It is particularly busy with city folk at lunchtime, when the upstairs grill room is also open. In the evening this *grenier* (attic) room is available for private functions, and has its own staff and kitchen. Both sections of the restaurant offer a short three-course fixed-price menu, which includes a vegetarian dish of the day. The menus are written in French without translations, . The menus read well and the dishes are accurately executed, but our inspector felt that the flavours were understated. He sampled salt cod mousse with a garnish of cucumber, tomato brunoise and flaked prawn with vinaigrette, followed by grilled red mullet with tasty vegetable couscous on a pile of samphire surrounded by a pool of beurre blanc. The dessert, custard tart with marrons glacés, lacked flavour and was a bit disappointing. The all-French wine list is short and pretty pricey. Staffing levels are good and service is attentive.

Directions: Between Aldersgate and Smithfield Market. Nearest Tube – Barbican

Map no: 130
Charterhouse Mews, Charterhouse Square EC1
Tel: 0171-608 1609

Cost: Fixed-price lunch and dinner £19.75. H/wine £7.50. Service inc
Credit cards: 1 3

Menus: Fixed-price lunch and dinner

Times: Midday-Last L 2.30pm, Last D 10pm. Closed Sat lunch, Sun, BHs, Xmas-New Year

Chef: Simon Cottard
Proprietor: Charles Graham Wood

Seats: 65, 50. Air conditioned
Additional: Children permitted; children's portions; ❂ dishes; Vegan/other diets on request

Le Caprice ✱✱✱

A converted warehouse by the Thames, where the food is modern, the atmosphere lively and the views stunning

Le Caprice is part of a successful complex created from a warehouse on Butler's Wharf by Sir Terence Conran. It comprises the restaurant, a bakery, wine merchant, delicatessen, and a popular bar food operation. The site, beside the Thames with a view of Tower Bridge, is another attraction, making booking essential. This, together with the stylish modern decor, piano music, and the buzz of so many people at closely packed tables combines to create an up-tempo atmosphere.
   The interesting *carte* offers a choice of dishes to suit its hours of opening, including light suppers for theatre goers. Honest

Map no: A131

Arlington House, Arlington Street SW1
Tel: 0171-629 2239

Cost: Alc £23. H/wine £8.50 ♀ Service exc. Cover charge
Credit cards: 1 2 3 4

Menus: A la carte, Sun brunch
Times: Midday-Last L 3.pm (Sunday brunch 3.30pm), 6pm-Last D midnight. Closed Aug BH, 24 Dec–2 Jan

main courses range from Lincolnshire sausages with bubble and squeak and onion gravy, to grilled rabbit with rosemary, creamed polenta and black olives, following starters such as Thai spiced shrimp broth and tomato and basil galette (vegetarian options are limited). Vegetables and salads are priced separately, as are all the 'extras', amounting to a sizeable bill for a full meal. Our inspector sampled a tasty smoked haddock risotto, garnished with Parmesan, but lacking the promised coriander flavour. Breast of roast duck was cooked pink with a crisp, dry skin, and served on a croûton of foie gras with a braised leg of duck and port wine sauce. At the same meal, tournedos of beef with a wild mushroom crust was accompanied by a delicious cream-based sauce, delicately flavoured with morels. For dessert, the nutmeg and custard tart had an unevenly cooked base and a rather firm filling, but was enjoyed for its subtle flavours.

The Sunday Brunch menu offers an intriguing choice of dishes, from blueberry muffins to steak tartare, washed down, perhaps, with a pitcher of Bloody Mary. There is a varied selection of sensibly priced wines from around the world, and there are some good wines available by the glass.

Directions: From Green Park underground head towards Piccadilly, then turn right, past the Ritz. NCP adjacent to restaurant

Chefs: Mark Hix, Tim Hughes
Proprietors: Christopher Corbin, Jeremy King

Seats: 70. Cigars and pipes at discretion of management. Air conditioned
Additional: Children welcome. ◐ dishes; other diets on request. Pianist in evenings

Le Gavroche ✿✿✿✿✿

Consistent excellence maintained at the restaurant that pioneered the modern French approach to cooking in Britain

We British owe our gratitude to Albert and Michel (senior) Roux, not only for the standard-setting quality of their London and Bray restaurants, but also for having awakened a nationwide interest in good food that was all but moribund when they arrived on the scene in the 1960s. Albert Roux handed over the management of the Gavroche kitchens to his son Michel when his brother opened The Waterside at Bray in 1988 and it is a tribute to this remarkable family that the quality of the cooking has remained so consistently first rate.

Famous 'signature' dishes appear as old friends on the carte. As a starter, the soufflé suissesse, deliciously light, floating on a perfectly gratinated creamy Gruyère sauce, has lost none of its appeal. 'Pigeonneau de Bresse en vessie aux deux céleris' delivers the bird whole to your table, enclosed in a pig's bladder which is then deftly opened on request and the pigeon carved on to a bed of braised celery and fennel - a masterpiece of a dish with a deeply satisfying flavour. 'Terrine de foie gras au poivre vert' was a sensational presentation and La Marmite Bretonne brought together a medley of clear fish flavours in a delicious sauce. For dessert, the 'petit pot de chocolat' with fresh madeleines had not that intensity of flavour one expects from the best chocolate, but an imaginative array of petits fours did compensate for the slight disappointment at the end of an otherwise excellent meal.

Service, in keeping with club-like surroundings of the restaurant, is formal and can be so attentive that staff seem almost to fall over one another. The clientele is, as one would

Map no: 132

43 Upper Brook Street W1
Tel: 0171-408 0881

Cost: Minimum charge on alc is £50. Av £70. Menu Exceptionnel £75. Fixed-price lunch £36, fixed-price dinner £48
Credit cards: 1 2 3 4

Times: Mon-Fri Midday-Last L 3pm, 7pm-Last D 11pm. Closed Sat, Sun, BHs, Xmas-New Year

Chef: Michel Roux
Proprietor: Le Gavroche Ltd

Seats: 60. Air conditioned
Additional: Children permitted. ◐ dishes; Vegan other diets on request

expect in Mayfair, distinctly affluent and sprinkled with celebrities. Considering the fact that the menus state that service and VAT are included in the price, it was an unwelcome surprise to find the credit card slip total left blank. However, the fixed-price lunch menu, with three alternatives per course, includes a half bottle of wine and is excellent value at around half the cost of the full *carte*. There is also a MenuExceptionnel for a minimum of two persons.

The extensive wine list is outsanding in its range and quality of French wines. You will find a page of vintage champagne, 45 choices of first growth claret, eight vintages of Château Yquem among other treasures and if you look carefully 20 or so wines at under £20.

Directions: From Park Lane, into Upper Brook St (one-way), Le Gavroche is on the right. Nearest Tube – Marble Arch

Leith's ✸✸✸

A smart restaurant serving modern British cooking based on quality produce, much of it organically grown on its own farm

Prue Leith's original ideals still hold at this smart restaurant, and now wherever possible produce is supplied by Leith's own farm, most of it organic. Chef Alex Floyd came here six years ago as a commis, and for the last three years has led the kitchen brigade. There is a weekly fixed-price two course menu and a seasonal *carte*, although guests are welcome to mix and match between the two. Vegetarians are taken seriously, and are offered a separate menu – guaranteed to contain no gelatine or meat stocks – and staff can also advise on the suitability of starters from any menu. Layers of roasted aubergine and goats' cheese with ratatouille vinaigrette is a typical vegetarian main course from a list of three.

Breads are home-baked and there is a range of about five, all freshly made. The first course trolley - a full explanation of which is given to diners before ordering - should not be missed as it provides the opportunity of tasting a variety of dishes, such as delicious spicy onion filo tart, seafood cocktail with ginger and lemon grass dressing, and cheese balls with cherry tomatoes and basil, the choice extending to about eight items all of equal quality. Our inspector followed this with a main course of oven roast rump of lamb, cooked pink and served with Mediterranean vegetables, a herbed jus and tiny chateau potatoes and turnips, the flavours all individual and the freshness indisputable.

His final choice for dessert was a chocolate and cherry soufflé, well risen and moist, accompanied by a chocolate sauce and, in contrast, a small brandy-snap basket filled with cherry ice cream. A selection of coffees and teas is available served with an assortment of petits fours. The well chosen and sensibly prices wine list gives informative and chatty comments on the selection of mainly French and New World wines.

Directions: 500 yds north of Notting Hill Gate

Map no: P133

92 Kensington Park Road W11
Tel: 0171-229 4481

Cost: Alc £37, fixed-price dinner £22.50 (Vegetarian),£25. Wine £14.30 ♀ Service exc
Credit cards: 1 2 3 4 5

Menus: *A la carte,* fixed-price, fixed-price vegetarian

Times: 7.30pm–Last D 11.30pm. Closed 2 days Aug BH, 4 days at Xmas

Chef: Alex Floyd
Proprietor: Prue Leith

Seats: 75. No-smoking area on request
Additional: Children permitted over 7. ◐ menu; Vegan/other diets on request

Le Meridien, Oak Room ❋❋❋

A magnificent-oak panelled restaurant where French cuisine is produced by a creative collaboration of two French chefs

At the time of our most recent visits to Le Meridien hotel, just before going to press, new chef Alain Maréchal had only been in position for a few weeks. Clearly, he had not had time to make his mark and the menus were still largely those created by consultant chef Michel Lorain, who comes over several times a year from his renowned restaurant in Burgundy, La Côte Saint-Jacques at Joigny, to bring his personal style of cooking to diners at the Oak Room.

Our inspector was fortunate enough to be eating lunch during one of these visits, and was pleased to sample a light, chilled gazpacho, bursting with vibrant flavours, with three firm textured langoustines and quenelles of courgette mousse softening the overall effect. This was followed by roast fillet of new season's lamb, pink and juicy, on a bed of crushed potatoes flavoured with Roquefort, served with an excellent lamb and oregano jus. Dessert, chosen from the trolley, was a slice of delicious chocolate gateau, a delicate sponge base with layers of gooey chocolate ganache and a nougat mousse with nuts and cherries, accompanied by chocolate and crème anglaise sauces. The ingredients used were first class and the combinations daring, but they worked, showing great skill.

The menus, written in French with English descriptions, include a seasonal *carte*, a short fixed price lunch, a set three-course dinner with wine, and a six-course Menu Gourmand. New menus in the autumn will incorporate the Provençale influences of chef Maréchal, who hails from Le Meridien in Nice, and the exemplary service is efficiently overseen.

The extensive wine list concentrates on France and California and the quality is excellent. With many grande marque champagnes, and some of the best of Bordeaux, there is a also a selection of red and white Burgundies.

Directions: On the north side of Piccadilly close to Piccadilly Circus. Nearest Tube – Piccadilly Circus

Map no: 134

21 Piccadilly W1
Tel: 0171-465 1640

Cost: A/c £40; fixed-price lunch £24.50; fixed-price dinner £28. H/wine £14 ♀ Service exc
Credit cards: 1 2 3 4 5

Menus: *A la carte*, fixed-price lunch and dinner, Menu Gourmand (7 courses)

Times: Midday-Last L 2pm, 7pm-Last D 10.30pm. Closed Sun, Aug

Chefs: Alain Maréchal and Michel Lorain
Proprietors: Meriden. Manager: Jean Quero

Seats: 50. Air conditioned
Additional: Children permitted; ♥ dishes; Vegan/other diets on request. Live entertainment

Le Mesurier ❋❋

This small restaurant remains popular for its lunchtime-only menu of mainly French cuisine

Gillian Enthoven's small ground floor restaurant is in a less than desirable location but has suceeded here for nine years or so, operating to the same formula. It opens for lunch only with a small *carte* of mainly French cuisine offering a choice of three dishes per course. This is supported by a short but carefully selected wine list with no halves. The restaurant is a bit cramped but remains popular; service is provided by just one very competent waiter, and can of necessity be a little slow. Our inspector had the impression that the cooking has become more complicated and ambitious, not always to the best effect, despite the use of good raw materials. A summer inspection

Map no: 135

113 Old Street EC1
Tel: 0171-251 8117

Cost: A/c lunch £23. H/wine £9. Service exc
Credit cards: 1 2 3 4 5

Menu: *A la carte*
Times: Midday-Last L 3.pm. Open evening for party bookings only. Closed Sat, Sun, 3 weeks Aug,1 week Xmas

meal began with chilled borsch and baby vegetables set in a beetroot jelly. This was followed by fresh, well made tagliatelle with langoustine, scallops and asparagus in a creamy lemon sauce. A simple, unadorned lemon tart proved an excellent dessert and certainly the best part of the meal. Vegetarian dishes are usually available, but it is best to pre-order.

Directions: At the western end of Old Street, on the north side close to the junction with Central Street. Nearest Tube – Barbican

Chefs: Gillian Enthoven, Loic le Pape
Proprietor: Gillian Enthoven

Seats: 25. No pipes or cigars.
Additional: Children over 10 permitted; children's portions

Lemonia ✿

☺ *A very large Greek restaurant where owner Antonis Evangelou is also head chef. The cuisine is typically Greek and is wholesome and tasty. They produce fine examples of taramasalata, hummus and avgolemono, and main course dishes include moussaka and stuffed vine leaves.*

Cost: Fixed-price L £7.95 (weekdays only), Meze £9.50. Wine £9 (litre). Service exc. **Credit cards:** 1 3.
Additional: Children welcome; children's portions; ❂ menu
Directions: Nearest Tube – Chalk Farm

Map no: Q136
89 Regent's Park Road NW1
Tel: 0171-586 7454
Chefs: Antonis Evangelou, A Khalid
Proprietor: Antonis Evangelou
Seats: 140. Air conditioned
Times: Last L 3pm/D 11.30pm. Closed Sat L, Sun D, 25 Dec, 1 Jan

Le Petit Max ✿✿

Simple, French provincial cuisine served in a friendly restaurant from a good-value fixed-price menu

Our inspector enjoyed his visit to Le Petit Max, which is rather different from its sister restaurant in Fulham. It has a friendly, casual atmosphere with Marc Renzland serving and brother Max cooking with the help of a young chef. The cuisine is mainly French provincial in style, wholesome and full of flavour, and the dishes are freshly prepared so it is best to allow time for a leisurely meal. From the good-value fixed price menu, our inspector selected the terrine maison, a rich home-made pâté of pork, veal and duck with pistachio nuts, garnished with small French beetroot and green leaves. This was followed by tender chargrilled guinea fowl with a slightly crisp skin, served on a bed of wilted rocket with a tasty pepper sauce and a selection of vegetables. Vegetarian dishes are also available. The dessert, crème brûlée, was a good example of the dish, with a lovely flavour and crisp caramel topping. Wine is not served but guests may bring their own, subject to a corkage charge of £1.

Directions: On the A310 Teddington Road, by Hampton Wick Station

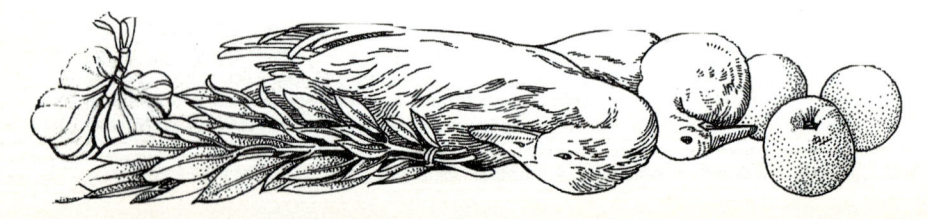

Map no: 137
Hampton Wick
Tel: 0181-977 0236

Chef: Max Renzland
Proprietors: Max Renzland, Marc Renzland

Le Pont de la Tour ❀❀

Popular riverside restaurant specialising in seafood and classic dishes

The personal touch may not be too apparent here, but the quality of the food far outweighs any criticism in that direction. This stylish Thames-side restaurant – Sir Terence Conran's latest gastronomic outlet, with stunning views of Tower Bridge and the Tower of London – offers a variety of menus featuring crustacean specialities from the coasts of Ireland and Scotland as well as classic French and Italian dishes. At lunchtime the short fixed-price menu might include starters such as wild mushrooms on toast or spinach and goat's cheese tart with red pepper sauce, and main choices like pan-fried calfs' liver with confit of red onions and sage. Rack of lamb in a herb crust was a tasty recent dish, and a chocolate marquise with rum crème anglaise was as rich and delicious as it sounds. A longer dinner *carte* offers more choice at a price, but the pre- and post-theatre menu provides excellent value for money. Home-made breads come fresh from the restaurant's own bakery, and there's always a wide range of seafood from the Crustacean Bar. This place tends to get busy and service can be a bit rushed, but a table out on the terrace is still a treat. The wide-ranging wine list offers wines from £11 to £850 for a1949 Mouton Rothschild.

Directions: On the river front, to the south-east of Tower Bridge

Map no: G138

36d Shad Thames, Butlers Wharf SE1
Tel: 0171-403 8403

Cost: *A/c* £55, fixed-price lunch £25. H/wine £10.75 ♀ Service inc
Credit cards: 1 2 3 4

Menus: *A la carte*, fixed-price lunch, pre-theatre, bar menu

Chef: David Burke
Proprietors: Sir Terence Conran, Joel Kissin, David Burke

Seats: 105
Additional: Children permitted. ✿ dishes/other diets on request

Les Associés ❀❀

A friendly little French restaurant serving well-flavoured food in a relaxed atmosphere.

A friendly, informal atmosphere pervades this intimate little French restaurant in Crouch End. Children are always welcome, and a separate menu reflecting their tastes is available on request; vegetarians are equally well catered for. The choice at lunchtime is restricted to a very limited set-price menu of fairly simple – though well presented – dishes, but the quality of the food equals that featured by chef Gilles Charvet on his more elaborate evening *carte*. In the course of an enjoyable dinner, a flavoursome duck liver pâté with onion marmalade might be followed by John Dory and basil sauce served 'en papillote'. Dessert could be a freshly prepared and tempting tarte tatin, its light soft pastry and tasty apple complemented by a well-made sauce anglaise, and the excellent coffee which completes the meal is accompanied by chocolate mints. The wine list, though not exceptional, contains a reasonable selection of French wines (though there are very few half bottles available) and prices are good. Service is attentive, and guests who arrive by car should have little difficulty in finding street parking nearby.

Directions: Half-way along Park Road, opposite the swimming pool. Nearest Tube – Finsbury Park

Map no: 139

172 Park Road N8
Tel: 0181-348 8944

Cost: *A/c* £27, fixed-price lunch £15.95. H/wine £9.80. Service inc
Credit cards: 1 3

Menu: *A la carte*

Times: 12.30-Last L 2pm, 7.30pm-Last D 10pm. Closed Sun, Mon, and Aug

Chef: Gilles Charvet
Proprietors: Gilles Charvet, Didier Bertran

Seats: 38
Additional: Children welcome, children's portions/menu. ✿ dishes/other diets on request

L'Escargot ●●●●

Vibrant French cooking from a skilled partnership of chefs in a well-established Soho restaurant

A long-established and well-known Soho restaurant, L'Escargot is divided between a downstairs brasserie and a revamped upper floor with bright harlequin decor and comfortable chairs. To be honest, the food is much the same – equally good – in both, but upstairs you get more personal attention, leisurely service and all the trimmings, such as petits fours (which, incidentally, are first rate). Our inspector ate upstairs on this occasion, where chefs David Cavalier and Gary Holihead offer a short *carte* with five items at each of three courses, a shorter fixed-price lunch, and a set dinner of five courses for two people. The style of cuisine is French with Mediterranean influences, and the menus are written, very briefly, in English.

Starters might include chicken and sweetbread terrine, salad of langoustine and artichoke, or bouillon of rabbit. Our inspector sampled an oyster tartlet with spinach, artichoke and superb glazed oysters, and a tagliatelle of cucumber and artichoke with warm vinaigrette and a rather superfluous bed of salad leaves. This was followed by corn-fed chicken with chicory - good crisp skinned chicken with a scattering of vegetables, set on a potato galette and served with a celeriac sweetened jus, a good foil to the sharpness of the chicory. Alternatives might be marmite of salmon or calf's' liver with sage jus. To finish there is a selection of farmhouse cheeses, or a choice of desserts such as pear condé, chocolate tart and ginger parfait. Our inspector opted for a raspberry soufflé, pronounced perfect, accompanied by a raspberry sorbet.

The wine list starts with some well chosen and keenly priced house wines, There is an excellent claret page, and some good red and white burgundies together with several wines from South Africa, Australia, New Zealand and the Americas.

Directions: Off Soho Square, half way up Greek Street on the right. Nearest Tubes – Tottenham Court Road, Leicester Square

Map no: 140

48 Greek Street W1
Tel: 0171-437 2679

Cost: *Alc* £30, fixed-price lunch £24, fixed-price dinner £39; H/wine £10 ♀ Service exc
Credit cards: 1 2 3 4 5

Menus: *A la carte*, fixed-price lunch and dinner

Times: 12.30-Last L 2.30pm, 7pm-Last D 11.15pm. Closed Sun, Mon, Easter, Xmas, BHs

Chefs: David Cavalier, Gary Holihead
Proprietor: Jimmy Lahoud

Seats: 32. Air conditioned
Additional: Children welcome. ❂ dishes; Vegan/other diets on request

L'Escargot Brasserie ●●

Nearly seventy years of traditional French cooking, now enhanced by the modern skills of two top chefs

Part of the Soho scene since 1927, L'Escargot bustles informally along as successfully as it ever did under Mme Salvoni. Chefs Gary Holihead and David Cavalier combine their talents to maintain a competitive edge over their many rivals, all clamouring for attention in this fashionable quartier. Surroundings are bright and cheerful and the staff are smart and friendly. Skilful innovation in the kitchen allows clear, natural flavours to enhance even further the mainly traditional French cooking; attractive presentation completes the picture. You'd expect escargots to be available and they are, as fritters with a bordelaise sauce. During our visit to the ground floor brasserie (there's a quieter restaurant upstairs), we chose a

Map no: 140

48 Greek Street W1
Tel: 0171-437 2679/6828

Cost: *Alc* £23; fixed-price lunch and dinner £16 (2 courses), £19. Wine £10 ♀ Service exc
Credit cards: 1 2 3 4 5

Menus: *A la carte*, fixed-price lunch and dinner, pre-theatre

Times: Midday-Last L 2.30 pm, 6pmLast D 11.15pm. Closed Sun, Sat lunch, Xmas, New Years day, Easter

scallop sous croute starter, served in the shell with a jus of olive oil, leeks and spinach. This was followed by mouth-wateringly pink slices of roast rump of lamb served on gratinée potatoes, surrounded by a tapénade vinaigrette containing baby broad beans and olives. Richly coloured, well-flavoured rhubarb compote finished the meal. The wine list offers a good French range augmented by a smaller international selection.

Directions: From Soho Square, about half way up Greek Street on right. Nearest Tubes – Tottenham Court Road, Leicester Square

Chefs: Gary Holihead, David Cavalier
Proprietors: Jimmy Lahoud

Seats: 90. No smoking-area. No pipes or cigars. Air conditioned
Additional: Children welcome; ❷ dishes; Vegan/other diets on request

Les Saveurs ✿✿✿✿

Exciting, inventive cooking from one of London's most highly praised chefs in very smart surroundings

Accolade has been piled on accolade for rapidly rising star of the London scene, Joël Antunès. After 20 years of cooking at some of the greatest restaurants in Europe - Troisgros, Bocuse, Robuchon - and a spell in the Oriental Hotel in Bangkok he still lives for innovation and is fascinated by experiments with flavours. When his inspirations come off his daring is inspired, but sometimes results are unbalanced, as in the overpowering flavour of dill that eclipsed both a lobster and salmon tartare topped with a creamy cauliflower mousse. Foie-gras terrines, when not served over-chilled, display the highest levels of culinary skill; at one recent lunch, layered with the freshest of leeks and just a hint of sea salt, at another, with aubergines confits, almost candied in texture, the dish given an oriental touch with balsamic vinegar, vanilla and coriander – an original and striking dish.

Another clever idea was red mullet served on chunky creamed celeriac with a salmis sauce, the mullet liver incorporated into its own stock with truffle oil, resulting in the big, gutsy flavours more often found in game dishes. A love of southern France shows through in classic dishes like rabbit salad à la niçoise and roast lamb à la provençal.

Joël Antunès admits to a love of sweet things, and delicately flavoured soufflés, among which is an outstanding one of lime with acacia honey, are a highlight of the dessert menu, where other interesting ideas include chocolate sorbet with tea syrup and croustillant of pears with liquorice. Keenly priced, his set lunch menu changes daily, as does the evening menu gourmand. The *carte* is seasonal. Service, expertly led by Emmanuel Menjuzan, has real grace and charm; as for wine, sommelier Yves Sauboua has enviable knowledge of his domain. Overwhelmingly French, the wine list, with over 850 bins, is rich in first-growth clarets, grand-cru burgundies, Sauternes and rare vintages.

Directions: Curzon Street is off Park Lane and parallel to Piccadilly. Next to the Curzon cinema. Nearest Tubes - Green Park, Hyde Park

Map no: 1141

37a Curzon Street W1
Tel: 0171-491 8919

Cost: Alc £36, fixed-price lunch £21, fixed-price dinner £32. H/wine £15. Service exc
Credit cards: 1 2 3 4 5

Menus: *A la carte,* fixed-price lunch and dinner

Times: Midday-Last L 2.30pm, 7pm-Last D 10.30pm. Closed Sat, Sun, 2 weeks Aug, 2 weeks Dec-Jan

Chef: Joël Antunès
Proprietor: Fujikoshi UK Ltd

Seats: 55. No-smoking area; no pipes. Air conditioned.
Additional: Children permitted; ❷ dishes; Vegan/other diets on request

Lexington ❋❋

Interesting eating at inexpensive prices in downtown Soho

New chef Mark Holmes has brought a flurry of new Mediterranean flavours – salsa verde, pesto, tapénade – to the sensibly limited *carte* of this trendy Soho diner. The decor is smart minimalist, the atmosphere informal and the service prompt, friendly and cheerful. On a *carte* with eight starters, three are vegetarian (offered as optional main courses) while of the four listed main courses, two are fish dishes. The set menu again caters for all tastes and at £10 per head is very good value. Our inspector's enjoyment of a recent meal increased with each succeeding dish, the first being a wild mushroom risotto, which arrived surprisingly quickly and, perhaps as a result, lacked any real flavour. A much more exciting crusted cod with green lentils was accompanied by a salsa verde of finely chopped parsley, with anchovy, garlic and olive oil and fresh al dente spinach bursting with flavour, colour and texture. Last came the highlight of the meal, a classic lemon tart, expertly constructed, light, eggy and tangy with the taste of lime and orange. Some wines on the international list are available by the half bottle or glass.

Directions: West Soho, between Brewer Street and Broadwick Street. Nearest Tubes – Oxford Circus, Tottenham Court Road, Piccadilly Circus

Map no: 142

45 Lexington Street W1
Tel: 0171-434 3401

Cost: *Alc* £19; fixed-price dinner £10 (2 courses). Wine from £8.75 ♀ Service exc
Credit cards: 1 2 3 4

Menus: *A la carte*, fixed-price dinner

Times: Midday-Last L 3pm, 6pm-Last D 11.30pm. Closed Sat lunch, Sun, BHs

Chef: Mark Holmes
Proprietors: Martin Saxon, Harriet Arden

Seats: 45. No-smoking area on request. No pipes or cigars
Additional: Children permitted; ❶ dishes; Vegan/other diets on request in advance. Panist in the evening

Lindsay House ❋❋

A Soho restaurant which knows that staying ahead means more than just good food

Chef Dean Rogers was away for our inspector's visit but the sous chef performed well, demonstrating that essential culinary ingredient - consistency. Soho spoils one for choice, but Lindsay House, with its intimate, antique-furnished dining room on the first floor, stays up with the leaders through its high standards of cooking and service. There are lunch menus and a dinner *carte*. In the evenings, game pie with Cumberland sauce, or wild mushrooms in a light puff pastry case with a rosemary cream sauce are typical starters. Main courses include roast sirloin of beef and Yorkshire pudding (although this is for two and takes 30 minutes to prepare), aubergine charlotte and, as our inspector discovered, good-tasting steamed monkfish with crab and sorrel sauce. On Sundays, an interesting lunch starter is crab, langoustine and coconut ravioli with a lemon balm butter sauce. A short selection of desserts includes bread and butter pudding and Welsh rarebit. Most of the wines are French, but Italy and the New World are not neglected. Theatre-goers will find it particularly convenient to begin dinner at 6 pm.

Directions: Close to Shaftesbury Avenue. Nearest Tube – Piccadilly Circus

Map no: 1143

21 Romilly Street W1
Tel: 0171-439 0450

Cost: *Alc* £26; fixed-price lunch £14.75. H/wine £9.50 ♀ Service exc
Credit cards: 1 2 3 4 5

Menus: *A la carte*, fixed-price lunch, Sunday lunch, pre-theatre

Times: 12.30pm-Last L 2.30pm (2pm Sun), 6pm-Last D midnight (10pm Sun, BHs). Closed Xmas

Chef: Dean Rogers
Proprietor: Roger Wren

Seats: 68
Additional: Children welcome; children's portions; ❶ menu; Vegan/other diets on request

The London Hilton on Park Lane 🏵🏵

A time of change for the Hilton flagship, with new management, chef and refurbishment

The Windows roof restaurant has long been famous for its panoramic views of London but with the arrival of top pedigree French chef Jacques Rolancey, this will hopefully become one of *the* places to eat. Unfortunately the duo hardly had time to settle before this guide went to print. At lunch there is a choice of three menus, two of which offer hors d'oeuvres as a starter and all inclusive of dessert and house wine. In the evening there is a *carte* and a five-course Menu Dégustation. There is always live music for which there is an extra charge. Influences are classic with a twist of innovation. Rolancey is fond of light soups, with the summer *carte* having no less than four including a chilled lobster bouillon of excellent clarity and fair flavour, enhanced by a julienne of beetroot, a poached quails egg and a crisp buckwheat pancake with a cool yoghurt filling. Panfried fillet of sea bream was topped with balsamic dressing and set on a bed of both baby and grown up leeks. The coffee shop style desserts such as Sachertorte were good. Service can be hurried at lunch, charm is more readily displayed in the evening.

Directions: Nearest Tube – Hyde Park Corner

Map no: 144

22 Park Lane W1

Tel: 0171-493 8000

Menus: *A la carte*, fixed-price, gourmet

Chef: Jacques Rolancey
Proprietors: Hilton International. Manager: Rudi Jagersbacher

The Lowndes 🏵

☺ *Belgravia-style Bangers and Mash is served in the Brasserie restaurant of this chic hotel, where the international menu also encompasses lobster bisque, mozarella and guacomole and warm Stilton pudding. The atmosphere is warm and welcoming, too.*

Additional: Children welcome; children's portions/menu; ◐ dishes; Vegan/other diets on request
Directions: From Sloane Street take first left into Lowndes Square, located on the bottom right hand corner. Nearest Tube – Knightsbridge (Sloane Street exit)

Map no: 145
21 Lowndes Street SW1
Tel: 0171 823 1234
Chef: Dennis Blokker and Schilo van Coetorden
Proprietors: Hyatt. Gen Manager: Miss Madelon Boom
Seats: 40. Air conditioned
Times: 7am-Last D 11.15pm (all day service)
Cost: *Alc* £20. Wine £10.50 ♀ Service exc
Credit cards: 1 2 3 4

Mandarin Kitchen 🏵🏵

☺ *A lively Chinese restaurant specialising in seafood, but offering plenty of meat alternatives.*

A simple, well used restaurant with unadorned white walls and smoked glass mirrors, the Mandarin Kitchen has a lively, very friendly atmosphere and a cosmopolitan clientele, including many families and friends. It is primarily a seafood restaurant, offering fresh lobster, crab, sea-bass, scallops, oysters and lesser-known Chinese fish. There is also a lengthy and unimaginative range of standard meat dishes, although the crispy aromatic duck looked good. Vegetarian food is available, but the menu has few options. Wind-dried oysters with black seaweed may not appeal to every palate, but the quail with paper-wrapped prawns, and crab with ginger and spring onions

Map no: R146

14-16 Queensway W2
Tel: 0171-727 9012

Cost: *A la carte* £15, fixed-price lunch and dinner £8.90. H/wine £7.50 ♀ Service exc
Credit cards: 1 2 3 4

Menus: *A la carte*, fixed-price lunch and dinner

Times: Midday-Last D11.30pm. Closed Xmas

were certainly good and demonstrated the freshness of the ingredients. Only the finest whole Scottish wild lobsters are served, and lobster with noodles is clearly popular, but it is advisable to check the cost as they are priced by weight. There are also four set dinners, each designed for parties of a specific size. The short wine list includes European and Australian wines, and good value French house wine at £6.50.

Chef: Mr Man
Proprietor: Helen Cheung

Additional: Children welcome.
❂ dishes; Vegan on request

Directions: Opposite Queensway Tube

Mas Café ❀❀

☺ *This strange but fascinating restaurant serves a range of Mediterrranean style dishes to a cosmopolitan clientele*

Map no: 147b

6-8 All Saints Road W11
Tel: 0171-243 0969

Multi-coloured, trendy and almost 'hip', this unusual restaurant in the cosmopolitan area around Westbourne Terrace and Ladbroke Grove raises eating to the level of spectator sport! Once past the bouncer on the door, you are in a world of colloquial London-speak and rap music where well-heeled young executives rub shoulders with local Rastafarians greeting friends at the bar; most of the customers are young, anthing goes in the way of dress and there is a real buzz of excitment in the atmosphere. The style of coooking is modern and the theme Mediterranean, the sensibly priced carte offering a choice of dishes at each course. An enjoyable test meal which began with good ravioli of oyster mushrooms went on to a main course of succulently pink roasted lamb fillet served with fresh seasonal vegetables (carefully cooked to retain their flavour) then a smooth cinnamon nd hazlenut mousse with praline. Vegetarian alternatives are provided, and children are welcomed – particularly at weekends, when there is a brunch menu. A value-for-money wine list contains some quality labels. There is some street parking in front of the restaurant.

Cost: *Alc* £17, fixed-price lunch £7.70 (2 courses), £9. Service charge 12.5%
Credit cards: 1 3 4 5

Menus: *A la carte*, fixed-price lunch, weekend brunch

Times: Midday-Last L 3pm, 7pm-Last D midnight (11.30pm Sun). Sat, Sun Brunch 11am-5pm

Chef: Philip Reynolds
Proprietors: Ian Alexander

Additional: Children welcome especially for weekend Brunch

Directions: Parallel to Portobello Road off Westbourne Park. Nearest Tubes – Ladbroke Grove, Westbourne Park

Matsuri ❀

In the heart of St James's, this new and flamboyant restaurant with cocktail and Sushi bars and Teppan counters, serves Teppan-yaki (grills on a hot plate), good Sashimi (assorted thinly sliced raw fish) and Tempura (deep fried in a light, rice flour batter). A popular restaurant.

Map no: 147
15 Bury Street SW1
Tel: 0171-839 1101
Chef: Kanehiro Takase
Proprietor: Shigemi Matsuda
Seats: 135. Air conditioned
Times: Last L 2.30pm/D 10pm. Closed Sun BHs

Cost: *Alc* £30, fixed-price L £33/D £34. Service exc.
Credit Cards: 1 2 3 4 **Additional:** Children welcome. ❂ dishes; Vegan/other diets on request
Directions: From Green Park Tube turn right down Piccadilly, right into St James's St, first left into Jermyn St, first right into Bury St

May Fair Inter-Continental ❀

Modern British cuisine with classical overtones and 'unstuffy' service make this hotel between Berkeley Square and Piccadilly so popular a place to eat that booking is essential; both carte and set-price menus offer a range of straightforward dishes made refreshingly different by unexpected flavour combinations.

Cost: Alc £25.50. Fixed-price L £22.50/D £29.50. H/wine £10 ♀ Opitional service12.5% **Credit cards:** 1 2 3 4 5
Additional: Children permitted. ❶ dishes; Vegan/others on request
Directions: Stratton St is off Piccadilly. Nearest Tube – Green Park

Map no: E148
Stratton Street W1
Tel: 0171-915 2842
Chef: Michael Coaker
Proprietor: Inter-Continental Hotels. Manager: Richard Griggs
Seats: 65. Air conditioned
Times: Last L 2.30pm/D 11pm. Closed Sat lunch & Aug

McClements Bistro ❀❀

☺ *An interesting variety of mainly rustic French cooking served in down-to-earth surroundings*

Rustic French dishes with an emphasis on offal sit comfortably side by side with some classics and a number of eclectic choices on the menu here. A small and rather stark room with bare floorboards houses this simple bistro, with crisp white linen napkins offering an unexpected touch of luxury amongst the basic black and white gingham tablecloths and mainly plain walls. The pig is another strong feature here, with dishes like 'tête de porc', 'kromeskie' and 'l'assiette du boucher' variously using all of that animal's parts. Our inspector began a recent meal with tourte of duck and foie gras - a puff pastry case filled with a chopped and moulded mixture of duck, garlic and foie gras - served with a delicate sauce and a leaf salad. 'Pot au feu' of pork was topped with a small piece of crispy cod, and served with braised chicory and sautéed new potatoes. Also on the varied *carte* might be risotto, home-made black pudding with Dijon mustard sauce, or lentil soup with Lyonnaise sausage, with main courses like tender shank of lamb, and pot roast of pheasant with liver dumplings. Service is variable.

Directions: In a small parade of shops, close to the station

Map no: 149

2 Whitton Road, Twickenham
Tel: 0181-744 9610

Cost: Alc £20. Service exc
Credit cards: 1 4

Menus: A la carte, Sunday lunch

Times: Midday-Last L 2.30pm, 7pm-Last D 11pm

Chef: John McClements
Propretor: John McClements

Additional: No cigars or pipes. Children welcome; ❶ dishes

McClements Petit Bistrot ❀❀

☺ *French provincial-style fish cookery is a speciality of this little bistro, where one-course meals may be taken*

Chef patron John McClements has returned to his roots, putting aside his more recent style of haute cuisine in favour of the straightforward approach he first adopted years ago. Many of his original recipes have since been copied by other chefs, but the French provincial fish cookery style is still very much his trade mark. Grilled sea scallops with home-made black pudding, cassoulet of shellfish, hot sea urchins on a pomme purée, and fish nobs (the cheeks of the skate fish, lightly pan-fried with lemon butter) are just some of the delights awaiting the more adventurous diner. The duck confit is worth trying, stuffed with chicken, crisply cooked and served with a duck fat

Map no: 150

12 The Green, Twickenham
Tel: 0181-755 0176

Cost: Alc £17.50
Credit cards: 1 3

Menus: A la carte

Times: Midday-Last L 2.30pm, 7pm-Last D 10.30pm. Closed Sun, Mon

Chef: John McClements
Proprietor: John McClements

jus reduction; and the red mullet, served with a tasty virgin olive oil butter paste textured with black olives and tomato concasse. Vegetarian dishes can also be provided on request. To finish, from a limited choice of sweets, the lemon tart remains a good example of the classic French dessert. A short list of carefully selected vintage wines is available by the bottle, and service is efficient and friendly, with no obligation to order more than one course.

Seats: 30
Additional: Children welcome: ❶ dishes on request

Directions: Leaving Twickenham town centre, the restaurant is opposite The Green and Hampton Road

Mijanou ❁❁

Original and eclectic cooking created with skill and imagination in a restaurant with a walled garden

Map no: J151

143 Ebury Street SW1
Tel: 0171-730 4099

Elaborate dishes full of pungent flavours are created by dynamic French chef/patronne Sonia Blech, whose rich, eclectic cooking makes an enjoyable alternative to current trends. Her popular, good-value fixed-price lunch menu is relatively restrained (for instance, mussels cooked in spices, lasagne basquaise), while at dinner her imagination and flair are allowed full rein with a seven-course 'Menu Dégustation' and a *carte* offering around five choices per course. An unusual and quite superb terrine of oxtail and foie gras on a muscat and passion fruit jelly served with an apple and onion relish was a recent first course typical of the house style. It was served, on this occasion, in the restaurant's small walled garden. Main courses can be equally exotic as in a pan of plump quails stuffed with wild rice and glazed with mango chutney and ginger, served with a Madeira sauce – a little too sweet for some, perhaps, but nonetheless delicious. As for puddings, be warned: they are rich and delicious, too! Co-patron Neville Blech is a genial host and his interesting wine list ranges from 'light dry white' to 'big scale fruity red'.

Cost: *Alc* £32.50, fixed-price L £13.50 (2 courses), £16.50 ♀ Service exc

Credit cards: 1 2 3 4
Menus: *A la carte*, fixed-price lunch

Times: Midday-Last L 2pm, 7pm-Last D 11pm

Chef: Sonia Blech
Proprietors: Sonia and Neville Blech

Seats: 30. No-smoking area. Air conditioned
Additional: Children permitted. ❶ menu

Directions: Ebury Street is between Sloane Square and Victoria Station. Nearest Tube – Sloane Square

Mims ❁❁

A cross between a boulevard café and a Caribbean coffee shop serving classical French cuisine with light sauces

Map no: 152

63 East Barnet Road, Barnet
Tel: 0181-449 2974

There's almost a Caribbean atmosphere to this informal French restaurant which fronts a busy shopping street. The relaxed and friendly service is favoured by the growing number of people who frequent this place, and booking is recommended, especially at weekends. The fixed-price lunch and dinner menus include a short choice of dishes for each course, while the *carte* offers a more elaborate evening selection, both from a solidly classical French repertoire, with chef Mr I Al-Sersy adding lighter and leaner sauces in the modern style. A moist and tender quail, well buttered and stuffed with barley, made a delicious recent starter, while monkfish fillet poached in a

Cost: *Alc* from £20, fixed-price lunch £9.50 (2 courses), £14. H/wine £8.95 ♀ Service exc
Credit cards: 1 3

Menus: *A la carte*, fixed-price lunch

Times: Midday-Last L 2.30pm, 6.30pm-Last D 11pm

thyme-flavoured stock with a selection of carefully-prepared and well-cooked vegetables was an enjoyable main course. Desserts come on a short list of simple creations, and the tarte tatin was an outstandingly well-flavoured choice. Other dishes might be fillet of beef with a mustard custard and wild mushrooms, and grilled veal sweetbreads with Jerusalem artichoke purée. The wine list offers a good range of popular wines with generous halves.

Directions: On the East Barnet Road, opposite Sainsbury's

Chef: Mr I Al-Sersy
Proprietors: Mr I Al-Sersy, Mr M Abouzahrah

Seats: 40. No cigars or pipes
Additional: Children permitted; no children under 6 at dinner.
❂ dishes, other diets on request

Ming ❂❂

☺ *The food at this Chinese restaurant stands head and shoulders above many others and is very good value*

A Chinese restaurant with a cool sea-green interior (and rather uncomfortable chairs), the Ming seems to have refined its cooking with improved presentation and lighter sauces. There has been no concomitant increase in the prices, however, and the food remains very good value for money. The menu offers four set meals priced from £12 to £19.50 per person, one a vegetarian option. Then there is a short list of special dishes, mostly market fresh fish and vegetables, with a dish for vegetarians such as fresh spinach in fermented beancurd sauce and chilli. The *carte* has a comprehensive selection of less usual dishes. Our inspector enjoyed the famous Ming scallops coated with black bean sauce and fresh chilli; fried dumplings (meat or vegetable) with lovely subtle flavours; 'Mr Edward's pork' flavoured with liquorice, and Ming special cauliflower, powerfully flavoured with salt and chilli, which should not be missed. Tibetan garlic lamb was another pungent dish with a good range of textures, including crunchy peppers and peanuts. A Gewürztraminer, especially recommended for Chinese food, is included in the wine list.

Directions: Behind Palace Theatre, 2-3 minutes' walk from Leicester Square and Piccadilly Circus

Map no: M153

35-36 Greek Street W1
Tel: 0171-734 2721

Cost: A/c £15, fixed-price lunch £10, fixed-price dinner £12, £19.50. H/wine £7.90. Service exc
Credit cards: 1 2 3 4

Menus: A la carte, fixed-price lunch and dinner

Times: Midday-Last D11.45. Closed Sun (except Chinese New Year), Xmas

Chef: E H Leu
Proprietor: Christine Yau

Seats: 65. No-smoking area. Air conditioned
Additional: Children welcome.
❂ dishes

Mirabelle ❂❂❂

A fine French restaurant in the traditional style with an additional Japanese teppanyaki room

A complete contrast of styles is offered at this fine old Mayfair restaurant, now under Japanese ownership. Traditional standards remain unchanged but a stylish Japanese teppanyaki room has been added, offering a teppan kaiseki (set course) menu which is available in both restaurants. The main restaurant is a haven of peace and refinement, where attentive staff provide unobtrusive service.
The menus, in French with an English translation, include a good-value fixed-price lunch and a set dinner in addition to the *carte*. There is also a daily changing, six-course Menu Surprise for the whole table. Some of chef Michael Croft's most popular dishes tend to remain on the *carte*, such as his starter of

Map no: I154

56 Curzon Street W1
Tel: 0171-499 4636

Cost: A/c £35, fixed-price Lunch £15 (2 courses) £18; fixed-price dinner £28. Wine £10. Service inc
Credit cards: 1 2 3 4 5

Menus: A la carte, fixed-price lunch and dinner,

Times: Midday-Last L 2pm, 6.30pm-Last D10.30 pm. Closed Sat lunch, Sun, BHs, 2 weeks

coquilles St Jacques - grilled scallops on a purée of watercress and parsley with a chive butter sauce, and another favourite, a potato, celeriac and foie gras galette with wild forest mushrooms and shallots in a Madeira and truffle essence. Main courses of pan-fried sea-bass with cabbage and caviar on a light langoustine sauce, and tournedos of beef poached in mushroom broth with wild mushrooms and fresh herbs have pleased our inspectors, though vegetables are used as garnishes to the main dish, and as such are not served in substantial quantities – disappointing to vegetable lovers. Vegetarian dishest can be provided on request.

For pudding, our inspector found the soufflé chocolat well worth the wait: a light soufflé of bitter chocolate served in a copper pot with a separate sauce boat of coffee cream sauce, described as a fitting end to an enjoyable meal. The mainly French wine list is outstanding, the major features being over twenty wines from Domaine de la Romanée-Conti and as many first growth clarets. Prices may seem high, but there are several recommended house wines at £10-£18.50 a bottle.

Directions: At Berkeley Square end of Curzon Street. NCP car parks close by. Nearest Tube – Green Park

Aug,1 week Xmas,

Chef: Michael Croft
Proprietor: Mr A Sekine

Seats: 100. No pipes. Air conditioned
Additional: Children over 6 permitted. ❂ menu

Mitsukoshi ●●

Superb examples of the simple art of Japanese cooking in an atmosphere of serenity and harmony

The entrance to this fine restaurant is to the right of the lobby of the Mitsukoshi department store – confusing when the department store is closed. Downstairs, subtle lighting, traditional lacquered furniture, and gentle Kimono clad waitresses emphasise the serenity of this Japanese restaurant. The set fixed-price complete meals can be ideal for the uninitiated, but the *carte* and sushi give an opportunity to try individually selected dishes. Chef Jiro Shimada San has brought to London some of the best of Japanese cooking, and by producing his own dashi (a delicate stock) and shuyu, (naturally brewed soy sauce), adds subtle flavours to any dish he has constructed. Our inspection meal began with sashimi – gleaming and succulent fresh raw fish, with a dipping ginger soy sauce which was followed by an excellent chawan mushi, a savoury cup custard. The meal was concluded in the traditional way with a fine miso soup, in which one could watch the bean paste still fermenting, fine sticky boiled rice, pickles and green tea, which has a distinctive flavour of tree bark. It is best to book as most of the Japanese clientele are regulars.

Directions: One minute's walk from Piccadilly Circus

Map no: 155

Dorland House, 14-20 Regent Street SW1
Tel: 0171-930 0317

Cost: Fixed-price L £20, fixed-price D £30. Service charge 15%. Cover charge £1.50
Credit cards: 1 2 3 4 5

Menus: *A la carte*, fixed-price lunch and dinner, pre-theatre

Times: Midday-Last L 2pm, 6pm-Last D 10pm. Closed Sun & BHs

Chef: Jiro Shimada San
Proprietor: Izumi Kudo San

Seats: 80. Air conditioned
Additional: Children over 5 permitted

Miyama ☺

☺ *A fairly healthy style of cooking is served at this Japanese restaurant, which offers a carte and set lunches, with specialities cooked at the table. Our inspector enjoyed his dobin-mushi (clear soup) but felt that some dishes lacked excitement.*

Cost: Alc £17, fixed-price L £11-£18; fixed-price D £32-£40. Service charge 15%
Credit cards: 1 2 3 4 5.
Additional: Children welcome; ❶ menu; Vegan on request
Directions: Nearest Tube – Green Park

Map no: 1156
38 Clarges Street W1
Tel: 0171-499 2443
Chef: F Miyama
Proprietors: F Miyama, T Miura
Seats: 65. No pipes. Air conditioned
Times: Last L 2.30pm/D 10.30pm. Closed Sat and Sun lunch

Monkeys ❀❀

Good value Anglo-French cooking is offered from a choice of menus at this friendly and intimate restaurant

Monkeys is a popular but intimate restaurant with a friendly atmosphere and a regular clientele who appreciate the hospitality, Brigitte Benham at front of house, and the uncomplicated yet thoughtfully prepared cooking of proprietor Tom Benham. A fixed-price lunch menu, a carte and two set dinners of Anglo-French cuisine are offered. This year our inspectors have sampled starters of scallop mousse with a fresh tasting lobster sauce, and a delicately flavoured terrine of brill, salmon and scallops with a light tomato sauce. Main course choices were grilled cod with a delicious crusty topping of herbs and breadcrumbs served in a generous portion with a béarnaise sauce, and a beautifully cooked roast bresse pigeon with wild mushrooms and another delightful sauce. At the pudding stage the crème brûlée, a bit overdone, was a slight disappointment, but the treacle tart with its crisp pastry and tasty filling was very much enjoyed. It was served with a choice of custard, cream or ice cream. A well balanced wine list is available, with a few nice clarets and Burgundies, and some New World wines.

Directions: Off the King's Road, on the corner of Markham Street and Cale Street. Nearest Tube – Sloane Square

Map no: 157
1 Cale Street,
Chelsea Green SW3
Tel: 0171-352 4711

Cost: Alc £26, fixed-price lunch £12.50; fixed-price dinner £22.50 (3 courses), £35. H/wine £11. Service exc
Credit cards: 1 3 5

Menus: A la carte, fixed-price lunch and dinner

Times: 12.30-Last L 2.30pm, 7.30pm-Last D 11pm. Closed Aug BH, 25 Dec, 1 Jan, 2 weeks Easter, 3 weeks Aug

Chef: Thomas Benham
Proprietor: Thomas Benham

Seats: 40. No pipes
Additional: Children permitted; children's portions

Montcalm, The Crescent ☺

☺ *The new Crescent contributes a commendable dimension to this recently refurbished discreet hotel. The interesting Anglo/French carte includes some flambé dishes and coquilles St Jacques with lobster butter and tournedos sauté with wild mushroom ravioli.*

Cost: Alc dinner £32, fixed-price L £14.50 (1 course), £17.50, £19.50/D £19.50 (inc wine). Wine £12 ♀ Service exc
Additional: Children welcome. ❶ dishes; Vegan/other diets on request. Pianist Fri/Sat evenings. **Credit cards:** 1 2 3 4 5
Directions: Great Cumberland Place is north of Marble Arch. Nearest Tube – Marble Arch

Map no: 158

Great Cumberland Place W1
Tel: 0171-402 4288
Chef: Gary Robinson
Proprietor: Nikko Hotels.
Manager: Gerhard Schaller
Seats: 60. No-smoking area. Air conditioned
Times: Last L 2pm/D 10pm. Closed Sat L, Sun

The Mountbatten ☻

☺ *A very pleasant small hotel with two fixed-price menus with a range of dishes centring on English ingredients. Starters might include wood pigeon terrine or Rossmore oysters, delivered twice weekly, poached in a saffron sauce. To follow, try rabbit with ginger or cod with parsley sauce.*

Cost: Alc £22, fixed-price L/D £15.50. H/wine £11.50 ♀ Service inc.
Credit cards: 1 2 3 4.
Additional: No children after 8pm. ◐ dishes; Vegan/other diets on request
Directions: In Covent Garden, next to Seven Dials

Map no: 159

Monmouth Street, Seven Dials,
Covent Garden WC2

Tel: 0171-836 4300
Chef: Keith Walker
Proprietors: Radisson Edwardian
Seats: 65. No-smoking area. Air conditioned
Times: Last L 2.30pm/D 11.30pm

Mulligans of Mayfair ☻☻

Honest cooking of wholesome dishes is offered at this, the only Irish restaurant in London

The only Irish restaurant in London, Mulligan's has a very busy lounge bar on the ground floor and a restaurant in the basement below. This is divided into sections with ornamental glass partitions, and portrait sketches of Irish personalities adorn the walls. As one might expect, the atmosphere is friendly and informal, with charming staff providing attentive and efficient service. Head chef Seamus McFaddon presents a short and frequently changing menu which includes Mulligan's home-made soup and home-made black pudding with apple chutney among the starters. Main courses offer braised beef and Guinness with 'boxty' potatoes, traditional Irish stew, and the wild Donegal salmon with creamed leeks and wild mushrooms enjoyed by our inspector. This he followed with a pudding of almond slice and vanilla sauce to finish. Vegetarian dishes are also available on request. The wine list is reasonably priced and well balanced, offering a few nice clarets and Burgundies.

Directions: Situated between Burlington Gardens and Clifford Street, just north of Piccadilly.

Map no: 160

13-14 Cork Street W1
Tel: 0171-409 1370

Chef: Seamus McFadden
Proprietor: Mulligans

Times: 12.30-Last L 2.30pm, 6.30pm-Last D 11pm. Closed Sat lunch, Sun, Xmas

Cost: Alc £22.50; H/wine £5.95 (half bottle). Service inc
Credit cards: 1 2 3 4.

Additional: Children welcome; children's portions; ◐ dishes

Museum Street Café ☻☻

☺ *A popular little café with a new look of understated chic serving imaginative dishes, many from the chargrill*

There have been some changes at this popular little café near the British Museum. A complete refit in early 1994 has created a spanking new dining area, and the galley kitchen is open to public scrutiny during service, which is performed in a cool and precise manner. A fixed-price menu has replaced the blackboard at lunchtime; an alcohol licence has been obtained, and the restaurant now takes credit cards. The small, sensibly chosen wine list marries well with the daily-changing lunch and weekly-changing dinner menus. A choice of two first courses at lunch might be red pepper soup or a well-rounded chicken liver pâté served on toasted slices of baguette. The chargrill is put to

Map no: 161

47 Museum Street WC1
Tel: 0171-405 3211

Cost: Fixed-price lunch £12 (2 courses), £15; fixed-price dinner £17 (2 courses), £21. Wine £7.90 ♀ Service exc. Corkage £4
Credit cards: 1 3 5

Menus: Fixed-price lunch and dinner

Times: 12.30pm-Last L 2.30pm, 6.30pm-Last D 9.30pm. Closed

good use for the main courses, which include warm goats' cheese salad, corn-fed chicken with pesto, swordfish with soy ginger, and a recently tested dish of bite-size chunks of freshest tuna and salmon, skewered and served with a dribble of lemon juice and a powerful green herb mayonnaise. For dessert our inspector sampled an olive oil and Sauternes cake with strawberries; the sponge weighted with the oil, but melting in texture.

Directions: Museum Street is off Bloomsbury Way. The café is on the right. Nearest Tubes – Tottenham Court Road, Holborn

Sat, Sun, BHs

Chefs: Mark Nathan, Gail Koerber
Proprietors: Mark Nathan, Gail Koerber

Seats: 34. No smoking
Additional: Children permitted; ◐ dishes/other diets on request with advance notice

Neal Street ✺✺✺

Italian cooking with many dishes reflecting owner Antonio Carluccio's passion for pasta and mushrooms

Santiago Gonzales has now retired as planned and in his place, perhaps surprisingly in this bastion of Italian cooking, there is an English chef, Nick Melmoth-Coombs. However, the menu format has not changed, nor has the quality of the ingredients or the cooking.

Mushrooms and pasta are the twin passions of charismatic owner Antonio Carluccio, who has written books about both, and many dishes on the menu feature one or the other, or a combination of the two, such as pappardelle with funghi, thick ribbons of egg-enriched pasta tossed with an intensely flavoured sauce of mixed field and wild mushrooms, and tagliolini with a truffle sauce. There is one price for pasta, which can be eaten as a starter or main course, and some of these dishes would be suitable for vegetarians. Mushrooms are also included in a mixed sauté as a starter, a soup, and a warm salad with bacon. There is a parcel of duck with funghi, beef with ceps, and an amazingly rich ragout of sweetbreads with fresh morels. Schiacciata of beef is similar to a carpaccio, although this one is briefly flashed in a hot oven and assembled at the table with plenty of Rucola, shavings of a memorable truffle cheese and a drizzle of virgin olive oil - a superb combination of textures and vibrant flavours. For those less keen on mushrooms there is still plenty to choose from, light buffalo Ricotta and spinach gnocchi with a summery basil and tomato sauce; marinated grilled swordfish and quails with grapes and grappa raisins, for example. Meals here begin with delicious focaccia, baked on the premises, and end with great espresso. Service is informed and charming – newcomers being welcomed with the same enthusiasm as the many regulars.

There is a first class selection of red and white wines on the list, backed up by some good ones from France.

Directions: Just north of where Shelton Street crosses Neal Street. Nearest Tube – Covent Garden

Map no: 162

26 Neal Street WC2
Tel: 0171-836 8368

Cost: A/c £37. H/wine £12.50 ♀
Service inc
Credit cards: 1 2 3 4 5

Menu: A la carte

Times: 12.30pm-Last L 2.30pm, 7.30pm-Last D 11pm. Closed Sun, Xmas–New Year, BHs

Chef: Nick Melmoth-Coombs
Proprietor: Antonio Carluccio

Seats: 60. Air conditioned
Additional: Children permitted; ◐ dishes; other diets on request

Nico at Ninety ●●●●●

Virtually faultless cooking in elegant surroundings, showing a mastery of the modern French style by one of Britain's great chefs

These Park Lane premises may occupy a part of the Grosvenor Hotel but Nico at Ninety is very much the domain of its owners, Nico and Dinah-Jane Ladenis. It is a discreet and elegant restaurant, admirably suited to the philosophy of a man now firmly established as a great chef. Here is where you will be able to savour excellent cooking in the French style coupled with impeccable presentation and service. Lunch menus are priced for two or three courses; the evening *carte* offers two courses for a fixed price and a separate dessert menu or the option of a superb gastronomic menu, available to a minimum of two diners.

Although dishes are very plainly described on the menus, make no mistake – the cooking is wonderful, and complemented by the very fine wine list of about 250 bottles and a good selection of halves. A dinner earlier this year began with thinly sliced noisettes of pig's trotter, stuffed with morels and sweetbreads, described by the inspector as an exquisite dish, and one which should now be the standard by which other interpretations are judged. A large ravioli of beautifully fresh sole, salmon and lobster followed, served with a sauce velouté flavoured with chives, and just slightly marred by a pinch of salt too many.

For dessert, a chocolate tart with an orange-flavoured custard, however, was the stuff of dreams, but so rich that our inspector was left with little appetite for the plate of blissful petits fours served with the coffee.

At another lunch, taken during the spring, the highlight was the essence of simplicity: faultlessly cooked, flavoursome chicken breast, stuffed with mushrooms and encased in a perfect butter pastry. Here is confident cooking of the highest standard, informed by a deep respect for the classical French tradition, but not so over-awed by it as to stifle innovation.

Directions: Adjoining the Grosvenor House Hotel, about halfway along Park Lane, between Upper Grosvenor Street and Mount Street. Nearest Tube – Marble Arch

Map no: 163

90 Park Lane W1
Tel: 0171-409 1290

Cost: Fixed-price lunch (3 courses) £25, dinner (2 courses) £42; Menu Gastronomic £40, £60 (both min 2 persons)
Credit cards: 1 2 3 4

Menus: Fixed-price lunch & dinner, Menu Gastronomic

Times: Last L 2pm, Last D 11pm. Lunch not served Sat. Closed Sun, BHs

Chefs: Nico Ladenis, Paul Rhodes
Proprietors: Nico and Dinah-Jane Ladenis

Seats: 80. No pipes allowed. Air conditioned
Additional: ♥ on request. No children under 5

Nico Central ●●●

☺ *A simple but elegant setting for classic dishes cooked with modern flair using first class ingredients*

Situated nearer the Oxford Circus end of Great Portland Street, this small, elegant restaurant is packed with customers from the local business community at lunchtime, while in the evening it has a more relaxed ambience. At lunch the dishes and vegetables are individually priced, but in the evening the formula has changed and is now more in line with its sister restaurant, Simply Nico, with a set price three-course menu. This includes good olives, fine bread, and excellent chips or creamy puréed potato. The menu content is similar at each

Map no: 164

35 Great Portland Street W1
Tel: 0171-436 8846

Cost: Fixed-price dinner £22. Wine £11.50 ♀ Service inc
Credit cards: 1 2 3 4

Menu: Fixed-price dinner

Times: Midday-Last L 2pm, 7pm-Last D 11pm. Closed Sun, Sat lunch, 4 days Easter, 10 days

meal, though, and many of the dishes are permanent features due to their popularity. Consequently this is not a restaurant at the forefront of food fads and fashion, but rather a place where one can enjoy classic dishes, competently cooked with modern flair using first class ingredients.

The 'boudin blanc', a sausage of chicken and foie gras, was light in texture but packed with flavour, served with a crisp caramelised apple galette and a lip-smacking grain mustard sauce. There is some doubling up, as the same mustard sauce followed with the pan-fried skirt of beef - a pink, chewy belly cut, layered on a crisp salardaise potato cake with oyster mushrooms. There is no stinting on luxuries with a menu that includes a gratin of langoustines and pasta, and even fried foie gras with brioche and caramelised orange (though this does carry a £6 supplement). Saucing is highly skilled, as demonstrated in the superb béarnaise served with chargrilled chicken and asparagus. Desserts include chocolate marquise, a hot ginger and walnut sponge and a classic lemon tart. Attentive service is provided by a fresh young team.

Although the compact wine list is restricted to about 35 wines, if offers a varied selection at prices up to £50 a bottle. Four good house wines are available by the glass.

Directions: Just of Oxford Circus, at southern end of Great Portland Street. Nearest Tube – Oxford Circus

Xmas, BH lunch

Chef: Andrew Jeffs
Proprietors: Nico and Dinah-Jane Ladenis

Seats: 50. No pipes or cigars. Air conditioned
Additional: Children permitted (over 3); ◐ dishes

Odette's ✸✸

Uncomplicated, subtle cooking from a talented, careful chef in a friendly neighbourhood setting

Little hints of the Far East creep into the talented modern British cooking of chef Paul Holmes, with results that are both refreshing and innovative. His clever use of spices and imaginative skill in producing subtle flavours greatly increase the diner's enjoyment, and show that he is capable of reaching the culinary heights. Our inspector was impressed with a recent meal which began with a delicious roasted fish soup, beautifully textured with fresh allumette of ribbon noodles, followed by lean and tender fillet of beef set on excitingly spiced aubergines – a perfectly balanced dish served with a delicately flavoured red wine sauce. Simply cooked vegetables had plenty of flavour, and apple and ricotta brioche crumble with crème fraîche was an enjoyable if unusual dessert. The separate lunch and dinner *cartes* also offer starters like breaded lambs brains', or sautéed foie gras, and main dishes of fillets of red mullet with pesto tagliatelle and gazpacho sauce, and confit of duck with vanilla butter beans and roasted Jerusalem artichokes. You can eat at tables on the pavement in warm weather.

Directions: At Primrose Hill end of Regents Park Road. Nearest Tube – Chalk Farm

Map no: Q165

130 Regents Park Road NW1
Tel: 0171-586 5486

Cost: A/c £24; fixed-price lunch £10. Wine £9.95 ♀ Service exc
Credit cards: 1 2 3 4

Menus: *A la carte*; fixed-price lunch, Sunday lunch, bar menu

Times: 12.30-Last L 2.30pm, 7pm-Last D 11pm. Closed Sat lunch, Sun dinner, 1 week at Xmas

Chef: Paul Holmes
Proprietor: Simone Green

Seats: 60
Additional: Children welcome; children's portions; ◐ dishes; Vegan/other diets on request

Odins ❂❂

☺ *A popular London restaurant famous for its paintings and a good standard of cooking*

A few new paintings have been added to the famous collection at this popular restaurant, but otherwise little has changed in the way of decor or atmosphere over the years. The food remains unfussy and straightforward, and chef Shaun Butcher has continued to maintain the same consistently high standards as his predecessor. A refreshingly chilled cucumber and mint soup thickened with yoghurt caught the attention of our inspector at a recent meal, and this tasty starter was successfully followed by a superbly cooked fillet of turbot, a speciality dish which was grilled with parsley butter and fully retained its moistness and flavour; the plain, fresh vegetables which accompanied this course were perfectly complementary. A long-time favourite dessert at Odins has been Mrs Langan's chocolate pudding, and the light sponge filled with cream and covered with heavy chocolate sauce was still enjoyable, although not quite as good as our inspector remembers it. The staff are friendly, but service is a little lacking in finesse. A mostly French wine list includes one or two New World choices.

Directions: At Marylebone High Street end of Devonshire Street. Nearest Tubes – Baker Street, Regents Park, Great Portland Street

Map no: 166
27 Devonshire Street W1
Tel: 0171-935 7296

Cost: Alc £23. Wine £8.50. Service inc
Credit cards: 1 2 3 4 5

Menu: A la carte

Times: 12.30-Last L 2.30pm, 7pm-Last D 11.30pm. Closed Sat, Sun

Chef: Shaun Butcher
Proprietors: Michael Caine, Richard Shepherd

Seats: 60. Air conditioned
Additional: ❂ dishes

The Old Delhi ❂

☺ *An intimate restaurant where the the chef is Indian but the owners Persian, so the cuisine is delightfully influenced by both these cultures. The spices and herbs are well balanced and not overpowering. There are a number of Persian desserts and a short wine list with some good wines.*

Cost: Alc £20. H/wine £8 (half bottle). Service inc.
Credit cards: 1 2 3 4 **Additional:** Children welcome; ❂ dishes
Directions: In Kendal Street, off Edgeware Road. Nearest Tube – Marble Arch

Map no: 167
48 Kendal Street W2
Tel: 0171-724 9580
Chef: Ram
Proprietors: Jay Shaghaghi, Hasser
Seats: 56

Olde Village Bakery ❂

Honest English cooking is served at this old world former bakery on the High Street dating from 1480. Our inspector sampled asparagus terrine with tomato coulis, tender medallions of pork with caramelised apples and Calvados sauce, and fig and almond tart with pistachio ice cream.

Cost: Alc £20. H/wine £8 (half bottle). Service inc
Additional: Children welcome; children's portions; ❂ dishes; Vegan/other diets on request
Directions: From Northwood (A404) turn right at Pinner Green into Bridge Street, then left into the High Street

Map no: 168
33 High Street, Pinner, Middx
Tel: 0181-868 4704
Chef: Simon Ault
Proprietors: Susan and Kevin Davies
Seats: 60. Separate room for smokers. No pipes or cigars
Times: Last L 3pm/D 10pm.

Olivo ◉◉

Map no: 169

☺ *A small, popular restaurant serving good-value authentic Sardinian dishes with lesser known Italian wines*

21 Eccleston Street SW1
Tel: 0171-730 2502

Honest cooking of well researched and authentic dishes is offered at this simple but colourful restaurant, designed to evoke memories of sultry Sardinian holidays. The formula works phenomenally well, with its friendly, informal atmosphere and value-for-money prices. Everything is produced daily by chef Giorgio Locatelli, who demonstrates his skill with excellent pasta and a special risotto made with carnaroli and vialone nano – very fine dwarf rice – which is cooked to order. Try the 'pappardelle con rucola e fave', fresh flat pasta with a broad bean purée and beurre blanc sauce; also grilled fillet of grey mullet with olive oil and chopped tomatoes. The 'torta di cioccolato e mandorle' should not be missed: a rich chocolate tart textured with finely chopped almonds and served with home-made chocolate ice cream. The lunch menu, changes daily and some dishes will find their way onto the dinner *carte*, and vegetarian options are always featured. Good value, lesser known Italian wines have been personally selected by proprietor Mauro Sanna. Early reservations are strongly advised.

Chef: Giorgio Locatelli
Proprietor: Mauro Sanna

Times: Last L 2.30pm/D 11pm. Closed Sat L, Sun, BHs, 3 weeks Aug, Xmas

Cost: *Alc* D £22.50; fixed-price L £15. No service charge
Credit cards: 1 2 3

Additional: Children welcome; ❸ dishes

Directions: From Buckingham Palace Road, opposite Victoria Station, turn into Eccleston Street. Olivio is on the left

Oriel ◉

☺ *A busy, informal brasserie with friendly service, good value food with a short, seasonally-changing menu. The cooking is careful and imaginative, with such dishes as seared tuna Niçoise, seafood tagliatelle, linguine or beef olives. Desserts range from sorbets to triple chocolate terrine.*

Map no: 170
51 Sloane Square SW1
Tel: 0171-730 2804
Chef: David Wilby
Proprietor: Forte. Manager: Lori Elmore
Seats: 75. No-smoking area
Times: Last D 10.30pm. Closed Xmas

Cost: *Alc* £15. Wine £9.95 ? Service exc. **Credit cards:** 1 2 3 4 5
Additional: Children welcome; children's portions. ❸ dishes; Vegan/other diets on request. Live jazz
Directions: From Sloane Square Tube turn right, Oriel is on the Royal Court Theatre side of the Square

Oriental House ◉

☺ *A mainly Cantonese restaurant where diners are well looked after by smartly uniformed waiters and fresh, quality ingredients and generous portions are the hallmarks.*

Map no: 171
251 Old Brompton Road SW5
Tel: 0171-370 2323
Chef: David Lu
Proprietors: Joe C K Lau, Stanley H K Lau
Seats: 60. Air conditioned
Times: Last L 2pm/D 11pm. Closed BHs

Cost: *Alc* £16; fixed-price D £16.50. Wine £8.50. Service inc
Credit cards: 1 2 3
Additional: Children welcome; ❸ menu; Vegan/other diets on request
Directions: Nearest Tube – Earls Court. Turn right at main entrance onto Earls Court Road, at traffic lights turn right again

Orso ❀❀

Popular basement Italian restaurant where distinctive flavours and authentic recipes are skilfully combined

Now well-established as one of the most accomplished Italian restaurants in this part of town, Orso's success is fed by chef Martin Wilson's skilful timing and handling of fresh, organically grown ingredients, a combination that can produce excellent results. Cooking here is authentic: everything that can be is home-made and the evolving menu changes twice daily, according to market availability. A range of Italian regional wines are listed on the back of the carte, which is sensibly presented in Italian and English parallel text. Exciting flavours leap out from dishes such as our inspector's first course of thin pasta with crab, courgettes and tomato, arguably one of the best starters of the year. Texture is equally expert: fresh and light in the ciabatta, tender and melting in succulent sautéed calfs' liver. Vegetables are notably good, the caponata especially recommended (ideal as a starter). Italian cheeses include Pecorino con pera and Taleggio and the apricot tart was most enjoyable. Booking is essential and busy periods mean an agreed release time; service is professional and efficient.

Map no: 172

27 Wellington Street WC2
Tel: 0171-240 5269

Cost: Alc £23. Wine £9. Service exc
Credit cards: None taken

Menu: A la carte

Times: Midday-Midnight

Chef: Martin Wilson
Proprietor: Joe Allen.
Manageress: Linda Thorne

Seats: 100. No-smoking area. Air conditioned
Additional: Children welcome; ❶ dishes

Directions: Wellington Street is at junction of The Strand and the Aldwych. Nearest Tube – Covent Garden

Osmani ❀

☺ *The cooking is North African and simple in this cosy little restaurant with cushioned chairs and fresh flowers. Couscous comes in five ways: lamb, chicken, vegetable, merguez and Royale and is served with a vegetable stew and a side dish of harissa. The meat is all charcoal grilled.*

Map no: 173
46 Inverness Street N6
Tel: 0171-267 4682
Chefs: A Osmani, B Karim
Proprietor: A Osmani
Seats: 28
Times: Last L 2.30pm/D 11.30pm. Closed BHs

Cost: Alc £16.50, fixed-price L/D £11.50. H/wine £8.50 ♀
Credit card: 2. **Additional**: Children welcome, children's portions. ❶ dishes
Directions: Inverness Street is off Camden High Street

Osteria Antica Bologna ❀❀

☺ *A typically Italian restaurant serving enjoyable food from the southern regions*

An Alpine chalet houses this enjoyable restaurant which specialises in Italian country cuisine using authentic staple ingredients. The cooking of Sicilian chef Raffaele Petralia leans heavily towards the southern regions, with dishes like 'conglio alla cacciatore', rabbit cooked in wine, tomato and mushrooms, served with black truffle crostino, or 'polipo in umido', casseroled octopus with olives, tomatoes, wine and chillies. Our inspector began a recent meal with 'radicchio con prosciutto', braised radicchio leaves with slices of ham but no sign of the promised rosemary pesto. 'Capretto alle mandorle', a house

Map no: B174

23 Northcote Road SW11
Tel: 0171-978 4771

Cost: Alc £15, fixed-price lunch £7.50. H/wine £6.90. Service exc. Cover charge 60p
Credit cards: 1 2 3 5

Menus: A la carte, fixed lunch

Times: Mon-Fri Midday-Last L 3pm, 6pm-Last D 11pm (11.30pm Fri); Sat Midday-

speciality of mild goat meat stewed in a rich tomato and almond pesto was enjoyable, but soggy mange-tout and overcooked spinach leaves with burnt pieces of garlic did not do justice to the meal. A delightfully succulent tiramisù was followed by hearty espresso coffee. Desserts like fresh strawberry and cream cake with a fresh strawberry sauce are verbally announced, and the seasonally changing *carte* is supported by a fixed-price menu at lunchtime. The wine list is confined to the regions of Italy.

Directions: Off Battersea Rise, between Wandsworth and Clapham Commons

11.30pm; Sun 12.30-10.30pm. Closed 10 days Xmas/New Year

Chefs: Aurelio Spagnuolo, Raffaele Petralia
Proprietors: Rochelle Porteous, Aurelio Spagnuolo

Seats: 75. Air conditioned
Additional: Children welcome; children's portions. ❖ dishes; Vegan on request

Overton's ❖❖

A re-vamped fish restaurant with a new image and new, innovative chef. Old favourites are still on the menu

Relaunched in July '93, this well-established fish restaurant has a new look. Gone is the ambience of a gentleman's club, in have come chairs with striking cushions, colourful coverplates on the well-spaced tables and a glass domed roof which adds newly found light. Al fresco dining in the lovely courtyard can be enjoyed on summer evenings. To complement the surroundings, the newly recruited Nigel Davies has brought innovation to the previously staid menu, although some regulars have asked for the return of old favourites like whitebait and melon! He has some interesting and gutsy combinations and Italian influences such as mussels with pesto and tomato toasts or plump Scottish scallops with smoked bacon risotto and a light veal jus. There are still crab and lobster salads, a traditional smoked haddock, spinach and egg pie and for carnivores pot-roasted venison and calves' liver with lentils. Portions are generous and vegetables are charged separately but are not always needed. Desserts are designed to please all tastes with spotted dick or a white chocolate and chestnut bavarois.

Directions: Off Piccadilly. Nearest Tube – Green Park

Map no: S175

5 St James's Street SW1
Tel: 0171-839 3774

Cost: Alc £27.50; fixed-price lunch £10.50, £23.75. H/wine £10.50 ♀
Credit cards: 1 2 3 4 5

Menus: *A la carte*, fixed-price lunch, bar menu

Times: Last L 2.45pm, Last D 10.45pm. Closed Sun, BHs, 4 days at Easter, 10 days at Xmas

Chef: Nigel Davies
Proprietor: Andrew Baker

Seats: 60. No pipes
Additional: Children over 5 permitted; children's portions. ❖ dishes; Vegan/other diets on request

Park Lane Hotel ❖❖

Formal English dining in the oak panelled restaurant of a long-established London hotel

For many generations this fine hotel has been in the same family ownership and a sense of tradition and elegance prevails in the Louis XIV decor of Bracewells restaurant. In keeping with the ambiance, the rather formal atmosphere sets the tone for the gastronomic dinner offering up to seven courses, though there are also a *carte* selection, weekly-changing fixed-price menu and regular items (typically chargrills). Chef Jon Tindall, cooking in English style, offers such first courses as Cornish lobster, warm English goats' cheese and smoked marinated Aylesbury duck. Rabbit loins in filo pastry accompanied by a marjoram sauce was a successful *carte* inclusion on our

Map no: F176

Piccadilly W1
Tel: 0171-499 6321

Chef: Jon Tindall
Proprietor: Clive Carr

Seats: 60. No-smoking area. Air conditioned

Times: Last L 2pm/D 10.30pm. Closed Sat L, Sun, BHs

Cost: Alc £28, fixed-price L £19.50/D £29. H/wine £16 ♀

inspector's visit. Main courses are mostly served with sauces and all 'married with their own vegetable garnishes'. Fillet of turbot was encrusted in a breadcrumb and herb topping, served on shredded savoy cabbage and complemented by a good shellfish sauce. A richly flavoured and freshly baked crème brûlée was chosen from the trolley; a cheese platter is also offered. More informal dining is available at the hotel's French-style Brasserie on the Park.

Directions: Nearest Tubes – Hyde Park Corner, Green Park

Service inc
Credit cards: 1 2 3 4 5.

Additional: Children welcome; children's portions; ❂ dishes; Vegan/other diets on request

Partners Brasserie ❀❀

☺ *Consistent, imaginative English cooking in an informal setting*

The atmosphere is informal and relaxed at this well established small restaurant which remains consistently good, with chef Timothy Franklin running the kitchen. A short, simple *carte* and a daily changing fixed-price menu offer good value and might include crispy duck parcels with oriental vegetables, chargrilled lamb's liver with olive oil mash, roast cod with sun-dried tomato and vegetable crust. Our inspector particularly enjoyed a hotpot of fish and shellfish which included lemon sole, grey mullet, cod, mussels and prawns cooked in good stock with a julienne of vegetables. Service was friendly and attentive.

Seats: 30. Air conditioned
Additional: Children welcome; children's portions. ❂ dishes
Directions: On the A24 between North Cheam and Morden

Map no: 177
23 Stonecot Hill, Sutton
Tel: 0181-644 7743

Cost: *Alc* £14, fixed-price L/D £9.95. H/wine £7.95. Service exc
Credit cards: 1 2 3 4

Menus: *A la carte*, fixed-price lunch and dinner

Times: Last L 2pm/D 9.30pm. Closed Sun, Mon, Xmas & New Year

Chef: Tim Franklin
Proprietors: Partners Restaurants

Pearl of Knightsbridge ❀❀

Mainly Cantonese cuisine, freshly prepared from quality ingredients, is served at this smart modern restaurant

A smart modern Chinese restaurant, the Pearl of Knightsbridge has a friendly atmosphere and mostly female waiting staff who provide efficient and helpful service. The cuisine is mainly Cantonese with a few dishes from the Peking region, such as the famous Peking duck which must be ordered in advance. There is a good selection of hot and cold appetisers: gourmet mixed hors d'oeuvre, deep-fried shredded squid, and sliced pork knuckle. Main courses include a number of fish, meat and poultry dishes; our inspector sampled steamed sea-bass with ginger, spring onions and black bean sauce, which he is happy to recommend, and shredded fillet of beef with fresh mango, well flavoured with a soy-based sauce. There are also some dishes suitable for vegetarians. Braised suprême shark's fin, and braised whole abalone with oyster sauce appear among the specialities, along with whole suckling pig, crispy Kwantung style, costing £120-£150, which must be ordered in advance. A list of reasonably priced, popular wines is also available.

Directions: On the north side of Brompton Road at the junction with Knightsbridge. Nearest Tube – Knightsbridge

Map no: 178
22 Brompton Road SW1
Tel: 0171-225 3888

Cost: *A la carte* £20, fixed-price £12.75. Service exc. Cover charge £2
Credit cards: 1 2 3 4

Menus: *A la carte*, fixed-price lunch and dinner

Times: Midday-Last L 3pm, 6pm-Last D 11.30pm. Closed Xmas

Chef: Hong Cheong
Proprietor: Anna Lam

Additional: Children welcome; ❂ dishes

Percy's ❀❀

☺ *Imaginative, liberated modern English cooking melding ultra-fresh ingredients with daringly original ideas*

An extraordinarily precocious talent unfettered by the constraints of tradition and formal training is behind the imaginative creations which emerge from this kitchen. Self-taught chef/patron Tina Bricknell-Webb has put North Harrow on the culinary map with her astonishingly original ideas, and entusiastically supportedby husband Tony. Much of the produce comes from the couple's farm in Devon, and vegetables in particular are tastier than usual. Our inspector enjoyed a simple starter of warm seafood salad with king scallops, smoked mussels, monkfish and John Dorey, all fresh and well cooked, and served with a decent red wine vinaigrette. Pan-fried haunch of Devon venison was perfectly cooked and attractively presented with a side plate of puréed baby turnip, brunoise of sautéed swede, steamed carrot batons and mange-tout. A very citrusy lemon tart combined beautifully with delicious rosemary ice cream, and intense espresso coffee came with pressed date and pistachio roulade. The short but wide-ranging wine list offers knowledgable comments.

Directions: Opposite North Harrow Tube

Map no: 179

66-68 Station Road, North Harrow
Tel: 0181-427 2021

Cost: Alc £20.50. H/wine £9.80
♀ Service charge
Credit cards: 1 2 3 4 5

Menu: A la carte

Times: Midday-Last L 3pm, 6.30pm-Last D 10.30pm. Closed Sun, Mon, 27 Dec-2 Jan

Chef: Tina Bricknell-Webb
Proprietor: Tina & Tony Bricknell-Webb

Seats: 70/80. No smoking
Additional: Children over 10 welcome. ◐ dishes; Vegan/other diets on request

Persad Tandoori ❀

A small, smart Indian restaurant in the busy shopping centre with an interesting cartewhich include the chef's specialities and a selection of Persian dishes such as shish kebab, the chef's thalia and tandoori chicken.

Cost: Fixed-price D £25, £40. H/wine £6 ♀ Service charge
Credit cards: 1 2 3 4. **Additional:** Children welcome, children's portions. ◐ dishes/other on request
Directions: In the High Street

Map no: 180
16 High Street, Ruislip
Tel: 01895 676587
Chef: Abdul Khoir
Proprietor: Mr H R Choudhury
Seats: 42
Times: Last L 2.30pm/D 11.45pm. Closed 25 Dec

Pied à Terre ❀❀❀❀

Inspired, innovative cuisine reaching the highest heights - but with occasional unpredictability

As soon as you spot the simple plate-glass and steel exterior of the Pied à Terre in Charlotte Street you realise that here is an establishment that is different from the surrounding restaurants - and so it is. The exterior has a stunning simplicity and once inside the white walls and grey slate flooring provide an excellent foil for some bright modern paintings and the bright handpainted plates on each table. Again simplicity and contrast are the keynote. The decor reflects the cooking of Richard Neat who has caused quite a stir in the culinary world in the last few years. His is creative experimental cuisine hastruly brilliant flashes but consistency is an occasional hostage to adventure and imagination. With David Moore, his partner, he set up this

Map no: 181

34 Charlotte Street W1
Tel: 0171-636 1178

Cost: Fixed-price lunch £16.50, fixed-price dinner £38. Wine £13 ♀ Service inc
Credit cards: 1 2 3 4 5

Menus: Fixed-price lunch and dinner

Times: Last L 2.15pm, Last D 10.15pm. Closed Sat lunch, Sun, last 2 weeks Aug, 2 weeks Xmas/New Year

Chef: Richard Neat

restaurant a couple of years ago and they created an atmosphere that is formal but friendly and the restaurant has built up a strong local clientele.

This year our inspection meals have been a little variable, with some dishes being quite stunning and others less so. One inspector felt that his meal was breathtaking, exciting and technically very capable while another felt that each course swung from first class to unbalanced flavours. A delicious appetiser of a plump oyster in a frothy mushroom-flavoured broth was well received and this was followed by a starter of roasted scallops with ginger purée and leaf spinach. The scallops were not a particularly good texture and the ginger purée overwhelmed their flavour. Another starter of confit of duck neck confit was, however, certainly worthy of Richard Neat's reputation. A main course of steamed veal fillet, endive and casserole of wild mushrooms had a good flavour enhanced by a veal-stock based sauce. Unfortunately a main course of sea-bass with a caviar and olive oil hollandaise was far less successful. The sea-bass itself was beautifully fresh and firm textured but its flavour was totally overwhelmed by the strong olive oil used in the hollandaise.

A particular treat followed the main course – a pre-dessert delicacy of a quite outstanding vanilla cream with a praline topping – rich, creamy and a real demonstration of the chef's skill. The clearly presented, reasonably-priced wine list is almost entirely French and draws on the talents of some of the best growers.

Proprietors: Richard Neat, David Moore

Seats: 40. No cigars or pipes in restaurant. Air conditioned
Additional: Children permitted

Directions: South end of Charlotte Street, parallel to Tottenham Court Road. Nearest Tube – Goodge Street

Poons ✹✹

☺ *A friendly, noisy, informal Chinese restaurant frequented by the young, where a wide choice of good-value dishes is served*

Recently renovated and now fashionably bright, Poons attracts a young clientele to its barely comfortable restaurant, which is scarcely less noisy than Leicester Square itself. The menu is long and surprisingly inexpensive, the seven set menus ranging in price from £14 for two people to £35 per head. The main menu offers a choice of old-fashioned dishes such as real Peking duck and sea-bass steamed with ginger and spring onion. The renowned Poons wind-dried meats are still also available but very few non-meat dishes are listed. The dishes sampled by our inspector demonstrated a good range of contrasts between crisp and moist, salt and sweet, hot and cold; an excess of any one flavour always tempered by another ingredient. This is not a restaurant to dress up for, staff strike an informal pose, kitted out in hand-knitted waistcoats, as they deal competently with the seemingly endless queue for tables. It should be noted that Poons does not accept credit cards.

Map no: 182

Leicester Street W1
Tel: 0171-437 1528

Cost: Set menus from £13 (for 2 people)-£35. H/wine £6.80
Credit cards: None taken
Menus: *A la carte*, 7 set menus

Directions: Leicester Street runs between Leicester Square and Lisle Street. Nearest Tubes — Leicester Square and Piccadilly

Quaglino's ❀❀❀

Dining à la mode at this large brasserie, a stunning designer conversion of the old Quaglino's ballroom

Dining at Quaglino's is still a marvellous experience, a year after its much hyped opening. Sir Terence Conran's transformation of the cavernous basement – Quaglino's ballroom in its earlier incarnation – is remarkable, with its giant columns decorated by named artists, subtly changing skylight, and stylish fixtures and fittings. From the mezzanine antipasti bar, where drinks and snacks are served all day, guests look down on the vast dining room – a 21st-century brasserie with a short, modish menu. The cooking is very good considering the scale of the operation, and the results are fresh. There is an abundant crustacea bar, and good use is made of the chargrill, herbs and simple garnishes.

Seafood figures prominently, with plenty of crab, oysters and lobster, and Sevruga and Beluga caviar (at a price). Other starters include chicken soup with cannelini beans and basil, foie gras and chicken liver parfait, and an endive, walnut and Roquefort salad. Our inspectors sampled a tartlet of crab and saffron, and seared tranche of salmon with a potato pancake. There is not much for vegetarians – a main course of spaghetti with roast tomatoes and rocket is listed – but dishes can be provided by arrangement. Our inspector enjoyed tender rabbit rolled in pancetta, with a light herby jus and chargrilled vegetables, and succulent charred swordfish steak with a rough salsa, good chips and a fresh cos salad with avocado and Pecorino. He chose, to follow, a fresh lime meringue tart, and a well made Sauternes custard with Armagnac marinated prunes. A small selection of cheeses is offered, and four coffee styles. The wine list is printed on the back of the menu card and offers a good choice from around the world at reasonable prices. A list of fine wines is available on request.

Directions: Near the Jermyn Street end of Bury Street (parallel to St James's Street). On the left. Nearest Tube – Green Park

Map no: S183

16 Bury Street, St James's SW1
Tel: 0171-930 6767

Cost: Alc £37.50. Fixed-price Sat and Sun lunch £12.95. H/wine £10.75 ♀ Service inc
Credit cards: 1 2 3 4

Menus: A la carte, fixed-price Sat and Sun lunch, bar menu

Times: Midday-Last L 3pm, 5.30pm-Last D midnight (Fri, Sat 1am, Sun 11pm). Closed Xmas

Chef: Martin Webb
Proprietor: Eric Garnier

Seats: 338. Air conditioned
Additional: Children permitted. ✿ dishes

Quality Chop House ❀❀

☺ *A unique blend of Le Caprice, where the chef came from, and upmarket working men's caff. Great fun*

This is in one of those parts of London that retains a Dickensian character. No famous landmarks, but well worth a wander round before lunch or dinner. As a 'progressive working class caterer', to use its own description, the Chop House is absolutely right for the Farringdon/Clerkenwell area. You might have to share your six-seater booth with someone from the *Guardian* or Sadler's Wells nearby, but that could be fun. Start with warm asparagus and Pecorino cheese or bang bang chicken and move on to grilled ox tongue with caper vinaigrette or . . . eggs, bacon and chips. Well, why not? Lamb chops, liver and bacon and corned beef hash are on the menu too. Bangers and mash is made with spicy Toulouse sausages

Map no: 184

94 Farringdon Road EC1
Tel: 0171-837 5093

Cost: Alc £16. Wine £9 ♀ Service exc
Credit cards: None taken

Menus: A la carte, Sunday lunch

Times: Midday-Last L 3pm (4pm Sun), 6.30pm (7pm Sun)-Last D 11.30pm. Closed Sat lunch, Xmas-New Year
Chef: Charles Fontaine

and even its onion gravy got a special mention in our inspector's report. The dessert list is easy to choose from – sorbet, caramel cheesecake, chocolate cake, apple crumble and crème brûlée. Bottles of HP, tomato ketchup and vinegar are on the tables. There is a short wine list and Bloody Mary and Buck's Fizz are served by the jug. Booking is essential and probably still will be when the extension next door is finished.

Proprietor: Fiona McIndoe

Seats: 48. Air conditioned
Additional: Children welcome; children's portions; ◑ dishes; other diets with prior notice

Directions: On the left-hand side of Farringdon Road, just before it meets Roseberg Avenue. Nearest Tube – Farringdon

Quincy's Restaurant ✿✿

British and French food at attractive prices in a friendly restaurant with enviable staying power

Map no: 185

675 Finchley Road NW2
Tel: 0171-794 8499

Restaurateurs who find the going tough must be quite perplexed that some of their peers never appear to struggle. David Wardle is one of these lucky people, although he would have every right to object to the word luck, when sheer hard work is really responsible for the popularity of his intimate, homely restaurant. Chef David Philpott is also, of course, a key player and it is his skills which ensure that even on a simple, monthly-changing, three-course, set dinner menu there is always sufficient variety and creativity. Fresh fish, according to the market, is a constant feature, as is a choice of meats such as breast of duck, roast rabbit, fillet steak and venison. Taking three different months' menus at random could produce the following meal – a starter of gravadlax and herring with a horseradish and dill sauce, then fillet of lamb, leeks, garlic and polenta and, before rounding off with a coffee and petits fours, try rhubarb gratin and fromage frais sorbet. Vegetarian dishes include French onion tart with leaf salad, and pimento soufflé Suissesse. A list of forty-odd wines includes bottles starting at £9 and halves at £6.50.

Cost: Fixed-price dinner £22. H/wine £9. Service exc
Credit cards: 1 2 3

Menus: Fixed-price dinner

Times: 7pm-Last D 11pm. Closed Sun, Mon, Xmas

Chef: David Philpott
Proprietor: David Wardle

Seats: 35. Air conditioned
Additional: Children welcome; children's portions. ◑ dishes; other diets on request

Directions: In Child's Hill, just north of junction of Finchley Road (A598) and Cricklewood Lane (A407). Nearest Tube – Golders Green

RSJ The Restaurant on the South Bank ✿✿

☺ *An unpretentious restaurant convenient for the South Bank offers a good range of dishes in bistro/brasserie style*

Map no: 186

13a Coin Street SE1
Tel: 0171-928 4554

Though set in unprepossessing surroundings in what was a row of terraced houses, this restaurant is completely full most of the time – its popularity due in part to the proximity of the National Theatre and LWT studios on the South Bank. Many customers, however, are just attracted by the delightful simplicity of its bright interior, by service which combines charm with efficiency, and by good-value fixed-price menus offering a varied choice in modern bistro/brasserie style. Enjoyable dishes sampled recently include a moist risotto generously topped with Parmesan cheese, a good cream of leek soup with a hint of ginger, salmon with braised red rice, shallots

Cost: Alc £20, fixed-price £15.95
Credit cards: 1 2 3

Menus: A la carte, fixed-price

Times: Midday-Last L 2pm; 6pm-Last D 11pm Lunch not served Sat. Closed Sun, BHs

Chef: Ian Stabler
Proprietor: Nigel Wilkinson

and a red wine sauce, and a suprême of sauté chicken on a grain mustard sauce flavoured with tarragon; a very interesting addition to the more predictable potato galette and broccoli that accompanied the chicken. A light, creamy, home-made bread and butter pudding was served with cardamom cream, hot rum custard enhanced the flavour of the fruit crumble.

Additional: No pipes or cigars.
❶ dishes

Directions: On the corner of Coin Street and Stamford Street. Near National Theatre and LWT studios

The Radisson Edwardian ❶

The main restaurant is a very plush, panelled room and the menu an interesting blend of modern French and English dishes. A selection from recent menus included sea-bream with Chardonnay and chervil, wild duck garnished with sprouts and chestnuts, and avocado parfait with lobster.

Additional: Children welcome. ❶ dish
Directions: On the A4, eastbound side

Map no: 187
Bath Road, Hayes
Tel: 0181-759 6311
Chef: Jean-Claude Sandillion
Proprietor: Radisson Edwardian
Manager: Paul Mansi
Cost: A/c £35, fixed-price £25
Credit cards: 1 2 3 4

Rani ❶❶

☺ *Good value dishes from north-west India in this family-run vegetarian restaurant in busy Finchley*

The quotes on the menu say it all. Supercritic Jonathan Meades judged it 'perhaps the best vegetarian Indian restaurant in London' and Paul Levy waxed even more lyrical with 'Who can set a price on paradise?'. At lunchtime and Monday evenings it is buffet only with bhajis, curries, rice and fruit. A good selection of dishes is available in the evening, including starters such as Bhel poori, a mixture of deep-fried crispy bread, puffed rice, sev, potato, onion, garlic and tamarind sauce or Dhai vada, spiced black lentil fritters in yoghurt sauce. Main courses include vegetable curries and daily specials like Saturday's Undhia, fried gram flour and fenugreek balls with exotic vegetables. There are plenty of breads, such as parathas, methis and chapatis. Sweet tooth hostages will find the desserts irresistible. Kulfi is a rich frozen milk delicacy with pistachios, almonds, cardamom and saffron; Gulab bambu is succulent sponge balls in a fragrant syrup. Animal fats, eggs, fish and meat are banned and all dishes indicate sugar, dairy product, wheat, nut, onion or garlic ingredients. All tips go to charity.

Directions: Situated at the north end of Long Lane at the junction with Ballards Lane. Nearest Tube – Finchley Central

Map no: 188
7 Long Lane N3
Tel: 0181-349 4386/2636

Cost: A/c £17; fixed-price buffet lunch £8; fixed-price dinner £20.90. Wine £8.40. Service inc
Credit cards: 1 2 3 5

Menus: A la carte, fixed-price dinner, buffet Sunday lunch
Times: 12.15pm Last L 3pm, 6pm-Last D 10.30pm. Closed Xmas day

Chefs: Mrs Kundan Pattni and Mrs Sheila Pattni
Proprietor: Mr Jyotindra Pattni

Seats: 90. No-smoking area (whole restaurant Mon and Sat). No pipes or cigars
Additional: Children welcome; children's menu; ❶ menu; Vegan/other diets on request

Ransome's Dock ❶❶

☺ *Cooking in modern European style at a relaxing, reasonably priced and popular riverside rendezvous*

Located south of the river in a peaceful waterside setting, this informal and friendly restaurant offers al fresco dining in fine

Map no: 189

35-37 Parkgate Road
Battersea SW11
Tel: 0171-223 1611

weather, while the bright, light interior reflects its watery surrounds sympathetically. The result is a relaxing venue in which to sample a varied and good value menu - especially the set-price lunch - complemented by a knowledgeable international wine list, with something to suit all palates and pockets, including several house wines. 'Warm salad of Innes goat's cheese, rocket and cherry tomatoes', Morecambe Bay potted shrimps, chargrilled quail and artichoke and mushroom lasagne are typical of the dishes served by cheery and helpful staff. Our inspector chose as first course filo pastry parcels filled with spinach, pine kernels and Fetta cheese, well-filled and evenly-cooked and served with a refreshing cucumber and dill salad. The lamb cutlets that followed were cooked pink, as requested, and served with a simple, rich and appetising jus and sweet onion tartlet. A zesty lemon and blueberry tart and good strong espresso coffee rounded off an enjoyable meal. Booking advised.

Directions: Between Albert Bridge and Battersea bridge. Nearest Tube – Sloane Square

Cost: Alc £20; fixed-price lunch £11.50 ♀ Service exc
Credit cards: 1 2 3 4 5

Menus: *A la carte,* fixed-price lunch, Sunday lunch, bar menu

Times: 11am–Last L 3.30pm, Last D 11pm (midnight Sat). Closed Sun eve, Xmas

Chef: Martin Lam
Proprietors: Martin and Vanessa Lam

Seats: 65. No pipes. Air conditioned
Additional: Children welcome; children's portions; ❿ dishes; Vegan/other diets on request

Red Fort ❀❀

Authentic Moghul cooking at one of London's best-respected Indian restaurants

Map no: 190

77 Dean Street W1
Tel: 0171-437 2115

The Mogul emperor Shah Jahan built the Taj Mahal in Agra as a memorial to his wife. Less romantically, he built Delhi's Red Fort for his government. Indirectly, therefore, he can be thanked for bringing chef Manjit Gill to London for six weeks each year to train the resident chefs how to prepare some of India's most appealing Mogul-style dishes. The menu is not over-long, so although there should be little need to keep asking the waiter to 'come back in another couple of minutes', everything is tempting. A starter of Murgh galouti, shallow-fried minced chicken, cloves, cinnamon and crushed pomegranate, could be followed by pomfret fish spiced with ajwain seeds cooked whole in the tandoor oven, or Lal maas from Rajasthan, hot spicy lamb simmered in a yoghurt-based gravy with black cardamoms and broken, dry red chillies. The non-superstitious could try Shah Jahan's Last Stew (maybe he simply gave up stews). At lunchtimes, try an ever-changing selection of hot and cold dishes served from the buffet. The vegetable dishes could well cause acute salivation at the first reading of the menu.

Directions: In Soho. Nearest Tube – Tottenham Court Road

Cost: Alc £25, buffet L £12.50. Wine £8.95 ♀ Service exc
Credit cards: 1 2 3 4 5

Chefs: Naresh Matta, M S Gill
Proprietor: Amin Ali

Times: Last L 3pm/D 11.30pm

Seats: 130. No-smoking area. Air conditioned
Additional: Children permitted. ❿ menu

The Regent ❀❀❀

Accomplished, mostly Italian-style cooking in the impressive surroundings of this stylish new hotel

Map no: 191

222 Marylebone Road NW1
Tel: 0171-631 8000

A former railway hotel, this classy establishment with spectacular Victorian architecture opened in 1993 and is

Chef: Paulo Simioni

enjoying increasing popularity and acclaim. Of particular note is the impressive Winter Garden lounge with its stunning atrium affording a glimpse of the clock tower through its glassy heights. In the comfortable dining room Paulo Simioni's cooking shows a lightness of touch and an emphasis on Italian recipes and ingredients, with risottos and pastas as a particular strength. At an inspection meal in June our inspector sampled a super creamy crab and leek risotto as a starter. This was followed by excellent lamb cutlets stuffed with ratatouille, breaded, and served with yet more ratatouille, green beans, and sliced potato with basil. With all this accomplished cooking it was a bit disappointing to find that the desserts came from a standard hotel trolley, but the alcoholic crème brûlée selected on this occasion was enjoyable enough, with good espresso to finish. For less formal meals there is the lounge and Cellar, the hotel's stylish basement pub. There are plenty of staff and service is bright and refreshingly courteous.

The Restaurant ✹✹✹✹✹

Assured, inventive cooking from an undisputed master in a very Knightsbridge ambience

Following the trend set by Nico Ladenis when he moved to Park Lane, Marco Pierre White has taken over the former Grill Room of the Hyde Park Hotel. Named simply The Restaurant, it has its own blue-canopied doorway at street level opposite Harvey Nichols. Downstairs, look for a discreet entrance on the left, leading to an elegant restaurant with stunning floral arrangements. Lunchtime seems geared to the set menu, a snip at half the price of the *carte* and only limited as to choice; otherwise the quality of cooking and presentation are identical. The full *carte*, also fixed-price, encompasses seven years of Marco's cooking in a dazzling array of some dozen first courses, 16 main courses and a separate dessert menu by Roger Pizey.

Old favourites, like a signature dish of tagliatelle of oysters and caviar rub shoulders with starters like ravioli of succulent langoustines and fresh truffle, served with an intensely flavoured foie gras sauce of wonderful sheen and consistency. The accompanying timbale of savoy cabbage perfectly demonstrated Marco's ability to carry off the most unexpected combinations of ingredients. Strong Mediterranean flavours brought excitement to a perfectly cooked red mullet set on boulangère potatoes and served with aubergine caviar, tomato, olives, basil and sauce vierge. The master-stroke of darnes of turbot, with a clever Sauternes jus and confit of garlic, was an intensely flavoured parsley purée. On a more classical note, braised oxtail, taken off the bone and served en crépinette, was served with excellent Vichy carrots and an intense red-wine fumet.

Among the desserts, the prune and Armagnac soufflé was highly recommended, and was preceded by a delicious little dessert appetiser of crème caramel with soaked raisins. All the other trimmings are good too, from the stunning appetisers like red mullet escabeche – although with mullet on the menu as a main course, it would be preferable not to double up ingredients – and a little cup of intense, fiery shellfish soup, to

Map no:192
66 Knightsbridge SW1
Tel: 0171-259 5380

Cost: Alc £71, fixed-price lunch £25. Wine £25 ♀ Service exc
Credit cards: 1 3 5

Menus: A la carte, fixed-price lunch

Times: Midday-Last L 2.30pm, 7pm-Last D 11.30pm. Lunch not served Sat. Closed Sun, 1st 2 weeks Aug, BHs, 10 days Xmas

Chef: Marco Pierre White
Proprietors: MCM Restaurants.
Managers: Nicholas Munier, Jean Cottard

Seats: 50. No pipes or cigars. Air conditioned
Additional: Children permitted.
❤ dishes; Vegan/other diets on request

the various breads and petits fours.

Service, led by Jean Cottard, is truly professional. If our inspectors had any criticism, it was that the maitre d' failed to inform about changes to the printed menu. An excellent wine list, mainly French and including the 1961 vintage of five premier crus – will significantly add to the expense – but cooking like this deserves a fine wine.

Directions: In the Hyde Park Hotel, Knightsbridge, with its own entrance opposite Harvey Nichols. Nearest Tube – Knightsbridge.

Restaurant 192 ❀

☺ *Despite how busy this bistro is, it has a very relaxed and casual atmosphere. The new chef Albert Clarke has made a few changes but dishes remain simple but effective. Starters include home-made soup, lemon butter and crispy leeks and, as a main course, there is pan-fried calf's liver.*

Cost: Alc £20, H/wine £8.75
Directions: At top end of Kensington Park Road between Elgin Crescent and Blenheim Crescent. Nearest Tube – Ladbroke Grove

Map no: D193
192 Kensington Park Road
Tel: 0171-229 0482
Chef: Albert Clarke
Proprietor: A Mackintosh,
Seats: 108
Times: Last L 3pm, Last D 11.30pm. Closed Xmas

Rhapsody ❀

☺ *Devoted to Latin American cooking (a rarity in London), most South American countries are represented. The menu changes according to availability and Argentinian chef/patron Alberto Portugheis has a sound reputation. Try the empanada (rissoles filled with meat, sweetcorn or cheese).*

Cost: Alc £18. Wine £8. Service charge 12.5% **Credit cards**: 1 2 3 4
Additional: Children permitted; ◐ dishes
Directions: Off Rockley Road at Shepherds Bush

Map no: 193b
25 Richmond Way W14
Tel: 0171-602 6778
Chef: Alberto Portugheis
Proprietor: Alberto Portugheis
Times: Midday-Last L 2.30pm, 7pm-Last D 10.30. Lunch not served Sat. Closed Sun

Ristorante L'Incontro ❀❀

This smart, modern restaurant on the edge of Chelsea is at the forefront of real Italian cooking

Stylish and popular Italian restaurants are not too hard to find in London but some, like L'Incontro, stand out for all the right reasons. The authenticity of the cooking is unmistakable, with Venetian dishes in evidence. A good idea is the one-dish lunch menu offering, for example, the unusual 'Casunzei', pasta parcels with beetroot in melted butter. A separate fixed-price lunch menu offers selections including lamb cutlets in a sweet and sour sauce, which was the highlight of our inspection meal. For lunch or dinner the *carte* spoils for choice, with Venetian-style scallops, or baked artichoke among the antipasti, and a selection of home-made pastas including 'Bigoli in salsa', thick spaghetti with anchovy and onion sauce. Cuttlefish, monkfish and sea-bass are among the main fish courses, and veal chops, roast quail, entrecôte of beef and calf's liver feature among the meats.

Map no: 194
87 Pimlico Road SW1
Tel: 0171-730 3663

Cost: Alc £32; fixed-price lunch £13.50 (2 courses), £16.80. Wine £12.50. Cover charge £1.50; Service charge 12%
Credit cards: 1 2 3 4

Menus: *A la carte*, fixed-price lunch

Times: 12.30pm-Last L 2.30pm (3pm Sat), 7pm-Last D 11.30pm. Closed Sun, Xmas

Chef: Nicola Celmanti
Proprietor: Santin Group.

Desserts include almond cake, Bavarois and chocolate délice. Most of the sixty or so wines are Italian with some quite expensive rarities, but reasonably priced house white and red. The service is professional and correct.

Directions: From Lower Sloane Street, left into Pimlico Road, the restaurant is on the right. Nearest Tube – Sloane Square

Seats: 55. No Pipes. Air conditioned
Additional: Children welcome; children's portions; ❷ dishes; Vegan/other diets on request

Ritz ❀❀❀

Suitably elaborate dishes presented in the magnificent restaurant of this internationally renowned hotel

Still one of London's most popular haunts for the rich, famous and fashionable, the Ritz is synonymous with all things opulent. Executive chef David Nicholls and his talented brigade are now well established and his elaborate style of cuisine is ideally suited to the breathtaking magnificence of the restaurant. Only the best quality, and wherever possible organic, produce is used in the kitchens for the continental-style cuisine. In addition to the *carte*, fixed-price lunch and dinner menus are offered, including Ritz blend coffee or a choice of fine teas with sweetmeats. For vegetarians there are dishes such as creamed woodland mushrooms in puff pastry with winter vegetables.

The dishes sampled this year, which led to a third rosette for the restaurant, were a complimentary appetiser – mille-feuille of sun-dried tomatoes, fish and pesto with balsamic dressing - and a salad of fiercely seared scallops and Alsace bacon with finely sliced tomato, intricately interleaved with truffle and flavoured with basil. This was followed by a strongly flavoured lobster and langoustine bisque with a sabayon topping. Southdown lamb fillets, pan-fried with courgette, Pecorino and basil cream was another artistic creation, served with the vegetables as an integral part of the dish, and at another meal a fillet of sea-bass, bursting with flavour, was delightfully presented with tiny potato scales. Desserts were chosen from an attractive trolley, soon to be replaced by a *carte* selection which will allow both early and late diners a similar choice. On this occasion, white and dark chocolate mousse, dome shaped in a dark chocolate shell, and a superb crème brûlée were chosen. The wine list was well-balanced and offered safe, reliable wines from France, California, Australia and New Zealand at reasonable prices.

Directions: Situated on south side of Piccadilly. Nearest Tube – Green Park

Map no: A195

Piccadilly W1
Tel: 0171-493 8181

Cost: *A/c* £55, fixed-price lunch £26, fixed-price dinner £39.50, £43.50. H/wine £16 ♀ Service inc
Credit cards: 1 2 3 4 5

Menus: *A la carte*, fixed-price lunch and dinner, pre-theatre, bar menu

Times: Last L 2.30pm, Last D 11.15pm

Chef: David Nicholls
Proprietor: Cunard. Manager: T R Holmes

Seats: 100. No pipes. Air conditioned
Additional: Children welcome; children's menu; ❷ menu; Vegan/other diets on request

Riva ❀❀

☺ *Serving substantial portions and big on flavour, this restaurant provides really authentic northern Italian cooking*

Andrea Riva, the cordial owner, wants greater recognition for his chef and partner, Francesco Zanchetta. With good reason, since this is one of the best Italian restaurants in town, specialising in dishes from the north, particularly Lombardy

Map no: H196

169 Church Road, Barnes SW13
Tel: 0181-748 0434

Cost: *A/c* £20. Wine £9.50. Service inc
Credit cards: 1 3

and Veneto. Most are commendable for their flavour, quality and freshness of ingredients. Fish dishes can include sea bream, baby squid, steamed sturgeon, freshwater crayfish and cuttlefish. Fresh pasta, soft maize polenta and pumpkin gnocchi produce some memorable flavours and fulfilling meals. On our inspection visit the cured pig's trotters, which should be eaten in their entirety, were a little undercooked. This made it difficult to get through the skin to the really succulent bits, although the Italian sausage meat filling was delicious. There are plenty of desserts to choose from but it was the ubiquitous tiramisù which made an indelibly positive impression. A well-selected short list of regional wines, includes Tokay white and a large selection of grappa. Service is informal, polite and personally supervised by Signor Riva.

Directions: At the southern end of Castelnau, opposite the Red Lion public house. Nearest Tube – Hammersmith

Menu: *A la carte*
Times: Midday-Last L 2.30pm, 7pm-Last D 11pm. Closed Xmas, Easter, last 2 weeks Aug

Chef: Francesco Zanchetta
Proprietor: Andrea Riva

Seats: 50. No cigars or pipes. Air conditioned
Additional: Children welcome; children's portions; ❶ dishes; other diets on request

River Café ❀❀❀

Modern Italian food using the freshest of ingredients in a celebrated converted warehouse restaurant

Now in their seventh year at the River Café, the enthusiasm of co-proprietors and chefs Rose Gray and Ruth Rogers is undiminished. Their restaurant, a celebrated conversion of a riverside warehouse, was due to be extended and refurbished at the time of our last visit, and of course they are lucky enough to have the services of a talented architect – Ruth's husband Richard Rogers.

The short *carte* changes daily at lunch and dinner, and the dishes read as appetisingly as they taste: asparagus with parmesan, prosciutto and sour dough bruschetta, chargrilled red mullet with braised mullet, roast duck stuffed with sage and rosemary, chocolate nemesis, and polenta lemon cake. Vegetarian options are included among the starters and pasta dishes, but not the main courses.

Shopping is a serious undertaking and the proprietors' commitment to finding the freshest and best of produce shows through in the well balanced blend of ingredients on the plate. The style is unashamedly Italian, in the recipes, ingredients and cooking techniques. Our inspectors have enjoyed a light pasta roll 'Rotolo di spinaci' filled with spinach, ricotta cheese and sage butter, and antipasta of best buffalo Mozzarella, marinated artichoke, coppa ham and olives – all with superb flavours. Succulent char-grilled scallops came with a tangy rosemary and anchovy sauce, lovely dressed spinach leaves and lightly battered deep-fried courgettes, and pink spring lamb with minty salsa verde. To finish, a macaroon-like Italian almond tart was served with a well-browned caramel ice cream, followed by good espresso.

Apart from champagne, the wine list is entirely Italian and does justice to the variety and quality this country can offer.

Directions: Turn off Fulham Palace Road at Rosedew Road, turn left into Rainville Road, the restaurant is on the left in a converted warehouse

Map no: 197

Thames Wharf Studios
Rainville Road
Hammersmith W6
Tel: 0171-381 8824

Cost: *Alc* £26. Wine £9 ♀
Service inc
Credit cards: 1 3 5

Menu: *A la carte*

Times: Last L 2.30pm, Last D 9.30pm. Closed Sun eve, BHs

Chefs: Rose Gray, Ruth Rogers, Theo Randall
Proprietors: Rose Gray, Ruth Rogers

Seats: 95. No pipes or cigars
Additional: Children welcome; children's portions. ❶ dishes; Vegan/other diets on request

Royal China ❀❀

☺ *An upmarket Chinese restaurant serving very decent food to families, fish-lovers and everyone else*

The dramatic black and gold uniforms of the Chinese staff match the decor at this well-managed restaurant, but neither is intimidating and the place is popular with well-heeled families. A genuine effort is made to provide good food and service, and on the whole it is successful. The dishes tried by our inspector elicited high praise, and the steamed fresh scallops with lots of garlic and soy sauce and the roasted baby squids with a mild sauce of chilli and tomato were both described as wonderful. Peking duck was slightly disappointing as the meat, although moist and tender, was tepid and the skin not crisp, but steamed strips of chicken breast with unusual mushrooms and ginger wrapped in lotus leaves was a lovely warm, fragrant dish. There were delicious chilli flavours too in the baked pork spare ribs in spicy salt, and sautéed Chinese broccoli stalks with ginger were glossy and crisp. The lengthy *carte* is divided into appropriate headings with over 20 entries under seafood, and in addition there are three set menus – one of them for vegetarians – and a lunchtime Dim Sum menu. A short wine list offers French and Italian wines plus sake.

Directions: Next to ice-skating rink. Nearest Tube – Queensway

Map no: R198

13 Queensway W2
Tel: 0171-221 2535

Cost: A/c £20; fixed-price dinner £20-£26; Wine £8.50. Service inc
Credit cards: 1 2 3 4

Menu: *A la carte*, fixed-price dinner

Times: Midday-Last D 11.15pm. Closed Xmas

Chefs: Simon Man, Wai Hung-Lan
Proprietors: Playwell Ltd. Manager: Ricky Au

Seats: 100. Air conditioned
Additional: Children welcome; ❍ menu; Vegan/other diets on request

Royal China ❀❀

A stylish Chinese restaurant serving well executed food which includes plenty of fresh fish

The same stylish black lacquered walls with gold flying ducks and roaring waves grace the interior of this restaurant as at its sister restaurant of the same name at Queensway. The interesting *carte* offers much in the way of fresh fish such as lobster, scallops , sea-bass and crab, together with unusual dishes such as 'chicken in lotus leaf'. At lunchtime a list of home-made Dim Sum is available. An inspection meal started with delicious 'golden scallops', deep fried fresh scallops sandwiched between slices of cucumber and coated in a light batter. This was followed by dumplings which had first been steamed, then fried. The steamed sea-bass was whole and fragrant with fresh ginger and spring onion. The 'hot and spicy' veal was tender and moist with a powerful flavour. the meal was remarkable for its freshness of ingredients and flavourings. The service was by cheerful smartly uniformed staff. The short wine list has a very drinkable house wine at £8.50.

Directions: Travelling north from the traffic lights in Putney High Street, Chelverton Raod is 2nd left. Nearest Tube – East Putney

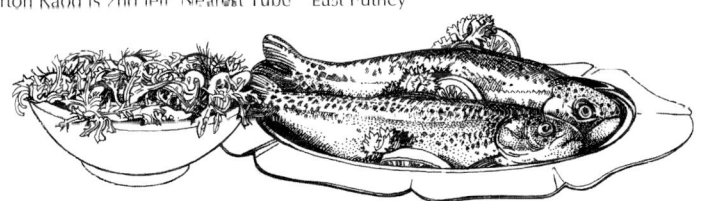

Map no: 199

3 Chelverton Road, Putney SW15
Tel: 0181-788 0907
Cost: A/c £26, Set menus £20, £26. Service charge 15%
Credit cards: 1 2 3 4

Menus: *A la carte*, set menus, Seafood Gourmet, Dim Sum

Times: Midday-Last L 4pm, 6.30pm-Last D 11.30pm

Chef: Siew Wing
Proprietors: Playwell Ltd

Additional: Children welcome

Royal Garden ❀❀

A tenth-floor hotel restaurant with spectacular views, offering classical French cuisine in a formal setting

The Royal Roof Restaurant, with one of the finest views of the London skyline, is located on the tenth floor of the Royal Garden Hotel, easily accessible from the hotel's main lobby by means of its own express lift. Chef Gunther Schlender has recently taken over in the kitchen, bringing with him a fine reputation established at the Restaurant Rue St Jacques. New menus are created each week, a Menu du Jour for lunch and a Menu du Chef for dinner, and these run alongside the *carte* which reflects chef Schlender's classic approach to serious cooking. An inspection meal began with a complimentary appetiser followed by 'soufflé d'advocat et saumon fumé au poivre vert', beautifully baked and textured with a separate butter and tomato concasse sauce. Our inspector then chose fillet of beef with potato rösti and a creamy veal stock sauce gently flavoured with cep juice. Vegetarian dishes are also featured. 'Piarde de pommes', from a good choice of desserts, was freshly prepared and well caramelised, served with lovely vanilla ice cream. The wine list offers a classic selection with some 114 bins to choose from, including some halves.

Directions: Adjacent to entrance to Kensington Palace. Nearest Tube – Kensington High Street

Map no: P200
Kensington High Street W8
Tel: 0171-937 8000

Cost: Alc £48.50, fixed-price dinner £33
Credit cards: 1 2 3 4

Menus: *A la carte*, fixed-price lunch and dinner

Times: Midday–Last L 2pm, 7pm–Last D 11pm. Closed Sat lunch, Sun, BHs, 3 weeks in Aug

Chef: Gunther Schlender
Proprietor: Rank

Seats: 50. Air conditioned
Additional: ◐ dishes

Royal Lancaster ❀

La Rosette restaurant overlooks the Italian gardens in this stylish, well-appointed modern hotel. A rather predictable carte might offer shellfish bisque or warm duck salad with quail's eggs, followed by Dover sole or steak. The fixed-price menu is good value, and the trolley desserts are enjoyable.

Cost: Alc £27.50, fixed-price L £22.50/D £25.75. H/wine £15. Service inc
Additional: Children welcome; children's portions. ◐ dishes; Vegan/other diets on request. Pianist in lounge
Directions: Above Lancaster Gate Tube Station

Map no: 201
Lancaster Terrace W2
Tel: 0171-262 6737
Chef: Nigel Blatchford
Proprietor: Lancaster Landmark.
Manager: Majid El Ghazal
Seats: 60. No-smoking areas. Air conditioned
Times: Last L 2.30pm./D 10.45pm. Closed Sat L, Sun, most BHs (except 25 Dec)

Royal Westminster Thistle ❀

A well-maintained hotel in an ideal location, where chef Bruce Smith practises his enterprising cooking. A new carte menu features pan-fried quail, served with fresh spinach with a honey and balsamic dressing and fillet of beef served with a tasty mixed whole peppercorn, veal jus and red wine sauce.

Cost: Alc £26. **Credit cards:** 1 2 3 4
Additional: Children welcome; children's menu; high chairs; ◐ dishes
Directions: Close to Victoria Station

Map no: 202
49 Buckingham Palace Road SW1
Tel: 0171-834 1821
Chef: Bruce Smith
Proprietor: Mount Charlotte Thistle
Times: Last D 10.30pm. Closed L all week, and Sun D

Rules ❀❀

One of London's oldest restaurants. Specialising in game cookery, the menu varies with the seasons

Rules still flourishes as one of the oldest and most celebrated restaurants in London. Recently refurbished under new ownership it retains all of its character. Specialising in classic game cookery, the *carte* features an array of feathered and furred, such as jugged hare, wild Highland red deer, wild duck, grouse and partridge, and last but not least roast breast of teal with parsnip purée and caramelised vegetables, which our inspector chose as a main course. The waiter will advise as to availability, as most of the game is seasonal. Chef Neil Pass, assisted by pastry chef Frank Wilkinson, are to be congratulated on the standard of cooking bearing in mind how busy this restaurant is, open throughout the day. Theatre-goers should look out for special deals on offer between 3pm and 6pm, any main course and any starter for £12.75, which must be the best value in the area? The *carte* is extensive and lists many popular dishes; the puddings alone are a special feature, ranging from treacle sponge to home made ice creams. The wine list is short, with half bottles, and some very good Sandeman claret 1988/90 at £8.50.

Directions: Maiden Lane is parallel with the Strand. Nearest Tubes – the Strand, Covent Garden

Map no: 203
35 Maiden Lane, Covent Garden WC2
Tel: 0171-836 5314

Cost: Alc £25. H/wine £8.50
Credit cards: 1 2 3 5

Menus: A la carte, Sunday lunch, pre-theatre

Times: Midday–Last D 11.15pm. Closed Xmas

Chef: Neil Pass
Proprietor: John Mayhew

Seats: 140. Air conditioned
Additional: Children welcome; children's portions

St Quentin ❀❀

☺ *A thoroughly French brasserie with freshly prepared, quality food and expertly supervised service*

Everything from the atmosphere to the expert service is thoroughly French at this popular brasserie opposite the Brompton Oratory, and not least the professional and skilful cooking of Nigel Davis. His Menu du soir offers particularly good value with a choice of two starters, two main courses, and cheese or dessert, while some good daily dishes and popular traditional dishes appear on the *carte*. Tables are conspiratorially close, and our inspector overheard several secrets while enjoying a recent meal. There was a good flavour to 'oeufs brouillés aux truffes', lightly souffléed eggs topped with wafer thin slices of truffle and set in a pastry tartlet, while 'confit de canard aux petits pois' was a beautifully tender, preserved duck dish served with delicious peas and diced carrots in a chicken stock flavoured with onion and mint. A dessert not to be missed is freshly baked pistachio soufflé served with a hot chocolate sauce. Other dishes might include steamed lemon sole with mussels, coquille St Jacques, and spicy Toulouse sausage with lentils. A vintage French wine list includes some good value bottles.

Directions: Opposite the Brompton Oratory on the corner of Brompton Road. Nearest Tube – South Kensington

Map no: 204
243 Brompton Road SW3
Tel: 0171-589 8005

Cost: Alc £25, fixed-price lunch and dinner £8 (2 courses). H/wine £8.60. Service inc
Credit cards: 1 2 3 4 5

Menus: A la carte and fixed-price menus

Times: Midday–3pm, 7pm–11.30pm (6.30pm-11pm Sun)

Chef: Nigel Davis
Proprietor: The Savoy plc. Manager: Patrick LaTouche

Seats: 65. Air conditioned
Additional: Children welcome; ❂ dishes; Vegan on request

Salloos ●●

Unique Pakistani cooking with subtle flavours from freshly spiced ingredients

Well-balanced flavours from the freshest of quality ingredients is what lifts this popular Pakistani restaurant way above the ordinary. Treasured recipes have been handed down from generation to generation, and then lovingly adapted to produce delicious and exotic Mughlai dishes. Our inspector had high praise for a recent meal which began with chicken tikka, a familiar dish with unusually subtle flavours and moist, well-marinated meat. 'Haleem akbari', shredded lamb cooked in whole wheatgerm, lentils and spices, was a strongly recommended speciality cooked from a unique recipe, and chicken 'taimura', a plain dish of marinated chicken cooked in special sauces then lightly battered and deep fried, was made fresh to order. Another much enjoyed dish was 'jheenga masala' – succulent prawns cooked in a subtly spiced dish. Desserts are limited to 'halwa gajar', hot and very sweet, and made from milk, almonds, pistachios and finely shredded carrot, and 'kulfi', a rich oriental ice cream. The prices are high, but the highly original food and very attentive service make a visit here a memorable one.

Directions: From Tube take first left into Wilton Place, first right opposite Berkley Hotel. Salloos on inside corner. Nearest Tube – Knightsbridge

Map no: 205
62-64 Kinnerton Street SW1
Tel: 0171-235 4444

Cost: *Alc* £27.50; Fixed-price lunch £16, fixed-price dinner £25. Wine £12.50. Service 15%; cover charge £1.50
Credit cards: 1 2 3 4

Menus: *A la carte* , fixed-price lunch and dinner

Times: Midday–Last L 2.30pm, 7pm–Last D 11.15pm. Closed Sun

Chefs: Abdul Aziz and Humayun Khan
Proprietors: Mr and Mrs F Salahuddin

Seats: 65. No pipes or cigars. Air conditioned
Additional: Children permitted (over 6 after 8pm); ◐ dishes; Vegan/other diets on request

San Lorenzo Fuoriporto ●

Decorated in a typical modern Italian style, this charming restaurant offers an interesting choice of dishes, all well prepared by chef Elizio, such as raw fillets of beef with Parmesan and rucola, and 'Cotolette di cinghiale', wild boar cutlets with beans, virgin oil and rosemary.

Cost: *Alc* £31. H/wine £10.50 ♀ Service exc
Credit cards: 1 2 3 4 5
Additional: Children welcome; ◐ dishes; other diets on request
Directions: Drive down Wimbledon Hill, turn right at the first set of traffic lights into Worple Road, then sharp left into Worple Mews

Map no: 206

Worple Road Mews SW19
Tel: 0181-946 8463
Chef: Elizio
Propietors: Ghigo and Angela Berni
Seats: 120
Times: Last L 2.45pm/D 10.45pm. Closed BHs

Santini ●●

A popular small Italian restaurant with particularly good pasta and fish. Meals can be pricey with extras

Santini is a popular Italian restaurant close to Victoria Station. The tables are quite closely packed, and once all the extras are added up a meal can prove quite pricey, but the food here does make a visit worthwhile. There is a wide selection of antipasti, such as soup, stuffed courgette flowers, a grilled vegetable platter, carpaccio, and Parma ham and melon. The pasta is especially recommended, and includes a skilfully made ravioli of Ricotta and spinach, and 'pasta mista' – four types of pasta

Map no: J207

29 Ebury Street SW1
Tel: 0171-730 4094

Cost: *Alc* £30, fixed-price lunch £16.50. H/wine £13.50. Service charge 12%. Cover charge £1.50
Credit cards: 1 2 3 4

Menus: *A la carte*; fixed-price business lunch

each with a different sauce. While no vegetarian main courses are listed on the *carte* , pasta can be taken as either a starter or a main dish. Fish is another strength, and swordfish, sea-bass and sea bream with olives might feature. Meat dishes range through veal escalopes with fresh orange sauce, roast quails with wine, herbs and polenta, and sliced sirloin steak with radicchio. To finish a small selection of desserts, cheese or fresh fruit is offered from the trolley, and our inspector enjoyed a freshly made tiramisù.

The wine list, naturally, includes a good choice of Italian wines, but also some fine clarets.

Directions: On the junction of Lower Belgrave Street and Ebury Street. Nearest Tube – Victoria

Times: 12.30–Last L 2.30pm, 7pm–Last D 11.30pm. Closed Sat and Sun lunch, Xmas

Chef: Guiseppe Rosselli
Proprietor: Gino Santin

Seats: 55. No pipes. Air conditioned
Additional: Children welcome; children's portions. ◐ dishes; Vegan on request.

The Savoy, River Restaurant ❀❀❀

Classical cooking with modern influences traditionally served in the smart surroundings of a renowned hotel

The grand old hotel on the Strand, the Savoy represents the pinnacle of British hotel-keeping. The first floor River Restaurant, with views over the gardens to the River Thames, provides traditional service, and our inspector was impressed with the staff's performance over a very busy luncheon. Smart dress is, of course, *de rigueur* and booking essential.

Chef Anton Edelmann is committed to excellence in all the hotel's food, and retains the classical style developed by the great Escoffier, though these days some lighter and healthier options are available. There is a choice of seasonal fixed-price and *carte* menus, in French with English descriptions. These include a 'Dejeuner en famille' at Sunday lunchtime, and a set meal with wines chosen to complement each course – the result of a collaboration between Anton Edelman and the sommelier Werner Wissmann.

The *carte* offers a selection of 'Regime Naturel' dishes, such as 'gnocchi de ricotta et d'espinard' which will appeal to vegetarians. Other typical dishes might be home-made ravioli filled with seafood and garnished with asparagus, char-grilled sea-bass perfumed with thyme, and breast of pigeon with wild mushrooms and savoy cabbage. From the attractively priced lunchtime fixed- price menu, our inspector selected a fine starter of red mullet with herbs, vegetables and a butter sauce, followed by paupiettes of sole, filled with lobster, sliced and served with a lobster sauce. Delicious sticky toffee pudding with butterscotch sauce and crème anglaise compled the meal.

The comprehensive wine list is well balanced. Some wines are expensive, but plenty are excellent value for money. Most Grande Marque champagnes are represented, and there is a good selection of claret in magnums.

Directions: From Embankment Tube, you can walk east through the riverside gardens to the hotel. See also below

Map no: 208

Strand WC2
Tel: 0171-836 4343

Cost: *Alc* £38.50, fixed-price lunch £26.50, fixed-price dinner £31 (Sun-Thu), £37 (Fri, Sat). H/wine £14.75. Service inc
Credit cards: 1 2 3 4

Menus: *A la carte*, Sunday Family lunch, fixed-price lunch and dinner
Times: 12.30-Last L 2.30pm, 6pm-Last D 11.30pm

Chef: Anton Edelmann
Manager: Luigi Zambon

Seats: 140. No pipes. Air conditioned
Additional: Children welcome; children's portions. ◐ menu; Vegan on request

The Savoy, Savoy Grill ●●●

A grand, panelled restaurant in a luxurious hotel setting serving grills and more adventurous modern French dishes

There are no major changes to report at the Savoy's famous wood panelled Grill Room, where David Sharland's solid cooking is well supported by Angelo Maresca's skilful restaurant brigade. The *carte* menu is divided between largely British 'plats du jour' and grills on one side and a more adventurous list of modern French dishes, with some Italian influences, on the other. Daily dishes range from sausages, creamed potatoes and onions for lunch to 'poularde de bresse grand mère' for dinner. Grills include lamb cutlets and kidneys, and vegetarian options can also be provided.

The more enterprising dishes are not always the most successful. At an early summer test meal, 'la salade de langoustines aux legumes frits, sauce epicée au vin rouge' didn't taste as well as it read, and the slightly soft prawns and rubbery fried vegetables were barely offset by a lively sauce. The roast pigeon breasts that followed were not as tender as they might have been, but the dish was again saved by a good rich sauce, mixed mushrooms and a small slice of excellent foie gras. (Vegetables are charged separately.) The trolley of desserts had great eye appeal, but our inspector felt that the heat of the room had affected his otherwise good crème brûlée. The wine list is shared with the Savoy's other restaurant, the River.

A theatre menu, priced for two or three courses is available from 6-7pm, with hors d'oeuvre such as salmon and tuna cured with spices and topped with caviar, egg and herb vinaigrette, and entrées of Savoy fish cake with parsley sauce, or roast saddle of lamb, from a choice of half a dozen. A few desserts are offered, but guests are invited to eat their first and main courses before the theatre, and return for coffee and pastries in the Thames Foyer.

Directions: Between Charing Cross and The Aldwych. The hotel, on the right, is set back from the Strand in a courtyard. See previous entry

Map no: 208
Strand WC2
Tel: 0171-836 4343

Cost: *Alc* £44, pre/post-theatre menu £29.75. H/wine £14.75
Service exc
Credit cards: 1 2 3 4

Menus: *A la carte*, pre/post-theatre menu

Times: 12.30 Last L 2.30pm, 6pm-Last D 11.15pm. Closed Sat L, Sun, Aug, BHs

Chef: David Sharland
Manager: Angelo Maresca

Seats: 100. No pipes. Air conditioned
Additional: Children permitted; children's portions. ◑ dishes/other diets on request

The Selfridge, Fletchers ●

☺ Original and interesting dishes, prepared with care, are presented with style in the welcoming setting of Fletchers, the restaurant of this smart and popular West End hotel. Our inspector appreciated his best end of lamb served with olive and tomato ravioli and a confit of lamb shoulder.

Costs: *Alc* £24; fixed-price L £16.50/D £19.59 (3 courses), £24.50. Wine £13 ♀ No service charge. **Credit cards:** 1 2 3 4
Additional: Children welcome; children's portions/menu; ◑ dishes; Vegan/other diets on request. Pianist
Directions: Entrance on Duke Street, off Oxford Street, behind Selfridges store. Nearest Tube – Bond Street

Map no: 209
Orchard Street W1
Tel: 0171-408 2080
Chef: Mark Page
Proprietors: Mount Charlotte Thistle. Manager: John Keating
Seats: 60 No smoking area. Air conditioned
Times: Last L 2.30pm/D 10.30pm. Closed Sat lunch, BHs

Shepherd's ◉◉

☺ *A chic restaurant, full of atmosphere, where good, freshly prepared food is efficiently served at reasonable prices*

In a good location below an apartment building a stone's throw from the Tate Gallery, this sophisticated, panelled restaurant and cocktail bar combines good food and wine with professional management and efficient service. The menu is very much in the Langan's mould, but offers exceptionally good value. Dishes are freshly prepared and skilfully cooked by James Rice and a team of capable chefs. The menu changes but long term favourites remain, such as jellied eels, mussel stew, steak and kidney pie, and lamb meatballs with turnips. Our inspector recently sampled a good smooth duck liver pâté with Cumberland sauce and hot toast, followed by tasty salmon fishcakes with a near perfect parsley sauce and fresh al dente vegetables. The pudding, rhubarb and ginger tart, was overcooked and didn't really work, but was enhanced by a good choice of home-made ice cream. A daily vegetarian dish is also featured. Alternatively there is a bar counter menu and a popular private dining room seating up to 30 people. Wines from around the world are offered, including some good house wines.

Directions: Near Tate Gallery and Westminster Hospital. Nearest Tube – Pimlico

Map no: 210

Marsham Court, Marsham Street SW1
Tel: 0171-834 9552

Cost: Fixed-price lunch and dinner £16.95 (2 courses), £18.95. H/wine £9.50. Service charge 12.5%
Credit cards: 1 2 3 4

Menu: Fixed-price *carte*

Times: 12.30pm-Last L 2.45pm, 6.30pm- Last D 11.30pm. Closed Sat, Sun, BHs

Chef: James Rice
Proprietors: Michael Caine, Richard Shepherd

Seats: 90, 14 Bar, 30 Private Room. Air conditioned
Additional: Children welcome; ◐ dish

Simply Nico ◉◉◉

An elegant restaurant in a prime location offering reasonably-priced menus of classic French food with modern influences

Its proximity to Westminster makes this small but elegant restaurant a popular spot with politicians, so it is wise to book a couple of days ahead. In the evening it is less busy, and the residents of nearby Belgravia predominate. Our inspector appreciated the simplicity of the narrow room and its appointments, as well as the charm and professionalism of the staff, although the tables are packed rather too closely for privacy. The fixed-price lunch and dinner menus offer very good value in view of the central location and the quality of both the cooking and the ingredients, and lunch is priced for two or three courses. The format for both menus is similar, with ten or so starters and main courses, a few of which are price supplemented. There is a happy mix of both classic dishes and more modern ideas, but no vegetarian main courses are featured.

Our inspectors sampled a full flavoured fish soup with rouille and croûtons; a rich risotto flavoured with cep cream and topped with a morsel of seared foie gras; and a whole grilled crottin (goats' cheese) with roasted red peppers. To follow, there was grilled red mullet with aïoli and olives; tender oxtail in a tasty red wine sauce; and duck - not as crispy as promised - with a sweet and sour plum sauce. All meals have a side dish of mixed vegetables, and there is the option of excellent chips or

Map no: 211

48a Rochester Row SW1
Tel: 0171-630 8061

Cost: Fixed-price lunch £20 (2 courses), £23.50, fixed-price dinner £25. H/wine £11.50 ♀ Service inc
Credit cards: 1 2 3 4

Menus: Fixed-price lunch and dinner

Times: Midday-Last L 2.pm, 7.pm-Last D 11pm. Closed Sat lunch, BH lunch, Sun, 4 days Easter, 10 days Xmas

Chef: Andrew Barber
Proprietors: Nico and Dinah-Jane Ladenis

Seats: 45. No pipes. Air conditioned
Additional: Children permitted,(over 4), ◐ dishes

fine creamed potatoes. For dessert the tart tartin with delicious home-made vanilla ice cream is recommended, but the nougat glacé was brittle and lacking in flavour. The extras, olives, breads and coffee, are all carefully selected and very good.

The compact wine list is varied and carefully selected, with a good range of countries and prices up to £48. Five good wines are available by the glass, including champagne.

Directions: Near Rochester Row police station. Nearest Tube – Victoria

Simpson's in the Strand ❀❀

Good quality traditional English cooking in one of central London's most famous restaurants. Always busy

Simpson's origins go back to 'The Grand Cigar Divan', or smoking-room, of 1828. Today this famous restaurant still recalls a bygone London, with its aproned waiters and attentive, efficient service. Its style is summed up by a Bateman cartoon on the menu in which a carver is aghast as a diner asks whether the meat is English or foreign. Indeed, foreign influences barely figure, except on the wine list. Our inspector began with well-prepared quails' eggs, haddock and cheese sauce and followed with a flavoursome steak, kidney and mushroom pudding (not pie, please note). He could also have chosen saddle of lamb or Aylesbury duck, carved at the table, Lancashire hot-pot or grilled Dover sole. Vegetables include bubble and squeak, although our inspector felt his pan-fried potato and spinach version lacked authenticity. If you have room, try a savoury such as Welsh rarebit or Scotch woodcock, or a pudding – spotted dick or treacle roll. The extensive wine list even has an index, listing English, German, Italian, Spanish and New World wines. The French wines include grand and premier cru Burgundies.

Directions: From Trafalgar Square follow the Strand almost to the end, Simpsons is on the right

Map no: 212
100 Strand WC2
Tel: 0171-836 9112

Cost: *Alc* £25, fixed-price lunch £10, fixed-price dinner (6-7pm) £10. H/wine from £12. Service exc
Credit cards: 1 2 3 4

Menus: *A la carte,* Sunday lunch, fixed-price lunch and dinner, bar menu

Times: Last L 2pm, Last D 11pm. Closed Good Friday, Xmas

Chef: Tony Bradley
Proprietor: Savoy Group. Manager: Brian Clivaz

Additional: Children permitted; children's portions. ❶ dishes; Vegan/other diets on request. Pianist in evenings

Singapore Garden ❀❀

☺ *Chinese, Singaporean and Malaysian specialities on a long exciting menu, served in a lively atmosphere*

The Lim family's first restaurant continues to attract a loyal following both from local Europeans and Asians so it is essential to book. The atmosphere is lively and the menu is long – combining many Chinese dishes with Singaporean and Malaysian specialities. There are also the usual dull set dinners (catering for the unadventurous European) or a handwritten list of specials dependent on market availability. Crispy Ikan Bilis makes a good accompaniment to the Tiger beer – shredded, sugared anchovies with peanuts roasted in their skins. Soft shell crab comes two ways – sautéed in bread crumbs or deep fried in a light batter with salt, garlic and chilli. The lobster and crab (still in their shells) are excellent, either with

Map no: 213

83 Fairfax Road NW6
Tel: 0171-328 5314

Cost: *Alc* £20, fixed-price lunch and dinner £16. H/wine £8.50. Service exc
Credit cards: 1 2 3 4

Menus: *A la carte,* fixed-price lunch and dinner

Times: Midday–Last L 2pm, 6pm–Last D 10pm (10.30pm Fri and Sat). Closed 5 days at Xmas

black pepper and butter or in the delicious sweet chilli sauce. For meat-eaters there are sizzling dishes or an authentic beef rendang, chunks of beef in a fragrant and spicy thick coconut sauce. If you don't fancy beer there is Chinese tea, a short wine list and the curious non-alcoholic grass jelly. Mrs Lim Senior cooks, while the family supervises the swift, friendly service.

Directions: Off the Finchley Road in Swiss Cottage. Nearest Tube – Swiss Cottage, exit Belsize Road

Chef: S K Lim
Proprietors: The Lim family, Mrs Lin Toh

Seats: 100. Air conditioned
Additional: Children welcome; ❷ dishes; other diets on request

Snows on the Green ❀❀

☺ *A full-flavoured taste of Southern Italy and France in a popular and busy restaurant*

The Mediterranean countries are the focus for the cooking at this popular restaurant, whose loyal following includes many customers from the BBC studios. Chef Sebastian Snow follows the same uncomplicated formula which has earned him success over the years, using good quality fresh ingredients to produce wonderfully true flavours. The *carte* lists recipes which are mostly repeated on the superbly priced, set lunch menu; starters like roasted squid with ink linguini, and potato fritters with snails, field mushrooms and gremolata may be followed by peppered breast of duck with turnip savoyard, or gratin of aubergine, Mozzarella and Parmesan. Our inspector enthused over a recent meal of tender baked capsicums filled with creamy cod brandade and sprinkled with roasted pine kernels, before stuffed pig's trotter with black pudding - beautifully cooked to a near perfect texture but slightly overpowered by the pudding - served with caramelised apples and stunningly flavoured mashed potato. A classic lemon tart made a sublime finish to the meal. Service is speedy and efficient.

Directions: Opposite Brook Green on Shepherds Bush Road. Nearest Tube – Hammersmith

Map no: T214

166 Shepherds Bush Road, Brook Green, Hammersmith W6
Tel: 0171-603 2142

Cost: *Alc* £20, fixed-price lunch £11.50 (2 courses), £13.50. H/wine £8.75. Service exc
Credit cards: 1 3 5

Menus: *A la carte*, Sunday lunch, fixed-price lunch

Times: Last L 3pm, Last D 11pm. Closed Sat lunch, Sun eve, 24 Dec-2 Jan, BHs

Chef: Sebastian Snow
Proprietor: Sebastian Snow

Seats: 70. No cigars or pipes. Air conditioned
Additional: Children welcome. ❷ dishes

Soho Soho ❀

A spacious, bustling West End restaurant offering French Provençal cuisine with an imaginative carte and small daily menu. Our inspector enjoyed salmon and French beans in pasta, and moist, tender red mullet in vine leaves. Chocolate marquise with roasted pistachio nuts proved tasty.

Cost: *Alc* £35, pre-theatre £14.95 (2 courses), £17.50 ♀ Service inc.
Credit cards: 1 2 3 4
Additional: Children permitted. ❷ dishes.
Directions: Frith Street is off Soho Square. Nearest Tubes – Tottenham Court Road and Leicester Square

Map no: 215
11 Frith Street W1
Tel: 0171-494 3491
Chef: Laurent Lebeau
Manager: Philippe Vachardpoulos
Seats: 65. No-smoking area. No cigars or pipes. Air conditioned
Times: Last L 2.45pm/D 11.45pm. Closed Sun. Telephone to check holiday closures

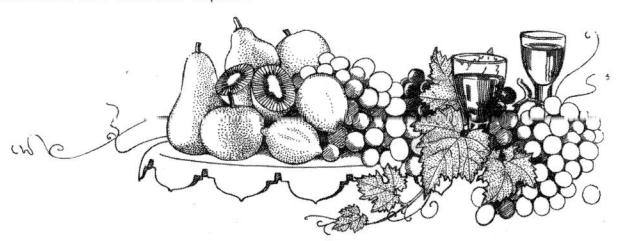

Sonny's ❀❀

☺ A talented new chef with a commendable reputation demonstrating his skilful modern British cooking

There's a light and airy feel to this informal modern restaurant in a parade of shops in fashionable Barnes. A popular café/bar at the front converts to more dining space in the evenings. New chef Redmond Hayward has brought with him a reputation for highly commendable modern British cooking, and in a short time he seems to be fulfilling all expectations. At a recent inspection meal flavours were fresh and distinct, and dishes were served by very helpful and attentive staff. Chicken liver parfait – a light and creamy creation served with home-made brioche and good apple and sultana chutney – was judged a firm success, followed by pan-fried liver with tarragon and red wine jus and a delicious lemon-flavoured potato cake. An excellent between-courses apple and celery soup was full-flavoured and freshly chunky, and the inspector still had praise for a crème brûlée with banana and rum. Fish dishes take up about half of the *carte* and short set menu. An interesting vintage wine list includes some New World and half bottles, some of which quality wines can be sampled by the glass.

Directions: From Castelnau end of Church Road, on left by shops

Map no: H216

94 Church Road, Barnes SW13
Tel: 0181-748 0393

Cost: *Alc* £18, fixed-price lunch and dinner £12.95 (2 courses). H/wine fr £7.95 ♀ Service exc
Credit cards: 1 2 3

Menus: *A la carte*, Sunday lunch, fixed-price lunch and dinner, café menu

Times: Last L 2.30pm (3pm Sun), Last D 11pm. Closed Sun eve & BH lunches

Chef: Redmond Hayward
Proprietor: Rebecca Mascarenhas

Seats: 100. Air conditioned
Additional: Children welcome. ❤ dishes

The Square ❀❀❀

An original and eclectic range of dishes enjoyed by a discerning clientele in a modern restaurant setting

A bright modern restaurant with clean decor and wooden floorboards, The Square is popular with a discerning clientele attracted by the cooking of Philip Howard, who is now a partner in the business. The lunch menu is confined to a choice of six starters and main courses, but an extended dinner menu, which changes every two months, is now in operation.

The cuisine falls into no clear category, but Howard's influences are drawn from the Mediterranean, America (where he has spent some time), and from other prominent chefs. What appears on the plate is an uncomplicated and, for the most part, successful blending of flavours, despite some inconsistencies in the seasoning and a penchant for black pepper. Among some original starters, such as saffron and mussel risotto with roasted pimento and Parmesan, and hot smoked eel with lightly curried lentils and horseradish chantilly, there will be an unusual soup - roast chicken, onion and chanterelle on one occasion.

Impressive main courses have included fillet of zander set on an intriguingly tasty bed of finely chopped ingredients with savoy cabbage and grain mustard, and pot roast kid with a ragout of white beans and rosemary. Vegetarian dishes are not featured, but are generally available on request. At the dessert stage, our inspector found the house's version of crème brûlée a bit of a disappointment. Service late at night can be uneven, but most of the time it is unobtrusive and efficient, in keeping with the food and decor, reflecting the unassuming modesty of Philip

Map no: S217

32 King Street
St James's, SW1
Tel: 0171-839 8787

Cost: *Alc* £35. Wine £15
Credit cards: 1 2 3 4 5

Menu: *A la carte*

Times: Midday-Last L 3pm, 6pm-Last D 11.45pm. Closed Sat and Sun lunch, BH lunch, 25 Dec-4 Jan

Chef: Philip Howard
Proprietors: Nigel Platts-Martin, Philip Howard

Seats: 70. Air conditioned
Additional: Children permitted. ❤ dishes, Vegan, other diets on request

Howard. The Square Selection offers some interesting wines at £12.50 to £30 a bottle. Other wines from around the world are listed by grape variety, and there is an excellent fine wine section, particularly strong in Burgundy and the Rhône.

Directions: Off Piccadilly; turn right into Duke Street, then left into King Street. Nearest Tubes – Piccadilly Circus, Green Park

Stafford ❀

An elegant and quietly located hotel where chef Armando Rodriguez shows his skill with delightful dishes. Amongst the tempting choices are fillet of red mullet and rosemary asparagus with lemon butter sauce or pan-fried lamb's liver, kidney and sweetbread with a rich Madeira sauce.

Cost: Alc £34, fixed-price £22.50. H/wine £14 **Credit cards:** 1 2 3 4
Additional. Children welcome; children's portions; ❂ dishes
Directions: Off St James's Street

Map no: 217a
16-18 St James's Place SW1
Chef: Armando Rodriguez
Proprietor: Armando Rodriguez
Times: Midday-Last L 2.30pm, 6pm-Last D 10.30pm. Lunch not served Sat

Stephen Bull Bistro ❀❀

☺ *A very popular eating place offering uncomplicated modern British cooking and value for money*

Bright, bold and bubbly is the order of the day at this popular Smithfield bistro, where imaginative cooking and a congenial atmosphere combine with good value for money. Cosy, intimate chat is out, but discreet eavesdropping is an easy perk at the closely packed tables. The cooking is naturally the biggest attraction, with the no-nonsense modern British dishes offering bright, honest textures and flavours. A very intense chicken liver parfait attractively served on julienne of courgette and diced tomatoes with crunchy onion marmalade was a typical recent starter, followed by fillet of red bream with a nage of small fresh mussels and feves – a light yet filling main dish with subtle flavours. A warm gingerbread pudding with apple and hazelnut marmalade and a powerful Calvados sauce was an enjoyable choice from a range also including brown sugar meringue with bananas, ice cream and hot fudge sauce. A pleasant, well-managed brigade looks after the guests with sociable efficiency and much agility. There's a good wine list of mainly French and New World wines, and an interesting selection of beers.

Directions: From Cowcross Street turn into St John Street, on the left-hand side after about 600 yards. Nearest Tube – Farringdon

Map no: 218
71 St John Street EC1
Tel: 0171-490 3127

Cost: Alc £17.50, Wine £9.50 ♀
Service exc
Credit cards: 1 2 3

Menus: A la carte

Times: Midday-Last L 2.15pm, 6.30pm-Last D 10.45pm. Closed Sat L, all day Sun, 10 days Xmas & BHs

Chef: Steven Carter
Proprietors: Stephen Bull, April Manley

Seats: 90. No cigars or pipes. Air conditioned
Additional: Children welcome; children's portions. ❂ dishes; Vegan/other diets on request

Stephen Bull ❀❀❀

A restaurant with minimalist-style decor and modern British cooking with strong European influences

Stephen Bull has continued to expand his activities with an establishment in the Fulham Road as well as his bistro, but in this, his original restaurant, he appears to be struggling to keep

Map no: 219
5-7 Blandford Street W1
Tel: 0171-490 1750

Cost: Alc £26. H/wine £10.50 ♀
Service exc
Credit cards: 1 2 3

its edge. The menus read well – the format much the same for lunch and dinner – and there is plenty of interest. Vegetarian starters are listed and main courses are available on request. European influences are apparent in dishes such as salad of chorizo, Pecorino and almonds, chicken breast with Serrano ham and lemon risotto, and a terrine of chicken confit with foie gras, rocket and good pear chutney. The latter was our inspector's choice, but was somewhat disappointing. Better was the stuffed globe artichoke with a mushroom duxelle, herbs and a vibrant citrus vinaigrette. Rib-eye of beef was competently grilled but the advertised foie gras butter was missing. Rare-grilled swordfish was actually cooked through but was very fresh and still moist, the samphire, asparagus and wilted spinach provided texture and the sauce vierge, flavour.

At the pudding stage the plate of chocolate desserts had a couple of real winners – the parfait and the pot au chocolat. The wine list is intelligently chosen and laid out, and several wines, like the good Menetou-Salon form Henri Pelle, come by the glass.

Directions: Off Marylebone High St, 75 yards down on the left. Nearest Tube – Bond Street

Menu: *A la carte*

Times: Last L 2.15pm, Last D 10.45pm. Closed Sat lunch, Sun, BHs, 1 week at Xmas

Chef: Enda Flanagan
Proprietors: Stephen Bull, Aiden Fahey

Seats: 53. No cigars or pipes in restaurant. Air conditioned
Additional: Children welcome; children's portions; ✿ dishes; Vegan/other diets on request

Suntory ✿✿

Traditional Japanese restaurant serving consistently good food made from fresh, quality ingredients

This long-established modern Japanese restaurant attracts a loyal corporate and social clientele to its traditional dining rooms which include a large teppan-yaki room and several small, discreet private salons. Chef Kato San produces consistently high standards of cooking from fresh quality ingredients, and the results can be sampled on his main *carte* as well as the list of chef's suggestions and various set menus. Our inspector started a recent meal with Sashimi, and enjoyed the mixture of sliced raw tuna, sea bream, squid, salmon and turbot with a bitter soy sauce. Prawn tempura, and chawan-mushi – a lightly set soup made from eggs, vegetables, chicken and seafood – were both enjoyable dishes, and the small crab fish cakes textured with yam, prawns, and fine strips of aubergine in a tasty mirin sake sauce were very successful. Freshly cooked and sticky boiled rice accompanied this satisfying meal, which ended with miso soup of fermenting bean paste with Japanese pickle and green tea. Service from traditionally dressed waitresses is polite and attentive, but misunderstandings can occur, and diners are urged to double check their order.

Directions: At the bottom of St James' Street, opposite St James' Palace. Nearest Tube – Green Park (turn right after Ritz Hotel)

Map no: 220

72 St James's Street SW1
Tel: 0171-409 0201

Cost: *Alc* from £32.50, fixed-price lunch £20, £35, fixed-price dinner £49.80, £65. Wine £14. Service inc

Credit cards: 1 2 3 4 5

Menus: *A la carte*, fixed-price lunch and dinner

Times: Midday-Last L 2pm, 6pm-Last D 10pm. Closed Sun, BHs, Xmas, New Year

Chef: Mr K Kato
Proprietor: Mr K Hamamoto

Seats: 120. Air conditioned
Additional: Children welcome. ✿ dishes; Vegan on request

Swallow International ❀

Inside this purpose-built and well managed hotel Blayney's restaurant features British cooking with Oriental and Asian influences skilfully produced by chef David Date. Starters include smoked salmon parcels filled with crème fraîche, and could be followed by roast lamb fillets with a tasty jus.

Cost: Alc £36.25, fixed-price dinner £17.25. H/wine £9.25
Credit cards: 1 2 3 4. **Additional:** Children welcome; children's menu; ❂ dishes
Directions: West side of the Cromwell Road

Map no: 220a
Cromwell Road, SW5
Tel: 0171-973 1000
Chef: David Date
Proprietors: Swallow. Manager: Geoffrey Gold
Times: Last D 11pm. Lunch not served. Closed Xmas

Tabaq ❀

☺ *A friendly, atmospheric Pakistani restaurant serving traditional family-style cooking from Lahore, with some dishes of Indian origin. Chef Manzoor Ahmed cooks to order and specialities include Palak Gosht, lamb cooked with spinach to an old village recipe.*

Cost: Alc £18.50. H/wine £7.25. Service charge **Credit cards:** 1 2 3 4
Additional: Children welcome; children's portions. ❂ dishes
Directions: On the South Circular. Nearest Tube – Clapham South

Map no: B221
47 Balham Hill, South Clapham SW12
Tel: 0181-673 7820
Chef: Manzoor Ahmed
Proprietor: Mushtaq Ahmed
Seats: 50. No-smoking area. Air conditioned
Times: Last D 11.30pm

Tatsusu ❀❀

Teppan and sushi menus supplement a traditional carte to provide a good range of tasty, authentic Japanese dishes

Quality authentic ingredients, all freshly prepared and professsionally cooked, produce dishes of a standard that keeps this restaurant constantly thronged with customers – its Teppan-yaki lunch counters, in particular, being extremely popular with Japanese city gentlemen; a Sushi menu and traditional *carte* are also available. One real attraction is the fact that chef Mr Yamanaki apparently makes all his own sauces and Dashi from scratch. A pickled prawn tempura in a tasty rice vinegar provided the appetiser to a recent inspection meal; this was followed by assorted Sashimi (turbot, salmon and yellow tail) served with a salad of green leaf, red cress, kelp, white radish and hot green mustard accompanied by a separate soy sauce. Other enjoyable dishes sampled included chawan-mushi (a delicate steamed egg curd textured with fresh chicken, spring onion and prawn) and ebi-tempura (fresh whole prawns dipped in a well-seasoned rice flour, lightly deep-fried and served with a light home-made soy-based sauce, radish and hot yellow mustard). The wine list offers both sake and Kirin beer.

Directions: Turn right out of Liverpool Street Station

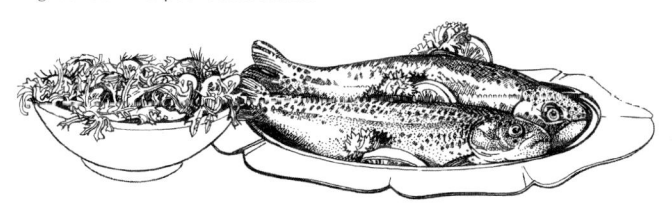

Map no: 222

32 Broadgate Circle EC2
Tel: 0171-638 5863

Cost: Alc £50, fixed-price £35. Service charge 13%
Credit cards: 1 2 3 4

Menus: A la carte, Teppan, Sushi, fixed-price

Times: 11.30-Last L 2.30pm, 6.30pm-Last D 9.45pm. Closed Sat, Sun, BHs
Chef: Yamanaki San
Proprietor: Nicholas Stern

Additional: Children welcome; children's portions; ❂ dishes

Thai Garden ❁

☺ *In the depths of the East End, this small but appealing Thai restaurant specialises in both vegetarian and seafood cookery with two separate menus. From the vegetarian, the satay of shitake mushrooms was good and from the seafood, fried pomfret, a dry fish with various toppings, was memorable.*

Cost: Alc £20, fixed-price £16.50. H/wine £5.95. Service charge
Additional: Children welcome; ❂ menu
Directions: Part of a small parade of shops at the Bethnal Green end of Globe Road

Map no: 223
249 Globe Road E2
Tel: 0181-981 5748
Chef: Mrs Pensri Vichit
Proprietors: Suthinee and Jack Hufton
Seats: 32. No-smoking upstairs
Times: Last L 2.45pm, Last D 10.45pm. Lunch not served Sat. Closed Sun

Thailand ❁

☺ *A small, unassuming but popular restaurant opposite Goldsmith's College offering Thai cuisine with some Laotian specialities. The extensive menu describes in English dishes ranging from soups to curries or stir fried squid. The short wine list also offers Chinese beer and over 50 malt whiskies.*

Cost: Alc £16, fixed-price D £20 (for parties). H/wine £8.50. Service exc. **Credit cards:** 1 2 3. **Additional:** Children permitted. ❂ dishes
Directions: Opposite Goldsmiths College. Five minutes' walk from New Cross and New Cross Gate Tubes

Map no: 224
14 Lewisham Way, Newcross SE14
Tel: 0181-691 4040
Chef: Kamkhong Kambungeot
Proprietor: Kamkhong Kambungeot
Seats: 25. Air conditioned
Times: 6pm-Last D 11pm. Closed Sun, Mon, 10 Apr-10 May

Thirty Four Surrey Street ❁

☺ *An American seafood restaurant producing blackened dishes (a southern US style of dry searing meat or fish with pungent spices), Mexican dishes, fajitas or chimichanga and easy snacks. Their fish pie was of succulent fish and prawns in a deliciously creamy sauce with a rich crust of pastry.*

Cost: Alc £17.85. **Credit cards:** 1 2 3 **Additional:** Children welcome; ❂ dishes
Directions: Behind the Fruit and Veg Market in the centre of Croydon

Map no: 225
34 Surrey Street, Croydon
Tel: 0181-686 0586
Chef: Malcolm John
Proprietor: Harry Coelho
Seats: 80. Air conditioned
Times: Last L 3pm/D 10.45pm. Closed Sat L, Sun, BHs

Thistells ❁

☺ *A mixture of French and Middle Eastern cuisine is served at this informal restaurant, which takes its name from the ornate Victorian (Scottish) tiling of its shop-style interior. Dishes range from falafel, hummus and zahtar toasts to pâté, moules marinières and duck cassoulet.*

Costs: Alc £20, fixed-price L £7.50. H/wine £7 ♀ Service inc
Additional: Children welcome; children's portions. ❂ dishes; Vegan/other diets on request
Directions: On Lordship Lane (A2216) just after junction with East Dulwich Grove

Map no: 226
65 Lordship Lane SE22
Tel: 0181-299 1921
Chef: Sami Youssef
Proprietors: Anne and Sami Youssef
Seats: 35-40
Times: Last L 2pm/D 10.30pm. Closed Sun eve

Tophams Ebury Court ❀

☺ *For many years now Tophams has been known for its Edwardian charm, and chef Philip Gonsalves offers traditional dishes alongside delicate modern fare (including a good vegetarian menu). Our inspector enjoyed sautéed ducks' livers with allumette of orange zest.*

Cost: A/c £20; fixed-price L/D £9.75 (2 courses). H/wine £8.50. Service exc
Credit cards: 1 2 3 4. **Additional:** Children welcome; children's portions. ✪ menu; Vegan/other diets on request
Directions: Three minutes' walk from Victoria Station

Map no: J227
28 Ebury Street SW1
Tel: 0171-730 8147
Chef: Phillip Gonsalves
Proprietors: Nicholas and Marianne Kingsford
Seats: 30. No smoking area. No pipes or cigars in restaurant.
Times: Last L 2pm/ D 9.30pm.
Closed 23 Dec-4 Jan

Tui ❀

A popular Thai restaurant offering straightforward cooking at reasonable prices, with an explicit menu of starters, soups, main courses, noodle dishes, curries and Yum dishes: a traditional method of cooking using fresh herbs, chillies and lime juice. Try Thai beer or ginger tea instead of wine.

Cost: A/c £22, fixed-price L £10. H/wine £7.95. Service 12.5%. Cover charge. **Credit cards:** 1 2 3 4. **Additional:** Children welcome for lunch. ✪ dishes; Vegan/other diets on request **Directions:** Near South Kensington Tube in direction of Victoria and Albert Museum

Map no: 228
19 Exhibition Road SW7
Tel: 0171-584 8359
Chefs: Mr and Mrs Kongsrivilai
Proprietor: Mr E Thapthimthong
Seats: 52. No cigars or pipes
Times: Last L 2.15pm (2.45pm Sun)/D 10.45pm (10.15pm Sun).
Closed 5 days Xmas, BHs

Turner's ❀❀❀

A comfortable restaurant serving good-value French cuisine carefully prepared from quality produce

Brian Turner, renowned for his northern hospitality, provides one of the best value lunches in the capital at his comfortable French restaurant at the west end of Walton Street. He may not spend so much time at the stove these days but he has a kitchen team who reflect his ideals, using the best of produce and retaining its natural flavours. Seating is close enough for one to become involved in a neighbour's conversation, and the blues and yellows favoured for the upholstery look a touch less than pristine, but comfort is the main priority.

The Menu du Jour, offering a choice at each of three courses (and priced for two or three), stints in neither quantity nor quality. Following canapés, our inspector chose a starter of pan-fried rabbit and strips of crispy bacon with various salad leaves lightly dressed in oil and served with slices of toasted brioche - a light and effective starter. 'Stuffed baby chicken' was the simple description of what turned out to be a wonderfully complex dish - boned poussin filled with mousse and set on a galette of shredded potato with a rich and aromatic sauce of stock and shitake mushrooms. Blueberry egg custard was a well-made dessert - a creamy custard with blueberries scattered on the top – followed by a strong well roasted blend of coffee and home-made petits fours.

The full menu, in French with English descriptions, is priced for two courses with dessert as an optional third course. It is

Map no: 229
87-89 Walton Street W3
Tel: 0171-584 6711

Cost: Fixed-price lunch £9.95 (2 courses), £13.50. Fixed-price dinner £32 (2 courses), £38.75. Service inc
Credit cards: 1 3

Menus: Fixed-price lunch and dinner

Times: 12.30-Last L 2.30pm, 7.30pm-Last D 10.45pm. Closed Xmas

Chefs: Brian Turner, Alan Thompson
Proprietor: Brian Turner

Seats: 52. Clients requested to smoke with consideration. Air conditioned

much more expensive but offers a wider choice and more time in which to enjoy it. Dishes might include chicken liver pâté with potato bread and oranges, Dover sole with pesto, baked beef fillet with a crust of black pudding and brioche, crème caramel with red berries, and tarte tatin with pears.

Directions: From Draycott Avenue, the restaurant is about 100 yards up Walton Street on the right. Nearest Tube – South Kensington

Two Brothers ✺

☺ *'Not just another chippy', is the claim of this busy fish restaurant – a really happy place with delightful staff – run by the Manzi brothers, Leon and Tony. Fish is freshly delivered each day and served fried, grilled or steamed, with excellent chips, home-made tartare sauce and good vinegar.*

Cost: *Alc* from £12. H/wine £8.10. Service exc. **Credit cards:** 1 2 3
Additional: Children permitted (no babies or push chairs after 6.30pm). ❷ dishes
Directions: Nearest Tube – Finchley Central

Map no: Q230
297 Regents Park Road, Finchley
Tel: 0181-346 0469
Proprietors: Leon and Tony Manzi
Seats: 90. No pipes or cigars. Air conditioned
Times: Last L 2.30pm/D 10.15pm. Closed Sun and Mon, Tues after BHs, Last 2 weeks Aug

The Veeraswamy ✺✺

Some of the best tastes of the sub-continent, all under one roof in the doyen of London's Indian restaurants

London's oldest Indian restaurant owes its name to a printer's error. Originally Veerasawmy's, it evolved from a spice-trading company established in 1927 by an Anglo-Indian whose great-grandfather was the Nizam of Hyderabad. Well-placed for Theatreland and the West End, this is not a restaurant into which one casually drifts after a leisurely drive from the country; trying to park round here will take the edge off any appetite. Find a more relaxed way of arriving to enjoy fully the well-prepared, but fairly standard, Indian dishes on the *carte* or pre- and post-theatre, fixed-price menu. Starters come from western India, Delhi (try the 'Alu tikki' – a favourite roadside snack of a minced potato, cheese and onion patty), Bombay and the southern mountains of Nilgiri. Tandoori specialities come from the north west and 'Murgh Kashmiri' is chicken in a rich, but mildly-spiced, creamy dry fruit sauce. Chunky pieces of cod in coconut milk with herbs and spices becomes Goan fish curry. A sorbet, or one of the Indian sweets, will round off the meal and an Indian beer might be a good alternative to wine.

Directions: Nearest Tube – Piccadilly Circus

Map no: 231
99-101 Regent Street W1
Tel: 0171-734 1401

Cost: *Alc* £60 (2 persons), fixed-price lunch £14.90. H/wine £13.50. Service charge 15%
Credit cards: 1 2 3 4
Menus: *A la carte*, fixed-price, pre-theatre, bar menu
Times: Miday-Last L 2.30pm, 6pm-Last D 11.30pm. Closed Sun, BHs
Chef: Sona Bedi
Proprietor: Paul Baretto
Seats: 110. No-smoking area. Air conditioned
Additional: Children welcome. ❷ menu; Vegan/other diets on request

Veronica's ✺✺

Soundly-cooked themed food of traditional British style, served in simple but pleasing surroundings

There's a friendly, informal atmosphere at this neat restaurant, helped, no doubt, by the chatty and descriptive menus which explain the themed food on offer. Veronica

Map no: R232
3 Hereford Road, Bayswater W2
Tel: 0171-229 5079

Cost: *Alc* £22.50; fixed-price lunch & dinner £11 (2 courses). Wine £9 ♀ Service 10%

Shaw and new chef Antonio Feliccio cook in traditional British style with a touch more spice than might be expected, but the results are very enjoyable. Recent menus have included selections from the best of past themes, with starters like grilled Wiltshire goats' cheese and elderflower syrup, and mushrooms with minted quails' eggs and smoked salmon. Main courses might be grilled calf's liver and Victorian benoiton sauce, or Tudor pye of salmon and mushroom. Our inspector enjoyed a freshly-made spinach soup, and a traditional smoked fish pie of haddock and cod topped with a cheesy potato purse and served with a side dish of crisp shredded leaks. Desserts are rich and tempting, and chocolate pudding with butterscotch and whisky sauce was heavy but tasty. Dishes are marked for low fat content, high fibre, vegetarian and vegan, and the *carte* is backed up by a short set menu offering two courses and coffee at fair prices.

Directions: On the south side of Hereford Road which runs parallel with Queensway. Nearest Tubes – Bayswater and Queensway

Credit cards: 1 2 3 4 5

Menus: *A la carte*, fixed-price lunch and dinner, pre-theatre

Times: Midday-Last L 2.30pm, 7pm-Last D 12am. Closed Sun, Sat lunch, Xmas, BHs

Chefs: Antonio Feliccio and Veronica Shaw
Proprietor: Philip Shaw

Seats: 60
Additional: Children welcome; children's portions; ◐ dishes; Vegan on request

Wagamama ✤

A very popular, up-beat fast food Japanese-style noodle bar, where diners sit at long communal tables and benches. The food is freshly prepared and skilfully cooked, with a frequently changing carte. Bookings are not accepted, and queues soon form but move briskly.

Cost: H/wine £6.80 ♀ Service exc. **Credit cards:** None taken.
Additional: Children welcome. ◐ dishes. Vegan on request
Directions: From New Oxford Street turn left into Bloomsbury and Streatham Street is first right. Nearest Tube – Tottenham Court Road

Map no: 233
4 Streatham Street WC1
Tel: 0171-323 9223
Chef:
Proprietors: Wagamama Ltd
Seats: 104. No smoking. Air conditioned
Times: Last L 2.30pm/D 11pm. Closed Sun, BHs

Waltons ✤✤

A smart restaurant with caring service offering mainly English cooking along with a good value wine list

Waltons is a smart restaurant attracting a good number of American visitors, who appreciate the friendly and professional service provided by Michael Mayhew and his team, as well as Paul Hodgson's fine cooking. The menus, a *carte*, fixed-price lunch and after-theatre supper, are not but offer a varied selection of English dishes, with some French influences apparent. This year our inspectors have enjoyed starters of seafood sausage filled with finely minced lobster and scallop, with a well-made lobster sauce, and a delicious chilled smoked salmon soup. A main course vegetarian dish is featured, such as home-made ravioli stuffed and topped with wild mushrooms in a brandy and Madeira cream sauce.
    Our inspectors opted for prime medallions of Scottish beef set on a celeriac and horseradish potato cake with a tasty truffle sauce, and a less successful dish of corn-fed guinea fowl with savoy cabbage and Madeira sauce. From a tempting dessert list the blackberry and apple charlotte

Map no: 234
121 Walton Street SW3
Tel: 0171-584 0204

Cost: *A/c* £35, fixed-price lunch £14.75, Sun lunch £16.50, after-theatre supper (9.30pm) £21. H/wine £9.50 ♀ Service exc
Credit cards: 1 2 3 4 5

Menus: *A la carte*, fixed-price lunch, Sunday lunch, after theatre supper

Times: 12.30pm-Last L 2.30pm (2pm Sun, BHs), 7.30pm-Last D 11.30pm (7pm-Last D 10pm Sun, BHs). Closed dinner 25 Dec, all day 26 Dec

Chef: Paul Hodgson
Proprietor: Roger Wren

proved a good choice. The wine list is excellent and modestly priced for this part of London.

Directions: On the corner of Walton Street and Draycott Avenue, just off Brompton Road. Nearest Tube – South Kensington

Seats: 85 inc private room. No pipes. Air conditioned
Additional: Children welcome; children's portions. ❷ dishes; Vegan/other diets on request

West Lodge Park ❀

☺ *Chef, Peter Leggat and his team offer a choice of tempting and varied dishes including a deliciously light salad of smoked chicken, salmon and tomato served with a walnut dressing, pan-fried breast of duck served with blackberries, pears and port, a pork fillet or Dover sole.*

Cost: Fixed-price L £15 (2 courses), £17.50; fixed-price D £19.50 (£21 Fri, Sat). H/wine £10.75. Service exc. **Credit cards:** 1 2 3 5
Additional: Children permitted; children's portions; ❷ dishes; Vegan/other diets on request
Directions: From Potters Bar and the M25 junc 24 follow signs to Cockfosters on the A111

Map no: 235
Cockfosters Road, Hadley Wood, Barnet
Tel: 0181-440 8311
Chef: Peter Leggat
Proprietors: The Beale family
Seats: 70. No smoking in dining room. Air conditioned
Times: Last L 2pm/D 9.45pm. Limited restaurant service 27-29 Dec

The White Tower ❀❀

Genuine Greek and Cypriot food in an old-established West End restaurant

If Barbara Cartland spotted our inspector, she didn't let on. He noticed her, though, just as he noticed the improvement in this long-established Fitzrovia restaurant since owners Mary Dunne and George Metaxas arrived in April 1993. They offer a good selection of Cypriot and mainland Greek dishes, with additional contributions from Turkey, Italy, France and Britain. Each day the chef prepares two special dishes such as 'Triade tour blanche' which combines moussaka, dolmades of baby marrows and chicken pilaff. Or there is 'Capana of lamb à la Morea', a Greek country casserole of lean meat, tomatoes and mushrooms with Greek dry white wine. The menu, with its quirky descriptions, makes no mention of desserts but Turkish coffee and Turkish delight could well be enough. About 60, mostly French, wines are available but only Cypriot or Greek, including that old holiday favourite Demestica, come in at less than £16 a bottle. On arrival you are likely to be greeted by the owners who will ensure you enjoy caring, professional service in an atmosphere that recalls the White Tower style of old.

Directions: Nearest Tubes – Tottenham Court Road, Goodge Street

Map no: 236
1 Percy Street W1
Tel: 0171-636 8141

Cost: A/c £35. H/wine £10.25. Service exc. Cover charge £2
Credit cards: 1 2 3 4

Menu: *A la carte*

Times: 12.30–Last L 2.30pm, 6.30pm–Last D 10.30pm. Closed Sat lunch, Sun, last 3 weeks Aug

Chef: Mauricio Ramos
Proprietors: George Metaxas, Mary Dunne

Seats: 80. Partially air conditioned
Additional: Children permitted at lunch. ❷ dishes

Wilson's ❀❀

☺ *A congenial atmosphere, confident cooking and good value for money in a restaurant with a Scottish emphasis*

A tremendously friendly atmosphere is generated by co-patron Bob Wilson at this small, homely restaurant which is very popular with regular diners. The accomplished cooking is based

Map no: T237
236 Blythe Road W14
Tel: 0171-603 7267

Cost: A/c £16.50, fixed-price lunch £7.50, fixed-price dinner £12. H/wine £8.95 ♀ Service

on high quality ingredients, nicely prepared and presented. The menu has a slight Scottish slant, featuring in the past haggis, haddock and lots of salmon. Indeed, crisp and tasty salmon fish cakes with parsley sauce were our inspector's chosen starter. First courses with an international flavour have included Parma ham rosette with Stilton mousse and lentil, lemon and cumin soup. Lightly cooked, the sauté of lambs' kidneys and cutlets was a tender meaty main dish. Other main courses typical of chef Robert Hilton's cooking have been duck breast stuffed with duck liver and red onions, and trout fillet with a langoustine mousse, while puddings have included tiramisù, chocolate crème brûlée and a refreshing strawberry sablé, served with fruit coulis. The house wines on the short, reasonably-priced list are particularly good value for money as are the fixed-price lunch and dinner menus. Booking here is advisable.

Directions: On the corner of Blythe Road and Shepherds Bush Road

charge exc
Credit cards: 1 2 3

Menus: *A la carte*, fixed-price lunch and dinner

Times: 12.30-Last L 3pm, Last D 11pm. Closed Sat lunch

Chef: Robert Hilton
Proprietors: Bob Wilson, Tony Jimenez

Seats: 50. Air conditioned
Additional: Children welcome; children's portions. ❂ dishes; Vegan/other diets on request

Yumi ❀❀

A long-established Japanese restaurant serving accomplished traditional cooking in an agreeable ambiance

As unadorned as a haiku, the tiled and wooden interior imparts a restful atmosphere complemented by welcoming and attentive treatment. Diners may sit cross-legged or at simple tables with western seating. A range of fixed-price lunch and dinner menus offers a variety of traditional Japanese dishes and methods of cooking, supplemented by a medium-length *carte* featuring seafoods such as 'Kaki furai' - deep-fried oysters coated in bread crumbs - pork, beef and chicken and a range of Sushi dishes (there is a small Sushi bar on the first floor). An enjoyable inspection meal began with Sashimi: fresh, raw and tender slices of tuna, brill, mackerel and salmon, served with a soy sauce. This was followed by a well-made 'Chawan mushi' egg custard, textured with kelp and chicken morsels and succulent 'Ebi Tempura' king prawns, lightly battered and deep fried. Dishes arrived out of sequence at times, though this did not impair their quality nor the enjoyment of the meal, highlights of which were the sauce flavours, including a fine primary dashi with the steamed egg custard. Drinks include Japanese beers and sake plus some European wines.

Directions: A few yards east of the junction of George Street with Gloucester Place. Nearest Tube – Marble Arch

Map no: 238

110 George Street W1
Tel: 0171-935 8320

Cost: *A/c* £30; fixed-price lunch £15.80; fixed-price dinner £26. H/wine £9.50. Service 12.5%. Cover charge
Credit cards: 1 2 3 5

Menus: *A la carte*, fixed-price lunch and dinner, Banquet dinner, pre-theatre

Times: 12.30pm-Last L 2pm, 5.30pm-Last D 10pm. Closed Sat lunch, Sun, BHs

Chef: M Sato
Proprietors: T Osumi

Seats: 76. No cigars or pipes. Air conditioned
Additional: Children over 9 permitted

Zen Central ❀❀

A good selection of Chinese dishes, including some more extravagant specialities, in a smart Mayfair setting

A modern Chinese restaurant in the heart of Mayfair, Zen Central is popular though pricey and it is essential to book. The menu is unchanging and offers an interesting selection of dishes with a few specialities, notably double boiled fluffy supreme

Map no: I239

20-22 Queen Street W1
Tel: 0171-629 8089

Cost: *A/c* £28, fixed-price dinner £35 (5 courses), £42, £50. Wine £25. Service exc. Cover charge £1

shark's fin at £70 for two, or a roasted whole Kwantung suckling pig, for which 24-hours notice is required. There is a good selection of hot and cold starters: fried crispy seaweed with pine kernels, a range of dumplings, and a platter of rice-marinated chicken and pig's trotter among them. Our inspector tasted main courses of crispy shredded beef with chilli, deep-fried paper-wrapped chicken, and crispy aromatic Szechuan duck, served with pancakes, shredded spring onion, cucumber and a well made plum sauce. There is also a choice of fish dishes and vegetarian options such as spinach sautéed with chilli and beancurd sauce, and monk's vegetables in a clay pot. A short dessert list features ice creams with fresh fruit salad, red bean paste pancakes (for a minimum of two), and almond tofu delight. Service is friendly and professional.

Directions: Off Curzon Street, Mayfair. Nearest Tube – Hyde Park Corner

Credit cards: 1 2 3 4 5

Menus: *A la carte*, fixed-price dinner

Times: 12.15-Last L 2.30pm, 6.30pm-Last D 11.30pm (11pm Sun). Closed 24-26 Dec

Chef: Michael Leung
Proprietor: William Lee

Seats: 100 No pipes or cigars. Air conditioned
Additional: Children permitted; ❷ dishes; Vegan/other diets on request

ZENW3 ❋❋

Fresh, healthy Chinese cooking with a good vegetarian selection in a busy High Street setting

A selection of 'healthy, evolved and delectable dishes' is on offer at this Chinese restaurant in busy Hampstead High Street. It is a popular place on two floors, the upper storey providing a more formal setting. The menu is not long but the selection is interesting with a good vegetarian choice. It is also a declared monosodium glutamate-free zone. Starters include cuttlefish cakes wrapped in green lettuce with herbs, 'hoi nam' satay, soups, a Dim sum package, and vegetable spring rolls; and there are pancake specialities, such as crispy fragrant and aromatic duck, or 'crispy duck' vegetarian. Our inspector sampled main course dishes of deep-fried crispy beef, double roast of boneless duck and pork served with Chinese cabbage, and good fresh steamed rice. Other options are fish and shellfish: fresh lobster, deep-fried and braised salmon with spring onion and ginger, steamed sea-bass with tangerine peel, sautéed prawns with cashew nuts in hot and sweet sauce, and charcoal grilled fish steaks. There are a few dessert options – toffee apples and bananas, fresh fruit and ice creams – and service is fairly formal but friendly.

Directions: From the main crossroads in Hampstead village centre, about 200 yards down Hampstead High Street on the right

Map no: O240

83 Hampstead High Street NW3
Tel: 0171-794 7863/4

Cost: *A/c* £22, fixed-price lunch £10.50, fixed-price dinner £26.50. Service charge 12.5%
Credit cards: 1 2 3 4

Menus: *A la carte*, fixed-price lunch and dinner

Times: Midday–Last D 11.15pm. Closed Xmas

Chef: Kwok-Lee Tangt
Proprietor: Dicken Chow

Seats: 140. Air conditioned
Additional: Children welcome; ❷ dishes; Vegan on request

Zoe ❋❋

☺ *Interesting Mediterranean cooking in a relaxed, colourful setting*

The trendy, pedestrianised setting of St Christopher's Place, tucked away discreetly behind the hubbub of Oxford Street, is home to a colourful café-cum-restaurant serving interesting modern Mediterranean food. There are two choices of eating places – ground floor level with an informal café-style menu

Map no: 241

St Christopher's Place W1
Tel: 0171-224 1122

Cost: *A/c* £20; fixed-price lunch and dinner £7.50 (2 courses), £10. Wine £8.25 ♀ Service exc
Credit cards: 1 2 3 4 5

and al fresco seating when the weather allows, and a basement restaurant offering a slightly more elaborate choice from seafood or Country and City menus. Portions are equally generous in both areas, and fresh, quality ingredients are handled with imagination and flair to produce some unusual dishes. French onion soup made from red onions with a tiny amount of cream and cider was surprisingly delicious at a recent meal, and fresh roasted cod with a herb crust served on a bed of plump cennelini beans was a very successful main dish. Other choices might include baked figs and pancetta with gorgonzola cream, or black ink ravioli filled with langoustines and a shellfish sauce. Tasty vegetarian dishes are plentiful, and there are irresistibly outsized sweets for those with enough room.

Directions: On the corner of Barrett Street and James Street which runs off Oxford Street near Selfridges. Nearest Tube – Bond Street

Menus: *A la carte*, fixed-price lunch and dinner, bar menu

Times: 1130am-11.30pm. Closed Sun, Bhs

Chef: Conrad Melling
Proprietor: Zen. Manager: Antony Worrall Thompson

Seats: 200. Smoking area. No pipes or cigars. Air conditioned
Additional: Children welcome; children's portions; ◊ dishes; Vegan/other diets on request

ENGLAND
AVON

ALVESTON, **Alveston House** ❀

☺ *A well-established commercial hotel with very conscientious service and continuing efforts from the kitchen. Imaginative menus offer well prepared and executed dishes including fresh scallops, pan-fried with crispy bacon or fillet of salmon and crab with dill sauce.*

Cost: Alc £21; fixed-price L/D £15.25. Wine £8.75. Service inc
Credit cards: 1 2 3 4 5. **Additional:** Children welcome; children's portions; ✪ dishes; Vegan/other diets on request
Directions: On the A38, 5 mins north of the M4/M5 junction

Map no: 3 ST68
Tel: 01454 415050
Chef: Julie Camm
Proprietor: Julie Camm
Seats: 75
Times: Last L 1.45pm/D 9.30pm

BATH, **Bath Spa** ❀❀

☺ *A luxury hotel on a hillside overlooking the city with a beautiful garden, supporting two restaurants*

This imposing Georgian property has an interesting history. It is set on a hillside overlooking the city and has a delightful garden as well as a croquet lawn. The two restaurants offer different styles; the Alfresco, set in the airy Colonnade is informal and offers a more eclectic carte mixing Far Eastern influences with the Mediterranean. The very much grander Vellore restaurant (named after the Indian home of the original owner) is situated in the elegant room that was once the ballroom. Here the cooking is more ambitious and the presentation is appealing without being pretentious. From the fixed-price menu our inspector selected a baked soufflé of smoked salmon, goats' cheese and spinach to start, which she found very tasty. Her companion selected a black ravioli filled with shellfish and set on a herb and butter sauce. To follow peppered duck breast with a broad bean 'cassoulet'and pink fillet of lamb with a punchy olive and aubergine ratatouille proved good choices. The imaginative patisserie of the desserts was clearly one of the restaurant's strengths.

Directions: From the A4 toChippenham road take left turn signposted A36 Warminster. Right at mini roundabout and pass fire and ambulance stations. Turn left into Sydney Place, hotel is on right

Sydney Road
Map no: 3 ST76
Tel: 01225 444424

Cost: Alc £17, Sunday lunch £19.50, fixed-price dinner £34. H/wine from £11.75 ♀ Service exc
Credit cards: 1 2 3 4 5

Menus: A la carte, Sunday lunch, fixed-price dinner

Times: Last Sun L 2pm, Last D 10pm

Chef: Jonathan Fraser
Proprietors: Forte. Manager Robin Sheppard

Seats: 36, 90. No-smoking area. Air conditioned
Additional: Children welcome; children's menu/portions; ✪ menu; Vegan/other diets on request

BATH, **Clos du Roy** ❀❀

☺ *Smart city-centre restaurant offering memorable French cooking at reasonable prices*

A wrought-iron dome stands prominently over this smart modern restaurant, providing a stunning setting in which to

1 Seven Dials, Saw Close
Map no: 3 ST76
Tel: 01225 444450

Cost: Fixed-price lunch £8.95 (2 courses), £11.95; fixed-price dinner £18.50 (3 courses),

enjoy the delights created by well-known French chef Philippe Roy. In the attractive upstairs dining room there's a musical theme, with the curved walls adorned with instruments and manuscripts. The fixed-price lunch and theatre menu offers a short, light selection of dishes, like salad of pigeon breasts garnished with noodles, and fillet of sole with fennel husks and a lemon butter sauce. Our inspector sampled the lengthier dinner *carte*, starting with a terrine of chicken livers studded with peppercorns and served with a tangy Cumberland sauce, and succulent pan-fried chicken breast sliced onto a bed of wild mushrooms with a smooth and delicately flavoured star anise sauce. Vegetables were fresh and crisp, and a very nutty iced nougat parfait contrasted well with a tart, red fruit purée. A few vegetarian dishes are always available, such as tartlet of wild mushrooms with hollandaise sauce. The interesting wines on a reasonably priced list are carefully chosen.

Directions: Under the wrought-iron dome of the Seven Dials centre, next door to the Theatre Royal

£22.50. Wine £9.50. Service exc
Credit cards: 1 2 3 4 5

Menus: *A la carte* dinner, fixed-price lunch and dinner, Sunday lunch, pre-theatre

Times: Midday–Last L 2.30pm, Last D 11.30pm

Chef: Philippe Roy
Proprietor: Philippe Roy

Seats: 80. No cigars or pipes
Additional: Children welcome; children's portions; ❂ menu; other diets on request. Pianist at weekends

BATH, Combe Grove Manor ❀❀

Beautifully sited Georgian hotel offering extensive leisure activities and creative modern English cooking

A combination of elegance and modern facilities blends well together at this delightfully situated 18th-century manor house just outside Bath. The extensive sports and leisure facilities are a major attraction in themselves, while the food served in the Georgian restaurant is of great interest to guests and non-residents alike. A choice of *carte* or fixed-price menu offers starters like smoked salmon and leek charlotte draped in hollandaise and served on a caviar sauce, and cured venison with juniper and passion fruit vinaigrette, while a main course might be loin of lamb sealed in an egg and bread crust on a mint-infused sauce. Our inspector recently tried a gateau of chicken and leeks – a fluffy, warm mousseline served with creamy chives and leeks, followed by fillet of turbot in a light and crisp filo pastry case with julienne of vegetables and another chive cream sauce. An elaborate Banoffi pudding of sticky toffee filling in a pastry case, topped with fresh banana and a whipped coffee-flavoured cream was surrounded by strawberry purée. The Manor Vaults offers a less formal atmosphere and menu.

Directions: Two miles south of Bath on A36. Turn sharp right at traffic lights up Brassknocker Hill

Brassknocker Hill
Monkton Combe
Map no: 3 ST76
Tel: 01225 834644

Cost: *Alc* £35; fixed-price lunch £13.50 (2 courses), £16.50; fixed-price dinner £25. Wine £9.50 ♀ Service inc
Credit cards: 1 2 3 4 5

Menus: *A la carte*, fixed-price lunch and dinner, Sunday lunch, bar menu

Times: 10.30am–Last lunch 2.30pm, Last dinner 9.30pm

Chef: Paul Mingo-West
Proprietors: Jack Chia Group. Manager: Antonio Parrilla

Seats: 48. No smoking in dining room
Additional: Children welcome; children's menu; ❂ dishes; Vegan/other diets on request

BATH, Garlands ❀❀

☺ *Superb cooking from a talented chef with a light touch and an eye for colourful, artistic presentation*

The bold and imaginative cooking of Tom Bridgeman continues to generate praise at this congenial little restaurant, where everything from the quality of ingredients to the

7 Edgar Buildings, George Street
Map no: 3 ST76
Tel: 01225 442283

Cost: *Alc* £21.45; fixed-price lunch £10.95 (2 courses), £13.95; fixed-price dinner £16.95 (2 courses), £19.50.

presentation of the food is first class. Tom's talented performance in the kitchen is backed up by Jo Bridgeman's genuine welcome and smiling service, a combination which makes Garlands one of the best restaurants in Bath. The fixed two and three-course menus offer great value for money, and the Friday night five-course gourmet dinner is an irresistible bargain. Our inspector enthused over a tasty crispy duck salad with oranges and balsamic vinegar, followed by tender, moist supreme of chicken boned and fanned on to a rich madeira sauce with wild oyster mushrooms. Other dishes like mignons of pork glazed with goats' cheese and salsa, and escalope of Cornish brill with crab and cucumber spaghetti have been equally successful. Delicious home-made chocolate terrine with a smooth coffee bean sauce, or poached pear with saffron sabayon might feature for dessert, and decent fresh coffee comes with tempting petits fours.

Additional: Children welcome; children's portions; ✪ dishes; other diets on request

Directions: George Street runs across the top of Milsom Street, in the centre of Bath

Wine £9.95 ⚲ Service exc
Credit cards: 1 2 3 4

Menus: *A la carte*, fixed-price lunch and dinner, Sunday lunch, pre-theatre, bar menu

Times: Midday–Last L 2.15pm, 7pm-Last D 10.30pm. Closed Mon

Chef: Tom Bridgeman
Proprietors: Tom and Jo Bridgeman

Seats: 28. No pipes or cigars

BATH, **The Hole in the Wall** ●●

☺ *Imaginative British cooking in a newly opened restaurant close to the city centre*

Old fashioned charm and elegance are brought together in this attractive restaurant, where one of the two dining areas is heavily beamed and the other is brightened with the clever use of mirrors. Colourfully upholstered benches and fresh flowers lend a cheerful appearance, and there's a pleasing balance to the menu which shows off chef Adrian Walton's flair for sympathetically blending different flavours. The *carte* offers a good range of meat, fish and poultry dishes, and a short fixed-price business lunch menu guarantees a meal within 50 minutes. Our inspector recently enjoyed a starter of soft, pink sautéed chicken livers in a light puff pastry case, served with a red wine sauce, and a main course of fillet of brill topped with a herb crust, which came with a creamy sauce delicately flavoured with smoked prawns. Vegetables were well cooked and full of flavour, while 'bara brith' and butter pudding was served with a smooth whisky ice cream. Other choices might be spicy pork kebab or roast rabbit, with a vegetarian dish like wild mushroom and thyme risotto. There are interesting French and New World wines.

Directions: George Street is at the top end of Milsom Street

16 George Street
Map no: 3 ST76
Tel: 01225 425242

Cost: *Alc* £20, fixed-price lunch £9.50. H/wine £9 ⚲ Service exc
Credit cards: 1 3 5

Menus: *A la carte*, fixed-price lunch, pre-theatre

Times: Midday–Last L 2pm, 6pm–Last D 11pm. Closed Sun, Xmas

Chefs: Christopher Chown, Adrian Walton
Proprietor: Christopher Chown

Seats: 72. No smoking room. Air conditioned
Additional: Children permitted. ✪ dishes

BATH, **New Moon** ●●

☺ *Enjoyable international restaurant-cum-brasserie cooking in the city centre*

A combination of restaurant and brasserie has proved successful at this congenial eating place near Bath's Theatre

Seven Dials, Saw Close
Map no: 3 ST76
Tel: 01225 444407

Cost: *Alc* £16, fixed-price lunch £6.25. H/wine £8.70 ⚲ Service exc

Royal. Part of the newish Seven Dials complex, it looks out on to a small courtyard with a cascading fountain which makes a natural point of interest for tourists. Diners can select from the *carte* or brasserie menu between 12-7pm, or just the *carte* after 7pm, and the dishes presented by chef Nick Peter are both inviting and imaginative. A recent inspection meal began with a tasty home-made duck sausage with braised lentils and a light Madeira sauce, followed by steamed fillet of salmon with a dry vermouth and dill cream sauce and a separate tomato concasse. Simple vegetables were cooked nicely al dente, and a smooth, light bread and butter pudding with vanilla custard was both wholesome and sweet. Other good dishes have been rack of lamb with onions, spicy green olives and rosemary sauce, fresh tagliatelle with white wine and pesto cream sauce, and Thai vegetable curry with coconut rice, with successful puddings like chocolate St Emilion, and orange and cardamon bavarois.

Credit cards: 1 2 3 5

Menus: *A la carte*, fixed-price lunch, pre-theatre

Times: Open all day 9am-11pm (10.30pm Sun). Closed Xmas, 1 Jan

Chef: Nick Peter
Proprietor: Keith Waring

Seats: 80. No-smoking area
Additional: Children welcome; ❂ dishes; Vegan/other diets on request

Directions: Within Seven Dials complex next to Theatre Royal

BATH, No 5 Bistro ❂

☺ *An interesting European-style carte is offered at this informal bistro, with a good range of dishes including fresh pasta, roasts, fillet steak and a choice of vegetarian dishes. This is supplemented by a list of specials – mostly fresh fish – and additional starters and desserts, plus snacks at lunchtime.*

5 Argyle Street
Map no: 3 ST76
Tel: 01225 444499
Chef: Steve Smith
Proprietors: Steve Smith and Charles Home
Seats: 38. No pipes or cigars in restaurant
Times: Last L 2.30pm/D 10pm (11pm Sat). Closed Sun and Mon lunch; 25–28 Dec

Cost: *Alc* £16.50. Wine £7.45 ♀ Service exc
Credit cards: 1 3 5. **Additional:** Children welcome; children's portions; ❂ dishes; other diets on request
Directions: Fifty yards past Pulteney Bridge towards Laura Place

BATH, Popjoys ❂

One-time home of Beau Nash's mistress Juliana Popjoy, there has now been an addition of a ground floor Brasserie to this restaurant. Upstairs, the more formal room has more depth to its menu with local wood pigeon salad and artichokes or loin of lamb with ratatouille and black olive and rosemary sauce.

Beau Nash House, Saw Close
Map no: 3 ST76
Tel: 01225 460494
Chef: John Simpson
Proprietor: Malcolm Buhr
Seats: 38. No pipes
Times: Last D 10.30pm. Closed Mon

Cost: *Alc* £25. H/wine £7.90. Service exc **Credit cards:** 1 2 3.
Additional: Children welcome; ❂ dishes; Vegan/other diets on request
Directions: Centre of Bath, immediately beside the Theatre Royal

BATH, Priory ❂❂

Classical French cooking in a stylish country house-style setting

There's more than just a slight country house feel to this gracious hotel, even though it is within walking distance of the centre of Bath. Set in a beautiful, elevated position in perfectly manicured grounds, the Priory offers old-fashioned standards of hospitality which easily extend into the very well-managed

Weston Road
Map no: 3 ST76
Tel: 01225 331922

Cost: *Alc* £32; fixed-price lunch £10 (2 courses), £13.50, £17; fixed-price dinner £22.50. Wine £16 ♀ Service inc
Credit cards: 1 2 3 4 5

dining room. Cooking is appealingly conservative in keeping with the setting, and chef Michael Collom augments his monthly-changing menu with a good value daily set menu. Starters range from simple melon with fresh fruit to chicken, bacon and chestnuts in filo pastry with tarragon sauce, while main dishes might include a straightforward chargrilled steak with horseradish relish, or roasted pigeon with apple galette and red wine sauce. There are several vegetarian options, like mille-feuille of goats' cheese, celeriac and field mushrooms baked in filo pastry. Our inspector enjoyed a delicately charred fillet of monkfish dressed with fresh herbs, anda good roast rack of lamb with a strong garlic crust. A hot sticky gingerbread pudding with toffee sauce brought the meal to a tasty, if slightly heavy, finish.

Directions: At the top of Park Lane on the west side of Victoria Park, turn left into Weston Road. The Priory is 300 yards on left

Menus: *A la carte*, fixed-price lunch/dinner, Sunday lunch, pre-theatre, bar menu, buffet

Times: 12.30pm-Last L 2pm, 7pm-Last D 9.15pm

Chef: Michael Collom
Proprietor: Select Country Hotels. Manager: Thomas Conboy

Seats: 65. No smoking in dining room
Additional: Children welcome/portions/menu; ❶ menu; Vegan/other on request

BATH, The Queensbury ❀❀

Interesting modern cooking using fresh local produce to create some robust Mediterranean flavours

A feeling of well-being pervades this tranquil Bath stone hotel close to the Royal Crescent and Assembly Rooms, much of it created by the hospitable owners. The focal point of this stylish hotel is the Olive Tree restaurant, an informal bistro on the lower ground floor where light-coloured floor tiles and crisp white tablecloths create a cool, uncluttered atmosphere. Chef and co-owner Stephen Ross cooks in modern English style, combining quality local produce with the robust flavours of the Mediterranean. Our inspector recently enjoyed a smoked salmon and fromage frais parfait garnished with an orange and chicory salad, and fillet of beef with a smooth red wine sauce, and crisp, fresh vegetables. A light, hot chocolate soufflé had a good bitter chocolate flavour, and richly roasted espresso coffee came with chocolate fudge. Other dishes on the *carte* might be braised shoulder of lamb, whole sea-bass baked with fennel and tarragon butter, and perhaps a vegetarian pancake galette with tomatoes, aubergine, cheese and herbs. There is also a verbal fixed-price three-course dinner menu.

Directions: 100yds north of Assembly Rooms in Lower Lansdown

Russell Street
Map no: 3 ST76
Tel: 01225 447928

Cost: *Alc* £26; fixed-price lunch £10.50; fixed-price dinner £17. Wine £10.50. Service exc
Credit cards: 1 2 3

Menus: *A la carte* dinner, fixed-price lunch and dinner, fish menu (Tues)

Times: Midday–Last L 2.pm, 7pm–Last D 10pm. Closed Sun, Xmas week

Chefs: Stephen Ross, Rupert Pitt
Proprietors: Stephen and Penny Ross
Seats: 45. No smoking
Additional: Children welcome; children's portions; ❶ dishes; Vegan/other diets on request

BATH, Rajpoot Tandoori ❀❀

☺ *Authentic Indian dishes cooked in a commendably classic style*

There's an authentic atmosphere at this stylish and welcoming Indian restaurant, helped by the imaginative decor and well-placed Indian artefacts. The food is no less genuine, and classic

Rajpoot House, 4 Argyle Street
Map no: 3 ST76
Tel: 01225 466833/464758

Cost: *Alc* £17.50; fixed-price dinner £15. Wine £7.50. Service exc
Credit cards: 1 2 3 4.5

Tandoori, Mughlai and Bengali dishes are carefully cooked to retain robust textures and subtly spiced flavours. The skilled and friendly staff are keen to help with choosing dishes if required, and a recent inspection meal of several small courses was highly successful. Moist, tender shish kebab and tandoori machlee (spiced, barbecued fish) were deliciously rich, and the accompanying nan and paratha (leavened and unleavened breads) and smooth raita were superb examples of their type. Tiny portions of lamb biriani were gently fried in ghees and served with an outstanding vegetable curry, while chicken Jaflang, tender meat with an abundance of delicate spices and herbs, surpassed even these highly praised offerings. Fluffy pilau rice and decent Indian puddings bring a meal here to an enjoyable end. Specialities like Navaratan pilau (a nutty, fruity vegetable pilau dish served with a sauce) are suitable for vegetarians.

Directions: Near city centre, by Pulteney Bridge

Menus: A la carte, fixed-price dinner

Times: Midday–Last L 2.30pm, 6pm–Last D 11pm, (11.30pm Fri and Sat). Closed Xmas

Chefs: H Zeraguai and A Ali
Proprietors: Ahmed Chowdhury and Mahmud Chowdhury

Seats: 98. Air conditioned
Additional: Children welcome; children's portions; ۩ menu; other diets on request

BATH, The Royal Crescent ✿✿✿

Modern English food served in a secluded garden setting to the rear of the celebrated Georgian crescent

Centrally situated in the glorious sweep of John Wood's Regency terrace, the Royal Crescent is a very handsome hotel. Its sumptuously furnished restaurant is located in the Dower House, a more recent building, just a short stroll across the enclosed garden on stone-flagged paths.

Cooking is in the hands of Stephen Blake and his team, and foreign travel has influenced the generally English menus with dishes such as tempura salmon with mussel liquor, pimento and olive oil, or tempura langoustines, enjoyed on this occasion as a light starter with a clear sauce of lobster stock with ginger and roast garlic. Following this, our inspector enthused about the superb presentation and flavour of lemon sole fillets sandwiching a layer of oyster soufflé, though the accompanying oyster cream sauce almost overwhelmed its delicacy. Highlights of 'a variety of apple desserts' from the five served were a lattice-topped apple pie and exotic cinnamon-flavoured miniature tarte tatin.

The daily changing two or three-course lunch menu, and three-course dinner menu, both fixed-price, offer a choice of three starters and main courses, supplemented in the evening by a longer *carte*. The latter might offer ballotine of rabbit, beef fillet or filo of pigeon and foie gras among a list of seven main courses. A vegetarian selection is readily available, with dishes such as lasagne of leek, courgette and pimento glazed with a mustard sauce, or Gruyère cheese omelette with spinach, wood mushrooms and chive butter, though advance notice is preferred to meet diners' specific dietary requirements. The large, comprehensive wine list includes a range of six house wines under £16. Champagnes and mature vintages of Burgundy and claret are more expensive, but there is something to suit all palates and pockets.

Directions: From city centre follow signs to Royal Crescent. In the Dower House, located in the garden at the rear of The Royal Crescent Hotel

16 Royal Crescent
Map no: 3 ST76
Tel: 01225 319090

Cost: Alc £38; fixed-price lunch £14.50 (2 courses), £18.50; fixed-price dinner £30. Wine £11.75 ♀ Service inc
Credit cards: 1 2 3 4

Menus: A la carte dinner, fixed-price lunch and dinner, Sunday lunch, pre-theatre, bar menu (lunch)

Times: 12.30pm–Last L 2pm, 7pm–Last D 9.30pm (Fri, Sat 10pm)

Chef: Steven Blake
Proprietors: Queens Moat. Manager: Simon Coombe

Seats: 60. No cigars or pipes
Additional: Children welcome; children's portions/menu; ۩ menu; Vegan/other diets on request. Pianist Fri, Sat eve

BATH, Woods ❁❁

9-13 Alfred Street
Map no: 3 ST76
Tel: 01225 314812

☺ *An elegant Georgian setting with a formal and informal dining choice for well cooked meals*

In one of Bath's many elegant Georgian buildings, just away from the bustle of the main shopping area, this deceptively spacious restaurant proves to be very popular. You can dine in the front bar-brasserie, or if you prefer, in the main dining area where tables are polished wood and the decor is bright, airy and attractive. The menus offer a good and varied choice and good value for money, as does the wine list with a special selection of wines under £12.00 as well as a good few available by the glass. In addition to the menu, there are also daily specials and these are written up on a blackboard. The recent meal taken here, on a sunny Saturday lunchtime, was most enjoyable. A good smoked mackerel pâté, served with a creamy horseradish sauce, was followed by roasted leg of lamb with an unusual but tasty Boursin sauce and the most excellent vegetables tasted for a long time, very bright in colour, full of flavour and cooked to retain all their crunch and crispness. Filo pastry parcels, filled with marinated fruits and a superb butterscotch sauce rounded off the meal very nicely. Staff are friendly and the atmosphere is relaxed.

Cost: *Alc* £11.25; Sunday lunch £10; fixed-price dinner £10.95 (Mon-Fri), £18.95 (Sat). H/wine £9 ♀ No service charge
Credit cards: 1 2 3

Menus: *A la carte*, fixed-price dinner, Sunday lunch, pre-theatre, bar menu

Times: 11am–Last L 3pm, 6pm–Last D 11pm. Closed Sun dinner, Xmas

Chef: Kirk Vincent
Proprietors: David and Claude Price

Seats: 120. No pipes or cigars
Additional: Children welcome/portions/menu; ❂ menu; Vegan/other on request

Directions: Opposite the Assembly Rooms

BRISTOL, Berkeley Square Hotel ❁❁

15 Berkeley Square, Clifton
Map no: 3 ST57
Tel: 0117 9254000

Expertly cooked modern English dishes in a stylish city-centre hotel

Set in a prime position right on the doorstep of Bristol University, and handy for the museum and art gallery, this stylish hotel restaurant remains as popular as ever. A hospitable team of keen, well-turned out staff offers a warm welcome and pleasing service throughout the meal, and the modern English cooking of Dermot Gale is full of interesting textures and bold flavours. Starters on the seasonal *carte* and fixed-price menu include pasta dishes, rich stock soups and chunky country terrines, while main courses might be breast of chicken scented with pesto wrapped in a pastry lattice and served on a fricassée of wild mushrooms, or pan-fried calf's liver served with sautéed onions and port wine jus. Our inspector enjoyed a rich home-made pastry tart filled with smooth ragout of mushrooms, bacon and lentils served with a distinct coriander broth, followed by delicious noisettes of tender lamb presented on a tasty potato cake crowned with a confit of provençal vegetables. The dessert was a treat: chocolate chip steamed pudding with a lovely rum chocolate sauce, and good quality coffee came with decent petits fours.

Cost: *Alc* £24; fixed-price lunch and dinner £14.85. Wine £8.75. Service exc
Credit cards: 1 2 3 4

Menus: *A la carte*, fixed-price lunch and dinner, Sunday lunch, bar menu

Times: Midday–Last L 2pm, 7pm–Last D 10pm. Closed Sat lunch, Sun eve

Chef: Dermot Gale
Proprietors: Clifton Group. Manageress: Sharon Love

Seats: 50
Additional: Children welcome; children's portions; ❂ menu; Vegan/other diets on request

Directions: Top of Park Street, turn left at traffic lights into Berkeley Square, hotel on right

BRISTOL, Bistro Twenty One ❀❀

☺ *A successful combination of classy French cooking and straightforward, welcoming surroundings*

Sophisticated yet robust cooking and a relaxed, unpretentious setting of French prints and posters, waxed tablecloths and comfortable captains chairs, make this typical bistro a great hit with a wide range of diners. Chef Alain Dubois has established a firm reputation for himself based on his honest, value-for-money dishes made from quality fresh produce and fish delivered overnight from Cornwall. Starters on the short *carte* and daily blackboard might include seafood terrine with garlic mayonnaise, and filo parcels filled with crab and coriander on a cream sauce, while main dishes range from grilled whole Dover sole to sauté of chicken in a red wine sauce with mushrooms and bacon. A recent successful inspection meal began with a rich confit of duck on a bright bed of dressed leaves, followed by little medallions of very fresh monkfish with a shallot and red wine sauce which perfectly enhanced the flavour of the fish. Iced white and dark chocolate parfait on a smooth coffee cream sauce was one of several rich home-made puddings. The small, well-balanced wine list is sensibly priced.

Directions: Off the B4051 onto St Michael's Hill. First right into Horfield Road, which becomes Cotham Road South

21 Cotham Road South
Kingsdown
Map no: 3 ST57
Tel: 0117 9421744

Cost: *Alc* £20; fixed-price lunch and dinner £12.95. H/wine £7.75. Service exc
Credit cards: 1 2 3 4 5

Menus: *A la carte* dinner, fixed-price lunch and dinner

Times: Midday-Last L 2pm, 7pm-Last D 11.30pm. Closed Sat lunch, Sun, BHs

Chef: Alain Dubois
Proprietors: Alain Dubois and Philippe Harding

Seats: 64
Additional: Children welcome; children's portions; ✪ dishes; other diets on request. Live jazz monthly

BRISTOL, Grange Hotel ❀

An elegant hotel with easy access to the centre of Bristol. Chef Richard Barker continues to show imagination in his production of the interesting dishes that make up the fixed-price and carte menus. The food is well prepared and presented with generous portions.

Cost: *Alc* £23; fixed-price L £13.95/D £16.95. H/wine £9.95 ♀ Service inc. **Credit cards:** 1 2 3 4 5
Additional: Children welcome; children's portions/menu; ✪ dishes; Vegan/other diets on request
Directions: From Winterbourne High Street take B4057, first right on B4427 in 1 mile

Northwoods, Winterbourne
Map no: 3 ST57
Tel: 01454 777333
Chef: Richard Baker
Proprietors: Jarvis. Manager: Greg Ballesty
Seats: 70. No smoking in dining room
Times: Last L 2pm (4pm Sun)/D 9.45pm. Closed Sat lunch

BRISTOL, Harvey's ❀❀❀

British cooking from a range of menus in the medieval cellar setting of the original Harvey's of Bristol

Extending his skills beyond the kitchen, Ramon Farthing has recently assumed the role of chef-manager in this long-established restaurant situated in medieval cellars. This is, of course, where the world-renowned Harvey's of Bristol was established back in 1796. At the time of our visit new seating was about to be installed, aiming for a fresher look, though the lilies, crisp linen, modern art and air conditioning already enliven what could be a rather dreary setting. Menus too are

12 Denmark Street
Map no: 3 ST57
Tel: 0117 9275034

Cost: *Alc* lunch £26.50, *Alc* dinner £33.50, fixed-price lunch £16.50, fixed-price dinner £28, gourmet dinner £38. H/wine £12 ♀ Service inc
Credit cards: 1 2 3 4 5

Menus: *A la carte* lunch/dinner, fixed-price lunch/dinner, surprise gourmet dinner menu constantly developing; there is now a set three-course lunch menu for £16.50 including coffee, as well as the *carte* which remains much the same for dinner, with a few additions. Other options in the evening are the six-course gourmet surprise menu (for a complete party), or a no-choice four-course dinner. A separate vegetarian menu is available on request.

With Paul Dunstan working with Ramon Farthing as head chef, cooking remains as accomplished as ever. Terrines are always first class, and at a test meal our inspector sampled a creamy mousse of salmon layered with the fish, sliced scallops and wild mushrooms, the whole encased in cabbage and served with a bacon and leek vinaigrette. Chunky croûtons, fried in bacon fat, added texture but marred the otherwise clean flavours. This was followed by wonderfully fresh sea-bass, on a bed of garlicky spinach leaves with a light but full-flavoured ratatouille butter infusion. Tangy orange soufflé came with a Drambuie and chocolate cream, confited kumquats and crisp biscuit twists. The cheese trolley and accompanying notes could easily inspire a further course.

Allow time to peruse the extensive wine list, which does full justice to Harvey's centuries of experience in the wine trade. The sections devoted to claret and vintage port are outstanding, but there are many other jewels too.

Directions: Denmark Street is off Unity Street which is at the bottom of Park Street, opposite the city hall and the cathedral

Times: Midday-Last L 1.45pm, 7pm-Last D 11pm. Lunch not served Sat. Closed Sun, BHs

Chef: Ramon Farthing
Proprietors: John Harvey & Sons

Seats: 120. Air conditioned
Additional: Children over 8 permitted; ❤ menu; Vegan/other diets on request

BRISTOL, **Henbury Lodge** ❀

☺ *A small family-run Georgian manor house with cooking from Teresa Mockridge making good use of fresh produce. Honest textures and flavours with her seasonal menus, including very smooth oak-smoked salmon terrine and the Scottish beef with a Burgundy and shallot sauce was exceptionally tender.*

Cost: Alc £16.80. **Credit cards:** 1 2 3 4
Directions: From junc 17 of the M5 take the A4018, turn right at the second roundabout, drive to the end of Crow Lane and turn right. The hotel is 50yds on the right

Station Road
Map no: 3 ST57
Tel: 0117 9502615
Chef: Teresa Mockridge
Proprietor: Mr D L Pearce
Times: Last L 2pm (by reservation); Last D 9pm

BRISTOL, **Howards** ❀❀

☺ *Comfortable and relaxed waterside restaurant with a reputation for fresh, honest cooking*

There are views of Clifton Suspension Bridge from this dockside restaurant which was converted from a shop and still retains many attractive old-fashioned features. The downstairs dining room has a cosy atmosphere, with its wide window ledges covered in Victoriana, while on the first floor there's a touch of grandeur enhanced by the lofty ceilings. Chef David Roast's cooking is refreshing and enjoyable, and the well-balanced *carte* is supported by short, good value set-price menus at lunch and dinner; a blackboard also lists any extra daily fish specials. Thin slices of marinaded beef served with

1A–2A Avon Crescent
Hotwells
Map no: 3 ST57
Tel: 0117 9262921

Cost: Alc £20, fixed-price lunch £13, fixed-price dinner £15. H/wine £7.25. Service exc
Credit cards: 1 2 3 4

Menus: *A la carte* and fixed-price lunch and dinner
Times: Midday-Last L 2.30pm, Last D 11.30pm. Closed Sun, Xmas

watercress salad made an attractively-presented if strongly-flavoured recent starter, with stir-fried breast of Barbary duck following as a deliciously rich main course. Other recommended dishes include home-made ravioli with tomato sauce, and wild sea trout, and there are vegetarian dishes like wild mushrooms, garlic and cream in a pastry case, or spinach and mushroom pancakes gratinéed with cream and Gruyère. Tempting desserts might be hot chocolate soufflé with Grand Marnier sauce or crème brûlée.

Chef: David Roast
Proprietors: Christopher and Gillian Howard

Seats: 65. No-smoking area
Additional: Children welcome; children's portions; ◐ menu; Vegan/other diets on request.

Directions: Follow Hotwells Road over the small swing bridge. Howards is on the dockside close to SS Great Britain

BRISTOL, **Hunt's** ●●

☺ *A pleasant, easy place to unwind with capable and enthusiastic cooking, interesting and a genuine welcome*

26 Broad Street
Map no: 3 ST57
Tel: 0117 9265580

Next to St John's Gate in the old city centre wall, Anne and Andrew Hunt three years ago established their unpretentious restaurant, offering a *carte* with good fish selection plus set-price lunches.

Simplicity is the keynote of the attractive decor which, combined with the affability of Andrew Hunt (who also cooks), creates a relaxing ambiance. Poetically-named dishes have included 'Veal cutlet with wild green lavender and lemon butter jus' and 'Three delicate white ice creams'. In contrast, smoked haddock soufflé sounds more basic and our inspector found its impact somewhat monopolised by the smoked salmon wrapping. On this occasion, main course fish dishes included halibut with grain mustard and Gruyere and sea-bass with sorrel sauce, while guinea fowl and calf's kidneys were among meat dishes. Tender breast of Hereford duck was cooked nicely pink with a crispy honey-glazed skin sporting a crust of chopped ginger and green peppercorns. Besides the white ices (angelica, coconut and vanilla and ginger), puddings included hazelnut parfait and a creme brûlée served with plums in cassis.

Cost: A/c £25, fixed-price lunch £11.50 (2 courses), £13.50. H/wine £9.50 ♀ Service inc
Credit cards: 1 2 3

Menus: *A la carte*, fixed-price lunch, pre-threatre

Times: Midday-Last L 2pm, 7pm–Last D 10pm. Closed Sun, Mon, 1 week Easter, 1 week summer, 1 week Xmas

Chefs: Andrew Hunt, Hayon Neal, Philip Devonshire
Proprietors: Andrew and Anne Hunt

Seats: 40
Additional: Children welcome; children's portions; ◐ dishes; Vegan/other diets on request

Directions: Next to St John's Gate in the old city centre wall

BRISTOL, **Markwicks** ●●

Interesting modern French/English cooking in an elegant basement setting

43 Corn Street
Map no: 3 ST57
Tel: 0117 9262658

Once used as the safety deposit vaults for the old commercial centre of the city, this tastefully converted restaurant near the covered market provides an elegant place to eat. The main dining room area is flanked by two smaller, wood-panelled rooms, one with a smart marble floor, and fresh flowers and subtle lighting add to the stylish atmosphere. Stephen Markwick offers daily-changing fixed-price lunch and dinner menus with various specials and several fish dishes, along with a well-balanced *carte*. Our inspector began a recent lunch with a perfectly cooked tagliatelle with lambs sweetbreads, three types of mushrooms, air-dried ham, pine kernels, broad beans, garlic

Cost: A/c £30; fixed-price lunch £12.50 (2 courses), £15; fixed-price dinner £19.50. H/wine £12. Service exc
Credit cards: 1 2 3

Menus: *A la carte*, fixed-price lunch and dinner
Times: Last L 2pm, Last D 10.30pm. Closed Sat lunch, Sun, 1 week Xmas, 1 week Easter, 2 weeks Aug, BHs

and herbs tossed in a tasty Madeira jus – all separately enjoyable but together rather over-complicating the dish. The delicate flavours of fillet of turbot were again slightly overpowered by the addition of cider, English mustard, sliced tomatoes and a pungent herb crumb, but the results were still enjoyable. Desserts are seasonal, and the chilled lemon soufflé was just right for a hot day. Judy Markwick is the perfect hostess.

Directions: Top end of Corn Street beneath Commercial Rooms

Chefs: Stephen Markwick and Sara Ody
Proprietors: Stephen and Judy Markwick
Seats: 40. **Additional:** Children welcome; children's portions; ❶ dishes; Vegan/other diets on request

BRISTOL, **Marriott** ❀

The rosette is awarded to the Chateau, one of the restaurants in the hotel. Under the direction of John Hitchen, the carte menu is supplemented by a changing menu of visiting chefs from around the world. A notable main course was medallions of monkfish with salmon ravioli.

Credit cards: 1 2 3 4. **Additional:** Children permitted; ❶ dishes
Directions: In the city centre, opposite the castle ruins

Lower Castle Street
Map no: 3 ST57
Tel: 0117 9294281
Chef: John Hitchen
Proprietor: Marriott. Manager: Stephen Dodwell
Times: Dinner only 7pm–11.45pm

BRISTOL, **Orchid** ❀

☺ An ever-popular family-run restaurant at the heart of the city's ethnic cuisine. A range of Singaporean, Thai, Chinese and Indonesian dishes permits all kinds of flavours, textures, aromas and colours in an oriental treasure trove. Imaginative noodle and rice dishes.

Cost: Alc £15; fixed-price L £8/D £14. Wine £7.50. Service exc
Credit cards: 1 2 3 5
Additional: Children welcome; ❶ menu; Vegan/other diets on request

908 Whiteladies Road
Map no: 3 ST57
Tel: 0117 9238338
Chef: M Lau
Proprietor: Margaret Dullah
Seats: 80. No pipes or cigars. Air conditioned
Times: Last L 2.30/D 11.30. Closed Mon lunch

BRISTOL, **Orient Rendezvous** ❀

☺ This smart family-run restaurant presents an extensive range of dishes from the Canton, Peking and Szechuan regions. Steamed prawns with rich black bean sauce, pork spare ribs with spicy sauce, and aromatic crispy duck are typical dishes from the carte, and there is a vegetarian option.

Cost: Alc from £15; fixed-price L £6.95/D £16.95 (3 courses), £19.95. H/wine £8.95. No service charge **Credit cards:** 1 2 3 4.
Additional: Children welcome; ❶ dishes; Vegan/other diets on request
Directions: From the city centre up Park Street, 200 yds from The Victoria Rooms

95 Queens Road, Clifton
Map no: 3 ST57
Tel: 0117 9239292
Chef: David Wong
Proprietors: Orient Rendezvous (Chinese Cuisine) Ltd
Seats: 150. No-smoking area. Air conditioned
Times: Last L 2.15pm/D 11.30pm. Closed Xmas

BRISTOL, **Restaurant Lettonie** ❀❀❀

Vibrant, intensely flavoured French and European cooking in an elegant suburban restaurant

Martin and Siân Blunos have been hiding their light for some time in this Bristol suburb. Their elegant little restaurant,

9 Druid Hill, Stoke Bishop
Map no: 3 ST57
Tel: 0117 9686456

Cost: Fixed-price lunch £15.95; fixed-price dinner £25. Wine £10.95. Service exc

tucked away in an unassuming row of shops, is a culinary gem. Siân provides a hospitable welcome to guests, assisted by a smart young French brigade. However it is Martin's cooking that is the hallmark here, with his adventurous concepts, intensity of flavours and superb saucing.

Fixed-price three-course menus are offered at lunch and dinner, with a choice of two or three mainly French dishes at each stage. A good value supper menu is also available from Tuesday to Thursday. Starters might include scrambled duck egg topped with Sevruga caviar and served with blini pancakes and a glass of vodka, or our inspector's choice, a richly flavoured terrine of chicken livers set in a smooth foie gras and chicken mousse accompanied by featherlight brioche and home-made pear and basil chutney. Tortellini of langoustine captured the very essence of the delicate fish, and was set off by a good olive oil dressing. Braised oxtail with tomatoes on a purée of butter beans, and pig's trotter stuffed with pork and chicken, both came to the table with wonderful sauces, and rolled fillet of brill was served with a commendable langoustine velouté. Vegetarian dishes can be provided, though they are not listed on the menus, and notice is preferred of guests' requirements.

Puddings are very impressive. The chocolate marquise with poire William sauce, and hazelnut and caramel biscuit ice with raspberry sauce are two quite distinct examples of excellence. And to finish, smooth high roast coffee is served with first class hand-made petits fours. The wine list is predominantly French including several mature vintages of claret and red Burgundy. Also lots of half-bottles.

Directions: North west of City Centre, other side of Clifton Downs

Credit cards: 1 2 3

Menus: Fixed-price lunch and dinner

Times: Last L 2pm, Last D 9pm. Closed Sun, Mon, 2 weeks Aug and Xmas

Chef: Martin Blunos
Proprietors: Siân and Martin Blunos

Seats: 24
Additional: Children welcome; children's portions; ✪ dishes; Vegan/other diets on request

BRISTOL, Swallow Royal ✹✹

☺ *An impressively restored hotel very much in the grand tradition*

Situated adjacent to the cathedral, this impressively restored hotel, faced in Bath stone, is very much in the grand hotel tradition from the moment one enters the spacious marble foyer. There is a choice of restaurants. The Terrace offers more informal dining at lunch and dinner, while the Palm Court, the former ballroom, is open for dinner only Monday to Saturday. Three storeys high, and with a stained-glass skylight, it can feel a little like a mausoleum. However, the food produced by Michael Kitts and Paul Bates is very much alive and shows flair and skill. A seasonally changing menu offers a choice of innovative dishes such as risotto of wild mushrooms garnished with baby asparagus, basil and Parmesan. Less adventurous items such as smoked salmon or grilled fillet steak are also available.

Additional: Children welcome; children's portions/menu; ✪ dishes; Vegan/other diets on request. Harpist (Palm Court)
Directions: In city centre adjacent to Bristol Cathedral

College Green
Map no: 3 ST57
Tel: 0117 9255100

Cost: *A/c* Terrace £22, Palm Court £32; fixed-price L £15/D £19. H/wine £9. Service inc
Credit cards: 1 2 3 4

Times: Last L 2.30pm/D 10.30pm. Palm Court closed lunch, Sun eve

Chef: Michael Kitts
Proprietors: Swallow. Manager: Philip Sager

Seats: 60 Palm Court, 140 Terrace. No-smoking area. Air conditioned

CHELWOOD, **Chelwood House** ☻

☺ *A charming little hotel. Owner Rudi Birk's cooking is robust with many dishes originating from his Bavarian homeland. Typical dishes like herrenhopt or goulash soup feature regularly. For the traditionalist, roast local pheasant, set on caramelised apples, or jugged hare, should please.*

Cost: Alc £22; Sun L £13.50; H/wine £9.50. Service inc
Credit cards: 1 2 3 4. **Additional:** Children permitted; children's portions; ❂ dishes; Vegan/other diets on request
Directions: On the A37 between Clutton and Pensford, 200 yds from Chelwood Bridge

Map no: 3 ST66
Tel: 0117 9490730
Chef: Rudi Birk
Proprietor: Rudi Birk
Seats: 24. No smoking in dining room
Times: Last L 1.30pm/D 9pm. Closed Mon–Sat Lunch, 1st 2 weeks Jan

FARRINGTON GURNEY, **Country Ways** ☻

☺ *A cosy hotel situated on the Avon/Somerset border with a well balanced menu. A range of rich home-made soups feature daily and breast of duck, cut into medallions with orange and redcurrant sauce scored very well. All dishes were served with generous portions of vegetables.*

Cost: Alc £22, H/wine £8.50. No service charge **Credit cards:** 1 3 4 5
Additional: Children permitted; ❂ dishes; other diets on request
Directions: From the A37 Bristol to Wells road go through the village and turn left down Marsh Lane

Marsh Lane
Map no: 3 ST65
Tel: 01761 452449
Chef: Janet Richards
Proprietor: Janet Richards
Seats: 20. No smoking in dining room
Times: Last L 1.45pm/D 8.45pm. Closed Sun, 1 week Xmas

HINTON CHARTERHOUSE, **Homewood Park** ☻☻

Beautifully presented Anglo-French cuisine in a comfortable Georgian country house

A delightfully unassuming yet stylish Georgian mansion is the lovely setting for this country house hotel situated between Warminster and Bath. Service is meticulous and professional if a little lacking in warmth, and a small team of well-trained staff attends diners in the pretty restaurant. The modern Anglo-French cooking uses fresh ingredients, and presentation is most attractive, but dishes tend to be a little over-fussy, and flavours sometimes clash. At a recent inspection meal a starter of sliced woodpigeon, cooked tender and pink, was tasty in itself, but complicated by a bundle of leaves with a basil dressing, a separate raspberry vinegar dressing, honey-glazed limes topped with walnuts and quenelles of caramelised beetroot purée. Panache of fresh grey mullet, John Dory and Cornish scallops came on a busy plate with trimmed asparagus tips, tomato, spring onion, puy lentils and a chervil butter sauce. On other occasions, dishes like double-baked soufflé with a creamy ragout of Cornish fish, and maize-fed guinea fowl filled with chervil mousse were thoroughly enjoyed.

Directions: Off the A36 Bath to Warminster road, 5 miles south-east of Bath

Map no: 3 ST75
Tel: 01225 723731

Cost: Alc £32; fixed-price lunch £19.50; fixed-price dinner £27.50. H/wine £12.50. Service inc
Credit cards: 1 2 3 4 5

Menus: A la carte; fixed-price lunch and dinner, Sunday lunch, pre-theatre by arrangement, restricted bar menu

Times: Last L 1.30pm, Last D 9.30pm

Chef: Tim Ford
Proprietors: Sara and Frank Gueuning

Seats: 55. No smoking
Additonal: Children permitted (early dinner only); children's portions; ❂ dishes; Vegan/other diets on request

HUNSTRETE, **Hunstrete House** ✪✪✪

Modern English cooking served in the elegant setting of an 18th-century country house hotel

All one would expect of a country house hotel, Hunstrete is an 18th-century property set in beautifully kept grounds overlooking rolling fields, deer parks and woodland. The interior has been lovingly furnished with antique pieces and recent refurbishment has in no way detracted from the warm and welcoming atmosphere of the house. In the main Terrace dining room, chef Robert Clayton demonstrates his skills in the production of appetising dishes offered from a choice of menus. There is a *carte* with half a dozen options at each course, a set three-course dinner, and a limited choice lunch menu at a very reasonable £15, including coffee and petits fours. Vegetarian dishes are not a feature of the menus, but can be provided on request.

At a test meal our inspector began with a tasty sausage of chicken and Madeira, served on a bed of puréed polenta with a creamy sauce delicately flavoured with ceps. His main course choice was breast of duckling with crisply roasted skin and slightly pink flesh set on a tagliatelle of leeks with a tangy dressing of cassis and shallots, served with an array of crunchy vegetables. Much of the kitchen's produce comes from the hotel's own garden, which grows an impressive 50 varieties of vegetables and herbs, introducing chilli peppers, stripey tomatoes, purslane, cape gooseberries and golden beetroot this year. The tempting dessert list includes hot orange and Grand Marnier soufflé, a selection of home-made ice creams and sorbets, and apple and pear tart, topped with crisp segments of apple and pear, surrounded by delicious caramel sauce and accompanied by chocolate ice cream. A separate cheese menu is also available. The carefully chosen wine list is easy to read and of convenient length, with good house wines and an excellent selection of Burgundy.

Directions: On A368 - 8 miles from Bath. If coming from Bristol take A37 (Wells) and turn left at Chelwood Bridge on to A368. The restaurant is 1.5 miles along, on the left

Chelwood
Map no: 3 ST66
Tel: 01761 490490

Cost: A/c £35, fixed-price lunch £15, fixed-price dinner £23.50. H/wine £10.50 ♀ Service exc
Credit cards: 1 2 3 4 5

Menus: *A la carte*, fixed price lunch and dinner, Sunday lunch

Times: Midday-Last L 3pm, Last D 9.30pm

Chef: Robert Clayton
Proprietors: Arcadian International. Manager: David Horton-Fawkes

Seats: 50. No smoking in dining room
Additional: Children welcome; children's portions; V dishes; other diets on request

NAILSEA, **Howard's Bistro** ✪

☺ *Chef Frank Luxton creates a selection of imaginative dishes for this modern bistro. Starters include asparagus en croute with lemon hollandaise or avocado and mango salad with raspberry vinaigrette and to follow choose a sirloin steak with red wine sauce or supreme of chicken.*

Cost: A/c £16, fixed-price D £12.50. H/wine £6.50 ♀ Service exc
Credit cards: 1 2 3 4
Additional: Children welcome; ◐ menu; Vegan/other diets on request
Directions: In the old village of Nailsea near the West End trading estate

2 King's Hill
Map no: 3ST47
Tel: 01275 858348
Chef: Frank Luxton
Proprietors: Christopher and Gillian Howard
Seats: 40
Times: Last Sun L 3pm/D 10.30pm (Tue Sat). Closed Mon, Xmas

AVON ENGLAND

PETTY FRANCE, **Petty France** ✹✹

A small hotel with a lot of character set in beautiful gardens with chefs Jason Burton and Jacqui Jones making good use of local produce. To start with try quail's egg and smoked bacon salad and follow with prawns with Pernod and walnut and herb rice.

Cost: Alc £22.50. H/wine £9.95. Service exc
Additional: Children welcome; ◐ menu; Vegan/other diets on request
Directions: On the A46, 5 miles north of the M4 junc 18

Map no: 3 ST78
Tel: 01454 238361
Chefs: Jason Burton, Jacqui Jones
Proprietor: Consort. Managers: W Fraser, ◐. Minnich
Seats: 55. No smoking in dining room
Times: Last L 2pm/D 10pm

RANGEWORTHY, **Rangeworthy Court** ✹

☺ An imposing manor house set in mature grounds with good access to Bristol. Personally operated by conscientious owners Mervyn and Lucia Gillett, a good choice of dishes is offered from the carte and set menus, using well prepared, fresh produce to create sound textures and identifiable flavours.

Cost: Alc £18; fixed-price L £11.50/D £16. Wine £8.50. Service inc
Credit cards: 1 2 3 4. **Additional:** Children welcome; children's portions/menu; ◐ dishes; Vegan/other diets on request
Directions: Signposted off B4058

Church Lane, Wotton Road
Map no: 3 ST68
Tel: 01454 228347
Chefs: Peter Knight, David Organ
Proprietors: Lucia and Mervyn Gillett
Seats: 52
Times: Last L 1.45pm/D 9pm (Sat 9.30pm)

THORNBURY, **Thornbury Castle** ✹✹

Classic English and French cuisine in an impressively grand setting

The striking architecture of Thornbury Castle makes a dramatic impact on most new arrivals, and a meal taken in the dining room can be an equally memorable experience. Light, fresh canapés and delicate appetisers herald the delights to come, and the dishes listed on Peter Brazil's interesting seasonal menus will not disappoint. The classic English and French cooking might produce dishes like oven-roast rack of lamb topped with an almond and rosemary crust served with a Madeira and mint sauce, or escalope of venison flavoured with juniper served on a bed of braised red cabbage with port and redcurrant sauce. Our inspector opted for a simple crisp salad of avocado and Cornish crab with sweet citrus vinaigrette, followed by a quality tournedos of Angus beef, cooked nicely pink with bold flavours, set off with two tasty mustard grain sauces. Al dente vegetables included light sautéed and boiled potatoes, mange-tout, baton carrots and puréed swede, while Thornbury treacle tart was refreshingly light and delicious. A daily vegetarian dish might be baked avocado filled with apple, walnuts and blue cheese. The wine list is extensive and comprehensive.

Directions: Bear left at bottom of High Street into Castle Street. The entrance to Thornbury Castle is to left of St Mary's Church

Map no: 3 ST69
Tel: 01454 281182

Cost: Fixed-price lunch £18.50; fixed-price dinner £31. Wine £12.50. No service charge
Credit cards: 1 2 3 4 5

Menus: Fixed-price lunch and dinner, Sunday lunch

Times: Closed 2 days early Jan

Chef: Peter Brazill
Proprietors: Pride of Britain, The Baron of Portlethen

Seats: 50. No smoking in the dining room
Additional: Children over 12 permitted; ◐ dishes; Vegan/other diets on request

WESTON-SUPER-MARE,
Commodore Hotel ⊛

Beach Road, Sand Bay,
Kewstoke
Map no: 3 ST36
Tel: 01934 415778

☺ *Bright, modern dishes with tasty sauces and good stock soups are offered at this friendly hotel. Head chef Paul Evans is still at the stove, producing very sound cooking, typically guinea fowl with chutney and nouvelle-style bread and butter pudding. Good value set-price meals.*

Chef: David Williams
Proprietor: John Stoakes
Seats: 82. No-smoking area
Times: Last L 2.30pm/D 9.30 pm

Cost: Alc £15. H/wine £6.95. Service exc. **Credit cards:** 1 2 3
Additional: Children welcome; children's menu/portions; ❂ menu; other diets on request
Directions: 1.5 miles north of Weston-super-Mare along the coast toll road

BEDFORDSHIRE

BEDFORD, **The Barns** ⊛

Cardington Road
Map no: 4 TL04
Tel: 01234 270044
Chef: Jeff Brimble
Proprietor: Country Club.
Manageress: Eva Duynham
Seats: 80. No-smoking area
Times: Last L 2pm/D 10pm.
Closed Sat lunch

☺ *The restaurant in this hotel overlooks the River Ouse. It has been developed around a 17th-century manor and medieval tithe barn. The fixed-price and carte menus are based on European dishes. Our inspector enjoyed pink chicken livers with stir-fried vegetables and roast pork with all the trimmings.*

Cost: Alc £18.50; fixed-price L £11.50/D £15. Wine £8.95 ? Service exc. **Credit cards:** 1 2 3. **Additional:** Children welcome; children's portions; ❂ dishes; Vegan/other diets on request
Directions: On A603, 2 miles out of town centre

FLITWICK, **Flitwick Manor** ⊛⊛⊛

Church Road
Map no: 4 TL03
Tel: 01525 712242

A country house setting for modern and classical-style cuisine offered from seasonally evolving set-price menus

Cost: Fixed-price lunch £16.50 (2 courses), £19.50, fixed-price dinner £35.50. H/wine £12.50. Service exc
Credit cards: 1 2 3 4

However turbulent the recent past has been at this country house hotel, little can detract from its peaceful, friendly atmosphere. Much character is lent by the grounds and surrounding countryside, and the building itself dates from the 17th century, featuring some fine pieces of furniture in keeping with the period.
 Chef Duncan Poyser presents seasonally evolving menus, now simpler in style, including a short lunch menu priced for two or three courses, with a wider choice in the evening. Set no-choice menus are also available for parties of eight or more, and a selection of vegetarian dishes is listed, with a risotto of wild mushrooms, or a tartlet of broccoli, sun-dried tomato and hazelnut draped in olive oil among the options.
 Meals are confidently prepared and reflect a growing maturity of approach in dishes such as lasagne of ox tongue and field mushrooms, or the terrine of pressed leeks, crab and lamb's sweetbreads enjoyed by our inspector during a July inspection

Menus: Fixed-price lunch and dinner, Sunday lunch

Times: Last L 1.30pm, Last D 9.30pm

Chef: Duncan Poyser
Proprietor: Mazard Hotel Management. Manager: Sonia Banks

meal. Main courses might offer pot roast guinea fowl with black pudding, or grilled John Dory set on a bed of wild rice and peas, accompanied by a selection of carefully cooked vegetables. Desserts include traditional bread and butter pudding, hot banana soufflé, and a fig 'tarte tartin' served with Chartreuse ice cream which, though a good idea, proved a slight disappointment. There is also a selection of traditional farmhouse cheeses served with home-made bread and biscuits. Chef Poyser excels at pastry, and his bread, canapés and petits fours have all impressed.

The main emphasis of the wine list is on good quality French wines from reputed estates and growers.

Seats: 40. No smoking in dining room
Additional: Children permitted (over 8 at dinner); children's portions; ◐ dishes

Directions: On A5120, two miles from junc 12 M1

LEIGHTON BUZZARD, **The King's Head** ❀

A traditional, timbered restaurant which groans with English gentility, but with French undertones. The carte is designed to please the more conservative palate and there is a monthly-changing, fixed-price menu. Daily specials are enthusiastically declared by the long-serving manger.

Cost: Alc £34; fixed-price L/D £20.25. Wine £13.25. Service inc
Credit cards: 1 2 3 4
Additional: Children welcome; ◐ dishes; Vegan/other diets on request
Directions: Ivinghoe is on B458 between Leighton Buzzard/Tring

Ivinghoe
Map no: 4 SP92
Tel: 01296 668388/668264
Chef: Patrick O'Keeffe
Proprietors: Forte Plc. Manager: Mr Georges de Maison
Seats: 55. No cigars or pipes in restautant. Air conditioned
Times: Last L 2.15pm/D 9.30pm

WOBURN, **The Bell Inn** ❀

☺ *The formal beamed restaurant of this well-established hotel offers bar meals and short, seasonal menus priced according to the number of courses. The new chef is maintaining good standards, with a clear emphasis on fresh ingredients, carefully prepared. There is a wide choice of 50 wines.*

Cost: Fixed-price L £13.95/D £16.95. H/wine £9.95. Service exc
Credit cards: 1 2 3 4 5
Additional: Children welcome; children's portions; ◐ dishes; Vegan/other diets on request
Directions: Northern end of the main street in Woburn, 5 minutes from junction 13 of M1

34 Bedford Street
Map no: 4 SP93
Tel: 01525 290280
Chefs: Grant Huntley
Proprietor: Best Western. Manager: Tim Chilton
Seats: 45. No pipes
Times: Last L 2pm/D 9.30pm. Closed Sat lunch, Sun eve, 25th–30th Dec

WOBURN, **Paris House** ❀❀

Classical French cuisine from a dedicated chef in a relaxed setting in Woburn Abbey grounds

An imposing setting beyond a Regency archway in the deer-grazed grounds of Woburn Abbey suggests a very grand eating place, but this is not the case. While the cooking is classically French prepared in bold and skilful style by a chef/patron with a faultless pedigree, there is nothing stiff or intimidating about the bright dining areas and relaxed atmosphere. Friendly staff are happy to elaborate on the bluntly worded *carte*, which is

Woburn Park
Map no: 4 SP93
Tel: 01525 290692

Cost: Alc £36; Sunday lunch £25, fixed-price lunch £23; fixed-price dinner £36. H/wine £10 ♀ Service exc
Credit cards: 1 2 3 4

Menus: *A la carte* dinner, fixed-price lunch and dinner, Sunday

supplemented by a daily-changing lunchtime menu and an evening gastronomic list. This is not food for trendy faddists, as a recent heavy and full-flavoured inspection meal proved: pig's trotters filled with mild chicken mousseline in a rich, strongly seasoned béarnaise sauce, was followed by ballotine of monkfish provençale – deliciously moist fish fillet with salmon mousse and basil-scented, finely cut vegetables. A soft, seductive pear frangipane tart with a pear liqueur sabayon was a dessert to savour. Among other recommended dishes have been wing of skate with nut-brown butter and capers. The well-notated wine list is mostly French and New World.

Directions: On the A4012 Woburn to Hockcliffe road, 1.5 miles out of Woburn. Through huge archway

lunch
Times: Midday-Last L 2pm, 7-Last D 9.30pm.

Chef: Peter Chandler
Proprietor: Peter Chandler

Seats: 44, 14 (private room). No pipes or cigars in restaurant
Additional: Children welcome; children's portions; ❂ dishes; other diets on request

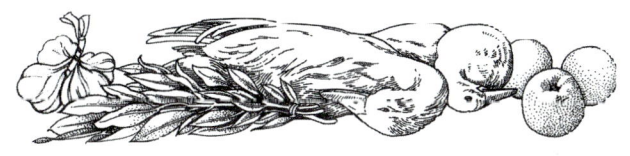

BERKSHIRE

ASCOT, Jade Fountain ❂

☺ *A smart high street restaurant with a loyal local following, the Jade Fountain has offered basically the same menu for the last decade, sticking to established western favourites. The main ingredients are chicken, prawns and beef, and the main flavours are light chilli, sweet, ginger and black bean.*

Cost: Alc £19; fixed price D £21. H/wine £7.90. Service inc
Credit cards: 1 2 3 4 5
Additional: Children over 2 welcome; ❂ dishes
Directions: A corner site in the middle of Sunninghill High Street

38 High Street, Sunninghill
Map no: 4 SU96
Tel: 01344 27070
Chef: C K Lee
Proprietors: H F Man and S Chiu
Seats: 90. Air conditioned
Times: Last L 1.45pm/D 10.30pm. Closed 24-27 Dec

ASCOT, The Royal Berkshire ❂❂

Imaginative use of ingredients including some Asian influences resulting in generously portioned dishes

There's a busy, lively atmosphere at this much-extended 18th-century hotel which centres around two attractive features: one is a popular leisure club, and the other is the quality restaurant. The latter is much frequented by locals as well as by resident visitors, and chef Robert Gibbins' classical English cooking received praise at a recent inspection visit. Using imaginative ingredients, many of them Asian, he creates interesting dishes which appear on the seasonal *carte* and a small 'bill of fare'. Portions are generous, and can occasionally be overwhelming, as our inspector discovered after ordering foie gras and duck rillette, and being served lots of stir-fried vegetables, two large potato rösti and a handful of mixed roast nuts. Monkfish and crab cakes with lobster sauce was a more restrained dish, served with manageable portions of potatoes, carrots and broccoli in a rich sauce. Tarte tatin was an

London Road
Map no: 4 SU96
Tel: 01344 23322

Cost: Fixed-price lunch £12.95-£19.95, fixed-price dinner £28. H/wine £14.95 ♀ Service inc
Credit cards: 1 2 3 4 5

Menus: A la carte, fixed-price lunch and dinner, bar menu

Times: Midday Last L 2pm, Last D 9.30pm

Chef: Robert Gibbins
Proprietors: Hilton Associate.
Manager: Simon Pearce

Seats: 45. No pipes or cigars

enjoyable dessert, followed by cafetière coffee and petits fours. The elegant public rooms are decorated with several different painting techniques, such as marbling, while the hotel is surrounded by parkland.

Directions: From the A30 take the A329 signed Ascot. The hotel entrance is on the right after 2 miles

Additional: Children welcome; children's portion/menu. ☻ menu; Vegan/other diets on request

BRACKNELL, **Coppid Beech** ❀❀

Modern English and French cooking highlighted by stunningly inventive sauces

A smart Alpine-style hotel next to a dry ski-slope is home to a chef with a promising future who already shows an original flair. Neil Thrift cooks English and Alsation dishes in modern style, and both *carte* and fixed-price menus offer examples of his cooking in dishes like saltimbocca of monkfish with peppers and creamed lobster gravy, and loin of lamb Niçoise. Diners are offered small herb-crusted rolls with slivers of sun ripe tomatoes inside to whet their appetites, and at a recent inspection meal a rather ordinary crab and cream cheese ravioli starter was given zest by the addition of a hot lemon and coriander vinaigrette. Farmhouse sausages (not home-made) were rich and herby, and came with puréed and new potatoes, minted peas, asparagus tips, spinach, braised leek and sweet carrots – a lovely selection of well-flavoured vegetables. A very lemony tart with a smooth, buttery texture was garnished with fresh fruit and a light covering of icing sugar. The rather plain restaurant continues the Alpine theme with glacier-style chandeliers like icicles. The wine list offers a very good choice with matching prices.

Directions: From M4 junction 10, follow A329(M) to first exit. At roundabout take first exit to Binfield, the hotel is 300 metres on the right

John Nike Way
Map no: 4 SU86
Tel: 01344 303333

Cost: *Alc* £30, fixed price lunch £14.50; dinner £25. H/wine from £11.50 ♀ Service exc
Credit cards: 1 2 3 4 5

Menus: *A la carte*, fixed-price lunch and dinner, Sunday lunch, bar menu

Times: 12.30pm–Last L 2pm, 6.30pm– Last D 10.30pm. Closed Sat lunch

Chef: Neil Thrift
Proprietor: Alan Blenkinsopp

Seats: 120. No-smoking area. No pipes or cigars. Air conditioned
Additional: Children welcome; children's portions/menu; ☻ dishes; Vegan/other diets on request. Live entertainment Sun lunch

BRAY, **Waterside Inn** ❀❀❀❀❀

First-class French cooking in the Roux brothers' inimitable style in a charming riverside setting

Its beautiful riverside setting has done much for the popularity of Michel Roux's restaurant, especially at lunchtime when the view lends enchantment to dishes expertly cooked from the finest ingredients in true French style. Guests have the choice of a fixed-price Menu Gastronomique, which offers an alternative at each of three courses and includes coffee; a Menu Exceptionnel for two or more also offers an alternative at each of five courses (one of which is a sorbet) or, of course, there is the *carte* which, at the top end of the price scale, may offer a starter of lightly fried slices of lobster in white port sauce to begin at £34.50! Most starters , however, are about half that price. Our Scottish inspector nevertheless decided to experience the Roux magic from the Menu Gastronomique and enjoyed a three-course lunch for the price of that lobster first course.

Ferry Road
Map no: 4 SU97
Tel: 01628 20691

Cost: *Alc* £65, fixed-price lunch £28.50 (£36 weekends), fixed-price dinner £62. Wine £25
Credit cards: 1 3 4 5

Menus: *A la carte*, fixed-price, Sunday lunch

Times: Midday-Last L 2pm (2.30pm Sun), 7pm-Last D 10pm. Closed all day Mon, Tue lunch, for dinner Sun (3rd week Oct - 2nd week Apr). Closed for 5 weeks from Boxing Day

After delicious canapés and an interesting appetiser of tuna mixed with white wine, the meal proper took off to an excellent start with a gourmandise of rabbit and duck with a truffle-scented vinaigrette. Succulent, tender thigh meat was nicely matched with a dense, rich slice of foie gras on a toasted brioche. A navarin of lamb à la beaujolais proved to be the Waterside's own interpretation of this classic meat stew, with beautifully flavoured pieces of shoulder in an intense sauce. The final touch was a mirabelle soufflé, just slightly runny in the middle, but well-risen and melting in the mouth. Dishes on this, the cheapest of the Waterside's menus, may be based on the less expensive raw materials, but there is no skimping on cooking skills or care of presentation. The extensive wine list is almost entirely French and of a quality to complement such excellent food, with the best vineyards and vintages represented.

Service under the direction of manager Diego Masciago, is delivered with charming efficiency by the French staff, who are happy to explain the make up of each dish. The Waterside has for some years lived, rather unfairly, in the shadow of Le Gavroche, and we are delighted this year to place it on an even footing with the award of a well-deserved fifth rosette.

In addition to the main restaurant, there is also a private cottage dining room, a motor launch for hire, and six luxurious bedrooms for guests wanting to stay the night.

Chef: Michel Roux, Mark Dodson
Proprietor: Michel Roux

Seats: 75. No cigars in dining room. Air conditioned
Additional: Children over 12 permitted; ❶ dishes

Directions: Take the Bray village road from the A308 Windsor/Maidenhead road. The restaurant is clearly signposted in the village

COOKHAM, **Cookham Tandoori** ❀❀

☺ *Distinguished Indian cooking full of fresh and subtle flavours in a cottage setting*

There's more than just a hint of the traditional English tea room about this pretty beamed and timbered cottage just up from the river and close to the village green. No scones or clotted cream are on sale in this cosy setting, however, but there is consistently good Indian food with a mainly East Bengali influence as well as many dishes with a more contemporary influence. Distinct and subtle flavours are the hallmark of Azad Hussain's home-taught cooking, and fresh produce, herbs and spices are liberally used. Mussels steamed and cooked with white wine, garlic, methi, coriander and a pasanda gravy were very tasty and juicy at a recent lunch, and other enjoyable dishes included chicken nawabi murgh Khyberi - tender, marinated meat chunks cooked with creamed coconut, almonds and sultanas; king prawn shashlick coloured red and served hissing and spitting on a skillet, with a sweet and sour flavour. Tandoori roti provided a fat-free alternative to nan bread; sag aloo spinach purée with firm potatoes was a tasty side dish, and the multi-coloured pilau rice was light and fluffy.

High Street
Map no: 4 SU56
Tel: 01628 522584

Cost: A/c £17.50, fixed-price Sun buffet L £12.95, fixed-price D £22.50. Wine £9.25
Credit cards: 1 2 3 4

Menus: A la carte , Sunday lunch buffet, fixed-price dinner

Times: Midday-Last L 2.30pm, 6pm-Last D 10.30pm. Closed Xmas

Chef: Azad Hussain
Proprietor: Bashir Islam

Seats: 80. No smoking
Additional: Children permitted, children's portions on Sundays; ❶ dishes; Vegan on request.

Directions: In Cookham village which is between Maidenhead and Marlow

HURLEY, Ye Olde Bell ✦

Reputedly England's oldest inn, this historic hotel is quietly located in the heart of the village and is popular with locals and residents alike. New chef David Moon offers imaginative and varied menus, with traditional seasonal dishes including game and fresh fish. The sweet trolley is not to be missed!

Cost: Alc £25; fixed-price L £14.95/D £18.95. H/wine £9.50. Service exc. **Credit cards:** 1 2 3 4. **Additional:** Children welcome; children's portions/menu; ◐ dishes; Vegan on request
Directions: Junction 8/9 of M4 motorway located on A423

Maidenhead
Map no: 4 SU88
Tel: 01628 825881
Chef: David Perron
Proprietors: Resort Hotels.
Manager: Michel Rosso
Seats: 80. No-smoking area
Times: Last L 2.30pm/D 9.30pm

MAIDENHEAD, Fredrick's ✦✦✦

Expensive traditional French and British cuisine served in a smart hotel restaurant where booking is essential

Fredrick's is a smart red-brick hotel set in its own attractive grounds on the outskirts of town, next to the golf course. Every aspect of the establishment reflects the style and personality of its owner, Fredrick Losel, for whom it is the realisation of a great ambition. The restaurant, in white and gold with chandeliers, fresh flowers and candlelight, is rather formal and gentlemen are required to wear jackets and ties. Service, as befits the establishment, is well managed, attentive and professional.

Chef Brian Cutler has been here for a number of years and his traditional French and English style of cooking is as popular as ever, in spite of the prices charged, and guests are well advised to book in advance. Short daily fixed-price lunch and dinner menus are offered in addition to the seasonally influenced *carte*, and the latter always has a vegetarian dish, such as vegetable gâteau Pithiviers. Good quality fresh, mostly local ingredients are used, and the vegetables, presented by silver service, are carefully cooked to retain firmness, colour and flavour.

A recent meal began with a terrine of smoked herring, which was smooth-textured, full-flavoured and enjoyable, though the accompanying melon chutney provided a somewhat unusual contrast to the fish. This was followed by fillet of rabbit served with tagliatelle, a light, well made port sauce and a selection of wild mushrooms. A wide choice of classic desserts is displayed on a trolley. Our inspector chose a lemon tart with crisp pastry and a zesty filling on a good raspberry coulis – the highlight of the meal.

The mainly French wine list is expensively priced but the quality is good. There are many fine vintages from all the classic areas, plus some excellent champagne.

Directions: From the A404M take the exit to Cox Green/White Waltham. At roundabout, turn left into Shoppenhangers Road.
From the A308 the turning next to the railway station bridge

Shoppenhangers Road
Map no: 4 SU88
Tel: 01628 35934

Cost: Alc £39; Sunday lunch £23.50; fixed-price lunch £19.50; fixed-price dinner £28.50. H/wine £13. Service exc
Credit cards: 1 2 3 4

Menus: *A la carte*, fixed-price lunch and dinner, Sunday lunch, bar/lounge menu

Times: Last L 2pm, Last D 9.45pm. Closed Sat lunch, 24-30 Dec

Chef: Brian Cutler
Proprietor: Fredrick W Lösel

Seats: 60. No cigars or pipes in dining room. Air conditioned
Additional: Children welcome; children's portions; ◐ dishes; Vegan/other diets on request

NEWBURY, Elcot Park ❀

Attractive menus are offered in the Orangery Restaurant of this country house hotel. Dishes include grills and vegetarian options, such as filo parcel of goats' cheese with pine kernels. Our inspector sampled a prawn and mussel casserole, lamb with lime and curry sabayon, and mandarin cheesecake.

Cost: Alc from £22; fixed-price L £12/D £15. ♀ Service exc
Credit cards: 1 2 3 4
Additional: Children welcome; children's portions/menu; ◐ dishes; Vegan/other diets on request.
Directions: Situated off the A4, halfway between Newbury and Hungerford

Elcot
Map no: 4 SU46
Tel: 01488 58100
Chef: Davide Paulische
Proprietors: Resort Hotels.
Manager: Frank Adams
Seats: 200. No-smoking area. Air conditioned
Times: Last L 2pm/D 9.30pm (Sat 10pm)

READING, Upcross Hotel ❀

At this large Victorian house a small, committed kitchen team produces simply crafted dishes based on traditional recipes, such as salmon and sole terrine with Chablis sauce, beef emincé in a grain mustard and shallot sauce, and a fresh fig mousse. A separate vegetarian menu is also available.

Cost: Alc £27; fixed-price L £10.50 (2 courses), £15/D £10.50 (2 courses), £15. Wine £10.50. Service inc
Credit cards: 1 2 3. 5 **Additional:** Children welcome; children's portions/menu; ◐ menu; Vegan/other diets on request
Directions: On main A4 within walking distant of town centre

68 Berkeley Avenue
Map no: 4 SU77
Tel: 01734 590796
Chef: Mr Adrian Offley
Proprietor: Mrs Jessica Cecil
Seats: 45 (restaurant), 75 (functions). No-smoking area. No pipes or cigars in restaurant
Times: Last L 2pm/D 10pm. Closed Sat lunch, 27 Dec–3 Jan

SHINFIELD, L'Ortolan ❀❀❀❀❀

An elegant country house setting for some exquisitely presented French cuisine from a very talented English chef

One of the few Englishmen at the top of his profession in this country, John Burton-Race's cooking is unmistakably French, and together with his French wife Christine he has created a fine French restaurant. L'Ortolan is an elegant brick-built former vicarage set in beautifully kept grounds within easy reach of Reading and the M4. The dining room is spacious and restfully decorated to provide a fitting backdrop for some exquisitely presented and exciting cuisine. John admits to being a classic chef, and he cooks with passion and creative flair, demanding the highest standards from his kitchen brigade and the predominantly French team of waiting staff.

A reputation for over-elaboration was refuted by one inspector at an early summer visit. He found no gratuitous complexity in any of the dishes he sampled, declaring all the constituents seasonal and relevant in concept and flavour. His meal began with a sensuous terrine of sliced foie gras and chicken, moist strips of the latter providing a good counter to the richness of the liver. The terrine was set on a clear and full-flavoured Madeira jelly; lamb's lettuce drizzled with truffle oil, providing a fresh and piquant balance. Fresh turbot followed, with a creamy light fish jus seasoned with herbs and chives, and a stir of little mushrooms and baby asparagus – a seasonal dish

The Old Vicarage, Church Lane
Map no: 4 SU76
Tel: 01734 883783

Cost: Alc £45 (2-courses); fixed-price lunch and dinner on weekdays only. £22 and £31.50 (both 3 courses). H/wine from £15.50
Credit cards: 1 2 3 4

Menus: A la carte all week, two fixed-price weekday lunch and dinner menus

Times: Midday-Last L 2.15pm, 7pm-Last D 11.pm. Closed Sun eve, Mon, last 2 weeks Aug, last 2 weeks Feb

Chef: John Burton-Race
Proprietor: Burton-Race Restaurants plc

Seats: 60
Additional: Vegetarian dishes by arrangement. Children permitted

full of delicate flavours. For dessert a poached peach was set on a vacherin base with creamy vanilla ice cream and marinated strawberries, topped with a haze of spun sugar around two or three mint leaves. It could not be described as a 'sugar basket' since these are invariably clumsy but this was ethereal, appropriate and eye-catching.

Sauces are particularly well constructed, and at an earlier meal a butter sauce spiked with chives proved the perfect complement to a starter of succulent scallops. The fillet of lamb chosen as a main course was roasted pink, topped with a light quenelle, spiked with its sweetbreads, wrapped in spinach leaves and served with a smooth reduction of the juices enriched with port. To finish, a tangy lemon tart with a brûlée topping was partnered by a good crème anglaise.

A choice of fixed-price menus is offered with a list of daily specials, all in French with detailed English descriptions. Vegetarian dishes are not featured but are available on request. Prices are high, but from the dainty canapés served with aperitifs in the lounge or conservatory, to the colourful array of petits fours with the coffee, one can be certain of a memorable gastronomic experience.

Directions: From M4 exit 11 take A33 towards Basingstoke. At the next roundabout, left to Three Mile Cross, then turn left to Shinfield, right at Six Bells pub. L'Ortolan is up the hill on the left

SLOUGH, **The Copthorne** ✣

A striking modern hotel close to Windsor with two eating options: the upbeat, informal Verandah, and the smarter Reflections restaurant serving fine French cuisine. The creative talents of chef Graham Riley are shown in dishes like terrine of foie gras and leeks, and pan-fried wood pigeon.

Cost: *Alc* £26; fixed-price L £17.50/ D £18. H/wine £12. Service inc.
Credit cards: 1 2 3 4 5
Additional: Children welcome; children's portions/menu; ♥ menu; Vegan/other diets on request
Directions: From junction 6 M6 turn into Tunns Lane, take first left at roundabout into Cippenham Lane

400 Cippenham Lane
Map no: 4 SU97
Tel: 01753 516222
Chef: Graham Riley
Proprietor: Patrick Maw
Seats: Reflections 40, Veranda 110. No-smoking area (Veranda). Air conditioned
Times: Veranda Last L 2pm/D10pm. Reflections Last D 10pm. Closed Sun

STREATLEY, **Swan Diplomat** ✣✣

A smart riverside restaurant with idyllic views and quality cooking to match

This attractive hotel occupies an idyllic spot alongside the Thames, and the restaurant is positioned to make the very most of the lovely riverside views. Inside, a delightfully charming young French team ensures that everything flows smoothly, and the food itself was virtually faultless during a recent visit. The cooking style is classic French, and there's a choice of menus from the light set lunch offered in summertime to the rather pricey fixed-price menus and *carte*.

The produce of local markets as well as speciality ingredients from London and Paris feature in recommended dishes like

High Street
Map no: 4 SU58
Tel: 01491 873737

Cost: *Alc* from £32; fixed-price lunch £19.25; fixed-price dinner £27.50. Wine £10.50. Service exc
Credit cards: 1 2 3 4

Menus: *A la carte*, fixed-price lunch and dinner, Sunday brunch, bar menu, classic lunch (Mon–Sat)
Times: 12.30pm-Last L 2pm,

lightly poached chicken ravioli surrounded by buttered oyster mushrooms with tomato vinaigrette, and steamed fillet of salmon in a creamy vermouth sauce with pieces of firm monkfish, topped with a tarragon herb crust. A separate vegetarian menu offers selections such as fricassée of woodland mushrooms with chives, tomato, and a raspberry vinegar sauce. Desserts and coffees are very good, and the interesting wine list is reasonably priced and affordable.

Directions: Follow A329 from Pangbourne. On entering Streatley, turn right at traffic lights. The hotel is on the left before the bridge

7.30pm-Last D 9.30pm

Chef: Philip Clarke
Proprietor: Borge Karlsson

Seats: 75. No cigars or pipes
Additional: Children welcome; children's portions; ◑ menu; Vegan/other diets on request

THATCHAM, Regency Park ◉◉

Lovely surroundings complement excellent fresh cooking of modern English/French cuisine

This independently owned, and much extended small hotel on the outskirts of town provides excellent individual service. To the rear of the hotel are particularly beautiful landscaped gardens with water gardens and wildlife ponds. The Terraces restaurant is a modern, pretty room decorated in peaches and pinks with summer prints. It is here that chef Michael Carney demonstrates his skills with his seasonally-changing fixed-price and *carte* menus featuring modern English/French cuisine. Our inspection meal started with a feuilleté of pheasant in a creamy green peppercorn sauce and whilst June is hardly the best time for game, the meat's dryness was otherwise compensated for. The monkfish was altogether more successful, braised in herbed warm vinaigrette, it was extremely fresh and tasty. This was followed by a delightful dessert of poached pear slices topped with a glazed pistachio sabayon.

Directions: From Thatcham turn right into Northfield Road, then left, hotel is on the right

Bowling Green Road
Map no: 4 SU56
Tel: 01635 871555

Cost: Alc £27.50; fixed-price L £13.95/L £18.50. Wine £11.95 ♀ Service inc
Credit cards: 1 2 3 4 5

Times: Last L 2.30pm/D 10.30pm

Chef: Michael Carney
Proprietor: Independent.
Manager: Timothy Bramhall

Seats: 65. Air conditioned
Additional: Children welcome; children's portions/menu; ◑ dishes; Vegan/other diets on request. Live entertainment Sat eve

WINDSOR, Aurora Garden ◉

A small hotel within a few minutes' walk of Windsor Great Park and with easy access to the castle. Chef Denton Robinson produces fresh and flavoursome dishes which are very well presented. Vegetarian dishes are strong and the team places great emphasis on individual care and attention.

Cost: Alc £25; fixed-price L/D £13.95. H/wine £8.50 ♀ Service exc
Credit cards: 1 2 3 4. **Additional:** Children welcome; children's portions/menu; ◑ menu; Vegan/other dishes on request
Directions: From the Castle turn left down High Street, then into Sheet Street. At the traffic lights straight on, turn right into Francis Road, 2nd exit off roundabout, 500 yds on right

14 Bolton Avenue
Map no: 4 SU97
Tel: 01753 868686
Chef: Denton Robinson
Proprietor: Clare House.
Manageress: Josephine Currie
Seats: 45. No cigars or pipes
Times: Last L 2pm/D 9pm.
Closed Xmas

WINDSOR, Oakley Court ❀❀

Classic French and modern English cooking in a neo-Gothic, Thames-side hotel restaurant

Used as Dracula's castle in the making of many films, this splendid neo-Gothic mansion with modern wings hides no horrors nowadays. It is set in extensive grounds that run down to a quiet stretch of the Thames, and the stylish and comfortable public rooms include the main Oakleaf restaurant. In here the traditional and more modern ideas of British cooking can be sampled in dishes that are produced with great skill and care, and shown on various set-price menus, a short *carte* and a vegetarian list. A recent inspection meal began with attractively browned scallops, langoustines and salmon with crisp slivers of asparagus, served with an intensely flavoured langoustine sauce. Pink duck magret with a sweet prune chutney and a creamy parsnip purée topped with deep-fried strands of swede was a well-balanced dish, followed by a rich brûlée on a mélange of banana and meringue in a chocolate case, with vanilla ice cream and a sliced, caramelised banana and caramel sauce. In September a new chef came to Oakley Court – Michael Croft whose extensive experience at the Mirabelle and the Royal Crescent will no doubt sustain the high standard of cuisine already set.

Directions: Beside the River Thames, off the A308 between Windsor and Maidenhead

Windsor Road, Water Oakley
Map no: 4 SU97
Tel: 01628 74141

Cost: Alc £37.50; fixed-price lunch £19.50; fixed-price dinner £29.50. Wine £13.90 ♀ Service exc
Credit cards: 1 2 3 4

Menus: *A la carte*, fixed-price lunch and dinner, Sunday lunch, pre-theatre, bar menu, Brasserie

Times: 12.30pm–Last L 2pm, 7.30pm–Last D 10pm

Chef: Michael Croft
Proprietors: Queens Moat. Manager: Jolyon Gough

Seats: 80. No-smoking area. No pipes or cigars in dining room
Additonal: Children welcome; children's portions; ❂ dishes; Vegan/other diets on request

YATTENDON, Royal Oak ❀❀❀

A good range of carefully cooked dishes are available in the bars and restaurant of this lovely old village inn

A 17th-century village inn of great character, the Royal Oak is staffed by a team of charming individuals well managed by Jeremy Gibbs. The bar and restaurant areas are at the heart of the hotel and are so popular that booking for meals is essential. An extensive choice of food is available in both, and chef Murray Chapman cooks with great care and skill, using good quality fresh ingredients, allowing their full flavours to come to the fore without over-elaboration.

Bar food dishes are individually priced and include a selection of breads: sun-dried tomato, garlic or olive, and starters such as coarse chicken liver pâté, home-made pasta with smoked salmon and fresh basil, and deep-fried Stilton and ham on a tomato sauce. Main courses range from spiced vegetables and mushroom ravioli with yoghurt for vegetarians, to lamb stew and parsley with spinach and game chips for omnivores, or another traditional favourite, grilled sausages, Yorkshire pudding and onion gravy. The fish section offers John Dory and bubble and squeak with mushroom sauce, and plain fish and chips. Vegetables and salads are available as side orders, and there is a good list of desserts, with bread and butter pudding and a cheesecake so wicked the management will accept no responsibility for it.

In the restaurant there is a fixed-price three-course menu for lunch and dinner. Our inspector enjoyed a summer lunch which

The Square
Map no: 4 SU57
Tel: 01635 201325

Cost: Alc £20; fixed-price lunch £19; fixed-price dinner £29. Wine £10.95 ♀ Service exc
Credit cards: 1 2 3 4 5

Menus: *A la carte*, fixed-price lunch and dinner, Sunday lunch, bar menu

Times: Midday-Last L 2.30pm, Last D 10pm

Chef: Murray Chapman
Proprietor: Regal Plc. Manager: Jeremy Gibbs

Seats: 70. No smoking in dining room
Additional: Children welcome; children's portions; ❂ menu; Vegan/other diets on request

began with a tasty salmon and sole mousseline, followed by rich, strongly flavoured loin of venison with a well made wild mushroom sauce and a delicate spinach timbale. To finish she chose a trio of hot soufflés which proved to be the highlight of the meal, with light textures and excellent flavours. Although predominantly French, the wine list includes a good choice of New World wines. There are some mature vintages of red Burgundy and claret.

Directions: In the centre of the village

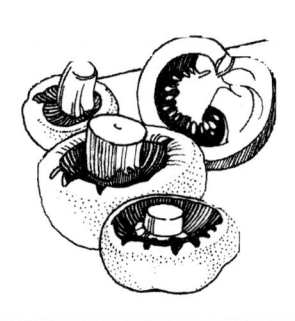

BUCKINGHAMSHIRE

ASTON CLINTON, **Bell Inn** ❀❀

Classical French and traditional English cookery in a village centre hotel setting

Several buildings on either side of the road make up this village centre hotel, but the main red-brick building houses the character bar and extensive restaurant – a long-acknowledged venue for good food. The restaurant can be cleverly divided by the use of a heavy curtain to suit the number of diners, and the first part is known as Regent Street because of its distinctive curve. Chef Jean-Claude MacFarlane offers a range of menus in the classic French style with English influences. There are daily fixed-price lunch and dinner menus, a set traditional meal and a *carte*. Aylesbury duck is a feature and may appear simply roasted, as a consommé, or as a plated selection of seven delicacies, sampled as a starter by our inspector. It included a confit, a coarse terrine, duck shredded in a rich rillette, and air-dried like ham, with a wonderful colour. This was followed by duo of lamb, rack and canon, with a purse of diced sweetbreads and a well made sauce. Sweets might include a soufflé, such as rum and banana, and a chocolate tower with macerated black cherries. Vegetarian dishes are also available.

Directions: Between Aylesbury and Tring. Situated in the centre of the village on the A41

Near Aylesbury
Map no: 4 SP81
Tel: 01296 630252

Cost: *Alc* £37.50; fixed-price lunch £13.50 (2 courses), £17; fixed-price dinner £22.50. Wine £9.50 ♀ Service exc
Credit cards: 1 2 3 5

Menus: *A la carte*, fixed-price lunch and dinner, Sunday lunch, bar menu

Times: Last L 1.45pm, Last D 9.15pm

Chef: Giles Stonehouse
Proprietor: Michael and Patsy Harris

Seats: 120. No smoking in dining room
Additional: Children welcome; /menu; ❶ menu; Vegan/other diets on request

AYLESBURY, **Hartwell House** ❀❀

A sumptuous country house hotel serving traditional British cooking from a bygone age

A meticulously restored Jacobean and Georgian stately home, this hotel offers stylish and luxurious accommodation in the most delightful of settings. The historic buildings were badly damaged by fire some years ago, but now the former splendours provide traditional country house living at its best. The two formal dining rooms are the perfect place to enjoy the

Oxford Road
Map no: 4 SP81
Tel: 01296 747444

Cost: *Alc* £38; fixed-price lunch £16.50 (2 courses), £22.40; fixed price dinner £38. Wine £11.90 ♀ Service inc
Credit cards: 1 2 3 4 5

Menus: *A la carte*, fixed-price

ENGLAND BUCKINGHAMSHIRE

old-fashioned British cooking of chef Alan Maw, with its emphasis on good country ingredients and rich, creamy sauces. Starters like terrine of foie gras with a Sauternes wine jelly, and cream of potato and leek soup with oysters might appear on the *carte*, with such main choices as roast mallard with braised endive and a truffle flavoured sauce, and fine slices of venison with spinach and a sauce of wild berries. Our inspector tried a full-flavoured warm pigeon breast salad with lentils, followed by rabbit salad with olive niçoise on a bed of crushed potatoes. Rich vegetable dishes like gratin dauphinois and cauliflower with hollandaise were enjoyable as were the more simple carrots. A long, expensive wine list offers mainly French varieties.

Directions: Two miles from Aylesbury on the right of the A418 to Oxford

lunch and dinner, Sunday lunch, Buttery

Times: 12.30pm-Last L 2pm, 7.30pm-Last D 9.45pm

Chef: Alan Maw
Proprietors: Historic House Hotels. Manager: Jonathan Thompson

Seats: 88. No smoking in dining room. Air conditioned
Additional: Children over 8 permitted; ◐ dishes; other diets on request

BURNHAM,
Burnham Beeches Moat House ❀

An extended Georgian country residence in a peaceful rural setting convenient for the M4 and M40. The imaginative set and seasonal menus include a carte, comprising game terrine or snow pea and warm duck breast salad, sea trout, guinea fowl or venison, and home-made desserts and sorbets.

Cost: *Alc* £29; fixed-price L £16/D £19 Wine £11. Service exc
Credit cards: 1 2 3 4
Additional: Children welcome; children's portions/menu; ◐ dishes; Vegan/other diets with prior notice
Directions: Off A355 via Farnham Royal roundabout

Grove Road
Map no: 4 SU98
Tel: 01628 603333
Chef: Lawrence Bryant
Proprietors: Queens Moat Houses. Manager: Michael Dewey
Seats: 90
Times: Last L 1.50pm/D 9.50pm. Closed Sat/BH Mon lunch

DINTON, La Chouette ❀❀

☺ *A pretty country cottage restaurant with a genial Belgian chef/patron*

The lively presence of the chef/patron makes a meal here an entertaining experience, but be prepared to exchange banter with M. Desmette or you might suffer a sudden loss of appetite. At a recent inspection meal the menu appeared to be redundant as the chef reeled off a list of available dishes and then raced off to cook what he had recommended. The result was not as rushed as it might sound, and a starter of goose liver terrine had a crisp, clean flavour but not a consistently smooth texture, and came with an unseemly large rustic white loaf. Breast of duck with morel sauce was surprisingly lacking in real flavour, but the profusion of vegetables that accompanied it were well cooked and fresh. Chocolate dominates the dessert menu, and the chosen hot chocolate soufflé was light, mild in flavour and enjoyable. Other choices might be 'Blanc de volaille a l'estragon' – chicken breast with tarragon, or 'Magret de canard au thym' – breast of duck with thyme. In addition to the expensive *carte*,

Near Aylesbury
Map no: 4 SP71
Tel: 01296 747422

Cost: *Alc* £19.50; fixed-price lunch £10; fixed price dinner £10 (3 courses), £19.90, £25, £35. Wine £10 ♀ Service 12.5%
Credit cards: 1 3

Menus: *A la carte*, fixed-price lunch and dinner

Times: Midday-Last L 2pm, 7pm-Last D 9pm. Closed Sat Lunch

Chef: Frederic Desmette
Proprietor: Frederic Desmette

there are a few set menus of varying length and price which offer better value for money. The wine list is mainly French.

Directions: Follow signs to Dinton on the A418

MARLOW, **The Compleat Angler** ✿

Situated on the bank of the river Thames, this well-known hotel has a lovely waterside terrace. Chef, Ferdinand Testka, offers French cuisine with modern influences all served in the Valaisan restaurant. Try foie gras terrine with warm brioche or red mullet with scampi mousse, leeks and tomato sauce.

Cost: A/c £40, fixed-price L £17.95 (2 courses), £22.95; fixed-price D £29.50. H/wine £15 ♀ Service inc. **Credit cards:** 1 2 3 4 5
Additional: Children welcome; children's menu/portions; ❾ menu. Pianist Fri and Sat
Directions: Located in centre of village by Marlow Bridge

TAPLOW, **Cliveden** ✿✿✿

This grand country house hotel provides a stunning setting and impeccable service for a memorable occasion

A stately home by the Thames, set in 376 acres of National Trust gardens and parkland, Cliveden is a unique hotel of unrivalled grandeur. It has two main restaurants, the Terrace, overlooking the formal garden, and Waldo's, a more intimate dinner venue. Chef Ron Maxfield's menus of mainly British dishes, integrated with Italian and French flavours, together with the stunning surroundings and attentive brigade of formal staff, make for a memorable dining experience.
In May our inspector took dinner in the Terrace Dining Room, beginning with a risotto of Provence vegetables and pesto, which had a wonderful flavour. Provence vegetables were more evident in the main course, fillet of sea-bass, with chargrilled aubergine, tomato, courgette, corn and mange-touts. The fish, moist and full of flavour, topped with couscous and a sprinkling of sesame seeds. Dessert was unusual; a lemon tart, with delicious pastry and a sharply flavoured filling, served with a ball of Mascarpone ice cream.
  Later in the year a visit was made to Waldo's, where the dinner menu is priced for three or four courses, with an alternative set six-course meal. A starter of crab with lime, pimento, scallops and three salads had a rather prissy 'nouvelle' presentation but good flavours. The main course 'lamb four ways' with fresh tomato, olive and basil sauce, came in only three ways: decent loin, liver and fried sweetbreads. Dessert was the highlight – a mirabelle soufflé, very light, with poached yellow plums and good liquorice ice cream. Vegetarian dishes are available on request in both restaurants. The splendid wine list is common to both dining rooms and offers the very best from all the classic areas of Europe, together with excellent wines from Australia, California and New Zealand.

Directions: On the B476, 2 miles north of Taplow

Additional: No cigars or pipes. Children welcome; children's portions/menu; other diets on request. Live entertainment

Marlow Bridge
Map no: 4 SU88
Tel: 01628 484444
Chef: Ferdinand Testka
Proprietors: Forte Grand.
Manager: David Warren
Seats: 100. No-smoking area; no cigars or pipes
Times: Last L 2.30pm/D 10pm

Map no: 4 SU98
Tel: 01628 668561

Cost: A/c £45; fixed-price lunch £26 (Mon–Fri), £34 (Sat, Sun); fixed-price dinner £36. Wine £16 ♀ Service exc
Credit cards: 1 2 3 4 5

Menus: A la carte, fixed-price lunch and dinner, Sunday lunch, Pavilion menu

Times: 12.30pm-Last L 2.30pm, 7.30pm-Last D 10pm
Waldo's 7pm-Last D10pm.
Closed Sun, Mon

Chef: Ron Maxfield
Proprietor: John Tham

Seats: 72. No pipes or cigars in the restaurant
Additional: Children welcome; children's portions/menu; ❾ dishes; Vegan/other diets on request. Pianist

WOOBURN COMMON, Chequers Inn ❀

Kiln Lane
Map no: 4 SU98
Tel: 01628 529575
Chef: Ian Price
Proprietor: Peter Roehrig
Seats: 60
Times: Last L 2.30pm/D 9.30pm

A very popular village inn, full of atmosphere. A wide choice of English and French cuisine is offered in the restaurant, with a good value fixed-price menu and a comprehensive carte. Our meal included shellfish bisque, venison with a port sauce, then iced parfait of walnuts and Grand Marnier.

Cost: Alc £25; fixed-price L £14.95/D £17.95 ♀ Service exc
Credit cards: 1 2 3. **Additional:** Children welcome; ❂ menu; Vegan/other diets on request
Directions: From High Wycombe, 2 miles along A40 turn left into Broad Lane, hotel 2.5 miles on right

CAMBRIDGESHIRE

ALWALTON, Swallow ❀

Lynchwood, Alwalton, Peterborough
Map no: 4 TL19
Tel: 01733 371111
Chef: Sydney Aldridge
Proprietor: Richard Scoble
Seats: 70, 80. No-smoking area. Air conditioned
Times: Last L 2pm/D 9.45pm

Situated opposite the East of England Showground, this hotel's rosette goes to the Emperor restaurant which offers serious modern French cuisine prepared by chef Sidney Aldridge. He also changes the menu every week unless you choose the fixed-priced menu, adding variety to the restaurant's assets.

Cost: Alc £36, fixed-price L £13.50, £14.50/D £18.50, £20.50. H/wine £9 ♀ Service exc. **Credit cards:** 1 2 3 4
Additional: Children welcome; children's menu/portions; ❂ menu; vegan/other diets on request
Directions: Situated on A605 opposite East of England Showground

BYTHORN, Bennett's ❀

The White Hart
Map no: 4 TL07
Tel: 01832 710 226
Chef: William Bennett
Proprietor: William Bennett
Seats: 50. No smoking in the dining room
Times: Last L 2pm/D 10pm. Closed Mon

☺ In the friendly, relaxed atmosphere of a restaurant that is part traditional bar and part conservatory dining area, guests can enjoy a short straightforward three-course menu which exhibits sound basic culinary skills. The wine list is both conservative and short, but draught beer is available.

Cost: Alc £23.50. Service inc
Credit cards: 1 3
Additional: Children welcome; children's portions; ❂ dishes; Vegan/other diets on request
Directions: Take A14 to Bythorn, centre of village on right

CAMBRIDGE, **Cambridge Lodge** ❀

A small, elegant hotel with a range of places for eating, from bar snacks in the lounge bar to the more formal restaurant. Chef Peter Reynolds offers an imaginative range of dishes through the daily and carte menus, including roulade of chicken with creamed horseradish sauce.

Cost: *Alc* £25; fixed-price L £9.95 (3 courses), £14.95/D £19.95. Wine £8.95. Service exc
Credit cards: 1 2 3 4 5
Additional: Children permitted before 8.30pm; children's portions; ❍ menu; Vegan/other diets on request
Directions: One mile north west of city on A1307

139 Huntingdon Road
Map no: 5 TL45
Tel: 01223 352833
Chef: Peter Reynolds
Proprietors: Sheila Hipwell and Darren Chamberlain
Seats: 74. No smoking in dining room before 9pm. No pipes or cigars in restaurant
Times: Last L 1.45pm/D 9.30pm. Closed 27–31 Dec

CAMBRIDGE, **Garden House** ❀

Sitting by the River Cam near the city centre, the hotel's restaurant Le Jardin has a good selection of modern and classical international dishes prepared by Alan Fuller from the freshest ingredients. An example main course is pastry horn cascading with shellfish in a seaweed and saffron sauce.

Cost: *A la carte* from £24; fixed-price L £17.95/D £21.50. Wine £10.95 ♀ Service exc. **Credit cards:** 1 2 3 4
Additional: Children permitted; ❍ dishes; Vegan/other diets on request
Directions: Down Trumpington Street, turn left into Mill Lane

Granta Place, Mill Lane
Map no: 5 TL45
Tel: 01223 63421
Chef: Alan Fuller
Proprietors: Queens Moat Houses. General Manager: Paul Breen
Seats: 130
Times: Last L 2pm, Last D 9.45pm

CAMBRIDGE, **Midsummer House** ❀❀❀

A serious place to eat and have a good time, with skilful cooking, exciting combinations and a great wine list

What might be a hungry student's loss is definitely a local foodie's gain, since the conversion of this unassuming house into a fine restaurant. Most of the ground floor, with its large conservatory extension, and the first floor are occupied by various eating rooms. The formally dressed staff are friendly and will readily provide explanations and suggestions from the well researched wine list - the result of conscientious efforts by sommelier John Gilchrist.
  Major plaudits are reserved for German-trained chef and co-owner Hans Schweitzer, whose dishes show a precision of flavours and an innovative, slightly risky combination of ingredients which cannot fail to please. The menu changes every six weeks and offers nine starters, such as aumônières of snails with garlic and herb butter baked in filo pastry or scallops fried in star anise butter, or our inspector's choice, suprême of pigeon with foie gras in beetroot gelée with onion confit, a lovely, busy combination. This was followed, from a choice of six main courses, by bean cassoulet with braised salmon, young leeks and mashed potato, the dish moistened with a tomato, Chardonnay and butter sauce. Other options include fillet of beef on a hermitage sauce infused with horseradish, and grilled best end of lamb with ratatouille on a rosemary jus, but there are no vegetarian dishes listed. Desserts

Midsummer Common
Map no: 5 TL45
Tel: 01223 69299

Cost: Fixed-price dinner £24 (2 courses), £30, £36. Wine £18 ♀ Service exc
Credit cards: 1 2 3

Menus: Fixed-price dinner

Times: 12.15-Last L 2pm, 7.15-Last D 10pm. Closed Sat lunch, Sun eve, Mon

Chef: Hans Schweitzer
Proprietor: Hans Schweitzer

Seats: 65
Additional: Children welcome; ❍ dishes

show a practised continental skill and confidence which shines through to the wonderful petits fours served with coffee. Our inspector sampled spiced bread pudding with apples and sultanas, toffee sauce, and a light cardamom-flavoured ice cream – a heavenly combination of flavours.

The wine list is long, comprehensive, but clearly set out, with helpful descriptions. Prices are quite high, but the quality is exceptional and 18 wines are available by the glass.

Directions: Park (if possible) in Pretoria Road, off Chesterton Road, then walk across the footbridge to Midsummer House

DUXFORD, **Duxford Lodge** ☻

☺ *A red-brick house within a short distance of the M11 and the renowned Imperial War Museum. The reasonably priced menus show touches of originality. Above average commitment and skill on the part of the chef/proprietor combine to produce imaginative and popular meals.*

Cost: Alc £17; fixed-price L/D £15.65. Wine £9. Service exc
Credit cards: 1 2 3 4 5
Additional: Children welcome; children's portions; ☻ dishes; Vegan/other diets on request
Directions: Take A505 eastbound then 1st turning on right to Duxford. Take right fork at T-junction, Lodge 80 yds on left

Ickleton Road
Map no: 5 TL44
Tel: 01223 836444
Chef: Ronald Henry Craddock
Proprietors: Ronald Henry and Suzanne Joyce Craddock
Seats: 36. No smoking in dining room before 9pm. No pipes or cigars in restaurant
Times: Last L 2pm/D 9.30pm. Closed Sat lunch

ELY, **Old Fire Engine House** ☻

☺ *A well-established English restaurant combined with an art gallery, run by a family team. Roasts, pies and casseroles stay on the menu seasonally with an emphasis on local game and produce. British cooking, including an unusual salmon and mushroom gratin, attracts a loyal clientele.*

Cost: Alc £21; H/wine £7 ♀ Service exc. **Credit cards:** 1 3
Additional: Children welcome; children's portions; ☻ dishes; Vegan/other diets on request
Directions: Just off A10 from Cambridge about 200yds west of cathedral

25 Saint Mary's Street
Map no: 5 TL58
Tel: 01353 662582
Chef: Terri Kindred, Olive Fison
Proprietors: Ann Ford and Michael Jarman
Seats: 60. No-smoking area. No pipes or cigars in restaurant
Times: Last L 2pm/D 9pm. Closed Sun dinner, BHs, 2 weeks from 24 Dec

FOWLMERE, **The Chequers Inn** ☻

☺ *A fine old 16th-century inn which in years gone by has played host to the likes of Samuel Pepys and wartime RAF and American aircrews. Louis Gambie continues to cook a short set menu at lunch, plus blackboard bar meal choices. At dinner a more sophisticated choice of dishes is available.*

Cost: Alc £20; fixed-price L £14.35. Wine £8.95. Service exc. Cover charge 80p **Credit cards:** 1 2 3 4 **Additional:** Children welcome/ portions; ☻ dishes; Vegan/other diets on request
Directions: On B1368 between Royston and Cambridge, accessible by A10 and A505

Near Royston
Map no: 5 TL44
Tel: 01763 208369
Chef: Louis Gambie
Proprietors: Norman Stephenson Rushton
Seats: 70
Times: Last L 2pm/D 10pm. Closed Xmas Day

KEYSTON, Pheasant Inn ❀

☺ *A delightful thatched village inn with a new chef, Roger Jones, who has changed the menu to reflect his modern British style of cooking. Well prepared, interesting dishes concentrate on strong flavours and quality local produce, with fish well represented and a choice of vegetarian dishes.*

Cost: Alc £20.25. H/wine £10 ♀ Service exc
Credit cards: 1 2 3 4 5. **Additional:** Children permitted (no babies); children's portions; ◐ dishes; Vegan/other diets on request
Directions: Take the B663 off the A14 into village, the Inn sits behind the church

Near Huntingdon
Map no: 4 TL07
Tel: 01832 710241
Chef: Roger Jones
Proprietors: Poste. Manager: Roger Jones
Seats: 100. No smoking
Times: Last L 2pm/D 10pm

MELBOURN, Sheen Mill ❀❀

A peaceful waterside restaurant with rooms serving enjoyable, uncomplicated modern cooking

A beautiful, restored 17th-century watermill offers an idyllic setting for a meal in truly peaceful surroundings. The large, attractive restaurant, nestling in secluded countryside on the Cambridgeshire/Hertfordshire borders, looks out over the River Mel which is floodlit by night. There's a professional, no-frills approach to the food which is displayed on a monthly-changing fixed-price menu and a seasonally-adjusted carte; dishes like French onion soup or terrine of calf's livers with onion confit might begin a meal, followed perhaps by leg of lamb steak with a red wine and rosemary jus, or ballotine of chicken stuffed with wild mushrooms and garlic. Our inspector enjoyed a fresh and well-made leek and basil tartlet with Parmesan and a faultless chive butter sauce, and rather tough tenderloin of pork with Meaux mustard sauce attractively served with a tiny brunoise of tomato. A crème brûlée was rich and creamy, with alternatives such as terrine of chocolate with fresh figs and a mint syrup, and hot peppered pineapple in caramel with vanilla ice cream. Vegetarian and flambéed dishes are also served.

Directions: Take 2nd exit on A10 Melbourn by-pass signed Melboourn. Sheen Mill is 300yds down Station Road on the right

Station Road
Map no: 5 TL34
Tel: 01763 261393

Cost: Alc £25, fixed-price lunch £14.95, fixed-price dinner £21.50. H.wine £8.35. Service exc
Credit cards: 1 2 3 4

Menus: A la carte, fixed-price lunch and dinner, Sunday lunch, bar lunch menu

Times: Midday-Last L 2pm, 7pm-Last D 10pm. Dinner not served Sun. Closed BHs

Chef: Jonathan Curtis
Proprietor: C G D Cescutti

Seats: 110. No pipes or cigars
Additional: Children welcome; children's portions; ◐ menu; Vegan/other diets on request

MELBOURN, The Pink Geranium ❀❀

Superb classic cooking in an unusual 'pink' environment, where the service smacks of a formal training

This pink, thatched and timbered cottage nestles near the centre of the quiet village. The ground floor is largely occupied by comfortable armchairs where guests are encouraged to linger before and after a meal. Steven Saunders, trained in the Savoy group and France, is an energetic individual who presides over a busy establishment and still finds time to write informative articles for a magazine. The daily-changing menus (lunch and dinner) and a short carte reflect the use of classic skills. The dedicated kitchen brigade clearly enjoy working with

Station Road
Map no: 5 TL34
Tel: 01763 260215

Cost: Alc £41.25, fixed-price £24.95
Credit cards: 1 2 3 5

Menus: A la carte, fixed-price, Sunday lunch

Times: Midday-Last L 2.30pm, 7pm-Last D 10.30pm. Closed all day Mon, Sun eve

ingredients such as fresh tuna which is seared and served as an original salade Niçoise or globe artichokes served with mushroom and corn salad. Main courses are served with well executed sauces have extra flourishes which stamps some character on the dishes: for example salmon with pimento butter sauce or tender slices of lamb with a rich olive jus. The desserts do not disappoint nor does the patissier skimp on the appetising petits fours. The wine list reads like a roll call of French nobility, along with a few from the New World.

Chef: Philip Guest
Proprietors: Steven and Sally Saunders

Seats: 65. No smoking in the dining area
Additional: Children welcome; ❂ dishes

Directions: On A10 between Royston and Cambridge. In the centre of the village, opposite the church

SIX MILE BOTTOM, **Swynford Paddocks** ❀

Map no: 5 TL55
Tel: 01638 570234
Chef: Patrick Collins
Proprietor: P Evans
Times: Last L 2pm/D 9.30pm. L not served Sat

An elegant mansion surrounded by paddocks and well tended gardens. Chef Patrick Collins offers imaginative menus of country Irish and French cuisine. Starters include cassoulet of snails with salad and prawn cocktail and try ragout of duckling with cranberry and orange sauce as a main course.

Cost: Alc £32, fixed-price £28. H/wine £8.95 **Credit cards:** 1 2 3 4
Directions: Six miles south-west of Newmarket on A1304

CHESHIRE

ALDERLEY EDGE, **Alderley Edge** ❀

Macclesfield Road
Map no: 7 SJ87
Tel: 01625 583033
Chef: Brian Joy
Proprietors: Ahmet Kurcer
Seats: 80. No pipes in restaurant
Times: Last L 2pm/D 10pm

Home-made breads, robustly flavoured soups and classic French dishes served with fresh seasonal vegetables are the strengths of this attractive restaurant - part of a beautiful house set in large landscaped gardens. Both carte and fixed-price menus are available, and the wine list is extensive.

Cost: Alc £26; fixed-price L £11.50 (2 courses), £16.50/D £20.50. Wine £11.95 ♀ Service 12.5% **Credit cards:** 1 2 3 4
Additional: Children permitted; children's portions; ❂ menu; Vegan/other diets on request
Directions: Follow signs for Alderley Edge on the B5087 Macclesfield Road

BOLLINGTON, **Mauro's** ❀❀

88 Palmerston Street
Map no: 7 SJ97
Tel: 01625 573898

☺ *Enjoyable Italian cooking served in a cheerful setting with a Mediterranean ambience*

There's a light, Mediterranean atmosphere at the new-look Mauro's now, where a sunny yellow background provides a

Cost: Alc £21, Sunday lunch £14.75. H/wine £8.30. Service exc

cheerful foil for the stunning green furniture hand-painted with floral and fruit designs. In this attractive setting, where arches have been strategically added to enhance the warm Continental ambience, chef/proprietor Vincenzo Mauro's authentic Italian cooking continues to please. A new bar is proving popular with lunch-time diners who find the bar snacks speedy and inexpensive, while in the evening the extra table space is quickly taken up. Vincenzo offers an interesting *carte* which covers the usual range of 'pollo' (chicken), 'carne' (meat), and 'pesci' (fish), as well as pasta which can be taken either as starters or main courses. In addition, there are a couple of daily specials at each course, which might be 'ravioli al funghi selvaggie' – home-made ravioli stuffed with wild mushrooms and cheese in a creamy sauce, and 'vitello del fiume' – escalopes of veal with smoked salmon in a delicate dill and white wine sauce. A good selection of wines covers all the Italian regions.

Credit cards: 1 2 3

Menus: *A la carte* , Sunday lunch

Times: Midday-Last L 2pm, Last D 10pm. Closed Sun except first Sun of every month for lunch

Chef: Vincenzo Mauro
Proprietor: Vincenzo Mauro

Seats: 55
Additional: Children welcome; children's portions ◐ dishes; Vegan/other diets on request

Directions: Situated on the main street of the village, at the Pott Shrigley end

BROXTON, **Broxton Hall** ❀

☺ *A half-timbered Tudor house set in five acres of grounds south of Chester. Chef Jim Makin displays an imaginative international cuisine with a fixed-price menu, and a carte available at lunch only. Dishes might include fish soup, carbonnade of beef and an inviting array of desserts.*

Cost: *Alc* £18; fixed-price L £12.90/D £22.90. Wine £9.75. Service exc. **Credit cards:** 1 2 3 4
Additional: Children permitted; children's portions; ◐ dishes; Vegan/other diets on request. Pianist Sat eve
Directions: On A41 between Whitchurch and Chester, where the A41 crosses the A54

Whitchurch Road
Map no: 7 SJ45
Tel: 01829 782321
Chef: Jim Makin
Proprietor: Rosemary Hadley
Seats: 60. No pipes or cigars in restaurant
Times: Last L 2pm/D 9.30pm. Closed Xmas Day

CHESTER, **The Chester Grosvenor** ❀❀❀

Artistically presented French and modern British cuisine in an elegant hotel restaurant with a brasserie alternative

At this magnificent old hotel in the centre of Chester, the Arkle restaurant has achieved a reputation for outstanding cuisine under chef Paul Reed. The style of food keeps well abreast of trends, and the carte is a thoughtful interpretation of modern cooking. The menu changes with the seasons, and the fish dishes are dependent on the daily markets. There is something for everyone, though seafood and offal are strong suits, and portions are healthy. Fixed-price lunch menus are also offered, and a six-course Menu Gourmand.
In the cocktail bar there are good hot and cold canapés, and at the table an impressive trolley of home-made breads is served with lovely butter. Our inspectors have tasted starters of mushroom risotto with a creamy sauce, and salad of local rabbit, cooked and presented in three separate ways and dressed with different oils. Among the main courses beautiful steamed sea-bass was a clear highlight, served on a bed of

Eastgate Street
Map no: 7 SJ46
Tel: 01244 324024

Cost: *Alc* £46.25; fixed-price lunch £18 (2-courses), £22.50; fixed-price dinner £37. Wine £10.50 ♀ Service exc
Credit cards: 1 2 3 4

Menus: *A la carte*, fixed-price lunch and dinner, Sunday lunch, Brasserie, pre-theatre

Times: Midday-Last L 2.30pm, 7pm–Last D 9.30pm. Closed Sun dinner, Mon lunch, Xmas eve, 2 weeks (excluding New Year's Eve)

macaroni flavoured with Parmesan and accompanied by good girolles, plump langoustines and a smooth shellfish sauce. On another occasion, baked red mullet, marginally overcooked but nonetheless enjoyable, came on a lightly spiced couscous with coriander. For dessert, 'gâteau chaud au chocolat' was attractively presented, covered in a dark chocolate sauce and set on a white chocolate sauce. An apricot soufflé sprang, full of flavour, from a pastry case and was served with ginger ice cream and a wicked concoction of caramelised nuts and apricots. Less formal dining is provided by Le Brasserie, along the front of the hotel. The extensive wine list is first class. A lot of space is devoted to Champagne, Burgundy and Bordeaux, but most other wine regions are represented too. The reduced list for the Brasserie is less expensive and entirely French.

Chefs: Paul Reed, Simon Radley
Proprietors: Small Luxury Hotels of the World. Managing Director: Jonathan W Slater

Seats: 45. No cigars or pipes in restaurant. Air conditioned
Additional: Children permitted; children's menu; ♥ menu; Vegan/other diets on request. Pianist in the evening.

Directions: In city centre adjacent to the Eastgate Clock

CHESTER, **Crabwall Manor** ❀❀

A successful combination of English and French dishes in an elegant manor house setting

Traditional English cooking with a classical French influence aptly describes the food served at this country manor house hotel which began its days as a Tudor farmhouse. Now a much-extended Grade II listed building, it offers elegant accommodation, and an attractive restaurant with views out over the garden. Chef Michael Truelove has produced a well-balanced *carte*, which ranges through meat and game to a strong emphasis on fish and a serious consideration for vegetarians. Starters might include thinly sliced scallops dressed with fruity olive oil and sweet basil, or salad of goat's cheese and pine kernels, dressed with walnut oil. Main course meat choices could be roast best end of lamb served with thyme jus and onion and shallot confit, or medallions of matured Scottish beef fillet with asparagus and red wine sauce, with perhaps poached salmon with hollandaise, and fillets of red mullet. There's no set menu, and lunch is only served on Sundays; such is this place's popularity that booking for non-residents is always essential.

Parkgate Road, Mollington
Map no: 7 SJ46
Tel: 01244 851666

Cost: *A*l*c* £25, Sunday lunch £14.50, H/wine £12. Service exc
Credit cards: 1 2 3 4 5

Menus: *A la carte,* Sunday lunch

Times: Midday-Last L 2pm, 7pm-Last D 9.30pm

Chef: Michael Truelove
Proprietor: Carl Lewis

Seats: 85. No smoking in dining room. Air conditioned

Directions: Set back from the A540 north of Chester

CHESTER, **Moat House International** ❀

The large Paddocks restaurant in this modern, city centre hotel enjoys views towards the hills and mountains of North Wales. The short fixed-price menu offers a good choice, priced by the number of courses. There is an appetising carte selection of grills, roasts, flambé and vegetarian dishes.

Trinity Street
Map no: 7 SJ46
Tel: 01244 322330
Chef: Paul Kerr
Proprietor: Manager: Bruce Wragg
Seats: 150. No-smoking area. Air conditioned
Times: Last L 2pm (Sun only)/D 10.30pm. Closed Xmas, New Year

Cost: *A*l*c* £25; fixed-price lunch £13.50 (2 courses), £18; fixed-price dinner £13.50 (2 courses), £18. Wine £9.45 ♀ Service exc
Credit cards: 1 2 3 4. **Additional:** Children welcome portions/menu; ♥ menu; Vegan/other diets on request. Live entertainment (Dec)
Directions: Off main road through Chester, next to Gateway Theatre

CHESTER, **Mollington Banastre** ❀

A formal, but relaxed, setting at The Garden Room restaurant, where classic and modern menus offer a comprehensive choice of dishes complemented by an extensive international wine list.

Cost: Alc £25.50; fixed-price L £10.95/D £20.50. Wine £9.95. Service inc **Credit cards:** 1 2 3 4. **Additional:** Children welcome; children's portions/menu; ❂ menu; Vegan/other diets on request. Pianist (Fri, Sat)
Directions: Bear left at end of M56 onto A5117, left at roundabout onto A540, the hotel is 2 miles on the right

Parkgate Road
Map no: 7 SJ46
Tel: 01244 851471
Chef: Ron Knox
Proprietor: Best Western.
Manager: John Mawdsley
Seats: 80. No-smoking area
Times: Last L 2pm/D 9.45pm

CHESTER, **The Gateway To Wales** ❀

☺ *The hotel's Regency restaurant offers carte, flambé and fixed-price menus in an uncrowded and relaxing setting. A blend of traditional and modern cooking gives a range of dishes such as chilled cucumber and mint soup with pork fillet wrapped in bacon with a spiced berry sauce to follow.*

Cost: Alc from £18; fixed-price L £6.99/D £14.50. H/wine £8.25. Service exc. **Credit cards:** 1 2 3 4 5. **Additional:** Children welcome/portions/menu; ❂ menu; Vegan/other diets on request
Directions: Three and a half miles outside the city centre near the junction of the A550 and A494. Close to RAF Sealand

Welsh Road, Sealand, Deeside
Map no: 7 SJ46
Tel: 01244 830332
Chef: Patrick Schmider
Proprietor: Deborah K Harford
Seats: 50. No smoking in dining room. Air conditioned
Times: Last L 2.30pm/D 9.30pm

KNUTSFORD, **La Belle Époque** ❀

Paris's 'beautiful age' lives on in this lovingly restored Edwardian showpiece, its intimate alcoves and art nouveau deco, a romantic setting for a meal. Typically British cuisine includes regional dishes like black pudding, tripe cooked in cider and fish with chips and mushy peas.

Cost: Alc £24. ♀ Service exc. **Credit cards:** 1 2 3 4 5
Additional: Children over 7 permitted at dinner; children's portions; ❂ dishes; Vegan/other diets on request
Directions: 2 miles from junction 19 on motorway (M6)

60 King Street
Map no: 7 SJ77
Tel: 01565 633060
Chefs: Graham Codd and David Mooney
Proprietors: Keith and Nerys Mooney
Seats: 100. No pipes
Times: Last L 2pm/D 10.30pm. Closed Sun, BHs

KNUTSFORD, **The Longview** ❀❀

☺ *Some very good value food with authentic flavours and more than a touch of individuality*

A charming end-of-terrace house with views across Knutsford Heath is the setting for this attractive Victorian style restaurant with an ever-growing reputation for fine food. Once the home of a local merchant, it is now a comfortable period hotel, serving quality British and Continental food reflecting the individuality of chef James Falconer-Flint. His frequently changing, set three-course menus offer good value and variety, with starters like mussels filled with smoked bacon or grilled oysters with a mango, lumpfish roe and spinach sauce, and main

Manchester Road
Map no: 7 SJ77
Tel: 01565 632119

Cost: Alc £19. Wine £7.25 ♀
Service exc
Credit cards: 1 2 3 4

Menus: A la carte, fixed-price dinner, bar menu (supper)

Times: 7pm Last D 9pm. Closed Sun, Xmas and New Year

courses such as a richly traditional fillet of venison with brandy, cream and wild mushrooms, or grilled fillet of pork. Our inspector enjoyed a delicious dish of crab meat and scallops in a garlic cream sauce served on a bed of rice, followed by tender slices of French duck breast in a very good sauce of plums, Madeira and angostura bitters. An enticing dessert was a layered chocolate sponge with a coffee cream sauce, chosen from a generous list including rich Bakewell tart and luxury cream and seasonal fruit shortbread.

Directions: Overlooking Knutsford Heath, left of the A50 travelling in a southerly direction, just before the town square

Chefs: James Falconer-Flint, Yvonne Burke
Proprietors: Pauline and Stephen West

Seats: 40. Guests requested to refrain from smoking in dining room
Additional: Children welcome; children's portions; ✿ menu; Vegan/other diets on request

KNUTSFORD, The Toft, Dick Willett's ✿

☺ *A good range of imaginative dishes is offered from the entirely vegetarian menu at Dick Willett's, the hotel restaurant. The carte has fulsome descriptions of each item, such a delicious nut and wine pâté served with toasted olive oil bread, and tasty 'burrito refritto' filled tortillas.*

Cost: Alc £16.95; fixed-price dinner £16.95. H/wine £10 ♀ Cover charge 10% for parties of 6 and over. Service exc
Credit cards: 1 2 3 5 **Additional:** Children over 10 permitted; ✿ menu
Directions: One mile south of Knutsford on the A50

Toft Road
Map no: 7 SJ77
Tel: 01565 634443
Chef: Jean Davies
Proprietors: Jean and Tony Davies
Seats: 50. No Smoking
Times: Last D 9.30pm. Closed Mon, Tues, Wed, Sun

NANTWICH, Churche's Mansion ✿✿

☺ *Modern British cooking with French and Italian influences, and a healthy obsession with perfect ingredients*

Hand-picked ingredients from the very best local suppliers form the raw material for Graham Tucker's cooking, and the results are remarkable. He uses Welsh lamb, Black beef, asparagus from a local farmer, a French neighbour who grows authentic Gallic vegetables and salad leaves, a cheese enthusiast who buys top-quality unpasteurised produce from all over the country – the list is endless. In the historic setting of an ornately timbered house which survived a fire and narrowly avoided being shipped to America, it is no surprise that diners are enchanted by the pronounced flavours of the modern British food they enjoy. The fixed-price menus change monthly to take account of fresh seasonal produce, and French and Italian undertones can be detected in the attractive dishes. Winter and early spring might see home-made black pudding with mashed potatoes, and shank of lamb on parsnip purée with flageolet beans, while summer choices might be tortellinis of crayfish with citrus vinaigrette, and seared red mullet on a Caesar salad with polenta croûtons. Puddings are highly imaginative.

Directions: Near the town centre at a roundabout on the junction of the Crewe/Stoke-on-Trent road

Hospital Street
Map no: 7 SJ65
Tel: 01270 625933

Cost: Fixed-price lunch £11.50 (2 courses), £14; fixed-price dinner £22. H/wine £9.25. Service exc
Credit cards: 1 3 4

Menus: Fixed-price lunch and dinner, light lunch

Times: Last L 2.30pm, 7pm-Last D 9.30pm. Dinner not served Sun. Closed Mon, 2nd week J

Chef: Graham Tucker
Proprietors: Robin Latham, Amanda Latham

Seats: 50. No cigars or pipes in the dining room
Additional: No children under 10 at dinner; children's portions; ✿ menu

NANTWICH, **Rookery Hall** 🌸

An impressive mansion surrounded by 200 acres of parkland, this hotel offers a fixed-price menu and a carte. The chef cooks imaginative dishes such as Brie and wild mushrooms on a lime pine kernel salad and, as a main course, suprême of chicken with capsicum honey sauce.

Cost: Alc £25, fixed-price dinner £25. H/wine from £11.95
Additional: 🌣 dishes
Directions: On the B5074 north of Nantwich

Worleston
Map no: 7 SJ65
Tel: 01270 626027
Chef: David Alton
Proprietors: P E Parker

PUDDINGTON, **Craxton Wood** 🌸🌸

☺ *Classic French cooking with English descriptions served in a relaxed country house setting.*

At night the streams and woods are floodlit, while in the daytime the beautiful rose gardens and spacious lawns can be enjoyed at this delightful country house hotel. The restaurant is decorated in delicate colours to provide an unobtrusive setting for the French cooking of James Minnis, a classically-trained chef who has perfected his craft in several countries. Fish always features on the *carte* and fixed-price four course menus, selected in the early hours at Liverpool fish market twice a week.

There is also an appealing vegetarian menu, offering such dishes as 'mille-feuille de poireau et carottes', layers of filo pastry filled with leeks and carrots with a bitter orange sabayon, and 'lasagne de lentilles'; layers of pasta filled with lentil purée and a fresh tomato sauce. Non-veggies might enjoy roasted monkfish tails with puréed leeks and spinach and a red pepper sauce, or fillet of beef with a truffle-flavoured mushroom sauce. Classic French desserts are tempting like 'mousse au chocolate' on a pistachio sauce, and a fine choice of English and French cheeses like Chèvre and Tomme.

Directions: Entrance on the A540 Chester to Hoylake road shortly after crossing the A550

Parkgate Road
Map no: 7 SJ37
Tel: 0151-339 4717

Cost: Fixed-price lunch and dinner £19.85. H/wine £12.85 ♀
Service inc
Credit cards: 1 2 3 4 5

Menus: A la carte, fixed-price lunch and dinner

Times: Midday-Last L 2pm, Last D 10pm. Closed Sun and BHs, last 2 weeks Aug, 1st week Jan

Chef: James Minnis
Proprietor: Médard-Anthony Petranca

Seats: 85. No pipes
Additional: Children welcome; children's portions; 🌣 menu, other diets on request.

SANDIWAY, **Nunsmere Hall** 🌸🌸🌸

An elegant country house setting for imaginative modern menus of elaborately presented, multi-sauced dishes

A sympathetically extended country house, this elegant hotel is set in wooded grounds on a peninsula surrounded on three sides by a lake. A striking feature of the house is the extensive use of wood, including the handsome new oak panelling. There is a formal atmosphere in the attractive dining room, and service is attentive and correct.

Chef Paul Kitching presents a fixed-price lunch menu, an interesting three-course dinner menu, priced according to the main course choice, and a set seven-course Menu Dégustation. His style is modern, emphasising the delicate flavours of good seafood in dishes such as confit of smoked salmon, smoked

Tarporley Road
Map no: 7 SJ67
Tel: 01606 889100

Cost: Alc from £26; fixed-price lunch £14.95 (2 courses), £17.50; fixed-price dinner £42.50. Wine £12.25. Service exc
Credit cards: 1 2 3 4 5

Menus: A la carte, fixed-price lunch, Sunday lunch, lounge/terrace menu, bar menu

Times: Midday-Last L 2pm,

haddock and poached salmon with three dressings, and grilled baby Cornish sea-bass with pea purée, herb noodles, grilled scallops and a beetroot and herb cream sauce. More robust flavours are developed in a game terrine bound with a chicken and orange mousse, served with a confit of apricots, chives and shallots; and roast fillet of Scottish beef with a rich port sauce, chive and Dijon mustard cream sauce. Vegetarian dishes can be provided on request.

Our inspector sampled a poached fillet of Cornish turbot with a Russian salad in a chive cream sauce topped with Sevruga caviar. This was followed by roast saddle of venison with a ragout of winter vegetables and a truffle and Madeira sauce. An enjoyable dish, though the farmed venison lacks the gamey flavour of its wild counterpart. The pudding was a rich, marbled chocolate truffle torte with raspberry cream sauce and a garnish of whole raspberries in their own syrup.

The wine list is good and of about the right length, containing selections from most regions. The house wines start at £12.25 a bottle and the Connoisseurs Selection lists some fine Burgundy and claret.

Directions: From Sandiway take the A49, Nunsmere Hall is one mile on the left

7pm-Last D 10pm

Chef: Paul Kitching
Proprietors: Malcolm and Julie McHardy

Seats: 48. No smoking in the dining room
Additional: Children welcome; children's portions; ✪ menu; Vegan/other diets on request. Harpist (Sat eve)

WILMSLOW, **Stanneylands** ✤

This much-extended country house dates back to the turn of the century. Chef Matthew Barrett's carte is imaginative, including fresh lobster on young spinach leaves with a warm Viennoise dressing. There is a good selection of interesting vegetables, including spinach mousse.

Cost: Alc £32; fixed-price L £12.50/D £25. H/wine £9 ♀ Service exc.
Credit cards: 1 2 3 4
Additional: Children welcome; children's portions/menu; ✪ menu; Vegan/other diets on request. Harpist
Directions: Junction off A34 between Wilmslow and Handforth, bear right to the find hotel just after crossing River Dean

Stanneylands Road
Map no: 7 SJ88
Tel: 01625 525225
Chef: Matthew Barrett
Proprietor: Mr G L Beech
Seats: 80. No cigars or pipes in restaurant. Partially air conditioned
Times: Last L 2pm/D 10pm. Closed 26 Dec2 Jan

CLEVELAND

EASINGTON, **Grinkle Park** ❀

☺ *At this Victorian mansion set in woody parkland, the elegant dining room makes an ideal backdrop for meticulously presented English/French cooking of high quality based on local produce.*

Cost: Fixed-price L £9/D £15.95. Wine £8. Service exc
Credit cards: 1 2 3 4
Additional: Children welcome; children's portions; ❂ dishes; Vegan/other diets on request
Directions: Between Guisborough and Whitby off A171

Saltburn-by-the-Sea
Map no: 8 NZ71
Tel: 01287 640515
Chef: Tim Backhouse
Proprietor: Bass. Manageress: Mrs Jane Norton
Seats: 80
Times: Last L 1.45pm/D 9pm (Sun–Thurs) 9.30pm (Fri, Sat)

HARTLEPOOL, **Krimo's** ❀

☺ *Good value Mediterranean cuisine is offered at this popular seafront restaurant. Dishes might include Algerian Boureks (filo pastry parcels of spicy minced fillet beef), sole stuffed with trout mousse with a creamy tomato sauce, a vegetarian dish of mushroom paesano, and light apple pancakes.*

Cost: Alc £19, fixed-price L £6/D £13.95 (parties of 8 or over). Wine £6.95. Service exc
Credit cards: 1 3. **Additional:** Children welcome; children's portions; ❂ dishes; Vegan/other diets on request
Directions: Two miles from Hartlepool, on the A178, situated on the seafront

8 The Front, Seaton Carew
Map no: 8 NZ53
Tel: 01429 266120
Chef: Krimo Bouabda
Proprietors: Krimo and Karen Bouabda
Seats: 56. Air conditioned
Times: Last L 1.30pm/D 9pm. Closed Sun, Mon, Sat lunch, first 2 weeks Aug, Xmas, New Year, BHs

STOCKTON-ON-TEES, **Parkmore** ❀

☺ *Popular with visiting business guests, this hotel is located at Eaglescliffe near Stockton. It offers international cuisine with a good selection of extensive menus, ranging from samosas and tacos to Whitby cod or beef and prawn chow mein. Carte choices are imaginative and include fish and chargrills.*

Cost: Alc £19.70; fixed-price L £12.25/D £16.75. Wine £7.25. Service exc
Credit cards: 1 2 3 4 5
Additional: Children permitted; children's portions/menu; ❂ menu; Vegan/other dishes on request
Directions: On the A135 between Yarm and Stockton-on-Tees

636 Yarm Road, Eaglescliffe
Map no: 8 NZ41
Tel: 01642 786815
Chef: Dennis Ginsberg
Proprietor: Best Western. Manager: Brian Reed
Seats: 70. No smoking in dining room
Times: Last L 2pm/D 9.45pm

CORNWALL & ISLES OF SCILLY

BLACKWATER, **Pennypots** ❁❁

Adventurous modern British cooking with interesting flavours and combinations

A quick glance at the carte at this pretty 18th-century restaurant shows the extent to which unusual and often exotic flavours are introduced into otherwise mainstream dishes. Chef/proprietor Kevin Viner cooks in an adventurous manner under the banner of 'modern British', and judging by the popularity of this place and the consequent need to book, his recipes are very well received. Dishes like chicken liver pâté with toasted brioche, served with pear chutney and caramelised oranges might number amongst the starters, or perhaps pan-fried scallops on a tagliatelli of cucumber with a fresh garlic and basil butter might demonstrate the freshness of locally-caught sea food. Other main courses may be red mullet grilled in sesame seed oil, on a light soy sauce flavoured with fresh coriander and ginger or fillet of pan-fried beef with a Madeira and wild mushroom sauce. Desserts are a speciality of the restaurant, and might include cinnamon soufflé with plums sautéed in brandy, served with apricot-flavoured ice cream, or light lemon mousse with blueberry sauce and Amaretto ice cream.

Directions: Just off the A30, under a mile from village centre

Near Truro
Map no: 2 SW74
Tel: 01209 820347

Cost: Alc £23. H/wine £7.50. Service exc

Menu: A la carte

Times: 7pm-Last D 10pm. Lunch not served. Closed Sun and Mon and 4 weeks in winter

Chef: Kevin Viner
Proprietors: Kevin and Jane Viner

Seats: 30. No smoking in dining room until after 10pm
Additional: Children welcome; children's portions; ♥ dishes

CALSTOCK, **Danescombe Valley** ❁❁

Unpretentious food with a variety of influences, served in a tiny dining room in a secret hidden valley

Set on one of the most beautiful stretches of the River Tamar on a wooded bend facing south, this hotel is tucked into a hidden valley imbued with peace and tranquillity. Views over the river - with its distant Tamar viaduct – the woods and pasture can be enjoyed from all of the rooms, and bedrooms on the first floor have access on to a verandah. The exquisite cooking of Italian-born Anna Smith is largely self-taught, and dinner is undoubtedly the highlight of a stay here; when all the rooms are full the tiny restaurant cannot take non-residents. The four course no-choice fixed-price menu is perfectly balanced, and reflects the English, French and Italian influences which the chef acknowledges as Elizabeth David, Michel Guérard, and her mother. A typical meal might comprise locally smoked Tamar salmon, followed by guinea fowl stuffed with fennel and potatoes, and roasted with olives and garlic; fresh vegetables are locally grown. A choice of West Country unpasteurised farmhouse cheeses comes next and, to finish, compote of fruit with a ramekin of baked custard. The lengthy wine list is very well described.

Directions: Turn off the A30 to Calstock, under viaduct, past chapel, turn sharp right. Hotel on right after about 0.75 miles

Lower Kelly
Map no: 2 SX46
Tel: 01822 832414

Cost: Fixed-price dinner £27.50. H/wine £9
Credit cards: 1 2 3 4

Menus: Fixed-price

Times: 7.30pm. Closed Wed, Thu and Nov-end March

Chef: Anna Smith
Proprietors: Martin and Anna Smith

Seats: 12. No smoking in dining room
Additional: Children over 12 permitted

CONSTANTINE BAY, Treglos ❀

☺ Whoever built Treglos did so for the view along the spectacular coastline. Chef Paul Becker's five-course lunch and six-course dinner menus of traditional English dishes with Cornish specialities, continue to please, especially with more locally caught fish available.

Cost: Alc £21.50; fixed-price L £11.50/D £19.50. Wine £8.20. Service exc. **Credit cards:** 1 3 **Additional:** Children permitted (over 6 at dinner); children's menu; ❂ menu; Vegan/other diets on request
Directions: Take the B3276 and follow signs for Constantine Bay. At Constantine Bay stores turn left, hotel 50 yds on left

Map no: 2 SW87
Tel: 01841 520727
Chef: Paul Kevin Becker
Proprietors: Crown Consort.
Managers: Ted and Barbara Barlow, Jim and Rose Barlow
Seats: 100. No smoking in the dining room. Air conditioned
Times: Last L 2pm/D 9.30pm. Closed 6 Nov–12 Mar

FALMOUTH, Greenbank ❀

☺ Reputedly Falmouth's first hotel, situated in a delightful position right on the water's edge. Nightingale's restaurant, named after former guest Florence Nightingale, serves a fixed-price menu with unusual seasonal choices and an extensive carte which includes fish, game, grills and flambé dishes.

Cost: Alc £20, fixed-price L £9.50/D £17.50. H/wine £7.50. Service inc **Credit cards:** 1 2 3 4 5 **Additional:** Children welcome; children's portions; ❂ dishes; other diets on request
Directions: 500yds past Falmouth Marina overlooking the water

Harbourside
Map no: 2 SW83
Tel: 01326 312440
Chef: Mr Paul Prinn
Proprietors: Mr Nigel Gebhard/Mr N Tongue
Seats: 70
Times: Last L 2pm/D 9.45pm. Closed 24 Dec–15 Jan

FALMOUTH, Royal Duchy ❀

A fine period hotel ideally situated to enjoy south-facing views across the bay, close to the beaches and within walking distance of the town centre. An extensive selection of menus offer dishes for all tastes, including a good vegetarian choice, and an imaginative carte.

Cost: Alc £25; Fixed-price L £8.95/D £15.50. Wine £7.75. No service charge **Credit cards:** 1 2 3 4 5
Additional: Children welcome; children's portions/menu; ❂ menu; other diets on request. Live entertainment most evenings
Directions: Go through the town. At the Green Lawn Hotel turn right, at the end turn left towards seafront. Hotel is at castle end of promenade

Cliff Road
Map no: 2 SW83
Tel: 01326 313042
Chef: Desmond Turland
Proprietors: Brend. Manager: Darryl Reburn
Seats: 150
Times: Last L 2pm/D 9pm

FOWEY, Food for Thought ❀❀

Fine river and seafood, superb views, exposed stone and solid beams in a popular Cornish holiday town

A stevedore's image of a quayside would differ from that of Martin and Caroline Billingsley. To the former, it is a place for cranes and containers; to the Billingsleys it is a prime spot for a restaurant, especially one with a glorious view of the Fowey River. Unsurprisingly, fresh seafood features prominently, such as fish and shellfish soup, or fresh crab meat ravioli with a

The Quay
Map no: 2 SX15
Tel: 01726 832221

Cost: Alc £22, fixed-price dinner £16.95. H/wine £6.95
Credit cards: 1 3

Menus: A la carte, fixed-price dinner, Menu Exceptionnel lobster cream sauce – both possible starters. Bass from the river is grilled with hollandaise sauce and the sea delivers the John Dory, turbot, salmon, scallops and sole for a rendezvous cooked with white wine sauce. As a daily extra, tuna is brought in from the troubled Bay of Biscay and simply grilled with an olive oil sauce. Meats are cooked with just as much thought and care. There are usually three meat dishes on the *carte*, such as Scotch fillet steak with mushroom duxelle, hollandaise and Madeira sauce, rack of Cornish lamb, with a rosemary herb sauce and French duck breast, thinly sliced with a blackcurrant liqueur sauce. Clotted cream features on the dessert list and there are several house wines among the three score and ten bins.

Times: 7pm-Last D 9pm. Closed lunchtimes, Sun, Jan and Feb

Chef: Martin Billingsley
Proprietor: Martin Billingsley

Seats: 38
Additional: Children permitted; ❶ dish

Directions: Walk down to the quay from the town centre car park

FOWEY, **Marina Hotel** ❀

☺ *A charming Georgian residence where the elegance of the period has been retained, with a spectacular view from the Marina Restaurant. A range of interesting local seafood dishes are offered, such as pan-fried red snapper with lemon butter sauce or steak, kidney and oyster pie in a Guinness sauce.*

Cost: Alc £20, fixed-price D £16. H/wine £6.75. Service exc
Additional: Children over six at dinner; children's portions. ❶ dishes; Vegan/other diets on request
Directions: In Fowey, drive down Lostwithiel Street, turn right into the Esplanade by Mace grocers. Hotel 50yds on left

The Esplanade
Map no: 2 SX15
Tel: 01726 833315
Chef: Dean Rodgers
Proprietors: David and Sheila Johns
Seats: 28. No smoking in dining room
Times: Last D 8.30pm. Closed Nov-Feb

GOLANT, **Cormorant** ❀❀

Freshly produced French cooking, with shellfish always available, in a stunning setting above an estuary

In a picturesque riverside setting on the edge of the small fishing village of Golant, this peaceful hotel offers unforgettable views set high above the Fowey Estuary, with full length picture windows in the public rooms. The food here is another powerful magnet, however, and guests and non-residents alike are drawn to the candle-lit dining room to sample the day's dishes. The accent is on daily-caught seafood and the freshest local produce and French chef Gilles Gaucher prepares a carte and fixed-price menus with an imaginative choice. The six course Menu Gastronomique might feature slices of foie gras and apples lightly fried in butter and flamed in Calvados, and lightly roasted rack of lamb with a white wine and rosemary jus, while the four-course menu could offer chicken liver parfait, and fried calf's kidneys with a Dijon mustard sauce. Lobster and other shellfish are always available even when not shown on the menu, and to finish there's a rich selection of desserts like bread and butter pudding studded with apricots marinated in Cognac.

Directions: Off A390 (Lostwithiel to St Austell) turn to Golant. Go right to end (almost to water's edge), entrance on right

Near Fowey
Map no: 2 SX15
Tel: 01726 833426

Cost: Alc £30, fixed-price dinner £21.50 (4 courses), £29. Service exc
Credit cards: 1 2 3

Menus: *A la carte,* light lunch, fixed-price dinner

Times: Midday-Last L 2pm, 7pm-Last D 9pm. Closed Jan

Chef: Geoffrey Buckie, Gilles Gaucher
Proprietor: Sharon Buckle

Seats: 25. No smoking in restaurant
Additional: Children over 12 permitted; ❶ dishes; Vegan/other diets on request

HELFORD, **Riverside** ✹✹

A small intimate restaurant in a delightful location serving French dishes made from the freshest ingredients

Reached after a pretty journey down narrow Cornish lanes, and set in a picture postcard position above a tidal creek, this intimate restaurant is well worth discovering. The freshness of the food, especially the fish, is remarkable, and owner Susie Darrell converts it with great skill into enjoyable provincial French dishes which are often praised. Our inspector recently enjoyed a simple but well-made salmon tart starter with chive butter sauce, followed by pink breast of Barbary duck with a garlic and thyme red wine sauce which really complemented the meat flavour. A medley of spring vegetables, all with their natural flavour and colour intact, included new potatoes cooked in their skins, baby corn, mange-tout and sugar snap peas. The meal ended with a rich chocolate mousse flavoured with whisky and chopped hazelnuts, and coffee and petits fours served in the lounge area. Other dishes might include roast monkfish wrapped in Parma ham on a bed of creamed leeks, or baked fillet of hake topped with a potato and sesame seed crust with a horseradish and mustard sauce.

Directions: This restaurant is clearly signposted in Helford village

Map no: 2 SW72
Tel: 01326 231443

Cost: Fixed-price dinner £30. Wine £10 ♀ Service inc
Credit cards: None

Menu: Fixed-price dinner

Times: Last D 9.30pm

Chef: Susie Darrell
Proprietor: Edward and Susie Darrell

Seats: 32. No pipes or cigars
Additional: Children permitted (over 9); Vegetarian dishes on request

HELSTON, **Nansloe Manor** ✹

☺ *Dating back to 1735, this charming small hotel is set in four acres of wooded grounds and gardens. The carte changes daily, featuring local produce including meat, fish and game, all carefully prepared, with a good choice. Traditional desserts come with bowls of Cornish clotted cream.*

Cost: Alc £19; Sun L £10.50. Wine £8.50. No service charge
Credit cards: 1 3 **Additional:** Children permitted (over 10); ◐ dishes; Vegan/other diets on request
Directions: Off the A394 Helston–Lizard Road down a well-signed drive

Meneage Road
Map no: 2 SW62
Tel: 01326 574691
Chefs: Martin Jones, Wendy Pyatt
Proprietors: John and Wendy Pyatt
Seats: 30. No smoking in dining room
Times: Last bar L 1.45pm (Mon-Sat)/Sun L 1.15pm/D 8.30pm

LISKEARD, **Well House** ✹✹✹

A polished and professional approach to food in a delightfully rural setting

Quietly tucked away down a small lane deep in the Looe Valley, this lovely country house enjoys an idyllic setting in mature gardens and grounds. It was built at the turn of the century by a tea planter with an understanding of Cornish sunlight, and the rooms are bright and airy with their original refinement and character still intact. The restaurant enjoys a fine reputation for good food, and new chef Wayne Pearson produces dishes of outstanding quality using ingredients for which Cornwall is famous: fish and seafood appear on the two, three or four-course fixed-price menus, along with wild boar, partridge and local cheeses.

St Keyne
Map no: 2 SX26
Tel: 01579 342001

Cost: Alc £24.95, fixed-price lunch £19.95. H/wine £8.50
Credit cards: 1 3

Menus: A la carte, fixed-price lunch, Sunday lunch

Times: Last L 2pm, Last D 9pm

Chef: Wayne Pearson
Proprietor: Nick Wainford

Our inspector appreciated the chef's serious and professional approach to cooking during a recent meal, which began with tasty appetisers of warm puff pastry filled with crab mousse, and savoury tartlet of mushroom duxelle. A beautifully constructed ballottine of quail made a very enjoyable starter, the meat poached, boned and rolled, and stuffed with chicken and herb mousse, then served with various leaves and a sun-dried tomato with olive oil balsamic sauce. Medallions of monkfish topped with pesto and surrounded by a deliciously rich red pepper purée was another creation which earned praise, and came with vegetables cooked al dente to retain all their natural flavours.

Other available dishes might be steamed fillet of sea-bass with creamed spinach and chervil sauce, or for meat lovers perhaps pan-fried calf's liver with creamed tarragon potatoes and caramelised shallots, or roast magret of duck breast with braised red cabbage. Puddings offer further home-made temptation, and the marbled chocolate marquise with a coffee bean sauce was another culinary triumph. Owner Nick Wainford heads a dedicated and involved team.

Seats: 32. No pipes or cigars

Additional: Children under 8 not permitted at dinner; children's portions; ❂ dishes; Vegan/other diets on request

Directions: At St Keyne village church follow signs to St Keyne Well, where the restaurant is situated

MARAZION, **Mount Haven** ❂

☺ There are views over Mounts Bay and St Michael's Mount from this hotel, and the restaurant offers imaginative modern dishes with vegetarian choices. Chef Andy Smith cooks with some style, using fresh local produce, including fish from Newlyn and a tasty beef Stroganoff.

Cost: Alc £17.75; fixed-price L £7.75/D £15.25. Wine £6. Service exc **Credit cards:** 1 2 3. **Additional:** Children welcome; children's portions; ❂ dishes; Vegan/other diets on request
Directions: Approaching Penzance on the A30, take the turning for Marazion. Through the village, on the right at the end of the built-up area

Turnpike Road
Map no: 2 SW53
Tel: 01736 710249
Chef: Andy Smith
Proprietors: Minotels. Managers: John and Delyth James
Seats: 50. No smoking
Times: Last L 2pm/D 9pm (8.30pm NovMar). Closed L Nov–Mar, Xmas

MAWNAN SMITH, **Trelawne Hotel** ❂

☺ An atmospheric hotel situated on the beautiful Cornish coastline, where chefs Grant Mather and Nigel Woodland produce a varied carte. The food is imaginative, especially their salads. Main courses include butter-fried suprême of chicken served on a Stilton sauce.

Cost: Alc £22.50, fixed-price D £18.90. H/wine £7.50. Service inc **Additional:** Children welcome; children's menu/portions. ❂ dishes; Vegan/other diets on request
Directions: 3 miles S of Falmouth on coast road to Mawnan Smith

Near Falmouth
Map no: 2 SW72
Tel: 01326 250226
Chefs: Grant Mather, Nigel Woodland
Proprietor: G Paul Gibbons
Seats: 40. No smoking
Times: Last L 1.30pm/D 8.30pm. Closed Jan

MOUNT HAWKE, Tregarthen Country Cottage ☻

A delightful cottage-style hotel on the edge of the village providing a warm welcome. The accent is on comfort and the beamed lounge has deep armchairs set around a real fire. Traditional home-cooked dishes are chosen from a set menu and served in the well-appointed dining room.

Map no: 2 SW74
Tel: 01209 890399
Proprietors: Mr & Mrs C P Hutton

Directions: On the edge of the village

NEWBRIDGE, Enzo of Newbridge ☻

☺ The restaurant is housed in a plant-filled conservatory attached to a stone house owned and run by the Blows. Ann Blow cooks in full view of diners while her son cooks other dishes in the kitchen behind. A typical Italian menu, but everything is cooked with care and attention to flavour.

Cost: Alc £17; fixed-price D £17. H/wine £8.95. Service inc
Credit cards: 1 2 3 4. **Additional:** Children welcome; children's portions; ❶ dishes; Vegan/other diets on request
Directions: On A3071 in village of Newbridge

Map no: 2 SW43
Tel: 01736 63777
Chefs: Sybil Anne and Hamish Blows
Proprietors: W and S A Blows
Seats: 60. No–smoking area. No pipes or cigars in restaurant
Times: Last D 9.30pm. Closed Sun winter, 2 weeks early Nov

NEWQUAY, Whipsiderry ☻

☺ The imaginative use of fresh produce in this friendly little holiday hotel's fixed-price menus of English and continental dishes reflects chef Gabriel Patrick Evans's extensive travels. Advance booking is advisable (and essential for vegetarians). Fortunate guests could see badgers being fed at dusk.

Cost: Fixed-price dinner £18. Wine £7.50. Service exc
Credit cards: 1 3
Additional: Children welcome; children's portions; ❶ dishes; Vegan/other diets on request. Live entertainment
Directions: Half mile outside Newquay on coastal road to Padstow

Trevelgue Road, Porth
Map no: 2 SW86
Tel: 01637 874777
Chef: Gabriel Patrick Evans
Proprietors: R E and A H Drackford
Seats: 50. No smoking in dining room
Times: Last D 8pm. Closed Oct-Dec

PADSTOW, Old Custom House Inn ☻

☺ In an idyllic harbour-side setting this busy pub-style hotel offers a choice of eating in either the spacious and popular public bar or the restaurant, where competently cooked traditional dishes include fishy main courses such as fresh marlin steak and seafood créole.

Cost: Fixed-price D £17.95. H/wine £5.75. Service exc
Credit cards: 1 2 3 4. **Additional:** Children welcome; children's menu; ❶ dishes; Vegan/other diets on request
Directions: Adjacent to South Quay, 2 minutes' from harbourside car park

South Quay
Map no: 2 SW97
Tel: 01841 532359
Chef: Guy Pompa
Manageress: Linda Allen
Seats: 60. Air conditioned.
Times: Last D 9pm

PADSTOW, St Petroc's ✿✿

☺ *A lively bistro restaurant with a simple short menu*

Very recently awarded a second rosette for its delightful food, St Petroc's is a lively bistro with a simple interior – its white decor enhanced by colourful daubed oil paintings. The dishes are of new-generation bistro with distinct natural flavours. Typical dishes may be a substantial home-made rustic soup with vegetables and haricot beans, and Chinese noodles with braised chicken in a lively sauce.

Seats: 30. No smoking in dining room. **Additional:** Children welcome; children's portions; ❷ dishes; other diets on request

Directions: Follow one-way around harbour, take first left, situated on the right

4 New Street
Map no: 2 SW97
Tel: 01841 532700

Cost: *Alc* £15; fixed-price lunch/dinner £13.50. H/wine £9.50 ♀ No service charge
Credit cards: 1 2 3 5

Menus: *A la carte*, fixed-price lunch and dinner
Times: 12.30pm–Last L 2pm, 7pm–Last D 9.30pm. Closed Mon, 24–29 Dec, 4 Jan–1 Feb

Chef: Paul Hearn
Proprietors: Rick and Jill Stein

PADSTOW, Seafood Restaurant ✿✿✿

A modern approach to seafood cookery in a contemporary-style quayside restaurant with ingredients fresh from the boats

A quayside restaurant with splendid rooms above, this is one of those places that strikes a balance between being casual and sophisticated. Like the food, the interior is smartly modern and there is a buzz of exquisite anticipation.

As you would expect from the name and the location, the menu is strong on fish with only a token meat dish (grilled sirloin steak), and a vegetarian alternative can be prepared to order. Fixed-price three-course lunch and dinner menus are offered along with the *carte*, and at lunch there is no minimum spend so you can pop in for a single course. Fish soup and oysters, Helford and Loch Fyne, are perennials served in many different and inventive ways. One starter was of local oysters and fat spicy little chorizo-style sausages garnished with seaweed. Fruits de mer – cockles, mussels, razorfish and scallops – is served hot with oil and lemon.

Monkfish coated in matzo meal and braised in cloves of garlic, fennel and celery was a superb introduction to the main zourses. The fish, dazzlingly white, went gamely into combat with the potentially overpowering opponents and came out the winner. Lobsters come fresh from the local boats and are kept in chilled sea water tanks until ordered. They are served with a light shellfish fumet flavoured with chervil, parsley, chives and tarragon. Freshly boiled crabs are served whole, with mayonnaise, to be eaten with the fingers. Sticky toffee pudding and crème brûlée are among the favourite sweets, but our inspector was a little disappointed with the deliciously light but rather boring plum fool, though delighted with its hazelnut shortbread.

The wine list offers a large selection of white wines from around the world, but there are good reds too. Amongst the halves is a lovely Manzanilla sherry.

Directions: Situated on South Quay

Riverside
Map no: 2 SW97
Tel: 01841 532485

Cost: *Alc* £35; fixed-price lunch £20.25; fixed-price dinner £27.85. H/wine £9.50 ♀ Service exc
Credit cards: 1 2 3 5

Menus: *A la carte*, fixed-price lunch and dinner.

Times: Last L 2.15pm, Last D 10pm. Closed Sun, 18 Dec1 Feb

Chef: Rick Stein
Proprietor: Jill Stein

Seats: 70. Air conditioned
Additional: Children welcome; children's portions; ❷ dishes, Vegan/other diets on request

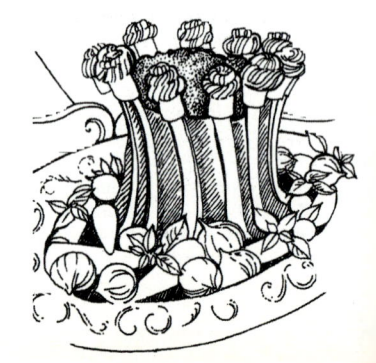

PENZANCE, Tarbert ❀

☺ *There is friendly hospitality in the restaurant of this terraced Georgian house. Chef Philip Thomas has a choice of three or four-course fixed-price menus and a carte. Smoked salmon croquettes and sautéed lambs kidneys are popular dishes. There is also a daily-changing fish special.*

Cost: Alc £16; fixed-price D £12.50. Wine £7.75. Service exc
Credit cards: 1 2 3 5
Additional: Children permitted; children's portions; other diets on request
Directions: At top of Market Jew Street continue into Alverton Street. At traffic lights turn right into Clarence Street

11–12 Clarence Street
Map no: 2 SW43
Tel: 01736 63758
Chef: Philip Thomas
Proprietors: Logis/Minotels.
Managers: Patti and Julian Evans
Seats: 32. No pipes or cigars in restaurant
Times: Last D 8.30pm. Closed 23 Dec–26 Jan

POLPERRO, Claremont ❀

☺ *A relaxed small hotel in the centre of this lovely fishing village, offering French cuisine that concentrates largely on seafood. Starters include Scallops Normande, scallops in their shell with a white wine sauce, and to follow red mullet chargrilled Mediterranean style.*

Cost: Alc £14, fixed-price D £10.95. H/wine £4.85 (half litre)
Additional: Children welcome; children's menu/portions. ❂ dishes
Directions: Village main street

Fore Street
Map no: 2SX25
Tel: 01503 72241
Proprietors: G Couturier, N Peyrin
Seats: 18
Times: Last L 2.30pm/D 8.30pm. Closed Wed and 5 Oct–Easter

POLPERRO, The Kitchen ❀❀

☺ *An inviting little restaurant specialising in seafood and international dishes*

Locally caught fresh fish and shellfish are the speciality of this pretty restaurant, and no heavy sauces or complicated cooking methods are allowed to interfere with natural flavours. Only one meaty starter appears on the *carte*, but there are several poultry and one or two meat dishes for the main course, and a decent selection of interesting vegetarian choices. Our inspector sampled very light, hot cheese puffs of deep-fried choux pastry with strong cheddar, served with a spiced chutney, and chargrilled lemon sole with rosemary and a tasty herb and lemon sauce. Fishy starters might be garlic mussels, deep-fried prawns or Cornish smoked fish, while main choices could include swordfish steak baked with cream, coriander and lemon, or pan-fried scallops with a sweet yellow pepper sauce. Many dishes have an oriental flavour to them, like chicken jalfrezi in a spicy tomato sauce, or lamb korma in an almond sauce with rice. Proprietors Ian and Vanessa Bateson cook with great skill and inventiveness, and service in their inviting pink and pine restaurant is attentive and professional.

Directions: Between the harbour and the car park

The Coombes
Map no: 2 SX25
Tel: 01503 72780

Cost: Alc £20. Wine £8.60 ♀
Service exc
Credit cards: 1 3

Menus: A la carte

Times: Holiday season Tues–Sat and BHs Last D 9.30pm. Other times please telephone

Chefs: Ian and Vanessa Bateson
Proprietors: Ian and Vanessa Bateson

Seats: 24. No cigars or pipes in restaurant
Additional: Children over 9 permitted; ❂ menu

POLZEATH, Pentire Rocks ☻

☺ *A small atmospheric hotel on the coast of North Cornwall, which offers imaginative cooking. Chef Graham Holder offers cuisine that shows his dedication and initiative. Like many seaside restaurants, the menu is definitely inclined towards seafood with calamari and whitebait for starters.*

Cost: Fixed-price D £20. H/wine £10. Service exc
Additional: Children over 8 welcome; children's portions; ❷ menu; Vegan/other diets on request
Directions: From Wadebridge/Camelford pass the 'Bee Centre' and take the right fork. The hotel is 300yds on the right

Near Rock
Map no: 2 SW97
Tel: 01208 862213
Chef: Graham Holder
Proprietors: Clive and Christine Mason
Seats: 45. No smoking in dining room
Times: Last D 9pm. Closed Jan

PORT GAVERNE, Port Gaverne Hotel ☻

☺ *Situated on the county's north coast, this hotel restaurant's menu specialises in seafood, all cooked with imagination by Ian Brodey. The specials depend on the local catch offering dishes such as Port Isaac lobster thermidor. A summer main course might be fillet steak with Stilton and port sauce.*

Cost: Alc £18.50. H/wine £5.90
Additional: Children over 7 permitted at dinner; children's portions. ❷ menu; Vegan/other diets on request
Directions: Signposted from B3314

Near Port Isaac
Map no: 2 SX08
Tel: 01208 880244
Chef: Ian Brodey
Proprietor: Mrs Midge Ross
Seats: 40. No smoking in dining room
Times: Last L 2pm/D 9.30pm. Closed mid Jan-mid Feb

PORTHLEVEN, Critchards ☻

☺ *A harbourside restaurant specialising in imaginatively cooked fish using herbs and spices. Fillet steak with a choice of sauces, duck and vegetarian dishes are also available. An inspection meal included mushroom soup, and smoked haddock with asparagus and a yoghurt and herb soufflé.*

Cost: Alc £18.20. Wine £7.95. Service exc **Credit cards:** 1 3
Additional: Children welcome; children's menu; ❷ menu; Vegan/other diets on request
Directions: Overlooking the harbour

The Harbour Road
Map no: 2 SW62
Tel: 01326 562407
Chef: Jo Critchard
Proprietors: Steve and Jo Critchard
Seats: 44. No smoking in dining room
Times: Last D 10pm. Closed Sun, Jan

PORTSCATHO, Gerrans Bay ☻

☺ *The restaurant of this relaxing family-run hotel provides traditional English cooking using home-grown herbs and local produce. The dishes are freshly prepared including home-made breads and patisserie. Recent dishes include avocado mousse and tomato and red pepper soup.*

Cost: Fixed-price menu £15.50. H/wine £6.45. **Credit cards:** 1 2 3
Additional: Children welcome, children's portions
Directions: Follow signs to Gerrans, the hotel is 100yds after the church on the road to St Anthony Head

Gerrans
Map no: 2 SW83
Tel: 01872 580338
Chef: Ann Greaves
Proprietors: Mr and Mrs B Greaves
Times: Closed Nov-Mar (open Xmas), Sun L from 1pm, Dinner 7.30pm-8pm

PORTSCATHO, Roseland House ☻

☺ *This hotel sits on a cliff top looking over magnificent views. The chef/proprietor Carolyn Hindley offers a set five-course dinner including home-made soup followed by dill-cured salmon The main course might be fillet of sea-bass with a wine cream and herb sauce..*

Cost: Fixed-price D £12 (2 course) £16; Sun L £9.50. H/Wine £4.50 (carafe). Service exc. **Credit cards:** 1 3
Additional: Children welcome; children's menu/portions; ◊ dishes; Vegan/other diets on request
Directions: Off A3078, hotel signposted about 5 miles from St Mawes

Rosevine
Map no: 2 SW83
Tel: 01872 580644
Chef: Mrs Carolyn Hindley
Proprietors: Mr and Mrs Hindley
Seats: 50. No smoking in dining room
Times: Last L 2.30pm/D 8.30pm

PORTSCATHO, Rosevine Hotel ☻

☺ *Authentic international additions bring variety to the traditional British fare featured on three and five-course fixed-price menus in the spacious modern restaurant of this hotel, a Georgian country house quietly set in 3.5 acres of mature sub-tropical gardens overlooking Porthcurnick Beach.*

Cost: Fixed-price L £8.50/D £16.50 (3 courses), £20. Wine £6.75. Service exc **Credit cards:** 1 3
Additional: Children welcome; children's portions/menu; ◊ dishes; Vegan/other diets on request
Directions: Turn south of the A390 for Tregony, take the A3078 to St Mawes. After passing through Ruan High Lanes take the 3rd turning left

Porthcurnick Beach
Map no: 2 SW83
Tel: 01872 580206/580230
Chef: Ian Andrew Thomson Picken
Proprietors: Pat and Roger Hearnden
Seats: 50. No pipes or cigars in the restaurant
Times: Last L 1.45pm/D 8.30pm. Closed Nov-Easter

RUAN HIGH LANES, The Hundred House ☻

☺ *This small hotel has an informal and relaxing style. Kitty Eccles prepares the fixed-price menu using home-grown vegetables and local produce. Hot brown home-made rolls are a delicious accompaniment to the carrot and artichoke soup, topped with crème fraîche and chopped chives.*

Cost: Fixed-price D £19.50. **Credit cards:** 1 3
Directions: On the A3078 at Ruan High Lanes

Map no: 2 SW93
Tel: 01872 501336
Chef: Kitty Eccles
Proprietors: Mr and Mrs Eccles
Times: D 7.30pm. Closed Nov-Feb and 2 weeks in Mar

ST AGNES, The Beach ☻

☺ *A family-run hotel situated on a cliff side overlooking Porthtowan Bay. The owner Howard Benson cooks his fixed-price dinner menu with imagination. His starters include mint marinated mushrooms and to follow perhaps roast quail stuffed with chicken pistachio cream.*

Cost: Fixed-price D £16. H/wine £5.95. Service inc
Credit cards: 1 2 3 4. **Additional:** Children permitted; children's portions; ◊ dishes
Directions: Take beach road up the west cliff

Porthtowan
Map no: 2 SW75
Tel: 01209 890228
Chef: Howard W Benson
Proprietors: Minotels.
Managers: The Benson family
Seats: 40. No pipes or cigars in the dining room
Times: Last D 8pm

ST AUSTELL, **Boscundle Manor** ❀

☺ *A short fixed-price four-course menu is served at this handsome 18th-century manor house hotel. Proprietor Mary Flint cooks with the best ingredients including local fish, meat and dairy produce. Our inspector enjoyed smoked salmon, roast lamb, fruit salad with clotted cream, and cheese to finish.*

Cost: Fixed-price D £22.50. Wine £9.50. Service exc
Credit cards: 1 2 3 **Additional:** Children welcome; children's portions on request; ❍ dishes;Vegan/other diets on request
Directions: Tregrehan signed 2m E of St Austell off A390

Tregrehan
Map no: 2 SX05
Tel: 01726 813557
Chef: Mary Flint
Proprietors: Andrew and Mary Flint
Seats: 20. No smoking in dining room
Times: Last D 8.30pm. Residents only Sun

ST AUSTELL, **Carlyon Bay** ❀

☺ *A well run hotel with a fabulous cliff-top position giving fine views over the coastline, set in 250 acres of mature grounds and gardens. A good selection of fixed-price and carte menus of modern English cuisine is offered in the attractive restaurant, including flambé specialities.*

Cost: Alc £19; fixed-price L £10.50/D £20. Wine £7.75. Service exc
Credit cards: 1 2 3 4 5
Additional: Children welcome; children's menu; ❍ menu; Vegan/other diets on request
Directions: Towards St Austell on the A390, take Charlestown Road at Mount Charles. Turn left into Church Road, over mini-roundabout into Beech Road, turn right for Sea Road. Hotel 100m on the left

Sea Road
Map no: 2 SX05
Tel: 01726 812304
Chef: Paul
Proprietors: Brend. Manager: Peter Brennan
Seats: 150
Times: Last L 2pm/D 9pm

ST IVES, **Chy-an-Dour** ❀

☺ *Proprietor David Watson is also the chef at this family hotel providing dishes of quality, honesty and with care in preparation. Examples are stir-fried tiger prawns with bean sprouts, grilled fillet of Megrim sole, and duckling with orange and Cointreau sauce.*

Cost: Fixed-price D £16.50. H/wine £5.40. Service exc
Credit cards: 1 3 5
Additional: Children permitted; no under 5's at dinner; ❍ dishes; Vegan/other diets on request
Directions: On A3074 into St Ives

Trelyon Avenue
Map no: 2 SW54
Tel: 01736 796436
Chef: David Watson
Proprietor: David Watson
Seats: 50. No smoking in dining room
Times: Last D 8pm

ST IVES, **Pig 'n' Fish** ❀❀

A wide array of beautifully cooked fish and shellfish dishes in a simple seaside setting

You will find the odd meat dish at this unsophisticated little restaurant near the sea, but fish is primarily its raison d'être, and the *carte* and fixed-price lunch menu reflect this fact. The kitchen revolves around the daily catch landed by local fishing boats, and anything from pot-roast skate to grilled cod with mashed potato might be available each day. Chef/co-proprietor·

Norway Lane
Map no: 2 SW54
Tel: 01736 794204

Cost: Alc £24, fixed-price lunch £14 (2 courses), £17.50. H/wine from £8. Service exc
Credit cards: 1 3

Menu: *A la carte*, fixed-price lunch

Paul Sellars keeps his mainly French and Italian recipes simple, and starters might include warm mussel salad with parsley pesto, crab pancakes with chilli, lemon grass and coriander, or an open ravioli of shellfish with olive oil, lemon and garlic. Main choices reflect the same policy of letting the ingredients speak for themselves, and there might be fillet of lemon sole with ginger, spring onion and a soya butter sauce, grilled tronçon of brill with hollandaise sauce, or perhaps bourride of red mullet, Dover sole, John Dory and mussels with aïoli. For meat eaters a sirloin steak with a cep and shallot butter sauce could be offered. Puddings are a treat – hot apple in filo pastry with fudge sauce or home-made crème brûlée.

Directions: From the Tate Gallery turn right, follow main road approx 300yds. Restaurant on the right

Times: 12.30-Last L 1.30pm, 7pm-Last D 9.30pm. Closed Sun, Mon, Nov-mid Mar

Chef: Paul Sellars
Proprietors: Debby Wilkins, Paul Sellars

Seats: 30. No cigars or pipes
Additional: Children welcome; children's portions

ST IVES, **Skidden House** ❀

☺ *Dating back many centuries, this is reputedly the oldest hotel in St Ives. In the intimate dining room enjoyable French cooking making good use of fresh produce is served. Dishes might include home-made soup, tournedos with a mushroom, cream and brandy sauce, and raspberry fool.*

Cost: Alc £19.50; fixed price D £15.95. Wine £9.50. Service inc
Credit cards: 1 2 3 4 5 **Additional:** Children welcome; ❶ menu; other diets on request
Directions: On entering St Ives take first right by the Catholic Church

Skidden Hill
Map no: 2 SW54
Tel: 01736 796899
Chef: Dennis Stoakes
Proprietors: C D Stoakes and Michael Hook
Seats: 22. No smoking
Times: Last L 1.30pm/D 9pm

ST MAWES, **Idle Rocks** ❀❀

Smart harbour-side restaurant serving a variety of modern and traditional French dishes including local seafood

Superbly situated right on the water's edge overlooking the sheltered harbour, this fine hotel offers outstanding sea views from most of its rooms. The smart restaurant, appropriately called the Water's Edge, offers an imaginative range of dishes on the *carte* and short fixed-price menu, including fresh fish from the River Fowey, and locally caught seafood. Our inspector sampled grilled lamb's liver in a puff pastry pillow with a warm tomato and rosemary dressing, and delicious steamed fillet of John Dory served with an unglazed thermidor sauce – a fresh and full-flavoured dish. The meal's highlight was an excellent hot chocolate soufflé on a fruity kumquat coulis, from a selection of tasty home-made sweets. Other recommended dishes from talented chef Alan Vickops have included potted duck and chicken liver pâté sealed in herb butter and served with toasted date and almond bread; fillet of sea trout topped with a seafood mousse and surrounded by sherry sauce; and a crisp filo pastry tulip filled with pan-fried scallops and wild mushrooms. A cheese board offers local farmhouse selections.

Directions: Take the A3078 to St Mawes. Hotel is on the left as you enter the village

Tredenhan Road
Near Truro
Map no: 2 SW83
Tel: 01326 270771

Cost: Alc £22.50; fixed-price dinner £18.75. Wine £7.95. Service exc
Credit cards: 1 3

Menus: A la carte, fixed price dinner, Sunday lunch, bar menu

Times: Last L 2.30pm, Last D 9.15pm

Chef: Alan Vickops
Proprietor: Mr E K Richardson

Seats: 60. No-smoking area. No cigars or pipes in restaurant
Additional: Children welcome; children's portions/menu; ❶ dishes, Vegan/other diets on request

ST MAWES, **Rising Sun** ✺

Seafood comes straight from the quayside to the attractively appointed restaurant of this bustling hotel on the harbour. Chef Paul Groves' enticing carte is supplemented by good-value bar meals in a casually relaxed pub-style ambience.

Map no: 2 SW83
Tel: 01326 270233
Chef: Paul Groves
Proprietors: Colin and Jacqueline Phillips
Seats: 40
Times: Last L 2.25pm/D 9pm

Cost: Sunday L £8.50. H/wine £7.75 ♀ Service exc **Credit cards:** 1 2 3 5
Additional: Children welcome. Children's menu/portions. ◑ menu; Vegan/other diets on request
Directions: On entering the village the hotel is on the right-hand side

ST MAWES, **The St Mawes** ✺

☺ A distinctive 17th-century house situated on the seafront overlooking the harbour. A simple selection of freshly cooked English and French dishes are offered in the cosy restaurant, which make good use of the local seafood, including Cornish lobster. The home-made desserts are not to be missed.

The Seafront
Map no: 2 SW83
Tel: 01326 270266
Chef: Juliet Burrows
Proprietor: Mr and Mrs C Burrows
Seats: 20. No cigars or pipes
Times: Last L 1.30pm/D 8.30pm

Cost: Alc £24, fixed price L £11.50/D £16. Wine £4.50 (half litre). Service inc **Credit cards:** 1 3
Additional: Children welcome; children's portions/menu; ◑ menu; Vegan/other diets on request
Directions: Opposite the Quay in centre of village

TALLAND BAY, **Allhays** ✺

This attractive family home is set in its own well-tended gardens on a gently sloping hillside overlooking Talland Bay. Meals from the short but well-executed menu are served in the conservatory dining room, with fresh local fish and home-made pudding specialities.

Near Looe
Map no: 2 SX25
Tel: 01503 72434
Chef: Lydia Spring
Proprietors: Mr and Mrs B Spring

Directions: West of Looe, off A387

TALLAND BAY, **Talland Bay** ✺

A fine Cornish house with sweeping views of Talland Bay. Friendly, professional service enhances enjoyable homemade meals. Colourful desserts are served with lashings of clotted cream.

Near Looe
Map no: 2 SX25
Tel: 01503 72667
Chef: Paul Kingswood
Proprietors: Mr and Mrs Rosier
Times: 7.30pm-Last D 9pm and Sunday lunch. Closed Jan

Cost: Alc £28, fixed-price D £19.75. **Credit cards:** 1 2 3 4
Additional: No children under 5 at dinner; ◑ dishes
Directions: Signposted from Looe/Polperro road

TRESCO, New Inn ❀

This attractive stone-built inn, at the centre of a scattered village just 400 yards from the quay, has earned a good reputation for well-prepared food. A four-course fixed-price and carte choice of English/French dishes is supplemented by separate menus for children and vegetarians.

Cost: Alc £24; fixed-price D £18.50. H/wine £4.50 ♀ Service exc
Credit cards: 1 3. **Additional:** Children welcome (before 8pm); children's portions/menu; ❶ menu; other diets on request. Live entertainment
Directions: 250yds from the harbour (private island – contact hotel for details)

Isles of Scilly
Map no: 2
Tel: 01720 422844
Chef: Steven Griffiths
Proprietor: Tresco Estate.
Manager: Graham Thomas Shone
Seats: 32. No smoking in dining room
Times: Last L 2pm/D 9.15pm

TRESCO, The Island ❀❀

An idyllically set hotel restaurant serving imaginative food cooked in modern English style.

There are magical qualities to Tresco – known as 'England's Island of Flowers' – which extend to this smart hotel set in an idyllic position beside the sea. Visitors arrive by helicopter or boat to a warm and genuine welcome from the friendly staff. The stylish restaurant has outstanding views to the tiny islands of Tean and St Helens, and makes a perfect setting for the imaginative cooking of Christopher Wyburn-Ridsdale. Not surprisingly local seafood and fish feature on the fixed-price dinner menus, and a recent inspection meal began with fresh Bryher crab meat simply shaped into a quenelle and served with mint and chive mayonnaise. A perfectly balanced chilled melon, ginger and mint soup followed and then a moist and very tasty fillet of black bream, served on a medley of Provençal vegetables with a second side dish of potatoes, courgette dauphinoise and carrots. The chosen pudding was a superb crème brûlée of excellent texture, deep colour and exquisite flavour, served with strawberries in Grand Marnier. Cafetière coffee and home-made petit fours served in the lounge made a fitting end to the meal.

Directions: Situated on north-eastern tip of island

The Isles of Scilly
Map no: 2
Tel: 01720 22883

Cost: Alc £24.95; fixed-price dinner £27.50. Wine £9.95
Credit cards: 1 2 3

Menus: A la carte, fixed-price dinner, bar menu

Times: Last L 2.15pm, Last D 9.30pm. Closed Nov-Feb

Chef: Chris Wyburne-Ridsdale
Proprietors: Tresco Estates.
Manager: Ivan Curtis

Seats: 110. No smoking in dining room
Additional: Children welcome; children's portions/menu; ❶ dishes; Vegan/other diets on request

TREYARNON BAY, Waterbeach Hotel ❀

☺ *A quietly located hotel, with glorious views, improving year by year due to owners, Vicky and Tony Etherington. Vicky, also the chef, cooks generous, wholesome dishes with skill and flair. The menu comprises six courses and is prepared with fresh local produce.*

Cost: Fixed-price D £12.50. Wine £6.50. Service inc
Credit cards: 1 3 5
Additional: Children welcome; children's menu; ❶ menu; other diets on request
Directions: Well signposted in Treyarnon Bay

Near Padstow
Map no: 2 SW87
Tel: 01841 520292
Chef: Mrs V Etherington
Proprietor: Mr A Etherington
Seats: 40. No smoking in the dining room
Times: Last D 8.15pm. Closed Nov-Easter

TRURO, **Alverton Manor** ✿

A former convent quietly set in terraced grounds, with a candle-lit restaurant offering typical modern British dishes from an enthusiastic chef such as fresh leek terrine, salmon and plaice roulade, and fillet of beef with artichoke cream.

Cost: Alc £28.50; Sunday L £10.75; fixed-price D £16.85. Wine £8.25. Service inc **Credit Cards:** 1 2 3 4 5 **Additional:** No smoking. Children welcome/portions/menu; ◐ dishes; Vegan/other on request **Directions:** Off the A390 Truro to St Austell

Tregolls Road
Map no: 2 SW84
Tel: 01872 76633
Chef: Mr M A Smith
Proprietor: Mr M Sagin
Times: Last L 1.45pm/D 9.30pm

VERYAN, **Nare** ✿

This hotel is in a perfect location overlooking a secluded beach. The fixed-price and carte menus are pricey but offer good modern Anglo-French cooking with a selection of fresh fish, grills, flambé specialities and traditional hot puddings.

Cost: Alc £28; Sunday lunch £14; fixed price L £12/D £27. Wine£9.25. Service exc **Credit cards:** 1 3 **Additional:** Children over 8 at dinner/portions/menu (lunch); ◐ menu; Vegan/other on request **Directions:** Go through Veryan passing New Inn on left, continue for a mile to sea and hotel

Carne Beach
Map no: 2 SW93
Tel: 01872 501279
Chef: Malcolm Sparks
Proprietors: Mr and Mrs T N Gray. Manageress: Mrs D Burt
Seats: 70. No pipes or cigars in restaurant
Times: Last L 2pm/D 9.30pm.
Closed 4 Jan-13 Feb

CUMBRIA

ALSTON, **Lovelady Shield** ✿✿

☺ A pleasant country house setting for an excellent choice of competently cooked food

With its gardens running beside the River Nent, this delightful country house hotel offers an attractive setting in quiet, secluded countryside. Inside – the atmosphere is unpretentious and relaxed, with lovely views of the gardens and warming log fires in winter. Barrie Garton's four-course dinner menu offers a good choice of dishes with an emphasis on quality local produce. Starters might include smooth chicken liver parfait or old English potted beef, followed by a home-made soup such as cream of sweet potatoes or tomato with tarragon, with perhaps Hungarian veal goulash, or grilled double breast of pigeon. Our inspector plumped for a delicate filo pastry cup filled with smoked salmon and topped with a mustard grain hollandaise, and spicy vegetable soup with a mildly curried flavour. Folded fillet of plaice went surprisingly well with a thick tomato sauce, and duchesse potatoes, broccoli, warm purée of red cabbage and diced turnip were all well cooked. The ever-favourite house speciality of hot baked sultana and butterscotch sponge served with a rich sauce and fresh cream proved irresistible.

Directions: Off the A689, 2.5 miles from East Alston

Map no: 12 NY74
Tel: 01434 381203

Cost: Fixed-price dinner £24.25. Wine £9.65. No service charge
Credit cards: 1 2 3 4

Menus: Fixed-price dinner, bar lunches

Times: 7.30pm-Last D 8.30pm. Closed 4 Jan–5 Feb

Chef: Barrie Garton
Proprietors: K S and M W Lyons

Seats: 26. No smoking in dining room
Additional: Children permitted (over 5); children's portions; ◐ dishes, Vegan/other diets on request

AMBLESIDE, **Borrans Park** ☺

☺ *A peacefully situated small hotel set back from the road, very convenient for the town centre. The set menu offers a four-course choice of well-produced English food which may feature the best local lamb, pork or trout, with a good home-made soup. The freshly made desserts are tempting.*

Cost: Fixed-price D £15.50. Wine £6.39 ♀ Service inc **Credit cards:** 1 3
Additional: Children permitted (over 7); children's portions/menu; ✿ menu; other diets on request
Directions: On the A5075 Borrans Road, opposite the Rugby Club

Borrans Road
Map no: 7 NY30
Tel: 015394 33454
Chefs: Barbara Lewis and Jane Whitehead
Proprietors: Brian Lewis and Andrew Whitehead
Seats: 30. No smoking
Times: Last D 8pm

AMBLESIDE, **Nanny Brow** ☺

A charming country house situated in beautiful grounds and gardens. Dinner is served in an intimate dining room with chef David Atkinson's menu providing a choice of tantalising dishes, finishing with a selection of English and Continental cheeses.

Cost: Fixed-price D £29.50. H/wine £11.99 ♀ Service exc
Credit cards: 1 2 3 4 5. **Additional:** Children permitted (over 11); ✿ menu; Vegan/other diets on request
Directions: 1.50 miles from Ambleside on A593 to Coniston

Clappersgate
Map no: 7 NY30
Tel: 015394 32036
Chef: David J Atkinson
Proprietor: Michael W Fletcher
Seats: 42. No smoking in dining room
Times: Last D 8.45pm

AMBLESIDE, **Rothay Manor** ☺

An elegant Regency-style house, which the mainly English menu is very well suited to. Dinner is the main meal with a fixed-price menu of three, four or five courses. An example of a main course being wild duck covered in smoked bacon braised in red wine with fresh herbs.

Cost: Fixed-price L £11.50, £14.50 (Sun)/D £22 (2 courses), £25, £28. H/wine £9.00. Service exc **Credit cards:** 1 2 3 4
Additional: Children welcome; children's portions/menu; ✿ menu; other diets on request
Directions: Quarter of mile out of Ambleside on the Coniston road

Rothay Bridge
Map no: 7 NY30
Tel: 015394 33605
Chefs: Jane Binns and Colette Nixon
Proprietors: Nigel and Stephen Nixon
Seats: 70. No smoking. Air conditioned
Times: Last L 2pm (1.30pm Sun)/D 9pm. Closed 2 Jan-10 Feb

AMBLESIDE, **Wateredge** ☺

Originally two fishermen's cottages, this elegant comfortable hotel stands on the shore of the lake. The delightful beamed, panelled restaurant is on two levels in the older part of the house. Excellent six-course set dinners are carefully prepared and presented, featuring mainly English food.

Cost: Fixed-price D £25.90. Wine £10. Service exc
Credit cards: 1 2 3 5
Additional: Children permitted (over 7); children's portions; ✿ menu; Vegan/other diets on request
Directions: On A591, at Waterhead Bay, adjacent to Steamer Pier

Borrans Road, Waterhead
Map no: 7 NY30
Tel: 015394 32332
Chefs: Michael Cosgrove, Mark Cowap and Kathryn Cosgrove
Proprietors: Mr and Mrs Derek Cowap
Seats: 50. No smoking. Partial air conditioning
Times: Last D 8.30pm. Closed mid Dec-early Feb

APPLEBY-IN-WESTMORLAND, Appleby Manor ❀

Roman Road
Map no: 12 NY62
Tel: 017683 51571
Chef: Dave Farrar
Proprietors: Best Western. Managers: Nick and Rachel Swinscoe
Seats: 70. No smoking in dining room
Times: Last L 2pm/D 9pm. Closed 24-26 Dec

☺ *The dining room of this hotel - a manor house with views over castle and rooftops to the Lake District's peaks - overlooks attractive gardens. Four fixed-price menus of British dishes include regional specialities like black pudding, served here with dates and blackcurrant liqueur.*

Cost: Fixed-price L/D £17.95 to £23.95. Wine £11.50 (litre). No service charge **Credit cards:** 1 2 3 4 5
Additional: Children welcome; children's portions/menu; ❤ dishes; Vegan/other diets on request
Directions: From B6260, through town, over bridge to T-junction. Turn left, then first right

APPLEBY-IN-WESTMORLAND, Tufton Arms ❀

Market Square
Map no: 12 NY62
Tel: 017683 51593
Chef: David Milsom
Proprietors: Consort. Manager: W D Milsom
Seats: 60. No-smoking area. Air conditioned
Times: Last L 2pm/D 9.30pm

☺ *This family-run hotel's Conservatory restaurant has a fixed-price and carte menus offering a wide variety of dishes, many based on local ingredients. The carte offers mostly grills with a delicious smoked haddock, mushroom and cheese hot-pot and, from the fixed-price menu, pan-fried guinea fowl.*

Cost: Alc £19, fixed-price D £16.50. H/wine £7.50 ⚲ Service exc
Credit cards: 1 2 3 4 5 **Additional:** Children welcome; children's portions. ❤ dishes; other diets on request
Directions: In the centre of Appleby in the main street

BASSENTHWAITE, Overwater Hall ❀

Ireby
Map no: 11 NY23
Tel: 017687 76566
Chef: Adrian Hyde
Proprietors: Adrian Hyde, Angela Hyde and Stephen Bore
Seats: 60. No smoking in dining room
Times: Last L 1.30pm/D 9pm

☺ *A 215-year-old mansion, 18 acres of gardens and woodland and the unspoilt Cumbrian countryside are some of the ingredients. Then take a five-course, fixed-price dinner menu, offering a wide choice of French and Modern English dishes, and the result is a fine Lakeland restaurant.*

Cost: Sunday L £9.50; fixed-price D £18.95. H/wine £7.50. Service exc **Credit cards:** 1 3. **Additional:** Children permitted; children's portions; ❤ dishes; other diets on request
Directions: Take the A591 from Keswick to Carlisle, after 7 miles turn right at the Castle Inn and hotel is signposted after 2 miles

BORROWDALE, **Borrowdale Gates** ☺

☺ *A charming country house set in two acres of gardens with picturesque views of the surrounding hills and mountains in this beautiful valley. Chef/patron Terry Parkinson's five-course evening meals are served in the elegant restaurant, with a wide choice of English/French dishes providing very good value.*

Cost: Fixed-price Sun L £12.50/D £20. H/wine £8.50 ♀ Service exc
Credit cards: 1 3 5
Additional: Children permitted (over 6 after 7pm); children's portions (lunch); ✿ dishes; other diets on request
Directions: From Keswick on B5289, in Grange village turn right at double humpback bridge. Hotel quarter of a mile on right

Grange, Keswick
Map no: 11NY21
Tel: 017687 77204
Chef: Terry Parkinson
Proprietors: Mr and Mrs T H Parkinson
Seats: 50. No smoking in dining room
Times: Last L 1.30pm/Last D 8.45pm. Closed first week Dec, first 3 weeks in Jan

BRAMPTON, **Farlam Hall** ☺☺

Original and imaginative English cooking in a delightful, welcoming country house hotel

The two experienced families who run this luxurious country house hotel know a thing or two about hospitality, and guests are treated to the personal touch from the moment they arrive. A meal in the elegant dining room offers further proof that quality is of the essence here, and chef Barry Quinion presents a short fixed-price dinner menu with the emphasis on fresh local ingredients cooked with imagination. Starters like roast tomato soup with garlic and black olives show plenty of originality, followed perhaps by fresh langoustine cooked with herbs, white wine and cream, or medallions of pork on a potato and apple cake, with apple and Calvados sauce topped with a mushroom duxelle. Our inspector was impressed with herb croûton topped with West Cumberland ham, avocado and tomatoes and glazed with hollandaise, and baked fillet of halibut set on a bed of leeks under a crunchy herb and saffron crust, served with a saffron and white wine sauce. A blackcurrant crème brûlée was very tasty, and coffee, like the delicious canapés and home-made rolls, was of superior quality. The wine list offers a good variety.

Directions: 2.5 miles south-east of Brampton on A689

Hallbankgate
Map no: 12NY56
Tel: 016977 46234

Cost: Fixed-price dinner £28. Wine £9.75 ♀ Service exc
Credit cards: 1 3

Menus: Fixed-price dinner

Times: Last D 8.30pm. Closed 26 Dec–31 Dec

Chef: Barry Quinion
Proprietors: Relais et Château.
Managers: Quinion and Stevenson families

Seats: 40. No pipes or cigars in restaurant
Additional: Children permitted (over 5); ✿ dishes; other diets on request

CARTMEL, **Aynsome Manor** ☺

☺ *A country house hotel in a delightful rural setting. The panelled dining room has lovely views and provides well produced English cuisine. Choices on the set menu may include smoked rainbow trout or roast poussin served with Madeira sauce and home-made soups and puddings.*

Cost: Sun L £10.50, fixed-price D £18.50. Wine £10. Service exc
Credit cards: 1 2 3 5. **Additional:** Children permitted (over 5 at dinner); children's portions; ✿ dishes; Vegan/other diets on request
Directions: Leave A590 signed Cartmel. Hotel is 2.5 miles on the right, before the village

Near Grange over Sands
Map no: 7SD37
Tel: 015395 36653
Chef: Victor Sharratt
Proprietor: P Anthony Varley
Seats: 28. No smoking in dining room
Times: Last Sun L 12.30pm/D 8.30pm. Closed L (except Sun), Sun eve; 2-26 Jan

CARTMEL, **Uplands** ◉◉◉

Haggs Lane
Map no: 7 SD37
Tel: 015395 36248

A well-established restaurant with a refreshing lack of pomposity, serving perfectly balanced food

There's an appealing lack of pretension at this friendly restaurant, which renders the food all the more remarkable for its outstanding quality. Tom Peter's consistently classy and talented cooking is much admired by the loyal and contented regulars who frequent this well-established restaurant. There are fine views over the surrounding countryside towards Morecambe Bay to be enjoyed too, and the warm welcome and chatty service provided by Di Peter are an added attraction for those who dislike the pomposity that is sometimes inseparable from fine food. Meals are served at set times – 12.30 for 1pm, and 7.30 for 8pm.

A hot, malty sweet loaf and carving knife are placed at each table, and a recent inspection meal began with a hot sole soufflé stuffed with mushroom pâté, served with a vibrant, full-flavoured watercress sauce. A tureen of excellent parsnip and ginger soup came next, with a lovely balance between the flavours, while the main course offered another unlikely but successful combination of flavours: breast of chicken stuffed with cheese and herb pâté and wrapped in air-cured ham with a tomato and mustard cream sauce. Vegetables are a strength, and whether plain or with added ingredients their true flavours come through. Puddings are in the country house mould, and the chocolate and Grand Marnier mousse was well made and rich. The short fixed-price menu offers little choice except at dessert stage, and other recommended dishes have been marinated breast of wood pigeon on pineapple salad with Cumberland sauce, tasty mushroom and apple soup, and pan-fried medallions of venison with blackcurrant and juniper sauce. The wine list is reasonably priced and offers a well-balanced selection from around the world.

Cost: Fixed-price lunch £14, fixed-price dinner £25. H/wine £8. Service exc
Credit cards: 1 2 3

Menus: Fixed-price lunch and dinner, Sunday lunch

Times: Last L 12.30pm (for 1pm), Last D 7.30pm (for 8pm). Closed 1 Jan-24 Feb

Chef: Tom Peter
Proprietor: Diana Peter

Seats: 28. No smoking
Additional: Children over 8 permitted; ◉ dishes; Vegan/other diets on request

Directions: Take the road signed Grange opposite the Pig and Whistle pub in Cartmel. Uplands is a mile on the left

CONISTON, **The Old Rectory** ◉

Torver
Map no: 7 SD39
Tel: 015394 41353
Chef: Carolyn Fletcher
Proprietors: Paul and Carolyn Fletcher
Seats: 14. No smoking in dining room
Times: Last D 7.30pm

A charming small country house hotel a short way from Torver village. Chef Carolyn Fletcher's cooking can best be described as honest and well produced using only fresh local produce, such as fillet of pork Normandy, cooked in creamy cider and Calvados sauce, garnished with apple rings.

Cost: H/wine £8.25. Service exc
Additional: Children welcome; children's portions; ◉ dishes; Vegan/other diets on request
Directions: 2.5 miles south of Coniston on the A593, just before Torver

CROOKLANDS, Crooklands ❀

☺ An attractive stone-built hotel, dating back in parts to 1750. The Hayloft restaurant features original beams and farming bric-a-brac, and enjoys a good reputation for its international cuisine. Both fixed-price and carte menus are offered, with good value and quality provided by the set menu.

Cost: Alc £22; fixed-price D £16.95. Wine £7.95. Service inc
Credit cards: 1 2 3 4. **Additional:** Children welcome in Carvery; children's portions; ❷ dishes; Vegan/other diets on request
Directions: 1.5 miles from junction 36 of M6. Hotel rurally located on the old A65 Kendal Road

Near Milnthorpe
Map no: 7 SD58
Tel: 015395 67432
Chef: Colin Scott
Proprietor: Best Western.
Manager: Neil Connor
Seats: 45. Air conditioned
Times: Last L 2pm/D 9.30pm Mon-Sat. Carvery L/D Mon-Sun

CROSBY-ON-EDEN, Crosby Lodge ❀

This hotel has been in the same family for over 20 years and maintains very high standards. The menus offer an extensive range of dishes, and a test meal comprised duck terrine with a cranberry and orange confit, ragout of wild venison served with rowan jelly, and a cream-laden pudding from the trolley.

Cost: Alc £28; fixed-price L £15/D £25.50. Wine £9. Service exc
Credit cards: 1 2 3
Additional: Children permitted (over 5 dinner); children's portions; ❷ dishes; other diets on request
Directions: Just off the A689 between Brampton and Carlisle

High Crosby
Map no: 12 NY45
Tel: 01228 573618
Chef: Michael Sedgwick
Proprietors: Michael and Patricia Sedgwick
Seats: 50. No smoking in dining room
Times: Last L 1.30pm/D 9pm. Closed Xmas eve–20 Jan

ELTERWATER, Langdale ❀

An established Tudor-style, family-run hotel with Polly's wine bar and the congenial wood-panelled Oak Room restaurant. Effort and imagination goes into the food, such as the terrines and pâtés, the bright, unfussy main courses and the generous home-made puddings.

Cost: Alc £30; fixed-price D £24.95. Wine £10 ♀ Service exc
Credit cards: 1 2 3 4 5
Additional: Children welcome; children's portions/menu; ❷ menu; Vegan dishes. Pianist

Map no: 7 NY30
Tel: 015394 37302
Chef: David Rodgie
Proprietors: Granville Graham
Seats: 100. No smoking in dining room. Air conditioned
Times: Last D 9.45pm

ESKDALE GREEN, Bower House Inn ❀

☺ An interesting menu with an international flavour is available every evening in the beamed restaurant of this character Lakeland inn. Only best quality produce is used in dishes such as our inspector's tomato, apple and celery soup, and pan-fried chicken with spicy apple sauce.

Cost: Alc from £17; fixed-price D £17; Wine £5.50. Service inc
Credit cards: 1 2 3 5
Additional: Children welcome; children's portions; ❷ menu; Vegan/other diets on request
Directions: From A595 follow signs to Eskdale Green

Holmrook
Map no: 6 NY10
Tel: 019467 23244
Chef: Margaret Johnson
Proprietors: Derek and Beryl Connor
Seats: 40. No cigars or pipes in restaurant
Times: Last L 2.30pm/D 9.30pm

GRASMERE, Gold Rill ✾

☺ *A pleasant hotel situated in two acres of gardens with an elegant restaurant enjoying lovely Lakeland views and a good standard of modern English cooking. Well produced soups and puddings are all home-made*

Additional: Children permitted (over 5); children's portions/menu; ❂ dishes; other diets on request
Directions: Turning opposite St Oswalds Church. Hotel on left

Red Bank Road
Map no: 11 NY30
Tel: 015394 35486
Chef: Ian Thompson
Proprietor: Paul Jewsbury
Seats: 50. No smoking
Times: Last L 1.45/D 8.30pm
Cost: A/c £18; fixed-price D £18. Wine £8. Service inc
Credit cards: 1 3

GRASMERE, Michael's Nook ✾✾✾

Creative modern cooking showing a light touch and true flavours in an indulgent country house setting

Visitors to this delightful country house hotel are treated more like treasured house-guests than the paying public, and several small quirks support this impression. Staff are summoned to the front door by a ringing bell to welcome visitors. The country house atmosphere extends into the dining room, where guests are seated promptly at 8pm to enjoy the delicious extravagances of the evening, and chef Kevin Mangeolles does not disappoint. His menus of modern English and French cooking are creative, demonstrating a lightness of hand combined with true flavours. A special six-course gourmet menu shows off the best of his skills
  Salmon tartar canapés awakened our inspector's appetite for a most enjoyable meal which began with mille-feuille of langoustine - delicate pastry layers with fresh langoustines and a julienne of sharp vegetables. Chicken liver mousseline was a delightfully light dish with lovely rich flavours, served hot with a rosemary flavoured butter sauce, and the main course of boned and shaped oxtail topped with foie gras came with salsify, parsnips and wild mushrooms on a Madeira sauce; the deliciously tender meat was perfectly complemented by the smooth foie gras, though the sauce was rather thin. Strawberry soufflé was airily light and fruity, set on a shortbiscuit base with a full-flavoured strawberry sorbet and quartered berries in a purée of the same fruit – a gratifying finish to the meal. Smiling staff provide attentive, unobtrusive service throughout.
  The wine list is both outstanding and reasonably priced. There are plenty of mature vintages of Burgundies and Bordeaux, and a good selection from all the major areas around the world.

Map no: 11 NY30
Tel: 015394 35496

Cost: Fixed-price lunch £17.50; fixed-price dinner £30. Wine £10. Service exc
Credit cards: 1 2 3 4

Menus: Fixed-price lunch and dinner, Sunday lunch

Times: 12.30pm-Last L 1pm, 7.30pm-Last D 8.30pm

Chef: Kevin Mangeolles
Proprietors: Reg Gifford

Seats: 36. No smoking in the restaurant
Additional: Children permitted (over 6 at dinner); ❂ dishes/other diets on request

Directions: Turn off the A591 at The Swan, bear left for 400 yds

GRASMERE, Grasmere Hotel ✾

☺ *A family-run Victorian house in the centre of village. The daily changing menu offers dishes such as turkey escalope stuffed with Stilton and roasted with smoked bacon*

Cost: Fixed-price D £18.50. **Credit cards:** 1 3
Additional: No smoking, children welcome

Broadgate, Grasmere
Map no: 11 NY 30
Tel: 015394 35277
Chef: Annette Mansie
Proprietors: Mr & Mrs Mansie
No smoking
Times: D 7.30-8.30

GRASMERE, Oak Bank ❀

☺ *This friendly family-run hotel is situated close to the centre of the village. Mrs Sharon Savasi produces a four-course menu which includes a choice of main dishes and a vegetarian dish. Some Continental influence is evident, but the theme is British.*

Cost: Fixed-price D £16.50. H/wine £1.60 glass. Service exc
Credit cards: 1 3 5. **Additional:** Children permitted (over 5); ❍ menu; other diets on request
Directions: Centre of village

Broadgate
Map no: 11 NY30
Tel: 015394 35217
Chefs: Mrs Sharon Savasi
Proprietors: Mr and Mrs A L Savasi
Seats: 36. No smoking in dining room
Times: Last D 8pm

GRASMERE, White Moss House ❀❀

Imaginative cooking including excellent soups and enjoyable dishes made from perfectly combined ingredients

William Wordsworth once owned this lovely Lakeland house which dates from 1730 and stands in well-tended gardens overlooking Rydal Water. It is now run as a hotel with great enthusiasm by owners Susan and Peter Dixon, who offer a place to relax with excellent hospitality and good English food. Our inspector was impressed by the imaginative cooking of Peter Dixon, which is shown off on the daily-changing five-course dinner menu: starters like wild Argyll salmon poached with champagne, and Wastwater wild trout and char baked with whiteBurgundy, follow a home-made soup such as woodland mushroom, marjoram and Marsala. Main courses might be roast fillet of Charolais beef, or goose breast marinated in stout. A delightful soufflé of salmon, leeks, asparagus, sea trout and smoked cheese, with all the flavours separately pronounced yet perfectly combined. Roast saddle of venison had a deep, rich flavour and was very tender, while apple and blackcurrant Grasmere made a superb dessert. A selection of British cheeses that would be hard to beat finished off this enjoyable meal.

Directions: On A591 at north end of Rydal Water, halfway between Grasmere and Ambleside

Rydal Water
Map no: 11 NY30
Tel: 015394 35295

Cost: Fixed-price dinner £27.50
♀ Service inc
Credit cards: 1 3

Menu: Fixed-price dinner

Times: D 8pm (one sitting). Closed Sun

Chefs: Peter Dixon, Colin Percival
Proprietors: Peter and Susan Dixon

Seats: 18. No smoking
Additional: Children permitted (no toddlers); ❍ dishes/other diets on request

GRASMERE, Wordsworth ❀

An attractive hotel in its own landscaped grounds where chef Bernard Warne artistically creates dishes with an emphasis on seasonal produce. Served in the stylish Prelude restaurant, a main course may be a lobster pot of seafood and sea vegetables finished with a black olive and tomato dressing.

Cost: Fixed-price L £18.50/D £28 (3 courses), £29.50. Wine £9.50. Service exc
Credit cards: 1 2 3 4
Additional: Children welcome; children's portions; ❍ menu; Vegan/other diets on request. Live entertainment Sat
Directions: In the centre of the village

Near Ambleside
Map no: 11 NY30
Tel: 015394 35592
Chef: Bernard Warne
Proprietor: Mr R A Gifford
Seats: 65. No smoking in dining room
Times: Last L 2pm/D 9pm (9.30pm Fri/Sat)

HOWTOWN, Sharrow Bay ✪✪✪

Every meal is an occasion, celebrated with rich and extravagant dishes, at this idyllically located country house hotel

Opened in 1949, Sharrow Bay is the grandfather of English country house hotels. The main house, Italianate-Lakeland built in 1840, is right on the shore of Lake Ullswater, surrounded by immaculate gardens and woodland. There are two dining rooms, the Lakeside room with its splendid views or the darker, panelled Studio, both with splendidly set tables of gleaming cutlery and crystal. The daily five-course lunch and six-course dinner menus offer a bewildering choice, and the long-established format pays scant regard to the food fashions of the day. There has always been a balance between tradition and creativity, and while many of the dishes are extravagantly rich it is possible to eat more simply, and vegetarian dishes are available on request.

The evening performance is well rehearsed and runs like clockwork, commencing with aperitifs and canapés in the lounge before guests are paraded past the tempting array of desserts. From the 13 or so starters, one might choose a smoked chicken consommé, Cumbrian ham, or a delicious ravioli of lobster mousseline in lemon pasta, served with fried julienne of vegetables and a full-flavoured lobster sauce garnished with fresh asparagus spears. A fish course always follows, accompanied by a cheesy Suissesse soufflé. A refreshing sorbet comes next, then the main course, perhaps roast sirloin of beef, noisettes of lamb or excellent local venison. Desserts are a great strength, such as the original and much-imitated sticky toffee pudding and a correctly made 'old English Regency syllabub'. For those who can manage it, there is also a trolley of 'Great British Cheeses'.

The wine list is reasonably priced and of excellent quality; there are three 1961 first growth clarets. An unusually large number of good wines are available by the glass

Directions: Turn off A592 to Pooley Bridge. On leaving village turn right and follow the signs to Howtown

Map no: 12 NY41
Tel: 017684 86301/86483

Cost: *Alc* £26; fixed-price L £30.75; fixed-price D £40.75. H/wine £11.95
Credit cards: None taken

Menus: Fixed-price lunch and dinner, Sunday lunch

Times: Last L 1.45, Last D 8.45pm. Closed Dec, Jan, Feb

Chefs: Johnnie Martin, Colin Akrigg, Philip Wilson, Christopher Bond
Proprietors: Relais et Chateaux. Managers: Francis Coulson and Brian Sack

Seats: 65. No smoking in dining room
Additional: Children permitted (over 12); ❂ dishes, Vegan/other diets on request

KESWICK, Brundholme ✪

An elegant 18th-century country house situated in wooded grounds above the River Greta and the town. Ian Charlton produces classical English/French dinners, with a carte offering such dishes as wild mushroom and Gruyère tart, monkfish, roast breast of goose and local Cumbrian cheeses.

Cost: H/wine £8.50. Service exc **Credit cards:** 1 2 3
Additional: Children permitted (over 12 at dinner); ❂ menu; Vegan/other diets on request
Directions: At A66 roundabout take first left to Keswick, left again, hotel on right

Brundholme Road
Map no: 11 NY22
Tel: 017687 74495
Chef: Ian Charlton
Proprietor: Ian Charlton
Seats: 40. No smoking in dining room
Times: Last L 1.30pm/D 8.30pm. Closed Xmas

KESWICK, **Dale Head Hall** ❀

☺ A charming hotel offering a very good value five-course meal prepared by Caroline Bonkenburg. The meal may begin with a salad or fruit then a soup. An example of a main course is guinea fowl on a bed of oysters and mushrooms, with a red wine sauce; followed by desserts and cheeses.

Cost: Fixed-price D £19.50. H/wine £9.75 ♀ Service exc
Credit cards: 1 3. **Additional:** Children permitted over 10; ❂ dishes
Directions: Halfway between Grasmere and Keswick, 400yds off A591

Map no: 11 NY22
Tel: 017687 72478
Chef: Caroline Bonkenburg
Proprietors: Alan and Shirley Lowe
Seats: 18. No smoking in dining room
Times: Last D 8.30pm

KESWICK, **Grange** ❀

☺ A well produced five-course dinner is provided at this country hotel. The fixed-price menu offers a short choice of traditional home cooking, with dishes such as salmon pâté, mushroom and walnut soup, moist turkey breast with a bilberry and orange sauce, and spicy apple pie to finish.

Cost: Fixed-price dinner £17.90. Wine £8.25 ♀ Service inc
Credit cards: 1 3 **Additional:** Children permitted (over 7); children's portions; ❂ dishes; other diets on request
Directions: Take A591 towards Windermere for half a mile, first right, hotel 200 yds on right

Manor Brow, Ambleside Road
Map no: 11 NY22
Tel: 017687 72500
Chef: Colin Brown
Proprietors: Mr and Mrs D M Millar
Times: Last D 8pm. Closed mid Nov-mid Mar
Cost: Fixed-price dinner £17.90. Wine £8.25 ♀ Service inc
Credit cards: 1 3

KESWICK, **Swinside Lodge** ❀❀

A charming hotel with a warm, relaxing atmosphere and very good British food

A delightful Victorian Lakeland house surrounded by hills, meadows and woodland offers a perfect retreat for those in search of peace and seclusion. Indoors the atmosphere is just as charming, with soft colours, fresh flowers and antiques creating a restful ambience, and friendly staff add to the warmth. The evening menu is another topic of interest, and chef Chris Astley has raised the standard of cooking by several notches since his recent appointment. His food is essentially British, and the daily-changing five-course menu offers no choice except at dessert. Our inspector recently enjoyed an exceptionally light and fluffy courgette soufflé, and tomato and red pepper soup, followed by chicken breast cooked in tarragon with a Madeira cream sauce which perfectly complemented the meat flavours. Guards pudding with a wine sauce was rich and delicate, while other dessert choices might be more hearty, like steamed ginger pudding with ginger caramel sauce. English cheeses and home-made biscuits was followed by coffee and petits fours in the lounge. The hotel is unlicensed, but sherry is offered before dinner.

Directions: 3 miles south-west of Keswick. Take the A66 for Cockermouth, left at Portinscale, follow road to Grange

Newlands
Map no: 11 NY22
Tel: 017687 72948

Cost: Fixed-price dinner £25.75. Service exc. No corkage charge
Credit cards: None

Menus: Fixed-price dinner

Times: Last D 7.30pm

Chef: Mr Chris Astley
Proprietor: Graham Taylor

Seats: 18. No smoking in dining room
Additional: Children permitted (over 11). ❂ dishes/other diets on request

KIRKBY LONSDALE, **Cobwebs** ❀

A major feature of this restaurant is the impressive wine list providing a wide choice of wines to accompany any dish. Main courses such as game trio – widgeon, pheasant and venison – with pink peppercorn sauce are offered, and to finish a meal, a range of Cumbrian and Lancastrian cheeses.

Leck Cowan Bridge
Map no: 7 SD67
Tel: 015242 72141

Directions: Take A65 east to Skipton – 8 miles into Cowan Bridge, turn left, restaurant 150yds on the left

MUNGRISDALE, **The Mill** ❀

☺ *This former mill cottage is a charming retreat. Chef and proprietor Eleanor Quinlan's imaginative cooking continues to draw praise; her five-course dinner challenges even the heartiest Lakeland appetite. Lovers of desserts will enjoy the mouthwatering selection served by Richard Quinlan.*

Near Penrith
Map no: 11 NY33
Tel: 017687 79659
Chef: Eleanor M Quinlan
Proprietors: Richard and Eleanor Quinlan
Seats: 20. No smoking
Times: Last D 8pm

Cost: Fixed-price D £19.75; H/wine £3.95. Service exc
Credit cards: Non. **Additional:** Children welcome; children's portions; ❂ menu; Vegan/other diets on request
Directions: On A66; follow signs for Mungrisdale and Caldbeck

NEWBY BRIDGE, **Lakeside** ❀

☺ *Esthwaite trout and Waberthwaite ham are typical of the fresh local produce served at this waterside hotel, with a choice of elegant restaurant or less elaborate brasserie-style dining.*

Ulverston
Map no: 7 SD38
Tel: 015395 31207
Chef: Konrad Howlett
Proprietor: Clive Wilson
Seats: 70. No smoking. Air conditioned
Times: Last L 3pm/D 9.30pm

Cost: Brasserie £17; Sunday lunch £9.95; fixed-price dinner £22.50. Wine £12 ♀ Service inc **Credit cards:** 1 2 3 4 5
Additional: Children only before 7.30pm; children's portions/menu; ❂ menu; Vegan/other diets on request. Live entertainment
Directions: On A590 to Newby Bridge, left over bridge and follow Hawkeshead Road for 1 mile to hotel

RAVENSTONEDALE, **Black Swan** ❀

☺ *A popular hotel with an attractive dining room offering a four-course dinner menu. Dishes are uncomplicated with oven-baked hake in a chervil sauce found to be a particularly good main course. Simple fresh vegetables with distinctive flavours – flavours being one of the strengths of the cooking here.*

Near Kirkby Stephen
Map no: 7 NY70
Tel: 015396 23204
Chefs: Graham Bamber, Mrs N W Stuart
Proprietors: G B and N W Stuart
Seats: 40. No smoking in dining room
Times: Last L 2pm/D 9.15pm

Cost: Alc £15; fixed price L £9.50/D £20. Wine £5.50 ♀ Service exc
Credit cards: 1 2 3 4 5
Additional: Children welcome; children's portions; ❂ menu; Vegan/other diets on request
Directions: From A685 towards Brough take road to Ravenstonedale

TEMPLE SOWERBY,
Temple Sowerby House ❀

The restaurant of an elegantly furnished former farmhouse, set in two-acre walled gardens east of Penrith, offers value for money in a range of skilfully prepared traditional English dishes. Daily-changing four and five-course menus give an ample choice which includes vegetarian options.

Cost: Fixed-price L £12.95/D £22. H/wine £7.50. Service exc
Credit cards: 1 2 3 4 5
Additional: Children welcome; children's portions; ◑ dishes; Vegan/other diets on request
Directions: On A66 in centre of village

Near Penrith
Map no: 12 NY62
Tel: 017683 61578
Chefs: Paul Rodgers, Joanne Wharton
Proprietors: Anne and Peter McNamara
Seats: 50. No smoking in dining room
Times: Last L 2pm/D 8.45pm

ULVERSTON, Bay Horse ❀❀

☺ *Delicious food showing plenty of imagination, served in a conservatory overlooking the sea*

John Tovey and the Miller Howe may have inspired this delightful country-style inn on the banks of the Leven Estuary, but the heart and soul of it belong to Robert Lyons. His creativity and innovation are much in evidence in the delicious dishes listed in the fixed-price lunch menu, or in the *carte* offered each evening at 7.30 for 8pm; many of the recipes come from John Tovey's cookbooks, signed copies of which are on sale here. Our inspector was impressed with an exotic-looking recent starter of prawns and avocado marinated in lemon juice and hazelnut oil, wrapped in smoked salmon and served with an attractive salad. Pan-fried lamb medallions filled with fried breadcrumbs, garlic and shallots made a tender and full-flavoured main course, served with a tasty mint and apple sauce and a beautiful presentation of interesting vegetables. Desserts like chocolate wholemeal slice with butterscotch sauce and cream and the orange and Grand Marnier mousse with a shortbread were a great success. The wines have been carefully chosen, and there's a separate New World list.

Directions: Leave A590 at sign for Canal Foot. Pass Glaxo Works

Map no: 7 SD27
Tel: 01229 583972

Cost: Alc £20; fixed-price lunch £14.50. H/wine £1.85 glass ♀ Service exc
Credit cards: 1 3

Menus: A la carte, fixed-price lunch, bar menu (lunch)

Times: 11am–Last L 1.30pm, Last D 8pm

Chefs: Robert Lyons
Proprietor: Robert Lyons

Seats: 50. No smoking in dining room
Additional: Children permitted (over 12); ◑ dishes; Vegan/other diets on request

ULVERSTON, Virginia House ❀

☺ *Alistair and Patricia Sturgis are delightful hosts to this pleasant small hotel. Alistair is an excellent chef and provides a good choice of well produced dishes. Only fresh produce is used and there is almost always a Colombian dish on the menu as Patricia comes from there*

Cost: Alc £13; fixed-price dinner £14.50. Wine £7.50. Service exc
Credit cards: 1 2 3 4 5
Additional: Children welcome; children's portions; ◑ dishes; other diets on request
Directions: Take A590 to Ulverston, after roundabout right turn at 2nd traffic lights; 150 yds on left

Queen Street
Map no: 7 SD27
Tel: 01229 584844
Chef: Alastair Sturgis
Proprietors: Alastair and Patricia Sturgis
Seats: 35. No smoking in dining room
Times: Last D 8.45pm. Closed Sun

WATERMILLOCK, Leeming House ◉◉

An elegant lakeside hotel offering equally high standards of hospitality and cooking

An attractive conservatory links this elegant Lakeland country house with a sympathetically-styled modern wing, creating a grand and sumptuously decorated hotel. On the western shore of Ullswater the hotel offers a high standard of courtesy and hospitality which extends into the dining room. Here chef Adam Marks produces a daily-changing fixed-price menu which shows off his culinary skills, especially with fish dishes like scallops in ginger and lemon, and steamed steak of Cornish halibut. Our inspector began a recent meal with smooth and full-flavoured duck liver parfait with a tangy Cumberland sauce, followed by turbot in a cream saffron sauce, garnished with fresh spinach and almonds. Chocolate marquise with a dark chocolate sauce and cream made a satisfying dessert. The menu also offers meat dishes like breast of Lancashire guinea fowl with blackberry stuffing, and roast loin of Welsh lamb, while a vegetarian choice might be spiced vegetable crumble with tomato and herb sauce, or fricassée of button mushrooms and cherry tomatoes on saffron noodles with Stilton sauce.

Directions: Follow signs for Patterdale on the A592. Hotel is on western shore of lake in Watermillock

Near Penrith
Map no: 12 NY42
Tel: 017684 86622

Cost: *A/c* lunch £21.95; Sunday lunch £16.25; fixed-price dinner £28.50 (3 courses), £35.50. Wine £12.95 ℜ. Service exc
Credit cards: 1 2 3 4 5

Menus: *A la carte* lunch, fixed-price dinner, Sunday lunch

Times: 12.30pm–Last L 1.45pm, 7.30pm–Last D 8.45pm

Chef: Adam Marks
Proprietors: Forte Hotels.
Manager: Christopher L Curry

Seats: 80. No smoking in dining room **Additional:** Children permitted (not babies or the very young at dinner); children's portions/menu; ◎ dishes; Vegan/other diets on request

WATERMILLOCK, Rampsbeck ◉◉

An interesting selection of innovative dishes cooked in a modern English style

A richly furnished restaurant with stunning views of Lake Ullswater is the ideal setting for some equally superb food. Chef Andrew McGeorge has rare skills, and he demonstrates them with consummate ease in dishes like roasted quail and woodland mushroom lasagne, and pan-fried loin of Cumbrian farmed venison served with a game jus flavoured with celeriac. His menus offer a selection of such interesting dishes, and a recent inspection meal produced a beautifully presented saddle of rabbit filled with sun-dried tomatoes and wrapped in air-dried ham, served with crunchy baby vegetables. A full-bodied oxtail soup followed, and the main course of roasted sea-bass with oyster butter sauce was highly praised. Very freshly tasting vegetables came in a filo basket, and poached peach filled with a creamy nougat ice-cream made an enjoyable dessert. Vegetarians are given equally imaginative choices like deep fried goat's cheese and sultana délice, and baked feuillete of creamed woodland mushrooms and globe artichokes scented with tarragon. Service is delightfully enthusiastic.

Directions: From M6, junction 40, follow signs for Ullswater. Turn right at water's edge. Hotel is 1.25 miles on the right

Map no: 12 NY42
Tel: 017684 86442

Cost: Fixed-price lunch £19.95; fixed-price dinner £28.50. Wine £8.95. Service exc
Credit cards: 1 3

Menus: Fixed-price lunch and dinner, Sunday lunch, bar menu

Times: 12pm–Last L 1.45pm, 7pm–Last D 8.30pm. Closed 4 Jan–mid Feb

Chef: Andrew McGeorge
Proprietors: T I and M M Gibb

Seats: 40. No smoking in dining room
Additional: Children permitted (over 5); children's portions; ◎ menu; Vegan/other diets on request

WETHERAL, Fantails ❀

☺ *An attractive restaurant that was previously a barn and blacksmith's is the atmospheric setting for a delicious meal from one of three menus including a vegetarian choice. Look for dishes such as chicken with stilton and mushroom stuffing, or breast of chicken in Marsala with roast almonds.*

Cost: Fixed-price D £15.95. H/wine £8.95. Service exc
Credit cards: 1 3
Additional: Children permitted; ❂ dishes; Vegan/other diets on request
Directions: Leave M6 at junction 42, follow signs for Wetheral

The Green
Map no: 12 NY45
Tel: 01228 560239
Chef: Peter Bowman
Proprietors: Gillian Tod, Bob and Jennifer Bowman
Seats: 85. No smoking in dining room
Times: Last D 9.30pm. Closed Mon

WINDERMERE, Burn How Garden House ❀

☺ *An appealing hotel, set in attractive well-tended gardens. Chef Joanna Byrne, who has quite recently taken over, cooks with simplicity and honesty and uses good quality fresh produce. A variety of the chef's home-made condiments are served with salads, and other dishes.*

Cost: Alc £18.50; fixed-price D £18.50, H/wine £9 ♀ Service inc
Credit cards: 1 2 3 5
Additional: Children permitted (over 5 dinner); children's portions/menu; ❂ dishes; other diets on request
Directions: 200m south of Bowness Bay on A591

Back Belsfield Road, Bowness
Map no: 7 SD49
Tel: 015394 46226
Chef: Joanna
Proprietors: Best Western.
Manager: Michael Robinson
Seats: 50. No smoking in dining room
Times: Last L 1.30pm/D 9pm

WINDERMERE, Cedar Manor ❀

This recently refurbished hotel takes its name from a magnificent Indian Cedar which stands in the grounds. Dinner is the responsibility of Mrs Lynn Hadley who provides imaginative, daily-changing, fixed-price menus with both British and Continental dishes featured.

Cost: Alc £22.50; fixed-price D £16.50. H/wine £10.80. Service exc
Credit cards: 1 3
Additional: Children permitted (over 5 at dinner); children's portions; ❂ dishes; Vegan/other diets on request
Directions: Situated on A591, quarter mile north of village

Ambleside Road
Map no: 7 SD49
Tel: 015394 43192
Chef: Lynn Hadley
Proprietors: Martin Hadley
Seats: 30. No smoking in dining room
Times: Last D 8.30pm. Lunch by arrangement

WINDERMERE, Gilpin Lodge ❀❀

A lovely hotel in a country setting serving an interesting choice of classical dishes with modern influences

No fewer than three cosy and elegant dining rooms provide a fitting setting in which to savour some delightful classical cooking with modern influences. This charming small hotel set in lovely grounds near Bowness has a relaxed cottage atmosphere which belies a serious approach to food. Chef Christopher Davies produces a five-course fixed-price menu

Crook Road
Map no: 7 SD49
Tel: 015394 88818

Cost: Alc £15; Sunday lunch £14; fixed-price dinner £26. Wine £9.95 ♀. No service charge
Credit cards: 1 2 3 4

Menus: *A la carte* lunch (Mon-Sat), fixed-price dinner, Sunday

each night (at lunch-time there's a carte) which offers several interesting choices at most courses: caramelised onion and black pudding 'tarte fine' on a tomato and coriander sauce to start, perhaps, followed by flaked smoked haddock with shallot beurre blanc on saffron and tomato pasta, and roast loin of lamb on a bed of piperade with tarragon sauce. Our inspector enjoyed feuillete of ducks' livers and lambs kidneys with shallots and smoked bacon and a grain mustard sauce, then a light sole mousseline served with a strongly brandy-flavoured lobster sauce, all with authentic flavours. Ragout of monkfish with a tasty mussel and Provençal sauce had a lovely perfume. Coffee and petits fours are served in the main lounge with a blazing log fire in winter.

Directions: On the B5284 Kendal to Bowness on Windermere Road, opposite golf course

lunch, bar menu (Mon–Sat lunch)
Times: 7.30am-Last L 2.30pm, Last D 8.45pm

Chefs: Christopher Davies
Proprietors: Christine and John Cunliffe

Seats: 45. No smoking in dining room
Additional: Children permitted (over 6); ❷ menu; other diets on request

WINDERMERE, Holbeck Ghyll ❀❀

Very fine and imaginative cooking from a talented chef who regularly excels herself

Once the country retreat and hunting lodge of Lord Lonsdale, this fine old house is now a charming and restful hotel sitting in a majestic location overlooking Lake Windermere. Many of the traditional country house comforts are still offered today, and dinner in the majestic oak-panelled restaurant is certainly one of them. Chef Sarah Ingleby's skills are very much in evidence from her imaginative three or four-course set menus, and only the best quality ingredients go into her traditional English cooking. Our inspector admired a recent meal which started with very fresh and tasty grilled sardines on a bed of beef tomatoes with leaf spinach in a warm lemon balm dressing. Cream of carrot and ginger soup was slightly less satisfying, but roast guinea fowl with a plum and shallot sauce, a dariole of basmati rice and a tartlet of apple and plum purée was a tender and full-flavoured dish that came with delicate portions of vegetables. Bread and butter pudding with prunes and sauce anglaise, and a garnish of prunes and apricots marinated in brandy, was surprisingly light and irresistible.

Directions: 3 miles north of Windermere on A591, turn right into Holbeck Lane. Hotel 0.5 mile on left

Holbeck Lane
Map no: 7 SD49
Tel: 015394 32375

Cost: Fixed-price dinner £27.50 (4 courses), £30. H/wine £10.50 ♀ Service exc
Credit cards: 1 2 3

Menus: Fixed-price dinner, bar menu
Times: 7pm-Last D 8.45pm

Chef: Sarah Ingleby
Proprietors: Small Luxury Hotels. Managers: David and Patricia Nicholson

Seats: 40. No smoking
Additional: Children permitted (over 8); children's portions; ❷ dishes; Vegan/other diets on request

WINDERMERE, Langdale Chase ❀

A charming country hotel, with some of the finest views in the Lake District, whose cuisine is in the capable hands of Wendy Lindars. The fixed-price and carte menus offer a good choice of mainly British dishes cooked classically or in a cuisine nouvelle style.

Additional: Children welcome; children's portions/menu; ❷ dishes; Vegan/other diets on request
Directions: Three miles north of Windermere on the lakeside

Map no: 7 SD49
Tel: 018394 32201
Chef: Wendy Lindars
Proprietor: Helmut Kircher
Seats: 80. No smoking in dining room. Air conditioned
Times: Last L 1.45pm/D 8.45pm
Cost: Alc £28; fixed-price L £14/D £22. Wine £11.30 ♀ Service exc
Credit cards: 1 2 3 4

WINDERMERE, Lindeth Fell ❀

☺ *Fine lake views are enjoyed from this charming hotel restaurant, where capable new chef Alison Thompson presents a fixed-price five-course dinner menu. Typical dishes might be mille-feuille filled with ham on an asparagus sauce, and pan-fried monkfish with a mild curry sauce.*

Cost: Sunday L £10; fixed-price D £19. H/wine £4.25 ♀ Service exc
Credit cards: 1 3
Additional: Children permitted (over 7 dinner); children's portions/menu; ◐ dishes, Vegan/other diets on request
Directions: 1 mile south of Bowness on A5074

Upper Storrs Park Road, Bowness
Map no: 7 SD49
Tel: 015394 43286
Chefs: Alison Thompson, Emma Sharman
Proprietors: Pat and Diana Kennedy
Seats: 35. No smoking in dining room
Times: Last L 1.30pm/D 8.30pm. Closed mid Nov–mid Mar

WINDERMERE, Linthwaite House ❀

This delightful hotel with its commanding views of Lake Windermere is the setting for a four-course daily-changing menu prepared by chef, Ian Bravey. The choice may include baked tail of monkfish wrapped in smoked salmon with a red wine butter sauce and garnished with collops of lobster.

Cost: Fixed-price D £27. H/wine £12 ♀ Service inc
Credit cards: 1 2 3 5
Additional: Children permitted (over 7 at dinner); children's portions (lunch only); ◐ dishes; Vegan/other diets on request
Directions: On B5284, 1 mile west of Golf Club going towards lake

Crook Road, Bowness
Map no: 7 SD49
Tel: 015394 88600
Chef: Ian Bravey
Proprietors: Michael Bevans
Seats: 40. No smoking in dining room
Times: Last L 1.30pm (Sun only)/D 9pm

WINDERMERE, Miller Howe ❀❀

Highly acclaimed and renowned Lake District hotel serving ever-enjoyable English cuisine

Some of the most spectacular views of the Lake District can be enjoyed from this Edwardian hotel perched high above Lake Windermere. The accommodation is comfortable and the main rooms richly furnished and decorated, but for most people the food is of primary importance. Dinner follows a time-honoured pattern, with the lights dimmed promptly at 8pm as the five-course meal is ceremoniously carried in. The standard of cooking remains high, and our inspector enjoyed a starter of sliced duck served warm on a cold salad of asparagus tips, sun-dried tomatoes, brown lentils and herbs, with a watercress and balsamic orange dressing, followed a delicious cream of sweetcorn and red pepper soup with deep fried crispy sprouting beans. The next course was a delicate fillet of sole wrapped around a banana, baked in cream and coated with savoury breadcrumbs, and the highlight of the meal was pork chop baked on apple and sage, served with a port wine sauce; the meat had been marinated for four days, and was deliciously tender. Desserts are a stunning feature, and the white chocolate orange tart was unmissable.

Directions: On A592 between Windermere and Bowness

Rayrigg Road
Map no: 7 SD49
Tel: 015394 42536

Cost: Fixed-price dinner £32. Wine £15 ♀ Service 12.5%
Credit cards: 1 2 3 4

Menu: Fixed-price dinner
Times: Dinner 8.30pm (one sitting). Closed early Dec-early Mar

Chefs: Christopher Blaydes
Proprietor: John Tovey

Seats: 70. No smoking. Air conditioned
Additional: Children permitted (over 8); ◐ dishes; other diets on request

WINDERMERE, Porthole Eating House ❀❀

A popular and busy Italian restaurant run by owners with a passion for good food and wine

A bustling, intimate Italian bistro, this place oozes atmosphere. Owners Gianni and Judy Bertoni continue to provide a flamboyant presence in the three low-ceilinged rooms with rough-cast walls and lighted candles, while Mike Metcalf is more than capable in the kitchen. His two *cartes* include a choice of weekly specials, and a more extensive menu with many Italian favourites like spaghetti bolognese, and suprême of chicken saltimbocca. Our inspector chose 'lasagne alla zia ancilla' to start, and enjoyed the very tender pasta layered with bolognese and topped with mushrooms and baked ham. The rare Windermere char – a cross between salmon and trout – was lightly grilled and served with a fresh dill and herb reduction, and made a delicate and tasty main dish. Several excellent deserts include a hot pudding of the day and various home-made sorbets and ice creams, and the sampled zuppa inglese was a moist Tuscan-style trifle layered with cherry brandy-soaked biscuits, crème patissiere and chocolate. An outstanding wine list offers many rarities and a good range of halves.

3 Ash Street, Bowness
Map no: 7 SD49
Tel: 015394 42793

Cost: *Alc* £25. Wine £9.50.
Service exc
Credit cards: 1 2 3 4

Menus: *A la carte*, fixed-price dinner and Sunday lunch (by request), pre-theatre

Times: 6pm-Last D 11pm.
Closed Tue, mid Dec

Chef: Mike Metcalfe
Proprietors: Gianni Bertoni

Seats: 40
Additional: Children welcome; children's portions; ❖ dishes; Vegan/other diets on request

Directions: In Bowness town centre near parish church

WINDERMERE, Quarry Garth ❀

☺ *Excellent food from a country house hotel and restaurant in eight peaceful acres on Lake Windermere's shore*

Celebrated not just for the lakes themselves but for its fells, its lonely clouds and its daffodils, Lakeland's restaurants are also essential to the repertoire; Quarry Garth is one of them. The mainly Anglo-French *carte* changes daily and all dishes are presented with great flair. Selecting examples is not easy when there are so many worthy contenders, but starters could include charlotte of chicken and pork filled with a ragout of potato and avocado and a balsamic vinaigrette; or diamonds of mackerel grilled with black pepper and served with vegetable spaghetti and pesto sauce. Fillet of West Coast cod grilled in garlic butter, topped with a herb crust and a basil sauce could be a main course, as could the rather unusual fillet of lamb wrapped in a mint farcie, presented on sautéed liver with parsley sauce. Sweets could include iced Armagnac parfait, bread and butter pudding or baked apple tart with toffee and butterscotch ice cream. Wines from the New World and Europe are helpfully grouped by taste eg. 'smooth and mellow'. Well-chosen staff assist owners Huw and Lynne Phillips with the attentive service.

Troutbeck Bridge
Map no: 7 SD49
Tel: 015394 88282

Cost: Fixed-price dinner £21.50.
Wine £9.75. Service exc
Credit cards: 1 2 3 4 5

Menus: Fixed-price dinner

Times: Last D 9pm

Chef: Huw Phillips
Proprietors: Huw and Lynne Phillips

Seats: 36. No smoking in dining room
Additional: Children permitted; ❖ dishes/other diets on request

Directions: On A591, 2 miles from Windermere travelling towards Ambleside

WINDERMERE, Rogers Restaurant ❀❀

☺ *An intimate restaurant where the proprietor's individual style of cooking has stood the test of time.*

Roger Pergl-Wilson and his wife Alena opened their intimate little restaurant on the edge of Windermere village, opposite the railway station, some fourteen years ago and have made few changes since then. Roger's individual style of cooking, though firmly rooted in classical French cuisine, is simply presented, very much his own and has stood the test of time. His interesting *carte*, three-course fixed-price, and no-choice French provincial menus attract a faithful clientele of regular customers, as well as visitors to the area. Popular main courses include crisply cooked honey-glazed Gressingham duck with blackcurrants, fillet of hake in flakey pastry and roast rack of spring lamb with a herb crust and Madeira gravy; an attractively served selection of vegetables could comprise dauphinoise potatoes, sliced and lightly buttered carrots, mange-tout and shredded cabbage with finely diced ham, and for dessert one might choose a dark chocolate marquise complemented by Irish coffee cream. Petit fours accompany the Italian blended coffee that completes the meal. A carefully chosen wine list covers all major areas, including the New World.

Directions: Opposite the Tourist Office, near the railway station

4 High Street
Map no: 7 SD49
Tel: 015394 44954

Cost: Fixed-price D £15.75.
H/wine £9.95 ♀ Service exc
Credit cards: 1 2 3 4

Times: Last D 9.30pm. Closed Sun (except BHs), 1 week summer/winter

Chef: Roger Pergl-Wilson
Proprietor: Roger Pergl-Wilson

Seats: 42. No cigars or pipes
Additional: Children welcome; children's portions; ✿ dishes; Vegan/other diets on request

WITHERSLACK, Old Vicarage ❀

Speciality gourmet dinners are a regular feature at this country house hotel, but almost equally tempting are the everyday fixed-price menus with a choice of starters and desserts with a set main course - perhaps a succulent rare Chateaubriand - though an alternative can be requested.

Cost: Fixed-price L £13.50/D £22.50. H/wine £12.50 ♀ Service exc
Credit cards: 1 3 5 **Additional:** Children permitted (no babies); children's portions; ✿ dishes, Vegan/other diets on request
Directions: Take turning in village signposted to church

Near Grange-over-Sands
Map no: 7 SD48
Tel: 015395 52381
Chef: Stanley Reeve, Paul Axford
Proprietors: Burrington-Brown and Reeve families
Seats: 35. No smoking in dining room
Times: Last L (Sun only) 12.30pm/D 7.30pm

DERBYSHIRE

ASHBOURNE, Callow Hall ❀❀

A country house hotel in a beautiful setting, offering a wide range of English and French dishes and imaginative menus.

The Spencer family are justifiably proud of their lovely country house hotel, set in 44 acres of neat gardens and grounds, surrounded by beautiful open countryside. Chef/patron David Spencer offers a four-course daily fixed-price menu or good *carte* choices that reflect traditional and modern French and

Mappleton Road
Map no: 7 SK14
Tel: 01335 343403

Cost: A/c £26, fixed-price dinner £27.50. H/wine £8.95 Service exc
Credit cards: 1 2 3 4

Menus: A la carte, fixed-price

English dishes. Good quality, personally selected produce is put to noticeable use throughout, with a particularly tasty starter of sautéed calf's liver with sesame seed topping, accompanied by shallots, bacon and a rich port sauce. Boned, roast guinea fowl with button onions, mushrooms, bacon and croûtons served with a red wine sauce proved a piquant main course. A superb tarte tatin demonstrated a magical combination of apple and caramel, topped by a delicate pastry. The comprehensive wine list specialises in French wines but the New World is also represented, together with a good selection of half bottles.

Directions: 0.75 mile from Ashbourne. Take A515 for Buxton, sharp left by Bowling Green Pub, first right to Mappleton Road

dinner, Sunday lunch
Times: Last L 1.45pm/D 9.15pm

Chefs: David and Anthony Spencer
Proprietors: David, Dorothy and Anthony Spencer

Seats: 60. No smoking
Additional: Children welcome; children's portions; ◐ dishes; Vegan/other diets on request

ASHFORD-IN-THE-WATER, Riverside ❀

☺ *An elegant, yet comfortable Georgian house hotel is the setting for modern English cuisine prepared by chef, Simon Wild, from fresh local produce. There is a five-course set menu of three larger courses, for example fillet steak, and some less filling extras, including Chef's Surprise Savoury.*

Cost: A/c £19, fixed-price D £19.50, £29
Credit cards: 1 2 3 5. **Additional:** Children welcome at lunch; children's portions (5.30pm-6.30pm). ◐ dishes; Vegan/other diets on request
Directions: On main street of village

Fennel Street
Map no: 7 SK16
Tel: 01629 814275
Chef: Simon Wild
Proprietors: Roger and Susan Taylor
Seats: 50. No smoking in dining room
Times: Last L 2.30pm/D 9.30pm. All day Lite Bite in Terrace Room 9.30am-9.30pm

BAKEWELL, Croft House ❀

A welcoming hotel situated in the unspoilt village of Great Longstone, whose restaurant offers good quality food. Lynne Macaskill prepares the dishes from the freshest produce, honest flavours and careful presentation of a short set menu. Alternative main course dishes are available on request.

Cost: Fixed-price dinner £21.50. Wine £7.75. Service exc
Credit cards: 1 3. **Additional:** No smoking in dining room. Children permitted (no babies); ◐ dishes; Vegan/other diets on request
Directions: Take A6020 signposted Chesterfield, after 0.75 miles turn left to Great Longstone. Hotel on the right entering village

Great Longstone
Map no: 8 SK26
Tel: 01629 640278
Chef: Mrs Lynne Macaskill
Proprietors: Mr R A and Mrs L Macaskill
Times: Last D 7.30pm

BAKEWELL, **Rutland Arms** ❀❀

☺ *A stone-built town centre hotel with the attractive Four Seasons Restaurant offering carefully prepared food.*

Fixed-price and *carte* menus reflect a balanced mix of modern and traditional British dishes with occasional French influences. Top quality produce is put to good use in seasonal dishes. The quality of the cuisine has consistently improved and this year the AA inspectors have awarded Rutland Arms an additional rosette.

Additional: No smoking in dining room. Children welcome; children's portions/menu; ❍ dishes; Vegan/other diets on request

The Square
Map no: 8 SK26
Tel: 01629 812812
Cost: *Alc* £18; fixed-price L £9.95/D £14.95 (2 courses), £17.50. Wine £8.95. Service exc
Credit cards: 1 2 3 4 5
Times: Last L 2.30pm/ D 9.30pm
Chef: Peter Sanderson
Proprietor: Best Western.
Manager: Roberto Ramirez

BASLOW, **Cavendish** ❀❀

Impressively presented food from an imaginative chef, served in a delightful setting

Sensational views over the Chatsworth estate – of which it is a part – can be enjoyed from most of the rooms in this 200-year-old inn. An enthusiastic and friendly welcome awaits visitors, and the delightfully furnished public rooms provide a relaxing atmosphere, with their chintzy furniture and objets d'art. Soft pinks and blues form the background to the elegant restaurant, where chef Nick Buckingham never fails to interest and delight even the most experienced of diners. His varied and imaginative dishes are impressively presented in a series of fixed-price menus, with an additional list of 'favourite' dishes at a supplementary price. Foie gras in a light pastry case with braised wild mushrooms and truffle was a satisfying recent starter, followed by a daily special dish of fresh turbot with oysters in a well-flavoured champagne sauce. The short list of desserts includes a daily hot choice and a 'surprise' mixture of sweets, while the chosen passion fruit soufflé with ice cream was very light and tasty. Chargrilled salmon, baked tuna steak and corn-fed chicken are typical dishes on the menu.

Directions: On the A619 in the village

Map no: 8 SK27
Tel: 01246 582311

Cost: Fixed-price lunch £20.75 (2 courses), £24.75, fixed-price dinner £24.75. H/wine £14.50. Service exc
Credit cards: 1 2 3 4 5

Menus: *A la carte*, fixed-price lunch and dinner, Sun lunch, all day Garden Room menu

Times: 12.30-Last L 2.pm, 7pm-Last D 10pm

Chef: Nick Buckingham
Proprietor: Eric Marsh

Seats: 50. No smoking in dining room
Additional: Children welcome; children's portions; ❍ menu; Vegan/other diets on request

BASLOW, **Fischer's** ❀❀❀

Classical French and modern European cuisine in an elegant country house restaurant, with a good value café alternative

The description 'restaurant with rooms' does little justice to this fine Edwardian manor house on the edge of the Chatsworth estate. Though it is true to say that the stylish restaurant and the informal Café Max dominate the hotel, and that food is of prime importance to the proprietors, Max and Susan Fischer.
Max presents a monthly-changing fixed-price dinner menu, which includes appetisers, a surprise hot savoury, three courses, coffee and petits fours, while at lunch the menu is priced for two or three courses. He cooks in an imaginative European style, offering a balance of simply prepared dishes and more complex

Baslow Hall, Calver Road
Map no: 8 SK27
Tel: 01246 583259

Cost: Fixed-price lunch £14.50 (2 courses), £17.50; fixed-price dinner £36. H/wine £9.50 ♀ Service exc
Credit cards: 1 2 4 5

Menus: Fixed-price lunch and dinner, Sunday lunch. *A la carte* (Café Max)

Times: 8am-Last L 2pm, Last D

creations. Vegetarian dishes may appear on the menu or can be specially requested. Our inspector's starter was a straightforward dish of British goat's cheese ravioli on a bed of full-flavoured tomatoes. This was followed by a delicious main course of tender pink spring lamb in a delicate aubergine wrapping with a farci of herbs and breadcrumbs. Dark chocolate gonache provided a rich finale to the meal, served with white and dark chocolate truffle cream and a delightful chocolate ice cream.

Café Max is a good value, informal alternative. The *carte* menu offering a range of dishes, with soups, terrines, antipasti and omelettes among the starters, and entrées such as bangers and mash, Fischer's fishcakes (cod and salmon with a hint of curry and coriander in a crisp crumb coating), or home-made cannelloni with ricotta cheese and Neapolitan sauce, which can also be taken as a starter. Desserts include their renowned lemon tart with home-made vanilla ice cream or Sharrow Bay sticky toffee pudding. The wine list is compact, easy to read and sensibly priced. Most wines are French, with good selections from Italy, Spain and Germany.

10pm. Closed Sun dinner, Xmas. Café Max closed all day Sun

Chef: Max Fischer
Proprietors: Max and Susan Fischer

Seats: 77. No smoking in dining room
Additional: Children permitted (over 12 after 7pm); children's portions; ❂ dishes; Vegan/other diets on request

Directions: On right of A623 as you leave Baslow towards Calver

BELPER, Makeney Hall ❂❂

A good choice of traditional French cuisine and vegetarian alternatives in a country house setting

An extensively refurbished country house hotel, Makeney Hall has a large restaurant divided between a light conservatory and a richly panelled room with a fabulous open fire. Chef Ronnie Wyatt-Goodwin offers a good selection of dishes cooked in traditional French style from good value fixed-price menus and a more extensive carte. His dedicated approach and use of the finest quality ingredients ensures dependable results. Our inspector particularly enjoyed a starter of local game terrine, a rich, well balanced dish served with a contrasting jelly of winter berries. Fish is well-represented, and a main course of monkfish and crab with a champagne sauce was interesting, though the sauce was a touch over-seasoned. The *carte* also offers half a dozen vegetarian dishes, including a vegetable lasagna, and filo parcels of feta and spinach on a tomato and basil coulis. For pudding, the hot Bramley apple soufflé proved a good choice, with a golden colour, well-flavoured apple base and unusual custard filling. French wines predominate on a list of 60 bottles, with some halves, and dessert and after dinner wines.

Directions: Join A6 north of Derby and turn right into village of Milford. Hotel is 0.25 miles

Milford
Map no: 8 SK34
Tel: 01332 842999

Cost: *Alc* from £30.25; Sunday lunch £13; fixed-price lunch £12; fixed-price dinner £17. H/wine £10. Service exc
Credit cards: 1 2 3 4 5

Menus: *A la carte*, fixed-price lunch and dinner, Sunday lunch

Times: 12.30pm–Last L 1.45pm, 7pm–Last D 9.45pm. Closed Sat lunch

Chef: Ronnie Wyatt-Goodwin
Proprietor: Mrs Sonia Holmes and David Hunter

Seats: 70
Additional: Children welcome; children's portions; ❂ menu; Vegan/other diets on request. Live entertainment Sat eve

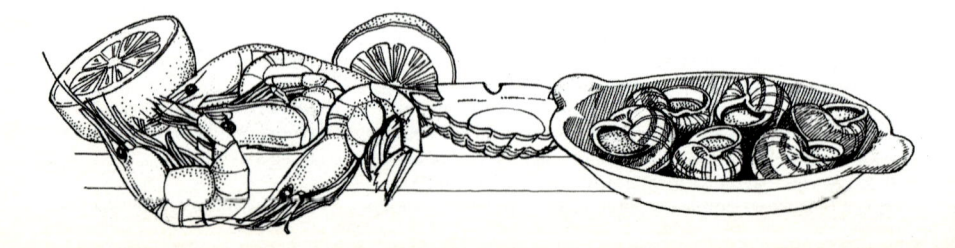

ENGLAND DERBYSHIRE 215

BUXTON, Lee Wood ☸

☺ *Chef Sean Ballington offers a comprehensive fixed-price menu together with a small speciality menu in the light airy conservatory restaurant. Dishes are predominantly modern British and classical French, using good quality produce, carefully and imaginatively prepared.*

Cost: Alc £21; Sunday L £12.50; fixed-price D £18 (3 courses), £19.95. Wine £10.75 ♀ Service exc. **Credit cards:** 1 2 3 4 5.
Additional: Children welcome; children's portions; ♥ menu; Vegan/other diets on request
Directions: Follow A5004 from Buxton town centre. Hotel 300 yds on left above Devonshire Royal Hospital

13 Manchester Road
Map no: 7 SK07
Tel: 01298 23002
Chef: Sean Ballington
Proprietor: Best Western.
Manager: John Millican
Seats: 80
Times: Last L 2pm/D 9.30pm

BUXTON, Portland ☸

☺ *Chef Brian Simmonds presents a good range of imaginative modern English dishes in the pleasant conservatory restaurant at the Portland Hotel. A hot and cold buffet is available at lunch, and a fixed-price and carte menu at dinner. Vegetarian options are always available.*

Cost: Alc £20; fixed-price L £5.50/D £18. H/wine £9. Service exc
Credit cards: 1 2 3 4 5 **Additional:** Children welcome; children's portions/menu; ♥ menu; Vegan/other diets on request
Directions: On A53 opposite the Pavilion Gardens

32 St John's Road
Map no: 7 SK07
Tel: 01298 22462
Chefs: Brian Simmonds, Tony Bennett
Proprietors: Logis. Managers: Brian and Linda Millner
Seats: 100. Air conditioned
Times: Last L 2pm/D 9pm

MATLOCK, Riber Hall ☸

A beautiful manor house sitting high up adjacent to Riber Castle with chef Jeremy Brazelles continuing to produce an interesting selection of modern British dishes through a fixed-price lunch menu and an evening carte. Seasonal menus with good game and vegetarian dishes.

Cost: Alc £27; fixed-price L £14.50. H/wine £10.90. Service exc
Credit cards: 1 2 3 4 5 **Additional:** Children welcome; children's portions; ♥ menu; Vegan/other diets on request
Directions: In Tansley left at filling station, 1 mile up lane to T junction. Drive straight ahead

Map no: 8 SK35
Tel: 01629 582795
Chef: Jeremy Brazelle
Proprietor: Alex Biggin
Seats: 60. No-smoking area
Times: Last L 1.30pm/D 9.30pm

MELBOURNE, The Bay Tree ☸

A small beamed restaurant with a friendly and intimate atmosphere and interesting, carefully prepared classic cooking. Dishes, lovingly described on the monthly-changing menu, recently included a light, warm duck liver mousse, salade nicoise and Lunesdale duckling

Cost: Alc £27, fixed-price Sun L £14.50. H/wine £8.95. Service exc
Credit cards: 1 2 3 5. **Additional:** Children welcome; children's portions
Directions: In the centre of town

4 Potter Street
Map no: 8 SK32
Tel: 01332 863358
Chef: Rex William Howell
Proprietors: Rex William Howell, Victoria Ann Talbott
Seats: 45. No-smoking area. No pipes or cigars. Air conditioned
Times: Last L 2pm/D 9.45 pm. Closed Sun eve, all day Mon, 1st week Jan, last 2 weeks Aug

RIDGEWAY, **The Old Vicarage** ✤✤✤

Map no: 8 SK48
Tel: 0114 2475814

A haven of civilised dining in an early-Victorian house where the city meets the country

Cost: Fixed-price menu £32
Credit cards: 1 2 3

In Derbyshire by a whisker, on Sheffield's south-eastern edge, is an 1840's village house in its own grounds. For a change, the Bramley proprietorial team is mother Tessa (chef) and son Andrew (front of house). Andrew is also the one who knows his way around the extensive choice of wines. These are featured on a substantial principal list, from which are drawn 'recommendations', offering a good spread of prices and origins. Guests are looked after with great care in the friendly, though slightly formal, atmosphere in the main dining room.

Mother Tessa's fixed-price menu changes weekly and could be the reason for making not just a first but at least one repeat visit here. Her ever-roving, ever-improving cuisine marries the best of local (often as local as the garden) and other British produce with an array of imaginative influences, such as Thai spices with piquant crab cakes on soft saffron rice and full-flavoured shellfish sauce, pesto with fresh turbot, filo parcel of mooli and lemon grass on black bean sauce and stir-fried oriental vegetables, served with spiced aubergine pancakes. Or roast fillet of lamb, served with pan-fried sweetbreads in a Sauternes sauce. Desserts, usually with a British bias, are as competent as everything that precedes them, such as delicately-flavoured trio of warm strawberry soufflé, tart and soft iced parfait. Only British cheeses are offered.

There is also the less expensive Bistro in the conservatory, with simpler, daily-changing dishes displayed on a blackboard. Those who have eaten at The Old Vicarage will be particularly interested in Tessa Bramley's new book *The Instinctive Cook* which adds another dimension to her talent-laden repertoire.

Menus: Fixed-price menu, bistro lunch

Times: 12.30-Last L 2pm, 7.pm-Last D 9.30pm

Chef: Tessa Bramley
Proprietors: Tessa Bramley and Andrew Bramley

Seats: 50 dining room, 30 bistro. No smoking in dining room
Additional: Children welcome.
ⓥ dish

Directions: South-east of Sheffield, off the A616. At the edge of the village follow the sign for Ridgeway Cottage Industries (Marsh Lane) and the restaurant is about half a mile on the left

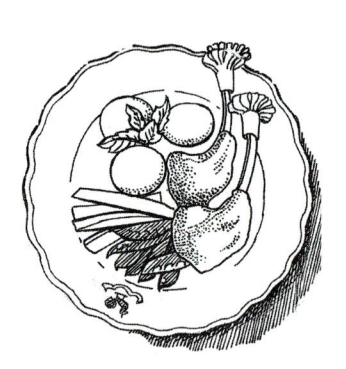

DEVON

ASHBURTON, **Holne Chase** ✤

Newton Abbott
Map no: 3 SX 77
Tel: 01364 631471
Chef: Edward Nuttall
Proprietors: Mr and Mrs K Bromage
Seats: 40. No smoking in dining room
Times: Last L 1.45pm/D 9pm

A family run hotel in a unique location, this 11th-century hunting lodge offers imaginative food cooked with produce from the walled kitchen garden. Choose from starters such as chilled smoked salmon soufflé or duck liver pâté and follow with stuffed suprême of chicken or poached salmon.

Cost: Alc £25, fixed-price L £14.50/D £20. H/wine £7. Service inc
Credit cards: 1 2 3 4 5. **Additional:** Children welcome; children's portions. ⓥ dishes; Vegan/other diets on request
Directions: Three miles north of Ashburton on the Two Bridges road

BARNSTAPLE, **Halmpstone Manor** ●●

Relaxed but attentive service accompanies enjoyable food which makes good use of fresh local produce

The atmosphere here is more like that of a friend's country house than a hotel, which is precisely what owners Jane and Charles Stanbury want to achieve. They manage to combine a relaxed informality with excellent attention to customer care, and all areas show evidence of the personal touch. The candle-lit dining room makes an appropriate setting for Jane Stanbury's impressive cooking, which draws on fish from Bideford Quay, herbs from the garden, home-made preserves and local produce where possible. A recent inspection meal began with a delicious hot crab soufflé with a crusted topping of baked egg white, followed by a complementary champagne sorbet, and then fillet of Devonshire beef served with caramelised shallots and a sweet Madeira wine sauce. The beautifully cooked vegetables were fresh and tasty. A dessert trolley displays some scrumptious creations from Sarah Ford, and the sampled brandy and cocoa mousse was a good example. Other dishes on the fixed-price dinner menus might be roasted fillet of monkfish with a seed mustard sauce, and roast venison with peppercorn sauce.

Bishop's Tawton
Map no: 2 SS53
Tel: 01271 830321

Cost: Fixed-price dinner £27.50. Wine £9.50. Service exc
Credit cards: 1 2 3 4

Menus: Fixed-price dinner

Times: Lunch by arrangement. 6.30pm-Last D 9pm. Closed Jan

Chef: Mrs Jane Stanbury
Proprietor: Charles and Jane Stanbury

Seats: 24. No smoking
Additional: Children permitted (over 12); ◐ dishes; Vegan/other diets on request

Directions: From Barnstaple take A377 to Bishop's Tawton. At end of village turn left; after 2 miles turn right as signposted

BOVEY TRACEY, **Edgemoor** ●

☺ *Monthly changing fixed-price menus are prepared with flair and imagination by chef Edward Elliot in this creeper-clad country house. Our inspector enjoyed cream of chicken and watercress soup, followed by breast of chicken stuffed with leek and ham.*

Haytor Road
Map no: 3 SX87
Tel: 01626 832466
Chef: Edward Elliott
Proprietors: Mr and Mrs Day
Times: Last L 1.45pm/D 9.30pm

Cost: Fixed-price menu £16.50. **Credit cards:** 1 3
Additional: No smoking in dining room. ◐ dishes
Directions: One mile out of Bovey Tracey on the Haytor road

BROADHEMBURY, **Drewe Arms** ●

☺ *The emphasis is very much on food at this stone-built pub and chef/patron Kerstin Burge's speciality is fresh fish and seafood. Dishes change with availability and the fish is delivered three times a week from Newlyn in Cornwall.*

Map no: 3 ST10
Tel: 01404 841267
Chef: Kerstin Burge
Proprietors: Kerstin and Nigel Burge
Seats: 40. No cigars or pipes in restaurant. Air-cleaning
Times: Last L 2pm/D 10pm

Cost: A/c £16.95; fixed-price L/D £16.95. Wine £6.95. Service exc
Credit cards: None taken
Additional: Children permitted (only lunch); children's portions; ◐ dishes; Vegan/other diets on request
Directions: From junction 28 (M5), 5 miles on A373 Cullompton to Honiton

BURRINGTON, **Northcote Manor** ✺

☺ *Chef/patron Glenda Brown shows imagination in the kitchen of her gabled stone manor house where the hearty five-course set dinner changes daily. Traditional, achievable and well-executed, her cooking draws on local produce including vegetables grown in the garden of this peaceful, relaxing hotel*

Cost: Fixed-price D £20.50. H/wine £8.50. No service charge
Credit cards: 1 2 3 4 5
Additional: No children under 12. ❂ dishes/other diets on request
Directions: Hotel drive opposite Portsmouth Arms pub, on A377 12 miles south of Barnstaple

Umberleigh
Map no: 3 SS61
Tel: 01769 60501
Chef: Glenda Brown
Proprietors: Best Western. Managers: Glenda and Peter Brown
Seats: 30. No smoking in dining room
Times: Last D 8.30pm. Closed Nov-Feb

CHAGFORD, **Easton Court** ✺

☺ *The thatched part of this hotel dates back to the 15th century and in its dining room you can choose from an imaginative fixed-price menu. Five courses are offered, using local fish and game. Meals are freshly cooked and our inspector's avocado and seafood cocktail was delicious.*

Cost: Fixed-price menu £16. **Credit cards:** 1 2 3
Additional: Children over 12 permitted
Directions: On the A382 by the main crossroads to Chagford

Easton Cross
Map no: 3 SX78
Tel: 01647 433469
Chef: Lynne Dan
Proprietors: Graham and Sally Kidson
Times: Closed Jan

CHAGFORD, **Gidleigh Park**

Paul and Kay Henderson have created this superb hotel, set in idyllic surroundings. They have designers' eyes for antiques, fabrics and colours and special skills in training one of the most naturally friendly and attentive teams of staff to be found in any hotel. The standard of cuisine has always matched their other standards and although their inspired chef, Shaun Hill, left during the summer of 1994 another chef, Michael Caines, has been appointed. Having worked with Raymond Blanc at Le Manoir aux Quat'Saisons and then subsequently with Bernard Loiseau in Burgundy and Joël Robouchon in Paris, he has the very best experience. Michael is a creative chef with an excellent reputation and we have no doubt that he will maintain the same level of excellence for our inspectors to report on during the coming year.

Near Newton Abbot
Map no: 3 SX78
Tel: 01647 432367

ENGLAND DEVON 219

CHAGFORD, **Mill End** ❀

This former flour mill's wheel is still turning in the peaceful courtyard. Hazel Craddock uses fresh, good quality ingredients to prepare dishes. Fresh Lunsdale duck can be followed by something from their superb award-winning cheese selection.

Cost: Alc £25.25; fixed-price L £16.50. H/wine £8.50. Service exc
Credit cards: 1 2 3 4 5. **Additional:** Children welcome; children's portions; ❂ dishes; Vegan/other diets on request. Live entertainment occasionally
Directions: From Exeter take A30 to Whiddon Down, turn south on A382 signposted Moreton Hampstead – do not turn into Chagford at Sandy Park the hotel is at Dogmarsh Bridge

Sandy Park
Map no: 3 SX78
Tel: 01647 432282
Chef: Hazel Craddock
Proprietors: Nicholas Craddock
Seats: 40. No smoking
Times: Last L 1.45pm/D 9pm.
Closed 5–15 Dec, 10–20 Jan

CHARDSTOCK, **Tytherleigh Cot** ❀

A thatched 14th-century building once used as a cider house, now a cottage hotel with a smart conservatory restaurant. There's a choice of interesting fish, meat and game dishes, including perhaps twice-baked goat's cheese soufflé, and braised rabbit with herb dumplings.

Cost: Alc £25.50; fixed-price L £10.50/D £17.95. Wine £10.50 ♀ Service inc. **Credit cards:** 1 3
Additional: Children permitted (over 10); children's portions; ❂ dishes; Vegan/other diets on request
Directions: One mile off A358, on right in village centre

Map no: 3 ST30
Tel: 01460 221170
Chef: Mrs Patricia Grudgings
Proprietors: Mr and Mrs F D Grudgings
Seats: 40. No smoking in dining room. Air conditioned
Times: Last L 1.30pm/Last D 9.30pm

COLYFORD, **Swallow Eaves** ❀

☺ *An elegant hotel overlooking the Axe Valley where Jane Beck's self-taught cuisine goes down very well. Meals are carefully prepared and dishes include cheesy prawns, as a starter, and pork with prunes in a white wine sauce or sirloin steak with green peppercorn and white wine sauce.*

Cost: Fixed-price D £17.90. H/wine £7.95 ♀ Service inc
Credit cards: None taken
Additional: No children
Directions: On the A3082 in the centre of the village

Swan Hill Road
Map no: 3 SY29
Tel: 01279 553184
Chef: Jane Beck
Proprietors: Mr and Mrs J Beck
Seats: 16. No smoking
Times: Last D 8pm. Closed Jan

DARTMOUTH, **Carved Angel** ❀❀❀

There is an emphasis on fish and a Mediterranean style of cooking at this long-established quayside restaurant

In 1995 Joyce Molyneux will be celebrating her 21st anniversary at this quayside restaurant, whose loyal clientele are tribute to its great appeal. Now in partnership, Joyce, Meriel Matthews, chef Nick Coiley and David Shephard (well known in the area for his wine expertise), are entering a third decade of good food on a very positive note.
   Lunch is chosen from the *carte* or a short fixed-price two or

2 South Embankment
Map no: 3 SX85
Tel: 01803 832465

Cost: Alc L £38.50; fixed price lunch £24 (2-courses), £29, Sunday £30; fixed-price dinner £40 (2 courses), £45. H/wine £14. No service charge
Credit cards: None taken

three-course menu. The *carte* appears again at dinner, but as a fixed-price selection of three courses plus a sorbet or cheese. Fish dishes take up half the menu, and Dart salmon and turbot are regulars in season. Only the finest local produce is selected, and cooked with inspired creativity.

At one meal our inspector was impressed by an 'aubergine plate', the universal vegetable prepared in four different ways: spiced, marinated with honey and thyme, prepared with coconut and honey, and with a sesame brochette. Other starters might include bresaola with vegetables à la grecque, or smoked eel with oatmeal pancakes and horseradish cream. For his main course our inspector opted for a trio of lamb's offal: sweetbread fritters on a bed of simple tomato, onion and garlic sauce, lightly pan-fried liver with a lovely sharp sauce of fresh limes and gin, and, the best of the bunch, sliced kidney with mustard butter. Iced honey and quince nougatine made a lovely light ending to the meal. Alternatives might be Russian pashka, lime leaf and lemon grass crème brûlée, or a selection of Ticklemore cheeses.

The wine list is first class; a very strong and reasonably priced section from Bordeaux, Burgundy and the Rhône and an excellent selection from New Zealand, Australia and America. Look too, at the list of bin-ends.

Guests should note that credit cards are not accepted.

Directions: Situated on the water's edge in the centre of Dartmouth

Menus: *A la carte* lunch, fixed-price lunch and dinner, Sunday lunch

Times: 12.30pm-Last L 2pm, 7.30pm-Last D 9.30pm. Closed Sun eve, Mon, 6 weeks from 2 Jan

Chefs: Joyce Molyneux, Nick Coiley
Proprietor: Joyce Molyneux

Seats: 45. No cigars or pipes
Additional: Children welcome; children's portions; ❶ dishes; Vegan/other diets on request

DARTMOUTH, **The Exchange** ❊❊

☺ *International cooking with a broad appeal in an informal, stylish setting, masterminded by a world-travelled patron and chef*

An attractive centuries-old listed building near the church, The Exchange, now a smart, two floor restaurant, was formerly a Job Centre. Its chef/proprietor David Hawke has a similarly unusual background in that he spent the last eight years as chef on a private yacht sailing the world. His brasserie-style operation has an informal and relaxed atmosphere offering a selection of light dishes at lunch-time and an evening *carte* reflecting his travels. First courses include scallops Provençal, black bean soup and our inspector's choice of crab cakes with avocado butter, an outstanding success, the spiciness of the crab set off by the coolness of the avocado. The following poached ┼halibut, served with a warm vinaigrette, was lightly cooked and freshly caught, full of that straight-from-the-sea-flavour. Char-grilled swordfish, blackened tuna and teriyaki sirloin steak were also on the menu. On this occasion, the chosen pudding was a chocolate pot flavoured with brandy, garnished with flaked almonds. The wine list is simple and reasonably priced, service friendly and easy.

Directions: In town centre near parish church

5 Higher Street
Map no: 3 SX85
Tel: 01803 832022

Cost: Alc £20. H/wine £7.50. Service exc
Credit cards: 1 3

Menus: *A la carte*, Sun lunch in winter

Times: Last L 2pm, Last D 10pm. Closed Tue and Xmas

Chef: David C Hawke
Proprietor: David C Hawke

Seats: 50
Additional: ❶ dishes; Vegan/other diets on request

ERMINGTON, Ermewood House ❀

☺ *The kitchen is the heart of Ermewood House, and Jack Mellor's short fixed-price daily menu attracts residents and non-residents alike. It offers four courses of traditional British cooking with some French influences, and dishes such as smoked fish pâté and roast duck with honey and whisky.*

Cost: Fixed-price D £17.50. H/wine £8.95 ♀ Service exc
Credit cards: 1 3. **Additional:** Children permitted; ❂ dishes; Vegan/other diets on request
Directions: Driveway to hotel off the A3121

Totnes Road
Map no: 2 SX65
Tel: 01548 830741
Chef: Jack Mellor
Proprietors: Jack and Jennifer Mellor
Seats: 22. No smoking in dining room
Times: Last D 8.30pm. Closed Sun, Xmas and New Year

EXETER, Buckerell Lodge ❀❀

Two rosette food in a recently refurbished family-run hotel

Raffles is the setting for Melvin Rumbles, the chef, to create imaginative and well prepared dishes. He and his team have maintained very high standards and have recently been awarded a second rosette. An example of the dishes on offer is escalope of Scottish salmon served with champagne and saffron sauce and garnished with baby leeks and artichoke bottoms. From the desserts a selection of light mango mousse with a raspberry sauce or a trio of English cheeses with walnuts and celery may be made.

Additional: Children welcome; children's portions; ❂ dishes; Vegan/other diets on request. Live entertainment
Directions: Follow signs for city centre then R D & E hospital, located on B3182

Topsham Road
Map no: 3 SX99
Tel: 01392 52451
Chef: Melvin Rumbles
Proprietors: Bruce and Pat Jefford
Seats: 70. Air conditioned
Times: Last L 2pm/D 10pm
Cost: Alc £22.50; fixed-price L £12.50/D £17.50. H/wine £9.95 ♀ Service exc
Credit Cards: 1 2 3 4

EXETER, Ebford House ❀

☺ *Horton's restaurant offers sophisticated modern cuisine in a formal setting; Frisco's Bistro has a simpler blackboard menu, but even here you can expect dishes like boneless chicken stuffed with prawns in a chasseur sauce. Meats and fish are locally produced; bread, soups and sauces are home made.*

Cost: Alc £20; fixed-price L £12.95/D £18.50. H/wine £8.10 ♀ Service exc **Credit Cards:** 1 2 3 5
Additional: Children welcome; children's portions/menu; ❂ dishes; Vegan/other diets on request
Directions: Situated on A376 Exmouth road near Topsham

Exmouth Road
Map no: 3 SX99
Tel: 01392 877658
Chefs: Don Horton, Paul Bazell
Proprietors: Logis. Manager: Don Horton
Seats: 50. No smoking in dining room
Times: Last L 1.30pm/D 9.30pm. Closed Sun lunch, 24–30 Dec

EXETER, St Olaves Court ❀❀

A friendly, busy restaurant in an attractive setting with an interesting selection of modern English dishes

The intimate feel of this cosy Georgian hotel is greatly enhanced by the relaxed and friendly manner in which it is run. St Olaves can be found close to the cathedral, attractively set in a small courtyard with a feature fountain and well-tended garden. The Goldsworthy restaurant has a fine reputation for modern

Mary Arches Street
Map no: 3 SX99
Tel: 01392 217736

Cost: Alc £24; fixed-price lunch and dinner £14.50. Wine £10.50. Service exc
Credit cards: 1 2 3 4

English cooking, and joint chefs Jason Horn and Colin Liddy work well together to produce some imaginative and interesting ideas. Their hand-written *carte* and Friday night gourmet menu offer a pleasing balance of fish, meat and game, with dishes like roasted local quail with home-made game sausage, and pork fillet on a compote of prune and apple proving popular. Our inspector recently sampled a light and delicate roulade of Scottish salmon and Dover sole with chives served with a chervil butter sauce, followed by fillet of home-smoked beef which was rather overwhelmed by a thin pommery mustard sauce. Spinach and oyster mushrooms in a puff pastry case, and a selection of fresh vegetables, accompanied this dish. The dessert of beautifully smooth and tangy lime tart came with a berry syrup and a tartlet of poached strawberries.

Directions: In city centre follow directions to Mary Arches car park. Hotel is opposite car park entrance

Menus: *A la carte*, fixed-price lunch and dinner, pre-theatre

Times: Midday–Last L 2pm, 6.30pm-Last D 9.30pm. Closed Sat, Sun L, 26 Dec-New Year

Chef: Jason Horn, Colin Liddy, Jos Davey
Proprietors: R and V. Wyatt, P Collier

Seats: 60. Guests requested to smoke only in bar
Additional: Children welcome; ❤ dishes; Vegan/other diets on request

GITTISHAM, **Combe House** ❀❀

English country house style cuisine in distinguished surroundings, in a fine Elizabethan manor house set in the heart of East Devon.

An impressive Elizabethan manor house set in parkland, with extensive views over the Blackmore hills to Exmoor. The Boswell family have run the hotel for almost 25 years, with the emphasis on creating a relaxed, house party style. Evidence of Therese Boswell's artistic skills are apparent throughout Combe in the form of paintings, sculptures and murals, and her culinary skills are evident from her supervision of the kitchen. A choice of short fixed-price or *carte* menus featuring country house English cuisine is offered, together with a light lunch menu priced according to courses taken and a traditional fixed-price lunch served on Sundays. The *carte* choice of starters includes slices of chargrilled duck breast spread with tapénade, layered with rosti potatoes and a crisp dressed salad. This could be followed by a plump roasted Combe pigeon served on a crouton of celeriac, surrounded by Strasbourg sauce. Lemon and passion fruit tart proved an enjoyable dessert. John Boswell's son Mark owns a wine shop in Ilminster and a selection of these wines comprises the wine list at Combe.

Directions: In village off the A30 south of Honiton

Map no: 3 SY19
Tel: 01404 42756

Cost: *A/c* from £27.50; fixed-price lunch from £12.75, fixed-price dinner from £19.50. H/wine £8.20 ♀ Service charge 12.5%
Credit cards: 1 2 3 4 5

Menus: *A la carte*, fixed-price lunch and dinner, Sunday lunch

Times: Last L 1.45pm, Last D 9.30. Closed 27 Jan-9 Feb

Chef: Thérèse Boswell
Proprietors: John and Thérèse Boswell

Seats: 56. No pipes or cigars
Additional: Children permitted; no children under 10 at dinner; ❤ dishes

GULWORTHY, **The Horn of Plenty** ❀❀❀

A Georgian property set in acres of gardens and orchards, this restaurant with rooms serves modern international cuisine

The proprietors of The Horn of Plenty, Ian and Elaine Gatehouse, have found a preference among their guests for the simplicity of the new policy of only an extended fixed-price menu, with some price-supplemented dishes. The Monday night 'Pot Luck' menu, begun last winter to enliven an

Map no: 2 SX47
Tel: 01822 832528

Cost: Fixed-price lunch £14.50 (2 courses), £17.50; Pot Luck Mon dinner £17.50; fixed-price dinner £25.50. Wine £10 ♀ Service exc
Credit cards: 1 2 3

Menus: Fixed-price lunch and

otherwise dreary evening, has proved a great success, with regular full houses to sample the three-course dinner at £16.50. Though the menu is shortened, there is a choice and the standard is as high as on any other day of the week.

And so it was on a Monday evening that our inspector enjoyed a tasty meal commencing with salmon and prawns in a pastry case served with red pepper sauce. The main course, roast loin of lamb with a garlicky herb filling and Madeira sauce, was beautifully cooked with a real lamb taste enhanced with natural flavours. Creamy coffee parfait with superb chocolate sauce completed the experience.

Peter Gorton is in charge of the kitchen and is particularly well regarded for his full-flavoured, unfussy style of food created from prime local ingredients. Examples from a typical evening menu, with seven dishes at each of three courses, might be pan-fried sea-bass on a bed of braised leeks with sweet and sour sauce or medallions of venison with apple compôte and black pepper cider sauce.

The hotel is a substantial Georgian property in four acres of gardens and orchards on the foothills of Dartmoor with splendid views over the Tamar Valley, which may be enjoyed from the restaurant. Though the approach to cooking is serious, the atmosphere is relaxed and service friendly and attentive. The wine list is well balanced and very reasonably priced – for example J. Faiveley's Bourgogne Pinot Noir (one of the carefully chosen house wines) is a snip at £11.75.

Directions: 3 miles from Tavistock on the A390. Turn right at Gulworthy Cross then first left. Horn of Plenty 400yds on right

dinner, Sunday lunch, Pot Luck menu (Mon dinner)

Times: Midday-Last L 2pm, 7pm-Last D 9pm. Closed Mon lunch, Xmas

Chef: Peter Gorton
Proprietors: Ian and Elaine Gatehouse

Seats: 50. No-smoking area. No cigars or pipes in restaurant
Additional: Children permitted at owners discretion (over 13 at dinner); ✿ dishes; Vegan/other diets on request

HAWKCHURCH, Fairwater Head ✿

A welcoming Edwardian hotel set in well-tended gardens with panoramic views across the Axe valley. Both simple and more adventurous tastes are satisfied by the country house style dishes on the carte and fixed-price menu, like terrine of salmon, halibut and spinach or lamb en croûte.

Cost: Alc £30; fixed-price L £11/D £18.50. Service exc
Credit cards: 1 2 3 4
Additional: Children welcome; children's portions/menu; ✿ dishes, Vegan/other diets on request. Live entertainment
Directions: Signposted from B3165. On outskirts of village

Near Axminster
Map no: 3 ST30
Tel: 01297 678349
Chefs: Ian Carter, Robert Renshaw
Proprietors: Harry and Rita Austin, John and Judith Lowe
Seats: 40. No smoking in dining room
Times: Last L 1.30pm/D 8.30pm. Closed Jan, Feb

HAYTOR, **The Bel Alp House** ✿

A Swiss-chalet style Edwardian hotel in the Dartmoor National Park. Dinner follows the family-home atmosphere in that it is styled like a dinner party with a limited choice but delicious five-course meal. Dishes include smoked salmon or watercress soup, guinea fowl suprême or fillet of beef.

Map no: 3 SX77
Tel: 01364 661217
Chef: Sarah Curnoch
Proprietors: Roger and Sarah Curnoch
Seats: 24. No smoking in dining room
Times: Last D 7.30pm

Cost: Fixed-price D £33, H/wine £9. Service exc
Credit cards: 1 3 5
Additional: Children over 7 permitted; children's portions; ❂ dishes
Directions: 2.5 miles west of Bovey Tracey off B3387 to Haytor

HAYTOR, **Rock Inn** ✿

Peacefully situated in the village of Haytor, the atmosphere is relaxed and welcoming. Our inspector enjoyed the Stilton pâté with crudités with warm toast squares, followed by very tender pieces of Devon beef flavoured with Guinness and bay leaves.

Near Newton Abbot
Map no: 3 SX77
Tel: 01364 661305
Chef: Neil Elliot
Proprietor: C Graves

Directions: In village

HOLBETON, **Alston Hall** ✿

☺ This turn-of-the-century hotel in its four acres of lightly wooded grounds epitomises the Edwardian era's gracious life-style. The restaurant's short but well-balanced fixed-price menus offer both traditional and innovative French/English dishes which make maximum use of fresh local ingredients.

Alston
Map no: 2 SX65
Tel: 01752 830555
Chef: Malcolm Morrison
Proprietor: Tim Pettifer
Seats: 50. No smoking in dining room
Times: Last L 1.45pm/D 9.30pm

Cost: Fixed-price L £12.50/D £22. H/wine £9.75. Service exc
Credit cards: 1 2 3 4
Additional: Children permitted (over 7 at dinner); children's portions/menu; ❂ dishes; Vegan/other diets on request
Directions: Follow A 379 through Yealmpton, turn right for Alston, the Hall is signposted on the right

HORRABRIDGE, **Overcombe** ✿

☺ Fresh local produce is used wherever possible in the interesting dishes that make up the good value dinner menus at this small hotel. A limited choice is offered for the set four courses, which might include garlic mushrooms; breast of duck with Cumberland sauce, and a steamed pudding.

Near Yelverton
Map no: 2 SX56
Tel: 01822 853501
Chef: Brenda J Durnell
Proprietors: Maurice and Brenda Durnell
Seats: 23. No smoking in dining room
Times: Last D 7.30pm

Cost: Fixed-price D £12. Wine £8.25 litre. Service inc
Credit cards: 1 3. **Additional:** Children welcome; children's portions; ❂ dishes; Vegan/other diets on request
Directions: Off the A386 past Yelverton roundabout travelling towards Tavistock. Take first left after sign Horrabridge

ILFRACOMBE, **Elmfield** ❀

Enjoyable home-cooked fare is served at this attractive Victorian property, which is peacefully located with a rural outlook. The good-value menus offer a vegetarian choice, with dishes such as veggie toad-in-the-hole, but our inspector advises that the steak and kidney pie should not be missed.

Cost: Alc £25; fixed-price D £12.00. Wine £7.50 ♀. Service exc
Credit cards: 1 3 **Additional:** Children permitted (over 7); ❂ menu; Vegan/other diets on request
Directions: From Barnstaple on A361, at first lights left into Wilder Road, left at next lights, left again into Torrs Park, hotel at top of hill on the left

Torrs Park
Map no: 2 SS54
Tel: 01271 863377
Chef: Ann Doody
Proprietors: Ann and Derek Doody
Seats: 30. No smoking in dining room
Times: Last L 2pm/D 8pm

IVYBRIDGE, **Glazebrook House** ❀

The cosy dining room of an elegant hotel set in lovely four-acre grounds on the southern edge of Dartmoor offers a choice of two interesting menus – one a limited carte, the other a good-value set meal. English dishes carefully prepared from fresh produce are attractively presented in nouvelle style.

Directions: Located on the southern edge of Dartmoor

Map no: 2 SX65
Tel: 01364 73322
Chef: David Merriman
Proprietors: Mr and Mrs Cowley

KINGSBRIDGE, **Buckland-Tout-Saints** ❀❀

A short selection of pleasing modern dishes served in elegant, tranquil surroundings

Narrow country lanes lead to this elegant Queen Anne hotel in the heart of the South Hams. In this tranquil position guests are treated to a relaxing visit, which includes the delights of Jeremy Medley's modern English cooking with hints of a classical French background. His short fixed-price menu includes a daily special for each course, and our inspector was impressed with a successful recent test meal: a slice of cold leek terrine laced with asparagus was a soft and light starter, served with a tasty shallot dressing and two crunchy asparagus spears; chargrilled calf's liver was somewhat overpowered by a strong grain mustard sauce, but vegetables were well cooked and full of flavour. Dessert came in the shape of a small chocolate pastry case filled with crème patissiere and topped with sliced strawberries with a raspberry sauce. Cannelloni of Devon scallops and leeks is a typical starter, while roast breast of Gressingham duck with braised cabbage, or baked fillet of cod, lobster and spinach might be offered as main courses. The wine list has a good selection of clarets and a few New World wines.

Directions: Two miles north-east of Kingsbridge, off the A381

Goveton
Map no: 3 SX74
Tel: 01548 853055

Cost: Fixed-price L £14.50, fixed-price D £25. Service exc
Credit cards: 1 2 3 4

Menus: Fixed-price lunch and dinner, Sun lunch

Times: Last L 1.45pm, Last D 9.30pm

Chef: Jeremy Medley
Proprietors: John and Tove Taylor

Seats: 54. No smoking in dining room
Additional: Children permitted; no babies at dinner; children's portions; ❂ menu

LEWDOWN, **Lewtrenchard Manor** ❀❀

Interesting dishes cooked from fresh local produce where possible, in a charming old manor house

Surrounded by well-tended grounds and the soft Devonshire countryside between Dartmoor and the Cornish borders, this handsome stone manor house has all the atmosphere of a large family home. It dates from around 1600, and is run as a small hotel with bags of character and charm by Sue and James Murray. Dinner is an important part of a stay here, and the fixed-price three-course menu and four-course gourmet menu offer a range of interesting dishes, all created from the best of fresh produce. A recent inspection meal began with a ragout of noodles and fresh wild mushrooms, followed by a light, well-cooked stew of brill in a Pernod sauce on a bed of fennel. The seasoning of these two dishes was not especially accurate, but the vegetables served were full of flavour. A hot raspberry soufflé, and then a tangy raspberry sorbet, brought the meal to a very sweet close. Other dishes on the menu might be pan-fried fillet of cod with a parsley butter sauce, and roast breast of guinea fowl stuffed with a thyme forcemeat, and served with a lemon butter sauce. An extensive and interesting wine list includes several halves.

Directions: From A386 turn right, then immediately left for Lewdown, after 6 miles turn left for Lewtrenchard

Near Okehampton
Map no: 2 SX48
Tel: 01556 783256

Cost: Fixed-price lunch £16; fixed-price dinner £25 (3 courses), £32. Wine £8 ♀ Service exc
Credit cards: 1 2 3 4

Menus: Fixed-price lunch and dinner, Sunday lunch, bar menu

Times: Last L 1.45pm, Last D 9.30pm

Chef: Patrick Salvador
Proprietors: Pride of Britain. Managers: James and Sue Murray

Seats: 35. No smoking in dining room
Additional: Children permitted (over 8 at dinner); children's portions; Vegan/other diets on request

LIFTON, **Arundell Arms** ❀❀

Modern British food with classical French influences at a country hotel renowned for its fishing

The Arundell Arms is a popular fishing hotel, with 20 miles of its own water on the River Tamar. However, the former coaching inn is equally attractive to those in pursuit of good food in a relaxing environment.

Chef Philip Burgess and his young team offer interesting and carefully prepared dishes using first class ingredients. The cooking has a pleasing simplicity with the emphasis on flavour, as in a salad of cold roasted peppers with anchovies, shaved parmesan and a basil infused oil – a vibrant combination. Marinated venison was meltingly tender, served with a robust crushed peppercorn sauce and a more subtle spiced pear. A light hand is evident in the home-made breads, indulgent truffles and an orange and white chocolate terrine served with caramelised oranges and vanilla cream. Daily fixed-price lunch and dinner menus are offered in the restaurant, along with a weekly *carte*, the latter with a vegetarian option such as crisp potato straw-cakes with wood mushrooms and creamed leeks. There are some inexpensive house wines, plenty of half bottles and wines by the glass.

Directions: Just off A30 in village of Lifton, 3 miles east of Launceston

Map no: 2 SX35
Tel: 01566 784666

Cost: Alc £27.40; fixed-price lunch £15.75; fixed-price dinner £21.50. Wine £9.50 ♀. Service exc
Credit cards: 1 2 3 4 5

Menus: *A la carte*, fixed-price lunch and dinner, Sunday lunch

Times: 12.30pm-Last L 2pm, 7.30pm-Last D 9.30pm

Chef: Philip Burgess
Proprietor: Best Western. Manageress: Anne Voss-Bark

Seats: 70. No smoking in dining room
Additional: Children permitted; children's portions; ✿ dishes; Vegan/other diets on request

LYMPSTONE, River House ◎◎

☺ *A village setting, river views, paintings on the walls and fine cuisine in one of Devon's finest restaurants*

If Exe marks the spot, the treasure is in Lympstone. Seeing the river estuary on entering the first-floor restaurant is a surprise in itself, since it is not visible at ground level. While undoubtedly inspiration for the artists whose work is displayed here, co-owner/chef Shirley Wilkes draws hers from a more global scene – France, Italy, Spain, the Orient and, of course, England. This explains dishes like spinach and Budleigh Salterton crab-filled ravioli, fillet of plaice Spanish-style (with a sherry, orange, currant and olive sauce) and Indonesian grilled chicken (served on rice with peanut and lime sauce). An inspection meal comprised velvety cream of leek and celery soup, and a fresh-flavoured Stilton and walnut tart, served with dressed mixed leaves and finely-diced apples, celery and grapes. Fillet of brill in a wine and herb stock, garnished with lightly-cooked scallops and prawns, came with a help-yourself selection of garden-fresh vegetables. Most wines are French, but lovers of varieties from elsewhere have a reasonable choice. House wines come by the glass, the bottle and in full or half litres.

Directions: From the A376 towards Exmouth, follow signs for Lympstone. Through village, restaurant near post office, on right

The Strand
Map no: 3 SX98
Tel: 01395 265147

Cost: *Alc* £18; fixed-price lunch and dinner £23.95 (2-courses), £27.50, £32.50. H/wine £8.95 ♀
Service exc
Credit cards: 1 2 3

Menus: *A la carte*, fixed-price lunch and dinner, Sunday lunch

Times: Midday-Last L 1.30pm, 7pm-Last D 9.30pm/10.30pm Sat. Closed Mon, Sun eve, BHs, 3 days Xmas, 2 days New Year

Chef: Shirley Wilkes
Proprietor: Michael Wilkes
Seats: 34. No smoking in dining room
Additional: Children permitted (over 6); children's portions; ◐ dishes; Vegan/other diets on request

LYNMOUTH, Rising Sun ◎

Skilful use is made of regional produce in preparing the range of English/French dishes featured on carte and fixed-price menus by the attractive restaurant of this harbour-front inn. Locally smoked trout, for example, and suprême of Exmoor pheasant or a sautéed fillet of Devon beef.

Cost: *Alc* £28; fixed-price L/D £21.50. H/wine £8.75. Service exc
Credit cards: 1 2 3 4 5
Additional: Children permitted (over 5); children's portions; ◐ menu; Vegan/other diets on request
Directions: A39 to Lynmouth. Located on the harbour-side

Harbourside
Map no: 3 SS74
Tel: 01598 53223
Chef: David Lamprell
Proprietor: Hugo Jeune
Seats: 34. No smoking in dining room
Times: Last L 2pm/D 9pm

LYNTON, Combe Park ◎

☺ *An attractive hotel situated at the head of the Watersmeet Valley offering generous portions in its restaurant. Guests choose from a list of starters at the bar but the main course is set. Our inspector had a delicious pork fillet en croute with an orangey sauce. The best of local produce is used.*

Cost: Fixed-price D £18. H/wine £8. Service exc
Credit cards: None taken
Additional: Children over 12 permitted
Directions: At Hillsford Bridge, 0.25 miles from junct of A39/B3223

Hillsford Bridge
Map no: 3 SS74
Tel: 01598 52356
Chef: Mrs S J Barnes
Proprietors: Mr & Mrs Barnes, Mr Walley
Seats: 20. No-smoking area
Times: Last D 7.15pm. Closed Nov-March

LYNTON, **Hewitts** ●●

☺ *Some irresistible dishes from a carefully planned and good-value set menu and carte*

The Hoe, North Walk
Map no: 3 SS74
Tel: 01598 52293

Cost: *Alc* £22.50; fixed-price lunch £14.50; fixed-price dinner £21.50. Wine £10.25 ♀ Service inc
Credit cards: 1 3 5

Guests at this warm, happy hotel are treated more like friends of the family than paying punters, and much effort goes into pleasing them in the dining room. Chef Robert Schyns takes a great deal of care with the fresh local ingredients at his disposal, and adds a touch of imagination and natural skill to produce some very tempting dishes. Our inspector began a recent meal with bacon and chicken parfait with peppercorns and a delicious vermouth vinaigrette, and went on to very tender slices of pan-fried venison with a rich sauce of red wine, onions and garlic, served with a good selection of vegetables. Desserts are simply not to be missed, and the chosen one of Belgian chocolate mousse with tangy orange sauce and dash of crème anglaise was light, tasty and effortless to eat. Coffee is served in the lounge, and there is more temptation in the shape of irresistible home-made petits fours. Other dishes offered on the very well priced menus might include chicken and king prawn crépinette in a morel sauce, and halibut steak coated in egg and cheese, baked and served with salmon caviar.

Menus: *A la carte*, fixed-price lunch and dinner, Sunday lunch, bar menu

Times: Last L 2pm, Last D 9pm

Chef: Robert Schyns
Proprietor: J E Bishop

Seats: 30. No smoking in dining room
Additional: Children permitted lunch only (over 8); childrens menu; ❂ menu; other diets on request

Directions: North Walk off Lee Road

LYNTON, **Lynton Cottage** ●

High in the hills overlooking Lynmouth Bay, the restaurant of this charming hotel offers a good choice of dishes from a fixed-price menu. Care and skill goes into the preparation of the food by chef and proprietor Mr Jones. Service is friendly and informal, and the atmosphere relaxing.

North Walk
Map no: 3 SS74
Tel: 01598 52342
Chef: John Jones
Proprietors: John and Maisie Jones

Directions: Off main street (Lee Road) towards sea

LYNTON, **Neubia House** ●

☺ *Honest, carefully prepared dishes in traditional British style are served in the attractively appointed no-smoking dining room of this friendly hotel. A five-course fixed-price dinner menu offering a particularly varied selection of vegetables and some old-fashioned puddings also gives vegetarians a good choice.*

Lydiate Lane
Map no: 3 SS74
Tel: 01598 52309
Chef: Brian Murphy
Proprietor: Brian Murphy
Seats: 30. No smoking in dining room
Times: Last D 9pm. Closed 2–31 Jan

Cost: Fixed-price D £15.50. Wine £7.50. Service inc
Credit cards: 1 3. **Additional:** Children permitted (over 3 at dinner); children's portions; ❂ dishes; Vegan/other diets on request
Directions: Go down Cross Street (opposite Town Hall), left at end then left again; few yards down on left

MARTINHOE, Old Rectory ❀

Nestling amidst three acres of natural gardens, this hotel is owned and personally run by John and Suzanne Bradbury. The menu is deceptively undescriptive and undersold, and quality dishes are served using fresh local produce. The home-made puddings must not be missed.

Cost: Fixed-price D £22. **Credit cards:** None taken
Additional: Children welcome; children's menu/portions. Vegetarian dishes on request.
Directions: Right at Blackmore Gate onto A39 (Parracombe and Lynton). Use Parracombe by-pass, turn left at Martinhoe Cross to Woody Bay and Martinhoe

Parracombe, Barnstaple
Map no: 3 SS64
Tel: 015983 368
Chef: Suzanne Bradbury
Proprietors: John and Suzanne Bradbury
Seats: 25. No smoking in dining room
Times: Last D 7.30pm

MARY TAVY, The Stannary ❀❀

A creative vegetarian chef producing a popular range of dishes in a restaurant with rooms on the edge of Dartmoor

A dedicated vegetarian restaurant which is a magnet for large numbers of meat eaters is the unusual but proud boast of chef/patron Alison Fife and her partner Michael Cook. The success of this elegant 16th-century and Victorian restaurant on the edge of Dartmoor is chiefly due to Alison's creative skill with unusual and exotic ingredients, and the strong flavours found in organic vegetables. Animal products are nowhere to be found. Our inspector enjoyed delicious canapés served with a home-made elderflower wine aperitif, before starting a recent meal with a sweetcorn tart filled with creamed corn topped with baby cobs with a lotus petal relish. 'Helios' was a filling main course, consisting of vine leaves stuffed with sun-dried tomatoes, sunflower seeds and quinoa (grain of the gods), served with savoy cabbage and coconut, purple Cape cauliflower and spicy aubergine. The overall flavour of the date and muscatel samosas – filo pastry filled with grapes and a sauce of the same wine – was much enjoyed. Speciality coffees and teas are offered, along with home-produced drinks and an extensive wine list.

Directions: 4 miles north-east of Tavistock on A386 Tavistock to Okehampton road

Map no: 2 SX57
Tel: 01822 810897

Cost: Fixed-price dinner £24 (2 courses), £30. H/wine £9.20 ♀
Service inc
Credit cards: 1 2

Menus: Fixed-price dinner

Times: 7pm-Last D 9pm. Closed Sun, Mon

Chef: Alison Fife
Proprietors: Michael Cook and Alison Fife

Seats: 20. No smoking in dining room
Additional: Children permitted (over 12); exclusively ✿;
Vegan/other diets on request

NORTH HUISH, Brookdale House ❀❀

A richly furnished country house hotel serving food with an emphasis on fresh, superior produce

In a delightful riverside setting in wooded grounds near a beautiful Victorian waterfall, this stunning stone-built hotel makes a very pretty picture. The Gothic-style buildings have been restored to their former glory, while the interior is richly furnished with antiques and decorated in a fresh, light style. Now being run as a country house hotel with a friendly and unpretentious atmosphere, it is quickly gaining a reputation for food. Fresh local fish is a speciality, and herbs from the garden

South Brent
Map no: 2 SX75
Tel: 01548 821661

Cost: Alc £30, fixed-price £22.50
Credit cards: 1 2 3

Menus: A la carte, fixed-price

Times: Midday-Last L 2pm, 7pm-Last D 10pm. Closed 2nd and 3rd week Jan

feature in many of the interesting dishes on the extensive *carte* and fixed-price menu. Our inspector began a meal with a deliciously rich oxtail soup packed with meat and diced vegetables, followed by stir-fried fillet of beef and king prawns with a very spicy sweet chilli and ginger sauce, served around a bed of rice. Other recommended dishes have included a basket of mushrooms with a creamy fennel sauce, and very fresh monkfish with a slightly overpowering sauce made from hot mustard and plenty of cheese. A long list of home-made puddings might include a tasty apple crumble, and a chewy ginger and apricot steamed pudding.

Chef: Mike Mikkelsen
Proprietors: Gill and Mike Mikkelsen

Additional: Not suitable for young children; ❂ dishes

Directions: Signposted from the village of Avonwick, beside the A38

PARKHAM, **Penhaven Country House** ❂

☺ *A peaceful former rectory where badgers can frequently be seen playing in the grounds. The carte offers a good choice of dishes including A Purse of Fillet; prime fillet steak filled with succulent prawns, sautéed in butter with cognac.*

Cost: Alc £20; fixed-price L £8.50/D £12.95. Wine £9.50 litre. Service exc
Credit cards: 1 2 3.4. **Additional:** Children permitted (over 10); ❂ menu; Vegan/other diets on request
Directions: From Bideford turn left of A39 at Honns Cross, follow signs to Parkham. On entering village, after church on right, take next left.

Bideford
Map no: 2 SS32
Tel: 01237 451711
Chef: Michael Kibby
Proprietors: Maxine and Alan Wade
Seats: 40. No smoking in dining room
Times: Last L 1.45pm/D 9pm

PLYMOUTH, **Chez Nous** ❂❂❂

A small town centre restaurant serving French 'cuisine spontanée' using the best of local produce

A unit in a modern shopping precinct in the centre of the town, this small French restaurant has plenty of character. The decor is predominantly red, white and blue and the walls are hung with framed menus and music hall posters. The atmosphere is that of a provincial bistro, and the restaurant is renowned for its friendly informality.
  Chef Jacques Marchal uses the best of produce, including fish from the Barbican, cooked in classical style to produce interesting dishes full of natural flavours. The fixed-price menu, offered at lunch and dinner, is handwritten in French and displayed on a blackboard. Mrs Marchal welcomes guests, escorts them to their tables and talks them through the dishes, describing the ingredients and methods of cooking.
  'Le petit bouillabaisse du Barbican', served in traditional style, is full of flavour. 'Saumon maimé aux herbes' is Jacques' version of gravadlax and was preferred by our inspector who considered it tastier and less sweet. 'Suprême de Caneton aux lentilles' was sliced and attractively presented duck with chewy lentils. set on a thin reduction of duck stock and port with blackcurrant, which worked very well. Vegetables, served on a separate plate, were good: a creamy purée of root vegetables, new potatoes cooked in their skins, crunchy slices of leek and

13 Frankfort Gate
Map no: 2 SX45
Tel: 01752 266793

Cost: Fixed-price lunch and dinner £28.50. H/wine £10.50. Service exc
Credit cards: 1 2 3 4

Menus: Fixed-price lunch and dinner, pre-theatre by arrangement

Times: 12.30-Last L 2pm, 7pm-Last D 10.30pm. Closed Sun, Mon, BHs, 3 weeks Feb & Sep

Chef: Jacques Marchal
Proprietors: Jacques and Suzanne Marchal

Seats: 28. No pipes
Additional: Children welcome. Other diets on request

calabrese cooked al dente.
   Our inspector's choice of dessert, a smooth orange parfait with segments of orange and pink grapefruit, provided a light finish to a rich meal. Coffee was served with home-made sweetmeats, including fudge, Turkish delight and nougat.
   As might be expected, the wine list is mainly French, with some really fine vintages of claret and red Burgundy. There are also five good house wines priced at £9-£10 a bottle.

Directions: Frankfort Gate is a pedestrianised street between Western Approach and Market Avenue

POUNDSGATE, Leusdon Lodge ☯

☺ *This stone-built Victorian house offers a panelled dining room with an impressive carved fireplace. Here, a simple fixed-priced menu, based on fresh local produce, delivers some tasty dishes such as moist breast of chicken in a creamy tarragon sauce, and a delicious Grand Marnier soufflé.*

Cost: Fixed-price D £22.50. Wine £10. Service inc **Credit cards:** 1 3
Additional: Children permitted lunch only; children's portions; ☯ dishes; Vegan/other diets on request
Directions: After passing through Poundsgate turn right signposted Leusdon, fork right at the Jubilee Stowe, then right down hill

Leusdon, Ashburton
Map no: 3 SX77
Tel: 01364 631304
Chef: Mary Miranda Russell
Proprietor: Ivor Russell
Seats: 20. No smoking in dining room
Times: Last L 2pm/D 8.45pm

SALCOMBE, Soar Mill Cove ☯

☺ *Overlooking what is often described as the most beautiful cove in Britain, this hotel's guests return again and again. Keith Makepeace (junior) is in charge of the kitchen using the finest of local produce including fish from Looe and locally farmed beef and lamb to create imaginative and traditional dishes.*

Cost: Alc L £20; fixed-price D £29. H/wine £10.30. No service charge **Credit cards:** 1 3 5
Additional: Children permitted (no babies at dinner); children's portions/menu; ☯ dishes; other diets on request
Directions: Leave A381 at Malborough, through village fork left after church, signposted Soar

Soar Mill Cove, Malborough
Map no: 3 SX73
Tel: 01548 561566
Chef: Keith Stephen Makepeace
Proprietors: Makepeace family
Seats: 48. No smoking
Times: Last L 2.30pm/D 9pm

SALCOMBE, Tides Reach ☯

Locally landed fish features on the menu of the Garden Room restaurant of this shoreline hotel, where the freshness and quality of ingredients is complemented by accomplished cooking in modern English/Continental tradition

Costs: Alc £26.25; fixed-price D £19.75. H/wine £9.25. Service exc
Credit cards: 1 2 3 4. **Additional:** Children permitted (over 8); ☯ dishes; Vegan/other diets on request
Directions: At South Sands Cove, take Cliff Road out of Salcombe towards the sea and Bolt Head

South Sands
Map no: 3 SX73
Tel: 01548 843466
Chef: Finn Ibsen
Proprietor: John Edwards
Seats: 90. No smoking
Times: Last L 2.15pm/D 9.30pm. Closed Nov-Feb

SIDMOUTH, **Brownlands** ☀

Sid Road
Map no: 3 SY18
Tel: 01395 513053

☺ *A country hotel prominently situated on the wooded slopes of Salcombe Hill, Brownlands offers a fixed-price five-course menu of imaginative dishes in its elegant dining room. Our inspector enjoyed prawns in a spicy sauce, bacon and lentil soup, escalopes of pork in a port sauce, and crème brûlée.*

Chef: Laurence J Barber, Janice May
Proprietors: Peter, Diane and Steven Kendall-Torry
Seats: 40. No smoking in dining room
Times: Last L 1.15pm/D 8pm. Closed Nov–Mar

Cost: Sunday L £9.50; fixed-price D £17.95. Wine £7.95. Service exc. **Credit cards:** None taken **Additional:** Children permitted (over 8); ❂ dishes; Vegan/other diets on request
Directions: Signposted, in Brownlands Road which is off Sid Road

SOUTH MOLTON, **Marsh Hall** ☀

Map no: 3 SS72
Tel: 01769 572666
Chef: Judy Griffiths
Proprietors: Tony and Judy Griffiths
Seats: 24. No smoking in dining room
Times: Last D 8.30pm

☺ *Dating from the 17th century, Marsh Hall is rumoured to have been built by the local squire for his mistress. Food is carefully prepared by Judy Griffiths using the best of fresh produce and, where possible, local meat. The herbs, fruit and vegetables are from the garden.*

Cost: Fixed-price D £18.50. H/wine £7. Service exc
Credit cards: 1 2 3 4 **Additional:** Children permitted (over 12); ❂ dishes/other diets on request
Directions: Off A361 signposted North Molton. Take first right, then right again

SOUTH MOLTON, **Whitechapel Manor** ☀☀☀

Map no: 3 SS72
Tel: 01769 573377

An Elizabethan manor house setting for beautifully presented traditional French-influenced cooking

Cost: Fixed-price lunch and dinner £26. Wine £10 ♀ Service inc
Credit cards: 1 2 3 4

Patricia and John Shapland's Grade I listed Elizabethan manor house is set in beautiful terraced gardens on the edge of Exmoor. It is run as a country house hotel, and very much a family enterprise with both sons involved. The house is stylishly furnished with antiques, and its greatest prize is the Jacobean carved oak screen in the Great Hall.
  In the hotel's dining room Patricia Shapland and new chef Martin Lee share the cooking duties. A fixed-price menu, with the option of three or four courses, is offered at lunch and dinner, and a few dishes are reduced in price. The food is French in style, and our inspector was impressed by the freshness of the flavours and the attractive presentation of the dishes. At an inspection meal his starter looked as good as it tasted: a ravioli of fresh pasta filled with white crab meat served on a fine spaghetti of fresh vegetables garnished with tomato concasse and finely chopped chives. The main course, roasted best end of lamb with puréed aubergine and lamb jus, was cooked deliciously pink. Celeriac, french beans and carrots were an integral part of the artistically presented plate, with just the potatoes served separately.
  Other dishes might include confit of duck, sandwiched between layers of crisp potato with shallots; and steamed fillet

Times: Midday–Last L 1.45pm, Last D 8.45pm
Menus: Fixed-price lunch and dinner, Sunday lunch
Chefs: Patricia Shapland and Martin Lee
Proprietors: John and Patricia Shapland
Seats: 24. No smoking in dining room
Additional: Children welcome; children's portions/menu; ❂ dishes, Vegan/other diets on request

of brill with mussels and a mussel and saffron sauce. A selection of cheeses, mostly from the south west, is offered, and our inspector concluded his meal with caramelised apple tart served with caramel ice cream. Vegetarians can be catered for by prior arrangement.

The compact wine list covers all the major wine producing countries of the world and is reasonably priced. There are mature vintages of claret, and the selection from Australia, California and New Zealand is of excellent quality.

Directions: From Tiverton take A361, then last turning off roundabout signposted Whitechapel. After 1 mile turn right

STOKE CANON, **Barton Cross** ❀

Barton Cross is an attractive thatched hotel, set in rural surroundings, with an unusual galleried restaurant. Chef Stuart Fowles' menu, based on local fish and meats, is priced for two and three courses, with a sorbet. A good choice is offered at each stage including some vegetarian dishes.

Cost: Alc £21. Wine £9.25. Service exc. **Credit cards:** 1 2 3 4 5
Additional: Children welcome; children's portions; ◐ dishes; other diets on request
Directions: 0.5 mile off the A396 Exeter to Tiverton road

Huxham
Map no: 3 SX99
Tel: 01392 841245
Chef: Stuart Fowels
Proprietors: Russell and Sheila Ball
Seats: 40. Smoking discouraged
Times: Last L 1.45pm/D 9.30pm. Closed Sun

TAVISTOCK, **Moorland Hall** ❀

☺ A delightful Victorian country house situated on the edge of Dartmoor. Every evening proprietor Gillian Farr produces a well balanced menu. A variety of dishes are cooked with care and attention to seasoning including seafood provençal – seafood with a tomato and herb sauce.

Cost: Fixed-price D £15. Service exc. **Credit cards:** 1 3
Additional: Children welcome; children's portions. ◐ menu; Vegan/other diets on request
Directions: Signposted from the centre of Mary Tavy on the A386

Brentnor Road
Map no: 2 SX47
Tel: 01822 810466
Chef: Gill Farr
Proprietors: Mr and Mrs Farr
Seats: 18. No smoking
Times: Last D 8pm. Reservations only

TEIGNMOUTH, **Coombe Bank** ❀

☺ The chef here has worked with Keith Floyd and uses only the best of fresh produce, including local meat and fish. Our inspector tried delicious leek and potato soup, lamb cutlets on a bed of puréed parsnips with a smooth Madeira sauce, followed by a delicious treacle tart for dessert.

Cost: Fixed-price D £16. **Credit cards:** 1 3
Additional: No smoking. Children welcome
Directions: Off Landscore Road

Landscore Road
Map no: 3 SX97
Tel: 01626 772369
Chef: Mathew Sherratt
Proprietors: Mr and Mrs P Vernall
Times: Last D 9.30pm

TORQUAY, The Imperial ❀

The cooking is described as classical French and chef David Berry offers a set menu or carte, which include seasonal dishes, grills and fish. From the set menu there is usually a choice between two dishes to have as a main course, for example, guinea fowl with juniper and cognac, or roast lamb.

Cost: Fixed-price L £16/D £32. H/wine £13.50 ♀ Service inc
Credit cards: 1 2 3 4 . **Additional:** Children welcome; children's portions/menu; ❂ menu; Vegan/other diets on request
Directions: Park Hill Road is off Torwood Street/Babbacombe Road, just north of the new harbour

Park Hill Road
Map no: 3 SX96
Tel: 01803 294301
Chef: David Berry
Proprietors: Forte Grand.
Manager Harry Murray
Seats: 300. No-smoking area. Air conditioned
Times: Last L 2.30pm/D 10pm

TORQUAY, Orestone Manor ❀❀

Some elaborate Anglo-French cooking from an ambitious chef

There are distant views of the sea from this Georgian country lodge hotel, but diners in the restaurant are likely to be oblivious to such distractions, once presented with the menu. Chef Ashley Carkeet is nothing if not ambitious, and his elaborate and extravagant dishes are vividly described in the pricey set four-course menu. His serious approach to cooking is evident in dishes like a recently enjoyed steamed paupiettes of lemon sole filled with flaked cod and celery leaves, served with mussels and a white wine and lavender green peppercorn sauce. This main course followed a starter of braised breast of pheasant with a leaf salad textured with lardons of bacon and orange segments, with a vinaigrette of fresh chopped walnuts, tarragon and lemon. Watercress and caramelised parsnip soup made a satisfying interim course, and rice pudding with prune crème brûlée was one of half a dozen or so rich and complicated desserts. A vegetarian choice is offered daily. The carefully selected wine list has some very good value house wines and interesting New World and young vintage wines.

Directions: From Torquay take B3199 towards Teignmouth. At top of Watcombe Hill is Brunle Manor, take turning opposite into Rockhouse Lane

Rockhouse Lane, Maidencombe
Map no: 3 SX96
Tel: 01803 328098

Cost: Fixed-price lunch £12.50; fixed-price dinner £27.50. Wine £9. Service exc
Credit cards: 1 2 3 4 5

Menus: Fixed-price lunch and dinner, Sunday lunch, bar menu (Mon–Sat lunch)

Times: Last L 1.30pm, Last D 8.30pm. Closed Jan

Chef: Ashley Carkeet
Proprietors: Mike and Gill Staples

Seats: 50. No smoking in restaurant
Additional: Children permitted (over 10); ❂ dishes; Vegan/other diets on request

TORQUAY, The Table ❀❀❀

A one-man kitchen providing a high standard of creative modern cookery in a tiny restaurant

A pretty little restaurant on the border of Torquay and Babbacombe, The Table continues to delight visitors with the high standard of cooking provided by Trevor Brooks, who works on his own in a minute kitchen. Jane Corrigan looks after the five tables front of house with great charm and consideration, but at the time of our last visit she was planning maternity leave and training a replacement. The menu describes dishes simply, but what appears on the plate is the result of some complex preparation.

135 Babbacombe Road
Map no: 3 SX96
Tel: 01803 324292

Cost: Fixed-price dinner £27.75. H/wine £9.50 ♀ Service exc
Credit cards: 1 3

Menu: Fixed-price dinner

Times: 7.30pm-Last D 10pm. Closed Mon, 1-18 Feb & 1-18 Sep

Our inspector was impressed by a galatine of salmon, comprising folded spinach leaves buried in a salmon mousseline with long slices of salmon and scallops, placed back in the salmon skin to reform the fish, then poached and sliced. This proved to be a beautifully flavoured and attractive starter, the spinach creating little zig-zags in the sliced portion, which was served with seared scallops, salad leaves and a lemon butter sauce. The main course was saddle and neck fillet of lamb, the former cooked pink and the latter braised slowly with five-spice powder and cardamom, a delicious dish with two totally different textures. Our inspector's dessert – rhubarb and ginger crème brûlée – was a fitting conclusion to a very enjoyable meal, along with a good coffee served with fresh petits fours.

The restaurant is open for dinner only, offering a fixed-price three-course menu. Vegetarian dishes can be provided, but by prior arrangement only. Seafood figures prominently and fresh fish dishes are announced daily according to market availability. The meal is served at a leisurely pace, and it is best to make a night of it. The compact, reasonably priced wine list is drawn mainly from the vineyards of Europe. It is grouped according to style rather than area.

Directions: Take B3189 (Torwood Street) from Torquay Harbour area for about 2 miles to Babbacombe, the restaurant is on the left

Chef: Trevor Brooks
Proprietors: Trevor Brooks

Seats: 20. No smoking
Additional: Children over 10 permitted

TWO BRIDGES, **Prince Hall** ☺

☺ *This small family-run hotel is remotely set in the Dartmoor National Park amid beautiful scenery. While menus are distinctly French in style, chef/patron Jean-Claud Denat has been joined by his son-in-law Todd who has introduced some flavours of his native Louisiana.*

Cost: Fixed-price D £19.95. Wine £7.50. Service exc.
Credit cards: 1 2 3 4
Additional: Children by prior arrangement; other diets on request
Directions: From Two Bridges take B3357 Dartmeet Road. The hotel is 1 mile on the right (cannot be seen from the road)

Near Yelverton
Map no: 2 SX96
Tel: 01822 89403
Chef: Jean-Claude Denat
Proprietors: Jean-Claude and Tessa Denat
Seats: 20. No smoking in dining room
Times: Last D 8.30pm. Closed 4–6 weeks Xmas/New Year (phone to check)

WHIMPLE, **Woodhayes** ☺☺

A country house hotel serving a set six-course dinner of carefully cooked and imaginative dishes

Situated in the cider apple village of Whimple, Woodhays is a charming Georgian country house, where Frank and Katherine Rendle and their son Michael provide friendly and attentive service. Mrs Rendle discusses the set six-course menu with guests, taking into account their preferences and aversions, including vegetarian requirements. At a test meal the starter of avocado mousse with prawns proved to be slightly lacking in flavour, but the velvety tomato and orange soup that followed certainly made up for it. The fish course, fillet of sea-bass on buttered spinach, was enjoyable, and the main course, rack of lamb with garlic and thyme, delicious. The lamb, cooked slightly pink, was served with dauphinoise potatoes and a

Map no: 3 SY09
Tel: 01404 822237

Cost: Fixed-price dinner £25. H/wine £9.90 ♀ Service inc
Credit cards: 1 2 3 4 5

Menus: Fixed-price dinner

Times: Last D no set time

Chefs: Katherine Rendle, Michael Rendle
Proprietors: Frank, Katherine and Michael Rendle

medley of vegetables creating a colourful dish full of natural flavours. A choice is offered for pudding and our inspector opted for a good crème brûlée with a thin caramel topping. A small selection of local cheeses is also available. Katherine and Michael cook with care and imagination and, judging from the compliments of diners, their efforts are greatly appreciated.

Directions: Whimple sign on the A30 midway between Honiton/Exeter. Straight down Whimple Road, hotel is first building on the right

Seats: 14. No smoking
Additional: Children permitted (over 12); ❂ dishes; Vegan/other diets on request

WINKLEIGH, **Pophams** ❂❂

☺ *A tiny café and delicatessen serving fabulous meals cooked within sight of the customers – a memorable experience*

This tiny café-cum-delicatessen open for lunch only and with seating for just ten has become renowned in the West Country, not only for the quality of the cooking but also for the warm welcome assured by proprietors Dennis Hawkes and Melvyn Popham. Winkleigh lies between Exmoor and Dartmoor but diners come to Pophams from much further afield. Originally a take-out delicatessen, the restaurant is not licensed but corkage is not charged on wines brought in. Guests can watch perfectionist chef Melvyn Popham at work in his small, open plan kitchen. Every dish from the blackboard menu is prepared and cooked to order . The chicken liver terrine was full of flavour and served with a smooth, sweet and spicy Cumberland sauce. A succulent chicken breast, cooked in the oven and coated with Parmesan had a crispy coating, was sitting on a bed of crunchy cabbage and served with creamy curry sauce. The lemon tart was rich and smooth and the sticky toffee pudding second to none. All in all Pophams was a memorable experience.

Directions: In the centre of the village of Winkleigh, about 9 miles from Okehampton

Castle Street
Map no: 3 SS60
Tel: 01837 83767

Cost: *Alc* £16. Un-licensed, no corkage charge. Service exc.

Menu: *A la carte*

Times: Last L 3pm. Closed Sun, Feb

Chef: Melvyn John Popham
Proprietors: Dennis Hawkes, Melvyn Popham

Seats: 10. No smoking. Air conditioned
Additional: Children permitted (over 13); ❂ dishes; other diets on request

WOOLACOMBE, **Little Beach** ❂

☺ *A five-course, limited choice, fixed-price menu of traditional English dishes is served in the very attractive dining room of this Edwardian seafront property; fresh produce is used to good advantage, and both the wholesome soups and old-fashioned puddings are all home-made.*

Cost: Fixed-price D £14.50. Wine £6.95. Service exc
Credit cards: 1 3
Additional: Children permitted (over 6); children's portions; ❂ dishes; other diets on request
Directions: From village centre 0.5 miles along seafront on right-hand side

The Esplanade
Map no: 2 SS44
Tel: 01271 870398
Chef: Mrs N B Welling
Proprietors: B D Welling
Seats: 24. No smoking in dining room
Times: Last L 1.30pm/D 8pm. Closed Nov–Mar

WOOLACOMBE, **Watersmeet** ●●

An ideal coastal setting in which to enjoy superb sea views and accomplished, unpretentious cooking

Standing on the cliff edge at Mortehoe with splendid sea views and vistas across the rocks towards the town, this smart hotel offers a convivial, friendly atmosphere. The light and airy dining room makes the most of the glorious views, and while tasty bar meals only are served at lunch-time, dinner is an occasion to sample a mixture of traditional and modern cooking. Chef John Physick – often joined in the kitchen by owner Brian Wheeldon – produces varied and imaginative dishes which demonstrate his skill and the use of quality ingredients, especially in sauces. Our inspector was full of praise for a recent starter of miniature pancakes interleaved with seafood fricassee in a cream and vermouth sauce, followed by marinated medallions of Exmoor venison on a bed of egg noodles with a red wine and mushroom sauce. Bakewell tart was a little hard on the outside but full of flavour, and the chef's flair for sauces was again demonstrated in the delicious custard that went with it. Also enjoyed have been duck liver pâté with Cumberland sauce, and lemon sole with a flawless tartare sauce.

Directions: Follow signs to Woolacombe, turn right at beach car park, restaurant 300 yards on right

Mortehoe
Map no: 2 SS44
Tel: 01271 870333

Cost: Alc £21, fixed-price dinner £25.50. H/wine £9.85. Service inc
Credit cards: 1 2 3

Menus: *A la carte*, fixed-price dinner, bar menu

Times: Midday-Last L 2.30pm, 7pm-Last D 8.30/9pm. Closed Dec & Jan

Chefs: J Physick, J B Wheeldon
Proprietors: Mr J B and Mrs P A Wheeldon

Seats: 60. No smoking in dining room
Additional: Children over 8 permitted at dinner; children's portions; ◐ dishes; Vegan/other diets on request

YARCOMBE, **The Belfry** ●

☺ *A converted Victorian village school, this small hotel offers home-cooked dishes from an interesting menu in its wood panelled restaurant. The set menu will usually include a tasty soup, a dish with fresh pasta, and delicious home-made puddings – the lemon meringue pie is a must.*

Cost: Alc £19.45; fixed-price D £12.75. Wine £8.50. Service exc
Credit cards: 1 2 3
Additional: Children permitted (over 11); ◐ dishes; Vegan/other diets on request
Directions: On A30 in centre of Yarcombe

Map no: 3 ST20
Tel: 01404 861234/861588
Chef: Jackie Rees
Proprietors: Jackie and Tony Rees
Seats: 18. No smoking in dining room
Times: Last D 9pm. Closed mid 2 weeks Nov and Feb

DORSET

BEAMINSTER, Bridge House ☻☻

3 Prout Bridge
Map no: 3 ST40
Tel: 01308 862200

☺ *Reliable, much-praised cooking from a chef with a touch of class*

Chef Lindsay Wakeman has a growing reputation for the quality of his cooking, and the attractive restaurant at this charming old hotel is usually busy. Diners greatly appreciate the variety and freshness of the dishes offered on the *carte* and good value set menu, and the British cheeses at a recent dinner elicited high praise from several guests. Our inspector enjoyed a lovely fluffy celeriac soufflé with a delicate flavour, served with a watercress sauce, followed by delicious roast West Country lamb, cooked pink and succulent, with a tangy lemon and mint sauce. Raspberry bavarois with a raspberry puree was bursting with fresh, fruity flavour, and cafetière coffee came with chocolate truffles. Fish features prominently on the menus, and might include Dover sole grilled whole on the bone, John Dory stuffed with orange and mushrooms and baked in wine, or paupiettes of brill and salmon with a mild curry sauce. Meat dishes such as duck braised with lemon grass in sherry, and lamb's liver sautéed with onions in red wine are also part of the repertoire. The charming staff present a quality, mainly French, wine list.

Cost: *Alc* £18.80; fixed-price lunch £11.95; dinner £15.95. Wine £7.50. Service exc
Credit cards: 1 2 3 4 5

Menus: *A la carte*, fixed-price lunch and dinner, Sunday lunch,

Times: 12.30pm-Last L 1.45pm, 7-Last D 9pm

Chef: Lindsay Wakeman
Proprietor: Best Western.
Manager: Peter Pinkster

Seats: 40. No smoking in dining room
Additional: Children permitted; children's portions; ♥ menu; other diets on request

Directions: 200m down the hill from the main town square

BOURNEMOUTH, Hotel Piccadilly ☻

Bath Road
Map no: 4 SZ09
Tel: 01202 552559
Chef: Wilfred Beckett
Proprietors: Marie and Don Cowie
Seats: 85. No smoking in dining room
Times: Last L 2pm/D 9pm

☺ *A popular East Cliff hotel where the cooking style reflects simple but best use of good, fresh produce combined with a genuine desire to please. An inspection meal of fresh fillets of lemon sole in a creamy white wine sauce, although slightly under-seasoned, attracted good marks.*

Cost: *Alc* £18.50; fixed-price L £7.95/D £14.50. Wine £7.95. Service exc. Credit cards: 1 2 3 4 5. Additional: Children welcome/portions/menu; ♥ menu; Vegan/other on request. Live entertainment
Directions: Lansdowne end of Bath Road, off roundabout

BOURNEMOUTH, Langtry Manor ☻

26 Derby Road, East Cliff
Map no: 4 SZ09
Tel: 01202 553887
Chef: Christian Lemmer
Proprietor: P Hamilton Howard
Seats: 50. No smoking in dining room
Times: Last D 9pm

☺ *The Edwardian era is a recurrent theme at this hotel, which was once the love nest of Lillie Langtry and Edward VII, and on Saturdays there is a six-course Edwardian banquet. Otherwise there is an extensive fixed-price menu of English and French dishes prepared from fresh, quality produce.*

Cost: Fixed-price D £19.75. Wine £7.95. Service inc
Credit cards: 1 2 3 4 5
Additional: Children permitted (over 7); children's portions; ♥ dishes, other diets on request

BOURNEMOUTH, Norfolk Royale Hotel ☻

☺ *A varied and enjoyable range of dishes is featured on chef Tony Gill's cosmopolitan carte and reasonable-choice fixed-price menus in the attractive Orangery Restaurant of this smart hotel. Good luncheons and afternoon teas are served in the lounge.*

Cost: Alc £15; fixed-price L £7.95 (2 courses), £9.95/D £18. H/wine £9.50. Service exc
Credit cards: 1 2 3 4
Additional: Children welcome; children's portions/menu; ◐ menu; Vegan/other diets on request
Directions: Near town centre. Half way down Richmond Hill which is just off Wessex Way

Richmond Hill
Map no: 4 SZ09
Tel: 01202 551521
Chef: Tony Gill
Proprietor: Thomas Fromm
Seats: 120. No-smoking area. Air conditioned
Times: Last L 2.30pm/D 10.30pm

BOURNEMOUTH, Queens ☻

☺ *Chef Will Summerell cooks in the modern British style with some Mediterranean influences. He presents fixed-price menus at lunch and dinner, with some supplementary dishes. Our inspector particularly enjoyed roasted quails with cider sauce and an interesting selection of vegetables.*

Cost: Fixed-price L £8.25/D £16.95. Wine £8.95. Service exc
Credit cards: 1 2 3 4 5
Additional: Children welcome; children's portions/menu; ◐ menu; Vegan/other diets on request
Directions: Off the Lansdowne, at the corner with Gervis Road

Meyrick Road, East Cliff
Map no: 4 SZ09
Tel: 01202 554415
Chef: Will Summerell
Proprietors: Arthur Young.
Manager: David Burr
Seats: 200. Smoking discouraged in restaurant
Times: Last L 1.45pm/D 8.45pm

BOURNEMOUTH, Royal Bath ☻☻

A friendly hotel of grand old style, serving carefully cooked Anglo-French cuisine and more informal options

Located high on the cliff top with fine views out to sea, this grand old hotel is handy for the town centre, and within easy reach of the promenade. It is popular with everyone from conference delegates to families, and one of its attractions is the relaxed atmosphere created by willing and cheerful staff. Another plus is the variety of food available in the hotel's different eating outlets, and in particular the high standard of Anglo-French cuisine offered at Oscar's Restaurant. Chef Wayne Asson cooks with care, and offers guests an imaginative *carte* as well as a short daily-changing fixed-price menu. Our inspector recently sampled the *carte*, and tried melon and crawfish terrine set in a passion fruit jelly, followed by pan-fried fillet of lamb on saffron potatoes with shitake mushrooms and sorrel jus; the lamb was tender and nicely cooked, and tastily enhanced by the potatoes and jus. The sweet offers only fruit, but a daily dessert menu included a delicious rice pudding with

Bath Road
Map no: 4 SZ09
Tel: 01202 555555

Cost: *Alc* £33.60; fixed-price lunch £15.50; fixed-price dinner £26. H/wine £10.75
Credit cards: 1 2 3 4

Menus: *A la carte*, fixed-price lunch and dinner, leisure club menu

Times: 12.30pm–Last L 2.15pm, 7.30pm–Last D 10.15pm.
Closed Sun, 23–31 Dec

Chefs: Wayne Charles Asson, Gerard Puigdellivol
Proprietors: De Vere. **Manager:** Philip Russell

a toffee topping, and a smooth and creamy bavarois of passion fruit and other fruit. The Garden restaurant and pool-side brasserie are more informal.

Directions: Within the Royal Bath Hotel which is just above the Pavilion and Promenade

Seats: 40. No pipes or cigars
Additional: Children permitted (over 10); children's portions; ❷ dishes; Vegan/other diets on request

BOURNEMOUTH, Sophisticats ❀

By popular demand this restaurant's menu remains fairly static, featuring the favourites of its loyal clientele, though daily specials ring the changes. The classic French and international dishes include a skilfully made cheese soufflé, old English venison pie and a wonderfully rich chocolate marquise.

Cost: Alc £23.50. H/wine £7.95. Service exc
Credit cards: None taken
Additional: Children permitted; ❷ dishes; other diets on request
Directions: One mile from town centre

43 Charminster Road
Map no: 4 SZ09
Tel: 01202 291019
Chef: Bernard J Calligan
Proprietors: B J Calligan, J E Knight
Seats: 34
Times: Last D 9.30pm. Closed Sun, 2 weeks Feb, 1 week July, 2 weeks Nov

BOURNEMOUTH, Wessex ❀

☺ Standing on the prestigious West Cliff, this hotel offers a choice of fixed-price or carte menus. From the former you can enjoy wild mushroom pancakes or veal Viennoise, and from the latter a good choice is the roast tenderloin of Dorset lamb with grain mustard, and a redcurrant and orange sauce.

Cost: Fixed-price D £14.95, £16.95. H/wine £8.95. Service inc
Credit cards: 1 2 3 4
Additional: Children welcome; children's menu/portions; ❷ dishes; Vegan/other diets on request
Directions: On the West Cliff

West Cliff Road
Map no: 4 SZ09
Tel: 01202 551911
Chef: Paul Riddiaigh
Proprietor: Mark Haslingdon
Seats: 120. No smoking in dining room
Times: Last D 9.15pm

BRIDPORT, Bridge House ❀

☺ Dating back to the 18th century this attractive property is personally managed by Mr and Mrs Badger. Simon Badger cooks enjoyable food in the basement restaurant with a choice of fixed-price and carte menus. A starter of tomatoes filled with hot stilton is one of the delicious choices.

Cost: Alc £17.50; fixed-price D £14.25. Wine £6.50. Service exc
Credit cards: 1 2 3. **Additional:** Children welcome; children's portions; ❷ dishes; other diets on request
Directions: Take A35 to roundabout in Bridport, straight over into East Street. Hotel is 1st building on right

115 East Street
Map no: 3 SY49
Tel: 01308 423371
Chef: Simon Jonathan Badger
Proprietors: Simon Jonathan Badger
Seats: 30. No smoking
Times: Last D 9.30pm. Closed Sun, Mon, Xmas and New Year

BRIDPORT, Innsacre ❀❀

A pretty country restaurant with a successful blend of enjoyable modern cooking and hospitable atmosphere

In a relatively short time this pretty restaurant with rooms has built up a fine reputation for a high standard of cooking and hospitality that is warm and welcoming. The Davies family are responsible for the friendly, informal atmosphere and attentive service, while the cooking is in the domain of the talented new young chef Tim Emberley. His modern British cooking is not complicated, but the care he takes in the preparation shows in the results: starters like filo pastry parcels of local crab meat delighted our inspector at a recent meal, while noisettes of English spring lamb with olive oil mashed potatoes and a port sauce was a particularly inspired main dish. Fresh fish, either as a main dish, or a separate fish course is always available, and the short fixed-price menu might also include roast venison with redcurrants and cassis, or breast of maize-fed chicken glazed with foie gras and served with a wild mushroom sauce. The dessert list shows a tempting choice which includes at least one hot pudding, and traditional steamed suet duff filled with raisins, currants and peel proved irresistible.

Directions: Take A35 from Bridport eastwards. In 2 miles take signposted turn to Shipton Gorge; Innsacre is signposted

Shipton Gorge
Map no: 3 SY49
Tel: 01308 456137

Cost: Fixed-price dinner £21.50. H/wine £10.50 ♀ Service exc
Credit cards: 1 3 5

Menus: Fixed-price dinner

Times: Last D 9pm. Lunch for party bookings only. Closed Sun, Mon and two weeks in Nov

Chef: Tim Emberley
Proprietor: Sydney Davies

Seats: 36. No smoking in dining room
Additional: Children welcome; children's portions; ❀ dishes; other diets on request

BRIDPORT, Riverside ❀❀

☺ *A bustling seafood restaurant in a pretty waterside setting, popular with a clientele from Londoners to local fishermen*

A very busy, delightfully un-fussy café/restaurant serving a lengthy and varied carte menu of fresh fish, with daily specials according to the catch, together with light meals and snacks. Situated in West Bay in a pretty waterside setting beside the river, it is popular with the local fishermen for breakfast, as well as locals and visitors who all flock here to enjoy the freshest fish cooked with the minimum of fuss and fancy sauces; reservation are advisable! On a recent visit, a very enjoyable meal began with delicious fish soup served with crunchy croutons along with whole mussels, prawns and scallops. The main course might be a whole brill baked in its skin with herbs, garlic, olive oil, white wine and onions. Fresh, nicely cooked vegetables, a choice of potatoes and salads are served as an accompaniment. Desserts are not to be neglected, with a wicked sticky toffee pudding or treacle tart as possible temptations. The well researched, keenly priced wine list includes New World wines along with the French favourites and offers good value for money. It is best to ring and check opening dates and times as they are complicated.

Directions: In the centre of West Bay next to the post office

West Bay
Map no: 3 SY49
Tel: 01308 422011

Cost: A/c £21. H/wine £10.50 (litre). Service inc
Credit cards: 1 3

Menu: A la carte

Times: Last L 2.30pm, Last D 8.30/9pm. Closed Sun eve, Mon (ex BHs) late Nov-early Mar. Seasonal variations Mar-May, Oct-Nov

Chefs: Natalie Ansell-Green, Janet Watson, Julian Bolton
Proprietors: Janet and Arthur Watson

Seats: 70. Customers asked not to smoke until after meals. No cigars or pipes
Additional: Children welcome; children's portions; ❀ dishes

BRIDPORT, Roundham House ❦

A small, well maintained hotel with a bright dining room is the setting for a fixed-price menu. Proprietor and chef, Betty Moody, produces a reasonable choice of dishes that changes daily and includes Somerset Pork, local pork chops cooked in cider with apples and served with honey and cider sauce.

Cost: H/wine £7.50. **Credit cards:** 1 3 4 5
Additional: ❂ dishes; other diets on request
Directions: From roundabout on A35 south of Bridport take road signposted West Bay, then 2nd turning on left into Roundham Gardens

Roundham Gardens
West Bay Road
Map no: 3 SY49
Tel: 01308 422753
Chef: Betty Patricia Moody
Proprietors: Robert David Moody and Betty Patricia Moody
Seats: 20. No smoking in dining room
Times: Last D 8pm. Closed Nov-Jan

BRIDPORT, Three Horseshoes Inn ❦

☺ A busy and popular local inn run by Mr and Mrs Ferguson. When our inspector visited, the wide-ranging menu included a very tasty leek and potato soup and salmon wrapped in pancake with ricotta cheese and spinach all encased in a brioche case with hollandaise sauce.

Cost: Alc £20, fixed-price menu £15. **Credit cards:** 1 2 3
Additional: No smoking in restaurant. Children welcome, children's portions, high chairs
Directions: In the village of Powerstock, 5 miles north-east of Bridport

Powerstock
Map no: 3 SY49
Tel: 01308 485328
Chef: Will Longman
Proprietors: Mr and Mrs Ferguson
Times: Last L 2pm/D 10pm

CHRISTCHURCH, Splinters ❦❦

A smart, cosy restaurant offering a good choice of well-prepared modern French dishes

Set in a cobbled courtyard close to the church, this long-established restaurant offers a choice of cosy and intimate dining rooms each with polished wood-panelled walls, flagstone floors and attractive tables. Guests are offered tasty aperitifs in the warmly decorated bar, where they may peruse the good value fixed-price menu or study the lengthy and interesting *carte*. Delicious modern French cooking produces starters like hot roast pigeon salad with garlic croutons and smoked bacon, and main courses such as pan-fried haunch of venison with a juniper sauce, or a vegetarian choice like risotto of mushrooms, tomato and herbs. Our inspector praised the delicate flavour of an onion tart with a herb butter sauce, and a tasty beef sirloin with a light red wine sauce, and a topping of delicious blue cheese hollandaise sauce. A dessert of home-made milk and dark chocolate mousse with a bitter orange sauce successfully rounded off an enjoyable meal. Guests are invited to relax in the comfortable first-floor lounge for coffee and truffles, if they wish. A reasonably priced wine list offers a fair choice.

Directions: Take road into Christchurch from A338 slip road. Located at end of the High Street in a cobbled area

12 Church Street
Map no: 4 SZ19
Tel: 01202 483454

Cost: Fixed-price lunch £8.60.
Wine £9 ♀ Service exc
Credit cards: 1 2 3 4 5
Menus: *A la carte*, fixed-price lunch, Sunday lunch
Times: 10.30am–Last L 2.30pm, 7pm–Last D 10.30pm. Closed Sun dinner, Mon, 2 weeks mid Jan, 26–30 Dec
Chefs: Robert Rees and Kerry Oliver
Proprietors: Timothy Lloyd, Robert Wilson
Seats: 40. No pipes or cigars in restaurant
Additional: Children welcome; ❂ dishes; other diets on request

CHRISTCHURCH, **Waterford Lodge** ☻☻

☺ *A delightful hotel that is a real family operation with the talented son as chef producing superb meals*

In the comfortable surroundings of the delightful family-owned hotel is a smart and popular restaurant. Ian Badley is a keen chef and along with his talented second chef, Mark Davies, they offer guests a varied and seasonally changing *carte* of interesting and well planned dishes. Recently enjoyed meals have begun with lovely home-baked breads and included a marbled salmon and shallot terrine or fillets of red mullet with a delicious herb infused sauce and a pasta rösti which was topped with two succulent scallops. Desserts such as lemon tart had plenty of zest and zing. Light and tasty appetisers are served in the bar.

Directions: Two miles east of Christchurch on A337, turn left towards Mudeford

87 Bure Lane, Friars Cliffe Mudeford
Map no: 4 SZ19
Tel: 01425 278801

Cost: Alc £19.95; fixed-price L £12.95. Wine £9.60. Service exc
Credit cards: 1 2 3 4
Times: Last L 2pm/D 9pm
Chef: Ian Badley
Proprietors: Best Western. Managers: David and Ian Badley
Seats: 40. No cigars or pipes in restaurant
Additional: Children permitted (over 5); children's portions/menu; ❻ dishes

CORFE CASTLE, **Mortons House** ☻

A beautiful manor house with tunnels linked to Corfe Castle where chef Pierre Mathiot prepares simple dishes with plenty of flavour; pasta with mussels, prawns and a Dorset Cheddar cheese sauce and guinea foule, bacon and mushroom presented Bourguignonne style.

Cost: Fixed-price L £15/D £22.50, Sun L £9.50. H/wine £11. Service exc. **Credit cards:** 1 2 3 4. **Additional:** Children permitted (no very young children at dinner); children's portions. ❻ dishes; other diets on request
Directions: In centre of village on A351

East Street
Map no: 3 SY98
Tel: 01929 480988
Chef: Pierre Mathiot
Proprietors: Mr and Mrs David Langford
Seats: 45, 20. No smoking in dining rooms
Times: Last L 2pm/Last D 10.30pm

DORCHESTER, **The Mock Turtle** ☻☻

☺ *Honest and uncomplicated new English cooking in a warm and friendly ambience*

There's a warm, friendly atmosphere at this restaurant which owes much to the fact that it's a family-run affair. Vivien Hodder looks after guests in the three separate dining areas - including one on a small balcony – while Raymond uses care and skill to prepare his uncomplicated new English dishes. The good value set lunch menu, and longer evening version with added specials and fish dishes, offer a well-balanced range: linguini with fresh mussels in a saffron and dill sauce, perhaps, or chicken liver, bacon and mushroom filo cup with a creamy Madeira sauce to start, with lamb in Greek pastry or monkfish Provençal as a main dish. Our inspector chose a nicely flavoured turbot terrine with a lemon and saffron sauce with prawns, followed by sauté of pork fillet with Grand Marnier sauce – a tender, well-cooked dish. All the vegetables were exceptionally good, and a short selection of desserts yielded a light and fluffy raspberry sablé served on crisp wholemeal

34 High West Street
Map no: 3 SY69
Tel: 01305 264011

Cost: Fixed-price lunch £10; fixed-price dinner £15.95 (2 course), £18.95. Wine £7.95. Service exc
Credit cards: 1 3

Menus: Fixed-price lunch and dinner

Times: Midday-Last L 2pm, 7pm-Last D 9.30pm. Closed Sat/Mon lunch, Sun (except BHs)

Chef: Raymond Hodder
Proprietors: Raymond, Alan and Vivien Hodder

shortbread. A vegetarian option is always available, such as a spinach, avocado, artichoke and walnut salad to start, followed by oriental vegetable pancakes.

Directions: At the western end of High West Street near Top 'o' Town roundabout

EVERSHOTT, **Summer Lodge** ❀❀❀

An attractive country house setting for some elaborately presented classic Anglo-French cuisine

A Georgian dower house, parts of which were designed by Thomas Hardy, Summer Lodge has been run by proprietors Nigel and Margaret Corbett for over 15 years. Attention to detail and dedication to customer care are evident and a well trained team of young staff provides consistently high levels of service. Attractive public rooms include a bar and small lounge, where canapés are served, leading into the attractive candlelit restaurant which has recently been extended. Chef Edward Denny, lately of the Box Tree, Ilkley, has taken over in the kitchen and is planning to introduce his own menu.

Our inspectors have reported favourably on starters including a well constructed terrine of calfs' sweetbreads textured with cep mushrooms, and a fresh flavoured celery and apple soup. A vegetarian main course is prepared each day. Our inspectors followed with roast quail served on tasty puy lentils with smoked lardons and a good Madeira and cep jus, and on another occasion, roast Bresse pigeon, again on puy lentils, with a fricassée of wild mushrooms and a rich truffle flavoured jus, (the latter somewhat complicated by an excess of contrasting flavours and unnecessary garnishes). A delicious rich dark chocolate marquise was also rather over-garnished with sliced fruits and icing sugar.

The kitchen makes good use of local produce, with herbs from the hotel's own garden, wild game from the nearby Melbery Estate and seafood direct from Looe in Cornwall. A short daily menu is offered plus a *carte,* which changes every few months, and children are particularly well catered for.

The wine list is first class, with plenty from some of the best estates around the world. While making your choice, enjoy a glass of fine sherry from an excellent range.

Directions: From the A37 from Dorchester turn left into Summer Lane. Hotel is on right

GILLINGHAM, **Stock Hill House** ❀❀❀

Generous portions of robust European cooking are served in the opulent surroundings of this country house hotel

Renowned for the warmth of its hospitality, the comfort of its appointments and its excellent cuisine, this fine country house hotel is set in ten acres of gardens and woodland and has been run for a decade by Peter and Nita Hauser. Peter is a skilled chef with a confident and robust style of cooking, and many of

Seats: 60
Additional: Children permitted; children's portions; ◐ dishes; Vegan/ other diets on request

Evershot
Map no: 3 ST50
Tel: 01935 83424

Cost: *Alc* £35, fixed-price lunch £17.50, fixed-price dinner £29.50. H/wine £11.75. Service exc
Credit cards: 1 2 3 5

Menus: *A la carte,* fixed-price lunch and dinner

Times: Last L 1.45pm, Last D 9pm

Chef: Edward Denny
Proprietors: Nigel and Margaret Corbett

Seats: 50. No smoking in dining room
Additional: Children permitted (over 8 at dinner); children's portions; ◐ dishes; Vegan/other diets on request

Stock Hill
Map no: 3 ST82
Tel: 01747 823626

Cost: Fixed-price L £19; fixed-price dinner £28. Wine £9.95 ♀ Service exc
Credit cards: 1 3 4

his dishes reflect his middle European roots. He offers a sensibly sized fixed-priced menu – three courses at lunch and four at dinner – making good use of quality fresh ingredients, much of the produce coming from his own kitchen garden. Great respect is shown in the cooking of the vegetables, which retain their texture, colour and flavour.

Our inspector's meal began with tasty canapés and home-baked bread rolls, and an enjoyable starter of grilled Somerset goats' cheese on a bed of cabbage, dressed in a light vinaigrette. Alternatives might be warm smoked haddock on watercress dressed with hazelnut oil, or chicken galantine with celery remoulade. Main courses could include grilled cevapcici on Bosnian rice; casseroled French guinea fowl with paprika sauce and spätzli, or the Aga-roasted new season rack of lamb sampled on this occasion, which had a superb flavour, cooked nicely pink and succulent with a strong but complementary rosemary jus. Vegetarian dishes are not generally a feature among the main courses, but can be provided on request.

A tempting choice of desserts is offered, such as banana tart with a sugar basket and caramel sauce, or the rhubarb and ginger soufflé described by our inspector as 'simply a dream'. The predominantly French wine list is of a convenient length, with particularly strong selection from the Rhône and the Loire. There are two good house wines as well as some attractive wines from Austria.

Directions: 3 miles off A303 on B3081

Menus: Fixed-price lunch and dinner, Sunday lunch
Times: Last L 1.45pm, Last D 8.45pm. Closed Mon lunch
Chefs: Peter Hauser, Lorna Connor
Proprietors: Peter and Nita Hauser
Seats: 24 main dining room, 14 Lancaster Room. No smoking in dining rooms
Additional: Children permitted (over 6); children's portions; ❶ dishes; Vegan/other diets on request

HIGHCLIFFE, **The Lord Bute** ❀❀

A restaurant with a difference, popular with locals and visitors attracted by well-prepared food and choice wines

It doesn't take much to work out who used to live in Highcliffe Castle; the restaurant was, in fact, an entrance lodge to the former home of the Marquesses of Bute, now a seminary. The young proprietors have built up a regular and appreciative local clientele, including businessmen and 'ladies who lunch'. There is much for them to appreciate, including the warmth of the welcome, the sensibly priced fixed-price menu (featuring chicken Rothesay – breast in filo pastry served with white wine cream sauce) and the *carte* on which the Bute home of the present Marquess crops up again as venison Rothesay – pan-fried mignons, garnished with glazed pear and served in redcurrant sauce. On an inspection visit the meal began with a good-tasting scallop and artichoke terrine with a creamy lemon mayonnaise and was followed by thinly-sliced, sautéed pork with a delicious creamed brown sauce, given extra bite by adding plenty of peppercorns. The subtly-flavoured lemon mousse, served in a crisp chocolate shell with a lemon and passion fruit sorbet, fittingly rounded off the meal.

Directions: Follow the A337 to Lymington, situated opposite St Mark's churchyard in Highcliffe

Lymington Road
Map no: 4 SZ29
Tel: 01425 278884

Cost: Alc £23, fixed-price lunch £11.95
Credit cards: 1 2 3 4
Times: Closed Sat lunch, Sun eve, Mon all day
Chefs: Christopher Denley, Tim Hoyle
Proprietors: Christopher Denley, Stephen Caunter, Simon Denley
Seats: 75-80. No pipes or cigars in restaurant
Additional: ❶ dishes. No children under 10

LYME REGIS, **Kersbrook** ◉

☺ *A charming hotel with a warm country house atmosphere, and fine views of the town and bay. Skilfully prepared food is served in the two dining rooms: perhaps mussels à la crème, or smoked salmon platter, with steak Camilla or tournedos Rossini. Vegetarians are catered for.*

Cost: Alc £20; fixed-price L £5.50/D £16.50. Wine £8. Service exc
Credit cards: 1 2 3. **Additional:** Children permitted (over 11 at dinner); children's portions; ◐ menu; Vegan/other diets on request
Directions: Pound Road joins Pound Street which is off the main road to Axminster. Opposite old hospital

Pound Road
Map no: 3 SY39
Tel: 012974 42596
Chef: Norman Arnold
Proprietors: Eric Hall Stephenson
Seats: 48. No-smoking area
Times: Last L 2pm/D 9pm. Closed Xmas and New Year

MAIDEN NEWTON, **Le Petit Canard** ◉◉

☺ *A friendly village restaurant where the light, gratifying food reflects some of the world's more exciting tastes*

Pacific Rim with French/Chinese overtones is a cooking style description with a difference. It is how the Chapmans, a Canadian husband and wife team, like to sum up the way Geoff (for it is he who cooks) demonstrates his early experience working with Oriental and European chefs. Not that they are a one-skill couple, though. Lin is well on her way to becoming a Master of Wine and stocks her cellar with great care, so her wine list comment ' Not yet tasted – I'm sure it's very good' is fully trustworthy. But back to the food. There is only a three-course, fixed-price dinner menu, changed monthly. It features half-a-dozen starters like rabbit stir-fried with mushrooms, roasted pepper, mange-tout and ginger/chilli/orange oil, or filo parcels of goat's cheese and tapénade with a sweet pepper jelly. There are six main courses, such as baked hake fillet with slivers of smoked halibut and a light tarragon cream sauce or – and here is a Pacific Rim candidate – char-grilled kangaroo fillet with mustard and shallot sauce. Desserts are of the 'I'm pretty full but I think I can just manage...' variety.

Directions: On the A356 in the centre of Maiden Newton

Dorchester Road
Map no: 3 SY59
Tel: 01300 320536

Cost: Fixed-price dinner £19.95, Wine £9.95. Service exc
Credit cards: 1 3

Menu: Fixed-price dinner

Times: 7.pm-Last D 9pm. Closed Sun, Mon

Chef: Geoff Chapman
Proprietors: Geoff and Lin Chapman

Seats: 28. No cigars or pipes
Additional: Children over 6 permitted; ◐ dishes

POOLE, **Harbour Heights** ◉

☺ *In a superb hill-top location with glorious views over the harbour, this hotel offers accomplished cooking. The menus are imaginative, with fresh produce used in a wide variety of dishes including pan-fried wild boar steak in a red wine and mushroom sauce.*

Cost: Alc £20; Sunday L £10.95; fixed-price D £15.50. Wine £8.95. Service exc
Credit cards: 1 2 3 4 5
Additional: Children welcome; children's portions/menu; ◐ menu; other diets on request
Directions: Midway between Poole and Bournemouth, overlooking Poole Harbour and the Purbeck Hills

73 Haven Road, Sandbanks
Map no: 4 SZ09
Tel: 01202 707272
Chef: Nino Satorello
Proprietor: Paul Shee
Seats: 120. No-smoking area
Times: Last L 2pm/Last D 9.30pm

POOLE, **Haven** ✿✿

Enjoyable food cooked and presented with flair in a waterside location with enviable views

In a delightful position at the water's edge and close to the Swanage ferry, this well-managed hotel has glorious sea views across the bay towards Brownsea Island. With its excellent business and leisure facilities it attracts a wide range of visitors, and the various eating outlets are also popular with all kinds of diners. A brasserie-style menu is offered on the terrace, while traditional food is served in the restaurant, and a more complicated cuisine is available from the *carte* in La Roche restaurant. High quality ingredients cooked with flair are common to all three, and our inspector enjoyed a recent meal at La Roche which began with pressed terrine of halibut and salmon flavoured with basil and served with a piquant tomato salad. An unusual poached beef fillet with a peppercorn and Madeira sauce was full of flavour, and came with well-cooked and fresh-tasting vegetables. Highly recommended from a tempting array of desserts was a light and fluffy chocolate soufflé with delicious strawberry purée and vanilla sauce. Service is pleasantly professional, and there is a well-balanced sensibly-priced wine list.

Directions: From Poole or Bournemouth follow signs to Sandbanks Peninsula

Banks Road, Sandbanks
Map no: 4 SZ09
Tel: 01202 707333

Cost: A/c £24; fixed-price lunch £15; fixed-price dinner £22. Wine £9.50 ♀ Service exc
Credit cards: 1 2 3 4

Menus: A la carte, fixed-price lunch/dinner, Sunday lunch, Brasserie, pre-theatre, bar menu

Times: A la carte open 7pm–Last D 10pm. Closed Sun

Chef: Heinz Karl Nagler
Proprietors: F J B Managers: I G Butterworth, Christopher Smith

Seats: A la carte 40, main restaurant 150. No smoking in main restaurant
Additional: Children welcome (main restaurant); children's portions/menu; ◐ menu; Vegan/other diets on request

POOLE, **Mansion House** ✿✿

☺ *A busy, popular hotel dining club serving a variety of quality modern British cooking*

Set close to Poole Quay and St James' Church, this friendly hotel is reached through an attractive entrance and imposing staircase. The older part of the building is beamed and cottagey, while the restaurant is in an elegant wood-panelled room which is invariably busy. This is partly due to a popular dining club which is open to non-members for a small supplement, but also to the imaginative, good-value menus of chef Gerry Godden. Hot onion tart made an enjoyable recent starter, followed by roast lamb from the carving trolley which offered a choice of well-cooked or pink meat, served with lightly cooked vegetables with good natural flavours. A creamy kumquat soufflé was a successful dessert, and decent coffee and petit fours came after. Various fixed-price menus are available for lunch and dinner, with typical dishes like fillet of salmon in a tomato and chive sauce with green peppercorns, and breast of guinea fowl with a red wine sauce and grilled corn cakes. Vegetarian choices might be vegetable lasagne glazed with goats' cheese and basil, and nut cutlets with a fresh tomato and herb sauce.

Directions: Follow the signs for Poole Quay. Turn left just before the Lipting Bridge, first road on left is Thames Street

Thames Street
Map no: 4 SZ09
Tel: 01202 685666

Cost: Fixed-price lunch £11.50; fixed-price dinner £19.25. Wine £11.50. Service exc
Credit cards: 1 2 3 4

Menus: Fixed-price lunch and dinner, Sunday lunch, bar menu

Times: 12.30-Last L 2pm, 7.30pm-Last D 9.30pm. Closed Sat lunch, Sun eve, 28–30 Dec

Chef: Gerry Godden
Proprietor: Robert Leonard

Seats: 85. No smoking area by arrangement; no pipes or cigars in restaurant. Air conditioned
Additional: Children permitted (over 5); children's portions; ◐ dishes; Vegan/other diets on request. Live entertainment once a month

POOLE, **Mez Creis** ✹

☺ *Named after the Breton fishing boat where Italian proprietor Nicola Dogana learned her trade, this restaurant specialises in local crustaceans, cooked well and at reasonable prices. Fishing ropes and nets hang from the beams giving an easy atmosphere to this informal bistro.*

Cost: Alc £13.50. H/wine £7.65. Service exc. **Credit cards:** 1 2 3 4 5
Additional: Children welcome; children's portions
Directions: 200yds from the Quay which runs parallel to the High Street

16 High Street
Map no: 4 SZ09
Tel: 01202 674970
Chef: Karen Brailsford
Proprietors: Karen Brailsford, Nicola Dogana
Seats: 38
Times: Last D 10.30pm (11pm Sat). Lunch not served. Closed 2 weeks Xmas, Sun in winter

POOLE, **Salterns** ✹✹

A locally-renowned waterside restaurant where customer satisfaction is the top priority

It wins glowing accolades from guide books, and its guests keep returning to eat and to stay, so Salterns must have something special – and indeed it does. On the edge of a marina, it offers fine views of Poole Harbour and Brownsea Island. New chef John Sanderson is behind a revised fixed-price *carte* which, like that of his predecessor, is strong on variety and value for money. Seafood-lovers will home in fast on a starter of ragoût of crayfish in langoustine sauce with a macedoine of vegetables and spring onions or, to follow, a trio of roast salmon, sea-bass and turbot on thyme-flavoured Provençale sauce. Main courses are well balanced between fish and meat – four of each on Sanderson's first production. He makes his own version of cock-a-leekie with poached suprême of chicken, onions, pearl barley, leeks and prunes. For those with a sweet tooth, there is a good choice of home-made desserts which includes some for the health and calorie-conscious too – our inspector (not strong on either virtue, she says) enjoyed the wickedness imbued by chocolate mousse. There is a fine wine list. Staff are charming and professional.

Directions: From Poole take B3369 for Sandbanks. In Lilliput turn right into Salterns Way. Restaurant on right at end

38 Salterns Way, Lilliput
Map no: 4 SZ09
Tel: 01202 707321

Cost: Alc £25, fixed-price lunch £25, fixed-price dinner D £16.50. H/wine £9.50 ♀ Service exc
Credit cards: 1 2 3 4

Menus: *A la carte*, fixed-price lunch and dinner

Times: Last L 2pm, Last D 9.30pm

Chef: John Sanderson
Proprietors: Best Western. Managers: Beverley and John Smith

Seats: 50. No smoking. Air conditioned
Additional: Children permitted; children's portions; ❤ menu; Vegan on request

POOLE, **Sandbanks** ✹

A well managed hotel with glorious views across the bay. A carte has recently been created which is interesting and well balanced. The quality and freshness of the ingredients is high and dishes, including scallops of monkfish garnished with bananas and toasted almonds, are very enjoyable.

Cost: Alc £22.50; fixed-price L £12/D £17. Wine £9.50. Service exc
Credit cards: 1 2 3 4. **Additional:** Children permitted (main restaurant); children's portions/menu; ❤ menu; Vegan/other diets on request. Live entertainment in summer
Directions: From Poole or Bournemouth follow signs to Sandbanks Peninsula

Banks Road, Sandbanks
Map no: 4 SZ09
Tel: 01202 707377
Chef: Robert Alan Jones
Proprietors: F J B. Managers: Mr J G Butterworth, Mr John Belk
Seats: *A la carte* 38, main restaurant 200. No smoking in dining rooms
Times: *A la carte* restaurant Last D 9.30pm. Closed Sun

SHAFTESBURY, La Fleur de Lys ❀❀

An impressive standard of French and modern English cooking with pronounced flavours

This little restaurant is easily living up to its early promise by continuing to serve deceptively simple dishes with outstanding flavours and attractive presentation. Chef David Shepherd combines elaborate care with his imaginative skills to produce dishes like chicken and sweetbread terrine with basil and a tomato puree, and pan-fried escalope of veal with wild mushrooms and devilled kidneys in a creamy Dijon mustard sauce. Our inspector enthused over a starter of shellfish tartlet, crisp pastry filled with succulent whole scallops, mussels and prawns and served with julienne of vegetables and a tasty saffron sauce. Pan-fried calf's liver was lightly cooked and tender, served on a crisp potato galette with another well-made sauce – raspberry this time. A good selection of vegetables was perfectly cooked, and a dessert of brandy snap with Calvados ice cream and apple was original and mouthwatering. A similar style of dishes appears on both the *carte* and the fixed price menu, but the latter offers better value for money while only the *carte* provides a vegetarian choice.

Directions: Near the post office in town centre, on the main road

25 Salisbury Street
Map no: 3 ST82
Tel: 01747 853717

Cost: Alc ££25; Lunch from £9; fixed-price dinner £15.50 (2 course), £18.95. Wine £9.50 ♀. Service exc
Credit cards: 1 2 3 4

Menus: A la carte, fixed-price lunch and dinner, Sunday lunch
Times: Midday–Last L 2.30pm, 7pm–Last D 10.30pm. Closed Sun eve, Mon lunch

Chefs: David Shepherd, Marc Preston
Proprietors: David Shepherd, Mary Griffin and Marc Preston

Seats: 40. Air conditioned
Additional: Children welcome; children's portions (pre-ordered); ❤ dishes; other diets on request. Live entertainment occasionally

SHAFTESBURY, Royal Chase ❀

☺ *Originally a Georgian monastery, this friendly hotel has two restaurants – the more formal of which, the Byzant, has the rosette. Typical dishes include warm chicken livers and bacon with a tarragon cream sauce and a breast of duck with green peppercorn and Grand Marnier sauce.*

Cost: Alc £13.75; fixed-price L £14.75 (2 courses), £16.75/D £19.90 ♀ Service inc
Credit cards: 1 2 3 4.5. **Additional:** Children permitted (not in Byzant at dinner); children's portions/menu; ❤ menu; Vegan/other diets on request
Directions: Set back from roundabout at A30 and A350 intersection to east of town

Royal Chase Roundabout
Map no: 3 ST82
Tel: 01747 853355
Chefs: Andrew Wheatcroft, Donna Bird
Proprietors: Best Western. Managers: George and Rosemary Hunt
Seats: 56 Byzant, 30 Country. No-smoking area; no cigars or pipes in restaurants
Times: Last L 2pm/D 9.45pm (Byzant), 830pm (Country)

SHERBORNE, Eastbury ❀

In a delightful Gerogian town house in the centre of this small town, the restaurant serves dishes such as steamed suprême of chicken, or cheese and spinach parcels in puff pastry.

Directions: In town centre just off A30 (Salisbury to Yeovil)

Long Street
Map no: 3 ST61
Tel: 01935 813131

SHERBORNE, Pheasants ❋❋

☺ *Imaginative and sometimes inspired contemporary English cooking in a cosy, unpretentious atmosphere*

A charming and genuinely warm welcome awaits visitors to this unpretentious town house restaurant at the top of Sherborne high street. Andrew and Michelle Overhill are delightful hosts, while in the kitchen Neil Cadle cooks with obvious enthusiasm and flair to produce some imaginative food. An extensive *carte* and good value fixed-price lunch menu show off his repertoire, such as a recently enjoyed home-cured Cornish cod marinated with dill, fresh herbs and citrus juices, and breast of wild duck in a sherry and green peppercorn-scented sauce. Our inspector enjoyed an inspired starter of sweet pan-fried scallops served with steamed fresh asparagus and a light, clean dressing of orange, dill, peppercorns and hazelnut oil. Roasted breast and thigh of guinea fowl stuffed with a chicken and corn farcie was moist and roundly flavoured, served with baby artichoke bottoms, baby turnips and a julienne of vegetables. Dessert was a very rich slices of praline parfait on chantilly cream in a crisp brandy snap basket with a light chocolate sauce feathered with fruit coulis. The wine list is knowledgeable.

Directions: On A30 at the top of the High Street., on the right from Yeovil direction

24 Greenhill
Map no: 3 ST61
Tel: 01935 815252

Cost: Alc £20; fixed-price L £12.85; fixed-price dinner £18.95, £19.50. Wine £8.20 ♀. Service exc
Credit cards: 1 3

Menus: A la carte, fixed-price lunch and dinner, Sunday lunch
Times: Midday-Last L 2pm, 6.30-Last D 10pm. Closed 2 weeks mid Jan
Chef: Neil D Cadle
Proprietor: Andrew L Overhill

Seats: 40. No cigars or pipes
Additional: Children welcome; children's portions; ♥ menu; Vegan/other diets on request

STUDLAND, Manor House ❋

☺ *A bright conservatory restaurant is an added addition to this rambling old gothic building with panoramic views of Studland Bay. The cooking is simple but sound with home-made soups, a good selection of fresh local fish and shellfish and meat dishes such as honey roast ham or noisettes of lamb.*

Cost: Fixed-price D £18.50. Wine £7.95. Service exc
Credit cards: 1 2 3. **Additional:** Children welcome; children's portions/menu; ♥ dishes; Vegan/other diets on request
Directions: In centre of village

Map no: 4 SZ08
Tel: 01929 44 288
Chefs: David Rolfe, John Thompson
Proprietor: Richard Rose
Seats: 80. No smoking in dining room
Times: Last L 2pm/D 8.30pm. Closed Xmas, Jan

STURMINSTER NEWTON,
Plumber Manor ❋❋

A Jacobean manor house where guests are treated as old friends and the cooking is highly recommended

It is hardly surprising that so many people return again and again to this mellow Jacobean manor house, offering as it does a haven of peace, good food, and really welcoming service. The hotel is very much a family business, with Richard Prideaux-Brune playing the charming host while his brother is the talented force in the kitchen. Brian cooks with care, and uses quality ingredients to create culinary delights for an appreciative audience. Starters include the boned and stuffed

Hazelbury Bryan Road
Map no: 3 ST71
Tel: 01258 472507

Cost: Sunday lunch £17.50; fixed-price dinner £20/£25 (3 courses), £22/£27. H/wine £10 ♀ Service inc
Credit cards: 1 2 3 4 5

Menus: Fixed-price dinner, Sunday lunch

Times: Last L 2pm (Sun), Last D 9.30pm. Closed Feb

quail our inspector recently enjoyed, filled with a Stilton and walnut mousse and served with wild rice and a deliciously rich sauce. Fillet of brill with a light mustard sauce was another recommended dish, as was tender spring lamb with a garlic and herb crust and a strongly flavoured sauce. Our expert on sticky ginger pudding with sweet butterscotch sauce was delighted with this version of the popular dessert. The three or four course set dinner menus of varying prices offer choices that may include medallions of venison with orange and apple sauce, and fillet of veal with basil mousse folded in Parma ham and wrapped in filo pastry, and there is always a vegetarian dish.

Directions: Turn off A357 into Hazelbury Bryan Road opposite the Red Lion

Chef: Brian Prideaux-Brune
Proprietor: Richard Prideaux-Brune

Seats: 65. Smoking discouraged
Additional: Children welcome; children's portions; ❶ dishes; Vegan/other diets on request. Pianist occasionally

SWANAGE, **The Cauldron** ❀

☺ *Good-value, enjoyable food prepared from fresh local ingredients is offered at this small High Street restaurant. Dishes might include smooth chicken liver pâté, breast of hen pheasant with a coriander and herb topping, bread and butter pudding with real custard, and a 'without meat' option.*

Cost: Alc £17.50; fixed-price D £10.95. Wine £7.50. Service exc
Credit cards: 1 2 3 4 5
Additional: Children permitted (early dinner); children's portions; ❶ menu; Vegan/other diets on request
Directions: At lower end of the main high street opposite The Old Quay

5 High Street
Map no: 4 SZ07
Tel: 01929 422671
Chef: Mr T Flenley
Proprietors: Margaret and Terry Flenley
Seats: 36. No cigars or pipes
Times: Last L 2pm/D 9.30pm. Closed Mon, Tues lunch (Summer) and Mon, Tues all day (Winter), last 3 weeks Jan

SWANAGE, **Grand** ❀

☺ *Enjoying an enviable position atop a cliff with spectacular views across Swanage Bay, the Renaissance restaurant offers particularly imaginative dishes from a daily-changing menu, as well as a more traditional carte. Warm poppy seed, Feta cheese and tomato tart was a pleasant starter.*

Cost: Fixed-price D £14.40. **Credit cards:** 1 2 3 4
Additional: Children welcome; ❶ dish
Directions: In a residential street on the cliff top

Burlington Road
Map no: 4 SZ07
Tel: 01929 423353
Chef: Theresa Read
Proprietor: Mr Kingham
Times: Last D 9.30pm

WAREHAM, Kemps ❀

☺ *Situated in unspoilt Dorset countryside this welcoming hotel offers a set-priced menu and a carte both served in the bright garden-style restaurant. The cooking is sound, flavoursome and well prepared. Starters include quails' eggs in a curry sauce, and main courses, roulade of veal filled with spinach and prawns.*

Cost: A/c £18, fixed-price L £8.95/D £17.95. H/wine £7.95 ♀ Service exc. **Credit cards:** 1 2 3 4
Additional: Children permitted; children's portions; ❂ dishes; Vegan/other diets on request
Directions: On A352 midway between Wareham and Wool

East Stoke
Map no: 3 SY98
Tel: 01929 462563
Chef: Phil Simpkiss
Proprietors: Paul and Gill Warren
Seats: 60. No smoking in dining room
Times: Last L 1.30pm/D 9.30pm

WAREHAM, Priory ❀❀

A glorious setting, charming staff and good food and wine in a comfortable and warm atmosphere make eating at this historic hotel a delight

Medieval monks were renowned for keeping a good table and the habit lives on at this 16th-century priory turned hotel, on the banks of the river Frome. While lunch is served in the light, airy Greenwood dining room, dinner guests descend to the vaulted Abbot's Cellar restaurant, very atmospheric by candlelight. The fixed-price and *carte* menus offer interesting selections of classic cooking, chef Michael Rust taking advantage of regional produce such as local lobster and Dorset ham. Main courses major on traditional dishes and may include lamb roasted with garlic, venison and poached pears and, at Sunday lunch, beef with Yorkshire pudding and horseradish sauce. Our inspector sampled a tasty game terrine successfully served with tangy mango chutney. The roast breast of guinea fowl on a bed of leaf spinach and pimentos was notable for its creamy sherry sauce. Somerset Brie and Dorset Blue Vinney are typical of the English cheeses offered while home-made puddings may include iced Grand Marnier parfait or rhubarb fool. The quality cooking is complemented by a sound wine list and attentive service.

Directions: To the east of Wareham beside River Frome

Church Green
Map no: 3 SY98
Tel: 01929 551666

Cost: A/c £33.50; fixed-price lunch £12.95, £14.95; dinner £24.50 (Sun–Fri), £28.50 (Sat). Wine £10.50. Service exc
Credit cards: 1 2 3 4

Menus: *A la carte*, fixed-price lunch and dinner, Sun lunch, bar menu

Times: 12.30pm–Last L 2pm, 7.30pm–Last D 10pm

Chef: Michael Rust
Proprietors: Stuart and John Turner

Seats: Greenwood 24, Cellar 48. No smoking in dining rooms
Additional: Children welcome; ❂ dishes; Vegan/other diets on request. Live entertainment

WAREHAM, Springfield ❀

☺ *An elegant hotel with an attractive restaurant where chef Andrew Cannon serves classic French cuisine. Starters include breadcrumbed deep-fried mushrooms stuffed with cream cheese which could be followed by slices of veal with a raspberry sauce or a mixed grill.*

Cost: A/c £18.50, fixed-price D £15. H/Wine £8.50. Service inc
Credit cards: 1 2 3 **Additional:** Children welcome; children's portions/menu; ❂ menu; Vegan/other diets on request
Directions: Off the A351 just outside the village, signed Creech, Steeple and Kimmeridge

Grange Road, Stoborough
Map no: 3 SY98
Tel: 01929 552177
Chef: Andrew Cannon
Proprietors: Mr J Alford
Seats: 55
Times: Last L 2pm/D 9pm

WEST BEXINGTON, **Manor** ❀

☺ *Yards from Chesil Beach, this handsome hotel offers a reasonably priced menu with a choice of two or three courses and a sorbet. There is a wide variety of dishes, including a vegetarian option. Walnut and Stilton pâté, and escalope of pork with grape and elderberry sauce are recommended.*

Cost: Fixed-price L £12.50 (2 courses), £14.50/D £16.85 (2 courses), £19.85. Wine £7.25 ♀ Service exc
Credit cards: 1 2 3 4 5
Additional: Children welcome; children's portions/menu; ❶ dishes; other diets on request
Directions: On B3157 west of Dorchester

Beach Road
Map no: 3 SY58
Tel: 01308 897616
Chef: Clive Jobson
Proprietors: Richard and Jaynie Childs
Seats: 65. No smoking area
Times: Last L 1.30pm/D 9.30pm. Closed Xmas eve

WEYMOUTH, **Perry's** ❀❀

☺ *A relaxed and friendly quayside restaurant offering fresh fish and interesting meat dishes*

A test of a really good restaurant is perhaps how the kitchen functions when the first two chefs are absent, and a recent inspection meal cooked by third chef Wayne Cramp was well worth two rosettes. This attractive restaurant opposite the Old Quay has a reputation for its fresh fish and seafood dishes, and the day's specials are written on the blackboard. There are plenty of meaty choices too, and our inspector's starter of avocado and Stilton tartare would have pleased any vegetarian. This colourful dish had a tasty combination of flavours, and was followed by a really fresh cod fillet with herb crust and a creamy, buttery sauce with Chardonnay and sweet mussels. A white and dark chocolate délice with a light coffee-flavoured sauce successfully rounded off this meal, and espresso coffee was richly dark. Other dishes on the *carte* and daily fixed-price menu might be moules marinière, crab thermidor, and medallions of venison and pigeon with a port sauce and cranberries, while vegetarian choices could include mushroom samosa with a spicy tomato and coriander sauce, and pithivier of leeks with Gruyère cheese.

Directions: On south side of harbour. Follow signs for Brewers Quay

The Harbourside
4 Trinity Road
Map no: 3 SY67
Tel: 01305 785799

Cost: *Alc* £19.50; fixed-price lunch £10 (2 courses), £12.50. Wine £7.50. Service exc
Credit cards: 1 3

Menus: *A la carte*, fixed-price lunch, Sunday lunch
Times: Midday-Last L 2pm, 7pm-Last D 9.30pm. Closed Sat/Mon lunch and Sun eve Oct-Mar (except BHs)

Chef: Andy Pike
Proprietors: Raymond, Alan and Vivien Hodder

Seats: 60
Additional: Children permitted; children's portions; ❶ dishes; Vegan/other diets on request

WEYMOUTH, **The Sea Cow** ❀

☺ *Relaxed and friendly, this simple waterside restaurant is deservedly popular, so booking is advisable at weekends. Fresh fish – perhaps locally-caught skate in a lemon and wine sauce – is a speciality, though the evening carte also offers plenty of meat.*

Cost: *Alc* L £10/D £19.50; Sunday L £8.93. Wine £9.75 litre. Service exc. **Credit cards:** 1 3
Additional: No-smoking area; no pipes or cigars in restaurant. Children welcome; children's portions; ❶ dishes; Vegan/other diets on request
Directions: On the Quay

7 Custom House Quay
Map no: 3 SY67
Tel: 01305 783524
Chef: Mr Terence Michael Woolcock
Proprietors: Terry and Susan Woolcock
Times: Last L 2pm/D 10.15pm. Closed Sun eve Oct–Jun

WIMBORNE, Les Bouviers ❀❀

Quality French cooking from a talented chef, supported by an impressive team of staff

A most impressive meal is what our inspector enjoyed recently at this cottage-style restaurant, where chef/patron James Coward can be relied upon to produce outstandingly good food. Great care and skill go into the preparation of his dishes, and a particular strength is the exceptional saucing. Perfectly fresh produce was much in evidence at a recent inspection meal, which began with a crisp puff pastry case filled with creamed spinach and topped with wild mushrooms cooked in a veal stock with herbs. Saddle of fresh local rabbit served with braised cabbage and lardons was an excellent main course, served with nicely cooked vegetables, and the apple and mango tart with blackcurrant sorbet which brought the meal to a finish was delightful. There's a fixed-price Menu Gourmand of five courses which changes often, and a seasonal *carte* offering fish, meat and a couple of vegetarian options. The young staff provide a friendly welcome and efficient service throughout, which easily matches the quality of the cooking. The unadventurous wine list consists mainly of French and New World wines.

Directions: 0.5 miles south of A31 Wimborne by-pass on junction of A349 and unclassified road to Ashington

Oakley Hill, Merley
Map no: 4 SZ09
Tel: 01202 889555

Cost: Alc £26; fixed-price lunch £8.95; fixed-price dinner £21.95. Wine £7.95 ₽. Service exc
Credit cards: 1 2 3 4

Menus: *A la carte*, fixed-price lunch and dinner, Sunday lunch, children's, bar menu

Times: Midday–Last L 2pm, 7pm–Last D 10pm. Closed Sat lunch and Sun dinner

Chef: James Coward
Proprietor: James Coward

Seats: 50. No-smoking area
Additional: Children welcome; children's portions; ❂ menu; Vegan/other diets on request

WIMBORNE MINSTER, Beechleas ❀❀

☺ *A professionally-run country house hotel using only the best produce and applying the highest standards*

A short walk from the town and the River Stour, Beechleas is a well-restored, Grade II-listed, Georgian house with an attractive, conservatory-style restaurant. Much of the produce used in the kitchen comes from a local farm, a partnership which benefits customers as well, since fresh and natural flavours are very evident in the cooking. The short dinner *carte*, from which two and three-course fixed-price meals may also be selected, changes regularly and features simple dishes, mainly Anglo-French in style. Our inspector enjoyed a starter of salmon fish cakes with a buttery dill sauce, medallions of beef fillet with peppercorn, cognac and cream sauce with perfectly-cooked vegetables. He finished with home-made pineapple crumble in which the sweetness of the topping was well balanced by the fruit's tartness. A thoughtfully-constructed wine list offers a good choice of bottles for less than £20, although more expensive varieties are available. Proprietor Josephine McQuillan and her charming staff care well for the locals, business executives and tourists who eat here.

Directions: On A349 at Wimborne

17 Poole Road
Map no: 4 SZ09
Tel: 01202 841684

Cost: Fixed-price dinner £15 (2 courses), £17.50. H/wine £8.95. Service exc
Credit cards: 1 2 3

Menu: Fixed-price dinner
Times: 7.30pm–Last D 9.30pm. Closed Sun, Mon, 24 Dec-24 Jan

Chef: Paulina Humphrey
Proprietor: Josephine McQuillan

Seats: 20. No smoking in dining room
Additional: Children welcome; children's portions; ❂ dishes/other diets on request

COUNTY DURHAM

BEAMISH, **Beamish Park** ❀

☺ *Situated in open countryside this modern hotel is well positioned for all the heritage sites of the North East. The rosette is awarded here to the restaurant at dinner where chef Clive Imber produces his well chosen menu. The puddings are all home-made and worth leaving room for.*

Cost: Fixed-price D £14.95 (2 courses), £17.95. H/wine £8.95.
Credit cards: 1 2 3 4. **Additional:** Children welcome; ◐ dishes.
Directions: Just off A6076 Newcastle to Stanley road

Beamish Burn Road, Marley Hill, Newcastle-upon-Tyne
Map no: 12 NZ25
Tel: 01207 230666
Chef: Clive Imber
Proprietor: William Walker
Seats: 38. No smoking in dining room
Times: Last L (Sun only) 2pm, Last D 9.30pm. Closed Sun eve

DURHAM, **Hallgarth Manor** ❀

☺ *On the edge of Durham City, a friendly country house-style hotel in large gardens. The Continental cuisine is typified by main courses from the carte such as spicy tournedos of Aberdeen Angus beef and lightly grilled darne of halibut. For dessert, ask for the pastry chef's daily specials.*

Cost: Alc £18.50, fixed-price L £12.50/D £15.50. H/wine £6.95. Service exc. **Credit cards:** 1 2 3 4. **Additional:** Children welcome; children's portions/ dishes; ◐ menu; Vegan/other diets on request
Directions: 3 miles north-east of Durham off the A690

Pittington
Map no: 12 NX24
Tel: 0191 372 1188
Chef: Thuya Winn
Proprietor: Terry Robson
Seats: 70
Times: Last L 2pm/D 9.15pm. Closed Sat L

REDWORTH, **Redworth Hall** ❀❀

Adventurous and exceptionally well prepared food can be enjoyed in the two restaurants of this superb country house.

This very impressive Jacobean country mansion, surrounded by 25 acres of gardens and woodland, offers two restaurants – the Blue Room featuring a more adventurous *carte* in classical French style while the larger Conservatory provides a carvery as well as its variety of traditional dishes. Chef Scott MacRae is a perfectionist who takes a great deal of pride in his cooking, and a recent inspection meal was very much above average: trio of warm fillets (duck, chicken and lamb, accompanied by a salad with mango and quails' eggs and given interest and balance by a balsamic vinaigrette) was followed by fresh sea-bass fillet filled with spinach mousseline and set on a picturesque capsicum fish reduction, the accompanying al dente vegetables retaining both their good colour and vibrant taste; a freshly cooked blackcurrant and apple charlotte was served with a notable vanilla-flavoured egg custard sauce, and there were home-made sweetmeats with the richly flavoured coffee. Children and vegetarians have their own separate menus. The wine list is extensive, and a smart staff provides professional service.

Directions: Situated on the A6072 (off A68) near Newton Aycliffe

Near Newton Aycliffe
Map no: 8 NZ22
Tel: 01388 772442

Cost: Alc £28.50, fixed-price L £9.50 (2 courses), £11.50/D £16.95
Credit cards: 1 2 3 4

Times: Last D 10pm

Chef: Scott MacRae
Proprietor: Brian Phillpotts

Seats: 40 (Blue Room), 86 (Conservatory Restaurant). No smoking in dining room

Additional: Children welcome, children's menu/portions; ◐ menu; Vegan/other diets on request

ROMALDKIRK, **Rose & Crown** ✺✺

☺ *Some sublime English cooking in a charming beamed and panelled setting*

There is little to fault in the cooking of chef/patron Chris Davy, and a meal at this delightful old country inn is a truly enjoyable experience. Only the freshest of ingredients go into the short selection of dishes on the fixed-price menu, and the only effort required is in making a choice. The chicken liver parfait at a recent inspection meal was pronounced superbly smooth and full of flavour, served with a tangy port and orange sauce. A good home-made soup is always offered between courses, and monkfish tails with a mild mustard grain sauce were brightly white in colour, and gently flattered by the subtle mustard flavours. Interesting vegetables like creamed carrots with walnut, stick beans wrapped in bacon, honey roasted parsnips and potatoes cooked in stock made an unusual change. A deceptively simple lemon pie was outstandingly tasty and refreshing. Other choices on the four-course dinner menu might be salad of quails' eggs, croutons and smoked bacon, and chargrilled slices of calf's liver and bacon with an onion confit. The wine list is well-chosen, and entries come with good descriptions.

Directions: In the centre of the village, near the church

Map no: 12 NY92
Tel: 01833 650213

Cost: Fixed-price lunch £10.95, fixed-price dinner £22. H/wine £8.50 ♀ Service inc
Credit cards: 1 3 5

Menus: Fixed-price lunch and dinner, Sun lunch, bar menu

Times: Midday–Last L 1.30pm, 7pm–Last D 9pm. Closed Sun eve, Xmas

Chef: Christopher Davy
Proprietors: Christopher and Alison Davy

Seats: 24. No smoking in dining room
Additional: Children permitted (early supper preferred), children's portions; ◐ dishes/other diets on request

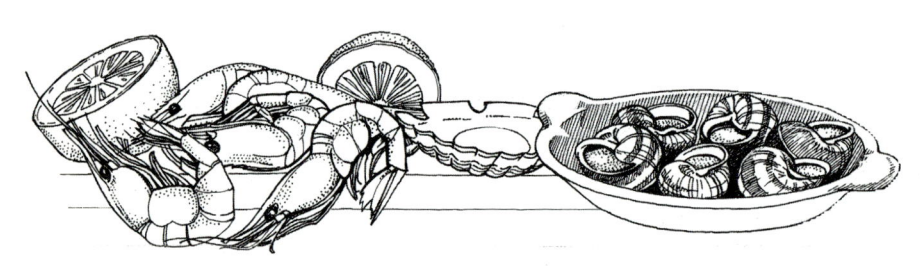

EAST SUSSEX

ALFRISTON, **Moonrakers** ✺✺

☺ *This delightful cottage restaurant offers personally-run service, good food and an interesting wine list.*

A long-established, 16th-century, oak-beamed inglenook cottage restaurant and bar personally run by the proprietor Norman Gillies. The fixed-price menu runs alongside a short *carte* which features on Saturday. A new chef, Mark Goodwin, has been installed and whilst he is clearly showing a dedicated approach, some uninteresting vegetables came in for some criticism this year. Our inspector chose the carrot and coriander soup, after enjoying a delightful tartlette appetiser, and followed with the grilled breast of Barbary duck, which was served with a

High Street
Map no: 5 TQ50
Tel: 01323 870472

Cost: *A/c* from £19.50, fixed-price dinner £16.95. H/wine £8.50. Service inc
Credit cards: 1 2 3

Menus: *A la carte,* fixed-price dinner, Sun lunch

Times: Last D 9.45pm. Closed Sun eve, last 2 weeks Jan

ginger and lime flavoured jus. Plain vegetables and the broccoli, carrots, mushrooms and new potatoes lacked excitement. A raspberry and Mascarpone brûlée was well made, but needed a little longer under the salamander to caramelise all the demerara sugar. Freshly brewed coffee is offered from the pot, and comes with some tasty chocolates. The wine list lincludes Old and New World, mostly recent vintages, and service is very attentive and efficiently polite. There are plans to move the bar lounge upstairs, to create a larger and additional dining area.

Chef: Mark Goodwin
Proprietor: Norman Gillies

Seats: 48. No-smoking area
Additional: Children over 6 welcome; children's portions. ✪ dishes; Vegan/other diets on request

Directions: Alfriston is about 3 miles from Seaford, just off the A259. Moonrakers is on the right-hand side of the High Street

BATTLE, **Netherfield Place** ❀❀

Enjoyable, uncomplicated English cooking in a relaxed and caring country house setting

A rather special, pampered atmosphere is an attractive feature of this peaceful, isolated hotel where staff are faultlessly considerate. Warm-looking stripped pine predominates in this 1920s country house, and the majestic dining room is a fine setting for the solid, uncomplicated English food served there. A short, reasonably priced 'executive' menu is offered at lunchtime, while in the evening the choice of food can be taken from a daily-changing fixed-price menu, a longer *carte* or a vegetarian list. Our inspector had no trouble choosing a starter of roasted quail with a zesty orange sauce and plenty of natural flavours, followed by red sea bream and samphire with a lemon butter sauce. Some elaborate vegetables included batter-covered fried courgettes, a mousse trio of spinach, swede and turnip, tomato stuffed with wild mushrooms duxelles, rösti, and asparagus with hollandaise sauce. Any room left afterwards should go on a dessert like the three chocolate mousses with individual sauces, or perhaps apple and peppermint parfait sliced onto a cinnamon cream.

Netherfield
Map no: 5 TQ71
Tel: 01424 774455

Cost: Alc £26, fixed-price L £15.95, fixed-price D £22. H/wine £8.95 ♀ Service exc
Credit cards: 1 2 3 4

Menus: *A la carte*, fixed-price lunch and dinner, Sunday lunch, bar menu

Times: 12.30-Last L 2pm, 7pm-Last D 9.30pm. Closed last week Dec and 1st 2 weeks Jan

Chef: Michael Collier
Proprietors: Michael and Helen Collier

Seats: 80. No pipes or cigars
Additional: Children permitted (before 7pm); children's portions/menu; ✪ dishes; Vegan/other diets on request

Directions: Turn off A2100 for Netherfield. The hotel is situated on the left-hand side after about 1.5 miles

BATTLE, **Powdermills** ❀

This converted 18th-century manor house provides a contemporary-style restaurant in the orangery. It has an interesting carte and two set meals, one for vegetarians. Dishes include roasted ballotine of rabbit with smoked bacon and Dijon sauce, and loin of lamb with a mixed bean panache.

Cost: Alc £28, fixed-price lunch £13.50/D £16. Service inc
Credit cards: 1 2 3 4. **Additional:** Children permitted at lunch; ✪ menu; Vegan/other diets on request
Directions: Go through Battle towards Hastings, turn right into Powdermills Lane, the hotel is on the right after a sharp bend

Powdermills Lane
Tel: 01424 775511
Map no: 5 TQ71
Chef: Paul Webbe
Proprietors: Douglas and Julie Cowpland
Seats: 85. No smoking
Times: Last L 2pm/D 9.30pm

BRIGHTON, Black Chapati ❀❀

☺ *Interesting dishes are the main feature of this charming restaurant, influenced by the patron's time in India*

12 Circus Parade
New England Road
Map no: 4 TQ30
Tel: 01273 699011

The interesting and very eclectic style of chef/patrons Stephen Funnell and Lauren Alker has created a very unusual dining experience in this unassuming little restaurant, with its minimalist black furnishings, by combining Indian sub-continent recipe, (which Stephen Funnell learnt living in India), with a variety of 'home spun' dishes which reveal the kitchen's ability to produce innovative and imaginative cooking with flair and real flavour. Dishes from India come in for the highest praise, whilst others, like breast of wood pigeon with udon noodles and coriander pesto, still need to be developed to become as exciting. Our inspector was very impressed with the vegetable samosas, with excellent filo pastry, minted yoghurt, and sweet pepper sauce. Another good dish was the fresh cod, baked in coconut milk with chillies and ginger, beautifully aromatic with cumin, cardamom, and creamed coconut, chilli chutney, timbale of best Basmati rice and black mustard seeds. Desserts usually include home made ice-creams. The wines are complemented by some interesting farmhouse ciders, and beers.

Cost: Alc £20. H/wine £8.50.
Service inc
Credit cards: 1 2 3 5

Menus: *A la carte*, Sunday lunch

Times: Last L 2pm, Last D 10.30pm. Closed Sun eve, Mon, 1 week Xmas

Chefs: S Funnell, L Alker
Proprietors: S Funnell, L Alker

Seats: 30
Additional: No children after 9pm, no babies; ❶ dish

Directions: Directions are complex. Readers are advised to use a local map

BRIGHTON, Brighton Thistle ❀❀

☺ *A very formal French restaurant in a smart and spacious seafront hotel*

Kings Road
Map no: 4 TQ30
Tel: 01273 206700

A dramatic and luxuriant atrium greets visitors to this large modern hotel right on Brighton's seafront, and the spacious public areas are only slightly less impressive. There are two restaurants, but it is the very formal La Noblesse which is attracting comment. Here chef Andrew Furrer cooks in a traditional French manner, producing interesting dishes which he presents with elaborate style. The set three-course lunch and dinner menus offer seven or eight choices at each course; a fish meal might begin with halibut and lobster terrine with a light tomato vinaigrette, followed by poached red snapper on a bed of vegetable julienne and spring onion sauce, and there are meaty choices like pan-fried sweetbread with pastry fleuron and a port wine sauce to start, and sautéed calf's liver with red onion and strips of smoked bacon. A recent inspection meal began with chicken timbale with a vibrantly fresh tomato purée, and then beef fillet with its own vegetables, finishing with a very nutty walnut tart. The only complaint was that the beautiful presentations can sometimes overwhelm delicate flavours.

Cost: Fixed-price lunch and dinner £17.50. H/wine £11.50 ⚲
Service inc
Credit cards: 1 2 3 4

Menus: Fixed-price lunch and dinner

Times: Last L 2pm, Last D 10pm. Lunch not served Sat. Closed Sun

Chef: Andrew Furrer
Proprietor: Thistle. Manager: Hugh F Hilary

Seats: 50. Air conditioned
Additional: Children welcome; ❶ dishes; Vegan/other diets on request

Directions: From Palace Pier roundabout take Kings Road. Hotel in half a mile on the left

ENGLAND EAST SUSSEX 259

BRIGHTON, **Grand** ❀

Opened in 1864, the Grand continues to offer luxury accommodation and good food. Sampled dishes include scallops in a sweet vermouth cream sauce, and slices of beef fillet, venison and duck breast with a tasty plum and mushroom sauce.

Cost: Alc £34, fixed-price L £16/D £24. H/wine £11.50 ♀ Service exc
Credit cards: 1 2 3 4. **Additional:** Children welcome before 9pm; children's portions/menu; ❶ menu; Vegan/other diets on request
Directions: Located on Brighton seafront (A259) adjacent to the Brighton Centre

Kings Road
Map no: 4 TQ30
Tel: 01273 321188
Chef: Ivan Parnell
Proprietors: De Vere. Manager: Richard Baker
Times: Last L 2.30pm (3pm Sun)/D 10pm

BRIGHTON, **Langan's Bistro** ❀❀

Famous name, famous town and food which is well on its way to the same accolade

Six years have elapsed since Langan's opened its doors to Brighton's *bons viveurs*. It is, of course, a direct descendant of the brasserie in Mayfair owned by Michael Caine, Richard Shepherd and, originally, the late Peter Langan himself. Pictures, prints and plates fill the elegant French-style restaurant, where at front of house Nicole Emmerson insists on the finest table appointments and top-notch service; her husband Mark is the chef. An advocate of subtle flavours, colours and textures, he changes menus two or three times a week, in order to get the best from the produce available. They are kept short, brutally so at lunchtime, when each course is down to two dishes. Crab ravioli, which our inspector had, are served with Japanese seaweed and a delightful fish fumet. A main course of noisettes of venison with a refined pepper sauce left a pleasant, lingering taste and the vegetables showed the care taken in the kitchen. The dessert – apple and plum paillard, served with honey ice cream – was good, but suffered a little from the odd tough plum skin. French wines are all from top producers, including the house wines.

Directions: Just off the seafront about halfway between the Palace Pier and the Marina

Map no: 4 TQ30
1 Paston Place
Tel: 01273 606933

Cost: Fixed-price lunch £12.50 (2 courses), £14.50. Wine £7.70. Service inc.
Cover charge 75p
Credit cards: 1 2 3 4

Menus: *A la carte*, fixed-price lunch, Sunday lunch

Times: Last L 2.15pm, Last D 10.15pm. Closed Sat lunch, Sun dinner, Mon, 1st 2 weeks Jan and last 2 weeks Aug

Chef: Mark Emmerson
Proprietor: Nicole Emmerson

Seats: 40. Air conditioned
Additional: Children welcome; ❶ dishes; Vegan/other diets on request

BRIGHTON, **Le Grandgousier** ❀

Owner Lewis Harris and Chef Nial Allbeury produce a simple yet very successful format of a six-course meal including a baguette crudités, pâté de foie de volaille with cornichons followed by a choice of main course, examples of which are, trout sauce Nantaise and fillet steak au poivre.

Cost: Alc £34, fixed-price L £16/D £24. H/wine £11.50 ♀ Service exc
Credit cards: 1 2 3 4. **Additional:** Children welcome before 9pm; children's portions/menu; ❶ menu; Vegan/other diets on request
Directions: Located on Brighton seafront (A259) adjacent to the Brighton Centre

15 Western Street
Map no: 4 TQ30
Tel: 01273 772005
Chef: Nial Allbeury
Proprietor: Lewis M Harris
Seats: 38. No cigars or pipes
Times: Last L 1.30pm/D 9.30pm. Lunch not served Sat. Closed Sun, 24 Dec-4 Jan

BRIGHTON, Topps ☻☻

17 Regency Square
Map no: 4 TQ30
Tel: 01273 729334

☺ *A well-balanced and interesting menu offering uncomplicated traditional cooking*

A beautifully restored Regency hotel close to Brighton's seafront houses this delightful basement restaurant. The cooking is a mixture of traditional English and French with an emphasis on simplicity, and self-taught chef/patron Pauline Collins puts great thought and care into producing her fixed-price dinner menu. Our inspector recently praised chicken livers in a spinach pastry tart, the livers fresh and tender and lightly cooked in wine with cream and herbs, with fresh spinach purée in a shortcrust tartlet. Dover sole with a prawn stuffing was also very fresh, and came with an excellent fish sauce, and tasty vegetables. A treacle tart of light buttery pastry and soft-textured treacle topping vied for favour with the now renowned bread and butter pudding. Other choices on the menu might be scampi in filo parcels, and rack of new season's lamb with onion sauce, and there are vegetarian options like cream cheese and spinach pancakes, and stuffed aubergine which can be served as a starter or main course. The standard of service is high, and the wine list includes some interesting New World varieties.

Cost: Fixed-price dinner £18.95 (2 courses), £21.95. H/wine £7.50. No service charge
Credit cards: 1 2 3 4 5

Menu: Fixed-price dinner

Times: Last D 9.30pm. Closed Wed, Sun, Xmas and Jan

Chef: Pauline Collins
Proprietors: Paul and Pauline Collins

Seats: 25
Additional: Children permitted, children's portions; ❖ dishes

Directions: In Regency Square which is opposite the West Pier

BRIGHTON, Whytes ☻☻

33 Western Street
Map no: 4 TQ30
Tel: 01273 776618

☺ *A friendly little restaurant offering high standards of modern cooking*

The continuing success of this small restaurant close to the seafront is due to two factors: consistently reliable and uncomplicated cooking and a friendly and attentive approach to customer care. Chef/patron Ian Whyte shows off his skills and flair for modern cooking in a set menu which changes every six weeks and makes the best use of locally caught seafood and local produce. Dishes like pan-fried medallions of fillet steak with a stout and mushroom sauce, and chicken supreme wrapped in smoked bacon with a chive sauce are popular with regulars, and Ian's home-made desserts are equally tempting. Our inspector opted for devilled crab and smoked bacon gratin, a good smoky starter served in a scallop shell. Roast fillet of lamb, cooked pink and served with a delightfully tasty garlic and cumin sauce was another success, and the carefully cooked vegetables came crisp and full of flavour. A pancake filled with Grand Marnier and rum and topped with cream, followed by coffee and chocolate truffles would leave most people feeling happily replete. The wine list has an extensive house selection.

Cost: Fixed-price dinner £14.50 (2 courses), £17.95. H/wine £7.50. Service exc
Credit cards: 1 2 3

Menus: Fixed-price dinner

Times: 7pm-Last D 10pm. Closed Sun

Chef: Ian Whyte
Proprietors: Ian and Jane Whyte

Seats: 36. Smokers asked to consider other diners
Additional: Children permitted; ❖ dishes

Directions: On the Brighton-Hove border, opposite the seafront. First right after the Norfolk Resort Hotel

EASTBOURNE, Downland ❀

Chef Patrick Faulkner has an eclectic and professional style of cooking, and he offers an interesting carte at this popular hotel restaurant. Dishes include terrine of duckling with Parma ham and passion fruit, charcoal-grilled fillet of beef topped with a strong cheese mousse, and traditional hot apple pudding.

Cost: Alc £22.50, fixed-price dinner £17.50. H/wine £8.50. Service exc. **Credit cards:** 1 2 3 4 5
Additional: Children permitted (over 7 at dinner); children's menu/portions; ❶ menu; Vegan/other diets on request
Directions: On A2021 about half a mile from the town centre

37 Lewes Road
Map no: 5 TV69
Tel: 01323 732689
Chef: Patrick Faulkner
Proprietors: Minotels.
Managers: Patrick and Stephanie Faulkner
Seats: 35. No cigars or pipes
Times: Last D 9pm (8.30pm Sun). Closed 26 Dec-20 Jan

EASTBOURNE, Grand ❀❀

Carefully-prepared modern English cooking using traditional skills

In a resplendent white Regency building, the Grand Hotel is an imposing presence on the western side of town across from the seafront. Smartly dressed staff offer a cheerful service, while the food in the Mirabelle restaurant continues to attract praise. The traditional skills of chef Neil Wiggins are perfectly demonstrated in the modern English dishes on the *carte* and daily-changing fixed-price menu. Starters like terrine of duck and foie gras with pistachio nuts, salad mâche and hot toasted brioche might be followed by saddle of rabbit stuffed with spinach and herbs served with a timbale of endives, or gratin of turbot with wild mushrooms. Our inspector recently sampled the hot chicken liver mousse wrapped in spinach and served on a rich cream sauce, and salmon with mushroom and tomato covered in a herb and Parmesan crust; vegetables were full of flavour. A fresh, rich, classic Marjolaine gateau with layers of puff pastry packed with hazelnut, chocolate and coffee cream is a must for the sweet-toothed. The canapés, petit fours and delicious cafetière coffee all received the same skilful treatment.

Directions: On the seafront at the western end of town

King Edward's Parade
Map no: 5 TV69
Tel: 01323 412345

Cost: Alc £30, fixed-price lunch £17.50, fixed-price dinner £25.50. H/wine £10.75 ♀
Service inc
Credit cards: 1 2 3 4

Menus: A la carte, fixed-price lunch and dinner
Times: Last L 2.30pm, Last D 10pm. Closed Sun, Mon, 1 week in Jan

Chefs: Neil Wiggins
Proprietors: De Vere. Manager: Peter Hawley

Seats: 50. No smoking before 2pm or 9pm. No pipes. Air conditioned
Additional: Children welcome; children's portions; ❶ menu; Vegan/other diets on request

EASTBOURNE, Lansdowne ❀

☺ *The rather drab exterior belies the outstanding quality and friendly service of this seafront hotel. Traditional English fare such as grilled rainbow trout with almonds and lemon butter, on a fixed-price menu is capably prepared by George Thompson, resident chef for 20 years.*

Cost: Fixed-price D £14. H/wine £8.25. Service inc
Additional: Children welcome; children's portions/menu; ❶ menu; Vegan/other diets on request

King Edward's Parade
Map no: 5 TV69
Tel: 01323 725174
Chef: George Thompson
Proprietors: Best Western.
Manager: Tony Hazell
Seats: 130
Times: Last L 2pm/D 8.30pm.
Closed 1-14 Jan

FOREST ROW, Ashdown Park ❋❋

A beautiful mansion with many ecclesiastical touches, serving modern international dishes with classical origins

There's still an ecclesiastical air about this grand mansion which was once a convent. Now completely refurbished to provide a high standard of spacious and elegant accommodation, even the former chapel has been cleverly converted into conference rooms. In the large Anderida restaurant a pianist plays most evenings, providing a relaxed yet formal setting for some classical cuisine which receives a modern touch from chef John McManus. A short *carte* and daily-changing set menu are offered, and our inspector chose a recent meal from the latter, enjoying the strong, distinctive flavours of pigeon breast with celeriac and port wine sauce. Breast of duck with crushed peppercorns and spätzli was a decent main course, served with tasty roasted shallots and some well-cooked vegetables. The attractively presented dessert of white chocolate mousse encased by a dark chocolate mousse and served with a double chocolate sauce was an excellent choice. Dishes from the *carte* might include terrine of sole and muscat grapes in a lemon verbena jelly, and grilled chicken with orange, honey and mustard glaze.

Directions: From A22 at Wych Cross take Hartfield turning. Ashdown Park is half a mile on the right

Wych Cross
Map no: 5 TQ43
Tel: 01342 824988

Cost: *Alc* from £30, fixed-price L £15/D £25. Wine £12.75. Service inc.
Credit cards: 1 2 3 4 5.

Chef: John McManus
Proprietor: Graeme C Bateman

Times: Last L 2pm/D 9.30pm (10pm Fri, Sat)

Seats: 100. No pipes or cigars
Additional: Children permitted (over 7 at dinner); children's portions; ❂ dishes; Vegan/other diets on request

HAILSHAM, The Olde Forge ❋

☺ *This beamed and candlelit restaurant was once the old forge. Chef Jean Daniels is a reliable and skilful cook and our inspector enjoyed 'meaty pâté' and local fillets of plaice and found the sweet trolley well stocked with interesting home-made desserts.*

Cost: *Alc* £15, fixed-price dinner £12.50. H/wine £8. Service exc
Credit cards: 1 2 3 4
Additional: Children welcome; children's portions by prior arrangement; ❂ menu; Vegan/other diets on request.
Directions: On the A271 Bexhill road, north-east of Hailsham

Magham Down
Map no: 5 TQ50
Tel: 01323 842893
Chef: Mrs Jean Daniels
Proprietors: Mr J P Bull, Miss Tracey Bull
Seats: 28. No cigars or pipes
Times: Last D 9.30pm

HASTINGS & ST LEONARDS, Rösers ❋❋❋

Classic French cuisine with Mediterranean influences in an unlikely seafront setting opposite the pier

Described by our inspector as 'a restaurant I'd go out of my way for', this unassuming seafront establishment, almost opposite Hastings pier, is now in its 10th year. Here, chef proprietor Gerald Röser provides consistently improving standards of cooking with unfaltering dedication and professional skill, making this an oasis of haute cuisine. The classical recipes featured on his *carte* reflect this serious approach. These include super fresh fish, home-smoked and home-marinated scallops, carp, chicken and salmon, and

64 Eversfield Place
Map no: 5 TQ80
Tel: 01424 712218

Cost: *Alc* £25, fixed-price lunch £15.95, fixed-price dinner £18.95. H/wine £8.95. Service inc
Credit cards: 1 2 3 4 5

Menus: *A la carte*, fixed-price lunch and dinner

possibly the best cod in the south, crusted with salsa. Chef Röser offers a short fixed-price lunch menu in addition to the carte and a monthly set gourmet dinner with wines to complement each course. Vegetarian main courses are not generally listed but can be provided on request.

Dishes that have impressed our team this year are complimentary appetisers of angels on horseback and foie gras, and starters of home-made and very fragrant wild boar sausage and a beautifully constructed cauliflower terrine with a fine langoustine sauce. Rack of local Romney Marsh lamb came crusted with coriander, fresh ginger and garlic, with a rich jus gravy and lightly cooked vegetables – delightful. A faultless dessert, a mille-feuille layered with apples and crème patisserie flavoured with Calvados, was served with excellent butterscotch sauce. Full-flavoured Italian coffee with petits fours completed an outstanding meal, which is all the more remarkable when one considers that Gerald Röser was working almost single-handedly in the kitchen.

The wine list is long and of excellent quality, its greatest strength being the selections for the classic areas of France. There are also three good house wines.

Times: Midday-Last L 2pm, 7pm-Last D10pm. Closed Sat lunch, Sun, Mon

Chef: Gerald Röser
Proprietors: Gerald and Jenny Röser

Seats: 40. No cigars or pipes
Additional: Children permitted. ❷ dishes; Vegan/other diets on request

Directions: Opposite Hastings pier

HERSTMONCEUX, Sundial ❀❀

The classic dishes of France are served in a setting which invokes the atmosphere of a typical French rural restaurant.

For more than 26 years Giuseppi Bertoli and his charming wife have run this restaurant in a delightful 17th-century country cottage, their attention to detail and genuine concern for customers' well-being earning them a regular and very loyal local following. A friendly atmosphere pervades the dining room, its oak beams, crisp Basque table linen and sparkling silver and copper all combining to create a typically French rural ambience – the illusion furthered by terraced gardens where guests can eat on summer days. Menus, too, are classically French, changing regularly to make effective use of market-fresh produce. An enjoyable meal might begin with mousseline aux trois poissons (a combination of fresh scallops, crab and salmon topped with lobster and served with an expertly constructed fish velouté sauce), this followed by two whole quails roasted and surrounded by a rich meat glacé flavoured with truffles and Calvados; home-made desserts include ice creams, crème brûlée and chocolate mousse, and an extensive wine list includes some fine vintages from reputable producers.

Map no: 5 TQ81
Tel: 01323 832217

Cost: Alc £32.50, fixed-price lunch £15.50, £19.50; fixed-price dinner £24.50. Wine £10.75. Service exc
Credit cards: 1 2 3 4

Menus: A la carte, fixed-price lunch and dinner, Sunday lunch

Times: Last L 2pm (2.30pm Sun),Last D 9pm (9.30pm Sat). Closed Sun eve, Mon, 2nd week Aug-1st week Sep, Xmas-20 Jan

Chef: Giuseppi Bertoli
Proprietors: Giuseppi and Laurette Bertoli

Seats: 60. No smoking in dining room
Additional: Children welcome; children's portions; ❷ dishes; other diets on request

Directions: In the centre of the village, on the main road

HOVE, Quentin's ☻

☺ *The hallmark of this simply decorated restaurant, with scrubbed tables and hardback chairs, is dishes combining modern English, Mediterranean and Oriental recipes. Quentin Fitch is self-taught and shows his flair with potato and crab fish cake or Indian style tiger prawns, to name but two.*

Cost: Alc £16, fixed-price L £4.95 (1 course), fixed-price dinner by arrangement from £12.95. H/wine £8.30 ♀ Service exc **Credit cards:** 1 2 3 4 **Additional:** Children welcome. ✪ dishes; other diets on request
Directions: On the south side of Western Road between Brunswick Square and Palmeira Square

42 Western Road
Map no: 4 TQ30
Tel: 01273 822734
Chef: Quentin Fitch
Proprietors: Candy and Quentin Fitch
Seats: 42. No pipes or cigars. Air conditioned
Times: Last L 2.30pm/D 10.30pm. Lunch not served Sat. Closed Sun, Mon, last week Aug, 1st week Sep

JEVINGTON, Hungry Monk ☻☻

☺ *Reliable, enjoyable cooking in a candlelit restaurant with a long-standing reputation*

Celebrating its 27th year under the same ownership, this delightful popular restaurant attracts a very loyal and celebrated clientele. The lounges create the perfect setting for aperitifs, and on warm summer days the terrace garden can be used. Original oak beams and flickering candlelight capture an atmosphere of days gone by and, with the attentive service, this can be the perfect setting for the 'bon vivant'. Cooking is shared by Claire Burgess and Mr Thai la Roche, who consistently provide reliable and enjoyable standards of cooking. Warm appetisers are offered, and our inspector kicked off with a Provençale onion tart, followed by the rabbit wrapped in prosciutto, roasted and stuffed with prunes, and set on a bed of flageolet beans, beautifully cooked; this came with a creamed jus and fresh rosemary. We had to have the banoffee pie, (which was first created here in 1972), and to no one's surprise it was perfect. Wines are coded A, B, C for flavour and style; with over 200 wines to choose from, and three pages of half bottles, it's worth studying the list before making a hurried selection.

Directions: Follow the A22 towards Eastbourne. Turn right on to the B2105. The restaurant is situated between Polegate and Friston

Polegate
Map no: 5 TQ50
Tel: 01323 482178

Cost: Fixed-price lunch and dinner £20.90. Wine £8 ♀
Service charge for parties over 8
Credit cards: 2

Menus: Fixed-price lunch and dinner
Times: Midday-Last L 2.15pm, Last D 10.30pm. Lunch not served Mon, Sat. Closed BHs (except Good Fri)

Chefs: Claire Burgess, Thai La Roche
Proprietors: Nigel and Sue Mackenzie

Seats: 40 (also 3 private dining rooms). No smoking
Additional: Children permitted (not under 3 in dining room); ✪ dishes; other diets on request

MAYFIELD, Rose and Crown ☻

☺ *Chef Kevin Shaw offers extensive and varied menus, including chef's 'specials' which are extremely popular, such as crispy-coated field mushrooms and Thai grilled caramelised fish with lime. On the carte there may be Stilton and bacon salad or aromatic honey and ginger duck.*

Cost: Alc from £12.50. H/wine £7.35 ♀ No service charge
Credit cards: 1 3. **Additional:** Children permitted; ✪ dishes; Vegan/other diets by arrangement
Directions: Turn off A267 into village, then left by garage, inn is on the left by a small green

Fletchling Street
Map no: 5 TQ52
Tel: 01435 872200
Chef: Kevin Shaw
Proprietors: Peter and Jackie Seely
Seats: 30. No pipes or cigars. Air conditioned
Times: Last L 2.15pm/D 9.45

RYE, **Landgate Bistro** ●●

The quintessential bistro where simplicity and informality are the keynotes to success

Rye was once a port, but today it stands two miles inland overlooking wild Romney Marsh. The sea's presence remains strong, though, and the old cliffs are still evident around part of the town. Equally evident is the flourishing partnership of chef Toni Ferguson-Lees and Nick Parkin, committed as ever to a winning fusion of good food and polite service. With everything freshly prepared and cooked to order, delays may occur but the wise customer is patient and has another glass of wine. Furnishings are hardly captivating, although oil-cloth table covers have a certain rustic charm. The Bistro is open only for dinner with a daily *carte*, and a fixed-price, three-course (plus coffee) menu available midweek. The *carte* features the old favourite, Very Fishy Stew, a selection of local fish poached in stock and served with aöli, garlic bread and a salad. Another is salmon and haddock fish cakes with parsley sauce, followed, say, by sautéed calf's liver with white wine and fresh sage. The menu never totally changes and, sensibly, vegetables are now priced and served separately. Seventy good value wines are available, many by the glass.

Directions: From the High Street head towards the Landgate. The Bistro is in a row of shops on the left-hand side

5-6 Landgate
Map no: 5 TQ92
Tel: 01797 222829

Cost: Alc £22; fixed-price dinner £14.20 (Tue-Thu) ♀
Credit cards: 1 2 3 4

Menus: A la carte, fixed-price dinner Tue-Thu

Times: 7pm-Last D 9.30pm. Lunch not served. Closed Sun, Mon, Xmas, & also 1 wk Jun

Chef: Toni Ferguson-Lees
Proprietors: Toni Ferguson-Lees, Nick Parkin

Seats: 30
Additional: Children welcome; ❶ dishes

RYE, **Mermaid Inn** ●

An ancient inn rebuilt in 1420, and one of the oldest in the country, full of creaking floorboards and medieval character. The restaurant is next to an inner courtyard and fountain, and serves some exciting dishes cooked to a high standard. Try French onion soup and baked local codling.

Cost: Alc from £23, fixed-price L £13.95/D £16.50 (£19 Sat). H/wine £7.95 ♀ Service exc. **Credit cards:** 1 2 3 4 5
Additional: Children welcome; children's portions; ❶ dishes; other diets on request
Directions: Centre of town. Car park through archway

Mermaid Street
Map no: 5 TQ92
Tel: 01787 223065
Chef: Brian Murray
Proprietors: Robert Pinwill, Judith Blincow
Seats: 64
Times: Last L 2.15pm/D 9.30pm

UCKFIELD, **Hooke Hall** ●

☺ *Since our last visit by an inspector Hooke Hall has changed to an Italian restaurant and we have been unable to visit again. Chefs Michele Pavanello and Silvano Gambetta specialise in food from Veneto and Liguria. Pasta dishes include an unusual asparagus ravioli with asparagus sauce.*

Cost: Alc £17. H/wine £7.75. Service exc. **Credit cards:** 1 3
Additional: Children welcome; ❶ dishes
Directions: Northern end of High Street

250 High Street
Map no: 5 TQ42
Tel: 01825 766844
Chef: Michelle Pavanello, Silvano Gambetta
Proprietors: Juliet and Alister Percy
Seats: 28
Times: Last L 1.45pm/Last D 9.15. Lunch now served Sat. Closed Sun, Xmas to New Year

UCKFIELD, **Horsted Place** ❀❀❀

A gracious country house setting with formal service for rather expensive Anglo-French cuisine, including a vegetarian menu

Set in the heart of the Sussex Downs, adjoining the East Sussex National Golf Course, this imposing Victorian mansion is a haven of gracious living with a level of discreet and formal service seldom found outside London. Head chef Allan Garth offers both fixed price and *carte* menus. The cuisine is predominantly French and English though other influences from Italy and Thailand are evident. Only the best quality produce is used, but what impresses most is the lack of pretension, the success of each dish depending on the skilful blending of flavours to enhance rather than overpower the basic ingredient. A good example of this was succulent new season's lamb with brown lentils and two vegetables (vegetables are always served as an integral part of the main course) – it needed no more as it could not have been improved upon. Starters have included a salad of crab with a light grain mustard dressing, and a memorable ballantine of foie gras.

A separate vegetarian menu is also available with a choice of two starters and main courses, such as a salad niçoise with a tapénade of olives, figs and capers and, as a main course, cannelloni of spinach, ricotta and almonds. To finish there is a selection of traditionally made British farmhouse cheeses, home-made ice creams and sorbets, or a choice of rich puddings: perhaps the unusual Austrian 'Kairershmarren', a souffléd pancake with raisins served on a strawberry sauce.

This is by no means a cheap place to eat, but perfect for a special occasion when one wishes to be cosseted and to enjoy fine food in a wonderfully calm atmosphere. Although French wines are in the majority, all other countries are represented on the wine list, including an excellent selection from Germany.

Little Horsted
Map no: 5 TQ42
Tel: 01825 750581

Cost: *Alc* £35, fixed-price lunch £14.95, fixed-price dinner £28.50. H/wine £9.95 ♀ No service charge
Credit cards: 1 2 3 4

Menus: *A la carte*, fixed-price lunch and dinner, Sunday lunch, pre-theatre

Times: Midday-Last L 2pm, 7.30pm-Last D 9.30pm

Chef: Allan Garth
Proprietor: Jonathan Ritchie

Seats: 40. No smoking in the dining room
Additional: Children over 8 permitted; children's portions; ❂ menu; other diets on request

Directions: Two miles south of Uckfield on the A26

WADHURST, **Spindlewood** ❀❀

An imaginative and confident cooking style in a comfortable, traditional setting

In contrast to the traditional setting in which it is served, the cooking here by chef Harvey Lee Aram follows a confident, modern approach. Home-made soups, game and fish dishes and well-crafted desserts are all particular strengths, and they appear on the fixed-price dinner menu and lunchtime *carte* in various imaginative guises. Starters might include hot mushroom mousse in a leek and almond broth, or tropical fruits with blue curacao sorbet, while main courses could be grilled fillet of beef with apple, grapes and red wine sauce, or loin of hare with peppercorn cream sauce. A selection of fish dishes is also offered. Our inspector chose fresh, well-cooked mushroom brunoise inside salmon parcels, served with a lemon beurre blanc with chives that was pronounced perfect. Lamb fillet was tender and sweet, and came with an interesting variety of fresh,

Wallcrouch
Map no: 5 TQ63
Tel: 01580 200430

Cost: *Alc* lunch £20, fixed-price dinner £23.20. H/wine £7.60. Service exc
Credit cards: 1 3

Menus: *A la carte* lunch, fixed-price dinner, Sunday lunch, bar menu
Times: Last L 1.30pm, Last D 9pm. Lunch not served BHs. Closed 4 days Xmas

Chef: Harvey Lee Aram
Proprietor: Robert V. Fitzsimmons

colourful vegetables. The dessert menu offers delights for the sweet-toothed, like a delicious coffee and ginger cheesecake served with coffee crème anglaise, and freshly ground coffee comes with four different petits fours. The wine list is compiled of over 80 mainly European wines.

Seats: 40. No cigars or pipes in the restaurant
Additional: Children welcome; children's portions; ❷ dishes; Vegan/other diets on request

Directions: About 2 miles south-east of Wadhurst on the B2099

ESSEX

BROXTED, **Whitehall** ❀❀

Elaborate, modern country-style cooking from a dedicated team

A timber-vaulted restaurant in a lovely Elizabethan country house hotel is home to the soundly-prepared modern English cooking of chef Paul Flavell. For the adventurous there's a 'surprise' six-course menu offering delicate gourmet dishes at a price. Otherwise the choice from the *carte* is still emphatically elaborate, and a generous and attractive selection of canapés and wan tun prepares the palate for what is to come. Starters might be hot soufflé of haddock, champ and whole grain mustard, or pan-fried foie gras with orange brioche and caramelised orange, while main courses could be roast breast of chicken with carrots and scallops in a Thai cardamom sauce, or fillet of turbot with Savoy cabbage and a whole grain mustard sauce. Our inspector was not entirely happy with a lobster tortellini with Parma ham, dried tomatoes and Parmesan for the lobster was overwhelmed, but monkfish tail in a black ink sauce was more effective. A ginger mousse with caramelised orange sauce and chocolate maple leaves, and bracing coffee with home-made chocolates ended the meal in style.

Church End
Map no: 5 TL52
Tel: 01279 850603

Cost: *Alc* £34, fixed-price lunch£19.50, *Menu Surprise* £37.50, H/wine £12
Credit cards: 1 2 3 4

Menus: *A la carte*, fixed-price lunch, *Menu Surprise*

Times: Last L 1.30pm, Last D 9.30pm

Chef: Paul Flavell
Proprietors: Pride of Britain.
Manager: Harold Tijssen

Seats: 40. No cigars or pipes
Additional: Children welcome; children's portions. ❷ dishes; other diets on request.

Directions: Leave the M11 at junction 8. Follow signs for Stansted Airport and then for Broxted

CHELMSFORD, **Pontlands Park** ❀

A well-looked-after Victorian hotel on the fringes of Chelmsford with chef Stephen Wright in the kitchen producing a wide variety of dishes. Starters include confit of duck and as a main course they offer medallion of venison in apple and peppercorn sauce or Chateaubriand from the grill.

West Hanningfield Road
Great Baddow
Map no: 5 TL70
Tel: 01245 476444
Chef: Stephen Wright
Proprietors: Robert Bartella, Jason Bartella
Seats: 70. No smoking area. No cigars or pipes
Times: Last L 2.30pm/D 10pm.
Cosed Sat L, Sun D, 27-30 Dec

Cost: *Alc* from £25, fixed-price L from £10/D from £17. H/wine £9.75 ♀ Service exc. **Credit cards:** 1 2 3 4 5
Additional: Children welcome (early at dinner); children's menu/portions; ❷ menu; Vegan/other diets on request
Directions: Leave the A12 (Chelmsford by-pass) at Great Baddow (A130), take first slip road, bear left for Great Baddow and first left

COGGESHALL, **Baumann's** ✿✿

4-6 Stoneham Street
Map no: 5 TL82
Tel: 01376 561453

☺ *Confident European cooking producing some hearty dishes served in an easy atmosphere*

With its wooden floorboards, white linen and assortment of antique chairs, this is a comfortable, gentrified brasserie. Staff are experienced and relaxed, and the pace is pleasantly unhurried. At lunchtime there's a well-priced two-course business lunch, and the monthly changing *carte* offers hearty dishes with some international influences like beef bresaola and rösti. There's also a daily fish dish which depends on the catch at Billingsgate market. At a recent inspection meal the delicate flavour of a creamy Jerusalem artichoke soup was overpowered by pungent, crispy barbecued croûtons and black pepper. Grilled lamb fillet was succulent and full-flavoured, and served on a bed of spicy, tangy green tomato chutney. A hot soufflé of caramelised apples served with runny Calvados crème anglaise was a very tasty choice from a richly tempting dessert selection. Other examples of Mark Baumann's and Doug Wright's confident cooking might be mussel and onion stew, or braised pheasant with Savoy cabbage and cranberries. A short wine list provides a broad choice under headings of colour and characteristics.

Cost: *Alc* £21, fixed-price lunch £9.95, Sunday lunch £13.95. H/wine £8.50 ♀ No service charge
Credit cards: 1 2 3 5

Menus: *A la carte*, fixed-price lunch, Sunday lunch

Times: 12.30-Last L 2pm, 7.30pm-Last D 10pm. Closed Sun eve, Mon, 2 weeks Jan

Chefs: Mark Baumann, Doug Wright
Proprietors: Baumanns

Seats: 75. No pipes or cigars
Additional: Children welcome; children's portions; ❷ dishes; other diets on request

Directions: In the centre of Coggeshall opposite the clock tower

COGGESHALL, **White Hart** ✿✿

Market End
Map no: 5 TL82
Tel: 01376 561654

☺ *Rich Italian cooking with refreshingly honest flavours in an old world setting*

Heavy oak beams dominate the stone-flagged rooms of this historic inn which dates in part from 1420. The original town guildhall forms part of the high-ceilinged first-floor lounge, and everywhere the past is apparent with all its character and charm. The split-level bar is popular for lunchtime snacks, and the blackboard showing daily specials is also available in the elegant restaurant where a lengthy *carte* lists the dishes on offer. Chef Fausto Mazza cooks traditional Italian food with panache and indulgence, and the results are rich but refreshingly honest. Our inspector had nothing but praise for a recent meal, which began with home-made tortelloni filled with a full-flavoured meat ragu sauce and oyster mushrooms. Another very rich dish was fillet of turbot with a buttery anchovy sauce, topped with mozzarella and bread crumbs, which came with tender baked chicory, properly sautéed potatoes, and nicely cooked florets of broccoli. A light version of the popular Italian trifle tiramisu was quite delicious, as was the espresso coffee. The wine list includes some excellent Italian bottles and a good Sicilian house wine.

Cost: *Alc* £20, Sunday lunch £13.95. Wine £9.25. Service exc
Credit cards: 1 2 3 4

Menus: *A la carte*, Sunday lunch, bar menu

Times: Midday-Last L 2pm, 7pm-Last D 10pm. Dinner not served Sun

Chef: Fausto Mazza
Proprietor: Mario Casella

Seats: 80
Additional: Children permitted; children's portions; ❷ dishes; other diets on request.

Directions: From the A12 towards Ipswich take the A120, left towards Braintree; at the B1024 crossroads turn left again

COLCHESTER, **Martha's Vineyard** ❀❀

☺ *An unlikely combination of sleepy English village and highly recommended, delicious American-style cooking*

A restaurant like Martha's Vineyard is probably the last thing you would expect to find in a sleepy village six miles outside Colchester. But local lovers of good food have embraced this informal little restaurant, where Ohio-born Larkin Rogers cooks an eclectic array of dishes with the emphasis firmly on her native America. A very short, fixed-priced menu shows the day's options, with perhaps starters like shredded barbecued duck salad served warm with a 'Q' sauce, or 'cioppino', a California-style mixed fish stew with red wine, tomatoes, red pepper, mayonnaise and croûtons. Main courses might include spicy braised lamb shoulder chops with haricot beans, cumin and chipolte peppers, or pan-seared chicken breast marinated in lime juice, allspice and coriander. Larkin makes her own delicious bread and pasta which might appear in a dish like buckwheat fettucine with mustard cream sauce, goat's cheese and arugula. The home-made puddings are highly recommended – perhaps rhubarb Linzertorte – a nut pastry filled with rhubarb compôte served with vanilla anglaise.

Directions: 6.5 miles north of Colchester, just off the A134, in the middle of Nayland High Street

High Street, Nayland
Map no: 5 TL92
Tel: 01206 2628888

Cost: Fixed-price dinner £15 (2 courses), £17. H/wine £8.95. Service exc
Credit cards: 1 3

Menu: Fixed-price dinner

Times: 7.30pm-Last D 9.30pm. Closed Sun, Mon, 2 weeks in winter, 2 weeks in summer

Chef: Larkin Rogers
Proprietors: Larkin Rogers, Christopher Warren

Seats: 41. No smoking
Additional: Children welcome; ❂ menu

DEDHAM, **Le Talbooth** ❀❀

A successful blend of straightforward cosmopolitan cooking in a comfortable riverside setting

Uncomplicated cooking that specialises in popular favourites is proving a great success at this delightful riverside restaurant. Chef Henrik Iversen has evolved a style that aims to please in an understated way, and judging by the increase in the number of people eating here he's on to a winner. Both the short, weekly-changing fixed-price menu and the lengthier seasonal *carte* offer a well-balanced choice, with dishes like steak and kidney pudding, and calf's liver and bacon, both served with tasty herb sauces. Our inspector sampled a warm ravioli of venison with béarnaise, and pink and tender slices of duck breast with a full-flavoured smoked duck's leg sausage, and black olive and coriander sauce. Other choices might be poached cod fillet wrapped in lettuce, and steamed breast of chicken with a citrus butter sauce. A simple, well-made Grand Marnier soufflé over orange segments made a light and tasty dessert, was chosen from amongst traditional summer pudding with clotted cream, and black cherry and Mascarpone torte with kirsch and a black cherry syrup. Attentive staff provide a well-paced service.

Directions: Located 6 miles from Colchester. Follow signs from the A12 to Stratford St Mary. Le Talbooth is on left, before the village

Gun Hill
Map no: 5 TM03
Tel: 01206 323150

Cost: *A/c* from £25.50, fixed-price lunch £12.50 (2 courses), £15; fixed-price dinner £16.50 (2 courses), £19.50. H/wine £10-£12. Service exc
Credit cards: 1 2 3 5

Menus: *A la carte*, fixed-price lunch and dinner, Sunday lunch

Times: Midday-Last L 2pm, 7pm-Last D 9.30pm

Chef: Henrik Iversen
Proprietor: Gerald Milsom

Seats: 80. No cigars or pipes
Additional: Children welcome; children's portions; ❂ dishes; Vegan/other diets on request.

FELSTED, **Rumbles Cottage** ✾

A delightful cottage restaurant where Joy Hadley prepares simple but delicious food. Starters include smoked chicken in egg white halves served on tarragon mayonnaise or as main course pork fillet Ardennaise, pork casserole in wine, gammon and onion with a cream and mustard sauce.

Cost: Alc £21, fixed-price L £12.50, fixed-price dinner pasta menu £10, guinea pig menu £12.50. H/wine £7.40. **Credit cards:** 1 3
Additional: Children welcome; children's portions. ✿ dishes; Vegan/other diets on request
Directions: From A120 or the A130. In centre of village

Braintree Road
Map no: 5 TL62
Tel: 01371 820996
Chef: E Joy Hadley
Proprietor: E Joy Hadley
Seats: 50
Times: Last Sun L 2pm, Last D 9pm. Closed Sun D, Mon

GREAT CHESTERFORD, **Crown House** ✾

☺ A listed Tudor building where chef John Pearman has established a reputation for delicious food using the freshest produce. Our inspector recommended a trio of pâtés, (avocado, chicken liver and salmon), followed by breast of English duck with a tasty lime and orange sauce.

Cost: Alc £16.20, fixed-price dinner £10.75. **Credit cards:** 1 2 3.
Additional: Children welcome; ✿ dishes on request

Map no: 5 TL54
Tel: 01799 530515
Chef: John Pearman
Proprietor: F D Ebdon
Seats: 70
Times: Last D 9.30pm

GREAT DUNMOW, **Starr** ✾✾

Consistently honest and uncomplicated cooking in a smart brasserie-style restaurant

An attractive, well-tended restaurant-with-rooms, the Starr offers civilised, uncomplicated cooking which appeals to a largely conservative clientele. The heavily beamed dining room is surprisingly light and airy, and there's a smart brasserie atmosphere which enhances the relaxed setting. The dishes are described on a somewhat confusing array of specials, mobile blackboard and main menu, but there's nothing muddled about the cooking: chef Mark Fisher produces solid, no-nonsense food that is reliably consistent. At a recent inspection meal a starter of mildly curried parsnip and courgette soup had a lovely, warming effect, while chicken suprême with rosemary and lemon stuffing and lemon sauce was moist and honestly simple. Fresh, crisp vegetables can be somewhat surprising: new potatoes roasted in Marmite, for example, were very effective. Desserts may feature tasty-sounding steamed sponge, fruit and filo pastry, or chocolate staples, but the chosen apple and ginger sponge with syrup and crème anglaise was a little dry.

Directions: At Junc 8 on the M11, take the A120 towards Chelmsford

Market Place
Map no: 5 TL62
Tel: 01371 874321

Cost: Alc lunch £25, fixed-price dinner £21.50, £32.50; Sun lunch £21.50. Wine £10.50. Service inc
Credit cards: 1 2 3 5

Menus: A la carte lunch (weekdays), fixed-price dinner, Sunday lunch
Times: Last L 1.30pm, Last D 9.30pm. Closed Sat lunch, Sun dinner and 1 week after New Year

Chef: Mark Fisher
Proprietor: Brian Jones

Seats: 50. No smoking in dining room
Additional: . Children welcome; children's portions; ✿ menu; Vegan/other diets on request

HARWICH, **The Pier at Harwich** ☺

☺ *An attractive building that promotes a relaxed and friendly atmosphere from its prominent position overlooking the harbour. The house speciality is fish and chips – a very popular dish – and a range of other seafood items and traditional dishes are available in the a la carte restaurant.*

Cost: Alc £18, fixed-price L £9 (2 courses) £11.75/D £12.75 (2 courses), £16. H/wine £7.95. Service exc
Additional: Children welcome; children's menu/portions. ❶ menu; Vegan on request. Pianist
Directions: On the quayside

The Quay
Map no: 5 TM23
Tel: 01255 241212
Chef: C E Oakley
Proprietors: Milsom. Manager: C E Oakley
Seats: 80. No cigars or pipes
Times: Last L 2pm/D 9.30pm

MANNINGTREE, **Stour Bay Café** ☺☺

☺ *For something a little different, try one of the typically Californian dishes on this restaurant's varied menu*

American chef Sherri Singleton brings a touch of California to this small Essex town, the inclusion on her fixed-price lunch menu or evening *carte* of such dishes as crab chowder or cioppino (a seafood stew with mussels, squid, monkfish and tuna) giving a hint of her Los Angeles origins; confirmation might be found in the buckwheat pancakes accompanying home-cured gravlax and the fact that oysters can be enjoyed Rockefeller style! Classics like honey-glazed roast leg of pork or rack of English lamb with fresh mint vinaigrette are also featured, however, and there is a hint of oriental influence in such dishes as poke tuna salad – fresh yellowfin tuna, marinated in sesame, soy, ginger and chilli then served on baby spinach with cucumber and radishes. Desserts include a delicious pecan waffle with home-made vanilla ice and 'drunken' bananas, and an assortment of teas and herbal infusions provide an alternative to coffee. A reasonably priced wine list has its contents grouped by area and helpfully described. This welcoming, out-of-the-ordinary café attracts a loyal following, so booking is advised.

Directions: Take the A137 from Colchester or Ipswich

39-43 High Street
Map no: 5 TM13
Tel: 01206 396687

Cost: Alc £16, Sunday lunch £13.95. Wine £8.55 ♀ Service exc **Credit cards:** 1 2 3

Menus: A la carte , Sunday lunch

Times: Midday-Last L 2.30pm, 7pm-Last D 10pm. Lunch not served Mon-Thu, Dinner not served Sun. Closed 2 weeks Jan, 2 weeks Sep

Chef: Sherri Singleton
Proprietors: David McKay, Sherri Singleton

Seats: 65. No smoking in dining room
Additional: Children welcome; children's portions; ❶ dishes; Vegan/other diets on request.

ROCHFORD, **Hotel Renouf** ☺

Pressed duck is the house speciality in this French-run hotel and restaurant and several variations on the theme are on offer. The carte also includes a good range of fish and modern French dishes. Examples include sole fillets Melvin on a bed of leeks and dill, and Chateaubriand au poivre.

Cost: Alc £30, fixed-price £19.50
Credit cards: 1 2 3 4 5.
Additional: Children welcome; children's portions; ❶ dishes
Directions: A127 into Rochford, reservoir on left, turn right at mini-roundabout, right again into car park

Bradley Way
Map no: 5 TQ89
Tel: 01702 544393
Chef: Derek Renouf
Proprietor: D J Renouf, J Edwards
Seats: 40. Air conditioned
Times: Last L 1.45pm/D 9.45pm. Closed Sun D, 26-30 Dec

SAFFRON WALDEN, Saffron ☺

☺ A listed building in the High Street of this market town. Nigel Few in the kitchen offers imaginative dishes as well as grills, flambés and a separate vegetarian menu. The chicken liver pâté with toast and onion marmalade, and the monkfish with a garlic, ham and mushroom sauce were both praised.

10-18 High Street
Map no: 5 RL53
Tel: 01799 522676
Chef: Nigel Few
Proprietor: David Ball
Seats: 50. No smoking
Times: Last L 2pm/D 9.30pm

Cost: Alc £20, fixed-price L/D £12.95 (2 courses), £14.95. H/wine £7.99. Service exc. **Credit cards:** 1 2 3 4. **Additional:** Children welcome; children's menu/portions. ❂ dishes; Vegan/other diets on request.
Directions: In the High Street

SOUTHEND-ON-SEA, Schulers ☺

☺ Manfred Schuler's restaurant has graced Southend's seafront for many years. The long menu includes lots of fish and seafood specialities and other interesting dishes – typical examples are tartlet with wild mushrooms, salmon strudel and skate (very fresh) with green lentils and coriander.

161 Eastern Esplanade
Map no: 5 TQ88
Tel: 01702 610172
Chef: Manfred Schuler
Proprietor: Manfred Schuler
Times: Last L 2pm/D 10pm.
Closed Sun D, Mon L, 25-28 Dec

Costs: Alc £20, fixed-price L/D from £8.75. H/wine £9.50 Service exc. **Credit cards:** 1 2 3 4. **Additional:** Children welcome; ❂ menu; other diets on request
Directions: From A127 into Southend follow seafront signs, then Eastern Esplanade B1016 (east of pier). Schulers is on the left

WEST MERSEA, Le Champenois (Blackwater Hotel) ☺

☺ This ivy-covered former Victorian coaching inn houses a pleasant French family restaurant, offering a wide variety of traditional French dishes, although some English dishes are also available. Typical dishes include snails or frog legs starters and pork Dijonais or coq au vin main courses.

20-22 Church Road
Map no: 5 TM01
Tel: 01206 383038
Chef: R Roudesli
Proprietor: Mrs M Chapleo
Seats: 45. No cigars or pipes
Times: Last L 2pm/D 10.pm.
Closed Tue L, Sun D, 1st 3 weeks Jan

Cost: Alc £20, fixed-price L/D £14.80 (2 courses), £17.80. H/wine £7.95 ♀ No service charge. **Credit cards:** 1 2 3. **Additional:** Children welcome; children's portions; ❂ dishes; other diets on request.
Directions: Drive through village, turning right at main church

WETHERSFIELD, Dicken's ☺☺

☺ Mainly Mediterranean-style cooking in a restaurant on the village green in rural Essex

The Green
Map no: 5 TL73
Tel: 01371 850723

Cost: Alc £18, fixed-price lunch £8-£15. H/wine £8.75. Service exc
Credit cards: 1 3 5

Menus: A la carte, Sunday lunch
Times: Last L 2pm, Last D

Dicken's overlooks its pretty village green and inside there is a cosy bar, with a display of old kitchen utensils, and a compact dining room. The large back room, with a vaulted ceiling and minstrel's gallery, is also sometimes used. The short menu (supplemented by daily specials) leans strongly towards the Mediterranean, with dishes such as spicy charcuterie and Parmesan cheese salad, and grilled suprême of salmon on roasted peppers, tomato and basil. In a recently-sampled special of rabbit and scallop salad, the shellfish was fresh and tender, but the meat was a little tough and garlic-heavy; the same eager garlic hand had struck at the vegetables too. But on a later inspection visit, more balanced flavours were apparent in a smooth, light-textured fish soup, and in the flesh of a slowly-braised lamb shank, cooked with pulses, which fell willingly from the bone into a tarragon-herbed jus. A handful of simple desserts completes the picture. The mainly French wine list is of excellent quality. It is keenly priced throughout, from the imaginatively chosen house wines to the 1970 classified clarets.

9.30pm. Closed Mon, Tue, and Sun D

Chef: W John Dicken
Proprietor: W John Dicken

Seats: 47. Smoking with consideration for other guests
Additional: Children welcome; children's portions. ❂ dishes; Vegan/other diets on request.

Directions: Overlooking the green, in the centre of Wethersfield

GLOUCESTERSHIRE

BIBURY, **The Swan** ❂❂

A charming village setting for this beautiful hotel serving pricey but enjoyably extravagant food

There has been an inn on this site almost since records began, and from its idyllic position on the banks of the River Coln the Swan remains a centre of hospitality hundreds of years later. Recent extensive refurbishment has brought it up to an extremely high standard, and the striking decor follows the twin themes of the Victorian and Edwardian periods. There are two choices of food style – a brasserie which offers informal, all-day eating, and an elegant restaurant where the food is pricey but the ingredients used are often extravagant and unusual. Chef Guy Bossom produces a fixed-price three-course menu in the evening with interesting and unexpected combinations: starters for example might include braised oxtail wrapped with tarragon mousseline and Madeira juices, or soft poached egg with a blanquette of chicken and truffle. Among the half dozen or so main courses might be offered veal escalope and kidney wrapped in crépinette served with its braised trotter and rosemary juices, or perhaps fillet of sea-bream with couscous, langoustine tails and globe artichokes with nage butter sauce. Puddings are rich and tasty.

Map no: 4 SP10
Tel: 01285 740695

Cost: Fixed-price lunch £17.50, fixed-price dinner £37.50.
H/wine £12.50 ♀ Service inc
Credit cards: 1 2 3 5

Menus: *A la carte,* fixed-price lunch and dinner, bar menu

Times: Midday-Last L 2pm, 7.30pm-Last D 9.45pm

Chef: Guy Bossom
Proprietors: Mrs E Hayles, Mr J Furtek

Seats: 65. No smoking in dining room
Additional: Children welcome; children's portions/menu; ❂ menu; Vegan/other diets on request

Directions: On B4425 between Cirencester (7 miles) and Burford (9 miles). Beside bridge in centre of Bibury

BIRDLIP, **Kingshead House** ☸

☺ *This 17th-century former coaching inn serves wholesome food from a fixed-price three- or four-course menu at dinner, and a flexible lunchtime carte. Our inspector enjoyed home-made breads, chicken breast with spinach and fresh pasta, fillet steak with Stilton and walnuts, and mocha truffle.*

Cost: *Alc* from £15, fixed-price D £22.50, Sun L £15.50. H/wine £9.80 ♀ Service exc. **Credit cards:** 1 2 3 4
Additional: Children welcome; children's portions. ◊ dishes
Directions: In Birdlip on the B4070

Map no: 3 SO91
Tel: 01452 862299
Chef: Judy Knock
Proprietors: Warren and Judy Knock
Seats: 34. Smoking restricted to after meal. No pipes or cigars
Times: Last L 1.45pm/D 10pm. Closed Mon, Sat L, Sun D, 26 Dec, 1 Jan

BLOCKLEY, **Crown** ☸

☺ *A charming coaching inn at the centre of a Cotswold village offering the choice of bistro-style or formal dining, where imaginative dishes are prepared with expertise and flair and served in a congenial ambience*

Cost: *Alc* £19.95, fixed-price L £11.95. H/wine £8.50 ♀ Service exc
Additional: Children welcome; children's portions. ◊ dishes; Vegan/other diets on request
Directions: In the High Street

High Street
Map no: 4 SP13
Tel: 01386 700245
Chef: Richard Smith
Proprietor: John Champion
Times: Last L 2pm/D 10pm

BOURTON-ON-THE-WATER, **Dial House** ☸

☺ *The candlelight, flagstones and inglenook fireplace of this hotel dining room create an inviting setting for chef Stephen Jones' sensibly sized fixed-price and carte menus. Dishes, based on quality fresh produce, are honest in texture and flavour and include some interesting vegetarian choices.*

Cost: *Alc* £18.50, fixed-price L £9.95/D £17. H/wine £9.50. Service exc. **Credit cards:** 1 2 3 5
Additional: Children over 5 welcome at lunch. ◊ menu; other diets on request
Directions: Village centre

The Chestnuts, High Street
Map no: 4 SP12
Tel: 01451 822244
Chefs: Stephen Jones, Mark Green
Proprietors: Lynn and Peter Boxall
Seats: 30. No smoking in dining room
Times: Last L 2pm/D 9.15pm

BUCKLAND, **Buckland Manor** ☸☸☸

A lovely country house setting for modern, French-influenced English food, with rather exclusive prices

Exactly as one would imagine a Cotswold manor house, a large golden stone building in a pretty village setting next to the church, this attractive country house hotel has it all. There are sumptuous interiors and acres of grounds with immaculate gardens providing fresh produce for the kitchen. The restaurant is a magnificent room with dark wood tables, upholstered chairs and views over the Cotswold hills.
 The food here is described as English with a French influence. Starters, from a choice of six hors d'oeuvre and three soups at dinner, might be oak-smoked Scottish salmon with fine capers, or Lunesdale duck liver pâté with truffles and pistachios. The

Near Broadway
Map no: 4 SP03
Tel: 01386 852626

Cost: *Alc* £36, fixed-price lunch £18.50, Sun lunch £20.50. H/wine from £9.30 ♀
Credit cards: 1 3

Menus: *A la carte*, fixed-price lunch, Sun lunch, bar menu
Times: Last L 2pm, Last D 9pm

Chef: Martyn Pearn
Proprietors: Roy and Daphne Vaughan

latter was sampled and found to be very meaty and solid, served on a pool of Cumberland sauce with toasted brioche. The food is not cheap, with main courses ranging from £18.55 for sautéed fillet of lamb (served deliciously pink with two mint sauces) to £25.50 for poached Cornish lobster presented with caviar 'sous cloche', and vegetarian dishes are not generally offered. For dessert our inspector chose a hot chocolate and Armagnac soufflé. This was served well risen and dusted with icing sugar, and had chocolate sauce poured into the centre, though on this occasion the soufflé was slightly under-cooked. Other options might be a thin apple tart with cinnamon ice cream and caramel sauce or a selection of British and French cheeses.

The restaurant is formal and gentlemen are required to wear jackets and ties, but the staff are charming with a natural warmth and ease.

The long and comprehensive wine list, carrying full descriptions of each wine, is dominated by the large Bordeaux and Burgundy sections, which include some rare vintages, with alternatively priced wines from other areas.

Directions: Through Broadway, turn on to the B4632 (Cheltenham). After 1.5 miles left turn to Buckland. The Manor is through the village on the right-hand side

Seats: 38. No smoking
Additional: ◐ dishes

CHARINGWORTH,
Charingworth Manor ❋❋

A blend of traditional cooking with modern influences set in stylish historical surroundings

Once, estate agents could have described Charingworth as a lovely Cotswold stone-built manor house standing in its own 54-acre estate. Now a law forbids them from using a subjective description like this but, let's face it, this house and its well-tended gardens are lovely. Dining is formal here and it is advisable to book. The compact *carte* offers sufficient variety starting, perhaps, with John Dory, ratatouille and tomato dressing, or fried herb pasta with chicken livers and tarragon sauce. Move on, possibly, to tournedos of beef and salsa verdi, fillet of venison and wild mushroom ravioli, or ragoût of sea bass with mussels and asparagus. An enjoyable inspection meal included pan-fried brill and scallops with grainy mustard sauce, served with crisp baby leeks. Desserts include red berry parfait, honey and whisky brûlée and sticky toffee pudding. Fixed-price lunch and dinner menus are available and vegetarian dishes may be arranged. The long wine list, leans strongly towards France although Italy and the New World all get a good look in. Well-trained staff provide attentive service.

Directions: On the B4035 (Shipston to Chipping Campden), 4 miles west of Shipston-on-Stour. Ignore signs to Charingworth

Map no: 4 SP13
Tel: 01386 593555

Cost: Fixed-price lunch £15.50, fixed-price dinner £29.50. H/wine £12.50 ♀ Service exc
Credit cards: 1 2 3 4

Menus: Fixed-price lunch and dinner, Sunday lunch
Times: Midday-Last L 2pm, 7pm-Last D 9.30pm

Chef: William (Bill) J Marmion
Proprietor: Simon Henty

Seats: 48. No smoking in the dining room
Additional: Children welcome at lunch; children's portions; ◐ dishes; other diets by arrangement

CHELTENHAM, Bonnets Bistro at Staithes ❀❀

12 Suffolk Road
Map no: 3 SO92
Tel: 01242 260666

☺ *Light, full-flavoured dishes and a classy setting offer an irresistible invitation to dine*

High standards of food in classy surroundings continue to provide appeal at this bistro-style restaurant close to the town centre. Quality table settings are one of the hallmarks which provide an irresistible invitation to dine. The cooking of Paul Lucas is no less tempting, and he achieves a fullness and depth of flavour in light, modern dishes using fresh ingredients and seasonal produce; rare and excessively expensive items are a thing of the past. The seasonal *carte* might offer starters like poached fillet of smoked haddock with a light curry and mango sauce, while main dishes could include thin slices of Barbary duck breast garnished with marinated blackcurrants, and pan-fried lambs' kidneys and sautéed spinach in a light puff pastry case with a grain mustard sauce. Fish lovers will enjoy the escalope of fresh tuna with capers, shallots and lemon and a brown butter sauce, while vegetarians might be offered a basket of filo pastry filled with aubergine purée and ragout of mushrooms and peppers on a saffron cream sauce. The range of home-made puddings include mango torte and peach crème brûlée.

Cost: Alc from £15.60. H/wine £9.95. Service exc
Credit cards: 1 2 3 4

Menu: *A la carte*

Times: Lunch by reservation. 7.30pm-Last D 10pm. Closed Sun, 1 week Xmas, 2 weeks summer, BHs

Chef: Paul Lucas
Proprietors: Heather and Paul Lucas

Seats: 24. No smoking in dining room
Additional: Children by arrangement. V, Vegan/other diets by arrangement

Directions: South of town on Suffolk Road (A40), close to junction with Bath Road

CHELTENHAM, Cleeveway House ❀❀

Bishops Cleeve
Map no: 3 SO92
Tel: 01242 672585

A country house 'restaurant with rooms' serving an à la carte menu of traditional cooking based on local produce

The best of local produce is used in traditional country house style cooking at John and Susan Marfell's 'restaurant with rooms' – a delightful period house on the edge of the village. A comfortable lounge and a separate bar are available for guests before and after the meal, and from the dining room guests have a partial view of the activities in the kitchen. John is the chef and his *carte* menu offers around 10 to 12 starters and main courses, mostly straightforward dishes with little in the way of gimmickry. Fresh crab, used for the crab au gratin and served in its shell, proved a tasty start to a summer test meal. This was followed by beautifully cooked rack of lamb, just pink, the six cutlets carved and presented with a gooseberry and mint sauce. Vegetables could not have been fresher – with spinach served fresh from the garden – and a vegetarian dish is always available. Sweets and cheeses are presented on a trolley, our inspector opting for coffee meringue cake on this occasion. The only disappointment in an otherwise enjoyable meal was the thick and bitter coffee. The wine list is mostly French with a few New World wines.

Cost: Alc £21, Sunday lunch £13.50. Wine £8. Service exc
Credit cards: 1 2 3

Menus: *A la carte*, Sunday lunch, bar snacks

Times: Midday-Last L 1.45pm, 7pm-Last D 9.45pm. Closed Sun D, Mon L, Xmas, 2 weeks Feb

Chef: John Marfell
Proprietors: Susan and John Marfell

Seats: 38. No cigars or pipes in dining room. Air conditioned
Additional: Children welcome; children's portions; ❖ menu

Directions: Take A435 towards Evesham. Turn right at 2nd roundabout on Bishop's Cleeve bypass. Cleeveway House is 200 yards on left

CHELTENHAM, **Epicurean**

81 The Promenade
Map no: 3 SO92
Tel: 01242 222466

Patrick and Clare McDonald's move to the Promenade should prove exceptionally popular. Our inspectors have visited, but unfortunately have been unable to make a formal assessment of this new operation before going to print. However, they are confident that Patrick will maintain his three rosette standards of previous years. The elegant building has been transformed into a superb eating establishment. Run by an efficient and enthusiastic team, the wine bar/café which is open all day and evening, serves imaginative snacks; the attractive bistro more elaborate meals and the formal dining room at the top of the house, Patrick's imaginative *carte*. The cooking throughout is carefully prepared but the *carte* dishes truly express the depth and expertise in his cooking. A recent inspection praised a delicately light, full flavoured lobster and langoustine ravioli and salmon tartar with a caviar crust and an exceptionally robust confit of duck with haricot beans on a bed of spinach. Desserts include a first-class pyramid of prune and vanilla parfait and a scrumptious glazed lemon tart.

CHELTENHAM, **Greenway** ❀❀❀

Shurdington
Map no: 3 SO92
Tel: 01242 862352

A lovely country house setting for some French influenced modern cooking served in healthy portions

A delightful ivy-clad Elizabethan house with later additions, the Greenway is set back from the road in colourful gardens surrounded by parkland and rolling Cotswold countryside. Public rooms are gracious and comfortable with antique furnishings, and include a bright conservatory restaurant. Chef Christopher Colmer, runner-up in the 1994 Young Chef of the Year competition, has stamped his own mark of authority on the hotel's cooking. Some over-elaboration here and there can be put down to youthful enthusiasm, as the food is now firmly in the upper echelons. There has been a conscious move away from the country house cooking of the 80s to a more robust style with a clear French influence, served in generous portions.

An enticing *carte* is offered along with a good value fixed-price dinner menu with just two items at each course, and a longer lunch menu priced for two or three courses. Some old favourites have returned – prawn cocktail, steak and chips, and black forest gateau – but with a Greenway interpretation, and the *carte* includes three vegetarian dishes, such as brioche buns filled with Somerset brie, pistachio nuts and spring onions on a tomato coulis.

A spring meal began with a bite-size appetiser of king prawn and sole mousseline with a tasty Thai dressing. This was followed by a hearty mille-feuille of chicken liver, foie gras and potato galette, all bursting with flavour, and a rich Madeira sauce. Sea bass and scallops came with mange-touts, home-dried tomatoes, deep-fried basil, potatoes and a first-class pesto dressing. To finish, a lemon curd tart with a 'brûléed' top was served with a raspberry coulis and a few good imported berries.

Cost: *Alc* £30, fixed-price lunch £15 (2 courses), £17, fixed-price dinner £25. H/wine £11.25 ♀ No service charge
Credit cards: 1 2 3 4

Menus: *A la carte*, fixed-price lunch and dinner, Sunday lunch.

Times: Midday-Last L 2.30pm, 7pm-Last D 9.30pm. Closed L Sat and BHs; 3-7 Jan

Chef: Christopher Colmer
Proprietor: Tony Elliott

Seats: 40. No pipes or cigars
Additional: Children over 7 welcome; ✪ dishes; Vegan/other diets on request

Directions: 2.5 miles south of Cheltenham on A46

CHELTENHAM, **Hotel On the Park**

38 Evesham Road
Map no: 3 SO92
Tel: 01242 518898

The restaurant at On the Park Hotel has ceased to be called The Epicurean, which has moved to another location in the city. Instead during the summer of 1994, a new chef, Eamonn Webster, has come to the hotel. After his last post as head chef at the Rampsbeck Hotel in Ullswater he became a consultant for some years, but has decided to return to the kitchen! He hopes to maintain the very high standards of his predecessor – and with his past track record we feel confident that he will achieve this – but unfortunately at the time of going to press we have been unable to make a formal assessment. For those who are already familiar with the hotel, The Restaurant's pricing policy is to be more in line with hotel's own than previously.

CHELTENHAM,
Le Champignon Sauvage ❀❀❀

14 Suffolk Road
Map no: 3 SO92
Tel: 01242 573449

Imaginative, French country-style dishes and friendly service from a small, popular town restaurant

'Sauvage' in this context means wild so dispel quickly any mental image of a marauding meadow cap, for David and Helen Everitt-Matthias take their French terroir cooking very seriously indeed. They have run this small restaurant, bedecked with fungi illustrations and situated among antique shops, galleries and other eating places, for over seven years. Helen looks after front-of-house in a friendly and relaxed yet efficient manner, while David's talents shine through in his creation of unusual dishes and in his original presentations. Fixed-price lunches from £12.50 to £17.50 are excellent value for money; the two-course Menu Rapide, with a glass of wine and mineral water, is popular with office staff.

Dinner menus are more extensive (and more expensive) but maintain the theme of combining flavours and textures in surprising ways, such as pot roast lamb on a basil barley risotto and an aubergine 'tikka'. Where else does that appear on a menu? Braised pork belly with Chinese spices, served on mixed leaves with sauté potatoes and fried onions, delighted one of our inspectors. The richness of his chocolate terrine dessert was well complemented by the prunes that studded it, and a prune and Armagnac ice cream was superb.

France leads the field on the wine list but it is varied with a reasonable selection from other countries, helpfully annotated and containing some unusual bins. There are six house wines selling at under £12 a bottle.

Directions: To south of town centre, close to the Boys' College on A40 (Oxford). Check local details when booking

Cost: Fixed-price lunch £12.50-£17.50; fixed-price dinner £18.50-£28.50. H/wine £8.50. Service exc
Credit cards: 1 2 3 4

Menus: Fixed-price lunch and dinner

Times: 12.30-Last L 1.30pm, 7.30pm-Last D 9.30pm. Dinner on served Sat. Closed Sun

Chef: David Everitt-Matthias
Proprietor: David and Helen Everitt-Matthias

Seats: 30. No pipes or cigars. Air conditioning
Additional: Children welcome

CHELTENHAM, **Mayflower** ❀

☺ *Robustly-flavoured Cantonese cuisine forms the basis of this neat restaurant's extensive carte and set-meal menus – though Szechuan and sizzling dishes are popular too. Service is swift but attentive, with no language problems, and an impressive wine list includes examples from the New World.*

Cost: *Alc* £15.50, fixed-price L £6.50/D £17.50. H/wine £8.25 ♀ Service exc. **Credit cards:** 1 2 3 4
Additional: Children welcome; ❂ menu; Vegan on request
Directions: Town centre opposite Eagle Star building

32-34 Clarence Street
Map no: 3 SO92
Tel: 01242 522426
Chefs: C F Kong, M M Kong
Proprietors: The Kong Family
Seats: 80, 50 Air conditioned
Times: Last L 1.45pm/D 10.45pm. Closed Sun L, 25-27 Dec

CHELTENHAM, **Regency House** ❀

☺ *In a Regency town, can there be a better name for a hotel? Even if there is, this is the one where the home-made cream of onion soup is recommended, and where stir-fry turkey with orange and chives and poached salmon were two of the four main courses on the seasonally-changing, fixed-price menu.*

Cost: Fixed-price L/D £15.95. H/wine £6.20. Service inc
Credit cards: 1 2 3. **Additional:** Children welcome at lunch; children's portions; ❂ dishes; other diets on request
Directions: Clarence Square is in Pitville just north of the town centre

50 Clarence Square
Map no: 3 SO92
Tel: 01242 582718
Chef: Barbara Oates
Proprietor: John Oates
Seats: 16. No smoking in dining room
Times: Last L 2pm/D 8pm

CHIPPING CAMPDEN, **Cotswold House** ❀❀

☺ *Accomplished British cooking in the beautiful setting of a country house style hotel*

A beautiful country house style hotel dating from the 17th century, this building occupies a prominent position in the town's high street. Gardens at the rear are overlooked by the formal restaurant where chef Scott Chance offers his menus: the main fixed-price one gives a well-balanced choice of British dishes with a continental influence, while a special daily set menu offers a short selection of similar dishes at a much reduced price. Starters from the main list might include a lightly poached sausage of brill with a mussel sauce scented with chives, or a meatier timbale of veal filled with young asparagus in a light tarragon gravy. Main choices might be medallions of beef fillet topped with creamed shallots and served with a port and truffle sauce, or roast loin of new season lamb surrounded by early vegetables and a light garlic jus. There are vegetarian dishes too, like the salad of baby spinach leaves, orange, melon and crumbled Stilton starter, and compôte of wild mushrooms with grilled polenta. Puddings are mostly cold like mango parfait and paw-paw sorbet, or bitter chocolate mousse on Kahlua sauce.

Directions: On B4081 (Chipping Campden), 1 mile north of A44 between Moreton-in-Marsh and Broadway

The Square
Map no: 4 SP13
Tel: 01386 840330

Cost: *A la carte* £25, fixed-price dinner £15.50, Sunday lunch £15, H/wine from £8.50. No service charge
Credit cards: 1 2 3

Menus: *A la carte*, fixed-price dinner, Sunday lunch

Times: Last Sun L 2pm, Last D 9.30pm. Closed 24-27 Dec

Chef: Scott Chance
Proprietors: Robert and Gill Greenstock

Seats: 35-40. No smoking in restaurant
Additional: Children over 8 permitted; children's portions on request; ❂ dishes

CHIPPING CAMPDEN, **Noel Arms**

High Street
Map no: 4 SP13
Tel: 01386 840317
Chef: Stephen Fitzpatrick
Proprietor: Neil John
Seats: 60. No-smoking area
Times: Last D 9.45pm

☺ *In the panelled Gainsborough Restaurant, head chef Stephen Fitzpatrick offers a table d'hôte menu of originality priced for two or three courses. Dishes, using fresh local produce, might include garlic and pork pâté, sirloin of beef with Yorkshire pudding, and a vegetarian alternative.*

Cost: Fixed-price D £13.95 (2 courses), £15.75, £19.95. H/wine £9.50 ♀ Service inc. **Credit cards:** 1 2 3 4 5
Additional: Children welcome; children's portions; ❷ dishes; Vegan/other diets on request

CHIPPING CAMPDEN, **Seymour House**

High Street
Map no: 4 SP13
Tel: 01386 840429
Chef: Serge Puyal
Proprietor: Mr Felice Tocchini
Times: Last L 2.30pm/D 10pm

☺ *A character Cotswold hotel where the cuisine shows effort in preparation by chef Serge Puyal. The menu is international but favours Italy with pasta specialities as starters and Filetto al piatto, a Tuscan favourite, of slices of beef sizzled in virgin oil, with sage, rosemary and garlic, on the list of main courses.*

Cost: Fixed-price L £12.95/D from £19.50. H/wine £9.95 (litre). Service inc
Credit cards: 1 2 3 5. **Additional:** Children welcome; children's portions; ❷ dishes; Vegan/other diets on request.
Directions: In the heart of village along the High Street

GLOUCESTER, **Hatton Court**

Upton Hill
Upton St Leonards
Map no: 3 SO81
Tel: 01452 617412
Chef: Alan Pierce
Proprietor: Anthony Davis
Seats: 80. No smoking in dining room. Air conditioned
Times: Last L 2pm/D 10pm

The hotel was originally a manor house, and Carrington's restaurant commands spectacular views across the Severn valley. A wide range of modern English and French dishes is prepared including loin of venison, roulade of chicken with cream and tarragon, enhanced by an extensive wine list.

Cost: Alc £27, fixed-price L £14.50/D £19.95. H/wine from £9.95 ♀ Service exc. **Credit cards:** 1 2 3 4 5
Additional: Children welcome; children's portions/menu; ❷ menu; Vegan/other diets on request
Directions: Three miles from Gloucester on B4037

LOWER SLAUGHTER,
Lower Slaughter Manor ❀❀❀

A listed manor house hotel where good value modern French cuisine is served by attentive French waiting staff

The home of Audrey and Peter Marks, this 17th-century manor house stands in neatly kept gardens beside the village church and the shallow Slaughter Brook. It is a fine hotel, renowned for its warm hospitality, the comfort of its appointments and the quality of the service it provides. The public rooms are filled with antiques and fresh flowers, and in this elegant setting, head chef Julian Ehlers presents a good range of modern French dishes from fixed-price menus at lunch and dinner, using good quality British ingredients.

Meals begin with a selection of tiny canapés, with the addition on one occasion of mini smoked salmon sandwiches and a chef's surprise of salmon in filo with Chardonnay sauce. A starter of layered terrine of foie gras and chicken was dramatically presented on a jelly made of Californian orange muscat. At another meal, good small ravioli of parsley and shallots came with a delicious langoustine sauce and three rather sappy fried prawns.

Our inspectors particularly enjoyed a main course of carefully fried sea-bass with asparagus and a thin truffle sauce, and best end of lamb, marinated in herbs, sugar and rice vinegar, with a tasty sauce made from the marinade. A well kept selection of British cheeses is offered, and a choice of desserts which might include a trio of chocolate, a hot soufflé of Cotswold honey and lime, served with a salad of citrus fruit and an orange sorbet, and pear galette with vanilla ice cream and warm caramel sauce.

In 1994 Lower Slaughter Manor received the 'Californian Cellar of the Year' Award, and there is certainly an enormous selection of wines from that area. France, however is not overlooked, as there are plenty of Burgundies and clarets from good growers, including many mature vintages.

Directions: Off the A429 signposted 'The Slaughters'. Half a mile into village on the right

Map no: 4 SP12
Tel: 01451 820456

Cost: Fixed-price lunch £17.95, fixed-price dinner £29.50. H/wine £15.50. Service exc
Credit cards: 1 2 3

Menus: Fixed-price lunch and dinner, Sun lunch

Times: Last L 2pm (2.30pm Sun), Last D 9.30pm (10pm Fri, Sat). Closed 2 weeks Jan

Chef: Julian Ehlers
Proprietors: Audrey and Peter Marks

Seats: 36. No smoking in dining room
Additional: No children under 10; ✪ menu

LOWER SLAUGHTER,
Washbourne Court ❀

Youthful enthusiasm lies behind the creation of the simply prepared dishes at this Cotswold hotel, and good use is made of seasonal produce. There is a limited menu at lunchtime and a broader choice in the evening, supplemented by a daily changing table d'hôte and separate vegetarian selection.

Cost: Alc from £25, fixed-price L £3.50-£8.50, fixed-price D £23.95. H/wine £9.75. Service inc
Credit cards: 1 2 3. **Additional:** Children welcome (no babies); ✪ menu; Vegan/other diets on request
Directions: In the centre of the village by the river

Map no: 4 SP12
Tel: 01451 822143
Chef: Scott Hunter
Proprietor: Michael Pender
Seats: 40 (50 outside on riverside terrace). No smoking in dining room
Times: Last L 2.30pm/D 9.15pm

MORETON-IN-MARSH, **Manor House** ❀

☺ *Situated in this beautiful Cotswold town, the hotel dates back to the 16th century. Chef Luc Gabard continues to offer table d'hôte and a sensibly short carte, which prove popular with residents and non-residents alike, for example, timbale of prawns wrapped in smoked salmon.*

Cost: *A/c* from £21, fixed-price L £8.50/D £18.50. H/wine £9.75 ♀ No service charge. **Credit cards:** 1 2 3 4 5
Additional: Children welcome; children's portions. ❤ dishes; Vegan/other diets on request
Directions: Situated on the A429 (Fosse Way) as it passes through Moreton-in-Marsh

High Street
Map no: 4 SP23
Tel: 01608 650501
Chef: Luc Gabard
Proprietor: Duncan Williams
Seats: 50. No smoking in dining room
Times: Last L 2pm (2.30pm Sun)/D 9.30pm (9pm Sun)

MORETON-IN-MARSH, **Marsh Goose** ❀❀

Robust modern cookery with good natural flavours served in an attractive village-centre restaurant

Situated in the busy main street of Moreton, opposite the war memorial, the Marsh Goose is made up of three interconnecting rooms with an additional balcony dining area. There is also a small bar, the only place where smoking is permitted. Sonya Kidney's cooking continues to please a varied clientele. At lunchtime there is a good-value set meal as well as the short *carte*. The fixed-price dinner menu presents a varied choice, featuring fish and local game in season, and a vegetarian dish such as filo parcel of cheese and mushrooms served with mixed pulses.

At a test meal our inspector praised the selection of freshly baked rolls and his starter of spinach roulade with poached quails' eggs. This was followed by pork fillet with a robust grain mustard sauce, attractively presented and full of natural flavours. A delicious dessert completed the meal – chocolate parfait served in an almond tuile with glazed bananas. There is an extensive wine list of Old and New World wines, and service is provided by an attentive waiting team, smartly turned out in colourful waistcoats and bow ties.

Directions: In the High Street opposite the war memorial

High Street
Map no: 4 SP23
Tel: 01608 652111

Cost: *A/c* lunch from £18, fixed-price lunch £13.50, fixed-price dinner £23, Sun lunch £17. H/wine £8.50. Service exc
Credit cards: 1 2 3
Menus: *A la carte* lunch, fixed-price lunch and dinner, Sunday lunch
Times: 12.30-Last L 2.30pm, 7.30pm-Last D 9.45pm. Closed Sun D, Mon
Chef: Sonya Kidney
Proprietors: Sonya Kidney, Leo Brookes-Little, Gordon Campbell-Gray
Seats: 60. No smoking in dining room **Additional:** Children permitted; children's portions; ❤ dishes; other diets on request

PAINSWICK, **Painswick Hotel** ❀❀

A delightful country house hotel offering short, balanced menus with an emphasis on fish

Painswick has more than 100 listed buildings; one is an elegant Palladian-style former rectory, now this country house hotel, containing what could be the archetypal 18th-century dining room. A team of young, award-winning chefs specialise in New English cooking, using Cotswold-raised meats, salmon from the Severn and Vale of Evesham game and vegetables. A two-dish, light lunch menu offers shellfish and vegetable broth, game terrine, pigeon salad, grilled tiger prawns, oysters or smoked salmon, and a traditional hot pudding. Finances will dictate

Kemps Lane
Map no: 3 SO80
Tel: 01452 812160

Cost: *A/c* £23.50, fixed-price lunch £8.50, fixed-price dinner £23.50. Wine £11.50 ♀ Service inc
Credit cards: 1 2 3 5
Menus: *A la carte,* fixed-price lunch and dinner, Sunday lunch

whether fixed-price dinner extends to two, three or four courses. On the *carte*-cum-seafood menu, starters largely replicate the lunch menu, but the ten main courses take us into new territory with, for example, lobster (cold or Thermidor) from the hotel's own sea-water tank and medallions of venison. No major surprises among the desserts, except maybe the hot Cumbrian apple pudding with a clear case of wanderlust. The wine list is comprehensive, ranging from £6 for a half bottle of Muscadet to £75 for a Château Latour.

Directions: Painswick is on A46, the Stroud/Cheltenham road. The turning into Kemps Lane is just near the church

Times: 12 30-Last L 2pm, 7.30pm-Last D 9.30pm

Chef: Robert Mauchan
Proprietor: Somerset Moore

Seats: 60. No-smoking area
Additional: Children welcome; children's portions/menu; ❶ menu; other diets on request

STONEHOUSE, **Stonehouse Court** ❀

A Grade II listed property, this hotel presents imaginative fixed-price and carte menus of Anglo-French cuisine. Our inspector sampled ravioli of langoustines with sweet vermouth sauce, canon of venison with rosemary set off with a black truffle mousse, and crème brûlée with home-made shortcake.

Cost: Alc £24.20, fixed-price D £15. H/wine £11. Service inc
Credit cards: 1 2 3 5. **Additional:** Children permitted; children's portions; ❶ menu; Vegan/other diets on request
Directions: On A417

Bristol Road
Map no: 3 SO80
Tel: 01453 825155
Chef: Alan Postill
Proprietors: Arcadian International. Manager: Louise Dunning
Seats: 60
Times: Last L 2pm/D 9.30pm

STOW-ON-THE-WOLD, **Fosse Manor** ❀

☺ *An imposing Cotswold manor house on the ancient Fosse Way which links Sidmouth and the Humber. Part-English, part-Continental is the best description for the varied choice of dishes on offer. Poached trout with kiwi fruit, maybe, for the diet-conscious or pan-fried pork loin for the less concerned.*

Cost: Fixed-price L £12.95/D £15.95. H/wine £8.95 (litre) ♀ Service exc. **Credit cards:** 1 2 3 4 5
Additional: Children welcome; children's portions/menu; ❶ menu; Vegan/other diets on request
Directions: One mile south of Stow on the A429

Map no: 4 SP12
Tel: 01451 830354
Chef: Clare Dockerty
Proprietors: Consort. Managers: Mr and Mrs Johnson
Seats: 70. No smoking
Times: Last L 2pm/D 10pm.
Closed 22-29 Dec

STOW-ON-THE-WOLD, **Grapevine** ❀

☺ *The eponymous grapevine is a feature of the hotel's restaurant, and dates from the last century. Chef Matt Rollinson's good-value fixed-price menus provide a varied choice of carefully prepared dishes, and demonstrate some modern influences. A vegetarian menu is also available.*

Cost: Fixed-price L £9.95/D £18.45. H/wine from £7.35 ♀ Service exc. **Credit cards:** 1 2 3 4 5. **Additional:** Children permitted at lunch, at dinner at hotel's discretion; Children's portions/menu; ❶ menu; Vegan/other diets on request
Directions: Leave A429 (Fosseway) at Stow-on-the-Wold and take A436 to Chipping Norton, 150 yards on right facing small green

Sheep Street
Map no: 4 SP12
Tel: 01451 830344
Chef: Matthew Rollinson
Proprietor: Best Western. Manager: Sandra (Sam) Elliott
Seats: 60. No smoking in dining room
Times: Last L 2pm/D 9.30pm.
Closed 24 Dec-11 Jan

STOW-ON-THE-WOLD, Old Farmhouse ❀

☺ *Generous portions are served in the cosy restaurant of this converted farmhouse hotel. Good use is made of local game, fish and poultry, and the dishes are well executed with honest flavours and textures. The fixed-price seasonal menus offer good value and a varied choice, including a vegetarian option.*

Cost: Fixed-price D £14.50. H/wine £7.50 ♀ Service inc
Credit cards: 1 3. **Additional:** No children at dinner. ◐ dishes; Vegan/other diets on request
Directions: In the village on the B4068

Lower Swell
Map no: 4 SP12
Tel: 01451 830232
Chef: Graham Simmonds
Proprietor: Erik Burger
Seats: 25-30. No smoking in dining room
Times: Last L 2pm/D 9pm. Closed 2 weeks Feb

STOW-ON-THE-WOLD, Wyck Hill House ❀❀❀

A wide range of dishes from the exotic and spicy to the simple and tasty is offered at this stylish country house hotel

Wyck Hill is a stylish country house hotel set in fine grounds with glorious views. The ornate restaurant, one of a number of elegant public rooms, provides friendly formal service. There really is something for everyone in the imaginative choice of dishes offered from the fixed price-lunch and *à la carte* dinner menus at Wyck Hill House. In the evening there is a choice of nine starters and main courses, which might include the tartlets of sautéed pheasant taken by our inspector, served with a confit of shallots and chestnuts, or one might opt for a spicy chowder of Cornish shellfish with toasted chilli corn bread. Chef Ian Smith's cooking is generally rich in flavour, and this was amply demonstrated in our inspector's main course of medallions of monkfish baked 'en croute' with saffron and tarragon vegetables on a gratin of Cornish mussels. For those who prefer more plainly cooked food there is a selection of grills, such as fillet steak with béarnaise sauce, or sole with herb and lemon butter.

A separate vegetarian menu of three starters and main courses is also offered, with tempting dishes such as grilled avocado on a casserole of Italian tomatoes and mushrooms, served with a cheese and oregano fondue, or Thai-style rice with vegetable and water chestnut spring rolls, spring onion and chilli sauce.

Mouth-watering desserts include hot coffee fondant pudding filled with cappuccino cream; pavlova of toffee bananas with Baileys and banana ice cream *and* vanilla cream; and fresh pineapple and fig fritters dusted with spiced sugar and served with a warm casserole of tropical fruits and a mango sorbet. The straightforward wine list is clearly presented and reasonably price, with all major areas represented.

Directions: About 1.5 miles south of Stow-on-the-Wold, on the A424 Stow to Burford road

Burford Road
Map no: 4 SP12
Tel: 01451 831936

Cost: Alc dinner £31, fixed-price lunch £9.50 (2 courses), £11.95. H/wine £11.95. Service exc
Credit cards: 1 2 3 4 5

Menus: *A la carte* dinner, fixed-price lunch, Sunday lunch

Times: Last L 2pm, Last D 9.30pm

Chef: Ian Smith
Proprietor: Lyric. Manager: Peter Robinson

Seats: 70. No smoking. Air conditioned
Additional: Children welcome; children's portions; ◐ menu; Vegan/other diets on request

STROUD, Oakes ●●●

169 Slad Road
Map no: 3 SO80
Tel: 01453 759950

Honest and accomplished cooking served in a friendly, recently refurbished restaurant

From a compact, pristine kitchen in a converted girls' school house, Chris Oakes turns out some of the best food to be found in this corner of the country. There have been a few changes in the past couple of years, including a partial refurbishment of the restaurant, the addition of a cosy little bar, and a move to a varied and fairly priced *carte*. However, the warmth of the welcome from Caroline Oakes and the popularity of the accomplished cooking are much the same.

Starters range from sautéed soft roes on horseradish toast to home-made venison sausage with braised lentils, bacon and onion gravy, and main courses from grilled skate wing with caper, lemon and anchovy butter to fillet of beef with garlic butter and oyster mushrooms. A vegetarian option is available at each course, such as fetta ravioli, with spinach and a tomato vinaigrette (which can also be taken as a main course), followed by Appenzeller cheese and onion tart, with endive, celeriac and mange-touts. Tempting home-made desserts might include a hot pistachio soufflé with chantilly cream and steamed apple pudding with warm cinnamon sauce (both with a cooking time of 15 minutes).

A test meal began with good herbed olives and a competent foie gras terrine (though it was an end slice and insufficiently chilled) served with a nicely dressed corn salad and sliced pink potato, an unusual but successful accompaniment. Next, a good fillet of pike was simply garnished with cucumber and ginger and served with a creamy sauce. The vegetables were a highlight – shredded parsnip, cabbage and puréed carrot with soured cream. To finish, good pastry formed the basis of a prune and custard tart served with decent Armagnac sauce. There is a compact and straightforward wine list starting with eight house selections, which offer excellent value.

Cost: *Alc* from £22.50. H/wine £8.50 ♀ No service charge
Credit cards: 1 2 3

Menus: *A la carte*

Times: Last L 1.45pm/D 9.30pm. Closed Sun D, Mon

Chef: Christopher Oakes
Proprietors: Christopher and Caroline Oakes

Seats: 34
Additional: Children welcome; children's portions; ♥ dishes; Vegan/other diets on request

Directions: On B4070, half a mile north-east of Stroud town centre

TETBURY, Calcot Manor ●●

Map no: 3 ST89
Tel: 01666 890391

A family-run country house hotel/restaurant in farm-like surroundings where culinary ingenuity is strong

Although technically under new ownership, Calcot is still in the safe hands of the Ball family, namely son Richard, who is now established as manager. Since our last visit considerable capital investment has been made with the construction of a new restaurant and bar, a kitchen extension and four new family suites in a former barn. But the charm of the place remains intact and it still, at first glance, resembles a group of Cotswold-stone farm buildings rather than a hotel. Alex Howard, the new chef, has brought a different perspective to the cooking with a short, imaginative *carte* displaying how well he uses the finest produce and ingredients. Among his star turns are pressed foie gras terrine with complementary fig relish, set off with brioche, and double goat's cheese soufflé. Main courses of note are roasted sea bass with celeriac purée and pesto, and free-range

Cost: *Alc* £28
Credit cards: 1 2 3

Menu: *A la carte*

Times: Last D 9.30pm

Chef: Alex Howard
Proprietors: Mr and Mrs Stone

Seats: 42. No smoking in dining room
Additional: Children permitted

chicken grandmère. Desserts like banana soufflé with toffee ice cream and scrumptious bread and butter pudding with cinnamon custard should round things off well.

Directions: From M4 take Jnct 18. Follow A46 towards Stroud. After 12 miles take A4135 (Tetbury). Hotel on left

TETBURY, **Close** ●●

Well-executed and full-flavoured English cooking served in a stylish garden-side restaurant

Charming, professional staff preside over the running of this distinguished old hotel, where a discreet façade belies the rich furnishings and luxurious accommodation inside. The dining room is appealingly elegant, and diners can look out over a secluded, mature, walled garden. The cooking of chef Paul Welch is in a class of its own too, with the *carte* and fixed-price menu offering a well-balanced range of imaginative seasonal dishes. At a recent meal our inspector praised a bright and full-flavoured starter of monkfish tails with a tasty honey and cumin vinaigrette, and deliciously moist breast of Gressingham duck fanned onto a tangy orange and redcurrant sauce. Medallions of beef fillet on a buttery savoy cabbage with a sweet garlic sauce was also highly recommended, and vegetables were simple but fresh and crunchy. The tempting range of home-made desserts will delight the sweet-toothed, and a light warm tarte tatin with a rich but smooth butterscotch and walnut sauce was a real winner. A good vegetarian choice includes mixed bean and mushroom kurmah, and filo parcel of stir-fried vegetables.

8 Long Street
Map no: 3 ST89
Tel: 01666 502272

Cost: *Alc* from £35, fixed-price lunch £9.99 (2 courses), £13.99, fixed-price dinner £25. Wine from £11.95. Service inc
Credit cards: 1 2 3 4 5

Menus: *A la carte*, fixed-price lunch and dinner, Sunday lunch

Times: Last L 2pm, Last D 9.45pm

Chef: Paul Welch
Proprietors: Voyager. Manager: Sean Spencer

Seats: 36. No smoking in dining room
Additional: Children welcome at lunch, under 8s before 7pm at dinner; ❷ dishes; Vegan/other diets on request

Directions: Located in the centre of Tetbury

TETBURY, **Hunters Hall Inn** ●

☺ *A popular, character inn with an intimate country restaurant where chef Kevin Stokes produces imaginative and well executed dishes using fresh local produce, especially game. Sirloin steak is served with a Stilton cheese and port cream sauce and plentiful al dente vegetables.*

Kingscote
Map no: 3 ST89
Tel: 01453 860393
Chef: Kevin Stokes
Proprietors: Kevin Stokes, Joanna Stokes
Seats: 40. No-smoking area
Times: Last L 2pm/D 9.30pm

Cost: *Alc* £18.50. H/wine £7.25 ♀ Service exc
Credit cards: 1 2 3 4 5. **Additional:** Children welcome; children's portions/menu; ❷ dishes; Vegan/other diets on request
Directions: On the A4135

TETBURY, **Snooty Fox** 🏵

This warm stone hotel in a Cotswold market town offers an appetising mix of traditional and contemporary French dishes, such as a large field mushroom filled with Stilton and wrapped in filo pastry, followed by charcoal grilled rump steak with roasted shallots and a Dijon mustard sauce.

Cost: Alc £26.50, fixed-price L £14/D £18. H/wine £10.50 ♀ Service exc. **Credit cards:** 1 2 3 4 5
Additional: Children welcome; children's portions ; ❤ menu; Vegan/other diets on request
Directions: Town centre opposite the Town Hall

Market Place
Map no: 3 ST89
Tel: 01666 502436
Chef: Stephen Woodcock
Proprietor: Colin Parcell
Seats: 50
Times: Last L 2pm/D 9.45pm

TEWKESBURY, **Puckrup Hall** 🏵🏵

A much-extended Regency hotel offering excellent facilities, and serving highly praised, interesting food

A former Regency country mansion set in its own extensive grounds which include a golf course, this hotel close to the M50 has undergone considerable changes recently. A large extension now houses a leisure complex and health facilities among other upmarket amenities. The smartly turned out staff continue to offer a high standard of service, while head chef Geoffrey Balharrie shows off his flair and imagination in the kitchen. A recent very tasty starter of potato gnocchi with gorgonzola, oyster mushrooms and a lentil-based tomato concasse sauce was much enjoyed, as were poached medallions of lamb cooked moist and pink and served with delicate little mint dumplings and a port wine sauce. Very generous portions of simply cooked vegetables come with the main course, and the deliciously tempting puddings included a light strawberry and Drambuie shortcake with a bright raspberry purée. Decent filter coffee follows with rich petit fours. Other recommended dishes include a cold kipper and onion pie with honey mustard, and the fillet of beef with a garlic crust, onion confit and rosemary sauce.

Directions: On A38 north of Tewkesbury, near junction of the M50. Entrance is just on the turning for Puckrup

Map no: 3 SO83
Tel: 01684 296200

Cost: Fixed-price dinner £25. H/wine £10 ♀ Service inc
Credit cards: 1 2 3 4 5

Menus: A la carte, fixed-price dinner, brasserie menu, bar menu

Times: Thu, Fri, Sat 7pm-Last D 9.30pm

Chef: Geoff Balharrie
Proprietors: Country Mansion Hotels

Seats: 45. No smoking in dining room
Additional: Children over 5 welcome; children's portions; ❤ dishes; other diets on request

UPPER SLAUGHTER,
Lords of the Manor ❀❀❀

An original approach to modern country house cooking in an ancient Cotswold manor house hotel

A Cotswold stone manor house dating from the 1650s, this hotel is peacefully set in eight acres of gardens and parkland on the edge of the village. Antiques, chintz and Victorian water colours are features of the interior, and in the restaurant formal dress is requested, attentive service is provided, and booking is essential.

Chef Robert-Clive Dixon has been here for over a year now and continues to attract compliments for his fixed price menus – a three-course market menu offering two choices at each stage, plus lunch and more extensive dinner menus priced for two or three courses. His imaginative use of fresh ingredients and modern style of cooking appeals to a growing number of clients, and his original approach is evident in the selection of canapés (fish cake, tartlet of ratatouille, home-made sausage and black pudding); the variety of freshly made rolls (white, granary with walnuts and apricots, and Italian with black olives), and the unusual combinations of ingredients in the dishes offered. Vegetarian and other special diets can also be accommodated.

At a test meal our inspector sampled a slice of salmon and brill terrine. This was solid and meaty, layered with herbs and finely diced shallots. Caesar salad, served separately, was also thoroughly enjoyed. The main course, fillet of new season's lamb, was cooked pink as requested and set on a bed of creamy potato surrounded by shredded spring cabbage. Topping the dish was a strudel 'hat' which looked a bit odd but enhanced the balance of textures. Rich chocolate marquise, with raspberries and pistachio nuts on a pool of orange coulis, proved a superb ending to the meal.

Directions: Follow the sign towards The Slaughters off the A429. The restaurant is located in the centre of Upper Slaughter

Map no: 4 SP12
Tel: 01451 820243

Cost: *A/c* £37, fixed-price lunch £10.95 (2 courses), £12.95, fixed-price dinner £29.50. H/wine £12.95. Service charge 12.5%
Credit cards: 1 2 3 4 5

Menus: *A la carte*, fixed-price lunch and dinner, Sunday lunch, bar menu

Times: Last L 2pm, Last D 9.30pm. Closed 1-15 Jan

Chef: Robert-Clive Dixon
Proprietor: James Gulliver

Seats: 60. No smoking
Additional: . Children welcome; children's menu/portions. ♥ dishes; Vegan/other diets on request

WINCHCOMBE, Wesley House ❀❀

☺ *Imaginative cooking with honest flavours offering good value in hospitable surroundings*

The preacher John Wesley is reputed to have stayed in this half-timbered merchant's house, and his visit has been permanently recorded. Nowadays his charismatic presence has been replaced by that of genial host Matthew Brown, who looks after guests while partner Jonathan Lewis takes charge of the kitchen. This bustling little restaurant, which also offers five pretty bedrooms, is open for meals all day, and simplicity and good value are its keynotes. The set two- and three-course menus change with the seasons, and supported by blackboard specials offer a range of imaginative dishes: perhaps rich and tasty chicken liver terrine wrapped in Parma ham, or marinated carpaccio of duck breast for starters, followed by

High Street
Map no: 4 SP02
Tel: 01242 602366

Cost: Fixed-price lunch £12.50, fixed-price dinner £19.50. H/wine £8.95 ♀ Service exc
Credit cards: 1 2 3 5

Menus: Fixed-price lunch and dinner, Sunday lunch, bar menu
Times: Last L 2.30pm, Last D 10pm. Closed Sun D

Chef: Jonathan Lewis
Proprietors: Jonathan Lewis, Matthew Brown

maize guinea fowl breast with basmati risotto and roast shallots. A recent inspection meal praised a simple asparagus dish served with crunchy dressed leaves and a mild green peppercorn sauce, and lightly poached American seabass on pasta with a creamy saffron sauce. Apricot and butterscotch steamed pudding with a vanilla sauce was a scrumptious classical British dish.

Directions: In centre of Winchcombe on the main road

Seats: 50. No-smoking area; no pipes or cigars
Additional: Children permitted (over 8 at dinner); children's portions; ✿ menu; Vegan/other diets on request

GREATER MANCHESTER

BURY, **Normandie** ✿✿✿

A well-established French hotel restaurant in Old Birtle at the foot of the Pennines

Back in the 1950s a collection of buildings at Old Birtle, in the foothills of the Pennines to the east of Bury, then known as the Crown Inn, were acquired by a talented Frenchman. The property was renamed Normandie and developed into a restaurant which soon became renowned for its French cuisine. The Normandie was later converted into a hotel. Now owned by the Moussa family, its reputation for fine food is undiminished, perpetuated to this day by the talents of head chef Pascal Pommier and his skilled team. They offer a good variety of dishes from the *carte* and a fixed-price daily menu with a choice of two dishes at each of three courses.

Starters might include tongue and ham shank terrine, ravioli of Dublin Bay prawns, or our inspector's choice, 'potage printannier au jarret de porc', a creamy spring vegetable soup with ham hock and lots of crisp diced vegetables. This was followed by 'mignon de boeuf gratiné, sauce vin rouge parfumée à l'oignon', a tender fillet of beef with horseradish and served with a robust red wine sauce. Vegetables, an integral part of the dish, comprising turned carrot, courgette and turnip,

Elbut Lane, Birtle
Map no: 7 SD81
Tel: 0161-764 1170

Cost: *Alc* £32, fixed-price lunch £12.50, £15, fixed-price dinner £18.95. H/wine £12.25 ♀
Credit cards: 1 2 3 4 5

Menus: *A la carte*, fixed-price lunch and dinner

Times: Midday-Last L 2.pm, 7pm-Last D 9.30pm. Lunch not served Sat and Mon. Closed Sun, 1 week Easter and 2 weeks after 25 Dec.

Chef: Pascal Pommier
Proprietors: Gillian Moussa, Max Moussa

Seats: 45. No cigars or pipes

and roast onions, all young and full of flavour.
  Other options might be scallops with black noodles and coriander or the featured vegetarian dish, perhaps a tartlet of pulses with mushrooms, spinach and poached egg. 'Croustillant de riz au lait et fruits éxotiques' proved to be a beautifully presented dessert of creamy warm rice pudding in a crisp basket accompanied by a variety of exotic fresh fruits. There is also a selection of French and British farmhouse cheeses.
  The lengthy wine list, complete with useful descriptions, is skilfully chosen and reasonably priced. It is mainly French, complemented by a few of the best wines from other countries.

Additional: Children welcome; children's portions if requested; ❤ dishes

Directions: From the M66, jnct 2, turn right into Wash Lane, right into Willows Street. Right at B6222, left into Elbut Lane, up hill 1 mile

MANCHESTER, **Little Yang Sing** ❀

☺ *Situated in the heart of Manchester's Chinatown, this restaurant specialises in Cantonese cuisine with the usual enormous choice specific to Chinese restaurants. Chef, Au Ting Chung, cooks delicious Dim Sum and main courses ranging from steamed King prawns to braised sliced duck.*

17 George Street
Map no: 7 SJ89
Tel: 0161-228 7722
Chef: Au Ting Chung
Proprietor: Christine Yeung
Seats: 90. Air conditioned
Times: Last L 4.30pm/D 11.15pm. Closed Xmas day

Cost: Alc £14, fixed-price L £8.95/D £13. H/wine £7.95. Service exc. **Credit cards:** 1 2 3 5. **Additional:** Children welcome; children's portions/menu; ❤ dishes; Vegan/other diets on request.
Directions: Behind Piccadilly Plaza on the corner of George and Charlotte Street (parallel with Mosley Street/Portland Street

MANCHESTER, **Market** ❀❀

☺ *A refreshingly relaxed restaurant opposite the old fish market serving an interesting variety of cooking styles*

This informal, relaxing and unpretentious restaurant has been part of the Manchester food scene for more than a decade, and its value-for-money cooking is as popular as ever. A mixture of styles and influences enlivens the monthly-changing *carte*: perhaps Thai sweetcorn fritters with cucumber relish to start, or 'Strata', a savoury Italian bread and butter pudding with prawns, herbs and mayonnaise, and main dishes like 'Torta Pasqualina', an Easter pie from Genoa with artichokes, spinach and dolcelatte cheese, or Cajun black-baked turkey breast with mango salsa. Our inspector opted for a conventional smoked salmon and asparagus tart that made a light and tasty starter, followed by breast of duck sliced and wrapped in a sorrel pancake, served with a delicate brown sauce and onion chutney. Buttered shredded cabbage, fried potato wedges and aubergines with onions were full of flavour if lacking in refinement, while walnut meringues with lemon curd cream and caramel sauce was a delicious and imaginative dessert. The wine list includes New World, organic and alcohol-free choices.

Edge Street, 104 High Street
Map no: 7 SJ89
Tel: 0161-834 3743

Cost: Alc £17.50 ♀ Service exc
Credit cards: 1 2 3 4 5

Menus: A la carte

Times: 6pm-Last D 9.30pm. Closed Sun, Mon, Tues, 1 week Xmas, 4 weeks Aug

Chefs: Mary-Rose Edgecombe, Paul Mertz, Dawn Wellens
Proprietors: Peter O'Grady, Anne O'Grady, Mary-Rose Edgecombe

Seats: 40. Cigars and pipes discouraged
Additional: Children welcome; children's portions; ❤ dishes; Vegan on request

Directions: On the corner of Edge Street and High Street, close to Craft Village. Nearest Metro station – High Street

MANCHESTER, **Moss Nook** ❀❀

A smart and expensive restaurant with a good reputation serving classical French cooking

A sophisticated style of classical French cooking in a plush Edwardian setting are an appealing combination at this well-established restaurant. High prices have not proved to be a deterrent, and the reliable and consistent cooking of Kevin Lofthouse remains an attraction to serious lovers of good food. The regularly changing *carte* offers half a dozen well-balanced choices at each course, while a 'menu surprise' delivers seven dishes chosen by the chef to tempt the palate. Our inspector opted for shelled tiger prawns baked in a sweet and citric sauce with toasted almonds, followed by a tiny bowl of tasty potato and leek soup. Medallions of beef fillet, grilled and topped with cucumber cream and served with a rich herb butter sauce was a succulent main dish, which came with an interesting variety of crisp and delicate vegetables. Several delicious fresh fruits studded the ice cream-filled summer fruit meringue, including strawberry, raspberry, redcurrant, kiwi fruit, blackcurrant, melon and apple, and pleasant coffee came with petist fours. The wine list contains some mainly French vintages, and good value house wines.

Directions: Close to Manchester airport – at junction of Ringway with B5166

Ringway Road
Map no: 7 SJ89
Tel: 0161-437 4778

Cost: A/c £35, fixed-price lunch £16.50, fixed-price dinner £28. Wine £9.90 ♀ Service exc
Credit cards: 1 2 3 4

Menus: *A la carte*, fixed-price lunch and dinner

Times: Last L 1.30pm, Last D 9.30pm. Lunch not served Sat. Closed Sun, Mon, 2 weeks Xmas

Chef: Kevin Lofthouse
Proprietors: Pauline and Derek Harrison

Seats: 65. No pipes
Additional: No children under 8; ❻ dishes; other diets on request

MANCHESTER, **Victoria & Albert** ❀❀

Highly acclaimed cooking from an enthusiastic chef, in a luxury hotel opposite Granada Studios

Converted from an early Victorian warehouse on the banks of the River Irwell, this luxury modern hotel can be found easily by following the ubiquitous signs for Granada Studio Tours. Many of the original features have been cleverly absorbed into the new building and the result is a series of elegant and stylishly thematic areas. The Sherlock Holmes restaurant is the most serious of three eating options, where dedicated chef John Benson-Smith and his team produce their colourful, creative and imaginative cuisine. Particularly popular is the gourmet menu, with its varied miniature dishes, but there are also fixed-price menus at lunch and dinner, and a serious *carte*. A recent inspection meal began with deep-fried fish cake and spicy tomato vinaigrette, with an interim course of Goosnargh chicken on a rosemary and raisin toast wedge, served with salad and a honey and lime dressing. Eggy bread lamb – a piece of meat inside French toast – was a mass of flavours heightened by the red wine, port and shallot sauce. A selection of mini sweets included special delicacies like pink blancmange and jelly.

Directions: Head for the city centre and follow signs for Granada Studios Tour. Hotel is opposite the Studios

Water Street
Map no: 7 SJ89
Tel: 0161-832 1188

Cost: A/c £34, fixed-price lunch £9.95 (2 courses), £12.95, fixed-price dinner £28.50. H/wine £12.20 ♀ service inc
Credit cards: 1 2 3 4 5

Menus: *A la carte*, fixed-price lunch and dinner, Sunday lunch, pre-theatre, bar menu

Times: Midday-Last L 2pm, 7pm-Last D 9.30pm. Dinner not served Sun

Chef: John Benson-Smith
Proprietors: Granada. Manager: James R Diamond

Seats: 120. Air conditioned
Additional: Children permitted; children's portions; ❻ menu; Other diets on request. Pianist

MANCHESTER, Woodlands ❀❀

33 Shepley Road, Audenshaw
Map no: 7 SJ89
Tel: 0161-336 4241

A reliably consistent French restaurant producing well-made dishes with an emphasis on good saucing

Once the home of the owners, this attractive Victorian house is now a friendly family-run restaurant with bedrooms where daughter Lesley looks after guests while son-in-law William Jackson provides inspiration in the kitchen. His fine skills as a chef are responsible for the high standard of French cooking, and dishes with a minimum of frills are beautifully presented at table; fish is a prominent feature, and sauces are a real strength. A fixed-price, three-course menu is produced both at lunch and dinner, while the well-balanced *carte* offers more choice. Our inspector thoroughly enjoyed a recent sample meal, which began with very light pasta in a sauce made with ham, mushrooms, peppers, garlic and cheese. Fresh plaice in a mushroom, cream and parsley sauce was a carefully made main dish, which came with tasty vegetables including green beans and new potatoes. The *carte* also offers choices like fillet of lamb with a rich tarragon sauce, and venison steak with chestnuts, mushrooms and glazed onions. Puddings might be a refreshing light and tangy lemon soufflé with a citron sauce, served in a thick brandy snap basket.

Cost: *Alc* £21.50, fixed-price lunch and dinner £15.65. H/wine £8.25. Service exc
Credit cards: 1 3

Menus: *A la carte*, fixed-price lunch and dinner, Sunday lunch on last Sunday of each month

Times: Last L 2pm, Last D 9.30, (10pm Sat). Lunch not served Sat. Closed Sun, Mon

Chef: William Mark Jackson
Proprietors: Mr and Mrs Dennis Crank

Seats: 36. No cigars or pipes
Additional: Children welcome Sunday lunch. ❂ dishes

Directions: From the M67 take A6017 to Ashton, after half a mile turn left at traffic lights, then right into Shepley Road. Woodlands is on the left

MANCHESTER, Yang Sing ❀❀

34 Princess Street
Map no: 7 SJ89
Tel: 0161-236 2200

This universally acknowledged Cantonese restaurant in the heart of Manchester's Chinatown offers a wide range of authentic dishes.

Credit cards: 1 2 3

Situated in the city centre, just west of the Chinese quarter, the Yang Sing is universally acknowledged as one of the best Cantonese restaurants in the country. One of Manchester's leading restaurants for many years, its move to the present larger basement premises has enabled many more people to enjoy its bustling atmosphere and the wide range of Cantonese dishes. The extensive *carte* menu offers a wide selection of beef, pork, fish, chicken, duck and barbecue dishes, accompanied by a variety of sauces and crisp fresh vegetables. Banquet and set dinner menus are also available, together with an impressive selection of Dim Sum served at lunchtime. Our inspector enjoyed two examples of Dim Sum: delicious fried Wan Tun (prawn dumplings) and steamed beef dumplings served with spring onion and ginger. This was followed by sweet and sour pork Cantonese style, fresh fillet of fish served with an excellent black bean sauce and tasty steamed duck with Chinese vegetables. Wines have been specially chosen to accompany the Chinese dishes and the house wines in particular represent good value for money.

Menus: *A la carte*

Times: Midday-Last D 11.15pm. Closed Xmas day

Chef: Harry Yeung
Proprietors: Yang Sing

Seats: 140, 110. Air conditioned
Additional: Children welcome; ❂ dishes; Vegan/other diets on request

Directions: Princess Street is a one way street leading from the Town Hall to the A57M and Wilmslow

ENGLAND GREATER MANCHESTER **293**

RAMSBOTTOM, The Village Restaurant ❀

16 Market Place
Map no: 7 SD71
Tel: 01706 825070
Chef: Ros Hunter
Proprietors: Ros Hunter, Chris Johnson
Seats: 32. No smoking
Times: Last L 2.30pm (Sun 1.30pm)/D 7.45. Closed Mon, Tue

☺ *An inexpensive bistro offering everyday food with personal service and traditional cooking in an unpretentious setting. Concentration is focused on showing the natural flavours of the dishes, and organic ingredients are used when possible. A regular main course is roast beef and Yorkshire pudding.*

Cost: Alc L £11, fixed-price supper £9.95, £12.95, £14.95. H/wine £8.50 ♀ Service exc. Corkage £4.95 on wines from shop
Credit cards: 1 2 3 4 5 **Additional:** Children permitted; ❿ dishes; Vegan/other diets on request
Directions: In the centre of the village

ROCHDALE, French Connection ❀

Edenfield Road, Cheesden, Norden
Map no: 7 SD81
Tel: 01706 50167
Chef: Andrew Nutter
Proprietors: Rodney Nutter
Seats: 52. No smoking
Times: Last L 2.30pm/D 9.30pm (Sun 9pm). Closed Mon; first 2 weeks Aug

Located on top of a lonely moor, this family restaurant produces French dishes cooked by Andrew Nutter. The best local produce is used to create beautifully presented dishes. Starters include snails sautéed in garlic cream on tagliatelle; main courses, turbot with asparagus and rocket sauce.

Cost: Alc £23.50, Menu dégustation £24.95. H/wine £7.80. Service exc. **Credit cards:** 1 2 5. **Additional:** Children welcome; children's portions; ❿ dishes; Vegan/other diets on request
Directions: on the A680 between Rochdale and Edenfield

STANDISH, Kilhey Court ❀

Chorley Road
Map no: 7 SD50
Tel: 01257 472100
Chef: Stephan Murphy
Proprietor: A Corlett

Elaborately presented food, but good, tasty food is served in the Conservatory restaurant, which looks out over the extensive grounds and adjoining lakes. A wide choice of food is available, and worth a special mention is the range of cheeses on offer and home-made bread.

Directions: On A5106 at Worthington

HAMPSHIRE

ALRESFORD, **Hunters** ◉◉

A relaxed, informal country restaurant offering skilfully cooked and imaginative menus of Anglo-French cuisine

A sister restaurant to Hunters in Winchester, this establishment has the same friendly atmosphere, with country-style decor and furnishings. Young chef Michael Greenhalgh cooks with skill and imagination to create nicely balanced menus. A daily fixed-price menu is displayed on a blackboard and a short *carte* is also presented. Starters might offer ravioli of spinach and prawns served in a sweet orange sauce, or our inspector's choice, a delicately flavoured terrine of salmon filled with a roulade of scallops and dill accompanied by a tasty tomato and chive vinaigrette. A vegetarian dish is featured among the main courses (such as a bake of aubergine, courgette, cheese and tomatoes) which might otherwise include roasted turbot with garlic and thyme accompanied by a red wine and shallot sauce, or the tender loin of rabbit enjoyed on this occasion, wrapped in spinach and a wild mushroom mousseline with fresh noodles and turned vegetables. The dessert selection lists summer pudding with cassis sauce, and mango ice cream and tatin.

West Street
Map no: 4 SU53
Tel: 01962 732468

Cost: *A/c* £21, fixed-price dinner £11.95 (2 courses), £14.95
Credit cards: 1 2 3 4

Menus: A la carte, fixed-price dinner, light lunch, Sunday lunch (winter only)

Times: Midday-2pm, 7pm-10pm. Closed Sun (but open for Sunday lunch in winter)

Chef: Michael Greenhalgh
Proprietor: Michael Birmingham

Seats: 30

Directions: In the centre of village in West Street

BARTON-ON-SEA, **The Cliff House** ◉

☺ *A popular little hotel with glorious sea views from a bracing cliff-top position. Traditional, hearty food is served in the restaurant, and booking is always essential. Dishes include a strong-flavoured Dorset pâté, home-made steak and mushroom pie with puff pastry, and creamy desserts.*

Cost: *A/c* £20, fixed-price L £10.95/D £16.50, Sunday L £11.95. H/wine £8.95 ♀ Service exc **Credit cards:** 1 2 3. **Additional:** Children welcome; children's portions; ❷ dishes; Vegan/other diets on request
Directions: From New Milton take A337 Lymington road, turn left by garage towards sea. The hotel is on the cliff edge overlooking the sea

Marine Drive West
Map no: 4 SZ29
Tel: 01425 619333
Chefs: James Simpson, Martin Cooper
Proprietors: James Simpson, Isobel Simpson
Seats: 50. No smoking
Times: Last L 2pm/D 9pm

BASINGSTOKE, **Audleys Wood** ◉

Chef Terence Greenhouse offers a carte and daily fixed-price menus in the restaurant of this luxurious country hotel. The ambitious and attractively presented dishes might include duck liver parfait on a redcurrant and port sauce, salmon on a chervil and cream sauce, and an elaborate treacle tart.

Cost: *A/c* £29, fixed-price L £17.95/D £23. H/wine £13.85 ♀ Service inc. **Credit cards:** 1 2 3 4 . **Additional:** Children welcome; children's portions. ❷ dishes; Vegan/other diets on request
Directions: On A339 from Basingstoke to Alton, on the right

Alton Road
Map no: 4 SU65
Tel: 01256 817555
Chef: Terence Greenhouse
Proprietor: Mount Charlotte Thistle
Seats: 70
Times: Last L 1.45pm/D 9.45pm. Lunch not served Sat, BHs (except Xmas and New Year)

BASINGSTOKE,
Basingstoke Country Hotel ❀

☺ *A well staffed and deservedly popular business hotel just off the M3 with every modern creature comfort in a country house setting. Chef Iain McCormack offers a wide choice of contemporary English dishes: impressive looking but veering toward the fussy. Nevertheless, the food is carefully prepared.*

Cost: Alc £25, fixed-price L £11.50 (2 courses), £14.50/D £19.50. H/wine £9.95 ♀ Service inc. **Credit cards:** 1 2 3 4 **Additional:** Children welcome; children's portions; ❶ dishes; Vegan/other diets on request
Directions: On A30 between Nately Scures and Hook

Nately Scures, Hook
Map no: 4 SU65
Tel: 01256 746161
Chef: Iain McCormack
Proprietors: Andrew Weir Hotels. Manager: Gavin Elliott
Seats: 90. Air conditioned
Times: Last L 2pm/D 9.45pm

BEAULIEU, Beaulieu Hotel ❀

☺ *Situated on an isolated heath in the New Forest the hotel's 'Hungry Horse' restaurant offers a daily fixed-price menu which could include New Zealand Greenlip mussels or smoked trout and salmon platter as a starter and sautéed venison steak as a main course.*

Cost: Fixed-price D £15. H/wine £9.30. Service exc
Credit cards: 1 2 3 4. **Additional:** Children welcome; children's menu; ❶ dishes; Vegan/other diets on request
Directions: On the B3056 between Lyndhurst and Beaulieu, opposite the Railway Station

Beaulieu Road
Map no: 4 SU30
Tel: 01703 293344
Chef: N Cole
Proprietor: Bryan Davies
Seats: 42. No smoking
Times: Last D 8.45pm

BEAULIEU, Montagu Arms ❀❀

An extensive range of excellent French and English dishes is featured on the menus of this exclusive country house hotel.

Elegant and exclusive, this creeper-clad hotel in English country house style stands in the centre of the village; a wood-panelled candlelit restaurant features fine cuisine, chef Simon Fennell offering fixed-price menus of two and three courses as well as the *carte*. A noteworthy inspection meal chosen from the gourmet menu included tasty confit of New Forest duckling wrapped in crispy filo then set on orange segments and accompanied by a sweet redcurrant sauce, tender medallions of Scottish fillet steak served on chopped spring onions and sliced Parma ham with a dark, rather bitter, meat glacé, and a good crème brûlée elaborately garnished with feathered mango purée, fresh strawberries and swan meringues and cream. Lightly cooked vegetables retain their flavour, and the coconut creams and shortbreads brought with coffee are home-made, as is a range of breads including walnut, caraway seed and raisin. Vegetarians are provided with a separate menu. An extensive (but pricey) wine list contains some New World labels, fine vintages, good estate and domaine bottled examples, and some halves.

Directions: From Southampton take A326 (Fawley), follow signs to Beaulieu (B3054). The hotel is on the left as you enter the village

Place Lane
Map no: 4 SU30
Tel: 01590 612324

Cost: Alc £35, fixed-price lunch £14.95, fixed-price dinner £18.90 (2 courses), £23.90. H/wine £12.50 ♀ Service exc
Credit cards: 1 2 3 4 5

Menus: A la carte, fixed-price lunch and dinner, Sunday lunch

Times: 12.30-Last L 2pm, 7.30pm-Last D 9.30pm (10pm Sat)

Chef: Simon Fennell
Proprietor: Green Close Ltd

Seats: 80-100. No smoking in dining room
Additional: Children welcome; children's portions; ❶ dishes; Vegan/other diets on request

HAMPSHIRE ENGLAND

BOTLEY, **Cobbett's** ☺☺

☺ *French country cooking from a native chef, in a small, affably run restaurant just outside Southampton*

According to our inspector's report, proprietor Charles Skipwith has a laid-back, friendly manner; how laid-back he didn't say, but it is a style which obviously helps to nourish the popularity of the restaurant. His co-proprietor, chef and wife, Lucie, generates the real nourishment with a near-ceaseless flow of high standard French provincial dishes from her long-established cottage kitchen. Since she came from St Emilion in the Bordeaux wine region, she had a head start in this respect. There is no attempt to bewilder customers with a long list of dishes – the *carte* is tightly assembled, but the choice is still good. One could follow our inspector's well-chosen lead and begin with brown and white crab meat and mussels in a light, crisp pastry case served in a cream basil sauce with tomato and mushroom. Then 'Poitrine de pigeon en croûte', tender breast stuffed with forcemeat encased in puff pastry with a hunky red wine sauce. And finally, chocolate mousse on a sponge with vanilla and orange liqueur sauce. Charles Skipwith has chosen his short wine selection well and prices them within sensible limits.

Directions: From the A27 follow signs to Botley to centre of village

15 The Square
Map no: 4 SU51
Tel: 01489 782068

Cost: Fixed-price £20. Wine £9.25
Credit cards: 1 3

Menu: Fixed-price

Times: Midday-Last L 2pm, 7.30-Last D 10pm. Closed Sat, Mon lunch, all day Sun, 2 weeks summer

Chef: Lucie Skipwith
Proprietors: Lucie and Charles Skipwith

Seats: 48. No cigars or pipes
Additional: Children welcome, (over 12 at dinner); ❂ dish

BROCKENHURST, **Careys Manor** ☺☺

Imaginative and skilful, classically based cooking in an elegant New Forest hotel

A former Victorian gentleman's residence, built in the style of a hunting lodge, and standing in five acres of mature grounds and landscaped gardens, Careys Manor is run as a country house hotel. Chef Kevin Dorrington continues to produce modern classically based cooking, applying his imagination and skill to the best quality ingredients with impressive results. A choice of hot or cold first courses is offered, recent dishes including 'New Forest mushrooms and sweet peppers sautéed with fresh herbs and finished with double cream', creamed smoked haddock in a pancake, and game terrine, blended with collops of rabbit and studded with Pistachio nuts. Poached fillet of brill set on fresh and well-seasoned spinach leaves was a successful main course as was fillet of pork topped with mushrooms, presented in filo pastry and served with Madeira sauce. Puddings are served from a dessert trolley. Fixed-price lunch and dinner menus are also available and the external Le Blaireau Café Bar offers an informal eating venue. The wine list includes a reasonably priced house selection.

Directions: On the A337 between Lyndhurst and Lymington

Brockenhurst
Map no: 4 SU30
Tel: 01590 23551

Cost: *Alc* £25, fixed-price lunch £13.50, fixed-price dinner £19.95. H/ wine £11.95
Credit cards: 1 2 3 4 5

Times: Last L 2pm/D 10pm

Chef: Kevin Dorrington
Proprietors: Christopher Biggin

Seats: 90. No smoking
Additional: Children permitted; children's portions; ❂ menu; Vegan/other diets on request

BROCKENHURST, Le Poussin ❀❀❀

A small restaurant, simple but tasteful in style, with a short list of dishes cooked to order from daily fresh produce

It is some years since Alex and Caroline Aitken took the decision to move to smaller premises in order to enjoy family life to the full. The idea was that Alex Aitken could concentrate on providing a straightforward short choice menu to relatively few tables, which could be written up at the start of each day. This simple format, priced for two or three courses, has proved successful, bringing about a high standard of cooking composed entirely of daily fresh ingredients. Chief among these must be the local New Forest venison, unbeatable at times for quality and price, and fresh seafood from Brixham and Keyhaven.

Alex excels in a simple modern approach to some favourite old recipes, such as fillet of turbot with leeks served with a light fish fumet and mustard seed sauce, and roasted marinated monk fish tail on a bed of sweet peppers, aubergines and fennel. Our inspector was particularly impressed by the braised venison, beautifully cooked and enhanced with a tasty jus. The venison is also offered as a rare roast with a good port wine sauce. A simple dish of creamy mashed potato, topped with fresh cream and glazed under the salamander, was quite outstanding. Just two puddings are listed, with cheese as an alternative, which allows the kitchen to prepare the dish to order. Hot banana soufflé, sampled by our inspector, proved worth the wait.

Son Justin Aitken attends to customers' needs. He is the sommelier and he personally decants and serves the wines with great skill and flair. Vegetarian and other special diets can only be accommodated by prior arrangement.

Directions: Through an archway between 'Best Sellars' book shop and a hairdressers

The Courtyard
Brookley Road
Map no: 4 SU30
Tel: 01590 23063

Cost: Fixed-price lunch £10(2 courses), £15; fixed-price dinner £20 (2 courses), £25. H/wine from £9.75 ♀ Service exc
Credit cards: 1 3 5

Menus: Fixed-price lunch and dinner, Sunday lunch

Times: Midday-Last L 2pm, 7pm-Last D 10pm. Dinner not served Sun. Closed Mon, Tue

Chef: Alex Aitken
Proprietors: Alex and Caroline Aitken

Seats: 24. No smoking
Additional: Children permitted

BROCKENHURST, New Park Manor ❀

An historic hunting lodge in the beautiful New Forest where chef Matthew Tilt produces a high standard of cooking. Our inspector sampled the sautéed langoustine and red mullet with Pernod and chive sauce followed by fillet of beef topped with a strong cheese mousse and spinach.

Cost: Alc £26, fixed-price £19.50
Additional: No smoking. Children welcome; ❂ dishes
Directions: Turn off the A337 between Lyndhurst and Brockenhurst and follow the hotel signs

Lyndhurst Road
Map no: 4 SU30
Tel: 01590 23467
Chef: Matthew Tilt
Proprietor: A Walden
Times: Last L 2.30pm/D 9.30pm

BROCKENHURST, Rhinefield House ●●

A handsome New Forest hotel restaurant offering a good range of dishes from a choice of menus

The present owners have done much to develop this outstanding 19th-century building, which is set amid the natural splendour of the New Forest. The hotel has many impressive original features, notably the Alhambra Room with its pillars and mosaic floor, now part of the cocktail bar, and the Armada Restaurant with its carved wooden panelling. The cooking is confidently in the modern style, and at dinner there is a choice between the daily fixed-price menu or the seasonal gastronomic menu, priced for two or three courses. Starters may include lobster and leek terrine with sherry dressing, or mackerel fillet poached and marinated in white wine and herbs. The latter proved quite delicious at a recent meal. There are main courses to suit all tastes, from plain grilled Dover sole to beef with a wild mushroom fricassee, and a vegetarian option. Our inspector chose tender, pink venison with glazed apples and a well-judged cinnamon scented jus, and to finish mint crème brûlée, which was more successful than it sounds. A reasonable wine list complements the food.

Directions: From Brockenhurst centre follow signs to Rhinefield. Hotel is on the left

Rhinefield Road
Map no: 4 SU30
Tel: 01590 622922

Cost: A/c £30, fixed-price lunch £14, fixed-price dinner £19.95. H/ wine £10 ♀ Service exc
Credit cards: 1 2 3 4 5

Menus: A la carte, fixed-price lunch and dinner, Sunday lunch

Times: Midday-Last L 2pm, 7pm-Last D 10pm. Lunch not served Sat

Chef: Mark Wadlow
Proprietor: Virgin Hotels. Manager: David London

Additional: Children welcome; children's portions. ♥ menu; Vegan/other diets on request

BROCKENHURST, Thatched Cottage ●

A pretty cottage hotel with plenty of charm is the setting for elaborate and enjoyable food. The fixed-price menu may include King Tiger prawns flavoured with garlic and chillies or roasted Barbary duck breast with a port and cassis sauce and accompanied by wild berries.

Cost: Fixed-price L £13/D £22.50. H/wine £9 ♀ Service charge for D
Credit cards: 1 3 5. **Additional:** Children permitted at lunch. ♥ dishes; Vegan/other diets on request
Directions: In village centre

16 Brookley Road
Map no: 4 SU30
Tel: 01590 23090
Chef: Michiyo Matysik
Proprietors: The Matysik Family
Seats: 20
Times: Last L 2.30pm/D 9.30pm. L not served Sat, D not served Sun. Closed 4 Jan-31 Jan. D by arrangement Feb, Mar

BROCKENHURST, Whitley Ridge ●●

A New Forest country house hotel with an attractive restaurant serving good-value English and French cuisine

A former royal hunting lodge in the heart of the New Forest, this country house hotel has attractively decorated public rooms. In the restaurant, chef Karen Tilt offers a short daily fixed-price menu and a more comprehensive *carte*. A choice from the additional vegetarian selection (perhaps aubergine and walnut provençale) can be taken as part of a fixed-price or an *à la carte* meal. Karen cooks with great care and attention to detail, using fresh produce to create tempting dishes. A test meal began well with a choice of home-made canapés in the bar, followed by tasty field mushrooms in a tangy home-made marinade. The main course was brill fillets poached in white

Beaulieu Road
Map no: 4 SU30
Tel: 01590 22354

Cost: A/c £22.40, fixed-price lunch £10.50, fixed-price dinner £18. H/wine £9.50 ♀ Service exc
Credit cards: 1 2 3 4 5

Menus: A la carte, fixed-price lunch and dinner, Sunday lunch, pre-theatre, bar menu

Times: Midday-Last L 2pm, 6.30pm-Last D 9pm

wine and court bouillon, with a puff pastry case filled with seafoods and a delicious creamy sauce of celery and fennel. The pudding, chocolate mousse with white chocolate sauce, provided a fitting finale to an enjoyable meal. The wine list, with wines from around the world, offers useful descriptions, a few half bottles, and house wines by the glass. Service is friendly and the proprietors, Rennie and Sue Law, are attentive hosts.

Directions: A337 (from Lyndhurst) turn left towards Beaulieu on B3055, approx 1 mile

Chef: Karen Tilt
Proprietors: Mr and Mrs R Law

Seats: 36. No smoking in dining room
Additional: Children permitted; under 10s before 7pm at dinner; ❶ menu; Vegan/other diets on request

BROOK, **Bell Inn** ❀

☺ *Previous high standards of classic French and English cooking continue with chef Malcolm Lugg's skilful approach producing interesting results – game pasty with Madeira sauce for example. Fixed-price or speciality menus and a good selection of wines are offered in this popular golfing hotel.*

Lyndhurst
Map no: 4 SU21
Tel: 01703 812214
Chef: Malcolm Lugg
Proprietor: Gavin Scott
Seats: 50. No smoking in dining room
Times: Last L 2.30pm/D 9.30pm

Cost: Fixed-price L £9.50/D £23.50. H/wine £8.50 ♀ Service inc
Credit cards: 1 2 3 4 5. **Additional:** Children welcome at lunch; children's menu/portions; ❶ dishes; Vegan/other diets on request
Directions: One mile north of jnct 1 of M27 (Cadnam)

BUCKLERS HARD, **Master Builders House** ❀

A pleasant 18th-century riverside house, styled with a nautical atmosphere, is the setting for fine English cooking where seasonal specialities include local game – venison with pepper sauce, saddle of rabbit – and fresh seafood. A selection from the local vineyard is included in the wine list.

Beaulieu
Brockenhurst
Map no: 4 SU40
Tel: 01590 616253
Chef: Simon Berry
Proprietors: Ring and Brymer. Manager: C Plumpton
Seats: 80. No pipes or cigars in dining room
Times: Last L 2pm/D 9.30pm

Cost: A/c from £20; fixed-price L/D £12.50 (2 courses), £15.95. H/wine £9.75. Service exc. **Credit cards:** 1 2 3 4
Additional: . Children welcome; children's portions. ❶ dishes; Vegan/other diets on request
Directions: Bucklers Hard is signposted from Beaulieu

CADNAM, **Bartley Lodge** ❀

☺ *Situated in the delightful New Forest, this former hunting lodge was built in 1759. The menu is traditional English, with a good mix of fish, meat and game dishes. The carte includes half roast pheasant with raspberry vinegar, and grilled cod fillet with prawn mousse and a tomato sauce.*

Lyndhurst Road
Map no: 4 SU31
Tel: 01703 812248
Chef: Mr Gary Watling
Proprietors: Care Hotels
Seats: 50. Guest are requested not to smoke
Times: Last L 2pm/D 8.45pm

Cost: A/c £18, fixed-price L £13.50/D £15. H/wine £9.15 Service exc. **Credit cards:** 1 2 3 4. **Additional:** Children welcome; children's portions/menu; ❶ dishes; Vegan/other diets on request
Directions: From exit 1 M27 New Forest, Bartley Lodge signed just off A337

DENMEAD, **Barnards** 👄👄

☺ *Confident Anglo-French cooking with an imaginative flair in a friendly and relaxed setting*

David and Sandie Barnard have now moved from Cosham into new premises in Denmead, taking with them their successful formula of classic Anglo-French cooking and short menus incorporating tried and tested favourites such as Swiss cheese soufflé and smooth chicken liver pâté. While David runs the kitchen with style, Sandie organises the dining room with capability and charm; an unusual and welcome note on the menu indicates that a service charge is neither included nor expected! There is usually a choice of meat, fish and perhaps game plus a vegetarian main course; past dishes have included fillet steak with mushroom pâté and Madeira sauce, suprême of duck and lime sauce and lobster with cheese sauce – all reflecting David Barnard's flair for a properly constructed and imaginative sauce. His lightly cooked vegetables are exceptionally good too. A terrine of home-made fresh fruit sorbets and meringue and strawberry mousse are a couple of recent inclusions on the mouthwatering puddings menu. Wines are very reasonably priced and service friendly and unhurried.

Directions: Opposite village church

Hambledon Road
Map no: 4 SU61
Tel: 01705 257788

Cost: A/c £25, fixed-price dinner £13.50. H/wine £8.25. No service charge
Credit cards: 1 2 3

Menus: *A la carte*, fixed-price dinner

Times: 7.30pm-Last D 10pm. Lunch not served. Closed Sun, Mon, 2 weeks Aug, 1 week Xmas

Chef: David Barnard
Proprietor: David Barnard

Seats: 30. No smoking in dining room
Additional: Children welcome; children's portions; ❤ dishes, other diets on request

EMSWORTH, **36 On The Quay** 👄👄👄

Fine food prepared with considerable flair, imagination and originality in an elegant quayside restaurant

A pretty restaurant with good views, 36 On The Quay is, as its name suggests, situated close to the water's edge. Guests are warmly greeted by the proprietor, Raymond Short, and Claire Eckerman (wife of the talented chef), who ensure that service is smooth, professional and extremely polite. Frank Eckerman has been here more than three years now and in that time has gained a well deserved reputation for the superb quality of his cooking. The restaurant is popular with locals and foodies from London – anyone who enjoys excellent food and fine wine.

There is a fixed-price dinner menu with plenty of choice, including some price-supplemented dishes and daily specials, and a shorter lunch menu also of three courses. Starters might include local oysters served naturally, poached in champagne or gratinated, or tartare of salmon – fresh salmon and marinated salmon bound with avocado pear in a colourful and tasty combination, served with a cucumber and dill dressing – a simple dish with good quality ingredients shining through. Among the main courses there is a vegetarian option such as baked tomato filled with mushrooms and aubergine, served on a bed of buttered rice with garden herbs.

Our inspector sampled a beautifully flavoured and succulent breast of Barbary duck, cooked pink, sliced and presented with a tomato and basil glaze. The dessert menu may offer a hot soufflé for a minimum of two people, a white and dark chocolate mousse or, as on this occasion, a lemon tart with a shortcake base, an enjoyable variation on a popular recipe, set

47 South Street
Map no: 4 SU70
Tel: 01243 375592

Cost: A/c £31, fixed-price lunch £19.55 Wine £11.50 ♀ Service exc
Credit cards: 1 2 3 4

Menus: *A la carte*, fixed-price lunch, Sunday lunch

Times: Midday-Last L 1.45pm, 7pm-Last D 9.45pm. L served Tue-Fri, D served Mon-Sat.. Closed Sun. Oct-Mar closed Tue, open Sun L

Chef: Frank Eckermann
Proprietor: Raymond Shortland

Seats: 46. No-smoking area, no cigars or pipes until after 2pm, 10.30pm
Additional: No children under 11; ❤ dishes; Vegan/other diets on request

on a carefully made clear red fruit coulis. To finish there is a choice of coffees and teas served with tempting truffles and petits fours.

Directions: The restaurant is the last building on the right in South Street before you reach the water. South Street runs from the Square in centre of Emsworth

EVERSLEY, **The New Mill** ❋❋

Accomplished traditional cooking is offered by a new chef in this beautifully located and welcoming restaurant

A delightful riverside setting in extensive grounds on the Blackwater race makes this 16th-century former mill an ideal location for special dining occasions. Its comfortably furnished, oak beamed bar has a blazing log fire in winter months, and, in summer a terrace on which to enjoy aperitifs. The Grill Room offers a more informal alternative to the Riverside Restaurant, where new chef Stephen Read now offers both *carte* and fixed-price menus, cooking in traditional style: his steak and kidney pudding is consistently recommended by regular diners. Our inspector chose duck liver pâté which came with an excellent warm brioche, lightly flavoured with sun-dried tomato. To follow, rolled fillets of sole, stuffed with crab meat, were served with a delightful lemon butter, and crab meat sauces. Though the vegetables were, on this occasion, unexciting, the pudding – caramelised pear tart with honey ice cream and chocolate sauce – was altogether enjoyable. The wine list has been thoughtfully compiled and service is attentive and friendly, supervised by the helpful proprietor, Anthony Finn.

Directions: From Eversley take A327 towards Reading. Cross the river, left at crossroads into New Mill Road and to end by a deep ford

New Mill Road
Map no: 4 SU76
Tel: 01734 732277

Cost: Riverside:*Alc* £30, fixed-price £19.50; Grill Room: *Alc* £15, fixed-price lunch and dinner £10 (Mon-Fri); H/wine £9.75
Credit cards: 1 2 3 4 5

Menus: *A la carte,* fixed-price price lunch and dinner, Sunday lunch, bar menu
Times: Midday-Last L 2pm, Last D 10pm

Chef: S Read
Proprietor: Anthony Finn

Seats: 80 (Grill Room 36). No pipes or cigars
Additional: Children welcome; children's portions; ❂ dishes, Vegan/other diets by special arrangement.

FAIR OAK, **Noorani** ❋❋

☺ *Consistently good cooking, in a north Indian and Bangladeshi style, is assured at this fine restaurant.*

The Noorani restaurant is on of the best Indian restaurants in the region and the cooking is so consistently good that it has recently been awarded a second rosette. The sauces are skilfully made,the spices carefully balanced and it is obvious from the quality of the foodthat the best of fresh ingredients are used, the sauces skilfully made and the spices carefully balanced. The quality of the meat is good and it is not over cooked as is often the case elsewhere. The menu offers a wide choice, including a selection of tandoori, vegetarian dishes and chef's specials. Our inspector enjoyed a wel-flavoured and well-prepared chicken tikka masala in a light sauce accompanied by Bhoona gosht – large pieces of tender lamb with fresh tomatoes, peppers and onions – accompanied by a Chineri sag which had plenty of large succulent prawns in a tasty spicy sauce.

Directions: In village square opposite war memorial

465 Fair Oak Road
Map no: 4 SU41
Tel: 01703 601901

Cost: *Alc* £15. H/wine £6.60. Service exc
Credit cards: 1 2 3 5

Menus: *A la Carte,* Sunday/Monday lunch buffet
Times: Midday-Last L 2pm, 6pm-Last D 11.30pm. Closed Xmas

Chefs: S Meah, M Ali
Proprietor: S Meah

Seats: 75. No-smoking area. Air conditioned
Additional: Children welcome; ❂ dishes

FAREHAM, Lysses House ❃

☺ *An efficient business hotel which nevertheless maintains its Georgian character and a friendly, personal atmosphere. Fresh local produce is skilfully and carefully prepared to create a wide choice of interesting French and English dishes; the wine list will suit most palates and pockets.*

Cost: Alc £23, fixed-price L £13.75/D £17.95. H/wine £9.25 ♀ No service charge
Additional: Children welcome; children's portions; ❂ menu; Vegan/other diets on request.
Directions: From M27 follow signs to Fareham Central and town centre. The hotel is on the left

51 High Street
Map no: 4 SU50
Tel: 01329 822622
Chef: Clive Wright
Proprietor: Prosig Computer Consultants
Seats: 70. No cigars or pipes. Air conditioned
Times: Last L 1.45pm/D 9.45pm. Closed Sun, BHs

FAREHAM, Solent ❃❃

A stylish but comfortable modern hotel offering quality English cooking and some local specialities

There's a country house feel to this tasteful, modern hotel in spite of its location on the edge of a new business park. Cherry wood panelling, polished stone floors and huge old beams all contribute to the relaxed and comfortable atmosphere, and well-trained staff offer friendly, professional service. There's a good choice of local specialities on the *carte* and set menu, like New Forest loin of venison with port wine and raspberries, and Dorset smoked pork sausages and apple chutney with mashed potatoes, spinach and gravy. Vegetarian dishes also feature, such as filo parcels of aubergine and brie with fettucine and tomato sauce. Our inspector tried Brixham market fish soup with rouille, and a very tasty chargrilled best end of lamb with provençale vegetables and tomato and basil sauce. The *carte* is supplemented by a few daily market specials like escalope of salmon and sorrel, pan fried with a white wine and sorrel cream sauce, and Chinese duck with garlic and yellow bean sauce. Desserts might be brandy snap basket filled with passion fruit sorbet, and there's a well constructed wine list.

Directions: Midway between Southampton and Portsmouth close to Junction 9 of M27

Solent Business Park
Rookery Avenue, Whitely
Map no: 4 SU50
Tel: 01489 880000

Cost: Alc £32.50, fixed-price lunch £13.95, fixed-price dinner £20. H/wine £11.50 ♀ Service inc
Credit cards: 1 2 3 4 5

Menus: A la carte, fixed-price lunch and dinner, Sunday lunch, 'all day' menu

Times: 12.30pm-Last L 2pm, no L Sat. 7pm-Last D 10pm.

Chef: David Fitzpatrick
Proprietors: Shire Inns.
Manager: George A Wortley

Seats: 106. No-smoking area. Air conditioned
Additional: Children welcome; children's portions/menu. ❂ dishes; Vegan/other diets on request

FORDINGBRIDGE, Ashburn ❃

☺ *On a hillside with views over the New Forest, the restaurant is in the capable hands of French chef Walter Heitz. At a test meal, our inspector enjoyed carrot and coriander soup, suprême of chicken on a crisp filo pastry base and a zesty passion fruit mousse.*

Cost: Alc from £15.75, fixed-price D £12.75. H/wine £6.95. Service exc. **Credit cards:** 1 3. **Additional:** Children welcome; children's portions/menu; ❂ dishes; Vegan/other diets on request
Directions: On the B3078

Damerham Road
Map no: 4 SU11
Tel: 01425 652060
Chef: Walter Heitz
Proprietors: Minotels.
Managers: Mr and Mrs Robinson, Mr and Mrs Harman
Seats: 50. No smoking
Times: Last L 1.45pm/D 9pm

FORDINGBRIDGE, Hour Glass ❀

☺ *A simple, pretty cottage restaurant with charming proprietors Mrs Collins and chef husband John. The fixed-price menus feature daily specialities of English/French cuisine. Dishes might include crab mousse with lime yoghurt and breast of chicken with grain mustard sauce.*

Cost: Fixed-price L £8.95 (2 courses), £10.95/D£17.95. H/wine £8.95. Service exc. **Credit cards:** 1 3 4
Additional: No children under 5 at lunch/under 13 at dinner; children's portions; ❶ dishes; Vegan/other diets on request
Directions: On main A338 (Salisbury/Ringwood road) just outside Fordingbridge

Burgate
Map no: 4 SU11
Tel: 01425 652348
Chef: John Collins
Proprietors: John and Jean Collins
Seats: 42 (60 in function suite). No-smoking area
Times: Last L 1.45pm/D 9.45. Dinner not served Sun. Closed Mon, 2 weeks Feb

FORDINGBRIDGE, Moonacre ❀❀

An imaginative and serious approach to food with dependable results, and some tantalising desserts

Modern country cooking with a strong emphasis on extracting real flavour from quality ingredients is behind this unpretentious restaurant's success. Chef/patron Barbara Garnsworthy has a fresh, imaginative approach to cooking which results in uncomplicated and fulfilling dishes: typical starters might be salmon fish cakes with spinach sauce, with main dishes like roast boned quail stuffed with rice, apricots and pistachio with a thyme and garlic sauce. A mid-week blackboard menu offers marvellous value for money, while there's more choice on the still very reasonable *carte*. Our inspector relished moist, rich pigeon breast terrine studded with pistachio and served with a very tasty damson sauce, followed by salmon fillet with a lightly spiced and creamy prawn and ginger sauce; fresh and lightly cooked vegetables included an excellent creamed potato purée. The chef's puddings are an undoubted strength – the apple frangipane tart with cinnamon ice cream was delicious. Service is skilful, especially at weekends, and the wine list complements the food with highly recommended house wines.

Directions: In Alderholt which is off the A338 south-west of Fordingbridge

Alderholt
Map no: 4 SU11
Tel: 01425 653142

Cost: Alc £21, fixed-price dinner £9 (2 courses), £11; Sun lunch £10. H/wine £7.50. Service exc
Credit cards: 1 3

Menus: A la carte; Sunday lunch, fixed-price dinner

Times: Last L 2pm, Last D 10pm. Dinner not served Sun. Closed Mon, 3 weeks early Mar

Chef: Barbara Garnsworthy
Proprietor: Barbara Garnsworthy

Seats: 38
Additional: Children permitted; children's portions; ❶ dishes

FORDINGBRIDGE, The Three Lions ❀❀

A consistently high standard of North European cooking in a popular country restaurant

Two blackboards greet visitors to this country pub restaurant, one listing an impressive array of starters and the other a similarly attractive range of main courses. Anyone straying in by mistake could be forgiven for thinking this was a chalked up pub menu, but once the food has been sampled its quality is instantly revealed. Chef/patron Karl Wadsack takes great care with his dishes with consistently good results. At a recent inspection meal the baked seafood and mushroom gratinée was

Stuckton
Map no: 4 SU11
Tel: 01425 652489

Cost: Alc lunch £20, dinner £27. Wine from £8.95 ♀ Service exc
Credit cards: 1 3 5

Menus: A la carte, blackboard
Times: Last L 1.30pm, Last D 9pm (9.30pm Sat). Dinner not served Sun. Closed Mon, Xmas,

praised, with its succulent prawns and scampi in a tasty cheese sauce. Roast breast of wood pigeon served with braised lentils on sliced mushrooms with a sweet onion and blackcurrant marmalade and a gamey sauce was an excellent dish, while equally superb was the Three Lions bread and butter pudding – a lovely tasting egg custard with a light, firm texture. Other dishes on the regularly changing menus might be steamed fillet of salmon with gooseberry sauce, and Wiener schnitzel. Friendly and helpful staff help June Wadsack with the service. Some fine German and Australian wines feature in the interesting list.

1/2 weeks Jul/Aug, 2 weeks Oct, 2 weeks Feb

Chef: Karl H Wadsack
Proprietors: Karl and June Wadsack

Seats: 55. Smoking not encouraged in dining room; no pipes or cigars. Air conditioned
Additional: No children under 14. ❷ dishes by arrangement

Directions: Turn off A338 at Fordingbridge on to B3078 Cadnam road, then turn right into minor road to Stuckton

GRAYSHOTT, Woods Place ❀❀

A friendly restaurant full of character offering excellent food and set in a delightful village

In the village of Grayshott, this restaurant was once the butcher's shop. The wall tiles are the authentic ones, as are the ham racks, which now have creeping ivy growing about them. The style of the place is unfussy, relaxed and friendly. On a quiet day chef/patron, Eric Norrgren, both cooks and serves and chats easily with his guests. Whilst it tends to be fairly quiet for lunch, it is busy and popular in the evenings. A recent meal was enjoyed here. Starting with gravlax with a sweet mustard sauce, and blinis with lumpfish caviar, smoked salmon and sour cream the meal got off to a good start. The main courses of breast of pan-fried pheasant with a creamy, walnut sauce and the fillets of brill, with aubergine marinated in honey and vinegar were very enjoyable and carefully prepared. The lemon tart (the recipe is one of the Roux brothers') was excellent, with plenty of fresh, zesty and tangy flavour to the filling, whilst the pastry base was thin, crisp and well dusted with icing sugar. A mocca bavarois with an apricot sauce was also tasted and pronounced good. The wine list is small but nicely balanced and sensibly priced .

Headley Road
Map no: 4 SU83
Tel: 01428 605555

Cost: Alc £21.50; H/wine £7.90. Service exc
Credit cards: 1 2 3 4

Menu: A la carte

Times: Midday-Last L 2.30pm, 7pm-11pm. Closed Sun, Mon

Chef: Eric Norrgren
Proprietor: Eric Norrgren

Seats: 36
Additional: Children welcome; children's portions

Directions: From A3 turn off on to B3003 towards Grayshott. The restaurant is on the left after 0.5 miles

HEDGE END, Botleigh Grange ❀

☺ *Cheery, helpful staff enhance the pleasures of Botleigh Grange, a hotel full of charm and history set in well-tended grounds. Its reputation is further advanced by the attractive restaurant: a fine backdrop to Martin Nash's interesting and carefully prepared classic English and French cooking.*

Map no: 4 SU41
Tel: 01489 787700
Chef: Martin Nash
Proprietor: Best Western.
Manager: Philip Audrain
Seats: 90. No smoking in dining room
Times: Last L 2pm/D 10pm

Cost: Alc £22, fixed-price L £10.50/D £16.50. H/wine £8.95 ♀
Service inc. **Credit cards:** 1 2 3 4 5. **Additional:** Children welcome; children's menu/portions. ❷ dishes
Directions: On the A334, 1 mile from junc 7 of M27

HIGHCLERE, **Hollington House** ❀❀

A delightfully friendly atmosphere and a very unusual wine list are part of the eating experience at this hotel

This wonderful house dating to 1904 has the appearance of being very grand, with its fine architectural features and gardens designed by Gertrude Jekyll, but the atmosphere of the hotel is very much a relaxed and friendly one with staff and owners, Mr and Mrs Guy, welcoming guests warmly. On a recent visit, the chef was about to change. The standard of cooking is enjoyable, with offerings such as a very tasty chilled carrot and almond soup or a succulent chicken breast with a stuffing of black olives, couscous and tomato. This is a part of the hotel dear to Mr Guy's heart and he and his new chef, David Lake, are keen to improve the standards still further. For those who love and enjoy good wines, the wine list here is a true delight. Not only are there very good quality French and European wine, the list of over 200-odd Australian wines must be the finest in the country. Mr Guy is an expert and will happily advise guests on a style of wine they may care to try. He is happy to offer any wine at £30 or under by the glass so it is an ideal opportunity to try many new and exciting wines without running up a huge bill!

Directions: Take Andover road (A343) from Newbury. Follow signs for Hollington Herb Garden. Restaurant is next door

Woolton Hill
Map no: 4 SU45
Tel: 01635 255100

Cost: *Alc* £35, fixed-price lunch £13.75 (2 courses), £16.75; fixed-price dinner £25. Wine £12 ♀ Service exc
Credit cards: 1 2 3 4

Menus: *A la carte*, fixed-price lunch and dinner

Times: Last L 2pm, Last D 9.30pm

Chef: David Lake
Proprietors: Mr and Mrs John Guy

Seats: 45/50. No cigars or pipes
Additional: Children welcome; children's portions; ❂ dishes; Vegan/other diets on request

HURSTBOURNE TARRANT, **Esseborne Manor** ❀

A family-owned and managed hotel with a cosy atmosphere and attentive service. Chef Andrew Norman offers good value menus with a range of dishes including traditional favourites such as home-made sausages and mash, as well as more refined dishes.

Cost: *Alc* £26, fixed-price L/D £15.50 (2 courses), £17.50. Service exc. **Credit cards:** 1 2 3 4 5. **Additional:** Children welcome (over 12 at dinner). ❂ dishes; vegan/other diets on request
Directions: 1.5 miles North of Hurstbourne Tarrant on A343

Map no: 4 SU35
Tel: 01264 736444
Chef: Andy Norman
Proprietor: Simon Richardson
Seats: 40. No cigars or pipes
Times: Last L 2.pm/D 9.30pm

LIPHOOK, **Nippon Kan at Old Thorn** ❀

Authentic, reliable Japanese cooking with typically attentive service. Traditional dishes – tempura, sushi, sashimi, shabu shabu – also include Teppen Yaki (Japanese griddle cooking) which the chef visibly enjoys preparing. Sanma, a sword-like fish, is imported directly from Japan.

Cost: *Alc* from £25, fixed-price dinner £20. Service exc
Credit cards: 1 2 3 4 5. **Additional:** Children welcome; children's portions/ menu
Directions: Approx. 500 yards from Griggs Green exit off A3

Longmoor Road
Map no: 4 SU83
Tel: 01428 724555
Chef: Mr T Suzuki
Proprietor: London Kosaido.
Manager: G M Jones
Seats: 36
Times: Last L 2pm/D 9.30pm. Closed Mon, and day after BH Mon

LYMINGTON, **Gordleton Mill** ✱✱✱

A beautifully situated converted mill house hotel in the New Forest serving elaborately presented French cuisine

A secluded hotel within the New Forest National Park, this former mill house has a lovely riverside setting with its own mill pond, rustic bridges, formal gardens, fields and woods. There is also a walled kitchen garden where fresh herbs and vegetables are grown for the Provence Restaurant Gastronomique Française, which is the mainstay of the establishment. Chef Didier Heyl originates from Strasbourg and has brought a little bit of the Alsace to the menu, and some fine classical recipes now feature on the *carte*. Other menu options are the fixed-price three-course lunch and the Menu Gastronomique, a set six-course dinner.

This year our inspectors have sampled a range of starters, including pan-fried duck breast and smoked duck foie gras with a truffle dressing and fried polenta on a salad of mixed leaves, served with lovely home-made brioche, and a delicious combination of fresh anchovies and tomato on a potato purée flavoured with garlic and olive oil. From the fish section, monkfish 'osso buco' (cooked on the bone), set on a bed of tasty sauerkraut with smoked duck foie gras and a spicy gravy, caught our inspector's attention. Enjoyable main courses have been 'St Jacques aux girolles', pan-fried scallops with a sauce of New Forest girolles and, a highlight of one meal, 'crêpinette de chevreuille', a fillet of venison wrapped in green cabbage and served with Alsatian dumplings and a vegetable purée. Presentation can be quite elaborate,; a simple dessert of lavender parfait came as a little mushroom in a patchwork of sauces. This and a chocolate soufflé with passion fruit sauce, proved worth the wait.

The wine list is first class, with a long list of half bottles and Burgundies from some of the best growers, and the Alsace selection is good.

Silver Street, Hordle
Map no: 4 SZ39
Tel: 01590 682219

Cost: A/c £30, fixed-price lunch £15, fixed-price dinner £39. H/wine £13. Service exc
Credit cards: 1 2 3 4 5

Menus: *A la carte*, fixed-price lunch and dinner, Sun lunch

Times: Midday-Last L 2.30pm, 7pm-Last D 10pm. Closed 2 weeks Jan

Chef: Didier Heyl
Proprietor: W F Stone

Seats: 50 (30 in private dining room). No smoking in dining room
Additional: Children over 7 permitted; children's portions; ♥ dishes; Vegan/other diets on request

Directions: About 2 miles north-west of Lymington on the Lymington/New Milton Road

LYMINGTON, **Passford House** ✱

For 25 years Passford House has built a reputation on high standards of service and its tranquil forest setting. New chef Adrian Waterton's competent French cooking – a 'Soupe des Poissons' was much enjoyed – has added a further dimension to the enjoyment of a meal here.

Cost: Fixed-price L £11.95/D £21. H/wine £9.50. Service exc
Credit cards: 1 2 3. **Additional:** Children permitted (over 5 at dinner); children's portions/menu
Directions: Take Sway road of A337 (by Tollhouse Inn), bear right into Mount Pleasant Lane, hotel on right after half a mile

Mount Pleasant Lane
Map no: 4 SZ39
Tel: 01590 682398
Chef: Adrian Waterton
Proprietor: Patrick Heritage
Seats: 100. No pipes or cigars. Air conditioned
Times: Last L 2pm/D 9pm

LYMINGTON, **Stanwell House** ❀

☺ *An elegant town centre hotel with a delightful walled garden and terrace to the rear of the restaurant. A fine setting for the reliable, freshly prepared modern English cooking – the parfait of chicken liver and roast Barbary duck were much enjoyed – and a choice a good quality wines.*

Cost: *Alc* £20, fixed-price L £10.50 (2 courses), £12.50; D £13.50 (2 courses), £15.50. H/wine £9.50 ♀ Service exc. **Credit cards:** 1 2 3 4 5. **Additional:** Children welcome; children's menu/portions. ❂ dishes; Vegan on request.
Directions: In the High Street

High Street
Map no: 4 SZ39
Tel: 01590 677123
Chef: Mark Hewitt
Proprietors: Arcadian International. Manager: Andrew Woodland
Seats: 60. No-smoking area. No pipes or cigars
Times: Last L 2pm/D 9.30pm

LYMINGTON, **String of Horses** ❀

Set in four acres of mature grounds, the intimate atmosphere of Gillian Reardon's delightful small hotel is the perfect place for adults to enjoy peace and quiet. Good classic food, freshly prepared by Mrs Reardon and Spanish chef Julio Robles, is served in the cosy, beamed dining-room.

Cost: *Alc* from £20, Sun L £11.95, fixed-price D £17.95. H/wine £8.50 (litre). Service exc. **Credit cards:** 1 2 3 4 5. **Additional:** Children permitted; over 14 at dinner; ❂ dishes; other diets on request
Directions: From village centre with Post Office on your left, cross Station bridge and take 2nd left, 350yds on left

Mead End Road, Sway
Map no: 4 SZ39
Tel: 01590 682631
Chef: Julio Frias Robles
Proprietor: Gillian A Reardon
Seats: 30. No smoking
Times: Last Sun L 2pm/Last D 9pm. Lunch served only on Sun, D not served Sun. Closed Mon, Tue

LYNDHURST, **Crown Hotel** ❀

☺ *Straightforward dishes (described to us as 'eclectic European') with the emphasis on fresh local ingredients – the home-made soups are recommended – from either a daily fixed-price menu or more extensive carte. This comfortable and attractive hotel has many faithful regulars.*

Cost: *Alc* £20, fixed-price L/D £12.75 (2 courses), £16. H/wine £8.50. Service inc
Credit cards: 1 2 3 4 5. **Additional:** Children welcome; children's menu/portions. ❂ dishes; other diets on request
Directions: Follow one-way traffic system, opposite village church in High Street

High Street
Map no: 4 SU30
Tel: 01703 282922
Chef: Paul Putt
Proprietors: Best Western. Managers: Mr and Mrs A J S Green
Seats: 80. No pipes or cigars
Times: Last L 1.45pm/D 9.30pm

LYNDHURST, **Parkhill Hotel** ❀❀

Classic English and Modern British dishes in a country house restaurant overlooking the New Forest

Every child knows that Sir Walter Raleigh introduced the potato to Britain but who brought in the first pineapple? He was, apparently, a one-time resident of this former 13th-century hunting lodge rebuilt in 1740 and still decorated with stone versions of his discovery. The *carte* and fixed-price lunch and dinner menus change regularly. On a spring visit our inspector

Beaulieu Road
Map no: 4 SU30
Tel: 01703 282944

Cost: *Alc* from £26.05, fixed-price lunch £15, fixed-price dinner £23.50. H/wine £9.25 ♀ Service exc
Credit cards: 1 2 3 4

began with home-smoked sliced duck breast under a glazed puff pastry fleuron with quenelles of duck liver pâté, served with caramelised kumquats. Two roast boneless quail followed, filled with a tasty chicken mousse and chopped onion, served with a basket of straw potatoes filled with caramelised pearls of apple, in a pink peppercorn sauce. An autumn starter could have been cassolette of sautéed shellfish and baby vegetables with a main course of grilled New Forest pheasant with a vegetable trellis. There is a choice of sweets and cheeses. The wine list has many modestly priced varieties, alongside others of greater vintage. This area is busy with tourists in the summer and booking is essential, but locals enjoy Parkhill all year round.

Directions: From Lyndhurst take B3056 signposted Beaulieu. After about 1 mile turn right at Parkhill sign

Menus: *A la carte,* fixed-price lunch and dinner, Sun lunch, bar menu

Times: Midday-Last L 2pm, 7pm-Last D 9pm

Chef: Richard Turner
Proprietors: Mr and Mrs G P Topham

Seats: 120. No smoking in dining room
Additional: Children welcome; children's menu; ◐ menu; Vegan/other diets on request

MIDDLE WALLOP, Fifehead Manor ❀❀

Interesting and delicately cooked food in a beamed setting where minstrels once played

A delightful manor house with reputedly 11th-century foundations is the historic setting for some surprisingly simple but delicately executed cooking. A well-balanced selection of meat, game and market-fresh fish every day features on the fixed-price menu, and chef Mark Robertson skilfully creates a range of eclectic dishes from these ingredients. Our inspector enjoyed a delicious meal in the heavily beamed dining room where the remains of a minstrel's gallery are still in place: a starter of superb red pepper mousse with a light texture and lovely flavour was followed by breast of chicken with a smooth and tasty sauce of cream, brandy and tarragon. Bread and butter pudding was richly filling but slightly on the heavy side, and home-made chocolates were served with good fresh coffee. Other dishes offered might be 'kilaw' – a salad of marinated fish in a creamed coconut dressing with red and green peppers, and noisettes of lamb topped with a herb and olive mousse. Vegetarians are given options like casserole of black eyed beans with mushrooms. The wine list offers a decent choice.

Directions: On the A343, 5 miles south of Andover

Map no: 4 SU23
Tel: 01264 781565

Cost: Fixed-price lunch £18.50, fixed-price dinner £26. H/wine £9 ♀ Service exc
Credit cards: 1 3

Menus: Fixed-price lunch and dinner, Sunday lunch, pre-theatre, bar menu

Times: Last L 2.15pm, Last D 9.15pm. Closed 2 weeks Xmas

Chef: Mark Robertson
Proprietor: Margaret Van Veelen

Seats: 40. No smoking in dining room
Additional: Children welcome; children's menu; ◐ dishes; Vegan/other diets on request

MILFORD ON SEA, Rocher's ❀❀

Well-balanced dishes created with care and enthusiasm plus good value for money make this small French restaurant appealing

After a complete refurbishment, this popular restaurant is looking very attractive with its refreshing new decor. Chef/patron Alain Rocher continues to produce a high standard of French cooking, his menu well balanced, his dishes prepared with care and skill. Typical first courses could include 'Cocktail Imperatrice', a prawn, chicken and pineapple cocktail topped with tomato and brandy mayonnaise, and 'Mousse de

Map no: 4 SZ29
69-71 High Street
Tel: 01590 642340

Cost: Fixed-price dinner £16.50, £19.40, £22.90. Sunday lunch £13.50. H/wine from £8.50. Service exc
Credit cards: 1 2 3 4

Menus: Fixed-price dinner, Sunday lunch

saumon au beurre blanc', light, fluffy and delicately flavoured, served with shallots and vinegar, their sharpness balancing the richness of the dish. Fish is a strength of the kitchen, a recent menu featuring scallops, monkfish with red pepper sauce and salmon and creamy garlic sauce while 'Filet de flétan au curry' utilised a good, moist piece of halibut, excellently cooked, served with a lightly flavoured sauce. Lamb, guinea fowl and beef are also typical menu items. A short list of puddings has featured crème brûlée and home-made iced chocolate dessert with a vanilla sauce. The interesting French wines include some fine clarets and Burgundies plus cheaper, good-value bottles.

Directions: On the B3058, 3 miles south-west of Lymington

Times: Sunday lunch Midday-1.45pm, 7.15pm-Last dinner 9.45pm. Dinner not served Sun. Closed Mon, Tue

Chef: Alain Rocher
Proprietors: Alain and Rebecca Rocher

Seats: 30 No cigars or pipes
Additional: No children under 10 (under 13 at dinner)

MILFORD ON SEA, **South Lawn** ❀

☺ *There is continuity in the cooking at the restaurant in this former dower house with David Gates as chef. Dishes include soups, local fish specialities – 'Catch of the Day' such as sea bream poached in white wine with cream, mushrooms and tomatoes – and a dessert like Bavarian coffee cake.*

Cost: Alc £16.75, fixed-price D £16, Sun L £10.50. H/wine £7.50. Service exc **Credit cards:** 1 3
Additional: No children under 7; children's portions; ❶ dishes
Directions: On A337. Approx 3 miles from Lymington turn left (B3058 Milford-on-Sea), about 0.75 miles on right

Lymington Road
Map no: 4 SZ29
Tel: 01590 643911
Chef: David Gates
Proprietors: E D Barten
Seats: 90. No smoking in dining room
Times: Closed 20 Dec-15 Jan

NEW MILTON, **Chewton Glen** ❀❀❀

A world famous hotel, health & country club whose chef provides an eclectic choice of imaginative modern dishes

A lovely Palladian-style country house, and one of Britain's top hotels, Chewton Glen is constantly changing and improving to achieve the highest standards. In the restaurant chef Pierre Chevillard's cuisine maintains a satisfying consistency, and the seasonally changing menus include a fixed-price lunch priced for two or three courses, and a short fixed-price dinner menu in addition to the comprehensive *carte*. Guests are welcome to take one simple course from the latter, or two starters in preference to a full meal.

Chef Chevillard draws on modern and classical traditions with starters such as red pepper crostini, and layered crispy potato galette with hot foie gras and a compôte of pear. Among the main courses may be fricassée of local scallops and horn-of-plenty mushrooms dressed with Madeira jus; and medallions of New Forest venison with black pepper sauce and winter fruits. Our inspector also sampled a succulent savarin with poached fruit, and some excellent local cheese.

Vegetarian dishes are clearly marked in all the menus, and the *carte* offers three vegetarian starters and main courses, these might include a wafer thin pastry tart filled with leeks and truffles, and mille-feuille of crispy polenta layers, tomatoes and aubergine. The restaurant uses only the best quality produce and proudly acknowledges its suppliers of fish, meat (including

Chewton Farm Road
Map no: 4 SZ29
Tel: 01425 275341

Cost: Alc £45, fixed-price lunch £17.50 (2 courses), £22.50, fixed-price dinner £25, £39.50; H/wine from £12.50 ♀ Service inc
Credit cards: 1 2 3 4 5

Menus: A la carte, fixed-price lunch and dinner, Sunday lunch

Times: 12.30pm-Last L 2pm, 7.30pm-Last D 9.45pm

Chef: Pierre Chevillard
Proprietors: Martin and Brigitte Skan

Seats: 180. No smoking in dining room
Additional: Children over 7 permitted; children's portions; ❶ dishes; Vegan/other diets on request

traditional New Forest sausages), vegetables, eggs and cheeses, most of whom are local.

The list of wines and the service of them are first class. Every country and region is represented, with full pages devoted to different vintages of some classic estates. There are also fifteen grande marque champagnes.

Directions: On A35 towards Lyndhurst take right turn signed Walkford, Highcliffe and New Milton. Once through Walkford, take 2nd left, which is Chewton Farm Road, then right into hotel drive

OLD BURGHCLERE, Dew Pond ❀❀❀

Sublimely simple, perfectly executed English food in a whitewashed farmhouse setting

Our inspector described eating at the Dew Pond as a real treat. A converted whitewashed farmhouse in a pretty green landscape, the restaurant is in sparkling order, inspiring confidence, and the service is welcoming but never intrusive. Food is simple but very good, using quality ingredients prepared with care and no unnecessary fuss. There are two menus, the cheaper one (not available on Saturday night) has three balanced choices, and the more expensive one, double the number. These change every eight weeks or so. Descriptions are straightforward and only hint at the level of expertise employed and the fabulous flavours to come. Keith Marshall has a particular affinity with his sauces – it takes a great deal of time and patience to achieve this purity.

Our inspector's meal began with nutty brown home-baked rolls, followed by a crisp buttery pastry sandwich of tender red slices of squab and juicy oyster mushrooms, its accompanying sauce creamy and delicate with just a hint of Madeira. Next came Lunesdale duckling, the breast served pink and the leg crisped, with a purée of apples and a perfectly judged Calvados sauce, rich yet subtle. Best end of lamb was pronounced 'wonderful', crusted with a tarragon and parsley mustard paste, set on a concentrated jus.

The dessert, a slightly different sticky toffee pudding was light and moist and came with a brandy snap basket filled with a ball of lovely honey ice cream. The lemon tart was good too, but for those tempted by all the puddings the plated assortment of all the listed desserts (supplement £2) is recommended. Vegetarian dishes do not generally appear on the menus but can be provided on request. The whole wine list is well chosen; the house selection of 12 wines at under £15 has several good quality wines, with helpful descriptions.

Directions: Six miles south of Newbury. Take the Burghclere turn off A34 (Winchester), and follow signs for Old Burghclere

Map no: 4 SU45
Tel: 01635 27408

Cost: A/c £25, fixed-price dinner (Tue-Fri) £16.50. H/wine £8. Service exc
Credit cards: 1 3

Menus: *A la carte*, fixed-price dinner

Times: Last D10pm. Closed Sun, Mon, 1st 2 weeks Jan, 2 weeks Aug

Chef: Keith Marshall
Proprietor: Keith Marshall

Seats: 44. No smoking in dining room
Additional: ❂ menu; Vegan/other diets on request

PORTSMOUTH & SOUTHSEA,
Bistro Montparnasse ❀❀

☺ *An authentic French bistro combining various cooking styles, in a Victorian seaside resort*

You can watch the Channel ferries crossing between Portsmouth and France from the road outside this smart restaurant, and then experience a real taste of France inside. Gillian and Peter Scott have created an authentic bistro in this seaside town, with a frequently changing *carte* and a very good-value weekday fixed-price blackboard menu. There is also a daily fish dish which varies according to market yield. While Peter provides a cheerful presence amongst diners, Gillian is a force in the kitchen, and her sound cooking is always enjoyable, with some Italian and other international influences to add spice. Home-made breads and focaccia served with tapénade and hummus can whet the appetite for starters like tatin of goat's cheese, leeks and roasted red peppers, or terrine of duck marinated in port with pistachio and orange. Crisp duck breast with prune and Armagnac jus is a typical main course, or oak-smoked fillet of beef with Roquefort polenta and caramelised onions, served with a leaf salad or vegetables. Puddings range from hot treacle sponge and custard to Grand Marnier crème brûlée.

103 Palmerston Road
Southsea
Map no: 4 SU60
Tel: 01705 816754

Cost: Alc £19.50, fixed-price dinner £12.50 (weekdays only). H/wine £9.90. Service exc
Credit cards: 1 2 3 5

Menus: A la carte, fixed-price weekday dinner

Times: 7pm-Last D 10pm (later by arrangement). Closed Sun, Mon, Tue following BHs, 2 weeks Jan

Chef: Gillian Scott
Proprietor: Peter Scott

Seats: 36, 20. No cigars or pipes
Additional: Children welcome; ❤ dishes; Vegan/other diets on request

Directions: Follow signs to D-Day Museum and Southsea Castle, then take Castle Avenue to Esplanade crossroads, the restaurant is on the right

RINGWOOD, Moortown Lodge ❀❀

Delightfully uncomplicated cooking from fresh local produce

An attractive restaurant is a delightful feature of this small country style hotel on the outskirts of the town. Owner Jilly Burrows-Jones cooks with flair and imagination, and produces simple, uncomplicated dishes which attract a loyal following. Her four-course fixed-price menu, with a daily special, changes regularly, and offer great value for money, while a couple of gourmet dishes are offered at an additional price: perhaps duck on a Calvados apple purée, or pan-fried veal with a creamy orange and rum sauce. Our inspector sampled the floating cheese island – a superbly made light cheese soufflé with a lovely flavour, followed by chicken breast with lime and local mushrooms served with a light cream sauce. Pavlova with fresh fruit and cream was an unmissable dessert. Other regular dishes, all made where possible from fresh local produce, include pan-fried tenderloin of pork with a Stilton and cream sauce and escalope of turkey breast with a sausage and bacon roll and home-made cranberry orange relish. Vegetarians are catered for on request. Service by Bob Burrows-Jones is friendly.

244 Christchurch Road
Map no: 4 SU10
Tel: 01425 471404

Cost: Alc £21.95, fixed-price dinner £14.95. H/wine £7.95. Service exc
Credit cards: 1 2 3

Menus: A la carte, fixed-price dinner, gourmet dishes at weekend

Times: 7pm-Last D 8.30pm. Closed Sun, 2 weeks Jan. Lunch not served

Chef: Jilly Burrows-Jones
Proprietors: Jilly and Bob Burrows-Jones

Seats: 24. No smoking in dining room
Additional: Children welcome; ❤ dishes; Vegan/other diets by arrangement

Directions: From Ringwood centre take B3347 towards Christchurch for about 1.5 miles

RINGWOOD, **Tyrrells Ford** ❀

Ideally located for explorers of the New Forest, Dorset or Hampshire, this country house offers a selection of menus. Chef Brian Dale cooks using local fresh produce, and there is a good choice of dishes including medallions if beef fillet in a Stilton and port sauce.

Cost: Alc £25, fixed-price L £10.95 (2 courses), £12.95/D £16.95. H/wine £7.95 ♀ Service exc. **Credit cards:** 1 2 3 4 5
Additional: Children welcome at lunch; children's portions; ❂ dishes; Vegan/other diets on request
Directions: On the B3347 6 miles north of Christchurch

Avon
Map no: 4 SU10
Tel: 01425 672646
Chef: Brian Dale
Proprietor: Ivan Caplan
Seats: 50 (100 in function room)
Times: Last L 2pm/D 9.30pm

ROMSEY, **Old Manor House** ❀❀❀

Italian and regional French cooking in a beautifully appointed beamed cottage-style restaurant

More period cottage than manor house, Mauro and Esther Bregoli's Tudor restaurant is full of character, with huge fireplaces, beams, and beautifully laid tables gleaming with fine glassware and crisp linen. The Bregolis have been here for over ten years now, and Esther welcomes guests in a brisk and friendly manner. The small bar has been extended over the years, but there is only enough room for everyone in summer, when the pretty little courtyard is used. The menu offers both French and Italian dishes, the latter best reflecting Mauro Bregoli's skills and enthusiasm. He hunts, fishes, gathers local woodland produce and prepares his own salami and cured meats. The cotechino (a spicy Italian sausage) is pungently flavoured, the fettucine light and fresh, and the bresaola smoked on the premises.

Our inspectors enjoyed two very different venison dishes in the spring: roe deer marinated with garlic, olive oil and herbs and quickly grilled, which was tender and full of flavour, and a knuckle pot-roasted for some hours, the rich meat falling off the bone. Sweets can be rather creamy but are well constructed, such as a smooth panna cotta (a crème caramel without eggs), well balanced with mango slices, and a warm pear tart with excellent pastry. Pressures of business have brought a few subtle changes, some good, some less so. The prices have softened, and the two or three course fixed menu is now available at dinner as well as at lunchtime, along with the *carte*. However, the choice of breads has given way to crisp rolls, and there were no appetisers before the meal.

It is worth spending time perusing the magnificent list of wines for great vintages from the very best estates abound, including Château Yquem, Domaine de la Romanée-Conti, Grange Hermitage and some exceptional Italian wines.

Directions: Opposite the entrance to Broadlands House, which is clearly signed in the town

21 Palmerston Street
Map no: 4 SU32
Tel: 01794 517353

Cost: Alc £25, fixed-price lunch and dinner £13.50 (2 courses), £17.50. H/wine £9.50. Service exc
Credit cards: 1 2 3

Menus: *A la carte*, fixed-price lunch and dinner

Times: Midday-Last L 2pm, 7pm-Last D 9.30pm. Dinner not served Sun. Closed Mon, 1 week Xmas and New Year

Chef: Mauro Bregoli
Proprietor: Mauro Bregoli

Seats: 45. No cigars or pipes
Additional: Children welcome; ❂ dishes

ROTHERWICK, Tylney Hall ❀❀

Exceptionally warm and hospitable staff in an attractive hotel serving a good selection of enjoyable dishes

Gertrude Jekyll designed much of the beautiful grounds at this attractive and impressive listed property, and guests are encouraged to walk around the lakes, woodland and rose gardens to enjoy her creations. The charming and friendly staff are also anxious to please in the dining room where the modern Anglo-French cooking rarely fails to delight. A choice of enjoyable dishes can be selected from the short, daily-changing set menu and much longer seasonal *carte*: starters such as terrine of duck and foie gras with a fragrant apricot and sage compote, and main dishes like rosette of beef on a celeriac and potato pancake, or fillet of veal and braised sweetbreads. Fish lovers are treated to their own section of the menu. Our inspector began a recent meal with terrine of guinea fowl and rabbit studded with pistachio nuts which produced a good flavour, and then enjoyed a fresh and meaty fillet of turbot with a butter vermouth sauce topped with deep-fried leeks. A lovely selection of British cheeses was well described by knowledgeable staff, and puddings include fresh and fruity apricot mousse, and lemon tart.

Map no: 4 SU75
Tel: 01256 764881

Cost: Alc £36, fixed-price L £19/D £27. H/wine £12.60. Service inc
Credit cards: 1 2 3 4 5

Times: Last L 2pm/D 9.45pm

Chef: Stephen Hine
Proprietor: Rita Mooney

Seats: 100. No-smoking in dining room
Additional: Children welcome; children's portions. ❶ dishes; Vegan/other diets on request

Directions: From Hook take B3349, left to Rotherwick at sharp bend, left again and left in village to Newnham, 1 mile on right

SILCHESTER, Romans ❀

☺ *A privately-owned hotel where chef Shelley May produces Modern English cuisine featuring imaginative fish, meat and game dishes. Our inspector enjoyed a starter of tagliatelle with fresh pesto sauce and herbs followed by poached fillet of salmon with a chive butter sauce.*

Little London Road
Map no: 4 SU66
Tel: 01734 700421
Chef: Shelley May
Proprietors: Mr and Mrs Tuthill
Seats: 40

Cost: Fixed-price £18
Additional: Children permitted. Vegetarian dishes on request
Directions: In the centre of the village

SOUTHAMPTON, Brown's Brasserie ❀❀

The chef's commitment to good cooking ensures high quality meals at this personally run restaurant

A dedicated and serious approach combined with an individual style characterises Patricia Brown's cooking at this small restaurant situated beneath an office complex. Husband Richard ensures a welcoming atmosphere and though the attentive service can be rather slow when he is on his own, the results from the kitchen are well worth waiting for. The regular *carte* may include starters such as grilled goat's cheese, spinach soufflé and roasted loin of rabbit, the meat moist and tasty, the accompanying rabbit boudin equally flavoursome, and the dish completed by a nicely balanced and textured Dijon mustard sauce. The selection of fish can be chosen as either main course

Frobisher House, Nelson Gate, Commercial Road
Map no: 4 SU41
Tel: 01703 332615

Cost: Alc from £29, fixed-price lunch and dinner £16.50. H/wine £9.50. Service exc
Credit cards: 1 2 3 4 5

Menus: A la carte, fixed-price lunch and dinner, Sunday lunch, pre-theatre

Times: Closed 2 week Aug

dishes or as an extra course, while meat dishes could include oxtails in crépinette, and loin of lamb, served pink, tender and well seasoned. Vegetarian dishes display greater imagination than usually found, and a good range of puddings is offered. The mainly French wine list includes a house selection. At lunchtime a supplementary *carte* and set meal are also offered while in the evening the Menu surprise can be designed to customers' tastes.

Directions: In Wyndham Place, between Commercial Road and entrance to main line railway station (north side)

Chef: Patricia Brown
Proprietors: Patricia and Richard Brown

Seats: 26. No smoking in dining room
Additional: No children under 12; ❂ dishes; Vegan/other diets on request

SOUTHAMPTON, Golden Palace ❁

An unpretentious Chinese restaurant in the city centre, offering eight set menus and the usual lengthy carte. Portions are large and prices low, and recommended dishes include the big and meaty spare ribs in a sweet, syrupy sauce, and beef with charcoal black bean and green pepper sauce.

17a Above Bar Street
Map no: 4 SU41
Tel: 01703 226636
Chef: Tony Shek
Proprietor: David Lai
Seats: 80
Times: Last D 11.45pm

Costs: Fixed-price L £4.30 (£4.60 Sat). Service exc
Credit cards: 1 2 3 4
Additional: Children welcome; ❂ menu; Vegan on request
Directions: Above shops in pedestrian area near the Bar Gate

STOCKBRIDGE, Peat Spade Inn ❁❁

Freshly prepared, uncomplicated cooking of a very high standard, from a self-taught chef/patron

This delightful pub-restaurant is amazingly a one-woman effort, with owner Julie Tuckett taking the orders, cooking the food, and then serving it with only occasional help. Some delay from the kitchen is inevitable as everything is cooked to order, but the results are well worth waiting for. Local game in season and locally grown herbs feature on the blackboard menu along with daily selected produce from the market, and the self-taught chef creates delicious, uncomplicated dishes that constantly delight. At a recent meal our inspector had an excellent seafood soup served with a garlic aïoli, and moved on to sautée of kidneys with Madeira wine, a fresh and tender dish of lightly pan-fried meat topped with assorted fresh herbs. Vegetables were plain and simple with lovely flavours, and a beautifully baked gratin dauphinoise came straight out of the oven. Desserts are limited to ice creams and a daily hot traditional pudding, like sticky toffee pudding with a butterscotch sauce and crème fraîche. Other main choices might be rillettes of pork, or chargrilled breast of Barbary duck.

Directions: Longstock is one and a half miles north of Stockbridge, left turn off A3057

Longstock
Map no: 4 SU33
Tel: 01264 810612

Cost: Alc £22, fixed-price L/D £11.85 (2 courses), £16.50. H/wine £9.75 ♀ Service exc.
Credit cards: 2 4

Times: Last L 2pm/D 10pm. Dinner not served Sun. Closed Xmas

Chef: Julie Teresa Tuckett
Proprietor: Julie Teresa Tuckett

Seats: 30. No pipes
Additional: Children permitted; children's portions; ❂ dishes; Vegan dish; other diets on request

SWANWICK, Yew Tree Farm ❀

A peaceful rural setting close to the River Hamble adds to the friendly atmosphere. New owners offer lunch and dinner menus featuring seasonal fish and game dishes, plus blackboard specials. Smoked ham mousse with asparagus sauce, and grilled sturgeon are worth trying A well-chosen wine list.

Cost: Fixed-price L £14 (2 courses), £16.50/D £21 (2 courses), £23.50. H/wine from £8.95 ♀ Service exc. **Credit cards:** 1 2 3 5
Additional: Children welcome; children's portions; ❂ dishes; Vegan/other diets on request
Directions: Leave M27 at jnc 9. Follow signs for A27 (Fareham) then A27 (Southampton), then Botley signs. Restaurant is after Swanwick railway station on the right

152 Botley Road
Map no: 4 SU50
Tel: 01489 577291
Chef: Mark Anthony DeReding
Proprietors: Carolyn Jenkins, Robert Ball
Seats: 36. No smoking in dining room
Times: Last L 2.15pm/D 9.45pm. L not served Sat, D not served Sun. Closed 2 weeks middle of Aug

WARSASH, Nook and Cranny ❀❀

☺ *In a quiet hamlet, a well-established restaurant with a reliable format and a loyal following*

An 18th-century restaurant and bar in a quiet hamlet setting, which has been successfully run by husband and wife team Colin and Pamela Wood for several years now. It enjoys a very loyal local following by keeping to the same reliable format, of offering uncomplicated dishes, carefully prepared by Colin Wood. The fixed-price menu offers a choice of two or three courses, with increased prices at dinner. Recent recommendations have included a watercress soup that was full of flavour and a soufflé Suissesse, a hot twice-baked cheese soufflé coated with ground almonds. The highlight of our inspector's meal was a 'fillet de barbue et mousse de saumon aux Noilly', beautifully fresh brill steamed in fish stock and vermouth, with a mousseline of salmon and pink grapefruit and a very tasty creamed reduced cooking sauce. Among the delicious desserts were home-made nougat ice cream with crystallised fruits flavoured with Cointreau and profiteroles filled with coffee cream and served with a warm dark chocolate sauce. Some interesting house wines are also offered by the glass including an English Lamberhurst.

Directions: Turn off Warsash road into Fleet End Road, restaurant within 1 mile

Hook Lane, Hook Village
Map no: 4 SU40
Tel: 01489 584129

Cost: *Alc* £19, fixed-price lunch £11.95 (2 courses), £13.50. H/wine £7.95 ♀ Service inc
Credit cards: 1 3

Menus: *A la carte*, fixed-price lunch

Times: Midday-Last L 1.45pm, 7pm-Last D 9.30pm. Closed Sun, Mon, 25 Dec-2 Jan

Chef: Colin Wood
Proprietors: Colin and Pamela Wood

Seats: 50. No-smoking area
Additional: Children welcome; children's portions; ❂ dishes; other diets on request

WICKHAM, Old House ❀❀

Enjoyable French cooking in a delightfully relaxed setting with hospitable staff

Character, charm, and a host of original features, make this Georgian hotel a friendly place to visit. The delightful staff have a strong sense of involvement, and guests are made to feel that their presence is all-important whether they are staying for a week or just an evening. On top of all this the food is outstanding, with chef Nick Harman losing none of his magic in seven years of working here. High quality fresh produce is

The Square
Map no: 4 SU51
Tel: 01329 833049

Cost: Fixed price lunch and dinner £15, £17.50, £20, £25. H/wine £11.50. Service inc
Credit cards: 1 2 3 4

Menus: Fixed-price lunch and dinner

handled with skill and imagination by Mr Harman and his team, and the result is enjoyable French cooking at its best. Our inspector relished delicious Barbary duck rillettes cooked with white wine and green peppercorns, while grilled fillet of local fresh seabass with a sauce of olive oil mixed with tomato concasse, herbs, garlic and coriander had plenty of excellent, clear flavours. Dessert was a smooth, soft-textured chocolate marquise served with a creamy pistachio-scented sauce. A short fixed-price menu offers really good value for money, while a longer menu offers a choice of two or three courses. A nicely balanced wine list has a strong French selection and some New World wines.

Directions: In the centre of Wickham, 3 miles north of Fareham at the junction of A32 and B2177

Times: 12.30-Last L 1.30pm, Last D 9.30pm. L not served Sat and Mon. Closed Sun, BHs, 10 days Xmas, 2 weeks Aug

Chef: Nicholas Harman
Proprietors: Richard and Annie Skipworth

Seats: 35. No cigars or pipes in dining room
Additional: Children welcome; children's portions; Vegetarian dishes on request.

WINCHESTER, **Hunters** ❀❀

Close to Winchester's ancient heart, a popular restaurant with a twin in a nearby small country town

Winchester's Jewry Street is well served by restaurants, Hunters itself having two of them as neighbours. The dishes are mainly modern English with shorter selections available at lunchtime, and in the evenings when the light supper menu offers two and three-course, fixed-price options. Starters from the *carte* could include wild mushroom and soft cheese quiche, or chef's salad of fresh tuna with quails' eggs and a gazpacho purée. Most tastes should be satisfied by the broad range of main courses such as grilled sea bream with a vegetable butter sauce, or roasted wood pigeon on a bed of lentils and baby onions with a red wine sauce, or spinach and Stilton ravioli on a beef tomato with a white wine, cream and chive sauce. Desserts here are a serious matter – prune and Armagnac parfait with crème anglaise and a raspberry purée, to spotlight just one. A 'connoisseur's' list of rather special Bordeaux and Burgundies supplements well-chosen wines more suited to eating out just for the sheer pleasure of it. Similar fare is available in a sister restaurant a few miles away in Alresford.

Directions: Facing St Georges Street at the top of the town, near the library and car park

5 Jewry Street
Map no: 4 SU42
Tel: 01962 860006

Cost: *Alc* £22.50, fixed-price lunch £12, fixed-price light supper £7.95 (2 courses), £11.50. H/wine £8.95 ♀ Service exc
Credit cards: 1 2 3 4 5

Menus: *A la carte*, fixed-price lunch, fixed-price light supper, pre-theatre

Times: Midday-Last L 2.30pm, Last D 10pm. Closed Sun, 25-30 Dec

Chef: Paul Revill
Proprietor: David Birmingham

Seats: 60. No-smoking area
Additional: Children welcome; children's portions; ❀ dishes.; other diets on request

WINCHESTER, **Lainston House** ❀❀

An classical setting is the backdrop for chef Friedrich Litty's highly regarded Anglo-European cooking

An exquisite William and Mary manor house, set in 70 tranquil acres, this is a quintessential country house hotel, traditional, charming and friendly. The entrance lobby features an impressive open fire, while in the panelled bar warm appetisers are served to guests at The Avenue restaurant which takes its name from the lime avenue visible from its windows. Chef Friedrich Litty, who has established a reputation as a capable and consistently good cook in the Anglo-European tradition,

Sparsholt
Map no: 4 SU42
Tel: 01962 863588

Cost: *Alc* £36, fixed-price lunch £13.50, fixed-price dinner £34.50. H/wine £13 ♀ Servic exc
Credit cards: 1 2 3 4 5

Menus: *A la carte*, fixed-price lunch, gourmet dinner, Sun lunch, pre-theatre

offers a *carte* which could include a venison and rabbit terrine, pan-fried scallops and shellfish soup. Honest and sound main dishes like baked fillet of turbot with herb crust are enhanced by well-made sauces, in this case saffron sauce; roast breast of wood pigeon was served with a morel and brandy sauce, lamb with basil sauce. Fish is well represented with possibly Dover sole and salmon plus a market selection. A shorter *carte* and fixed price lunch menu are also offered and a well balanced wine list includes some half bottles.

Directions: Three miles from the centre of Winchester, off the A272 road to Stockbridge. Signposted

Times: 12.30-Last L 2pm, 7pm-Last D 10pm

Chef: Friedrich Litty
Proprietor: Richard Fannon

Seats: 70. No cigars or pipes
Additional: Children welcome; children's portions; ❶ dishes; vegan/other diets on request

WINCHESTER, **Old Chesil Rectory** ❀❀

Exciting and accomplished modern cooking in an ancient, atmospheric setting

Proprietors Nicholas and Christina Ruthven-Smith have preserved admirably the historic charm of this 16th-century rectory, where their restaurant is housed on two storeys, both with oak beams, wooden floors and exposed brickwork. Guests are invited to chose from the extensive blackboard menu or *carte* while enjoying an aperitif in the cosy bar. Nicholas, also chef, cooks with talent and individual style, combining classic and international recipes to create exciting and interesting dishes. Seafood is especially well represented and our inspector started with light and well-flavoured fish quenelles served with a tasty shellfish sauce. Sauté of guinea fowl and pigeon breast with wild rice pilaff and rich game jus was a successful main course. Sauces were the highlights of this meal, showing the kitchen's good approach to flavour, balance and texture. Puddings usually include a traditional glazed French apple tart or sticky toffee pudding. Chocolate St. Émilion was enjoyable, but not as the menu described. The wine list includes some very good bin ends and attentive service is supervised by Christina Ruthven-Smith.

Directions: From the centre of Winchester (King Alfred's statue) at the bottom end of The Broadway take the exit over the bridge. The restaurant is immediately in front on the mini roundabout

1 Chesil Street
Map no: 4 SU42
Tel: 01962 851555

Cost: A/c lunch £18, alc dinner £25. H/wine £8.50 ♀ Service exc
Credit cards: 1 3 5

Menus: A la carte, pre-theatre

Times: Midday-Last L 2pm, 6pm-Last D 9.30pm. Closed Sun, Mon, 2 weeks from Xmas, last 2 weeks Jun

Chef: Nicholas A Ruthven-Stuart
Proprietors: Nicholas A Ruthven-Stuart, Christina Ruthven-Stuart

Seats: 60. No-smoking area
Additional: Children welcome; children's portions. ❶ dishes; Vegan/other diets on request

WINCHESTER, **Royal** ❀

A quietly situated hotel in the heart of this historic city, where chef Sean Ennis cooks a good variety of imaginative dishes. Starters include broccoli soup, trio of fish mousses with yoghurt and perhaps to follow, roast duck with black cherry sauce or pork in an Asian crumb with mango sauce.

Cost: A/c £25; fixed-price L £12.25/D £17.50. H/wine £9.25 ♀ Service exc. **Credit cards:** 1 2 3 4 5
Additional: Children welcome; children's portions; ❶ dishes
Directions: Take one-way system through Winchester, turn right off St George's St into St Peter's St. Hotel is on the right.

Saint Peter Street
Map no: 4 SU42
Tel: 01962 840840
Proprietors: Best Western. Managers: Tony and Pamela Smith
Seats: 80. No smoking in dining room
Times: Last L 12.30pm/D 9.30pm

HAMPSHIRE – HEREFORD & WORCESTER ENGLAND

WINCHESTER, **Wykeham Arms** ❀

☺ *One of the most popular inns in the area, situated in the very heart of this historic city. Chef Vanessa Booth offers a good choice of simple but well- prepared dishes. Starters include country pork and green peppercorn pâté and as a main course there is fried calves liver served on a bed of garlic sautéed potatoes with an onion and Madeira sauce.*

Cost: *Alc* £17, fixed-price L £8. H/wine £8.45 ♀ Service inc
Credit cards: 1 2 3 5. **Additional:** Children over 14 only; ❂ dishes
Directions: Head south out of Winchester via Southgate St, take 3rd turning left (Canon Street). The pub and car park are at end on right.

73 Kingsgate Street
Map no: 4 SU42
Tel: 01962 853834
Chefs: Vanessa Booth, Belinda Watson, Nicola Jacques
Proprietors: Graeme and Anne Jameson
Seats: 75. No-smoking dining rooms
Times: Last L 2.30pm, Last D 8.45pm

HEREFORD & WORCESTER

ABBERLEY, **Elms** ❀❀

French and British food of an increasingly high standard in elegant surroundings

Beautifully maintained formal gardens line the approach to this Queen Anne mansion and its elegant Brooke Room restaurant. Michael Gaunt offers a fixed-price three-course British menu, or a more elaborate French menu and a *carte*. Michael is also an accomplished seafood cook – mussels and monkfish are amongst his specialities. The cooking here is so good that during the preparation of the guide, the hotel was awarded an additional rosette.

Additional: Children welcome; children's portions; ❂ dishes; Vegan/other diets on request
Directions: On A443 between Worcester and Tenbury Wells. Do not go into Abberley village

Map no: 3 SO76
Tel: 01299 896666

Cost: *Alc* £26.50, fixed-price L £11.95 (2 courses), £14.95; fixed-price D £16, £22. H/wine £11.50. Service exc
Credit cards: 1 2 3 4

Times: Last L 2pm/D 9.30pm

Chef: Michael Gaunt
Proprietors: Queens Moat Houses. Manager: Shaun Whitehouse

Seats: 75. No cigars or pipes in restaurant

BRIMFIELD, **Poppies** ❀❀❀

A typical village inn with a serious restaurant serving good-value modern British cooking

Poppies Restaurant is part of the Roebuck, a typical village inn with rooms. Proprietor Carole Evans is a self-taught cook who takes her place among the top British chefs with acknowledged skill, an assured touch and some very imaginative cooking. Her dedication to quality and good value is commendable. Our inspector enjoyed a three-course set lunch of baked queenie scallops topped with mushrooms and shallots served on a bed of home-made noodles and a sauce (brilliantly yellow from

The Roebuck
Map no: 3 SO56
Tel: 01584 711230

Cost: *Alc* £27, fixed-price lunch £18. Wine £12. Service inc
Credit cards: 1 2 3 5

Menus: *A la carte*, fixed-price lunch

Times: Last L 2pm, Last D 10pm. Closed Sun, Mon, Xmas,

saffron) of fish stock, Noilly Prat and crème fraîche. This was followed by steak and kidney pudding with tender meat, mushrooms and a proper suet crust. The dessert, caramel pyramid, was a spectacular creation, with clear toffee triangles surrounding delicious spiced brown bread ice cream.

The longer *carte* might include starters of lobster ravioli with lemon grass sauce, and local asparagus with a red and yellow pepper bavarois, and main courses such as fillet of Hereford beef served on a purée of walnuts and peas with pickled walnuts and shallots, or peppered Trelough duck breast with a brandy and orange sauce on a bed of puy lentils. A comprehensive dessert list ranges over chocolate pots, bread and butter pudding with apricot sauce, and a number of home-made ice creams. Alternatively, there is a good selection of British cheeses with home-made oatcakes and walnut and sultana bread. Vegetarian and other diets can be accommodated, but prior notice is preferred.

Good bar food, from cheese and pickles to cushion of Shetland salmon on a bed of hop shoots, is also available.

The wine list offers plenty of variety, together with value for money, without being too long. There is a good selection of half-bottles and some interesting bin-ends.

2 weeks Feb, 1 week Oct

Chef: Carole Evans
Proprietor: Carole Evans
Seats: 36. No-smoking area. No pipes or cigars
Additional: Children welcome; ❂ dishes; Vegan/other diets on request

Directions: 4 miles south of Ludlow in the village of Brimfield

BROADWAY, **Collin House** ❂

A delightful 16th-century Cotswold stone house in a quiet country setting 1 mile north-west of Broadway. An interesting selection of dishes is available from the carte, priced according to main course choice, or the daily specials on the blackboard, plus a good range of bar lunches and Cotswold suppers.

Cost: Fixed-price L £14.50. **Credit cards:** 1 3
Additional: No children under 7 at dinner; children's portions at lunch; ❂ dishes; Vegan/other diets on request.
Directions: North-west on A44 for 1 mile from village, turn right at Collin Lane. The restaurant 300yds on right

Collin Lane
Map no: 4 SP03
Tel: 01386 858354
Chefs: Mark Brookes, Antony Ike
Proprietor: John Mills
Seats: 24. No smoking in dining room
Times: Last L 1.30pm/D 9pm

BROADWAY, **Dormy House** ❂❂

A country house atmosphere in which to enjoy high quality Anglo-French cooking

Perched above the village of Broadway, this former 17th-century farmhouse has been transformed into a smart and popular hotel. Flagged floors, stone walls, beamed ceilings and open log fires create a country house atmosphere, where the elegant restaurant is professionally managed by Saverio Buchicchio, a past winner of the *Caterer's* Head Waiter of the Year award. The atmosphere is fairly formal, upholding the tradition that gentlemen diners wear a jacket and tie. Chef John Sanderson's more imaginative dishes display bold distinctive flavours and textures. A variety of menus is offered with separate ones for children and vegetarians. A recent meal

Willersley Hill
Map no: 4 SP03
Tel: 01386 852711

Cost: A/c from £36.50, fixed-price lunch £14 (2 courses), £16; fixed-price dinner £25.50. H/wine £9.85 Service exc
Credit cards: 1 2 3 4

Menus: A la carte, fixed-price lunch and dinner, gourmet

Times: Midday-Last L 2pm, 7.30pm-Last D 9.30pm (9pm Sun). Closed Sat L and Xmas

included a well-rounded tian of Cornish crab bound with yoghurt and a main course of a moist, pink suprême of duckling, lean and full of rich flavour, served on a bed of julienne vegetables with a soy, honey and sherry sauce, which had good depth, but avoided heaviness. Steamed sea-bass with a tarragon mousse served with pan-fried scallops was another successful dish. There is a menu of home-made puddings and a classic comprehensive wine list.

Chef: Alan Cutler
Proprietor: Mrs Ingrid Philip-Sorensen
Seats: 80. No-smoking area
Additional: No children after 7.30pm; children's portions/menu; ❶ menu; Vegan/other diets on request

Directions: At the junction of A424 and A44 follow the road towards Broadway for 3 miles. Take the 3rd right signposted Saintbury. In 1 mile turn left at the crossroads. The hotel is on the left

BROADWAY, **Hunter's Lodge** ❀

A classic style of well-prepared food is offered in this delightful vine-covered Cotswold town-house setting. Main courses may include a pair of boned quails with sage stuffing and cider, or blanquette of spring lamb with vegetable julienne.

Cost: Alc £25, fixed-price L £14 (Sat), £15 (Sun); fixed-price D £17.50. H/wine £7.70. Service exc
Credit cards: 1 2 3 4. **Additional:** No children under 8 at dinner; children's portions; ❶ dishes; Vegan/other diets on request

High Street
Map no: 4 SP03
Tel: 01386 853247
Chef: Kurt Friedli
Proprietor: Kurt Friedli
Seats: 45. No cigars or pipes
Times: Last L 1.45pm/D 9.45pm. L served Sat, Sun. D served Wed, Thu, Fri, Sat. Closed Mon, Tue, 3 weeks Feb, 3 weeks Aug

BROADWAY, **Lygon Arms** ❀❀

A good choice of modern English country cooking in a mellow Cotswold setting

The popularity of this mellow, honey-coloured Cotswold inn continues to grow, partly due to its genuine period character and partly because of the consistently good food. The style of cooking is modern English with an emphasis on country recipes and a touch of French skill, and chef Clive Howe has developed menus with a very good range of choices. Starters like baked cod on a creamed kipper sauce have been enjoyed, along with main choices like Cornish lobster and Dover sole in a saffron spiced chowder, or baked saddle of Cotswold lamb with kidney and an oatmeal and walnut crust. A disappointing inspection meal began with country rabbit and pickled celeriac that took ages to arrive, and some red and angry looking venison cutlets that were redeemed by a novel bread sauce made with gingerbread. A wartime dessert of wine and rhubarb blancmange was very enjoyable, and good strong coffee came with well-made chocolate petit fours. In addition to the *carte* there are fixed-price vegetarian, seasonal and standard three-course menus. The staff are smart and courteous, and the wine list offers a good range.

Directions: In the centre of Broadway's High Street

High Street
Map no: 4 SP03
Tel: 01386 852255

Cost: Fixed-price L £19.50. H/wine £11 ♀ Service exc
Credit cards: 1 2 3 4

Menus: *A la carte*, fixed-price, pre-theatre, bar menu

Times: Last L 2pm, Last D 9.15pm

Chef: Roger Narbett
Proprietors: The Savoy Group.
Manager: Kirk Ritchie

Seats: 100-120. No smoking in dining room requested
Additional: Children permitted; no children under 3 at dinner; children's menu/portions; ❶ menu; Vegan/other diets on request

BROMSGROVE, Grafton Manor ❀❀

☺ *Innovative cooking that covers a wide range of styles, in a friendly, hospitable hotel*

In a peaceful setting in beautiful grounds which include a lake, this country house hotel is easily accessible. The house dates from the 16th century, but was largely rebuilt two hundred years later, and 15 years ago the hospitable Morris family opened it as a hotel. Nowadays life at the manor revolves around the dining room, where the innovative cooking of chef Simon Morris knows no bounds. His various fixed-price menus feature dishes which come under the heading of 'modern British', but in reality the range is much wider. A typical meal on the three-course dinner menu might be chicken terrine encased in bacon, served with onion purée and a Dijonaise sauce, and spring lamb's liver with a tarragon and green peppercorn sauce and a chive sausage. Vegetarians have their own menu perhaps listing dishes like tomato and bergamot terrine with tomato sauce, and goat's cheese grilled on a croûton with black olives and thyme. A cafetière of quality coffee comes with home-made petit fours, and the Morrises provide a caring but unobtrusive service in and out of the dining room. There is also a well-described wine list.

Directions: South of Bromsgrove, off the B4091

Grafton Lane
Map no: 7 SO97
Tel: 01527 579007

Cost: Fixed-price L £19.95, fixed-price D £22.50 (3 courses), £31.50. H/wine £10.50. Service inc
Credit cards: 1 2 3 4 5

Menus: Fixed-price lunch and dinner, Sunday lunch

Times: Last L 1.30pm, Last D 9pm

Chef: Simon Morris
Proprietors: Stephen Morris

Seats: 45
Additional: Children welcome; children's portions; ❂ menu; other diets on request

CHADDESLEY CORBETT,
Brockencote Hall ❀❀

☺ *Exciting and innovative French cooking offered on a variety of menus*

Lovely countryside surrounds the large landscaped grounds of this impressive country house hotel which offers good old-fashioned hospitality. The pine and maple-panelled bar is the setting for pre-dinner drinks, canapés and after dinner coffee, while the two spacious rooms which comprise the restaurant are a pleasant place to enjoy the exciting French food. Chef Eric Bouchet offers a good balance of innovative dishes which appear on his three differently-priced set menus, and the French descriptions are supported by full English translations. A typical meal from the cheapest menu might be a sole and prawn tails terrine with a chilled turmeric cream, followed by a light fish medley on a provençal vegetable ragoût. For those who want to spend more, pan-fried slice of foie gras on mixed bean sprouts with a Sauterne butter sauce might precede baked fillet of sea-bass with onion purée flavoured with green olives. Puddings are standard for all menus, and the range could include meringue swans flavoured with rose water and filled with champagne ice cream, or pancake with prune cream and an Armagnac sauce.

Directions: The village is on the A448 between Kidderminster and Bromsgrove

Map no: 7 SO87
Tel: 01562 777876

Cost: Fixed-price lunch £16.50, fixed-price dinner £21.50. H/wine £12.40. Service inc

Credit cards: 1 2 3 4
Menus: Fixed-price lunch and dinner, Sunday lunch

Times: 12.30-Last L 1.30pm, 7pm-Last D 9.30pm. Closed Sat lunch

Chef: Eric Bouchet
Proprietors: Alison and Joseph Petitjean

Seats: 50. No smoking in dining room
Additional: Children welcome; children's portions

CORSE LAWN, **Corse Lawn House** ❀❀

A listed property with a restaurant and less formal bistro offering a range of French, English and vegetarian dishes

A handsome Queen Anne property, Corse Lawn House is set back from the village green behind its own ornamental duck pond. Cleverly extended and restored by the Hine family, the hotel now has a bistro in addition to the restaurant, to provide a less formal and more moderately priced alternative. Chef Baba Hine is English and her husband Denis is French, so they provide three separate menus of British, French and vegetarian fare so that guests may mix and match. In the restaurant, a choice of fixed-price or *carte* menus is available, including a separate vegetarian selection with dishes such as French onion tart with hollandaise followed by sauté of avocado and chestnuts with tarragon and noodles. The main *carte* might list starters of Mediterranean fish soup with garlic rouille, or hot crab sausage with tomato sauce and chick peas, and main courses of fillet of beef with wild mushrooms, Madeira and polenta, or shellfish platter with lobster, oyster, langoustine, prawns and cockles. Among the tempting desserts there is 'chocolate indulgence' and hot butterscotch pudding. The wine list is extensive.

Directions: 5 miles south-west of Tewkesbury on B4211 in the village centre

Map no: 3 SO83
Tel: 01452 780771

Cost: *Alc* £32.50, fixed-price lunch £15.95, fixed-price dinner £23.50. H/wine £9.50 ♀ Service inc
Credit cards: 1 2 3 4

Menus: *A la carte*, fixed-price lunch and dinner, Sunday lunch, bar menu

Times: Last L 2pm, Last D 10pm

Chef: Baba Hine
Proprietors: Denis and Giles Hine

Seats: 50
Additional: Children welcome; children's portions/menu; ❂ menu; Vegan/other diets on request

EVESHAM, **Evesham Hotel** ❀

☺ *A very pleasing hotel with some great touches of humour from the family owners, the Jenkinsons. The menu offers a variety of enjoyable international dishes with good textures and flavours and definite imagination such as a starter of curried banana soup which we are assured is very popular!*

Cost: *Alc* £19, fixed-price buffet L £6.65. H/wine £9. Service inc
Credit cards: 1 2 3 4 5. **Additional:** Children welcome; children's menu/portions; ❂ dishes; other diets on request.
Directions: Coopers Lane is off the road alongside the River Avon

Coopers Lane, off Waterside
Map no: 4 SP04
Tel: 01386 765566
Chef: Ian Mann
Proprietors: Jenkinson family
Seats: 55. Smoking not encouraged. No cigars or pipes
Times: Last L 2pm/D 9.30pm

EVESHAM, **Mill At Harvington** ❀

Good, interesting food – monkfish and mushroom layers topped with béarnaise sauce – reasonably priced quality wines and a warm atmosphere continue at the Mill at Harvington. The secluded riverside location of this splendid former malting mill is a further attraction.

Cost: *Alc* £22.50, fixed-price L £13.95, fixed-price dinner £22.50. H/wine £8.75 ♀ **Credit cards:** 1 2 3 4 5.
Additional: Children over 8 permitted; children's portions at Sun L; ❂ dishes; Vegan/other diets on request
Directions: Turn south off B439, heading away from the village, down Anchor Lane

Anchor Lane, Harvington
Map no: 4 SP04
Tel: 01386 870688
Chef: Jane Greenhalgh
Proprietors: Simon and Jane Greenhalgh
Seats: 40. No smoking in dining room
Times: Last L 1.45pm/D 9pm
Closed 24-29 Dec

EVESHAM, **Riverside** ❂

☺ *Rosemary Willmott's daily fixed-price menus offer tempting choices: an enjoyable inspection meal included home baked bread, tender calf's livers and treacle pudding. Nothing special about the wine list but attentive service and notable views in a pleasing 'restaurant with rooms' setting.*

Cost: Fixed-price L £15.95/D £21.95. Sun L £17.95. H/wine £9.95. Service inc. **Credit cards:** 1 3 5
Additional: Children welcome; children's portions; ❂ dishes/Vegan on request
Directions: Situated 2 miles from town centre on B4510 towards Offenham. At end of narrow lane marked 'The Parks'

The Parks, Offenham Road
Map no: 4 SP04
Tel: 01386 446200
Chef: Rosemary Willmott
Proprietors: Rosemary Willmott, ❂ M Willmott
Seats: 45. No smoking in dining room
Times: Last L 2pm/D 9pm. Dinner not served Sun. Closed Mon

HEREFORD, **Merton** ❂

☺ *Not the most inspiring place from the outside, the Merton is relaxed and friendly within. The cooking is British and French in style: a game terrine came with a tasty pear and orange relish, and calf's liver was done in batter. An interesting menu, though the cooking sometimes fall short of perfection.*

Cost: *Alc* from £15. H/wine £8.30 ♀ Service exc
Credit cards: 1 2 3 4. **Additional:** Children welcome; children's portions; ❂ dishes; other diets on request
Directions: In the city on the main Worcester road, near the station and opposite the cinema

28 Commercial Road
Map no: 3 SO53
Tel: 01432 265925
Chefs: Nick Brown, Scott Partridge
Proprietors: Nick Brown, Cliff Jackson
Seats: 70. No-smoking area; air conditioned
Times: Last L 2pm/D 9.45pm

LEDBURY, **Hope End** ❂❂

A restaurant where the food is in perfect harmony with the delightful surroundings

The sight of a minaret alongside Elizabeth Barrett Browning's former home, deep inside 40 acres of restored 18th-century parkland, is almost as unreal as pink elephants. Nevertheless, minaret it is and it overlooks a walled garden where an extraordinary range of fruit, vegetables and herbs is grown; for more than 16 years this garden has inspired Patricia Hegarty's cooking. Beef, lamb, fish and game are also locally produced, fresh, home-made brown bread is always served and the hotel has its own fine spring water. In such a classically English setting (Turkish-style folly apart) one would expect the food to be completely compatible – and it is. Our inspector commended his confit of Trelough duck with chicory and orange salad, enjoyed his lightly baked fillet of turbot with a bay leaf and lime sauce (but wished the portion was larger) and saved his highest praise for the smooth textured, bitter chocolate and Calvados terrine. A selection of rare English farmhouse cheeses, such as Double Berkeley and Devon Blue, is usually available. There is an impressive wine cellar.

Directions: From the centre of town, take B4214 Bromyard road, then first right after railway bridge, signed. Entrance on left

Hope End
Map no: 3 SO73
Tel: 01531 633613

Cost: Fixed-price dinner £30. H/wine from £8. No service charge
Credit cards: 1 3 5

Menus: Fixed-price dinner

Times: Last D 8.30pm. Closed mid Dec to 1st week in Feb

Chef: Patricia Hegarty
Proprietors: Patricia and John Hegarty

Seats: 24. No smoking in dining room
Additional: No children under 12. ❂ dishes

LEOMINSTER, Marsh ☺☺

☺ *Historic but homely, this country hotel offers a balanced menu of honest British dishes based on quality fresh ingredients*

A 14th-century timbered house is one of the three buildings that go to make up this homely hotel, neatly tucked away in picturesque rural surroundings just outside the town. The bright, attractive country-style dining room provides an appropriate setting in which to enjoy honest British cooking, a well balanced fixed-price menu offering imaginative dishes which make good use of quality ingredients – many of them either from local suppliers or the hotel's own kitchen garden. Freshly made canapés and good walnut and olive bread might be followed by a full-flavoured goats' cheese, leek and hazelnut soufflé, then, as a main course, saddle of local lamb stuffed with apricots and set with fennel-topped button mushrooms and a good onion sauce. Alsace rhubarb tart with a refreshing orange ripple ice cream and good coffee accompanied by home-made chocolates could bring the meal to a successful conclusion. A short wine list with a fair choice of half bottles includes New World labels as well as those from the traditional wine-growing areas. Vegetarian options are provided.

Directions: Two miles north-west of Leominster. Follow signs for Eyton and Lucton

Eyton
Map no: 3 SO45
Tel: 01568 613952

Cost: Fixed-price D £18.50. H/wine from £7.50
Credit cards: 1 2 3 4 5

Menus: Fixed-price dinner, Sunday lunch

Times: Last Sun L 2pm, Last D 9pm

Chef: Jacqueline Gilleland
Proprietors: Jacqueline and Martin Gilleland

Seats: 24. No smoking in dining room
Additional: Children permitted; ❂ dishes; other diets on request

MALVERN, Cottage in the Wood ❂

A charming hotel set high above the Malvern hills, with superb views. The carte offers a good range of modern English food which might include beef cannelloni, followed by medallions of loin of lamb, with pumpkin pie as an unusual finale. The large international wine list is informative.

Cost: Alc £25, fixed-price L £9.95. H/wine £11. Service inc
Credit cards: 1 2 3 5
Additional: Children permitted; children's portions; ❂ dishes; Vegan/other diets on request
Directions: 3 miles south of Great Malvern off A449. Signed turning virtually opposite petrol station

Holywell Road, Malvern Wells
Map no: 3 SO74
Tel: 01684 573487
Chef: Kathryn Young
Proprietors: John and Sue Pattin
Seats: 50. No smoking in dining room
Times: Last L 2pm/D 9pm

MALVERN, Holdfast Cottage ❂

☺ *A delightful little cottage hotel, dating from the 17th-century. Its three or four choice fixed-price menu offers imaginative traditional and continental cooking. A meal may well start with carrot and apple soup or avocado mousse with prawns followed by honey and mustard chicken.*

Cost: Fixed-price D £17. H/wine £8.95 ♀. **Credit cards:** 1 3
Additional: Children welcome; children's portions. ❂ dishes; other diets on request
Directions: 4 miles south-east of Malvern

Little Malvern
Map no: 3 SO74
Tel: 01684 310288
Chef: Jane Knowles
Proprietors: Mr and Mrs S Knowles
Seats: 24. No smoking in restaurant
Times: Last D 9pm

ROSS-ON-WYE, Chase ❀

Polite service and a relaxed atmosphere are the hallmarks of this impressive Regency hotel. A smart peach-and-gold dining room provides the ideal setting in which to enjoy your choice from interesting carte and fixed-price menus of honest-flavoured, first-class fare soundly based on quality ingredients.

Gloucester Road
Map no: 3 SO52
Tel: 01989 763161
Chef: Ken Tait
Proprietors: John and Ann Lewis
Seats: 70
Times: Last L 2pm/D 10pm

Cost: Alc £28, fixed-price L £12.50/D £21. H/wine £8.75. Service inc **Additional:** Children welcome; children's portions/menu; ✪ dishes; Vegan/other diets on request
Directions: From centre of town follow A40 to Gloucester. Approx 200yds on right

ROSS-ON-WYE, Pengethley Manor ❀

Dining in the grand manner poses no problem at Pengethley: it boasts a Tudor oak panelled hall and stands in 15 acres of mature grounds. The cooking is unpretentious – poached salmon tranche, skate wing in black butter – but not lacking in imagination or flavour. An unstuffy atmosphere prevails.

Map no: 3 SO52
Tel: 01989 730211
Chef: Ferdinand Van der Knaap
Proprietors: Geraldine and Patrick Wisker
Seats: 40. No smoking in dining room
Times: Last L 2pm/D 9pm

Cost: Alc £25, fixed-price L £16/D £24. H/wine £12.75 ♀ Service exc
Credit cards: 1 2 3 4 5. **Additional:** Children welcome; children's portions/menu; ✪ dishes; Vegan/other diets on request
Directions: A49 (Ross-on-Wye to Hereford road); 2nd turning on right after Peterstow Common

ROSS-ON-WYE, Peterstow ❀❀

An elegant former rectory in fine pastoral surroundings offering Modern English-based cooking

Eighteenth century rectors liked plenty of breathing space. A good thing too, now that many of their former properties, like Peterstow with 28 acres of woods and pasture, are country house restaurants. The reasonably new head chef, Andrew Thomas, is maintaining his predecessor's high standards. The centre-piece of the old house is the elegant dining room offering daily-changing, fixed-price menus. Terrines often feature as starters – chicken and raisin with glazed kumquats, perhaps – or maybe hot fish sausage with coriander dressing, or avocado salad with pine-nuts, goat's cheese and other goodies. The intermediate fish course could be steamed squid with tomato and dill sauce. Main courses normally feature salmon, lamb, chicken, duck and beef, the last on one recent inspection being a foie gras-topped fillet with a dense-flavoured vegetable faggot, all on a rich shallot and red wine sauce. A warm prune tart with almond filling was a touch heavy for our inspector, but the flavour was there all right. Wines come from all over France, a few from Italy and Spain, plus foot-in-the-door candidates from the Antipodes.

Peterstow
Map no: 3 SO52
Tel: 01989 562826

Cost: Fixed-price L £12.50, fixed-price D £24.50. H/wine £8.90. No service charge
Credit cards: 1 2 3 4

Menus: Fixed-price lunch and dinner, Sunday lunch

Times: Last L 2pm, Last D 9pm. Closed 1st 2 weeks Jan

Chef: Sacha Ferrier
Proprietors: Mike and Jeanne Denne

Seats: 46. No smoking in dining room
Additional: Children over 8 permitted; ✪ dishes; Vegan/other diets on request

Directions: On A49 in Peterstow village, next to the church

ULLINGSWICK, **The Steppes** ❀❀

Eclectic cooking in the pretty setting of a rural retreat

Tucked away in the hamlet of Ullingswick, Henry and Tricia Howland's country house hotel has a distinctive character and charm. The 17th-century building has been personally and painstakingly restored by the owners, preserving many of its quaint and original farmhouse features. The Howlands are most congenial hosts, with Tricia's cooking one of the hotel's strengths. Making good use of quality produce, she offers an eclectic *carte* and set gourmet menu, the latter featuring recent starters such as chilled cheese and cider soup, avocado pear with chilli tomato ice and smooth chicken liver mousse of a pleasingly light consistency. Noisette of lamb with paloise sauce and medallions of venison with cherry and juniper cream sauce are past main course from Tricia's repertoire. Our inspector chose beef olive, presented with a mustard sauce, the meat lean and moist, with a fresh strong texture and satisfying flavour, served with cauliflower and broccoli topped with a savoury meringue. Tempting puddings have included black treacle jelly with nuts and cream. The selection of wines is interesting.

Directions: Off the A417 Gloucester to Leominster road

Nr Hereford
Map no: 3 SO54
Tel: 01432 820424

Cost: A/c £25, fixed-price dinner £22.50. H/wine £8.95 (litre) ♀ Service inc
Credit cards: 1 2 3

Menus: A la carte, fixed-price dinner, bar menu
Times: Last D 8.30pm. Closed 2 weeks before Xmas, 2 weeks after New Year

Chef: Tricia Howland
Proprietors: Henry and Tricia Howland

Seats: 12. No smoking in dining room. Air conditioned
Additional: Children over 12 permitted; ◐ dishes; Vegan/other diets on request

VOWCHURCH, **Poston Mill** ❀❀

☺ *Good value carefully prepared modern British cooking served in a converted 16th-century mill with just six tables*

A 16th-century stone-built flour mill has been converted to create this charming little restaurant, a 15-minute drive from Hereford. There are just six tables and caring service is provided by Samantha de Feu. Dedicated chef proprietor, John Daniel, demonstrates his skill with a modern style of British cooking, offered from a fixed price three-course menu with no extras other than drinks. Starters might include pike and spinach sausages on a bed of leeks with tarragon sauce, and a pastry case filled with chicken livers cooked with Madeira and mushroom stock scented with garlic. A vegetarian dish is always featured, perhaps a strudel of filo pastry and vegetables seasoned with curry. Other main courses could be breast of pheasant set on a potato and apple cake flavoured with honey, or roast Trelough duckling coated with a lime sauce and served with walnut stuffing. To finish there is the renowned rum flavoured crème brûlée, almond flan with coconut ice cream and mango sauce, or a selection of British cheeses. A good choice of teas and coffees is available, and an international wine list.

Directions: On the B4348 between Hereford and Hay-on-Wye

Map no: 3 SO33
Tel: 01981 550151

Cost: Fixed-price lunch/dinner £20. H/wine £9.75. Service exc
Credit cards: 1 2 3

Menus: Fixed-price lunch and dinner
Times: Midday-Last L 2pm, 7pm-Last D 9pm. D not served Sun, L not served Tue. Closed Mon, 3 weeks Xmas

Chef: John F Daniels
Proprietor: John F Daniels

Seats: 30. No smoking dining room
Additional: Children welcome; children's portions; ◐ dishes; Vegan/other diets on request

WORCESTER, Brown's ❀❀

A converted corn mill provides an attractive setting for a range of English and French influenced dishes

Brown's enjoys a central location alongside the River Severn, not far from a car park. It is a converted corn mill with a light, high ceilinged interior and simply decorated brickwork as a backdrop for many prints and pictures. Above the restaurant there is a mezzanine floor where pre-dinner drinks are served, and which is also used as an overflow eating area. Fixed-price menus are offered at lunch and dinner, and though the evening menu is longer it is twice the price. Dishes might include soup of the day, fresh oak-smoked salmon, and diced kidney and bacon on mushroom tapénade with brioche toast, as starters. Vegetarian options might be tagliatelle with walnut and cream sauce, followed by feuillete of leeks and mushrooms. Other main course dishes have included sirloin of beef with a wine, tomato and herb sauce, and suprême of chicken stuffed with a crayfish mousseline and sauce. To finish there is cheese or puddings such as 'chocolate rye', a chewy chocolate cake with a dark chocolate sauce and cream, and rum-soaked brioche and butter pudding. The wine list also offers a good choice.

Directions: Left at bridge, along the riverside towards the cathedral

The Old Cornmill, South Quay
Map no: 3 SO85
Tel: 01905 26263

Cost: Fixed-price lunch £15 (Mon-Fri); fixed-price dinner £30, Sunday lunch £20. H/wine £9.90. Service inc
Credit cards: 1 2 3 4 5

Menus: Fixed-price lunch and dinner, Sunday lunch
Times: 12.30-Last L 2.45pm, 7.30pm-Last D 9.45pm. L not served Sat, D not served Sun. Closed BH Mons, 1 week Xmas

Chef: W R Tansley
Proprietors: W R and P M Tansley

Seats: 80. No-smoking area
Additional: Children over 10 permitted; ❂ dishes; Vegan/other diets on request

WORCESTER, Fownes ❀

☺ *International cuisine is served in the restaurant of this hotel, converted from a Victorian glove factory. A typical meal might begin with a home-made soup, followed by strips of pork Chinese-style with sesame and ginger sauce.*

Cost: Alc £23, fixed-price L £8.95/D £14.95. H/wine £9.50. Service inc. **Credit cards:** 1 2 3 4 5 **Additional:** Children welcome; children's portions/menu; ❂ dish; Vegan/other diets on request
Directions: 100yds from the Commandery and the Cathedral

City Walls Road
Map no: 3 SO85
Tel: 01905 613151
Chef: John Holden
Proprietor: Mr Swire
Seats: 50. No pipes
Times: Last L 2.30pm/D 9.45pm. L not served Sat

HERTFORDSHIRE

BISHOP'S STORTFORD, The Mill ❀

Lying next to the River Stort, this 19th-century converted mill enjoys a lovely setting, complemented by the mill machinery restored and turning inside. Modern English cuisine is offered on the carte with successful dishes including fresh asparagus terrine, a rendezvous of seafood and lemon and lime mousse.

Cost: Alc £27, fixed-price L £10.95/D £14.95. H/wine £10.95 ♀ Service exc. **Credit cards:** 1 2 3 5. **Additional:** Children welcome; children's portions; ❂ menu; Vegan/other diets on request
Directions: Three miles from Bishop's Stortford, just off the A1060 to Hatfield Heath

Old Mill Lane, Gaston Green, Little Hallingbury
Map no: 5 TL42
Tel: 01279 726554
Chefs: Andrew Phillips, Chris Pulfer
Proprietor: David Coopersmith
Seats: 120
Times: Last L 2pm/D 10pm. L not served Mon, D not served Sun. Closed 1 week after Xmas

BOVINGDON, The Bobsleigh Inn ☻

☺ *Built in 1898 as a country residence, this is now a privately owned and run hotel with a popular restaurant offering international cuisine with fixed-price and carte menus. Enjoyable dishes include succulent fillet steak, rack of lamb and Aylesbury duckling, with home-made desserts.*

Cost: Alc £20.50, fixed-price L £12.95/D £16.95, H/wine £9.95. Service inc
Credit cards: 1 2 3 4 5. **Additional:** Children permitted; children's portions/menu; ❷ menu; Vegan/other diets on request
Directions: On A41 (Aylesbury) past Hemel Hempstead station, turn left at Swan (B4505 to Chesham) 1.5 miles on left

Hempstead Road
Map no: 4 TL00
Tel: 01442 833276
Chef: Stuart Ambury
Proprietors: Celia Derbyshire, Arthur Rickett
Seats: 80
Times: Last L 2pm/D 9.30pm. Closed Sun, BH Mons, 26 Dec-6 Jan

ST ALBANS, Noke Thistle ☻

Sweet pepper terrine, mousseline of gingered pike, char-grilled poussin or more traditional cooking – roast of the day and steamed ginger pudding – are typical dishes at the much extended 19th century Noke Thistle Hotel. High standards are evident throughout and staff are exceptionally friendly.

Cost: Alc £25, fixed-price L £14 (2 courses), £17.70; fixed-price D £17.50 (2 courses), £21. H/wine £10.85 ♀ Service exc
Credit cards: 1 2 3 4
Additional: Children welcome; children's menu/portions; ❷ menu; Vegan/other diets on request
Directions: On A414, Watford road

Watford Road
Map no: 4 TL10
Tel: 01727 854252
Chef: Derek Abbot
Proprietors: Mount Charlotte Thistle. Manager: Gerard L Virlombier
Seats: 90. No cigars or pipes. Air conditioned
Times: Last L 2pm/D 10pm. L not served Sat

ST ALBANS, Sopwell House ☻☻

Enjoyable and creative modern cooking in a traditional country setting

The showpiece of this elegant Georgian hotel is undoubtedly the Magnolia conservatory restaurant, where modern English cooking continues to excite the palates of guests. Chef Andrew Bennett offers a creative style of cooking which combines interesting and sometimes unusual ingredients with great success, and there's an international flavour to some of the dishes. A recent inspection meal began with an enjoyable mousse of scallops wrapped in spinach with a cucumber and dill sauce, while a main course of rack of lamb with spinach and chicken mousse and a tomato and basil sauce was a tasty, hearty dish. Vegetables came in individual parcels – one of glazed baby onions and duxelles wrapped in filo pastry, the other of buttered cabbage enclosed in cabbage leaves. The chosen sweet of warm lemon tart with baked bananas in rum was disappointing, but filter coffee with freshly made petit fours compensated. Chinese duck with stir-fried vegetables, and saddle of rabbit Provencal, are two typical main choices, and vegetarians are offered dishes like roast globe artichoke with wild mushrooms in puff pastry.

Directions: On London road from St Albans follow signs to Sopwell, over mini-roundabout, hotel on left

Cottonmill Lane
Map no: 4 TL10
Tel: 01727 864477

Cost: Alc £25, fixed-price lunch £14.95 (2 courses), £18.50; fixed-price dinner £19.50. H/wine £11.50 ♀ Service exc
Credit cards: 1 2 3 4 5

Menus: *A la carte*, fixed-price lunch and dinner, Sunday lunch, bar menu

Times: Last L 2.30pm, Last D 10pm. Lunch not served Sat, D not served Sun

Chef: Andrew Bennett
Proprietor: Martyn Lawson

Seats: 90
Additional: Children welcome; children's menu; ❷ dishes; Vegan/other diets on request. Pianist

TRING, **Rose & Crown** ◉

☺ *A Tudor style building in the centre of Tring, the hotel's cuisine is traditional, but not lacking in imagination. Chef Greig Barnes offers from the carte a typical starter and main course: parcels of Stilton wrapped in bread crumbs followed by calf's liver served with a piquant jus.*

Cost: Fixed-price L £9.95/D £15.95. H/wine £7.95 ♀ Service exc
Credit cards: 1 2 3 4 5
Additional: Children welcome; children's menu/portions; ❂ dishes; Vegan/other diets on request
Directions: Centre of Tring, opposite the church

High Street
Map no: 4 SP91
Tel: 01442 824071
Chef: Greig Barnes
Proprietor: Alison Phillips
Seats: 60. No smoking in dining room
Times: Last L 2pm/D 10pm

WARE, **Hanbury Manor** ◉◉◉

Some of the best food outside London, French in style, offered from a choice of restaurants in a country house setting

A 19th-century country house in the grand style, Hanbury Manor is set in 200 acres of parkland, much of it given over to a championship golf course. Chef Rory Kennedy oversees three restaurants, each with its own distinctive style. The Zodiac, the smartest of the three, presents an extensive classic *carte*, in both French and English, and a seven-course Menu gourmand. Dishes might include a hochepot of mussels, clams and shrimp with mushrooms and garden herbs to start; foie gras terrine with braised oxtail and warm brioche from among the hors d'oeuvre, and saddle of rabbit in vine leaves with red wine and chestnuts as a main course. Portions can be on the generous side, and there is a tendency to over-elaborate and add just one more tasty morsel, but the chef's skill and the quality of the ingredients shine through.

In early summer our inspector praised a fish dish of steamed brill with spring onion bulbs, mange-touts, lemon zest and new potatoes, with a light vegetable, fish stock and cream sauce infused with ginger. A separate vegetarian menu is available on request, listing a choice of three starters and main courses, such as grilled avocado with tagliatelle and basil butter, followed perhaps by a ragout of vegetables with cabbage, walnuts and a velouté sauce scented with rosemary.

To finish orange bavarois in a brandy snap basket with a well balanced sauce suzette, and a rather disappointing under-caramelised brûlée of pecan nuts. The two other restaurants, the Conservatory with its light and healthy approach to cooking, and Vardons offering a brasserie-style selection, are less expensive but no less enjoyable.

The wine list is outstanding – long, comprehensive with plenty of first growth claret, premier cru Burgundy or Krug champagne. There are six house wines by the glass.

Directions: On the A10, just past the sign for Ware North

Thundridge
Map no: 5 TL31
Tel: 01920 487722

Cost: *Alc* from £33, fixed-price lunch £19.50, fixed-price dinner £25. H/wine £13 ♀ Service inc
Credit cards: 1 2 3 4 5

Menus: *A la carte*, fixed-price lunch and dinner, Menu du Jour, Menu Gourmand

Times: Last L 2pm, Last D 9.30pm (9.45pm Fri, Sat). Lunch not served Sat, dinner not served Sun

Chef: Rory Kennedy
Proprietors: Poles Ltd. Manager: Jean-Jaques Pergant

Seats: 40. No cigars or pipes
Additional: Children under 8 encouraged to dine in Vardon's; children's menus and portions; ❂ menu

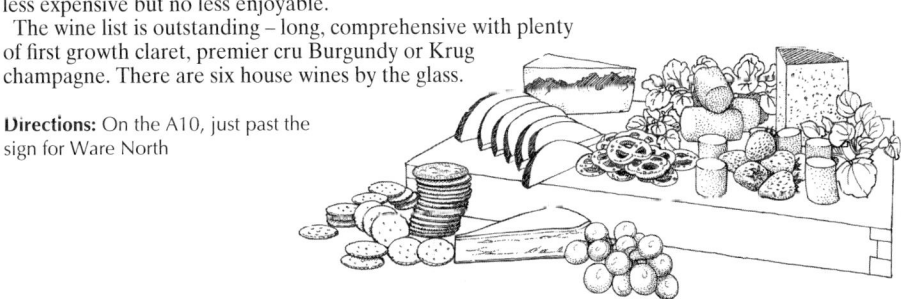

HUMBERSIDE

CLEETHORPES, **Kingsway** ❀

Four generations of the Harris family have run the Kingsway, and the restaurant has a traditional feel, serving up classic French and British cuisine. Hare and smoked bacon tart might be followed by tournedos and devilled kidneys, and then raspberry bavarois.

Cost: Alc £22, fixed-price L £8.75 (2 courses), £11.50/D£15.50. H/wine £8.75. Service exc. **Credit cards:** 1 2 3 4
Additional: Children over 5 permitted; children's portions; ♥ menu
Directions: On the sea front

Map no: 8 TA30
Chef: Ivon Trushell
Proprietor: John Harris
Seats: 80
Times: Last L 2pm/D 9pm. Closed Xmas

HULL, **Cerutti's Restaurant** ❀

A long established restaurant overlooking the estuary where chef Tim Bell creates dishes using the freshest of local produce, predominantly fish. Starters include herring and anchovy salad and as a main course you could have a seafood rendezvous served in a creamy chive sauce.

Cost: Alc £22.50; H/wine £10.80 ♀ **Credit cards:** 1 3
Additional: Children welcome; children's portions; ♥ dishes; Vegan on request
Directions: Follow signs to Victoria Pier from the town centre

10 Nelson Street
Map no: 8 TA02
Tel: 01482 28501
Chef: Tim Bell
Proprietor: A J Cerutti
Seats: 40. No-smoking area
Times: Last L 2pm/D 9.30pm L not served Sat. Closed Sun, BHs, Xmas

WILLERBY, **Willerby Manor** ❀

Young chef Adam Richardson, previously at the exceptional Winteringham Fields restaurant, brings a modern touch to classic cuisine. A combination of fresh fish was topped with a mousseline sauce; steak came with a chestnut and apricot sauce, followed by an excellent lemon tart dessert.

Cost: Alc £20, fixed-price L £12/D £14. H/wine £7.85
Additional: Children welcome: children's portions; ♥ dishes; Vegan/other diets on request. Trio Fri, Pianist Sat
Directions: Willerby is west of Hull off the A1105

Map no: 8 TA03
Chef: Adam Richardson
Proprietor: Alexandra Townend
Seats: 60
Times: Last L 2pm/D 9.30pm. L not served Sat, D not served Sun. Closed BHs

WINTERINGHAM, **Winteringham Fields** ❀❀❀

A 16th-century country house 'restaurant with rooms' serving a good choice of Swiss and French provincial cooking

It is not so many years since Germain and Annie Schwab established their restaurant in the centre of Winteringham village, a few minutes from the southern end of the Humber Bridge. It comprises a cluster of low buildings with pantile roofs in a courtyard setting with a lovely garden. The 16th-century

Map no: 8 SE92
Tel: 01724 733096

Cost: Alc £39, fixed-price lunch £15.75, fixed-price dinner £27 (3 courses), £42. H/wine £11 ♀ Service inc
Credit cards: 1 2 3

Menus: A la carte, fixed-price lunch and dinner

house retains much of its original character with exposed timbers, oak panelling and period fireplaces, and a complete refurbishment of the small dining room was being planned at the time of our visit. Restaurant manager John O'Connor and Annie Schwab oversee the dedicated staff, who, it is interesting to note, have their own dining club to visit major restaurants around Britain.

Germain Schwab is a classically trained Swiss chef who uses modern techniques to lighten dishes. In addition to the *carte* menu there is a fixed no-nonsense menu du jour, two fish market specials and a chef's menu surprise of six courses served to complete tables. (Vegetarian dishes on request.)

Our inspector had a wonderfully light lunch of incredibly good value. He was unable to choose between gratinée of smoked haddock or chilled apple and ginger soup to start, and was delighted to be served both. These were followed by cod (landed that morning at nearby Grimsby). A thick slice of the fish pan-fried on one side only to keep it as white as possible, set on fresh pasta tossed in an oil of the chef's own creation, giving it an intriguingly spicy flavour. The dish was topped off with deep-fried shreds of carrot. Summer fruits soufflé was a splendid dessert for such a modestly priced menu, small but exquisitely flavoured, accompanied by an almond tuile cup with a ball of ice cream made from the same soft fruits.

Times: Midday-Last L 1.30pm, Last D 9.30pm. Closed 2 weeks Xmas, 1st week Aug

Chef: Germain Schwab
Proprietors: Germain and Annie Schwab

Seats: 36. No smoking
Additional: Children permitted; ✿ dishes; Vegan/other diets on request

Directions: South bank of the Humber, off the A1077 in the centre of the village

ISLE OF WIGHT

SEAVIEW, **Seaview** ❀❀

☺ *A much-loved little hotel in a yachting village serving good quality food including local fish and vegetables*

A pretty seaside village frequented by the yachting fraternity is the setting for this popular hotel which attracts visitors back time after time. Owned by the friendly Nicola and Nicholas Hayward, and personally run by them in relaxed and cheerful style, the hotel's heart is the dining room where local seafood and asparagus often feature on the *carte* and daily specials menu. Chef Charles Bartlett and his enthusiastic young team use only the best quality fresh ingredients to produce famous dishes

High Street
Map no: 4 SZ69
Tel: 01983 612711

Cost: *Alc* from £18.50, Sun lunch £10.95, H/wine £7.60. No service charge
Credit cards: 1 2 3 4

Menus: *A la carte*, Sunday lunch
Times: 12.30-Last L 1.30pm, 7.30pm-Last D 9.30pm. Dinner not served Sun

like baked hot crab ramekin with cream and tarragon and a topping of cheese, or scallops and mussels sautéed in garlic and saffron. Our inspector recently praised duck liver pâté served with a tangy Cumberland sauce and pickled vegetables, and a special dish of fresh and succulent lamb cooked pink with a creamy rosemary sauce, and simply cooked vegetables of carrots, broccoli and buttered New potatoes. Desserts like bread and butter pudding with custard are unmissable, and the mango mousse on a blackberry purée was very smooth and creamy, and full of fruity flavour. There is always a vegetarian dish.

Chef: Charles Bartlett
Proprietors: N W T and N D Hayward

Seats: 30. No-smoking dining room
Additional: No children under 5 at dinner; children's portions/menu; ❂ dishes; Vegan/other diets on request.

Directions: B3330 from Ryde to Nettlestone. Turn on to B3340 to Seaview. Hotel on left near seafront

KENT

ASHFORD, **Eastwell Manor** ❂❂❂

Eastwell Park, Boughton Lees
Map no: 5 TR04
Tel: 01233 635751

Modern British cooking with distinct French influences offered from a range of menus in a lovely manor house setting

Eastwell is a magnificent manor house in a secluded setting, yet not far from the motorway and Channel Tunnel. The hotel's grounds include walled and sunken gardens, and in the public rooms there are many fine architectural features, including ornate plaster ceilings and large fireplaces.

Chef Ian Mansfield shows dedication and assured skill in his choice of menu styles. These include weekly three-course fixed-price lunch and dinner menus, a more comprehensive seasonal menu, and a set six-course speciality menu designed to be taken by the entire table. His cooking has a classical basis with a modern lightness. There are no outrageous combinations or ostentatious garnishes, yet his imagination shines through in the flavour of the ingredients.

At a spring meal our inspector enjoyed a light ravioli of crab and ginger as a starter, from a choice that included quail salad with foie gras and artichokes, and nage of scallops spiked with Thai spices. Main courses could offer roast monkfish with cumin, aubergine caviar and juice of red peppers or, our inspector's choice, a full flavoured succulent wild duck, the skin well crisped, served with leg confit, roast endive and a rich jus. The weekly menus offer a vegetarian option, such as fettucine with assorted mushrooms and tarragon, or cannelloni of artichoke, spinach and pearl barley. For pudding, our inspector plumped for a re-worked tiramisù: rich flavoured coffee mousse with a light texture, enriched with a topping of Mascarpone cheese and layered with delicate rounds of bitter chocolate

The wine list is comprehensive, with a good selection of wines from all the classic areas of France, as well as other major wine producing countries around the world.

Cost: *Alc* £36.50, fixed-price lunch £14.50, fixed-price dinner £24.50. H/wine £12.50 ♀
Service exc
Credit cards: 1 2 3 4

Menus: *A la carte*, fixed-price lunch and dinner, Sunday lunch, bar menu

Times: 12.30-Last L 2pm, 7pm-Last D 9.30pm

Chef: Ian Mansfield
Proprietor: Queens Moat Houses. Manager: Tony Shone

Seats: 80. No smoking in dining room
Additional: Children welcome; children's portions/menu; ❂ dishes; Vegan/other diets on request

Directions: From M20, junc 9 follow A251 towards Faversham. Hotel about 3 miles just before Boughton Aluph

BRANDS HATCH, **Brandshatch Place** ❀❀

Fawkham
Map no: 5 TQ56
Tel: 01474 872239

An interesting selection of modern British dishes is featured in the pleasant restaurant of this busy commercial hotel

In the Hatchwood restaurant – the main feature of a busy commercial and conference hotel with good leisure facilities – head chef Mike Rieder presents an interesting range of meals in modern British style, the quality of the tasty dishes featured on both his *carte* and daily fixed-price menus giving ample proof of the expertise and care expended in their preparation. A recent inspection meal, for example, began with a light pancake filled with delicately flavoured crab mousse and accompanied by a rich crayfish sauce; this was followed by excellent fillet of beef set on a bed of fresh leaf spinach and potato pancake and served with a morel and mushroom sauce, and for pudding a delicious, light crème brûlée. Well supervised service is both friendly and attentive, and a carefully balanced, reasonably priced wine list including some New World labels complements the meal. Vegetarians are well catered for. Extension and refurbishment of the restaurant is planned by the new owners, Arcadian Hotels, and these improvements are expected to be completed early in 1995.

Cost: Alc £32, fixed-price L £14.95/D £18.50. H/wine £10.95 ♀ Service exc
Credit cards: 1 2 3 4 5

Times: Last L 2pm/D 9.30pm. L not served Sat. Closed 27-31 Dec

Chef: Michael Rieder
Proprietor: I S Wynne

Seats: 60. No smoking in dining room
Additional: Children welcome; children's portions/menu; ❂ menu

Directions: Off the A20

CANTERBURY, **County Hotel, Sully's** ❀❀

High Street
Map no: 5 TR15
Tel: 01227 766266

A charming restaurant with friendly staff offering quality food in pleasant surroundings

Hidden away behind the mock Tudor frontage of the County Hotel is arguably Canterbury's best restaurant, Sully's, where French chef Eric Gavignet produces French and Mediterranean-inspired dishes that display his classic training at Le Gavroche. The set menu at lunch and dinner offers four choices per course; a meal may start with a feuillete of mussels with saffron sauce or smoked salmon terrine with cucumber and brill. The main course choices could include daube of beef with olives and marrow, or guinea fowl with creamed ginger sauce. The *carte* changes with the seasons and offers a very satisfying range of dishes, like our inspector's choice of sautéed scallops with bacon and a fine tomato and olive oil dressing. Boudon blanc with pistachios had a good texture and a nice Madeira sauce, but its flavours were overpowered by the accompanying braised Puy lentils. Patisserie was the strength among the puddings. Service is friendly and interested.

Cost: Alc £25, fixed-price L £12.50 (2 courses), £15/D £15.50 (2 courses), £18. H/wine £10.50
Credit cards: 1 2 3 4 5

Times: Last L 2.30pm/D 10pm

Chef: Eric Gavignet
Proprietor: J B Penturo

Seats: 60. No pipes. Air conditioned
Additional: Children welcome; children's portions; ❂ menu; Vegan/other diets on request

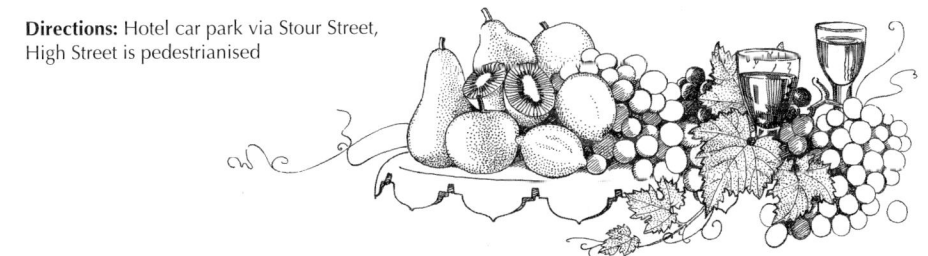

Directions: Hotel car park via Stour Street, High Street is pedestrianised

CANTERBURY, **Ristorante Tuo e Mio** ❀

☺ *A bright and modern, straightforward Italian restaurant in the city centre serving mainly traditional dishes at lunch and dinner, with daily specials extending the choice. Popular with locals and tourists.*

Cost: Alc £16, fixed-price D from £20. H/wine £7.50 ♀ Service inc. Cover charge 50p. **Credit cards:** 1 2 3 4 5
Additional: Children welcome; ◐ dishes
Directions: Opposite Kings School

16 The Borough
Map no: 5 TR15
Tel: 01227 761471
Chef: M Orietti, Y Mula
Proprietors: R P M Greggio
Seats: 70. No pipes
Times: Last L 2.30pm/D 10.45pm. Closed Mon and Tue L, last 2 weeks Feb, last 2 weeks Aug

EDENBRIDGE, **Honours Mill** ❀❀

Accomplished French cooking is presented in tasteful surroundings at this smart waterside restaurant

This former working water mill has been carefully restored, with parts of the wheel mechanism preserved on the ground floor while the smart dining area above boasts a complicated vaulted wooden ceiling. Menus are less complicated: the same short, three course fixed-price menu is offered at lunch and dinner, with half a bottle of house wine included in the price at the latter sitting. This menu changes fortnightly while the main menu (again fixed-price) changes twice yearly, and can show a disregard for the seasons. Chef Martin Radmall produces well-timed meals, and especially good, full-tasting sauces. A recent meal consisted of mussels and monkfish served in a fennel, saffron and cream nage and chicken stuffed with seasoned wild rice, which was greatly enhanced by an orange juice, veal stock and Roquefort cheese reduction. Puddings might include Sussex Pond Pudding (traditional steamed lemon suet) or iced soufflé of prunes and Armagnac. On a recent visit, the lemon cheesecake was disappointing, served after its flavour had faded. The wine list is mainly French with some New World additions.

Directions: In the centre of the High Street, opposite a car park

87 High Street
Map no: 5 TQ44
Tel: 01732 866757

Cost: Fixed-price lunch £14.50, £31.75; fixed-price dinner £25, £31.75; Sun lunch £22.50. H/wine £9.95. Service inc
Credit cards: 1 2 3

Menus: Fixed-price lunch and dinner, Sunday lunch

Times: 12.15-Last L 2pm, 7.15pm-Last D 10pm. L not served Sat, D not served Sun. Closed Mon, 2 weeks after Xmas

Chef: Martin Radmall
Proprietors: Neville, Duncan and Giles Goodhew

Seats: 38. No cigars or pipes
Additional: Children permitted at Sun lunch only

FAVERSHAM, **Read's** ❀❀❀

The best place to eat in Kent for civilised service and British cooking with a light touch and honest flavours

The exterior of this restaurant is not the most inviting, but the interior is both smart and comfortable, with a recently added lounge and dispense bar. Prices have gone up since last year so the restaurant is no longer cheap, though the fixed-price lunch offers good value for money. There is a dinner menu priced for three courses and a traditional menu, available Tuesday to Friday, lunch and dinner, comprising nibbles, a surprise appetiser, three courses including a choice of dessert or cheese, and coffee and sweetmeats.

The food is predominantly British with some French influences, and the general style reflects the personality and approach of enthusiastic chef owner David Pitchford, a modest and

Painters Forstal
Map no: 5 TR06
Tel: 01795 535344

Cost: Alc £32, fixed-price lunch £14.50, fixed-price dinner £23.50. H/wine £12 ♀ Service exc
Credit cards: 1 2 3 4 5

Menus: A la carte, fixed-price lunch and dinner

Times: Last L 2pm, Last D 10pm. Closed Sun, Mon, 2 weeks Aug

unassuming chap who is at last getting the recognition he deserves. There is nothing flashy or pretentious here, where the emphasis is on clear and honest flavours. Starters are particularly appealing, such as fresh crabmeat and salmon fish cakes set on a tomato and lemon balm sauce, twice baked cheese soufflé on a ratatouille of Provence vegetables, and fillet of pink trout grilled in an envelope of courgettes on a creamed lobster sauce.

From a choice of seven main course dishes (vegetarian by arrangement) our inspector plumped for Lunesdale duckling served on an oriental plum sauce with ginger stir-fried vegetables, a dish that reminded our inspector of how duck used to taste. Among the tempting desserts the most popular is surely 'Chocoholics Anonymous', a combination of chocolate mousse, chocolate marquise and chocolate truffle cake served with chocolate ice cream. There is a carefully chosen condensed wine list with reasonably price wines (£12-£16) or a larger list including fine claret vintages and some red Burgundy from the late '40s.

Directions: Exit 6 from M2. Turn left onto A2, then left into Brogdale Road, signposted Painters Forstal

Chef: David Pitchford
Proprietors: David and Rona Pitchford

Seats: 40
Additional: Children welcome; children's portions/menu; ♥ dishes; other diets on request

HYTHE, Hythe Imperial ❀

A turn-of-the-century sea front palace, offering a restaurant menu with seasonal influences. Chef David Lintern competently prepares the food and produces a wide variety of dishes. Choices include a starter of a half-dozen snails, and a main course of medallions of venison with a rich game sauce.

Cost: A/c from £22.25, fixed-price L £15/D £19. H/wine £9.95 ♀ Service exc. **Credit cards:** 1 2 3 4. **Additional:** children welcome; children's portions/menu; ♥ dishes; Vegan/other diets on request
Directions: In Hythe follow signs to Folkestone, turn right into Twiss Road opposite Bell Inn, go towards sea front and hotel

Princes Parade
Map no: 5 TR13
Tel: 01303 267441
Chef: David Lintern
Proprietors: Marston. Manager: David Nott
Seats: 100. No smoking in dining room. Air conditioned
Times: Last L 2pm/D 9.30pm (10pm Fri and Sat)

LITTLEBOURNE, King William IV ❀

☺ *A character country inn situated in the centre of the village where chef Nick Perkins cooks good simple and wholesome food. Our inspector recommended home-smoked salmon with scrambled egg followed by a well prepared and delicious dish of braised rabbit with leeks and ale.*

Cost: A/c £13, fixed-price L £9/D £10. H/wine £5.95. Service inc
Credit cards: 1 3. **Additional:** Children over 12 permitted; ♥ dishes; Vegan/other diets on request
Directions: In centre of village

4 High Street
Map no: 5 TR25
Tel: 01227 721244
Chef: Nick Perkins
Proprietors: Lynn and Paul Thurgate
Seats: 40
Times: Last L 2.30pm/D 9.30pm

MAIDSTONE, Tanyard ⚫

A charming, beamed country house in the peaceful Kent countryside where the restaurant offers modern English style cuisine. Dishes might include smoked fish with a cucumber and basil timbale, pan-fried monkfish with crabcakes and a shellfish sauce or lamb with mint and Madeira sauce.

Directions: From A247 turn on to B2163 for 6 miles. At The Cock pub turn left down Weirton Hill to the bottom of the hill on the left

Weirton Hill, Boughton Monchelsea
Map no: 5 TQ75
Tel: 01622 744705
Proprietor: Jan Davies

ROYAL TUNBRIDGE WELLS, Cheevers ⚫⚫

Some confident modern cooking that successfully follows a tried-and-tested formula

Tim Cheevers has developed a recipe for success at his town centre restaurant which satisfies local tastes, and he's sticking to the formula. Good seasonal ingredients are chosen according to price and availability, and converted with confidence into some pleasing modern dishes: hot calf's liver mousse with peppercorn sauce, and mussel and fennel broth are two typical starters, while main courses might be monkfish sautéed with Pernod, and roast guinea fowl with celeriac. A keenly priced lunchtime menu offers a short choice from three courses, while in the evening a similar menu is available at a fixed price. Our inspector enjoyed a leek and almond soup with a strong nutty flavour that was warm and satisfying, but detected a slightly heavy-handed interference with the sautéed noisettes of venison with apple and raisins which were rather overpowered by a red wine and stock reduction. Dessert was a simple but delicious bread and butter pudding, and some excellent home-made shortbread and flapjack biscuits came with fresh-tasting filter coffee. There's a traditional, mainly French wine list.

Directions: From the railway station, the restaurant is halfway down the High Street on the right

56 High Street
Map no: 5 TQ53
Tel: 01892 545524

Cost: *Alc* L £19, *Alc* D (Tue-Thu) £19, fixed-price D (Fri, Sat), £25. H/wine £8.75 ♀ Service exc
Credit cards: 1 2 3 5

Menus: *A la carte*, fixed-price dinner

Times: 12.30-Last L 2pm (Sat 1.45pm), 7.30pm-Last D 10.30pm. Closed Sun, Mon, 1 week Xmas

Chef: Timothy Cheevers
Proprietors: Timothy Cheevers, Martin Miles

Seats: 32. Air conditioned
Additional: Children welcome; children's portions/menu

ROYAL TUNBRIDGE WELLS, Royal Wells Inn ⚫⚫

An attractive Victorian hotel serving sound Anglo-French cooking in the modern vein

There is an undeniable air of Victorian elegance at this imposing hotel, and it comes as no surprise to learn that Queen Victoria was a frequent visitor during her childhood. The first floor Conservatory restaurant remains the epitome of gracious style, and the wide choice of food offered in these magnificent surroundings proves an attraction to hotel residents and locals alike: a speciality fish menu and good value fixed-price menu supplement the frequently changing *carte*, ably produced by Robert Sloan with some help from his brother David. Mainly modern dishes such as beef carpaccio with basil sauce and vegetarian choices like mushroom and broccoli pancakes with

Mount Ephraim
Map no: 5 TQ53
Tel: 01892 511188

Cost: *Alc* £26.25, fixed-price L £16.25/D £19.25. H/wine £9.25. Service inc

Credit cards: 1 2 3 4 5

Times: Last L 2.15pm/D 10pm Closed Sun, Mon, Good Fri, Xmas

Chef: Robert Sloan
Proprietor: David Sloan

Seats: 50

Gruyère might be served alongside the classic moules marinière and chicken in tarragon. Our inspector plumped for warm salad of crispy duck with a sweet oriental dressing, and fillets of brill on a thick beurre blanc with a julienne of leeks, and a side plate of crisp roast parsnips and fine beans. Desserts are a high point, and a memorable warm lemon pie had a lovely smooth zesty filling and a topping of lightly caramelised icing sugar.

Directions: Situated 75yds from the juction of the A21 and A264

Additional: Children welcome; children's portions; ❶ dishes; other diets on request

ROYAL TUNBRIDGE WELLS,
Thackeray's House ❀❀❀

A smart restaurant with literary associations offering a good choice of modern European/British cooking

The former home of 19th-century novelist William Makepeace Thackeray provides a smart setting for this popular restaurant, where evening booking is essential. In the elegant dining room the tables are intimately spaced and attractively laid with crisp linen and fresh flowers. A lounge is provided for aperitifs, service is pleasant, and Thackeray's books are on prominent display.

Chef patron Bruce Wass has been here nearly 10 years, and he continues to plough his own furrow with unpretentious cooking in a modern European/British style with clean, honest flavours. The menu structure is quite complicated. There is a fixed-price lunch and in the evening a mid-week menu (Tuesday, Wednesday and Thursday) priced for two or three courses, an additional, more expensive, four-course fixed-price menu, a *carte* and a separate vegetarian menu. However, this does lead to a wide choice of dishes and prices.

At a spring meal our inspectors sampled a fine salmon mousseline with mussels and a slightly disappointing crab bisque, served in a generous portion with a good crab flavour but lacking 'bisqueness'. A main course of duck confit with puy lentils and a tasty duck jus was greatly enjoyed, as was the steak au poivre from the *carte* menu, cooked exactly as ordered. Tempting desserts include some old favourites of the house such as apricot, walnut, ginger and toffee pudding, with all the ingredients present and clearly identifiable in a delightfully gooey creation, and an equally impressive chocolate Armagnac loaf with coffee sauce.

The 'House Selection' offers twenty wines from five countries at prices ranging from £11 to £20 bottle. The remainder of the list is interesting and varied and concludes with a great choice of half-bottles.

Directions: At corner of London Road/Mount Ephraim Road by Tunbridge Wells Common

85 London Road
Map no: 5 TQ53
Tel: 01892 511921

Cost: Alc £35, fixed-price lunch £14.75, fixed-price dinner (Tue-Thu) £21.50. H/wine £12.50 ♀ Service exc
Credit cards: 1 3 5

Menus: *A la carte*, fixed-price lunch and dinner, Sun lunch

Times: 12.30-Last L 2.30pm, 7pm-Last D 10pm. Dinner not served Sun. Closed Mon, 5 days at Xmas

Chef: Bruce Wass
Proprietor: Bruce Wass

Seats: 40. No pipes or cigars
Additional: Children welcome; children's portions; ❶ menu

SEVENOAKS, **Royal Oak** ❀

An attractive 17th-century property with a restaurant that offers imaginative menus. Chef James Butterfill cooks with flair, and often uses local produce. Enjoy a delicious mushroom and leek lasagne starter followed by fresh salmon with a herb crust, both from the carte.

Cost: Alc £25, fixed-price L £8.95 (2 courses), £10.95/D £10.95 (2 courses), £13.95. H/wine £8.95 ♀ Service exc
Credit cards: 1 2 3 4
Additional: Children welcome; children's portions; ❂ menu; Vegan/other diets on request
Directions: Situated at the far end of the High Street, opposite Sevenoaks school, within easy walking distance of the town centre

Upper High Street
Map no: 5 TQ55
Tel: 01732 451109
Chef: James Butterfill
Proprietors: Brook Hotels.
Manager: Lisa Butterfill
Seats: 80. No-smoking area; no cigars or pipes. Air conditioned
Times: Last L 2pm/D 10pm

SISSINGHURST, **Rankins** ❀❀

☺ *Quality food served in a small spot of isolated culinary splendour in the Kentish heartland*

An unassuming little beamed house sandwiched between the post office and the village general stores houses this restaurant which enjoys a good reputation for serious food. In an area with few quality restaurants, this early Victorian property with its large picture windows draws on a wide spread of clients. The cooking range is based on English, French and Italian recipes, and chef/patron Hugh Rankin produces his uncomplicated dishes with assurance. Different fixed-price menus with two courses are offered at dinner and Sunday lunch, and desserts are charged as extras. Typical evening meals start with curried crab pot with coriander, served with mint chutney and fried poppadom, or perhaps spinach and nutmeg terrine with prawns and chive hollandaise. Main courses might be halibut steak baked in a parcel, on creamy mashed potatoes with parsley sauce, or roast Lunesdale duck legs on red cabbage with smoked sausage and apple, and enriched cooking juices. Desserts include choices like sticky toffee pudding with toffee ice cream and pecan fudge sauce, and frozen chocolate terrine.

Directions: Located between the post office and general store in centre of village

The Street
Map no: 5 TQ73
Tel: 01580 713964

Cost: Fixed-price lunch £16.95, fixed-price dinner £18.95. H/wine £7.80. No service charge
Credit cards: 1 3

Menus: Fixed-price lunch and dinner, Sunday lunch

Times: 12.30-Last L 1.30pm (Sun), 7.30pm-Last D 9.pm (Wed-Sat). Closed Mon, Tue, BHs

Chef: Hugh Rankin
Proprietors: Hugh and Leonora Rankin

Seats: 26 **Additional:** Children permitted, over 7s at dinner; children's portions; ❂ dishes; other diets on request

ST MARGARET'S AT CLIFFE, **Walletts Court** ❀❀

☺ *A memorable dining experience in candle-lit surroundings, with interesting dishes from a competent chef*

Dining in the candle-lit restaurant at this Jacobean manor house is a truly unique experience. Dating back to the Domesday Book and restored in the early 17th century, its peaceful atmosphere is enhanced by the exposed beams and inglenook fireplaces. Chef/proprietor Christopher Oakley brings a serious dedication to the cooking, which combines the

West Cliffe
Map no: 5 TR34
Tel: 01304 852424

Cost: Fixed-price dinner £20 (Mon-Fri), £25 (Sat, Sun). H/wine £8.75. Service inc

Credit cards: 1 3

Menus: Fixed-price dinner 3 and 5 courses

French recipes of the Roux brothers with the robust dishes of medieval times. A set three-course menu operates during the week, while on Saturday there are five courses at a slightly higher price. A typical meal from the latter might begin with a Huntsman's platter of smoked duck breast and venison terrine with a compote of kumquats, followed by a second course of wild salmon with smoked haddock on a spinach mayonnaise, and then a refreshing apple sorbet. The main dish might be sautéed pork loin steak with old-fashioned mustard sauce and oyster mushrooms, or roast breast of Barbary duck served in a port wine sauce with Cumberland jelly. Enjoyable desserts have been bread and butter pudding, coffee and Belgian chocolates to follow.

Times: 7pm-Last D 9pm. Closed 4 days Xmas, 1 week late Jan
Chef: Christopher Oakley
Proprietors: Christopher and Lea Oakley and family

Seats: 50. No smoking
Additional: Children permitted; children's portions; ◐ dishes; other diets on request

Directions: Take A258 from Dover, left at roundabout then B2058 to St. Margaret's at Cliffe. The hotel is on the right

WESTERHAM, Kings Arms ❀

There is a good choice from a monthly changing fixed-price menu and seasonal carte at this attractive Georgian hotel. A simple salmon and dill terrine with horseradish mayonnaise followed by rabbit stew was quite acceptable, with a smart team providing good service.

Market Square
Map no: 5 TQ45
Tel: 01959 562990
Chef: Richard Duckworth
Proprietors: Hallett and Breen
Seats: 76. No cigars or pipes
Times: Last L 2pm/D 10pm. L not served Sat

Cost: Alc £25.50, fixed-price L £11.95 (2 courses), £15.75/D £18.50. H/wine £9.60. Service exc. **Credit cards:** 1 2 3 4
Additional: Children welcome; children's portions. ◐ dishes.
Directions: On main High Street

WHITSTABLE,
Whitstable Oyster Fisher Co ❀

☺ *This restaurant is a find for fish lovers, situated in a Victorian warehouse with lobster tanks in the basement and a dining room, oyster bar and open kitchen above. Blackboard menus change daily according to the fishermen's catch, and cooking of the fish is fresh-as-fresh and straightforward.*

Horsebridge Beach
Map no: 5 TR16
Tel: 01227 276856
Chefs: Nikki Billington, Chris Williams
Proprietors: Whitstable Oyster Fishery Co
Seats: 150
Times: Last L 2pm/D 9pm. Closed Xmas, New Year's Day

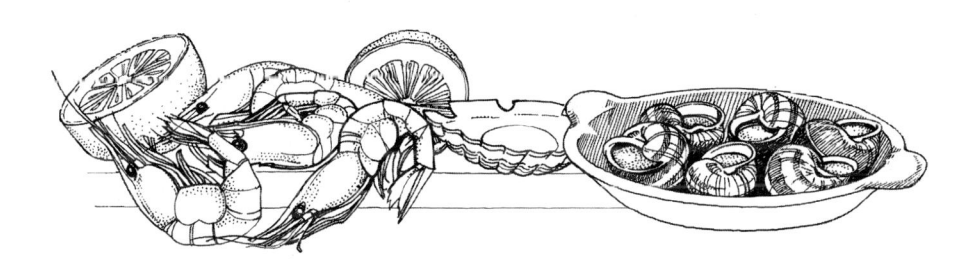

Cost: Alc £15. H/wine £9 ♀ Service exc. **Credit cards:** 1 2 3 4 5
Additional: Children welcome; children's portions; ◐ dishes; other diets on request

LANCASHIRE

BILLINGTON, **Foxfields** ❀

☺ *A modern, spacious restaurant offering a combination of classical English and French dishes. The carte offers a range of chef's specials such as deep-fried beignets of mixed English cheeses with raspberry coulis, followed by gratinated goujons of salmon with port, truffle and chive butter sauce.*

Cost: *Alc* £22, fixed-price L £11.95/D £16.95. H/wine £9.95. Service inc. **Credit cards:** 1 2 3 4. **Additional:** Children welcome; children's portions; ❂ menu; Vegan/other diets on request
Directions: Off A59 at Langho roundabout. One mile on right on road to Whalley

Whalley Road
Map no: 7 SD73
Tel: 01254 822556
Chef: Peter Desmet
Proprietors: Lyric Hotels.
Manager: Stuart Chirnside
Seats: 90. No pipes or cigars; air conditioned
Times: Last L 1.30pm/D 9.30pm

BLACKBURN, **Millstone** ❀

An attractive stone-built hotel where chef Mark Wilkin provides interesting and enjoyable meals that might include a starter of pan-fried mushrooms, duck breast, pine nuts and bacon followed by tender best end of lamb with a rustic ratatouille. Portions are hearty.

Cost: *Alc* £22, fixed-price L £11.50 (2 courses), £13.50/D £18. H/wine £10.45 ♀ Service exc. **Credit cards:** 1 2 3 4 5
Additional: Children welcome; children's portions/menu; ❂ dishes; Vegan on request
Directions: Three miles west of Blackburn at the juction of Mellor Lane and Church Lane

Church Lane, Mellor
Map no: 7 SD62
Tel: 01254 813333
Chef: Mark Wilkin
Proprietors: Shire Inns.
Manager: Anthony Whiteley
Seats: 34. No-smoking area
Times: Last L 2pm/D 9.45pm

BLACKPOOL, **September Brasserie** ❀❀

Simple cooking with outstandingly fresh flavours in a delightful first-floor restaurant

Amid all the vibrancy and noise of Blackpool, this little restaurant stands out as a delightful and refreshing oasis of good taste. It's really just a bistro above a town centre hairdressers, with bare tables at lunchtime covered with tablecloths for the more formal evenings. The honest flavours of Michael Golowicz's cooking is popular with discerning local diners, and our inspector was impressed with his skills at a recent meal. The monthly changing menu offers three or four choices including a vegetarian section, and there are blackboard specials with local fish catches, and a summer special fixed-price menu. Chopped spinach and Lancashire cheese rarebit was a decent starter with a crunchy base, followed by delicious veal sausage with puréed potato flavoured with olive oil – bangers and mash really, but several notches up from the usual version. Sweets might include baked banana in puff pastry with toffee sauce, or dark chocolate

15-17 Queen Street
Map no: 7 SD33
Tel: 01253 23282

Cost: *Alc* £21, fixed-price dinner £15.95. H/wine £8.50 ♀ Service exc
Credit cards: 1 2 3 4

Menus: *A la carte*, fixed-price dinner, pre-theatre

Times: Midday-Last L 2pm, 7pm-Last D 9.30pm. Closed Sun, Mon, 2 weeks Summer, 2 weeks Winter

Chef: Michael Golowicz
Proprietors: Michael Golowicz, P Wood

Seats: 40

marquise in between sablé biscuits, and there's a good choice of local cheeses. The kitchen is open to the restaurant, and the chef seems to enjoy being on display.

Directions: 100 yards from the promenade, opposite the cenotaph by the North Pier

Additional: Children permitted; children's portions; ❂ dishes; other diets on request

GISBURN, **Stirk House** ❂

☺ *The restaurant in this lovely 16th-century manor house is renowned for its high standard of English and French cuisine. On our visit, tournedos of beef in a truffle and forest mushroom sauce had good flavour and was tender, with contrasting colour of vegetables.*

Cost: Alc £20, fixed-price L £8.95/D £18. H/wine £9. Service inc
Credit cards: 1 2 3 4. **Additional:** Children welcome; children's portions/menu; ❂ menu; Vegan/other diets on request. Pianist
Directions: West of village on A59, Clitheroe Road

Near Clitheroe
Map no: 7 SD84
Tel: 01200 445581
Chef: Keith Blackburn
Proprietor: David Raistrick
Seats: 80. No smoking
Times: Last L 2pm/D 9.30pm

LANGHO, **Northcote Manor** ❂❂

A Victorian manor house with a friendly atmosphere provides the setting for traditional regional cooking

There is always a friendly welcome and a relaxed atmosphere at this Victorian manor house hotel, where enthusiastic young owners Craig Bancroft and Nigel Haworth have just completed their first 10 years of business. The restaurant is hung with chandeliers and furnished with well laid tables (its decor more restful than its nondescript muzak).

Nigel is a classically trained chef whose interest lies in promoting traditional regional fare. The menus are likely to feature dishes such as Pendle lamb shank, pot roasted with onions on a crisp layer of potato; Bury black pudding, and Hindle Wakes (corn fed breast of Goosnargh chicken with a plum and basil stuffing wrapped in bacon and roast gravy). There is also local game in season, fresh fish, and vegetarian alternatives on request. A good choice of dishes is available at both lunch and dinner, but the market menu of daily dishes offers particularly good value. It might include tasty pan-fried salmon fish cakes with a caper and gherkin butter sauce; tender mallard with braised lentils and potato rösti, and Swiss plum tart with delicious home-made ice cream.

Directions: From M6 take A59, follow signs for Clitheroe. At first traffic lights left on to Skipton/Clitheroe road for 8 miles. Left into Northcote Road. The hotel is on the right

Northcote Road
Map no: 7 SD73
Tel: 01254 240555

Cost: Alc £28, fixed-price lunch £14.95. H/wine £8.80 ♀ Service inc
Credit cards: 1 2 3 4 5

Menus: A la carte, fixed-price lunch

Times: Last L 1.30pm, Last D 9.pm. Closed 1, 2 Jan

Chef: Nigel Haworth
Proprietors: Nigel Haworth, Craig Bancroft

Seats: 90
Additional: Children welcome; children's portions; ❂ dishes; Vegan/other diets on request

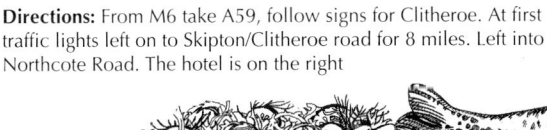

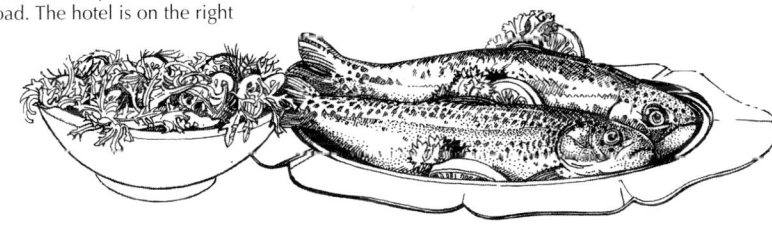

LONGRIDGE, **Heathcotes** ❀❀❀❀

Higher Road
Map no: 7 SD63
Tel: 01772 784969

Regional British cooking for the 1990s, produced by a dedicated chef in Lancashire's foremost restaurant

These delightful cottage-style premises have recently been extended to provide a comfortable lounge area to make eating at Heathcotes an even more pleasant experience. Paul Heathcote's passion for top quality produce, which he cooks with consistent flair and attention to detail, has led to a well-deserved award of a fourth rosette. Such is his concern for his ingredients that local Goosnargh duckling and corn-fed chicken, raised specially for him, make regular appearances on his menus – and now on other menus up and down the country. Duck is sometimes served as a main course on cider potatoes with a confit of parsnips and chestnuts; chicken may be lightly stuffed with truffle and thyme and served with a casserole of wild mushrooms, asparagus and juices scented with truffle oil.

A hallmark here is judicious balance of tastes, as in a main course sampled at a test meal – fillet of beef with braised oxtail and smoked bacon to produce a rich, powerfully flavoured, but not over-powering, sauce. On this occasion the starter of John Dory fillet was perfectly matched by its butter red-wine sauce and deep-fried herbs. At an earlier meal, slices of pig's trotter, stuffed with ham hock and sage, served with a pea purée tartlet, successfully brought together robust country flavours.

Nothing but praise for puddings, too, from a velvety terrine of dark and white chocolate with a dark chocolate sorbet, pistachio nuts and mint-flavoured chocolate sauce, or a first-rate banana soufflé with vanilla ice cream. Last but not least, the breads, including one studded with diced black pudding, came in for special praise.

The clearly presented wine list offers a wide and varied selection from all over the world, starting with nine house wines ranging from £14-£26. Most of the clarets and red burgundies are drawn from the good vintages of the 1980's and there are some interesting choices from Italy and Spain.

Cost: *Alc* £37, fixed-price lunch £22.50, fixed-price dinner £32. H/wine £14. Service inc
Credit cards: 1 2 3 5

Menus: *A la carte*, fixed-price lunch and dinner, Sunday lunch

Times: Last L 2pm (Fri and Sun), Last D 9.30pm (Tue-Sun). Closed Mon

Chefs: Paul Heathcote, Andrew Barnes
Proprietor: Jeremy Bewick

Seats: 55. No smoking
Additional: Children over 5 permitted. ❤ dishes; Vegan/other diets on request

Directions: Follow signpost for Jeffery Hill. Higher Road is beside White Bull pub in Longridge. Heathcotes 0.5 mile on right

POULTON-LE-FYLDE, **Mains Hall** ❀

Mains Lane
Map no: 7 SD33
Tel: 01253 885130
Chef: Mark Mench
Proprietors: Pamela and Roger Yeomans
Seats: 14, 26
Times: Last L 2pm/D 9pm

This 16th-century building stands in 4 acres of grounds and is reached down a long drive. A typical menu might include chicken liver parfait dressed on a Cumberland sauce followed by fillet of beef plain grilled with a beef jus or pepper sauce.

Cost: *Alc* £30, fixed-price L £15/D £25. H/wine £10.50. Service inc
Credit cards: 1 2 3 4. **Additional:** Children welcome; children's menu/portions. ❤ dishes; Vegan/other diets on request
Directions: On A585 between Singleton and Cleveleys

PRESTON, **Broughton Park** ⚜⚜

A welcoming country house restaurant offering imaginative and competent English/French cuisine at a reasonable price

Local residents and business people rub shoulders in the restaurant of this extended Victorian country house in its own mature grounds – all drawn there by chef Neil McKevitt's enterprising *carte* and daily-changing fixed price menus of English/French dishes. Skilfully produced and sometimes elaborately presented traditional favourites like potted game with a fruit jelly, seared raviolis of lobster and roast sirloin with red wine sauce and candied shallots are complemented by freshly cooked, imaginative vegetables and a trolley of home-made breads which includes foccaccia and curried loaf; a range of British and French cheeses (served with celery, fruit and nuts) provides a virtuous alternative to such tempting desserts as rich chocolate mousse or apple and ginger tart tatin with caramel ice cream, and a vegetarian option is always available. Staff are both welcoming and attentive, and the fairly predictable list of wines offers some by the glass as well as several half bottles. Though smoking is not permitted in the restaurant itself, it is allowed in the lounge (where a selection of Havana cigars is on sale).

Directions: Three miles north of Preston on A6

Garstang Road, Broughton
Map no: 7 SD52
Tel: 01772 864087

Chef: Neil McKevitt
Proprietor: Paul Le Roi

Times: Last L 2pm/D 9.45pm. L not served Sat

Cost: Alc £25, fixed-price L £13.25/D £18.95.
H/wine £9.95 ♀
Credit cards: 1 2 3 4.

Additional: Children welcome; children's portions; ♥ dishes; Vegan/other diets on request

RAWTENSTALL, **The Rose** ⚜

The artistically elegant Victorian decor, full of flowers, pictures and rose-patterned fabrics, makes a sumptuous and relaxed setting for accomplished new British cooking served in style. Recent dishes include boned roast quail with root vegetables and a notable bread pudding.

Costs: Alc £11, fixed-price dinner £21.50. H/wine £7.95. Service exc. **Credit cards:** 1 3. **Additional:** Children welcome; children's portions; ♥ menu; Vegan on request
Directions: Waterfoot is situated between Rawtenstall and Bacup. Turn into car park in Bacup road, opposite the Royal Hotel, the restaurant is behind the neighbourhood office, through the car park

Rose Cottage, Waterfoot
Map no: 7 SD82
Tel: 01706 215788
Chef: Lee Martin Page
Proprietors: Regina and John Arkwright
Seats: 32. No smoking in dining room
Times: Last L 2pm (4pm Sun)/D 9.30pm. D not served Sun. Closed Mon, 4th week July, 1 week after New Year

SLAIDBURN, **Parrock Head** ⚜

☺ *Worth a journey before you even start eating: the restaurant is part of a farmhouse hotel in gorgeous scenery. Chef/patronne Vicky Umbers provides food to match with dishes such as 'Filo pastry purses of wild and button mushrooms set on a pink peppercorn and chive butter sauce'*

Cost: Fixed-price L £12.50/D £18. H/wine £7.50 ♀ Service exc
Credit cards: 1 2 3 4. **Additional:** Children welcome; children's portions/menu; ♥ dishes; Vegan/other diets on request
Directions: Take B6478 from Clitheroe to Slaidburn. Parrock Head is one mile north-west of village on the left

Near Clitheroe
Map no: 7 SD75
Tel: 01200 446614
Chefs: Lorraine Chapman, Vicki Umbers
Proprietor: R and V. Umbers
Seats: 36. No smoking in dining room
Times: Last D 9pm

THORNTON, **Victorian House** ☺☺

☺ *A wide choice of dishes in the French style*

Map no: 7 SD34
Tel: 01253 860619
Chef: Didier Guerin
Proprietors: Mr and Mrs D Guerin
Seats: 60
Times: Last L 1.30pm/D 9.30pm. Closed Sun, first 2 weeks Feb

A monthly changing fixed-price menu offers a generous choice of French dishes. Our inspector enjoyed his delicious-sounding starter of filo pastry parcels filled with pieces of fresh salmon and shredded courgette, accompanied by chopped tomatoes and a lemon butter sauce. The cooking here is so good that duing the preparation of this guide the Victorian House was awarded a second rosette.

Cost: Fixed-price L £10/D £21. H/wine £9.50 ♀ Service inc
Credit cards: 1 3 5. **Additional:** Children permitted; ◐ dishes; Vegan/other diets on request
Directions: On A585

WRIGHTINGTON, **High Moor** ☺

High Moor Lane
Map no: 7 SD51
Tel: 01257 252364
Chef: Darren Wynn
Proprietor: John Nelson
Seats: 90
Times: Last D 10pm/Sun L 2pm

Two, three and four-course fixed-price menus are reasonable value in this isolated restaurant looking down on the lights of Wigan and Skemersdale at night. On this occasion a puff pastry case of smoked haddock with cucumber butter sauce was enjoyable. Cooking is modern English.

Cost: Alc £23.50, fixed-price D £18.50 (2 courses), £28. H/wine £8.90. **Credit cards:** 1 2 3 4 5
Additional: Children welcome; children's portions; ◐ dishes; Vegan/other diets on request
Directions: From M6 Junction 27 take B5239

LEICESTERSHIRE

CASTLE DONINGTON,

Donington Thistle ☺

East Midlands Airport
Map no: 8 SK42
Tel: 01332 850700
Chef: Philip O'Hagan
Proprietors: Mount Charlotte Thistle. Manager: David Friesner
Seats: 85. No-smoking area
Times: Last L 2pm/D 10pm. L not served Sat

An international style of cooking affords a varied choice of dish to the diner with main courses like roast leg of lamb with rosemary and an apple and berry confit, or breast of chicken with white crab and pink peppercorn butter on a bed of leeks.

Cost: Alc £26, fixed-price L £14/D £18. H/wine £10.25 ♀ Service exc. **Credit cards:** 1 2 3 4.**Additional:** Children welcome; children's portions/menu; ◐ menu; Vegan/other diets on request
Directions: At East Midlands International Airport, 2 miles from junc 24 of M1 and 1 mile from M1/A42 interchange

HINCKLEY, **Sketchley Grange** ❀

The popular Willow Restaurant overlooking the garden in this pleasant building offers a good-value business lunch and a carte and fixed-price menu. Colin Bliss produces some interesting dishes but excessive use of cream sometimes masks the true flavour. Staff are very attentive.

Sketchley Lane, Burbage
Map no: 4 SP49
Tel: 01455 251133
Chef: Colin Bliss
Proprietor: Nigel I Downes
Seats: 90. Air conditioned
Times: Last L 1.45pm/D 9.45pm

Cost: Alc from £20, fixed-price D £16.95, Sun L £10.75. H/wine £8.50. Service exc **Credit cards:** 1 2 3 4 **Additional:** Children's menu/portions; high chairs available Children welcome; children's portions; ❂ menu; Vegan/other diets on request. Pianist
Directions: From M69 junc 1 take B4109, at mini roundabout turn left, then first right

LEICESTER, **Belmont House** ❀

☺ Close to the city centre in a Victorian conservation area, Belmont House offers the Cherry restaurant for formal dining and a brasserie for those after a more casual meal. The fixed-price lunch and the carte in the Cherry offer so many appealing dishes that return visits are likely.

De Montfort Street
Map no: 4 SK50
Tel: 01533 544773
Chef: Mark Crockett
Proprietor: Best Western.
Manager: James Bowie
Seats: 60
Times: Last L 2pm/D 10pm. L not served Sat. Closed 25-28 Dec

Cost: Alc from £16.50, fixed-price L £11.95/D £16.50. H/wine £8.50 ♀ Service exc. **Credit cards:** 1 2 3 4 **Additional:** Children welcome; children's portions; ❂ dishes; Vegan on request
Directions: Head for railway station, first right off A6 heading south

MARKET HARBOROUGH, **Three Swans** ❀

☺ The restaurant is one of the attractions of this old coaching inn. With its formal, attentive service and imaginative food by Richard Payne, the restaurant is busy. Our inspector enjoyed celery and chestnut soup, Chicken Magdalene that was moist and tasty, and a very good crème brûlée.

21 High Street
Map no: 4 SP78
Tel: 01858 466644
Chef: Richard Payne
Proprietor: Best Western.
Manager: Josef Reissmann
Seats: 85. Air conditioned
Times: Last L 2.15pm/D 10pm. D not served Sun

Cost: Fixed-price L £11.95/D £17.95. H/wine £9.45 ♀ Service exc **Credit cards:** 1 2 3 4 5
Additional: Children welcome; children's portions; ❂ menu; Vegan/other diets on request

MELTON MOWBRAY, **Stapleford Park** ❀

A stately home in 500 acres, complete with lake, stables, church and gardens laid out by Capability Brown. The hotel offers a traditional English carte with some old-fashioned American and Mediterranean additions. The wine list has been arranged by grape variety.

Map no: 8 SK71
Tel: 01572 787522
Chef: Malcolm Jessop
Manager: Mark Scott
Seats: 60
Times: Last L 2.30pm/D 9.30pm (weekends 10.30

Cost: Alc L£20/D £35. H/wine £12.5. **Credit cards:** 1 2 3 4
Additional: ❂ menu
Directions: Three miles east of Melton Mowbray on the B676

NORMANTON, **Normanton Park**

☺ *On the shores of Rutland Water, the Orangery restaurant in this converted coachhouse is fashioned with greenery and fruity Christopher Wray light fittings. The food is served in generous portions, tasty and wholesome with home-baked bread and ice creams.*

Cost: *Alc* £18, Sun L £13.95. H/wine £7.95 ♀ **Credit cards:** 1 3 5
Additional: Children welcome before 8.30pm; children's portions/menu; ❂ menu; Vegan/other diets on request
Directions: South shore of Rutland Water near Edith Weston

Rutland Water, South Shore
Map no: 4 SK90
Tel: 01780 720315
Chef: Paul Huxtable
Proprietors: Daniel Hales, Robert Reid
Seats: 80. No smoking
Times: Last L 2.30pm/D 9.45pm

OAKHAM, **Barnsdale Lodge**

☺ *There are three separate rooms in which you can choose to eat your meal, each different yet all Edwardian. The carte is mostly interesting farmhouse fare with a few international dishes as well, all carefully prepared by chef Robert Knowles.*

Cost: *Alc* £18, Sun L £13.95. H/wine £7.95 ♀ **Credit cards:** 1 3 5
Additional: Children welcome; children's portions/menu; ❂ dishes; Vegan/other diets on request
Directions: On the A606 (Oakham-Stamford) 2 miles outside Oakham

The Avenue, Rutland Water
Map no: 8 SK80
Tel: 01572 724678
Chef: Robert Knowles
Proprietor: Robert Reid
Seats: 30
Times: Last L 2pm/D 9.45pm

OAKHAM, **Hambleton Hall** ✽✽✽✽

Polished modern British cooking in a fine country-house retreat on Rutland Water where booking is essential

Our inspectors are full of praise for Aaron Patterson's accomplished cooking which achieves levels of complexity that stand comparison with London's best restaurants and have this year earned Hambleton Hall its coveted fourth rosette. The seasonal *cartes* are supplemented by a set, fixed-price menu of three courses and coffee and a 'gourmet corner'.

Good hot and cold canapés in the bar put our inspector in the mood for a delightful pre-lunch appetiser of jellied langoustines with nicely dressed ratatouille. An excellent braised fillet of brill with a poached courgette flower and shellfish, garnished with asparagus, made a beautifully balanced starter to lead into his main course, in which a flavoursome sauce enriched with aged sherry and morels accompanied a moist, crisply cooked local chicken. The meal finished with a refreshing vanilla-flavoured fromage frais with a good berry compôte.

Earlier in the year, on another visit, a 'palate pleaser' of lobster and ginger bisque drew high praise. Morels (a favourite ingredient at Hambleton) and baby asparagus accompanied a starter of light, fine foie gras mousse with a cheese enhancer served on a full-tasting liver sauce. On this occasion the main course was a wonderful, elaborate creation in which flavours were expertly balanced – saddle of rabbit topped with forcemeat mousse, enclosed in a lattice pastry basket, and served on a bed of cabbage.

An extensive and carefully chosen wine list begins with about 30 wines recommended as 'drinking well now', arranged in

Hambleton
Map no: 8 SK80
Tel: 01572 756991

Cost: *Alc* £50, fixed-price lunch/dinner £29.50. H/wine £16 ♀ Service inc
Credit cards: 1 2 3 5

Menus: *A la carte*, fixed-price lunch/dinner, Sunday lunch, snack menu

Times: Last L 2pm, Last D 9.30pm

Chef: Aaron Patterson
Proprietors: Tim and Stefa Hart

Seats: 60. No cigars or pipes
Additional: Children welcome; children's portions; ❂ menu; Vegan/other diets on request

three price bands: under £16; from £17.50 to £25; over £25 (expensive but worth it). The remainder of the list concentrates on the traditional areas of France, though there are some good bottles from California, South Africa and Australia.

Directions: From A1 take A606 Oakham road. One mile before Oakham turn left to Hambleton village. Restaurant is on the right off the main street

OAKHAM, **Whipper-in Hotel** ✿

Carl Bontoft continues to produce simple and well prepared meals in this 17th-century hotel which is recognised as being one of the best eating places in the area. At lunchtime the chicken pie with a light puff pastry lid went down easily, followed by apple tartlet.

Market Place
Map no: 8 SK80
Tel: 01572 756971
Chef: Carl Bontoft
Proprietor: David Tofiluk
Seats: 50. No-smoking area
Times: Last L 2.30pm/D 9.30pm

Cost: Alc £22, fixed-price lunch £6.95 (2 courses), £9.95, fixed-price dinner £12.95. H/wine £8.95 ♀ Service exc
Credit cards: 1 2 3. **Additional:** Children welcome; children's portions/menu; ✿ dishes
Directions: On the right in the Market Place in town centre

QUORN, **Quorn Grange** ✿

☺ Imaginative, robust English cooking is served in the restaurant of this lovely country-house style hotel. The carte offers dishes such as confit of duckling with port and orange as a starter, followed by a main course of pot roasted pigeon with smoked bacon rösti and toasted pine kernels.

88 Wood Lane
Map no: 8 SK51
Tel: 01509 412167
Chef: Gordon Lang
Proprietor: E Jeremy Lord
Seats: 45
Times: Last L 2pm/D 9.30pm. L not served Sat

Cost: Alc £24.50, fixed-price L £9.95/D£15.95. H/wine £9 ♀ Service Inc. **Credit cards.** 1 2 3 4 5
Additional: Children welcome; children's portions; ✿ menu; Vegan/other diets on request
Directions: From Loughborough take 1st right in Quorn after police station, into Wood Lane

STRETTON, **Ram Jam Inn** ✿

☺ An unusual inn with a good selection of bar food and a short carte in the restaurant, with daily blackboard specials catering for travellers. From Algerian marinated chicken breast chargrilled with tabouleh to steak and kidney pudding to ground rump steak burger, there's something for everyone.

Great North Road
Map no: 8 SK91
Tel: 01780 410776
Chef: Gregory Power
Proprietor: Tim Hart
Seats: 29. No-smoking area
Times: Last D 10pm. Closed Xmas Day

Cost: Alc £16. H/wine £8. Service exc
Credit cards: 1 2 3 4 5. **Additional:** children welcome; children's portions/menu; ✿ dishes; other diets on request
Directions: On northbound carriage of A1. Well signposted off B668, through Texaco Service Station

UPPINGHAM, Lake Isle ❀

High Street East
Map no: 4 SP89
Tel: 01572 822951

Proprietor David Whitfield does much of the cooking, producing a short, choice menu of mainly French dishes from high quality produce. A savoury brioche might be followed by ragout of fish, with interestingly prepared vegetables and a dessert of chocolate and walnut tart topped by spun sugar.

Chefs: David Whitfield, Beverly Price
Proprietors: David and Claire Whitfield, Nicola Goden
Seats: 40. No pipes or cigars
Times: Last L 2pm/D 10.30pm. L not served Mon, D not served Sun

Cost: Fixed-price L £10.50 (2 courses), £13.50/D £21 (2 courses), £24. H/wine £8.75 ♀ Service exc. **Credit cards:** 1 2 3 4
Additional: Children permitted; children's portions; ✿ menu; Vegan/other diets on request
Directions: Proprietors suggest ask when booking

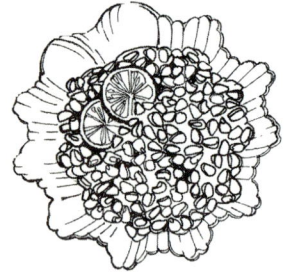

LINCOLNSHIRE

BECKINGHAM, Black Swan ❀❀

Hillside
Map no: 8 SK85
Tel: 01636 626474

☺ *A cosy inn with an attractive riverside location, this restaurant offers two fixed-price menus of imaginative dishes*

Chef Anton Indans has always maintained sound cooking practices at this small riverside inn, and though the *carte* has disappeared a range of imaginative dishes is offered from two differently priced but interchangeable set menus. Anton has taken up the position of executive development chef with a major food company, which means that on quieter evenings he may not be cooking and that his personally trained young staff will be in charge of the kitchen. This was the case at the time of our inspector's visit, and Anton's absence did tell in a few minor areas. Overall, though, our inspector enjoyed his meal, beginning with a pigeon salad followed by an impressive Beef Wellington, with golden melt-in-the-mouth pastry, the combined flavours of the pâté and duxelle filling enhancing the good cut of beef fillet. The 'assorted plate of Black Swan sweets' provided the opportunity to taste all the sweets on the menu, including the house favourite, hot rum and raisin soufflé, which really packs a punch. Vegetarian dishes include cashew nut cutlet on tomato vinaigrette, and the wine list has useful descriptions and plenty of halves.

Cost: Fixed-price lunch £14.75, fixed-price dinner £14.75, £19.90. H/wine £7.20. Service exc
Credit cards: 1 3

Menus: Fixed-price lunch and dinner, Sunday lunch

Times: Midday-Last L 2pm, 7pm-Last D 10pm. Booking essential for lunch. D not served Sun. Closed Mon, 1 week Aug, 4 days Xmas

Chef: Anton Indans
Proprietors: Alison and Anton Indans

Seats: 35. No smoking in dining room **Additional:** Children permitted; ✿ dishes

Directions: East of Newark off the A17

BELTON, **Belton Woods** ⊛

In the formal surroundings of the first floor Manor Restaurant overlooking the golf course, Geoff Wellbeloved and his team offer an extensive carte and fixed-price menu of mainly modern British dishes, all carefully prepared. Informal meals at a more reasonable price are available all day in Plus Fours.

Cost: *Alc* £30, fixed-price L £16.95/D £19.50, H/wine £9.95 ♀ Service inc. **Credit cards:** 1 2 3 4 5
Additional: Children welcome; children's portions/menu; ⊙ menu; Vegan/other diets on request
Directions: Follow A607 through Manthorpe, approx 1 mile on left, well signposted

Near Grantham
Map no: 8 SK93
Tel: 01476 593200
Chef: Geoff Wellbeloved
Proprietors: De Vere Hotels.
Manager: Roland Ayling
Seats: 100. No-smoking area. Air conditioned
Times: Last L 2.30pm, Last D 10pm

GRANTHAM, **Harry's Place** ⊛⊛

'French eclectic' is what the owners call their cooking in a village restaurant where excellence is vigorously pursued

'What seems to be the trouble?' is not the way customers are greeted by the eponymous Harry (Hallam), or his wife Caroline. One could be forgiven for expecting to be, though, as the small detached house, with its brass plaque, looks more like a doctor's surgery than a restaurant. Inside, the surroundings are much more restaurant-like and the only medical condition requiring treatment is a chronic case of desire for perfectly-cooked food. The Hallams are sticklers for quality, first indicated by the hand-written, two-choice per course *cartes* designed around the day's available produce, and then by the food itself. At lunchtime, there could be sautéed lobster in butter, Cognac and Madeira sauce, filleted loin of baby roe deer in a tarragon and white wine sauce, or sliced Orkney king scallops in a leek, mushroom and basil sauce, wrapped in a pancake. An evening visit might find monkfish or wild boar, roast grouse or wild salmon, turbot or grey partridge – and more. Each will be prepared with a distinctive, complementary sauce. Desserts, like the rest, are quite pricey but worth it.

Directions: Two miles north-west of Grantham on the B1174

17 High Street, Great Gonerby
Map no: 8 SK93
Tel: 01476 61780

Cost: *Alc* lunch £30, dinner £35. Wine £17.50. Service exc
Credit cards: 1 3

Menus: *A la carte* lunch and dinner

Times: Last L 2pm, Last D 9.30pm. Closed Sun, Mon, Xmas

Chef: Harry Hallam
Proprietors: Harry and Caroline Hallam

Seats: 10. No smoking
Additional: Children over 5 permitted; children's portions

LINCOLN, **Wig & Mitre** ⊛

☺ *A delightful 14th-century building situated in the heart of Lincoln right by the cathedral. A mixture of French, Italian and traditional English dishes make for a varied menu including items such as roast Lincolnshire duck with lemon and walnut stuffing.*

Cost: *Alc* £17.70. H/wine £9.40 ♀ Service exc
Credit cards: 1 2 3 4. **Additional:** Children permitted; ⊙ dishes; Vegan/other diets on request
Directions: Adjacent to Lincoln Cathedral, Lincoln Castle and the castle car park at the top of Steep Hill

29 Steep Hill
Map no: 8 SK97
Tel: 01522 535190
Chef: Paul Vidic
Proprietor: Tobias Hope
Seats: 60-70
Times: Last D 11pm. Closed 25 Dec

STAMFORD, George of Stamford

☺ The restaurant menu has essentially traditional English dishes but also incorporates a variety of international ideas. Main dishes include pan-fried pigeon breast on char-grilled polenta with lentil and port sauce, and traditional roast duck with peaches and brandy.

Cost: Fixed-price L £15.50, £18.50. H/wine £8.45
Additional: Children welcome; children's portions; ❂ dishes; Vegan/other diets on request.
Directions: From the A1 take B1081 to traffic lights, hotel is on left

St Martin's
Map no: 8 TF00
Tel: 01780 55171
Chefs: Chris Pitman, Matthew Carroll
Proprietors: Poste Hotels. Manager: Chris Pitman
Seats: 80-90
Times: Last L 2.30pm/D 10.30pm

SUTTON ON SEA, Grange & Links

☺ Handy for the Sandilands Golf Club, this is a popular restaurant for golfers. The carte offers plenty of fish, shellfish and steaks done in varying ways with an irresistible sweet trolley. The whole environment of the hotel is lively.

Cost: Alc £20, fixed-price L £6.50. H/wine £8 ♀ Service exc
Credit cards: 1 2 3 4 5
Additional: Children welcome; children's menu; ❂ menu; Vegan/other diets on request
Directions: From Sutton on Sea follow signs to Sandilands

Sea Lane, Sandilands
Map no: 9 TF58
Tel: 01507 441334
Proprietor: Ann Askew
Seats: 100
Times: Last L 1.30pm/D 8.45pm

MERSEYSIDE

BIRKENHEAD, Beadles

A well presented range of mainly British dishes is offered by this friendly little restaurant on the main street of Oxton village. Owners Bea and Roy Gott share the workload – she cooking, while he enthusiastically guides customers through a monthly-changing carte with five choices at each course.

Cost: Alc £22. H/wine £6.50. Service exc. **Credit cards:** 1 3 5
Additional: Children over 7 welcome; ❂ dishes; other diets on request
Directions: Centre of village

5 Rosemount, Oxton
Map no: 7 SJ38
Tel: 0151-653 9010
Chef: Bea Gott
Proprietors: Roy and Bea Gott
Seats: 34. Smoking permitted only after coffee served
Times: Last D 9pm. Closed Sun, Mon, 2 weeks in Aug/Sep

BIRKENHEAD, Capitol ❀

☺ *This popular Chinese restaurant is said to be Birkenhead's oldest and meals continue to confirm its good reputation. Menus consist of various banquets, including one of seafood and a vegetarian one. The carte lists Cantonese and Pekinese dishes including the renowned Roast Peking Duck.*

Cost: Alc £13; fixed-price L £4.95/D £12. H/wine £8.25. Service inc.
Credit cards: 1 2 3 5. **Additional:** Children welcome; children's portions; ❂ menu; Vegan/other diets on request
Directions: At the corner of Hamilton Square

29 Argyle Street
Hamilton Square
Map no: 7 SJ38
Tel: 0151-647 9212
Chef: Mr Tam
Proprietor: Steve Tam
Seats: 80. Air conditioned
Times: Last L 1.45pm/D 11pm.
Closed Xmas

ST HELENS, Chalon Court ❀❀

There is nothing transparent about the high quality of the cooking in the most modern hotel in town

St Helens is the home of British glass, thanks to Pilkington's; unsurprising then, that the modern Chalon Court uses glass so imaginatively, inside and out. Children will really love it for the chance at lunchtime to make their own pizzas and sundaes, and because of the various forms of entertainment. Dinner – a more serious affair – can be chosen from the two to five-course *cartes* with their abundant selections of starters and main dishes, or from a five-course 'speciality menu'. After a complimentary appetiser of turbot mousse and green-leaf in vinaigrette, our inspector opted for smoked salmon and turbot roulade marinated in lemon juice and sea salt, served with mango sauce; in all but the salmon, flavours came through well. This was followed by tender, sliced fillet of lamb, served on a bed of braised green lentils with a rosemary jus and garnished with mint mousse in a filo pastry parcel. An extensive vegetarian menu is always available. Just reading the desserts had this office-based editorial team drooling. The wines come mainly from smaller domaines and estates all over the world, but especially France.

Directions: From M62 take junc 7 and linkway to St Helens. Hotel is at the end of linkway on the right and signed

Chalon Way, Linkway West
Map no: 7 SJ59
Tel: 01744 543444

Cost: Alc £24.95, fixed-price D £19.95. H/wine £9.50. No service charge.
Credit cards: 1 2 3 4

Times: Last L 2pm/D 9.45pm. D not served Sun

Chef: John Branagan
Proprietors: Celebrated Hotels.
Manager: Jeremy Roberts

Seats: 65. No smoking in dining room. Air conditioned
Additional: Children welcome; children's menu/portions; ❂ menu; Vegan/other diets on request

THORNTON HOUGH, Thornton Hall ❀

Once the home of a shipping magnate and now a hotel, it retains the wood carving and panelling which is the setting for the restaurant. The carte offers an international type of choice. At a sample meal, the shrimp and sweetcorn soup with saffron aromatics and chopped green and red peppers was good.

Cost: Alc £27, fixed-price L £8.25/D £17.25. H/wine £9.25. Service inc. **Credit cards:** 1 2 3 5. **Additional:** Children welcome; children's portions; ❂ dishes; Vegan/other diets on request
Directions: From Chester take A540, then right turn onto B5136. Hotel on the right just before the village

Neston Road
Map no: 7 SJ38
Tel: 0151-336 3938
Chef: David Cooke
Proprietor: Colin Fraser
Seats: 50
Times: Last L 2.15pm/D 9pm (Sun), 9.30pm (Mon-Thu), 10pm (Fri, Sat). L not served Sat

NORFOLK

BLAKENEY, **Morston Hall** ❀❀

A wonderfully friendly and relaxed restaurant with rooms serving imaginative cooking

Natural hospitality is extended to all guests at this informal country house, whether their stay is residential or simply to sample the culinary delights on offer. This tranquil refuge dates back to the 17th century, and still retains many original features. A new conservatory has created a pleasant place to foregather at 7.30pm for drinks before dinner at 8pm, and to study the set four-course menu which offers no choices until the dessert stage. The food is the product of the imaginative mind and competent cooking skills of chef and co-owner Galton Blackiston, formerly of the Miller Howe, and a recent inspection meal verified his credentials: fillet of smoked haddock topped with Welsh rarebit on plum tomatoes, was followed by duck breast teriyaki with lardons and spring onions, served with olive oil, mashed potatoes, leeks with red peppers and diced carrots with orange. There were good flavours to a warm apple soufflé with a small side portion of poached rhubarb and a pot of whipped cream, and cafetière coffee came with freshly made chocolate truffles. The wine list, arranged by grape variety, is spread across the world.

Directions: 2 miles west of Blakeney in the small village of Morston on A149 Kings Lynn to Cromer road, well signposted

Map no: 9 TG04
Tel: 01263 741041

Cost: Fixed-price dinner £21, Sun lunch £13. Wine from £8.50 ♀ Service exc
Credit cards: 1 2 3

Menu: Fixed-price dinner, Sunday lunch

Times: Last Sun L 12.30 for 1pm, Last D 7.30pm for 8pm. Closed weekday lunch; Jan-Feb

Chef: Galton Blackiston
Proprietors: Galton and Tracy Blackiston, Justin Fraser

Seats: 40. No smoking in dining room
Additional: Children permitted (over 10 at dinner); children's portions; ❂ dishes; Vegan/other diets on request

BURNHAM MARKET, **Hoste Arms** ❀

☺ *An up-market inn in a fashionable 'weekenders' village. Real ale, jazz nights and pictures by local artists give the inn a good atmosphere. The menu is currently mainy fish but may diversify with the arrival of new chef Glen Purcell.*

Cost: Alc £15.75. **Credit cards:** 1 2 3 4. **Additional:** ❂ dishes
Directions: In the centre of the village

The Green
Map no: 8 TF84
Tel: 01328 738257
Chef: Glen Purcell
Proprietor: Paul Whittome

COLTISHALL, **Norfolk Place** ❀❀❀

A good-value menu of honest and creative dishes served in generous portions at this new village restaurant

After many years earning acclaim as an executive chef (more paperwork than pastry work), Nick Gill has returned to the kitchen, sleeves rolled up, in his own fresh little restaurant in the centre of the village. His fiancée Philippa Atkinson looks after the front of house in a pleasant and observant fashion, and apart from them and a general assistant in the kitchen, there is no other help. The limited number of well spaced tables and the short menu, priced for three or four courses including an aperitif and coffee, allows this to work without much upset.

Point House
Map no: 9 TG21
Tel: 01603 738991

Cost: Fixed-price dinner £23.50 (3 courses), £26.50. H/wine £7.75. Service inc
Credit cards: 1 2 3 4

Menus: Fixed-price dinner

Times: 7.30pm-Last D 9pm. Closed Sun, Mon, Tue, Jan

The food is simple, honest and good, and a full appetite is essential to appreciate the generous portions. The fish, meat and vegetables will more than likely come from within a short radius of the village, the cheese from Boulogne and the wine from a well established wine merchant in Suffolk. The short wine list is well-balanced and attractively priced, with three house wines at £7.75

At a recent test meal there were appetisers of black olives and mini tartlets of cockles with garlic and tarragon at the table. The meal proper beginning with asparagus and a sweetened chive dressing, followed by whole Mediterranean prawns covered in garlic and ginger. The more serious main course comprised a perfectly timed tender fillet of beef covered in a fine but pungent layer of ceps and white truffle. It was a shame, though, that this simple delicacy was marred by a sea of demi-glace. A varied selection of soft, hard and unusual goats' and cows' cheeses came next with raisin bread, and discomfort notwithstanding, a full flavoured but light raspberry syllabub for dessert. Finally, coffee was served with chocolates, and all for a very reasonable price. Vegetarian dishes can also be provided with notice, and lunch by special arrangement.

Chef: Nick Gill
Proprietor: Nick Gill

Seats: 26
Additional: children welcome; children's portions. ◐ dishes; Vegan/other diets on request

Directions: Travelling north from Norwich on the B1150, enter village of Coltishall and take the 2nd left after the humpback bridge

DISS, Salisbury House ❀❀

Dependable food standards and a tranquil atmosphere make a meal at this town-centre restaurant a pleasant experience

A tranquil, homely atmosphere always prevails in this restaurant pleasantly housed in a Georgian building on the fringe of the town centre. Food standards are dependably good, too, the monthly-changing *carte* of English and French dishes offering a set fish course with a limited choice at each of the other three. Dishes, though served in a straightforward manner, are attractively presented, and the mousse appearing at each course indicates the good use that the kitchen makes of fresh raw ingredients. An enjoyable inspection meal beginning with creamy asparagus mousse (served with a powerful tomato vinaigrette) also included mousseline of salmon with a chive sauce and thyme-coated lamb fillet set on a bracing sauce lifted by balsamic vinegar and brown sugar. The preparation of vegetables shows some interesting touches, and simply-crafted desserts such as mango parfait with blackcurrant sauce are followed by refreshing coffee (or tisanes) and freshly made petits fours. A children's menu is available on request, and dishes for vegetarians are on every menu. Three rooms are available for guests.

84 Victoria Road
Map no: 5 TM18
Tel: 01379 644738

Cost: Fixed-price lunch/dinner £18.50 (2 courses), £22, £27. H/wine £7.55. Service exc
Credit cards: 1 3

Menus: Fixed-price lunch and dinner

Times: Last L 1.45pm, Last D 9.15pm. Closed Sun, Mon, 2 weeks Aug, 1 week Xmas

Chef: Barry Davies
Proprietors: Barry Davies

Seats: 36. No smoking in dining room
Additional: Children welcome; children's portions; ◐ dishes; other diets on request

Directions: Situated on the A1066 Thetford to Scole road, a quarter of a mile east of Diss town centre

ERPINGHAM, The Ark ❀❀

The Street
Map no: 9 TG13
Tel: 01263 761535

☺ *Wonderfully honest and uncomplicated cooking using the best available ingredients*

A flint stone cottage in a rural retreat is the charming setting for some wonderful straightforward cooking and friendly service. Chefs Sheila and Becky Kidd use their own organic garden, which produces sometimes startlingly fresh and tasty vegetables and herbs. Other ingredients come from the quality local suppliers, and the daily-changing fixed-price menu offers two, three or four courses which reflect seasonal variations. Squid and Mediterranean vegetable ragout is a typical starter, along with buckwheat crêpes with mushroom and sour cream filling, and crab, grapefruit and orange salad with avocado sauce. Main courses offer a short choice between fish and meat, with perhaps monkfish with cucumber and mint and a lightly spiced cream sauce, or herb roast leg of lamb with flageolet purée. Vegetarians are offered tantalising choices like dark mushroom roulade with asparagus and pine nuts, and spinach layer with cashews and parmesan. Puddings can be adventurous, like pears poached in blackcurrants with home-made vanilla ice cream, or iced orange soufflé with caramel sauce.

Cost: *Alc* £20, Sunday lunch £12.25, fixed-price dinner £16.25 (2 courses), £19, £21. Service exc
Credit cards: None taken

Menus: *A la carte*, fixed-price lunch and dinner, Sunday lunch
Times: Last Sun L 2pm, Last D 9.30pm. L not served Mon-Sat, D not served Sun. Closed Mon
Chefs: Sheila Kidd, Becky Kidd
Proprietors: Sheila and Michael Kidd
Seats: 36. No smoking in dining room **Additional:** Children permitted; no young children after 8pm; Children's portions; ❂ dishes; Vegan/other diets with prior notice

Directions: From Norwich take A140, just north of Aylsham take 2nd sign to Erpington. This leads directly to restaurant which is on the right

GREAT YARMOUTH, Imperial ❀

North Drive
Map no: 5 TG50
Tel: 01493 851113

☺ *The restaurant has the feel of a French brasserie: expect French specialities as well as fish (as you'd expect of the seaside) and vegetarian choices. Well prepared dishes like cod with horseradish are occasionally let down by use of less than fresh tasting ingredients. The wine list is long and informative.*

Chefs: Roger Mobbs, Stephen Duffield
Proprietor: Nicholas Mobbs
Seats: 70. Air conditioned
Times: Last L 2.30pm, Last D 10pm

Cost: *Alc* £19, fixed-price L £8.50/D £14.50. H/wine £9.50 ♀ Service exc
Additional: Children welcome; children's portions; ❂ menu; other diets on request
Directions: Situated on the seafront 100 yds north of the Britannia Pier

GRIMSTON, Congham Hall ❀❀

Lynn Road
Map no: 9 TF72
Tel: 01485 600250

A restaurant ideal for diners who love the special appeal of good food and caring service in a country house setting

Everywhere, Georgian mansions make excellent country house hotels and restaurants. Here is another, tucked away in parkland on the edge of a quiet village, where owners Trevor and Christine Forecast have fostered a relaxing atmosphere and nurtured a caring team of staff, while their fine garden provides much of the produce for the kitchen. Choose from three menus in the evening: a light three-course, fixed-price

Cost: Fixed-price lunch £15, fixed-price dinner £21.50 (3 courses), £29.50. H/wine £11.50 ♀ Service exc
Credit cards: 1 2 3 4

Menus: *A la carte*, fixed-price lunch and dinner, bar menu

dinner, a seasonally-changing four-course *carte*, plus dishes of the day, and Hobson's Choice, a set dinner of seven light courses. Taking the *carte* as an example, a starter could be ravioli of veal sweetbreads with spinach and forest mushrooms, baked fillet of salmon with a crab crust in a delicate shellfish cream sauce with baby vegetables and, for dessert, caramelised pear tartain and cinnamon ice cream. Set Sunday lunch could begin with a warm salad of Chinese-style chicken with sesame seed dressing, then embrace roast loin of pork with basil and tomato gravy, and finish with baked raspberry soufflé with lemon sorbet. There is a full wine list with most of the world's key producing areas represented.

Directions: Take A148 (Sandringham), after 100 yards right to Grimston. Congham Hall is on left after 2.5 miles

Times: 12.30-Last L 2pm, 7.30pm-Last D 9pm. L not served Sat

Chef: Jonathan Nicholson
Proprietors: Christine and Trevor Forecast

Seats: 50. No smoking in dining room
Additional: Children over 12 permitted; ✪ dishes; Vegan/other diets on request

HETHERSETT, **Park Farm** ✤

☺ *This sprawling hotel built around the existing Georgian manor house is approached along a tree-lined drive. Modern French-style cooking provides a range of well-prepared meals including braised rabbit in red wine or mushroom stroganoff with saffron rice.*

Cost: *Alc* £20, fixed-price L £10.75 /D £15. H/wine £8.25 ♀ Service exc. Min charge Sat £15
Credit cards: 1 2 3 4 5. **Additional:** Children permitted; children's portions; ✪ menu; Vegan/other diets on request
Directions: Six miles south of Norwich off A11

Heathersett
Map no: 5 TG10
Tel: 01603 810264
Chef: Peter Rogers
Proprietors: Mr and Mrs P G Gowing and partners
Seats: 50. No smoking in dining room. Air conditioned
Times: Last L 2pm/D 9pm (9.30pm Fri, Sat)

KING'S LYNN, **Rococo** ✤

A chic restaurant in the Old Town, run by chef Nick Harrison and his wife, whose art adorns the walls. Fillet of brill rolled round seaweed with lobster bisque typifies the modern Anglo-French style, and there is also a simpler quick lunch menu. Vegetables are good.

Cost: Fixed-price L £9 (2 courses), £12/D £19.50 (2 courses), £24.50. H/wine £9.50 ♀ Service exc. **Credit cards:** 1 2 3 5
Additional: Children welcome; children's portions; ✪ dishes; other diets on request
Directions: Follow signs to 'The Old Town'

11 Saturday Market Place
Map no: 9 TF62
Tel: 01553 771483
Chef: Nick Anderson
Proprietors: Nick and Anne Anderson
Seats: 35-40. No-smoking area
Times: Last L 2.30pm/D 10.30pm. L not served Mon. Closed Sun

NORWICH, **Adlard's** ✤✤✤

Modern Anglo-French cuisine with bold flavours served in a relaxed atmosphere

The occasional appearance of chef owner David Adlard bearing plates to the tables, reflects the relaxed atmosphere of the restaurant, with its deep green decor, wooden floors and white linen. This approach is also apparent in the style of cooking, which can be a little too relaxed at times, revealing some inconsistency, though most dishes are skilfully executed with

99 Upper St Giles Street
Map no: 5 TG20
Tel: 01603 633522

Cost: Fixed-price L £10 (2 courses), £13/D £29.50 (3 courses), £32. H/wine £9
Credit cards: 1 2 3

Menus: Fixed-price lunch and dinner

robust and clearly defined flavours.

At lunch there is a reasonably priced seasonal menu with a limited choice at each course. In the evening the menu is more elaborate, offered as a fixed-price three or four-course meal, or with the dishes individually priced, including optional cheese, salad, and tea/coffee and petits fours.

Our inspectors have sampled a pretty tart of buttery pastry filled with a black duxelle of mushrooms and topped with three softly boiled quails' eggs, and another starter of many flavours, char-grilled marinated salmon with a butter based sauce, braised endive enhanced with pesto, and cucumber with crème fraîche. Spring lamb, tender and lightly flavoured as one would expect, was barely recognisable in its flattened state, coated in bread crumbs. A rich demi-glace didn't help, but certainly benefited the fresh mushrooms, including the quaintly named 'chicken of the woods'. At another meal, tender roasted and sliced pigeon breast on a tasty essence was served with a perfectly contrasting mound of smooth onion marmalade and a lightly oiled leaf salad with nasturtiums. Desserts have been a bit of a disappointment: a rather runny crème brûlée, and a cream based dessert marred by a less than fresh rhubarb compote, making the lime sorbet with roast pears look all the more inviting.

The wine list is of good quality and reasonably priced. It is long but represents the best vineyards and wine makers.

Directions: In the city centre, 200 yards behind the City Hall. From the Grapeshill roundabout head towards the city, then go left into the one-way system

Times: 12.30-Last L 1.45pm, 7.30pm-Last D 10.30pm. Closed Sun, Mon

Chef: David Adlard
Proprietors: David Adlard

Seats: 40. Smoking after the main course only
Additional: Children welcome; children's portions; ❷ dishes; other diets by arrangement

NORWICH, **Brasted's** ❀❀

Visually amazing but serious in intent, this city restaurant uses quality fresh ingredients in its range of simple dishes

The small ante-room bar of this city-centre restaurant close to both castle and cathedral offers aperitifs, bowls of freshly roasted nuts and a chance to study lunchtime fixed-price menus or the evening *carte*; in the dining room the boldly striped wall and ceiling covering with wooden floorboards brings childhood memories of the circus flooding back! Food is regarded seriously here, however, and service is cheerful. Chef Adrian Clarke bases his range of simply-presented dishes on quality fresh ingredients. A range of appetising starters – for example, deep-fried filo 'purses' of cheese accompanied by a thick, aromatic apple jelly flavoured with thyme – precede such substantial main courses as medallions of pork loin cooked in bread crumbs and served with an apple sauce fortified with Calvados and diced prunes, or Beef Stroganoff; dessert can be as light as iced coffee soufflé or as filling as old-fashioned bread and butter pudding, and a choice of savouries will please guests who haven't a sweet tooth. The wine list has a good selection of French wines and a few from the New World.

Directions: In the city centre, close to the castle and cathedral

8-10 St Andrews Hill
Map no: 5 TG20
Tel: 01603 625949

Cost: *Alc* £25, fixed-price lunch £8.50 (2 courses), £12.50, £15. Wine £10.50

Menus: *A la carte*, fixed-price lunch, pre-theatre

Times: Last L 2pm, Last D 10pm. L not served Sat. Closed Sun, BHs

Chef: Adrian Clarke
Proprietor: John Brasted

Seats: 22
Additional: Children welcome; children's portions; ❷ dishes; other diets on request

NORWICH, By Appointment ❀

A small restaurant masquerading as an antique shop, reached via an alleyway. Chef and co-owner Timothy Brown competently uses a traditional cooking style to fill the carte with dishes such as medallions of beef with a red burgundy and oyster mushroom sauce.

Cost: Alc £24. H/wine £9 ♀ Service exc
Credit cards: 1 3
Additional: Children over 12 welcome; ✪ dishes by arrangement
Directions: From St Andrews Hall, down St Georges Street, into Colegate then first right into courtyard

27-29 St George's Street
Map no: 5 TG20
Tel: 01603 630730
Chef: Timothy David Brown
Proprietors: Timothy David Brown, Robert Culyer
Seats: 45. No smoking in dining room
Times: Last D 9.45pm. L not served. Closed Sun, Mon

NORWICH, Greens Seafood ❀❀

Principally a seafood restaurant, obviously – and very good seafood it is – but enough choice for meat eaters too

The name may reflect the colour scheme, or vice versa – it really doesn't matter. There's no doubt that it is a seafood restaurant, though, and the management are steadfast in their aim to keep freshness at the top of their list of objectives. This was convincingly illustrated by a recent main course of sea-bass stuffed with a fish mousse, whose fresh flavour was helped along by a tarragon sauce and a garnish of delicious scampi tails. Confidence is another great culinary virtue which our inspectors can spot pretty swiftly and at Green's it also showed through in the thin strips of home-cured salmon accompanying a savoury tomato and Guyère tart. In any group there is usually someone who is not a great fish eater, but that's not a problem – some meat dishes, such as duck and steak, are available. Desserts vary daily and rely on more traditional rather than contemporary recipes, one example being poached pear and apple mousse with cassis sauce. Anyone wishing to see a production at the nearby Maddermarket Theatre or Theatre Royal can interrupt their meal for the show and return for the main course.

Directions: Near St John's RC Cathedral

82 Upper St Giles Street
Map no: 5 TG20
Tel: 01603 623733

Cost: Alc £28, fixed-price £12.50.
Credit Cards: 1 3

Menus: Last L 2.15pm/D 10.30pm Closed Sat L, Sun, Mon

Chef: Dennis Crompton
Proprietor: Dennis Crompton

Menus: Last L 2.15pm/D 10.30pm Closed Sat L, Sun, Mon

Seats: 48
Additional: Children permitted (over 6)

NORWICH, Marco's ❀❀

Real Italian food and all-Italian wines in a small, popular city centre restaurant

'The sunshine is wonderful, no matter which country it shines on', says Marco Vessalio, who offers only Italian wines. He is not in the least dismissive of other countries' wines; it's just that he is, after all, offering food from his own So, look in vain for a Bordeaux, just as you will for pizza, and lasagne – he leaves those to the big 'Italian' chains, focusing on less ubiquitous dishes which reflect the true culinary kaleidoscope of Italy. Among his numerous antipasti are rice terrine with sole fillet and pesto sauce, long thin pasta (tagliolini) with smoked salmon sauce, and quill-shaped pasta (garganelli) with shallots, red

17 Pottergate
Map no: 5 TG20
Tel: 01603 624044

Cost: Alc £28, fixed-price lunch £14. H/wine £9.50. Service exc
Credit cards: 1 2 3 4

Menus: A la carte, fixed-price lunch

Times: Midday-Last L 2pm, 7pm-Last D 10pm. Closed Sun, Mon

wine and courgettes. All his pastas are made on the premises. Secundi piatti include some wonderful fish dishes, including sturgeon with leeks and oyster sauce, and sea-bass fillet with Belgian endives. Fillet of beef on a potato bed with Barbera wine sauce is another possibility. Not all desserts are Italian, but bread and butter pudding billed as 'Budino di pane', might just as well be. Actually, Marco's version is called 'Italian style' because it comes with a glass of white Prosecco wine.

Directions: From the market place, facing the Guildhall, take the turning on the right-hand side, then left into Pottergate

Chef: Marco Vessalio
Proprietor: Marco Vessalio

Seats: 22. No smoking in the dining room
Additional: children welcome; children's portions; ◐ dishes; Vegan/other diets on request

NORWICH, **Pinocchio's** ❂

☺ *A warm, pine-furnished brasserie serving a traditional Italian menu with 'New Wave' leanings in an informal manner with background jazz. A daily changing list of specials supplements the menu. Straightforward skills in the kitchen with friendly service make this place enjoyable.*

Cost: *Alc* £16, fixed-price L £3.50 (1 course), £4.95. H/wine from £6.95 ♀ Service exc. **Credit cards:** 1 3 5
Additional: Children welcome; children's portions; ◐ dishes; Vegan/other diets on request. Jazz Mon and Thu evenings
Directions: From Norwich city centre follow Castle Meadow to traffic lights. Take 1st left into Bank Plain, which leads to St Andrews Street then St Benedicts Street. Pinocchio's is on the right

11 St Benedicts Street
Map no: 5 TG20
Tel: 01603 613318
Chef: Nicola Parsons
Proprietors: Nigel and Jane Raffles
Seats: 96. No-smoking area
Times: Last L 2pm/D 11pm. D not served Sun. Closed 25 Dec, 1 Jan

NORWICH, **St Benedicts Grill** ❂

☺ *Set in the city centre this bistro offers European and one or two Oriental dishes which chef/proprietor Nigel Raffles cooks with good flavours and seasoning. Starters include tempura of giant prawns with an Oriental dipping sauce and roast lamb with saffron mash and rosemary sauce to follow.*

Cost: *Alc* £20. H/wine from £6.95. Service exc. **Credit cards:** 1 2 3 5
Additional: Children welcome; ◐ dishes; Vegan/other diets on request
Directions: Nearest car park, Duke Street. Street parking difficult

9 St Benedicts
Map no: 5 TG20
Tel: 01603 765377
Chef: Nigel Raffles
Proprietors: Jayne Raffles, Nigel Raffles
Seats: 64. No cigars or pipes
Times: Last L 2pm/D 10.30pm

TITCHWELL, **Titchwell Manor** ❂

A professionally run hotel where chefs Roger Skeen and Peter Bagge cook simple but effective dishes with an emphasis on seafood. Starters include local oysters or fillets of smoked trout and could be followed by lobsters or a fillet steak with mushrooms, fried with brandy, cream and peppercorns.

Cost: *Alc* £25, fixed-price L £10.95/D £18.95. H/wine £10.50. Service exc. **Credit cards:** 1 2 3 4
Additional: Children welcome; children's menu/portions; ◐ menu; other diets on request
Directions: On the A149 coast road

Nr Kings Lynn
Map no: 9 TF74
Tel: 01485 210221
Chefs: Roger Skeen, Peter Bagge
Proprietors: Margaret and Ian Snaith
Seats: 45. No smoking in dining room
Times: Last L 2pm/D 9.30pm

WELLS-NEXT-THE-SEA, **Moorings** ✿✿

☺ *Local fish feature throughout many dishes carefully prepared by the American chef*

At this unassuming establishment you are assured of a combination of fresh ingredients and imaginative seasoning which are the creations of American-born Carla Phillips who draws on many years of cooking experience preceded by a stint as a recipe writer. The tightly hand-written menu, which is helpfully annotated, is supplemented by an informative sheet with recipes and lists of suppliers. Full explanations are freely given, but the flavours eventually speak for themselves. As expected, fish dominates and a spicy fish soup turned out to be quite gentle. Other starters might include local cockles or a local coarse terrine aptly called Norfolk pork brawn. The main courses display more thought and great activity as in the fillet of brill steamed over fennel, served on an aubergine puree and coated with a Niçoise sauce. There are surprises in the vegetable selection which at a recent meal produced a stuffed courgette flower. The desserts are more subdued and some pride is placed in the assortment of a predominantly British cheese board. The atmosphere is relaxed, the service informal and the local reputation strong.

Directions: Situated on the quay, well signposted from all directions

6 Freeman Street
Map no: 9 TF94
Tel: 01328 710949

Cost: Fixed-price lunch £9.95 (2 courses), £12.95/D £12.95 (2 courses), £15.95. H/wine £6.95 ♀ Service inc
Credit cards: None taken

Menus: Fixed-price lunch and dinner
Times: Last L 1.45pm, Last D 8.45pm. L not served Thu. Closed Tue, Wed, also early Jun, early Dec, 24-26 Dec

Chef: Carla Phillips
Proprietors: Carla and Bernard Phillips

Seats: 35. No smoking in the dining room
Additional: Children welcome; children's portions; ❻ menu; other diets on request

WYMONDHAM, **Number Twenty Four** ✿

☺ *This popular restaurant provides good food at reasonable prices. There's a blackboard menu for lunch and a regularly changing carte for dinner. Thai and Japanese cooking influences the preparation of local produce. Coffee and cakes are served in the morning*

Cost: Fixed-price L £10.50/D £15.95. H/wine £7.50 ♀ Service exc
Credit cards: 1 3. **Additional:** Children welcome; children's portions; ❻ menu; Vegan/other diets on request.
Directions: Town centre opposite War Memorial

24 Middleton Street
Map no: 5 TG10
Tel: 01953 607750
Chefs: Richard Hughes, Nigel Crane
Proprietors: R Hughes
Seats: 70. Smoking permitted after 9pm
Times: Last L 2.30pm/D 9.30pm. D not served Tue. Closed Sun, Mon, 24-30 Dec

NORTHAMPTONSHIRE

CASTLE ASHBY, **Falcon** ❀

The restaurant in this peaceful village inn with stone walls covered with flowering shrubs is the attraction. Its menu is inventive, mainly British but with a French influence and features local game and dishes such as scallops with tuna or skate wings. Watch out for their seasonal festival of asparagus!

Map no: 4 SP85
Tel: 01604 696200
Chef: Neil Helks
Proprietors: Neville and Josephine Watson
Seats: 55
Times: Last L 2pm/D 9.30pm

Cost: Alc £23, fixed-price L/D £19. Service exc. **Credit cards:** 1 2 3 5 **Additional:** Children permitted; no children under 8 after 8pm; children's portions; ❂ dishes; Vegan/other diets on request
Directions: From A428 Northampton-Bedford road turn off at Castle Ashby sign, hotel ahead

HELLIDON, **Hellidon Lakes** ❀

☺ A modern hotel with lovely views over the valley and golf course. The restaurant, where Chef Edward Stephens cooks, has a good reputation for generous portions – just what is needed after a round of golf!

Map no: 4 SP55
Tel: 01327 62550
Chef: Edward Stephens
Proprietors: G S and J A Nicoll
Seats: 80
Times: Last L 2.30pm/D 9.30pm

Cost: Alc £20, fixed-price D £15.95. H/wine £9.50. Service exc.
Cost: 1 2 3 4 5 **Additional:** Children permitted at lunch; children's portions; ❂ dishes.
Directions: Turn off A361 at Charwelton for Hellidon/Daventry

HOLDENBY, **Lynton House** ❀❀

Italian cuisine and a traditional English setting are the twin strengths of a restaurant housed in an old country rectory

Quintessentially English, this old country rectory features print-hung cream walls, fresh flower posies on pink tablecloths and reproduction button-back Queen Anne chairs; a wisteria-clad terrace sheltered by an awning leads onto the lawns, providing guests with a pleasant area where they can linger over an aperitif in summer. Cuisine is Italian, but not self-consciously so, both fixed-priced menus and the evening carte displaying originality and the modern readiness to mix styles. Frittata (an egg-based dish like a baked omelette) with onions, peppers and tomatoes might be followed by lamb cooked in Marsala and topped with goats' cheese and parsley, grilled sardines with a sharp salsa verde or pan-fried pigeon breasts with oyster mushrooms; a home-made caramel meringue, its chewy crispness filled with almond cream and fresh berries, then a good brew of ground coffee served with florentine and almond fudge could complete an enjoyable meal. The wine list is worthy of note, boasting a good selection of new vogue Tuscany wines, and tips are neither included nor sought.

Directions: On Church Brampton/East Haddon road, follow the signs for Holdenby House Gardens. 200 yards from village

The Croft
Map no: 4 SP66
Tel: 01604 770777

Cost: Alc from £23, fixed-price lunch £11.50, fixed-price dinner £19.75. H/wine £9.75 ♀ Service exc
Credit cards: 1 2 3

Menus: A la carte, fixed-price lunch and dinner

Times: 12.30-Last L 1.45pm, Last D 9.45pm. Closed Sat & Mon lunch, Sun

Chef: Carol Bertozzi
Proprietors: Carol and Carlo Bertozzi

Seats: 45
Additional: Children over 6 permitted at dinner; children's portions; ❂ dishes

HORTON, French Partridge ☺☺

☺ *A well-loved restaurant serving deliciously tempting food in an unhurried atmosphere*

This is not a restaurant for those in a tearing hurry, as service follows the dictates of the kitchen and can sometimes be a little measured, but for those without a deadline the experience of eating here is one they will want to repeat. David Partridge still cooks with confidence and enthusiasm after 30 years, and is now assisted by his son Justin. The cooking style is described as eclectic, with an occasional foray into places like Morocco (Kofta – spicy lamb meat balls), and Malaya for baked chicken breast with coconut cream and citrus juice. Our inspector savoured gently-fried slices of moist scallops on a mouth-watering beurre blanc with chopped chives, and was equally delighted with the roast jointed quail with grapes and bacon on potato galette – the meat had a full game flavour and the potatoes were richly imbued with juice, vegetables were competently cooked. Californian 'tarte tatin' made with poached pears steeped in spiced red wine was a tasty dessert. The modestly priced four-course menu reads simply and temptingly, and the wine list shows an interest in French and German wines.

Directions: In centre of village on the B526, Northampton to Newport Pagnell road

Map no: 4 SP85
Tel: 01604 870033

Cost: Fixed-price dinner £23. H/wine £10.50. Service inc
Credit cards: None taken

Menus: Fixed-price dinner

Times: 7.30pm-Last D 9pm. Closed Sun, Mon, 2 weeks Xmas, 2 weeks Easter, 3 weeks Aug

Chefs: Partridge
Proprietors: Partridge

Seats: 50. No-smoking area
Additional: Children welcome; ❶ dishes; other diets on request

KETTERING, Kettering Park ☻

A modern hotel with a very agreeable atmosphere, where chef Darren Winder produces a range of interesting dishes with above average flair. Our inspector enjoyed smoked bacon with asparagus and hollandaise sauce and a successful roast cod with provençal vegetables and pesto dressing.

Cost: Alc £28, fixed-price £20. **Credit cards:** 1 2 3 4
Additional: Children permitted; ❶ dishes
Directions: At the intersection of the A509 and A14

Kettering Parkway
Map no: 4 SP87
Tel: 01536 416666
Chef: Darren Winder
Proprietor: Gordon Jackson
Menus: Last L 1.45pm/D 9.30pm. Closed Sat L

ROADE, Roadhouse Restaurant ☻

☺ *Situated on the village high street, and offering honest, affordable French country cooking. Chef Christopher Kewly creates dishes that, despite being original and contemporary, are classic, very much in the tradition of haute cuisine, and sometimes inspired from further afield than France.*

Cost: Alc £23, fixed-price L £14.50. H/wine £9.50. Service inc
Credit cards: 1 2 3
Additional: Children permitted; children's portions
Directions: Take A508 to Milton Keynes; after 2 miles left at the George Inn. Roadhouse is 300yds on the left

16 High Street
Map no: 4 SP75
Tel: 01604 863372
Chef: Christopher Kewley
Proprietors: Christopher and Susan Kewley
Seats: 45
Times: Last L 1.45pm/D 9.30pm. L not served Sat, D not served Sun. Closed Mon, 2 weeks Jul/Aug, 1 week Dec

TOWCESTER, Vine House ❂❂

☺ *Fresh seasonal produce is put to good use in the preparation of uncomplicated English dishes by this village-centre restaurant*

Tasty, value-for-money English cooking is the hallmark of this restaurant which overlooks the school from its pleasant setting in an attractive stone cottage at the centre of the village. Neither surroundings nor food aspire to be fashionable, but the short, amazingly well balanced fixed-price menu offers a competently prepared choice of relatively uncomplicated English dishes where the emphasis is on clean, bold flavours based on the effective use of fresh seasonal produce. The smoked salmon is a hybrid of gravlax and oak-smoked – tender and moist, with any oiliness taken out by marinating – while Auntie Hilda's roast rabbit dumpling turns out to be a large ball of herbed rabbit mince served with roasted shallots, tiny fresh peas and a purée of potatoes; desserts include a delicious marmalade rice pudding served in a thin, crisp basket on a bed of vanilla-peppered cream. The wine list currently comprises nearly 80 bins (many of them available by the glass) and the inclusion of more New World labels is planned.

Directions: Just south of Towcester and signposted from the A5

100 High Street, Paulerspury
Map no: 4 SP64
Tel: 01327 811267

Cost: Fixed-price lunch £13.95, fixed-price dinner D £19.50. H/wine £8.95. Service exc
Credit cards: 1 3

Menus: Fixed-price lunch and dinner

Times: Last L 2.30pm/D 10.15pm. Closed Sun

Chef: Marcus Springett
Proprietors: Marcus and Julie Springett

Seats: 45. No-smoking area. No pipes or cigars
Additional: Children welcome; children's portions

NORTHUMBERLAND

ALNWICK, Blackmores ❂

John and Penny Blackmore's cosy restaurant occupies two floors of the second oldest building in the town. The cooking is honest and generously sauced. Baked chicken came with bacon and garlic in port sauce, and mignons of venison with sautéed apples, mushrooms and creamed cider sauce.

Cost: Alc £28, fixed-price D £16. H/wine £7.80. Service exc
Credit cards: 1 2 3 4. **Additional:** Children over 5 permitted; children's portions; ❂ menu; other diets on request
Directions: Follow signs for castle, park at castle and walk down 'Narrowgate' – 200 yds

1 Dorothy Foster, Narrowgate
Map no: 12 NU11
Tel: 01665 604465
Chef: John Blackmore
Proprietors: John and Penny Blackmore
Seats: 28. No smoking in dining room
Times: Last D 9pm. Closed Sun, Mon

BERWICK-UPON-TWEED, Funnywayt'Mekalivin ❂❂

☺ *First class food in a popular, homely restaurant (and a name that may need repeating before the penny drops)*

The complete dinner menu for one day in May was carrot and apple soup with poppy seed rolls, tarte au soufflé with tomato and mustard sauce, coq au vin with Jersey new potatoes and

41 Bridge Street
Map no: 12 NT95
Tel: 01289 308827

Cost: Alc lunch £10, fixed-price dinner £22.50. H/wine £8.25 ♀ Service inc

Credit cards: 1 3 5

fine beans and desserts (the only course for which you get a choice) of chocolate pavlova with Cointreau cream, tipsy trifle or iced apricot parfait – all written on a blackboard. One soon realises that this is a different sort of restaurant. From the street, it is easy to miss but, once inside, with its hefty wooden tables and characterful bric-a-brac – even a Post Office mailbox is set into one wall – this restaurant is quite irresistible. Lunch offers more choice than dinner and there are also theatre suppers comprising a starter, dessert and coffee – for example, smoked Tweed salmon or Dijon egg mayonnaise, bread and butter pudding or iced apricot parfait – all for a really good-value £7. Backing this display of charming individuality are Elizabeth Middlemiss's delectable home cooking, a great little wine list and the cheery service of a lone waitress. It seems like an ideal way to make a living.

Menus: *A la carte*, fixed-price dinner, pre-theatre

Times: 11.30am-Last L 2.30pm, Last D 8.30pm. Closed Sun, Mon

Chef: Elizabeth Middlemiss
Proprietors: Elizabeth and Robert Middlemiss

Seats: 36. No smoking in dining room
Additional: children welcome; ✪ menu; other diets on request

Directions: From the main street go down Hide Hill and turn into Bridge Street. The restaurant is half way along on the left

BLANCHLAND, **Lord Crewe Arms** ✪

An historic inn, dating back to medieval times, where one can enjoy interesting four-course menus in the spacious dining room. Local produce is used to create dishes such as smoked goose breast with kiwi and raspberry coulis as a starter, and a vegetarian main course of Nut Wellington.

Nr Consett
Map no: 12 NY95
Tel: 01434 675251
Chef: Ian Press
Proprietors: Alexander Todd, Peter Gingell and Ian Press
Seats: 50
Times: Last Sun L 2pm. Last D 9.15pm

Cost: Alc D £26, Sun L £14. H/wine £10. Service exc
Credit cards: 1 2 3 4
Additional: Children welcome; children's portions; ✪ menu; Vegan/other diets on request
Directions: 10 miles south of Hexham on B6306

CHOLLERFORD, **George Hotel** ✪

☺ *Joe Hetherington's menus are popular with locals and visitors alike at this country hotel restaurant. Dishes, including a vegetarian choice on the carte, are based on fresh produce. Our inspector enjoyed a main course of turbout on a ragout with wild mushrooms and red wine sauce.*

Nr Hexham
Map no: 12 NY97
Tel: 01434 681611
Chef: Joe Hetherington
Proprietors: Swallow. Manager: Dennis Fulford-Talbot
Seats: 82. No-smoking area
Times: Last L 2pm/D 9.30pm

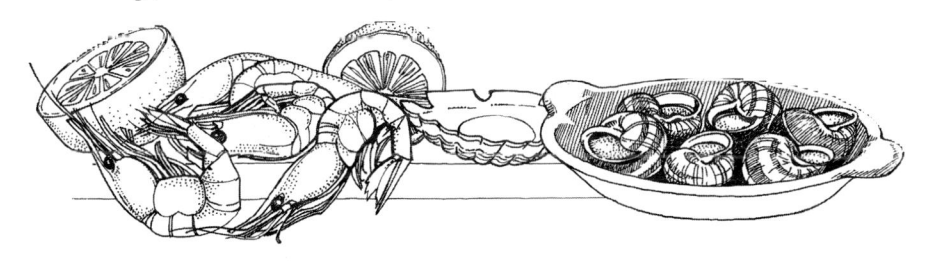

Cost: Alc £24, fixed-price L £14.50/D £19.50. H/wine £11.50 ♀ Service inc. **Credit cards:** 1 2 3 4
Additional: Children welcome; children's menu/portions; ✪ menu; Vegan/other diets on request
Directions: At crossroads on B6318 turn left. The hotel is 0.25 miles over the bridge, on the banks of the River Tyne

HEXHAM, **Black House** ❀

Situated in a rural position, the cuisine at this 18th-century house is assured and accurate. Chef Hazel Pittock uses good quality products and the helpings are generous. An example of a main course is roast lamb with glazed onions and Shrewsbury sauce.

Cost: Alc £25, H/wine £8.75. Service exc. **Credit cards:** 1 3
Additional: Children over 12 permitted; ❖ dishes; Vegan/other diets on request
Directions: From Priestpopple take Eastgate turning, after 0.25 mile at 'Y' junction fork right to crossroads, turn left to Black House

Map no: 12 NY96
Tel: 01434 604744
Chef: Hazel Pittock
Proprietors: Christopher and Hazel Pittock
Seats: 26. No smoking in dining room
Times: Last D 9.30pm. Closed Sun, Mon

LONGHORSLEY, **Linden Hall** ❀

☺ *The Dobson Restaurant at Linden Hall Hotel is the setting for chef Keith Marshall's modern style of cooking. Our inspector sampled lobster and sole terrine on saffron noodles, suprême of Magret duckling on a marmalade and shallot syrup, finishing with coffee and walnut sponge with fudge sauce.*

Cost: Fixed-price L £16.50/D £23.40. H/wine £11.50 ♀ Service inc
Credit cards: 1 2 3 4. **Additional:** Children under 12 before 7.30pm; children's portions/menu; ❖ menu; Vegan/other diets on request. Pianist at weekends
Directions: Situated on A697 Coldstream road. Linden Hall is 1 mile north of Longhorsley

Map no: 12 NZ19
Tel: 01670 516611
Chef: Keith Marshall
Proprietor: Jon Moore
Seats: 80. No smoking in dining room
Times: Last L 2pm/D 9.45pm

POWBURN, **Breamish House** ❀❀

☺ *English cooking with an emphasis on simplicity and honest flavours, served in a traditional country setting*

In traditional country house style dinner is at 7.30 for 8pm at this elegant Georgian hotel, when guests congregate to begin the serious task of selecting their courses. Doreen Johnson's English menu offers five courses of full-flavoured, adventurous dishes where simplicity is of the essence. Starters might be terrine of pork and veal layered with prunes served with a crab apple jelly, or smoked fish creams – a light mousse of haddock and salmon served warm with a chervil sauce, while main choices could include roast wild boar marinated in red wine, served with glazed chestnuts and shallots in a wine sauce, or fillet of Amble cod with a parsley crust and lemon sauce. Our inspector was not disappointed with a light and creamy watercress mousse with dressed prawns and tomato concasse, followed by a tasty cream of fennel and tarragon soup, and then fresh king scallops that almost melted in the mouth, served with a butter and chervil sauce. Vegetables were simply cooked and delicious, including the first baby carrots from the garden. There's a well-balanced wine list with good halves.

Directions: In the village on the A697

Map no: 12 NU01
Tel: 01665 578266

Cost: Fixed-price dinner £21.50, Sun lunch £13.50. H/wine £10.90 per litre. No service charge
Credit cards: 1 3 5

Menus: Fixed price dinner, Sunday lunch

Times: Dinner 7.30pm for 8pm, Sun L 12.30 for 1pm

Chef: Doreen Johnson
Proprietors: Alan and Doreen Johnson

Seats: 30. No smoking in dining room
Additional: Children permitted, under 12 by arrangement at dinner

NORTH YORKSHIRE

APPLETON-LE-MOORS, **Appleton Hall** ❀

☺ *A delightful Victorian country house set in spacious, well tended gardens, surrounded by beautiful countryside. Graham and Norma Davies offer a very good value five-course fixed-price menu with a choice of three starters, home-made soup or sorbet, five main courses, sweet and cheese*

Map no: 8 SE78
Tel: 01751 417227
Chef: Norma Davies
Proprietor: Graham Davies
Times: 7pm–last D 8.30pm; also Sun L

Cost: Fixed-price D £18.95. H/wine £8. Service exc.
Credit cards: 1 2 3 5. **Additional:** No children under 12; ❍ dishes by arrangement; no smoking in restaurant
Directions: On the edge of the village

ARNCLIFFE, **Amerdale House** ❀

The small menu changes daily at this elegant country house, where offerings have included home-made ribbons of pasta with smoked ham and Gruyère cheese followed by roast breast of Barbary duck with Cumberland sauce. Puddings are all home-made and the wine list is well chosen.

Map no: 7 SD97
Tel: 01756 770250
Chef: Nigel Crapper
Proprietors: Mr & Mrs Nigel Crapper
Times: 7.30pm–last D 9pm

Cost: Fixed-price D £23 **Credit cards:** 1 2 **Additional:** Children permitted; ❍ dishes; no smoking in dining room
Directions: On edge of village

ASKRIGG, **King's Arms** ❀❀

Some delightful-sounding food that lives up to expectations, served in an elegant panelled restaurant

James Herriot and his fellow vets may have left this small Dales village, but his reputation lingers and draws a steady stream of tourists in its wake. Another excellent reason for visiting Askrigg is to enjoy the charms of this lovely old inn, and in particular the good food for which it is renowned. New chef John Barber also comes with a good reputation, and his short four-course menu offers an interesting choice of tantalisingly described and beautifully presented dishes. Typical starters might be warm salad of black pudding cocktail lacquered by a Dijon vinaigrette, and braised squid piped with a mosaic of seafood complemented by a chive cream, with main dishes like feuillete of calf's liver, edged by a crème cassis sauce, or a ragout of seafood in a trio of filo baskets with a gratinée of hollandaise sauce. Very sweet king scallops with pink quail breast on colourful leaves with a sesame oil dressing delighted our inspector, as did fillet of turbot with a herb nut filling and a honey and vermouth sauce. Vegetables were fresh and plain, and bread and butter pudding was deliciously creamy.

Directions: In centre of village

Market Place
Map no: 7 SD99
Tel: 01969 650258

Cost: The Clubroom - fixed-price L £14/D £27.50; Silks Grill – alc £12.50. H/wine £8 ♀
Service exc. **Credit cards:** 1 2 3

Menus: A la carte, fixed-price, Sunday lunch, bar menu
Times: 11am–last L 2pm, 6.30pm–last D 9.30pm

Chef: John Barber
Proprietors: Liz and Ray Hopwood

Seats: Clubroom30; Silks40. No smoking area. No cigars or pipes
Additional: Children welcome in Grill; over 10 in Clubroom (except Sun L); Children's menu in Grill; ❍ dishes; Vegan/other diets on request.

BILBROUGH, Bilbrough Manor ◉◉

Inspired new classical French cooking in a comfortable manor house not far from York

Just five miles from the centre of York, this delightful manor house sits in peaceful seclusion on the edge of an attractive conservation village. Comforts abound in the tastefully furnished public rooms, and the manor's oak-panelled dining room makes an impressive setting for a meal. The cooking of Andrew Pressley is inventive and carefully executed, and his *carte* with its special vegetarian section, and a choice of two, three or four courses from a set Menu Exceptionnel, offers an exciting range of dishes. Our inspector particularly enjoyed a starter of saffron ravioli filled with succulent langoustines with a cream mussel sauce. Main courses are well balanced across meat, fish and game, and the chosen poached chicken breast sausage with a tomato and basil farce on a lemon grass sauce was skilfully prepared. A sharp, hot lemon soufflé with raspberry sauce and fresh strawberries made a refreshing end to the meal, with fresh coffee and petits fours served in the lounge. Dishes from the set menu might include salad of pan-fried chicken livers, roast pork fillet with a lentil and bacon purée, and banana and strawberries with a Cointreau sabayon.

Directions: In main street near the church

Map no: 8 SE54
Tel: 01937 834002

Cost: *Alc* from £20, fixed-price L £10.50 (2 courses), £14.50, fixed-price D £20 (2 courses) £25, £30. H/wine £11.95 ♀
Service exc
Credit cards: 1 2 3 4

Menus: *A la carte*, fixed-price, Sunday lunch, pre-theatre, bar menu and OAP menu
Times: Last L 2pm/D 9.30pm

Chef: Andrew Pressley
Proprietors: Susan and Colin Bell

Seats: 50. No smoking in dining room
Additional: Children welcome; children's portions; ❶ menu; Vegan/other diets on request; piano music

BOLTON ABBEY, Devonshire Arms ◉

Once a coaching inn, this quality hotel is owned and run by the Chatsworth estate. The food is worthy of note, and recommended dishes have been excellent cannon of lamb with redcurrant sauce, and interesting puddings like apple and blackcurrant money-bag with custard.

Cost: *Alc* £32.50, fixed-price L £17.95/D £28.95. H/wine £11.95 ♀
Service inc **Credit cards**: 1 2 3 4. **Additional**: Children permitted (over 12 at dinner); children's menu/portions; ❶ menu; other diets on request; piano music Fri & Sat
Directions: On the B6160 to Bolton Abbey, 250yds north of its roundabout junction with the A59

Near Skipton
Map no: 7 SE05
Tel: 01756 710441

Chef: Gavin Beedham
Proprietors: Duke and Duchess of Devonshire
Seats: 75. No smoking in dining room
Times: Midday–last L 2pm, 7pm–last D 10pm

BUCKDEN, Buck Inn ◉

☺ *The charming restaurant at this Georgian coaching inn has been created from a courtyard where local wool auctions were once held. The carte includes fresh fish, Dales-bred meat and locally grown vegetables, all upholding the inn's reputation for good food. Bar meals are also popular.*

Cost: *Alc* £17. H/wine £6.50. Service exc **Credit cards**: 1 3
Additional: Children welcome; children's menu/portions where possible; ❶ dishes
Directions: In centre of village

Near Skipton
Map no: 7 SD97
Tel: 01756 760228
Chef: Marco Cording
Proprietors: Roy, Marjorie and Nigel Hayton
Seats: Restaurant 40, Dining Room 40. No smoking
Times: Midday–last L 2.30pm, 7pm–last D 9pm

ENGLAND NORTH YORKSHIRE

CRATHORNE, **Crathorne Hall** ❀❀

Interesting original and traditional food in a hospitable and peaceful Edwardian setting

A warm welcome and high levels of courtesy distinguish this fine Edwardian hall set in a peaceful location not too far from Teesside International Airport. New chef Phillip Pomfret offers an interesting *carte* supported by a reasonably priced four-course dinner menu, with choices such as wild boar and venison terrine studded with pistachio nuts, with a home-made date chutney, and rabbit stew with apple dumpling. The only slight criticism is that some dishes are a little fussy, and a perfectly cooked blue cheese soufflé at a recent meal was spoilt by the unnecessary – and overpowering – addition of cold lobster pieces. Fillet of Aberdeen Angus beef was tender and very tasty, and surrounded by succulent mushrooms and home-made mini-black puddings, including one in a tortellini. Vegetables were fresh and well cooked, and a warm chocolate tart was very flavoursome. Vegetarians are offered dishes like baked flat cap mushrooms with a leek and Brie filling and tomato sauce, and asparagus and mozzarella soufflé.

Directions: Off A19 opposite junction with A67; signposted Crathorne. Crathorne Hall is on the left

Map no: 8 NZ40
Tel: 01642 700398

Cost: *Alc* from £22.75, fixed-price L £14.50, fixed-price D £22.75. H/wine £12.50 ♀
Service exc
Credit cards: 1 2 3 4

Menus: *A la carte*, fixed-price, Sunday lunch, bar menu
Times: Last L 2.30pm/D 9.45pm

Chef: Philip Pomfret
Proprietors: Voyager. Manager: Julian Ayres

Seats: 60. No cigars or pipes in dining room
Additional: Children welcome; children's menu/portions; ❂ menu; Vegan/other diets on request; live entertainment

ESCRICK, **Parsonage** ❀

A 19th-century parsonage standing close to the church it once served, its intimate dining room making a fine setting for lunch or dinner. Chef Martin Griffiths' Anglo-French cuisine is inventive and the variety-filled, fixed-price dinner menu can be supplemented by additional dishes for a small supplement.

Cost: *Alc* £27.50, fixed-price L £9.50/D £18.50. H/wine £8.95. No service charge **Credit cards**: 1 2 3 4 5 **Additional**: Children welcome; children's menu/portions; ❂ dishes; Vegan/other diets on request
Directions: In village centre

Main Street
Map no: 8 SE64
Tel: 01904 728111
Chef: Martin Griffiths
Manager: Peter Taylor
Seats: 40. No smoking in dining room
Times: Midday–last L 2pm, /pm–last D 9.30pm

GOATHLAND, **Mallyan Spout** ❀

A moorland village hotel of great character, the Mallyan Spout is named after a nearby waterfall. It has a spacious restaurant where well-produced dinners are served using local produce wherever possible. The menu of mainly British dishes is priced for two and three courses.

Cost: *Alc* £21; Sunday L £12; fixed-price D £18.00 (3 courses), £21.50; H/wine £8.50. service exc. **Credit cards**: 1 3 4 5
Additional: Children permitted (over 6 at dinner); children's portions; ❂ dishes; Vegan/other diets on request
Directions: In village, opposite church

Map no: 8 NZ80
Tel: 01947 86486
Chefs: David Fletcher, Peter Heslop, Martin Skelton
Proprietors: Peter and Judith Heslop
Seats: 60. No cigars or pipes
Times: 7pm–last D 8.30pm; Sun L midday–last L 2pm. Closed Xmas and sometimes Jan

GRASSINGTON, **Grassington House** ❀

☺ *A good-value fixed-price dinner is offered at this 18th-century house in the centre of the village. From an interesting choice, our inspector sampled deep-fried monkfish with a lime butter sauce, noisettes of lamb on an apricot purée bordered with rich Madeira sauce, and a tangy lemon tart.*

Cost: Fixed-price D £17.95. H/wine £7.45 ♀ Service exc
Credit cards 1 3. **Additional** children welcome; children's portions; ❂ dishes; Vegan/other diets on request
Directions: In centre of village

5 The Square
Map no: 7 SE06
Tel: 01756 752406
Chefs: Peter Chevin, Phillip Hatfield
Proprietors: G and L Elsworth
Seats: 50
Times: Last L 2pm/D 9.30pm

HARROGATE, **Balmoral** ❀❀

☺ *A town-centre hotel with a country-house feel with good but slightly fussy menus*

Although situated in the town centre, the Balmoral Hotel manages to create a pleasant country-house atmosphere. In Henry's restaurant two choices of menu are offered (including vegetarian selections) and there is an interesting wine list. At one inspection meal, somewhat over-complicated vegetables and a lobster timbale that lacked flavour were let-downs, but breast of duck with truffle, shallot and wild mushroom and Madeira sauce were good, with the sauce well reduced and the meat tender. On another visit fillet of lamb also proved a good choice, and poached pears with honey ice cream were excellent and there was also a good lemon tart with a sauce anglaise. The meal was finished off with coffee and petits fours, both of which were very good. An unusual offering in the bar were Dim Sum.

Directions: Near Conference Centre on corner of Franklin Mount and Kings Road

Franklin Mount
Map no: 8 SE35
Tel: 01423 508208

Cost: Alc £23.50, fixed-price D £17.50. H/wine £8.30. Service inc **Credit cards**: 1 2 3
Menus: *A la carte*, fixed price, pre-theatre on request
Times: 7pm–last D 9.30pm

Chef: Graham Fyfe
Proprietors: Keith and Alison Hartwell
Seats: 45. No smoking in dining room
Additional: Children over 2 permitted up to 8pm; children's portions; menu on request; ❂ menu; Vegan/other diets on request; magician Sat evening

HARROGATE, **Boar's Head** ❀❀

Consistently high standards of food in a comfortable and relaxed setting

It was in 1919 that Sir William Ingilby of Ripley Castle ordered that the Star Inn, now the Boar's Head, should be closed on the Sabbath. The publican promptly left. Three years ago the Ingilbys, who own this hotel, had a change of heart and restored this buff, square stone building standing in the cobbled market square. Much of the furnishing and paintings at the hotel are from the Castle and this is the setting for a first-class restaurant. Chef David Box and his team offer a three-course fixed-price lunch and a four-course seasonally-changing dinner menu where the price of the meal is set against the main course. With a modern English approach, typical dishes you can expect are breast of chicken with braised green lentils and wild mushrooms, or grilled salmon with curly kale and champagne sauce. For lunch, our inspector chose confit of duck terrine,

Ripley
Map no: 8 SE35
Tel: 01423 771888

Cost: Alc D £27; L £12 ♀ Service exc
Credit cards: 1 2 3

Menus: *A la carte*, Sunday lunch, pre-theatre, bar menu

Times: Last L 2pm/D 9.30pm

Chef: David Box
Manager: Paul Tatham

Seats: 40. No cigars or pipes
Additional: Children welcome; children's menu/portions; ❂

with a meaty texture and good flavour, followed by Shetland salmon and a tomato and pepper sauce which complemented the fish. Fresh and vibrant vegetables accompanied this. To finish – a chocolate and black cherry terrine.

Directions: On A61, 3 miles north of Harrogate

HARROGATE, Grundy's ✿

A varied choice of interesting modern English dishes from either carte or fixed-price menu is offered at this stylish little restaurant. Try Welsh goats cheese in filo, or roast duckling with a sweet kumquat and lime sauce. Puddings like sticky toffee pudding with creamy ice cream cannot fail to delight.

Cost: Alc £20 fixed-price £10.95 (2 courses), £12.95. H/wine £8.50 ♀ Service exc **Credit cards**: 1 2 3 5. **Additional**: No children under 10; children's portions; ◐ dishes; Vegan/other diets on request
Directions: Close to Royal Hall. At the bottom of Parliament Street turn right at lights and right again (signposted 'Leeds'); 40 yds on right

dishes; Vegan/other diets on request

21 Cheltenham Crescent
Map no: 8 SE35
Tel: 01423 502610
Chef: Val Grundy
Proprietors: Val and Chris Grundy
Seats: 40. No pipes
Times: 6.30pm–last D 10pm.
Closed Sun, BHs, 2 weeks end Jan/early Feb, 2 weeks end Jul/early Aug

HARROGATE, Millers, The Bistro ✿✿✿

A modern French brasserie-style menu of outstanding cooking at remarkably reasonable prices in pleasant surroundings

Marvelling at the freshness and excitement of the cooking, our inspector described his lunch at this pleasing little bistro as quite the best meal he'd had in months. The restaurant's modern decor, small tables and wooden floor are very attractive, but the most obvious signs that it is something out of the ordinary come from the warmth of the welcome, the aroma wafting through the door from the tiny kitchen, and the thoughtful table settings, each with a bowl of good olives, sherry vinegar and Spanish olive oil.
  Simon and Rena Gueller transformed Millers from a traditional restaurant in 1993. Simon Gueller is a protégé of the *enfant terrible* himself, Marco Pierre White, and he has brought to Millers a style of food that is both uncomplicated and eclectic, with no equal in this part of the country. With starters at £5 and main courses under £10 it is also remarkably good value for money. Followers of Marco Pierre White will notice

1 Montpelier Mews
Map no: 8 SE35
Tel: 01423 530708

Cost: Fixed-price £16.50 (2 courses). H/wine £8.95 ♀ Service exc. Cover charge £1
Credit cards: 1 2 3

Menus: Fixed-price, Sunday lunch (seasonal) and pre-theatre by arrangement

Times: 6.30/7pm–last D10pm.
Closed Sun and Mon except during conferences

Chef: Simon Gueller
Proprietors: Simon and Rena Gueller

some similarities between the menu at Millers and The Canteen in London's Chelsea Harbour, but anyone about to accuse Simon of lacking original thought should consider that, dish for dish, his cooking is at least as good. (Vegetarian by request only.)

An early-year test meal began with a terrine of pressed duck and foie gras, so good that our inspector imagined he was eating in Strasbourg rather than Yorkshire. Fresh fish is, of course, readily available, but none could have been fresher than the fillets of turbot that came with a stunning mushroom velouté, fresh noodles and crisp spinach that day. An innovative iced tiramisû, excellent espresso and Valrhona chocolate concluded a very special meal.

Seats: 40. Smoking not encouraged
Additional: Children welcome; children's portions; ✪ dishes on request

Directions: Situated in the town centre, just to the west of Parliament Street (A61) near the cenotaph

HARROGATE, Nidd Hall ✪

An elegant Georgian manor house with its own lake, where well-produced dishes are created by chef Glenn Elie. Our inspector recommended a starter of terrine of asparagus and wild mushrooms followed by sea-bass on a bed of garlic potatoes and accompanied by a vierge sauce.

Map no: 8 SE35
Tel: 01423 771598
Chef: Glenn Elie
Proprietors: Leisure Holdings. Manager: Mr Watson

Cost: Alc £30, fixed-price £18.50. **Credit cards**: 1 2 3 4
Additional: Children welcome; ✪ dishes
Directions: On B6165 between Ripley and Knaresborough

HARROGATE, White House ✪

A graceful hotel, eye-catchingly ornamented, where chef Jennie Forster creates excellent, imaginative food such as starters of tiny jacket potatoes filled with crème fraîche and Beluga caviar or broiled swordfish steak with mustard for a main course.

10 Park Parade
Map no: 8 SE35
Tel: 01423 501388
Chef: Jennie Forster
Proprietor: Jennie Forster
Seats: 46. No smoking in dining room
Times: Midday–last L 2.30pm, 7.30pm–last D 9.30pm

Cost: Alc £23.50, fixed-price L £16.50. H/wine £8.95. Service exc **Credit cards**: 1 2 3 4. **Additional**: Children permitted; children's portions; ✪ dishes; Vegan/other diets by arrangement
Directions: Opposite Christchurch, just off the A59 close to Wetherby Road

HELMSLEY, Black Swan ✪

The spacious restaurant at this attractive hotel offers a carte and short set-price menu of tasty dishes prepared by chef Nigel Wright. These might include mushrooms with cream and Stilton sauce, and roast fillet of turbot with lobster sauce. A choice of vegetarian dishes is also available.

Market Place
Map no: 8 SE68
Tel: 01439 770466
Chef: Nigel Wright
Proprietors: Forte. Manager: Steven Maslen
Seats: 70. No smoking in restaurant
Times: 12.30pm–last L 2pm; 7.30pm–last D 9.30pm

Cost: Alc £30; fixed-price L £11.75 (2 courses), £15/D £25. H/wine £12.75 ♀ Service inc **Credit cards**: 1 2 3 4 5
Additional: Children welcome, children's menu/portions; ✪ menu; Vegan/other diets on request
Directions: In centre of village

HELMSLEY, Feversham Arms ❀

The Goya Restaurant at the Feversham Arms Hotel provides an attractive setting for well-produced dinners. Our inspector sampled a dish of three pâtés, sole with asparagus sauce, and baked apple with honey sauce. The menu is backed by a good wine list which includes many great clarets and Riojas.

Cost: A/c from £18, fixed-price L £12/D £18. H/wine £9.50 ♀ Service exc **Credit cards**: 1 2 3 4 **Additional**: No children under 7; children's menu/portions; ◐ dishes; Vegan/other diets on request
Directions: 200 yds north of Market Place

1 High Street
Map no: 8 SE68
Tel: 01439 770766
Chefs: Martin Steel & Linda Barker
Proprietor: Gonzalo Aragues y Gaston
Seats: 44
Times: Midday–last L 2.30pm, last D 9.30pm

HETTON, Angel Inn ❀❀

A thriving inn offering real Yorkshire hospitality and interesting menus. Booking essential

Located just on the edge of the Yorkshire moors and in the small village of Hetton, the attractive greystone building has long attracted a regular following of discerning diners. The restaurant *carte* is now offering three courses for £12.95 which proves to be excellent value for money, and an interesting and well-balanced choice is always on offer. The menu always features a daily 'market fresh' fish and only the best of local produce is used. A recent inspection dinner started with a pressed salmon and scallop terrine. The salmon had an excellent flavour and the scallops were light and juicy. The main course of roast duck with a tatin of apple and an orange and thyme sauce, was well made and presented. The vegetables were notably fresh and tasty. A light, hot sticky toffee pudding completed the meal. The inn is extremely popular and is likely to be full on any night, so it is essential to book. Service offers warm Yorkshire hospitality and is so professional that Andrew Pratt, the Assistant Head Waiter was recently awarded the title 'Young Waiter of the Year' by the Restaurateurs Association of Great Britain.

Directions: In village centre

Map no: 7 SO95
Tel: 01756 730263

Cost: Fixed-price L £16.75, fixed-price D £21.95 ♀ Service exc
Credit cards: 1 3 5

Menus: Fixed-price, Sunday lunch, bar menu

Times: Midday–last L 2.30pm, last D 9.30pm. Closed 3rd week Jan

Chefs: Denis Watkins, John Joseph Topham
Proprietors: Denis and Juliet Watkins, John Joseph Topham

Seats: 54. No-smoking area
Additional: Children permitted; children's portions Sunday lunch only; ◐ dishes, Vegan/other diets on request

KNARESBOROUGH, Dower House ❀

Well established as a charming, family-run traditional hotel, the Dower House has a new attraction now that Paul Desport has taken over the kitchen. Hazelnut-dressed smoked chicken with mango and celeriac salad typifies his interesting combinations of flavours.

Cost: A/c £24, fixed-price L £10./S/D £18.50. Service exc
Credit Cards: 1 2 3 4 5. **Additional:** Children welcome; children's menu/portions; ◐ menu; other diets on request
Directions: 3 miles from Harrogate on the A59 York road

Map no: 8 SE35
Tel: 01423 863302
Chef: Paul Desport
Proprietors: N R & M J Davies
Seats: 100. No smoking in dining room. Air conditioned
Times: Midday–last L 1.45pm, 7pm–last D 9.15pm. Closed Sat lunch

MALTON, **Burythorpe House** ❀

☺ *A friendly, family-run Georgian country house hotel in horse-racing country, offering a good standard of cooking and a commendably wide choice of dishes from an undaunting menu. Most tastes, including the plainer palate and vegetarian, are catered for.*

Burythorpe
Map no: 8 SE77
Tel: 01653 658200
Chef: Mrs S M Austin
Proprietors: Mr and Mrs T Austin
Times: Last L 1.30pm/D 9.30pm

Cost: Alc £15, fixed-price L £9.75/D £14.95. H/wine £8.50. Service exc. **Credit cards**: 1 3. **Additional**: Children permitted before 7.30pm; children's menu and portions; ❂ dishes; Vegan dishes by arrangement, other diets on request
Directions: On the edge of the village, 4 miles south of Malton on minor roads

MALTON, **Newstead Grange** ❀

☺ *An elegant Georgian country house where Paul Williams provides delightful hospitality and Pat, his wife, a delicious four-course dinner for their residents. Rosettes of tender pork and mustard sauce followed by very enjoyable chocolate torte formed part of a good four-course meal.*

Norton
Map no 8 SE77
Tel: 01653 692502
Chef: Pat Williams
Proprietors: Mr & Mrs Pat Williams
Times: D served at 7.45pm to residents only

Cost: Fixed-price D £13.50. **Credit cards**: 1 3. **Additional**: ❂ dishes; no smoking
Directions: On the Beverley road

MARKINGTON, **Hob Green** ❀

☺ *A delightful country house surrounded by beautiful Yorkshire countryside where chef Andrew Brown produces an excellent dinner using fresh local produce with vegetables coming from the kitchen garden. Our inspector had a delicious rack of venison with creamed mustard sauce.*

Map no: 8 SE26
Tel: 01423 770031
Chef: Andrew Brown
Proprietor: Gary Locker
Seats: 30. No cigars or pipes in dining room
Times: Last L 2pm/D 9.30pm

Cost: Alc £19, Sun L £11.95. H/wine £9.75. Service exc
Credit cards: 1 2 3 4. **Additional**: Children welcome; children's portions; ❂ dishes; other diets on request
Directions: One mile from village of Markington off A61

MASHAM, **Jervaulx Hall** ❀

☺ *Close to Jervaulx Abbey, the hotel has a real country-house feel. Menus are very restricted and feature local produce such as Whitby crab and Wensleydale lamb. The cooking doesn't always quite come off: roast duck proved dry, for example, but was followed by a fine fresh summer pudding.*

Map no: 8 SE28
Tel: 01677 460235
Chef: Margaret Sharp
Proprietors: John and Margaret Sharp
Seats: 20. No smoking in dining room
Times: Last D 8pm. Closed Nov–Mar

Cost: Fixed-price D £20. H/wine £7.80 (litre). Service exc
Credit cards: None taken. **Additional**: No children under 10; ❂ dishes; other diets on request
Directions: A6108, midway between Masham and Leyburn, adjacent to Jervaulx Abbey

MIDDLEHAM, **Millers House** ☺

☺ *An attractive, Georgian-house restaurant on a cobbled market square in Wensleydale, where local produce forms the basis of well-prepared dishes such as poached fillet of salmon and three-bean goulash. The hotel earned an AA Courtesy and Care Award for its friendly, helpful service.*

Map no: 7 SE18
Tel: 01969 22630
Chefs: Mark Gatty, Judith Sunderland
Proprietors: Crossley and Judith Sunderland
Seats: 15. No smoking area
Times: 7pm–last D 8.30pm; closed Jan

Cost: Fixed-price D £19.50. H/wine £5.15. No service charge
Credit cards: 1 3. **Additional**: No children under 10; ✿ menu; Vegan and other diets on request
Directions: Off the market place

MOULTON, **Black Bull Inn** ☺

Various eating areas – including a Pullman coach – are available at a charming old village pub run by the same couple for almost 30 years. Carte and set-price menus strong in imaginatively prepared fish dishes, together with relaxed but attentive service, have made the inn popular.

Map no: NZ20
Tel: 01325 377289
Chef: Stuart Birkett
Proprietors: G H and A M C Pagendam
Seats: 100. Air conditioned areas
Times: Midday–last L 2pm; last D 10.15pm. Closed Sun evening and 24–27 Dec

Cost: Alc £24, Sunday L £15, fixed-price L £13.75. H/wine £7.25. Service exc. **Credit cards**: 1 2 3. **Additional**: Children over 7 permitted; ✿ dishes; Vegan and special diets on request
Directions: Off the A1, a mile south of Scotch Corner

NORTHALLERTON, **Solberge Hall** ☺

The Garden Room restaurant of this hotel – a very attractive Victorian house set in extensive grounds – provides a pleasant setting in which to take your pick from a wide-ranging selection of well-produced English/French dishes in country style; predictably, its popularity makes reservations essential.

Newby Wiske
Map no: SE39
Tel: 01609 779191
Chef: Peter Wood
Proprietor: Michael Hollins. General Manager: Linda Mercer
Seats: 70. No smoking in dining room
Times: Last L 2pm/D 9.30pm

Cost: Alc £25, fixed-price L £10–£15/D £19.50. H/wine £9.95. Service exc. **Credit cards**: 1 2 3 4 5. **Additional**: Children welcome, but no very young children at dinner; children's portions; ✿ menu; other diets on request; pianist Sunday lunchtimes
Directions: 2 miles south of Northallerton, turning right off the A167

NUNNINGTON, **Ryedale Lodge** ☺

Once the village railway station, the converted Ryedale Lodge offers a good selection of dishes. Seafood from the Scottish Isles, produces from London and Paris, and local game, meats and cheese are the order of the day. Main courses include fillet of beef with a red burgundy wine sauce.

Map no: 8 SE67
Tel: 01439 748246
Chef: Janet Laird
Proprietors: Jon and Janet Laird
Seats: 30. No smoking in dining room
Times: 7pm–last D 9pm

Cost: Fixed-price £26.75. H/wine £9.95 ♀ Service exc
Credit cards: 1 3. **Additional**: Children welcome; children's menu/portions; ✿ menu; Vegan/other diets on request
Directions: Take Oswaldkirk road to pass Nunnington Hall on left. In 400 yds turn right at crossroads, pass church, 1 mile further on right

PATELEY BRIDGE, Sportsman's Arms ✣

Generously proportioned dishes, soundly based on such fresh local produce as Dales lamb or Nidderdale trout, are accompanied by an all-world choice of wines at this restaurant – a mellow stone building dating back to the 17th century and set in its own grounds in the small village of Wath.

Cost: H/wine £9.50. Service exc **Credit cards**: 1 3
Additional: Children welcome; children's portions; ◐ dishes, Vegan/other diets on request
Directions: 2 miles north of Pateley Bridge on minor road

Wath-in-Nidderdale
Map no: 7 SE16
Tel: 01423 711306
Chefs: Ray Carter, Chris Williamson
Proprietors: Jane and Ray Carter
Seats: 50. No smoking in dining room
Times: Midday-last L 2.30pm, 7pm-last D 10pm. Closed Xmas Day

PICKERING, Forest & Vale ✣

An attractive 18th-century building where chef Tony Spittlehouse creates well-prepared dishes. Main courses include breast of chicken with strawberries in a pepper and brandy sauce, medallions of fillet of beef in wild mushroom and Madeira sauce or oak-smoked Pickering trout.

Cost: Alc £23.25, fixed-price L £8.15/D £14.15. H/wine £8.95. Service exc. **Credit cards**: 1 2 3 4. **Additional**: Children welcome; children's menu/portions; ◐ menu; Vegan/other diets on request
Directions: On the main roundabout in Pickering; access to car park on Malton road

Malton Road
Map no: 8 SE78
Tel: 01751 472722
Chef: Tony Spittlehouse
Proprietors: Paul Flack
Seats: 50. Air conditioned
Times: Midday-last L 2pm, 7pm-last D 9pm. Closed 25 & 26 Dec evenings

PICKERING, Fox & Hounds ✣

☺ *A relaxed, country-style restaurant in a picturesque village, offering a mix of French, Italian and English dishes for evening diners. Bar meals only at lunch times. Scampi from Whitby and locally produced fresh meats are among the attractions, supplemented by chef's daily specials.*

Cost: Alc £15, fixed-price L £8.90. H/wine £7.15. Service exc **Credit cards**: 1 3 **Additional**: Children welcome; children's menu/portions; ◐ menu; Vegan and other diets on request
Directions: In centre of Sinnington

Main Street, Sinnington
Map no: 8 SE78
Tel: 01751 431577
Chef: John Skilbeck
Proprietors: Paul and Jennifer Cusworth
Seats: 60. No smoking in dining room
Times: 11.45am-last L 1.45pm, 6.30pm-last D 9pm

RAMSGILL, Yorke Arms ✣

☺ *Ideal for country-lovers, this charming creeper-clad hotel deep in Nidderdale boasts a very attractive restaurant where skilfully prepared meals are served in a relaxed and friendly atmosphere. Head chef Nicholas Robertson makes good use of locally reared lamb, Dales cheeses and Whitby fish.*

Cost: Fixed-price L £11.95/D £17.95. H/wine £8.95. Service exc **Credit cards**: 1 3. **Additional**: Children over 10 permitted at lunch, over 14 at dinner; ◐ dishes; Vegan/other diets on request
Directions: At head of Gouthwaite Reservoir

Map no: 7 SE17
Tel: 01423 755243
Chef: Nicholas Robinson
Managers: Pauline and Peter Robinson
Seats: 34. No smoking in dining room
Times: 11am-last L 1.45pm, last D 9pm. Closed first week Feb

ROSEDALE ABBEY, **Blacksmiths Arms** ◉

This charming 16th-century farmhouse – now a well-furnished hotel – has two dining areas, the restaurant and a country bar/dining room. There is a choice of a carte or blackboard menus giving an interesting range of well presented and carefully produced dishes.

Hartoft End
Map no 8 SE79
Tel: 01751 417331
Chef: Greg Dewhurst
Proprietors: Mr A T Foot
Times: Last L 1.30pm/D 8.30pm

Cost: Alc £22.50. **Credit cards**: 1 2 3 4. **Additional**: No children in restaurant; ❶ /Vegan dishes; No smoking in dining room
Directions: At Wrelton turn right and follow signs for Cropton and Rosedale Abbey. Approx 3 miles past Cropton

ROSEDALE ABBEY, **Milburn Arms** ◉

☺ The imaginative Anglo-French carte offered in the restaurant of this delightful hotel changes regularly to take advantage of such fresh regional produce as Whitby fish and local game. Ampleforth venison, for example, might appear in a ragout flavoured with ginger wine and juniper berries.

Map no 8 SE79
Tel: 01751 417312
Chef: Andrew Pern
Proprietor: Terry Bentley
Seats: 60. No smoking in dining room. Air conditioned
Times: Midday-last L (Sun) 2pm, 7pm-last D 9.30pm

Cost: Alc £20, fixed-price Sunday L £8.75/D by prior arrangement. H/wine £7.95. Service exc. **Credit cards**: 1 3 4
Additional: Children welcome; children's menu/portions; ❶ menu; Vegan/other diets on request
Directions: In village centre

SETTLE, **Royal Oak Hotel** ◉

☺ A friendly, family-owned hotel dating back to 1686 situated in the centre of the town. A very good menu is provided in the oak-panelled restaurant and the cooking is now in the capable hands of Sue Rayner now that Philip, the owners' son, has acquired his own hotel.

Market Place
Map no: 7 SD86
Tel: 01729 822561
Chef: Sue Rayner
Proprietors: W B and S M Longrigg
Seats: 36
Times: Last L 2pm/D 10pm. Closed Xmas Day evening

Cost: Alc £15, fixed-price D £12, Sunday L £11.95. H/wine £9 (litre). Service inc. **Credit cards**: None taken
Additional: Children welcome; children's menu/portions; ❶ menu; Vegan/other diets on request
Directions: In north-west corner of Market Square

SKIPTON, **Randell's** ◉

☺ A large hotel on the Leeds and Liverpool canal where chef Malcolm Whybrow creates an interesting menu for the Waterside restaurant. A starter might be Chinese deep fry with oriental dip which could be followed by venison steak with a peppered cream.

Keighley Road, Snaygill
Map no: 7 SD95
Tel: 01756 700100
Chef: Malcom Whybrow
Proprietor: United Hotels.
General Manager: Chris Hull
Seats: 70. No smoking area. Air conditioned
Times: Last D 10pm, L Sun only

Cost: fixed-price D £15.95. H/wine £8.50 ♀ Service inc
Credit cards: 1 2 3 4 5. **Additional**: Children welcome early evening; children's menu/portions; ❶ menu; Vegan/other diets on request
Directions: On A629 on the outskirts of Skipton, beside trans-Pennine waterway

STADDLE BRIDGE,
McCoys (Tontine Inn) ❀❀

The Tontine Inn
Map no: 8 SE49
Tel: 01609 882671

The McCoy brothers continue to produce good modern eclectic cooking to great effect in this popular restaurant and cellar bistro

Cost: Alc £30. H/wine £9.95 ♀
Service exc
Credit cards: 1 2 3 4 5

A long-established restaurant located at the junction of the A19 and A172 which continues to attract the crowds. The *carte* menu of modern British cuisine is served in both the restaurant, which features mirrored walls, and the more informal cellar bistro. Starters may include langoustine pasta with a shellfish sauce or perhaps six Irish oysters with home-made soda bread. Enjoyable main courses include pan-fried venison with wild mushrooms and smoked bacon or roasted quail, boned and stuffed, served with a potato rösti, grapes and Madeira sauce. Puddings are all home-made and range from Cointreau ice cream and prunes soaked in Armagnac to 'choc o block Stanley': chocolate fondant and sponge soaked in Tia Maria with coffee bean sauce. The wine list now extends to 50 bins, with New World wines well represented, and a range of half bottles. Service is friendly and varies in style, depending on the venue.

Menu: A la carte

Times: Last L 2pm, 7pm-last D 10pm. Closed Sun & Mon, 25-26 Dec & 1 Jan

Chef: Tom McCoy
Proprietors: McCoy Brothers

Seats: 50. Air conditioned
Additional: Children welcome; children's portions; ❂ menu; Vegan/other diets on request

Directions: At the junction of the A19 and A172

THIRSK, Sheppard's ❀

Once a barn – being part of a hotel created from a farm and its outbuildings – this restaurant retains the original flagstone floors, mangers and tack. Dinner offers an interesting choice of fresh, well-produced dishes which include a variety of fish and seafood, while lunch is served to a separate bistro menu.

Church Farm, Front Street, Sowerby
Map no: 8 SE48
Tel: 01845 523655
Chef: William C Murray
Proprietors: Olga and Roy Sheppard
Seats: Restaurant 40/Bistro 75. No pipes in dining areas
Times: Midday-last L 2pm, 7pm-last D 10pm. Restaurant closed Sun, Mon

Cost: Alc Restaurant £24, Bistro £14, Sunday L £8.95. H/wine £9.75 (litre) ♀ Service exc. **Credit cards:** 1 3. **Additional:** Children welcome; children's portions; ❂ menu; Vegan/other diets on request
Directions: off A61 Ripon road towards Sowerby

YORK, Ambassador ❀

☺ *A former merchant's residence situated near the city centre where chef Robert McQue produces an interesting menu in the Gray's restaurant. Starters include smoked salmon mousse in a dill and lemon crêpe which could be followed by roast duckling with gooseberry and port sauce.*

125 The Mount
Map no: 8 SE65
Tel: 01904 641316
Chef: Robert McQue
Proprietor: David Miller.
Manager: Sallie Gray
Seats: 70. No smoking in dining room
Times: 7.30-last D 10pm, Sun L by arrangement

Cost: Fixed-price D £17 Service exc. **Credit cards:** 1 2 3
Additional: Children welcome; children's menu/portions; ❂ dishes; Vegan/other diets on request; piano music Sat evenings
Directions: On A1036 near racecourse

YORK, Grange ☻

☺ *A Regency town-house hotel with a formal restaurant serving modern British cooking, and a cellar brasserie alternative. Dinner offers roast quail with confit of rabbit cannelloni followed by medallions of beef fillet with a crust of mushrooms on a bed of braised onion in a red wine sauce.*

Cost: Alc £21.50, fixed-price L £12.50/D £21.50. H/wine £9. Service inc. **Credit cards**: 1 2 3 4 5. **Additional**: Children welcome; children's portions; children's menu by arrangement; ❻ menu; other diets on request
Directions: On A19 north of York, 400 yds from City walls

Clifton
Map no: 8 SE65
Tel: 01904 644744
Chef: Christopher Falkas
Proprietors: Jeremy Cassel
Seats: 50
Times: Midday-last L 2.30pm, 7pm-last D 10pm. Closed for lunch Sat & BH Mons

YORK, Melton's ☻☻

☺ *A solid, dependable restaurant offering a wide variety of dishes from some of the world's favourite cuisines*

Reviews do not normally begin by highlighting one of the restaurant's bottled beers, but this exception is because the beer in question is Timothy Taylor's Landlord. It must be touches like this which help Michael and Lucy Hjort maintain their fine reputation. She runs front-of-house with natural charm and friendliness, while he cooks. His time with the Roux brothers undoubtedly influences his style and his monthly-changing *carte* allows ample scope for his accumulated skills. Watch out for his rillettes, if available; our inspector chanced upon a really stunning rabbit one. The regular *carte* could offer corn-fed chicken with sherry and morels, or roast quails with walnuts, grapes, spiced pilau rice and red cabbage. Certain evenings feature speciality dishes – seafood on Tuesdays, puddings on Wednesdays, and vegetarian on Thursdays. A Tuesday could offer pan-fried skate wing and black butter as a starter, and ragout of salmon and Dover sole with crab sauce, broccoli and plain rice. For dessert, try pear and frangipani. The wine list groups by colour, strength and price range.

Directions: From the town centre/Coppergate, head south across Skeldergate Bridge towards Bishopthorpe. Scarcroft Road is the 3rd turning on the right

7 Scarcroft Road
Map no: 8 SE65
Tel: 01904 634341

Cost: Alc £21. Sun L £13.90. H/wine £10.60 ♀ Service inc
Credit cards: 1 3 5

Menus: A la carte, Sunday lunch, pre-theatre

Times: Midday-last L 2pm, 5.30-last D 10pm. Closed Sun eve, Mon lunch, 3 weeks Xmas/New Year & last week in Aug

Chefs: Michael Hjort, Elizabeth Cooper
Proprietors: Michael and Lucy Hjort

Seats: 40. No smoking area
Additional: Children welcome; children's menu/portions; ❻ dishes; Vegan/other diets available with prior notice

YORK, Middlethorpe Hall ☻☻

A magnificent country house hotel where a talented chef produces some delightful, well presented dishes

A magnificent William III country house in delightful grounds close to York racecourse and only a mile and a half from the city. The house has been carefully restored, offering quality and comfort throughout the elegant public rooms with particular attention to keeping the decor and furnishings in keeping with the period of the house. The elegantly panelled dining rooms compliment the talents of the chef, Kevin Francksen, who offers an interesting array of beautifully presented dishes. The menu format has changed to fixed-price three or four course

Bishopthorpe Road
Map no: 8 SE65
Tel: 01904 641241

Cost: Fixed-price L £14.90 (2 courses) £16.90, D £24.95 (3 courses), £27.95, Gourmet £35.80. Wine £11. Service inc
Credit cards: 1 2 3 4 5

Menus: Fixed-price, Gourmet, Sunday lunch
Times: 12.30-last L 1.45pm, 7.30-last D 9.45pm

Gourmet and daily menus that are readily interchangeable. Our inspector particularly enjoyed his starter of poached sea-fish and tarragon sausage set on a potato and leek rösti. This was followed by a classical tournedos Rossini – a quality cut of beef fillet set on a rich mushroom, truffle and Madeira sauce. Desserts are worthy of note and generally a hot soufflé is available. On our inspection visit this was a hazelnut soufflé accompanied by a carmelised pear and chantilly cream – a good finish to a thoroughly enjoyable meal.

Chef: Kevin Francksen
Proprietors: Historic House Hotels. Manager: Stephen Browning

Seats: 60. No smoking in dining room
Additional: No children under 8; ❂ dishes; Vegan/other diets on request

Directions: 1.5 miles from city centre, beside the racecourse

YORK, **Mount Royale** ❀

Set in a hotel of character where antiques and objets d'art abound, this delightful restaurant overlooking the garden augments its fixed-price dinner menu with such daily specialities as fresh asparagus and lobster – the variety of dishes matched by a wine list covering most areas of the world.

The Mount
Map no: 8 SE65
Tel: 01904 628856
Chef: Karen Brotherton
Proprietor: Stuart Oxtoby
Seats: 85
Times: Last D 9.30pm. Closed 23-31 Dec

Cost: Fixed-price D £24.95. H/wine £9.95 ♀ Service exc
Credit cards: 1 2 3 4 5 **Additional**: Children welcome; children's menu/portions; ❂ menu; Vegan/other diets on request; live entertainment
Directions: On B1036 near the racecourse

YORK, **19 Grape Lane Restaurant** ❀❀

Uncomplicated modern English cooking offering a good range of enjoyable dishes

This cosy little restaurant is tucked away in a narrow cobbled street in the heart of York, close to the Minster. The historic timbered building with its low-beamed ceilings is furnished in cottage style, and guests have a choice of dining upstairs or on ground floor level. Chef Michael Fraser cooks in modern English style without fuss or complication, and the well-balanced results can be chosen from three menus – a *carte*, a fixed-price menu and a blackboard selection of daily-changing dishes. Our inspector went for duck terrine with tarragon jelly served in little pastry cases, and enjoyed the good flavours of both meat and jelly. Lightly pan-fried medallions of hare with field mushrooms were tender and tasty, and served with a good Madeira sauce, while vegetables included delicious new potatoes. Desserts combine cold sweets like fresh fruit terrine with bread and butter pudding and sticky toffee pudding, and a selection of teas makes a refreshing alternative to coffee. The light lunch menu offers mainly hot and cold salad dishes and snacks. Well-priced wines from all over the world feature on the wine list.

19 Grape Lane
Map no: 8 SE65
Tel: 01904 636366

Cost: Alc £26.70, fixed-price D £19.95. H/wine £8.95. Service exc
Credit cards: 1 3

Menus: *A la carte*, fixed-price dinner, light lunch menu

Times: Midday-last L 1.45pm, 7-last D 9.30/10.30pm. Closed Sun, Mon, 25-28 Dec, 1st 2 weeks Feb, last 2 weeks Sep

Chef: Michael Fraser
Proprietors: Gordon and Carolyn Alexander

Seats: 34. No-smoking area, no pipes or cigars
Additional: Children permitted, must be over 5 at dinner; children's portions; ❂ dishes; Vegan/other diets on request

Directions: Walking away from Minster down Petergate, take 2nd right into Grape Lane; No 19 is at end on right

YORK, **Town House** ❀

☺ *Fixed-price and carte menus offer a range of imaginative dishes in this hotel, a conversion of several Victorian town houses near the city; venison, beef and pork medallions are served with a trio of accompaniments – blackcurrant sauce, horseradish butter and caramelised apple.*

Cost: A/c £17.50, fixed-price D £12.50. H/wine £8.25 (litre) ♀ Service exc. **Credit cards**: 1 3. **Additional**: Children welcome; Children's menu/portions; ✪ dishes; Vegan/other diets on request
Directions: On the A59 10 mins walk from City Walls

98-104 Holgate Road
Map no: 8 SE65
Tel: 01904 636171
Chef: Neil Cook
Proprietors: R A Hind, H Rolf, S J Howe
Seats: 60
Times: 6.30pm-last D 9.30pm. Closed Xmas week

YORK, **York Pavilion** ❀

☺ *Booking is advisable in the restaurant of this hotel run in country-house style and set in gardens on the edge of the city. Modern English cuisine shows some French influence, and an interesting carte is supplemented by daily-changing set-price menus offering two courses at lunch and four at dinner.*

Cost: A/c £23.95, fixed-price L £7.95 (2 courses), £9.95/D £17.95. H/wine £9.95 ♀ Service inc. **Credit cards**: 1 2 3 4 5
Additional: Children permitted; children's menu/portions; ✪ dishes; Vegan by arrangement; other diets on request
Directions: 1.5 miles from city centre on A19 Selby road

45 Main Street, Fulford
Map no: 8 SE65
Tel: 01904 622099
Chef: Shaun Harris
Proprietors: Andrew and Irene Cossins
Seats: 95 (in 3 rooms). No smoking in dining room
Times: Midday-last L 2pm, 6.30pm-last D 9.30pm. Closed Xmas Day evening and all Boxing Day

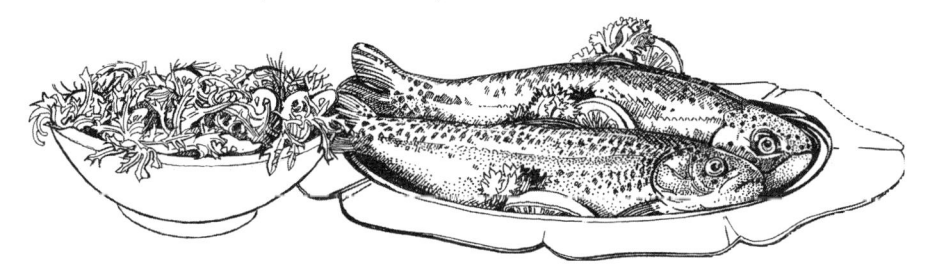

NOTTINGHAMSHIRE

LANGAR, **Langar Hall** ❀

Here, in a comfortable country hotel set in large gardens beside the church, a balanced wine list offering some unusual choices accompanies an imaginative short carte of classic British dishes which reveal a hint of Mediterranean influence. Vegetarian menus are tempting.

Cost: A/c £23, fixed-price L £10-£20. H/wine £8.50. Service exc
Credit cards: 1 2 3. **Additional**: Children welcome at lunchtime; children's portions; ✪ dishes; Vegan/other diets on request; live entertainment last Friday of month
Directions: In village, behind the church

Map no: 8 SK73
Tel: 01949 860559
Chefs: Douglas Stevens and Toby Garratt
Proprietor: Imogen Skirving
Seats: 30. No smoking area; no cigars or pipes
Times: Last L 2pm; 7.30-last D 9.30pm weekdays; 7pm-last D 10pm weekends. Closed Sun, 25 Dec

NOTTINGHAM, **Sonny's** 🌸

3 Carlton Street, Hockley
Map no: 8 SK53
Tel: 0115 9473041
Chef: Graeme Watson
Proprietor: Arten Janmaat
Seats: 80. No cigars or pipes. Air conditioned
Times: Midday–last L 2.30pm, 7pm–last D 10.30pm (11pm Fri & Sat, 10pm Sun). Closed BHs

A popular restaurant in the oldest part of the city, Sonny's offers honest cooking in the café/brasserie style. The surroundings are simple, the atmosphere lively, and the service friendly. New chef Graeme Watson concentrates on classical French dishes with Californian influences.

Cost: Alc £20, fixed-price L £10.95 (2 courses), £13.95/D £13.95, Sunday L £10.95. H/wine £8.95 ♀ Service exc. **Credit cards**: 1 2 3
Additional: Children permitted; ✿ dishes; Vegan/other diets on request
Directions: In city centre, close to Market Square and Victoria Centre

OXFORDSHIRE

ADDERBURY, **Red Lion** 🌸

The Green, Oxford Road
Map no 4 SP52
Tel: 01295 810269
Chef: Andy Wood

☺ *This popular eating place offers blackboard choices of snacks, light meals and a more extensive dining menu. The style is claimed to be of home cooking, but there is a definite Mediterranean influence, much of the fish coming from the proprietors' own Cornish fishing boat.*

Cost: Alc £12.50. **Additional**: Children welcome; ✿ dishes
Directions: Opposite village green

BICESTER, **Bignell Park** 🌸

Chesterton
Map no: 4 SP52
Tel: 01869 241444/241192
Chef: Mark Pearce
Proprietor: Erling K Sorensen
Seats: 45. No-smoking area
Times: Midday-last L 1.30pm, 7pm-last D 9.30pm. Closed Sun eve

Set in large gardens, a Cotswold-stone restaurant with a minstrels' gallery offering interestingly varied, well-prepared dishes. Temptations from the lunch and dinner menus include Cajun spice prawns with peanut dip and roast collop of pork in bacon. Fresh produce is used as much as possible.

Cost: Alc £23, fixed-price L £12.50 (2 courses), £15. H/wine £9.90. Service exc **Credit cards**: 1 2 3 4 **Additional**: Children over 6 permitted; children's portions; ✿ menu; other diets on request
Directions: On edge of town on the A4095

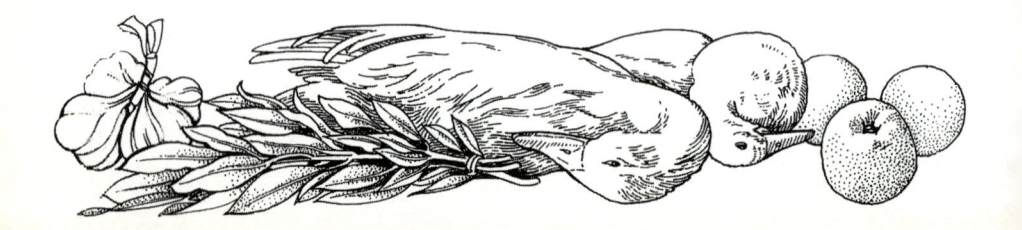

BURFORD, Bay Tree ✤

12-14 Sheep Street
Map no: 4 SP21
Tel: 01993 822791
Chef: Steve Chiverton
Proprietor: Mr R Haisley
Seats: 45. No smoking in dining room
Times: Last L 2pm/D 9.30pm

A pretty, ancient hotel in an elegant setting producing modern English cuisine from a choice of menus. Starters include casserole of wild mushrooms in herbs and white wine, and for main course local trout, or loin of lamb baked with a herb and garlic crust on a port wine jus.

Cost: Alc £27.50, fixed-price L £11.50 (2 courses), £12.95/D £19.95. H/wine £9.95 ♀ Service exc. **Credit cards**: 1 2 3 4
 Additional: Children welcome; children's portions on request; ❂ dishes; Vegan/other diets on request
Directions: Off main road in centre of Burford

BURFORD, Inn For All Seasons ✤

The Barringtons
Map no: 4 SP21
Tel: 01451 844324
Chef: Matthew Sharp
Proprietor: Matthew Sharp

☺ *A beautiful old 16th-century coaching inn where chef Matthew Sharp cooks good food with generous portions and fresh vegetables. Wiltshire ham terrine with green peppers and lime pickle was our starter, followed by skate-wing, nut-buttered with capers and prawns.*

Cost: Fixed-price £15.75. **Credit cards**: 1 2 3 4
Additional: Children permitted; ❂ dishes
Directions: On the A40 west of Burford

CHADLINGTON, The Manor ✤

Map no: 4 SP32
Tel: 01608 676711
Chef: Chris Grant
Proprietor: David Grant
Seats: 20. No smoking in dining room
Times: Last D 8.30pm

A country house hotel situated adjacent to the church where Chris Grant produces a well-balanced menu. Starters include hazelnut roulade with herb cream cheese and tomato vinaigrette and could be followed by calves' liver with blackcurrants and cassis or red mullet with a chive cream.

Cost: Fixed-price D £25.50. H/wine £9. Service inc
Credit cards: 1 3. **Additional**: Children permitted; children's portions; ❂ /Vegan/other diets on request
Directions: In village centre, beside church

CHARLBURY, The Bell ✤

Church Street
Map no: 4 SP31
Tel: 01608 810278
Chef: Salvador Fernandez
Proprietor: Juan Claramonte
Seats: 30. No smoking in dining room
Times Midday–last L 2.30pm, last D 9.15pm

☺ *A picturesque village inn of mellow Cotswold stone where the food has a particularly Spanish feel to it due to owner Juan Claramonte's Catalan origins. Starters include kidneys sautéed in sherry and main course of poached fillet of plaice with white wine and almond sauce.*

Cost: Fixed-price L £9.50 (2 courses), £13.50/D £13.50. H/wine £6.50 ♀ Service exc. **Credit cards**: 1 2 3 4
Additional: Children welcome; children's portions; ❂ menu; other diets on request
Directions: In town centre

CLANFIELD, **The Plough at Clanfield** ●●

A fine 16th-century house serving richly satisfying food at prices to suit everyone

Food of a consistently high quality is the proud boast of this restaurant, and chef Stephen Fischer has a robust, earthy style of cooking which produces honest flavours from fresh ingredients. The 16th-century inn also offers comfortable accommodation, and the warmth and friendliness of the staff help to create a very special atmosphere here. A choice of small menus includes the 'Gourmand', offering seven courses of speciality dishes, and the 'Epicure' with its choice of three or four courses. Delicious hot canapes, like creamed chicken tart, and ham and mustard croissant recently whetted the appetite for a fresh pasta ravioli on a sharp, buttery beurre blanc. A richly satisfying main course was breast of chicken stuffed with diced sweetmeats and toasted pine kernels, roasted with shallots, garlic and various mushrooms. A side plate of vegetables tasting only of their own flavours nicely complemented this dish. Poached pears with crispy toffee topping and honey ice cream were delicious, and huge cafetières of extra strong coffee come with a dish of home-made fudge and gooey chocolate petits fours.

Directions: In village centre

Bourton Road
Map no: 4 SP20
Tel: 0136 781222

Cost: Alc £29, fixed-price L £10.95 (2 courses), £14.50, fixed-price D £19.50. H/wine £9.95. Service exc
Credit cards: 1 2 3 4 5

Menus: A la carte, fixed-price, Sunday lunch, Gourmand, Epicure, bar menu

Times: Last L 2pm/D 10pm (9.30pm Sun)

Chef: Stephen Fischer
Proprietors: Hatton Hotels.
Manager: Jean Dunstone

Seats: 30. No smoking in the restaurant
Additional: Children welcome; children's portions; ۞ menu; Vegan/other diets on request

DEDDINGTON, **Holcombe** ●

☺ *A Cotswold-stone 17th-century inn with a popular restaurant offering fixed-price and carte menus featuring classical French and traditional English cuisine. The set menu offers a wide choice at each course, ranging from smoked salmon roulade, Dover sole, venison and mushroom pudding to steaks.*

Cost: Alc £21.45, fixed-price L £14.95/D £19.95. H/wine £10.50. No service charge **Credit cards:** 1 2 3 5 **Additional:** Children welcome; children's menu/portions; ۞ dishes; Vegan/other diets on request
Directions: In village centre by traffic lights

High Street
Map no: 4 SP43
Tel: 01869 38274
Chef: Alan Marshall
Proprietors: Mr and Mrs C Mahfoudh
Seats: 50. No-smoking area. No cigars or pipes
Times: Midday-last L 2.15pm, last D 10.45pm. Closed 2-14 Jan

DORCHESTER-ON-THAMES, **White Hart** ●●

☺ *Skilful English cooking with a hint of French influences, in a lovely old coaching inn*

A heavily-beamed restaurant with gleaming brasses is the setting for some enjoyable English cooking with French influences and a touch of panache. This old coaching inn is where chef John Wills demonstrates his skills in a sensibly short *carte* which changes with the seasons. There is usually a fixed-price menu too. Dishes like snails flamed with green Chartreuse, shallots, walnuts and cream, and mixed leaf salad with avocado, olives and quail's eggs might be offered as starters, with main courses like pan-fried medallions of veal

High Street
Map no: 4 SU59
Tel: 01865 340074

Cost: Alc from £19.65, fixed-price L £9.50 (2 courses), £13.50/D £13.50. H/wine £8.95. Service inc
Credit cards: 1 2 3 4

Menus: A la carte, fixed-price, Sunday lunch, bar menu

Times: Last L 2pm/D 9.30pm.

served with poached pear and port sauce, and roast breast of Barbary duck on leeks with an orange sauce. Our inspector tried delicious fresh asparagus with puff pastry and a white wine and chive butter sauce, followed by tender rack of lamb, herb-crusted and roasted, with a lovely flavour. Crème brûlée flavoured with a coffee liqueur was a long way from the traditional version, and not very successful either. Vegetarian options might be mushroom and pepper stroganoff with saffron rice, or layered aubergine, goa'ts cheese and fried courgette with a tomato and basil sauce.

Directions: In village centre

GORING, **The Leatherne Bottel** ✹✹

Enjoying a beautiful riverside setting, this delightful restaurant features imaginative modern English cuisine

A charming restaurant with a delightful setting beside the River Thames offering modern, exciting English cooking of a high standard. The terrace leads to the water and is a peaceful spot for drinks or dinner. Inside there are two cosy dining rooms and a bar with log fires in the winter. The imaginative *carte* offers a good choice at each course, with a Mediterranean/Italian influence characterised by light oil-based sauces, unusual fresh vegetables and liberal use of fresh herbs. An inspection meal started with delicious home-made tomato and black olive, or spinach and walnut bread which can be ordered in advance to take home. Crab cakes flavoured with coriander and mild Asian galangal served with bean sprouts, plum tomato and a julienne of snow peas provided an exciting combination of textures and . flavours. Breast of local chicken steamed with tarragon dumplings over chicken stock with herbs and spring vegetables proved tender and full of flavour. British cheeses come with crisp home-made biscuits and chutney. The wine list covers seven countries but prices are high and the choice is limited.

Directions: Signposted off B4009 Goring to Wallingford road

GREAT MILTON,
Le Manoir aux Quat' Saisons ✹✹✹✹✹

Memorable French cooking by an acknowledged master in a superb hotel with a friendly, relaxing atmosphere

'Light, beautifully presented and full of flavour, exciting without being outlandish' - such, writes our inspector, are the characteristics of the food at Le Manoir, where Raymond Blanc still pursues his quest for perfection. At all levels a guest will find excellence: luxurious bedrooms equipped with every little extra, relaxing, spacious lounges, and a restaurant that has been a mecca for food lovers for more than a decade.
    It consists of three rooms, the first decorated in sunny, harmonious yellows, then the smaller Loxton room, with clever lighting and mouth-watering displays of bottled fruits, and

Closed Xmas Day

Chef: Jon Wills
Proprietors: Raceoak.
Managers: Mr & Mrs Jack Bradley

Seats: 35
Additional: Children welcome; children's portions; ❶ dishes; other diets on request

Map no: 4 SU68
Tel: 01491 872667

Cost: Alc £27.50. H/wine £10.50 ♀ Service exc
Credit cards: 1 2 3

Menu: A la carte

Times: Midday-last L 2pm (2.30pm Sat & Sun), 6.30-last D 9pm (9.30 Sat). Closed Xmas Day

Chefs: Keith Read and Clive O'Connor
Proprietors: Keith Read and Annie Bonnet

Seats: 60. Air conditioned
Additional: Children permitted occasionally at restaurant's discretion; ❶ dishes; Vegan/other diets on request

Church Road
Map no: 4 SP60
Tel: 01844 278881

Cost: Alc £75, fixed-price L £29.50, Menu Gourmand (L and D) £65. H/wine £20 ♀
Credit cards: 1 2 3 4 5

Menus: A la carte, Menu Gourmand, fixed-price lunch Menu du Jour

Times: 12.15pm-last L 2.15pm, 7.15pm-last D 10.15pm

finally the conservatory, which is the largest area, furnished in spring-like greens and pinks. This is also the setting for delicious breakfasts with freshly-baked viennoiseries (croissants, brioches, etc).

Our inspector had nothing but praise for the dinner he sampled, beginning with an intensely-flavoured and light-textured chilled watercress soup that packed a punch of vitamin and iron to set the taste buds zinging. A perfect starter of morels, stuffed with the lightest of chicken mousse, poached in Gewürztraminer and served with the best-flavoured asparagus he had tasted for years – doubtless the product of the hotel's almost legendary herb and vegetable gardens. Succulent breasts of quail formed the main course, perched on fondant potato, with an aromatic sauce flavoured with pineau des charentes, ceps and smoked bacon and, as the *pièce de résistance* of the presentation, a nest of fried leek and potato containing two soft-centred quail's eggs.

Desserts include Raymond's famous café crème – a wonderful conceit of a cup and saucer made of wafer-thin bitter chocolate and filled with intense coffee ice cream and a Kirsch sabayon – but our inspector chose a warm chocolate fondant served with almond cream and delicious pistachio ice cream to round off his evening. Menus consist of a seasonally-changing *carte*, with about seven choices at each stage, a set Menu Gourmand of seven courses, and a lunchtime fixed-price menu with a limited choice that represents a real bargain and would certainly inspire one to go back for dinner. There is also a reasonably priced and sensibly chosen children's menu.

The wine list is suitably impressive and comprehensive. It is good to see that beside the famous names and great vintages – Château Pétrus 1970, Château Latour 1961, four vintages of La Tâche, etc. – it also lists some very fine French regional wines, especially those from the Jura. There are more than 100 bottles costing less than £30 and a good range of half bottles.

Directions: From M40 junction 7 follow A329 towards Wallingford. In 1 mile turn right, signposted Great Milton Manor

Chefs: Raymond Blanc and Clive Fretwell
Proprietor: Raymond Blanc. General Manager: Simon Rhatigan

Seats: 95. No smoking areas. Air conditioned
Additional: Children welcome; children's menu/portions; ❂ menu; Vegan/other diets on request

HENLEY-ON-THAMES, Red Lion ❂

Ideally situated beside the River Thames and the famous Regatta course, this 16th-century red-brick coaching inn is family owned. Chef Emil Forde offers a carte featuring Modern British cuisine which includes vegetarian choices and a pleasing balance of interesting fish and meat dishes.

Cost: *Alc* £25, fixed-price L £18.50, Sunday L £17.50. H/wine £10.50. Service exc. **Credit cards**: 1 2 3 5. **Additional**: Children welcome; children's menu/portions; ❂ dishes; Vegan/other diets on request

Hart Street
Map no: 4 SU78
Tel: 01491 572161
Chef: Emil Forde
Proprietors: Durrani's Hotel. Manager: J P Leveque
Seats: 70. No cigars or pipes
Times: 12.30pm– last L 2pm, last D 10pm. Closed 27-29 Dec

ENGLAND OXFORDSHIRE

HORTON-CUM-STUDLEY,
Studley Priory ❀❀

Beautifully presented food which pleases the eye as much as the palate, in an equally lovely setting

Vestiges of a gilded past still cling to this Elizabethan monastery which dates back to the 12th century and is magnificently steeped in history. The beauty of Studley Priory is reflected in the food served in the smart restaurant, and meticulous care is taken with the presentation of every dish. The hotel is keen to promote new English cooking with the use of top-quality traditional English ingredients. Typical dishes on the well-written daily *carte* and fixed-price menus may include a starter of braised whole stuffed quail, or grilled fillets of mackerel, with main courses such as fillet of brill with woodland mushrooms and a tarragon sauce, or black-leg chicken with a blue sauce, walnuts and grapes. A recent inspection meal included some perfect-looking pan-fried Cornish scallops with a tomato and basil dressing, and moist breast of guinea fowl served with some very pretty vegetables. The chosen dessert was a smooth sticky toffee pudding, picked from an attractive selection. A good wine list is separated into the reasonable and the expensive.

Directions: At top of hill in the village

Map no: 4 SP51
Tel: 01865 351203

Cost: *Alc* £30, fixed-price L £19.50, fixed-price D £22.50. H/wine £10. Service inc
Credit cards: 1 2 3 4 5

Menus: *A la carte*, fixed-price, Sunday lunch, bar menu

Times: Last L 1.45pm/D 9.30pm

Chef: Trevor Bosch
Proprietor: Jeremy Parke

Seats: 60. No cigars or pipes
Additional: Children welcome (over 5 at dinner); children's portions; ◐ menu; Vegan/other diets on request

KINGHAM, Mill House ❀❀

Its attractive setting, relaxed atmosphere and imaginative menus make this restaurant understandably popular

Part of a delightful little hotel – a sensitively restored and extended building on the edge of the village, its seven-acre grounds bounded by a trout stream – this restaurant shares the relaxed yet efficient atmosphere that pervades the whole establishment. Head chef Stephen Lewis' imaginative fixed-price menus offer a well balanced choice (plus specialities with a supplementary charge). In the course of a typically enjoyable meal, cream of carrot and caraway soup with crisp golden croûtons might be followed by pan-fried loin of veal with a Madeira sauce and wild mushrooms; traditional rice or bread and butter puddings offer an alternative to lighter desserts like iced walnut parfait, or a choice of three cheeses comes with grapes and celery, as well as biscuits. Fresh vegetables are lightly cooked to preserve their flavour, but if you prefer them less crisp the menu invites you to make this known when placing your order; there is a separate vegetarian menu, and dishes suitable for children are always available. A fairly extensive wine list includes a good selection of half bottles as well as some New World labels.

Directions: On southern outskirts of village

Map no: 4 SP22
Tel: 01608 658188

Cost: *Alc* £28.95, fixed-price L £10.95, fixed-price D £19.95. H/wine £10.50 ♀ Service exc
Credit cards: 1 2 3 4 5

Menu: *A la carte* extras to fixed prices, fixed-price, Sunday lunch, bar menu

Times: Midday-last L 2pm, last D 9.45pm

Chef: Stephen Lewis
Proprietors: Mr and Mrs J Barnett. Manager: Simon Ellis

Seats: 70. No cigars or pipes
Additional: Children welcome; children's menu/portions; ◐ dishes; Vegan/other diets on request

MIDDLETON STONEY, Jersey Arms ✿

The restaurant of a former coaching inn retaining much of its 17th-century character and charm offers a seasonally-changing carte of sensible length. Dishes in modern style show a degree of originality, and the intrepid guest might choose a starter of kidney and snail ragout served in a pastry case.

Cost: Alc £21. H/wine £9.50 ♀ Service exc. **Credit cards:** 1 2 3 4
Additional: Children welcome; children's portions; ❽ dishes
Directions: 10 miles north of Oxford on the B430

Near Bicester
Map no: 4 SP52
Tel: 01869 343234
Chef: John Corbett
Proprietor: Consort. **Manager:** Donald Livingston
Seats: 50. No smoking in dining room
Times: Midday-last L 2pm, 7.30pm-last D 9.30pm. Closed Sun eve

MINSTER LOVELL,
Lovells at Windrush Farm ✿✿✿

A farmhouse 'restaurant with rooms' serving a no-choice lunch and dinner menu of classically cooked dishes

A period farmhouse in the Windrush Valley, this delightful restaurant with just three letting rooms is newly opened this year and is already attracting quite a following. Chef Robert Marshall-Slater offers a set three-course lunch and seven-course dinner with no choice at either, but the menus are discussed with guests on booking so that suitable alternatives can be provided if necessary. Vegetarians can also be catered for on this basis. Each of the dishes is classically cooked, and at a test lunch our inspector found them as near perfect as imaginable.

Meals, beginning with an appetiser of deep-fried cheese beignets, have continued with a regular starter of spinach soup, flavoured once with basil and finely grated parmesan and on another occasion with lime leaf. This was followed by chump of herb-crusted lamb, with a full-bodied minted jus and vegetables served as an integral part of the dish – turned courgette, swede, mange-touts, cauliflower and a crisp rösti. While at another meal the main course comprised fillet of beef rolled in cracked peppercorn, with a splendid colour and true Scottish flavour. This was set on a bed of shredded leek, lightly braised in white wine with grain mustard and cream, and accompanied by a tasty rösti of grated potato and carrot fried in duck fat. The stock sauce was finished with redcurrant jelly and vinegar, with plum tomato concasse as a garnish. The puddings sampled were a simple lemon tart with fine buttery pastry and a smooth lemon filling served with a thin strawberry coulis, and a trio of apple, including apple soufflé, roasted apple on filo pastry, and iced nougat with diced apple, all in an Italian meringue.

Directions: From the Witney–Minster Lovell road, take the first turning to the Old Minster

Map no: 4 SP31
Tel: 01993 779802

Cost: Alc £13.50, fixed-price £27.50
Credit cards: 1 2

Menus: A la carte, fixed price

Times: Closed Mon, Sat lunch, Sun eve

Chef: Robert Marshall-Slater
Proprietors: Mark Maguire, Norma Cooper

Additional: ❽ dishes; no smoking in dining room

MOULSFORD, Beetle & Wedge ❀❀❀

A delightful setting on the banks of the Thames for a choice of two fine restaurants in contrasting styles

A gem of a place situated on the banks of the Thames, this hotel is run by charming owners Richard and Kate Smith and their team of naturally friendly staff. The restaurant has recently been extended and converted into a light conservatory-style room with lovely garden views down to the river. In addition to the restaurant there is the ever-popular Boathouse, a less formal venue with an exciting *carte* menu. The quality of ingredients and the general standard of cooking is excellent, and though simpler in style than the restaurant food, it is no less enjoyable. The fish soup was wonderful, the best our inspector had tasted this year, and the duck liver terrine, flavoured with cognac, also delicious. An attractively presented dish of monkfish with baby onions, scallops and sun-dried tomatoes tasted as good as it looked, and a superb lemon tart with crème anglais and lemon ice cream rounded off the meal. Skilled saucing, simple vegetables and an unfussy style of cooking bring the freshness and flavour of the food to the fore, and as meals are freshly prepared vegetarians can discuss their requirements for adapted dishes at the time of ordering.

The Dining Room (restaurant) offers a more sophisticated *carte* and fixed-price lunch menus. Here, at an early summer dinner, our inspector sampled a Stilton soufflé with mushroom sauce described as 'absolute heaven', followed by chargrilled sea-bass with a tomato, basil and olive oil sauce. It has to be admitted that she chose lemon tart again for dessert (she couldn't resist it) but other options might have been chocolate rum truffle cake, hot Cointreau soufflé with hot raspberry sauce or a selection of farmhouse cheeses.

The wine list is of a convenient length and drawn almost entirely from the classic areas of France, including many mature vintages of Burgundy and claret. House wines are available by the glass and part of a bottle.

Directions: In village turn towards river via Ferry Lane

Ferry Lane
Map no: 4 SU58
Tel: 01491 651381

Cost: *Alc* Dining room £30, Boathouse £25, fixed-price (Dining Room only) L £17.50, Sun L £27.50. H/wine £10.75 ♀ Service exc
Credit cards: 1 2 3 4 5

Menus: *A la carte*, fixed-price lunch, Sunday lunch

Times: 12.30-last L 2pm, 7.30-last D 10pm. Closed 25 Dec. Dining Room closed Sun eve & all day Mon

Chef: Richard Smith
Proprietors: Kate and Richard Smith

Seats: Dining room 40, Boathouse 60. No smoking in Dining Room
Additional: Children permitted; children's portions on request; ❷ dishes; Vegan/other diets on request

OXFORD, Bath Place ❀❀

The Parisian effect of this small restaurant's exterior is echoed in the continental influences which shape its cuisine.

Neo-classical dishes are given a Mediterranean interpretation by this cottage-style restaurant tucked away down a cobbled city alley. Occupying three sides of the alley's end, it makes excellent use of its position – a profusion of hanging baskets and potted shrubs creating a positively Parisian effect on sunny days – and the small bar and adjoining dining room are equally full of character. A typical first course like ravioli of scallop and salmon flavoured with saffron oil might be followed by roast wood pigeon set on a bed of spinach and artichoke hearts and served with a robust, spicy gravy, the meal perhaps ending with an apricot-glazed savarin of raspberries, then good espresso coffee with truffles and petits fours. The wine list offers a good

4 & 5 Bath Place, Holywell Street
Map no: 4 SP50
Tel: 01865 791812

Cost: *Alc* £33, fixed-price L £12 (2 courses), £16.50, Sun L £19.50, fixed-price D (residents only) £16.50. H/wine £10.50 ♀ Service exc
Credit cards: 1 2 3
Menus: *A la carte*, fixed-price, Sunday lunch
Times: Midday–last L 2pm, 7pm–last D 10pm (10.30pm Fri & Sat). Closed Sun eve, all day Mon & Tue lunch

selection of French regional and New World wines which has something to suit most pockets, and low-key service helps to create a relaxed atmosphere. True vegetarians should note that there are a restricted number of dishes meeting their requirements – but those among them who eat fish are well catered for.

Directions: Off Holywell Street in the city centre, opposite Holywell Music Room

Chef: Jeremy Blake O'Connor
Proprietors: Kathleen and Yolanda Fawsitt
Seats: 30. No smoking in dining room
Additional: Children welcome; children's portions; ❶ menu; Vegan dishes by arrangement; other diets on request

OXFORD, '15' ✿✿

☺ *A totally transformed restaurant with an abbreviated name, minimalist decor and an eclectic international menu*

Fifteen North Parade, established by Georgina Wood in 1988, has undergone a complete transformation, affecting its look, ambience and menu, and is now known simply as '15'. The kitchen has been taken over by Georgina's son Sean and his colleague Ben Gorman, both of whom trained under Sonia Blech at Mijanou, Belgravia. The cool modern decor of the reconstituted restaurant provides an appropriate setting for their eclectic new *carte* menu. Dishes include starters of 'salmorejo', a chilled tomato soup with basil, egg and cured ham, and wild salmon carpaccio with fresh radishes, mouli and home-made horseradish. Main courses range from hamburger with spicy yellow catsup, red onion relish and chunky chips, to lamb with saffron, zucchini and marjoram tajine, and a three-rice timbale. Vegetarian options are available, perhaps borlotti beans and chestnuts stewed in red wine with garlic crostini. Tempting desserts such as light summer pudding or hot chocolate brownie are offered, or cheese with home-made biscuits, followed by coffee or mint tea with crystallised pecan nuts. There is a short wine list.

Directions: Off the Banbury road

15 North Parade Avenue
Map no: 4 SP50
Tel: 01865 513773

Cost: *Alc* £18.50, fixed-price L £10 (2 courses), £12, Sun L £13.75. H/wine £9.75. Service exc
Credit cards: 1 3 5

Menus: *A la carte*, fixed-price lunch, Sunday lunch
Times: Midday-last L 2pm, 7pm-last D 11pm. Closed Sun eve and all day Mon

Chefs: Sean Wood and Ben Gorman
Proprietor: Georgina Wood

Seats: 55-60. No-smoking area. Air conditioned
Additional: Children welcome; children's portions; ❶ dishes; Vegan and other diets on request

OXFORD, **Hawkwell House** ✿

A period country house enjoying a pretty village riverside location. A short fixed-price and carte menus are offered in the Orangery restaurant, featuring tasty, modern English cuisine. Carte dishes might be chicken, mushroom and herb mousse followed by roast venison and summer pudding.

Cost: *Alc* L £28, Sunday L £11.50, fixed-price D £15. H/wine £8.75. Service exc. **Credit cards**: 1 2 3. **Additional**: Children welcome; children's portions; children's menu by arrangement; ❶ menu; Vegan dishes by arrangement; other diets on request
Directions: 2 miles from city centre into Iffley village

Church Way, Iffley
Map no: 4 SP50
Tel: 01865 749988
Chef: Dean Collins
General Manager: Stephen G Carter
Seats: 60. No smoking in dining room
Times: 7pm-last D 9.45pm (9.30pm Sun), last Sun L 2.30pm

OXFORD, Liaison ❀

Specialising in Dim Sum, the carte also contains dishes from many Asian countries such as Malaysian satay and Mongolian lamb. Also available are the traditional favourites such as crispy aromatic duck in pancakes with plum sauce as well as hotter dishes like the pork dish Jarjoy.

Cost: *Alc* £30, fixed-price £14.80. H/Wine £8.50. **Credit cards:** 1 2 3 4
Directions: The restaurant is behind the main shopping centre

29 Castle Street
Map no: 4 SP50
Tel: 01865 242944
Times: Midday-last L 2.45pm, 6pm-11.15pm. Closed Xmas

OXFORD, Munchy Munchy ❀

☺ *A bistro-style restaurant offering a choice of six or seven Asian dishes which are skilfully seasoned. Dishes, principally from Sumatra, include chicken with turmeric, cinnamon, nutmeg, mint and apricot, or King prawns with aniseed, red pepper, black mushrooms and a ginger wine sauce.*

Cost: *Alc* £13.50. H/wine £7.15. Service exc. **Credit cards:** 1 3 5
Additional: Children permitted (not under 6 on Fri & Sat evenings); one daily ❂ dish
Directions: West of city centre, between Nuffield College and the station

6 Park End Street
Map no: 4 SP50
Tel: 01865 245710
Chef: Ethel Ow
Proprietors: Tony and Ethel Ow
Seats: 60. No-smoking area; no pipes or cigars
Times: Midday-last L 2pm, 5.30pm-last D 10pm. Closed Sun, Mon, 3 weeks Dec/Jan

OXFORD, Whites ❀❀

Quality fresh produce handled skilfully and served in an enjoyable ambience

One of Oxford's honey-coloured terraced houses, this is an interesting restaurant where plum and cerise decorations provide a rich background for the enjoyably unfussy cooking. An attractive choice of fixed-price menus offers a glass of wine with each course, carefully chosen to complement imaginative creations such as leek, black pudding and parmesan tart, or spiced coconut mussels; alternatively there is a short *carte* of mainly meat and game dishes with a fresh fish option when it is available. Our inspector opted for the latter menu, and enjoyed a moist and gamey roast breast of pigeon with chestnut polenta and a redcurrant jus for starters. Simply steamed monkfish was tasty and firm, and served on a bed of tagliatelle with a light chive and saffron butter sauce and tasty glazed vegetables, and an individual bread and butter pudding made to the restaurant's own recipe was very good. The staff are friendly and there is an excellent wine list with plenty of good vintages, halves and by-the-glass choices. A vaulted cellar from part of the city wall houses the owner's wine shop.

Directions: In city centre, next to Jesus College, opposite Exeter College

Turl Street
Map no: 4 SP50
Tel: 01865 793396

Cost: *Alc* from £25, fixed-price L £12.95, fixed-price D £23.95. H/wine £8.50 ♀ Service exc
Credit cards: 1 2 3 4

Menus: A la carte, fixed-price, Sunday lunch

Times: 12.30pm–last L 2pm, 6.30pm–last D 10.15pm. Closed Sun eve during University vacations and 1 week at Xmas

Chef: Christopher Bland
Proprietor: Michael White

Seats: 45. No–smoking area. No pipes
Additional: Children permitted; children's portions; ❂ dishes; Vegan/other diets by arrangement

SHIPTON-UNDER-WYCHWOOD, **Lamb Inn** ⊛

☺ *A cross between Cotswold inn and country house, the Lamb offers a comfortable venue for both buffet lunches and restaurant dinners. Cooking is English in style – dishes like field mushrooms stuffed with Stilton or pan-fried veal kidneys with mustard sauce make good use of local produce.*

Cost: Fixed-price D £19.50. H/wine £8 ♀ Service exc **Credit cards:** 1 2 3 **Additional:** No children under 14; ❂ dishes
Directions: In village centre

High Street
Map no: 4 SP21
Tel: 01993 830465
Chef: Robin Bancroft
Proprietor: Mr L Valenta.
Manager: Mr R Ansell
Seats: 30. No smoking in dining room
Times: Last L 2pm/D 9.30pm. Closed Mon

STONOR, **Stonor Arms** ⊛⊛⊛

Charming staff serve a good choice of European dishes in the restaurant or brasserie of this former village inn

Once the village inn, this attractive hotel and restaurant is in a rural setting close to Henley-on-Thames. The hotel has developed a fine reputation, not only for its comfort and hospitality, but also for the quality of its food. Chef-proprietor Stephen Frost and his talented team offer an imaginative and sensibly priced range of dishes in the more formal Stonor Restaurant, or Blades Brasserie which is located in a conservatory overlooking the vegetable garden.

Three-course fixed-price and *carte* menus are presented in the restaurant and the style of cooking is mostly English and French with Italian and other influences. A test meal began with canapés served with drinks in the bar, and at the table there was a good choice of breads, including sun-dried tomato and walnut. The starter of ratatouille timbale with a pesto vinaigrette was lovely, fresh and colourful with good flavours reminiscent of the Mediterranean. The mussel and saffron soup was also worthy of note. Main courses include loin of rabbit stuffed with prunes, much enjoyed by our inspector, with mashed potato and wild mushrooms, and, also good, pan-fried breast of duckling served in a pastry galette with apple purée and lightly flavoured ginger sauce. Vegetarian options are also available.

Desserts include hazelnut mousse with praline biscuits and passion fruit sauce, poached fruit savarin glazed with a Chartreuse sabayon with a raspberry sauce, or a well-recommended dark chocolate soufflé. Alternatively, there is a plate of British cheeses, with oatcakes and cheese and herb biscuits. Coffee comes with a good array of petits fours.

Standing out from the excellent wine list are seven vintages of Château Batailley dating back to 1947, and a lovely range of white Burgundy from Olivier Leflaive. Also offered is an interesting selection of recommended wines.

Directions: In centre of village

Near Henley-on-Thames
Map no: 4 SU78
Tel: 01491 638345/638866

Cost: *Alc* £21.50, fixed-price D £29.50. H/wine £8.75. Service exc
Credit cards: 1 2 3

Menus: *A la carte,* fixed-price dinner, bar menu

Times: Last L 2pm/D 9.30pm

Chefs: Stephen Frost, Stuart Morrison
Proprietors: Stonor Hotels.
Manager: Stephen Frost

Seats: 60. No cigars or pipes
Additional: Children welcome; children's portions; ❂ dishes; Vegetarian menu on request; Vegan/other diets on request

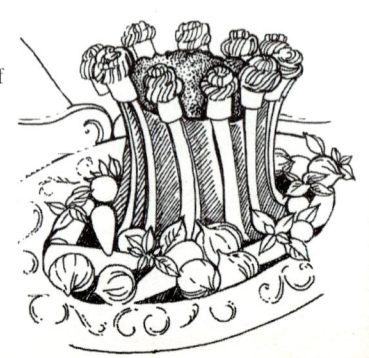

THAME, Spread Eagle ❀

☺ *A refreshingly different Spiced Spring menu – its distinctive flavours and textures superior to those achieved by many Chinese and Indian restaurants – supplements the well-balanced carte and fixed-price choices of English/French dishes available at this characterful coaching inn.*

Cost: *A/c* £20.95, fixed-price L up to £16.45/D £18.95. H/wine £8.75 ♀ Service inc. **Credit cards:** 1 2 3 4 5
Additional: Children welcome; children's menu/portions; ❂ menu; Vegan/other diets on request
Directions: In town centre

Cornmarket
Map no: 4 SP70
Tel: 01844 213661
Chef: Michael Thomas
Proprietors: D M L Barrington
Seats: 65
Times: 12.30–last L 2pm (2.30pm Sun), 7pm (7.30 Sat)-last D 10pm (9pm Sun). Closed 28-30 Dec

WALLINGFORD, Springs ❀

A mock-Tudor hotel with a balcony-style restaurant, overlooking a lake. The menus offer a good choice of grills, fish and vegetarian dishes. Chef Jamie Jones creates such delicious dishes as six large Cornish oysters, or escalopes of salmon wrapped in salmon with a herb crust.

Cost: *A/c* from £20, fixed-price L £14 (2 courses), £17/D £21.50. H/wine £12. Service exc. **Credit cards:** 1 2 3 4. **Additional:** Children permitted; half-portions; ❂ dishes; Vegan/other diets on request
Directions: On B4009 between Crowmarsh and Goring, on outskirts of North Stoke

Wallingford Road, North Stoke
Map no: 4 SU68
Tel: 01491 836687
Chef: Jamie Jones
Proprietor: Michael Cavilla
Seats: 80. No cigars or pipes
Times: Last L 2pm/D 9.45pm

WANTAGE, Foxes ❀

A cosy restaurant in a 16th-century beamed cottage where chef Karen Sweeney produces a good variety of dishes including vegetarian choices. To start try baked bantam and quail's eggs and follow with sea-bream served with cockles and vermouth sauce or an asparagus pancake.

Credit Cards: 1 3. **Additional:** Children permitted; ❂ menu; Vegan dishes with advance notice; other diets on request
Directions: Just off market square on Newbury/Reading road

8 Newbury Street
Map no: 4 SU38
Tel: 01235 760568
Chef: Karen Sweeney
Proprietors: Karen Sweeney and Nicholas Offen
Seats: 30/35. No smoking until all meals served
Times: Midday-last L 1.45pm, 7pm-last D 9.30pm. Closed Sun eve, Mon lunch; Mon eve pre-booking only; 3 weeks Jan

WESTON-ON-THE-GREEN, Weston Manor ❀

The manor has lovely gardens, and guests eat in a splendid baronial hall (but don't expect baronial portions of Andrew Cunningham's modern cuisine). A ravioli of mushroom and chicken proved tiny but tasty, and a dessert of iced banana parfait was also highly praised. There is a vegetarian option.

Cost: Fixed-price L £15.50/D £24.50. H/wine £10.50. Service exc
Credit cards: 1 2 3 4 **Additional:** Children welcome; children's menu/portions; ❂ dishes; Vegan/other diets on request
Directions: In village centre

Map no: 4 SP51
Tel: 01869 350621
Chef: Andrew Cunningham
Proprietor: Dudley Osborn
Seats: 40
Times: 12.30pm–last L 2pm, 7.30pm–last D 9.45pm. Closed Sat lunch

WOODSTOCK, **Bear** ❀

Dinner menus change daily, lunches and Sundays change weekly and there are seasonal revamps too, but a British emphasis is maintained throughout, with dishes such as lamb steak with wild mushroom and Madeira sauce. Beams, tapestries and huge fireplaces provide a traditional setting.

Cost: *Alc* £35, fixed-price L £14.95 (2 courses), £16.95/D £22.95. H/wine £14.95. Service inc. **Credit cards:** 1 2 3 4 5
Additional: Children permitted; children's menu/portions; ❂ menu; Vegan/other diets on request
Directions: At end of High Street

Park Street
Map no: 4 SP41
Tel: 01993 811511
Chef: Ian Morgan
Proprietor: Forte. Manager: Helen Rich
Seats: 90. No smoking in dining room
Times: 12.30pm–last L 2.30pm, 7pm–last D 9.45pm

WOODSTOCK, **Chef Imperial** ❀

☺ *Peking and Szechuan specialities in a very British location. Some unusual choices such as the 'Leave-it-to-us Feast' - selected by the chef, or three-course 'Just duck special'. Over 100 items appear on the varied carte, in generous portions and with reasonable prices.*

Cost: *Alc* £15, fixed-price L £5.95/D £14-£14.75 (2 courses), £16.50, £17.50, £20. H/wine £8.50. Service exc
Credit cards: 1 2 3. **Additional:** Children welcome; ❂ menu, Vegan/other diets on request
Directions: In centre of Woodstock, opposite car park near Blenheim Palace

22 High Street
Map no: 4 SP41
Tel: 01993 813593
Chef: P C Wong
Proprietor: Alan Shek
Seats: 100. No-smoking area. Air conditioned
Times: Midday–last L 2.30pm, 6pm–last D midnight. Closed 25-27 Dec

WOODSTOCK, **Feathers** ❀❀

A converted 17th-century inn offering progressive English cooking that shows much imagination

Winding passages and steep staircases confirm the 17th-century origins of this country inn close to the imposing entrance to Blenheim Palace. The Feathers offers comfortable accommodation and good food, together with a high standard of hospitality. Delicious titbits are laid out for diners in the flagstoned bar where orders are taken, and the light and elegant restaurant makes a pleasant setting for chef David Lewis's imaginative cooking. He has a certain flair for adapting popular Mediterranean and classic dishes, and the various set and *carte* menus might offer chargrilled smoked salmon with sweet peppers and lime, or confit of leg of duck with braised red cabbage and soy and ginger dressing. A recent enjoyable inspection meal began with marinated New Zealand mussels wrapped in Parma ham – a version of angels on horseback which produced a delicious combination of flavours but was rather dry. Braised chicken in thyme was tasty and moist, and vegetables were naturally full of flavour. A steamed ginger sponge with a good caramel sauce came with a dollop of vanilla ice cream.

Directions: In centre of Woodstock, off the A44; from the south take 2nd left after Blenheim Palace gates

Market Street
Map no: 4 SP41
Tel: 01993 812291

Cost: *Alc* from £29, fixed-price L £16.50 (2-course), £19.95, fixed-price D £23.50. H/wine £11.60 ♀ Service 15%
Credit cards: 1 2 3 4

Menus: *A la carte*, fixed-price; Sunday lunch, bar menu

Times: Last L 2.15pm (2.30pm Sun)/D 9.30pm

Chef: David Lewis
Proprietor: Tom Lewis

Seats: 60. No cigars or pipes. Air conditioned
Additional: Children welcome; children's portions on request; ❂ dishes/Vegan/other diets on request; live entertainment Wed evenings

SHROPSHIRE

BRIDGNORTH, **Haywain** ●●

☺ *An interesting and enjoyable eating experience in an atmosphere of tangible well-being*

A smart cottage-style restaurant in a secluded rural position near the River Severn is the delightful setting for an unusual eating experience. Chef David Browning provides a cold table for the second course from which diners can try a little of everything – including salads, smoked and fresh meats, and crab and various fish – and the idea has proved very popular. The seven-course gourmet menu also offers home-made soup, sorbet, a choice of five main courses, dessert and cheese, and our inspector thoroughly enjoyed a recent meal which began with a smooth nettle soup with an appealing flavour. Five rosettes of juicy lamb needed no improvement, but were surprisingly enhanced by a sharp damson sauce, while an open apple tart was a tasty dessert. There is also a shorter fixed-price menu and a separate one for vegetarians, and both are frequently changed. Typical main courses might be piccatas of tuna with ginger and red wine, and marinaded pheasant cooked with mushrooms and baby onions. There's a relaxed, informal atmosphere in which to enjoy this modern English cooking, and service is friendly and attentive.

Directions: 4 miles south of Bridgnorth off the A442

Hampton Loade
Map no: 7 SO79
Tel: 01746 780404

Cost: Fixed-price D £15.50 (4 courses) £25, Sunday L £11.95. H/wine: £6.95 ♀ Service inc
Credit cards: 1 2 3 4

Times: 12.30-last L 2pm, 7.30pm-last D 9.30pm. Closed Sun eve and all day Mon

Chef: Carl B Withey
Proprietor: David R Browning

Seats: 50. No smoking in dining room
Additional: Children welcome; children's portions; ✿ menu; Vegan/other diets on request

CLEOBURY MORTIMER, **Redfern** ●

☺ *A small and pleasant family-run hotel, with the proprietor's son, Richard, providing good, wholesome food. The food is unpretentious, with jumbo whole crevettes as a starter from the supplementary carte, and grilled whole trout with prawn sauce, a main course from the daily-changing fixed menu.*

Cost: Alc £18, fixed-price £15.95. Service inc. **Credit cards**: 1 3
Additional: Children permitted; ✿ dishes; no smoking in dining room
Directions: On eastern side of town centre

Map no: 7 SO67
Tel: 01299 270395
Chef: Richard Redfern
Proprietors: Jon and Liz Redfern

DORRINGTON, Country Friends ❀❀

A long-established village restaurant serving a short but balanced selection of well-made British food

A black and white timber-framed building houses this popular village restaurant set in pleasant gardens, and exposed ceiling beams and an inglenook fireplace create an attractive atmosphere inside. Guests are looked after by the very experienced Pauline Whittaker, while her husband Charles produces a short but varied fixed-price menu from seasonal ingredients, including a daily fresh fish dish and a vegetarian choice; the price varies according to the number of courses taken, and is the same at lunch and dinner. A typical meal might be twice-baked courgette soufflé, followed by Trelough duck breast with spiced plum and ginger sauce, and traditional bread and butter pudding. At a recent meal our inspector chose delicately flavoured fish quenelles with a light smoked prawn sauce, and lean and tender lamb served with a tartlet of flageolet beans, baby onions and bacon. Apple galette had a good fruit filling inside well-made pastry, and came with a creamy custard sauce which showed little evidence of the mint flavour it promised. Fresh, strong coffee and petits fours brought an enjoyable meal to a close.

Directions: In centre of village

Map no: 7 SJ40
Tel: 01743 718707

Cost: Fixed-price L & D £20.50 (2 courses), £24.50. H/wine £10.50 ♀ Service exc
Credit cards: 1 2 3

Menus: Fixed-price, bar menu

Times: Last L 2pm/D 9pm (9.30pm Sat). Closed Sun, Mon, 2 weeks Jul, last week Oct & Xmas

Chef: Charles Whittaker
Proprietors: Charles and Pauline Whittaker

Seats: 45. No smoking in dining room
Additional: Children welcome; ❂ dish; other diets on request

LUDLOW, Dinham Hall ❀

☺ *A delightful stone-built Georgian house situated opposite Ludlow Castle, where chef David Osler produces a short but imaginative menu. Dishes include smoked chicken and asparagus salad as a starter which could be followed by breast of guinea fowl with coarse-grain mustard sauce.*

Cost: Fixed-price D £18.50. H/wine £8.75 ♀ Service exc
Credit cards: 1 2 3 4 5. **Additional**: Children permitted; children's portions; ❂ dishes; Vegan/other diets on request
Directions: In town centre, opposite castle gardens

Map no: 7 SO57
Tel: 01584 876464
Chef: David Osler
Proprietors: Jean-Pierre and Jen Mifsud
Seats: 30. No smoking in restaurant
Times: 12.30pm–last L 2.30pm, 7pm–last D 9.30pm

LUDLOW, Feathers at Ludlow ❀

A distinguished hotel with 17th-century origins, featuring an impressive façade of carved timber work and arches. The Housman Restaurant offers fixed-price and carte menus with dishes covering a wide price range. Good English cooking is the theme, ranging from lamb cutlets to the daily roast.

Cost: Alc £25, buffet L £7.50, fixed-price L £9 (1 course) £11, £13/D £19.50. H/wine £9 ♀ No service charge **Credit cards**: 1 2 3 4 5
Additional: Children welcome; children's portions; ❂ dishes; other diets on request
Directions: In town centre

Bull Ring
Map no: 7 SO57
Tel: 01584 875261
Chef: Philip Woodhall
Proprietor: O Edwards.
Manager: Peter Nash
Seats: 60. No smoking in dining room. Air conditioned
Times: 7.30pm–last D 9.30pm

MARKET DRAYTON, **Goldstone Hall** ●

A country house with an intimate atmosphere where chef Nigel Huxley produces various menus including a 'Thank Fish It's Friday' menu which is almost entirely fish. Starters of asparagus could be followed by casserole of rabbit with fungi and cream or fillet of beef with peppercorn sauce.

Cost: A/c £22, fixed-price L £14.95/D £28.50. H/wine £8.30 ♀ Service exc. **Credit cards**: 1 2 3 4 5. **Additional**: Children permitted; children's portions; ◊ dishes; Vegan/other diets on request
Directions: 4 miles south of Market Drayton, follow tourist signs for Goldstone Hall Gardens

Goldstone
Map no: 7 SJ63
Tel: 01630 661202
Chef: Nigel Huxley
Proprietors: John Cushing and Helen Ward
Seats: 60. Smoking discouraged in dining room; no cigars or pipes
Times: Midday–last L 2.30pm, last D 10.pm

SHREWSBURY, **Albright Hussey** ●●

A superb hotel which offers a delightful dining experience in a memorable setting

Set in landscaped gardens with an original moat crossed by a stone bridge and inhabited by stately black swans, this impressive hotel simply exudes character. The black and white building dates from the early 16th century, and the interior has been meticulously restored by its committed owners. The hospitable Subbiani family provide guests with a warm welcome which, far from fading with familiarity, continues in the form of constant caring attention. It comes as no surprise to learn that the food is of the same consistently high standard, and visitors can expect to sample enjoyable meals cooked to order using only fresh quality ingredients. The French *carte* with English translations offers an extremely well-balanced choice, with fish and shellfish sitting comfortably beside meat, game and the odd vegetarian dish. Starters might include 'terrine de fruits de mer au sabayon' – seafood paté in a light lobster sauce, followed, perhaps, by 'foie de veau berrichonne' – calf's liver tossed in Tio Pepe, or 'mignonettes de chevreuil aux myrtilles' – pan-fried marinated venison fillets sliced in a blueberry sauce.

Directions: On A528 2.5 miles from centre of Shrewsbury

Ellesmere Road
Map no: 7 SJ41
Tel: Bomere Heath 01939 290571

Cost: A/c from £20, fixed-price L from £12/D £15. H/wine £9.30. Service exc
Credit cards: 1 2 3 4

Menu: *A la carte*, fixed-price, Sunday lunch

Times: Midday–last L 2.15pm, last D 10.15pm

Chefs: Paul Davies, Neil Marriot, Nick Shingles
Proprietor: Franco Subbiani

Seats: 80. No smoking
Additional: No children under 3; children's portions; ◊ menu; Vegan/other diets on request

TELFORD, **Holiday Inn** ●

Situated adjacent to the exhibition centre, this modern low-rise hotel offers an eclectic mix of cuisine in Courts Restaurant. Chef John Mitchell provides an extensive range of menus with a wide selection of Japanese and healthy eating dishes to complement the English and international cuisine.

Cost: A/c £23.65, fixed-price L £10.95/D £15.95, set Japanese menu £14.50. H/wine £8.95 ♀ Service exc. **Credit cards**: 1 2 3 4
Additional: Children welcome; children's menu/portions; ◊ menu; Vegan/other diets on request
Directions: 1/2 mile south-east of town centre, just off the St Quentin roundabout

St Quentin Gate
Map no: 7 SJ60
Tel: 01952 292500
Chef: John Mitchel
Proprietor: Holiday Inn.
Manager: James Ford
Seats: 110. No smoking area. Air conditioned
Times: Last L 2pm/D 10pm

SHROPSHIRE ENGLAND

TELFORD, **Madeley Court** ❀

An impressive 13th-century house lying next to a lake set in mature parkland, where chef Paul Davis-Clarkson produces good imaginative food. Our inspector recommended salmon and spinach en croûte with a velouté of ginger, preceded by a smooth garlic and liver pâté with cranberry purée.

Credit cards: 1 2 3 4
Additional: Children welcome; ❂ dishes.

Map no 7 SJ60
Tel: 01952 680068
Chef: Paul Davis-Clarkson

WORFIELD, **Old Vicarage** ❀❀❀

A hotel restaurant offering a good variety of dishes, including a vegetarian option, based on top-quality fresh ingredients

A fine hotel, this Edwardian former vicarage was acquired by Christine and Peter Iles in 1979, and sympathetically restored with no loss of charm and character. The comfortable public areas are enhanced by a collection of paintings.

Young chef John Williams has a well-deserved reputation for his good food. His menu, priced for three or four courses, is a sensible size offering half-a-dozen options at each stage, and it changes frequently to take account of the best available fresh produce. Local lamb, pork, beef, poultry, fish and game all feature, along with shell and sea fish from the West Country. All the breads, ice cream, sorbets and preserves are home-made, and an excellent selection of hand-made traditional British cheeses is offered, including Shropshire Blue, Bonchester, and several vegetarian cheeses such as Yarg from Cornwall, a semi-hard cheese wrapped in nettle leaves. Vegetarians are taken seriously here, with an appropriate starter and main course always available, such as carrot and coriander soup, followed by baked aubergines with pesto, tomato with goat's cheese and roast shallots.

An enjoyable May inspection meal began with creamy leek and potato soup served with crisp, buttery croûtons. The main course was a hearty and thoroughly enjoyable dish of braised shank of Shropshire lamb, the tender meat falling off the bone, accompanied by mashed potato with chives and a robust Madeira jus. The refreshing and attractively presented dessert comprised half a baby pineapple filled with rice soufflé and served with pineapple ice cream.

The extensive wine list is representative of some of the best estates and growers around the world, and keenly priced throughout. The Bordeaux and Burgundy and half-bottle sections are particularly strong.

Directions: From Wolverhampton take A454 Bridgnorth road, turning right after Hilton; from Telford take the A442 Kidderminster road, turning left beyond Norton

Map no: 7 SO79
Tel: 01746 4497

Cost: Fixed-price L £17.50, fixed-price D Mon-Thu £21.50, Fri & Sat £26.50 (3-course), £5 for extra course. H/wine £11.50 ♀ Service exc
Credit cards: 1 2 3 4

Menus: Fixed-price, Sunday lunch

Times: Last L 2pm/D 9pm. Closed Sat lunch

Chef: John Williams
Proprietor: Peter Iles

Seats: 50. No-smoking area
Additional: Children permitted (not under 8 at dinner); children's menu/portions; ❂ dishes; Vegan/other diets on request

SOMERSET

AXBRIDGE, **Oak House**

The Square
Map no: 3 ST45
Tel: 01934 732444
Chef: P A Cook
Proprietor: P W Cook
Seats: 40. No smoking in dining room
Times: Midday–last L 2.15pm, last D 9.15pm

☺ Set in the square of the town of Axbridge, this property dates back to the 13th century. The hotel offers a choice of either a formal restaurant or a popular bistro. Good quality produce is cooked with honesty and fresh textures and flavours.

Cost: Alc £20, fixed-price L & D £12.95. H/wine £6.50. Service exc
Credit cards: 1 2 3 5. Additional: Children permitted; children's portions; ❻ dishes
Directions: On east side of town square

BECKINGTON, **Woolpack Inn**

Near Frome
Map no: 3 ST85
Tel: 01373 831244
Chef: David Woolfall
Proprietors: Martin E W Tarr and Paul A Toogood
Seats: 100. No-smoking area
Times: Midday–last L 2.30pm, 7pm–last D 10pm

This small 16th-century coaching inn was a worthy winner of the Best Newcomer Award for 1994. Head chef David Woolfall offers a carte menu of modern English dishes with a French influence, such as chicken liver parfait, loin of lamb and a tangy lemon tart.

Cost: Alc L £15/D £24. Credit cards: 1 3
Additional: Children welcome; ❻ dishes
Directions: In village centre

BRUTON, **Truffles**

95 High Street
Map no: 3 ST63
Tel: 01749 812255
Chef: Martin Bottrill
Proprietors: Denise and Martin Bottrill
Seats: 20. No smoking whilst others guests are eating; no pipes
Times: Last L 2pm/D 9.30pm. Closed Mon except BHs

☺ Imaginative and predominantly French cuisine features in this atmospheric cottage restaurant. Snail and garlic pâté or roasted ratatouille wrapped in an aubergine jacket could be followed by suprême of chicken provençale with spicy sausage, sun-dried tomatoes and olives in paprika sauce.

Cost: Alc £21.70, fixed-price L £12.95 (3 courses)/D £12.50 (2 courses). H/wine £8.50 ♀ No service charge. Credit cards: 1 3
Additional: No children under 6; children's portions; ❻ menu; Vegan dishes to order only; other diets on request
Directions: At start of one-way system, on left-hand side next to car showroom

DULVERTON, **Ashwick House**

Map no: 3 SS92
Tel: 01398 23868
Chef: R Sherwood
Proprietor: R Sherwood
Seats: 35-40. No smoking in dining room
Times: Last L 1.45pm/D 8.30pm

A charming Edwardian house generally offering a set four-course dinner. Prepared from the best fresh produce, dishes may include local fish, meat and game when in season. For example: thin slices of smoked venison as a starter, and fillet of salmon with a Vermouth sauce as a main course.

Cost: Fixed-price L £13.95/D £21.35. H/wine £10. Service exc
Credit cards: None taken. Additional: No children under 8; ❻/Vegan/other diets with prior notice
Directions: Off B3223 Lynton road, turn left after second cattle grid

DUNSTER, **Exmoor House** ❀

☺ *Phyl Lally cooks simple but delicious food in this small Georgian hotel with its cosy atmosphere. Starters include pears with Stilton sauce or apple and prawn salad, and main courses include lamb en croûte, venison in red wine, carbonnade of beef or pork chop cooked in cider and topped with cheese.*

Cost: Fixed-price D £14.50. H/wine £8. Service inc
Credit cards: 1 2 3 4. **Additional**: No children under 12; children's portions; ⓥ dishes; other diets on request
Directions: Off High Street, 75 yds from church

12 West Street
Map no: 3 SS94
Tel: 01643 821268
Chef: Phyl Lally
Proprietors: Brendan and Phyl Lally
Seats: 24. Exclusively non-smoking
Times: Last D 8pm. Closed Nov–Jan

EXEBRIDGE, **Anchor Inn** ❀

☺*The inn, mentioned in 'Lorna Doone', is in a quiet hamlet by the River Exe. The restaurant, in a converted stable block offers trout from the river and local game whenever possible. There is a range of delicious home-made puddings.*

Cost: D £15.95, Sunday L £9.50. H/wine £6.95. **Credit cards**: 1 3
Additional: ⓥ dishes. Children's menu/portions;
Directions: Situated on B3222 just off the Minehead road

Near Dulverton
Map no: 3 SS92
Tel: 01398 23433
Chef: Jane Osbourne
Proprietors: John and Judy Phripp
Times: Last L 2pm/D 9pm

HOLFORD, **Combe House** ❀

☺ *A beautifully situated former tannery where chef Lynn Gardener creates a balanced menu of delicious dishes. Amongst the temptations are baked aubergines with tomato and mozzarella and, to follow, calf's liver with fresh herbs or poached fillet of salmon with hollandaise sauce.*

Cost: Fixed-price D £15.25. H/wine £6.95 ♀ Service inc
Credit cards: 1 2 3 5. **Additional**: Children welcome; children's portions; chldren's menu on request; special diets on request
Directions: Half a mile from A39, turn up lane between garage and Plough Inn, then left at fork

Map no: 3 ST14
Tel: 01278 741382
Chef: Lynn Gardner
Proprietor: Richard Bjergfelt
Seats: 36. No smoking in dining room
Times: Last L 2pm/D 8.30pm

MINEHEAD, **Periton Park** ❀❀

☺ *Modern British cuisine using fresh local produce in the kitchens of this superbly situated country hotel*

The air of a country gentleman's house pervades this secluded hotel on the edge of Exmoor, and after trying traditional rural pursuits such as hunting, shooting and fishing – or even just relaxing in the garden – guests peruse the dining room's fixed-price menus with particular enthusiasm! Individually prepared dishes in modern British style are soundly based on fresh local produce (including game in season), and the chef's soup of the day might be followed by loin of Somerset lamb with a fragrant tarragon sauce or medallions of Exmoor venison, pan-fried and served with a green peppercorn sauce. There is always a vegetarian option (perhaps aubergine galette, its oven-baked

Middlecombe
Map no: 3 SS94
Tel: 01643 706885

Cost: Fixed-price D £20. H/wine £7.95. Service exc
Credit cards: 1 2 3

Menus: Fixed-price dinner

Times: 7pm-last D 9pm

Chefs: Angela Hunt
Proprietors: Angela and Richard Hunt

layers of aubergine, tomato, onion and ricotta cheese enhanced by a tomato and herb sauce), and the desserts include such old favourites as sticky toffee pudding alongside lighter sweets like meringue heart with fresh fruit sorbet. Coffee and mints can be served either at your table or in front of the drawing room fire. A descriptive wine list has 52 bins, including the product of a good Somerset vineyard, Wootton Courtenay.

Seats: 24. No smoking in dining room
Additional: No children under 8; ◐ dishes; Vegan dishes with advance notice; other diets on request

Directions: Off A39 signposted Porlock and Lynmouth. Hotel about 1 mile on left

MONTACUTE, **Kings Arms Inn** ❀

☺ *This 16th-century inn contains the Abbey Room Restaurant for which dishes are produced with flair and imagination. Starters on offer are grape, prawn and mango salad or seasonal melon, and a main course is asparagus crêpe in a cheese and wild mushroom sauce.*

Cost: Alc £16. H/wine £6.70–£7.20. Service exc
Credit cards: 1 2 3 4. **Additional**: Children permitted; children's portions; ◐ dishes; other diets on request
Directions: In village centre, next to church

Map no: 3 ST41
Tel: 01935 822513
Chef: Diane Warren
Proprietors: Michael and Vicki Harrison
Seats: 50. No smoking in dining room
Times: Midday–last L 2pm, 7pm–last D 9.30pm. Closed 25-26 Dec

MONTACUTE, **Milk House** ❀❀

☺ *A historic little restaurant in a pretty village, serving delicious food with outstanding natural flavours*

Everything is made on the premises at this 15th-century restaurant, including the mustard, and the natural intensity of flavours is instantly noticeable. An evolving menu of French-influenced dishes reflects the seasonal produce used, and fish in particular is never farmed but depends on the catch of the day. This delightful restaurant in an idyllic village of golden-stone buildings, sold milk from its stables for centuries until just 20 years ago. Now boasting a fine reputation for its food, diners are lured to the polished antique tables by the promise of something special. The fixed-price menu, which can be adapted as a *carte*, does not disappoint. Starters like spiced and braised mushrooms with a chopped nut topping might be offered, or sliced pear marinated in walnut oil and served with cream cheese and avocado slices, followed by braise-roasted guinea fowl with a fresh herb sauce, or green sorrel roulade with a cep, onion and pistachio filling. Desserts are positively sinful, and include choices like honeyed crêpes flambéed in brandy, or hot chocolate and raisin sponge pudding with a rum, honey and chocolate topping.

Directions: Follow National Trust signs to Montacute House. The Milk House is in the square opposite

The Borough
Map no: 3 ST41
Tel: 01935 823823

Cost: Fixed-price D £11.50 (1 course), £16, £19.80, Sunday L £12.50. H/wine £9 ♀ Service inc
Credit cards: 1 3

Menus: Fixed price dinner, Sunday lunch

Times: 7.30–last D 9pm, last Sun L 1.30. Closed Sun eve, Mon, Tue & 25-26 Dec

Chef: Lee (Elizabeth) Dufton
Proprietors: Lee and Bill Dufton

Seats: 36. No smoking in dining room
Additional: No children under 12; children's portions; ◐ dishes; Vegan/other diets on request

NUNNEY, George at Nunney ❂

☺ *A traditional 17th-century coaching inn, The George offers an extensive range of menus to suit all pockets and palates. Caroline Filder-Barker in the kitchen produces imaginative dishes from the carte with a good use of quality local produce and she is backed up by a friendly team of local staff.*

Cost: Alc £20, fixed-price L £5.50/D £9.90. H/wine £8 ♀ Service exc
Credit cards: 1 3. **Additional:** Children permitted lunchtime only; children's menu/portions; ◊ dishes; Vegan/other diets on request
Directions: In village centre

11 Church Street
Map no: 3 ST74
Tel: 01373 836458
Chefs: Caroline Filder-Barker, Mark Humphreys
Proprietor: David Page
Seats: 60. Cigars and pipes discouraged
Times: Midday-last L 2pm, 6.30pm-last D 9.30pm (10.30pm weekends)

PORLOCK, Oaks ❂

☺ *A sensibly short fixed-price four-course dinner menu is offered at this hospitable small hotel. The food is simply prepared and enjoyable, with dishes such as home-made soup, smoked haddock mousse, lamb cutlets with an apricot, mint and horseradish sauce, and apple and cider cake with cream.*

Cost: Fixed-price D £20. Service inc. **Credit cards:** 1 2 3 4
Additional: Children permitted; children's portions; ◊ dishes/other diets on request

Doverhay
Map no: 3 SS84
Tel: 01643 862265
Chef: Anne Riley
Proprietor: Tim Riley
Seats: 24. No smoking in dining room
Times: 7pm–last D 8.30pm. Closed Jan and Feb

SHEPTON MALLET, Bowlish House ❂

Situated close to the town centre in a beautiful 17th-century building, Bowlish House offers delicious food prepared by Linda Morley. Start with a warm courgette and almond mousse set on a glazed béarnaise sauce and follow with braised rabbit flamande with sultanas and prunes.

Cost: Fixed-price D £22.50, Sunday L (1st Sunday of month only) £12.95. H/wine £8.25 ♀ Service exc. **Credit cards:** 1 3
Additional: Children welcome; ◊ dishes (menu by arrangement); Vegan/other diets on request
Directions: A quarter of a mile from town centre on A371 Wells road

Wells Road, Bowlish
Map no: 3 ST64
Tel: 01749 342022
Chef: Linda Morley
Proprietors: Bob and Linda Morley
Seats: 24. No smoking while others are eating
Times: Last D 9.30pm, L by appointment. Closed 1 week autumn, 1 week spring

SHEPTON MALLET, Shrubbery ❂

☺ *A bright, comfortable, unpretentious hotel with a congenial small restaurant, and a small wine bar open mainly at weekends. Menus feature English, French and Italian cuisine which ranges from shelled tiger prawns or sautéed lamb kidneys to loin of local venison or breast of duck.*

Cost: Alc £16.50, fixed-price D £10.95. H/wine £7.50 ♀ Service exc
Credit cards: 1 3 5. **Additional:** Children welcome; children's menu/portions; ◊ menu; other diets on request; live entertainment
Directions: On main A361 through town, next to police station

Commercial Road
Map no: 3 ST64
Tel: 01749 346671
Chefs: Jon Dors, Stephanie Ward, Hamish Curwen-Reed
Proprietors: Stephanie Ward, Hamish Curwen-Reed
Seats: Restaurant 36, Bistro 40. No smoking in dining room
Times: Last L 2.15pm/D 10pm

SHIPHAM, **Daneswood House** ☸☸

At this charming Edwardian house you can enjoy meals competently prepared in predominantly English style.

The cosy restaurant of this hotel – a lovely Edwardian house with breathtaking views across surrounding countryside to the distant coastline – provides a congenial setting in which to enjoy the carefully prepared dishes featured on chef John Dawson's seasonally-changing set-price menus. Though basically modern English, his style also betrays distinct French and Italian influences: a recent inspection meal began with fresh Dorset mussels marinière with a hint of fresh ginger and garlic, this followed by lightly roasted Gressingham duck accompanied by a complementary lavender and port wine sauce and served with simply presented al dente vegetables; a selection of delicious desserts includes old favourites like bread and butter pudding – here given a glazed apricot topping and sauce flavoured with a vanilla pod. The well-balanced wine list features a good range of clarets and New World labels. Special theme events (a Saint Patrick's Day dinner or an Italian gourmet weekend, for example) are held throughout the year.

Directions: Just outside the village centre

Cuck Hill
Map no: 3 ST45
Tel: 01934 843145

Cost: Alc £21.50, fixed-price £17.50 (2 courses), £21.50. H/wine £8.95
Credit cards: 1 2 3 4

Menus: A la carte, fixed-price

Times: Midday-last L 1.45pm, 7pm-last D 9.30pm. Closed 26-31 Dec

Chef: John Dawson
Proprietors: David and Elise Hodges

Seats: 40. No-smoking area; no cigars and pipes
Additional: Children permitted; ❶ dishes

SIMONSBATH, **Simonsbath House** ☸

☺ *A delightful white-painted 17th-century house overlooking a valley. Sue Burns cooks imaginative food using fresh produce creating such delicious dishes as a platter of artichoke hearts, cherry tomatoes, egg and mixed peppers as a starter, and strips of fillet steak in a mushroom cream sauce as a main course.*

Cost: Fixed-price D £20.50. H/wine £7.95. No service charge **Credit cards:** 1 2 3 4 **Additional:** No children under 10; ❶ dishes/other diets on request
Directions: Situated on B3223 in the village

Map no: 3 SS73
Tel: 0164 383259
Chef: Sue Burns
Proprietor: Mike Burns
Seats: 24. No smoking in dining room
Times: 7pm–last D 8.30pm. Closed Dec & Jan

SOUTH PETHERTON, **Oaklands** ☸

A fine Georgian house promoting a little touch of Corsica right in the heart of Somerset. Chef Pascal Salmon cooks bright French regional dishes with honest textures and flavours. For example fillet of lamb wrapped in spinach leaves flavoured with mint sauce.

Cost: Fixed price dinner £20.25, Sunday lunch £11.50. H/wine £8.75. Service exc. **Credit cards:** 1 2 3. **Additional:** Children permitted; children's portions; ❶ dishes; other diets on request

Directions: 100 yards from village centre on Shepton road

8 Palmer Street
Map no: 3 ST41
Tel: 01460 240272
Chef: Pascal Salmon
Proprietors: F & A Merlozzi
Times: Last D 9pm. Closed Sun eve, Mon, Nov-Dec
Seats: 25. No cigars or pipes

STON EASTON, **Ston Easton Park** ✾✾✾

An elegant country-house setting for some fine classical French cooking with English influences

Situated in the Mendip Hills between the cities of Bath and Wells, Ston Easton Park is one of England's finest country houses and provides a unique opportunity to experience the elegance and splendour of the 18th century. Approached by a tree-lined drive, through landscaped gardens and parkland, with the River Norr running through, this stone-built house is of exceptional architectural interest and the interiors have been restored with exquisite taste using period antiques. An impeccably trained team of naturally friendly management and staff are a major ingredient in the overall ambience of charm and well being.

Head chef Mark Harrington offers a fixed-price menu, three courses at lunch and four at dinner (including a light hors d'oeuvre), using the best of fresh produce. Indeed many of the vegetables, fruits and herbs come from the hotel's kitchen gardens, and a vegetarian dish is always featured, such as open ravioli of wild mushrooms with a balsamic dressing.

This year our inspectors have sampled a deliciously smooth terrine of chicken liver parfait and foie gras, and an intensely flavoured confit of duck with lentils and orange as starters. Their main course choices were succulent fillet of Scottish beef served with a timbale of wild mushrooms and a rich truffle sauce, and rosette of turbot with lobster mousseline and a stuffed courgette flower, served with a good shellfish sauce and enjoyable vegetables. Desserts offer a hot and cold choice including a banana tartlet served hot with banana ice cream and crème anglaise, and a teardrop of two chocolates on a coulis of Grand Marnier and oranges.

The extensive wine list has particularly strong selections of red and white Bordeaux, and also a wide choice of wines from Australia and New Zealand.

Directions: On A37 from Bristol to Shepton Mallet, about 6 miles from Wells

Map no: 3 ST65
Tel: 01761 241631

Cost: Fixed-price L £26, fixed-price D £38.50. H/wine £14.50. No service charge
Credit cards: 1 2 3 4 5

Menus: Fixed-price lunch and dinner, Sunday lunch, light meals

Times: 12.30pm-last L 2pm, 7.30-last D 9.30pm (10pm Fri & Sat)

Chef: Mark Harrington
Proprietor: Peter Smedley.
Manager: Kevin Marchant

Seats: 40. No smoking in dining rooms
Additional: No children under 7; ✪ dishes; Vegan/other diets with advance notice

TAUNTON, Castle ✿✿✿✿

Appetising presentation of technically faultless cooking in the modern British style at a long-established, red-star hotel

Four rosettes this year for Phil Vickery's assured cooking which, sensibly based on intelligently chosen ingredients from mainly local suppliers, continues a well-established policy at the Castle. His fixed-price lunch and dinner menus (two or three courses at lunch, three or four at dinner), may be understated, but every dish offers something exciting and really lovely flavours in some of his dishes show an equal mastery of delicacy and intensity.

Delicious fresh fettucine, lightly marinated in vinaigrette and garnished with chive flowers, served with fennel and asparagus, was a real breath of spring at the start of one inspection meal, and at another, his perennially popular crisp pastry tart filled with crab and capsicum mousseline under a glazed hollandaise, was described as memorable. A meaty, marbled duck terrine with spiced pears led into a main course with a hint of Mediterranean flavours – succulent sea-bass with softly roasted garlic, saffron potatoes and spinach, served with a light cream sauce. A duck suprême was perfumed with the flavours of ginger and lemon grass; braised shoulder of lamb, redolent with garlic and thyme, had excellent flavour and came with a lovely jus and boulangère potatoes. For pudding, two inspectors on separate occasions independently chose, and highly commended, a clear-flavoured clementine blancmange served with a light coriander syrup. On Sundays, the traditional lunch is very good value, and children under 12 years old eat for half the adult price.

The extensive wine list, a labour of love on the part of Mr Chapman senior, is helpfully annotated and begins with a useful short list of about 30 inexpensive (under £15) bottles and seven house wines. There are some very good sherries to sip while you peruse the list which represents all the best wine areas of the world. There is an abridged version of reasonably priced bottles

Directions: In town centre, off Corporation Street and Castle Way, turning right at Castle Green Hotel

Castle Green
Map no: 3 ST22
Tel: 01823 272671

Cost: Fixed-price L £14.50 (2 courses), £15.90, fixed-price D £25.90 (3 courses), £29.90. H/wine £9.70 ♀ Service exc
Credit cards: 1 2 3 4 5

Menus: Fixed-price lunch and dinner, Sunday lunch

Times: 12.30pm-last L 2pm, 7.30pm-last D 9pm

Chef: Philip Vickery
Proprietors: Kit Chapman, Andrew Grahame

Seats: 70. No smoking in dining room
Additional: No children under 12; children's portions; ❂ dishes; Vegan/other diets on request

TAUNTON, Farthings ✿✿

☺ *Enjoyable modern English food in a quietly positioned popular hotel*

The peaceful village of Hatch Beauchamp just outside Taunton is the setting for this charming Georgian hotel. Evidence of good taste is everywhere, from the pretty bedrooms to the small lounge and bar, although it may be a bit of a struggle to find a seat in the evenings. The restaurant has a healthy non-resident trade, and Mark Miller's serious and interesting modern English cooking is the reason for its popularity. The food is well priced, and comes on a fixed-price menu with a choice of course numbers. At a recent inspection meal the home-made watercress soup was a well-flavoured starter, followed by large

Hatch Beauchamp
Map no: 3 ST22
Tel: 01823 480664

Cost: Fixed-price £16
Credit cards: 1 2 3 4

Menus: Fixed-price

Times: Midday-last L 2pm, 7pm-10pm

Chef: Mark Miller
Proprietors: Mr & Mrs Barker

and succulent medallions of pork served with a Calvados and cinnamon juice and garnished with caramelised plum and apple slices. Vegetables were simply cooked but full of natural flavour, and dessert came in the shape of a rich, smooth lemon tart with a deliciously tangy citrus taste, served with a honey and orange sauce. A team of uniformed staff provides a friendly but pleasantly professional service in the two freshly decorated dining rooms. There's a well-explained wine list.

Additional: Children welcome; ❂ dishes; no smoking in restaurant

Directions: In village centre

TAUNTON, Nightingales ❂

☺ *Chef Mark Lawson-Smith cooks imaginative dishes using fresh produce. Starters include tomato and tarragon soup with orange-scented chicken dumplings and as a main course choose Barbary duck with cassis sauce or fillet of beef with a port and Stilton sauce.*

Cost: Fixed-price D £16.90, Sunday L £12.95. H/wine £7.95 ♀
Service exc. **Credit cards**: 1 3. **Additional**: Children welcome; children's portions; ❂ dishes; Vegan/other diets on request
Directions: On A358 opposite Hatch Beauchamp turning

Bath House Farm, Lower West Hatch
Map no: 3 ST22
Tel: 01823 480806
Chef: Mark Lawson–Smith
Proprietors: Mark and Amanda Lawson–Smith
Seats: 40. No smoking in dining room
Times: Last Sun L 1.45pm/D 10pm. Closed Mon, 1st 2 weeks Feb

WELLS, Ancient Gate House ❂

☺ *Set in the grounds of Wells Cathedral, this hotel's Rugantino restaurant offers good Italian food using fresh produce. The chef's speciality starter is squid, mussels and prawn salad which could be followed by escalope of veal fried with onions, white wine, mushrooms and cream.*

Cost: Alc £13.75, fixed-price L £6.20/D £13.75. H/wine £8.90.
Service exc. **Credit cards**: 1 2 3 4 5
Additional: Children welcome; children's portions; ❂ dishes
Directions: Situated on west side of Wells Cathedral, backing on to the Cathedral Green

Sadler Street
Map no: 3 ST54
Tel: 01749 672029
Chefs: Luigi Abbis
Proprietor: Franco Rossi
Seats: 45. No cigars or pipes
Times: Last L 2pm/D10.30pm

WELLS, Fountains Inn, Boxers ❂

☺ *Situated extremely close to Wells Cathedral, Boxers offers a set menu to suit all palates and pockets. Julie Pearce in the kitchen creates very worthy and imaginative dishes. Delicious Poole mussels and a sea-bass, monkfish and salmon medley are served with velouté stock sauce.*

Cost: Alc £12.50, fixed-price L £5.50 (2 courses), £7.50. H/wine £6.75 ♀ Service exc. **Credit cards**: 1 2 3 5
Additional: Children welcome; children's menu/portions; ❂ menu; Vegan/other diets on request
Directions: In city centre at junction of A371 and B3139, 50 yds from Cathedral

1 St Thomas Street
Map no: 3 ST54
Tel: 01749 672317
Chef: Julie Pearce
Proprietors: Adrian and Sarah Lawrence
Seats: 30. No pipes in restaurant
Times: 11am-last L 2pm, 6pm-last D 9.30pm. Closed 25 & 26 Dec

WILLITON, **Curdon Mill** ☻

☺ *Set in the beautiful, tranquil area of the Quantock Hills, the Royal Oak Inn offers a cosy atmosphere and country cuisine cooked by chefs Daphne Criddle and Lorraine Seldon with good use of made local produce. Examples of main courses are salmon en croûte, beef Wellington and sirloin of beef.*

Cost: Fixed-price D £19.50, Sunday L £11.50. H/wine £7.80 ♀ Service inc. **Credit cards**: 1 3. **Additional**: Children permitted; children's portions; ◐ menu; Vegan/other diets on request
Directions: On the Stogumber road (A358)

Vellow
Map no: 3 ST04
Tel: 01984 56522
Chefs: Daphne Criddle, Lorraine Seldon
Proprietors: Richard and Daphne Criddle
Seats: 50. No-smoking area
Times: Last D 8.30pm, last Sunday L 2.30pm

WILLITON, **White House** ☻☻☻

A dinner-only hotel restaurant in a village setting serving simply presented honest British cooking

The White House is a well established village hotel owned and run by husband and wife team Dick and Kay Smith for over 27 years. The restaurant is at the heart of the establishment, and opens for dinner only at 7pm for 7.30pm. The food is cooked to order with guests making a choice from the menu on their return to the hotel each day. It is a short menu priced for three, four or five courses offering mainly British cooking with influences from France, Italy and California. There is always a soup to begin, perhaps sorrel and potato or Provençal fish soup, followed by a choice of starters, including the ever-popular soufflé Suissesse, a tasty cheese soufflé, twice baked and finished with Gruyère, parmesan and cream – delicious. Our inspector enjoyed a main course of fillet of lamb cooked pink and served sliced around a minted hollandaise sauce with another small pool of meat juices, attractively presented but in no way fussy. Others could be roast Gressingham duck with mulberry sauce and caramelised apples, or escalope of salmon on a julienne of leeks, carrots and mushrooms, topped with chive-flavoured crème fraîche and lumpfish roe, and served with saffron-mashed potatoes. Meatless starters can also be adapted to provide vegetarian main courses. Among the desserts is a selection of chocolate puddings – a marquise, a profiterole with a good chocolate sauce, and a mousse in a chocolate sponge case. The plate of local cheeses and home-made oatmeal biscuits is also recommended, Mr Smith describing each of the cheeses and where it comes from. To finish, coffee is served in the sitting room or bar.

The wine list contains many interesting and unusual items. There are half-a-dozen house wines followed by two pages of the proprietor's recommendations.

Directions: On the A39 in the centre of village

Long Street
Map no: 3 ST04
Tel: 01984 632306

Cost: Fixed-price D £26.50. H/wine £11. No service charge
Credit cards: No cards taken

Menus: Fixed-price dinner
Times: 7pm for 7.30pm

Chefs: Dick and Kay Smith
Proprietors: Dick and Kay Smith

Seats: 26. No smoking in dining room
Additional: Children welcome; children's portions

WINSFORD, Royal Oak Inn ❀

A beautiful 12th-century thatched inn situated on the edge of Exmoor National Park. The daily-changing menus offer a selection of traditional English dishes, all served with fresh vegetables. A main course of venison steak with mushrooms and chives is served with a port and redcurrant sauce.

Cost: Alc from £22.50, fixed-price L £12.50 Service exc
Credit cards: 1 2 3 4 5. **Additional**: Children permitted; children's portions; ❻ menu; other diets on request
Directions: From the A396, turn left to Winsford, then left in the village

Map no: 3 SS93
Tel: 0164 385455
Chef: Kevin Smokum
Proprietor: Charles Steven
Seats: 34
Times: 12.30pm–last L 1pm, last D 9.30pm

WITHYPOOL, Royal Oak Inn ❀

An Exmoor property full of character and charm where chef Peter Norris cooks with care and style and a refreshing lack of unnecessary flamboyancy. Vegetarians have a separate menu. Dishes include poached mushrooms in oyster sauce and brandy-flamed tenderloin of pork with orange sauce.

Cost: Alc £25, fixed-price D £19.50, Sun L £13.50. H/wine £8.50 ♀ Service exc. **Credit cards**: 1 2 3 4 5. **Additional**: No children under 8; children's portions; ❻ menu; Vegan dishes with advance notice; other diets on request
Directions: Off B3223 between Dulverton and Simonsbath

Map no: 3 SS83
Tel: 0164 383506/7
Chef: Peter Norris
Proprietor: Michael Bradley
Seats: 32. No pipes in dining room
Times: 11am–last L 2pm, 6pm–last D 9pm. Closed 25-26 Dec

WITHYPOOL, Westerclose ❀

☺ A converted hunting lodge with views over the moor, this hotel offers a fixed-price menu of three or four courses in the Barle restaurant. An interesting range of dishes is prepared from local produce and organic vegetables from the kitchen garden, and vegetarian options are always available.

Cost: Alc L £15.50, Sunday L £12.50, fixed-price D £19 (3 courses), £21. H/wine £7.95. Service exc. **Credit cards**: 1 2 3
Additional: Children welcome; children's menu/portions; ❻ menu; Vegan dishes one day's notice; other diets on request
Directions: Turn right by the inn in the village and follow hotel signs

Map no: 3 SS83
Tel: 0164 383302
Chef: Joanna Foster
Proprietors: Ben, Joanna and Mrs R P Foster and Blue Walshe
Seats: 16–25. No smoking in dining room
Times: Last L 2.30pm/D 9.15pm. Closed Mon to non-residents (except BHs), Jan and Feb

WIVELISCOMBE, Langley House ❀❀

A delightful small hotel and restaurant with a welcoming atmosphere and modern English cooking of some depth

This charming little hotel and restaurant, dating from the 16th century, has acquired a Georgian elegance over the years. and is now boldly decorated and richly furnished along classical lines. Owner Peter Wilson cooks with depth and skill, and his interesting set dinner menu shows evidence of quality produce being converted into modern English dishes: if diners are not happy with anything on the menu an alternative can be instantly arranged. Our inspector was more than satisfied with a

Langley Marsh
Map no: 3 ST02
Tel: 01984 623318

Cost: Fixed-price D £24.50 (3 courses), £28.50. H/wine £8.50 ♀ Service inc
Credit cards: 1 2 3

Menu: Fixed-price dinner

Times: Last D 8.30–8.45pm

tasty warm quail breast salad, nicely dressed with pinenuts in walnut oil, which came before a superb fish course of grilled baby turbot sprinkled with a glazed topping of fresh crab and served with a lightly-flavoured tomato purée. The main course of gently pan-fried rosettes of fillets of Somerset new-season suckling lamb was deliciously tender, moist and full of flavour, and served with a tartlet of onion and cassis purée, plus bright al dente vegetables. The home-made puddings are hard to choose between, but the smooth and creamy chocolate terrine layered with almond and hazelnut meringue was a winner.

Chef: Peter Wilson
Proprietor: Peter Wilson

Seats: 18. No smoking in dining room
Additional: No children under 7; children's portions; ❷ dishes; Vegan by prior arrangement/other diets on request

Directions: Half mile from centre of Wiveliscombe on Langley Marsh road

YEOVIL, **Little Barwick House** ❀❀

Accomplished British cooking at a popular but peaceful Georgian hotel

British country cooking at its best, with fresh, natural flavours carefully extracted from quality local produce, is the order of the day here. A full house during midweek shows the popularity of this tranquil Georgian restaurant, where chef-owner Veronica Colley demonstrates her skills in an interesting set menu supplemented by daily-changing dishes, especially fish and pies. Our inspector enjoyed the simplicity and lovely flavours of roast red pepper with cherry tomato, shallots and feta cheese, while Little Barwick pie was a rich mixture of fillet and venison inside a crisp, nutty pastry case. Vegetables were particularly bright and fresh, and shortbread and mango with passion fruit purée – a real joy to eat – was the chosen dessert from a range that included old-fashioned French apple and almond tart, and a very light steamed treacle sponge. Other typical imaginative dishes might be avocado and chicken tikka salad with Greek yoghurt and lime sauce, and roast loin of venison with a blackcurrant and port sauce. Service is natural and easy and there is an interesting wine list with affordable prices.

Barwick Village
Map no: 3 ST51
Tel: 01935 23902

Cost: Fixed-price D £17.50 (2 courses), £23. H/wine £9.20. Service exc
Credit cards: 1 2 3

Menus: Fixed-price dinner

Times: 7-last D 9pm (9.30pm Sat). Closed Sun to non residents, 3 weeks in Jan

Chef: Veronica Colley
Proprietors: Veronica and Christopher Colley

Seats: 40. No smoking in dining room. Air conditioned
Additional: Children permitted; children's portions, ❷ menu; Vegan/other diets on request

Directions: One mile from Yeovil on Dorchester road (A37), turn left opposite Red House pub. Hotel is 450yds on left

YEOVIL, **Yeovil Court** ❀

☺ *A conveniently positioned hotel on the western fringe of the town. Howard Mosley in the kitchen is a very capable cook. Our inspector recommends the field mushroom filled with chicken and Stilton mousse to start, followed by crispy roast duckling in a plum and brandy sauce.*

Cost: Alc £17. H/wine £7.50 ♀ Service inc. **Credit cards**: 1 2 3 4 5
Additional: Children permitted; children's portions (menu by arrangement); ❷ menu; Vegan/other diets on request
Directions: On A30, 2.5 miles west of Yeovil

West Coker Road
Map no: 3 ST51
Tel: 01935 863746
Chef: Howard Mosley
Proprietor: Brian Devonport
Seats: 50
Times: Last L 1.45pm/D 9.45pm. Closed Sat lunch, Sun eve, BHs except Xmas Day

SOUTH YORKSHIRE

BARNSLEY, **Armstrongs** ❀❀

☺ *Mediterranean ingredients are used to good effect in the preparation of a range of interesting continental dishes here*

This well-established restaurant in the heart of the town centre – just across the road from the imposing town hall – continues to offer interesting dishes in modern continental style, making good use of many Mediterranean ingredients; some Thai influence is also discernible. Diners can choose either the very good value early evening *carte* served between 7 and 8pm (Tuesday to Friday) or a more extensive and sophisticated range of dishes available after that time. The lunch menu tends to be shorter and lighter in style; our inspector recently enjoyed a flavoursome salmon escalope coated with sesame seeds and set on a red wine and soy sauce, then lightly cooked noisettes of lamb sliced and set round a central mix of olives and dried Moroccan lemon with a basil jus and, finally, the iced butterscotch meringue cake for which the place is renowned, its sweetness effectively countered by a zesty orange sauce. Vegetarian dishes are readily available, with Vegan on request. Italy, Spain and the New World are all represented on a mainly French wine list.

Directions: In the town centre by the Town Hall

6 Shambles Street
Map no: 8 SE30
Tel: 01226 240113

Cost: *Alc* £19, fixed-price D £12.95 (7–8pm only). H/wine £8.85. Service exc
Credit cards: 1 2 3

Menus: *A la carte*, fixed-price dinner early evening

Times: Midday–last L 2pm, 7pm–last D 9.30pm (10pm Sat). Closed Sat lunch, all day Sun & Mon

Chef: Nick Pound
Proprietor: Nick Pound

Seats: 60
Additional: Children welcome; children's portions; ❂ dishes; Vegan/other diets on request

BARNSLEY, **Restaurant Peano** ❀❀

☺ *Well-balanced French and Italian cooking with strong individual flavours from fresh ingredients*

Set on the outskirts of Barnsley in a spacious Victorian house, this restaurant has built up a well-deserved regular and local following over the years. Lemon silk walls make a fresh background for the well-spaced polished tables in the dining room, and a pleasant setting for the careful cooking of chef/patron Michael Peano. His skilful handling of fresh quality ingredients results in well-balanced Italian and French dishes with distinctive flavours. A recent inspection meal started with a filling home-made tagliatelle with tomato and meat balls coated in a tangy sauce with freshly grated parmesan. This was followed by a successful fillet of beef topped with melted pesto and set on a polenta cake, served with a light red wine sauce and crisp vegetables. A must for chocolate lovers was the very smooth, rich dark chocolate terrine which contrasted beautifully with a refreshingly tasty citrus sauce, while mellow coffee and home-made petits fours completed an enjoyable meal. Other dishes might be wood pigeon breast and wild mushroom mousse wrapped in puff pastry, and pan-fried saddle of lamb topped with a herb crust.

Directions: From M1 Jct 37 follow signs to Barnsley town centre. Restaurant is 1 mile on the right

102 Dodworth Road
Map no: 8 SE30
Tel: 01226 244990

Cost: *Alc* £22.50, fixed-price L & D £11.95. H/wine £9.50. Service inc
Credit cards: 1 2 3 5

Menus: *A la carte*, fixed-price

Times: Last L 1.30pm/D 9.30pm. Closed Sun, Mon, Sat lunch, 1 wk Jan, 1 week May or June

Chef: Michael Peano
Proprietors: Michael and Tracey Peano

Seats: 50. No cigars or pipes in the dining room
Additional: Children welcome; children's portions; ❂ dishes

CHAPELTOWN, **Greenhead House** ❀❀

A cottage-style restaurant with a warm, friendly atmosphere offers imaginative menus of French country cuisine

Dedicated attention on the part of the proprietors has turned this old stone house into a friendly, warm-hearted restaurant – the cottage-like ambience of its restful green and white dining room providing the ideal setting in which to enjoy an exciting choice of earthy, full-flavoured dishes in French country style. The main course chosen governs the cost of your set-price meal, and there is a rich variety in the four or five alternatives offered at each stage. Crab meat tartlet with mushroom hollandaise or rillettes of lamb with juniper, for example, might be followed by watercress and potato soup or melon, then options based on salmon, veal, duck, sea-bass and fillet steak; sweets range from strawberry tarts to mango with pineapple sorbet, and a selection of English and continental cheeses is served with grapes, apples and celery. Vegetarian dishes are always available, though there is no separate menu. Children are welcome at lunchtime. A descriptive list of predominantly French wines includes some bin ends and half bottles.

Directions: From M1 Jct 35 follow signs to Huddersfield. Continue over two roundabouts. Restaurant is on right

84 Buncross Road
Map no: 8 SK39
Tel: 0114 2469004

Cost: Fixed-price D £27.50 ♀
Service exc
Credit cards: 1 3

Menu: Fixed-price dinner

Times: Last D 9pm. Closed Sun, Mon, 2 weeks Easter, 2 weeks Aug, 23 Dec - 1 Jan

Chefs: Neil Allen
Proprietors: Neil Allen

Seats: 32. No smoking in dining room
Additional: Children welcome; children's portions; ❂ dishes; Vegan/other diets on request

CHAPELTOWN, **Staindrop Lodge** ❀

☺ *The restaurant dominates the public areas of this comfortable small hotel, and is popular with guests and locals alike. Chef John Olerenshaw offers mainly modern British cooking from good value menus. Dishes include timbale of salmon and lobster, and baked breast of guinea fowl with game forcemeat.*

Cost: Alc £17.95, fixed-price L £8.10 (2 courses), £9.10/D £17.90. H/wine £8. No service charge. **Credit cards**: 1 2 3 4 5
Additional: Children welcome (except New Year's Eve); children's portions; ❂ dishes; Vegan/other diets on request
Directions: Half mile from Chapeltown, following signs to High Green

Lane End
Map no: 8 SK39
Tel: 0114 2846727
Chef: John P Olerenshaw
Proprietor: Mark A Bailey
Seats: 70
Times: Midday-last L 1.45pm, last D 9.30pm. Closed Sat and Mon L, Sun eve and BH Mons

SHEFFIELD, **Charnwood** ❀❀

Listed Georgian hotel with a reputation for a plentiful and elegant table

Once the home of a Sheffield master cutler this restored and converted hotel still retains more than a trace of its origins. The original Georgian building has been extended to provide spacious accommodation, and two eating options: the lively and popular Brasserie Leo which is open all day, and the more formal Henfrey's restaurant where chef Stephen Hall offers a short menu of imaginative classical European dishes. Game is a firm favourite here, with perhaps quail, partridge and venison appearing with a couple of meat and a fish dish. Our inspector started a recent meal with vegetable pancakes filled

10 Sharrow Lane
Map no: 8 SK38
Tel: 0114 2589411

Cost: Alc Henfreys £32, fixed-price D £25. H/wine £11.95; Brasserie Leo alc £17, fixed-price £11. H/wine £8.50 ♀
Service exc
Credit cards: 1 2 3 4
Menus: Henfrey's - *a la carte*, fixed-price dinner; Brasserie Leo - *alc*, fixed-price, Sun L, Sunday brunch
Times: Henfrey's 7pm-last D

with foie gras on a dark Madeira sauce, before going on to partridge stuffed with marinated cabbage and wrapped in golden crisp butter pastry, served on a red wine and herb sauce. Vegetables had a good colour and tasty, earthy flavour, while crêpe soufflé maltaise was deliciously filled with orange soufflé and set on a caramel orange sauce. Also on the menu might be loin of monkfish roasted with mussels and saffron on spinach, or medallion of venison on a potato rösti with port and chestnuts.

Directions: 1.5 miles south-west of city centre, off London Road (A621)

10pm, Brasserie Leo 7am-11pm. Closed Sun & Mon, 25 & 26 Dec
Chef: Stephen Hall
Proprietor: Chris King
Seats: Henfrey's 28; Brasserie Leo 59. Air conditioned
Additional: Children welcome; children's menu in Brasserie Leo; ◐ dishes; other on request; pianist Sat eve (Henfreys)

SHEFFIELD, **Harley** ✤

A carte and fixed-price menu provide a good choice of interesting modern dishes from Monday to Thursday at this elegant hotel restaurant, with a set-price menu only Friday to Sunday (closed Sunday evening). Our inspector sampled an enjoyable sautée of game, and turbot cooked en papillote.

Cost: Alc £25, fixed-price L £9.75/D £15. H/wine £10.75 ♀ Service exc **Credit cards**: 1 2 3 4. **Additional**: No children under 12; ◐ dishes; Vegan/other diets with advance notice; pianist & singer Friday and Saturday eve
Directions: Half mile from city centre at junction of West Street (A57) and Hanover Street (Inner City Ring Road)

334 Glossop Road
Map no: 8 SK38
Tel: 0114 2752288
Chef: Ian Morton
Proprietor: P Womack
Seats: 54. No pipes in dining room. Air conditioned
Times: 11.30am–last L 2pm, last D 9.45pm. Closed Sat lunch, Sun and BHs

STAFFORDSHIRE

WATERHOUSES, **Old Beams** ✤✤✤

☺ *A cottage-style restaurant in a village setting offering daily set price menus of modern British cooking*

Dedicated husband and wife team Nigel and Anne Wallis are now in their 15th year at Old Beams, a mid-18th-century property in a village setting on the edge of the Staffordshire moorlands. During their time here they have transformed the simple cottage-style restaurant into a charming establishment characterised by its low beamed ceilings and the conservatory extension which overlooks the lovely rear garden. For those who wish to extend their stay a separate building has been converted to provide six bedrooms.

No matter how busy they are, the friendliness and attentiveness of the service, supervised by Anne, never falters. Nigel, the chef, works incredibly hard, cooking late into the night and shopping at the Birmingham market in the early morning, selecting the best available fresh produce for his daily-changing set price menus. These include a good-value plat du jour during the week, with just two items at each course, a short lunchtime selection, and a comprehensive six-course dinner menu. Vegetarian dishes do not generally feature but

Leek Road
Map no: 7 SK05
Tel: 01538 308254

Cost: Fixed-price L £10.95 (2 courses), £17.50, fixed-price D £18.50 (4 courses), £32.50, service exc
Credit cards: 1 2 3 4

Menu: Fixed-price, Sunday lunch

Times: Midday-last L 2pm, 7pm-last D 9.30pm. Closed Sat L, Sun eve, all day Mon

Chef: Nigel Wallis
Proprietors: Nigel and Ann Wallis

Seats: 45-50. No smoking in dining room

can always be provided on request.

At an early summer test dinner, when the restaurant was extremely busy, our inspector ate an enjoyable meal. Appetisers of olives and home-made crisps were offered with the aperitifs, and there were warm home-made rolls at the table. The starter, ravioli of Dublin Bay prawns, was served piping hot with a rich lobster sauce. This was followed by mille-feuille of chargrilled fillet steak and venison covered with a port wine sauce. The meal concluded with a perfectly risen pistachio soufflé and hot chocolate sauce.

The wine list concentrates on the classic areas of France, but also include an interesting New World selection. The two house wines at about £15 are of very good quality.

Directions: On A523, Leek to Ashbourne road

Additional: Children welcome; ❂ dishes; Vegan dishes by arrangement; other diets on request

SUFFOLK

ALDEBURGH, **Regatta** ❂

☺ *Part restaurant, part wine bar, the Regatta has a blackboard menu supported by a list of specials. The main menu offers duck, oysters, fish soup, chicken with sesame sauce, cod with champagne sauce and a vegetarian dish. Desserts are a strong point, with crème brûlée, ice creams and chocolate pudding.*

Cost: A/c £17, fixed-price L £4.95. H/wine £6.95 ♀ Service exc
Credit cards 1 2 3 **Additional**: Children welcome; children's menu/portions; ❂ dishes; Vegan/other diets on request
Directions: In centre of town

171 High Street
Map no: 5 TM45
Tel: 01728 452011
Chef: Christopher Hyde
Proprietors: Robert and Johanna Mabey
Seats: 80. No smoking area in dining room
Times: Midday–Last L 2pm, Last D 10pm; all times flexible during summer. Closed Mon & Tue Oct to Mar, but open over Xmas & New Year

BURY ST EDMUNDS, **Angel** ❂❂

An atmospheric, vaulted restaurant serving light modern food cooked with care and skill

Mr Pickwick enjoyed an excellent roast dinner at this medieval hostelry, according to his creator Charles Dickens, and the tradition continues over 100 years later. Nowadays English and French food is cooked by chef Graham Mallia in a modern style, and his speciality set menus and *carte* show evidence of skill and imagination. Starters like sliced foie gras seared with shallots and wild mushrooms and served on a crisp potato cake are followed by a fruit sorbet, and then perhaps a main dish like turbot poached in red Bordeaux with shallots, garnished with asparagus and chervil, or perhaps a meaty one like breast of Lunesdale duck cooked with ginger and raspberry vinegar flamed with cognac. British cheeses are an optional extra. Our inspector was satisfied with a well-crafted chicken and vegetable terrine with honest flavours, and fresh-tasting plaice and mussels in a tasty butter sauce. Poached pear in syrup with strong honey-flavoured ice cream and butterscotch and vanilla sauce was a

Angel Hill
Map no: 5 TL86
Tel: 01284 753926

Cost: A/c £25, fixed-price L £11.95 (2 courses), £13.95, fixed-price D £19.35. H/wine £8.85 ♀ service exc
Credit cards: 1 2 3 4

Menus: A la carte, fixed-price, Sunday lunch, pre-theatre, bar menu

Times: Midday–Last L 2pm, 7.30pm–Last D 10pm

Chef: Graham Mallia
Manager: Gerry Skinner

Seats: 30–40. No smoking in

delicious dessert. The food can be sampled in the medieval vaulted restaurant which has a grandly historic atmosphere.

Directions: In town centre, opposite the abbey gates

BURY ST EDMUNDS, **Priory** ❀

Set within its own walled grounds, this hotel has a country house feel. A selection of fixed-price and carte menus is offered in the restaurant. Skilful, simply crafted meals are served, such as seafood pancakes, fillet of Welsh lamb or breast of duck.

Cost: Alc £24, fixed-price L £12.50 (2 courses), £17.50/D £17.50. H/wine £8.50 ♀ Service inc. **Credit cards**: 1 2 3 4
Additional: Children permitted; children's menu/portions; ❶ dishes; Vegan/other diets on request
Directions: Leave A45 at Bury Central turn-off and follow 'Mildenhall Hotel' signs for 1 mile

dining room
Additional: Children welcome; children's portions; ❶ dishes; Vegan/other diets on request

Tollgate
Map no: 5 TL86
Tel: 01284 766181
Chef: Didier Piot
Proprietor: Edward Cobbold
Seats: 70. No cigars or pipes in dining room
Times: Midday-Last L 2pm, 7pm-Last D 9.30pm

BURY ST EDMUNDS, **Ravenwood Hall** ❀

Chef David White's daily changing menu, for the restaurant of this large Tudor building, shows effort and competence, and includes fresh salmon strudel and home-smoked duck as main courses, preceded by Norfolk nut brown mushrooms filled with Suffolk ham mousse served on a marsala sauce.

Cost: Alc £22, fixed-price L and D £16.95. H/wine £8.95 ♀ Service exc. **Credit cards**: 1 2 3 4 .**Additional**: Children welcome; children's portions; ❶ dishes; Vegan/other diets on request
Directions: 3 miles east of Bury St Edmunds off A14 (formerly A45) signposted Rougham

Rougham
Map no: 5 TL86
Tel: 01359 270345
Chef: David White
Proprietor: Craig Jarvis
Seats: 45. No-smoking area; no cigars or pipes in dining room
Times: 12.30pm–Last L 2pm, 7.30pm–Last D 9.30pm

EARL STONHAM, **Mr Underhills** ❀❀❀

A 200-year-old former inn, this cosy restaurant serves a no-choice menu of modern British cooking

Incongruously situated on a busy road, this cosy private restaurant with a no-choice menu is run by committed restaurateurs Christopher and Judy Bradley. The menu is discussed on booking so alternatives can be arranged for any unsuitable dishes. Likewise vegetarians can be catered for. Christopher is the chef and he cooks in a tiny galley kitchen, demonstrating his creativity in the use of flavours and textures, which are distinct but harmonise to create a well balanced meal. The formula does not allow for much adventure but it has led the kitchen to a point of perfection in dishes produced on a regular basis according to the seasons.

A winter inspection meal began with thick, heated slices of smoked salmon served with lentils, ginger and basil, followed by fillet of beef with a trusted demi-glace, white truffle paste and tarragon – an enjoyable version of the staple salmon and beef meal. The Italian olive oil breads, such as ciabatta and focaccia, and a sublime bread and butter pudding made with

Norwich Road
Map no: 5 TM15
Tel: 01449 711206

Cost: Fixed-price D £26.50 (3-courses), Sun L £19.50 (2-courses), £23. H/wine £9.95 ♀ No service charge
Credit cards: 1 3 4

Menus: Fixed-price, Sunday lunch

Times: Last D 8.45pm, Last Sun L 1.30pm (Tue-Fri by arrangement), Closed Sat lunch, Sun eve, all day Mon

Chef: Christopher Bradley

Proprietors: Christopher and Judy Bradley

Italian panettone show a willingness to stray.
At a later meal in June, our inspector enjoyed black olives with herbs and hot cheesy beignet tartlets as appetisers, and a selection of warm home-baked breads. Tender asparagus, as a starter, was coated in a tangy beurre blanc and broad bean purée. The main course comprised slow-cooked Barbary duck in an accurate essence flavoured quite sharply with wine vinegar herbes de provence. This was accompanied by wafer thin sweetcorn pancakes which soaked up the jus and tasted wonderful. Again the lovely Italian bread and butter pudding was served with crème anglais, peppered with crushed vanilla seeds, and a dash of cream.

There are many interesting and unusual wines on the list, as well as more well-known varieties from the classic areas.

Directions: On A140, 300 yds south of the junction with the A1120

Seats: 24. No smoking in dining room
Additional: Children welcome; children's portions; ❶ dishes; Vegan/other diets on request

FRESSINGFIELD, **Fox & Goose** ❶❶❶

☺ *A friendly country pub setting for an eclectic menu of creative international dishes using the very best of ingredients*

With the look and the feel of a real country pub, situated between a duck pond and a graveyard, this restaurant offers a creative style of cooking using best quality, carefully sourced ingredients. Indeed, most of the salads, asparagus and herbs come from chef/proprietor Ruth Watson's own garden. Fish is from the Suffolk coast, vegetables are locally grown, and dairy products and soft fruit come from a nearby farm. Chinese food is bought in China town, and Thai, Indian, Greek and Italian items are all from specialist suppliers – giving some indication of the eclectic nature of the menu. The stated philosophy of the establishment is to leave good food alone, and so it is presented – simple and delicious.

The lunch menu is priced for two or three courses, and there is a *carte*, with some dishes available as starters or main courses. Blackboard specials, mostly fish, have recently included red mullet fillets wrapped in Spanish ham (acorn-fed black footed pigs at £296 a leg!) with grilled fennel and salsa verde, and stir-fried mussels with chilli, garlic, basil and oyster sauce. Vegetarians can also be accommodated.

At a test meal our inspector sampled tender griddled squid and coriander masala with Indonesian spices, followed by rump of English lamb marinated and served with a sauce of white lamb stock, shallots and rosemary. Crème caramel and apricot compote, from a list of traditional puddings, completing the meal. Bar snacks provide a good-value alternative, and could include crispy Peking duck with spring onions, cucumber, hoisin sauce and pancakes, or six escargot in garlic butter with French baguette and a side salad.

The wine lists have been compiled with great care. One is long and comprehensive and notable for many fine vintages of Burgundy and claret; the other is a shorter, well-balanced and keenly priced version which includes house wines from the proprietor's vineyard in France.

Directions: In village centre by the church

Map no: 5 TM27
Tel: 01379 586247

Cost: Alc £20, fixed-price L £9.95. H/wine £8.50 ♀ Service exc
Credit cards: No cards taken

Menus: *A la carte*, fixed-price lunch, Sunday lunch

Times: Last L 2.15pm/D 9.15pm. Closed Mon, Tue, 25-27 Dec, 2 weeks Nov

Chefs: Ruth Watson, Brendan Ansbro, James Perry and Max Dougall
Proprietor: Ruth Watson. Manager Tim O'Leary

Seats: 50. No cigars or pipes in dining room
Additional: Children welcome; children's portions; children's menu in summer; ❶ dishes; Vegan/other diets on request

HINTLESHAM, **Hintlesham Hall** ✸✸✸

An elegant country house setting for good value seasonal menus of modern English cooking

Viewed from the rear, Hintlesham Hall is resplendent in the red brick of Tudor England, but it's public image is that of the handsome colour washed Georgian façade, which varies dramatically with the changing light. The Hall stands in parkland with mature trees and has its own golf course. Great changes have been made to the interior in recent times, but the restaurant remains at the heart of the hotel's appeal.

Chef Alan Ford presents a seasonal *carte* and fixed-price menus of real interest, and these offer surprisingly good value for quality cooking in such gracious surroundings. The spring *carte*, with a choice of eight starters, included 'breast and thigh of pigeon served in a field mushroom with bitter chocolate sauce', and the marinated seafood, selected by our inspector, served with crisp vegetables in a cool oriental-style dressing with coriander noodles. 'In between' dishes might be a grape and tarragon granité or chicken and tomato consommé. Our inspector's main course was escalopes of veal, beaten a little too thin, with sweetbread croquettes and a creamy mushroom sauce infused with Marsala. An alternative from the separate, short vegetarian menu might be baked filo pastry vegetable 'moneybags' set on a sesame and coriander butter sauce. The *carte* has some warm puddings, such as apricot and cinnamon soufflé with an orange Curaçao sorbet, and a selection of British and French cheeses is available, but on this occasion the iced lemon parfait, topping a sweet carrot cheesecake was sampled.

The very extensive wine list starts with four pages of house recommendations rising in price from £12.50. The rest of the list is dominated by an excellent selection of fine claret, though the inclusion of five vintages of the magnificent Gran Coronas from Torres is an unusual feature.

Directions: On the A1071 Ipswich to Hadleigh road

Map no: 5 TM04
Tel: 01473 652268

Cost: A/c £29.25, fixed-price L £18.50. H/wine £12.50 ♀ No service charge
Credit cards: 1 2 3 4 5

Menus: *A la carte*, fixed-price, Sunday lunch

Times: Last L 2pm/D 9.30pm

Chef: Alan Ford
Proprietors: Small Luxury Hotels. General Manager: Timothy Sunderland. Restaurant Manager: Andrew Lester

Seats: 120. No smoking in dining room
Additional: No children under 10 at dinner; children's portions; ❂ menu; Vegan/other diets on request

IPSWICH, **Kwoks Rendezvous** ✸

☺ *Situated in the city centre, this Chinese restaurant specialises in Peking and Szechwan dishes. Chef/patron Thomas Kwok creates a huge choice of dishes. Starters include Shanghai spicy beef, and as a main course they offer Cantonese-style crab meat with straw mushrooms.*

Cost: A/c £15, fixed-price L & D £13.95 (4 courses), £15.95. H/wine £7.30 Service exc. **Credit cards**: 1 2 3. **Additional**: Children welcome; children's portions; ❂ dishes; other diets on request
Directions: From Civic Drive, turn into Frais Road, left into St Peter Street and then St Nicholas Street. Kwoks is opposite public car park

23 St Nicholas Street
Map no: 5 TM14
Tel: 01473 256833
Chef: Thomas Kwok
Proprietor: Thomas Kwok
Seats: 50
Times: Midday-Last L 1.45pm, 7pm-Last D 10.45pm. Closed Sun, BHs, 2 weeks late Mar/early Apr

IPSWICH, **Marlborough** ❦❦

Elaborate, well sauced dishes attract lovers of traditional French cuisine to the restaurant of this small hotel

Meals in the classical French style are the strength of this small, privately run hotel situated in a residential area to the north of the town centre. The complex dishes featured on two fixed-price menus are enhanced by confident saucing, and almost everything – including several types of flavoured bread rolls and a rich assortment of petits fours – is made on the premises. In the course of a typical meal, monkfish wrapped in parma ham and served on a bed of sauerkraut with a beurre blanc sauce might be followed by lamb fillet well seasoned with black pepper and garlic and accompanied by gratin dauphinoise, broccoli with toasted almonds, baby turnips filled with leaf spinach and cold turned carrots; dessert could be a strawberry tartlet with a pungent strawberry purée and vanilla sauce, and there might be candied rose petals among the petits fours that come with cafetière coffee. Vegetarian and vegan dishes are available, and the 'calorie conscious' section of the menu gives weight-watchers no excuse for lapses! A shortened, mainly French wine list includes examples from the New World.

Directions: Take the A12/14 toward Felixstowe and Yarmouth. Right at the brow of hill at traffic lights. The hotel is 500yds along on right

Henley Road
Map no: 5 TM14
Tel: 01473 257677

Cost: *Alc* £23, fixed-price L £10.50 (2 courses), £13.50, fixed-price D £16.95. H/wine £8.95 ♀ Service exc
Credit cards: 1 2 3 4

Menus: *A la carte*, fixed-price lunch and dinner, Sunday lunch, Pre-theatre, bar menu

Times: 12.30pm-Last L 2pm, Last D 9.30pm. Closed Sat lunch

Chef: Simon Barker
Proprietor: Robert Gough

Seats: 60. No smoking in dining room
Additional: Children permitted; children's portions; ❂ menu; Vegan/other diets on request

IPSWICH, **Old Boot House** ❦❦

☺ *Once a pub, this informal village restaurant offers straightforward menus of cosmopolitan dishes*

A refreshing new lease of life has been given to this converted pub at the edge of Shotley village on the south bank of the Orwell estuary. The style of operation is informal, the avowed aim of the establishment being the provision of good food in an unfussy manner. Light lunches and snacks are served, and the two-page *carte* – changed daily as chef/owner Ian Chamberlain deems most advantageous – offers a choice of six starters, main courses and desserts. Efficiently prepared and attractive dishes include innovative starters like smoked salmon cheesecake, while fish main courses are equally attractive, with such seasonal variations as monkfish chilli or grilled sea trout; alternatives could include baked Norfolk guinea fowl with wild mushrooms or medallions of pork topped with avocado and goats' cheese. Vegetables are lightly cooked, and your meal might perhaps end with an old-fashioned summer pudding served with cream. Vegetarian dishes are available. Disappointing coffee is more than compensated for by the accompanying miniature croissant – fresh, piping hot and oozing chocolate.

Directions: 7 miles south-east of Ipswich on the B1456, through Chelmondiston and 0.25 mile beyond Shotley sign on right (not to be confused with The Boot pub at Freston)

Shotley
Map no: 5 TM14
Tel: 01473 787755

Cost: *Alc* from £15.85, light lunches from £2.95. H/wine £7.25. Service exc
Credit cards: 1 3

Menus: *A la carte*, Sunday lunch, light lunches, bar menu

Times: Midday–Last L 2pm, 7pm–Last D 9pm (10pm Sat). Closed Sun eve, all day Mon

Chef: Ian Chamberlain
Proprietors: Ian and Pamela Chamberlain

Seats: 40. No smoking in dining room
Additional: Children permitted; children's portions; ❂ dishes; Vegan/other diets on request

IPSWICH, **Orwell House** ✸

☺ *Chef Jonathan King has a well-balanced menu of international dishes in this comfortable family run restaurant. Fish is strong on the menu, with King Prawn tempura, moules marinière and lobster thermidor – fresh lobster in a mustard, brandy, shallot and cheese sauce.*

Cost: *Alc* £20, fixed-price L and D £9.45. H/wine £7.95 ♀ Service exc
Credit cards: 1 2 3 4. **Additional**: Children welcome; children's portions; children's menu on request; ✪ menu; Vegan/other diets on request
Directions: South-east of town centre between Tacket Street and Upper Orwell Street, opposite St Pancras Church and Cox Lane car park

4A Orwell Place
Map no: 5 TM14
Tel: 01473 230254
Chef: Jonathan King
Proprietors: Rosemary King
Seats: 50. No smoking in dining room
Times: Midday-Last L 2pm, 7pm-Last D 10pm. Closed Sun, Mon, BHs

IPSWICH, **St Peter's** ✸✸

☺ *Enjoyable modern brasserie cooking catering for those who appreciate good food*

A rather drab corner of Ipswich has been transformed by the bright yellow-painted corner building which now houses this informal brasserie. Varnished pine, tiled floors and blue carpets make the interior as inviting as the outside is striking, and a hotch-potch of modern international dishes are chalked up on various blackboards. The menu changes every few weeks, and offers typical brasserie fare, like deep-fried mussels with garlic and herb butter, and main dishes like grilled calf's liver with bacon and an onion gravy, or Chinese grilled chicken with black bean sauce and rice. Warm, crusty bread came with the escalope of smoked salmon and dill sauce recently sampled by our inspector, while fillet of beef was topped with mushroom purée and ginger butter, and served with chunky chips. All ingredients were fresh and of good quality, and flavours were satisfying. Crème brûlée was a rich and creamy dessert, and the lack of promised cinnamon flavour was no drawback to its complete enjoyment. There is a wine bar at one end of the building for those not eating a full meal.

Directions: On outskirts of town centre, corner of St Peter's Street and Star Lane, near St Peter's Church

35–37 St Peter's Street
Map no: 5 TM14
Tel: 01473 210810

Cost: *Alc* £17.50. H/wine £6.95 ♀ Service exc
Credit cards: 1 2 3 5

Menus: *A la carte*, pre-theatre, bar menu

Times: Midday–Last L 2pm, 6pm–Last D 10pm. Closed Sun, Mon, 25–29 Dec

Chef: Robert Mabey
Proprietors: Robert Mabey, Justin Cain

Seats: 85. No-smoking area
Additional: Children welcome; children's menu/portions; ✪ menu; Vegan/other diets on request

IXWORTH, **Theobalds** ✸✸

A heavily beamed period restaurant serving an attractive blend of fine English and French cooking

A splendid period property dating back to 1650, complete with heavy oak beams and huge inglenook fireplace, houses this friendly restaurant. Simon and Geraldine Theobald converted the old building 14 years ago, and have built up a fine reputation for good food which ranks among the best in the area. A blend of English and French cooking is offered on the fixed-price menu which varies according to the main course taken, there's a short lunch menu, and regular Friday evening fish supper which includes half a bottle of Chablis in the cost. A

68 High Street
Map no: 5 TL97
Tel: 01359 231707

Cost: *Alc* L & D £24.50-£28.50, fixed-price L £15.95. Service exc
Credit cards: 1 3

Menus: *A la carte* lunch & dinner, fixed-price lunch & Sunday lunch

Times: Last L 1.30pm, Last D

typical dinner might begin with parfait of chicken livers with a port and redcurrant sauce served with toasted brioche, followed by noisettes of hare wrapped in bacon, served on croûtons with a game sauce laced with blackberry juice. Desserts might be iced Grand Marnier mousse with chocolate sauce, or caramelised lemon tart with strawberry sauce. The popular fish suppers offer perhaps warm mousseline of salmon with a buttered sauce, grilled scallops in bacon on a bed of spinach, and sea-bass with ginger and a white wine and soy sauce.

Directions: 7 miles from Bury St Edmunds on A143, Bury to Diss road

9.30pm. Closed Mon, Sat lunch, Sun eve & BHs
Chef: Simon Theobald
Proprietors: Simon and Geraldine Theobald

Seats: 36. No cigars or pipes; no smoking in dining room while others are eating
Additional: Children permitted (over 7 at dinner); ◐ dishes

LAVENHAM, Swan ❀

☺ *Traditional and skilful British cooking – Scottish salmon, English lamb, venison – in classic Elizabethan grandeur, complete with beams on the ceiling and logs on the fire. Warm, peaceful atmosphere in which to savour the short, tasteful carte or fixed-price dinner*

Cost: Fixed-price L £12.95 (2 courses), £14.95/D £19.95. H/wine £12.75 ♀ Service exc. **Credit cards**: 1 2 3 4 5
Additional: Children welcome; children's menu/portions; ◐ dishes; Vegan/other diets on request
Directions: In main street of village

High Street
Map no: 5 TL94
Tel: 01787 247477
Chef: Andrew Barrass
Proprietor: Forte. Manager: Michael Grange
Seats: 75. No smoking in dining room
Times: 12.30-Last L 2pm, 7pm-Last D 9.30pm

LONG MELFORD, Chimneys ❀❀

A simple, friendly restaurant in typically Suffolk style serves a good range of honest dishes based on quality ingredients

The charming interior of this busy town centre restaurant is totally in keeping with its whitewashed timbered exterior, and both – like the friendly greeting given to guests as they arrive – are typical of Suffolk. Three-course fixed-price meals are selected from a good range of modern English dishes. From the weekly-changing lunch menu you might choose cream of carrot, celery and swede soup or a warm salad of smoked bacon, lentils and mushrooms, following this by a hearty dish like braised oxtail in a red wine sauce or roast leg of lamb with thyme and garlic. The dinner menu offers slightly more exotic fare: a salad of quails' eggs and asparagus with cheese and herb fritters might precede guinea fowl filled with wild mushrooms and encased in puff pastry. Fresh vegetables are simply prepared and lightly cooked, and a selection of cheeses served with apricot and walnut bread may divert you from the tantalising array of desserts! You will still be tempted, however, when home-made fudge and petits fours accompany the robust cafetière coffee. An extensive wine list accompanies the meal.

Directions: In the centre of the village

Hall Street
Map no: 5 TL84
Tel: 01787 379806

Cost: Fixed-price L £14.50, fixed-price D £27.50. H/wine £9.85 ♀ Service exc
Credit cards: 1 2 3 4

Menus: Fixed-price lunch and dinner, Sunday lunch

Times: Midday-Last L 2pm, 7pm-Last D 9pm

Chef: Steven Wright
Proprietor: Samuel Chalmers

Seats: 50. No cigars or pipes
Additional: Children permitted; children's portions; ◐ dishes; Vegan/other diets on request

LONG MELFORD, Countrymen Restaurant at the Black Lion ❀

☺ This family-run 17th-century inn has a 'home from home' atmosphere, in relaxed informal surroundings. The Countrymen Restaurant reflects this, and is a popular local restaurant offering a monthly changing fixed price menu together with a good selection of wines.

Cost: Fixed-price L £11.25/D £13.25. H/wine £8.25 ♀ Service exc
Credit cards: 1 2 3 5. **Additional**: Children welcome; children's menu/portions; ✿ dishes; Vegan dishes usually available; other diets on request
Directions: Situated on the village green

The Green
Map no: 5 TL84
Tel: 01787 312356
Chef: Stephen Errington
Proprietor: Stephen Errington
Seats: 50. No-smoking area; no cigars or pipes
Times: Last L 2pm/D 9.30pm
Closed Mon

LONG MELFORD, Scutchers ❀

☺ It is difficult to pinpoint the ethos of the kitchen in this relaxed restaurant but it could be described as European/Italian. Classically trained chef Nicholas Barrett creates tempting dishes, for example avocado and smoked chicken salad followed by roast fillet of lamb on a minty couscous salad.

Cost: Alc from £15. H/wine £7.75 ♀ Service exc. **Credit cards**: 1 2 3
Additional: Children welcome; children's portions; ✿ dishes; other diets on request
Directions: About one mile from Long Melford on the road to Clare

Westgate Street
Map no: 5 TL84
Tel: 01787 310200/310620
Chef: Nicholas Barrett
Proprietor: Nicholas Barrett
Times: Last L 2pm/D 9.30.
Closed Sun

NEWMARKET, Heath Court ❀

☺ An excellent selection of meals prepared from fresh seasonal ingredients is available in the bar and restaurant of this modern red brick hotel. From the good value fixed-price dinner menu our inspector enjoyed gazpacho, chicken suprême with spinach roulade, and strawberry and vanilla bavarois.

Cost: Fixed-price £15.95. H/wine £9.50. Service exc
Credit cards: 1 2 3 4. **Additional**: Children welcome; ✿ dishes; Vegan/other diets on request; smoking area
Directions: At east end of town

Moulton Road
Map no 5 TL66
Tel: 01638 667171
Chef: Paul Bolt
Proprietor: Stephen Gross
Times: 7.30pm-Last D 9.30pm

ORFORD, Butley Orford Oysterage ❀

☺ Not a typical restaurant, but with a reputation decades long attributed to local support, freshness of seafood and simplicity of preparation. Popular dishes are smoked salmon pâté and Butley oysters. The smoke-house at the back produces smoked mackerel, cod-roe, chicken and salmon.

Cost: Alc £15. H/wine £8. Service exc. **Credit cards**: None taken
Additional: Children welcome; children's portions
Directions: In market square, next to town hall

Map no: 5 TM45
Tel: 01394 450277
Chefs: Mr J Knights and Mrs J Pinney
Proprietors: William Pinney and M P Pinney
Seats: 95
Times: Midday-Last L 2.15pm, Last D 9pm. Closed 25 & 26 Dec

SOUTHWOLD, **Crown at Southwold** ❀

☺ *Simply crafted meals (including lots of fish) make up the daily changing bar and restaurant menus here. Typical dishes are mussels bonne femme, and brill fillet with slices of sea trout on a Chablis sauce. Adnam's beers are served in the popular bar, and there is an outstanding wine list.*

Cost: Fixed-price L £12.75 (2 courses), £14.75/D £17.25 (2 courses), £19.95 ♀ Service exc. **Credit cards:** 1 2 3 4 5. **Additional:** Children welcome; children's portions; ❶ dishes; other diets with advance notice
Directions: At top of High Street, just before market place

90 High Street
Map no: 5 TM57
Tel: 01502 722275
Chef: Andrew Mulliss
Proprietors: Adnams. Manager: Anne Simpson
Seats: 22 (Restaurant), 22 (Parlour). No smoking in dining room. Air conditioned (restaurant)
Times: 12.30pm-Last L 1.30pm, 7.30pm-Last D 9.30pm. Closed 1 week Jan

SUDBURY, **Mabey's Brasserie** ❀❀

☺ *Tempting blackboard menus with good-value daily specials and plenty of local fish attract a loyal band of regulars here*

Local residents rub shoulders with businessmen and tourists in the cheerful, unpretentious atmosphere of this restaurant just off the market place; smokers are banished to a section near the front of the building, but other guests have a good view of the kitchen staff's skill as they prepare a predominantly classic range of dishes in a mixture of traditional and modern styles. Blackboard menus offer a balanced choice of tempting options and feature three value-for-money daily specials as well as a lot of fresh local fish (including mussels and oysters in season). Desserts, both traditional and innovative, are too good to miss, and unlimited fresh coffee served with home-made fudge will bring the meal to a fitting close. Vegetarians are provided with three alternatives, while vegan dishes are readily available. Youngsters are positively welcomed – high chairs and children's cutlery are provided. There is a moderately priced and helpfully annotated wine list of some 35 bins from both Old and New Worlds.

Directions: 150yds from Market Hill, next to Gainsborough House Museum

47 Gainsborough Street
Map no: 5 TL84
Tel: 01787 374298

Cost: L £8, D £16. H/wine £6.95 ♀ Service exc
Credit cards: 1 2 3

Menu: Blackboard

Times: Midday–Last L 2pm, Last D 10pm. Closed Sun, Mon, 25 & 26 Dec

Chef: Daniel McClelland
Proprietors: Robert and Johanna Mabey

Seats: 40. No smoking in dining room. Air conditioned
Additional: Children welcome; children's portions; ❶ dishes; Vegan/other diets on request

WOODBRIDGE, **Captain's Table** ❀

☺ *Simple but effective are the by-words of this long established seafood restaurant. The menu hardly changes, but the seafood variety depends on suppliers. Chef/patron Tony Prentice offers seafood soup and crab mousse and fillet of brill in a langoustine sauce or a mixed seafood grill as main courses.*

Cost: Alc £20, fixed-price L & D £11.95. H/wine £9.55. Service inc
Credit cards: 1 2 3 4 5. **Additional:** Children permitted; children's portions; ❶ dishes; Vegan dishes by arrangement; other diets on request
Directions: Quay Street is opposite the cinema. The restaurant is 100yds on left

3 Quay Street
Map no: 5 TM24
Tel: 01394 383145
Chef: Tony Prentice
Proprietor: Tony Prentice
Seats: 46. No smoking in dining room
Times: Last L 2pm/D 9.30pm Closed Sun, Mon, 1st 2 weeks Feb

SURREY

BAGSHOT, **Pennyhill Park** ●●●

London Road
Map no: 4 SU96
Tel: 01276 471774

Attentive service and quality cooking with some rather elaborate presentation in an elegant hotel restaurant

A sympathetic amalgam of several architectural periods, Pennyhill Park is an extensive hotel set in beautifully maintained gardens. Limited public areas, due for expansion this year, include the elegant Latymer Restaurant where professional service and fine cuisine from chef Karl Edmunds combine to provide a memorable dining experience. Choices range from traditional roasts from the trolley to more complex dishes from an extensive *carte*, fixed-price 'symphony' menu, lunch and children's menus.

An inspection meal began with an appetiser of salmon tartare, and a starter of lobster salad, with a sour cream and chive dressing, served with warm sautéed strips of sole. Other options included terrine of leeks layered with red pepper and accompanied by a truffle and walnut oil dressing and pan-fried ecrevisse, or home-smoked duck breast, thinly sliced and arranged on a light seasonal salad with a citrus fruit vinaigrette. Main courses might offer stuffed calves' liver with Cumberland sausage, on creamed mashed potato and a lemon and thyme jus garnished with black pudding; our inspector's choice, beef wellington with a good truffled Madeira jus, or a vegetarian option such as stuffed globe artichoke with baby vegetables and lime butter sauce topped with a puff pastry cage.

The highlight of our inspector's meal was an excellent hot pear and cinnamon strudel served with fruit compote and home-made cinnamon ice cream. Alternatives might be coconut bavaroise with a compote of strawberries on a Malibu and strawberry coulis, or for a savoury finish, a selection of British and French cheeses with a range of savoury breads.

Cost: *Alc* £35, fixed-price L £17.95, Sunday lunch £19.50, fixed-price D £28. Service inc
Credit cards: 1 2 3 4

Menus: *A la carte*, fixed-price lunch and dinner, Sunday lunch

Times: 12.30pm-Last L 2.30pm, 7.30-Last D 10.30pm

Chef: Karl Edmunds
Proprietor: Laura Hotels.
Manager: Dermot Fitzpatrick

Seats: 45. No cigars or pipes
Additional: Children welcome; children's menu; ◐ dishes by arrangement

Directions: On A30 between Bagshot and Camberley

BRAMLEY, **Bramley Grange** ●

Horsham Road
Map no 4 TQ04
Tel: 01483 893434
Chef: David Skan
Times: Midday-Last L 2.30pm, 7pm-Last D 10pm

☺ *Hamiltons restaurant at Bramley Grange has some very ambitious and interesting recipes on its menu, including an Around the World in Seven Dishes option. Other dishes may include roast stuffed quail with dried wild mushrooms and port wine jus – as well as innovative variations.*

Cost: *Alc* £19.95, fixed-price £10. H/wine £9.95.
Credit Cards 1 2 3 **Additional**: Children welcome; children's portions; ◐ dishes
Directions: In village centre

ENGLAND SURREY 421

BRAMLEY, **Le Berger** ☻

☺ *A cosy restaurant where chef and owner Peter Hirth creates a variety of well prepared dishes . Choices include venison and port terrine and roast courgettes with prawns in puff pastry as starters and fish symphony in dry Martini sauce or pork medallions in an orange sauce as main courses.*

Cost: Alc £16.50, Sunday L £9.95. H/wine £8.50 ♀ Service exc
Credit cards: 1 3. **Additional:** No children under 12; ❻ dishes; Vegan dishes with advance notice; other diets on request
Directions: 3 miles south of Guildford on A281

4a High Street
Map no 4 TQ04
Tel: 01483 894037
Chef: Peter Hirth
Proprietors: Peter and Mary Hirth
Seats: 26. No-smoking area. Air conditioned
Times: Last L 3pm/D 9.30pm. Closed Mon–Thu, Fri lunch, Sun eve & 2 weeks Jan

CLAYGATE, **Le Petit Pierrot** ☻☻

☺ *Jean-Pierre and Annie Brichot's comfortable little restaurant presents dishes in the French provincial style*

This small comfortable restaurant is situated in a parade of shops in well-heeled Claygate. Jean-Pierre and Annie Brichot have been established here for some four years now – Annie offers warm, smiling hospitality and leads the informal and professional service while Jean-Pierre prepares carefully-cooked meals of French provincial origin but with some modern touches of refinement. The fixed-price menu served at both lunch and dinner (though priced slightly higher in the evening) is supplemented by a good-value short choice menu at lunchtime. A recent inspection meal began with a taster of breadcrumbed deep-fried king prawns with a spicey tomato concasse, and a starter of creamy crab mousse served with an artichoke salad. The main course of pink boned quails, stuffed with a farce of walnuts, foie gras and celery was declared to be 'tender, succulent and tasty' and was followed by crème brûlée infused with saffron and pieces of rhubarb. The wines are French, varied in range and fair in value.

Directions: In Claygate follow signs for The Parade

4 The Parade
Map no: 4 TQ16
Tel: 01372 465105

Cost: Fixed-price L £9.95 (2 courses), £14.45, £16.85, fixed-price D £18.95. H/wine £8.25. Service exc
Credit cards: 1 2 3 4

Menus: Fixed-price lunch and dinner
Times: 12.15pm-Last L 2.30pm, Last D 10.30pm. Closed Sat L, Sun & BHs

Chef: Jean-Pierre Brichot
Proprietors: Jean-Pierre and Annie Brichot

Seats: 32. No pipes in dining room. Air conditioned
Additional: No children under 9; ❻ dishes

CLAYGATE, **Les Alouettes** ☻☻

Well-balanced flavours and inspired saucing are hallmarks of the food at this smart modern restaurant

An attractive gabled house in the centre of a peaceful village houses this smart restaurant with a regular local following. The atmosphere is friendly and relaxed in spite of the serious, professional approach to both service and food, and chef Simon Young's cooking is consistently good. His exceptional talent with sauces guarantees the success of his interesting modern European dishes, and the *carte* and fixed-price menus offer a balanced choice; fish dishes might include baked fillet of Scotch salmon wrapped in spinach and pastry on a lime butter sauce, with meaty choices like roast chump of lamb, or pan-fried calf's liver. Our inspector chose delicious breast of chicken wrapped in smoked ham with a rich red wine sauce, which came after a starter of casserole of king scallops and mussels braised with

High Street
Map no: 4 TQ16
Tel: 01323 464882

Cost: Alc £25, fixed-price L £9.99, fixed-price D £14.95. H/wine £11 ♀ Service 12.5%
Credit cards: 1 2 3

Menus: *A la carte*, fixed-price, Sunday lunch, specials

Times: Midday-Last L 2pm, Last D 10pm. Closed Sat lunch, Sun eve, 2 weeks Aug, 1 week Xmas

Chef: Simon Young
Proprietor: Steve Christov

smoked bacon, vermouth and chives. Both dishes were carefully prepared and full of flavour, with the expected excellent saucing. Bread and butter pudding was a delicious treat for our expert, with its tasty cardamon flavoured custard sauce. Two separate wine lists are offered.

Directions: On main A244 in Claygate

Seats: 70. Air conditioned
Additional: Children welcome; children's portions and Sunday lunch menu; ◐ dishes; Vegan/other diets on request; piano music

CRANLEIGH, **La Barbe Encore** ✺

This upmarket French-style bistro boasts a regular following of guests attracted time and again by its consistently good food and friendly atmosphere. A board of daily 'specials' broadens the choice offered on interesting two and three-course menus of flavoursome dishes based on fresh quality ingredients.

Cost: Fixed-price L £14.95 (2 courses), £16.95/D £17.95 (2 courses), £19.95. H/wine £9.25 ♀ Service exc. **Credit cards**: 1 2 3 5
Additional: Children welcome; children's portions on request; ◐ dishes; Vegan/other diets on request
Directions: Opposite St Nicholas's Church and next to the hospital

High Street
Map no: 4 TQ03
Tel: 01483 273889
Chef. Jean Pierre Bonnet
Proprietors: Jean Pierre and Ann Bonnet
Seats: 60. No-smoking area; no cigars or pipes
Times: Midday–Last L 2pm, 7pm–Last D 10.30pm. Closed Sat and Mon lunch, Sun dinner

CROYDON, **Coulsdon Manor** ✺

A fine Victorian manor in 140 acres of Surrey parkland. The menu may offer ravioli of wild mushrooms with a vegetable jus, and a main course sea-bass migonette with white and black peppercorns and beurre blanc. Since our visit a new chef has been appointed.

Cost: Alc £26, fixed-price dinner £16.50.H/wine from £9.75
Credit cards: 1 2 3 4 5. **Additional**: Children welcome; children's menu; ◐ menu; no-smoking area
Directions: Turn off A23 signposted Old Coulsdon B2030, hotel is 1 mile up the hill on the left

Coulsdon Road
Tel: 0181-668 0414
Chef: Michael Neil
Manager: Richard Rhodes
Times: Last L 2pm (2.30pm Sun)/D 9.30pm (10pm Fri, Sat). D not served Sun

DORKING, **Partners West Street** ✺✺

A new menu format and cooking team at a smart restaurant which did not quite meet expectations

Transformations have taken place at this popular restaurant during the last twelve months which have resulted in a different menu format and a change in the kitchen brigade. The carte is now available at lunchtime as well as in the evening, and new fixed-price menus make for a more versatile selection. In spite of high expectations of some interesting-sounding dishes, however, our inspector was slightly disappointed with a heavy-handedness that had not been present before, but was willingly put down to first night inconsistencies. The meal began with a charred salmon terrine and tarragon mayonnaise that had rather overpowering flavours but was otherwise fresh and well presented, followed by poached fillet of English lamb with new carrots, braised celery and ricotta dumplings. Chocolate and

2, 3 & 4 West Street
Map no: 4 TQ14
Tel: 01306 882826

Cost: Alc £30.40, fixed-price L £11.95 (3 courses) £19.95, Sunday L £11.95, £14.95, fixed-price D £19.95. H/wine £10.95. Service inc
Credit cards: 1 2 3 4

Menus: A la carte, fixed-price, Sunday lunch
Times: 12.15pm-Last L 2pm, 7.30-Last D 9.30pm

Chefs: Tim McEntire, Nathan Darling, Stuart Cauldwell,

hazelnut torte with hot cherries was a tiny but rich dessert with plenty of nuts and poached fresh cherries, and filter coffee with a good flavour came with excellent chilled chocolate truffles. Professional staff hover without being intrusive.

Additional: Children welcome; children's portions; ❷ dishes; other diets on request

Directions: In town centre on main street

Anthony Robinson, Paul Boyland
Proprietors: Partners Restaurants plc. Manager: Andrew Thomason

Seats: 45. No-smoking area; no pipes

EAST HORSLEY, **Thatchers** ❀

Thatchers Hotel is an extended timbered 30s property with a beamed restaurant. Here chef Paul O'Dowd's set price and carte menus offer a range of dishes cooked with care and style, from straightforward grills to pot roast, best end of lamb with thyme, or ragout of seafood, plus a vegetarian dish of the day.

Cost: *Alc* £24, fixed-price L £14.50/D £18.50. H/wine £9.40. Service exc. **Credit cards:** 1 2 3 4 5. **Additional:** Children welcome; children's menu/portions; ❷ dishes; Vegan/other diets on request
Directions: On main road through village

Epsom Road
Map no: 4 TQ05
Tel: 01483 284291
Chef: Paul O'Dowd
Proprietor: Resort. Manager: James Levick
Seats: 50–80
Times: 12.30pm-Last L 2pm, 7.30pm-Last D 9.30pm. Closed Sat L, some BHs & part of Xmas week

EGHAM, **Runnymede** ❀

A very busy riverside hotel catering for conferences, meetings and functions. The formal split-level River Room restaurant offers a carte as well as a choice of fixed-price meals, with dishes like roast monkfish with Welsh rarebit, and sausage and onion toad with shallot gravy. Treacle tart is a tasty dessert.

Cost: *Alc* from £22, fixed-price L £16.95/D £19.95. H/wine £11.75. Service inc. **Credit cards:** 1 2 3 4
Additional: Children welcome; ❷ /Vegan dishes; other diets on request; pianist weekday evenings
Directions: On A308 Windsor road off junction 3 of M25

Windsor Road
Map no: 4 TQ07
Tel: 01784 436171
Chef: Laurence Curtis
Proprietor: Daniel Pedreschi
Seats: 100. Air conditioned
Times: 12.30pm-Last L 2.15pm, 7pm-Last D 9.45pm (9.30 Sun). Closed Sat lunch

EPSOM, **Le Raj** ❀❀

Creative and exciting Bangladeshi cooking from a seriously innovative chef

Creative and innovative Bangladeshi cooking from a very talented and dedicated chef is proving to be a great attraction for lovers of good food. Chef Enam Ali has brought a new style to Indian cuisine, and using traditional cooking techniques has adapted recipes which are now entirely his own. His specialities are creative and exciting, and everything is cooked to order. Our inspector's best Indian meal for a long time began with samosa, crisp and lightly deep-fried filo pastry filled with fresh vegetables, and pakura – shredded onion and Bringal green pepper, lightly spiced and deep-fried. Fresh and succulent chicken tikka garnished with allumette of grilled onion was very

211 Firtree Road
Map no: 4 TQ26
Tel: 01737 371371/371064

Cost: *Alc* L £23, D £40. H/wine £6.95. Service exc
Credit cards: 1 2 3 4 5

Menus: *A la carte*

Times: Midday-Last L 2.30pm, 5.30pm-Last D 11pm. Closed 25 & 26 Dec

Chef: Enam Ali
Proprietor: Tipu Rahman

enjoyable, while 'sag ghost' – fresh spinach cooked in ghee with lean lamb was delicately flavoured and delicious. Peshwari nan was light and puffy, and a plain version tasted equally mouth-watering. Only lamb passanda was slightly disappointing. Other speciality dishes on the *carte* include 'Bahar-e-Summunder' (tropical Indian fish cooked with North Indian spices), and 'Sali Boti' (mutton cooked with dried apricots in a spicy sauce garnished with crisp straw potato).

Directions: Off the A217, near the racecourse

Seats: 50. No cigars or pipes. Air conditioned
Additional: Children welcome; children's menu on request; ❂ dishes; Vegan/other diets on request

ESHER, Good Earth ❂❂

A popular high street restaurant includes Mandarin, Szechuan and Pekinese dishes in its predominantly Cantonese menus

The generic term 'Chinese' is the fairest description of this smart, air-conditioned restaurant, for though chef Cheng's cuisine is predominantly Cantonese he also offers Mandarin, Szechuan and Pekinese specialities, this year making further amendments to his long established *carte* of some 160 items (which includes a good vegetarian section). Fixed-price meals, including a gourmet menu, are available for two or more persons. A recent meal beginning with rather disappointing plain boiled prawns accompanied by soya sauce to which a few chillies had been added continued with excellent, well cooked crispy fragrant duck with pancakes, chopped cucumber and a good hoi sin sauce; Szechuan Dover sole (the fillets battered and served in a sweet and sour sauce) was delicious, and beef with sweet pickled ginger (thin, tender pieces of steak with pickled ginger, red and green peppers and a pleasant sauce) also met with our inspector's approval. Smartly decorated and comfortable, the split-level dining room is much used by businessmen at lunchtime and is popular with groups in the evening.

14-18 High Street
Map no: 4 TQ16
Tel: 01372 462489

Cost: *Alc* £20, fixed-price L £12.50, fixed-price D £17.25. H/wine £7.50. Service 15%
Credit cards: 1 2 3 4

Menus: *A la carte*, fixed-price

Times: Midday-Last L 2.15pm, 6pm-Last D 11pm. Closed 23-26 Dec

Chef: Mr Wong
Proprietors: Mr Cheung and Mr Lau

Seats: 90. Air conditioned
Additional: Children welcome; ❂ menu; Vegan dishes on request

Directions: Sandown Park end of the High Street

GUILDFORD, Angel Posting House ❂

A charming old inn with a well-deserved reputation for its interesting and unusual cuisine. Main courses include suprême of salmon with crab mousse served with a fish sauce flavoured with Pernod and dill.

Cost: *Alc* £23.50, fixed-price L £8.50 (2 courses), £10.95/D £14.50. H/wine £8.75. Service exc. **Credit cards**: 1 2 3 4 5
Additional: Children welcome; children's menu/portions; ❂ dishes; Vegan by arrangement; other diets on request
Directions: In town centre (one-way street)

91 High Street
Map no: 4 SU94
Tel: 01483 64555
Chef: Anthony O'Hare
Proprietor: Hazel Smith
Seats: 42
Times: Midday–Last L 2.30pm, 7pm–Last D 10.30pm

GUILDFORD, Manor ✸✸

In a convenient parkland setting, Squires Restaurant features Anglo-French cuisine with a good choice of menus and wines

Usefully located directly off the A25 Guildford-Dorking road at Newlands Corner, this hotel is quietly situated in six acres of mature parkland. Squires Restaurant and Bar are very popular locally, with good value two and three-course daily fixed-price menus offered alongside the main *carte*. Chef Andrew Males previously worked in London and the Channel Islands, and his professional skills are very evident when choosing the more interesting dishes featuring his Anglo/French cuisine, which also includes a choice from the char grill. Our inspector enjoyed a flaked haddock, potato and leek terrine served warm with a white wine sauce, followed by tournedos of beef fillet with creamed wild mushrooms and a rich gravy. Traditional steak and mushroom pie and braised oxtail are also recommended, along with the bread and butter pudding. Service is very attentive and well supervised by a cordial head waiter. The well chosen wine list has some good examples of Domaine and Grand Cru, along with a good choice of New World wines and some half bottles.

Directions: Just outside the town to the east, on the A25

Newlands Corner
Map no: 4 SU94
Tel: 01483 222624

Cost: *A/c* £25, fixed-price L & D £12 (2 courses), £15, Sunday L £9.95. H/wine £8.95. Service exc
Credit cards: 1 2 3 4 5

Menus: *A la carte*, fixed-price, pre-theatre, bar menu, Sunday jazz brunch
Times: Midday-Last L 2.15pm, 7pm-Last D 9.45pm. Closed Sun eve

Chef: Andrew Males
Proprietor: Peter Davies
Seats: 45. No cigars or pipes
Additional: No children under 5; children's menu/portions by arrangement; ✪ /Vegan dishes; other diets by arrangement; jazz Sun lunchtime

HASLEMERE, Lythe Hill ✸✸

Classic French cuisine in a 15th-century hotel with tasteful modern additions

In a listed building which partly dates from 1475 with modern additions, this pretty hotel is set on a hillside overlooking a lake and parkland. The historic accommodation includes the Henry VIII room dating from 1614, while the Auberge de France restaurant which serves classical French cooking is housed in the oldest building. Chef Roger Clarke brings natural flair and skill to his cooking, and his interesting recipes attracted the praise of our inspector at a recent meal. Butterfly-shaped tiger prawns in a light lemon and garlic soy sauce made a fresh and tasty starter, while roast sea bass with a pinenut crust and red wine sauce was a fresh and enjoyable dish. The highlight of the meal was a memorable roast cannon of lamb served pink and tender with an aubergine and courgette gateau, and various freshly cooked vegetables. Desserts like the hot soufflé of the day are well worth waiting for, and come flavoured with a liqueur creme anglaise of one's choice. The *carte* and seasonal set menus include dishes like tournedos of tuna in a caper and lemon oil, and fillet of pork topped with black pudding mousse.

Directions: 1 mile east of Haslemere on the B2131

Petworth Road
Map no: 4 SU94
Tel: 01428 651251

Cost: *A/c* from £30.75, Sun L £14.50 (2 courses), £17.50, fixed-price D £17.50 (2 courses), £22.50. H/wine £11.75. No service charge
Credit cards: 1 2 3 5

Menus: *A la carte*, fixed-price, Sunday lunch, bar menu
Times: Last D 9.30pm/Sun L 2.15pm. Closed Mon

Chef: Roger Clarke
Manager: Kevin Lorimer

Seats: 60
Additional: Children welcome; children's portions; ✪ dishes; Vegan/other diets on request; piano music Fri, Saturday dinner and Sunday lunch

HASLEMERE, Morels ❀❀❀

Classic French cuisine along with some new wave Mediterranean flavours at an elegant cottage restaurant

Morel's location on a high pavement above the main road makes it necessary to park first in the town's pay and display car park before setting out for the terraced 17th-century beamed cottage. The restaurant comprises a comfortable lounge, where aperitifs and appetisers are served, and a well appointed dining room with crisp linen, gleaming tableware and fresh flowers, combining with pastel decor to create an elegant setting for some fine French cuisine. Chef patron Jean-Yves Morel has retained his successful recipes for many years while introducing new dishes with a Mediterranean flavour, more seafood, and the 'chef's fish dish of the day'. Among the new style dishes are the layered ballotine of omelette, scented with fresh provencal vegetables, and a grilled breast of chicken with black olives, tapénade and basil, offered alongside old favourites such as blinis filled with smoked salmon, yoghurt and lashings of Danish caviar.

At an inspection meal, following a complimentary ballotine of duck with puy lentils and shallot confit, our inspector thoroughly enjoyed a starter of Mediterranean fish soup, served with a mayonnaise garlic rouille and toasted croûtons. The main course, grilled breast of chicken, came with a delightful stock-based balsamic vinegar and virgin olive oil sauce, textured with chopped Greek black olives, shallots and fresh basil. Each main dish comes with its own fresh vegetables from a local farm. The dessert, a perfectly constructed 'grandmother's version' of crème brûlée, demonstrated the chef's skills to the full, and was served with a selection of fresh fruit sorbets.

The wine list has strong selections from all the classic areas of France, including excellent vintages of Burgundy and claret.

Directions: In the town centre on the Liphook road

23/27 Lower Street
Map no: 4 SU94
Tel: 01428 651462

Cost: *Alc* £31, fixed-price L £17, fixed-price D £19.30. H/wine £12. Service exc
Credit cards: 1 2 3 4

Menus: *A la carte*, fixed-price lunch and dinner

Times: Last L 2pm/D 10pm. Closed Sat lunch, all day Sun & Mon, 3 weeks end Sep

Chef: Jean-Yves Morel
Proprietors: Jean-Yves and Mary-Anne Morel

Seats: 50. No smoking
Additional: Children welcome; children's portions; ❂ dishes; Vegan dishes by arrangement

HERSHAM, Dining Room ❀

☺ *The name might be simple, but not the layout which results from two cottages combined into one, leaving small interconnecting dining rooms, giving this popular restaurant an unusual character. It serves classic English dishes like toad-in-the-hole, steak and kidney pudding and bubble and squeak.*

Cost: *Alc* £18.50, fixed–price L £11.75, Sunday L £11, fixed-price D £12.75. H/wine £7.50. Service exc **Credit cards:** 1 2 3
Additional: Children permitted; children's Sunday lunch menu; ❂ dishes; other diets on request
Directions: Off the village green

10-12 Queens Road
Map no: 4 TQ16
Tel: 01932 231686
Seats: 90. No cigars and pipes in dining rooms. No smoking area
Times: Midday-Last L 2pm (2.30pm Sun), 7pm-Last D 10.30pm. Closed Sat L, Sun eve, BHs & 10 days at Xmas

HORLEY, **Langshott Manor** ❀❀

Freshness and simplicity are the keys to chef Christopher Noble's choice seasonal menus

This charming property stands in its own well-tended garden and grounds, just a short distance from Gatwick Airport. However, the hotel is hidden along a narrow country lane and you couldn't feel further removed from a busy airport area. Personally-run by the Noble family, the atmosphere is a relaxed and cheery one and nothing appears to be too much trouble. Guests are invited to take a pre-dinner drink in the lounge whilst browsing through the menu and this provides a perfect opportunity to get to know the other guests staying at the hotel. Blazing fires roar in the grate and the ambience is truly special. The home-cooked fare is prepared with care, using quality, fresh produce and guests delight in the delicious puddings, including the very excellent gooseberry crumble with custard – just like grandma used to make. Booking is essential and vegetarians should advise when booking.

Directions: At Horley, take Ladbroke Road, turning off Chequers roundabout to Langshott, proceed to end, entrance is about 3/4 mile on right

Ladbroke Road
Map no: 4 TQ24
Tel: 01293 786680

Cost: Fixed-price L £22, fixed-price D £25. H/wine £9.50 ♀
Service exc
Credit cards: 1 2 3 4 5

Menus: Fixed-price, Sunday lunch and private dining by arrangement

Times: Last D 9.30pm

Chef: Christopher Noble
Proprietors: Geoffrey Noble

Seats: 14. No smoking in dining room
Additional: Children permitted; ✿ dishes

NUTFIELD, **Nutfield Priory** ❀❀

Imaginative and skilfully prepared dishes in modern English style are served in the restaurant of this striking hotel

Extravagantly magnificent in style, an hotel which originated as a Victorian folly overlooks the Surrey countryside from a fine setting in 40 acres of mature grounds on the Nutfield Ridge. The Cloistered Restaurant features both a fixed price menu and seasonal *carte*, chefs Stewart Dunkley and Jo Moore working in complete harmony to achieve a most imaginative and very individualistic interpretation of modern English cuisine which includes particularly impressive patisserie: breads are fresh, petits fours excellent and a perfect chocolate tart was the highlight of a recent inspection meal. Starters might include cream of pesto soup or quail and spinach salad, this perhaps followed by tender, tasty noisettes of English lamb wrapped in smoked bacon and served with a peach and ginger relish. A good regional selection of wines (which comprises some 97 bins and includes a selection of half bottles) complements the food, and well supervised service is particularly friendly and attentive. A Special Events Diary details theme dinners held throughout the year.

Directions: On A25 Redhill road

Map no: 4 TQ35
Tel: 01737 822066

Cost: Alc £32, fixed-price L £13 (2 courses), £16.00, fixed-price D £19.95. H/wine from £10.50 ♀
Service inc
Credit cards: 1 2 3 4 5

Menus: A la carte, fixed-price lunch and dinner, Sunday lunch, bar menu
Times: Last L 2pm/D 10pm. Closed Sat lunch

Chef: Stuart Dunkley
Proprietor: Arcadian. Manager: John Pearmain

Seats: 60. No-smoking area
Additional: Children permitted; ✿ dishes; Vegan/other diets on request

REIGATE, **Bridge House** ❂

A popular hotel and restaurant on a hillside with excellent panoramic views over Reigate valley where chef David Dunn produces traditional cooking. Our inspector tried a delicious main course of monkfish wrapped in sorrel leaves and puff pastry, served with a creamed shell-fish and vermouth sauce.

Cost: Alc £27, fixed-price £24. H/wine £9.50 **Credit cards**: 1 2 3 4
Additional: Children welcome; ❂ dishes

Reigate Hill
Map no 4 TQ25
Tel: 01737 246801
Chef: David Dunn
Times: 12.30pm-Last L 2.15pm, 7.30pm-Last D 10pm

RIPLEY, **Michels** ❂❂❂

Delicately prepared dishes with great flavours in a stylish town house

An attractive town centre restaurant with decor that has a feminine touch and tables spaced to give privacy. Erik Michel's cooking is a revelation, with his delicately prepared dishes and balanced flavours. The menu is not large but interesting, with starters such as nettle soup, scallops baked in their shells with lime butter, and chicory with a pastry lid, or ragout of wild blue boar with root vegetables mixed with marrow, roasted and served with a peppery roquette salad. The latter was a tasty dish to set before the inspector and he followed it with sea-bass and wild mushrooms cooked in veal juice, succulent and moist, served on a bed of creamed potatoes. In fact, he described his whole meal as 'quite delicious'. Prices are fairly high but the quality of the meal makes it good value. Karen Michel helped by pleasant staff, gives friendly and unobtrusive service. An inviting wine list includes popular wines with some from the New World – at reasonable prices.

Additional: Children welcome; one ❂ dish; other diets on request
Directions: In village centre

13 High Street
Map no: 4 TQ05
Tel: 01483 224777/222940

Cost: Alc L £28, D £30, fixed-price L £19.50, fixed-price D £21 (4 courses), £28. H/wine £9 ♀ Service exc
Credit cards: 1 2 3

Menus: A la carte, fixed-price, Sunday lunch

Times: 12.30-Last L 1.30pm, Last D 9pm. Closed Sat L, Sun eve & all day Mon, 1st week Jan

Chef: Erik Michel
Proprietors: Erik and Karen Michel

Seats: 45/50. No cigars or pipes

SOUTH GODSTONE, **La Bonne Auberge** ❂❂

A popular French restaurant offering carefully cooked food at reasonable prices

There's a pleasant atmosphere at this busy restaurant where attentive staff offer just the right amount of interested service. The food is no less inviting, and there are various choices to suit all pockets, ranging from the six-course mystery menu to a short fixed-price one that offers excellent value for money. Soundly cooked game and meat dishes dominate the menus, and at any time these might feature goose, pigeon, guinea fowl, pheasant and venison cooked in modern French style: 'pigeon des bois parfume aux truffes' (whole roast wood pigeon served with a truffle jus), and 'noisettes de chevreuil en croute' (loin of venison baked in pastry with chestnuts, juniper berries and gin sauce) are two such examples. A light and smooth 'terrine de maquereau et saumon fumé' appealed to our inspector, with its good mackerel flavour and tasty avocado sauce, followed by 'tournedos Poele, sauce Roquefort', quality, tender fillets of

Tilburstow Hill
Map no: 5 TQ34
Tel: 01342 892318

Cost: Alc £28.50, fixed-price L £15, fixed-price D £17.75. H/wine £9.80. Service inc
Credit cards: 1 2 3 4 5

Menus: A la carte, fixed-price, Sunday lunch
Times: Last L 2pm/D 10pm. Closed Sun eve, all day Mon, 26–30 Dec

Chef: Martin Bradley
Proprietor: Antoine Jalley

Seats: 70. No cigars or pipes in dining room

steak served with a well-made blue cheese sauce. The fruit mousse dessert was a light and creamy delight served with a fruit purée and fresh fruits. The wine list features clarets and Burgundies.

Directions: Just off A22, 3.5 miles from M25 Jnct 6. Turn left at the Bell Inn in Godstone

Additional: Children welcome; children's portions; children's menu by arrangement; ◊ dishes; Vegan/other diets on request

STOKE D'ABERNON, **Woodlands Park** ❀

☺ *A grand Victorian mansion offering menus by Nigel Beckett whose cooking is modern with some creations that are quite unusual. Starters include gallotine of quail and apricots, and main dishes, monkfish wrapped in Bayenne ham with peppers and lentils.*

Cost: Fixed-price L £10.75/D £14.35. 1 l/wine £7.95 ♀ Service exc.
Credit cards: 1 2 3 4. **Additional**: Children welcome; children's menu/portions; ◊ menu; Vegan/other diets on request
Directions: On the A245 Cobham-Leatherhead road

Woodlands Lane
Map no: 4 TQ15
Tel: 01372 843933
Chef: Nigel Beckett
Proprietors: Select. Manager: Michael Dickson
Seats: 35. No cigars or pipes
Times: 12.30–Last L 2pm, 7.30pm–Last D 9.30pm. Closed Sat lunch, 24–31 Dec

WEYBRIDGE, **Oatlands Park** ❀

An impressive hotel with a marble pillared entrance where Chef John Hayes produces good, uncomplicated dishes with an emphasis on fish. House speciality is salmon quartet: smoked salmon with Sevrunga caviar gravadlax, potted salmon and tartar of salmon with imperial caviar.

Cost: Alc from £25, fixed-price L £15/D £17.50. H/wine £10.95 ♀ Service exc. **Credit cards**: 1 2 3 4. **Additional**: Children permitted; children's portions; children's menu on request; ◊ dishes; Vegan/other diets on request; live entertainment Friday and Saturday evening and Sunday lunchtime
Directions: From High Street proceed up Monument Hill and turn left into Oatlands Drive

146 Oatlands Drive
Map no: 4 TQ06
Tel: 01932 847242
Chef: John Hayes
Proprietor: Stephen Craner
Seats: 120
Times: 12.30pm-Last L 2pm, 7.30pm-Last D 10pm (9pm Sun). Closed Sat lunch, Xmas–New Year

WEYBRIDGE, **Ship Thistle** ❀

Popular and long established, this town centre hotel's restaurant has an extensive carte of classical and modern French cuisine. A highly recommended starter is the carrot and coriander soup laced with Sauternes, and for main course, the beef fillet with wild forest mushrooms.

Cost: Alc £26.50, fixed-price £15.95. H/wine £11.45
Credit cards: 1 2 3 4. **Additional**: Children welcome; children's menu; games & fun-packs; ◊ dishes; no smoking in dining room
Directions: In town centre

Monument Green
Map no 4 TQ06
Tel: 01932 848364
Chef: Stephen Santin
Proprietors: Mount Charlotte Thistle. Manager: Simon Scarborough
Times: Midday-Last L 1.45pm, 7.30pm-Last D 9.45pm

TYNE & WEAR

BOLDON, **Forsters** ❀❀❀

One of the north east's leading restaurants serving good-value, light modern cooking in generous portions

Forsters is a small but smart restaurant located in a shopping parade in the village of East Bolden. It has quickly become one of the leading restaurants in the north east and chef patron Barry Forster can be justifiably proud of the high standard he has set. The *à la carte* menu retains is familiar format with eight starters and six main dishes plus fish from 'today's market', and there is a good-value set dinner available Tuesday to Friday displayed on a blackboard and presented at each table in turn. Cooking is modern, light and delicate, but as our inspector commented, the portions are more generous than on previous visits.

There is no bar, but aperitifs are served at the table with olives and a good variety of crusty rolls. Starters might include fresh mussels marinière with parsley, cream and white wine, snails sizzling in garlic butter, or pork and chicken liver pâté with home-made apricot chutney. On this occasion our inspector sampled a tasty cheddar cheese and chive soufflé, served freshly made and very hot. He followed this with roast loin of venison with braised cabbage, bacon and caraway. The meat pink, tender and full of flavour in a rich demi-glace. Other options might be roast beef, with mustard, fresh herbs and red wine; lamb with basil and tomato, and duck with black pudding and olive oil mash or, perhaps, grilled fillet steak with creamy pepper sauce or a béarnaise. Vegetarian dishes can be provided though they are not generally featured on the menus. Sweets include favourites such as sticky toffee pudding with cream and vanilla ice cream, chocolate marquise with coffee bean sauce, and our inspector's choice, a traditional, lightly caramelised lemon crème brûlée.

Directions: In village of East Bolden, just off main Newcastle-Sunderland road

2 St Bedes, Station Road
Map no: 12 NZ36
Tel: 0191-519 0929

Cost: Alc £22, fixed-price D £15. H/wine £7.65. Service exc
Credit cards: 1 2 3 4

Menu: A la carte, fixed-price

Times: 7pm-Last D 10.30pm. Closed Sun, Mon & BHs

Chef: Barry Forster
Proprietors: Barry and Sue Forster

Seats: 28. No cigars or pipes
Additional: No children under 12; children's portions; ◐ dishes

GATESHEAD, **Eslington Villa** ❀❀

High quality British cuisine offering original dishes served with particular friendliness

Essentially British dishes cooked with great innovation and served in generous portions is the chief attraction at this elegant Edwardian hotel overlooking the Team Valley. Hospitality is also a priority, and owners Melanie and Nick Tulip are renowned for the courtesy and care they extend to guests. Chef Ian Lowery produces a fixed-price menu with five choices at each course and a longer evening *carte*, with a choice of two or three set courses at lunchtime, and our inspector had high praise for a recent meal chosen from the latter: grilled Scottish scallops in herb butter with a fresh flavour and good

8 Station Road, Low Fell
Map no: 12 NZ26
Tel: 0191-487 6017

Cost: Alc £27.50, fixed-price L £9.95 (2 courses), £13.95, fixed-price D £21.95. H/wine £8.95. Service exc
Credit cards: 1 2 3 4 5

Menus: A la carte, fixed-price, Sunday lunch

Times: Midday-Last L 2pm, 7pm-Last D 10pm. Closed Sat

texture was followed by Northumberland game torte in a refined, delicate red wine sauce. The *pièce de résistance* was a light, mousse-like chocolate truffle cake spiked with brandy and served with a delicious crème anglaise. Alternatives from the *carte* might be supreme of salmon with crab and ginger mousse and a white wine sauce, and puddings like white chocolate and Grand Marnier bombe studded with apricots and pecan nuts and apricot purée, or strawberry sponge pudding with custard. There's a small select wine list.

Directions: Off A1(M) along Team Valley, turning right at Eastern Avenue, then left into Station Road

lunch, Sun eve, BHs, 1 week at Xmas
Chef: Ian Lowery
Proprietors: Melanie and Nick Tulip

Seats: 55. No smoking in dining room
Additional: Children welcome; children's portions; ◐ dishes; Vegan/other diets on request

NEWCASTLE UPON TYNE, Copthorne ✤

Le Rivage restaurant overlooks the Tyne, the Copthorne enjoying a riverbank position near the city centre. A carte of well presented French dishes includes elaborate combinations like quail stuffed with veal forcemeat, topped with puff pastry and served on a Madeira sauce with truffles and foie gras.

Cost: Alc £23. H/wine £9.95. Service inc. **Credit cards**: 1 2 3 4
Additional: Children welcome; children's menu/portions; ◐ menu; Vegan/other diets on request; live entertainment
Directions: From north side of Tyne bridge turn left into Mosley Street, left at traffic lights into Dean Street and at bottom of hill turn right at roundabout, continue to find hotel on left.

The Close, Quayside
Map no: 12 NZ 26
Tel: 0191-222 0333
Chef: Abdelhamid Afia
Proprietor: Copthorne.
Manager: Stefan Drechsler
Seats: 18. No smoking area. Air conditioned
Times: 7pm-Last D 10.30pm.
Closed Sun

NEWCASTLE UPON TYNE, Courtneys ✤

Stylish but friendly, this split-level restaurant beneath the Tyne Bridge offers a wide range of dishes from carte, fixed price and daily blackboard menus. These might include goats' cheese and leek filo, tomato and cheese gratin, beef fillet with sherry and truffle sauce, and Lindisfarne mead posset.

Cost: Alc £22.75 fixed-price L £12.50 (2 courses), £14.50. H/wine £10. Service exc. **Credit cards**: 1 2 3 5. **Additional**: Children permitted; children's portions on request; ◐ dishes; Vegan/other diets by prior arrangement.
Directions: Bottom of Dean Street on right before roundabout at Quayside

5-7 The Side
Map no: 12 NZ 26
Tel: 0191-232 5537
Chef: Michael Carr
Proprietors: Michael Carr and Kerensa Courtney
Seats: 26. No cigars or pipes in dining area. Air conditioned
Times: Last L 2pm/D 10.30pm.
Closed Sat lunch, Sun, BHs, 2 weeks May, 1 week Xmas

NEWCASTLE UPON TYNE, Fishermans Lodge ✤✤

A highly recommended, mainly seafood restaurant, in a peaceful spot outside the city

As the name suggests, this smart, friendly restaurant specialises in fresh fish and seafood, although meat dishes too are sprinkled throughout the menus. Chef Steven Jobson's cooking emphasises natural and individual flavours, and his food is renowned for its beautiful presentation. Oysters baked with

Jesmond Dene, Jesmond
Map no: 12 NZ 26
Tel: 0191-281 3281

Cost: Alc £36, fixed-price L £17, fixed-price D £25. H/wine £10. Service inc
Credit cards: 1 2 3 4

Menus: *A la carte*, fixed-price, bar lunch

garlic butter rub shoulders with pan-fried scallops in langoustine sauce for starters, and there are main dishes like chargrilled sea bass and red mullet, and lightly oak-smoked salmon fillet with butter cream and cucumber sauce. On the meat side, Northumbrian lamb might be served as a medley of roast shoulder with rosemary, cutlet with a herb crust, and sliced fillet with Madeira sauce. Our inspector opted for an attractively garnished foie gras and ham terrine, followed by delicious salmon with scallops and asparagus, grilled and served with sorrel sauce. A selection of stewed vegetables was served in a small pastry cup, while dessert consisted of three chocolate mousses – dark, milk and white – all presented differently with fresh strawberries and raspberries. The new lunchtime snack menu is popular.

Times: Midday-Last L 2pm, 7pm-Last D 11pm. Closed Sat lunch, Sun, BHs

Chef: Steven Jobson
Proprietors: Franco and Pamela Cetoloni

Seats: 65. No smoking in dining room
Additional: Children welcome (not under 10 at dinner); children's portions; ◐ menu; Vegan/other diets on request

Directions: In centre of Jesmond Dene Park, about 2.5 miles from city centre, turning right off the A1058 Tynemouth road at Benton Bank

NEWCASTLE-UPON-TYNE,
Fisherman's Wharf ✲

15 The Side
Map no: 12 NZ 26
Tel: 0191-232 1057
Chef: Simon Tennet
Proprietor: Alan Taylor
Seats: 50. Air conditioned
Times: 11.30am-Last L 2pm, 7.30pm-Last D 11pm. Closed Sat lunch, all day Sun and BHs

A predominantly seafood restaurant using only the best supplies of fish and game in the wide variety of dishes on the carte and fixed price menus. An example of a main course from the carte is casserole of lobster, cooked with vegetables and cream in a fish stock, created by Chef Simon Tennet.

Cost: Alc £35, fixed-price L £10 (2 courses), £15.75/D £25. H/wine £11 ♀ **Service exc Credit cards**: 1 2 3 4 **Additional**: Children welcome; ◐ dishes; Vegan/other diets on request
Directions: From north side of Tyne bridge, turn left into Mosley Street, left into Dean Street and left again into The Side

NEWCASTLE-UPON-TYNE,
21 Queen Street ✲✲✲

21 Queen Street, Quayside
Map no: 12 NZ 26
Tel: 0191-222 0755

A smart restaurant in the shadow of the Tyne Bridge where a good choice of modern dishes is served

Cost: Alc £30, fixed-price L £15.00 (2 courses), £17. H/wine £10.80 ♀ Service exc
Credit cards: 1 2 3 4

Pale decor, attractive prints and fresh flowers create a relaxed modern atmosphere at this smart city restaurant, situated close to the quayside below the famous Tyne Bridge. Chef patron Terence Laybourne's excellent cooking can be enjoyed at lunch or dinner, with the same high standards at each meal. At lunchtime a fixed price menu of two or three courses is available in addition to the *carte*, both menus offering a varied and interesting selection of modern French influenced dishes. Fresh fish features prominently in the 'today's market' section, with dishes such as fillet of turbot with lobster mousse and cucumber, or sauté of salmon and asparagus with chervil butter.
  Meals begin with tasty canapés in the bar, and a good variety of bread at the table – raisin and walnut, sun-dried tomato and plain white on this occasion – with delicate unsalted butter. Starters might include bavarois of Scotch smoked salmon with

Menus: A la carte, fixed-price lunch

Times: Midday-Last L 2pm, 7pm-Last D 10.45pm. Closed Sun, BHs and Last 2 weeks Aug

Chef: Terence Laybourne
Proprietor: Terence Laybourne

Seats: 50. No pipes
Additional: Children permitted;

two caviars, Shanghai shellfish risotto with crispy ginger, and a delightful shin of beef soup with horseradish dumplings. Among the main courses are medallions of Keilder venison with compote of lentils and spices; assiette of duck cooked in five different ways, and a classic tournedos Rossini – beef fillet, griddled foie gras and a truffle and Madeira sauce. The tempting range of desserts might offer lemon brûlée with fresh fruits, white chocolate truffle cake with brandied cherries, and a very good pear and almond soufflé.

The wine list is predominantly French, though the house selection of over 20 wines selling at under £18 a bottle includes interesting wines from other countries. The top growth clarets and Burgundies are real bargains.

Directions: Queen Street runs parallel to and just behind Newcastle Quay – almost under the Tyne Bridge on north side of river

children's portions on request;
◐ dishes/other diets on request

NEWCASTLE-UPON-TYNE, **Vermont** ❋❋

A winning combination of superbly cooked and presented food in a delightfully warm and friendly city-centre hotel

Housed in the former county hall buildings close to the castle and the swing bridge, this newly opened city centre hotel is already gaining a reputation for its food. There are two eating options, but the one which has aroused excitement is the Blue Room where Jonathan Brown displays his fine cooking skills. A very wide range of superbly presented dishes can be chosen from the *carte* or fixed-price menu, and our inspector was impressed by a recent meal which was served with tasty apricot and walnut bread. A very light chicken mousse delicately flecked with tarragon, and floating on a very rich Madeira and wild mushroom sauce gave the meal a delicious start, while panache of fresh fish – the chef's daily special – was indeed an extraordinary main course; halibut, brill, langoustines and salmon were beautifully cooked and served with a perfect chive butter sauce. Vegetables were an integral part of the dish, and included a tart filled with julienne of root vegetables, and a small bed of home-made pasta. To finish there was an impressive dessert of red berries in puff pastry with a tangy raspberry sauce. Enchanting service.

Directions: In city centre, by the castle and swing bridge

Castle Garth
Map no 12 NZ26
Tel: 0191-233 1010

Cost: *Alc* £35, fixed-price £25
Credit cards: 1 2 3 4

Menus: *A la carte*, fixed-price dinner

Chef: Jonathan Brown
General Manager: Paul McIntyre

Additional: Children permitted;
◐ dishes; No smoking area

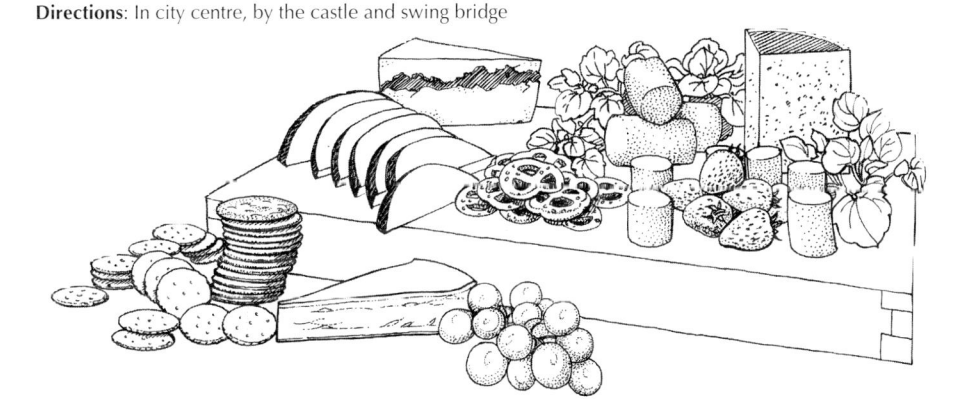

WARWICKSHIRE

ABBOT'S SALFORD, **Salford Hall** ❀

A beautifully restored manor house dating back in parts to the 15th century, with much of the original charm and architecture of the period retained. One of the hotel's strengths is the cooking of Rob Bean who offers, in the Stanford Restaurant, a fixed-price menu of modern English cuisine.

Map no: 4 SP05
Tel: 01386 871300
Chef: Rob Bean
Proprietors: Charter Hotels Ltd
Seats: 50. No smoking in dining room
Times: Last L 2.00pm/D 9.45pm

Cost: *Alc* £21.50, fixed-price L £14.95/D £21.95 H/wine £10.95
Credit cards: 1 2 3 4. **Additional**: Children permitted; ✪ dishes
Directions: On the A439 8 miles west of Stratford-upon-Avon

ATHERSTONE, **Chapel House** ❀

A delightful former dower house, dating from 1720, this hotel provides friendly and professional service. Food is central to the operation, and an imaginative set price menu of three or four courses (two Monday-Thursday) is offered in the elegant restaurant, featuring French and English cuisine.

Friar's Gate
Map no: 4 SP39
Tel: 01827 718949
Chef: Gary Thompson
Proprietor: Pat and David Roberts
Seats: 50. No cigars or pipes in dining room. Smoke filtration system
Times: Last D 9.15pm. Closed Sun, 25-26 Dec

Cost: *Alc* £22, fixed-price D £16 (2 courses), £24. H/wine £9 ♀ Service exc. **Credit cards**: 1 2 3 4 5. **Additional**: No children under 10; ✪ dishes; Vegan/other diets on request

BARFORD, **Glebe at Barford** ❀

☺ The Glebe is a former rectory dating from the 1820s. French, English and some Italian dishes are served in the attractive conservatory restaurant, and the menu includes a vegetarian section. Our inspector sampled mariner's omelette, sauté of calf's liver au poivre, and strawberry cheesecake.

Church Street
Map no: 4 SP26
Tel: 01926 624218
Chef: Andrew Wheeler
Manager: David Jones
Seats: 80. Air conditioned
Times: 11.30am–Last L 2.30pm, Last D 10pm

Cost: Fixed-price D £14.95, Sunday L £12.50. H/wine £9.50. Service exc. **Credit cards**: 1 2 3 4 5 **Additional**: Children welcome; children's menu/portions; ✪ menu; Vegan/other diets on request
Directions: In village centre, near the church

HENLEY-IN-ARDEN, **Le Filbert Cottage** ❀❀

Well-executed French cooking and charming Gallic service in a typically English village setting

64 High Street
Map no: 4 SP16
Tel: 01564 792700

Set right in the heart of a typical English village, this cottage restaurant with oak beams and quarry tiled floors really looks in place. The robust and colourful cooking of chef/patron Maurice Ricaud is undeniably French, however, and his wife Elva offers a characteristically Gallic service. Simplicity and honesty are the key notes here, and the rich, fresh flavours of the dishes indicate the classical training of the chef. 'Magret de

Cost: *Alc* £18.80, fixed–price L £18.50-£20, fixed–price D £20–£25. H/wine £8. Service exc
Credit cards: 1 2 3 4

Menu: *A la carte*, fixed-price

canard landais au poivre noir', duck with black pepper, and 'noisettes d'agneau avec sauce piquante aux Cassis', collops of lamb, are typically unfussy dishes that might appear on the *carte*, and there's a fixed-price three-course menu at lunch and dinner. At a recent inspection lunch delicious Cornish crab bisque with a distinct depth of flavour made a first class starter, followed by 'troncon de barbue' – three delicate fillets of Cornish brill lightly poached in a mustard and herb sauce with cream and white wine. Home-made crème caramel of light texture with a smooth vanilla sauce was followed by decent filter coffee. The wine list offers a good range of French wines.

Directions: In town centre, at junction of High Street and Station Road

Times: Midday-Last L 1.30pm, 7pm-Last D 9.30pm. Closed Sun, Mon & BHs

Chef: Maurice-Jean–Gaudens Ricaud
Proprietor: Maurice-Jean–Gaudens Ricaud

Seats: 30. No smoking in dining room
Additional: No children under 5; children's portions; ◐ dishes

KENILWORTH, **Restaurant Bosquet** ❁❁

Unpretentious but reliably good, this peaceful restaurant offers a good choice of honest-flavoured French dishes

Though inconspicuously sandwiched between other restaurants and small hotels in a terrace of houses beside the main road, this is one of the most consistently reliable eating places in the Midlands. A very popular fixed-price menu offers good, full-flavoured dishes in predominantly French style, but it is on the *carte* that you will find special occasion choices – perhaps saddle of venison with chestnuts and mandarins in a port and game sauce, or breast of duck thinly sliced with pear and ginger and served with a lime sauce. Noteworthy home-made desserts include a deep, warm lemon tart accompanied by a sharp lime sorbet, and good cafetière coffee with delicious petits fours completes the meal. The well balanced list of mainly French wines has a range that should suit every pocket. Both vegetarian and Vegan meals can be provided on request, and children are welcome if they will eat from the adult menu. Guests are assured of a charming welcome which, together with the calm, peaceful atmosphere that pervades the establishment, adds much to the pleasure of a visit here.

Directions: Located towards the southern end of the High Street in Kenilworth

97a Warwick Road
Map no: 4 SP27
Tel: 01926 52463

Cost: Alc £27, fixed-price L & D £19.80. H/wine £10.80. Service exc
Credit cards: 1 2 3

Menus: A la carte and fixed-price
Times: Last L 1.15pm/D 9.30pm. Closed Sun, Mon, 1 week Xmas & 3 weeks Aug

Chef: Bernard Lignier
Proprietors: Bernard and Jane Lignier

Seats: 26. No pipes
Additional: Children welcome; children's portions; ◐ Vegan/other diets on request

ROYAL LEAMINGTON SPA, **Lansdowne** ❁

☺ *A Regency-style hotel in the heart of town, the Lansdowne offers simple but effective cooking full of natural flavours. Particular pride is taken in the excellent Aberdeen Angus beef which is regularly featured, and a ginger sorbet (bought in) was the best our inspector had ever tasted.*

Cost: Fixed-price £16.95. H/wine £7.95. No service charge
Credit cards: 1 3. **Additional**: No children under 5; children's portions; ◐ dishes; Vegan/other diets on request
Directions: Town centre, corner of Clarendon Street and Warwick Street, near The Parade

87 Clarendon Street
Map no: 4 SP36
Tel: 01926 450505
Chef: Lucinda Button
Proprietors: David and Gillian Allen
Seats: 24. No smoking in dining room
Times: 6.30pm-Last D 8.30pm. Closed Sun eve to non-residents, 25-26 Dec

ROYAL LEAMINGTON SPA,
Mallory Court ✹✹✹

Harbury Lane, Bishop's Tachbrook
Map no: 4 SP36
Tel: 01926 330214

Creatively presented and expensive modern French cuisine served in the dining room of a country house hotel

Mallory Court is a lovely Lutyens styled manor house set in formal gardens surrounded by countryside. Proprietors Allan Holland and Jeremy Mort work hard to maintain the ambience of a private house, so there are no bars here but two lounges with fine rugs, open fires and floral displays.

The kitchen team, led by Allan Holland, cook lunch and dinner each day, and the meals are served in the elegant oak panelled dining room. Fixed-price menus are offered in addition to the *carte*, and these include a two or three-course lunch, a three-course dinner, and a no-choice five-course gourmet menu at £60, with coffee and petits fours.

A light touch with the cooking is evident in dishes such as scallop mousse with leeks, scallops and a delicately flavoured ginger sauce. Main courses, too, are light and creatively presented. A braised turbot with wild mushrooms was almost perfect, with a sauce of natural juices enhanced with just a touch of Madeira. Alternatives might be starters of spinach and ricotta cheese ravioli with a tomato and basil sauce, or pheasant and pigeon terrine with Cumberland sauce. While main courses include fillet of venison served on braised red cabbage with a poivrade sauce and blackcurrants, and sautéed breast of Gressingham duck with a confit of the leg and sautéed apples, honey and cider vinegar. Vegetarian main courses are not featured on the menus but can be provided on request. To finish, there are beautifully presented desserts such as hot passion fruit soufflé with its own sorbet, feuilleté of William pear poached in vanilla syrup with a caramel sauce, and a chocolate tear filled with a white chocolate mousse and served with raspberry coulis.

The wine list offers excellent quality and variety. The claret, Burgundy and dessert sections are particularly strong, and the house wines are imaginatively chosen.

Cost: *Alc* £50, fixed-price L £19.50 (2 courses), £23.50, fixed-price D £30. H/wine from £9.95. No service charge
Credit cards: 1 2 3 5

Menus: *A la carte*, fixed-price lunch and dinner, Sunday lunch, pre-theatre

Times: Last L 2pm/D 9.45pm. Closed 3–12 Jan

Chef: Allan Holland
Proprietors: Allan Holland and Jeremy Mort

Seats: 50. No cigars or pipes
Additional: No children under 9; ✿ dishes; Vegan/other diets on request

Directions: 2 miles south off the B4087 towards Harbury

ROYAL LEAMINGTON SPA, **Regent** ✹

77 The Parade
Map no 4 SP36
Tel: 01926 427231
Chef: Roland Clark
Proprietor: Mrs Cridlan
Times: Midday-Last L 2pm, 7pm-Last D 10pm

Built in 1819, this well-established hotel has a choice of two dining places and a range of menus. One of our inspector's dishes was the light and tasty monkfish set within a garlic, tomato and onion provençale sauce.

Cost: *Alc* £15.25, fixed-price £24. **Credit cards**: 1 2 3 4
Additional: Children permitted; ✿ dishes; no-smoking area
Directions: In town centre near Royal Priors Shopping Centre

STRATFORD-UPON-AVON,
Alveston Manor ☻

☺ *Set in seven acres of mature gardens and grounds, this hotel restaurant provides well-prepared dishes making good use of quality produce. A recently inspected meal included a moist and full flavoured baked fillet of salmon on a bed of julienne of leeks with a chive and tomato butter sauce.*

Cost: Fixed-price £21.50. **Credit cards**: 1 2 3 4
Additional: Children permitted; ❶ dishes; no smoking in dining room
Directions: Close to town centre, adjacent to Banbury and Evesham roads

Clopton Bridge
Map no: 4 SP25
Tel: 01789 204581
Chef: Simon Furey
Times: Midday-Last L 2pm, 6pm-Last D 10.30pm

STRATFORD-UPON-AVON,
Billesley Manor ☻☻☻

A historic Elizabethan manor house serving richly classical Anglo/French cooking with a modern twist

William Shakespeare was a frequent visitor to this charming Elizabethan manor house outside Stratford, and is reputed to have written *As You Like It* whilst staying here. The beautiful stone house, set in delightful grounds complete with topiary gardens, retains the qualities that must have enchanted the playwright, and remains a peaceful country retreat. Nowadays a French team under the direction of Christophe Gallot looks after the dining room, providing a professional service which is nicely tempered by genuine hospitality.

The superb cooking of Mark Naylor is a great strength of the hotel, and in particular his very fine saucing. The cuisine is richly classic Anglo/French with an occasional modern twist, and the four-course seasonal *carte* and daily changing fixed-price menus can be a bit of a challenge. Our inspector had little difficulty rising to it at a recent meal, beginning with an intensely coloured and flavoured red mullet soup which was subtly enhanced with coriander seed, and served with saffron aïoli, garlic croûtons and Gruyère cheese. Succulent breast of Gressingham duck came with a confit of its thigh, and a gin and juniper sauce; sweet parsnip and honey purée added another rich dimension to this stunning main course. Best end of Cornish lamb with tarragon mousse, tomato and salsify might be another choice, or pan-fried fillet of beef crusted with pine kernels, Parma ham and a horseradish jus. Vegetarians are given their own menu, which could include a leek and cheese kromesqis, or baked field mushrooms with walnuts and Brie, while fish lovers are offered a daily market dish. Soufflés are a house speciality, like the wonderful Grand Marnier version flecked with grated dark chocolate and served with clotted cream.

The clearly presented and well balanced wine list offers a broad range of wines from many countries.

Directions: On the A46, 3 miles west of Stratford-upon-Avon

Billesley, Alcester
Map no: 4 SP25
Tel: 01789 400888

Cost: A/c £35, fixed-price L £17, fixed-price D £26. H/wine £10.50. Service exc
Credit cards: 1 2 3 4 5

Menus: A la carte, fixed-price lunch and dinner, Sunday lunch, bar menu

Times: Last L 2pm/D 9.30pm (10pm Fri, Sat)

Chef: Mark Naylor
Proprietor: Queens Moat Houses. Manager: Peter Henderson

Seats: 70. No cigars or pipes
Additional: Children permitted, but very young children discouraged at dinner; Children's menu/portions; ❶ menu; Vegan/other diets on request

STRATFORD-UPON-AVON, Stratford House ❀

Dating back to 1823, this delightful small hotel is conveniently situated within a short walk of the theatre and the town centre. The attractive Shepherd's Garden restaurant has a conservatory extension, and imaginative, wholesome dishes are offered on the short international carte.

Credit cards: 1 2 3 4 5. **Additional**: Children welcome; children's portions; ❂ menu; Vegan/other diets on request
Directions: In town centre, 100 yds from Royal Shakespeare Theatre

Sheep Street
Map no: 4 SP25
Tel: 01789 268288
Chefs: N Paul, A Steele
Proprietor: Sylvia Adcock
Seats: 45. No cigars or pipes in dining room
Times: Last L 2pm/D 9.30pm. Closed Mon lunch

STRATFORD-UPON-AVON, Welcombe ❀❀

A high standard of British cooking with some innovative touches and generous helpings

Surrounded by its own golf course and extensive landscaped gardens, this newly-refurbished hotel is equally attractive to conference, business and holiday guests. Set in a rural position the hotel offers some superb accommodation as well as its own leisure facilities. As befits this area of great historical interest, the food is traditionally British, and portions are generous. A recent inspection meal began with marinated new potatoes with sliced breast of guinea fowl, an enjoyable starter with the meat moist and tasty. Game casserole was an innovative main dish: pheasant, pigeon, hare and rabbit in a herby sauce came in a puff pastry case, with three slices of tender fillet of venison served apart on the plate. Other recommended dishes have been consommé of root vegetables finished with garden herbs and grated ginger, and a garland of crab meat topped with medallions of sea bass with grilled scallops and a garnish of asparagus tips. Puddings might be a rich crème brûlée, or perhaps a duo of chocolate parfait with a crème anglaise sauce, chosen from the *carte* or fixed-price menu.

Directions: About 1 mile east of town centre on the A439

Warwick Road
Map no 4 SP36
Tel: 01789 295252

Cost: *Alc* £33, fixed-price £18
Credit cards: 1 2 3

Menus: *A la carte*, fixed-price

Chef: Michael Carver
General Manager: Brian Miller

Additional: Children permitted; ❂ dishes; no cigars or pipes in restaurant

WISHAW, Belfry ❀❀

An interesting variety of well-executed French cooking in an impressive hotel setting

The French Restaurant is one of several dining options at this impressive hotel and leisure complex, and the quality of its food marks it out above the others. Some fine and elaborate French dishes are prepared by long-serving chef Eric Bruce, who offers them on a series of menus: a well-balanced *carte* is supplemented by fixed-price four-course dinner and three-course lunch menus, a separate vegetarian selection and a set five-course gourmet menu. Our inspector recently sampled 'cassolette de fruits de mer', steamed seafood panache in a filo basket with crayfish sauce which made a full-flavoured, creamy starter, followed by very tender 'selle de chevreuil belle

Lichfield Road
Map no: 7 SP19
Tel: 01675 470301

Cost: *Alc* £29, fixed-price L £15.95, fixed-price D £25.50. H/wine £11.95 ♀ Service inc
Credit cards: 1 2 3 4

Menus: *A la carte*, fixed-price, Sunday lunch, Carvery, bar menu
Times: 12.30pm–Last L 2pm, 7.30pm–Last D 10pm. Closed Sat lunch, Sun eve
Chef: Eric Donaldson Bruce

forestière', a tasty venison fillet steak with a pungent game jus. Warm banana pancake with a sabayon sauce and a vanilla ice in a brandy snap basket was a typically elegant dessert, and very good cafetière coffee came with solid white truffles. The set menus might offer starters like pithivier of pan-fried duck livers, bacon and wild mushrooms with a Madeira wine sauce, or such main dishes as grilled lamb cutlets with smoked bacon.

Directions: At junction of A446 and A4091, one mile north-west of M42 junction 9

Proprietor: De Vere. General Manager: Mike Maloney

Seats: 80. No-smoking area

Additional: Children welcome; half-portions available; ⊘ dishes; Vegan/other diets on request; live entertainment

WEST MIDLANDS

BALSALL COMMON, **Haigs** ❀❀

☺ *Dedicated and creative cooking producing authentic flavours in a meticulously run hotel*

Within its classification this small, privately run hotel is quite simply a perfect specimen, and the owners cannot do enough to accommodate their guests. This unusual degree of professionalism extends into the kitchen where chef Paul Hartup shows a dedicated approach to his cooking. From the delectable home-made bread – of a texture and flavour to rival the best anywhere – right down to the delicious petits fours, his sound expertise and flair are well demonstrated. Dishes like baked halibut filled with asparagus mousse served with a sherry vinegar sauce, and grilled calf's liver with bacon and onions are listed on the *carte*, while the daily-changing set two or three course menu might offer grilled pork chops with mushroom sauce, or pan-fried rainbow trout with herb butter. Our inspector praised a starter of roasted red peppers filled with tomatoes and olives, and topped with melted ewes' cheese. Steamed red snapper fillet was enhanced by a pungent ginger and lime sauce, and there was a lovely flavour to the almond tart. Nut croquettes, and stir-fried vegetables with rice are offered for non-carnivores.

Directions: 4 miles north on A452

Kenilworth Road
Map no: 7 SP27
Tel: 01676 533004

Cost: *Alc* £21.50, Sun L £12.15, fixed-price D £14.15 (2 courses), £16.85. H/wine £8.75. No service charge

Credit cards: 1 3 5
Menus: *A la carte*, fixed-price, Sunday lunch

Times: 7.30-Last D 9pm (9.30pm Sat), Last Sunday L 2pm. Closed 26 Dec-4 Jan

Chef: Paul Hartup
Proprietors: Jean and John Cooper

Seats: 40. No cigars or pipes
Additional: Children welcome; children's portions; ⊘ dishes; Vegan/other diets by prior arrangement

BALSALL COMMON, **Nailcote Hall** ❀❀

An Elizabethan country house featuring a good fixed-price Anglo-French menu of classic and modern cuisine

A black and white timbered and gabled Elizabethan country house peacefully set in eight acres of mature grounds, yet conveniently located for the motorway network, NEC and airport. The beautiful Oak Room Restaurant features jade walls enhancing the rich timbers, emphasising the successful harmony between the original period features and both contemporary and antique furniture. A good fixed-price Anglo-French menu including grills demonstrated the well executed classic and

Nailcote Lane, Berkswell
Map no: 7 SP27
Tel: 01203 466174

Cost: *Alc* £26, fixed-price L £17.75, fixed-price D £26. H/wine £10. Service exc
Credit cards: 1 2 3 4

Menus: *A la carte*, fixed-price, Sunday lunch

Times: Midday-Last L 2.15pm,

modern cuisine from chef Mark Bradley, with the menu presented in French, with English translations. Typical starters might include wild mushrooms with fresh pasta in a pastry case or pan fried fillet of monkfish with lardons of bacon and dill. Main course choices include chargrilled pork loin dressed on a vegetable ratatouille, or pan fried calves liver with red onions and sage; grilled fillet of American sea bream with anchovy butter features in the grill choices. A short selection of desserts includes strawberry shortbread or black cherry custard tart.

Directions: 1.5 miles from Balsall Common on the B4101 Tile Hill/Coventry road, on the right

7.30pm-Last D 9.45pm. Closed 27 & 28 Dec

Proprietor: R W Cressman

Seats: 42. No cigars or pipes in dining room
Additional: Children welcome; children's portions by arrangement; ❼ menu; Vegan/other diets on request; live entertainment

BIRMINGHAM, Chung Ying Garden ❀

A large Chinese restaurant situated in China Town, near the Hippodrome Theatre. The lengthy carte includes an excellent selection of dim sum as well as many specialities such as steamed scallop stuffed with minced prawn or aromatic duck with pancakes. There are also set dinner menus.

Cost: H/wine £8.50 (litre). No service charge. **Credit cards**: 1 2 3 4 5
Additional: Children welcome; ❼ menu; Vegan/other diets on request
Directions: In city centre, off Hurst Street, near the Hippodrome Theatre

17 Thorp Street
Map no: 7 SP08
Tel: 0121–666 6622
Chef: Siu Chung Wing
Manager: Danny Chan
Seats: 350. Air conditioned
Times: Midday–midnight. Closed Xmas Day

BIRMINGHAM, Copthorne ❀

A stylish modern hotel in the heart of the city centre. The staff are highly trained and very efficient and Goldsmiths Restaurant has a menu for all tastes, including The All American Dream Burger and Baked Salmon with crab mousse. The ingredients are fresh and the skills competent.

Cost: Alc £29, fixed-price L £6.95. H/wine £8.95 ♀ Service inc **Credit cards**: 1 2 3 4 5. **Additional**: Children welcome; children's menu/portions; ❼ dishes; Vegan/other diets on request; live entertainment
Directions: In city centre, next to ICC

Paradise Circus
Map no: 7 SP08
Tel: 0121–200 2727
Chef: Terry Howland
Proprietor: Copthorne.
Manager: Stephen Price
Seats: 50 restaurant; 90 brasserie. No-smoking area. Air conditioned
Times: 7pm–Last D 10pm (restaurant), 11am–11pm (brasserie)

BIRMINGHAM, Shimla Pinks ❀

☺ It is said that in the 1930's the 'Shimla Pinks' were India's equivalent to the 'Sloane Rangers'. Chef Ganesh Shresta produces modern versions of popular Indian dishes using fresh ingredients, herbs and spices. Specialities include southern Indian garlic chilli chicken.

Cost: Alc £15, fixed-price L £6.95/D £12.95 (2 courses), £14.95. H/wine £7.95 ♀ Service exc. **Credit cards**: 1 2 3 4 5
Additional: Children welcome; children's portions; ❼ dishes; Vegan/other diets on request
Directions: In city centre, near the ICC and opposite Novotel

214 Broad Street
Map no 7 SP08
Tel: 0121-633 0366
Chef: Ganesh Shresta
Proprietor: Dhalinal and Pannum
Seats: 165. Air conditioned
Times: Midday-Last L 2.30pm, 6pm-Last D 11pm. Closed Sat and Sun lunch, 25-26 Dec

ENGLAND WEST MIDLANDS 441

BIRMINGHAM, Sloan's ❀❀

Once fine food that now lacks sparkle and quality, still popular with Birmingham business people

27-29 Chad Square, Hawthorne Road, Edgbaston
Map no 7 SP08
Tel: 0121-455 6697

Sloan's has been at the forefront of the city's eating scene for some years now, but recent visits have suggested that it has lost its sharp edge and faded somewhat. This restaurant is still busy and popular, especially at lunchtime when the city's business population descends on its unlikely location in a small, modern shopping precinct. Our inspector found the interior to be rather ageing and dated, while the food which once inspired superlatives was found to have less than its former appeal and polish. A recent meal began with a thick brown Thai chicken soup which was disappointingly overwhelmed by excessive amounts of coconut milk, served with a spicy dumpling that was more West Indian than Thai. Crispy confit of Norfolk duck with potato galette was dry and tasteless, and came with lukewarm gratin dauphinoise and tired vegetables. However, other recent meals have produced one or two successful dishes – ballotine of chicken and foie gras was deliciously juicy, and breast of wood pigeon was tender and tasty – but overall the former quality was missing, and even a dessert like crème brûlée was overcooked.

Cost: A/c £25, fixed-price £15
Credit cards: 1 2 3

Menus: A la carte, fixed-price

Times: Midday-Last L 2pm, 7pm-Last D 10pm. Closed Sun, BHs & Xmas

Chef: Simon Booth
Proprietor: John Narbett

Additional: Children permitted

Directions: From Five Ways roundabout take Calthorpe Road. Right at lights. Continue to White Swan pub; Sloan's is opposite

BIRMINGHAM, Swallow ❀❀❀

French Mediterranean cookery served with some aplomb in an attractive hotel restaurant

12 Hagley Road, Five Ways, Edgbaston
Map no: 7 SP08
Tel: 0121-452 1144

The Swallow Hotel is a skilfully converted Edwardian office block overlooking Five Ways roundabout, its quiet elegance a complete contrast to the urbanisation all around. The hotel's two restaurants offer widely different styles but equally good cooking from the young and enthusiastic chef de cuisine, Jonathan Harrison.
The Sir Edward Elgar is the main restaurant, and the more formal of the two, serving French Mediterranean cookery with classical influences from a seasonal *carte*. The menu is a handsome production in itself, incorporating biographical notes and photographs of Edward Elgar. Starters range from white bean soup with a confit of rabbit at £5.95, to Sevruga caviar with warm blini at £50 per 50g portion. There are three fish dishes, which can be taken as a fish course or a main dish, such as the fillet of sea bass with herb couscous, basil and olive tapénade sampled by our inspector. The choice of around seven main courses included fillet of pork wrapped in parma ham, with parmesan, macaroni and roasted peppers, or grilled maize-fed chicken on a bed of foie gras spätzel. A vegetarian option, though not listed on the *carte*, can be provided. Among the desserts were a terrine of chocolate and praline served with a soup of fresh strawberries, and a light mousse of clementines with a crisp orange tuile, which our inspector thought to be more of a parfait.

Cost: A/c £40, fixed-price L £16.50 (2 courses), £20.50, fixed-price D £25 (3 courses), £30. H/wine £15 ♀ Service exc
Credit cards: 1 2 3 4 5

Menus: A la carte, fixed-price, after theatre
Times: 12.30-Last L 2.30pm, 7.30-Last D 10.30pm (10.45pm after theatre, if pre-booked). Closed Sat lunch

Chef: Jonathan Harrison
Proprietor: Swallow. Manager: Hugh Patton

Seats: 60. Air conditioned
Additional: Children welcome; children's menu/portions; ♥ dishes; Vegan/other diets on request; pianist every evening and Sunday lunchtime

The waiting staff, mostly French, smartly uniformed and attentive, raise their cloches with a theatrical flourish; and the pianist is more likely to play *Smoke gets in your eyes* than anything by the restaurant's eponymous composer. The wine list offers a large selection of French and European wines, together with several from the New World. There are some lovely vintage champagnes, and a selection of half bottles.

Directions: At the city end of the A456, at the Five Ways roundabout

COVENTRY, **Brooklands Grange** ❀

☺ Behind its Jacobean façade, this hotel is thoroughly modern. The restaurant, Herbs Brasserie, has a new chef but the style remains much the same. The carte offers a huge and very varied choice with plenty of vegetarian dishes, supported by a short set price menu of two or three courses.

Cost: *Alc* £19.95, fixed-price D £12.95 (2 Courses), £15.95. H/wine £7.95 ♀ Service inc. **Credit cards**: 1 2 3 4
Additional: Children welcome; children's menu/portions; ❂ dishes; Vegan/other diets on request; live entertainment
Directions: Leave city westwards on the A4144; Brooklands Grange is on right, just before the Allesley roundabout

Holyhead Road
Map no: 4 SP37
Tel: 01203 601601
Chef: Stuart Hope
Manager: Lesley Jackson
Seats: 60. No cigars or pipes. No smoking area
Times: Midday-Last L 2pm, 7pm-Last D 10pm. Closed for lunch Sat & BHs

HOCKLEY HEATH, **Nuthurst Grange** ❀❀❀

Honest cooking embracing classical and modern, French and British styles served in a country house setting

An attractive country house, built more than 100 years ago, Nuthurst Grange is set in seven acres of landscaped gardens and woodlands, and is approached by a long tree-lined drive. Chef/patron David Randolph and his wife Darryl have been here for just over seven years and in that time have built up a fine reputation for their restaurant as well as developing the hotel. Food is very much at the heart of the operation and the spacious and well appointed restaurant is a fitting showcase for the honest food prepared by David, head chef Simon Wilkes and their team, for both lunch and dinner. There are two menus, an affordable three-course fixed price menu and a more ambitious and expensive *carte*.

Starters include sliced smoked goose breast with sautéed mushrooms and salad leaves garnished with bacon and croûtons; Indian spiced potatoes with cucumber and yoghurt, and broccoli and almond soup, the good stock base rather overwhelming the flavour of the broccoli at an inspection meal. Sauces are good, as demonstrated in the Dover sole sampled by our inspector, served off the bone with a chive and Champagne sauce coloured by a tomato concasse. Other choices could be breast of guinea fowl with sauerkraut and a smoked bacon sauce, or loin of pork with apples and cider. Vegetarian dishes can also be provided on request.

The dessert menu will delight those who enjoy hot puddings, and the steamed date sponge with toffee sauce was one of the best our inspector had tasted. Other classics are also offered,

Nuthurst Grange Lane
Map no: 7 SP17
Tel: 01564 783972

Cost: *Alc* £39.90, fixed-price L £16.50, fixed-price D £23.90. H/wine £9.95. Service exc
Credit cards: 1 2 3 4 5

Menus: *A la carte*, fixed-price, Sunday lunch

Times: Midday-Last L 2pm, 7pm-Last D 9.30pm. Closed Sat lunch

Chef: David Randolph
Proprietor: David Randolph

Seats: 50. No smoking in dining room
Additional: Children welcome; children's portions (menu by arrangement); ❂ dishes; Vegan/other diets on request

such as crème brûlée, and a light and dark chocolate mousse encased in blond caramel threads with a fresh coffee bean sauce. The wine list comprises a well balanced selection from around the world, its main strength being the red and white burgundy sections, and some reasonably priced claret.

Directions: Off A3400 1/2 mile south of Hockley Heath, turning at notice-board into Nuthurst Grange Lane

MERIDEN, Forest of Arden ❀

☺ *Meriden is reputed to be at the centre of England and the 1994 English Open was played on one of the hotel's two golf courses. Courses of another kind include fillet of red snapper, fillet of pork and, for two people, Chateaubriand, which are served in the hotel's restaurant.*

Cost: Fixed-price L and D £19.50. H/wine £10.95. Service inc
Credit cards: 1 2 3 4. **Additional**: Children welcome; ❍ menu; Vegan/other diets on request; pianist Sunday lunchtime
Directions: From M42 junction 6, take A45 Coventry road, straight on at Stonebridge Island. In 0.75 mile turn left into Shepherds Lane, hotel is in 1.5 miles on left.

Maxstoke Lane
Map no: 4 SP28
Tel: 01676 522335
Chef: Glyn Windross
Proprietor: Michael O'Dwyer
Seats: 130. No smoking in dining room
Times: 12.30 Last L 2pm, 7pm-Last D 9.45pm. Closed Sat lunch

OLDBURY, Jonathans ❀

The interior of this modern red brick hotel is an authentic re-creation of the Victorian era, absurd in places but great fun. The cuisine, characterised by much hyperbole, offers plentiful amounts of tasty old English or French dishes, in a choice of restaurants. Light dishes are available for the faint hearted.

Cost: Alc £25, fixed-price L £12.50, fixed-price D £24.90. H/wine £10.90. Service exc. **Credit cards**: 1 2 3 4 5
Additional: Children welcome; children's portions; ❍ menu; Vegan/other diets on request; live entertainment
Directions: At the junction of A456/A4123, 1 mile from M5 junction 2

16-24 Wolverhampton Road
Map no: 7 SO98
Tel: 0121-429 3757
Chef: Graham Bradley
Proprietors: Jonathan Baker and Jonathan Bedford
Seats: 140. No-smoking area
Times: Last L 2pm (4pm Sun)/D 10pm Closed 1 Jan

SOLIHULL, Solihull Moat House ❀

An attractively landscaped modern hotel situated in the town centre. Brookes Restaurant offers fixed-price and carte menus featuring fine cuisine in the modern English vein with French influences. Dishes might include a red pepper mousse, halibut steak with mushrooms, and lemon tart brûlée.

Cost: Alc £25, fixed-price L £11.75/D £15.75. H/wine £8.50. Service exc. **Credit cards**: 1 2 3 4
Additional: Children welcome; children's menu/portions; ❍ menu; Vegan/other diets on request; live entertainment
Directions: From M42 junction 5 take A41 signposted town centre, before 2nd traffic lights bear left, pass church and turn left into Church Hill Road, at roundabout take 3rd exit.

61 Homer Road
Map no: 7 SP17
Tel: 0121-711 4700
Chef: Mark Houghton
Proprietor: Queens Moat.
Manager: Mario Lolli
Seats: 75. No-smoking area. Air conditioned
Times: 12.30pm-Last L 2pm, Last D 10pm. Closed 27-31 Dec

SUTTON COLDFIELD, New Hall ●●

A historic country house hotel in a tranquil moat setting, serving quality food in a variety of styles

A lily-filled moat surrounds this 800-year-old manor house splendidly set in 26 acres of gardens and reputedly the oldest inhabited building of its kind. Many of the fine additions to the house over the years have been retained, like the Flemish glass and 17th-century fireplaces. The dining room itself is lined with 16th-century oak panelling, making an impressive setting. The *carte* and fixed-price menus offer a mixture of traditional British and some more contemporary ideas, and our inspector began a recent lunch with a fresh Caesar salad, followed by grilled salmon with new potatoes and a tomato and basil vinaigrette, and a warm date and almond tart with a well-made crème anglaise. The *carte* offers a more extensive selection, with starters like chargrilled king prawns on a ratatouille crostini, and pan-fried wild mushroom and Gruyère gnocchi, or main dishes such as tournedos of beef, or pan-fried fillet of monkfish with a scampi and spinach ravioli. Since our visit Simon Radley has become chef. The Parkes' are delighted with his menus and hope to raise the restaurant's status yet further.

Directions: On the B4148 east of Sutton Coldfield

Walmley Road
Map no: 7 SP19
Tel: 0121-378 2442

Cost: *Alc* from £35, fixed-priced D £21 (2 courses), £25.45. H/wine £11.75 ♀ Service exc
Credit cards: 1 2 3 4 5

Menus: *A la carte,* fixed-price, Sunday lunch, pre-theatre
Times: Last L 2pm/D 10pm. Closed Sat lunch
Chef: Simon Radleyl
Proprietors: Ian and Caroline Parkes

Seats: 60
Additional: No children under 8; children's portions; children's menu by arrangement; ◐ dishes; Vegan and other diets on request

WALSALL, Fairlawns ●

Chef Todd Hubble creates reliable dishes, at this country hotel, and his fish comes highly recommended. The choice is wide on a fixed-price menu and includes stuffed peppers and Bombay duck, or choose a rack of lamb with lovage and Madeira sauce from the carte.

Cost: *Alc* from £23.50, fixed-price L £12.95 (2 courses), £15/D £19.95. H/wine £9.95 ♀ Service inc. **Credit cards**: 1 2 3 4 5
Additional: Children welcome; children's portions; ◐ dishes; Vegan/other diets on request
Directions: Outskirts of Aldridge, 400yds from crossroads of A452 (Chester Road) and A454 (Little Aston Road)

178 Little Aston Road, Aldridge
Map no: 7 SP09
Tel: 01922 55122
Chef: Todd Hubble
Proprietor: John Pette
Seats: 70. No cigars or pipes. Air conditioned
Times: 12.30–Last L 2pm, Last D 10pm. Closed Sat Lunch, Sun dinner, BHs

WEST SUSSEX

AMBERLEY, Amberley Castle ●●

Here you can sample modern adaptations of old English dishes within the walls of a castle which has stood for 900 years

Probably one of the oldest English strongholds still inhabited, Amberley Castle has stood for over 900 years in this peaceful part of the South Downs. The present house – built within the walls of the original castle – has, over the last five years, been converted into a country house hotel. The grand first-floor

Map no: 4 TQ01
Tel: 01798 831992

Cost: *Alc* £50, fixed-price L £13.50 (2 courses), £16.50, fixed-price D £25.50, £40.00. H/wine £11.95 ♀ Service inc
Credit cards: 1 2 3 4

Menus: *A la carte*; fixed-price,

Queen's Room Restaurant with its high vaulted ceiling features a range of Castle Cuisine fare (recipes of Old England adapted for modern palates) alongside modern British dishes. Two set-price menus and a *carte* are offered, the 'chef's choice' representing best value for money in our inspector's opinion. After tasty hot canapés and a complimentary filo parcel of goats' cheese and avocado, he enjoyed quail and spinach ravioli in wild mushroom broth followed by medallions of pork with caramelised shallots and black pudding, this accompanied by creamed leaf spinach, mild flavoured carrots and a good braised fennel; dessert was a marbled chocolate terrine with orange sauce and hazelnuts. An extensive wine list is interestingly arranged in global areas.

Directions: Half-way between Amberley village and Amberley station on the B2139 Storrington–Bury Hill road, drive marked by flagpole

Sunday lunch
Times: Midday-Last L 2pm, 7pm-Last D 9.30pm

Chef: Nigel Boschetti
Proprietor: Martin Cummings

Seats: 60. No smoking in dining room
Additional: Children permitted (very young at manager's discretion); children's portions; ◐ dishes; Vegan/other diets on request

ARUNDEL, George & Dragon ✿✿

Standards are maintained under new ownership at this friendly country inn serving a balanced range of French/English dishes

A change of owners at this popular country inn has resulted in no changes to kitchen or restaurant staff and therefore no falling away from previous high standards. Kate Holle and her team continue to present a well balanced fixed-price menu of French and English dishes which follows such starters as smoked duck breast and salad or oven-baked Stilton and Brie filo parcels by main courses like roast fillet of lamb, sliced pink and garnished with Marsala sauce, or a brace of boned stuffed quails with a port sauce. Fish may include grilled halibut lightly brushed with Pernod and served with a delicate cream, mushroom and dill sauce, while the list of freshly made desserts could well contain both Italian trifle and dark and white chocolate mousse. Vegetarian alternatives are always available. Guests are warmly welcomed on arrival, and a friendly staff provides attentive service which includes such niceties as the clearing of the table before dessert. Both old and new worlds are well represented in a wine list of moderate length.

Directions: Off A27 near Arundel railway station, signposted Burpham, continue for 2.5 miles on country lane

Burpham
Map no: 4 TQ00
Tel: 01903 883131

Cost: Fixed-price D £15.50 (2 courses), £18.50, Sun L £14.50. H/wine £7.80 ♀ Service exc
Credit cards: 1 3

Menus: Fixed-price, Sunday lunch, bar menu

Times: Midday-Last L 1.45pm, 7.15-Last D 9.45pm. Closed Sun eve

Chefs: Kate Holle, David Futcher, Gary Scott
Proprietors: James Ross and Kate Holle

Seats: 34. No cigars or pipes. Partial air conditioning
Additional: Children permitted; ◐ dishes

ASHINGTON, Willows ✿✿

A welcoming cottage-style restaurant offering competent cooking and efficient service

A high degree of professionalism marks out this attractively beamed restaurant, and both cooking and service are reliable and enthusiastic. Chef Carl Illes offers an interesting, long-established menu from which can be selected two or three courses for lunch and a three-course dinner; one or two daily specials are also available. Typical starters are marinated anchovy fillets on toasted brioche with basil oil, sun-dried gooseberries and capers, and cheese and spinach gnocchi with a cheese and cream sauce, while main dishes range from light

London Road
Map no: 4 TQ11
Tel: 01903 892575

Cost: Fixed-price L £12.50 (2 courses), £15.50, fixed-price D £18.25. H/wine £7.35. Service exc
Credit cards: 1 2 3

Menus: Fixed-price, Sunday lunch

Times: Midday–Last L 2pm,

medallions of monkfish and scallops with tomato sauce on fresh noodles to a traditional half roast duck with sage and onion stuffing and apple sauce. Our inspector sampled fresh ravioli envelopes filled with tasty salmon mousse which were slightly spoilt by a sharp lemon sauce. Two mignons of tender fillet steak, pan-fried and served with a Madeira sauce and a shallot cream sauce respectively was a very enjoyable dish, served with fresh and crunchy vegetables. One of the chef's own dessert creations – an extravaganza of meringue, hard caramel, almonds and crème anglaise – brought the meal to a fulfilling finish.

Directions: Set back from the A24, midway between Horsham and Worthing

7pm–Last D 10pm. Closed Sat lunch, Sun eve, all day Mon

Chef: Carl Illes
Proprietors: Carl and Julie Illes

Seats: 30. No cigars or pipes in the dining room
Additional: Children welcome; children's portions by prior arrangement; ✿ menu; Vegan/other diets on request.

BILLINGSHURST, Gables ✿

Low ceilings, inglenook fireplaces and a friendly atmosphere make this a delightful restaurant. The mainly English cuisine is uncomplicated but well prepared such as roast rack of lamb with julienne of tomato and basil sauce.

Map no 4 TQ02
Tel: 01403 782571
Chef: Nicky Illes
Proprietors: Nicky Illes and Becky Gilroy

Cost: Fixed-price L £14.95/D £17.95. H/wine £6.50. Service exc
Credit cards: 1 3. **Additional**: Children over 8 welcome; ✿ dishes
Directions: Half a mile south on the A29

BOSHAM, Millstream ✿

A three-course fixed-price menu of English and French dishes is featured in the no-smoking ground floor restaurant of this charmingly located hotel, the lawns of which are bounded by the former millstream from which it takes its name. Particularly good provision is made for vegetarian guests.

Bosham Lane
Map no: 4 SU80
Tel: 01243 573234
Chef: Bev Boakes
Proprietor: Mr D Rodericks
Seats: 80. No smoking in dining room. Air conditioned
Times: 12.30-Last L 2pm, 7pm-Last D 9.30pm

Cost: Fixed-price L £11.50/D £17.25. H/wine £9.15. No service charge. **Credit cards**: 1 2 3 4 5. **Additional**: Children welcome; children's portions; ✿ menu; Vegan dishes by prior arrangement; other diets on request
Directions: In village centre near church and quay

BRACKLESHAM, Cliffords Cottage ✿✿

Good value, mainly French-style food

Bracklesham Lane
Map no: 4 SZ89
Tel: 01243 670250

A charming cottage with a low beamed ceiling and open log fires which add to the cosiness. The atmosphere is warm and informal and Mrs Shanahan is a charming hostess who, together with her helpful staff, provides an efficeint service. Chef/patron Tony Shanahan continues to maintain his high standard of cooking, with carefully and thoughtfully prepard dishes. His fixed-price and *carte* menus feature a mix of English and French cuisine, with a good choice of dishes on each menu. On this occasion our inspector chose a starter of seafood pancake with diced tomatoes which was followed by tender fillets of beef served with a Madiera and forest mushroom sauce. The selection of desserts included delicious bread and

Chef: Tony Shanahan
Proprietor: Brenda Shanahan

Seats: 30. No-smoking area on request; no cigars or pipes in dining room. Air conditioned
Times: Last D 9.15pm, Last Sun L 1.30pm. Closed Mon, Sun eve, first 2 weeks Nov, Last week Feb

Cost: *Alc* £25, fixed-price L £12,

butter pudding and kiwi and mango pancakes. The wine list complements the food and has a reasonable selection of French and New World wines. Just before going to press Cliffords Cottage was awarded a well deserved second rosette.

Directions: On B2179 Birdham road

CHICHESTER, Comme Ça ●●

☺ *Good, honest, French provincial style cooking is served at this comfortable restaurant close to the Festival Theatre*

Friendly French staff recommend dishes from the *carte* and set menus plus daily specials, like fish soup or 'roulade de saumon fumé' and main course dishes such as 'magret de canard au cassis'. Chef/patron Michel Navel continues to produce interesting and well prepared dishes in a good, honest French provincial style. His goats' cheese and honey in filo pastry starter was served with a creamy tomato and tarragon sauce. The peppered fillet of halibut steak for the main course was nicely cooked and rested on a bed of fresh spinach. It was accompanied by a tasty béarnaise sauce. The dessert of white and milk chocolate mousse was refreshingly light and fluffy. The enlarged wine list offers a short selection of fine French clarets and a few New World wines.

Additional: Children welcome; children's portions; ● dishes; Vegan/other diets on request
Directions: On the A286 near Festival Theatre

CHICHESTER, Droveway ●●

Consistently good Anglo-French cooking in a bright and welcoming restaurant

A continuing high standard of cooking is the boast of this bright and friendly restaurant above a shop in the centre of Chichester. Jonas Tester offers nicely-prepared dishes made from good fresh produce, and if the sauces are a little rich and creamy nobody seems to mind. The imaginative *carte* offers fish dishes including a daily choice from the market, and five meat dishes, as well as a separate vegetarian menu on request. Starters like charlotte of sea bass wrapped in smoked salmon might be followed by noisettes of milk-fed spring lamb with buttered spinach, or pirouette of chicken and smoked ham with a basil-flavoured cream sauce. Our inspector chose a croustade of poached eggs and camembert, and roasted monkfish – a very well cooked dish, moist and full of flavour. Desserts such as baked banana with a rum sabayon, and blancmange of vanilla and apricots, make tempting reading, but the chosen bread and butter pudding was a little disappointing, being a bit on the heavy side. The short set menu offers good value, and the well-balanced wine list has a separate list of fine wines at reasonable prices.

Directions: In centre of city, on the first floor above a shop called Soupson

fixed–price D £16.50. H/wine £8.20. Service exc
Credit cards: 1 2 3 4 5
Additional: Children over 3 welcome; children's portions; ● dishes; other diets on request

Broyle Road
Map no: 4 SU80
Tel: 01243 788724/536307

Cost: *Alc* £20, fixed-price L £13.75 (2 courses), £16.75/D £14.50, theatre menu £16.50. H/wine £8.20 ♀ Service exc
Credit cards: 1 2 3 5

Times: 11am-Last L 2pm, 5pm-Last D 10.30pm. Closed Sun eve, all day Mon

Chef: Michel Navet
Proprietor: Michel Navet

Seats: 48. No cigars or pipes in restaurant

30a Southgate
Map no: 4 SU80
Tel: 01243 528832

Cost: *Alc* £24, fixed-price L £11.50 (2 courses), £14, fixed–price D £19.50. H/wine £10 ♀ Service exc
Credit cards: 1 2 3

Menus: A la carte, fixed-price
Times: 12.30pm-Last L 2pm, 7pm-Last D 10pm. Closed Sun & Mon, first 2 weeks Jan

Chef: Jonas Tester
Proprietors: Jonas and Elly Tester

Seats: 38. Separate room for non-smokers
Additional: Children welcome; children's portions; ● menu; Vegan/other diets by prior arrangement; live entertainment

CHICHESTER, Ship ●

☺ *This fine Georgian building is the setting for Murray's Restaurant, offering a daily fixed-price menu and a carte. Chef Robin Castle's cooking is professionally constructed using good quality produce. Avocado pears and crab may be followed by saddle of venison, marinated in redcurrant gin.*

Cost: Alc £20, fixed-price L £9.95/D £14.50. H/wine £8.50. Service exc. **Credit cards**: 1 2 3 4 5. **Additional**: Children welcome; ♥ dishes; Vegan/other diets on request
Directions: From Festival Theatre roundabout, turn towards shopping centre. Hotel is on left

North Street
Map no: 4 SU80
Tel: 01243 778000
Chef: Robin Castle
Proprietor: Peter Cook
Seats: 54
Times: Midday-Last L 2pm, 6pm-Last D 9.30pm

CHILGROVE, White Horse Inn ●●

A warm and friendly country inn serving carefully prepared and enjoyable Anglo/French cooking

Two things can be relied on at this pretty, popular inn tucked under the Sussex Downs: one is the warmth of the welcome from owners Dorothea and Barry Phillips, who create an attractively relaxed and friendly atmosphere; the other is the consistently high quality of the cooking. Mainly modern English food with a dash of French is the forte of Neil Rusbridger. An inspection meal produced a superb dish of lightly grilled scallops with crisp bacon and lettuce leaves, followed by pan-fried Barbary duck with a tasty jasmine sauce. There are separate menus, lunch and dinner offering daily specials and fish dishes. Typical starters might be grilled collop of fresh salmon on a warm mixed bean salad, and Stilton and avocado pear mousse with caramelised apple and apricot, with main dishes like suprême of pheasant on a leek purée with wild rice, or artichoke, hazelnut and spinach filo. Home-made ice creams and desserts are offered verbally.

The wine list is as long, comprehensive and full of vintage claret as you will ever see, but also contains some good and reasonably priced house wines.

Directions: On the B2141

Map no: 4 SU81
Tel: 01243 535219

Cost: Fixed-price L £17.50, Sun L £6.95, D £23, theatre menu £21. H/wine £9.50 ♀ Service exc
Credit cards: 1 3 4 5

Menus: Fixed-price, Sunday lunch, pre- and after-theatre, bar menu
Times: 11am-Last L 2pm, 6pm-Last D 9.30pm (10.30pm if booked). Closed Sun eve, all day Mon, Last week Oct, 3 weeks Feb

Chef: Neil Rusbridger
Proprietors: Barry and Dorothea Phillips, Neil Rusbridger

Seats: 65. No cigars or pipes in restaurant. Air conditioned
Additional: Children permitted; ♥ dishes; other diets on request

CLIMPING, Bailiffscourt ●●●

A wide repertoire of inventive, premier league cooking from a chef with an impressive CV and an obvious desire to excel

In a land where it is almost obligatory for a country house restaurant to be a century old at the very least, here is a maverick. Despite the building's handsome appearance it is barely half that. Nothing is deceptive, though, about young chef Simon Rogan's cooking, clearly reflecting his training under Marco Pierre White and other such luminaries from the world of the whisk. He offers no *carte*, just a choice of fixed-price lunch menus and a three-course dinner plus coffee. Main courses are strong on seafood – panache of turbot, escalope of Scottish salmon, bass en croûte, fillet of sole, nage of lobster –

Littlehampton
Map no: 4 TQ00
Tel: 01903 723511

Cost: Fixed price lunch £17.50, fixed-price dinner £29.50. Service exc
Credit cards: 1 2 3 4

Menus: Fixed-price lunch and dinner

Times: Last D 9.30pm

Chef: Simon Rogan

all cooked in really imaginative ways. Fillet of red mullet, for example, comes with tempura of langoustine, piperade, sautéed potatoes and ginger sauce.

Meat dishes also betray Simon's past, as in braised stuffed pig's trotter with spices, potato purée with olive oil, fricassee of lentils and fumet of thyme. Arguably his style is still emerging, but his talent is indisputable, judging by an inspection meal which began with tartare of salmon and tuna and two sauces – a slightly salty, caviar-topped green one and a tangy gazpacho one. Then, cutlets of venison with wild mushrooms wrapped in a flat French sausage, a rich jus and fondant vegetables. A zingy, zesty lemon tart, served with a light, fluffy lemon soufflé is talked about still. Desserts tend to be intricate and take time to prepare, so are best ordered early in the meal.

House wines do not exceed £13.95 and the serious Bordeaux include both petits châteaux and crus bourgeois, while there are some fine Burgundies too. Other big wine-producing countries get a modest look-in and even England offers a medium dry white from Hampshire. Staff are charming and professional, yet remain approachable.

Additional: No smoking area. ✪ dishes.

COPTHORNE,
Copthorne Effingham Park ✪

This modern hotel, developed around a former stately home set in 40-acre grounds, offers two restaurants; the more formal and intimate Wellingtonia featuring three-course fixed-price menus of such traditional French dishes as beef fillet flamed in Cognac and served in a subtle garlic and rich meat sauce.

West Park Road
Map no: 5 TQ33
Tel: 01342 714994
Chef: Kevin Lindsay
Propietor: Copthorne. Manager: W Clifford
Seats: 90 Wellingtonia, 75 Terrace
Times: Last L 2pm/D 10pm

Cost: Fixed-price L £15.50/D £25. H/wine £10.25. **Credit cards:** 1 2 3 4 5. **Additional:** Children welcome; children's menu; ✪ dishes; other diets on request; live entertainment on Saturdays
Directions: From M23 junction 10 take A264 East Grinstead road, left at second roundabout onto B2028, 0.25 mile on right

CRAWLEY,
Holiday Inn London-Gatwick ✪

Within this hotel the Colonnade restaurant offers well-balanced, consistent cooking. Both the fixed-price menu and the carte are created by Chef David Woods with influences from around the world. For example, Thai inspired shellfish soup to start and Szechuan sizzling beef as a main dish.

Langley Drive
Map no: 4 TQ23
Tel: 01293 529991
Chef: David Woods
Proprietor: Holiday Inn. Manager: Alan Murphy
Seats: 100. No smoking area. Air conditioned
Times: 7pm–Last D 9.30pm, Sun L 12.30pm–2pm. Closed BH Mons

Cost: A/c £23, fixed-price D £9.95 (1 course), £14.50, £16.95, dinner dance £18.50, dinner disco £14.95, Sunday L £14.95. H/wine £9.95 ℚ Service exc. **Credit cards:** 1 2 3 4
Additional: Children welcome; children's menu/portions; ✪ menu; Vegan/other diets on request; dinner disco every Friday, dinner dance 1st Saturday of month
Directions: At junction of A23 and A264, Tushmore roundabout

CUCKFIELD, Ockenden Manor ●●

A historic, atmospheric setting for contrasting modern British and French cooking

Seafood from Newhaven and locally shot game are some of the fresh ingredients that chef Geoff Walsh lovingly converts into some highly recommended dishes. His enterprising modern cooking is one reason for the success of this peaceful old manor house, parts of which date back to 1520. Historic stained glass windows and an embossed ceiling lend an impressive atmosphere to the restaurant, and both the *carte* and daily fixed-price menu offer food to savour in this lovely setting. Steamed field mushrooms with tarragon mousse, wood pigeon breast and white wine truffle sauce made an enjoyable recent starter with plenty of good, strong flavours, and roast haunch of Ashdown venison, chestnuts and port wine sauce was a tender, well-cooked main dish. Vegetables were the only low point in the meal, being either bland or overpoweringly sweet, but clootie pudding, a Scottish version of spotted dick served with crème anglaise feathered with strawberry purée, was a satisfying dessert. A classic wine list offers excellent vintage French regional wines and decent house bottles at very reasonable prices.

Directions: Off main street

Ockenden Lane
Map no: 4 TQ32
Tel: 01444 416111

Cost: Alc £33, fixed-price L £16.50, fixed-price D £26.50. Service exc
Credit cards: 1 2 3 4 5

Menus: *A la carte*, fixed-price, Sunday lunch

Times: 12.30-Last L 2pm, 7.30-Last D 9.30pm

Chef: Geoff Welch
Proprietor: Mr & Mrs Goodman. Manager: Mr Kerry Turner

Seats: 45. No smoking in dining room
Additional: Children permitted (over 5 at dinner); children's portions; ◐ dishes; Vegan/other diets on request

EAST GRINSTEAD, Gravetye Manor ●●●

Classical English and modern French cooking professionally served in a 16th-century country house hotel

Gravetye, a stone-built Elizabethan manor house, stands at the end of a mile long drive amid magnificent gardens. Its beauty owes much to two of its owners: William Robinson the famous Victorian gardener and creator of the English natural garden, and since 1958, Peter Herbert, the doyen of country house hoteliers. Over the years Peter Herbert has continued to improve the hotel with period furnishings and quality fabrics, and the public rooms are warmly welcoming with oak panelling, log fires and fresh flowers. The food and wine are all one would expect at this level, and the dedicated team of staff provide professional and unobtrusive service.

Chef Stephen Morey offers a seasonal *carte*, and regularly changing set-price lunch and dinner menus. The best of ingredients are used, including fruit, vegetables and herbs from the kitchen garden. Modern and classical influences are evident in a Mediterranean-style aubergine and tomato tian with basil and tomato coulis; rich oxtail consommé; and our inspector's choice of twice baked goats' cheese soufflé. This was followed by a memorable dish of tortellini filled with a mousseline of scallop and crab, served with sliced pan-fried scallops and a tangy lemon sauce spiced with cinnamon. The *carte* also offers a vegetarian option of warm artichoke heart filled with mushrooms and quails' eggs and topped with hollandaise. Grand Marnier soufflé omelette with orange and lemon butter sauce, and a terrine of three chocolates figure among the

Map no: 5 TQ33
Tel: 01342 810567

Cost: Alc £35, fixed-price L £20, Sun L £28, fixed-price D £26. H/wine £15. Service inc
Credit cards: 1 3

Menus: *A la carte*, fixed-price lunch and dinner, Sunday lunch

Times: 12.30-Last L 2pm, 7.30-Last D 9.30pm. Closed Xmas Day eve to non-residents

Chef: Stephen Morey
Proprietor: Peter Herbert

Seats: 36. No smoking in dining room
Additional: No children under 7; half-portions where feasible; ◐ dishes; other diets with advance notice

desserts, but our inspector chose a glazed French apple tart served with a scoop of delicious cinnamon ice cream and a light vanilla anglaise.

The wine list is long, and prices are exclusive of VAT. There are many good vintages of claret and Burgundy, as well as excellent selections from Alsace, the Rhone and the Loire.

Directions: South-west of East Grinstead on B2110 Turners Hill road

EAST GRINSTEAD, **Woodbury House** ☻

☺ *This attractive gabled house situated about a mile from the town centre has both a bar-bistro and a more formal restaurant. The hotel has recently changed owner and chef, and dishes range from fillet of beef to breast of Barbary duck, the duck served with cranberry and orange relish sauce.*

Cost: Alc £20, fixed-price L and D £12.95. H/wine £8.50. Service exc. **Credit cards**: 1 2 3 4 5. **Additional**: Children welcome; children's portions; ۏ menu; Vegan/other diets on request
Directions: On the A22 0.5 mile south of town

Lewes Road
Map no: 5 TQ33
Tel: 01342 313657
Chef: Mark Cheesman
Manager: Stephen Eagle
Seats: 45. No-smoking area. No cigars or pipes
Times. Midday–Last L 2.15pm, 7pm–Last D 9.45pm. Closed Xmas Day evening, all day Boxing Day

GOODWOOD, **Goodwood Park** ☻

Inside this hotel is a characterful and atmospheric restaurant where Michael Oliver produces his menu of very enjoyable dishes that may include asparagus and hollandaise sauce or quenelles of crab mousse as starters, and fillet of pork with wine and saffron sauce to follow.

Cost: Alc £29.50, fixed-price L £8.50, Sunday L £12.95/D £18.50. H/wine £9.95 ♀ Service inc. **Credit cards**: 1 2 3 4 5
Additional: Children welcome; children's menu/portions; ۏ dishes; Vegan/other diets on request; live entertainment Friday & Saturday evenings
Directions: Off the A27, following signs for Goodwood House. Once on the estate, follow signs for hotel

Map no: 4 SU80
Tel: 01243 775537
Chef: Michael Oliver
Proprietor: Whitbread. General Manager: Stephen Fenwick
Seats: 100. No smoking in restaurant
Times: Midday–Last L 2pm (2.30 Sun), 7pm–Last D 9.30pm (10pm Fri/Sat). Closed Sat lunch

HORSHAM, **Random Hall** ☻

☺ *Dating from the late 16th century, this hotel retains much its period character. In the candlelit, Tudor-style restaurant, chef Jonathan Gettings offers modern British cooking from a good-value fixed price menu. Recommendations include the soups, fresh fish and seafood, and spit roasted duck.*

Cost: Fixed-price L £9.50 (2 course), £11.50/D £10.95 (1 course), £13.95, £15.95. H/wine £9.25 ♀ Service inc. **Credit cards**: 1 2 3 5
Additional: No children under 8; half portions; ۏ menu; Vegan/other diets on request
Directions: 4 miles west of Horsham on the A29, just outside Slinfold

Stane Street, Slinfold
Map no: 4 TQ13
Tel: 01403 790558
Chef: Jonathan Gettings
Proprietor: Nigel Evans
Seats: 36. No-smoking area. No cigars or pipes
Times: Last L 2pm/D 10pm. Closed Boxing Day

LANCING, **Sussex Pad** ◉

Old Shoreham Road
Map no: 4 TQ10
Tel: 01273 454647
Chef: Paul James Hornsby
Proprietor: Wally John Pack
Seats: 45. No smoking in dining room
Times: Midday–Last L 2pm, Last D 9.45pm

☺ *The restaurant at this friendly family-run hotel specialises in fresh fish. Chef Paul Hornsby produces enjoyable dishes using best quality ingredients. Our inspector sampled the chef's chicken liver pâté, seafood bisque, rack of lamb with a bread crumb, garlic and herb crust, and good baked Alaska.*

Cost: Alc from £17.50, fixed-price L and D £11.50 (2 courses), £13.50. H/wine £8.66 ♀ Service inc **Credit cards** 1 2 3 4
Additional: Children welcome; children's portions; ✪ dishes; Vegan/other diets on request
Directions: On the A27 by Lancing College, opposite Shoreham airport

LOWER BEEDING, **Jeremy's at the Crabtree** ❀❀

Brighton Road
Map no: 4 TQ22
Tel: 01403 891257

Enjoyable modern cooking with an international flavour in an old world atmosphere

A 17th-century house complete with wattle and daub frames and panels and log burning fires provides a rustic setting for some imaginative modern cooking with an international flavour. Interesting though this historic building is, it is unlikely to distract diners from the food that chef/patron Jeremy Ashpool creates for them. Recommended dishes have included roast loin of pork with Chinese vegetables and a red wine and ginger sauce, grilled monkfish with a watercress mousse and tarragon sauce, and for vegetarians the feta, spinach and olive tart with a tomato and coriander dressing. Our inspector recently sampled grilled haddock with tapénade topping which had a good combination of flavours, and pan-fried lambs' liver with a mustard and thyme sauce, set on fresh spinach leaves and noodles. The traditional hot desserts include a delicious hot syrup sponge with toffee sauce. A fixed-price menu offers a small choice including a vegetarian dish, and a mid-week special with no choices is available for half price. Young vintage wines and some worthy new world bottles are listed, and a good fruity house red.

Cost: Alc £19.50, fixed-price L £7.50, fixed-price D £19.50. H/wine £7.95 ♀ Service inc in dinner price
Credit cards: 1 3

Menus: *A la carte*, fixed-price lunch and dinner, Sunday lunch, bar menu
Times: 12.30–Last L 2pm, 7.30–Last D 9.45pm. Closed Sun eve

Chef: Jeremy Ashpool
Proprietors: Jeremy and Vera Ashpool, Nick Wege

Seats: 40. No-smoking area
Additional: Children permitted; children's portions; ✪ dishes; Vegan dishes on request

Directions: 4 miles south-east of Horsham on A281 Brighton road

LOWER BEEDING, **South Lodge** ❀❀

Brighton Road
Map no: 4 TQ22
Tel: 01403 891711

A luxury country house hotel with high standards of hospitality matched by the quality of the cooking

One of the finest rhododendron collections in the country graces the mature grounds of this lovely Victorian manor house with wonderful views of the rolling South Downs. Inside the luxury country house hotel all is comfortable and gracious, with antique furniture, log fires and wood panelling adding a relaxing dimension. The food is a very good reason for a visit, and John Elliott cooks in modern style with Mediterranean and

Cost: Alc £32.50, fixed-price L £15, Sun L £17.50, fixed-price D £25 (3 courses), £32. H/wine £13 ♀ Service exc

Credit cards: 1 2 3 4 5

Menus: *A la carte*, fixed-price

oriental influences which he shows off on a three or five-course signature menu, a set lunch menu and a lengthier *carte*. A delicious cream of leek and potato soup with added pieces of smoked salmon greatly appealed to our inspector, as did bresaola – a thin slice of Northern Italian dried salt beef served on a crisp bruschetta topped with garlic flavoured tomatoes, aubergine and peppers. Sautéed monkfish tail on fresh spinach leaves with a creamed fish and Noilly Prat sauce was a fresh and tasty main dish, but the attractively presented vegetables were spoilt by contrasting flavours. An unusual butter croissant pudding with an orange-flavoured crème anglaise was thoroughly enjoyed.

Directions: At junction of A279 (Horsham) and A281, turn onto the Cowfold/Brighton road. Hotel is 0.5 mile on right

lunch and dinner, Sunday lunch, bar menu
Times: Last L 2pm (3pm Sun)/D 10pm (10.30 Fri & Sat)

Chef: John Elliott
Proprietors: Exclusive Hotels. General Manager: David French

Seats: 40. No smoking
Additional: Children welcome; children's menu/portions; ✪ menu; Vegan/other diets on request; pianist Friday & Saturday eve and Sunday lunch

MIDHURST, **The Angel** ✦✦

☺ *A lovely old coaching inn where traditional French and modern English dishes blend beautifully together*

This 16th-century coaching inn has a convivial atmosphere that makes it popular with visitors from near and afar. One of the main attractions is undoubtedly the pretty restaurant, where a *carte* and set lunch menu offer a rich and imaginative choice of food. A recent inspection lunch began with a very smooth and well-made duck liver parfait on a brioche, followed by fillet of salmon with a fresh tomato sauce topped with pickled vegetables – very fresh and tasty. A delicious orange and chocolate terrine made an irresistible dessert from a choice that included toffee and pecan steamed sponge pudding with custard, and strawberry trifle, and a cup of strong cafetière coffee was also much enjoyed. The *carte* offers a wide range of dishes from a vegetarian pasta with wild mushrooms, parmesan and rosemary pesto, to meaty dishes like braised rabbit with haricot beans and sweet mustard, or canon of local roe deer with apple chutney and port sauce. The cooking by owner Peter Crawford-Rolt and Andrew Stephenson is a mixture of modern English and traditional French.

Directions: Halfway along Midhurst High Street (A286)

North Street
Map no: 4 SU82
Tel: 01730 812421

Cost: Alc £20, fixed-price L £11.50 (2 courses), £13.50, fixed-price D £16 (brasserie). H/wine £9.50 ♀ Service exc
Credit cards: 1 2 3 4
Menus: A la carte, fixed-price lunch and dinner, Sunday lunch, pre-theatre, bar menu
Times: Midday-Last L 2.30pm, Last D 10pm

Chef: Peter Crawford-Rolt, Andrew Stephenson
Proprietors: Peter Crawford-Rolt, Nicholas Davies
Seats: 50 restaurant, 50 brasserie
Additional: Children welcome; children's menu/portions; ✪ dishes; Vegan/other diets on request

MIDHURST, **Southdowns** ✦

☺ *Chef Darren Lunn offers a good range of modern English dishes at Southdowns, offering both fixed-price and carte menus in the Country Restaurant, and a good value alternative in the Tudor Bar. Fresh salmon, local game and a choice of grills all feature, along with vegetarian options.*

Cost: Alc from £18.85, fixed-price L/D £12.50. H/wine £10.45 ♀ No service charge. **Credit cards**: 1 2 3 4. **Additional**: Children welcome; children's menu/portions; ✪ menu; Vegan/other diets on request; live entertainment

Trotton
Map no: 4 SU82
Tel: 01730 821521
Chef: Darren Lunn
Proprietors: R Lion, D Vedovato
Seats: 40-120. No-smoking area. Air conditioned
Times: Midday-Last L 2pm, Last D 10pm

MIDHURST, Spread Eagle ❀❀

Serious and reliable Anglo-French cooking in a charming old world setting

Steeped in history dating back to 1430, this former coaching inn retains its charm and atmosphere with Tudor bread ovens, Flemish stained glass, and broad inglenook fireplaces. In this pleasing setting the Anglo-French cooking of chef Ken Jelfs is all the more enjoyable, with well-constructed and consistently good dishes offered on a fixed-price *carte* and set lunch menu. Pâtés are a renowned strength, and a recently sampled venison, pheasant and hare terrine had a good meaty flavour and firm, smooth texture. Salmon brioche with shellfish sauce had a slightly bland 'farmed' flavour, but the flesh was fresh and the prawn sauce tasty, and a blackcurrant mousse with white peach sauce was very satisfying. Other choices might be breast of pigeon cooked in filo pastry with a Stilton and port sauce, or braised oxtails with vegetables and herbs. Vegetarian options might include a red pepper mousse starter, and three filo parcels filled with creamed spinach, and a fricassee of mushrooms and vegetables on a red pepper sauce. Service is particularly attentive, and the wine list offers some good vintages and classified growths.

Directions: On A272 in town centre

South Street
Map no: 4 SU82
Tel: 01730 816911

Cost: Fixed-price L £16.00/D £25.75. H/wine £9.50. Service exc
Credit cards: 1 2 3 4 5

Menus: Fixed-price lunch and dinner, Sunday lunch, bar menu

Times: Last L 2.15pm/D 9.30pm

Chef: Ken Jelfs
Proprietors: Mr and Mrs Goodman

Seats: 70. No smoking in dining room
Additional: Children welcome; children's portions; ◐ dishes; Vegan/other diets on request

PETWORTH, L'Amico ❀

☺ *The conservatory restaurant of this Sussex farmhouse serves a traditional Italian menu. Two fixed-price menus are available, our inspector enjoyed Scaloppine al limone – veal coated with flour in a white wine and lemon sauce.*

Cost: *Alc* £20, fixed-price £12.75, £15.50. H/wine £8.75. Service exc
Directions: To the east of the town

Grove Lane
Map no 4 SU92
Tel: 01798 343659
Chef: Gino Tecchia
Proprietors: Gino and Barbara Tecchia
Times: 7pm-Last D 10pm; lunch also served. Closed Sun eve and all day Mon

PULBOROUGH, Stane Street Hollow ❀❀

A delightful little restaurant offering reliable international cooking and lovingly attentive service

Attentive personal service plus quality international cooking and a delightful little farmhouse restaurant is a recipe for ongoing success. René and Ann Kaiser have employed this formula for many years now, and their high standards are an example to other restaurants. While Ann offers a dedicated, caring approach to customers, René continues to produce delicious dishes that make his daily specialities a treat not to be missed. 'Filet de Barbue Joinville' – brill poached in white wine with prawns, mushrooms and cream, 'Saumon Poche' cooked with fresh sorrel, and 'Perdreau Roti' – partridge roasted with bacon, flared with brandy and served with sauerkraut are some examples of the delights available. Our inspector relished 'mousse de poisson au crevettes' which was warm and lightly

Codmore Hill
Map no: 4 TQ01
Tel: 01798 872819

Cost: *Alc* £22, fixed-price L £8.50, Sun L£13.50 (2 courses), £16.50. H/wine £12.50 ♀ Service exc
Credit cards: 1 3 4 5

Menu: *A la carte*, fixed-price lunch, Sunday lunch

Times: 12.30-Last L 1.30pm, 7.15-Last D 9.15pm. Closed Mon, Tue, 2 weeks early Jun, 2 weeks late Oct

textured, and 'Kasseler Dijonaise' – fresh loin of pork cooked in cider with a mild-flavoured mustard sauce. Home-grown vegetables like leeks and beetroot were full of flavour, and 'Kaiser Choux', a pastry swan filled with rum-flavoured cream chantilly and sliced bananas, and topped with a rich dark chocolate sauce, was delicious.

Directions: On the A29 at the northern end of village

Chef: René Kaiser
Proprietors: René and Ann Kaiser

Seats: 32. No smoking in dining room
Additional: Children welcome; children's portions; ✿ dishes

RUSPER, **Ghyll Manor** ✿

Chef Shane Wheelan offers a seasonal carte and daily fixed price menus in the elegant candlelit restaurant of this historic former monastery. His cooking demonstrates an imaginative and serious approach, resulting in a range of tasty British dishes with French and Italian influences

Cost: Alc £19, fixed-price L £13.95/D £17.25. H/wine £10.80. Service exc. **Credit cards:** 1 2 3 4 5. **Additional:** Children welcome; children's menu/portions; ✿ dishes; other diets on request
Directions: On main street, opposite church

Map no: 4 TQ23
Tel: 01293 871571
Chefs: Shane Wheelan
Proprietor: CSMA. Manager: Raymond Court-Hampton
Seats: 45 restaurant, 35 terrace. No smoking
Times: 12.30pm-Last L 2.30pm, 7pm-Last D 9.30pm

STORRINGTON, **Manleys** ✿✿✿✿

Excellent value from a family team producing confident, classically-based cooking with individual flair in delightful surroundings

The most attractive little restaurant, once a school-house, has been run with great charm by Karl Löderer and his family for the last 17 years. It has always won high praise from our inspectors and the cuisine has now reached such a high standard that they have been happy to award it a coveted fourth rosette. An Austrian by birth, Mr Löderer shows equal confidence in handling interpretations of classical French cooking and his own traditions, for instance on the menu may be 'Weiner-Paprika Huhn mit Butter Nokerln und Krem Spinat', a Viennese chicken in a piquant paprika sauce served with home-made noodles and creamed spinach.
   At recent meals our inspectors have been greatly impressed by his skill in balancing delicate flavours, as evidenced by a lemon sole wrapped round a mousse of crab and prawn and served with a mild mustard sauce. Equally successful was flavoursome lamb, cooked exactly as requested, and served with thin slices of parsnip in a perfect partnership, and a gâteau of carrot and courgette strips enclosing a kind of ratatouille. First courses like tagliatelle with smoked salmon and a light cream sauce, glazed with cheese, and tried scallops with braised leeks and crisp courgettes also worked well.
   Puddings are wickedly tempting and our inspectors fell for a complicated but successful creation of poached pear, filled with ice cream and set on sponge soaked in eau de vie, covered with a citrus cream and served with an excellent raspberry coulis, and a pancake filled with hot strawberries marinated in eau de vie and served with ice cream. The fixed-price lunch and dinner menus with three or four dishes at each stage including coffee

Manleys Hill
Map no: 4 TQ01
Tel: 01903 742331

Cost: Alc £34, fixed-price L £18.60, Sun L £23.50, fixed-price D £26.50. H/wine £13.80
♀ Service exc
Credit cards: 1 2 3

Menus: A la carte, fixed-price lunch and dinner menus, Sunday lunch

Times: Last L 2pm/D 9.15pm. Closed Sun eve, Mon and 1st 2 weeks Jan

Chef: Karl Löderer
Proprietor: Karl Löderer

Seats: 48. No cigars or pipes. Air conditioned
Additional: Children welcome; children's portions; ✿ dishes; Vegan/other diets on request

and petits fours, offer superb value. In the evenings you can also choose two courses from the full *carte* for an inclusive price, with dessert and coffee extra.

The wine list offers a good choice of mainly French and German wines, without being over powering. There are some mature vintages of claret from the 1970's; also two or three good Austrian wines.

Directions: On the main A283, just to the east of Storrington

STORRINGTON, **Old Forge** ❀❀

Good British cooking using quality produce, and excellent service

6a Church Street
Map no: 4 TQ01
Tel: 01903 743402

There are few restaurants which seem to get everything right, but here at this delightful 15th-century beamed cottage restaurant, Cathy and Clive Roberts succeed in doing just that; Cathy's personal style of service together with Clive's very innovative and imaginative modern British cooking sets standards for others to follow. Using only the best quality produce, including some home grown vegetables, home made breads, patisserie and ice creams, the results are commendable and full of flavour. Warm appetisers are offered to start, and recommendations this year include succulent steamed freshwater shrimp, served with a honey dressing flavoured with ginger and lemon, and tenderloin of pork wrapped in sage leaves encased with prosciutto, and set on a creamed purée of asparagus. Vegetables can be some of the best produced in the area, with home grown kohlrabi, Spanish flat beans, a paysanne of young carrots, with separate baked garlic potatoes served in a copper pot, all being highly praised by our Inspector. A round of baked rhubarb tart followed served with ginger flavoured cream. An excellent wine list includes some interesting New World wines.

Cost: *A/c* £23.50, fixed-price L £14.50, fixed-price D £20.50. H/wine £8.50. Service exc
Credit cards: 1 2 3 4

Menus: *A la carte*, fixed-price lunch and dinner, Sunday lunch
Times: 12.30-Last L 1.30pm, 7.15-Last D 9pm. Closed Tue & Sat lunch, Sun eve, all day Mon, 2 weeks late spring, 3 weeks autumn

Chefs: Clive and Cathy Roberts
Proprietors: Clive and Cathy Roberts

Seats: 24. No smoking while others are eating
Additional: Children permitted (very young at owners' discretion); children's portions; ❂ dishes; Vegan dishes on request; other diets by advance arrangement

Directions: On a side street close to the village centre

TURNERS HILL, **Alexander House** ❀❀

Elaborate French and more simple English dishes in a sumptuous country house setting

East Street
Map no: 4 TQ33
Tel: 01342 714914

A splendid country house, decorated and furnished in sumptuous style, unsurprisingly offers an elaborate choice of food which looks as ornate as its surroundings. Nothing is stinted on either inside or outside Alexander's restaurant, where a pricey French *carte* and more keenly priced daily set menu offer a range of classic and modern dishes with an emphasis on seafood: 'Soufflé Alexander' (fresh local lobster soufflé with brandy sauce) and 'Barquette de Champignons Sauvages' (wild mushrooms in puff pastry with truffle sauce) are typical starters on the *carte*, while main dishes might be 'Loup de Mer' – grilled seabass with a fresh crayfish and white wine sauce, and 'Foie de Veau Sauté' (pan-fried calf's liver with

Cost: *A/c* £40, fixed-price L £16.75 (2 courses), £18.75, fixed-price D £24.95. H/wine £14.50. Service exc
Credit cards: 1 2 3 4

Menus: *A la carte*; fixed-price lunch and dinner, Sunday lunch, bar menu
Times: 12.30-Last L 2pm, 7.30-Last D 9.30pm (9pm Sun)

Chef: Tim Kelsey

crispy bacon). Our inspector's starter of duck terrine with port, thyme and garlic was strongly flavoured and enjoyable, while a tasty, well-cooked fillet of red mullet came with a sea bass fillet which was less fresh and rather overcooked. No fewer than eight vegetables complicated this main dish, and a delicate leek and mussel butter sauce was almost completely overshadowed. A vegetarian menu offers a serious choice of well-priced dishes.

Directions: 1 mile east of Turners Hill on the B2110

Proprietor: International Hotels.
Manager: Sarah Varcoe

Seats: 45. No smoking in dining room
Additional: No children under 7; children's portions; ❂ menu; Vegan/other diets on request; pianist Saturday evening

WEST YORKSHIRE

BRADFORD, **Restaurant Nineteen** ❂❂❂

Out-of-city centre, 19th-century grandeur and the only Bradford restaurant we have awarded rosettes to

Our inspector began his report by saying it 'was clearly the best meal I have taken so far this year'. Admittedly, it was only March, but by then he would have already sampled more than a few lunches and dinners. What appealed was his full-flavoured, tender wood pigeon served with a shallot sauce and clever little ravioli made from a thin middle cut of celeriac containing a light mousse of the same vegetable. Next, a refreshing celery and fennel soup, followed by bright white scallops and pink salmon, sautéed to perfection with a faultless provençal sauce resting on a fresh-tasting bed of crispy noodles. The dessert – a trio of rhubarb-based dishes – was interesting. Element one was a light and tangy rhubarb jelly; two, rhubarb ice cream and three – the highlight – crème brûlée made just the way it should be – thick and creamy with a thin sugar crust which broke with just the lightest of taps.

Stephen Smith is the chef in this substantial Victorian house, standing by Lister Park in one of the city's leafier suburbs. He produces a four course, set-price menu on which the dishes with full citizenship are mainly English, Italian and French, although Oriental touches like stir-fried vegetables and curry flavouring slip in with work permits.

The wine list would prove no embarrassment to many a larger establishment. It is mainly French supported by two or three selections from most of the other countries around the world. Several of the clarets and Burgundies are from excellent mature vintages, and reasonably priced.

Directions: Take the A650 (Manningham Lane) out of Bradford, turn left at Manningham Park gates, then right into North Park Road. 350 yds on left

19 North Park Road, Heaton
Map no: 7 SE13
Tel: 01274 492559

Cost: Fixed-price D £26. H/wine £11.50 ♀ Service exc
Credit cards: 1 2 3

Menu: Fixed-price dinner

Times: 7pm-Last D 9.30pm (10pm Sat). Closed Sun, 1 week Xmas, 2 weeks Aug/Sep

Chef: Stephen Smith
Proprietors: Robert Barbour, Stephen Smith

Seats: 34. No cigars or pipes in dining room
Additional: No children under 8; ❂ /special diets on request

HALIFAX, **Holdsworth House** ❋❋

☺ *A well-cared for 17th-century hotel serving a balanced range of dishes from a young French chef*

Three beautifully furnished rooms complete with polished panelled walls, wooden beams and mullioned windows form the restaurant at this delightful 17th century manor house hotel. This is a haven of tranquillity to which guests return with confidence, with the added inducement of some very fine cooking. There is an interesting choice of modern British dishes with discreet French overtones, as might be expected from the young French chef, Eric Claveau, and the keynote to his cooking is its freshness of flavours from quality produce. Our inspector recently praised a Camembert and onion tartlet starter, made from a light pastry with a delicately flavoured cheese and onion filling, which came with tangy home-made apple chutney. Pistou soup was nicely peppery and full of fresh vegetables, while steamed scallops were natural and fragrant, and refreshingly served with a ginger and soy sauce. Apple and custard tart had the same melt-in-the-mouth pastry as the starter, with finely sliced sharp apples and a sweet sauce anglaise. A *carte* and fixed-price menu offer a good choice of fish, meat and game.

Directions: From Burdock Way roundabout in Halifax take A629 Keighley road for 1.5 miles, turn right at garage into Shay Lane. Hotel is 1 mile on right, opposite school

Holmfield
Map no: 7 SE02
Tel: 01422 240024

Cost: *Alc* £22, fixed-price L £12.50, fixed-price D £19.50. H/wine £9.50. Service inc
Credit cards: 1 2 3 4 5

Menus: *A la carte,* fixed-price lunch and dinner, Sunday lunch once a month

Times: Midday-Last L 1.30pm, 7pm-Last D 9.30pm. Closed 26-30 Dec

Chef: Eric Claveau
Proprietor: Gary Swarbrooke

Seats: 70. No-smoking area; no cigars and pipes in restaurant

Additional: Children permitted (not under 10 at dinner); children's portions; Funday Club Sunday lunch; ❤ dishes; Vegan/other diets on request

HAWORTH, **Weavers** ❋❋

☺ *Refreshingly honest and unstuffy British food in a converted cluster of weavers' cottages*

You can look out over the Brontë Parsonage and the moors beyond from this cosy restaurant with rooms, and soak up the atmosphere. Originally a group of traditional weavers' cottages, this popular restaurant in the centre of the village enjoys an ever-growing reputation for its food. Chef/patron Colin Rushworth uses only local supplies of fresh produce in his modern and traditional British cooking, and there is nothing stuffy or pretentious about the enjoyable results. Starters are hearty, and might include 'kofte', minced lamb and onion meatballs served warm with a cucumber and yoghurt dip, or sliced, smoked goose breast served with mango and apricot and a sage and gooseberry jelly; home-made soups are always available, like 'cullan skink' – smoked haddock soup with bacon and potatoes, and 'cock-a-leekie', a mixture of shredded chickens and leeks. Main courses could be quick-fried calf's liver with a gin and lime sauce and a portion of bubble and squeak, or fisherman's bake topped with mashed potatoes. Vegetarians might be offered parsnip and cashew nut loaf with a fresh herb and tomato sauce.

Directions: In the centre of Haworth, beside Brontë Parsonage Museum car park

15 West Lane
Map no: 7 SE03
Tel: 01535 643822

Cost: *Alc* £20, fixed-price L & D £9.95 (2 courses), £11.95. H/wine £8.25 ♀ Service exc
Credit cards: 1 2 3 4 5

Menus: *A la carte,* fixed-price, Sunday lunch in winter

Times: Midday–Last L 1.30pm, Last D 9.15pm. Closed Sun & Mon, 2 weeks July, 2 weeks Xmas

Chefs: Colin and Jane Rushworth
Proprietors: Colin and Jane Rushworth

Seats: 45. No smoking in dining room. Air conditioned
Additional: Children welcome; ❤ dishes; Vegan/other diets by prior arrangement

HORSFORTH, **Paris** ☻☻

☺ *Excellent French and modern English cooking with delightful presentation in a popular restaurant*

Good old Yorkshire hospitality is guaranteed at this popular restaurant, where the delightful atmosphere makes a splendid background for Thomas Mulkerrin's excellent cooking. The best value for money comes before 7.30pm when an early bird set menu offers a small but interesting choice of dishes; the main *carte* is chalked on a blackboard, and lists well-presented French and modern English dishes made from the best market produce. The results were approved by our inspector, who recently rhapsodised over a starter of scallop mousse with creamed morels and ginger, served warm and light and prettily topped with thin slices of deep-fried leeks. Welsh medallions of lamb cooked pink and coated with a meaty sauce kept to the same high standard, while plain vegetables were full of natural flavours and vibrant colours. A warm apple Charlotte with light texture and tangy apples floating on a light plum purée was the icing on the cake. Vegetarians are not ignored, being offered a few choices like ravioli of wild mushrooms, roast tomatoes and chives, and broccoli and Boursin cheese tart with Provencal vegetables.

Directions: From ring road on north-west edge of Leeds, turn onto Fink Hill, first right after supermarket, and right at T-junction onto Horsforth Town Street

36a Town Street
Map no: 8 SE23
Tel: 0113 2581885

Cost: *Alc* £16.50, fixed-price D (before 7.30pm) £12.95. H/wine £7.95 ♀ Service exc
Credit cards: 1 2 3 5

Menus: *A la carte*, fixed-price dinner, pre-theatre
Times: 6pm–Last D 10.30pm (11pm Fri & Sat). Closed 25 & 26 Dec & 1 Jan

Chef: Thomas Mulkerrin
Manager: Kimberley O'Rourke

Seats: 86. Air conditioned
Additional: Children welcome; children's portions; ❍ dishes; other diets on request

HUDDERSFIELD, **Bagden Hall** ☻

An elegant country house set in 40 acres of beautiful parkland. Chef Paul Davies continues to provide a good standard of well produced international cuisine with fixed-price and carte menus, offering such dishes as timbale of prawns and grilled swordfish from the very reasonably priced luncheon menu.

Cost: *Alc* £22, fixed-price L £8.95 (2 courses), £10.75/D £15.95. H/wine £8.25 ♀ Service exc. **Credit cards**: 1 2 3 4 5
Additional: Children permitted (not Saturday eve); children's portions; ❍ dishes; Vegan/other diets on request
Directions: 0.5 mile south of Scissett, on A363 Denby Dale road. Scissett is midway between Huddersfield and Barnsley

Wakefield Road, Scissett
Map no: 7 SE11
Tel: 01484 865330
Chef: Paul Davies
Proprietors: Mrs Braithwaite.
Manager: Mr C Storr
Seats: 60. No-smoking area. Air conditioned
Times: Midday-Last L 2pm, 7pm-Last D 10pm. Closed Sun eve

HUDDERSFIELD, Cote Royd ✦

☺ *An interesting selection of good value dishes is offered in the well appointed Victorian dining room of this converted mill owner's mansion. Dishes include home-made pâtés, trio of seafood, chicken suprême, ratatouille crumble, bread and butter pudding, and a dark and white chocolate terrine.*

Cost: Alc £15, Sunday L £9.95. H/wine £7.75. Service exc
Credit cards 1 2 3 4 5. **Additional**: Children welcome; children's portions; ✪ dishes; Vegan/other diets on request
Directions: On north-west outskirts of Huddersfield, on the left-hand side of the A629 Halifax road

7 Halifax Road, Edgerton
Map no: 7 SE11
Tel: 01484 547588
Chef: Edriss Marsh
Proprietor: Neville Phillips
Seats: 35. No-smoking area
Times: 7pm–Last D 9pm, Sun L. Closed Sun eve and BH Mons

HUDDERSFIELD, Lodge ✦

A fine Victorian house, this hotel has a richly decorated restaurant offering a good choice of modern British dishes. Our inspector sampled duck, leek and apricot sausage, turban of lemon sole, and a rich chocolate mousse with a ginger biscuit base on a bitter orange cream sauce.

Cost: Alc L £14.95, fixed-price L £11.95/D £21.95. H/wine £9.95 ♀ Servic exc. **Credit cards**: 1 2 3 **Additional**: Children permitted until 7pm; children's menu/portions; ✪ menu; Vegan/other diets on request
Directions: Follow Huddersfield signs from M62 junction 24, left at first lights (Birkby Road), turn right after Nuffield Hospital, 100yds on left

48 Birkby Lodge Road, Birkby
Map no: 7 SE11
Tel: 01484 431001
Chefs: Kevin and Garry Birley, Richard Hanson
Proprietors: Kevin and Garry Birley
Seats: 62. No smoking in dining room
Times: Midday–Last L 1.45pm, 7pm–Last D 9.45pm. Closed Sun eve, 25-27 Dec & 1 Jan

HUDDERSFIELD, Weavers Shed ✦✦

Well produced British food and a setting reminiscent of years long gone combine to make this a popular local rendezvous.

Housed in a converted weavers' mill, this friendly and down-to-earth restaurant retains much of its original charm and character, open stone walls, beamed ceilings, flagged floors and a wealth of memorabilia coming together to evoke nostalgic memories of a bygone age. Chef Ian McGunnigle, aided by owner Stephen Jackson, continues to attract a loyal following with his attractive presentation of well produced British dishes, a blackboard list of daily specials supplementing the *carte* and lunchtime fixed-price menus. Don't miss the traditional Yorkshire pudding filled with thick onion gravy (reputedly the best to be found in the entire country!), perhaps following this by sweet-flavoured baked halibut served with a delicate dill cream sauce and fresh, crisply cooked vegetables; dessert could be a light, airy lemon mousse sandwiched between thin layers of dark chocolate and floated on a tangy pool of orange purée, and the coffee that concludes the meal is rich and tasty. Vegetarian dishes are always available, but guests requiring the special children's menu should give prior notice.

Directions: Just outside Golcar village, 3 miles west of Huddersfield

Acre Mills, Knowl Road, Golcar
Map no: 7 SE11
Tel: 01484 654284

Cost: Alc £21, fixed-price L £10.95. H/wine £8.95. Service exc
Credit cards: 1 2 3

Menus: *A la carte* lunch and dinner, fixed-price lunch
Times: Midday-Last L 1.45pm, 7pm-Last D 9.15pm. Closed Sat lunch, all day Sun & Mon, first 2 weeks Jan & Last 2 weeks Jul

Chefs: Ian McGunnigle, Stephen Jackson
Proprietor: Stephen Jackson

Seats: 60–70
Additional: Children welcome; children's portions (menu with prior notice); ✪ dishes; Vegan/other diets with prior notice

ENGLAND WEST YORKSHIRE

ILKLEY, **Box Tree** ❀❀

A very stylish, established restaurant offering classic French food with top-quality ingredients handled by an expert chef

Originally an 18th-century Yorkshire farmhouse, this well-established restaurant has built up a reputation for providing top quality ingredients with classic French presentation. However, the team at The Box Tree has changed since the last edition of this guide, with Thierry Le Prêtre Granet now in control of the kitchen, which builds well from his previous experience at Whitechapel Manor where he held three rosettes. Our inspector found his dishes to be well worthy of high praise, with very attractive presentation and only the best produce put to good use in the preparation of the French/modern English dishes. He offers a choice of fixed-price classical menus, with starters such as hot duck foie gras salad with globe artichoke. Sea-bass with a mushroom crust and herb butter sauce or breast of Gressingham duck, leg confit, with prune and ginger sauce are popular main courses. Tempting desserts include hot passion fruit soufflé. We feel this current period of stability can only be to the benefit of both the restaurant and its customers.

Directions: On the A65, on the Skipton side of Ilkley near the parish church

27 Church Street
Map no: 7 SE14
Tel: 01943 608484

Cost: Fixed-price L £22.50, fixed-price D £29.50. H/wine £13 ♀ Service inc
Credit cards: 1 2 3

Menus: Fixed-price lunch and dinner, Sunday lunch
Times: Last L 2.30pm/D 10.30pm. Closed Mon, Sat lunch, Sun eve & Last 2 weeks Jan

Chef: Thierry Leprêtre Granet
Proprietor: Mme Avis. Manager: J Parker

Seats: 50–60. No smoking in dining room
Additional: Children permitted at lunchtime; ◐ dishes; Vegan/other diets on request

ILKLEY, **Rombalds** ❀

Set between the moor and the town this family owned and run hotel produces a classical style of cooking. Starters include confit duck salad with Stilton and croûtons, or seafood ravioli, and for main courses rack of lamb with couscous or salmon steak with teriyake sauce.

Cost: Alc £24, fixed-price (Mon–Fri only) L £9.95/D £10 (2 courses), £12.95. H/wine £8 ♀ Service exc. **Credit cards**: 1 2 3 4
Additional: Children welcome; children's menu/portions; ◐ dishes; Vegan/other diets with advance notice
Directions: From A65 traffic lights in centre of town, turn up Brook Street to the top, turn left then immediately right into Wells Road. 600yds on left

11 West View, Wells Road
Map no: 7 SE14
Tel: 01943 603201
Chef: Bruce Gray
Proprietors: Jill and Ian Guthrie. Manager: Gail Wadsworth
Seats: 40. No smoking in dining room
Times: Last L 2pm/D 9.30pm Closed 27-30 Dec

LEEDS, **Brasserie Forty Four** ❀❀

☺ *A fun place to eat, this restaurant offers a good choice of modern menus with a strong Mediterranean influence*

A hugely popular restaurant located in a smartly redeveloped area of town, Brasserie Forty Four has a lively atmosphere and friendly staff who provide relaxed but professional service. It now also opens for Sunday lunch when children's entertainment is a feature. There are several regularly changing menus to choose from, offering a wide variety of imaginative dishes, the three-course fixed price lunch menu giving particularly good value for money. Chef Jeff Baker cooks using quality fresh ingredients and the results are very tasty. Our inspector's wild

42-44 The Calls
Map no: 8 SE23
Tel: 0113 2343232

Cost: Alc £19, fixed-price L £7.50 (2 courses), £11.25, Sun L £14.70. H/wine £8.95 ♀ No service charge
Credit cards: 1 2 3
Menus: A la carte, fixed-price lunch, Sunday lunch, pre- and after-theatre
Times: Midday-Last L 2pm, 6.30pm-Last D 10.30pm (11pm

mushroom risotto was an excellent starter, full of earthy flavour. This was followed by chicken breast, roasted and served on a potato cake with a good shallot dressing, accompanied by carefully cooked vegetables. Bread and butter pudding with plenty of fruit completed the meal, though parties of two or more should try the chocolate fondue laced with Cointreau. A favourite vegetarian main course is grilled polenta, served with mushrooms and parmesan, or mozzarella, spinach and tomato fondue. The wine list reflects good quality growers from many countries and complements the menu well.

Directions: From Crown Point Bridge, turn left past church, then left into High Court Road which merges into The Calls. The restaurant is on the riverside by a new footbridge

Sat). Closed Sat lunch, Mon eve, 5 days Xmas & BH Mons
Chef: Jeff Baker
Proprietors: Jonathan Wix and Michael Gill

Seats: 125. No cigars or pipes. Air conditioned
Additional: Children welcome; children's portions/Sun L menu; ✪ dishes; Vegan/other diets on request; live entertainment Sunday lunchtime

LEEDS, **Haley's** ✪✪

☺ *Modern English cooking in a refined atmosphere at this stylish hotel on the city's edge*

Quietly situated in a residential part of Headingley, a couple of miles from Leeds city centre, this restored Victorian home is now a town house hotel, professionally run with considerable charm under the direction of Stephen Beaumont. The restaurant has a serious edge, offering at dinner a sensibly sized *carte* with daily-changing specialities. Representative first courses could include pear and Parmesan salad, aubergine and red pepper terrine and, our inspector's choice, a salad of crispy fried vegetables, dressed with a finely judged balsamic vinaigrette. A middle course of panache of fish comprised beautifully fresh sea-bass, sole, mullet and salmon topped with good ink spaghetti off-set by a slightly over-seasoned vermouth butter sauce. The main course of roast Barbary duck came very pink with a bland port sauce rescued by tip-top red cabbage. A choice of vegetarian main courses is offered and puddings could include the local favourite of curd tart or a seasonal dish of roulade of autumn fruit. There is an international wine list.

Directions: 2 miles north of city centre, off the A660 Otley road. In Headingley turn off main road between Midland and Yorkshire banks

Shire Oak Road, Headingley
Map no: 8 SE23
Tel: 0113 2784446

Cost: *Alc* £18.50. H/wine £10.50 ♀ Service inc
Credit cards: 1 2 3 4 5

Menus: *A la carte*, Sunday lunch, pre-theatre, bar menu

Times: 7.15-Last D 9.45pm, Sun midday-Last L 2.30pm. Closed Sun eve (except residents), 26-30 Dec

Chef: Chris Baxter
Proprietor: John Appleyard. General Manager: Moira Snape

Seats 45. No cigars or pipes in restaurant. Air conditioned
Additional: Children welcome; children's portions; ✪ dishes; other diets on request

LEEDS, **Leodis Brasserie** ✪

☺ *A smart brasserie in a converted warehouse, this popular restaurant presents an imaginative range of dishes. These might include black pudding, fish soup, bangers and mash, tandoori monkfish, oxtail and Madeira pudding, and a choice of vegetarian dishes. To finish, the lemon tart is recommended.*

Cost: *Alc* £18, fixed-price £10.95. H/wine £8.95 ♀ Service exc **Credit cards**: 1 2 3 5. **Additional**: Children welcome; children's portions; ✪ dishes; Vegan/other diets on request
Directions: From city square, go under station and turn left by Hilton Hotel onto Sovereign Street. 100yds on left

Victoria Mill, Sovereign Street
Map no: 8 SE23
Tel: 0113 2421010
Chefs: Steven Kendell, Dean Eccles
Proprietors: Martin Spalding, Steven Kendell
Seats: 160
Times: Last L 2pm/D10pm (11pm Fri & Sat). Closed Sat lunch, Sun, 25-26 Dec & 1 Jan

LEEDS, Olive Tree ☺

☺ *A new Greek restaurant providing all the expected dishes from the area with only the freshest produce to ensure great flavours. Starters include dolmades (stuffed vine leaves). There is a good selection of lamb, fish and chicken dishes as main courses whilst stafidhopitta is the house speciality sweet.*

Cost: Alc £16, fixed-price L & D £9.95. H/wine £7.95. Service exc
Credit cards: 1 2 3 5. **Additional:** Children welcome; children's portions; ❻ menu; Vegan/other diets on request; live entertainment Tue & Fri
Directions: By Rodley roundabout on outer ring road (A6120), north-west of city

Oaklands, 55 Rodley Lane
Map no: 8 SE23
Tel: 0113 2569283
Chefs: George Psarias, Andreas Lacovou
Proprietors: George & Vasoulla Psarias
Seats: 150
Times: Midday–Last L 2.30pm, 6pm–Last D 11.30pm. Closed Sat lunch, 25-26 Dec & 1 Jan

RIPPONDEN, Over The Bridge ☺

☺ *A charming restaurant standing beside a hump-backed bridge, which has been providing good food for about 20 years. The honest and solid cuisine may include dishes such as ramekin of smoked haddock and avocado or Lumesdale duck breast with caramelised onion confit.*

Cost: Fixed-price D £22.50. H/wine £8.50. Service inc
Credit cards: 1 2 3. **Additional:** Children permitted; children's portions; ❻ dishes; other diets on request
Directions: In village by church and pack-horse bridge

Millfold
Map no: 7 SE01
Tel: 01422 823722
Chef: Susan Tyer
Proprietor: Ian Beaumont
Seats: 45. No pipes in restaurant
Times: 7.30pm–Last D 9.30pm. Closed Sun & BHs

WETHERBY, Wood Hall ☺

A magnificent Georgian mansion overlooking the wooded valley of the River Wharfe, where there is a good choice of British dishes. Our inspector recommended ravioli of scallop and crab, followed by east-coast haddock topped with Welsh rarebit and floating on a good red pepper and chilli sauce.

Cost: Alc £27. **Credit cards:** 1 2 3 4. **Additional:** Children permitted; ❻ dishes; no smoking in dining room
Directions: In village, take turning opposite the Windmill pub signed Wood Hall and Linton

Trip Lane
Map no: 8 SE44
Tel: 01937 587271
Chefs: Andrew Mitchell
Proprietor: Miss A Lee (General Manager)
Times: Last L 2pm/D 9.30pm

WILTSHIRE

ALDBOURNE, Raffles ☺☺

☺ *A well-run village restaurant where the hard-to-please enjoy themselves and come back for more*

Chef/proprietor Jim Hannan trained at the Ritz, spent 15 years at the Caprice and Grosvenor House; his wife Mary looked after VIP's at other top London hotels. Some pedigree. But is all this experience evident today? Yes it is, although one small

The Green
Map no: 4 SU27
Tel: 01672 40700

Cost: Alc £19.45, Sunday L £9.95. H/wine £8.95. Service exc
Credit cards: 1 2 3 4

gripe (probably just bad luck) meant that our inspector had to endure long waits between courses, accentuated by the heartless half-hourly chiming of a clock. He started with a well-seasoned tagliatelle with home-made tomato and onion sauce, and then chose clear-flavoured boiled silverside with dumplings, a traditional dish of the day. Others could be beefsteak and kidney pie, osso buco with saffron rice, and ragout of selected fish and shellfish. Looking at the list of desserts, one might have a sense of mild déjà vu as the eyes take in apple strudel, crème brûlée, hazelnut and almond torte, and so on – but we Britons love them, so why change a winning formula? Swindon's business community tends to descend on Raffles, but they are obviously a discerning bunch who, having found a good restaurant, stick with it.

Directions: In the centre of the village overlooking the green

Menus: *A la carte*, Sunday lunch

Times: 12.30pm–Last L 2.15pm, 7pm–Last D 10.30pm. Closed Mon & Sat L, Sun eve, Last 2/3 weeks Aug, 25-31 Dec and BHs

Chef: James F Hannan
Proprietor: James F Hannan

Seats: 36. No cigars or pipes
Additional: Children welcome; children's portions; ◊ dishes; Vegan dishes by prior arrangement; piano music Wed and Thu

BOX, Box House ✿✿

Close to Bath, a country house hotel/restaurant where originality is the foundation of the stylish cooking

Head chefs always know best and the talented Darren Francis here is no exception. The *carte* advises that he prefers to cook his red meat pink or medium, but to tell the waitress if something more, or less, is wanted. Pink or medium sounds fine, actually. The hotel/restaurant is a handsome Georgian mansion in its own well-tended, walled garden. Some interestingly different dishes appear on both the *carte*, which changes seasonally, and the daily-changing, three course, fixed-price menu. Recent starters included home-made creamed broccoli soup, sliced salmon and langoustine terrine on a pesto sauce, and grilled avocado with caper vinaigrette. As a main course, Lunesdale duck served with a raspberry vinegar sauce was a candidate, as was whole onion filled with ratatouille on a bed of grilled aubergines with a warm tomato purée, or puff pastry filled with sautéed wild mushrooms and walnuts on rice with a chervil sauce. Desserts usually include a hot soufflé, but allow for half an hour's preparation time. Others could be Irish pear tart or sautéed peppered pineapple with vanilla ice cream.

Directions: In village, on the main A4

London Road
Map no: 3 ST86
Tel: 01225 744447

Cost: *Alc* £22, fixed-price L and D £9.95. H/wine £9.50. Service exc
Credit cards: 1 2 3 5

Menus: *A la carte*, fixed-price, Sunday lunch, pre-theatre, bar menu

Times: Midday-Last L 2.30pm, 7pm-Last D 10.30pm

Chef: Darren Francis
Proprietors: Tim & Kathryn Burnham

Seats: 60
Additional: Children welcome; children's portions; ◊ dishes (menu on request); Vegan/other diets on request

BRADFORD ON AVON, Woolley Grange ✿✿✿

An exceptionally special hotel, whose twin strengths are its fine food and its genuine desire to entertain children

Children are treated as important little people in their own right at this charmingly friendly hotel, and given the same serious and careful attention that their parents receive. There is a total lack of stuffiness in the lovely old Jacobean house set in equally attractive grounds, and while nannies, playrooms and the owners' own children quickly capture the attention of small

Woolley Green
Map no: 3 ST86
Tel: 01225 864705

Cost: Fixed-price D £28, Sun L £17. H/wine £9.85 ♀ Service inc
Credit cards: 1 2 3 4 5

Menus: *A la carte*, fixed-price dinner and Sun lunch, bar menu

Times: Last L 2pm/D 10pm

visitors, adults find plenty of their own pleasures. One of these is the fine food for which this hotel is becoming well known, and Colin White's dedicated country house cooking with its emphasis on honest flavours is well worth savouring. One of his secrets is the use of top quality produce, much of its grown in the hotel's gardens, where natural flavours are allowed to speak for themselves. With this emphasis on individual ingredients, it is no surprise that the simplest of dishes served here can taste extraordinary.

The daily-changing fixed-price menu offers tempting starters such as sweet chilli squid with pea and coriander pancakes, or terrine of smoked haddock, leeks and saffron with chive cream, with main dishes like saddle of lamb stuffed with walnuts and rosemary, or fillet of striped bass with roast fennel and saffron butter. Delicious mushroom risotto with shaved parmesan and truffle oil got a recent inspection meal off to a good start, with breast of chargrilled chicken to follow – a succulent, full-flavoured dish served with parsley pesto, ratatouille and polenta. To end the meal a vanilla bavarois proved to be light and creamy with a lovely fresh vanilla flavour, served with large juicy raspberries. Coffee and home-made petits fours followed. Staff are relaxed and very helpful. The wine list is clearly presented, of manageable length, and offers an interesting selection from Italy.

Chef: Colin White
Proprietors: Nigel and Heather Chapman

Seats: 54 restaurant, 20 conservatory. No smoking in dining room
Additional: Children welcome; children's portions; children's menu served in supervised nursery/playroom; ❻ dishes; Vegan/other diets on request

Directions: Off the Bath road, 1 mile north-east of town

BURBAGE, **Savernake Forest** ❀

☺ *Attractive Victorian country house on the edge of the forest, with a warm welcome from friendly owners. Capable chef Stephen Brough produces enjoyable dishes like chicken liver pâté, and breast of chicken filled with spring onions and ginger. Bread and butter pudding crammed with fruit is a must.*

Cost: Alc £13.50, fixed-price D £18.50. H/wine £7.95. Service exc
Credit cards: 1 2 3 4 5. **Additional:** Children welcome; children's menu/portions; ❻ dishes; Vegan/other diets on request
Directions: 0.25 miles off A346 just before Burbage bypass

Savernake
Map no: 4 SU26
Tel: 01672 810206
Chef: Stephen Brough
Proprietors: Richard Johnson and Lynne Gurney
Seats: 60 Great Western Room, 32 Green Room. No smoking area; no cigars or pipes
Times: 12.30pm-Last L 2.15pm, Last D 9.15pm

CASTLE COMBE, **Castle Inn** ❀❀

A hotel full of character serving inventive and professionally executed meals

This character inn which dates back to the 12th century has been carefully restored to a high standard retaining much of the charm of the original building. The public rooms are cosy and full of character and there is a conservatory and patio dining room for light lunches and breakfast. Dinner is also served in Olivers restturant, where chef Antony Smith produces commendable cooking with some depth and flair. His efforts with fresh, quality produce result in well-executed dishes. Recently inspectors praised the fresh scallops with a fine julienne of ginger starter. A scrumptious confit of duck

Map no: 3 ST87
Tel: 01249 783030

Cost: Alc £24, fixed-price L £12.50, fixed-price D £17.50. H/wine £9.95 ♀ Service exc
Credit cards: 1 2 3 4 5
Menus: A la carte, fixed-price lunch and dinner, Sunday lunch, bar menu
Times: Midday-Last L 2pm, 7.30pm-Last D 10pm (9.30 Sun)

Chef: Tony Smith
Proprietor: Darren Hiscock

with bacon and pine kernels was followed by a tasty roasted salmon with a herb crust, and a handsome home-made white chocolate mousse served with roasted almond biscuits and sprinkled with bitter chocolate concluded an excellent meal.

Directions: In village centre

CASTLE COMBE, Manor House ✸✸

An elegant stone-built country house serving classy English food in an atmosphere of well being

Modern improvements have not detracted from the original character of this unpretentious country house that dates in part from the 14th century, and the luxurious comforts and old-world atmosphere sit easily together. In the spacious restaurant an attentive team of staff watches over diners, while the carefully-prepared English dishes of chef Mark Taylor are brought out to tempt and satisfy. Food is as pricey as the surroundings might suggest, and may be chosen from the *carte* where a vegetarian menu can also be selected as a five-course gourmet meal, or a fixed-price lunch menu or short dinner menu offering seasonal selections: from the latter bouillon of asparagus and langoustine might be followed by sorbet of orange and anis, and loin of lamb sliced onto a purée of broad beans with garlic cream sauce. Our inspector chose a hot blue cheese and cauliflower soufflé, a light and airy starter enhanced by a butter sauce, and then fillet of brill cooked in paper with cepes, and served with a creamy mushroom sauce on a bed of soft tagliatelle. A brûlée of apricots in a pastry tartlet was followed by an interesting selection of English cheeses.

Directions: Near centre of village, signposted from market cross

CHIPPENHAM, Stanton Manor ✸

Set in five acres of gardens and woodland, the hotel's restaurant has both a carte and a fixed-price menu. The freshly cooked dishes use fresh produce, some of which is provided by the Manor's own kitchen garden.

Cost: Alc £22, fixed-price £18. **Credit cards**: 1 2 3
Additional: Children permitted by arrangement; ❂ menu; no smoking in restaurant
Directions: In village centre, next to church

COLERNE, Lucknam Park ✸✸✸

Modern English cooking based on best quality ingredients, organic where possible, in a country house setting

A mile long avenue of graceful beeches lines the driveway to Lucknam Park, a Georgian country house with all the grandeur and elegance of the period, and now an internationally recognised hotel. The public rooms are sumptuously furnished

Manager: Paul Thompson
Seats: 30 , 30 conservatory. No-smoking area.
Additional: Children welcome; children's portions; ❂ dishes; Vegan/other with notice

Map no: 3 ST87
Tel: 01249 782206

Cost: Alc £43, fixed-price L £16.95, fixed-price D £32. H/wine £16.50. Service exc
Credit cards: 1 2 3 4

Menus: *A la carte*, fixed-price lunch and dinner, Sunday lunch, pre-theatre, bar menu
Times: Last L 2pm/D 9.30pm

Chef: Mark Taylor
Proprietor: Martin J Clubbe

Seats: 70. No smoking in dining room
Additional: Children welcome; children's menu/portions; ❂ menu; Vegan/other diets on request

Stanton St Quintin
Map no 3 ST97
Tel: 01666 837552
Chef: Tony Ashton
Proprietors: Philip and Elizabeth Bullock
Times: 7pm-Last D 9.30pm. Closed 26 Dec-10 Jan

Map no: 3 ST87
Tel: 01225 742777

Cost: Alc £22.50, fixed-price D £39.50. H/wine £15.50 ♀ Service inc
Credit cards: 1 2 3 4

Menus: *A la carte*, fixed-price

and boldly decorated, and service is provided by an immaculately turned out team.

Head chef Michael Womersley, who has worked alongside great European chefs such as Raymond Blanc and Michael Guerard, produces imaginative and well balanced menus with first class produce, organic where possible. The lunch menu is priced for two or three courses, and the dinner menu for three courses with coffee and petits fours. Starters might include a whole roast quail with a green bean purée served with a salad; carpaccio of prime fillet steak with pickled baby vegetables, or, our inspector's choice, tasty glazed scallops and langoustine set off with a mousseline of spinach. He followed with wafer thin slivers of Trelough duck wrapped around a powerful sautéed foie gras with a rich classical sherry sauce (supplement £3). Alternatives might be roast monkfish with a crisp coating of sesame seeds and a soya ginger butter sauce, or lasagna of woodland mushrooms with a coriander sauce spiked with fine vegetables and lentils. Vegetarian dishes do not always appear on the menus but they can be provided on request.

Desserts are a treat, and many of them are warm – hot chocolate pudding with vanilla sauce, and pear soufflé with a home-baked macaroon both scoring well. Alternatively, there is a selection of English and French cheeses.

The wine list is long but clearly presented, and offers a world wide selection of good wines. The clarets are chosen from the best vintages going back to 1947, and there are some excellent Burgundies and Rhône wines too.

Directions: North of Colerne on the Ford road; 1 mile south of the A420 Chippenham-Bristol road at Ford

dinner and Sunday lunch

Times: 12pm-Last L 2pm, 7.30pm-Last D 9.30pm

Chef: Michael Womersley
Proprietor: Robert Carter

Seats: 80. No smoking
Additional: Children permitted (over 12 at dinner); ✿ dishes; Vegan dishes on request

CORSHAM, **Rudloe Park** ✿

☺ *This Victorian country house stands in four acres of beautifully kept gardens and grounds, the restaurant offering an extensive choice of dishes. Our inspector's main course was a succulent pan-fried chicken breast served with a thick and creamy asparagus sauce.*

Cost: *Alc* £15.95, fixed-price L £12.95/D £12.95 (2 courses), £15.95. H/wine £8.50. Service exc. **Credit cards**: 1 2 3 4 5
Additional: Children welcome; children's menu/portions; ✿ menu; Vegan dishes on request
Directions: 1 mile west of town on A4 Bath-Chippenham road

Leafy Lane
Map no: 3 ST87
Tel: 01225 810555
Chef: Geoffrey Bell
Proprietors: Steve and Ros Salter
Seats: 65. No smoking in dining room. Air conditioned
Times: Midday–Last L 2pm, Last D 10pm

FORD, **White Hart Inn** ✿

☺ *This attractive restaurant offers an interesting selection of dishes on the frequently changed carte menus. The inspector chose the flavoursome and well-seasoned spinach soup followed by medallions of pork on a smooth, tomato based sweet and sour sauce.*

Cost: *Alc* £16. **Credit cards**: 1 2 3 4
Additional: Children welcome; ✿ dishes
Directions: In village centre

Map no 3 ST87
Tel: 01249 782213
Chef: Lee Owen
Proprietors: Mr & Mrs C Phillips
Times: Midday-Last L 2pm, 7pm- Last D 9.30pm

WILTSHIRE ENGLAND

HINDON, **Lamb at Hindon**

A well established stone built 17th-century coaching inn standing in the centre of this picturesque village. A selection of interesting dishes is offered on the fixed-price menu, together with a choice of sophisticated bar snacks. Chef John Croft makes use of local meat and game when in season.

Cost: Fixed-price L £12.95/D £18.95. H/wine £6.95 ♀ Service exc
Credit cards: 1 2 3 5. **Additional**: Children welcome; children's portions; ♥ dishes; Vegan/other diets on request
Directions: In village centre

Map no: 3 ST93
Tel: 01747 820573
Chef: John Croft
Proprietors: John and Paul Croft
Seats: 40. No smoking in dining room
Times: Midday-Last L 2pm, 7pm-Last D 9.30pm

INGLESHAM, **Inglesham Forge**

This charming cottage-style restaurant has an extensive wine list and offers a choice of interesting dishes on its à la carte menus. In the past, main courses have included fillet steak béarnaise, fresh Scottish salmon and suprême of chicken Diane.

Cost: Alc £20–£24. H/wine £8.95 ♀ Service inc. **Credit cards**: 1 3
Additional: Children welcome; children's portions; ♥ dishes; other diets on request
Directions: In village centre

Near Swindon
Map no: 4 SU29
Tel: 01367 252298
Chef: Manuel Gomez
Proprietor: Manuel Gomez
Seats: 30
Times: Last L 1.45pm/D 9.30pm. Closed Sun, Mon & Sat lunch & BHs

LIMPLEY STOKE, **Cliffe Hotel**

☺ A former country house overlooking the Avon valley, within easy reach of Bath and Bristol. The dining room is attractive and guests are made to feel welcome. The menu features uncomplicated but appealing main courses such as breast of duck and fresh fish of the day.

Cost: Alc £19, fixed-price L £15. H/wine £7.85. Service exc
Credit cards: 1 2 3. **Additional**: Children welcome; children's menu/portions; ♥ menu; Vegan/other diets on request
Directions: At traffic lights in Limpley Stoke take B3108, fork right signposted Lower Stoke. At brow of hill turn right

Crowe Hill
Map no: 3 ST76
Tel: 01225 723226
Chef: Peter Clare
Proprietor: Richard Okill
Seats: 40. No smoking in dining room
Times: Midday-Last L 2pm, 7pm-Last D 9.30pm

MALMESBURY, **Knoll House**

A refurbished Victorian hotel offering imaginative dishes cooked in a modern style

Chef Andrew Stickings gained his experience while travelling around the world, and there is an unstuffy element to his cooking which is greatly appealing. Now settled at this extensively refurbished Victorian hotel, he displays his skills on a fixed price menu which offers two or three courses of modern English and French dishes. Our inspector recently enjoyed an innovative smoked sea trout lasagne layered with lightly cooked asparagus spears and leaf spinach and a chervil butter sauce – a colourful starter with good flavours and contrasting textures. Oven baked fillet of lamb was coated in a garlic and

Swindon Road
Map no: 3 ST98
Tel: 01666 823114

Cost: Alc £23, fixed-price D £15. H/wine £8.50 ♀ Service inc
Credit cards: 1 2 3 5

Menus: A la carte, fixed-price, Sunday lunch, bar menu

Times: Midday-Last L 2pm, 7pm-Last D 9.30pm

Chef: Andrew Stickings

herb crust and served with potato cake and meat juices, and fresh vegetables. A tasty crème brûlée and strawberry compote came sensibly in separate dishes, and freshly brewed coffee and delicious home-made truffles were a credit to the kitchen. Other choices from the menu might be breast of pheasant with a game farcie and port sauce, or a vegetarian casserole of Jerusalem artichokes, wild mushrooms, asparagus and spinach with goats' cheese in a pastry tartlet. At lunchtime the bar has a brasserie menu.

Proprietor: Simon Haggarty

Seats: 45. No smoking in dining room
Additional: Children welcome; children's menu/portions; ❶ Vegan/other diets on request

Directions: On the B4042 Swindon road

MARLBOROUGH, Ivy House ❀

This attractive ivy-clad Grade II Georgian residence started life in 1707 as the Marlborough Academy for boys. It is now a comfortable hotel with an elegant restaurant offering a menu with prices fixed by course and a carte featuring interesting dishes of modern English cuisine at reasonable prices.

High Street
Map no: 4 SU16
Tel: 01672 515333
Chef: David Ball
Proprietors: David Ball and Josephine Scott
Seats: 50. No cigars or pipes
Times: Midday-Last L 2pm, Last D 9.30pm

Cost: Alc £27.50, fixed-price L £10.50 (2 courses), £12.50/D £14.50 (2 courses), £16.50. H/wine £8.50 ♀ Service exc. **Credit cards**: 1 2 3
Additional: Children welcome; children's menu/portions; ❶ menu; Vegan/other diets on request
Directions: In the main street at centre of town

MELKSHAM, Beechfield House ❀

☺ *A delightful Victorian Bath stone hotel with a garden, which grows a lot of the fruit and vegetables chef Nicola O'Brien uses in the choice of interesting dishes on offer. Our inspector sampled pancakes filled with mushrooms and onions topped with a cheese sauce, followed by lamb's liver.*

Beanacre
Map no 3 ST96
Tel: 01225 703700
Chef: Nicola O'Brien
Proprietor: Macdonald Hotels. Manager: Lorna Bryden
Times: Midday-Last L 2pm, 7pm-Last D 9.30pm

Cost: Fixed-price £19.50. **Credit cards**: 1 2 3 4
Additional: Children welcome; ❶ dishes; no smoking in restaurant
Directions: In the village, on the A350 Melksham/Chippenham road

MELKSHAM, Shaw Country Hotel ❀

☺ *A 16th-century creeper-clad property where for the Mulberry restaurant, the proprietors' twin sons, Nicholas and Paul, create the interesting selection of dishes, including pan-fried mushrooms filled with Atlantic prawns and crab-meat starter followed by grilled venison loin.*

Bath Road, Shaw
Map no 3 ST96
Tel: 01225 702836/790321
Chefs: Nicholas & Paul Lewis
Proprietors: Mr & Mrs Lewis
Seats: 40. No smoking in dining room
Times: Midday-Last L 2pm, 7pm-Last D 9pm

Cost: Alc £16.95, fixed-price L £9.95/D£13.95. H/wine £7.25. Service exc. **Credit cards**: 1 2 3 5. **Additional**: Children permitted; children's portions; ❶ dishes; Vegan/other diets on request
Directions: 1 mile north-west of Melksham on A365

MELKSHAM, **Toxique** ⬤⬤

A strikingly different restaurant with an air of intrigue provides a friendly atmosphere and value-for-money meals

Not surprisingly, proprietors who are by training an architect and an interior designer have created a restaurant with a distinct style in this 17th-century farmhouse about a mile from the town centre. Two dining areas and a lounge have wooden floors, low ceilings, dark walls where unframed pictures provide the only splash of colour and simple modern furnishings. White-clothed tables lit by candles stuck into flowerpots give a hint of informality, however, and this is reflected in friendly, relaxed service. Value for money fixed-price menus offer a daily-changing choice of dishes (augmented at each stage by a few more at a supplementary charge), and the adventurous eater will be in his element! The intriguingly named Buffalo Mozzarella with sun-dried tomatoes and basil torino, for example, could be followed by red snapper with ginger, simmered in sake marinade and served with seaweed and Japanese saifun. Those of less exotic inclination, however, are not denied their fillet of beef, loin of venison or spring lamb. The extensive, predominantly French wine list contains a good selection of half bottles.

Directions: Take the Calne road from centre of Melksham. Turn into Forest Road, the restaurant is on the left after 0.75 miles

187 Woodrow Road
Map no 3 ST96
Tel: 01225 702129

Cost: Fixed-price L £13.50 (2 courses), £16.50, fixed-price D £24.50. H/wine £9.75. Service inc
Credit cards: 1 2 3 4 5

Menu: Fixed-price dinner, Sunday lunch
Times: Last D 10, Last Sun L 2pm. Closed weekday lunch, Sun eve, all day Mon & Tue

Chef: Helen Bartlett
Proprietors: Helen Bartlett, Peter Jewkes

Seats: 30. No smoking in dining rooms
Additional: Children welcome; children's portions; ⓥ dishes; Vegan/other diets on request

PURTON, **Pear Tree at Purton** ⬤

A former vicarage built of Cotswold stone, this hotel has a smart conservatory restaurant where guests can enjoy the best local meat, poultry and fresh fish, along with interesting vegetarian dishes. The fixed-price lunch and dinner menus offer imaginative and elaborately presented English cooking.

Cost: Fixed-price L £17.50/D £27.50. H/wine £11 ♀ Service exc
Credit cards: 1 2 3 4 5. **Additional**: Children welcome; children's portions; ⓥ dishes; Vegan/other diets on request; classical guitarist at weekends
Directions: On Lydiard Millicent road out of the village

Church End
Map no: 4 SU08
Tel: 01793 772100
Chef: Janet Pichel-Juan
Proprietors: Francis and Anne Young
Seats: 60. No cigars or pipes
Times: Midday-Last L 2pm, 7pm-Last D 9.15pm. Closed Sat L

REDLYNCH,
Langley Wood Restaurant ⬤

Hidden in woods beside Langley Wood Nature Reserve, this small restaurant offers a good range of dishes with honest uncluttered flavours. Our inspector recommended grilled goat's cheese, followed by slice Barbary duck on aubergine with coriander and yoghurt.

Cost: Alc £22, Sun L £13.75. H/wine £7.20 ♀ Service exc
Credit cards: 1 2 3 4. **Additional**: Children permitted Sunday lunch only; children's portions where feasable; ⓥ dishes; other diets with advance notice
Directions: In village

Map no: 4 SU22
Tel: 01794 390348
Chef: Sylvia Rosen
Proprietors: David and Sylvia Rosen
Seats 30. No smoking in dining room
Times: 7.30pm-Last D 11pm, Sun L 12.30-2pm. Closed Sun eve, all day Mon & Tue

ROWDE, George & Dragon ⚜

This friendly 17th-century village pub provides excellent quality food in relaxed surroundings. The cheese soufflé is a great favourite with many regular diners and the home-made fudge is another speciality of this delightful little place.

Cost: Fixed-price L £10. H/wine £8 ♀ Service inc. **Credit cards:** 1 3
Additional: Children permitted before 9.30pm; children's portions; ❂ dishes usually on menu; other diets with advance notice
Directions: On the A342 Devizes-Chippenham road

High Street
Map no: 3 ST96
Tel: 01380 723053
Chef: Tim Withers
Proprietors: Tim and Helen Withers
Seats: 35
Times: Midday-Last L 2pm, 7pm-Last D 10pm. Closed Sun & Mon, 25, 26 Dec and 1 Jan

SALISBURY, Milford Hall ⚜

Peter Roberts is responsible for the interesting and ambitious menus at this extended Georgian mansion. Our inspector sampled a tartlet of oyster mushrooms with a béarnaise sauce, rack of lamb with a garlic and herb crust on a bed of noodles, and a fluffy hot chocolate soufflé with Amaretto.

Cost: Alc £22, fixed-price L £9.95/D £12.50. H/wine £7.50 ♀ Service exc. **Credit cards:** 1 2 3. **Additional:** Children welcome; children's menu/portions; ❂ menu; Vegan/other diets on request
Directions: Half a mile north of city centre, off A30 ring road at junction with A345 and Castle Street

206 Castle Street
Map no: 4 SU12
Tel: 01722 417411
Chef: Peter Roberts
Manager: Mark Robertson-Walker
Seats: 70. No smoking in dining room
Times: Midday-Last L 2pm, 7pm-Last D 10pm

SWINDON, Blunsdon House ⚜

☺ Situated in a peaceful location, this hotel contains the Ridge Restaurant where the food is fresh, well presented and flavoursome. The choice is varied with five or six fish, poultry, flambé, grill or meat dishes. For example fillet of pork with Stilton flavoured with port and brandy sauce.

Cost: Fixed-price L £14.50/D £17.50. H/wine £9.50. Service inc
Credit cards 1 2 3 4 5. **Additional:** Children welcome; children's menu/portions; ❂ menu; Vegan/other diets on request; live entertainment
Directions: 3 miles north of town centre. From A419 take turning signposted Broad Blunsdon, then first left

Blunsdon
Map no: 4 SU18
Tel: 01793 721701
Chef: Elisley Haines
Proprietor: John Clifford
Seats: 70. Air conditioned
Times: 12.15pm-Last L 2pm, 7pm-Last D 10pm

SWINDON, Chiseldon House ⚜⚜

Enjoyable flavours and attractive presentation of modern English cooking in a tasteful hotel

Built in 1837 as a manor house for the village of Chiseldon, this tastefully-converted hotel retains the friendly atmosphere of a private home. Now a Grade II listed buildingit is set in three acres of lawned gardens. Elegant public rooms include the Orangery restaurant, where chef John Farrow produces an interesting array of well-cooked dishes on both a *carte* and a fixed-price menu. A well-presented and generally enjoyable recent inspection meal began with watercress soup that was slightly over-peppered, and was followed by succulent rack of

New Road, Chiseldon
Map no 4 SU18
Tel: 01793 741010

Cost: Alc £28, fixed-price £19.95
Credit cards: 1 2 3

Menus: A la carte, fixed-price

Times: Midday-Last L 2pm, 7.00-Last D 9.30pm. Closed Sat lunch

lamb that was cooked pink, and came with a creamy caper sauce, a subtle garlic-flavoured jus, and a tartlet of caramelised onions; the fresh vegetables were unfortunately over-cooked and tended to lack flavour. There's a good choice of hot and cold desserts, such as sticky toffee pudding, and a tasty parfait of blackcurrant served with dipped chocolate ice cream and an excellent blackcurrant purée. Service was seriously understaffed and slow, but pleasantly performed by a team of two. There's a short wine list with a few halves and some New World wines.

Chef: John Farrow
Proprietor: Sven Ehrnlund

Additional: Children welcome; ✪ dishes

Directions: In village centre

TEFFONT MAGNA, Howards House ✿✿

A wide range of English dishes based on good fresh produce is served in the restaurant of this delightfully situated hotel

Set amid two acres of glorious gardens in one of the most beautiful villages in Wiltshire, peacefully hidden in the lovely Nadder valley and little changed since the 17th century, this charming hotel features a well laid out, award winning restaurant. Accomplished chef and part owner Paul Firmin (a member of the Martell Cordon Bleu Association, an invitation-only association of some 40 of the best chef/patrons outside London) presents a two or three course fixed-price dinner menu which is predominantly English in style, though with some French influence. On a typical day you might enjoy marinated pigeon breasts with Calvados jus and an onion and apple compote, then grilled sea bream with a fresh basil and saffron sauce, and a hot passionfruit soufflé with ginger ice cream; a selection of unpasteurised cheeses is also available. Good, fresh produce forms the basis of all dishes, and it is hoped that eventually the hotel garden (which already provides herbs) will be able to supply many of the vegetables used. A predominantly French wine list offers seven house wines.

Map no: 3 ST93
Tel: 01722 716392

Cost: Fixed-price D £29.50 (3 courses), £32.50, Sunday L £17.50. H/wine £11 ♀ Service inc
Credit cards: 1 2 3 4 5

Menus: Fixed-price dinner, Sunday lunch
Times: Last D 9.30/10.30pm, Last Sun L 2pm

Chef: Paul Firmin, Michael Fox
Proprietors: Paul Firmin, Jonathan Ford, George Ford

Seats: 34. No smoking in dining room
Additional: Children welcome; children's menu/portions; ✪ dishes

Directions: Turn off the B3094 opposite the Black Horse in Teffont, signposted 'Chicksgrove'

WARMINSTER, Bishopstrow House ✿✿

Mellow stone country house hotel offering competent English cooking with many influences

A charming creeper-clad Georgian country house in its own grounds with a river flowing through makes a comfortable place to sojourn and a delightful setting for a meal. Standards of hospitality are extremely high, and the quality of the food has added to this lovely hotel's reputation. The English cooking with many influences is soundly competent, even when the head chef has a night off, and our inspector enjoyed a recent meal which began with macaroni cheese with sun-dried tomato purée and parmesan – faultless home-made pasta but the tomatoes were invisible! Roast pheasant had a delicate, farmed flavour, and came with spicy red cabbage compote and a richly-

Map no: 3 ST84
Tel: 01985 212312

Cost: Alc £31, fixed-price L £15, Sun L£17. H/wine £12.50 ♀ Service exc
Credit cards: 1 2 3 4

Menus: *A la carte*, fixed-price, Sunday lunch
Times: 12.30-Last L 2pm, 7.30-Last D 9pm (9.30pm Sat & Sun)

Chef: Christopher Suter
Proprietors: The Blandy family.
Manager: David Dowden

flavoured jus, but the meal's highlight was a black cherry steamed sponge of light and moist texture served with a generous helping of juicy black cherries and a smooth vanilla sauce. The set-price menu might also offer ravioli of crab and wild salmon, and main dishes like roast chump of lamb with herb crust, or vegetarian options such as bruschetta of chargrilled aubergine, and asparagus and wild mushroom pasta. Service is attentive and efficient.

Seats: 64. No smoking in dining room
Additional: Children permitted; children's menu from 6.30pm; ✪ menu; Vegan/gluten-free dishes on request; pianist at weekends

Directions: From Warminster take B3414 towards Salisbury. Hotel is signposted

CHANNEL ISLANDS
ALDERNEY

ALDERNEY, **Inchalla** ✿✿

☺ *A very hospitable hotel serving carefully cooked food including local fish and seafood*

Customer care is top of the priority list at this delightful hotel, along with the very good cooking for which the chef/patron is renowned. Valerie Willis takes a well-deserved pride in the friendly and helpful service she offers to guests, and no less delight in the food she prepares with chef Kevin Hyde, and which was recently praised by our inspector. An interesting *carte* with a good choice of fish, meat and vegetarian dishes is supplemented by a daily-changing fixed-price menu plus the 'catch of the day', while a large selection of delicious homemade sweets offers a source of temptation on the trolley. Shellfish ravioli was an enjoyable recent starter, with fresh pasta filled with juicy diced Alderney lobster and scallops, in a thick, creamy sauce with chopped tomato, chives and parsley. Six oysters came in their shells on ice with lemon, Tabasco sauce and a vinaigrette dressing, while pan-fried fillet of beef with whole roasted shallots and a rich red wine sauce was served with tasty and well-seasoned vegetables. Bread and butter pudding with a honey-flavoured crust and tasty vanilla flavour was an excellent dessert.

Directions: On the outskirts of St Anne

Le Val, St Anne
Map no: 16
Tel: 01481 823220

Cost: *Alc* £18, fixed-price D £12, Sun L£8.75. H/wine £7 Service inc for non-residents
Credit cards: 1 2 3

Menus: *A la carte*, fixed-price, Sunday lunch

Times: Last L 2pm/D 8.45pm. Closed Sun eve, 2 weeks Xmas

Chef: Valerie Willis
Proprietor: Valerie Willis

Seats: 35. No smoking in restaurant
Additional: Children welcome (over 2 at dinner); children's portions; children's menu on request; ✪ dishes; Vegan/other diets on request

GUERNSEY

CATEL, **Cobo Bay** ❁

☺ *You can eat meat and vegetarian dishes here, but the freshest of seafood dominates the menu - Herm oysters, Guernsey lobster and sea-bass for example. On our inspection meal excellent vegetables, interestingly prepared, were served with poached Guernsey plaice.*

Cost: *Alc* £18.95, fixed-price D £15.95, Sun L £9.95. H/wine £5.95. Service exc. **Credit cards**: 1 3. **Additional**: Children permitted; children's portions; ❻ dishes; other diets on request; live entertainment
Directions: On main Cobo coast road

Cobo
Map no: 16
Tel: 01481 57102
Chef: Christian Eickhoff
Proprietor: David Nussbaumer
Seats: 110. No cigars or pipes. Air conditioned
Times: Midday-last L 2pm, 7pm-last D 9.45pm

CATEL, **La Grand Mare** ❁❁

An innovative modern cuisine with Mediterranean influences is the hallmark of this new purpose-built complex's restaurant.

A major feature of a new purpose-built complex which is part hotel and part time-share – with a new 18-hole golf course being added – this restaurant boasts the combined talents of chef Adrian Jones and manager Vito Scaduto, a past winner of the 'Head Waiter of the Year' award. A modern approach to classical cuisine betrays Mediterranean influence in such innovative dishes as a warm goat's cheese ravioli served with a confit of sun-dried Italian tomatoes and surrounded by a lemon butter sauce infused with tomato oil. Our inspector followed this by fillet of venison with baby onions, pancetta and herb spätzle – the meat perhaps lacking the 'gamey' flavour that comes with hanging, but the sauce flavoursome and well reduced with port wine – then a light, crispy individual blackcurrant tart with a baked cream topping. Don't overlook the possibilities of a hot soufflé (best ordered in advance); candied lemon with banana ice cream and butterscotch sauce is well worth trying! A carefully selected list offers a range of Old and New World wines, some available by the glass.

Directions: On the coast road

Vazon Bay
Map no: 16
Tel: 01481 56576

Cost: *Alc* £24.90, fixed-price L £11.50 (2 courses), £14.95, fixed-price D £19.95. H/wine £9.50 ♀ Service exc
Credit cards: 1 2 3 4 5

Menus: *A la carte*, fixed-price, Sunday lunch

Times: Last L 2pm/D 9.30pm

Chef: Adrian Jones
Proprietor: Simon Vermeulen

Seats: 75. No-smoking area
Additional: Children welcome; children's menu/portions; ❻ menu; Vegan/other diets on request; live entertainment Wed and Fri

PERELLE, **L'Atlantique Hotel** ❁❁

An award-winning hotel restaurant offering imaginative modern English and continental dishes

Flanked by sandy beaches and overlooking Perelle Bay on the west coast road, this modern hotel provides commendable customer care in addition to a lovely seaside setting. The cooking is another considerable strength, and the Green Restaurant has achieved the Guernsey Restaurant of the Year award for 1994. Chef Gary Kenley's imaginative French and modern English dishes often feature locally caught seafood, as

Perelle Bay
Map no: 16
Tel: 01481 64056

Cost: *Alc* £21, fixed-price D £13.90, Sun L£9.50. H/wine £6.75. Service exc
Credit cards: 1 2 3 4

Menus: *A la carte*, fixed-price, Epicure Dinner 3rd Wed & Thu in month, Sunday lunch, bar

well as a good range of meat and game, and these appear on the daily fixed-price menu, a longer *carte*, and a monthly Epicurean menu. There's also a serious vegetarian menu, with choices like Indonesian vegetable casserole with cumin and leek risotto, and French bean, corn and cashew tart. Our inspector selected a meal from the recent prize-winning menu, and started with a well-made poached trout and brill sausage with a tasty fish fumet scented with fennel and Noilly Prat, followed by timbale of baked salmon with an asparagus sabayon and a scallop sauce. A marbled chocolate terrine flavoured with orange and Tia Maria was the meal's highlight.

Directions: Situated on the west coast road

menu
Times: Last D 9.30pm/Sun L 2pm

Chef: Gary Kenley
Manager: Michael Lindley

Seats: 55. No-smoking area; cigars and pipes discouraged
Additional: Children welcome; children's menu/portions; ❶ menu; Vegan/other diets on request

ST MARTIN, **Idlerocks** ❀

☺ *Overlooking the sea, Admirals restaurant at this family-run hotel continues to provide reliable standards of cooking, specialising in local seafood, with a carte and a fixed-price menu.*

Cost: *Alc* from £18, fixed-price D £13.50. H/wine £8.90. Service exc
Credit cards: 1 2 3 4. **Additional:** Children welcome; children's menu/portions; ❶ menu; Vegan/other diets on request
Directions: On cliffs above Jerbourg Point about 10 minutes' drive from St Peter Port and airport

Jerbourg Point
Map no: 16
Tel: 01481 37711
Chef: Kelvin Clarke
Proprietors: Paul and Janice Hamill
Seats: 80. No-smoking in dining room. Air conditioned
Times: Last L 2pm/D 9.30pm

ST MARTIN, **La Barbarie** ❀

A former 16th-century priory, the hotel stands in mature grounds. Chef Stuart Anderson offers good value meals. Local seafood is especially recommended; try a seafood platter (hot or cold), or a loin of lamb with spinach en croûte.

Cost: *Alc* £21.25; fixed-price D £16.50. **Credit cards:** 1 3
Additional: Children welcome; children's portions; children's fun packs; ❶ dishes; no-smoking area
Directions: At the traffic lights in St Martin take the road to Saints Bay; hotel is on the right at the end of Saints Road

Saints Road, Saints Bay
Map no: 16
Tel: 01481 35217
Chef: Stuart Anderson
General Manager: Andrew Coleman
Times: 6.15pm–last D 9.30pm

ST PETER PORT, **The Absolute End** ❀❀

☺ *An award-winning fish restaurant that caters well for meat eaters and vegetarians*

Freshly prepared food, a serious and dedicated approach to cooking, and attentive service all add up to award-winning standards, and it comes as no surprise that this is a recent Guernsey Restaurant of the Year. Seafood is the speciality, and the *carte* lists a great variety of fish dishes as well as several meaty choices and some good vegetarian suggestions. Our inspector opted for a rich fish soup with a full lobster coral flavour and plenty of fishy pieces in it, and turbot cardinale – fresh fillet of poached turbot with a lovely moist texture and taste, served with a creamy lobster velouté with fresh prawns,

Longstore
Map no: 16
Tel: 01481 723822

Cost: *Alc* £19, fixed-price L £11. H/wine £6.50. Service inc
Credit cards: 1 2 3 4 5

Menus: *A la carte,* fixed-price lunch

Times: Last L 2pm/D 10pm. Closed Sun and Jan

Chef: Antonio Folmi

mussels in the shell, and peppers. Vegetables came plain and cooked al dente, while an impressive apple brûlée with flaming Calvados was an attractive dessert. Espresso coffee is available and well worth asking for. Owner Gastone Toffanello is personally involved with looking after customers in the two eating levels of this friendly restaurant, and his careful attention provides the finishing touch to a fulfilling experience. A well-chosen wine list offers some good classified vintage claret and a well-priced house carafe.
Directions: At the far end of Longstore Street, past the harbour

Proprietor: Gastone Toffanello

Seats: 60. No cigars or pipes
Additional: Children permitted; children's portions; ❶ menu; other diets on request

ST PETER PORT, Café du Moulin ❷❷

Unusual dishes and top-rate puddings from a talented chef working in a charming location

It is well worth seeking out this restaurant in a granite-built former granary dating from the 1850s, which nestles in a tiny wooded valley. Robust cooking is offered by talented chef David Mann, whose creative and imaginative modern style is very appealing, shown off to best effect in the evening menus. Puddings and home-made breads are his particular strengths, though everything is of a very pleasing standard. A choice of eight first courses could be offered including hot seafood grill, melon and mixed berry sorbet and an enjoyable spinach and goat's cheese ravioli, featuring home-made pasta. As for main courses, 'Hindle Wakes', a 17th-century Lancashire chicken recipe, rubs shoulders with bourride, a four-fish dish from Provence, along with other exciting choices. Roast loin of lamb was served fairly pink, slightly crusted and with very tasty slices of home-made spicy lamb sausage and a lightly mint-flavoured clarified jus. The assorted stir-fried vegetables with a hoy sin sauce were also very enjoyable. The meal ended on a specially high note with a lemon tart. Wines are well chosen and the service very good.

Directions: Take the Forest road from St Peter Port, turn left at St Peters, signposted 'Torteval', take 3rd right, signposted 'Café du Moulin' and continue for half a mile

Rue du Quarteraine
Map no: 16
Tel: 01481 65944

Cost: Alc £22, fixed-price L £10.50 (2 courses), £13.50. H/wine £7.50. Service exc
Credit cards: 1 3 5

Menus: A la carte, fixed-price, Sunday lunch, bar menu
Times: 12.15pm-last L 1.45pm, 7.15pm-last D 9.30pm. Closed Sun eve, Mon, 2 weeks March

Chefs: David Mann, Guy Moinan
Proprietor: Gina Mann

Seats: 45. No smoking while others are eating
Additional: Children permitted (not under 7 at dinner); children's portions; ❶ menu; Vegan/other diets on request

ST PETER PORT, La Fregate ❷

☺ *The interesting carte and fixed-price menus offer an extensive choice of dishes making good use of fresh local fish. Dishes have included 'Timbale de crustaces à l'Amiral' – scampi, prawns and scallops with mushrooms in a short crust tartelette with a tasty shellfish sauce.*

Cost: Alc £20, fixed-price L £12.50/D £18.00. H/wine £8.50 ♀ No service charge. **Credit cards:** 1 2 3 4 5. **Additional:** No children under 8; ❶ menu; Vegan/other diets on request

Les Cotils
Map no: 16
Tel: 01481 724624
Chef: Oswald Steinsdorfer, Gunter Botzenhardt
Proprietor: Oswald Steinsdorfer
Seats: 80. Air conditioned
Times: Last L 1.30pm/D 9.30pm

ST PETER PORT, La Piazza Ristorante ☻

☺ *Since it opened in 1986, this all-Italian establishment has provided a reliable standard of authentic regional cooking. The restaurant is run by proprietor Gaetano Bianco, while brother and partner Emilio cooks. The daily fresh fish dishes on the blackboard menu are especially recommended.*

Cost: Alc £20. H/wine £5.70. Service exc. **Credit cards:** 1 2 3 5
Additional: No children under 6; children's portions; ❶ dishes; Vegan/other diets on request

Under the Arch, Trinity Square
Map no: 16
Tel: 01481 725085
Chef: Emilio Bianco
Proprietor: Gaetano Bianco
Seats: 54
Times: Last L 2pm/D 10pm. Closed Sun, 24 Dec-23 Jan

ST PETER PORT, Le Nautique ☻

☺ *This well-known restaurant overlooking the harbour has been serving traditional French food for over 33 years, the last 11 under the direction of chef Vito Garau. His menu, in French, relies mainly on locally caught seafood. Expert flambé cooking is a feature.*

Cost: Alc £19.50, fixed-price L/D £16.50. H/wine £7. Service inc
Credit cards: 1 2 3 4 5. **Additional:** No children under 5; ❶ dishes
Directions: Overlooking marina and Castle Cornet

Quay Steps
Map no: 16
Tel: 01481 721714
Chef: Vito Garau
Proprietor: Carlo Graziani
Seats: 68. No cigars or pipes in dining room
Times: Midday-Last L 2pm, Last D 10pm. Closed 25 Dec-10Jan

ST PETER PORT, St Pierre Park ☻☻

Elegant style and imaginative cuisine are the hallmarks of this hotel's neo-classical restaurant.

Mecca for the bon viveur, the Victor Hugo restaurant with its neo-classical decor and sumptuous furnishings also boasts modern air-conditioning. Live piano entertainment is provided each evening, and guests can enjoy a pre-dinner drink in an adjacent cocktail bar. New chef Christian Gilbert offers *carte* and fixed-price menus of contemporary British/European dishes (with flambé recipes still a speciality); a tasty seafood pancake soufflé filled with crab and lobster meat in a light, creamy sauce might perhaps precede beautifully tender lamb en croûte with a fine mushroom duxelle and good jus sauce. Vegetarian dishes range from Stilton and walnuts in a cheese sauce sprinkled with basil to the elaborate Bourguignonne of fresh mushrooms, sautéed in red wine with pearl onions and Quorn then served on a crown of risotto. Youngsters are welcome, though there are no special facilities but a children's menu is available by arrangement. Service is professionally efficient, and an extensive wine list details some fine vintage clarets and reputable labels from France and the New World.

Directions: 1 mile from the centre of St Peter Port on main route to the west coast

Rohais
Map no: 16
Tel: 01481 728282

Cost: Alc from £20, fixed-price L £9.95 (2 courses), £11.95, fixed-price D £16.95. H/wine £9.25 ♀ Service exc
Credit cards: 1 2 3 4 5

Menus: A la carte, fixed-price lunch and dinner, Sunday lunch, business lunch
Times: 12.15–Last L 2.15pm, 7pm–Last D 10pm. Closed Sat lunch, Sun eve

Chef: John Cruickshank
Proprietor: Tom C Castledine

Seats: 70. No-smoking area by arrangement; no cigars or pipes in dining room. Air conditioned
Additional: No children under 7; children's portions; ❶ menu; Vegan/other diets on request; piano music every evening

HERM

HERM, White House ☺

☺ *Chef Chris Walder offers good-value fixed price menus, with Herm oysters and other local seafood to the fore. Other dishes enjoyed here include medallions of beef fillet, pan-fried and set on celeriac pancake; vegetarians are offered delicacies such as a filo nest of stir-fried vegetables, fruit and nuts.*

Cost: Fixed-price L £10.50/D £15.25 (£16.25 Sat). H/wine £6.95 ♀ No service charge .**Credit cards**: 1 3. **Additional**: Children permitted (not under 8 at dinner); children's menu; children's portions at lunch; ❂ menu; other diets on request
Directions: Only hotel on island

Island of Herm
Map no: 16
Tel: 01481 722159
Chef: Chris Walder
Proprietors: Michael Hester
Seats: 118. No smoking in dining room
Times: 12.30-Last L 2pm, Last D 9.30pm. Closed Oct-Mar

JERSEY

GOREY, Jersey Pottery ☺☺

☺ *A popular restaurant specialising in local seafood*

The conservatory restaurant should stay as popular as ever – but beware the heat on sunny days – under new chef Anthony Dorris (from the Ritz). The style is modern British; local seafood is a speciality but our inspector also enjoyed tender duck, and found the crème brûlée superb. Service is excellent to. Our inspectors recently awarded a well-deserved second rosette for the quality cuisine

Seats: 300. No-smoking area. No pipes
Additional: Children welcome; children's menu/portions; ❂ menu; Vegan/other diets on request
Directions: In Gorey village, well signposted from main coast road

Gorey Village
Map no: 16
Tel: 01534 851119

Cost: Alc £21. H/wine £9.80 ♀ Service inc
Credit cards: 1 2 3 4 5

Menu: *A la carte*
Times: 9am-Last L 4.30pm. Closed Sun, 10 days Xmas

Chef: Anthony Dorris
Proprietor: Colin Jones.
Manager: Robert Jones

GROUVILLE, Hotel Kalamunda ☺

☺ *A modern hotel near the historic village of Gorey where a range of menus offer a selection of interesting dishes. Local fish is always used by Chef Arwell Williams to produce moules marinière or Dover sole and king prawns with a white wine sauce.*

Cost: Alc £20, fixed-price L £9.50/D £10.90. H/wine £5 ♀ Service exc. **Credit cards**: 1 3. **Additional**: Children welcome; children's menu/portions; ❂ menu; Vegan/other diets on request; live entertainment
Directions: On the seaward side of Gorey village

Gorey Village
Map no 16
Tel: 01534 856656
Chef: Arwell Williams
Proprietor: John Rice
Seats: 60/100. No-smoking area. No cigars or pipes
Times: Midday-Last L 2pm, Last D 10pm

L'ETACQ, Lobster Pot ❀❀

☺ *Overlooking St Ouen's Bay, this hotel restaurant has a reputation for good lobster and fish, making it popular with locals, although meat, poultry and game are also well represented on the extensive carte.*

Cost: Fixed-price L £9.95/D £14.50. H/wine £8.25. Service exc
Credit cards: 1 2 3 4 5. **Additional:** Children welcome; children's portions; ❂ menu; Vegan/other diets on request
Directions: From the main road from St Helier, turn left at St Ouen Parish Hall, then left onto the B64, and branch right onto B35

Map no: 16
Tel: 01534 482888
Chef: Gilbert Heliou
Proprietor: Gerald A Howe
Seats: 100. Air conditioned
Times: 12.30pm-Last L 2pm, 7.30-Last D 10pm

ROZEL BAY, Château La Chaire ❀❀

Local seafood and home-grown herbs are used to good effect in the modern British dishes served in this attractive restaurant.

On fine summer days you can lunch al fresco here, overlooking a quiet valley from this fine hotel's terraced hillside garden as you eat, and the panelled restaurant – candlelit in the evening – now has a conservatory extension reserved for non-smokers. Chef David Tilbury offers a range of menus, both fixed-price and *carte*, together with some flambé dishes cooked at the table. His cuisine reflects the modern British style, making good use of local seafood and home-grown herbs in recipes adapted to attract both guests and a local clientele. Notable luncheon dishes include duck confit with rocket and a twice-baked goat's cheese soufflé with a light beurre blanc sauce, while for dinner you might choose a starter of chicken and fennel terrine followed by fresh sea-bass served on a very tasty fricassée of flat field mushrooms garnished with salsa verde and courgette noodles, then a traditional sticky toffee pudding with a good butterscotch sauce and crème fraîche. A wine list of 136 vintage bins representing both Old and New Worlds offers five good house wines .

Directions: Take first left by Rozel Bay Inn on entering the village. Hotel is 100yds on right

Map no: 16
Tel: 01534 863354

Cost: Alc £28.50, fixed-price L £11.75 (2 courses), £14.25, fixed-price D £19.50. H/wine £8.90 ♀ service exc
Credit cards: 1 2 3 4 5

Menus: A la carte, fixed-price, Sunday lunch, bar menu

Times: Midday-Last L 2pm, 7pm-Last D 10pm

Chef: David Tilbury
Proprietor: Alan Winch

Seats: 65. No-smoking area
Additional: No children under 7; children's portions; ❂ dishes; Vegan/other diets on request

ST BRELADE, Hotel L'Horizon ❀❀

However elegant or informal you want your meal to be, one of this popular seafront hotel's three restaurants can oblige

The joys of eating should never pall here, for this popular hotel leading directly on to a sandy beach offers three very different options - the informal Brasserie and more sophisticated Crystal Room providing alternatives to the intimate Star Grill. All maintain high standards of cuisine, however, chef Peter Marek and his team making good seasonal use of locally caught fish and fine Jersey vegetables, the latter served slightly crisp to retain their full flavour. Seafood bisque with a hint of Cognac might be followed by roast cannon of lamb stuffed with asparagus and set on a rich redcurrant sauce; a choice of fresh

St Brelade's Bay
Map no: 16
Tel: 01534 43101

Cost: Alc £30, fixed-price L £14.50. H/wine £10.75
Credit cards: 1 2 3 5

Menus: A la carte dinner, fixed-price lunch, Sunday lunch

Times: 12.30-Last L 2.15pm, Last D 10.15pm

Chef: Peter Marek

480 JERSEY CHANNEL ISLANDS

fruit or cheese offers an alternative to more elaborate desserts, and vegetarian options are tempting – perhaps a timbale of wild mushrooms placed on a bed of spinach with cheese and lentil sauce, or layers of aubergine, courgette, asparagus, peppers and onions all covered with a cheese sauce and served gratinée. Most of the wines on an extensive wine list are French, but there is a good range of prices, so everyone should find something to suit taste and pocket.

Directions: Overlooking St Brelade's Bay

Proprietors: Arcadian International. Restaurant Manager: Augusto Travaglini

Seats: 50. No cigars or pipes in restaurant. Air conditioned
Additional: No children under 12; ♥ dishes; Vegan/other diets on request

ST HELIER, Grand ❀

Victoria's is a restaurant in the grand style with mirrors, chandeliers and marble pillars offering a splendid carte with flambé and a fixed-price Menu dégustation. Our inspector was in the pink with a fish soup and a suprême of chicken with rose wine, pink peppercorns and tarragon sauce

Cost: Alc £28, fixed-price L £14.75/D £21.50. H/wine £10. Service inc. **Credit cards**: 1 2 3 4. **Additional**: Children permitted; children's menu/portions; ♥ menu; other diets on request; live entertainment
Directions: On outskirts of town, overlooking Elizabeth Castle

The Esplanade
Map no: 16
Tel: 01534 22301
Chef: Adrian Doolan
Proprietors: De Vere. Manager: Timothy Brooke
Seats: 140. No-smoking area; no cigars or pipes. Air conditioned
Times: Last L 2.15pm/D 10pm. Closed Sun eve

ST HELIER, Pomme d'Or Hotel ❀

☺ Well located in the centre of the town, this family-owned hotel offers a choice of eating places. Our inspector dined in La Petite Pomme, beginning his enjoyable meal with a seafood mousse wrapped in smoked salmon. Following this were tasty fillets of beef in a rich Stilton and port wine sauce.

Cost: Fixed-price L £12.50/D £15.50. H/wine £5.50 ♀ Service inc
Credit cards: 1 2 3 4 5. **Additional**: Children welcome; children's portions; ♥ dishes; Vegan/other diets on request
Directions: Adjacent to main bus station

Liberation Square
Map no: 16
Tel: 01534 878644
Chef: Henri Fauconnier
Proprietors: Pomme d'Or Hotel. Manager: Italo Miorin
Seats: 170
Times: Midday-Last L 2.30pm (2pm Sat), 7pm-Last D 10pm

ST SAVIOUR, Longueville Manor ❀❀❀

A good choice of modern English menus is offered in the panelled medieval dining room of this 13th-century manor house

A wisteria-clad 13th-century stone-built manor house, Longueville is set in 40 acres of beautiful grounds, including an ornamental lake. The hotel has been run by the Lewis family for over 35 years, and they play an active role in the provision of skilful service, ably supported by a team of willing staff.
 A selection of menus is offered in the panelled, medieval dining room, and a separate room provided for those who wish to smoke. There is a light lunch and snack menu, and a full lunch menu. At dinner a short fixed-price four-course menu is presented in addition to the comprehensive carte. A vegetarian set meal is available at £25, comprising a soufflé, consommé, and a main course such as globe artichoke filled with a

Map no: 16
Tel: 01534 25501

Cost: Alc £35.25, fixed-price L £18, fixed-price D £28.50. H/wine £8 ♀ Service inc
Credit cards: 1 2 3 4 5

Menus: A la carte, fixed-price, Sunday lunch, bar menu

Times: 12.30pm-Last L 2pm, 7.30pm-Last D 9.30pm

Chef: Andrew Baird
Proprietor: Malcolm Lewis

casserole of woodland mushrooms and glazed quail eggs, followed by a choice of desserts. The chef has also prepared a Tasting menu of eight courses plus coffee and petits fours for £50, for a full table only.

At a spring meal our inspector sampled suprême of brill served with oysters and ginger in a creamy chive sauce. This was followed by rack of new season lamb, which was a little too young to have any great lamb flavour but was enhanced by the accompanying Provençal jus and ratatouille. Most of the herbs are home grown, and chef Andrew Baird is particular in his selection of fresh produce. Vegetables are carefully chosen to complement each dish – dauphinois potatoes with the lamb, and green beans, mange touts and aubergine on a side dish. Desserts include hot puddings, and 'three flavours of lemon' comprising a lemon soufflé, lemon tart and lemon sorbet with a good crème anglaise.

The wine list, predominantly French has a good selection of champagnes and mature vintages of Burgundy and claret.

Seats: 65. No-smoking area. Air conditioned
Additional: No children under 7; ✿ menu; Vegan/other diets on request

Directions: From St Helier take A3 to Gorey. The hotel is 3/4 mile on the left

SARK, **Stocks Island** ✿

☺ *Getting here – by boat from Guernsey, then by tractor-drawn bus, and foot! – is an adventure which may well whet your appetite for the seafood specialities of the hotel's bistro's light meals and for the interesting carte and five-course fixed-price menus of the Cider Press restaurant.*

Island of Sark
Map no: 16
Tel: 01481 832001
Chef: Peter Gottgens
Proprietor: Paul Armorgie
Seats: 70. No-smoking area; no cigars or pipes in dining room
Times: Midday-Last L 2.30pm, 7pm-Last D 9pm. Closed 1 Oct-1 Apr

Cost: Alc £19.50, fixed-price L £10.50/D £16.95. H/wine £5 ♀ No service charge. **Credit cards**: 1 2 3 4. **Additional**: Children permitted (must be over 8 at dinner); children's menu/portions; ✿ dishes; other diets on request
Directions: tractor-drawn bus from harbour, then 15-minute walk

ISLE OF MAN

DOUGLAS, **Mount Murray** ✿

A recently opened luxury hotel and leisure complex where Michael Wilkinson prepares dishes with precision and care for the main restaurant. Starters include crab salad or garlic prawns, and for a main course, chicken and avocado pear in puff pastry with a cream and garlic sauce.

Santon
Map no: 6 SC37
Tel: 01624 661111

NORTHERN IRELAND
ANTRIM

PORTRUSH, **Ramore Restaurant** ●●

☺ *A revamped style of operation but still with superb cuisine has brought this lively restaurant back to popularity*

A change in direction has meant packed tables at this waterside restaurant overlooking the harbour. The longer opening hours, more realistic pricing together with chef George McAlpin's reliable and uncomplicated cooking has proved a winner and brought his band of loyal followers back in droves. Menus are less adventurous but quality ingredients remain and the emphasis on seafood has not been lost. The interior, with its impressive black and white colour scheme and open plan kitchen, allows diners to view the young team at work. Music tends to be loud and may not be to everyone's taste but it still allows private conversation. The *carte* changes every three or four months with a reasonable choice at each stage plus a range of daily blackboard specials. A successful inspection meal from the blackboard started with delicious baby scallops lightly grilled in garlic and parsley butter, followed by tender, well-flavoured home-smoked brill with a somewhat heavy, but delicately flavoured cream and chive sauce. To finish, a delicious choux pastry mille-feuille, with fresh cream, strawberries and chocolate sauce.

Directions: Situated beside the harbour

The Harbour
Map no: 1 C6
Tel: 01265 824313

Cost: Alc £19. H/wine £7.50 ♀ Service exc
Credit cards: 1 3

Menus: *A la carte*

Times: 6.30pm-Last D 10.30pm. Closed Sun, Mon

Chef: George McAlpin
Proprietors: George and Jane McAlpin, John and Joy Caithness

Seats: 85. Air conditioned
Additional: Children permitted; ♥ dishes; Vegan/other diets on request

ARMAGH

WARINGSTOWN, **Grange Restaurant** ●

A 17th-century, former planter's house where chef and proprietor Robert Lynn cooks straightforward tasty dishes based on local produce like best end of Antrim lamb with walnuts, beef with port, Guinness and pickled walnuts, or wild Irish salmon with parsley butter.

Cost: Alc £22
Additional: Children permitted; children's portions; ♥ dishes
Directions: On the main road in the village

Main Street
Map no: 1 D5
Tel: 01762 881989
Chef: Robert Lynn
Proprietors: The Lynn Brothers
Times: Last L 1.45pm/Last D 9.30pm. Closed Sun eve, Mon, 2 weeks mid Jul

BELFAST, **Roscoff** ●●●

Good value French cooking with Italian, Asian, Californian and Irish influences, in a strikingly modern restaurant

Probably the best food in Northern Ireland is served at this bright, contemporary restaurant. Chef-patron Paul Rankin

7 Lesley House, Shaftesbury Square
Map no: 1 D5
Tel: 01232 331532

Cost: Alc £28; fixed-price lunch £14.50; fixed–price dinner

combines his modern French style of cooking with Californian and other international influences with the natural flair, imagination and attention to detail that have brought him to prominence. Not surprisingly, Roscoff is always busy with a large loyal following, and Paul Rankin's series of TV programmes for RTE as well as the sous chef Jane McMeekin's award of 'Young Chef of the Year' by the Restaurateurs Association of Great Britain, can only boost its popularity. Lunch, with its value-for-money fixed-price menu, has business people coming in droves, so you are well advised to book. In the evening the wider choice fixed-price menu, available Monday to Thursday, attracts a more varied clientele, so advance booking is again essential. The staff, kitted out in white aprons and multi-coloured ties and waistcoats, are friendly and willing to please.

The interesting *carte* and separate vegetarian menu are always available. An enjoyable inspection meal, selected from the *carte*, began with a gratin of prawns with beautifully cooked penne pasta, a delicious lobster cream sauce and a garnish of spinach. The main course, tender rack of lamb with a parsley and mustard crust, served with tasty haricot beans, mixed vegetables and the lamb jus, provided a good combination of honest flavours and is well recommended. To finish, the warm chestnut and Amaretto soufflé, though a little lop-sided, was exceptionally light and the chocolate sauce was the ideal accompaniment.

The comprehensive wine list is drawn from most major wine-producing countries, with Spain, Australia, New Zealand, and California well represented. Prices are very reasonable.

Directions: On entering the city, the restaurant is on the left side of Shaftesbury Square, just at the start of Great Victoria Street

£19.50. H/wine £11.25 ♀
Service exc
Credit cards: 1 2 3 4

Menus: *A la carte*, fixed-price lunch and dinner

Times: 12.15pm-Last L 2.15pm, 6.30pm-Last D10.15pm. Lunch not served Sat. Closed Sun, Xmas, Easter Mon & 12 Jul

Chef: Paul Rankin
Proprietors: Paul and Jeanne Rankin

Seats: 75. No-smoking area. Air conditioned
Additional: Children welcome; children's portions; ❻ dishes; Vegan/other diets on request

DOWN

ANNALONG, **Glassdrumman Lodge** ❀❀

A genial welcome and interesting dining awaits at this delightful hotel offering something a little different...

Well-deserving of the recognition it is now receiving, this small quality hotel offers first-class food and service. A former farmhouse, it is dramatically set between the sea and the magnificent Mourne Mountains and its appealing features include a stone fireplace with log burner and a lounge full of books and flowers. The restaurant has been enlarged, so non-residents can now, with advance booking, join house guests to sample chef Stephen Webb's innovative country cooking - based on fresh ingredients, many of which are produced on the adjoining farm. In addition to the communal refectory table, more intimate seating is available in the cosy extension. Dinner is served at 8pm and guests may choose either the English or the French menu, each offering four courses (no choice, although one may mix dishes from both). An unusual touch is the recommended glass of

85 Mill Road
Map no: 1 D5
Tel: 013967 68451

Cost: *Alc* from £25; fixed–price dinner £25. H/wine £10 ♀
Service exc
Credit cards: 1 2 3 4 5

Menus: *A la carte*, fixed-price dinner, pre-theatre

Times: Last D 8pm

Chef: Stephen Webb
Proprietor: Joan Hall

Seats: 50. No pipes or cigars
Additional: Children permitted;

wine served with each course. Our meal began with a light soup of local sea and shellfish, with a main course of baked salmon, moist, tender and full of flavour and concluded with home-made apple pie and ice cream, all served by friendly local staff.

Directions: From Newcastle take A2 coastal road to Kilkeel. 1 mile after Glassdrumman House, take first right at the pub into Mill Road. The Lodge is 1 mile on the right

HOLYWOOD, Culloden Hotel ✿

☺ *Some fine French-style dishes are prepared by the chef for the Culloden Hotel's Mitre restaurant. Most of the world's main grape-growing areas are featured on the well-balanced wine list. The Cultra Inn in the grounds is better for less formal dining.*

Cost: Alc £20, fixed-price L £14, £17/D £17, £19. H/wine £8.50. Service exc. **Credit cards:** 1 2 3 4. **Additional:** Children welcome; children's portions; ♥ menu; Vegan/other diets on request
Directions: On main A2 (Belfast-Bangor) on south shores of Belfast Lough 6 miles from city centre

children's portions; ♥ dishes; Vegan/other diets on request

Map no: 1 D5
Tel: 01232 425223
Chef: Paul McKnight
Proprietors: Hastings. Manager: Philip J Weston
Seats: 140. No-smoking area
Times: Last L 2.30pm/D 9.45pm (10.30pm Sun). Closed Sat L, 24-25 Dec

SCOTLAND
BORDERS

KELSO, Sunlaws House ✿✿

☺ *Grand surroundings for accomplished Scottish-French cooking with particularly good value fixed-price lunches*

This fine baronial mansion, owned by the Duke of Roxburghe, lies in 200 acres of woodland and gardens on the banks of the River Tweed. Blazing log fires in season create a welcoming atmosphere and staff are friendly and attentive to the hotel's clientele of shooters, fishers and tourists; non-residents must make advance restaurant reservations. The dinner menu, though not extensive, is carefully chosen and while cooking is in the modern style, care is taken to ensure that hearty appetites are satisfied. Past first courses have included pressed baby leeks with walnut and tomato oil, rich beef broth and, our inspector's choice, mille-feuille of venison with oyster mushrooms and bacon, visually very impressive, accompanied by oriental-flavour vegetables. This was followed by pan-fried fillet of Angus beef, a cracking piece of meat cooked exactly to taste, cutting easily, succulent and flavoursome. Baked loin of lamb in puff pastry and a brace of stuffed quails have been other recent main course choices. Exotic puddings could include a soufflé or fruit dish and the wine list is outstandingly good.

Directions: On the A698, 3 miles south of Kelso

Heiton, Roxburghshire
Map no: 12 NT73
Tel: 01573 450331

Chef: David Bates
Proprietor: The Duke of Roxburghe

Seats: 60. No smoking in dining room

Times: Last L 2pm/D 9.30pm

Cost: Alc £14, fixed-price D £23 (2 courses), £27. H/wine £11 ♀ No service charge.
Credit cards: 1 2 3 4.

Additional: Children welcome; children's portions/menu; ♥ dishes/Vegan/other diets on request

PEEBLES, Cringletie House ❀

☺ *A beautiful red-sandstone Scottish Borders baronial home offers carefully prepared and imaginative dishes. Good use is made of the walled kitchen garden for fresh vegetables. Main courses include medallions of venison with whisky cream sauce or pork stuffed with leeks.*

Peeblesshire
Map no: 11 NT24
Tel: 01721 730233
Proprietor: S L Maguire
Times: Last L 1.45pm/D 8.30pm. Closed Jan, Feb

Cost: Alc L £5.50 (1 course), Sun L £14, fixed-price D £24.50. H/wine £5.75 (half litre). Service inc. **Credit cards:** 1 3.
Additional: Children welcome; children's portions; ✿ dishes; Vegan/other diets on request. No smoking in dining room
Directions: 2.5 miles north of Peebles on A703

SWINTON, Wheatsheaf ❀

☺ *A country inn and restaurant where the Reids have built up a reputation for good food, with the emphasis on fresh Scottish produce. Our inspector recommended the chicken liver and brandy pâté, which could be followed by medallions of Scotch beef fillet in oyster and mushroom sauce.*

Berwickshire
Map no: 12 NT84
Tel: 01890 860257
Chef: Alan Reid
Proprietors: Alan and Julie Reid
Seats: 26, 18. No pipes or cigars
Times: Last L 2pm/D 9.30pm. Closed Mon; 2 weeks Feb, last week Oct

Cost: Alc £15.50. H/wine £7.95. Service exc
Credit cards: 1 3. **Additional:** Children permitted (over 7 after 7.30pm); children's portions; ✿ dishes; Vegan/other diets on request
Directions: On B6461 between Kelso and Berwick-upon-Tweed

CENTRAL

ABERFOYLE, Braeval Mill ❀❀❀

An attractive converted mill, where the well-balanced set menu is based on carefully cooked quality produce

Stirlingshire
Map no: 11 NN50
Tel: 01877 382711

Cost: Fixed-price dinner £27.50, Sun lunch £18.50. H/wine from £12 ♀ Service exc
Credit cards: 1 3

Nick Nairn loves food, and it shows in his dedicated pursuit of quality produce and its sympathetic treatment. Nine years ago he converted an old mill, close to Aberfoyle, into what is now an appealing small country restaurant, with exposed stone walls, flagstone floors and neatly laid tables. A cast-iron stove in the middle of the room provides welcome heat on chilly winter evenings, and the greeting, usually by Jean Bond, is always warm. There is no written menu, the set four-course *carte* being verbally recited by Jean. A telephone call in advance will inform guests of the likely dishes, and vegetarians can be accommodated by prior arrangement.

The format does not vary a great deal, beginning with tasty canapés, such as a deliciously smooth chicken liver parfait with liquid Cumberland sauce, followed by a very good home-made soup of intense flavour and colour – perhaps pea, lettuce and mint or wild mushroom. Pasta, made with dexterity, is a favoured intermediate course. It may be combined with fish or,

Menus: Fixed-price dinner, Sunday lunch

Times: Last Sun L 1.30pm, Last D 9.30pm. Closed Mon, 1 week Feb, Nov, May/June

Chef: Nick Nairn
Proprietors: Nick and Fiona Nairn

Seats: 34. No cigars or pipes
Additional: Children permitted

as on one stormy spring evening, guinea fowl and some warming pesto and olive oil. Main courses also often feature fish. At one meal a medley of wonderfully fresh and accurately cooked salmon, monkfish, langoustine and mussels was greatly enjoyed by our inspector. Saucing has a light touch and herbs are much in evidence, but nothing is allowed to overwhelm the main ingredient. A choice is offered at the pudding stage, usually three or four items such as crème brûlée, Armagnac parfait with Earl Grey tea syrup and prunes, or a wickedly rich hot chocolate soufflé with chocolate sauce. A selection of largely British unpasteurised cheeses is an attractive alternative.

The wine list offers an excellent choice from a variety of countries, without being overpowering. There is an interesting selection of house wines selling at £12-£15 a bottle and a wide range of half-bottles.

Directions: At junction of A81 (Callander/Stirling Road) and A821, left to Callander, restaurant 200 yards on left

(no very young children); ✪ dishes; other diets on request

BRIDGE OF ALLAN, Royal Hotel ✪

A popular business hotel in the main street of this small town. In the Rivendell restaurant Stuart Harrow produces British cooking in the modern style such as provençale of baked mushrooms and roast venison flavoured with Madeira.

Cost: Alc £23, fixed-price D £15.50   **Credit cards:** 1 2 3 4
Additional: ✪ dishes on request
Directions: Half-way down Bridge of Allan High Street

Henderson Street
Stirlingshire
Map no: 11 NS79
Tel: 01786 832284
Chef: Stuart Harrow
Proprietor: Mr A Scholar
Seats: 70
Times: Last L 2.30pm/D 9.30pm

CALLANDER, Lubnaig Hotel ✪

☺ *This delightful small hotel is a good base from which to explore the area. The food is prepared by Susan Low with fresh ingredients to make enjoyable dishes including bacon, prawn and cream cheese pâté as a starter and jugged pheasant, Burgundy beef or steak and pigeon pie as a main course.*

Cost: Residents only. Fixed-price D £10 (2 courses), £15, £16.50. H/wine £8.75 ♀ Service exc.   **Credit cards:** 1 3   **Additional:** Children over 7 welcome; children's portions. ✪ dishes on request
Directions: Through Callander to western outskirts. Right to Leny Feus

Leny Feus
Perthshire
Map no: 11 NN60
Tel: 01877 330376
Chef: Mrs Susan Low
Proprietors: Mr and Mrs Low
Seats: 20. No smoking in dining room
Times: Last D 8.30pm. Lunch not served. Closed mid Oct-Apr
Credit cards: 1 3

CALLANDER, Roman Camp ✪✪

Imaginative modern Scottish cooking in a charming old manor house set in delightful grounds

An attractive candlelit restaurant under a richly painted 16th-century ceiling is the marvellous setting for some enjoyable modern cooking. Chef Simon Burns achieves wonderful results with his imaginative treatment of the finest available fresh Scottish ingredients. Guests can opt either for the 'tasting menu' which offers five courses with no choice, or a short *carte*, and there is also a vegetarian menu with half-a-dozen or so

Perthshire
Map no: 11 NN60
Tel: 01877 330003

Cost: Alc £37.50; fixed-price lunch £13.50 (2 courses), £18; fixed price dinner £32. H/wine £12 ♀ Service exc
Credit cards: 1 2 3 4 5

Menus: *A la carte,* fixed-price lunch and dinner, Sunday lunch

choices which can be taken either as starters or main courses. Our inspector began with an enjoyable pan-fried salmon dish set on a bed of pasta biscuit with a delicious soy and shallot vinaigrette, followed by a warming vegetable broth with toasted oatmeal. Roast best end of lamb came moist and tender pink, with a delicate wild mushroom timbale, garlicky dauphinoise potatoes, and a very competent truffle and mint sauce. A sorbet was declined, but room was found for an iced praline parfait on a raspberry purée decorated with fresh raspberries and strawberries, and strong filter coffee and home-made petits fours rounded off the meal.

Directions: In town centre, turn left down a driveway at the east end of main street

Times: Midday-Last L 2pm, 7pm-Last D 9pm

Chef: Simon Burns
Proprietors: Eric and Marion Brown
Seats: 40. No smoking in the dining room

Additional: Children permitted (over 5 at dinner); children's portions/menu; ◑ menu; Vegan/other diets on request.

DUNBLANE, Cromlix House ❋❋

A homely but elegant hotel serenely set in 3,000 acres, serving beautifully cooked produce from its own estate

A fine Scottish mansion furnished and decorated as an Edwardian family home offers all the expected comforts, plus the added attraction of its own beautiful chapel. Set on a 3,000-acre estate, much of the produce used in the kitchen is home-bred or grown, including trout, salmon, game, beef and Jacob's lamb. The results of Stephen Robertson's handling of these fresh quality ingredients can be sampled on his fixed-price lunch and dinner menus, and a serious vegetarian list. Decisions are difficult even with only two choices to a course, and our inspector was pleased to have plumped for terrine of chicken liver and foie gras with plenty of garlic flavour, followed by very dark and well-hung beef fillet in a pastry lattice, moistened with Madcira sauce. Vegetables were not disappointing, and warm lemon tart with sauce anglaise had a subtle citrus flavour. Other choices might include collops of venison topped with a leek and garlic crust on a juniper berry and orange sauce, while vegetarians are offered dishes like lemon and parsley pancakes filled with asparagus spears, or a cabbage parcel with onion and mushroom stuffing on a leek cream sauce.

Directions: 4 miles north of Dunblane. From A9 take turning to Kinbuck, through village, 2nd left after small bridge

Kinbuck
Perthshire
Map no: 11 NN70
Tel: 01786 822125

Cost: Fixed-price lunch £17 (2 courses), £24; fixed-price dinner £35. H/wine £11. Service exc
Credit cards: 1 2 3 4

Menus: Fixed-price lunch and dinner, Sunday lunch
Times: 12.30pm-Last L 1.15pm, 7pm-Last D 8.30pm. Sat and Sun lunch only served Oct-Mar. Closed mid Jan-mid Feb

Chef: Stephen Robertson
Proprietors: David and Ailsa Assenti

Seats: 40, 22. No smoking in dining rooms
Additional: Children permitted (over 8 at dinner); children's portions; ◑ menu; Vegan/other diets on request

PORT OF MENTEITH, Lake Hotel ❋

☺ *An old-established hotel occupying a delightful lakeside position where chef and manager Mark Riva produces innovative dishes such as chilled apricot and champagne soup or more conventionally, saddle of lamb with rosemary and a hint of garlic.*

Cost: Alc £22, fixed-price L £14.95/D £20.90. H/wine £8. No service charge. **Credit cards:** 1 3. **Additional:** Children permitted; children's portions; ◑ menu; other diets on request. Live entertainment in winter
Directions: From Glasgow, take the A81 to Aberfoyle. Just before Aberfoyle, turn right onto the A873 to Port of Monteith.

Perthshire
Map no: 11 NN50
Tel: 01877 385258
Chef: Mark Riva
Proprietor: Douglas Little
Seats: 30. No smoking in dining room
Times: Last L 2pm/D 8.30pm

STIRLING, Stirling Highland 🌸🌸

Spittal Street
Stirlingshire
Map no: 11 NS79
Tel: 01786 475444

Modern Scottish cooking with a French influence, and an emphasis on good saucing and dazzling desserts

High above the town of Stirling and close to the famous castle, this imposing hotel has been cleverly converted from the old high school. There's a strong Scottish flavour to the cooking, but chef Kieran Grant is also influenced by modern French cuisine, and the results are extremely enjoyable. The *carte* and fixed-price menus are well balanced between fish, meat and game, and there is a separate list of interesting vegetarian choices: parsnip and apple soup might be followed by gateau of grilled aubergine and courgette layered with braised cabbage and an oriental sauce. Home-made fresh ravioli filled with queen scallop and salmon was full of flavour but still enhanced by a fishy Noilly Prat sauce at a recent meal. Good saucing again lifted an already delicious breast of duck with sautéed wild mushrooms – this time a nicely reduced rosemary one. The chosen dessert, layered orange and chocolate parfait was a *pièce de resistance* – perfectly textured parfait with distinctive orange and chocolate flavours, attractively presented with a spun dome and a mix of exotic fruits.

Cost: *Alc* £30; fixed-price lunch £10.50; fixed-price dinner £19.75. H/wine £9.50. Service inc
Credit cards: 1 2 3 4 5

Menus: *A la carte*, fixed-price lunch and dinner, Sunday lunch

Times: Midday-Last L 2pm, 7pm-Last D 9.30pm. Closed Saturday lunch and Sunday dinner

Chef: Kieran Grant
Proprietor: Scottish Highland.
Manager: Chris Hansen

Seats: 70. No smoking in dining room

Additional: Children welcome; children's portions; ◊ dishes; Vegan/other diets on request. Entertainment most Fri, Sat nights
Directions: Follow signs for Stirling Castle. Spittal St goes to castle

STRATHYRE, Creagan House 🌸

Map no: 11 NN51
Tel: 01877 384638
Chef: Gordon A Gunn
Proprietors: Gordon and Cherry Gunn
Seats: 15. No smoking in dining room
Times: Last L 1pm/D 8.30pm. Closed Feb, 1 week Oct

Patron Gordon Gunn combines French and Scottish cooking traditions in his original, creative dishes at this family-run former farmhouse, where guests are served generous portions at refectory tables in the baronial dining hall

Cost: *Alc* £21, Sunday lunch £14.25, fixed-price dinner £15.50. H/wine £8 ♀ Service exc. **Credit cards:** 1 2 3
Additional: Children permitted (over 10 at dinner); children's portions; other diets on request
Directions: 0.25 miles north of the village on A84

DUMFRIES & GALLOWAY

AUCHENCAIRN, Collin House 🌸🌸🌸

Castle Douglas
Kirkcudbrightshire
Map no: 11 NX75
Tel: 01556 640292

A superbly located restaurant offering carefully considered, well-prepared dishes from a short set menu

As Collin House's brochure points out, many people think Scotland starts at Loch Lomond. If this is why Dumfries and Galloway is still so tranquil and unspoilt, don't let them near

Cost: Fixed-price dinner £26. H/wine from £6.75 ♀ Service inc
Credit cards: 1 3

the road atlas. The listed house is nearly 250 years old and overlooks the Solway Firth and the Cumbrian Hills, a view that comes free with dinner, but is obviously best on a fine summer's evening. The fixed-price, four/five-course menu is short, but chef and co-owner John Wood's excellent preparation of just a few dishes each night is compensation enough. Each course offers two dishes, with a soup or maybe crème Florentine between the first and the second.

Our inspector judged a crab soup with rouille to be the best of his professional career and he also praised a warm mousse of Arbroath smokies. Main courses could be fillet of Galloway beef with Madeira sauce, venison noisettes with peppercorns, or scallops of halibut rolled in sesame seeds with a sorrel butter sauce. Desserts include something hot and traditional, such as bread and butter pudding, as well as cold sweets like hazelnut meringue or mango fool. The predominantly French wine list is not long, but it has obviously been carefully chosen and refined over the years. Some relatively unfamiliar wines from small growers will appeal to more adventurous customers. The house wines are keenly priced and there are some outstanding bin ends at about £30 a bottle.

Directions: Turn right off A711, 0.25 miles east of Auchencairn, Collin House is signposted

Menus: Fixed-price lunch and dinner

Times: 7.15pm- Last D 8.15 (or by arrangement). Closed lunch and 2/3 weeks Jan, Feb

Chef: John Wood
Proprietors: Pam Hall, John Wood

Seats: 18. No smoking in dining room
Additional: Children permitted; ❷ dishes/Vegan/other diets by arrangement

ESKDALEMUIR, **Hart Manor** ❀

☺ *Good cooking with well-maintained flavours and textures is available at dinner in the cosy restaurant of this small hotel. The home-made soups are strongly recommended, as are the local lamb and fresh fish. The menu offers a short choice and is reasonably priced for four courses and coffee.*

Cost: Alc £11; fixed-price D £16.50. H/wine £7.50 ♀ Service exc.
Credit cards: None taken. **Additional:** Children permitted before 8.30pm; children's portions; ❷ dishes on request
Directions: From the South, turn off at exit 44 of M6 onto A7 to Langholm. From Langholm take B709. Hart Manor is 2.5 miles north on Eltrick Road

Langholm
Dumfriesshire
Map no: 11 NY29
Tel: 01387 373217
Chef: John Medcalf
Proprietors: John and Pamela Medcalf
Seats: 20. No smoking in dining room
Times: Last L 2pm/Last D 8pm. Closed Tue in winter, 25 Dec

MOFFAT, **Beechwood** ❀

☺ *Originally a school for young ladies, this Victorian country house overlooks the town. Chef Carl Shaw's imaginative five-course fixed-priced menu offers a choice of mainly Scottish dishes at each course, including smoked salmon with dill mayonnaise as a starter or fillet steak as a main course.*

Cost: Fixed-price L £13/D £20. H/wine £8.25. Service exc
Credit cards: 1 2 3. **Additional:** Children welcome; children's portions/menu; ❷ dishes/other diets on request
Directions: Turn right by church into Harthope Place and follow 'Hotel 0.25 mile' sign

Harthorpe Place
Dumfriesshire
Map no: 11 NT00
Tel: 01683 20210
Chef: Carl S Shaw
Proprietors: J P and L M Rogers
Seats: 20. No smoking
Times: Last L 2pm/D 9pm. Closed 2 Jan-15 Feb

MOFFAT, Well View ❀❀

Ballplay Road
Dumfriesshire
Map no: 11 NT00
Tel: 01683 20184

A restful, welcoming hotel serving lovingly prepared food with a strong French influence

Guests are encouraged to feel at home in this delightful small hotel, and nowhere more so than in the restaurant where a lovingly prepared dinner awaits them. There's a strong French influence to chef/patron Janet Schuckardt's fine cooking, and dishes like breaded Camembert with salad and a gooseberry and elderflower sauce, or roast breast of duck with a mango sauce scented with a little ginger give a hint of the imaginative food on offer. A crisp filo cup filled with soft, fresh chicken livers, smoked bacon strips and mushrooms made an enjoyable recent starter, while lamb fillet with a tangy, piquant sauce was full of honest flavours. In between there may be a sorbet or a well-made soup, and the sampled grapefruit sorbet made a refreshing intervention. Al dente vegetables are cooked to retain bright colours and natural flavours, though they can also be cooked to taste if requested. The cheese board offers several full-flavoured Scottish products, and if there is any space left a pudding like iced soufflé with sauce anglais makes an enjoyable finish. The short five-course menu offers little choice but very good value.

Cost: Fixed–price lunch £10.50; fixed-price dinner £21.50. H/wine £8.20 ♀ Service exc
Credit cards: 1 2 3

Menus: Fixed-price lunch and dinner, Sun lunch

Times: Last L 1.15pm, Last D 8.30pm. Closed Sat lunch, 2 weeks Jan, 3 weeks Oct

Chef: Janet Schuckardt
Proprietor: John Schuckardt

Seats: 30. No smoking in dining room
Additional: Children permitted (over 5 at dinner); ❂ dishes/ other diets on request

Directions: From Moffat take A708 towards Selkirk, turn left after fire station, hotel is 300 yds on right

NEWTON STEWART, Kirroughtree ❀❀

Minnigaff
Wigtownshire
Map no: 10 NX46
Tel: 01671 402141

☺ *Much-acclaimed Anglo-French cooking in an impressive country setting with full use of fresh local produce*

An impressive 18th-century mansion standing in beautifully landscaped grounds is the fine setting for this peaceful, secluded hotel. Lovely views of the surrounding countryside can be enjoyed from the bedrooms, while the two elegant dining rooms, one on either side of the main lounge, are equally resplendent in their respective reds and blues – the latter reserved for non-smokers. Ian Bennett's cooking has received much acclaim, and he makes good use of the best local produce to create the sort of dishes that recently impressed our inspector: fillet of monkfish with a sauce vierge was grilled with a pleasant charcoal flavour, and breast of Barbary duck with a green peppercorn sauce came crisp-skinned, pink and tender, with the sauce doing much to bring out the meat flavour. A delicious sweet came in the form of poached peaches in champagne, on a thin shortbread and covered with a sugar-strand cloche, served in a tasty cream sauce with traces of strawberry puree. As well as the fixed-price dinner, Sunday lunch menu and the lunchtime *carte*, a creative vegetarian choice is offered on a four-course menu.

Cost: *Alc* £16; Sun lunch £12, fixed-price dinner £25. H/wine £10.05. Service inc
Credit cards: 1 3 5

Menus: *A la carte* lunch, fixed-price dinner, Sunday lunch, bar menu

Times: Midday-Last L 1.30pm, 7pm-Last D 9.30pm. Closed 3 Jan-3 Mar

Chef: Ian Bennett
Proprietor: Douglas McMillan

Seats: 30, 30. One dining room non-smoking
Additional: Children over 10 permitted; ❂ dishes/Vegan/ other diets on request. Pianist

Directions: From the A75, follow the signs for New Galloway (A712). The hotel entrance is 300 yards along this road on the left

PORTPATRICK, Knockinaam Lodge ❀❀❀

French cooking of note in a country house restaurant on the shores of the Irish Sea

Wigtownshire
Map no: 10 NW95
Tel: 01776 810471

Cost: Fixed-price lunch £22.50, fixed-price dinner £32. H/wine £9.50. Service exc
Credit cards: 1 2 3 4

It is easy to understand why Winston Churchill chose this house for a clandestine meeting with General Eisenhower during World War II. The setting is stunning – cliffs on three sides, and only the sea and a private, Gulf Stream-washed beach on the fourth. Today, talk is not of conflict but confit, for the food here is unequivocally French. The fixed-price lunch and dinner menus change daily, offering two dishes at each course.

Taking recent examples, there could have been starters of casseroled half guinea fowl or ragout of lobster, main courses of goujonettes of sole in sesame seeds, or noisette of venison, and a choice of sweets every bit as mouth-watering as the rest. Such prosaic descriptions are poor substitute for the rhapsodic French used throughout the menus, and the charmingly-illustrated paper on which they are printed. The Gallic influence may be unashamedly apparent, but the fresh produce used is Scottish. Everything is skilfully prepared by talented chef Stuart Muir, now in his second year here.

Wines are well chosen and described – there are even a few rarities from Switzerland, and although the majority of wines are French, there are some good selections from most other countries too. Prices are very reasonable.

M. and Mme Frichot have been perfect hosts here for nine seasons and their team of dedicated, friendly staff know just how to apply *le style Frichot*.

Menus: Fixed-price lunch and dinner, bar menu

Times: 12.30-Last L 2pm, Last D 9pm. Closed 2 Jan-20 Mar

Chef: Stuart Muir
Proprietors: Marcel and Corinna Frichot

Seats: 28
Additional: Children welcome; children's portions/menu; special diets on request

Directions: Turn left off A77 (Stranraer to Portpatrick) 3 miles south of Portpatrick on a well-signposted lane

FIFE

ANSTRUTHER, Cellar Restaurant ❀❀❀

A fishing village restaurant run by a man who loves his kitchen and of whom other Scottish chefs speak highly

Map no: 12 NO50
Tel: 01333 310378

Cost: Fixed-price dinner £25.50
Credit cards: 1 2 3

Anstruther is one of those picturesque Scottish fishing villages that appear on calendars. Locals call it 'Ainster', which might be a useful tip if you get lost in the East Neuk of Fife. The Cellar is tucked away among narrow streets in the village centre, between the harbour and the Scottish Fisheries Museum. On a wet and windy night, local girls served our inspector with great charm and warmth and their smiles were the perfect remedy for the Spring gales outside.

Chef/patron Peter Jukes's cooking loudly declares his natural skills; add the presence on his doorstep of some of the finest produce Scotland's seas can muster, and the world cannot be anything but his oyster. The fixed-price, three or four-course dinner menu is very seafood-oriented, chicken livers or

Menus: *A la carte* lunch, fixed-price dinner

Times: Last L 1.30pm, Last D 9.30pm. Closed Sun. Mon lunch, 1 week May, Xmas

Chef: Peter Jukes
Proprietors: Peter and Vivien Jukes

Perthshire beef often the only departures. A small lunch *carte* offers a good meal for about £15.

The inspector's dinner began with three types of salmon, all prepared on site. Traditional oak-smoked would be stunning on finger sandwiches at the finest hotels; 'hot kiln' roasted provided a different texture and flavour and a marinated gravlax gave a stronger flavour still – Scandinavians would love it. The main course of roasted monkfish tail was among the finest our inspector ('I could not get enough') had tasted. Freshness obviously has something to do with it, but Chef's coating of herbs, curry powder, crumbs and garlic gave it a perfect lift. More's the pity, then, that the vegetables were so ordinary – a real anti-climax. Delicacy returned with a pleasingly-textured chocolate layer mousse, a fitting end to an extremely good meal. For a restaurant that likes to keep matters simple, the wine list breaks the house rule – but very creditably.

Seats: 32. No smoking in dining room
Additional: Children permitted (over 5 at dinner)

Directions: From the harbour, turn left in to Hadfoot Wynd by the Scottish Fisheries Museum, then right into East Green

CUPAR, **Ostlers Close** ●●●

A simply-styled small restaurant where uncomplicated food is popular with locals and those from further afield

Ostlers Close is tucked up an alley, as great restaurants and pubs often are. The word unpretentious comes to mind and, although it is an overworked word in the lexicon of good eating places, here is one which really doesn't aspire to be something grander than it is. Jimmy and Amanda Graham, the friendly and dedicated restaurateurs, enjoy sharing their culinary passions with their customers. The simple Modern British food they serve is unadorned, in keeping with the here-to-stay, Mediterranean-style stuccoed surroundings. Scottish influences, such as West Coast scallops, make a discreet appearance every so often on the short, handwritten *cartes* but, if some of the dishes are not blatantly ethnic, much of the produce is.

Behind the simplicity of the menus are intricate combinations of flavours, especially in the sauces which accompany most main courses. Lovage, peppery and celery-like in flavour, may be combined with leeks, onion, garlic and white wine to make a delicate chicken and duck stock-based soup. A tureen of this was sorely tempting for our inspector, but he dutifully turned his attention to the day's seafood selection. That day there were bite-sized chunks of cod, monkfish, turbot, scallop and salmon, in the middle of which sat some fresh, crisp sea kale – just how fresh and crisp it could be, our inspector had long forgotten. Accompanying the dish was a thick, dark sauce reduced from langoustine and pesto-flavoured fish stocks. Amanda is the creator of most desserts, such as that old faithful, sticky toffee pudding, but on this occasion Jimmy Graham baked lemon tart and served it warm with lemon sorbet. The tart's delightful, rich taste reflected his desire to experiment with duck eggs. There is an excellent value-for-money wine list.

Bonneygate
Map no: 11 NO31
Tel: 01334 655574

Cost: *A/c* lunch £14.50/dinner £24. H/wine £7.75 ♀ Service exc
Credit cards: 1 2 3 5

Menus: *A la carte*

Times: 12.15pm-Last L 2pm, 7pm-Last D 9.30pm. Closed Sun, Mon, first 2 weeks Jun

Chef: James Graham
Proprietors: James and Amanda Graham

Seats: 26. Smoking allowed at end of evening
Additional: Children permitted (over 6 at dinner); children's portions; ◐ dishes; other diets on request

Directions: In small lane off main street of Cupar

ELIE, **Bouquet Garni** ❧❧

Quality fresh seafood, simply cooked to retain its individual flavours, is the speciality of this popular little restaurant.

It is easy to see why Andrew and Norah Keracher's delightful small restaurant is rapidly becoming very popular – they adopt a sensible pricing policy, use top quality ingredients and provide a welcoming atmosphere. Seafood figures prominently on their seasonally-changing *carte* of Scottish and French dishes, for Andrew's family are local fish merchants and he has the pick of the catch. This he cooks sympathetically and with care, allowing the natural flavours of the ingredients to predominate; his beautifully presented medley of seafood, for example, includes superbly plump oysters, mussels and scallops accompanied by a suitably delicate Muscadet sauce. Meat eaters are not neglected, and the same meal might offer warm breast of pigeon and oyster mushrooms encased in puff pastry and served with a rich and gamey Madeira jus, or pink lamb slices arranged around a mushroom-garnished bed of celeriac, this time with a fine rosemary sauce. A well-chosen wine list of 30 bins complements the food. Very reasonably priced light lunches are served in the bar.

Directions: From the A915 St Andrews road take the A917 to Elie. The restaurant is in the village centre

51 High Street
Map no: 12 NO40
Tel: 0333 330374

Cost: Alc £23, lunch £12.
Service exc
Credit cards: 1 2 3 5

Menus: *A la carte,* Sunday lunch, bar menu

Times: Midday-Last L 1.30pm, 7pm-Last D 9.30pm. Closed Sun eve, 2nd & 3rd weeks Jan, 2nd week Nov

Chef: Andrew Keracher
Proprietors: Norah and Andrew Keracher

Seats: 50. No smoking in dining room
Additional: Children permitted (over 12 at dinner); children's portions; ✪ dishes, Vegan and special diets by arrangement

GLENROTHES, **Rescobie** ❧

☺ *In the small dining room of this comfortable Edwardian house, chef Angus MacLeod offers a range of carefully prepared dishes based on traditional Scottish ingredients and lots of fresh herbs. An extensive carte is supported by a fixed-price and separate vegetarian menus.*

Cost: Alc from £16; fixed–price L £8-£15/D £16. H/wine £7.50.
Service exc. **Credit cards:** 1 2 3 4. **Additional:** Children welcome; children's portions/menu; ✪ menu; Vegan/other diets on request
Directions: At west end of Leslie High Street, turn left, then first left, hotel on left hand side

Valley Drive, Leslie
Map no: 11 NO20
Tel: 01592 742143
Chef: Angus MacLeod
Proprietor: Tony and Wendy Hughes-Lewis
Seats: 42
Times: Last L 2pm/Last D 9pm. Closed 24-26 Dec

LUNDIN LINKS, **Old Manor** ❧

A comfortable hotel overlooking Largs Bay and Lundin Links Golf Course offering an imaginative menu with a high standard of cuisine. Prawns and ginger in filo pastry followed by medallions of pork in Stilton sauce were an enjoyable inspection choice.

Cost: Alc £23, fixed-price £19.50. **Credit cards:** 1 2 3
Additional: Children not encouraged; ✪ menu
Directions: Overlooking golf course and sea

Leven Road
Map no: 12 NO40
Tel: 01333 320368
Chef: Alun Brunt
Proprietor: Alistair Clark
Times: Last L 2pm/D 9.30pm

MARKINCH, **Balbirnie House** ✿✿

☺ *Imaginative traditional and modern Scottish cooking in a relaxed and courteously-run hotel*

A combination of sophistication and informality is what sets this elegant Georgian mansion apart from other grand hotels. The Russell family, who own it, and their courteous staff offer a traditional and very personal service, and guests are free to relax and bask in the unpretentious atmosphere. Dining at Balbirnie is an experience not to be missed, and the stylish restaurant provides the perfect setting for Ian MacDonald's traditional Scottish cooking. Many dishes on the good value set four-course menu and lunch-time *carte* reflect a modern influence, such as the recently sampled smoked fish roulade served with a lemon and watercress cream sauce and a delightful little salad. Highland game consommé with woodland mushroom dumpling had a good rich colour and flavour, while collops of venison with poached pear and black pudding in a red wine sauce was a tasty and innovative main dish. A selection of al dente vegetables included carrots, mange-touts, haricots verts, swede purée and broccoli with two kinds of potatoes, and an orange and Grand Marnier crème brûlée came with a sugar-strand dome. The wine list includes exceptional as well as modest choices.

Directions: Take Junction 3 off M90. Follow A92 to Glenrothes. Continue north towards Tay Road Bridge. Turn right onto B9130 to Markinch just beyond Glenrothes

Balbirnie Park
Map no: 11 NO20
Tel: 01592 610066

Cost: *A/c* lunch £13.50, Sunday lunch £13.75, fixed-price dinner £25. H/wine £10.75. Service inc
Credit cards: 1 2 3 4

Menus: *A la carte* lunch, fixed–price dinner, Sunday lunch, bar menu

Times: Last L 2.30pm, Last D 9.45pm

Chef: Ian MacDonald
Proprietor: Alan Russell

Seats: 50. No-smoking in dining room
Additional: Children permitted; children's portions; ❂ menu; Vegan/other diets on request

PEAT INN, **The Peat Inn** ✿✿✿

A high quality restaurant serving some of the finest food in the region – well worth a drive to this rural spot

When road atlases show a restaurant's name, it must be a promotional advantage. The reason is that Peat Inn is also the name of a hamlet which grew up at the meeting of two roads heading for Cupar, an ancient market town in the middle of Fife. Apart from running the restaurant, chef/patron David Wilson also sells to his customers gaudy ties of the sort he likes to wear himself. His zest for fine quality food is not as easily emulated as his dress-sense, however, and the standards he sets leave lesser mortals trailing.

It took just one meal for our inspector to realise why customers travel long distances to eat at this famous old inn. His outstandingly-good value lunches cost less than £20, inclusive of canapés, coffee and petits fours (and no crafty add-ons like cover charges). Langoustine broth was finished with mixed fish and a few prawns, crushed by the chef at the last moment to release the flavour. The brandade of roast cod, as fresh-tasting as the moment it hit the trawler's deck, was served on a mash of potato, fennel, garlic and cream, and a succulent roast breast of duck in red wine sauce with honey and orange delivered a perfect balance of tastes.

There is a four-course fixed-price dinner for £28 and – an interesting idea this – a 'tasting menu' which, for £42, allows complete tables to try six of the house specialities, served in

Cupar
Map no: 12 NO40
Tel: 01334 84206

Cost: *A/c* £32, fixed-price lunch £18.50, fixed-price dinner £28 (4 courses), £42. Wine £12 ♀ Service inc
Credit cards: 1 2 3 4 5

Menus: *A la carte*, Tasting menu, fixed-price lunch and dinner

Times: L 12.30 for 1pm, Last D 9.30pm. Closed Sun, Mon, Xmas, 1 Jan

Chefs: David Wilson, Angus Blacklaws
Proprietors: David and Patricia Wilson

Seats: 48. No smoking in dining room
Additional: Children welcome; children's portions; ❂ dishes; Vegan/other diets on request

slightly smaller than normal portions. Eating from the *carte* would probably end up with a bill between the two figures, without wine, of course. The 30-page wine list includes David Wilson's 'view from the stoves', in other words, why and how he chooses the very comprehensive range on offer. The list has been chosen and presented with skill and imagination, and is keenly priced throughout. The selections from Alsace, Burgundy and Bordeaux are particularly strong.

Directions: At junction of B940/B941 6 miles south-west of St Andrews

ST ANDREWS, Parkland Hotel ❀

☺ *The restaurant is the focal point of this small mansion hotel. Good-value meals are offered from a short three-course fixed-price menu, and a 'Menu en Surprise' for parties of two or more. Chicken stuffed with local cheese, wrapped in bacon and presented on a whisky and oatmeal sauce is a typical dish.*

Cost: Fixed-price L £7/D £15. H/wine from £6.95. Service exc.
Credit cards: 1 2 3 5. **Additional:** Children permitted before 8pm; children's portions; ❂ dishes/Vegan/other diets on request
Directions: West of the centre of town, opposite Kinburn Park

Kinburn Castle, Double Dykes Road
Map no: 12 N051
Tel: 01334 73620
Chef: Brian J MacLennan
Proprietor: Brian J MacLennan
Seats: 50. No smoking in dining room
Times: Last L 2pm/D 8.30pm. Dinner not served Sun. Closed Mon, Xmas, 1-2 Jan

ST ANDREWS, Rufflets ❀

The recently refurbished Garden restaurant, overlooking award-winning gardens, is renowned for its modern Scottish cuisine. Poached East Coast sole, ragout of Perthshire lamb, grilled collops of Scottish beef fillet and local cheeses may be found on the fixed-price lunch menu or dinner carte.

Cost: Fixed price L £15/D £25. Service inc
Credit cards: 1 2 3 4 5. **Additional:** Children welcome; children's portions; ❂ dishes; other diets on request
Directions: 1.5 miles west on B939 St Andrews to Ceres road

Strathkinness Low Road
Map no: 12 NO51
Tel: 01334 472594
Chef: Robert Grindle
Proprietor: Scotland's Commended. Manager: Peter Aretz
Seats: 60. No smoking in dining room
Times: Last L 2pm/D 9pm

ST ANDREWS, St Andrews Golf Hotel ❀

The hotel enjoys a commanding position on the seafront and the famous Old Course is next door. The menu includes chef's Highland game pie, fresh Loch Fyne oysters and loin of Perthshire venison, to name three dishes from a kitchen which extends the description of its cuisine to Franco-Scottish.

Cost: Alc £26, fixed-price L £13.25/D £21.50 (3 courses), £25. H/wine £9.75 ♀ Service exc
Credit cards: 1 2 3 4. **Additional:** Children welcome at lunch; children's portions/menu; ❂ dishes; Vegan/other diets on request
Directions: Take 1st left at Golf Place, then 1st right into The Scores, hotel 200 yards on right

40 The Scores
Map no: 12 NO51
Tel: 01334 472611
Chef: Adam Harrow
Proprietor: Brian Hughes
Seats: 55. No smoking in dining room
Times: Last L 2.30pm/D 9.30pm

ST ANDREWS,
St Andrews Old Course ❀❀

Old Station Road
Map no: 12 NO51
Tel: 01334 474371

Good Taste of Scotland cooking offered in an attractive modern hotel overlooking the famous old golf course

The top floor cocktail bar and grill room of this modern resort hotel have splendid views over the famous Old Course to the sea beyond. The hotel is not only a golfing venue, it has many attractive features, not least of which is the high quality food served in the Grill Room There has been a change of chef, with Bruce Price taking overall responsibility in the kitchen, but he has been here for some time so continuity is assured. The imaginative menus are centred on local produce, especially seafood from the fishing villages of Fife and quality Perthshire meat. The *carte* features a Taste of Scotland selection, and there is a four-course fixed-price menu which includes a vegetarian option and a healthy 'Spa Cuisine' dish at each course. Starters of Crail fish-cake and citrus butter, or brill and potato with shallot and basil vinaigrette have attracted our inspector, and seared sirloin of beef or roast monkfish to follow. Tempting desserts are offered, or Scottish cheeses – Lanark Blue and Bonnet among them. Wines from all around the world are listed.

Cost: *A/c* from £40; fixed-price dinner £34.50. H/wine £14.50. Service exc
Credit cards: 1 2 3 4 5

Menus: *A la carte,* fixed-price dinner, all-day conservatory menu

Times: Last D 10pm. Closed Xmas week

Proprietor: Old Course Ltd.
Manager: Peter Crome

Seats: 80. No smoking in dining room
Additional: Children welcome; children's portions/menu; ❀ menu; other diets on request

Directions: Situated close to the A91 on the outskirts of the city

ST ANDREWS, Scores ❀

76 The Scores
Map no: 12 NO51
Tel: 01334 472451
Chef: Mark Trimble
Proprietor: Mr T Gilchrist
Times: Last D 9.15pm

The hotel enjoys views fine views over the sea and in the kitchen Mark Trimble cooks some very innovative dishes such as a highly enjoyable escalope of venison with an onion and marmalade sauce.

Cost: Fixed-price D £21. **Credit cards:** 1 2 3 4 5
Additional: Children welcome (can choose from coffee shop menu)
Directions: West of town. Turn into Golf Place then into The Scores

GRAMPIAN

ABERDEEN, Ardoe House ❀

Blairs, South Deeside Road
Aberdeenshire
Map no: 15 NJ90
Tel: 01224 867355
Chef: Ed Cooney
Proprietor: Macdonald.
Manager: Derek Walker
Seats: 60. No smoking in dining rooms Times: Last L 2pm/Last D 9.45pm. Closed Sat lunch

Here is a Scottish baronial hall with turrets, heraldic inscriptions, high ornate ceilings and splendid wood panelling-reached by a tree-lined drive. Its restaurant uses fresh Scottish produce and the carte and fixed-price menus feature plenty of local fish, game and meat.

Cost: *A/c* from £23.15; fixed-price L from £9.55/D £22.50. H/wine £11.95 ♀ Service exc. **Credit cards:** 1 2 3 4 5 **Additional:** Children welcome; children's portions/menu; ❀ dishes; other diets on request
Directions: 2 miles from Aberdeen on B9007, on left hand side

SCOTLAND GRAMPIAN 497

ARCHIESTOWN, **Archiestown Hotel** ●●

Fish is a speciality at this hotel, where all the food is based on local produce cooked in a country style

Fishermen predominate among the guests at this Victorian stone-built country hotel – here for the River Spey salmon – and not surprisingly fish is a speciality of the house. Proprietors Judith and Michael Bulger are the welcoming proprietors, and Judith is responsible for the cooking, which is country style with many international influences, prepared from the best local and seasonal produce available. A short choice menu is offered in the delightful restaurant, while for those who prefer a less formal environment there is the back room bistro-bar where diners can enjoy the same dishes as in the restaurant but with additional daily choices from the blackboard menus – fresh fish, shellfish and game figuring strongly. Our inspector's meal commenced with a thick crumbly slice of a good-flavoured pigeon terrine served with redcurrant jelly. This was followed by a robust dish of oxtail cooked in port, with tender meat and good cooking juices. Spiced apple tart, with lovely crisp pastry completed the meal. A fairly inexpensive wine list is offered with a supplementary list of vintage clarets.

Directions: Turn off A95 at Craigellachie on to B9102

Morayshire
Map no: 15 NJ24
Tel: 01340 810218

Cost: Fixed-price dinner £22.50. H/wine £10. Service exc
Credit cards: 1 2 3

Menus: Fixed-price dinner, Sunday lunch, bar menu

Times: Last L 2.30pm, Last D 8.30pm. Closed mid Oct–early Feb

Chef: Judith Bulger
Proprietors: Judith and Michael Bulger
Seats: 25. No smoking in dining room
Additional: Children permitted; children's portions; ◐ dishes; other diets on request

BALLATER, **Balgonie** ●

A fine Edwardian country house hotel, the Balgonie provides a fine setting for chef David Hindmarch's short but imaginative fixed-price four-course dinner menu. Dishes are prepared from the best of Scotland's meat, game and seafood: Orkney oysters, and medallions of Aberdeen Angus, for example.

Cost: Fixed–price L £15.50/D £27.50. H/wine £13.50. Service exc
Credit cards: 1 2 3. **Additional:** Children permitted (over 8 at dinner); children's portions/menu (5-7pm only); ◐ dishes/Vegan/other diets on request
Directions: On outskirts of Ballater, off A93 in the direction of Braemar

Braemar Place
Aberdeenshire
Map no: 15 NO39
Tel: 013397 55482
Chef: David J Hindmarch
Proprietors: John and Priscilla Finnie
Seats: 25. No smoking in dining room
Times: Last L 1.45pm/D 9pm. Closed Jan-Feb

BALLATER, **Craigendarroch** ●●

Fine views across Deeside from a popular family resort hotel with a choice of three restaurants

Royal Family-watchers will not be the only ones to love Craigendarroch, an old red-sandstone mansion near Balmoral. There are timeshare lodges, a country club, extensive leisure facilities and three restaurants, including the Clubhouse which children will like. Adults may head for the more formal Oaks where they can enjoy the standard of cooking that has earned our rosettes. Our inspector chose from both the fixed-price menu and the *carte*, saying of the venison liver parfait that it 'packed a wallop of a flavour'. He also approved of the sea-bass baked with root ginger, lemon thyme and vermouth, although

Braemar Road
Aberdeenshire
Map no: 15 NO39
Tel: 013397 55858

Cost: A/c £28; Sunday lunch £13.50 (2 courses), £17.50; fixed price dinner £24. H/wine £11.75. Service exc
Credit cards: 1 2 3 4 5

Menus: *A la carte*, fixed-price dinner, Sunday lunch, bar menu
Times: Last Sun L 2.30pm, Last D 10pm

the accompanying timbale of fennel and apple was a little intense for his taste. There were also tournedos of beef and veal and pan-fried rack of lamb, both served with intriguing sauces and fresh vegetables. Among the desserts were hot soufflé of mirabelle plums and apple and cherry crêpes. Naturally, Scottish farmhouse cheeses are available. The wine list is brimming with vintages, with some half bottles.

Directions: On A93 to Braemar, 0.5 mile from village centre

Chef: Andrew Tanner
Proprietor: Craigendarroch Ltd.
Manager: Eric Brown

Seats: 45. No smoking in dining room
Additional: Children permitted at Sun lunch only; ✿ dishes; Vegan/other diets on request

BALLATER, **Darroch Learg** ✾✾

☺ *Imaginative modern Scottish cooking in a fine setting*

This fine period house enjoys superb views across Deeside to Lochnager. The restaurant offers a well-balanced wine list and an imaginative fixed-price menu with dishes which have included roast monkfish tail, collops of Highland venison, and escalope of Scottish salmon. Such is the quality of the cuisine here tha,t as we were going to press, the inspectors have upgraded the Darroch Learg to two rosettes.

Cost: Fixed-price L £11.75/D £21.75. H/wine £9 ♀ Service inc
Credit cards: 1 3 4. **Additional:** Children permitted; children's portions; ✿ dishes, Vegan and special diets with prior notice
Directions: On A93 at the west end of village

Braemar Road
Aberdeenshire
Map no: 15 NO39
Tel: 013397 55443
Chef: Robert MacPherson
Proprietors: Nigel Franks
Seats: 48. No smoking in dining room
Times: Last L 2pm/D 8.30pm.
Closed Xmas

BANCHORY, **Banchory Lodge** ✾

☺ *Game and salmon feature prominently during the season in the Victorian-themed restaurant of this hotel – a Georgian house tranquilly set in 12 acres of well-tended grounds beside the River Dee. Hospitality is warm, service cheerful, and a four-course menu offers a choice of substantial dishes.*

Cost: Alc £9.50; Sunday lunch £15, fixed-price D £24.50. H/wine from £8.05. Service inc. **Credit cards:** 1 2 3 4 5
Additional: Children permitted (over 8 at dinner); children's portions/menu; ✿ dishes; Vegan/other diets on request
Directions: 18 miles from Aberdeen on A93

Kincardineshire
Map no: 15 NO69
Tel: 01330 822625
Chefs: Miss K Steven, Miss E Cooper
Proprietors: Mr and Mrs D Jaffray
Seats: 80-100. No cigars or pipes
Times: Last L 1.45pm/D9.30pm

BANCHORY, **Raemoir House** ✾

A beautiful 18th-century mansion in wooded grounds, and part of an extensive estate, where Chef Derek Smith offers the best of fresh Scottish produce in a range of imaginatively prepared dishes. Main courses include saddle of Highland venison, fillet steak Balmoral or poached Dee salmon.

Cost: Alc £30, fixed-price D £24.50, Sun L £14.50. H/wine £10. Service exc. Cover charge £15.**Credit cards:** 1 2 3 4
Additional: Children permitted (over 10 after 7.30pm); children's portions/lunch menu; ✿ menu/other diets on request
Directions: Follow A980, signed Torphins, and in 2 miles at T junction go straight ahead for hotel drive

Kincardineshire
Map no: 15 NO69
Tel: 01330 824884
Chef: Derek A Smith
Proprietors: Scotland's Commended. Manager: Mike Ollis
Seats: 60-80. No smoking in dining room
Times: Last L 2pm/D 9pm.
Closed first 2 weeks Jan

BRAEMAR, **Braemar Lodge** ❀❀

Glenshee Road
Aberdeenshire
Map no: 15 NO19
Tel: 013397 41627

☺ *Carefully prepared dishes feature at this hotel restaurant*

A friendly little hotel transformed from a Victorian shooting lodge where Caroline Hadley-Smith produces a short but carefully chosen fixed-price menu. Dishes include duck liver and mushroom crêpes with port and grape sauce, and pan-fried trout with fennel and prawns flavoured with Pernod.
During the preparation of this guide our inspectors awarded Braemar Lodge a second rosette for the quality of its cooking.

Chef: Caroline Hadley-Smith
Proprietors: Alex Smith, Caroline Hadley-Smith

Seats: 20. No smoking in dining room
Times: Last D 9.pm. Lunch by arrangement. Closed 31 Oct-23 Dec

Cost: Fixed-price D £21. H/wine £9.30 ♀ Service inc
Credit cards: 1 3. **Additional:** Children over 12 permitted; ❂ dishes, Vegan and other diets on request
Directions: On A9 near centre of village

BRIDGE OF MARNOCH, **The Old Manse of Marnoch** ❀❀

Aberdeenshire
Map no: 15 NJ55
Tel: 01466 780873

☺ *Fish features on the menu of this nautically-themed hotel restaurant*

A delightful country house hotel with four acres of gardens, set in secluded surroundings in lovely countryside. A set four-course Taste of Scotland dinner served in the nautically-themed dining room might include asparagus soup followed by Argyll ham with mustard dressing, local fresh salmon and chocolate truffle tart to finish. The quality of the cuisine is such that the inspectors have happily awarded the Old Manse a second rosette this year.

Cost: Fixed-price dinner £20. H/wine £12. No service charge
Credit cards: 1 3
Menus: Fixed–price dinner
Times: Last D 7.30pm for 8pm. Closed 2 weeks winter

Chef: Keren Carter
Proprietors: Patrick and Keren Carter

Seats: 16. No smoking in dining room

Additional: Children over 12 permitted
Directions: On B9117, just off the A97 (Huntly/Banff) road

CRAIGELLACHIE, **Craigellachie** ❀

Banffshire
Map no: 15 NJ24
Tel: 01340 881204
Chef: Robert Taylor
Proprietor: Cathryn Amor
Seats: 35. No smoking in dining room
Times: Last L 2pm/D 9.30pm

☺ *An appealing hotel where the menu has a distinct Scottish flavour, including such dishes as the local black pudding, cured Spey salmon and roast gigot of Scottish lamb. The well-chosen wine list includes several quality bins.*

Cost: Alc £13.50; fixed-price L £13.50/D £25.50. H/wine from £9.95 ♀ Service exc. **Credit cards:** 1 2 3 4 5 **Additional:** Children welcome; children's portions; ❂ dishes; Vegan/other diets on request
Directions: In the village centre

DRYBRIDGE, **The Old Monastery** ●●

A converted monastery offers some wonderful local produce beautifully cooked

You will find this delightfully converted monastery perched high on a hill, with spectacular views out over Spey Bay on the Moray Firth. Dinner is served in the Chapel Restaurant, offering Scottish cooking with French influences, imaginatively combining quality seasonal local produce, cooked by Douglas Gray and charmingly served by Maureen Gray and her young local staff. The menu follows a well-tried formula with local seafood and game featuring quite heavily. Our inspector enjoyed a good starter of fresh scallops cooked in a tomato and herb sauce, presented in a golden crisp pastry, followed by a moist tender guinea fowl, accompanied by the boned leg stuffed with smoked bacon and mushrooms, set on a rather sharp claret and mushroom sauce that did little to enhance the otherwise good flavours. The ambitious sweet of lemon mousse clafoutis, a light sponge-wrapped lemon mousse, was accompanied by a smooth strawberry ice-cream and an iced banana soufflé, the last flavours combined nicely, slightly at odds with the sharper lemon flavour.

Directions: Turn off A98 at Buckie on to Drybridge/Deskford road. Follow for 2.5 miles to top of hill. Do not turn right into Drybridge village

Buckie
Banffshire
Map no: 15 NJ46
Tel: 01542 832660

Cost: *Alc* lunch £15, dinner £25. H/wine from £8.50. Service exc
Credit cards: 1 2 3

Menus: *A la carte* lunch and dinner
Times: Midday–Last L 1.45pm, 7pm–Last D 9.30pm. Closed Sun, Mon, 3 weeks Jan, 2 weeks Nov
Chef: James Douglas Gray
Proprietors: J D and M G Gray

Seats: 40. No smoking in dining room
Additional: Children over 8 permitted; children's portions; ❷ dishes/other diets on request

ELGIN, **Mansefield House** ●

☺ *Formerly a manse, now converted to a stylish hotel. The restaurant is in the old stables whose original arches are today a wall of windows. Seafood is the speciality here and even well-known dishes are given imaginative treatment. Some might find a little too much emphasis is given to presentation.*

Cost: *Alc* £20, L £11. H/wine £6.95 ♀ Service exc
Credit cards: 1 2 3 5. **Additional:** Children welcome; children's portions; ❷ dishes; Vegan/other diets on request
Directions: A short walk from the town centre, well signposted

Mayne Road
Morayshire
Map no: 15 NJ26
Tel: 01343 540883
Chef: Robin Murray
Proprietor: Moray. Managers: Mr and Mrs T R Murray
Seats: 65. No smoking in dining room. Air conditioned
Times: Last L 2.30pm/D 10.30pm

ELGIN, **Mansion House** ●

☺ *A fine turreted baronial mansion beside the River Lossie where chef John Alexander produces an extensive range of dishes with a modern style. The freshest seafood, game, prime beef and lamb are used to create dishes such as tender lamb with kidneys on a croûton.*

Cost: *Alc* £18, fixed-price £19. **Credit cards:** 1 2 3 4
Additional: Children welcome; ❷ dishes

The Haugh
Morayshire
Map no: 15 NJ26
Tel: 01343 548811
Chef: John Alexander
Proprietors: Mr and Mrs Stirrat
Times: Last L 2pm/D 9pm

FORRES, Ramnee ❀

☺ *A large and distinguished old house where dishes are created with combined influences of Scotland and France. When our inspector visited, the fixed-price menu and carte offered such tempting dishes as large prawns in a brandy, mushroom onion and cream sauce and Chateaubriand with a béarnaise sauce*

Cost: Alc £19.50, fixed-price L £9.50/D £17.50. H/wine £8
Credit cards: 1 2 3 4 5. **Additional:** Children welcome; children's portions/menu; ❶ menu; Vegan/other diets on request
Directions: Turn into Forres off the A96 at the eastern side of town. Ramnee is 200yds on the right

Victoria Road
Morayshire
Map no: 14 NJ05
Tel: 01309 672410
Chef: James Murphy
Proprietors: Garry and Roy Dinnes
Seats: 34. No cigars or pipes
Times: Last L 2pm/D 9pm.
Closed 25 Dec and 1-3 Jan

INVERURIE, Thainstone House ❀❀

A splendid Palladian mansion setting for some highly acclaimed Scottish cooking

Chef Bill Gibb has deservedly won much acclaim for his splendid Scottish food, and guests are invited to sample the results from a choice of interesting fixed-price menus. His innovative, modern style of cooking uses only the finest raw ingredients to produce some distinctive and honest flavours. Simpson's restaurant, an elegant Georgian room in this imposing Palladian mansion, is the setting for this fine food, where even the vegetarian menu offers a feast of creative delicacies: sweet galia melon with white port sorbet and red berries on a persimmon sauce might be followed by cream of woodland mushroom and basil soup, then fettucine of vegetables set on a potato rösti with a lemon grass capsicum sauce, and a choice of dessert to finish. Our inspector chose a hearty terrine of duck, venison and pigeon with salad, and a smooth and tasty crab soup. Steamed salmon fillet with Keta caviar, pastry basket and delicate dill cream was an enjoyable main dish served with fresh vegetables, and a raspberry crème brûlée was well-recommended. The dearer set menu offers no choice, and the biggest variety of dishes comes at lunch.

Directions: 2 miles from Inverurie on the A96 Aberdeen road

Aberdeenshire
Map no: 15 NJ72
Tel: 01467 621643

Cost: Fixed-price lunch £9.50 (1 course), £14.50; fixed-price dinner £29. H/wine £12.50. No service charge
Credit cards: 1 2 3 4 5

Menus: A la carte, fixed-price lunch and dinner, Sunday lunch, bar menu

Times: Last L 2pm, Last D 9pm
Chef: Bill Gibb

Proprietor: Peter Medley
Seats: 45. No smoking in dining room

Additional: Children welcome; children's portions/menu; ❶ menu; other diets on request

KILDRUMMY, Kildrummy Castle ❀

A stone mansion in glorious countryside overlooking the 13th-century castle ruins. Fresh fish and game are well represented on the interesting carte and fixed-price menus, with the emphasis on traditional Scottish food together with fine wines, complemented by charming Scottish hospitality.

Cost: Alc £29, fixed-price L £14.50/D £26. H/wine £9. Service inc
Credit cards: 1 2 3. **Additional:** Children welcome; children's portions/menu; ❶ dishes; Vegan/other diets on request
Directions: Off A97 (Huntly-Ballater road)

Aberdeenshire
Map no: 15 NJ41
Tel: 019755 71288
Chef: Kenneth Whyte
Proprietor: Scotland's Heritage.
Manager: Thomas Hanna
Seats: 42. No smoking in dining room
Times: Last L 1.45pm/D 9pm.
Closed Jan

HIGHLAND

ARDELVE, **Loch Duich** ❀

☺ *Enjoyable Taste of Scotland cooking is offered at this former drovers' inn, which overlooks Loch Duich and Eilean Donan Castle. Dishes might include local scallops served with herb butter; monkfish tails with a creamy sauce lightly flavoured with whisky; and atholl brose for pudding.*

Cost: Fixed–price D £17.50. H/wine £7. No service charge
Credit cards: 1 3. **Additional:** Children permitted at lunch only; children's portions; ❖ dishes; other diets on request
Directions: Beside the A87 'Road to the Isles'. Across the Dornie Bridge, facing Eilean Donan Castle

Ross & Cromarty
Map no: 14 NG82
Tel: 0159985 213
Chefs: Steven Crockett, Hannah Fairley
Proprietors: Ian Fraser, Sonia Moore
Seats: 38. No smoking in dining room
Times: Last L 2pm/D 9pm. Closed Xmas day

ARISAIG, **Arisaig House** ❀❀

Desserts are a high spot but other dishes are well up to the mark at this remote Highland hotel

Breathtaking Highland scenery provides the backdrop for this remote country house, where views of the formal terraced gardens vie for attention with those of the rugged coastline. Indoors there's a peaceful atmosphere and in the dining room polished tables and wood panelling lend a mellow feel. Chef David Wilkinson maintains a consistently high standard of cooking which is good news for serious lovers of food, and his limited four-course menu offers some delightful dishes with a few extra choices. Sweetbreads in crisp filo pastry with a well-balanced sherry sauce was a recent successful starter, followed by a pleasant mixed-leaf salad with red pepper dressing: soup is also offered at this stage. Shetland salmon with lemon-oil dressing was fragrant and simple, and vegetables were well timed. Puddings were the high spot of this delicious meal, with a very good crème brûlée in fruit purée, and an excellent sticky toffee pudding. Other main course choices might be marinated loin of venison with green lentils and juniper sauce, or saddle of Scotch lamb with fresh herb and spinach stuffing.

Directions: On A830 Fort William to Mallaig road, 3 miles east of Arisaig village

Beasdale
Inverness-shire
Map no: 13 NM68
Tel: 016875 622

Cost: *Alc* lunch from £12.50, fixed-price dinner £29.50. H/wine £14.50. No service charge
Credit cards: 1 3

Menus: *A la carte* lunch, fixed–price dinner, bar lunch menu
Times: Last L 2pm, Last D 8.30pm. Closed Dec-Mar

Chef: David Wilkinson
Proprietor: Relais et Chateaux. Managers: Ruth, John and Andrew Smither

Seats: 36. No smoking in dining room
Additional: Children over 10 permitted; ❖ dishes; other diets on request

CONON BRIDGE, **Kinkell** ❀

☺ *A former farmhouse with beautiful views of Ben Wyvis and the Cromarty Firth is the setting for Marsha Fraser to create honest, enjoyable food with her uncomplicated treatment of local produce. Our inspector had delicious salmon and scallops with a lime and coriander sauce.*

Cost: Alc L £9/D £18.75, fixed-price D £18. H/wine £7.95. Service inc. **Credit cards:** 1 3. **Additional:** Children welcome; children's portions; ◐ dishes; other diets on request
Directions: One mile from the A9, on the B9169

Map no: 14 NH55
Tel: 01349 861270
Chef: Marsha Fraser
Proprietor: Marsha Fraser
Seats: 30. No smoking in dining room
Times: Last L 2pm/D 9pm. Closed Jan, Feb

CONTIN, **Coul House** ❀

A lovely Victorian mansion peacefully set in its own grounds where chef Chris Bentley's enjoyable Taste of Scotland dishes are prepared from fresh local produce. Our inspector enjoyed a game pâté followed by roast rack of lamb served with the pan juices and mint sauce.

Cost: Alc £24, fixed-price D £22. **Credit cards:** 2 4 **Additional:** No smoking in diningroom; no children under 6 at dinner; ◐ dishes
Directions: A long drive leads to the hotel from the A835 in the centre of the village

By Strathpeffer
Ross & Cromarty
Map no: 14 NH45
Tel: 01997 421487
Chef: Chris Bentley
Proprietor: Thomas MacKenzie
Times: Last D 9pm

DULNAIN BRIDGE, **Muckrach Lodge** ❀

This converted hunting lodge, set in 10 acres of grounds, has an attractive garden restaurant with a conservatory extension. Guests can choose from a daily fixed-price menu or the imaginative carte of Scottish and French cuisine, the latter offering a choice of three vegetarian main courses.

Cost: Fixed–price L £10.50/D £22.50. H/wine from £8.50. Service exc. **Credit cards:** 1 2 3 4 5. **Additional:** Children welcome; children's portions/menu; ◐ menu; Vegan/other diets on request
Directions: On A938, 0.5 mile from Dulnain Bridge

Morayshire
Map no: 14 NH92
Tel: 01479 851257
Chef: Paul McLaughlin
Proprietors: Captain R T & Mrs F P Watson
Times: Last L 1.45pm/D 9pm

DUNDONNELL, **Dundonnell Hotel** ❀

The Dundonnell's ambitious menus sometimes fall just short of perfection: a pork and nut terrine proved rather solid, for example. Such drawbacks are more than made up for by the general excellence of the Scottish ingredients, details like delicious home-made bread, and a welcoming atmosphere.

Cost: Alc £19.50, fixed-price D £22.75. H/wine £6.95. Service exc.
Credit cards: 1 3. **Additional:** Children welcome; children's portions/menu; ◐ dishes; Vegan on request
Directions: A 835 (Inverness/Ullapool), left on to A832 at Braemore. Dundonnell is 14 miles, hotel on roadside

Ross & Cromarty
Map no: 14 NH08
Tel: 01854 633204
Proprietor: Selbie Florence
Seats: 70. No smoking in dining room. Air conditioned
Times: Last L 2.15pm/D 8.30pm

HIGHLAND SCOTLAND

DUROR, Stewart ●●

Simple but highly effective modern British cooking in a lovely Highland hotel

The Oban to Fort William west coast road is the lovely setting for this Highland hotel which is charmingly run by the Lacy family. While Chrissie and a smart young team look after the elegant restaurant, Michael presides over the kitchen producing a daily-changing four-course menu with limited choice: the best of local produce is used, and dinner is based around fresh ingredients that might only become available at the last minute. At a recent inspection meal a pleasant feuilleté of smoked salmon was followed by carrot and orange soup, and then tasty and enjoyable medallions of pork with spinach and Gruyère – the meat tender and arranged in slices around the spinach with gruyere sauce over the top. A steamed ginger pudding with an apricot and Glayva liqueur sauce finished the meal off in style. Cafétière coffee or selected teas with chocolates can be served in the comfortable first floor lounge or the Unicorn bar. Other dinner choices might include fillet of Mallaig cod with a gin and juniper sauce, or fillet of Loch Linnhe salmon with a chive beurre blanc sauce, and there's a good value wine list.

Directions: On the A828 between Oban and Fort William, 7 miles south of Ballachulish

Appin
Map no: 14 NM95
Tel: 0163174 268

Cost: Fixed-price dinner £25. H/wine £9.50. Service exc
Credit cards: 1 2 3 4

Menus: Fixed-price dinner, bar menu
Times: 7pm-Last D 9pm. Closed mid Oct-Mar

Chef: Michael Lacy
Proprietor: Best Western.
Managers: The Lacy Family

Seats: 35. No smoking in dining room
Additional: Children over 4 permitted; ● dishes; other diets on request

FORT WILLIAM, Crannog ●

☺ *On the town pier beside Loch Linnhe is a pretty good place for a simply-styled seafood restaurant, but having a fishing boat and smokehouse too, really puts it in a class of its own. The nearly all-fish menus, with additional blackboard specials, are excellent value.*

Cost: Alc £18. H/wine £7.95 ♀ Service exc. **Credit cards:** 1 3
Additional: Children welcome; children's portions; ● dishes
Directions: On waterfront in town centre

Inverness-shire
Map no: 14 NN17
Tel: 01397 705589
Chef: Susan Trowbridge
Proprietor: Susan Trowbridge
Seats: 60. No-smoking area
Times: Last L 3pm (2.30pm winter)/D 10.30pm (9.30pm winter). Closed 25 Dec, 1 Jan

FORT WILLIAM, Inverlochy Castle ●●●

A grand country house hotel with a fixed-price dinner menu successfully combining traditional and modern styles

Inverlochy Castle is the hotel that has everything: an unrivalled location in 500 acres of magnificent grounds with Ben Nevis and all the splendour of the Highlands as a backdrop, the solid stone structure of the house itself, and an interior of unabashed luxury. Then, of course, there is the food, which is all one would expect in this setting.
Chef Simon Haigh is now well established and produces a daily changing four-course dinner menu that successfully combines the traditional and the innovative. Not surprisingly, the emphasis is on local produce, West coast fish, scallops and lobster, Angus beef and game in season.
Meals are preceded by clever canapés – mini-ravioli, toad-in-

Inverness-shire
Map no: 14 NN17
Tel: 01397 702177

Cost: Fixed-price dinner £40, £45. H/wine £12 ♀ No service charge
Credit cards: 1 2 3

Menus: Fixed-price dinner, Sunday lunch

Times: 12.15-Last L 1.45pm, Last D 9.45pm. Closed mid Dec-1 Mar
Chef: Simon Haigh

the-hole, croissant and baked potato at a test meal in spring – and some very good home-baked breads. From a choice of five starters our inspectors sampled a small pig's trotter filled with a tasty mousse of chicken and sweetbreads, served with a Madeira sauce, marred only by some gritty morels, and a confit of quail, tender and succulent, accompanied by braised lentils. There is always a soup course, pleasant cream of spinach, watercress and potato on this occasion. The main courses chosen were a superb fillet of beef topped with a tangy horseradish hollandaise and presented with braised root vegetables, and queen scallops with asparagus and a thin butter sauce. Dessert was the highlight of the meal, however, a spectacularly towering hot orange soufflé which tasted as good as it looked.

The wine list is long and of great quality, offering red and white wines from all around the world. The claret section is particularly strong, containing many mature vintages including three superb 1961's

Proprietor: Grete Hobbs

Seats: 40. No smoking in dining room
Additional: No children at dinner; ❍ dishes

Directions: 3 miles north of Fort William on the A82, just past the golf club. Ignore signs to Inverlochy Castle, which is a ruin

FORT WILLIAM, **Moorings** ❀❀

Imaginative Scottish cooking making the most of fresh local produce, served in a welcoming atmosphere

Banavie
Inverness-shire
Map no: 14 NN17
Tel: 01397 772797

The warmth of its hospitality is matched only by the fires that burn at this hotel on chilly days, and the Sinclair family deserve their reputation for friendliness. Set in the village of Banavie, the hotel overlooks Neptune's Staircase, a series of locks on the Caledonian Canal. The cooking of chef Michel Nijsten is another attraction here, his set four-course dinner menu offering an imaginative selection of dishes featuring local fish, meat and game. Past starters have been steamed whole Speyside quail, and terrine of turbot and leek, with main courses like casserole of Rannoch venison, and roast Mallaig monkfish tail. Our inspector enjoyed a casserole of very fresh Mallaig scallops and Loch Linnhe prawns served with a delicate dill cream sauce, followed by a perfectly clear and tasty chicken soup with leeks and lovage. Loin of Mamore lamb was attractively presented with a tartlet of rhubarb chutney and a rosemary sauce, served on a bed of rösti potatoes. Strawberry cranachan was a light and refreshing dessert chosen from a tempting array including hot apple and almond tart, and Mrs Sinclair's lemon flan.

Cost: Fixed-price dinner £24. H/wine £10.75. Service exc
Credit cards: 1 2 3 4

Menus: Fixed-price dinner, bar menu

Times: Lunch by arrangement only. 7pm-Last D 9.30pm. Closed Xmas

Chef: Michel Nijsten
Proprietor: Norman Sinclair

Seats: 80. No smoking in dining room. Air conditioned
Additional: Children welcome; children's portions/menu; ❍ dishes; other diets on request

Directions: Leave Fort William on A82 in the direction of Inverness for almost 2 miles. Then join the A830 Mallaig road for 1 mile. Immediately after crossing the Caledonian Canal, the hotel is on the right

HIGHLAND SCOTLAND

GARVE, **Inchbae Lodge** ❦

Good food with a hearty welcome is to be expected at this small hotel on the banks of the River Blackwater. The short, menu uses plenty of fresh local produce: rum-cured smoked salmon wrapped around smoked haddock mousse or venison with wild mushrooms and red wine are a few examples.

Cost: Fixed-price D £21. H/wine £7.95. Service exc
Credit cards: None taken. **Additional:** Children welcome; children's portions; ❍ menu; Vegan/other diets on request
Directions: 6 miles west of village on A835 Inverness-Ullapool road

Inchbae
Ross & Cromarty
Map no: 14 NH36
Tel: 019975 269
Chefs: Les and Charlotte Mitchell
Proprietors: Les and Charlotte Mitchell
Seats: 30. No smoking in dining room
Times: Last L 2pm/D 8.30pm. Closed Xmas

GRANTOWN-ON-SPEY, **Garth** ❦

Standing beside the historic square, this well-run family-owned hotel offers a taste of Scotland prepared by Chef Anthony Renjard. Some of his tempting dishes include Spey salmon served in prawn and dill sauce, venison steak hunter-style, and Grampian pork fillet au poivre vert.

Cost: A/c £21, fixed-price L £10/D £23. Service exc
Credit cards: 1 2 3 4. **Additional:** Children welcome; children's portions; ❍ dishes; Vegan on request
Directions: Overlooking town square

Castle Road
Morayshire
Map no: 14NJ02
Tel: 01479 872836
Chef: Anthony Renjard
Proprietor: Gordon D McLaughlan
Seats: 50. No smoking in dining room
Times: Last L 2pm/D 6.30pm

INVERNESS, **Bunchrew House** ❦

A beautiful turreted building set in a landscaped garden where Chef James Cappie creates imaginative dishes on a fixed-price four-course menu. Starters include baked avocado stuffed with mushrooms and bacon, and to follow baked fillet of wild salmon with a herb crust set on tomato and basil coulis.

Credit cards: 1 2 3. **Additional:** Children welcome; children's portions/menu; ❍ dishes; Vegan/other diets on request
Directions: 3 miles west off A862

Bunchrew
Inverness-shire
Map no: 14 NH64
Tel: 01463 234917
Chef: James Cappie
Proprietors: Stewart and Leslie Dykes
Seats: 90. No smoking in dining room
Times: Last L 2pm/D 9pm

INVERNESS, **Dunain Park** ❦

A cosy Georgian country house set in six acres of gardens and woodland off the A82 Loch Ness road. Run in a friendly, unassuming manner by the Nicoll family, imaginative country cooking is offered, with a five-course carte priced by course and a separate steak menu.

Cost: A/c dinner £28, fixed-price lunch £16.50. H/wine £10. Service exc. **Credit cards:** 1 2 3 4 5. **Additional:** Children permitted; children's portions; ❍ dishes; Vegan on request
Directions: One mile from town boundary on A82

Inverness-shire
Map no: 14 NH64
Tel: 01463 230512
Chef: Ann Nicoll
Proprietors: Ann and Edward Nicoll
Seats: 36. No smoking in dining room
Times: Last L 1.30pm/D 9pm. Closed 3 weeks Jan/Feb

KENTALLEN, Ardsheal House 🏵🏵

Modern cuisine offering an imaginative choice of soundly-cooked dishes in a spectacular setting

A spectacular outlook over Loch Linnhe to the Morvern Hills beyond is enjoyed from this elevated hotel. Game and seafood feature strongly on the fixed-price menu which offers a choice at each stage plus a refreshing salad after the main course. The smart dining room and conservatory extension make a delightful setting for the modern cooking of George Kelso, and our inspector enjoyed a recent meal which began with a delicate smoked chicken and bacon terrine laced with nuts and red peppers, served with a contrasting chutney of red cabbage and apple. A smooth mange-tout and ginger soup was an interesting and unusual dish, and this was followed by roast saddle of moist, tender fillets of venison with delicious flavour, on a bed of braised lentils and celeriac, with a tasty rosemary and redcurrant sauce. Plated vegetables were simple but full of flavour, and a tangy baked lemon tart with sweet caramel ice cream was sheer heaven. Other choices might be pavé of lamb with provençale vegetables and port wine sauce, or grilled fillet of turbot with braised fennel and a vermouth and chervil sauce.

Directions: 4 miles south of the Ballachulish Bridge on the A828 between Glencoe and Appin

Appin
Argyllshire
Map no: 14 NN05
Tel: 0163174 227

Cost: Fixed-price lunch £17.50; fixed-price dinner £32.50. H/wine £9. Service exc
Credit cards: 1 2 3

Menus: Fixed-price lunch and dinner

Times: Midday-Last L 1.50pm, D 8.45pm

Chef: George Kelso
Proprietor: Michelle Kelso

Seats: 30-40. No smoking in dining room
Additional: Children permitted; ❂ dishes/other diets on request

KINGUSSIE, Osprey Hotel 🏵

☺ *An ideal base for exploring the Spey Valley, this comfortable hotel offers competent cooking. Fresh produce is used to create thoroughly enjoyable Taste of Scotland dishes, including Scotch lamb noisettes with a haggis and mint crust set on a base of black pudding and swede.*

Cost: Fixed-price D £19.25. H/wine £8. Service exc
Credit cards: 1 2 3. **Additional:** Children over 10 welcome; children's portions; ❂ dishes/Vegan on request; other diets with prior notice
Directions: On main street in village

Ruthven Road
Inverness-shire
Map no: 14 NH70
Tel: 01540 661510
Chef: Aileen Burrow
Proprietors: Aileen and Robert Burrow
Seats: 20. No smoking in dining room
Times: Last D 8pm. Closed 2 weeks Nov

KINGUSSIE, The Cross 🏵🏵🏵

Delightfully located and friendly, this restaurant makes good use of local fish, meat and game

A charming restaurant with its original beamed ceiling and exposed stone walls provides the focal point of a hotel – once an old tweed mill – idyllically set beside the stream in a small glen just above the village. The four-course fixed-price dinner menu offers a limited but well-balanced range of tried and tested dishes which take full advantage of quality Scottish produce. Such is the quality of the cuisine that our inspectors have been happy to award an additional rosette this year.

Local fish and game are sympathetically treated to achieve deceptively simple results; hot, home-smoked Shetland salmon with avocado and a pesto dressing, for example, might be

Tweed Mill Brae, Arbroilach Road
Inverness-shire
Map no: 14 NH70
Tel: 01540 661166

Cost: Fixed-price lunch £12.50 (2 courses), £15, fixed-price dinner £27.50 (4 Courses), £35. H/wine £8.50 ♀ Service exc
Credit cards: 1 3 5

Menus: Fixed-price lunch and dinner

Times: Last L 2pm, Last D 9pm.

followed by fillet of wild red deer lightly cooked and served with a sauce of red wine, juniper and thyme, or perhaps tender saddle of hare with a rich game gravy. Desserts range from Chocolate Whisky Laird ('three and a half million calories per slice', warns the menu!) to a light individual lime cheesecake set alongside a compote of cherries.

The wine list is outstanding, both for its value and range, and help is always at hand ; the Menu gastronomique actually includes an abbreviated list appropriate to that evening's food.

Directions: 200 yards uphill from traffic lights along Ardbroilach Road, then left down Tweed Mill Brae

Closed Tue, 1-26 Dec, 5 Jan- 1 Mar

Chef: Ruth Hadley
Proprietors: Ruth and Tony Hadley

Seats: 28. No smoking in dining room
Additional: No children under 12; Vegetarian dishes by prior arrangement

KINLOCHBERVIE, **Kinlochbervie Hotel** ❁

A modern hotel with views over the sea and fishing harbour where chef and proprietor Rex Neame produces a menu featuring local seafood. Dishes include grilled brill with mushroom and herb sauce, as well as meat and game dishes to cater for other tastes.

Cost: Fixed-price dinner £27.50. H/wine £7.50. Service exc
Credit cards: 1 2 3 4 **Additional:** Children welcome; children's portions; ❂ dishes; Vegan/other diets on request
Directions: Overlooking harbour

Sutherland
Map no: 14 NC25
Tel: 01971 521275
Chef: Rex Neame
Proprietors: Rex and Kate Neame
Seats: 40. No smoking in dining room
Times: Last D 8.30pm. Closed Nov-Mar

ONICH, **Allt-Nan-Ros** ❁

☺ *Fresh Highland ingredients underpin the success of the imaginative, French-influenced dishes on chef Stuart Robertson's daily-changing fixed-price menu, and an extensive wine list offers some good bins. Originally a Victorian shooting lodge, the hotel overlooks Lochs Leven and Linnhe.*

Cost: Fixed–price D £19.50. H/wine £8.95. Service exc
Credit cards: 1 2 3 4 5 **Additional:** Children welcome; children's portions/menu; ❂ dishes; Vegan/other diets on request
Directions: On A82, 11 miles south of Fort William, on the left hand side

Inverness-shire
Map no: 14 NN06
Tel: 018553 210/250
Chef: Stuart Robertson
Proprietors: Lachlan, Fiona and James MacLeod
Seats: 45. No smoking in dining room
Times: Last L 2pm/D 8.30pm

PLOCKTON, **Haven** ❁

The hotel is situated in the centre of this picturesque village on the bank of Loch Carron. A shortish fixed-price menu of four courses changes daily, and is inspired by fresh local produce – roulade of smoked salmon and mackerel pâté, and scallops and scampi with rice made an enjoyable sample meal.

Cost: Fixed–price D £21. H/wine £7. Service exc
Credit cards: 1 3. **Additional:** Children permitted; children's portions; ❂ dishes
Directions: On the main road, on the left just before the lochside

Ross & Cromarty
Map no: 14 NG83
Tel: 0159 9544223
Chef: Ian James
Proprietors: Majorie Nichols, John Graham
Seats: 38. No smoking in dining room
Times: Last D 8.30pm. Closed Jan & Xmas

SHIELDAIG, **Tigh an Eilean** ❀

☺ *This attractive hotel restaurant has a short daily-changing fixed-price menu with interesting dishes carefully prepared from fresh local ingredients, including fish. Our inspector tried the fresh and tender fillets of monkfish, served with white wine and cream sauce with a tomato purée and olives.*

Cost: Fixed-price D £19.50. H/wine £4.20 (half litre). Service exc
Credit cards: 1 3. **Additional:** Children welcome; children's portions; ❶ dishes on request
Directions: In the centre of Shieldaig, at the water's edge

Ross-shire
Map no: 14 NG85
Tel: 01520 755251
Chef: Callum F Stewart
Proprietors: Callum F Stewart
Seats: 26. No smoking in dining room
Times: Last D 8.30pm. Closed Nov-Mar

SKYE, ISLE OF – ARDVASAR, **Ardvasar Hotel** ❀

☺ *This unpretentious hotel is located close to the Armadale-Mallaig ferry terminal and offers genuine hospitality, good food and a friendly atmosphere. The carte features fresh island produce, including seafood and game. Dishes might include smoked venison and some tempting desserts.*

Cost: Alc £20. H/wine £6 ♀ Service exc. **Credit cards:** 1 3 5
Additional: Children welcome; children's portions; ❶ dishes; other diets on request
Directions: From Armadale ferry turn left and on through village

Map no: 13 NG60
Tel: 014714 223
Chef: Bill Fowler
Proprietors: Bill and Gretta Fowler
Seats: 25. Smoking discouraged
Times: Last L 2pm/D 8.15pm. Dining room closed end Nov-Mar

SKYE, ISLE OF – PORTREE, **Rosedale** ❀

A tempting range of Scottish fare is featured in the restaurant of a charming hotel created from three adjoining nineteenth-century buildings beside the harbour. All five courses of the daily-changing menus are soundly based on quality fresh produce – much of it from Skye itself.

Cost: Fixed-price D £22 ♀ Service exc. **Credit cards:** 1 3
Additional: Children permitted; children's portions; ❶ dishes
Directions: From centre of village drive down Wentworth Street, over small crossroads and into the harbour area. Rosedale is at the bottom of the brae on the left facing the loch

Map no: 13 NG44
Tel: 01478 613131
Chef: Linda Thomson
Proprietor: Hugh Andrew
Seats: 36. No smoking in dining room
Times: Last D 8.30pm

HIGHLAND SCOTLAND

SKYE, ISLE OF – COLBOST,
Three Chimneys ❋

Located on the secluded southern shore of Loch Dunvegan, this characterful restaurant has views extending over The Minch to the Outer Isles. The emphasis here is very much on sea food, especially shellfish. A selection of fixed-price four-course menus includes an improved choice for vegetarians.

Cost: Alc L £15, fixed-price D £25, £27.50, £65 (seafood special for 2). H/wine £9.95. Service exc. **Credit cards:** 1 3 5
Additional: Children permitted (please phone to check for dinner); children's portions; ❍ menu; Vegan/other diets on request
Directions: From Dunvegan take B884 to Glendale. Restaurant is at Colbost 4.5 miles from main road turn off

Map no: 13 NG24
Tel: 01470 511258
Chef: Shirley Spear
Proprietors: Eddie and Shirley Spear
Seats: 30. No smoking in dining room
Times: Last L 2pm/D 9pm. Closed Sun, Nov-Mar

SKYE, ISLE OF – HARLOSH,
Harlosh House ❋❋

Modern cooking with honest flavours and simple but meticulous preparation, specialising in the fruits of the sea

Local seafood and fish are the specialities of this delightful little hotel, and meticulous attention is paid to their preparation and presentation. Prime beef, lamb and game also appear on the short but well-balanced carte, and everything from home-made bread to chocolates is handled with the same blend of finesse and loving care. Dishes are prepared to order as far as possible, and guests are ushered into the dining room in groups of four at half-hourly intervals. A recent inspection meal was thoroughly enjoyed, starting with very fresh-tasting crab claws served cold with a mayonnaise dip, followed by whole monkfish tail lightly studded with garlic and roasted, then served with finely shredded lettuce and a sharply flavoured mint and hazelnut salsa. Attractive vegetables included fine green beans and carrots, tasty leeks and well-made sauté potatoes. Desserts are another plus here, and the chosen nutty profiteroles filled with fresh cream and served with caramel sauce were a great success. With its spectacular setting overlooking Loch Bracadale this hotel offers a haven of peace and good food.

Directions: Four miles south of Dunvegan, turn right off A863, signed Harlosh

Dunvegan
Map no: 13 NG24
Tel: 01470 521367

Cost: Alc £21.50. H/wine £8.50. Service exc.
Credit cards: 1 3 5

Menu: A la carte

Times: 7pm-Last D 8.30pm. Closed Mon; mid Oct-Easter

Chef: Peter John Elford
Proprietors: Peter and Lindsey Elford

Seats: 18. No smoking in dining room
Additional: Children welcome; children's portions; other diets on request

SKYE, ISLE OF – ISLE ORNSAY,
Kinloch Lodge ❋❋

A relaxed and welcoming former lodge with commanding views and some very enjoyable cooking

In a completely secluded setting at the end of a long forest track stands this charming country house hotel, the home of Lord and Lady MacDonald. With its splendid outlook over

Map no: 13 NG71
Tel: 014713 214

Chefs: Lady MacDonald, Peter MacPherson, Claire Munro
Proprietors: Lord and Lady MacDonald

Seats: 30. No smoking in dining room

Loch na Dal to the mainland hills beyond, this civilised hotel has the atmosphere of a comfortable private home. The elegant dining room with its family portraits and silver is an appropriate setting for Lady Claire MacDonald's delicious cooking, and the short fixed-price menu changes daily: perhaps cheese tartlets filled with quail's eggs and garlic with tomato mayonnaise, followed by mushroom and leek soup, and chargrilled fillet of venison with port and redcurrant jelly. A recent inspection meal began with an intensely flavoured smoked mackerel and horseradish mousse, with a second course of very enjoyable pea, pear and mint soup – a successful combination of flavours. Devilled seafood including monkfish, prawns, scallops and salmon came with a delicate tomato and Tabasco sauce, with a superbly wicked dark chocolate terrine to finish. Strong coffee and home-made fudge are served in the drawing rooms.

Times: Last D by arrangement

Cost: Fixed-price D £25, £33. H/wine £8. Service exc
Credit cards: 1 3.

Additional: Children permitted (over 8 or by arrangement); children's portions; ❷ dishes; special diets on request

Directions: Six miles south of Broadford on A851

SPEAN BRIDGE, Old Station ❁

☺ *This charming little restaurant has a well-deserved local reputation. Owner Richard Bunney is the chef and his wife Helen looks after the customers. The menu is unpretentious and use is made of local produce in a style of cooking which is light and complemented by delicate saucing.*

Cost: Alc £18. H/wine £8.25. Service exc. **Credit cards:** 1 3 .
Additional: Children permitted; ❷ dishes; Vegan/other diets by arrangement
Directions: In centre of village, follow road signposted Corriechoillie for 100 yards. Then take first right signposted BR station, for 200 yards

Station Road
Inverness-shire
Map no: 14 NN28
Tel: 01397 712535
Chef: Richard Bunney
Proprietors: Richard and Helen Bunney
Seats: 30. No smoking in dining room
Times: Last D 9pm. Closed Sun-Wed (Oct-Apr), 2 weeks Oct, 2 weeks Mar, 25 Dec, 1 Jan

STRONTIAN, Kilcamb Lodge ❁❁

A family operation offering fine food and good hospitality in a striking setting

A mother and son partnership in the kitchen is a recipe for success at this charming small hotel, which nestles in 30 acres of grounds on the shores of Loch Sunart. The cooking of Ann and Peter Blakeway is going from strength to strength, and their sound, well-balanced menu reflects a reliable Scottish style of cuisine. The four set courses have featured starters like cucumber mousse with smoked salmon, and mousseline of lemon sole, while main courses might be roast noisettes of Scottish lamb with fresh mint sauce, or Scottish rainbow trout with mushroom stuffing. A soup is always served between courses – perhaps celery, almond and walnut, and tomato and orange.
  Our inspector enjoyed a delicious chicken and spinach pancake, with a creamy white wine sauce and a hint of parmesan, and a steak and kidney pie made from lean, tender meat and good pastry. Vegetables were plain and simple but very tasty, while an elaborate dessert was light coffee meringues with coffee-flavoured filling and chocolate sauce – a mini gâteau. The rest of the Blakeway family is fully involved

Argyllshire
Map no: 14 NM86
Tel: 01967 2257

Cost: Fixed-price dinner £24. No service charge
Credit cards: 1 3

Menu: Fixed–price dinner

Times: Last D 7.30pm. Closed 20 Nov-10 Feb

Chefs: Peter and Ann Blakeway
Proprietors: The Blakeway Family

Seats: 26. No smoking in dining room
Additional: Children over 10 permitted; children's portions; ❷ dishes; other diets on request

outside the kitchen, and their gracious hospitality ensures excellent service.

Directions: Over the Corran ferry off A82. Follow signs to Strontian. First left over bridge in centre of village

TORRIDON, **Loch Torridon Hotel** ●●

Innovative Cordon Bleu cooking in a loch-side Highland shooting lodge

A panelled dining room under a beautiful ornate ceiling, with views of mountain and loch, is the dramatic setting for some memorable Cordon Bleu cooking. This Victorian shooting lodge has recently undergone a complete transformation from run-down pile to country house hotel, and its grand Highland atmosphere is easily matched by the cuisine. Chef Timothy Morris relies on the best local ingredients to produce quality results with his innovative style of cooking: the short fixed-price menu features starters like sautéed rabbit on a bed of leek purée with a Madeira sauce, and a roast Gressingham duck main course with chicken liver mousse and a game stock sauce. At a recent inspection meal sautéed chicken livers with quail's eggs and mixed lettuce salad made a delightful starter – the livers all but melting in the mouth. Fresh local scallops were sautéed almost to perfection, and served on a bed of fennel with a delicate, creamy champagne sauce. Desserts are not for the faint-hearted, and an airy dark chocolate mousse flavoured with Grand Marnier was delectable.

Directions: On the A896 south of Torridon, ignore turning for Torridon village

Torridon
Ross & Cromarty
Map no: 14 NH15
Tel: 01445 791242

Cost: Fixed-price dinner £29.50. H/wine £9.50 ♀ No service charge
Credit cards: 1 3

Menus: Fixed-price dinner, bar menu
Times: Last D 8.30pm. Restricted service Jan and Feb
Chefs: Tim Morris, Geraldine Gregory
Proprietors: Geraldine and David Gregory

Seats: 40. No smoking in dining room
Additional: Children over 12 permitted; children's portions/menu; ❷ dishes; Vegan/other diets on request

ULLAPOOL, **Altnaharrie Inn** ●●●●

A place of pilgrimage for food lovers that lives up to its reputation with cooking of impeccable artistry and individual style

To eat here you must take a ferry from Ullapool (park at the Royal Hotel) across Loch Broom and after dinner stay overnight in one of the eight delightful bedrooms. Booking, therefore, is essential, and the evening's menu will be discussed when you make the reservation.
  Gunn Eriksen and Fred Brown have not made life easy for themselves by choosing such a remote location, but the cooking, the setting, and the atmosphere of this wonderful inn have created a mystique that has drawn in crowds of food worshippers for many years. Here is cooking of great artistry, and clear honest flavours that linger in the memory for months. Our inspector's spring meal this year began with aperitifs and canapés in the lounge while he waited to be seated in the attractive restaurant with its flagstone floors, antique tables and huge pots of flowers.
  That evening the meal began with the simple, exquisite taste of two scallops, split and gently cooked, served on a bed of

Ross & Cromarty
Map no: 14 NH19
Tel: 01854 633230

Cost: Check when booking. The meal cost -approximately £55 - is included in the overnight stay. H/wine £12 ♀ No service charge
Credit cards: 1 2 3

Menus: None, guests are consulted prior to arrival

Times: Dinner 8pm. No lunches

Chef: Gunn Eriksen
Proprietors: Fred Brown, Gunn Eriksen

Seats: 16. No smoking throughout
Additional: No children under 8

lightly dressed rocket over green lentils. A lobster broth followed, with the claw and pieces of meat in a crystal-clear liquid of remarkably intense flavour that bit back with ginger and chilli. The main course, roast saddle of rabbit was stuffed with a mousse of its own trimmings and herbs, artfully separated from the saddle by spinach leaves, and hiding the explosive taste of juniper berry in every piece. This came on a bed of rösti potatoes garnished with kidney, liver and strips of mushroom, with two sauces, one a juniper-flavoured cream, the other Burgundy-based.

A selection of cheeses in excellent condition followed and then desserts, the only course at which there is a choice, and our inspector opted for one of Gunn Eriksen's own favourites, cloudberry ice cream served in a pastry shell, topped with spun sugar.

The wine list starts with a dozen or so house wines of excellent quality from about £12 to £22. If you wish to look further, you will find many mature vintages of claret and Burgundy, plus some good choices from the other classic areas of France and the New World.

Directions: Follow A835 north to Ullapool. Telephone from Ullapool for directions to ferry. Advance booking at Altnaharrie essential

LOTHIAN

DUNBAR, **The Courtyard** ❀

☺ *Converted from fishermens' cottages, this pleasant small hotel is on the waterfront. Top quality seafood, game, prime beef and lamb feature, and the carte offers a range of Taste of Scotland dishes and a tempting choice of home-made desserts, with a more modest short fixed-price menu.*

Cost: Alc £19.65; fixed-price D £15. H/wine £8.50. Service inc.
Credit cards: 1 2 3 4. **Additional:** Children welcome; children's portions; ❀ dishes; other diets on request
Directions: Situated on the seafront close to the town centre

Wood Bush Brae
East Lothian
Map no: 12 NT67
Tel: 01368 864169
Chef: Peter Bramley
Proprietor: Peter Bramley
Seats: 26. No cigars or pipes
Times: Last L 2pm/D 9.30pm. Closed Xmas Day evening

EDINBURGH, **Atrium** ❀❀❀

☺ *An avant-garde setting in the heart of the city for modern Scottish cooking with cosmopolitan influences*

In his first venture as chef/proprietor, Andrew Radford (formerly of Waterloo Place and Hansel's restaurants) and his wife Lisa have set up shop in a corner site within the Traverse Theatre building, adjacent to the Usher Hall. Their relaxed and increasingly popular establishment may be considered Edinburgh's first avant-garde restaurant. Tables are crafted from old railway sleepers (appropriately enough for a chef first

Cambridge Street
Midlothian
Map no: 11 NT27
Tel: 0131-228 8882

Cost: Alc £20. H/wine £8.95 ♀
Service exc
Credit cards: 1 2 3 5

Menus: *A la carte*, snack lunch, pre-theatre

associated with the luxury Royal Scotsman train) and lit with odourless paraffin torches to give an almost medieval atmosphere. Canvas is not only used to cover the chairs but is stretched sail-like across part of the concrete ceiling. The branched ceiling lights and various metal sculptures are also a talking point, but the real star of the show is the food.

Prime ingredients are sympathetically handled and cleanly presented with no unnecessary flourishes, while flavours are well defined and textures thoughtfully balanced. Fish is especially successful as two lunchtime meals proved. A good piece of cod, simply cooked and accompanied by dressed greens and lemon butter made a sizeable but light starter, and beautifully cooked, moist salmon with baby spinach, leeks and butter sauce an enjoyable main course. At lunchtime there is a choice of four dishes at each course, all reasonably priced, while in the evening the range of dishes increases, as do the prices to some extent. Fillet of Scottish beef, venison or corn-fed chicken might appear, and a vegetarian dish, such as courgette and leek gratin with shaved goat's cheese.

Desserts are effectively straightforward, including banana crumble with toffee sauce and Amaretto chocolate mousse with shortbread. There are many interesting and unusual choices on the wine list, starting with house wines at £8.95.

Directions: From Princes Street take 2nd left off Lothian Road into Castle Terrace, 1st right into Cambridge Street. Atrium is next to Usher Hall

Times: Midday-Last L 2.30pm, 6pm-Last D 10.30pm. L not served Sat. Closed Sun, 1 week Xmas

Chef: Andrew Radford
Proprietor: Andrew Radford

Seats: 60. Air conditioned
Additional: Children welcome; children's portions; ✪ dishes; Vegan/other diets on request

EDINBURGH, **Balmoral** ✿✿

International standards in Scottish cooking at an impressive Edinburgh landmark

The Balmoral hotel blends old-fashioned elegance with the modern facilities of an international hotel. The spacious lobby with marble floor and plush carpets gives access to the Palm Court Lounge, ideal for morning coffee and afternoon tea, while Bridges Brasserie provides an informal all-day food option. In contrast, the Grill Room offers serious cooking in the grand style, the result of the kitchen team's creative flair combined with the freshest Scottish ingredients. A French influence is apparent in the stimulating *carte* which also features Taste of Scotland specialities, such as the 'Maize-fed baby chicken carved on to a braised savoy cabbage, adorned with black sausages and a Glayva whisky mousse'. Crab-filled courgette flowers and porterhouse steak have recently featured on the menu, which has a strong seafood component. This was investigated by our inspector who tried the seafood compote and soufflé of fresh scallops wrapped in lemon sole, ending an enjoyable meal with an airy blueberry mousse. Fixed-price lunch menus are also offered, whilst the wine list is extensive and knowledgeable.

Directions: In hotel next to Waverley Railway Station

Princes Street
Midlothian
Map no: 11 NT27
Tel: 0131-556 2414

Cost: *Alc* £45, fixed-price lunch £18.50 (2 courses), £21.50, fixed-price dinner £35. H/wine £16.50 ♀ Service exc
Credit cards: 1 2 3 4 5

Menus: *A la carte,* fixed-price lunch and dinner, pre-theatre

Times: Midday–Last L 2.15pm, 7pm–Last D 10.30pm. Closed Sat lunch, Sun lunch

Proprietor: Iain Archibald

Seats: 45. Air conditioned

Additional: Children welcome; ✪ menu; other diets on request

SCOTLAND LOTHIAN

EDINBURGH, **Caledonian Hotel** ●●

An elegant hotel with a traditional air and a choice of two restaurants

Affectionately known as the Caley, this former railway hotel with its magnificently restored facade dominates the west end of the city. An air of quiet elegance prevails and much of the hotel's original Victorian architecture is retained, especially in the superb staircase and impressive Pompadour restaurant. Carriages restaurant has archways leading to the old Caley railway station. In keeping with this traditional air, consistently attentive service continues to be provided. The formal but by no means stuffy atmosphere in the Pompadour, where a pianist plays in the evening, is the perfect platform for chef Tony Binks' cooking. Three menu themes are offered at dinner, from the French-influenced *carte* to a selection of 'classic' dishes of the past. A terrine of Barbary duck confit with mango and sultana chutney was noted for its moist texture and distinctive flavour. Roast saddle of lamb stuffed with spinach and rosemary with a mushroom and shallot sauce was less impressive, being a rather poor cut of meat. An orange bavarois was subtly flavoured and benefited by a powerful sabayon, one of several sauces from the trolley.

Directions: At western end of Princes Street

Princes Street
Midlothian
Map no: 11 NT27
Tel: 0131-225 2433

Cost: *Alc* £40, fixed-price lunch £21; fixed-price dinner £32.50. H/wine £13 ♀ Service exc
Credit cards: 1 2 3 4

Menus: *A la carte,* fixed-price lunch and dinner

Times: 12.30pm-Last L 2pm, 7.30pm-Last D 10.30pm. Closed Sat lunch, Sun dinner

Chef: Tony Binks
Proprietor: Queens Moat Houses. Manager: David Clarke

Seats: 60. No-smoking area
Additional: No children; ♥ menu; Vegan/other diets on request; pianist

EDINBURGH, **Carlton Highland** ●

The choice of eating options at this busy hotel near the Royal Mile includes Carlyle's patisserie with its delicious open sandwiches, the Carlton Court carvery serving all-day snacks and grills, and Quills, an elegant formal restaurant where varied menus offer a range of Scottish and international dishes.

Cost: *Alc* £20.45; fixed-price L £9.95 (2 courses), £11.95/ D £19.75. H/wine £9.95. Service exc. **Credit cards:** 1 2 3 4 5 **Additional:** Children welcome; children's menu; ♥ dishes; Vegan/other diets on request
Directions: At the east end of Princes Street, on the North Bridge

North Bridge
Midlothian
Map no: 11 NT27
Tel: 0131-567 277
Chef: Charles Price
Proprietor: Scottish Highland. Manager: Ilio Giovacchini
Seats: 45. No cigars or pipes. Air conditioned
Times: Last L 2pm/D 10pm. Lunch not served Sat. Closed Sun

EDINBURGH, **Channings** ●

☺ *A cosy club-like atmosphere prevails at this discreet conversion of five Edwardian terraced townhouses, quietly situated just north-west of the city. Fixed-price and carte menus are offered in the brasserie restaurant, with the emphasis on good quality fresh Scottish ingredients cooked in modern style.*

Cost: *Alc* £18.50, fixed-price L £7.50 (2 courses), £9.95/D £17.50. H/wine £8.95. **Credit cards:** 1 2 3 4 5 **Additional:** Children permitted; children's portions; ♥ dishes; Vegan/other diets on request
Directions: From city centre follow signs for A90 and Forth Road Bridge on to Queensferry Road. After passing Learmonth Terrace on the right, turn right into South Learmonth Gardens. The hotel is halfway along

South Learmonth Gardens
Midlothian
Map no: 11 NT27
Tel: 0131-315 2226
Chef: Colin Drummond
Proprietor: Peter Taylor
Seats: 70
Times: Last L 2pm/D 9.30pm (10pm Fri/Sat). Closed 26-28 Dec

EDINBURGH, **Dalmahoy** ❀

An impressive extended Georgian mansion with grounds including two golf courses. The Pentland restaurant offers Scottish/French cuisine with a fixed-price menu and an imaginative carte. Dishes might include a chicken liver pâté with smoked venison, or fresh turbot with a seafood sauce.

Cost: Alc £23.50, fixed-price L £14.50/D £23.50. H/wine £10.95 ♀ Service exc. **Credit cards:** 1 2 3 4
Additional: Children welcome; children's portions; ❶ menu; Vegan/other diets on request. Live entertainment
Directions: Follow A71 towards West Calder from Edinburgh, on left-hand side

Kirknewton
Midlothian
Map no: 11 NT27
Tel: 0131-333 1845
Chef: Gary Bates
Proprietor: Country Club.
Manager: Colin Mossman
Seats: 125. No-smoking in dining room. Air conditioned
Times: Last L 2pm/D 9.45pm. L not served Sat

EDINBURGH, **Ellersly House** ❀

☺ Seasonally-changing fixed-price menus make imaginative use of fresh Scottish produce in the comfortable traditional restaurant of this popular hotel – a creeper-clad Edwardian house in a residential area. Pan-fried venison may be served on vegetable spaghetti with a café au lait sauce.

Cost: Fixed-price L £12.75/D £22.50. H/wine £10.95 ♀ Service exc.
Credit cards: 1 2 3 4 5. **Additional:** Children welcome; children's portions/menu; ❶ dishes; Vegan/other diets on request
Directions: From Corstorphine road, pass Edinburgh Zoo heading for West End. Turn left at Western Corner into Ellersly Road.

4 Ellersly Road
Midlothian
Map no: 11 NT27
Tel: 0131-337 6888
Chef: Trevor Ward
Proprietor: Jarvis Hotels.
Manager: Paul Bean
Seats: 70. No smoking in dining room
Times: Last L 2.30pm/D9.30pm. L not served Sat

EDINBURGH, **George Inter-Continental** ❀

Behind a classical façade, this well-managed and long-established hotel offers a choice of restaurants. Our rosette goes to Le Chambertin. Chef Klaus Knust combines good Scottish produce with French-styled dishes complemented by a fine wine list and personable service.

Cost: Alc £35, fixed-price lunch £19, £21, £23, fixed–price dinner £19.94. H/wine £11.75 ♀ Service exc. **Credit cards:** 1 2 3 4 5
Additional: Children welcome; children's portions/menu; ❶ menu; Vegan/other diets on request. Sat dinner dance
Directions: At the east end of George Street

19-21 George Street
Midlothian
Map no: 11 NT27
Tel: 0131-459 2506
Chef: Klaus Knust
Proprietor: Inter-Continental.
Manager: Barnaby Hawkes
Seats: 54. No-smoking area; pipes and cigars only after coffee
Times: Last L 2pm/D 10pm. Closed Xmas, New Year, BHs

EDINBURGH, **King James Thistle** ✦

Dinner in the split-level Saint Jacques Brasserie of this busy hotel – part of a shopping complex off the east end of Princes Street – remains an enjoyable experience, chef David Veal taking pride in the creation of a range of interesting international dishes from fine Scottish and continental ingredients.

Cost: Alc £26; fixed-price L £9.50 (2 courses), £11.50/D £19.50. H/wine £11.30 ♀ Service exc. **Credit cards:** 1 2 3 4. **Additional:** Children welcome; children's portions/menu; ✪ menu; Vegan/other diets on request
Directions: Adjacent to St James shopping mall

107 Leith Street
Midlothian
Map no: 11 NT27
Tel: 0131-556 0111
Chef: David Veal
Proprietor: Mount Charlotte Thistle. Manager: Peter Ratcliffe
Seats: 90. Air conditioned
Times: Last L 2.15pm/D 10pm

EDINBURGH, **L'Auberge** ✦✦

A busy city-centre restaurant offering extremely good-value set menus and an interesting French carte

Contemporary French cooking styles using the best Scottish ingredients continue to be a successful formula at this long-established city restaurant. Chef Fabrice Bresulier produces an interesting signature *carte* as well as various fixed-price menus, and our inspector was highly impressed with a recent set lunch that offered quality and outstanding value. This meal began with a smooth and moist terrine of salmon and whitefish with a lemon, dill and garlic mayonnaise sauce, followed by very tender pigeon breast cooked pink on a bed of stewed onions, and served with a well-made redcurrant jus. A light and zesty French lemon tart with a gently caramelised topping was an ideal dessert for pudding lovers. The *carte* offers a choice of soups, and starters such as mousseline pâté of chicken and oyster mushroom, with main dishes like sauté of North Sea scallops with a crab and shellfish cream sauce, and vegetarian fricassée of parsnip navets and oyster mushrooms with a white wine cream sauce. Service is enthusiastic and attentive in this split-level restaurant, and a distinctly French wine list offers a good selection of halves.

Directions: In city centre, near John Knox House

56 St Mary's Street
Midlothian
Map no: 11 NT27
Tel: 0131-556 5888

Cost: Alc £23; fixed-price lunch £10; fixed-price dinner £19.85. H/wine £8.50 ♀ Service exc
Credit cards: 1 2 3 4

Menus: A la carte, fixed-price lunch and dinner, Sunday lunch, pre-theatre

Times: Last L 2pm, Last D 9.30pm

Chef: Fabrice Bresulier
Proprietor: Daniel Wencker

Seats: 60. No smoking until after meal; no pipes or cigars. Air conditioned
Additional: Children welcome; children's portions/menu; ✪ menu; other diets on request

EDINBURGH, **Le Marché Noir** ✦✦

☺ A lively restaurant offering mainly contemporary French dishes from a choice of fixed-price dinner menus

Lying just off Dundas Street, this cheerful little restaurant cooks French dishes in contemporary style. Proprietor Malcolm Duck does not consider it an out-and out French restaurant, and although its menu is in French, he and his friendly staff willingly offer translation and this establishes a nice rapport with the customers. There are two fixed-price dinner menus which differ in price but standards are consistent. An exceedingly good chicken liver parfait had plenty of flavour and proved an excellent starter. Roast fillet of lamb with a minted redcurrant sauce was capably cooked, although the herb en

2/4 Eyre Place
Midlothian
Map no: 11 NT27
Tel: 0131-558 1608

Cost: Fixed-price L £10 (2 courses), £11.50, £16.50/D £19.50 (3 courses), £25.50. H/wine £8.50 ♀ Service exc.
Credit cards: 1 2 3

Times: Last L 2.30pm/D10pm (10.30pm Fri, Sat, 9.30pm Sun). Closed Xmas, 1-2 Jan

croute was merely the lightest covering of crust. Vegetables are treated sympathetically. Other main courses included an unusual roast fillet of salmon with a smoked salmon cream with Cognac, whilst desserts ranged from the traditional poached pear and red wine to a hot lemon sponge with raisins. The restaurant was recently awarded a well-deserved second rosette for its excellent cuisine.

Directions: Turn off Dundas Street into Eyre Place

Chef: Neil Ross
Proprietor: Malcolm Duck

Seats: 40-45. Smoking allowed after meals

Additional: Children permitted; ❷ dishes; Vegan/other diets on request

EDINBURGH, **Martins** ❀❀❀

The friendliest of restaurants offering modern Scottish cooking using first-class produce and organic vegetables

Some of the best restaurants are tucked away in the oddest of corners, and this is certainly the case with Martins. Fear not, once inside the attractive little restaurant, the austere surroundings of the back street lane are instantly forgotten in the warmth of the greeting provided by Gay and Martin Irons. A short *carte* menu of well-chosen dishes is offered, based on the availability of first-class produce – fish and game figuring prominently. Vegetarian dishes are not generally featured on the menu but can be provided on request.

At an inspection meal, which began with a delicious cheese quiche appetiser, a starter of pan-fried monkfish on a bed of spring onion, olive and tarragon salsa brought a Mediterranean flavour to a winter's evening. A new dimension was given to a good saddle of venison by serving it chargrilled, though the accompanying purée of cumin and garlic was served unexpectedly cool. Vegetables are organically grown and this can limit the selection, but on this occasion a smoky-flavoured kale was particularly appreciated. Roast breast of Barbary duck, another main course sampled, was rated by our inspector as among the best he had tasted.

To finish, there is a choice of about five puddings. Our inspector opted for a well-made orange parfait, and if the orange flavour was slightly elusive, the accompanying zesty lemon soufflé certainly compensated, along with the sharp redcurrant coulis. Cheese lovers should beat a path here! There is a mouth-watering selection of unpasteurised cheeses from small independent Scottish and Irish producers. Martin will gladly give chapter and verse on each – pure theatre!

Directions: North Lane is off Rose Street, between Frederick Street and Castle Street. Cars enter via Frederick Street

70 Rose Street, North Lane
Midlothian
Map no: 11 NT27
Tel: 0131-225 3106

Cost: *Alc* £28.90, fixed-price lunch £10.95. H/wine £9.95. Service exc
Credit cards: 1 2 3 4

Menus: *A la carte* lunch and dinner, fixed-price lunch
Times: Midday-Last L 2pm, 7pm-Last D 10pm. L not served Sat. Closed Sun, Mon, 4 weeks from 24 Dec, 1 week Jun, 1 week end Sep

Chefs: Forbes Stott, Alan Mathieson
Proprietors: Martin and Gay Irons

Seats: 28. No smoking in dining room
Additional: Children over 8 permitted; ❷ dishes; Vegan/other diets on request

EDINBURGH, **Norton House** ❀❀

Ambitious dishes in the pretty and pleasant environment of a Victorian mansion

The attractive candlelit Conservatory restaurant at Norton House is the ideal setting for chef David Burns's creative modern cooking. *Carte* starters have included 'Home-cured "Duck Breast Ham" with warm salsa croutons and balsamic

Ingliston
Midlothian
Map no: 11 NT27
Tel: 0131-333 1275

Cost: *Alc* £33; fixed-price lunch £14.75; fixed–price dinner £20.50 ♀ Service exc
Credit cards: 1 2 3 4 5

vinegar' alongside Arbroath smokies and, our inspector's choice, a light, creamy soup of crab, prawns and squat lobster, which had an honest, shellfish aroma. Borders lamb served with a filo basket of shepherd's pie and a dish of venison with chocolate sauce are typical of the main course selections. The grill section may feature, for example, Angus beef, Scottish salmon and sea-cat while vegetarian dishes are well represented. Our inspector chose navarin of lamb, served with a very thin red wine gravy which, though uneven, (with some rather crude lumps of meat) was very tasty and tender. This was accompanied by simply and crisply cooked beans, carrots and small spring onions and firm new potatoes boiled in the skin. Rich and inspired puddings include chestnut charlotte with malt whisky and marbled chocolate mille-feuille. All is supported by willing service.

Directions: Near junc 2 of M8, off the A8, past Edinburgh Airport

Menus: A la carte, fixed-price lunch and dinner, business lunch Mon-Fri, Sun lunch, bar/lounge menu
Times: Midday-Last L 2pm, 7pm–Last D 9pm. Lunch not served Sat

Chef: David Burns
Proprietor: Voyager Group
Manager: Aileesh Carew

Seats: 80. No-smoking area
Additional: Children welcome; ❂ menu; Vegan/other diets on request. Entertainment Thu–Sat

EDINBURGH, **The Vintners Room** ❂❂

An original setting for a popular wine bar and an intimate candlelit restaurant

The dockland area of Leith is being steadily redeveloped, and fast becoming the 'in' place in the city. However, the Vintner Room has been established for several years now. Occupying the ground floor of an old Georgian warehouse, the wine bar was originally a bottle store and it retains an authentic functional appearance with its plaster walls, wooden floors and old furniture. The smaller, more intimate candlelit restaurant is similar, with smart table settings being its one concession to style. This no-frills theme extends to the cooking which has hearty French provincial roots, with chef/patron Tim Cumming preferring the flavours to do the talking, as with an intriguing starter of sautéed scallops with rhubarb butter sauce. It did work, but the rhubarb tended to dominate. Venison noisette with a plum purée and polenta was also a good marriage. Tim resists the temptation to sauce every dish. A white and dark chocolate parfait was beautifully smooth, but deserved a crème anglaise rather than custard. For cheese buffs there is an impressive selection in perfect condition; a Caerphilly was found to be outstanding.

Directions: Drive down Leith Walk, left into Junction Street, right into Henderson Street. Restaurant is part of old wine warehouse on the right

The Vaults
87 Giles Street, Leith
Midlothian
Map no: 11 NT27
Tel: 0131-554 6767

Cost: Alc £25; fixed-price lunch £8.75 (2 courses), £11.75.
H/wine £8.50. Service exc
Credit cards: 1 2 3

Menus: A la carte, fixed-price lunch, bar menu
Times: Midday–Last L 2.30pm, Last D 10.30pm. Closed Sun & 2 weeks Xmas

Chef: A T Cumming and J Baxter
Proprietors: A T and S C Cumming

Seats: 65. No smoking in dining room
Additional: Children welcome; children's portions; ❂ menu; other diets on request

EDINBURGH,
The Witchery by the Castle ❂❂

Artistic but unfussy Scottish cooking in two contrasting but interesting restaurants

An old kirk and the Whisky Heritage Centre flank this famous restaurant where the Hellfire Club was reputed to meet in medieval times, and which retains much of that original atmosphere. The ambience is quite relaxed, unlike the more

Castle Hill, Royal Mile
Midlothian
Map no: 11 NT27
Tel: 0131-225 5613

Cost: Alc £25; fixed–price lunch £10.40 (2 courses), £12.95; fixed–price dinner £19.95.
H/wine £10.95 ❂ Service exc
Credit cards: 1 2 3 4 5
Menus: A la carte, fixed-price

formal Secret Garden which shares the same menu and high standards of service. Here candlelight replaces electricity for an elegant and discreet setting for the fine Scottish food. Flavours are distinctive and accurate in both restaurants, as our inspector discovered with pan-fried venison livers with garlic dauphinoise and natural juices, followed by tender fillet of beef with a Madeira and thyme glaze, with a generous dish of excellent vegetables. A rather heavy bread and butter pudding with crème anglaise let the meal down slightly, but not enough to doubt the high standards normally achieved. Another dish on the *carte* or short set menus might be vegetarian carrot and walnut ravioli parcels on fried leeks. Allow yourself plenty of time to peruse the wine list for it is 100 pages long and contains good example, of every style and quality of wine.

Directions: At the entrance to Edinburgh Castle at the very top of the Royal Mile

lunch and dinner, Sunday lunch, after theatre

Times: Midday-Last L 4pm, Last D 11.30pm. Closed Xmas, 1 Jan

Chef: Andrew Main
Proprietors: James Thomson, Sid N Mattison

Seats: 120
Additional: Children permitted (over 8 after 8pm); ❂ dishes; Vegan/other diets on request

GULLANE, **Greywalls** ❂❂

A gracious country house of character and charm where the modern British cooking lives up to the standards set by staff

Directly overlooking the 9th green of the Muirfield golf course, this delightful Lutyens house is understandably popular with golfers – but is much more than a sporting hotel. Dating from 1901 it retains the relaxed and elegant ambience of Edwardian times, tastefully and sympathetically furnished down to the grand piano and wind-up gramophone. Complementing the house are glorious Gertrude Jekyll gardens, while another outstanding feature is the cooking of chef Paul Brown who offers a daily-changing four-course menu of sensibly limited choice. Dinner may start with canapés in the cosy bar and continue in the small dining room with perhaps pan-fried foie grasset on saffron brioche and accompanied by apple and thyme compôte, or a bright, fresh vegetable terrine with pink peppercorn vinaigrette. An accomplished soup or sorbet usually precedes the main course which, on a recent inspection visit, was rack of lamb with whole sweet garlic and red wine sauce – the highlight of the meal. Fruity or filling puddings include pear and ginger parfait and bitter chocolate torte. The good food is supported by well-chosen wines.

Directions: Signposted on the A198 North Berwick road in the village of Gullane

Muirfield
East Lothian
Map no: 12 NT48
Tel: 01620 842144

Cost: *Alc* lunch £18, Sun lunch £20, fixed-price dinner £33. H/wine £11.50. Service exc
Credit cards: 1 2 3 4 5

Menus: A la carte, Fixed-price dinner, Sunday lunch

Times: 12.30–Last L 1.45pm, 7.30pm–Last D 9.15pm. Closed Nov-Mar

Chef: Paul Baron
Proprietor: Giles and Ros Weaver

Seats: 50. No smoking in dining room
Additional: Children permitted at lunch; special diets on request

GULLANE, **La Potinière** ❂❂❂

Set lunchtime and weekend dinner menus of reasonably priced French cuisine prepared from Scottish ingredients

A former schoolhouse in the centre of the golf-dominated town, La Potinière is a charmingly unpretentious haven of good food and wine. For nearly 20 years proprietors Hilary and David Brown have been delighting their guests (the majority a loyal band of regulars) with their hospitality, service and

Main Street
East Lothian
Map no: 12 NT48
Tel: 01620 843 214

Cost: Fixed-price lunch £18.25, £19.25; fixed–priced dinner £28.50. H/wine £9.75 ♀ Service exc
Credit cards: None taken

reasonably priced meals. Lunches and dinners (the latter on Fridays and Saturdays only) comprise a set meal and the one, handwritten French menu is set in a frame under a flamboyant display of fresh flowers. The four-course lunch is served promptly at 1pm (and if you want an apéritif you are advised to arrive in good time). Dinner commences at 8pm and includes an extra course. Meals, served by David alone, are a leisurely affair, so allow plenty of time to enjoy the experience. Hilary's cooking is assured and accurate, uncomplicated in style with freshness of flavour as a clear priority.

Soups are always successful, and this spring our inspector tasted a brightly coloured 'potage St Germain', the flavours of peas and mint carefully balanced. Perhaps there were too many flavours in a fillet of sole stuffed with pesto and set on a bed of spinach, topped with deep-fried strands of courgette and accompanied by a caramel-based, more sweet than sour sauce. However, there were no reservations about the breast of tender duckling that followed, served with risotto-like pearl barley infused with the heady flavours of wild mushrooms, and individual rounds of pommes dauphinoise. At lunch, guests have the choice of dessert or cheese, but on this occasion our inspector could not resist a warm gratin of raspberries with a brittle brûlée-like topping.

The wine list offers an outstanding range of French wines and some excellent bottles from California and Italy.

Directions: On the main village street

Menus: Fixed-price lunch and dinner, Sunday lunch

Times: Last L 1pm, Last D 8pm. Dinner only Fri and Sat, lunch Sun-Tue, Thu. Closed Wed, 1 week Jun, Oct

Chef: Hilary Brown
Proprietors: David and Hilary Brown

Seats: 30. No smoking in dining room
Additional: Children permitted; ◐ dishes/other diets on request

LINLITHGOW, **Champany Inn** ❋❋❋

A period restaurant serving prime quality steaks – popular with business people and those simply out for an occasion

The idea of Mary Queen of Scots going for a picnic with her friends is intriguing. In her pre-Thermos world, did wasps come from all over The Lowlands for the jam scones? The answer is outside the scope of this Guide, but we do know that Mary, who was born in Linlithgow Palace, enjoyed her trips *à la campagne* and this, apparently, is how the inn got its name. The cocktail lounge retains a period charm and even boasts a sea-water pool from which customers may select unlucky lobsters and crayfish for the pot. An upward glance reveals one of the lofted wine cellars displaying some of the 1000 bins which fill a 300-page wine list – so we suggest you make time to study it! There are fixed-price, two-course lunch and three and four-course dinner menus, as well as a *carte*.

Champany has a reputation as a steak house, but that is like calling the QE2 a boat. Nevertheless, steak is important here and chef/proprietor Clive Davidson's former career as a beef farmer and butcher means he knows how perfect Aberdeen Angus can be after at least three weeks' hanging. Steaks are charcoal-grilled on and off the bone and quantity and quality are both excellent, but expect to pay for the privilege. A club steak portion might even be enough for two or, then again, it might not, so the steak-tailoring service is a good way of matching cut to capacity. Specialities include 'Carpet bagger' – a thick cut fillet stuffed with a fresh oyster and 'Salmon bagger'

Champany
Map no: 11 NS97
Tel: 01506 834532

Cost: *Alc* from £35.50, fixed-price lunch from £13.75, fixed-price dinner £27.50 (3 courses), £35. H/wine £9.50 ♀ Service exc
Credit cards: 1 2 3 4 5

Menus: A la carte, fixed-price lunch and dinner, bar menu
Times: 12.30-Last L 2pm, 7pm-Last D 10pm. Lunch not served Sat. Closed Sun, Xmas, 1-2 Jan

Chef: Clive Davidson
Proprietors: Clive and Anne Davidson

Seats: 50. No pipes
Additional: Children over 8 permitted; ◐ dishes; Vegan/other diets on request

sirloin stuffed with a pouch of smoked salmon. Lamb in season or chargrilled salmon are worthy alternatives. Main courses may be accompanied by a selection of eight self-service salads and the day's vegetables are presented in a basket for choosing at the order stage. The Davidsons' efforts to improve their desserts is now showing through and the results are good.

Directions: 2 miles north-east of Linlithgow at junction of A904/A803

ORKNEY

ST MARGARET'S HOPE, **Creel** ❀

Front Road
Map no: 16
Tel: 01856 83311
Chef: S Alan Craigie
Proprietors: S A Craigie and J M Craigie
Seats: 36
Times: Last Sun L 2pm/D 9pm. Open daily May-Oct; Fri, Sat and Sun L Nov-Apr

☺ *The use of fresh, local produce – especially fish – is a feature at this small intimate waterfront village restaurant. Successful main courses have included a moist tender fillet steak with a whisky sauce, or escalope of salmon stuffed with ginger and currants, wrapped in pastry.*

Cost: Alc £20, Sun L £12. H/wine £7.30. Service exc
Credit cards: 1 3. **Additional:** Children welcome; children's portions; special diets on request
Directions: Take A961 south from Kirkwall. Turn right at St Margaret's Hope. Parking on seafront

STRATHCLYDE

ARDUAINE, **Loch Melfort** ❀

Arduaine
Argyllshire
Map no: 10 NM71
Tel: 01852 200233
Chef: Philip Lewis
Proprietors: Philip and Rosalind Lewis
Seats: 70. No smoking in dining room
Times: Last L 2.30pm/D 9pm. Closed mid Jan–mid Feb

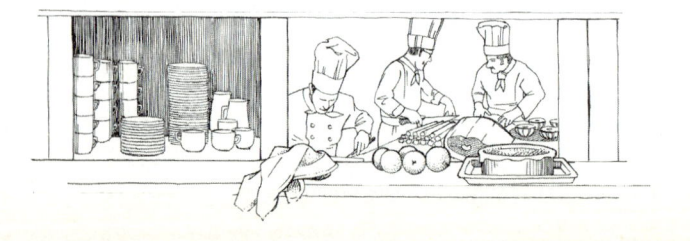

One of Argyll's most popular holiday hotels, the Loch Melfort has an attractive south-facing restaurant. Chef-patron Philip Lewis' daily fixed-price menu is supported by a range of seafood specialities, such as locally caught scallops, langoustines, oysters and, when available, lobster.

Cost: Fixed-price D £25. H/wine £11.95. Service exc
Credit cards: 1 3 5. **Additional:** Children permitted; children's portions; ❖ dishes; Vegan/other diets on request
Directions: On A816 midway between Oban and Lochgilphead

SCOTLAND STRATHCLYDE 523

AYR, **The Boathouse** ❀

Situated near the town centre, this restaurant offers a carte and chef's specials in an attractive environment. The innovative sausage of salmon and mussel with a sesame dressing, and the stuffed duck breast in a lattice of pastry are two dishes recently selected by our inspector.

Cost: Alc £22. H/wine from £8.50 ♀ Service exc **Credit cards:** 1 2 3 4
Additional: Children welcome; children's portions; ❂ dishes; Vegan/other diets on request
Directions: By the harbour close to Ayr leisure centre

Waterfront Quay
4 South Harbour Street
Ayrshire
Map no: 10 NS32
Tel: 01292 280212
Chef: Raymond Millar
Proprietors: Robert Jones, Heather Clark
Seats: 50
Times: Last L 2.30pm/D 9.30pm

AYR, **Fouters Bistro** ❀

Fine Scottish produce cooked in the French style, is the promise of this popular cellar bistro, with its vaulted ceiling, flagstone floors and stucco walls. Chef John Winton offers a range of good value menus and a flexible approach, giving an option of one, two or three courses.

Cost: Alc £23.50, fixed-price L £6.95/D £11.50. H/wine £9 ♀ Service exc. **Credit cards:** 1 2 3 4 5. **Additional:** Children welcome; children's portions/menu; ❂ menu; Vegan/other diets on request
Directions: Opposite Town Hall

2A Academy Street
Ayrshire
Map no: 10 NS32
Tel: 01292 261391
Chef: John Winton
Proprietors: Laurie and Fran Black
Seats: 38. No-smoking area. No pipes. Air conditioned
Times: Last L 2pm/D 10.30pm. Lunch not served Sun. Closed Mon, 1-4 Jan, 25-27 Dec

BALLOCH, **Cameron House** ❀❀

Modern Scottish cooking offering a good range of imaginative choices in a stylish setting

A splendid turreted Georgian mansion houses this sophisticated leisure hotel set in extensive grounds on the banks of Loch Lomond. Much of the original character has been retained and the stylish Georgian restaurant is an appropriate setting for the innovative modern cooking of chef Jeff Bland. Menus range from an imaginative carte and a daily-changing market menu to a popular celebration menu offering six surprise courses. Our inspector enjoyed a small warm pastry case filled with veal kidneys and wild mushrooms served with a tasty Arran mustard sauce, followed by langoustine bisque with a strong brandy flavour. A delicious pan-fried fillet of sea-bass was moist and very tender, served on spinach with a light and creamy nutmeg sauce, and accompanied by very fresh vegetables. A suitable ending to the meal came with a delicately-flavoured apple bavarois with a thin caramelised topping and Calvados anglaise. A separate vegetarian menu offers dishes like ravioli of broccoli and chestnut with garlic courgette cream. Service here is professional and enthusiastic.

Directions: From M8 follow A82 to Dumbarton. Take the road to Luss and 1 mile past Balloch hotel signed on right

Alexandria
Dunbartonshire
Map no: 10 NS38
Tel: 01389 55565

Cost: Alc £41, fixed-price lunch £16.50, fixed-price dinner £32.50. H/wine £11.65 ♀ No service charge
Credit cards: 1 2 3 4 5

Menus: A la carte, fixed-price lunch and dinner, Sunday lunch, bar menu
Times: Midday-Last L 2pm, 7pm-Last D 10pm. Lunch not served Sat

Chef: Jeff Bland
Proprietor: Craigendarroch Group. Manager: Michael Nalborczyk

Seats: 50. No smoking in dining room. Air conditioned
Additional: Children permitted; ❂ menu; Vegan/other diets on request

BIGGAR, **Shieldhill** ●●

Quothquan
Lanarkshire
Map no: 11 NT03
Tel: 01899 20035

A very old house amid lawns and gardens where good taste applies to everything from the cooking to the four-posters

The hotel logotype says simply 'Shieldhill established 1199AD', thus taking almost 800 years of existence in its stride. This is how long the former home of the Chancellor family has stood in the rich farmland and rolling hills of the Clyde Valley, although it only became a hotel in 1959. The small but tastefully appointed dining room is the perfect setting for Keith and Nicola Braidwood's cooking. Their compact, fixed-price dinner menu offers three or four courses, with a short choice at each stage. An enjoyable inspection meal began with a delicious timbale of superbly-flavoured Arbroath smokies and smoked salmon on a bed of creamed leeks. The following cream of tomato, red pepper and orange soup had a lovely texture and rich colour but the pepper came through a bit too strongly. Soft and fresh, lightly-baked scallops were superb, served on spaghetti vegetables with a tasty green olive and caper potato cake. And finally...sticky toffee pudding with caramel and cream sauce, accompanied by caramel ice cream in a small brandy snap basket.

Chef: Paul Whitecross
Proprietors: Joan and Neil Mackintosh

Seats: 28. No smoking in dining room
Times: Last L 1.30pm/D 9pm
Cost: A/c £25.50; fixed-price L £14.50/D £25.50. H/wine £9.30 ♀ Service exc.
Credit cards: 1 2 3 4 5.

Additional: Children permitted (over 11 at dinner); children's portions at lunch; ◑ dishes; Vegan/other diets on request

Directions: On B7016, signposted from centre of Biggar

BRODICK, **Auchrannie** ●

Map no: 10 NS03
Tel: 01770 302234
Chef: George Ramage
Proprietors: Iain Johnston
Seats: 60. No smoking in dining room
Times: Last L 2.30pm (bistro), Last D 9.30pm

Friendly, efficient staff and good food feature at this Victorian mansion hotel restaurant. The Bistro provides an informal alternative to the Garden Restaurant where the chef offers a range of tempting carefully-prepared dishes from the best ingredients including fresh island produce.

Cost: Fixed-price D £21. H/wine £9.75 Service exc
Credit cards: 1 3 5 **Additional:** Children welcome; children's portions; ◑ dishes; Vegan/other diets on request
Directions: Through Brodick village take second left past Brodick Golf Club, 250yds up this road

CLACHAN-SEIL, **Willowburn** ●

Argyllshire
Map no: 10 NM71
Tel: 018523 276
Chef: Maureen Todd
Proprietors: Archie and Maureen Todd
Seats: 30. No smoking in dining room
Times: Last L 2pm/D 8pm. Closed Nov–Mar (open New Year)

☺ *Maureen and Archie Todd's small holiday hotel has an attractive restaurant where Maureen offers a daily fixed-price menu with a choice of supplementary starters and main courses. Her uncomplicated cooking produces honest natural flavours and her range of seafood dishes is especially popular.*

Cost: Fixed-price D £18. H/wine £7. Service exc
Credit cards: 1 3. **Additional:** Children permitted at lunch; children's menu, ◑ dishes; other diets on request
Directions: South from Oban on A816 for 8 miles, then B844, signposted Easdale for 3 miles. Hotel on waterfront, 0.5 mile from Atlantic Bridge

DUNOON, Beverley's ◉

☺ A charming Victorian country house hotel set in 16 acres with fine views over the Firth of Clyde. The short fixed-price menu is due to be supported by a small carte specialising in fresh Argyll produce with the emphasis on seafood and game. The wine list has a superb collection of old rare wines.

Cost: Alc £20, fixed–price D £25. H/wine £11 ♀ Service exc
Credit cards: 1 2 3 4. **Additional:** Children welcome; children's portions/menu; ◐ dishes; other diets on request
Directions: At the west end of Dunoon overlooking West Bay

West Bay
Argyllshire
Map no: 10 NS17
Tel: 01369 2267
Chef: William McCaffrey
Proprietor: William McCaffrey
Seats: 40. No smoking in dining room
Times: Last D 10pm. Closed Sun or Mon in winter

DUNOON, Enmore ◉

☺ A family-run hotel on a coastal road where David Wilson cooks imaginative food influenced from around the world. Dishes include baked banana wrapped in bacon with curry mayonnaise and Japanese prawns with a crumb coating, or honey-roast duckling with an orange and brandy sauce.

Cost: Alc £13.50, fixed-price D £25. H/wine £9.50 ♀ Service inc.
Credit cards: 1 3 **Additional:** No children after 7.30pm; children's portions; ◐ dishes; Vegan on request
Directions: From Dunoon pier head north on coastal road, hotel is on the left in Kirn

Marine Parade, Kirn
Argyllshire
Map no: 10 NS17
Tel: 01369 2230
Chef: David Wilson
Proprietors: Angela and David Wilson
Seats: 30. No smoking
Times: 10am-10pm. L on request

EAST KILBRIDE, Westpoint ◉

☺ Westpoint is a modern purpose-built hotel with an open-plan American theme bar and grill room, offering a varied menu based on quality ingredients. The more sophisticated Simpsons Restaurant will appeal to the gourmet palate, with its carte and fixed-price market menu of mainly French-style dishes.

Cost: Alc £24, fixed–price D £24. H/wine £8.50 ♀ No service charge
Credit cards: 1 2 3 4 5. **Additional:** Children welcome; children's portions/menu; ◐ dishes; Vegan/other diets on request
Directions: Take A726 from Glasgow, towards East Kilbride

Stewartfield Way
Lanarkshire
Map no: 11 NS65
Tel: 013552 36300
Proprietor: Craigendarroch.
Manager: Roddy Whiteford
Seats: 30. No smoking in dining room. Air conditioned
Times: Last D 10pm. Closed Mon

ERISKA, Isle of Eriska ◉◉

An unspoilt island hotel which gives fresh, locally caught fish a high profile

Fresh, locally caught fish, carefully cooked with delicate flavours, is one of the recommended delights of this loch-side country house hotel. Set on its own island with access from the mainland by bridge, in unspoilt grounds and mature gardens, its peace and splendour are undisturbed. Dinner is one of the high spots of a visit here, and the daily-changing fixed-price menu offers two choices at most of the six courses: to start with perhaps pan-fried sweetbreads with a champagne and mustard sauce, with spiced prawn soup to follow, and then panache of

Ledaig, by Oban
Argyllshire
Map no: 10 NM94
Tel: 01631 72371

Cost: Fixed-price dinner £35.
H/wine £8.50 ♀ No service charge
Credit cards: 1 3 5

Menus: Fixed-price dinner
Times: Last D 9pm. Closed Dec-Mar

West Coast sea-fish on a chive butter sauce. Our inspector's recent meal was deliciously fish-biased, starting with succulent marinated scallops served with lemon vinaigrette, and a second course of sole paupiette filled with a very light lobster mousse - a lovely combination of fresh flavours. Baked monkfish on sauce Nero was moist and meaty, with deep-fried leeks and good plain vegetables. A classic lemon tart was faultlessly creamy and zesty, and for those with room left there's a first class selection of Scottish cheeses. Service is charming and courteous.

Directions: From Connel take A828, signposted Fort William, for Benderloch village. Follow signs to Isle of Eriska

Chefs: Mrs S M Buchanan-Smith, Mr A Clark
Proprietors: Pride of Britain. Managers: The Buchanan-Smith family

Seats: 40. No cigars or pipes
Additional: Children over 10 permitted; ❀ dishes; Vegan/other diets on request

GLASGOW, Buttery ❀❀

An unassuming exterior opens on to Victorian splendour offering good taste both literal and metaphorical

This restaurant is widely regarded as one of the city's institutions, and as such has remained unchanged for years. Housed in a tenement building in the shadow of Kingston Bridge, nothing could prepare newcomers for the splendid Victorian interior, or for the high-class Scottish and French cuisine served there. In the elegant panelled dining room a young team in long white aprons brings an imaginative array of dishes from the enticing *carte* and excellently valued fixed-price lunch menu: starters on the former might be pigeon and blackberry pie, or steamed Loch Hourn mussels in a scampi and prawn sauce, while main dishes could be shallow-fried fillet of beef with Guinness sauce and barley cream, or sliced fillet of pork with honey-glazed apples on a rosemary cream. Our inspector was impressed with the flavours of terrine of veal, mushroom, ham and parsley, while steamed fillet of salmon was moist and tender, and served with a delicate white wine and fresh vegetable butter sauce. Tasty raspberry crème brûlée came from a rich choice of desserts. A separate vegetarian menu offers serious and original options.

Directions: From city centre follow St Vincent Street west. Cross the M8, left at lights into Elderslie Street, left again into Argyle Street

652 Argyle Street
Lanarkshire
Map no: 11 NS56
Tel: 0141-221 8188

Cost: A/c £26, fixed-price lunch £14.75. H/wine £10.95. Service exc on *alc*
Credit cards: 1 2 3 4 5

Menus: *A la carte*, fixed-price lunch, bar menu
Times: Last L 2.30pm, Last D 10.30pm. Lunch not served Sat. Closed Sun, BHs

Chef: Stephen Johnson
Proprietor: Alloa. Manager: James Wilson

Seats: 50. Air conditioned
Additional: Children permitted; ❀ menu; Vegan/other diets on request

GLASGOW, Crannog Seafood Restaurant ❀

☺ *An increasingly popular speciality seafood restaurant with a bright, cheerful bistro atmosphere, offering the freshest seafood in tempting dishes at affordable prices. The two-course blackboard lunch is excellent value, supported by the carte, with more blackboard specials in the evening.*

Cost: A/c £18, fixed-price L £7.50 (2 courses), £8.50. H/wine £7.95 ♀ Service exc. **Credit cards:** 1 3. **Additional:** Children welcome; children's portions; ❀ dishes
Directions: Proceed along the Broomielaw, turn up Cheapside Street, 2 minutes from centre

28 Cheapside Street
Lanarkshire
Map no: 11 NS56
Tel: 0141-221 1727
Chef: Paul Laurie
Proprietor: Lisa Potter
Seats: 60
Times: Last L 3pm/D 10.30pm. Closed Sun, Mon, Xmas, 1-2 Jan

SCOTLAND STRATHCLYDE 527

GLASGOW, **Ewington** ❀

☺ *Part of a residential Victorian terrace overlooking Queens Park, this family-owned hotel is traditional, unpretentious and friendly. A fixed-price menu offering enjoyable Scottish and international dishes is served in the recently refurbished dining room, and staff are cheerful and hospitable.*

Cost: Fixed-price L £7.26/D £13.95. H/wine £8.55. Service exc
Credit cards: 1 2 3 4. **Additional:** Children permitted; children's portions; ❂ menu; Vegan/other diets on request
Directions: From M8 junc 20 follow A77 1.5 miles south of city centre. Pass through 8 sets of traffic lights then take 2nd left after Allison Street

132 Queens Drive
Lanarkshire
Map no: 11 NS56
Tel: 0141-423 1152
Chef: Robert Sturgeon
Proprietor: Best Western.
Manager: Marie-Clare Watson
Seats: 60. No smoking in dining room
Times: Last L 2pm/D 9pm

GLASGOW, **Glasgow Hilton** ❀

Scotland's tallest and largest hotel is an impressive 20 storeys of polished granite and mirrored glass situated to the west of the city centre. A Scottish country house style is the theme in the elegant Cameron's restaurant, featuring modern European cuisine using the best of Scottish produce.

Cost: Alc £29, fixed-price L £16.50 (2 courses), £19. H/wine £13 ♀ Service inc. **Credit cards:** 1 2 3 4 5. **Additional:** Children permitted; children's portions; ❂ menu; Vegan/other diets on request
Directions: Take Charing Cross exit off M8 at approach to Glasgow. Turn right at first set of traffic lights, then right again and follow signs for hotel

1 William Street
Lanarkshire
Map no: 11 NS56
Tel: 0141-204 5555
Chef: Michael Mizzen
Proprietor: David Gilius
Seats: 55
Times: Last L 2.30pm/D 10.30pm. Closed Sunday

GLASGOW, **Killermont Polo Club** ❀

☺ *The food prepared by Pawan is predominantly Rajastani and north Indian. However, strong connections with the game of polo here mean a different style from usual Indian restaurants. Dishes include Jaipuri curry with peppers, mushrooms and coriander or a tandoori combination.*

Cost: Alc £15, fixed-price L £6.95 (2 courses), £7.95; fixed-price buffet D Sun and Mon £9.95. H/wine £8.25. Service exc
Credit cards: 1 2 3 4 5 **Additional:** Children permitted; ❂ dishes; Vegan/other diets on request
Directions: From the city centre travel towards the West End, then Bearsden on the Maryhill Road. The driveway for the restaurant is before the Science parks

2002 Maryhill Road
Lanarkshire
Map no: 11 NS56
Tel: 0141-946 5412
Chef: Pawan
Proprietor: Jaz Saggoo
Seats: 22, 42, 32
Times: Last L 2pm/D 10.30pm. L not served Sun. Closed 1 Jan

GLASGOW,
Moat House International ❀❀

A friendly modern hotel beside the Clyde offering innovative and enjoyable cooking

A strikingly modern high rise building beside the River Clyde and the Scottish Exhibition Centre houses this friendly hotel. The restaurant is prominently placed on the ground floor, and

Congress Road
Lanarkshire
Map no: 11 NS56
Tel: 0141-204 0733

Cost: Fixed-price lunch £14.50 (2 courses), £16.50; fixed-price dinner £32.50. H/wine £12.50. Service inc
Credit cards: 1 2 3 4 5

here guests are well looked after by a team of smartly uniformed staff. The best of Scottish produce goes into the modern classical cooking of Thomas Brown, and his innovative dishes appear on the seasonal *carte* and fixed-price lunch menu: scallops of monkfish marinated in walnut oil and served with fresh fruits and sesame, or cream of chicken soup with lobster and chives might be followed by breast of Gressingham duck with Asian pears, pickle ginger and rosemary jus, or perhaps saddle of roe deer with a pumpkin and passion fruit charlotte and port wine essence. Our inspector recently sampled scallop and bacon salad with mustard and lime dressing, and moist and juicy salmon with warm potato salad, and fairly average vegetables. Bread and butter pudding with dates was pleasantly unusual, and chosen from a list which included warm chocolate pudding, and mandarin yoghurt torte. The wine list is mainly French.

Directions: Next to the Scottish Exhibition and Conference Centre

Menus: *A la carte,* fixed-price lunch and dinner

Times: 12.30pm–Last L 2.30pm, 7pm–Last D 11pm. Closed Sun, BHs

Chef: Thomas R Brown
Proprietor: Queens Moat Houses

Seats: 50. No-smoking area; no pipes. Air conditioned
Additional: Children over 12 permitted; ♥ menu; other diets on request. Pianist Fri and Sat

GLASGOW,
One Devonshire Gardens ❀❀

A distinctive hotel with a sumptuous interior and cooking to match

Dramatic colour schemes, boldly imaginative designs and sumptuous furnishings make this hotel one of the most distinctive in Glasgow, whilst the discreet and very personal service offered by the dedicated owner and his staff is highly regarded by guests. The fine cuisine is another major plus, and new chef Andrew Fairlie is more than living up to early expectations. His fixed-price menus offer a short but really well-balanced choice, and the intimate, elegant restaurant is the ideal place to sample his cooking. Our inspector enjoyed a recent starter of roasted scallops with an attractive and tasty garnish of couscous, fresh herbs and a warm gazpacho sauce, followed by pan-fried calf's liver that was soft and tender, served with sage-mashed potatoes and a green peppercorn sauce. A lovely dense chocolate marquise came with a smooth and freshly-made white chocolate ice cream, but was not enhanced by a hot hazelnut sauce. Other recommended dishes have been dressed crab with refreshingly true flavours, seared red mullet and sea-bass with aniseed butter sauce, and a hot raspberry soufflé dessert.

Directions: Take A82 (Dumbarton). On Great Western Road turn left at lights towards Hyndland. In 200 yards turn right and right again

1 Devonshire Gardens
Lanarkshire
Map no: 11 NS56
Tel: 0141-339 2001

Cost: Fixed-price lunch £21.50, fixed-price dinner £37.50. H/wine £16. Service exc
Credit cards: 1 2 3 4 5

Menus: Fixed-price lunch and dinner, Sunday lunch
Times: 12.30–Last L 2.30pm, 7.15pm–Last D 10.15pm. Lunch not served Sat

Chef: Andrew Fairlie
Proprietor: Ken McCulloch

Seats: 45
Additional: Children welcome; ♥ menu; Vegan/other diets on request

GLASGOW, **Rogano** ❀❀

An appealing and popular seafood restaurant in a fashionable part of the city

There's an air of quiet elegance in this famed Glaswegian restaurant, where the Art Deco style of the 1930s has been

11 Exchange Place
Lanarkshire
Map no: 11 NS56
Tel: 0141-248 4055

Cost: Alc £27.50, fixed-price lunch £16.50. H/wine £9 ♀

carefully preserved but food styles have been brought right up to date. Seafood is what this place is renowned for, and it remains widely appealing to the loyal local and international clientele; other tastes are also well catered for. At lunchtime there's a no-choice fixed-price menu and an inexpensive oyster bar menu, as well as a more pricey *carte*, while in the evening this really comes into its own. Fillet of Angus beef with peppercorns and Cognac, or breast of duckling with apricots, port and cinnamon might feature along with lobster grilled or thermidor, grilled supreme of salmon with orange and coriander, and scallops and monkfish with ginger and spring onions. Our inspector enjoyed Rogano fish soup served with small, crisp croutons, and lovely poached halibut with a delicate sorrel and scallop cream. Vegetables like crisp carrots and mange-touts, crunchy green beans and tasty courgettes were all plain and fresh. Mousse brûlée was a recommended dessert. The cafe is an informal alternative.

Directions: From Argyle Street turn left into Queen Street, then left into Royal Exchange Square. Rogano is in lane running from here to Buchanan Street

Service exc
Credit cards: 1 2 3 4 5

Menus: *A la carte*, fixed-price lunch, bar menu
Times: Midday-Last L 2.30pm, Last D 10.30pm. Lunch not served Sun. Closed BHs

Chef: Jim Kerr
Proprietor: Alloa. Manager: Gordon Yuill

Seats: 110 No smoking before 2pm or 9pm. Air conditioned
Additional: Children welcome; ❷ dishes; Vegan/other diets on request

GLASGOW, **The Town House** ❀

The splendid Music Room restaurant having been given over to function use, a smaller but nonetheless elegant restaurant has been created at this city centre hotel. It offers a range of imaginatively prepared modern British dishes from carte and fixed-price menus, including a separate vegetarian selection.

Cost: Alc £35; fixed–price L/D £16.95 (2 courses), £19. H/wine £9.75 ♀ Service exc. **Credit cards:** 1 2 3 4 5 **Additional:** Children welcome; children's portions/menu; ❷ menu; Vegan/other diets on request
Directions: On the corner of West George Street and Nelson Mandela Square

West George Street
Lanarkshire
Map no: 11 NS56
Tel: 0141-332 3320
Chef: John Shields
Proprietor: John P Campbell
Seats: 40. No-smoking area. No cigars or pipes
Times: Last L 2pm/D 10pm. Lunch not served Sat

KILCHRENAN, **Ardanaiseig** ❀❀

A splendid baronial mansion amidst spectacular scenery, serving adventurous and innovative Scottish cooking

Set close to the picturesque shore of Loch Awe this splendid 19th-century baronial mansion is a haven of peace and tranquillity. Many rooms offer superb views over the island-studded loch, and in the dining room candles and polished silver provide a civilised setting for some exceptional cooking. New chef Simon Bailey has found his niche here, and his adventurous adaptation of classical recipes is proving highly successful. A short daily changing fixed-price menu and a small *carte* offer a good balance of dishes, and our inspector praised a recent meal: warm salad of pan-fried fresh scallops with crisp salad leaves and a delicious vinegar, soya and French mustard sauce was an almost perfect starter, followed by the best cream of tomato and basil soup ever tasted, and oven-baked cannon of spring lamb with a brioche and herb crust. Vegetables were firm and fresh, but a brandy snap basket filled with sorbet and fresh

Argyllshire
Map no: 10 NN02
Tel: 018663 333

Cost: Alc £25; fixed-price lunch £12.50, fixed-price dinner £30, H/wine £9 ♀ Service exc
Credit cards: 1 2 3 4

Menus: *A la carte*, fixed-price lunch, Sunday lunch, bar menu
Times: Last L 2pm, Last D 9.30pm. Closed Nov-Mar

Chef: Simon Bailey
Proprietors: Nigel Liston, Seonaid Travers

Seats: 30. No smoking in dining room

fruit on a raspberry purée was a trifle disappointing. A meal here begins and ends on a high note, with delicious canapés and home-baked rolls, and good strong cafétière coffee with tasty petits fours.

Directions: From A85 take B845 south. At Kilchrenan village bear left. Hotel at end of this road

Additional: Children over 8 permitted; children's portions; ❶ dishes

KILCHRENAN, **Taychreggan** ❀❀

A peaceful hotel dedicated to the needs of guests, serving praiseworthy cooking from an innovative chef

For over 300 years this old stone house, once a drover's inn built around a cobbled courtyard, has stood beside the tranquil shores of beautiful Loch Awe. Nowadays this hotel remains a peaceful haven, where owner Annie Paul and her hand-picked team are unstinting in their efforts to care for their guests. In the kitchen, chef Hugh Cocker is continuing to earn praise for his innovative modern cooking based on the best available fresh Scottish ingredients, and his fixed-price five-course menu offers interesting dishes with no choice except at the sorbet/soup stage. Our inspector recently relished pan-fried wood pigeon with quail's eggs and crisp salad leaves with a raspberry and olive oil dressing, followed by a delicious if unusual curried parsnip and pear soup. Grilled fillet of halibut on a bed of spring cabbage and small chunks of smoked bacon was tender and full-flavoured, served with a well-matched dry vermouth and chive sauce. Sweets tend to be fruit-based, and the sampled light tartlet with mirabelle plums on pastry cream with a white chocolate and mint sauce was quite delicious.

Directions: One mile before Taynuilt, turn left on to B845. Follow single-track road to end

Argyllshire
Map no: 10 NN02
Tel: 018663 211

Cost: Fixed-price dinner £26.50. H/wine £7.75 ♀ Service exc
Credit cards: 1 2 3

Menus: A/c lunch, fixed–price dinner, bar menu
Times: Last L 2.15pm, Last D 8.45pm

Chef: Hugh Cocker, Michael Nicholson
Proprietor: Mrs Annie Paul

Seats: 40. No smoking in dining room
Additional: Children permitted; older children at dinner; ❶ dishes; other diets on request

KILFINAN, **Kilfinan** ❀❀

A successful marriage of French and Swiss cooking styles with the freshest available Scottish produce

The food is the main draw at this white-painted former coaching inn, although the comforts of the hotel and the spectacular scenery vie for equal second place. Chef/manager Rolf Mueller combines his Swiss training and natural skill with the best of local produce to create some superb dishes with an emphasis on game and fish. The short but imaginative fixed-price menu offers four interesting courses, which might include sautéed rabbit liver on apple and rösti potato perfumed with Madeira, followed by carrot, orange and chervil soup, then guinea fowl suprême with leaf spinach. Our inspector praised a smooth and tasty smoked trout pâté with small rolled slices of smoked salmon, and enjoyed a soup of vegetable purée with dainty garlic croûtons. 'Fondant d'agneau', three small noisettes of lamb, was tender and unusually flavoured with a thyme jus. Vegetables came fresh and crisp, and a Bavarian cream topped with Swiss roll and served with a strawberry and

Argyllshire
Map no: 10 NR97
Tel: 0170082 201

Cost: Fixed-price D £25. H/wine from £7 ♀ Service inc.
Credit cards: 1 2 3

Menus: Fixed-price dinner, Sunday lunch, bar menu
Times: Last L 2.30pm/D 9.30pm. Closed Feb

Chef: Rolf Mueller
Proprietors: Rolf and Lynne Mueller

Seats: 22. No smoking in dining room
Additional: Children welcome;

orange sauce was a delightful dessert. Other tested dishes were superb seafood pancakes, and delicious scallops with a saffron sauce.

Directions: On B8000 7 miles north of Tighnabruaich

children's portions/menu; ✿ dishes; other diets on request

KILMARTIN, Cairn ✤

☺ *Small and refreshingly unpretentious, this country bistro is popular with locals and visitors alike, its Victorian decor an attractive backdrop to the international and regional cuisine; a good-value bar menu operates at lunch, and the evening carte includes speciality steak and seafood dishes.*

Cost: A la carte from £13.35. H/wine £8.20 (litre). Service exc.
Credit cards: None taken. **Additional:** Children permitted (over 10 at dinner); children's portions; ✿ dishes; Vegan/other diets on request
Directions: On A816 Lochgilphead-Oban road

Argyllshire
Map no: 10 NR89
Tel: 01546 5254
Chef: Marion Thomson
Proprietors: Ian and Marion Thomson
Seats: 40-80. No cigars or pipes. Air conditioned
Times: Last L 3pm/D 10pm. Closed Mon, Tue, Wed during Oct-Mar

KILMUN, The Bistro at Fern Grove ✤

☺ *This small family-run bistro is part of a detached Victorian house overlooking Holy Loch. A range of light snacks and more substantial dishes reflect enthusiastic and uncomplicated cooking featuring game and salmon. Its homely atmosphere and local following mean that booking is advisable.*

Cost: Alc from £15, fixed–price L £12.50/D £15. H/wine from £5.95 ♀ Service exc. **Credit cards:** 1 2 3 **Additional:** Children welcome; children's portions/menu; ✿ dishes
Directions: 6 miles from Dunoon by the side of the Holy Loch, 50 yds past Kilmun Pier

Argyllshire
Map no: 10 NS18
Tel: 0136984 333
Chef: Estralita Murray
Proprietors: Ian and Estralita Murray
Seats: 24. No smoking in dining room
Times: Last D 9.30pm. Closed Feb & Nov

KILWINNING, Montgreenan Mansion ✤

A fine Scottish house surrounded by park and woodland, set in a rural area away from the town. The restaurant is well patronised by locals: generous portions and good fresh local produce being the attraction, with fixed-price and carte menus featuring sound Scottish cooking of a reasonable standard.

Cost: Alc £27; fixed–price L £13.75/D £23. H/wine £9.90. Service inc. **Credit cards:** 1 2 3 4. **Additional:** Children permitted; children's portions; ✿ dishes; Vegan/other diets on request
Directions: 4 miles north of Irvine on A736

Ayrshire
Map no: 10 NS34
Tel: 01294 57733
Chef: Alan McCall
Proprietor: Best Western. Manager: Darren Dobson
Seats: 60. No smoking in dining room
Times: Last L 2.30pm/D 9.30pm

532 STRATHCLYDE SCOTLAND

LANGBANK, Gleddoch House

This large hotel is popular with business people, offering both a carte and fixed-price menus featuring fresh produce in dishes that have included smoked chicken with passion fruit, avocado and poppy-seed salad.

Cost: Fixed-price L £15.50 (2 courses), £18.50,/D £29.50. H/wine £9.95. Service inc
Credit cards: 1 2 3 4. **Additional:** Children welcome: children's portions/menu; ❶ dishes; Vegan/other diets on request
Directions: From Glasgow take the M8 (Greenock) then the B789 Langbank exit. Follow signs to hotel

Renfrewshire
Map no: 10 NS37
Tel: 0147550 711
Chef: Brian Graham
Proprietor: Leslie W Conn
Seats: 80/90. Air conditioned
Times: Last L 2.30pm/D 9.30pm

LARGS, Brisbane House

☺ *Speciality seafood and Taste of Scotland selections supplement weekly-changing fixed-price menus and an imaginative carte of international dishes in the elegant restaurant of this comfortable hotel, a Georgian house overlooking the Firth of Clyde.*

Cost: Alc £18; fixed–price D £19.75. H/wine £9 ♀ Service inc
Credit cards: 1 2 3 4 5. **Additional:** Children welcome; children's portions/menu; ❶ dishes; Vegan/other diets on request
Directions: On main road, 200 yds from the Pier

14 Greenock Road
Ayrshire
Map no: 10 NS25
Tel: 01475 687200
Proprietors: Mr Maltby, Mr Bertschy
Seats: 100. Air conditioned
Times: Last L 2.30pm/Last D 9pm

MAYBOLE, Ladyburn

A charming home offering absolute tranquillity where Jane Hepburn's superb home-cooking creates an excellent menu. Smooth avocado mousse wrapped in smoked salmon made an enjoyable starter followed by roast sirloin of beef served with gravy, Yorkshire pudding and fresh vegetables.

Cost: Fixed-price D £23. **Credit cards:** 1 2 3
Additional: No smoking in dining room. No children under 14. ❶ dishes by arrangement

Ayrshire
Map no: 10 NS20
Tel: 01655 4585
Chef: Mrs Jane Hepburn
Proprietors: Mr and Mrs D J S Hepburn
Times: Last D 8.45pm. Closed 2 weeks Nov, 4 weeks Jan-Mar

MULL, ISLE OF – DERVAIG, Druimard

☺ *Enthusiastic owners Wendy and Hadyn Hubbard have settled in well at this small country house hotel. Wendy is producing an interesting range of mostly Taste of Scotland dishes from a daily fixed-price menu, served in the attractive and recently refurbished restaurant.*

Cost: Fixed-price D £15.50. H/wine £8.60. Service exc
Credit cards: 1 3. **Additional:** Children welcome; children's portions; ❶ menu; other diets on request
Directions: From the Craignure ferry turn right to Tobermory. Go through Salen, turn left at Aros, signposted Dervaig, on right hand side

Map no: 13 NM45
Tel: 01688 345/291
Chef: Wendy Hubbard
Proprietors: Mr and Mrs H R Hubbard
Seats: 32. No smoking in dining room
Times: Last D 8.30pm. Closed Sun

MULL, ISLE OF – TOBERMORY,
Strongarbh ●●

☺ *Fabulous views and a good choice of local seafood mark out this friendly Victorian hotel*

From the dining room of this delightful Victorian mansion guests can look out over the fishing grounds where much of their meal originated. Seafood features prominently on the attractively priced *carte*, along with local game and other meat dishes to suit most tastes. Owner Ian McAdam makes the best use of freshly caught produce such as Mull salmon and Tobermory trout, and our inspector enjoyed the flavour of local prawns grilled with garlic and served with a simple salad, and Isle of Mull scallops with tagliatelli and red peppers. The latter dish would have been preferred without the pepper sauce, allowing the natural flavours to flourish. Puddings like sticky toffee with butterscotch sauce and vanilla ice cream are always featured owing to popular demand, and this version in a brandy basket was very enjoyable. Other typical dishes might be smoked duck breast with orange and pecan salad, or Danish blue cheese pastry puff with asparagus sauce to start, and marinated honey and orange pork grilled with glazed apples, or local cheddar and broccoli soufflé. Service is friendly and attentive.

Map no: 13 NM55
Tel: 01688 2328

Cost: Alc £20; fixed-price lunch £12.50. H/wine £10.50. Service exc
Credit cards: 1 3 5

Menus: *A la carte*, fixed-price lunch
Times: 6pm–Last D 10pm.

Chefs: Graham Horne
Proprietor: Ian McAdam

Seats: 32. No pipes or cigars
Additional: Children welcome; children's portions; ◐ dishes; other diets on request

Directions: In the centre of town, signposted

OBAN, **Manor House** ●

This Georgian former dower house enjoys spectacular views over Oban Bay, and the dining room, featuring the original range, is elegant in pink linen and candlelight. There is a short fixed-price menu, and a longer carte with an emphasis on seafood. Vegetarians are also catered for.

Cost: Alc £24; fixed-price D £21.90. H/wine £7.50 ♀ Service exc.
Credit cards: 1 3 5. **Additional:** Children permitted; children's portions; ◐ dishes; Vegan/other diets on request
Directions: From south side of town follow signs for car ferry. Continue past ferry entrance for further half mile

Gallanach Road
Argyllshire
Map no: 10 NM82
Tel: 01631 62087
Chef: Patrick Freytag
Proprietors: Patrick and Margaret Freytag
Seats: 34. No smoking in dining room
Times: Last L 2pm/D 8.45pm. Closed Jan

PORT APPIN, **Airds** ●●●

A formal hotel restaurant, with beautiful loch and mountain views, serving some of the best food in Scotland

Airds is a small country hotel in a spectacular location overlooking Loch Linnhe. Once the ferry inn for the hamlet, it is now a welcoming hotel lovingly converted by owners Eric and Betty Allen. Food is at the heart of the establishment, and it is essential for non-residents to book in advance. The sparkling, formally appointed restaurant takes full advantage of the lovely view, and service, provided by Eric and his young team, is charming and attentive. Betty and son Graeme are

Argyllshire
Map no: 14 NM94
Tel: 0163173 236

Cost: Fixed-price lunch £9; fixed-price dinner £35. H/wine £12. Service exc
Credit cards: 1 2 3 5

Menus: Fixed-price lunch and dinner
Times: Last L 2pm, Last D 8pm

responsible for the refined style of cooking, which is based on the best quality produce prepared with the greatest care to bring out the natural flavours of the food.

A fixed-price three-course lunch and four-course dinner menu is presented and includes a short, well-balanced range of dishes with starters such as sautéed scallops with shitake mushrooms and sweet and sour sauce, and confit of duckling served between crisp potato wafers accompanied by a delightful prune and apple sauce. Soup will follow, perhaps cream of smoked haddock, and main courses could include fillet of monkfish on a bed of spinach with champagne and chervil sauce or, our inspector's choice, roast rack of lamb sliced thinly over an intensely flavoured onion confit with lightly cooked kidneys and sweetbreads - an instant success. Vegetarian options can be provided by prior arrangement. A tempting selection of desserts - maybe coffee and pistachio iced soufflé with coffee sauce, or a delicious mille-feuille of chocolate and raspberry mousses - can be made from a choice of five, plus Scottish and French farmhouse cheeses.

There is an interesting and attractively priced selection of house wines. Thereafter the list is long and carefully chosen. All the classic areas of Europe are well represented, especially Italy, as are the New World countries.

Chefs: Betty Allen, Graeme Allen
Proprietor: Eric Allen

Seats: 36. No smoking in dining room
Additional: Children welcome; children's portions; ◐ dishes/other diets on request

Directions: Leave the A828 at Appin. Airds is 2.5 miles after turning off on to unclassified road to Port Appin

RHU, **Rosslea Hall** ❀

☺ *Chef Colin Mason superimposes French style on the best of fresh produce - including the beef, game and seafood for which the area is renowned - in the dishes of his carte and fixed-price menus; the restaurant is part of an extended Victorian mansion near the Gareloch.*

Helensburgh
Dunbartonshire
Map no: 10 NS28
Tel: 01436 820684
Chef: Colin Mason
Proprietors: Echo/Queens Moat House. Manager: J Osborne
Seats: 60. No smoking in dining room
Times: Last L 2.30pm/D 9.30pm

Cost: Fixed-price L £15.50/D £17.50. H/wine £8.95. Service exc.
Credit cards: 1 2 3 4 5 **Additional:** Children welcome; children's portions/menu; ◐ menu; Vegan on request
Directions: On A814 past post office

COLONSAY, ISLE OF – SCALASAIG,
Colonsay Hotel ❀

☺ *A delightfully remote island hotel, ideal for the escapist. The timber-clad dining room is the setting for uncomplicated cooking featuring island produce, especially seafood. For example, roulade of whiting with white wine sauce with Colonsay oysters or seafood and pasta salad starters.*

Map no: 10NR39
Tel: 019512 316
Chef: Christa Bryne
Proprietors: Kevin and Christa Bryne
Seats: 28. No smoking in dining room
Times: Last L 1.30pm/D 7.30pm. Closed Nov-Feb

Cost: Fixed-price D £19.25. H/wine £9 ♀ No service charge
Credit cards: 1 2 3 4 5. **Additional:** Children permitted at lunch; children's portions; ◐ dishes; Vegan/other diets on request
Directions: 400yds from West Pier

SCOTLAND STRATHCLYDE

STEWARTON, **Chapeltoun House** ❀

Set in 20 acres of grounds, this small turn-of-the-century, country house hotel is committed to good food. The dinner menu offers carefully chosen dishes which have included a timbale of chicken and spinach pancake, baked loin of lamb with Madeira sauce, and raspberry crème brûlée.

Cost: Fixed-price L £15.50/D £23.90. H/wine from £9.90. Service exc. **Credit cards:** 1 2 3. **Additional:** Children over 12 permitted; ❂ dishes; special diets on request

Ayrshire
Map no: 10 NS44
Tel: 01560 482696
Chef: Tom O'Donnell
Proprietors: Colin McKenzie and Graeme McKenzie
Seats: 55. No smoking in dining room
Times: Last L 2pm/D 9pm. Closed first 2 weeks Jan

STRATHAVEN, **Strathaven** ❀

☺ A fine Adam house with a beamed dining room is the setting for chef Jason Henderson's carefully prepared Scottish and European dishes. Both carte and fixed-price menus are offered, the latter with an option of two, three or four courses. A vegetarian dish is always included.

Cost: Alc £19; fixed-price L £9/D £15.45 ♀ Service exc. **Credit cards:** 1 2 3 5. **Additional:** Children welcome; children's portions/menu; ❂ dishes; Vegan/other diets on request
Directions: On A723 Hamilton road, on outskirts of Strathaven

Hamilton Road
Lanarkshire
Map no: 11 NS74
Tel: 01357 21778
Chef: Jason Henderson
Proprietors: Malcolm MacIntyre, Shiela MacIntyre
Seats: 42
Times: Last L 2.30pm/D 10pm

TROON, **Highgrove House** ❀❀

Superb coastal views and the chance to enjoy modern British cuisine make a visit here an occasion to remember.

Set in its own gardens, in an elevated position that commands magnificent sweeping views of the Ayrshire coast and Isle of Arran, this small hotel draws to its restaurant a loyal following from a wide area; an excellent lunchtime carte (served both in the bar and split-level restaurant) is particularly popular, and booking is essential at weekends. Modern British cuisine reveals some French influence – especially in careful saucing – but its real strength lies in the skilful use of quality fresh ingredients. The main course at dinner (a more formal meal, offering a choice of fixed-price four-course menu and carte) could be two generous medallions of flavoursome beef, cooked exactly to order, topped with mushrooms and served with a peppercorn and whisky cream sauce containing sliced asparagus. This might be preceded by a smooth, tasty liver pâté with basil dressing and redcurrant marmalade, the meal brought to a successful conclusion by a well-made tarte tatin with good sauce anglaise. Vegetarian dishes are available at short notice. A carefully chosen wine list includes some half bottles.

Directions: On A78 from Prestwick to Irvine take right turn at Troon. In 1 mile turn right at mini roundabout

Old Loans Road
Ayrshire
Map no: 10 NS33
Tel: 01292 312511

Cost: Alc £20, fixed–price lunch £12.95, fixed–price dinner £21.50. H/wine £9.95. Service exc
Credit cards: 1 2 3 5

Menus: A la carte, fixed-price lunch and dinner, bar menu

Times: Midday-Last L 2.30pm, Last D 9.30pm

Chef: James Alyson
Proprietors: Bill and Catherine Costley

Seats: 80. No cigars or pipes
Additional: Children welcome; children's portions; ❂ dishes; Vegan/other diets on request

TROON, Lochgreen House ☻☻

Monktenhill Road, Southwood
Ayrshire
Map no: 10 NS33
Tel: 01292 313343

☺ *A comfortable, welcoming country house hotel where the cooking is taken seriously*

The Scottish lawyer who built this country house had an eye for beauty as well as a feel for comfort, and modern guests are still treated to plenty of both. Set in 16 acres of manicured grounds, this delightful old place creates a welcoming atmosphere, with staff offering courteous service. The cooking is another attraction, and seasonal Scottish produce is competently prepared and presented in modern style in the magnificent oak-panelled restaurant. The set three-course lunch and four-course dinner menus might offer assorted Highland game terrine with hazelnuts and a maple dressing for starter, and perhaps West Coast seafood nage with fresh herb noodles, white wine and tarragon as a main choice. Our inspector began a recent meal with spiced lobster ravioli with creamed leeks and garden herbs, followed by mild parsnip soup with Thai spices and coconut milk – a sound and very hot soup. Medallions of beef with wild mushrooms and shallots, and a blue cheese and leek crust, was delicious, but the meal's high spot was a light, fresh-tasting chocolate bavarois with candied orange for dessert.

Cost: Fixed-price dinner £25. H/wine £9.95. Service inc
Credit cards: 1 2 3 5

Menus: Fixed-price dinner, Sunday lunch, bar menu

Times: Last L 2.15pm, Last D 9pm

Chef: Andrew Hamer
Proprietors: William Costley

Seats: 80. No smoking in dining room
Additional: Children permitted (no under 12s at dinner); children's portions; ❂ dishes; Vegan/other diets on request

Directions: On B749 south-east of Troon

TROON, Marine Highland ☻

Ayrshire
Map no: 10 NS33
Tel: 01292 314444
Chef: Richard Sturgeon
Proprietor: Scottish Highland. Manager: Andrew M Overton
Seats: 100. No-smoking area
Times: Last L 2pm/D 10pm

☺ *On the west coast and near some of the world's best golf courses, this hotel restaurant offers a fixed-price and a carte menu rich in seafood. From the carte our inspector selected a symphony of seafood: sole, salmon, prawn and king prawn in lobster sauce with brown rice.*

Cost: Alc £22.50, fixed-price D £21. H/wine £9.75 ♀ Service inc
Additional: Children welcome; children's portions/menu; ❂ menu; Vegan/other diets on request
Directions: Overlooking 18th fairway of Troon's golf course

TROON, Piersland House ☻

Craigend Road
Ayrshire
Map no: 10 NS33
Tel: 01292 314747
Chef: John Newton
Proprietor: Aristo. Manager: Michael Lee
Seats: 50. No cigars or pipes
Times: Last L 2.30pm/D 9.30pm

☺ *A good choice is offered from a range of carte, fixed-price and vegetarian menus at this comfortable hotel restaurant. Our inspector enjoyed a smooth terrine of venison and pheasant, steamed Tay salmon with spaghetti of vegetables and lemon butter sauce, and an iced heather honey parfait.*

Cost: Alc £17.50; fixed–price L £10.95/D £16.95. H/wine £8.95 ♀ Service exc. **Credit cards:** 1 2 3 4 5. **Additional:** Children welcome; children's portions/menu; ❂ menu/other diets on request
Directions: Opposite Royal Troon Golf Club

TURNBERRY, **Turnberry** ❀❀

Ayrshire
Map no: 10 NS20
Tel: 01655 31000

Praise and awards continue to be heaped on this fine hotel, renowned as much for its cuisine and a new spa and leisure complex as its championship golf course.

Cost: *Alc* £27.50. H/wine £17
Credit cards: 1 2 3 4 5

As might be expected of such a high-ranking hotel, the levels of hospitality and luxury are outstanding, and in addition there are spectacular sea views towards Ailsa Craig and the snow-capped mountains of Arran. Food is taken seriously here, and three eating options offer a wide choice of excellent cuisine: the Bay restaurant produces light, modern dishes with a Mediterranean flavour, like grilled goat's cheese and gnocchi, scampi and mussel risotto, and figs and almonds with green walnut liqueur, while the Clubhouse provides food for those in a hurry, with a salad table and daily roast carved on the trolley. The third option, the formal main restaurant, was visited by our inspector who found classical dishes like smooth, strong duck liver parfait, and velouté of wild mushrooms enhanced by a hint of pesto. There was good flavour to both Ayrshire lamb and the new potatoes served with it, while hot pear and almond tart was served with a superb dark yellow vanilla sauce.

Menu: *A la carte,* daily lunch, bar menu
Times: Midday-Last L 2.30pm, 6.30pm-Last 9.30pm

Chef: D S Cameron
Proprietor: C J Rouse

Seats: 54. No cigars or pipes. Air conditioned
Additional: Children welcome; children's portions, ❍ menu; Vegan/other diets on request

Directions: On north side of the village on A719

TAYSIDE

ABERFELDY, **Guinach House** ❀❀

By the 'Birks', Urlar Road
Perthshire
Map no: 14 NN84
Tel: 01887 820251

☺ *A totally committed chef/patron with an evident love of cooking, backed up by a homely, cosy atmosphere*

Cost: Fixed-price lunch £15, fixed-price dinner £21. H/wine £9.50. Service inc
Credit cards: 1 3

It is for the food that most guests seek out this secluded little hotel. Chef/patron Bert Mackay is totally committed to his love of cooking, and the care he extends in the kitchen is matched by the hospitable and homely atmosphere created by Marian Mackay. The four-course dinner menu offers an impressive choice, with starters like locally smoked venison, and moules marinière, and main courses such as West Coast scallops on a Chablis cream sauce, or breast of wild widgeon duckling on a honey and cranberry sauce. Our inspector enjoyed a well-made avocado and seafood mousse on a lemon and chive mayonnaise, followed by a rich and hearty fish soup stuffed with delicious chunks of salmon, monkfish and seafood. The main course was a successful trio of fillets: tender and succulent lamb, beef and venison with a port wine and bramble sauce to nicely complement the three flavours. A smooth zabaglione parfait with a hazelnut sauce was chosen from amongst a tempting array including white peach bavarois with Amaretto biscuits, and home-made pistachio and Turkish delight ice cream bombe.

Menus: Fixed-price lunch and dinner
Times: Last L 2pm, Last D 9.30pm

Chef: Albert Mackay
Proprietor: Albert Mackay

Seats: 24. No smoking in dining room
Additional: Children welcome; children's portions; ❍ dishes; Vegan/other diets on request

Directions: Follow A826 Crieff road out of Aberfeldy, the restaurant is situated on the right-hand side beside the 'Birks'

AUCHTERARDER, Auchterarder House ✽✽

A delightfully personal hotel in a peaceful setting serving quality Scottish cooking

The essence and elegance of Scottish baronialism have been retained at this magnificent Victorian mansion, which also offers all the modern standards of a luxury hotel. Set in the gently rolling Perthshire hills and glens, Auchterarder is perfectly positioned to make use of the finest Scottish produce. Local lamb and Shetland salmon often feature on the *carte* and set no-choice menus, although guests ordering from the latter can choose other dishes more to their liking for an additional supplement. David Hunt is the capable chef who brings inspiration and innovation from the kitchen to the splendid dining room, and our inspector could scarcely fault a recent meal. Boned quail was a warm and full-flavoured starter, simply served with an eye-catching salad and a spicy lentil sauce, while the delicious salmon main course was served with juicy langoustines floating on a well-made lobster sauce; vegetables were simple and very fresh. Baked filo moneybag filled with warm diced pears and bananas was decorated with caramel-coated banana slices and served with scrumptious butterscotch sauce.

Directions: From Auchterarder follow B8062 Crieff road for 1.5 miles. Hotel is signposted on right

Perthshire
Map no: 11 NN91
Tel: 01764 663646

Cost: *Alc* from £37.50, fixed-price lunch £15, fixed-price dinner £27.50. H/wine £12.50 ♀
Service exc
Credit cards: 1 2 3 4

Menus: *A la carte*, fixed-price lunch and dinner, Sunday lunch
Times: Last L 2.30pm, Last D 9.30

Chef: David Hunt
Proprietor: Mr and Mrs Ian L Brown

Seats: 23. No smoking in dining room
Additional: Children over 10 permitted; ♥ dishes, Vegan on request

AUCHTERARDER, Duchally House ✽

☺ *A well-produced dinner is served in the dining room of this family-owned Victorian manor house, with its crisp linen and sparkling silverware. Dishes might include chicken liver terrine, Scottish salmon with white wine sauce, or brie and broccoli pithiviers. A simpler menu is offered in the bistro.*

Cost: *Alc* £23; fixed-price L £12.50/D £16.50. H/wine £8. Service inc. **Credit cards:** 1 2 3 4. **Additional:** Children welcome; children's portions/menu; ♥ menu; other diets on request
Directions: From A9 take A823 (Crieff/Dunfermline), after 1 mile turn left at sign for Duchally. Hotel in 0.25 mile

Perthshire
Map no: 11 NN91
Tel: 01764 663071
Chefs: Derek and Liz Alcorn
Proprietors: Maureen and Arne Raeder
Seats: 36. No smoking in dining room
Times: Last L 2.15pm/D 9.30pm

AUCHTERARDER, The Gleneagles ✽✽

More a national institution than a hotel, with a wide selection of food to suit all tastes

A resort destination in its own right, Gleneagles counts falconry, fishing, riding and shooting among the sports on offer in addition to its three championship golf courses. Not everyone goes there for the outdoor activities, however, and a team of forty chefs under the direction of Alan Hill ensures that food is at the top of the list of pleasures to be savoured. The Strathearn restaurant caters for all tastes as long as they

Perthshire
Map no: 11 NN91
Tel: 01764 662231

Cost: *Alc* £40, fixed-price lunch £26, fixed-price dinner D £39.50. H/wine £15.50 ♀
Credit cards: 1 2 3 4

Menus: *A la carte*, fixed price lunch and dinner, Sunday lunch, bar menu

are expensive, and a selection of fixed-price dinner menus offers a formidable choice; three Taste of Scotland menus give a range of typical Hibernian dishes, with haggis piped in ancient tradition. Our inspector began a recent lunch with a nicely-balanced dish of seared scallops and langoustines with étuvée of vegetables, and went on to poached fillet of first-class beef in mushroom broth. Enjoyable as these dishes were, the outstanding highlight of the meal was an iced parfait of pistachio and hazelnut with praline sauce. Other popular dishes might be saltimbocca of chicken with Marsala, and steamed halibut with crayfish mousseline and chervil sauce. A top-class wine list has prices to match.

Directions: Just off the A9, well signposted

Times: Midday–Last L 2.30pm, Last D 9.30pm

Chef: Alan Hill
Proprietor: Guinness. Manager: Peter Lederer

Seats: 150. No cigars or pipes
Additional: Children welcome; children's portions; ❡ dishes; Vegan/other diets on request. Pianist

AUCHTERHOUSE, **Old Mansion House** ❀

A delightfully attractive mansion house skilfully converted into a hotel by the present owners, with its own grounds and gardens that include a pool, croquet and tennis lawns. The food is in the very capable hands of Campbell Bruce with an interesting choice of dishes using fresh local produce.

Cost: Alc £25; fixed–price L £15. H/wine £9.95. Service exc
Credit cards: 1 2 3 4 5. **Additional:** Children permitted at lunch; ❡ menu; Vegan/other diets on request
Directions: Take A923 from Dundee, cross the Kingsway. From Muirhead take B954, hotel on left after 2 miles

Forfarshire
Map no: 11 N033
Tel: 0182626 366
Chef: Campbell Bruce
Proprietors: Nigel and Eva Bell
Seats: 40. No smoking in dining room
Times: Last L 1.45pm/D 9.15pm. Closed 25 Dec-4 Jan

BLAIRGOWRIE, **Kinloch House** ❀❀

Scottish cooking with an emphasis on game and natural, fresh produce

A charming Scottish country house overlooking parkland and reached along a drive lined with rhododendrons, is an ideal setting for a peaceful break. Lovely lounges and plenty of oak panelling lend much warmth and character to this hotel, enhanced by the hospitality of friendly owners and dedicated staff. Dinner offers another memorable experience, with Scottish dishes prepared with great skill by chef Bill McNicoll, and the fixed-price four-course menu shows off the range. Our inspector was enchanted with a starter of squid stuffed with seafood served with a tasty sweet sauce, and a creamy plum and champagne sorbet of mouth-watering freshness. Roast partridge had a good flavour, and came with bread sauce, game chips, fried breadcrumbs, strong game gravy and redcurrant jelly. By contrast, vegetables were rather ordinary, and Parisian gâteau looked more appealing than it tasted. Game always features on the menu, and other choices might be fillet of hare sautéed in garlic butter with tarragon and port sauce, and breast of guinea fowl with an orange, green peppercorn and brandy sauce.

Directions: Three miles west of Blairgowrie on A923

Perthshire
Map no: 15 NO14
Tel: 01250 884237

Cost: Fixed-price lunch £14.50; fixed-price dinner £25.90. H/wine £10.50 ♀ Service inc
Credit cards: 1 2 3 4

Menus: Fixed-price lunch and dinner, Sunday lunch, bar lunch
Times: 12.30-Last L 2pm, 7pm-Last D 9.15pm

Chef: Bill McNicoll
Proprietors: David and Sarah Shentall

Seats: 55. No smoking in dining room
Additional: Children permitted (over 7 at dinner); children's portions; ❡ dishes; Vegan/other diets on request

BRIDGE OF CALLY, Bridge of Cally ☻

☺ *Good food is central to the operation of this small hotel beside the bridge. Meals can be taken in the bar, or in the dining room where a four-course fixed-price dinner menu is served along with a good value supper and vegetarian carte. Game features in season among the mainly British dishes.*

Cost: Alc £10.50, fixed-price D £17.50. H/wine £7.50. Service exc.
Credit Cards: 1 3. **Additional:** Children welcome; children's portions/menu; ❻ dishes; other diets on request
Directions: Six miles north of Blairgowrie, on A93

Near Blairgowrie
Perthshire
Map no: 15 NO15
Tel: 01250 886231
Chefs: Michael Wright, William McCosh
Proprietor: William McCosh
Seats: 35
Times: Last D 9.30pm. Closed Xmas

CLEISH, Nivingston House ☻

A carefully extended former farmhouse dating back to the 18th century, standing in 12 acres of delightful grounds in a peaceful location. The well produced three-course fixed-price and carte menus feature Scottish cuisine using local fresh produce, and there is an imaginative bar lunch menu.

Cost: Alc from £20; fixed-price L £15.50/D £25. H/wine £10.95
Credit cards: 1 2 3 5. **Additional:** Children welcome; children's portions; ❻ menu; Vegan/other diets on request
Directions: Two miles from exit 5 of M90

Cleish Hills
Kinross-shire
Map no: 11 NT09
Tel: 01577 850216
Chef: Michael Thompson
Proprietor: Scotland's Commended. Managers: Pat and Allan Deeson
Seats: 50. Smoking discouraged
Times: Last L 2pm/D 9pm. Closed 1st 2 weeks Jan

DUNKELD, Kinnaird ☻☻☻

A grand country house hotel on a huge estate serving modern British cooking in gracious surroundings

An outstanding house, most of which dates from 1770, Kinnaird is the residence for an estate of around 9000 acres. It has been in the Ward family since 1927 and the present owner, Mrs Constance Ward, renovated the property in 1990, when the house was opened to the public for the first time. The interior has been appointed with great charm and good taste, with stunning public rooms and elegant antiques. Of the two dining areas, the principal room has original Italianate frescoed walls, and both have good views to the river and blazing log fires in cool weather.

John Webber is in charge of the cooking. He came here from Cliveden and, before that, Gidleigh Park. The food has to be consistently good to justify the high prices, but all our reports indicate that high standards are being maintained. Lunch can be taken as a two or three-course meal, and dinner is selected from a fixed-price menu of considerable range. Decent canapés and good bread set the scene, and a spring test meal began with an open ravioli of superb pigeon breast with a rich red wine sauce and Puy lentils. Another popular starter comprises sautéed slices of marinated salmon with a good vegetable butter sauce. Main courses sampled have included rich and tasty braised oxtail, boned and stuffed with spinach and set on a potato rösti; and charbroiled lamb with a tartlet of onion and coriander confit with a good lamb-flavoured sauce.

To finish there is a selection of cheeses from the trolley or a

Kinnaird
Perthshire
Map no: 11 NO04
Tel: 01796 482440

Cost: Fixed-price lunch £19.50 (2 courses); £19.50; fixed-price dinner £38. H/wine £15 ♀ Service exc
Credit cards: 1 2 3 5

Menus: fixed-price lunch and dinner

Times: Last L 1.45pm,D 9.30pm. Closed Feb

Chef: John Webber
Proprietor: Relais et Châteaux. Managers: Constance Ward and Douglas Jack

Seats: 35. No smoking in dining room
Additional: Children permitted (over 12); ❻ dishes; Vegan/other diets on request

choice of tempting desserts, such as hot marzipan soufflé with Amaretto ice cream, or our inspector's choice, a 'brûléed' lemon tart. The wine list starts with an interesting page of Kinnaird suggestions (£15 to £24 a bottle) followed by a tremendous choice of half-bottles. The remainder is mainly French, though all other countries are well represented, too.

Directions: Continue north past Dunkeld on A9 for about 2 miles, take exit on left, B898, signed Dalguise and Balnaguard. Kinnaird is 4.5 miles along

GLAMIS, Castleton House ❀

☺ *Lying south of the village, this Victorian mansion has been converted to a country house hotel. Chef/proprietor William Little offers fixed-price and carte menus cooked in the modern style, served in the elegant dining room or the less formal conservatory, where a menu is available all day.*

Cost: fixed-price lunch £11.75/D £19.50. H/wine £9.50
Credit cards: 1 2 3. **Additional:** Children permitted; children's portions/menu; ❹ dishes; Vegan/other diets on request
Directions: 3 miles west of Glamis on A94, between Forfar and Coupar Angus

Angus
Map no: 15 NO34
Tel: 01307 840340
Chef: James Thomson
Proprietor: William Little
Times: Last L 2.30pm/D 9.30pm

INVERKEILOR, Gordon's ❀

☺ *Good-value lunch, high tea, dinner and supper menus are offered at this delightful village restaurant. Gordon Watson's cooking is very capable, and includes dishes such as fish market soup, smoked wild venison, and chicken Devonshire with cider, apples and cream sauce.*

Cost: Alc £18.50. H/wine £8. Service exc. **Credit cards:** 1 3
Additional: Children welcome; children's portions/menu; ❹ menu; other diets on request
Directions: Situated north end of main street

Homewood House, Main Street
Angus
Map no: 15 NO64
Tel: 01241 830364
Chef: Gordon Watson
Proprietors: Gordon and Maria Watson
Seats: 25. No-smoking area. Air conditioned
Times: Last L 2pm/D 9.30pm. Closed Mon & last 2 weeks Jan

KILLIECRANKIE, Killiecrankie Hotel ❀❀

A charming little hotel with friendly staff and a reputation for good classical and traditional Scottish cooking

A reputation for fine food is the main reason behind the popularity of this small hotel which overlooks the lovely River Garry and the historic Pass of Killiecrankie. Other attractions include dramatic local scenery, and the charming staff who welcome visitors to this relaxed and comfortable place. A four-course dinner is the high point of each day, and an interesting set menu offers a good balance of classical and traditional Scottish dishes, all made from the best local produce. Our inspector sampled galantine of wild pheasant with duck, infused with orange and marjoram and served with a slightly sweet Cumberland sauce, and pan-fried rump of wild venison with whole chestnuts – perfectly cooked and tender venison with a

Pitlochry
Perthshire
Map no: 14 NN96
Tel: 01796 473220

Cost: Fixed-price dinner £25.50
♀ Service inc
Credit cards: 1 3 5

Menu: Fixed-price dinner

Times: Last D 8.30pm. Closed Jan & Feb

Chef: John Ramsay
Proprietors: Colin and Carole Anderson

first-class red wine and redcurrant jelly sauce and a delicious tartlet of wild summer berries. An excellent cheese trolley with a selection of Scottish and Continental varieties leaves just a little room to enjoy desserts like fresh gooseberry mousse with ginger-flavoured crème anglaise. Other dishes served here might be fricassée of hare and pigeon, or grilled rib-eye steak.

Seats: 34. No smoking in dining room
Additional: Children permitted (over 5); children's portions; ❹ dishes; other diets on request

Directions: Turn off A9 at sign for Killiecrankie. Hotel in 3 miles

KINCLAVEN, **Ballathie House** ❀

Ballathie House is a turreted mansion in a stunning setting on the River Tay, and the cooking lives up to expectations with lots of regional produce. A typical menu might include pan-fried West Coast scallops followed by pigeon breast with Madeira sauce. There are interesting vegetarian choices too.

Ballathie
Perthshire
Map no: 11 NO13
Tel: 01250 883268
Chef: Kevin McGillivray
Proprietor: C J Longden
Seats: 80. No smoking in dining room
Times: Last L 2pm/D 9pm

Cost: fixed-price L £10/D £25. H/wine £8.75 ♀ Service exc
Credit cards: 1 2 3 4 5 **Additional:** Children welcome; children's portions/menu; ❹ dishes; Vegan/other diets on request
Directions: Off A93 at Beech Hedges, follow signs for Kinclaven, approx 2 miles

KINNESSWOOD, **Lomond Country Inn** ❀

☺ A very popular hotel with lovely views of Loch Leven. A brisk bar trade and a well-attended restaurant serving interesting Scottish cuisine. Light and tasty Arbroath smokie mousse and pheasant breast in a well-made mushroom cream sauce were appreciated by our inspector.

Kinross-shire
Map no: 11 NO10
Tel: 01592 840253
Chef: Alex Deakin
Proprietor: David Adams
Seats: 80. No-smoking area
Times: Last L 2.30pm/D 9pm

Cost: Alc £13; fixed-price L £8/D £8 (2 courses), £10. H/wine £6.50 ♀ Service exc. **Credit cards:** 1 2 3 4 5 **Additional:** Children welcome; children's portions/menu; ❹ dishes; other diets on request
Directions: On the A911

KINROSS, **Croft Bank** ❀❀

Artistic but unfussy cooking by a talented chef in a friendly Victorian hotel restaurant

30 Station Road
Kinross-shire
Map no: 11 NO10
Tel: 01577 863819

There's nothing fussy or complicated about the artistic cooking of chef/owner Bill Kerr, and his undoubted talent for marrying together ingredients is one of his great strengths. The resulting fine balance of flavours has proved to be a great attraction at this Victorian villa hotel, and a recent inspection lunch was an enjoyable experience, while also offering tremendous value. A warm salad of turkey livers with a mustard seed dressing was a tender, succulent starter, while breast of pigeon on a bed of braised barley with a raspberry wine vinegar and port sauce ranked among the best our inspector had tasted. Filo pastry filled with pear and banana was an innovative hot dessert, and the meal ended with a pot of mint tea. As well as the fixed-price lunch menu there's a seasonal dinner menu supplemented by daily specials, and a carte offering starters like tureen of seafood

Cost: Alc £22, fixed-price lunch £9.95 (2 courses), £11.95; fixed-price dinner £22. H/wine £9.95. Service exc
Credit cards: 1 3

Menus: A la carte, fixed-price lunch and dinner, Sunday lunch, bar menu
Times: Midday-Last L 1.45pm, 6pm-Last D 9pm. Closed Mon

Chef: Bill Kerr
Proprietor: Bill and Diane Kerr

chowder topped with pastry, and chicken liver parfait, with main dishes like ragout of fresh fish and seafood with ribbon pasta, or roast saddle of venison. There is also an interesting bar menu at lunch time.

Directions: On west side of town

PERTH, **Huntingtower** ❀

A mock-Tudor country house set in attractive landscaped gardens where chef Lawrence Robertson produces modern British cuisine, regularly featuring seafood and game such as lobster bisque with Arbroath smokie ravioli or venison and lamb's livers on a bed of lentils with Madeira sauce.

Cost: Alc £22, fixed-price £18.95. **Credit cards:** 1 2 3 4 5
Additional: Children permitted. ❂ dishes
Directions: 1 mile west of Perth on A85 (Crieff road), 2nd turning on right

PERTH, **Murrayshall** ❀❀

An attractive golfers' hotel in a magnificent setting, renowned for its fine Scottish cuisine

The focal point of this magnificent mansion surrounded by 300 acres of parkland is undoubtedly the golf course. A Mecca for corporate golfers as well as smaller parties and individuals, this hotel offers a relaxed and friendly environment to players and non-players alike. High on its list of attributes is Andrew Campbell's modern style of Scottish cooking which is French by influence but lacking in any flamboyance of style. His appealing dishes have attracted much praise, and the *carte* and short fixed-price menus offer an interesting choice in the Old Masters restaurant: perhaps roulade of fresh salmon mousseline studded with prawns to start, followed by pan-fried breast of Angus chicken in a brandy and soft green peppercorn sauce. Our inspector tried a smooth, firm chicken liver parfait with gooseberry and mint jelly, and roast New Zealand lamb served with a Madeira reduction and a timbale of spinach and pine kernels. The dessert was a complicated affair of home-made apple pastry with caramel and Calvados sauce served with vanilla and honey ice cream in a brandy snap basket.

Directions: From Perth take A94 towards Coupar Angus, signed Murrayshall on the right before New Scone

Seats: 40. No smoking in dining room
Additional: Children permitted (over 4); children's portions/menu; ❂ dishes; Vegan/other diets on request

Crieff Road, Almondbank
Perthshire
Map no: 11 NO12
Tel: 01738 583771
Chef: Lawrence Robertson
Proprietor: Gordon Sneddon
Seats: 70. No cigars
Times: Last L 2pm/D 9.30pm (10pm weekends)

New Scone
Perthshire
Map no: 11 NO12
Tel: 01738 551171

Cost: Alc £23.50, fixed-price dinner £18.50. H/wine £12.50. Service inc.
Credit cards: 1 2 3 4 5

Menus: *A la carte*, fixed-price dinner, Sunday lunch, light lunch

Times: Midday-Last L 2.30pm, 7pm-Last D 9.30pm

Chef: Andrew Cambell
Proprietor: Antony Bryan

Seats: 60. Air conditioned
Additional: Children over 5 permitted; children's portions; ❂ dishes; other diets on request

PERTH, **Newton House**

A former dower house situated in the village of Glencarse, where chef Moira Macrae prepares predominantly Scottish food. Haggis is on offer as well as grilled breast of chicken with green peppercorn sauce and grilled Perthshire lamb cutlets.

Cost: Alc £21, fixed-price L £11.50/D £15.50. H/wine £9.95
Credit cards: 1 2 3 4. **Additional:** Children welcome; children's portions/menu; ❂ menu; Vegan/othr diets on request
Directions: Set back on the A90 4 miles from Perth, 13 miles from Dundee

Glencarse
Perthshire
Map no: 11 NO12
Tel: 01738 860250
Chef: Moira MacRae
Proprietors: Carole and Christopher Tallis
Seats: 48. No smoking in dining room
Times: Last L 2pm/D 9pm

PERTH, **Number Thirty Three**

Seafood predominates at this family-run restaurant, where Mary Billinghurst's honest cooking continues to attract praise. One can eat in the restaurant or the bar and the two menus are supplemented by daily blackboard specials. The interior is Art Deco in style, with comfortable banquette seating.

Cost: H/wine £9.60. **Credit cards:** 1 2 3. **Additional:** Children permitted (over 5); children's portions; ❂ dishes
Directions: In the city just off the High Street, near the river

33 George Street
Perthshire
Map no: 11 NO12
Tel: 01738 633771
Proprietors: Mary and Gavin Billinghurst
Seats: 24. No cigars or pipes
Times: Last L 2.30pm/D 9.30pm. Closed 10 days Xmas/New Year

PERTH, **Parklands**

Two townhouses were combined in 1991 to create this popular hotel overlooking North Inch Park. Fixed-price and carte menus feature modern British cuisine, with typical dishes including warm smoked halibut, pan-fried loin of fallow deer or rack of lamb. The wine list offers pricey traditional wines.

Cost: Alc £23, fixed-price L £15.50/D £24.95. H/wine £10.95
Credit cards: 1 2 3. **Additional:** No young children at dinner; children's portions; ❂ dishes
Directions: Overlooking South Inch Park, on the inner ring road

St Leonards Bank
Perthshire
Map no: 11 NO12
Tel: 01738 622451
Chef: Craig Wilson
Proprietor: Scotland's Commended. Manager: Allan Deeson
Seats: 30. No smoking in dining room
Times: Last L 2pm/D9pm. Closed Xmas and New Year

PITLOCHRY, **Knockendarroch House**

Home cooking at its best is the kitchen's strength at this secluded private country house hotel. Perthshire lamb, Tay salmon and roast quail are recent features of the mainly Scottish menu, supported by an economically-priced wine list.

Cost: H/wine £5.90. **Credit cards:** 1 2 3 4
Additional: Children welcome; ❂ dishes; Vegan/other diets on request
Directions: First right after the Atholl Palace Hotel, then second left, last hotel on left

Higher Oakfield
Perthshire
Map no: 14 NN95
Tel: 01796 473473
Chefs: Helen McKinnon, James McMenemie
Proprietor: Scotland's Commended. Manager: Francis Martin
Seats: 24. No smoking
Times: Last D 7.45pm

ST FILLANS, **Achray House** ❀

☺ *This popular hotel overlooking over Loch Earn has menus at a range of prices, all with vegetarian choices. Enjoyable starters have included a light savoury crêpe; a main dish of poached scallops was delicately flavoured but rather chewy. There is an extensive range of puddings.*

Cost: Alc £19, fixed–price L £10.50/D £15. H/wine £6.50. Service exc. **Credit cards:** 1 3 5. **Additional:** Children welcome; children's portions; ◐ menu; other diets on request
Directions: Five miles west of Comrie. St Fillans is by Loch Earn

Perthshire
Map no: 11 NN62
Tel: 01764 685231
Chef: Bernard Steinka
Proprietors: Tony and Jane Ross
Seats: 34. No smoking in dining room
Times: Last L 2pm/D 9pm. Closed Nov-Feb

ST FILLANS, **The Four Seasons** ❀❀

A loyal local following characterises a restaurant which has earned an additional rosette since last year

The Scott family (who must surely be represented at the Scottish Tartans Museum a few miles away) run the Four Seasons in a friendly and relaxing manner. The surrounding scenery is spectacular, with uninterrupted views down Loch Earn providing at least some inspiration, no doubt, for Andrew Scott's cooking style. He sums this up as Scottish with international influences. There is a short, daily-changing dinner menu on which home-team representatives, when in season, could be steamed lemon sole with Skye mussels and saffron, and West Coast scallops, bacon and garlic. Our inspector chanced upon an evening when a moist, tender lemon sole, rolled around a light lemon-flavoured stuffing, shared a platter with the scallops and saffron butter, as a main course. All the sweets from the trolley are home made, including rhubarb tart, Perthshire raspberry cranachan and triple chocolate marquise. Plenty of choice in the wine list which is strong on French, German and Italian, but also has a good showing from Australia. One can also dine in the lounge bar, choosing from an impressive supper menu.

Directions: On A85 at western edge of village overlooking Loch Earn

Perthshire
Map no: 11 NN62
Tel: 01764 685333

Chef: Andrew Scott
Proprietors: John A Scott, Barbara and Andrew Scott

Seats: 50. No smoking in dining room
Times: Last L 2.15pm/D 9.30pm. Closed mid Dec-early Mar

Cost: Fixed-price L £13/D £22. H/wine £9 ♀ Service exc
Credit cards: 1 2 3. **Additional:** Children permitted (no toddlers at dinner); children's portions; ◐ dishes; Vegan/other diets on request

STANLEY, **The Tayside** ❀

☺ *The Tayside is a popular sporting and holiday hotel in Edwardian style, and Liz Robinson's cooking is robust to match. Outdoor types enjoy the daily roast and hearty dishes such as lamb kidney turbigo; our inspector was particularly impressed by a 'delicious' home-made syrup sponge.*

Cost: Alc from £15.50, fixed-price D £15.50. H/wine £7.50. Service exc. **Credit cards:** 1 3 5. **Additional:** Children welcome; children's portions; ◐ dishes; Vegan/other diets on request
Directions: Five miles from Perth. In Stanley, on B9099, turn right at village green, then left

Mill Street
Perthshire
Map no: 11 NO13
Tel: 01738 828249
Chef: Peter Graham
Proprietor: Edgilton
Seats: 32. Smoking discouraged
Times: Last L 1.45pm/D 8.30pm

WALES
ANGLESEY, ISLE OF

BEAUMARIS, Ye Old Bull's Head ●●

An ancient inn oozing with character, offering good food and wine and superb views of the mountains and the sea

In Old French, *beau marais* was the 'fine marsh' where Edward I built the adjacent castle in 1295. The Grade 2-listed Bull is not quite that old, but it has notched up more than half a millennium – quite enough to give it a distinct cachet in the longevity stakes. Incidentally, it is a privately-owned member of the delightfully-named Welsh Rarebits Marketing Consortium. There are two dinner menus – a very simple three-course, fixed-price, and the *carte*. At first glance, neither is overtly Welsh, but closer inspection reveals regularly-appearing dishes such as Anglesey eggs, baked Arctic char from Lake Padarn below Snowdon, and parcels of galia melon with Carmarthen ham, to remind us where we are. Seafood salad, roast teal duck with puy lentils and juniper berries, and ballotine of game with a spiced aubergine relish, are all bedfellows of the red dragon too. The main restaurant is not open for lunch, except on Sundays when traditional roasts can be ordered. Ample bar meals are available the rest of the week. No-one should have difficulty finding something suitable from the well-stocked wine cellar.

Directions: The inn is on the main street in the town centre

Castle Street
Map no: 6 SH67
Tel: 01248 810329

Cost: *Alc* dinner £23.75, fixed-price D £18.95, Sun lunch £14.75. H/wine £12. No service charge
Credit cards: 1 3 5

Menus: *A la carte*, fixed-price dinner, Sun lunch, bar menu
Times: Last Sun L 2.30pm, Last D 9.30pm. Closed Xmas & 1 Jan

Chefs: Keith Rothwell, Anthony Murphy
Proprietor: David Robertson

Seats: 70. No-smoking area
Additional: Children permitted; no chidren under 7 at dinner; ◐ dishes; Vegan/other diets on request

LLANGEFNI, Tre-Ysgawen Hall ●●

☺ *Original ideas bring new life to the dishes here in the peaceful heart of Anglesey*

This guide sensibly overlooks the fact that Anglesey is part of Gwynedd by listing it separately. Not that it is noticeably different in cuisine from the mainland, but it is an island on the other side of the Menai Strait, after all. The house, built in 1882, has a beautiful oak staircase leading to spacious and opulent bedrooms, many containing antique furniture. There are two menus, a daily-changing, fixed-price and the *carte*; it would be a surprise if dishes chosen from either failed to please even the most jaded of palates. When our inspector visited (no jaded palate, his), roulade of smoked salmon with a caviar vinaigrette, magret of duck in a sherry and spice sauce and hot rum and raisin soufflé all earned his praise. Supreme of Conwy salmon, fillet of pan-fried Anglesey beef with garlic and shallots, and loin of Welsh lamb coated in a mint mousse, wrapped in spinach and served on a potato and onion bhaji with a mild curry sauce, acknowledge the region, but essentially the dishes are Anglo-French. A very good selection of European and New World wines is extended to include a Château Musar from Lebanon and a Director's Reserve from Russia.

Directions: A5 to Llangefni, take B5111 to Llanerchmedd through Rhosmeirch. After 1 mile turn right for Capel Coch. Restaurant signposted

Capel Coch
Map no: 6 SH47
Tel: 01248 750750

Cost: Fixed–price lunch £11 (2 courses), £14; fixed–price dinner £19.95. H/wine £9.80. Service exc.
Credit cards: 1 2 3 4 5
Menus: *A la carte*, fixed-price lunch and dinner, Sunday lunch, pre-theatre
Times: Midday-Last L 2.30pm, 7pm-Last D 9.30pm

Chef: Mark Colley
Proprietors: Ray and Pat Craighead
Seats: 64. No smoking area; no pipes or cigars in dining room
Additional: Children permitted (over 8 at dinner); children's portions; ◐ menu; Vegan/other diets on request

CLWYD

COLWYN BAY, Café Niçoise ❀❀

124 Abergele Road
Map no: 6 SH87
Tel: 01492 531555

Modern provincial French cooking using local fish and produce, run by friendly Francophiles in an informal setting

Designed to resemble a typical Nice cafe, this delightful restaurant serves a mixture of traditional and modern provincial French cooking learned in the kitchens of the Roux Brothers. Chef Carl Swift has hit on a successful recipe which greatly appeals to locals and tourists alike, and his various menus range from good value, light choices at lunch-time to an evening Menu Touristique and blackboard dishes, plus *carte*. Lynne Swift and a local team offer an informal and relaxed service at flower-adorned and candle-lit tables while French music plays in the background, and our inspector was impressed by the atmosphere at a recent visit. The food is attractively presented, and mouth-watering asparagus served in a chervil sauce was followed by locally caught sea bass poached in a light prawn bisque which had a superb flavour, and came with crisp and very fresh vegetables. A simple terrine of summer fruits was relished before coffee and home-made petits fours, providing the perfect ending to an enjoyable meal. Other dishes from the *carte* might include assiette of Welsh lamb or medley of seafood.

Chef: Carl Swift
Proprietors: Lynne and Carl Swift
Seats: 32
Times: Last L 2pm/D 10pm. L not served Mon. Closed Sun, 1 week Jan, 1 week Jun

Cost: *Alc* £21.50, Fixed-price L/D £10.50 (2 courses), £12.95. H/wine from £7.50 ♀ Service exc
Credit cards: 1 2 3

Additional: Children welcome; children's portions; ❂ dishes; Vegan/other diets on request

Directions: From A55 from Chester take exit signed Old Colwyn, turn left at slip road, right at mini roundabout, then right towards Colwyn Bay. Restaurant is on the left at the bottom of the hill, opposite Esso Garage

EWLOE, St David's Park ❀

St Davids Park
Map no: 7 SJ36
Tel: 01244 520800

A modern hotel, the St David's Park has a popular restaurant, where chef Graham Tinsley offers a carvery, gourmet menus and a carte with a list of alternative vegetarian main courses. Our inspector sampled smoked haddock topped with Welsh rarebit, pheasant on a rich Burgundy jus, and lemon tart.

Chef: Graham Tinsley
Proprietor: Hamish Ferguson
Seats: 120. No-smoking area. Air conditioned
Times: Last L 2pm(3pm Sun)/D 10pm
Cost: *Alc* £30, fixed-price L £10.95 /D £16.95. H/wine £9.50 ♀ Service exc. **Credit cards:** 1 2 3 4 5

Additional: Children welcome; children's portions/menu; ❂ menu; Vegan/other diets on request
Directions: Situated where A55 meets the A494, 10 minutes' drive from M56

HAWARDEN, Swiss Restaurant Imfeld ❀❀

68 The Highway
Map no: 7 SJ36
Tel: 01244 534523

☺ *Genuine Swiss dishes are served at this friendly and informal restaurant where gourmet evenings are a feature*

Markus Imfeld has brought his own brand of Swiss cooking to an unlikely setting in this small North Wales village. Such has his reputation spread, however, that diners travel from far and wide to enjoy his food. The restaurant is small and cosy with a separate section for smokers. Blackboards advertise the fish

Cost: *Alc* from £14.35, fixed-price D from £14.50, Gourmet £22. H/wine £8.20 ♀ Service exc
Credit cards: 1 3 5

Menus: *A la carte*, fixed-price

catches of the day, there is a fixed-price chef's selected menu, fondue specials and the *carte* choice. Food is influenced by the three main cultures found in Switzerland – Italian, French and German. Typical dishes are Zürigeschnetzettes – strips of veal with mushrooms and a sauce of white wine and cream, Berner Ratsherrentopf – fillets of beef, chicken and pork on a bed of rösti potatoes and Knöpfli 'n' Pilz – home-made pasta dumplings sautéed with mushrooms and leeks. Swiss chocolates and cheeses feature inevitably and gourmet evenings are held on the middle Wednesday of every month. The wines have been carefully chosen to complement Swiss food. Markus' wife Yvonne together with local staff looks after the bar and restaurant and the atmosphere is very friendly and informal.

Directions: Take A55 to North Wales; leave at Queensferry and take 2nd exit at roundabout to Hawarden. At top of hill, turn right at T-junction; restaurant is 0.25 mile on left

dinner, Gourmet menu 2nd Wed each month, Fondue menu each Fri and Sun
Times: 7pm-Last D 9pm (10pm Sat). Closed Mon, 2 weeks Feb, 2 weeks Sep

Chef: Markus Imfeld
Proprietors: Markus and Yvonne Imfeld

Seats: 40. No-smoking area
Additional: Children welcome; children's portions; ❷ dishes; special diets on request

HOLYWELL, **Kinsale Hall** ❀

A fine 17th-century building with views over the Dee estuary, where chef Kevin Steel produces enjoyable food in the attractive Raffles restaurant. Our inspector enjoyed a starter of scrambled egg with smoked salmon on a puff pastry base served with lemon butter sauce.

Directions: Off A548 near Mostyn

Map no: 7 SJ17
Tel: 01745 560001
Chef: Kevin Steel
Proprietor: Bill Johnson
Times: Last D 10pm
Credit cards: 1 2 3
Additional: Children permitted; ❷ dishes

LLANDRILLO, **Tyddyn Llan** ❀❀

The best of Welsh produce is skilfully transformed into imaginative dishes served in this charming restaurant

Guests who have spent their day fishing on the River Dee, exploring Snowdonia's magnificent scenery or visiting the historic city of Chester (some 35 miles away) peruse with gusto the inventive and constantly changing fixed-price menus offered by this attractive hotel's elegant restaurant. Freshly grown vegetables from the kitchen garden and a range of tasty sauces enhance a good balanced range of fish, meat, poultry and game, an enjoyable meal perhaps including such local specialities as Dee salmon and Welsh lamb or beef. Vegetarian options like mille-feuille of mushrooms, vegetables and nuts in a sherry sauce or a strudel of cream cheese, pine nuts and vegetables are equally tempting, then – for those not strong enough to cope with sticky toffee pudding at this juncture! – the meal can be rounded off with a light orange rosewater mousse. A good choice of house wines and a fairly wide selection of half bottles are featured on a reasonably-priced wine list which represents both Old and New Worlds very adequately.

Directions: Take B4401 from Corwen to Llandrillo. Restaurant is on the right as you leave the village

Map no: 6 SJ03
Tel: 01490 440264

Cost: Fixed-price L £10 (2 courses), £12.50, fixed-price D £21.50 (3 courses), £23.50. H/wine from £7. Service exc
Credit cards: 1 3 4

Menus: Fixed-price lunch and dinner, Sunday lunch, bar menu
Times: Last L 2pm, Last D 9.30pm. Closed 1st week Feb

Chef: Dominic Gilbert
Proprietors: Peter and Bridget Kindred

Seats: 60. No pipes or cigars in dining room
Additional: Children welcome; children's portions/menu; ❷ dishes; Vegan/other diets on request

LLANGOLLEN, **Bryn Howel** ☺☺

☺ *Daily-changing menus geared to market availability and quality produce in this delightful restaurant*

The Cedar Tree restaurant at Bryn Howel looks out over beautiful lawns running down to the canal and enjoys sweeping views of the Vale of Llangollen; guests' appreciation of this scenic splendour, however, could well take second place to their enjoyment of the area's produce – herbs freshly picked from the hotel garden enhancing the flavours of Dee salmon, Welsh lamb, local poultry and game in season. Fixed-price menus which change daily according to market availability have earned an excellent reputation for head chef Dai Davies – not least because of specialities like home-made bread (of which there are five or six different types available). For a real taste of Wales you might, perhaps, sample a baby quiche of Pant Ys Gawn goats' cheese infused with spring onions, then Welsh-farmed venison pudding topped with cream of leeks, an ice cream flavoured with locally made blackcurrant mead and, finally, coffee served with tiny Welshcakes. An extensive and predominantly French wine list contains only four half bottles.

Directions: Two miles east of Llangollen on A539

Map no: 7 SJ24
Tel: 01978 860331
Chef: Dai Davies
Proprietors: John E Lloyd
Seats: 90
Times: Last L 2pm/D 9pm. Closed 25 Dec
Cost: Fixed-price L £12.90/D £19.90. H/wine £10.90 ♀ Service exc
Credit cards: 1 2 3 5
Additional: Children welcome; children's portions/menu; ❷ dishes; Vegan/other diets on request

ROSSETT, **Llyndir Hall** ☺

Traditional English cuisine with a French influence is skilfully prepared at this imposing country house, and a vegetarian choice is always available.

Credit cards: 1 2 3 4 5. **Additional:** Children welcome before 8.30pm; children's portions/menu; ❷ menu; Vegan/other diets on request
Directions: South from Chester on A483 to Wrexham, follow signs for Pulford/Rossett B5445. Llyndir Hall signed on the right

Map no: 7 SJ35
Tel: 01244 571648
Chef: Mark Knowles
Manager: Keith Palfrey
Seats: 50. Guests requested not to smoke. No cigars or pipes
Times: Last L 2pm/D 9.30pm
Cost: Alc £25.50, fixed-price L £14.50/D £17.50. Service exc

ROSSETT, **Rossett Hall** ☺

The restaurant of this fine country house hotel offers good quality food including flambé and vegetarian dishes. Our inspector selected a distinctively flavoured calf's liver served with crisp vegetables. A home-made treacle tart concluded his enjoyable meal.

Directions: Situated between Chester and Wrexham off the A483

Map no: 7 SJ35
Tel: 01244 571000
Chef: Neil Baker
Proprietors: Mr and Mrs Craven

RUTHIN, Ye Olde Anchor Inn ❀

Rhos Street
Map no: 6 SJ15
Tel: 01824 702813
Chef: Rod England
Proprietor: Rod England
Seats: 40. No-smoking area
Times: Last L 2pm/D 9.30pm

☺ *The carte at this 18th-century town centre hostelry provides good choice and variety with the dishes featuring a far-eastern influence. Our inspector tried the rich dish of scallops and scampi sautéed in butter and flamed in brandy with garlic, parsley, lemon and served with rice.*

Cost: Alc £14, fixed-price D £11.95, Sun L £7.45. H/wine £7.45. Service exc. **Credit cards:** 1 3 5. **Additional:** Children welcome; children's portions/menu; ❂ dishes; Vegan/other diets on request
Directions: Situated in Ruthin at the junction of the A525 and A494

DYFED

ABERYSTWYTH, Conrah ❀❀

Ffosrhydygaled, Chancery
Map no: 6 SN58
Tel: 01970 617941

Skilful French-based cooking showing extreme freshness, simplicity and honest flavours from balanced menus

Chef: Stephen West
Proprietor: Welsh Rarebits. Manager: Frederick John Heading

A private kitchen garden yielding a ready supply of herbs and vegetables is part of the secret behind the exceptional freshness of the food served here. The hallmark of this immaculately kept country house hotel is care and attention, and nowhere is it more evident than in the dining room. Chef Stephen West uses newly caught salmon or game and young Welsh lamb to create his own blend of modern and classical dishes based on traditional French recipes, with well-executed and uncomplicated results. Our inspector recently tried a salad of samphire, Japanese seaweed, mussels and cockles, and walnut vinaigrette – an attractively presented starter of wonderful simplicity and honest flavours. Lamb fillet on wild mushrooms mixed with saffron noodles and served with Madeira sauce was a very enjoyable main course, and vegetables were full of flavour. The freshness of the dessert was also highly praised: palmiers with over ten varieties of fruit, like passion, mini fig, mango and red berries, came with white chocolate and red berry purée. The set three-course dinner menu and longer *carte* offer a well-balanced choice, and there are over 100 wines.

Seats: No-smoking in dining room
Times: Last L 2pm/Last D 9pm

Cost: Alc £25, fixed-price L £13.75/D £22.50. H/wine £9.50. Service exc
Credit cards: 1 2 3 4 5

Additional: Children permitted (over 5); children's portions; ❂ dishes; Vegan/other diets on request

Directions: On A487, 3 miles south of Aberystwyth

ABERYSTWYTH, Groves ❀

44-46 North Parade
Map no: 6 SN58
Tel: 01970 617623
Chef: Steve Albert
Proprietors: The Albert family
Seats: 60. No-smoking area. Air conditioned
Times: Last L 2pm/D 9pm

This pleasant and comfortable little town-centre hotel provides a good choice of Welsh dishes. The full flavoured home-made soup served with granary loaf is of a high standard as are the carefully prepared main courses.

Cost: Fixed-price D £14, Sun L £11.50. H/wine £7.50 ♀ Service inc
Credit cards: 1 2 3 4 5 **Additional:** Children welcome; children's menu; ❂ menu, Vegan/other diets on request
Directions: In town centre in tree-lined road. Take road opposite railway station, 2nd right and Groves is on the left

WALES DYFED

BRECHFA, Ty Mawr ✽

☺ *Standing by the bridge over the River Marlais, the restaurant at this lovely old stone building offers delicious home-made bread. The highlight of our inspector's meal, however, was the chocolate and almond puff with its excellent puff pastry and rich chocolate filling.*

Cost: Fixed-price L £12, £14/D £16, £18. H/wine £8.25 ♀ Service inc. **Credit cards:** 1 2 3. **Additional:** Children permitted at lunch; children's portions/menu; ◐ menu; Vegan/other diets on request; **Directions:** In the centre of the village 6.5 miles from the junction of A40/B4310

Map no: 2 SN53
Tel: 01267 202332
Chef: Beryl Tudhope
Proprietors: Dick and Beryl Tudhope
Seats: 35-50. No smoking in dining room
Times: Last L 2pm/D 9.30pm. Closed Tue, Xmas, last 2 weeks Jan

EGLWYSFACH, Ynyshir Hall ✽✽

A relaxing, peaceful restaurant where notable food is served by friendly, attentive owners and staff

Queen Victoria used to own the estate on which Ynyshir Hall was once a shooting lodge; today she might be wryly amused that most of it is now a bird reserve. Twelve acres of attractive grounds, however, still belong to the fine Georgian house where young chef Tony Pierce arrived in January 1994. His imaginative cuisine soon earned him a good reputation in west Wales. A first course from his fixed-price menu could be roast saddle of rabbit with carrot and chive salad, or pan-fried fillet of red mullet with home-made noodles and gazpacho sauce. Main course options include fillet of Welsh black beef with creamed potatoes and a truffle oil-scented sauce, paupiette of guinea fowl with poached apricots, bacon and thyme, and mille-feuille of salmon from the River Dyfi nearby, with steamed vegetables and a basil cream sauce. Our inspector's tender Welsh lamb was served on a bed of Puy lentils with a confit of shallots and a light rosemary sauce. Rhubarb and ginger soufflé or a light apple tart with Calvados parfait might follow. The wine list is beautifully hand-written and illustrated by co-owner Rob Reen.

Directions: Off the A487, 6 miles from Machynlleth and 11 miles from Aberystwyth

Near Machynlleth
Map no: 6 SN69
Tel: 01654 781209

Cost: Fixed-price dinner £25. H/wine from £10. Service exc
Credit cards: 1 2 3

Menus: Fixed-price dinner, Sunday lunch
Times: Last L 1.30pm, Last D 8.45pm

Chef: Tony Pierce
Proprietors: Rob and Joan Reen

Seats: 30. No smoking in dining room
Additional: Children permitted (over 9); ◐ dishes; other dishes on request

PEMBROKE, Court ✽

A good choice of dishes is provided at this elegant country house hotel, from the carte, fixed-price menu and vegetarian selection. Our inspector enjoyed a starter of prawns sautéed with bacon and finished with brandy and cream, followed by beef Cromwell, and a coffee flavoured trifle with whisky.

Cost: A/c from £20, fixed-price D £15.95. H/wine £8.95. Service inc. **Credit cards:** 1 2 3 4 5 **Additional:** Children welcome; children's portions; ◐ dishes; other diets on request
Directions: From Pembroke take coast road to Tenby. In the village of Lamphey, turn left onto private drive, signed

Lamphey
Map no: 2 SM90
Tel: 01646 672273
Chef: Wayne Wysoski
Proprietor: Best Western.
Managers: Tony and France Lain
Seats: 50. No smoking. Air conditioned
Times: Last L 1.45pm/D 9.45pm

ST DAVID'S, **Warpool Court** ❀

Originally built as the cathedral choir school, this hotel overlooks St Bride's Bay. Chef Mark Strangward produces enjoyable food using local fish and produce. Lobsters and crab are often available in season. Fillet of red mullet with béarnaise sauce is another delicious dish.

Additional: Children welcome; children's portions/menu; ❂ menu; Vegan/other diets on request
Directions: From Cross Square, left beside Cartref Restaurant, down Goat Street, at fork follow hotel signs

Map no: 2 SM72
Tel: 01437 720300
Chef: Mark Strangward
Proprietors: Peter Trier, Rupert Duffin
Seats: 60. No pipes or cigars
Times: Last L 2pm/D 9.15pm. Closed Jan
Cost: Alc £26, fixed-price L £15.95/D £22. H/wine £7.70. Service inc. **Credit crds:** 1 2 3 4 5

TENBY, **Penally Abbey** ❀

Overlooking Caldey Island and Carmarthen Bay, this restaurant has a small but interesting menu making good use of fresh, quality produce. Meals here have included the smooth and lightly textured salmon and trout terrine, and roast breast of Barbary duck in a port wine sauce.

Additional: Children over 7 permitted at dinner; children's portions/menu; ❂ dishes; Vegan/other diets on request
Directions: 1.5 miles from Tenby, just off Penally village green

Penally
Map no: 2 SN10
Tel: 01834 843033
Chef: Mrs Ellen Warren
Proprietors: Mr and Mrs S T Warren
Seats: 46. No smoking in dining room
Times: Last L 2pm/D 9.30pm
Cost: Fixed-price D £23.50. H/wine £9.80 ♀ Service inc
Credit cards: 1 2 3

GWENT

ABERGAVENNY, **Llanwenarth Arms** ❀

☺ *A welcoming inn overlooking the River Usk where D'Arcy McGregor cooks international style dishes using local game, trout and salmon. Our inspector recommended queen scallop and oyster mushrooms with garlic butter followed by local roasted breast of duck with sweet orange sauce.*

Cost: Alc £20. **Credit cards:** 1 2 3
Additional: ❂ dishes. Children permitted
Directions: On A40 midway between Abergavenny and Crickhowell

Brecon Road
Map no: 3 SO21
Tel: 01873 810550
Chefs: D'Arcy McGregor, Julie Jones, Julie Bull
Proprietors: Angela and D'Arcy McGregor
Seats: 60. No cigars or pipes
Times: Last L 2pm/D 9.45pm. Closed Boxing Day

CHEPSTOW, **Leadon's Brasserie** ❀❀

French-inspired, good value food and a worthy selection from the world's wine cellars

One-time Welsh Chef of the Year, Wayne Leadon made his reputation in other people's restaurants but he has consolidated it in his own. A move from his original cellar restaurant in the town has upped his seating capacity by a third. He knows his market well, supplying simple, light meals as well as more robust dishes, suiting most tastes and pockets in the process. Freshness is the watchword, as in the daily-arriving fish specials.

6 Station Road
Map no: 3 ST59
Tel: 01291 627402

Cost: Alc lunch £7, dinner £18, fixed-price early bird dinner £12.95. H/wine £8.95 ♀ Service exc
Credit cards: 1 2 3 4 5

Menus: A la carte, fixed-price early bird dinner, Sunday lunch

In a pre-move visit, an inspector's unerring instinct for quality led him to well-prepared mussels marinière-style, with tomato, fresh crab and croûtons. Then he chose succulent scallops, lightly flashed under the salamander and served in a filo pastry case, topped with a first-class hollandaise sauce, all on a bed of sherried mushrooms for added piquancy. One minor gripe with the menu – why describe chargrilled marinated chicken breast and Japanese butterfly king-prawns with thermidor as 'Feather and surf'? This is the tacky shorthand often used, shall we say, by less discerning establishments. A modicum of V-marked dishes will please vegetarians and a range of home-made puddings, like Wayne's tempting chocolate marbled terrine with caramel sauce, should please everyone.

Times: Midday-Last L 2pm, 6pm-Last D 10pm. L not served Sat

Chef: Wayne Michael Leadon
Proprietor: Wayne Michael Leadon

Seats: 48
Additional: Children welcome; children's portions/menu; ❷ dishes; special diets on request

Directions: From the Severn Bridge into Chepstow, turn left into Station Road. Restaurant is 400yds on the right adjacent to Coltharts Garage

CHEPSTOW, **St Pierre Park** ❀

☺ *A popular golfing and leisure hotel just by the Severn Bridge. The chef produces well-prepared dishes with honest textures and flavours using quality produce, such as warm pigeon breast salad and best end of lamb medallions with a jus of balsamic vinegar and rosemary.*

St Pierre Park
Map no: 3 ST59
Tel: 01291 625261
Chef: Mark Lindsey
Proprietor: D Beswick
Times: Last D 9.45pm (10pm Fri, Sat)
Cost: Fixed-price D £19.50.
Credit cards: 1 2 3 4

Additional: No smoking in dining room. ❷ dishes
Directions: Just off the A48 west of junc 22 M4 Chepstow

LLANDDEWI SKYRRID,
Walnut Tree Inn ❀❀❀

An informal country inn setting for a comprehensive menu of mainly Italian dishes

Franco Taruschio has been at the Walnut Tree for over 30 years. It is a pretty whitewashed inn, retaining much of its historic character, in a lovely rural setting. The tables are fairly closely packed and the atmosphere is lively and informal. A *carte* of mainly Italian dishes is offered, though some French influences are apparent, and the menu is the same for lunch and dinner. Lunch is served in the two bars, the restaurant opening only in the evening. Great store is set on the ingredients and Franco goes to a lot of trouble to source the best possible produce. He chooses tried and tested dishes prepared in a straightforward style with flavour as the main priority.
Our inspector's lunch began with delicious warm spinach quiche as an appetiser, followed by a starter of two crispy pancakes filled to overflowing with crab meat and served with a French salad. Alternatives, from a comprehensive list, could include soup, perhaps asparagus and tarragon, bresaola, bruschetta with seafood, Thai pork, and crostini of peppers with home-made Italian sausage. Fish and seafood figure prominently among the main courses, with dishes such as roast monkfish, laverbread, orange sauce and deep-fried seaweed; brodetto (mixed fish casserole), and cold lobster with tomato

Abergavenny
Map no: 3 SO31
Tel: 01873 852797

Cost: Alc £28. H/wine £9.75 (litre) ⁹ No service charge
Credit cards: None taken

Menu: A la carte
Times: Midday-Last L 3pm, 7pm-Last D 10.15pm. Closed Sun, Mon, Xmas, 2 weeks Feb

Chef: Franco Taruschio
Proprietor: Franco Taruschio

Seats: 40. Air conditioned
Additional: Children welcome; children's portions; ❷ dishes; Vegan/other diets on request

salsa. Our inspector went for a meat option – delicious Welsh lamb served pink with deep-fried artichoke, some wild mushrooms and a natural jus. Vegetarians are not forgotten, with their platter of fried artichokes, polenta, griddled courgettes, aubergine and Piedmontese peppers. There is a huge range of puddings, including several home-made ice creams. Our inspector chose an unusual crème brûlée, full of flavour, with stewed rhubarb beneath the thin caramel topping.

Directions: Three miles north-east of Abergavenny on B4521

NEWPORT, Celtic Manor ❀❀

A stylish manor house offering quality cooking in the formal restaurant

As we were going to press our inspectors confirmed that the Celtic Manor Hotel had been awarded a second rosette for the quality of its cuisine. There are two dining options at this stylish manor house; either Hedleys or the more informal patio restaurant. A recent inspection meal commenced with a tasty home-made ravioli of crab and avocado, followed by excellent roasted breast of Lunesdale duck presented with a delicate filo pastry parcel of candied onions.

Additional: Children permitted; children's portions/menu; ☻ menu; special diets on request
Directions: On A48 just off junc 24 of M4 towards Newport

Coldra Woods
Map no: 3 ST38
Tel: 01633 413000

Chef: Trevor Jones
Manager: David Morgan

Seats: 60. No-smoking area. No pipes
Times: Last L 2.30pm/D 10.30pm. Closed Sat L, Sun, BHs
Cost: Alc £26.95, fixed-price L £13.95 (2 courses), £15.95/D £18.50 (2 courses), £22.50. H/wine £10.50. Service exc
Credit cards: 1 2 3 4

TINTERN, Royal George Hotel ❀

☺ *An attractive 17th-century inn style hotel close to the famous abbey ruins. Here chef Lawrence Reed produces good honest food using quality local produce. Our inspector enjoyed chicken liver and Cumberland sauce and loin of lamb on a light but tasty port sauce.*

Cost: Fixed-price D £15.95. **Credit cards:** 1 2 3
Additional: Children permitted; ☻ dishes
Directions: On the main road, close to Tintern Abbey

Map no: 3 SO50
Tel: 01291 689205
Chef: Lawrence Reed
Proprietor: Mr A J Pearce
Times: Open for dinner all year

WHITEBROOK, Crown at Whitebrook ❀❀

A remote and beautiful retreat in the Wye Valley serving commendable French food cooked from the finest produce

Perched high up in a remote corner of the Wye Valley within wooded surroundings reached by a narrow lane, this restaurant with rooms offers a gem of a retreat. Sandra and Roger Bates personally run this charming place, and whilst he provides a hospitable welcome and attentive service, she is responsible for the commendable cooking which is behind the Crown's growing reputation. Everything from the bread rolls to the sorbets is home made from fresh local produce and quality Welsh ingredients, and a recent inspection meal elicited fulsome praise.

Map no: 3 SO50
Tel: 01600 860254

Cost: Fixed-price lunch £14.95, fixed-price dinner £24.95. H/wine £7.50 ♀ No service charge
Credit cards: 1 2 3 4 5

Menus: Fixed-price lunch and dinner, light lunches Tue-Sat
Times: Midday-Last L 2pm, 7pm-Last D 9.30pm. D not served Sun, L not served Mon. Closed 2

Delicious fresh canapés were followed by delicately smooth duck liver parfait with intense flavours, served on a toasted brioche with pickled vegetables. Succulent, tiny noisettes of lamb were chargrilled but moist, and served with a robust confit of shoulder of lamb and shallots, and a lovely rosemary and Madeira sauce. A really tasty 'tatin au poire' was hot and full of flavour, with a delicious caramelised sauce and fresh cream. The fixed-price lunch and dinner menus show much imagination and flair, with seven or so choices at each course, and there's a good selection of Welsh and border cheeses.

Directions: Turn west from A466 south of Bigsweir Bridge, signposted Whitebrook

weeks Jan, 2 weeks Aug

Chef: Sandra Bates
Proprietors: Sandra and Roger Bates

Seats: 36. No-smoking area; no cigars or pipes in restaurant
Additional: Children welcome; children's portions; ✪ dishes; special diets on request

GWYNEDD

ABERDOVEY, **Maybank** ✪

☺ The restaurant of this small hotel has views extending over the estuary and the hills beyond. The fixed-price menu changes regularly and local fish catches often appear on the blackboard list of specials. Sea-bass and sea trout are not to be missed and local lamb is also superb.

Credit cards: 1 3. **Additional:** Children permitted; under 5s from 5pm-6pm when children's portions/menu available; ✪ dishes
Directions: On A483 (Machynlleth-Aberdovey), 500yds from village sign on left

4 Penhelig Road, Penhelig
Map no: 6 SN69
Tel: 01654 767500
Chef: Elizabeth A Dinsdale
Proprietors: Elizabeth A Dinsdale, Paul C Massey
Seats: 26-32. No-smoking area; no pipes or cigars
Times: Last D 9pm/10pm. Closed 9 Nov-mid Dec, Jan-mid Feb
Cost: Fixed-price D £16.95. Service exc

ABERDOVEY, **Penhelig Arms** ✪

☺ With lovely views over the Dovey Estuary, this small hotel has a restaurant to be proud of. The cooking is quite sophisticated with plenty of fresh fish and other local produce. Our inspector enjoyed sea bass with garlic mayonnaise, venison pie and a rich bread and butter pudding

Credit cards: 1 3. **Additional:** Children welcome; children's portions; ✪ dishes; special diets on request **Directions:** At eastern end of village (A493) from Machynlleth. Car park opposite by sea wall

Map no: 6 SN69
Tel: 01654 767215
Chef: Jane Howkins
Proprietors: Robert and Sally Hughes
Seats: 34. Smoking not encouraged. **Times:** Last Sun L 2pm/D 9.30pm. Closed Xmas
Cost: Fixed-price D £17.50, Sun L £11.50. H/wine £8 ♀ Service exc

ABERSOCH, **Tudor Court** ✪

☺ An attractive hotel in a convenient location not far from the town centre and beaches. A carte of popular English and French dishes is offered in the pretty restaurant. Local fresh fish and produce is put to good use, and pork, poultry and beef dishes are accompanied by a range of well made sauces

Cost: Alc £20, fixed-price L £10.35/D £13.50. H/wine £7.95 ♀ Service exc. **Additional:** Children welcome; children's portions/menu; ✪ menu special diets on request. **Directions:** In the centre of the village

Lon Sarn Bach
Map no: 6 SH32
Tel: 0175871 3354
Chef: Jack Courtney
Proprietor: Jennifer Jones
Seats: 40. No-smoking area; no cigars or pipes
Times: Last L 2.30pm/D 9.30pm

BANGOR, **Menai Court** ✤

☺ *The owners, Judy and Elwyn Jones of Black and White Minstrels fame create a relaxed atmosphere at their hotel overlooking the Menai Straits. Chef Stephen Brown has a daily changing menu offering, for instance, filo pastry envelopes with fish and vegetables or duck breast with cherry sauce.*

Additional: Children permitted; children's portions; ❂ dishes; Vegan/other diets on request
Directions: Take A55 into Bangor. Turn right at railway station, and at top of hill turn right again by Midland Bank into College Road. Then take the first left into Craig y Don Road

Craig y Don Road
Map no: 6 SH57
Tel: 01248 354200
Chef: Stephen Brown
Proprietors: Judy and Elwyn Hughes
Times: Last L 2pm/Last D 9.30pm. Lunch not served Sun. Closed 26 Dec-2 Jan
Cost: Alc £17, fixed-price L £11.50/D £14.95. H/wine £9.20 (litre). Service exc
Credit cards: 1 3 5.

BARMOUTH, **Ty'r Graig** ✤

☺ *The Wright family have run this comfortable hotel for many years. Mrs Wright is responsible for the food, which is offered from a daily changing set price menu supplemented by a carte of popular dishes. Our inspector enjoyed sole mousseline, stuffed roast lamb, with apple pie to follow.*

Cost: Alc £15.50, fixed-price L £9.25/D £15.50. H/wine £8.95 ♀ Service exc. **Credit cards:** 1 2 3 **Additional:** Children permitted; children's portions; ❂ dishes; special diets on request
Directions: On coast road 1 mile outside Barmouth (towards Harlech) on seaward side

Llanaber Road
Map no: 6 SH61
Tel: 01341 280470
Chef: Jill Wright
Proprietors: Mr and Mrs Wright
Seats: 26-28. No smoking in dining room
Times: Last L 2pm/D 8.30pm. Closed Nov-mid Mar

BONTDDU, **Bontddu Hall** ✤

A large choice of dishes is available at this restaurant which has beautiful views of the Cader Idris range of mountains. A good selection of vegetables accompanied our inspector's dish of chicken breast stuffed with leeks with leek sauce, and the bread and butter pudding with vanilla sauce had good flavour.

Additional: Children over 3 welcome; children's portions/menu; ❂ dishes; Vegan/other diets on request
Directions: Turn off A470 north of Dolgellau on to A496 Barmouth road. Restaurant is on the right as you enter the village

Map no: 6 SH61
Tel: 01341 49661
Chef: Trevor Pharoah
Proprietor: Mike Ball
Seats: 70. No-smoking area
Times: Last L 2pm/D 9.30pm. Closed Nov-Mar
Cost: Fixed-price L £11.75/D £23.50. H/wine £9.25. Service exc

CAERNARFON, **Seiont Manor** ✤

☺ *The hotel is located in wood and pasture land. Our inspector tried the light lunch menu, which included a good terrine of mixed seafood as a starter. This was followed by a fine-flavoured small escalope of salmon in a tarragon butter sauce with a selection of superb vegetables.*

Cost: Gourmet £29.95, fixed-price L £7.50/D £19.50. H/wine £8.95. Service exc. **Credit cards:** 1 2 3 4 5. **Additional:** Children welcome; children's portions/menu; ❂ menu; Vegan/other diets on request
Directions: From Caernarfon follow A4086 toward Llanrug, hotel on left

Llanrug
Map no: 6 SH46
Tel: 01286 673366
Chef: Richard Treble
Manager: Philip Warren
Seats: 60. No smoking in dining room
Times: Last L 2.15pm/D 10pm. Closed Sat L

CONWY, **Castle Bank** ☺

☺ *This small, completely no-smoking hotel is run by the friendly Gilligans, and while Sean looks after the front of house Marilyn cooks the enjoyable meals. Her good value menus comprise popular choices, using local produce when possible, and great care is taken with the preparation.*

Credit cards: 1 3. **Additional:** Children welcome; children's portions; ❶ dishes; special diets on request
Directions: Drive through Conwy to Bangor Archway. Turn left into Mount Pleasant, then right through public car park

Mount Pleasant
Map no: 6 SH77
Tel: 01492 593888
Chef: Mrs Marilyn Gilligan
Proprietors: Mr and Mrs Sean Gilligan
Seats: 40. No smoking
Times: Last Sun L 1pm/D 8pm. Closed Jan-mid Feb
Cost: Fixed-price D £14, Sun L £9.25. H/wine £8. No service charge

CONWY, **The Old Rectory** ❀❀

Fresh Welsh ingredients cooked with outstanding skill, in a stylish Georgian hotel

A meal of rare quality served in a relaxed and very friendly atmosphere is guaranteed at this delightful hotel. Set in attractive gardens overlooking the Conwy estuary and castle, the Georgian hotel has been restored to the elegance of its period. Co-owner Wendy Vaughan is an outstanding chef, and only the finest local ingredients go into her light and delicate cooking. The four-course menu offers no choice except at dessert, and might include warm smoked sea trout with a tartlet of quail's egg and asparagus, with roast fillet of Welsh mountain lamb with a leek and laverbread timbale and tarragon jus. Our inspector waxed lyrical about a recent meal which began with a beautifully presented trio of salmon – dariol of smoked salmon with salmon caviar, salmon mousse, and salmon pyramids, garnished with pickled samphire. Pink slices of deliciously tender roast breast of Lunedale duck on a potato crust were served with chicory salad and ginger sauce. Welsh cheeses with oatmeal biscuits can be replaced by a green salad or a fruit sorbet, and a dessert of sweet coffee marquise with a light coffee sauce was the perfect finish.

Directions: In Conwy take the Bangor road to the west. Immediately after passing through the arch in the town wall turn left. Hotel 200yds on right

Llanrwst Road, Colwyn Bay
Map no: 6 SH77
Tel: 01492 580611

Cost: Fixed-price dinner £27.50. Wine £10.90. Service inc
Credit cards: 1 2 3 4 5

Menu: Fixed-price dinner
Times: D 7.15pm for 8pm. Closed 14 Dec-1 Feb

Chef: Wendy Vaughan
Proprietors: Wendy and Michael Vaughan

Seats: 16. No smoking
Additional: No children under 5; children's portions

DOLGELLAU, **Clifton House** ❀

☺ *Despite its former use as the County Gaol, contemporary visitors to Clifton House can look forward to a friendly welcome. High standards of cooking continue to credit the unusually imaginative menu of traditional and modern English dishes; a good selection of Welsh cheeses to finish.*

Cost: Alc £16.50, fixed-price D (Sun eve only) £11.25. Service inc
Credit cards: 1 3. **Additional:** Children permitted; children's portions; ❶ dishes; Vegan/other diets on request
Directions: On one-way system in town centre, 100yds from main square

Smithfield Square
Map no: 6 SH71
Tel: 01341 422554
Chef: Pauline Dix
Proprietors: Rob and Pauline Dix
Seats: 22. No smoking in dining room
Times: Last D 9.30pm. Closed Xmas & Jan

DOLGELLAU, **Dolmelynllyn Hall** ❀

☺ *The restaurant of this country house is half panelled and features stained glass windows. The daily-changing five course menu offers carefully prepared and presented dishes. Our inspector recently enjoyed a pancake of broccoli with smoked goose and a superb batter pudding of brazil nuts and peaches.*

Credit cards: 1 2 3 4 **Additional:** Children over 10 permitted; ❷ dish; Vegan/other diets on request
Directions: Entrance to hotel drive is at southern end of village of Ganllwyd on the A470, 5 miles north of Dollgellau

Ganllwyd
Map no: 6 SH71
Tel: 01341 440273
Chef: Joanna Reddicliffe
Proprietor: Jonathan Barkwith
Seats: 20. No smoking
Times: Last D 8.30pm. Closed Dec-Jan
Cost: Fixed-price D £22.50. H/wine £8.75 ♀ No service charge

DOLGELLAU, **Dolserau Hall Hotel** ❀

☺ *Set in five acres of beautiful countryside the restaurant of this Victorian mansion hotel overlooks the Wnion valley. The four-course fixed-price menu changes daily, offering dishes such as grilled fresh river trout or honey roast ham, and a vegetarian dish is always available.*

Additional: Children over 5 permitted; children's portions; ❷ dishes; special diets on request. **Directions:** 1.5 miles north of Dolgellau, between A470 and A494 to Bala

Map no: 6 SH71
Tel: 01341 422522
Chef: Huw Roberts
Proprietors: Marion and Peter Kaye
Seats: 40. No smoking
Times: Last D 8.30pm
Cost: Fixed-price D £18.50. H/wine £6.95. **Credit cards:** 1 3

DOLGELLAU, **Penmaenuchaf Hall** ❀

A magnificent house built as a summer and sporting residence. Local fresh produce features prominently and the hotel has its own herb garden. Chef Lee Jones produces a superb saddle of venison with blueberry, Canadian whisky and Hickory Smoke sauce.

Additional: Children permitted, under 10s before 7.30pm; children's portions; ❷ dishes; Vegan/other diets on request
Directions: From A470, take A493 (Tywyn/Fairbourne); entrance 1.5 miles on left by sign for Penmaenpool

Penmaenpool
Map no: 6 SH71
Tel: 01341 422129
Chef: Lee Jones
Proprietors: Mark Watson, Lorraine Fielding
Seats: 35. No smoking
Times: Last L 2pm (2.30pm Sun)/D 9.30pm
Cost: Fixed-price L £11.95 (2 courses), £13.95/D £21.50. H/wine from £9.85. Service exc

HARLECH, **Castle Cottage** ❀

☺ *Glyn Roberts has brought his considerable skills to this delightful little restaurant, situated near the castle. The fixed-price menu is regularly changing and Welsh lamb and locally caught fish feature strongly.*

Cost: Sun L £12, fixed-price D £16 (2 courses), £18.50. H/wine £7.95 ♀ Service exc. **Credit cards:** 1 2 3 5 **Additional:** Children welcome; children's portions/menu; ❷ dishes; Vegan/other diets on request
Directions: Just off the High Street (B4573) in view of Harlech Castle

Map no: 6 SH53
Tel: 01766 780479
Chef: Glyn Roberts
Proprietors: Glyn and Jacqueline Roberts
Seats: 45. No smoking in dining room
Times: Last L 2pm/D 9pm. Closed 2 weeks Jan

LLANBERIS, **Y Bistro** ✹

☺ *This popular village restaurant is run almost entirely by a husband and wife. The menu contains seven or eight choices with fixed prices according to the number of courses taken, and changes daily. Full use is made of local lamb, fish and poultry, and the home-made bread is fresh and crispy.*

Cost: Fixed-price D £21.50. H/wine £8.50. No service charge
Credit cards: 1 3 5 **Additional:** Children welcome; children's portions; ❶ dishes; Vegan/other diets on request
Directions: In middle of town

Glandwr
43-45 Stryd Fawr
Map no: 6 SH56
Tel: 01286 871278
Chef: Nerys Roberts
Proprietors: Danny and Nerys Roberts
Seats: 52. No smoking in dining room
Times: Last D 9.45pm

LLANDDEINIOLEN, **Ty'n Rhos** ✹

☺ *Nigel and Lynda Kettle have run this delightful farm hotel for over 20 years. Lynda cooks using fresh seasonal foods. She offers a set four-course menu but she is hoping to expand this. The quality of the food is high, shown in the slightly pink roast beef and excellent sticky toffee pudding.*

Cost: Alc £19, fixed-price D £17.50. H/wine £7.50. No service charge. **Credit cards:** 1 2 3. **Additional:** Children over 6 permitted; ❶ dishes; Vegan/other diets on request
Directions: In the hamlet of Seion between BB4366 and B4547

Map no: 6 SH56
Tel: 01248 670489
Chefs: Lynda Kettle, Bill Ashton
Proprietors: Nigel and Lynda Kettle
Seats: 30. No smoking in dining room
Times: Last D 8.30pm. Closed Sun

LLANDUDNO, **Bodysgallen Hall** ✹✹

An interesting selection of British cooking in a lovely, peaceful country house setting

A pianist plays during dinner at this lovely old country house hotel, while guests are encouraged to relax over the set three or four course bill of fare, and enjoy the fruits of their choice. A dedicated team of staff provides a discreetly attentive service in the two elegant dining rooms, while chef Mair Lewis creates many traditional country house dishes amongst a largely British style of cuisine. Starters like confit of duck with leeks, lentils and Cumberland sauce are widely enjoyed, while main courses might be marinated collop of veal with baby vegetables and a red wine jus, or poached salmon fillet topped with a herb crust on a dill butter. Our inspector chose an attractive baked parcel of monkfish served with tasty leek and chive butter, and a pink and succulent rack of lamb with deep-fried garlic and shallots. Scrumptious desserts might include brandy snap cornets filled with a coffee syllabub, served with a warm dark chocolate sauce, or hot lime tart set on a warm lemon custard, and the chosen one of raspberry charlotte with seasonal fruits and warm caramel was a success. A shorter lunch menu offers a similar choice.

Directions: 3 miles south of Llandudno on the A470. Bodysgallen Hall is 1 mile on right

Map no: 6 SH78
Tel: 01492 584466

Cost: Fixed-price lunch £15.90, fixed-price dinner £29.95. H/wine £11.75. Service inc
Credit cards: 1 2 3 4 5

Menus: Fixed-price lunch and dinner, Sunday lunch
Times: Midday-Last L 2pm, 7.30pm-Last D 9.45pm

Chef: Mair Lewis
Proprietor: Historic House Hotels. Manager: Andrew Bridgford
Seats: 80. Smoking permitted after coffee; no pipes or cigars
Additional: Children permitted (over 8); ❶ dishes; Vegan/other diets on request. Pianist

LLANDUDNO, Empire ☺

☺ *Echoes of a bygone age are part of the Empire's charm in a resort town between the Great and Little Orme headlands. In the striking main restaurant a daily-changing five-course dinner menu offers a good choice, including vegetarian dishes. Try the Poolside Coffee Shop for simpler meals.*

Cost: Fixed-price L £9.70/D £15.37. H/wine £9.95 (litre) ♀ Service inc. **Credit cards:** 1 2 3 4 5. **Additional:** Children welcome; children's portions; ❂ dishes, Vegan/other diets on request
Directions: At end of Pier, turn left into Church Walks, 150 yds on left

Church Walks
Map no: 6 SH78
Tel: 01492 860555
Chefs: Stephen Walker, Michael Waddy
Proprietors: Leonard and Elizabeth Maddocks
Seats: 110. No-smoking area. Air conditioned
Times: Last L 2pm/Last D 9.30pm. L served Sat and Sun only. Closed 17-29 Dec

LLANDUDNO, Imperial ☺

☺ *Set on an impressive Victorian sea front, the Imperial has the comfortable atmosphere of a professionally run establishment. Dishes from the menu are attractively presented and sometimes unusual – hot mushrooms and apples with crisp salad pleasantly surprised our inspector.*

Cost: Fixed-price L £9.50/D £19.50, Sun L £10.50. H/wine £8.95. Service inc. **Credit cards:** 1 2 3 4 5. **Additional:** Children welcome; ❂ dishes; Vegan/other diets on request
Directions: Centrally situated on the promenade

The Promenade
Map no: 6 SH78
Tel: 01492 877466
Chef: Andrew Goode
Proprietor: Geoffrey Lofthouse
Seats: 160. No pipes or cigars
Times: Last L 2pm/D 9.30pm

LLANDUDNO, St Tudno ☺☺☺

☺ *An award-winning small hotel serving quality modern British cooking with Welsh and classical French influences*

There's much to commend this delightful sea front hotel, which looks from the outside much the same as its neighbours but is seen to be special immediately on entering. Owners Janette and Martin Bland have a caring and friendly approach that makes for a welcoming atmosphere, and their young staff are equally attentive.
The cooking is another major attraction, and the set three and five course dinner menus offered by chefs David Harding and Ian Watson provide a lightly-prepared and well-balanced meal. Our inspector praised a recent meal which began with chicken livers and Madeira sauce with fresh pasta, followed by a tasty and hotly spiced mulligatawny soup with evident apple flavour, served with crisp, light croutons. Salmon baked with spinach and pastry and a tangy beurre blanc was a delightful main course, served with sweet young mange tout, parsnip and broccoli. Rather burnt Trinity College creams failed to excite, but the selection of Welsh cheeses was much more enjoyable. A daily chef's vegetarian dish is offered with starters like avocado pears with asparagus, and tomato and basil soup, and there are some good value wines.

Directions: On promenade opposite the pier entrance

The Promenade
Map no: 6 SH78
Tel: 01492 874411

Cost: Fixed-price lunch £11.50 (2 courses), £13.50, fixed-price dinner £22 (3 courses), £26. H/wine from £9.50. Service inc
Credit cards: 1 2 3 4 5

Menu: Fixed-price lunch and dinner, Sunday lunch, pre-theatre, bar menu
Times: 12.30-Last L 2pm, 7pm-Last D 9.30

Chefs: David Harding, Ian Watson
Proprietors: Janette and Martin Bland

Seats: 55. No smoking in dining room; air conditioned
Additional: Children welcome (no children in high chairs at dinner); children's portions/ menu; ❂ dishes; special diets on request

PORTMEIRION, **The Hotel Portmeirion** ❀

In the centre of this famous and unique Italianate village, the hotel restaurant overlooks the estuary and Snowdonia beyond. Menus here are imaginative and cover a wide range of meats and fish. The terrine of vegetables chosen by our inspector was light with good flavours and complemented his meal.

Cost: Fixed-price L £13.50/D £25. H/wine £9.50. Service inc
Credit cards: 1 2 3 4 **Additional:** Children welcome; children's portions; ♥ dishes; Vegan/other diets on request
Directions: Off A487 at Minffordd, signposted from main road

Portmeirion
Map no: 6 SH63
Tel: 01766 770228
Chef: Craig Hindley
Manager: Mrs Menai Williams
Seats: 100. No smoking in dining room
Times: Last L 2pm/D 9.30pm. Closed Mon L

PWLLHELI, **Plas Bodegroes** ❀❀❀

A smart country house 'restaurant with rooms' where a five-course dinner of light modern British cooking is served

Plas Bodegroes is a small Georgian manor house set in secluded grounds and gardens, featuring a magnificent avenue of beech trees, said to be 200 years old, which leAds to the house. It is really a restaurant with rooms, run by Christopher and Gunna Chown, and while Christopher is in charge of the kitchen Gunna looks after the front of house. The cuisine is light and modern in style, and the fixed-price five-course dinner menu, with a choice of four or five items at each course, gives good value for money.

Starters might include vegetable soup, smoked haddock fish-cake with tartare sauce, or the ballotine of guinea fowl, apricot and pistachios, described by our inspector as exemplary. Options for the fish course could include hotpot of mussels and scallops with lemon grass and chillies, or delicious baked fillet of brill with a herb crust and piquant tomato and basil sauce. There is also a non-fish alternative, such as tagliatelli with venison sauce and pine nuts.

Our inspector enjoyed a main course of roast saddle of venison with port and juniper berries, served pink and rich with delicate vegetables and finely sliced potatoes cooked in stock with lentils and shredded cabbage.

Next comes the cheese course – on this occasion, Stilton and biscuits, grilled goats' cheese with celery and walnut salad, or a selection of cheeses with biscuits and home-made walnut bread. A trio of chocolate with mango coulis completed our inspector's meal, comprising chocolate mousse, hot chocolate in a pastry cup and a white chocolate ice cream.

There is a comprehensive list of wines, with every country of note well represented. Prices, which start at £10 a bottle are reasonable throughout and there are many bargains to be had – also an interesting selection of house wines.

Directions: Head west on the A497, through Pwllheli, follow signs for Nefyn; bear right at the roundabout - the entrance is on the left behind a high stone wall

Map no: 6 SH33
Tel: 01758 612363

Cost: Fixed-price dinner £30. H/wine £10. Service inc
Credit cards: 1 2 3

Menu: Fixed-price dinner
Times: Last D 9.30pm. Closed Mon & Nov-Feb

Chef: Christopher Chown
Proprietors: Mr and Mrs C Chown

Seats: 35. No smoking in dining room
Additional: Children permitted

TAL-Y-LLYN, **Minffordd Hotel** ❀

☺ *Enjoying a spectacular location at the foot of Cader Idris, this restaurant offers the best of local produce. The dishes on the three-course menu are carefully prepared with pleasant flavours, such as the soufflé-style chocolate mousse.*

Cost: Fixed-price D £17.50. H/wine £7.75. No service charge
Credit cards: 1 3. **Additional:** Children over 9 permitted; children's portions; special diets on request **Directions:** At the junction of the A487 and the B4405, at the foot of Cader Idris

Minffordd
Map no: 6 SH70
Tel: 01654 761665
Chef: Jonathan Pickles
Proprietor: Jessica Gibbs
Seats: 24. No smoking in dining room
Times: Last D 8.30pm. Closed Sun to non-residents, & Nov-Mar

TALSARNAU, **Maes-y-Neuadd** ❀❀❀

Excellent British food making full use of local produce is the keystone of an occasion rich in the pleasures of good eating

The oldest part of the house is almost as old as Edward I's mighty Harlech Castle nearby. The view across Tremadoc Bay to the distant Lleyn Peninsula can scarcely have changed, except for the smoke from the *tràn bach* puffing its way from Portmadoc to Blaenau Ffestiniog. The house has been owned since 1981 by the Horsfalls and the Slatters who, with their staff, ensure that from the first sip of an apéritif on the terrace to the napkin's final dab of the lips, everything is a pleasure.

Dishes are mainly British, with starters like scallop and smoked duck salad with pickled pheasant eggs, or quenelles of smoked trout mousse on a pool of chive yoghurt sauce; soup could be carrot and kohl rabi. Fish dishes have included steamed fillet of lemon sole stuffed with pimento, with a Pernod and lime sauce, and roast monkfish with a waistcoat of poppy and sesame seeds. An obvious Welshness, such as laverbread mousse, might edge into a main course description, as when it accompanies breast of chicken wrapped in spinach, but much of the produce including, of course, the home-grown vegetables and herbs, is of Welsh origin anyway. Vegetarians should be happy with a main course like vegetable crumble glazed with Parmesan cheese. Why the final course is known as The Grand Finale (Diweddglo Mawreddog)) becomes clear when invited to sample each of the delicious sweets – Welsh cheeses, home-made ice creams and sorbets and maybe bread and butter pudding, a coconut charlotte and vanilla sauce, or a strawberry and vanilla mousse.

Directions: Situated 0.5 mile off B4573 between Talsarnau and Harlech (sign on corner of unclassified road)

Map no: 6 SH63
Tel: 01766 780200

Cost: Fixed-price lunch £10.75, Sun lunch £14.50, fixed-price dinner £19.95 (3 courses), £26.50. H/wine £8.45 ♀ Service inc
Credit cards: 1 2 3 4 5

Menus: Fixed-price lunch and dinner, Sunday lunch
Times: Midday-Last L 1.45pm, 7pm-Last D 9.15pm

Chef: Peter Jackson
Proprietors: June and Michael Slatter, Olive and Malcolm Horsfall

Seats: 50. No smoking
Additional: No children under 7 at dinner; children's portions; ❂ dishes; Vegan/other diets on request.

TREFRIW, **Hafod House** ❀

☺ *Converted from a 17th-century farmhouse, this hotel stands in the Conwy valley and enjoys superb views. The restaurant is in two parts with several alcoves, and the menus change regularly. Our inspector enjoyed asparagus crêpe baked in a cream sauce followed by lamb cutlets, and Spotted Dick.*

Credit cards: 1 2 3 4 5 **Additional:** Children over 11 permitted; ❂ dishes; special diets on request **Directions:** At the south end of the village on B5106 (Conwy/Betws-y-Coed)

Map no: 6 SH76
Tel: 01492 640029
Chef: Norman Barker
Proprietor: Norman Barker
Seats: 35. No smoking
Times: Last L 2pm/D 9.30pm. Closed Mon, Tue, Jan
Cost: Fixed-price lunch £8.95, fixed-price dinner £16.95 (3 courses), £18.95. H/wine £6.95. No service charge.

MID GLAMORGAN

BRIDGEND, **Coed-y-Mwstwr** ●●

An intoxicating blend of remote country retreat and classy cooking with flavours to savour

'Whispering Trees' is the attractive-sounding translation of this elegant hotel's name – fittingly so since its setting in the Vale of Glamorgan is heavily wooded. Perched high on the hillside overlooking the village of Coychurch, there's a peacefulness about the location which attracts seekers of silence and lovers of good food. Gareth Passey has set high standards in the kitchen which he has consistently surpassed over the years, with results to be savoured. The *carte* offers a delightfully well-balanced choice of dishes including fish and shellfish, and vegetarian options as well as poultry, game and meat, while the fixed-price menus provide a short but similarly interesting choice; the use of first class ingredients is clearly evident. Starters might include a chilled sausage of lemon sole and smoked trout with a capsicum relish, or pan-fried quail with chicken liver mousse and a blackcurrant and orange jus, with main courses like turbot rubbed with coarse grain mustard in a sherry cream sauce, or whole roast poussin stuffed with spinach, apricot and almonds with a light curry sauce. Enticing home-made puddings cannot be ignored.

Directions: Leave M4 Jct 35, take A473 towards Bridgend for 1 mile; turn into Coychurch, right at petrol station. Follow signs up the hill for 1 mile

Coychurch
Map no: 3 SS97
Tel: 01656 860621

Cost: *Alc* £29, fixed-price lunch £12.95 (2 courses), £16.95, fixed-price dinner £24. H/wine £8.95 ♀ Service exc
Credit cards: 1 2 3 4 5

Menus: *A la carte*, fixed-price lunch and dinner, Sunday lunch, bar menu
Times: Last L 2.30pm, Last D 9.30pm

Chef: Gareth Passey
Proprietor: Philip Thomas

Seats: 60
Additional: Children welcome; children's portions; ❂ dishes; Vegan/other diets on request

MISKIN, **Miskin Manor** ❂

Enjoyable modern Welsh cooking is served at this elegant country house hotel. Chef Tony Kocker uses quality local produce in dishes executed with some flair, such as game terrine with elderberry and pear relish, fillet of brill filled with scallops, and hot carrot pudding with crème anglaise.

Credit cards: 1 2 3 4 5. **Additional:** Children welcome; children's portions/menu; ❂ menu; Vegan/other diets on request
Directions: Signed from junc 34 of M4

Pontyclun
Map no: 3 ST08
Tel: 01443 224204
Chef: Tony Kocker
Proprietor: John Millard
Seats: 60
Times: Last L 2pm/D 9.45pm
Cost: *Alc* £23.50. H/wine £8.95 ♀ Service exc

PONTYPRIDD, **Llechwen Hall** ❂

A 17th-century farmhouse now a small hotel of character, set in an elevated position overlooking four valleys. The Llanfabon Dining Room offers a fixed-price menu, and the St Cynons Restaurant caters for more formal dining with a carte featuring well executed cuisine by the Swiss-trained chef.

Cost: *Alc* £26. H/wine £7.95 ♀ Service exc
Credit cards: 1 2 3 4 5. **Additional:** Children over 12 permitted; ❂ menu; Vegan/other diets on request
Directions: North-east of Pontypridd on the A4054 to Cilfynydd

Llanfabon
Map no: 3 ST08
Tel: 01443 742050
Chef: Louis Huben
Proprietors: L Huben, J Mackie
Seats: 36. No pipes or cigars
Times: Last L 2.30pm/D 10pm. D not served Sun

PORTHCAWL, **Heritage** ❀❀

☺ *Quality cooking using fresh produce – especially fish – hidden among unpretentious seafront guest houses*

This little gem of a restaurant is a delightful discovery tucked away amongst a host of small hotels and guest houses close to Porthcawl's sea front. In an area not especially noted for its fine cuisine, this small place has attracted a loyal and discerning band of good food lovers, and our inspector joined them for a recent meal. Chef/patron James Miller cooks with enthusiasm using only quality fresh ingredients, especially fish, and the results can be sampled on his seasonally changing menus. Smoked breast of pheasant with a piquant cassis sauce was a delicious starter, followed by escalope of veal and light chicken mousse with wild mushrooms and blackberry sauce, and fettucini of vegetables. A tempting array of puddings was offered, and the chosen filo pastry basket of hot caramelised apples and apricots with a cool sauce anglaise lived up to our inspector's expectations. Other recently recommended dishes have been coquilles St Jacques with creamed spinach and lemon and herb sauce, delicately poached skate with a smooth caper sauce, and spotted dick with custard.

Directions: St Mary Street leads off the seafront by the Grand Pavillion. Restaurant is on the right

24 Mary Street
Map no: 3 SS87
Tel: 01656 771881

Cost: *Alc* £18, fixed-price lunch £7.95, fixed-price dinner £11.75, Sun lunch £8.45. H/wine £7.75. Service exc
Credit cards: 1 3

Menus: *A la carte,* fixed-price lunch and dinner, Sun lunch, pre-theatre
Times: Last L 2pm, Last D 9pm (weekends 9.30pm). D not served Sun. Closed Mon, 2 weeks Jan

Chef: Jimi Miller
Proprietor: Jimi Miller

Seats: 36. No-smoking area. No pipes or cigars
Additional: Children welcome; children's portions; ❤ dishes; Vegan/other diets on request

POWYS

BRECON, **Peterstone Court** ❀❀

An elegant Georgian manor delightfully run and serving accomplished modern English cooking

There's an attractive atmosphere at this elegant 18th-century hotel which owes as much to its dedicated and friendly staff as to the relaxed, peaceful setting. Local regulars and holiday visitors are drawn by the excellent food for which it is renowned, and chef John Maynard Harvey does not disappoint: in the formal restaurant diners can sample his Menu Exceptionnel offering six courses of delicate and imaginative dishes, plus a *carte* and fixed-price menu, all cooked in modern English style. Our inspector chose the first, and praised a wonderful rich mushroom soup which was followed by a rather oily chicken and sun-dried tomato dish. A main course of roast guinea fowl came on a bed of braised cabbage, served with a mousse of leg meat and a very tasty sauce. Pear tart and a full-flavoured cinnamon ice cream were followed by cafetière coffee and a dish of freshly made petits fours. Typical dishes on the set menu include chicken liver parfait with warm brioche and Cumberland sauce, and supreme of salmon with ratatouille and a basil cream sauce. Informal bistro-style dining is served on the terrace.

Directions: On the A40 in the centre of the village

Llanhamlach
Map no: 3 SO02
Tel: 01874 86387

Cost: *Alc* £30, fixed-price lunch £11.95, fixed-price dinner £21.95. H/wine £9.25 ♀ No service charge
Credit cards: 1 2 3 4

Menus: *A la carte,* fixed-price lunch and dinner, Sunday lunch, pre-theatre, bar menu
Times: Last L 2.30pm, Last D 9.15pm. Closed 27-29 Dec

Chef: John Maynard Harvey
Proprietors: Michael and Barbara Taylor
Seats: 40 (dining room), 26 (bistro). No-smoking area. Air conditioned
Additional: Children welcome; children's portions; ❤ menu; vegan/other diets on request

CRICKHOWELL, **Bear** ☻☻

☺ *A well-established inn with a deservedly fine reputation for its cooking*

A 15th-century former coaching inn with flower-filled courtyard and beamed and flagstoned bars, this congenial hotel enjoys a growing reputation for its fine classical-based cuisine without resting on its laurels. Indeed the cooking of chef Shaun Ellis goes from strength to strength, and evidence of his special skills can be seen in the honest flavours and robust textures that are his hallmark. The quite lengthy *carte* offers a difficult choice between innovative and interesting dishes, and there is a trio of daily specials at each course to add to the anguish; bouillabaisse of fine seafood bound with tomatoes and herbs to start, perhaps, and loin of lamb wrapped in spring cabbage, rosemary and honey laced with a rich lamb juice. Recommended dishes have included a very tasty lobster terrine interlaced with pieces of fresh lobster on a bisque sauce, and escalope of veal with sauté mushrooms, a light cheese topping and a grain mustard sauce. A rich and creamy bread and butter pudding infused with brandy and served with home-made ice cream showed that desserts are another strength. Portions are copious, so be prepared.

Map no: 3 SO21
Tel: 01873 810408

Cost: *Alc* £19. H/wine £7.95. Service inc
Credit cards: 1 2 3 5

Menus: *A la carte*, Sunday lunch, bar menu
Times: Last D 9.30pm. Closed Sun

Chef: Shaun Ellis
Proprietors: Mrs J Hindmarsh, Stephen Sims-Hindmarsh

Seats: 60. No cigars
Additional: Children over 5 permitted; children's portions; ♥ menu; other diets on request

Directions: In the town centre on the A40

CRICKHOWELL, **Gliffaes** ☻

Situated beside the River Usk among 29 acres of mature garden and park land, this stylish restaurant makes good use of the tasty fresh salmon which features on the menu. The generously filled home-made steak and kidney pie is also worth a try and a good vegetarian menu is available.

Additional: Children welcome at lunch; children's portions/menu; ♥ menu; Vegan/other diets on request
Directions: 2.5 miles west of Crickhowell; turn left off A40, approx 1 mile, signposted

Map no: 3 SO21
Tel: 01874 730371
Chef: Peter Hulsmann
Proprietors: Nick and Peta Brabner
Seats: 75. No smoking
Times: Last D 9.15pm. Closed 5 Jan-24 Feb
Cost: *Alc* £25.50, fixed-price D £18.50, Sun L £17.50. H/wine £8.10. Service inc.
Credit cards: 1 2 3 4

HAY-ON-WYE, **Old Black Lion** ☻

☺ *Exposed timbers and beams, some possibly 700 years old, provide the setting for dining, while the skilled kitchen team produces myriad dishes from a range of menus which must keep local meat and fish suppliers very happy. A truly international array of well-prepared food and good wines.*

Cost: *Alc* £16, Sunday lunch £7.95. No service charge
Credit cards: 1 2 3. **Additional:** Children permitted (over 8); children's portions; ♥ menu; Vegan/other diets on request
Directions: In the centre, 30 yards from junction of Lion Street and Oxford Road

26 Lion Street
Map no: 3 SO24
Tel: 01497 820841
Chef: J Collins
Proprietor: J Collins
Seats: 30. No smoking in dining room
Times: Last L 2.30pm/D 9.15pm

KNIGHTON, **Milebrook House** ✿

☺ *The hotel is set in woodland that is a birdwatcher's paradise. Beryl Marsden produces home-cooked dishes such as local salmon in sorrel sauce with home-grown vegetables from the large garden, cooked al dente. Welsh farmouse cheeses or apple pancakes with Calvados may follow.*

Cost: *Alc* £19.95, fixed-price L £10.75/D £16.95. H/wine £8.40. Service exc **Credit cards:** 1 3 **Additional:** Children over 6 welcome at lunch; children's portions/menu; ❷ dishes; Vegan/other diets on request
Directions: 2 miles east of Knighton on A4113, Ludlow road

Milebrook
Map no: 7 SO27
Tel: 01547 528632
Chef: Beryl Marsden
Proprietor: Rodney Marsden
Seats: 30. No smoking in dining room
Times: Last L 1.45pm/D 8.30pm. Closed Mon L

LLANFYLLIN, **Seeds** ✿

☺ *Mark and Felicity Seager took over this pretty little restaurant a few years ago, where Mark practises his skills in the kitchen, buying local produce with an emphasis on Welsh lamb. Cooking is straightforward with good use made of clear flavours and dishes are not over elaborate.*

Cost: *Alc* L £12.50, fixed-price D £15.75 (3 courses), £17.75. H/wine £7.85. Service exc. **Credit cards:** 1 3 **Additional:** Children permitted (no babies at dinner); ❷ dishes; Vegan/other diets on request
Directions: Situated in the main street

Map no: 7 SJ11
Tel: 01691 648604
Chef: Mark Seager
Proprietors: Mark and Felicity Seager
Seats: 22. No smoking
Times: Last L 2.30pm/D 9.30pm. Closed Mon Sep-May (exc BH Mon)

LLANGAMMARCH WELLS, **Lake** ✿✿

A delightful country retreat serving food with an emphasis on natural flavours and herbs

Set in 50 acres of mature woodland with riverside walks and a large trout lake, this fine hotel offers a delightful country retreat. Guests are carefully cosseted, not least in the pretty restaurant, where a fixed-price five course menu created by chef Richard Arnold satisfies most tastes. Typical dishes are black olive pastry tartlet filled with fresh shellfish in a sun-dried tomato custard with a crayfish shellfish sauce, and crispy roast duckling with a baby spinach mousseline and a spicy sauce. Delicious potato bread and tomato and marjoram soup began a recent inspection meal, followed by an attractive dish of sautéed queen scallops and Cornish mussels around a timbale of wild rice and saffron. Fillet of turbot with crab meat was rated as superb, and came topped with a thin lattice of smoked salmon and lovage. A very unusual sweet of fennel and anise in a light pastry strudel with marjoram and toffee sauce made a surprisingly delicious talking point, and a selection of Welsh cheeses was followed by coffee and petits fours. The owners and staff promote an atmosphere of informality and tranquillity.

Directions: Take A483 to Garth, 6 miles west of Builth Wells. Turn left for Llangammarch Wells and follow signs to hotel

Map no: 3 SN94
Tel: 01591 620202

Cost: Fixed-price lunch £15.50, fixed-price dinner £25.50. H/wine £9.75 ♀ Service inc
Credit cards: 1 2 3 4 5

Menus: Fixed-price lunch and dinner, Sunday lunch
Times: 12.30-Last L 2pm, 7.30pm-Last D 9.30pm

Chef: Richard Arnold
Proprietor: Jean-Pierre Mifsud

Seats: 50. No smoking in dining room
Additional: Children permitted (over 8 at dinner); children's menu; ❷ dishes; Vegan/other diets on request

LLANWDDYN, **Lake Vyrnwy** ❀

In an elevated position overlooking the lake, this long established hotel is set in 24 acres of mature woodland. Chef Andrew Wood offers a four-course menu of traditional British cooking using produce from the hotel's garden, and he makes the bread and delicious canapés served before dinner.

Credit cards: 1 2 3 4 **Additional:** Children welcome; children's portions/menu; ◐ dishes; Vegan/other diets on request
Directions: On A495, 200 yards past dam

Lake Vyrnwy
Map no: 6 SJ01
Tel: 0169173 692
Chef: Andrew Wood
Proprietor: J P Talbot
Seats: 70. No smoking in dining room
Times: Last L 1.45pm/D 9.15pm
Cost: Fixed-price L £12.75/D £22.50. Sun L £13.75. H/wine £8.95 ♀ Service exc.

LLANWRTYD WELLS, **Carlton House** ❀❀

☺ *A gem of comfort and fine food where booking by non-residents is essential*

Highly distinguished cooking of depth and imagination is the forte of this cosy little hotel, although initial impressions may suggest otherwise. The tiny dining room holds only 12, so booking for non-residents is essential; the rewards for those obtaining a table are immense. Chef/patron Mary Ann Gilchrist is classically trained, and everything bears the hallmark of quality. The short *carte* and fixed-price dinner menu offer starters like baked goats' cheese and apple croustade, and cucumber mousse with peeled prawns, while main courses might be seared spiced salmon with lime, and old-fashioned steak and kidney pudding served with a jug of rich gravy. A recent inspection meal began with light pasta pillows stuffed with rich and creamy sherry mushrooms, followed by moist and exceptionally full-flavoured rack of Welsh lamb, set on a bold red pepper and pesto sauce which perfectly complemented the meat. Bright, simply cooked vegetables come with the meal, but room must be left for desserts: a blow-torch lemon tart of subtly tangy flavour was fascinatingly glazed at the table.

Directions: In the town centre

Dolycoed Road
Map no: 3 SN84
Tel: 01591 610248

Cost: A/c £19, fixed-price D £15. H/wine £8. Service inc
Credit cards: 1 3

Menus: A la carte, fixed-price dinner
Times: Last D 8.30pm. Closed Xmas, New Year

Chef: Mary Ann Gilchrist
Proprietor: Alan Gilchrist

Seats: 12. No smoking in dining room

Additional: Children permitted; ◐ dishes

LLYSWEN, **Griffin Inn** ❀

☺ *Traditional country-style cooking is on offer at this delightful old inn. Locally caught salmon and brook trout feature on the menu, with other firm favourites such as jugged hare, jugged venison and ratatouille pasta. Bar meals of home-made soup, pâté and local game are excellent value.*

Cost: A/c £20; fixed-price D £16.50. Sun L £12.50. H/wine £7.50 ♀ Service exc. **Credit cards:** 1 2 3 4 5. **Additional:** Children welcome; children's portions; ◐ dishes; Vegan/other diets on request
Directions: On A470

Map no: 3 SO13
Tel: 01874 754 241
Chef: Eileen Harvard
Proprietors: Richard and Di Stockton
Seats: 40. No smoking in dining room
Times: Last L 2pm/D 9pm. Closed Xmas

LLYSWEN, **Llangoed Hall** ●●●

Near Brecon
Map no: 3 SO13
Tel: 01874 754525

Beautifully presented modern British cooking in the sunny dining room of an Edwardian country house hotel

Llangoed Hall is the fulfilment of Sir Bernard Ashley's long-held ambition to create the perfect hotel, and to recreate the atmosphere of an Edwardian house party. The hotel, which opened in 1990, has been carefully restored and beautifully decorated with Laura Ashley wall coverings and fabrics, and furnished with fine antique and period pieces. It is also home to Sir Bernard's extensive art collection.

In 1993, at the end of the year in which Llangoed was awarded the AA's three rosettes for its cuisine, and the Care and Courtesy Award for its standard of service, the hotel saw some change of personnel. Head chef Mark Salter, along with general manager Tom Ward, left to join a sister hotel, The Inn at Perry Cabin, and Mark's sous chef, Nigel Morris (Welsh Chef of the Year), took his place.

Nigel's exciting cooking style has made new friends for the hotel while maintaining his predecessor's high standards. He offers a small *carte* of five items per course and a chef's five-course set menu.

A test meal began with red mullet Provençal, a delicious fillet, beautifully presented with fiercely grilled Provence vegetables drenched in olive oil. The main course, mille-feuille of crab and turbot, was slightly overpowered by the strong flavour of the dark crab meat but had a wonderful sauce. The mirabelle plum soufflé for dessert was one of the best our inspector had encountered, feather-light yet moist, and at the bottom the explosive flavour of the plums.

Many of the wines on the extensive and well presented list are expensive, but their quality is without question. Good vintages abound of wines produced on prestigious estates and many grape varieties are represented.

Cost: Alc £40, fixed-price lunch £13 (2 courses), £16, fixed-price dinner £35.50. H/wine £14.50 ♀ Service exc
Credit cards: 1 2 3 4

Menus: *A la carte,* fixed-price lunch and dinner, Sunday lunch
Times: Last L 2pm, Last D 9.30pm

Chef: Nigel Morris
Proprietor: Sir Bernard Ashley

Seats: 40. No smoking in dining room
Additional: No children under 8 at dinner; ◐ dishes; special diets on request

Directions: On A470, 2 mile from Llyswen heading towards Builth Wells

THREE COCKS, **Three Cocks Hotel** ●●

Map no: 3 SO13
Tel: 01497 847215

Both the decor and cooking style of this pleasant, value-for-money restaurant arouse memories of France and Belgium

The tastes of France and old Belgium are recreated in the kitchen of this hotel, an ivy-clad stone house which has stood in the shadow of the Black Mountains since the 15th century, and the continental motif is repeated in the lacy tablecloths and tapestry-covered walls of a dining room dominated by a massive armoire. Chef Michael Winstone offers a fixed-price menu, dishes skilfully prepared from quality fresh produce retaining individual flavours and textures: loin of venison, for example, served rare with pink peppercorns and wood mushrooms, the accompanying vegetables including bright, crisply al dente baby marrow, French beans and turned carrots. Soup served family-style from a large bowl (with second helpings available!) is accompanied by soft warm rolls, and

Cost: Alc £22.50, fixed-price lunch/dinner £23. H/wine £8. No service charge
Credit cards: 1 3

Menus: *A la carte,* fixed-price lunch and dinner, bar menu
Times: Midday-Last L 1.30pm, 7pm-Last D 9pm. L not served Sun. Closed Dec-2nd weekend Feb, and Tue mid Sep-mid Jul,

Chef: Michael Winstone
Proprietors: Michael and Marie-Jeanne Winstone

home-made puddings might include a delicious chocolate terrine accompanied by proper vanilla sauce and passion fruit sorbet. However, little provision is made for vegetarians. A short, mainly French wine list is available – but many dishes would be complemented equally well by the Belgian beer which is also available.

Seats: 28. No cigars or pipes
Additional: Children welcome; children's portions/menu; ❷ dish; Vegan/other diets on request

Directions: In the village of Three Cocks, 4 miles from Hay-on-Wye, 11 miles from Brecon

WELSHPOOL, **Golfa Hall** ✻

☺ *Honest, tasty dishes make up new chef/manager David Ostle's sensibly sized fixed-price and carte menus at this delightful little hotel overlooking the hills adjoining Powys Castle. Quenelles of salmon with hollandaise, for example, might be followed by fillet of beef with rösti potatoes and green peppercorn sauce.*

Llanfair Road
Map no: 7 SJ20
Tel: 01938 553399
Chef/manager: David Ostle
Proprietors: Mr and Mrs Bowen
Seats: 60. No cigars or pipes
Times: Last L 2pm/D 7pm

Cost: Fixed-price L £11.95/D £15.35. H/wine £6.95. Service inc
Credit cards: 1 2 3 4. **Additional:** Children permitted at dinner at management's discretion; children's portions; ❷ dishes; Vegan on request
Directions: On the A458, 1.5 miles west of Welshpool

SOUTH GLAMORGAN

BARRY, **Egerton Grey Hotel** ✻

☺ *At this elegant 19th-century former rectory, quality local produce provides the basis for a sensibly sized seasonal fixed-price menu prepared with flair and consistency. Main courses have included poached fillet of plaice wrapped in leek and pan fried noisettes of Welsh lamb.*

Porthkerry
Map no: 3 ST16
Tel: 01446 711666
Chefs: Craig Brookes
Proprietor: Anthony Pitkin
Seats: 40. No smoking in dining room
Times: Last L 2pm/D 9.30pm. Closed 1 Jan

Cost: Fixed-price L £12.50-£19.50/D £19.50 (3 courses), £22.50. H/wine £9.50. Service inc
Credit cards: 1 2 3 4. **Additional:** Children welcome; children's menu/portions; ❷ menu; other diets on request
Directions: Left at roundabout by Cardiff airport and left again, after 400yds down lane between thatched cottages

CARDIFF, **Chikako's** ❀

☺ *An authentic Japanese restaurant in a typical oriental style where chef and proprietor Chikako Cameron produces delicious dishes such as chicken teriyaki, boneless chicken with sake, soy sauce and ginger or a selection of seafoods and vegetables in a soup.*

Cost: Fixed-price D £11.80–£19.50. H/wine £7.50 ♀ Service exc
Credit cards: 1 2 3 5 **Additional:** Children welcome; children's portions; ❂ dishes; Vegan/other diets on request
Directions: In city centre immediately opposite Marriott Hotel near National Ice Rink and The Hayes shopping centre

10-11 Mill Lane
Map no: 3 ST17
Tel: 01222 665279
Chef: Mrs Chikako Cameron
Proprietor: Mrs Chikako Cameron
Seats: 52 (Western style), 20 (Japanese style). Air conditioned
Times: Last D 11.30pm. Closed Xmas Day

CARDIFF, **Le Cassoulet** ❀❀

A friendly little bistro serving robust provincial food that comes directly from Toulouse

A robust and full-flavoured style of provincial French cooking is the speciality of this charming little bistro. While guests are looked after with humour and efficiency by owner Gilbert Viader, the cooking is left in the exceptionally capable hands of chef Michael Wignall who handles the quality produce with style and flair. The result is a two or three course fixed-price menu that offers some memorable dishes: 'terrine de chevreuil' (venison and pistachio terrine with truffle vinaigrette) to start perhaps, with main choices like the famed 'cassoulet Toulousain' (white haricot bean stew with coarse pork sausage, confit of duck and neck end of pork), available only with prior notice. Our inspector enjoyed a delicious starter of warm lobster ravioli, delicately light and smooth, on a bed of ribbons of smoked salmon and ginger-spiked cucumber. Mille-feuille of lamb in feather-light puff pastry on a bed of wild rice was moist and boldly flavoured, and accompanied by bright al dente vegetables. Puddings and petits fours are all home made, and the hot mango tart with mango sauce was scrumptious.

Directions: Follow A48 and A4119 into city centre, then B4258 (Llandaff road). Turn left into Romilly Crescent. Restaurant next to Post Office

5 Romilly Crescent, Canton
Map no: 3 ST17

Tel: 01222 221905

Cost: Fixed-price lunch £16 (2 courses), £18; fixed–price dinner £19 (2 courses) £24. H/wine £8.95 ♀ Service exc
Credit cards: 1 2 3

Menus: Fixed-price lunch and dinner, selection of specials
Times: Last L 2pm, Last D 10pm. L not served Sat. Closed Sun, Mon, Aug & 2 weeks Xmas

Chef: Michael Wignall
Proprietors: Mr and Mrs G Viader

Seats: 40
Additional: Children welcome; children's portions; ❂ dishes; other diets on request

CARDIFF, **Manor Parc** ❀

Continental, mainly Italian dishes are offered from an extensive carte in the recently constructed conservatory restaurant of this hospitable small hotel. The emphasis is on quality fresh produce, and the well executed dishes are full of flavour and texture.

Credit cards: 1 2 3. **Additional:** Children permitted (no toddlers at dinner); children's portions; ❂ menu; other diets on request
Directions: On the outskirts of Cardiff on the A469 Cardiff to Caerphilly Road

Thornhill Road
Map no: 3 ST17
Tel: 01222 693723
Chef: Russell Palfrey
Proprietors: S Salimeni, E Cinus
Seats: 75. No cigars or pipes in dining room. Air conditioned
Times: Last L 2pm/D10pm. Closed Xmas eve-Boxing Day
Cost: Fixed–price L £13. H/wine £8.75 ♀ Service exc.

WEST GLAMORGAN

LANGLAND BAY, **Langland Court** ❋

An established Tudor-style hotel within walking distance of the bay. The wood-panelled Oak Room restaurant offers a short fixed-price menu and an interesting carte featuring pâtés, rich terrines, unfussy main courses and home-made puddings. Polly's Wine Bar provides more informal, equally good food.

Cost: A/c from £21, fixed-price L £11.95/D £18. H/wine £8.25. Service exc. **Credit cards:** 1 2 3 5. **Additional:** Children welcome; children's menu/portions; ❖ menu; Vegan/other diets on request **Directions:** A4067 Swansea to Mumbles road, take B4593 signposted Caswell, then left at St Peter's Church. Hotel signposted

Langland Court Road
Map no: 2 SS68
Tel: 01792 361545
Chef: Kevin Strangward
Proprietors: Best Western. Managers: C R Birt, C J Hamilton-Smith
Seats: 50. No smoking in dining room
Times: Last L 2pm/D 9.30pm

REYNOLDSTON, **Fairyhill** ❋❋

Seafood features prominently in a country house restaurant an easy drive from Swansea and Llanelli

New owners Jane and Peter Camm, Andrew Hetherington and Paul Davies have brought new determination to this characterful house at the heart of the Gower Peninsula. The improvements they have made to this charming 18th-century mansion, set in 24 acres of woodland and with its own trout stream, are already reaping rewards. Elegant lounges, a choice of dining rooms, and a cosy bar all create a welcoming feel. One of the hotel's strengths is the cooking of chefs and partners Paul and Kate Cole whose most inspirational seasonal menus make excellent use of local produce such as sewin (a young Welsh sea-trout), lobster, crab, cockles from nearby Penclawdd, of course, and laver bread. One of our inspectors reported favourably on a delicate squid ink-coloured fettucine and crayfish salad with tomato purée, followed by a roasted guinea fowl with lemon and tarragon stuffing, and a featherlight apple and tarragon tart for dessert. The wine list has classical depth with a sprinkling of New World and Welsh varieties.

Directions: Reynoldstown is off the A4118 from Swansea

Map no: 2 SS48
Tel: 01792 390139

Cost: Fixed-price £24.50
Credit cards: 1 2 3

Menu: Fixed-price
Times: Open all year for lunch and dinner

Chef: Paul Davies
Proprietors: Jane and Peter Camm, Paul Davies, Andrew Hetherington

Additional: No pipes or cigars in dining room. Children permitted; ❖ dishes

SWANSEA, **Beaumont Hotel** ❋❋

The New World is well represented in the extensive wine list which accompanies British, French and Italian dishes here

Good fresh ingredients transformed by the imaginative, yet classically based, culinary skills of experienced chef Brian Evans make the restaurant of this comfortable hotel a real find. Both the *carte* and fixed-price dinner menu offer a range of British, French and Italian dishes; simply cooked vegetables are supplied in generous quantity and home-made puddings are noteworthy. Typically, a savoury bacon and mushroom pancake with a port cream sauce might be followed by a prime Scotch

72 Walter Road
Map no: 3 SS69
Tel: 01792 643956

Cost: A/c £27.50, fixed-price dinner £19.75. H/wine £8.50. Service exc
Credit cards: 1 2 3 4 5

Menus: *A la carte,* fixed-price dinner

Times: Last D 9.30pm. D not

sirloin steak glazed with Burgundy then profiteroles topped by a very rich brandy-infused chocolate sauce, the meal ending with good filter coffee and petits fours. Vegetarians are well catered for with dishes such as mushroom and leek mille-feuille with garlic cream, or goats' cheese wrapped in filo pastry with creamed spinach and lentils, and vegan requirements can be met. The sizeable wine list – now extended to include many examples from the New World – contains twelve half bottles as well as three reasonably priced house wines, and a separate list of pudding wines accompanies the dessert menu.

served Sun
Chef: Jon Choolsen
Proprietors: J Wynne Jones, John Colenso

Seats: 40. No smoking
Additional: Children over 6 permitted; children's portions; ❷ menu; Vegan/other diets on request

Directions: On the A4118, opposite St James' Church in an area called Uplands, just to the north-west of the town centre

SWANSEA, **Windsor Lodge** ✤

☺ *Standards remain high at this delightful Georgian house with dishes providing quality produce, honest textures and pleasant flavours. Among the wide choice of dishes are fillet of red mullet with chive sauce and fresh salmon with mussel sauce.*

Mount Pleasant
Map no: 3 SS69
Tel: 01792 642158
Chef: Hervé Chataignere
Proprietors: Ron and Pam Rumble
Seats: 40. No smoking in dining room
Times: Last D 9.30pm. Closed Sun, Xmas

Cost: Fixed-price D £18.50. H/wine £5.95 ♀ Service exc
Credit cards: 1 2 3 4. **Additional:** Children welcome; children's portions/menu; ❷ dishes; Vegan/other diets on request
Directions: From the leisure centre go up Princess Way, across roundabout, left at T junc. On the right after the pedestrian lights

INDEX

A

The Absolute End, St Peter Port 475-6
The Academy, London WC1 25
Achray House, St Fillans 545
Adlard's, Norwich 355-6
Airds, Port Appin 533-4
Ajimura, London WC2 25
Alastair Little, London W1 26
Alba, London EC1 26-7
Albero and Grana, London SE3 27
Albright Hussey, Shrewsbury 395
Al Bustan, London SW1 27
Alderley Edge, Alderley Edge 172
Alexander House, Turners Hill 456-7
Allhays, Talland Bay 192
Allt-Nan-Ros, Onich 508
Al San Vincenzo, London W2 27-8
Alston Hall, Holbeton 224
Altnaharrie Inn, Ullapool 512-13
Alverton Manor, Truro 194
Alveston House, Alveston 140
Alveston Manor, Stratford-upon-Avon 437
Ambassador, York 376
Amberley Castle, Amberley 444-5
Amerdale House, Arncliffe 365
Anchor Inn, Exebridge 398
Ancient Gate House, Wells 404
Angel, Bury St Edmunds 411-12
Angel, London SE16 28
The Angel, Midhurst 453
Angel Inn, Hetton 371
Angel Posting House, Guildford 424
Anna's Place, London N1 28-9
Appleby Manor, Appleby-in-Westmorland 196
Appleton Hall, Appleton-le-Moors 365
Arcadia, London W8 29
Archiestown Hotel, Archiestown 497
Ardanaiseig, Kilchrenan 529-30
Ardoe House, Aberdeen 496
Ardsheal House, Kentallen 507
Ardvasar Hotel, Ardvasar, Isle of Skye 509
The Argyll, London SW3 29-30
Arisaig House, Arisaig 502
The Ark, Erpingham 354
Armstrongs, Barnsley 408
Arundell Arms, Lifton 226
Ashburn, Fordingbridge 302
Ashdown Park, Forest Row 262
Ashwick House, Dulverton 397
Athenaeum, London W1 30
Atrium, Edinburgh 513-14

Auberge de Provence, London SW1 30
Aubergine, London 30-1
Auchrannie, Brodick 524
Auchterarder House, Auchterarder 538
Audleys Wood, Basingstoke 294
Au Jardin des Gourmets, London W1 31-2
Aurora Garden, Windsor 163
Aynsome Manor, Cartmel 197
Ayudhya, Kingston upon Thames 32

B

Baboon, London W1 32
Babur Brasserie, London SE23 33
Bagden Hall, Huddersfield 459
Bahn Thai, London W1 33
Bailiffscourt, Climping 448-9
Balbirnie House, Markinch 494
Balgonie, Ballater 497
Ballathie House, Kinclaven 542
Balmoral, Edinburgh 514
Balmoral, Harrogate 368
Banchory Lodge, Banchory 498
Barnards, Denmead 300
The Barns, Bedford 155
Barnsdale Lodge, Oakham 346
Bartley Lodge, Cadnam 299
Barton Cross, Stoke Canon 233
Basil Street, London SW3 34
Basingstoke Country Hotel, Basingstoke 295
Bath Place, Oxford 387-8
Bath Spa, Bath 140
Baumann's, Coggeshall 268
Bay Horse, Ulverston 205
Bay Tree, Burford 381
The Bay Tree, Melbourne 215
The Beach, St Agnes 189
Beadles, Birkenhead 350
Beamish Park, Beamish 255
Bear, Crickhowell 565
Bear, Woodstock 392
Beaulieu Hotel, Beaulieu 295
Beaumont Hotel, Swansea 571-2
The Bedlington Café, London W4 34
Beechfield House, Melksham 469
Beechleas, Wimborne Minster 254
Beechwood, Moffat 489
Beetle & Wedge, Moulsford 387
The Bel Alp House, Haytor 224
Belfry, Wishaw 438-9
The Belfry, Yarcombe 237
Belgo, London NW1 34
The Bell, Charlbury 381
Bell Inn, Aston Clinton 165

Bell Inn, Brook 299
The Bell Inn, Woburn 156
Belmont House, Leicester 345
Belton Woods, Belton 349
Belvedere, London W8 35
Bennett's, Bythorn 168
Bentley's, London W1 35-6
The Berkeley, London SW1 36
Berkeley Square Hotel, Bristol 146
The Berkshire, London W1 36
Beverley's, Dunoon 525
Bibendum, London SW3 37
Bice, London W1 37-8
Bignell Park, Bicester 380
Big Night Out, London NW1 38
Bilbrough Manor, Bilbrough 366
Billesley Manor, Stratford-upon-Avon 437
Bishopstrow House, Warminster 472-3
The Bistro at Fern Grove, Kilmun 531
Bistro Montparnasse, Portsmouth & Southsea 311
Bistrot Bruno, London W1 38-9
Bistrot 190, London SW7 39
Bistro Twenty One, Bristol 147
Black Bull Inn, Moulton 373
Black Chapati, Brighton 258
Black House, Hexham 364
Blackmores, Alnwick 362
Blacksmiths Arms, Rosedale Abbey 375
Black Swan, Beckingham 348
Black Swan, Helmsley 370
Black Swan, Ravenstonedale 204
Blueprint Café, London SE1 39-40
Blunsdon House, Swindon 471
Boar's Head, Harrogate 368-9
The Boathouse, Ayr 523
The Bobsleigh Inn, Bovingdon 328
Bodysgallen Hall, Llandudno 559
Bombay Brasserie, London SW7 40
Bonnets Bistro at Staithes, Cheltenham 276
Bontddu Hall, Bontddu 556
Borrans Park, Ambleside 195
Borrowdale Gates, Borrowdale 197
Boscundle Manor, St Austell 190
Botleigh Grange, Hedge End 304
Bouquet Garni, Elie 493
Bower House Inn, Eskdale Green 199
Bowlish House, Shepton Mallet 400
Box House, Box 464
Box Tree, Ilkley 461
Boyd's, London W8 40-1

574 INDEX

The Brackenbury, London W6 41
Braemar Lodge, Braemar 499
Braeval Mill, Aberfoyle 485-6
Bramley Grange, Bramley 420
Brandshatch Place, Brands Hatch 333
Brasserie Forty Four, Leeds 461-2
Brasted's, Norwich 356
Breamish House, Powburn 364
Bridge of Cally, Bridge of Cally 540
Bridge House, Beaminster 238
Bridge House, Bridport 240
Bridge House, Reigate 428
Brighton Thistle, Brighton 258
Brisbane House, Largs 532
Britannia Inter-Continental, London W1 41
Brockencote Hall, Chaddesley Corbett 321
Brookdale House, North Huish 229-30
Brooklands Grange, Coventry 442
Broughton Park, Preston 343
Brownlands, Sidmouth 232
Brown's Brasserie, Southampton 313-14
Brown's, London W1 42
Brown's, Worcester 327
Broxton Hall, Broxton 173
Brundholme, Keswick 202
Bryn Howel, Llangollen 549
Buchan's, London SW11 42
Buckerell Lodge, Exeter 221
Buck Inn, Buckden 366
Buckland Manor, Buckland 274-5
Buckland-Tout-Saints, Kingsbridge 225
Bunchrew House, Inverness 506
Burnham Beeches Moat House, Burnham 166
Burn How Garden House, Windermere 207
Burythorpe House, Malton 372
Butley Orford Oysterage, Orford 418
Buttery, Glasgow 526
By Appointment, Norwich 357

C

Café des Arts, London NW3 43
Café du Moulin, St Peter Port 476
Café Fish, London SW1 43
Café Niçoise, Colwyn Bay 547
Café Royal Grill Room, London W1 43
Cairn, Kilmartin 531
Calcot Manor, Tetbury 285-6
Caledonian Hotel, Edinburgh 515
Callow Hall, Ashbourne 211
Cambridge Lodge, Cambridge 169
Cameron House, Balloch 523
Canal Brasserie, London W10 44
Cannizaro House,

London SW19 44
The Canteen, London SW10 44-5
Cantina del Ponte, London SE1 45
Capital, London SW3 45-6
Capitol, Birkenhead 351
Captain's Table, Woodbridge 419
Careys Manor, Brockenhurst 296
Carlton Highland, Edinburgh 515
Carlton House, Llanwrtyd Wells 567
Carlyon Bay, St Austell 190
Carved Angel, Dartmouth 219-20
Castle, Taunton 403
Castle Bank, Conwy 557
Castle Cottage, Harlech 558
Castle Inn, Castle Combe 465-6
Castleton House, Glamis 541
The Cauldron, Swanage 251
Cavendish, Baslow 213
Cecconi's, London W1 46
Cedar Manor, Windermere 207
Cellar Restaurant, Anstruther 491-2
Celtic Manor, Newport 554
Cerutti's Restaurant, Hull 330
Chalon Court, St Helens 351
Champany Inn, Linlithgow 521-2
Chandni Restaurant, Bromley 47
Channings, Edinburgh 515
Chapel House, Atherstone 434
Chapeltoun House, Stewarton 535
Chapter 11, London SW10 47
Charingworth Manor, Charingworth 275
Charnwood, Sheffield 409-10
Chase, Ross-on-Wye 325
Château La Chaire, Rozel Bay 479
Cheevers, Royal Tunbridge Wells 336
Chef Imperial, Woodstock 392
Chelsea Hotel, London SW1 47
Chelwood House, Chelwood 152
The Chequers Inn, Fowlmere 170
Chequers Inn, Wooburn Common 168
Chesterfield Hotel, London W1 48
The Chester Grosvenor, Chester 173-4
Chewton Glen, New Milton 309-10
Chez Max, London SW10 48
Chez Max, Surbiton 49
Chez Moi, London 49
Chez Nous, Plymouth 230-1
Chikako's, Cardiff 570
Chimneys, Long Melford 417
Chinon, London W14 50
Chiseldon House, Swindon 471-2
Christopher's, London WC2 50-1
Chung Ying Garden, Birmingham 440
Churche's Mansion, Nantwich 176
Churchill Inter-Continental, London W1 51
Chutney Mary, London SW10 51

Chy-an-Dour, St Ives 190
Cibo, London W14 52
City Miyama, London EC4 52
Claremont, Polperro 187
Claridge's, London W1 52-3
Clarke's, London W8 53
Cleeveway House, Cheltenham 276
Cliffe Hotel, Limpley Stoke 468
The Cliff House, Barton-on-Sea 294
Cliffords Cottage, Bracklesham 446-7
Clifton-Ford Hotel, London W1 54
Clifton House, Dolgellau 557
Cliveden, Taplow 167
Clos du Roy, Bath 140-1
Close, Tetbury 286
Cobbett's, Botley 296
Cobo Bay, Catel 474
Cobwebs, Kirkby Lonsdale 204
Coed-y-Mwstwr, Bridgend 563
Collin House, Auchencairn 488-9
Collin House, Broadway 319
Colonsay Hotel, Scalasaig, Isle of Colonsay 534
Combe Grove Manor, Bath 141
Combe House, Gittisham 222
Combe House, Holford 398
Combe Park, Lynton 227
Comma Ça, Chichester 447
Commodore Hotel, Weston-super-Mare 155
The Compleat Angler, Marlow 167
Congham Hall, Grimston 354-5
The Connaught, London W1 54
Conrah, Aberystwyth 550
Cookham Tandoori, Cookham 159
Coombe Bank, Teignmouth 233
Coppid Beech, Bracknell 158
Copthorne, Birmingham 440
Copthorne, Newcastle-upon-Tyne 431
The Copthorne, Slough 162
Copthorne Effingham Park, Copthorne 449
The Copthorne Tara, London W8 55
Cormorant, Golant 182
Corse Lawn House, Corse Lawn 322
Cote Royd, Huddersfield 460
Cotswold House, Chipping Campden 279
Cottage in the Wood, Malvern 324
Coul House, Contin 503
Coulsdon Manor, Croydon 422
Country Friends, Dorrington 394
Countrymen Restaurant at the Black Lion, Long Melford 418
Country Ways, Farrington Gurney 152
County Hotel, Sully's, Canterbury 333
Courtneys, Newcastle-upon-

INDEX

Tyne 431
Court, Pembroke 551
The Courtyard, Dunbar 513
Crabwall Manor, Chester 174
Craigellachie, Craigellachie 499
Craigendarroch, Ballater 497-8
Crannog, Fort William 504
Crannog Seafood Restaurant, Glasgow 526
Crathorne Hall, Crathorne 367
Craxton Wood, Puddington 177
Creagan House, Strathyre 488
Creel Restaurant, St Margaret's Hope 522
Cringletie House, Peebles 485
Critchards, Porthleven 188
The Criterion, London W1 55
Croft Bank, Kinross 542-3
Croft Hotel, Bakewell 212
Cromlix House, Dunblane 487
Crooklands, Crooklands 199
Crosby Lodge, Crosby-on-Eden 199
The Cross, Kingussie 507-8
Crown, Blockley 274
Crown at Southwold, Southwold 419
Crown at Whitebrook, Whitebrook 554-5
Crown Hotel, Lyndhurst 307
Crown House, Great Chesterford 270
Crowthers, London SW14 55-6
Culloden Hotel, Holywood 484
Curdon Mill, Williton 405

D

Dale Head Hall, Keswick 203
Dalmahoy, Edinburgh 516
Danescombe Valley, Calstock 180
Daneswood House, Shipham 401
Dan's, London SW3 56
Daphne's, London SW3 56-7
Darroch Learg, Ballater 498
Dell'Ugo, London W1 57
Devonshire Arms, Bolton Abbey 366
Dew Pond, Old Burghclere 310
Dial House, Bourton-on-the-Water 274
Dicken's, Wethersfield 272-3
Dinham Hall, Ludlow 394
Dining Room, Hersham 426
Dolmelynllyn Hall, Dolgellau 558
Dolserau Hall Hotel, Dolgellau 558
Donington Thistle, Castle Donington 344
The Dorchester, The Grill Room, London W1 58
The Dorchester, The Oriental, London W1 58-9
Dormy House, Broadway 319-20
Dower House, Knaresborough 371

Downland, Eastbourne 261
Downstairs at 190 Queensgate, London SW7 59
Drewe Arms, Broadhembury 217
Droveway, Chichester 447
Druimard, Dervaig, Isle of Mull 532
Drury Lane Moat House, London WC2 60
Duchally House, Auchterarder 538
Dunain Park, Inverness 506
Dundonnell Hotel, Dundonnell 503
Duxford Lodge, Duxford 170

E

The Eagle, London EC1 60
Eastbury, Sherborne 249
Easton Court, Chagford 218
Eastwell Manor, Ashford 332
Ebford House, Exeter 221
Edgemoor House, Bovey Tracey 217
Egerton Grey Hotel, Barry 569
Elcot Park, Newbury 161
Ellersly House, Edinburgh 516
Elmfield, Ilfracombe 225
Elms, Abberley 318
Empire, Llandudno 560
Empress Garden, London W1 60
English Garden, London SW3 61
The English House, London SW3 61
Enmore, Dunoon 525
Enoteca, London SW15 62
Enzo of Newbridge, Newbridge 185
Epicurean, Cheltenham 277
Ermewood House, Ermington 221
Eslington Villa, Gateshead 430-1
Esseborne Manor, Hurstbourne Tarrant 305
Evesham Hotel, Evesham 322
Ewington, Glasgow 527
The Exchange, Dartmouth 220
Exmoor House, Dunster 398

F

Fairlawns, Walsall 444
Fairwater Head, Hawkchurch 223
Fairyhill, Reynoldston 571
Falcon, Castle Ashby 360
Fantails, Wetheral 207
Farlam Hall, Brampton 197
Farthings, Taunton 403-4
Feathers at Ludlow, Ludlow 394
Feathers, Woodstock 392
Feversham Arms, Helmsley 371
Fifehead Manor, Middle Wallop 308
Fifteen North Parade, Oxford 388
Fifth Floor at Harvey Nichols, London SW1 62
Fischer's, Baslow 213-14

Fisherman's Lodge, Newcastle upon Tyne 431-2
Fisherman's Wharf, Newcastle-upon-Tyne 432
Flitwick Manor, Flitwick 155-6
Food for Thought, Fowey 181-2
Forest & Vale, Pickering 374
Forest of Arden, Meriden 443
Forsters, Boldon 430
Forum, London SW7 63
Fosse Manor, Stow-on-the-Wold 283
Fountains Inn, Boxers, Wells 404
Four Seasons, London W1 63
The Four Seasons, St Fillans 545
Fouters Bistro, Ayr 523
Fownes, Worcester 327
Fox & Goose, Fressingfield 413
Fox & Hounds, Pickering 374
Foxes, Wantage 391
Foxfields, Billington 340
The Fox Reformed, London N16 64
Fredrick's, Maidenhead 160
French Connection, Rochdale 293
French House Dining Room, London W1 64
French Partridge, Horton 361
Fulham Road Restaurant, London SW3 64-5
Fung Shing, London WC2 65
Funnywayt'Mekalivin, Berwick-upon-Tweed 362-3

G

Gables, Billingshurst 446
Garden House, Cambridge 169
Garlands, Bath 141-2
Garth, Grantown-on-Spey 506
The Gateway to Wales, Chester 175
Gay Hussar, London W1 65
George & Dragon, Arundel 445
George & Dragon, Rowde 471
George at Nunney, Nunney 400
George Hotel, Chollerford 363
George Inter-Continental, Edinburgh 516
George of Stamford, Stamford 350
Gerrans Bay, Portscatho 188
Ghyll Manor, Rusper 455
Gidleigh Park, Chagford 218
Gilbert's, London SW7 65-6
Gilpin Lodge, Windermere 207-8
Glasgow Hilton, Glasgow 527
Glassdrumman Lodge, Annalong 483-4
Glazebrook House, Ivybridge 225
Glebe at Barford, Barford 434
Gleddoch House, Langbank 532
The Gleneagles, Auchterarder 538-9
Gliffaes, Crickhowell 565
Golden Palace, Southampton 314

INDEX

Gold Rill, Grasmere 200
Goldstone Hall, Market Drayton 395
Golfa Hall, Welshpool 569
Good Earth, Esher 424
Good Earth Restaurant, London NW7 66
Good Earth Restaurant, London SW3 66
Goodwood Park, Goodwood 451
Gopal's, London W1 67
Gordleton Mill, Lymington 306
Gordon's, Inverkeilor 541
Goring, London SW1 67
Grafton Manor, Bromsgrove 321
Grand, Brighton 259
Grand, Eastbourne 261
Grand, St Helier 480
Grand, Swanage 251
Grange, Keswick 203
Grange, York 377
Grange Hotel, Bristol 147
Grange & Links, Sutton on Sea 350
Grange Restaurant, Waringstown 482
Grapevine, Stow-on-the-Wold 283
Grassington House, Grassington 368
Grasmere Hotel, Grasmere 200
Gravetye Manor, East Grinstead 450-1
Great Nepalese Restaurant, London NW1 67
Greek Valley, London NW8 68
Greenbank, Falmouth 181
Greenhead House, Chapeltown 409
The Greenhouse, London W1 68-9
Greens Seafood, Norwich 357
Greenway, Cheltenham 277
Greywalls, Gullane 520-1
Griffin Inn, Llyswen 567
Grinkle Park, Easington 179
Grosvenor House, Pavilion, London W1 69
Groves, Aberystwyth 550
Grundy's, Harrogate 369
Guinach House, Aberfeldy 537

H

Hafod House, Trefriw 562
Haigs, Balsall Common 439
Haley's, Leeds 462
The Halkin, London SW1 69-70
Hallgarth Manor, Durham 255
Halmpstone Manor, Barnstaple 217
Hambleton Hall, Oakham 346-7
The Hampshire, London 70
Hanbury Manor, Ware 329
Harbour City, London 70
Harbour Heights, Poole 246
Harley, Sheffield 410

Harlosh House, Harlosh, Isle of Skye 510
Harry's Place, Grantham 349
Hart Manor, Eskdalemuir 489
Hartwell House, Aylesbury 165-6
Harvey's, Bristol 147-8
Harvey's, London SW17 70-1
Hatton Court, Gloucester 280
Haven, Plockton 508
Haven, Poole 247
Hawkwell House, Oxford 388
Haywain, Bridgnorth 393
Heathcotes, Longridge 342
Heath Court, Newmarket 418
Hellidon Lakes, Hellidon 360
Henbury Lodge, Bristol 148
Heritage, Porthcawl 564
Hewitts, Lynton 228
Highgrove House, Troon 535
High Moor, Wrightington 344
Hilaire, London SW7 71
Hintlesham Hall, Hintlesham 414
Hob Green, Markington 372
Holbeck Ghyll, Windermere 208
Holcombe, Deddington 382
Holdfast Cottage, Malvern 324
Holdsworth House, Halifax 458
The Hole in the Wall, Bath 142
Holiday Inn London-Gatwick, Crawley 449
Holiday Inn Mayfair, London W1 72
Holiday Inn, Telford 395
Hollington House, Highclere 305
Holne Chase, Ashburton 216
Homewood Park, Hinton Charterhouse 152
Honours Mill, Edenbridge 334
Hooke Hall, Uckfield 265
Hope End, Ledbury 323
The Horn of Plenty, Gulworthy 222-3
Horsted Place, Uckfield 266
Hoste Arms, Burnham Market 352
Hotel Conrad, London 72
Hotel Inter-Continental, Le Soufflé, London W1 72-3
Hotel Kalamunda, Grouville 478
Hotel L'Horizon, St Brelade 479-80
Hotel on the Park, Cheltenham 278
Hotel Piccadilly, Bournemouth 238
The Hotel Portmeirion, Portmeirion 561
Hotel Renouf, Rochford 271
Hour Glass, Fordingbridge 303
Howards, Bristol 148-9
Howard's Bistro, Nailsea 153
Howard's House, Teffont Magna 472
Hudsons, London NW1 73
The Hundred House, Ruan High Lanes 189
Hungry Monk, Jevington 264

Hunstrete House, Hunstrete 153
Hunters, Alresford 294
Hunters, Winchester 316
Hunters Hall Inn, Tetbury 286
Hunter's Lodge, Broadway 320
Huntingtower, Perth 543
Hunt's, Bristol 149
Hyatt Carlton Tower, London SW1 73-4
The Hyde Park, The Park Room, London SW1 74
Hythe Imperial, Hythe 335

I

Idlerocks, St Martin 475
Idle Rocks, St Mawes 191
Imperial, Great Yarmouth 354
Imperial, Llandudno 560
The Imperial, Torquay 234
Imperial City, London EC3 74
Inchalla, Alderney 473
Inchbae Lodge, Garve 506
Indian Connoisseurs, London W2 75
Inglesham Forge, Inglesham 468
Inn For All Seasons, Burford 381
Innsacre, Bridport 241
Inverlochy Castle, Fort William 504-5
The Island, Tresco 193
Isle of Eriska, Eriska 525-6
The Ivy, London WC2 75
Ivy House, Marlborough 469

J

Jade Fountain, Ascot 157
Jeremy's at the Crabtree, Lower Beeding 452
Jersey Arms, Middleton Stoney 386
Jersey Pottery, Gorey 478
Jervaulx Hall, Masham 372
Jimmy Beez, London W10 76
Jin, London W1 76
Jonathans', Oldbury 443

K

Kai Mayfair, London 76-7
Kalamara's, London W2 77
Kastoori, London SW17 77
Kemps, Wareham 252
Ken Lo's Memories of China, London SW1 77-8
Ken Lo's Memories of China, London SW10 78
Kensington Place, London W8 78-9
Kersbrook, Lyme Regis 246
Kettering Park, Kettering 361
Kilcamb Lodge, Strontian 511-12
Kildrummy Castle, Kildrummy 501
Kilfinan, Kilfinan 530-1
Kilhey Court, Standish 293

INDEX 577

Killermont Polo Club, Glasgow 527
Killiecrankie Hotel, Killiekrankie 541-2
King James Thistle, Edinburgh 517
King's Arms, Askrigg 365
Kings Arms, Westerham 339
Kings Arms Inn, Montacute 399
Kingshead House, Birdlip 274
The King's Head, Leighton Buzzard 156
Kingsway, Cleethorpes 330
King William IV, Littlebourne 335
Kinkell, Conon Bridge 503
Kinlochbervie Hotel, Kinlochbervie 508
Kinloch House, Blairgowrie 539
Kinloch Lodge, Isle Ornsay, Isle of Skye 510-11
Kinnaird, Dunkeld 540-1
Kinsale Hall, Holywell 548
Kirroughtree, Newton Stewart 490
The Kitchen, Polperro 187
Knockendarroch House, Pitlochry 544
Knockinaam Lodge, Portpatrick 491
Knoll House, Malmesbury 468-9
Krimo's, Hartlepool 179
Kwoks Rendezvous, Ipswich 414

L

La Barbarie, St Martin 475
La Barbe Encore, Cranleigh 422
La Belle Époque, Knutsford 175
La Bonne Auberge, South Godstone 428-9
L'Accento, London W2 79
La Chouette, Dinton 166-7
Ladyburn, Maybole 532
La Fleur de Lys, Shaftesbury 249
La Fregate, St Peter Port 476
La Grand Mare, Catel 474
Laicram Thai, London SE3 79
Lainston House, Winchester 316-17
Lake, Llangammarch Wells 566
Lake Hotel, Port of Menteith 487
Lake Isle, Uppingham 348
Lakeside Hotel, Newby Bridge 204
Lake Vyrnwy, Llanwddyn 567
L'Altro, London W11 80
Lamb at Hindon, Hindon 468
Lamb Inn, Shipton-under-Wychwood 390
L'Amico, Petworth 454
Landgate Bistro, Rye 265
The Lanesborough, London SW1 80-1
Langan's Bistro, Brighton 259
Langan's Brasserie, London W1 81
Langar Hall, Langar 379
Langdale, Elterwater 199
Langdale Chase, Windermere 208

Langland Court, Langland Bay 571
Langley House, Wiveliscombe 406-7
Langley Wood Restaurant, Redlynch 470
Langshott Manor, Horley 427
Langtry Manor, Bournemouth 238-9
Lansdowne, Eastbourne 261
The Lansdowne, London NW1 81
Lansdowne, Royal Leamington Spa 435
La Piazza Ristorante, St Peter Port 477
La Potinière, Gullane 520-1
La Tante Claire, London SW3 81-2
L'Atlantique, Perelle 474-5
L'Auberge, Edinburgh 517
Launceston Place, London W8 82
Laurent, London NW2 83
Leadon's Brasserie, Chepstow 552-3
The Leatherne Bottel, Goring 383
Le Berger, Bramley 421
Le Boudin Blanc, London 83
Le Café du Jardin, London WC2 84
Le Café du Marché, London EC1 84
Le Caprice, London SW1 84-5
Le Cassoulet, Cardiff 570
Le Champenois (Blackwater Hotel), West Mersea 272
Le Champignon Sauvage, Cheltenham 278
Leeming House, Watermillock 206
Lee Wood Hotel, Buxton 215
Le Filbert Cottage, Henley-in-Arden 434-5
Le Gavroche, London W1 85-6
Le Grandgousier, Brighton 259
Leith's, London W11 86
Le Manoir Aux Quat' Saisons 383-4
Le Marche Noir, Edinburgh 517-8
Le Meridien, Oak Room, London W1 87
Le Mesurier, London EC1 87-8
Lemonia, London NW1 88
Le Nautique, St Peter Port 477
Leodis Brasserie, Leeds 462
Le Petit Canard, Maiden Newton 246
Le Petit Max, Hampton Wick 88
Le Petit Pierrot, Claygate 421
Le Pont de la Tour, London SE1 89
Le Poussin, Brockenhurst 297
Le Raj, Epsom 423-4
Les Alouettes, Claygate 421-2
Les Associes, London N8 89
Les Bouviers, Wimborne 254
L'Escargot, London W1 90
L'Escargot Brasserie, London W1 90-1

Les Saveurs, London W1 91
Le Talbooth, Dedham 269
Leusdon Lodge, Poundsgate 231
Lewtrenchard Manor, Lewdown 226
Lexington, London W1 92
Liaison, Oxford 389
Linden Hall, Longhorsley 364
Lindeth Fell, Windermere 209
Lindsay House, London W1 92
Linthwaite House, Windermere 209
Little Barwick House, Yeovil 407
Little Beach, Woolacombe 236
Little Yang Sing, Manchester 290
Llangoed Hall, Llyswen 568
Llanwenarth Arms, Abergavenny 552
Llechwen Hall, Pontypridd 563
Llyndir Hall, Rossett 549
Lobster Pot, L'Etacq 479
Loch Duich, Ardelve 502
Lochgreen House, Troon 536
Loch Melfort, Arduaine 522
Loch Torridon Hotel, Torridon 512
Lodge, Huddersfield 460
Lomond Country Inn, Kinnesswood 542
The London Hilton on Park Lane, London 93
Longueville Manor, St Saviour 480-1
The Longview, Knutsford 175-6
The Lord Bute, Highcliffe 245
Lord Crewe Arms, Blanchland 363
Lords of the Manor, Upper Slaughter 288
L'Ortolan, Shinfield 161-2
Lovelady Shield, Alston 194
Lovells at Windrush Farm, Minster Lovell 386
Lower Slaughter Manor, Lower Slaughter 281
The Lowndes, London 93
Lubnaig Hotel, Callander 486
Lucknam Park, Colerne 466-7
Lygon Arms, Broadway 320
Lynton Cottage, Lynton 228
Lynton House, Holdenby 360
Lysses House, Fareham 302
Lythe Hill, Haslemere 425

M

Mabey's Brasserie, Sudbury 419
Madeley Court, Telford 396
Maes-y-Neuadd, Talsarnau 562
Mains Hall, Poulton le Fylde 342-3
Makeney Hall, Belper 214
Mallory Court, Royal Leamington Spa 436
Mallyan Spout, Goathland 367
Mandarin Kitchen, London W2 93-4

578 INDEX

Manleys, Storrington 455-6
The Manor, Chadlington 381
Manor, Guildford 425
Manor, West Bexington 253
Manor House, Castle Combe 466
Manor House, Moreton-in-Marsh 282
Manor House, Oban 533
Manor House, Studland 250
Manor Parc, Cardiff 570
Mansefield House, Elgin 500
Mansion House, Elgin 500
Mansion House, Poole 247
Marco's, Norwich 357-8
Marina Hotel, Fowey 182
Marine Highland, Troon 536
Market, Manchester 290
Markwicks, Bristol 149-50
Marlborough, Ipswich 415
Marriott, Bristol 150
Marsh, Leominster 324
Marsh Goose, Moreton-in-Marsh 282
Marsh Hall, South Molton 232
Martha's Vineyard, Colchester 269
Martins, Edinburgh 518
Mas Café, London W11 94
Master Builders House, Bucklers Hard 299
Matsuri, London SW1 94
Mauro's, Bollington 172-3
Maybank, Aberdovey 555
May Fair Inter-Continental, London W1 95
Mayflower, Cheltenham 279
McClements Bistro, Twickenham 95
McClements Petit Bistrot, Twickenham 95-6
McCoys (Tontine Inn), Staddle Bridge 376
Melton's, York 377
Menai Court, Bangor 556
Mermaid Inn, Rye 265
Merton, Hereford 323
Mez Creis, Poole 248
Michael's Nook, Grasmere 200
Michels, Ripley 428
Middlethorpe Hall, York 377-8
Midsummer House, Cambridge 169-70
Mijanou, London SW1 96
Milburn Arms, Rosedale Abbey 375
Milebrook House, Knighton 566
Milford Hall, Salisbury 471
Milk House, Montacute 399
The Mill, Bishop's Stortford 327
The Mill, Mungrisdale 204
Mill at Harvington, Evesham 322
Mill End, Chagford 219
Miller Howe, Windermere 209
Millers House, Middleham 373
Millers, The Bistro, Harrogate 369-70

Mill House, Kingham 385
Millstone, Blackburn 340
Millstream, Bosham 446
Mims, Barnet 96-7
Minffordd Hotel, Tal-y-Llyn 562
Ming, London W1 97
Mirabelle, London W1 97-8
Miskin Manor, Miskin 563
Mitsukoshi, London SW1 98
Miyama, London W1 99
Moat House International, Chester 174
Moat House International, Glasgow 527-8
The Mock Turtle, Dorchester 243-4
Mollington Banastre, Chester 175
Monkey's, London SW3 99
Montagu Arms, Beaulieu 295
Montcalm, The Crescent, London W1 99
Montgreenan Mansion, Kilwinning 531
Moonacre, Fordingbridge 303
Moonrakers, Alfriston 256-7
Moorings, Fort William 505
Moorings, Wells-next-the-Sea 359
Moorland Hall, Tavistock 233
Moortown Lodge, Ringwood 311
Morels, Haslemere 426
Morston Hall, Blakeney 352
Mortons House, Corfe Castle 243
Moss Nook, Manchester 291
The Mountbatten, London WC2 100
Mount Haven, Marazion 184
Mount Murray, Douglas 481
Mount Royale, York 378
Mr Underhills, Earl Stonham 412-13
Muckrach Lodge, Dulnain Bridge 503
Mulligans of Mayfair, London W1 100
Munchy Munchy, Oxford 389
Murrayshall, Perth 543
Museum Street Café, London WC1 100-1

N

Nailcote Hall, Balsall Common 439-40
Nanny Brow, Ambleside 195
Nansloe Manor, Helston 183
Nare, Veryan 194
Neal Street, London WC2 101
Netherfield Place, Battle 257
Neubia House, Lynton 228
New Hall, Sutton Coldfield 444
New Inn, Tresco 193
The New Mill, Eversley 301
New Moon, Bath 142-3
New Park Manor, Brockenhurst 297

Newstead Grange, Malton 372
Newton House, Perth 544
Nico at Ninety, London W1 102
Nico Central, London W1 102-3
Nidd Hall, Harrogate 370
Nightingales, Taunton 404
Nineteen Grape Lane Restaurant, York 378
Nippon Kan at Old Thorn, Liphook 305
Nivingston House, Cleish 540
No 5 Bistro, Bath 143
Noel Arms, Chipping Campden 280
Noke Thistle, St Albans 328
Nook and Cranny, Warsash 315
Noorani, Fair Oak 301
Norfolk Place, Coltishall 352-3
Norfolk Royale Hotel, Bournemouth 239
Normandie, Bury 289-90
Normanton Park, Normanton 346
Northcote Manor, Burrington 218
Northcote Manor, Langho 341
Norton House, Edinburgh 518-19
Number Thirty Three, Perth 544
Number Twenty-Four, Wymondham 359
Nunsmere Hall, Sandiway 177-8
Nutfield Priory, Nutfield 427
Nuthurst Grange, Hockley Heath 442-3

O

Oak Bank, Grasmere 201
Oakes, Stroud 285
Oak House, Axbridge 397
Oaklands, South Petherton 401-2
Oakley Court, Windsor 164
Oaks, Porlock 400
Oatlands Park, Weybridge 429
Ockenden Manor, Cuckfield 450
Odettes, London NW1 103
Odins, London W1 104
Old Beams, Waterhouses 410-11
Old Black Lion, Hay-on-Wye 565
Old Boot House, Ipswich 415
Old Chesil Rectory, Winchester 317
Old Custom House Inn, Padstow 185
The Old Delhi, London W2 104
The Olde Forge, Hailsham 262
Olde Village Bakery, Pinner 104
Old Farmhouse, Stow-on-the-Wold 284
Old Fire Engine House, Ely 170
Old Forge, Storrington 456
Old House, Wickham 315-16
Old Manor, Lundin Links 493
Old Manor House, Romsey 312
The Old Manse of Marnoch, Bridge of Marnoch 499
Old Mansion House,

INDEX 579

Auchterhouse 539
The Old Monastery, Drybridge 500
The Old Rectory, Coniston 198
The Old Rectory, Conwy 557
Old Rectory, Martinhoe 229
Old Station, Spean Bridge 511
The Old Vicarage, Ridgeway 216
Old Vicarage, Witherslack 211
Old Vicarage, Worfield 396
Olive Tree, Leeds 463
Olivo, London SW1 105
One Devonshire Gardens, Glasgow 528
Orchid, Bristol 150
Orestone Manor, Torquay 234
Oriel, London SW1 105
Oriental House, London SW5 105
Orient Rendezvous, Bristol 150
Orso, London WC2 106
Orwell House, Ipswich 416
Osmani, London 106
Osprey Hotel, Kingussie 507
Osteria Antica Bologna, London SW11 106-7
Ostlers Close, Cupar 492
Overcombe, Horrabridge 224
Over The Bridge, Ripponden 463
Overton's, London SW1 107
Overwater Hall, Bassenthwaite 196

P

Painswick Hotel, Painswick 282-3
Paris, Horsforth 459
Paris House, Woburn 156-7
Park Farm, Hethersett 355
Parkhill Hotel, Lyndhurst 307-8
Parkland Hotel, St Andrews 495
Parklands, Perth 544
Park Lane Hotel, London W1 107-8
Parkmore, Stockton-on-Tees 179
Parrock Head, Slaidburn 343
Parsonage, Escrick 367
Partners Brasserie, Sutton 108
Partners West Street, Dorking 422-3
Passford House, Lymington 306
Pearl of Knightsbridge, London SW1 108
Pear Tree at Purton, Purton 470
The Peat Inn, Peat Inn 494-5
Peat Spade Inn, Stockbridge 314
Penally Abbey, Tenby 552
Pengethley Manor, Ross-on-Wye 325
Penhaven Country House, Parkham 230
Penhelig Arms, Aberdovey 555
Penmaenuchaf Hall, Dolgellau 558
Pennyhill Park, Bagshot 420
Pennypots, Blackwater 250
Pentire Rocks, Polzeath 188
Percy's, North Harrow 109
Periton Park, Minehead 398-9

Perry's, Weymouth 253
Persad Tandoori, Ruislip 109
Peterstone Court, Brecon 564
Peterstow, Ross-on-Wye 325
Petty France, Petty France 154
Pheasant Inn, Keyston 171
Pheasants, Sherborne 250
Pied à Terre, London W1 109-10
The Pier at Harwich, Harwich 271
Piersland House, Troon 536
Pig 'n' Fish, St Ives 190-1
The Pink Geranium, Melbourn 171-2
Pinocchio's, Norwich 358
Plas Bodegroes, Pwllheli 561
The Plough at Clanfield, Clanfield 382
Plumber Manor, Sturminster Newton 250-1
Pomme d'Or Hotel, St Helier 480
Pontlands Park, Chelmsford 267
Poons, London 110
Pophams, Winkleigh 236
Popjoys, Bath 143
Poppies, Brimfield 318-19
Port Gaverne Hotel, Port Gaverne 188
Porthole Eating House, Windermere 210
Portland Hotel, Buxton 215
Poston Mill, Vowchurch 326
Powdermills, Battle 257
Prince Hall, Two Bridges 235
Priory, Bath 143-4
Priory, Bury St Edmunds 412
Priory, Wareham 252
Puckrup Hall, Tewkesbury 287

O

Quaglino's, London SW1 111
Quality Chop House, London EC1 111-12
Quarry Garth, Windermere 210
Queens, Bournemouth 239
The Queensbury, Bath 144
Quentins, Hove 264
Quincy's Restaurant, London NW2 112
Quorn Grange, Quorn 347

R

The Radisson Edwardian, London 113
Raemoir House, Banchory 498
Raffles, Aldbourne 463-4
Rajpoot Tandoori, Bath 144-5
Ram Jam Inn, Stretton 347
Ramnee, Forres 501
Ramore Restaurant, Portrush 482
Rampsbeck, Watermillock 206
Randell's, Skipton 375
Random Hall, Horsham 451
Rangeworthy Court, Rangeworthy 154

Rani, London N3 113
Rankins, Sissinghurst 338
Ransome's Dock, London SW11 113-14
Ravenwood Hall, Bury St Edmunds 412
Read's, Faversham 334-5
Redfern, Cleobury Mortimer 393
Red Fort, London W1 114
Red Lion, Adderbury 380
Red Lion, Henley-on-Thames 384
Redworth Hall, Redworth 255
Regatta, Aldeburgh 411
Regency House, Cheltenham 279
Regency Park, Thatcham 163
The Regent, London NW1 114-15
Regent, Royal Leamington Spa 436
Rescobie, Glenrothes 493
The Restaurant, London SW1 115-16
Restaurant 192, London 116
Restaurant Bosquet, Kenilworth 435
Restaurant Lettonie, Bristol 150-1
Restaurant Nineteen, Bradford 457
Restaurant Peano, Barnsley 408
Rhapsody, London W14 116
Rhinefield House, Brockenhurst 298
Riber Hall, Matlock 215
Rising Sun, Lynmouth 227
Rising Sun, St Mawes 192
Ristorante L'Incontro, London SW1 116-17
Ristorante Tuo e Mio, Canterbury 334
Ritz, London W1 117
Riva, London SW13 117-18
River Café, London W6 118
River House, Lympstone 227
Riverside, Ashford-in-the-Water 212
Riverside, Bridport 241
Riverside, Evesham 323
Riverside, Helford 183
Roadhouse Restaurant, Roade 361
Rocher's, Milford on Sea 308-9
Rock Inn, Haytor 224
Rococo, King's Lynn 355
Rogano, Glasgow 528-9
Roger's Restaurant, Windermere 211
Roman Camp, Callander 486-7
Romans, Silchester 313
Rombalds, Ilkley 461
Rookery Hall, Nantwich 177
Roscoff, Belfast 482-3
The Rose, Rawtenstall 343
Rose & Crown, Mayfield 264
Rose & Crown, Romaldkirk 256
Rose & Crown, Tring 329
Rosedale, Portree 509
Roseland House, Portscatho 189
Rösers, Hastings & St

INDEX

Leonards 262-3
Rosevine Hotel, Portscatho 189
Rossett Hall, Rossett 549
Rosslea Hall, Rhu 534
Rothay Manor, Ambleside 195
Roundham House, Bridport 242
Royal, Winchester 317
Royal Bath, Bournemouth 239-40
The Royal Berkshire, Ascot 157-8
Royal Chase, Shaftesbury 249
Royal China, London SW15 119
Royal China, London W2 119
The Royal Crescent, Bath 145
Royal Duchy, Falmouth 181
Royal Garden, London W8 120
Royal George Hotel, Tintern 554
Royal Hotel, Bridge of Allan 486
Royal Lancaster, London W2 120
Royal Oak, Sevenoaks 338
Royal Oak, Yattendon 164-5
Royal Oak Hotel, Settle 375
Royal Oak Inn, Winsford 406
Royal Oak Inn, Withypool 406
Royal Wells Inn, Royal Tunbridge Wells 336-7
Royal Westminster Thistle, London SW1 120
RSJ The Restaurant on the South Bank, London SE1 112-13
Rudloe Park, Corsham 467
Rufflets, St Andrews 495
Rules, London WC2 121
Rumbles Cottage, Felsted 270
Runnymede, Egham 423
Rutland Arms, Bakewell 213
Ryedale Lodge, Nunnington 373

S

Saffron, Saffron Walden 272
St Andrews Golf Hotel, St Andrews 495
St Andrews Old Course, St Andrews 496
St Benedicts Grill, Norwich 358
St David's Park, Ewloe 547
The St Mawes, St Mawes 192
St Olaves Court, Exeter 221-2
St Peter's, Ipswich 416
St Petroc's House, Padstow 186
St Pierre Park, Chepstow 553
St Pierre Park, St Peter Port 477
St Quentin, London SW3 121
St Tudno, Llandudno 560
Salford Hall, Abbot's Salford 434
Salisbury House, Diss 353
Salloos, London SW1 122
Salterns, Poole 248
Sandbanks, Poole 248
San Lorenzo Fuoriporto, London SW19 122
Santini, London SW1 122-3
Savernake Forest, Burbage 465
The Savoy, River Restaurant, London WC2 123

The Savoy, Savoy Grill, London WC2 124
Schulers, Southend-on-Sea 272
Scores, St Andrews 496
Scutchers, Long Melford 418
The Sea Cow, Weymouth 253
Seafood Restaurant, Padstow 186
Seaview, Seaview 331-2
Seeds, Llanfyllin 566
Seiont Manor, Caernarfon 556
The Selfridge, Fletchers, London W1 124
September Brasserie, Blackpool 340-1
Seymour House, Chipping Campden 280
Sharrow Bay, Howtown 202
Shaw Country Hotel, Melksham 469
Sheen Mill, Melbourn 171
Shepherd's, London SW1 125
Sheppard's, Thirsk 376
Shieldhill, Biggar 524
Shimla Pinks, Birmingham 440
Ship, Chichester 448
Ship Thistle, Weybridge 429
Shrubbery, Shepton Mallet 400
Simonsbath House, Simonsbath 401
Simply Nico, London SW1 125-6
Simpsons in the Strand, London WC2 126
Singapore Garden, London 126-7
Sketchley Grange, Hinckley 345
Skidden House, St Ives 191
Sloan's, Birmingham 441
Snooty Fox, Tetbury 287
Snows on the Green, London W6 127
Soar Mill Cove, Salcombe 231
Soho Soho, London W1 127
Solberge Hall, Northallerton 373
Solent, Fareham 302
Solihull Moat House, Solihull 443
Sonny's, London SW13 128
Sonny's, Nottingham 380
Sophisticats, Bournemouth 240
Sopwell House, St Albans 328
Southdowns, Midhurst 453
South Lawn, Milford on Sea 309
South Lodge, Lower Beeding 452-3
Spindlewood, Wadhurst 266-7
Splinters, Christchurch 242
Sportsman's Arms, Pateley Bridge 374
Spread Eagle, Midhurst 454
Spread Eagle, Thame 391
Springfield, Wareham 252
Springs, Wallingford 391
The Square, London SW1 128-9
Stafford, London SW1 129
Staindrop Lodge, Chapeltown 409
Stane Street Hollow, Pulborough 454-5

The Stannary, Mary Tavy 229
Stanneylands, Wilmslow 178
Stanton Manor, Chippenham 466
Stanwell House, Lymington 307
Stapleford Park, Melton Mowbray 345
Starr, Great Dunmow 270
Stephen Bull, London W1 129-30
Stephen Bull Bistro, London EC1 129
The Steppes, Ullingswick 326
Stewart, Duror 504
Stirk House, Gisburn 341
Stirling Highland, Stirling 488
Stock Hill House, Gillingham 244-5
Stocks Island, Sark 481
Ston Easton Park, Ston Easton 402
Stonehouse Court, Stonehouse 283
Stonor Arms, Stonor 390
Stour Bay Café, Manningtree 271
Stratford House, Stratford-upon-Avon 438
Strathaven, Strathaven 535
String of Horses, Lymington 307
Strongarbh, Tobermory, Isle of Mull 533
Studley Priory, Horton-cum-Studley 385
Summer Lodge, Evershott 244
Sundial, Hertsmonceux 263
Sunlaws House, Kelso 484
Suntory, London SW1 130
Sussex Pad, Lancing 452
Swallow, Alwalton 168
Swallow, Birmingham 441-2
Swallow Eaves, Colyford 219
Swallow International, London SW5 131
Swallow Royal, Bristol 151
The Swan, Bibury 273
Swan, Lavenham 417
Swan Diplomat, Streatley 162-3
Swinside Lodge, Keswick 203
Swiss Restaurant Imfeld, Hawarden 547-8
Swynford Paddocks, Six Mile Bottom 172

T

Tabaq, London SW12 131
The Table, Torquay 234-5
Talland Bay Hotel, Talland Bay 192
Tanyard, Maidstone 336
Tarbert, Penzance 187
Tatsusu, London 131
Taychreggan, Kilchrenan 530
The Tayside, Stanley 545
Temple Sowerby House, Temple Sowerby 205
Thackeray's House, Royal Tunbridge Wells 337
Thai Garden, London E2 132

INDEX 581

Thailand, London SE14 132
Thainstone House, Inverurie 501
Thatched Cottage, Brockenhurst 298
Thatchers, East Horsley 423
Theobalds, Ixworth 416-17
Thirty Four Surrey Street, Croydon 132
Thirty-Six On The Quay, Emsworth 300-1
Thistells, London SE22 132
Thornbury Castle, Thornbury 154
Thornton Hall, Thornton Hough 351
Three Chimneys, Colbost, Isle of Skye 510
Three Cocks Hotel, Three Cocks 568-9
Three Horseshoes Inn, Bridport 242
The Three Lions, Fordingbridge 303-4
Three Swans, Market Harborough 345
Tides Reach, Salcombe 231
Tigh an Eilean, Shieldaig 509
Titchwell Manor, Titchwell 358
The Toft, Dick Willett's, Knutsford 176
Tophams Ebury Court, London SW1 133
Topps, Brighton 260
The Town House, Glasgow 529
Town House, York 379
Toxique, Melksham 470
Tregarthen Country Cottage, Mount Hawke 185
Treglos, Constantine Bay 181
Trelawne Hotel, Mawnan Smith 184
Tre-Ysgawen Hall, Llangefni 546
Truffles, Bruton 397
Tudor Court, Abersoch 555
Tufton Arms, Appleby-in-Westmorland 196
Tui, London SW7 133
Turnberry, Turnberry 537
Turners, London W3 133-4
Twentyone Queen Street, Newcastle-upon-Tyne 432-3
Two Brothers, Finchley 134
Tyddyn Llan, Llandrillo 548
Tylney Hall, Rotherwick 313
Ty Mawr, Brechfa 551
Ty'n Rhos, Llanddeiniolen 559
Ty'r Graig, Barmouth 556
Tyrrells Ford, Ringwood 312
Tytherleigh Cot, Chardstock 219

U

Upcross Hotel, Reading 161
Uplands, Cartmel 198

V

The Veeraswamy, London 134
Vermont, Newcastle-upon-Tyne 433
Veronica's, London W2 134-5
Victoria & Albert, Manchester 291
Victorian House, Thornton 344
The Village Restaurant, Ramsbottom 293
Vine House, Towcester 362
The Vintners Room, Edinburgh 519
Virginia House, Ulverston 205

W

Wagamama, London WC1 135
Walletts Court, St Margaret's at Cliffe 338-9
Walnut Tree Inn, Llanddewi Skyrrid 553-4
Waltons, London SW3 135-6
Warpool Court, St David's 552
Washbourne Court, Lower Slaughter 281
Waterbeach Hotel, Treyarnon Bay 193
Wateredge, Ambleside 195
Waterford Lodge, Christchurch 243
Waterside Inn, Bray 158-9
Watersmeet, Woolacombe 237
Weavers, Haworth 458
Weavers Shed, Huddersfield 460
Welcombe, Stratford-upon-Avon 438
Well House, Liskeard 183-4
Well View, Moffat 490
Wesley House, Winchcombe 288-9
Wessex, Bournemouth 240
Westerclose, Withypool 406
West Lodge Park, Barnet 136
Weston Manor, Weston-on-the-Green 391
Westpoint, East Kilbride 525
Wheatsheaf, Swinton 485
Whipper-in Hotel, Oakham 347
Whipsiderry, Newquay 185
Whitechapel Manor, South Molton 232-3
Whitehall, Broxted 267
White Hart, Coggeshall 268
White Hart, Dorchester-on-Thames 382-3
White Hart Inn, Ford 467
White Horse Inn, Chilgrove 448
White House, Harrogate 370
White House, Herm 478
White House, Williton 405
White Moss House, Grasmere 201
Whites, Oxford 389
The White Tower, London W1 136
Whitley Ridge, Brockenhurst 298-9
Whitstable Oyster Fisher Co, Whitstable 339
Whytes, Brighton 260
Wig & Mitre, Lincoln 349
Willerby Manor, Willerby 330
Willowburn, Clachan-Seil 524
Willows, Ashington 445-6
Wilson's, London W14 136-7
Windsor Lodge, Swansea 572
Winteringham Fields, Winteringham 330-1
The Witchery by the Castle, Edinburgh 519-20
Woodbury House, East Grinstead 451
Wood Hall, Wetherby 463
Woodhayes, Whimple 235-6
Woodlands, Manchester 292
Woodlands Park, Stoke d'Abernon 429
Woods, Bath 146
Woods Place, Grayshott 304
Woolley Grange, Bradford-on-Avon 464-5
Woolpack Inn, Beckington 397
Wordsworth, Grasmere 201
Wyck Hill House, Stow-on-the-Wold 284
Wykeham Arms, Winchester 318

Y

Yang Sing, Manchester 292
Y Bistro, Llanberis 559
Ye Olde Anchor Inn, Uthin 550
Ye Olde Bell, Hurley 160
Ye Olde Bull's Head, Beaumaris 546
Yeovil Court, Yeovil 407
Yew Tree Farm, Swanwick 315
Ynyshir Hall, Eglwysfach 551
Yorke Arms, Ramsgill 374
York Pavilion, York 379
Yumi, London W1 137

Z

Zen Central, London W1 137-8
ZENW3, London NW3 138
Zoe, London W1 138-9

KEY TO ATLAS

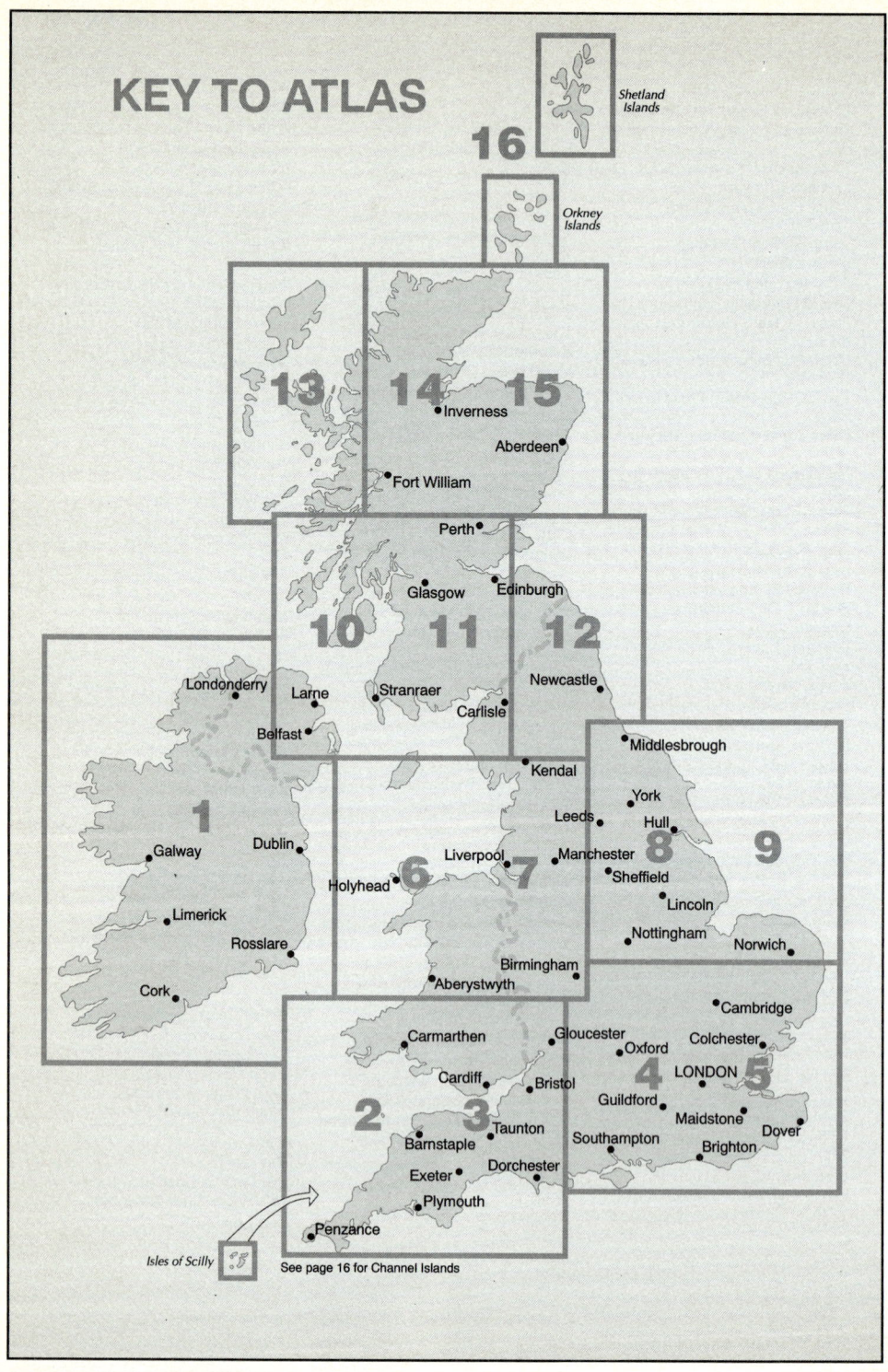

© The Automobile Association 1994

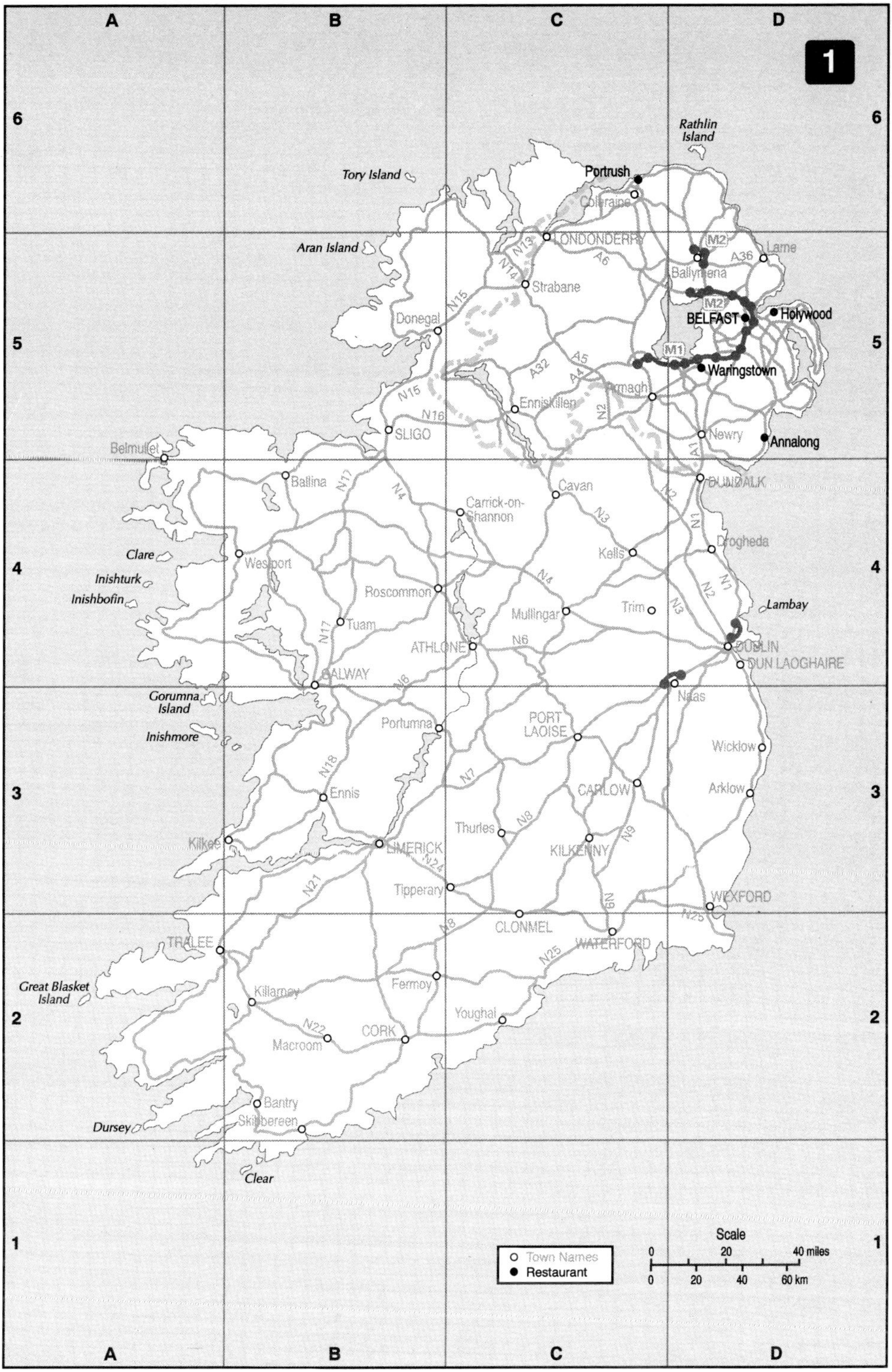

A
B
C
D
1
6
5
4
3
2
1
Rathlin Island
Tory Island
Portrush
Coleraine
Aran Island
LONDONDERRY
M2
Larne
A36
Ballymena
N13
A6
N14
Strabane
M2
Holywood
BELFAST
N15
Donegal
M1
A5
Waringstown
A32
A4
Armagh
N2
N15
Enniskillen
N16
SLIGO
Newry
Annalong
Belmullet
A1
DUNDALK
Ballina
N17
N4
Cavan
N2
Carrick-on-Shannon
N3
N1
Clare
Westport
Kells
Drogheda
Inishturk
N4
N1
Inishbofin
Roscommon
N2
Lambay
Trim
N3
Mullingar
Tuam
N17
N6
ATHLONE
DUBLIN
DUN LAOGHAIRE
GALWAY
N6
Gorumna Island
Naas
PORT LAOISE
Portumna
Inishmore
Wicklow
N18
N7
CARLOW
Arklow
Ennis
N8
Thurles
N9
Kilkee
KILKENNY
LIMERICK
N24
N21
Tipperary
WEXFORD
N9
N25
CLONMEL
N8
WATERFORD
TRALEE
N25
Great Blasket Island
Fermoy
Killarney
Youghal
N22
CORK
Macroom
Bantry
Dursey
Skibbereen
Clear
Town Names
Restaurant
Scale
0
20
40 miles
0
20
40
60 km

2

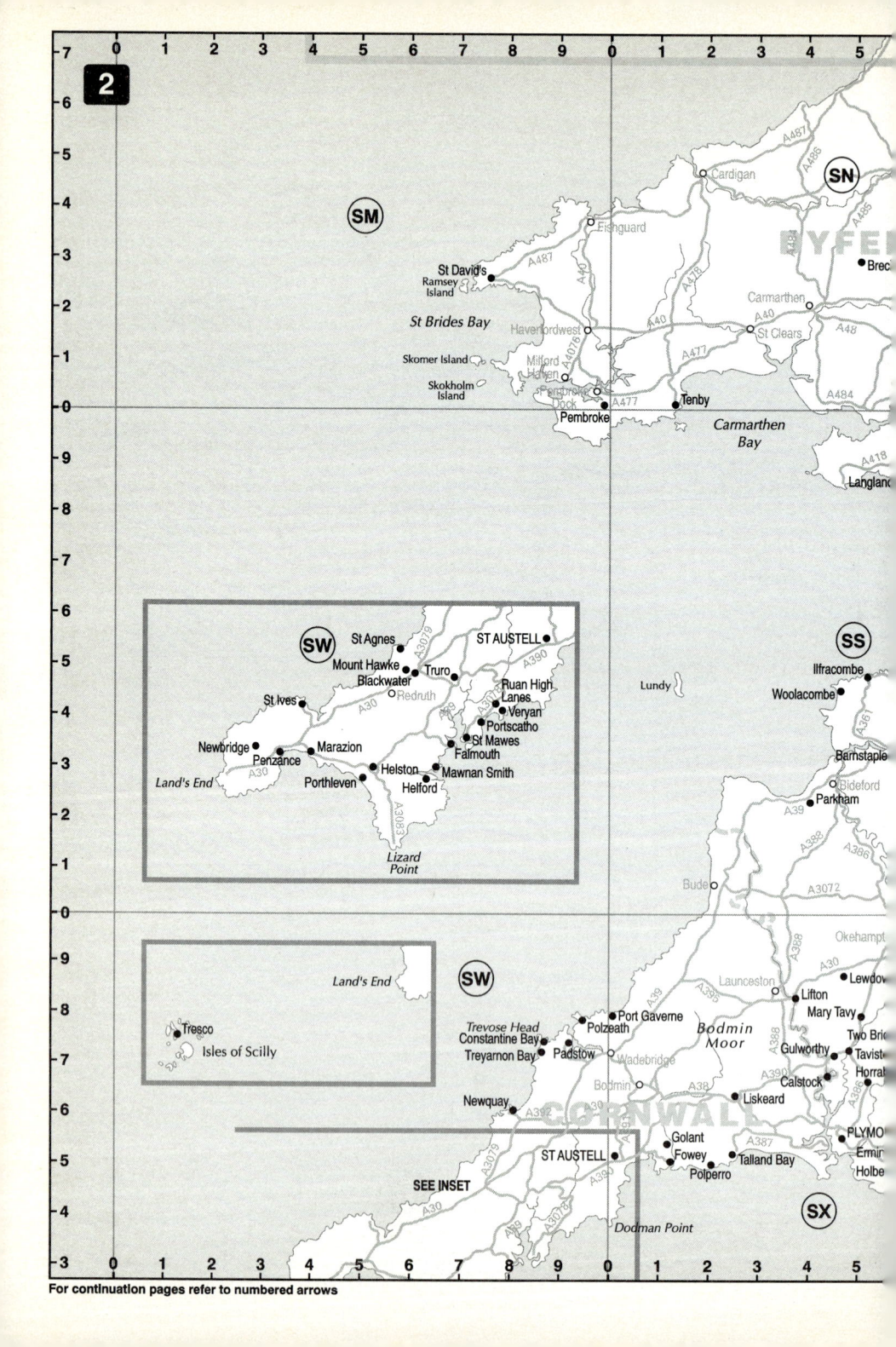

For continuation pages refer to numbered arrows

Map labels

- SM
- SN
- SW
- SS
- SX

Wales / Pembrokeshire area
- Cardigan
- Fishguard
- St David's
- Ramsey Island
- St Brides Bay
- Haverfordwest
- Skomer Island
- Skokholm Island
- Milford Haven
- Pembroke Dock
- Pembroke
- Tenby
- Carmarthen
- St Clears
- Carmarthen Bay
- Langland
- Brecon

Cornwall inset (SW)
- St Agnes
- Mount Hawke
- Blackwater
- Truro
- ST AUSTELL
- Redruth
- Ruan High Lanes
- Veryan
- St Ives
- Portscatho
- Newbridge
- Marazion
- St Mawes
- Penzance
- Falmouth
- Porthleven
- Helston
- Mawnan Smith
- Helford
- Land's End
- Lizard Point

Isles of Scilly inset
- Tresco
- Isles of Scilly
- Land's End

Cornwall / Devon
- Trevose Head
- Constantine Bay
- Treyarnon Bay
- Polzeath
- Port Gaverne
- Padstow
- Wadebridge
- Bodmin Moor
- Launceston
- Lewdown
- Lifton
- Mary Tavy
- Two Bridges
- Gulworthy
- Tavistock
- Horrabridge
- Bodmin
- Newquay
- Liskeard
- Calstock
- ST AUSTELL
- Golant
- Fowey
- Polperro
- Talland Bay
- PLYMOUTH
- Ermington
- Holbeton
- Dodman Point
- Lundy
- Ilfracombe
- Woolacombe
- Barnstaple
- Bideford
- Parkham
- Bude
- Okehampton

SEE INSET

CORNWALL

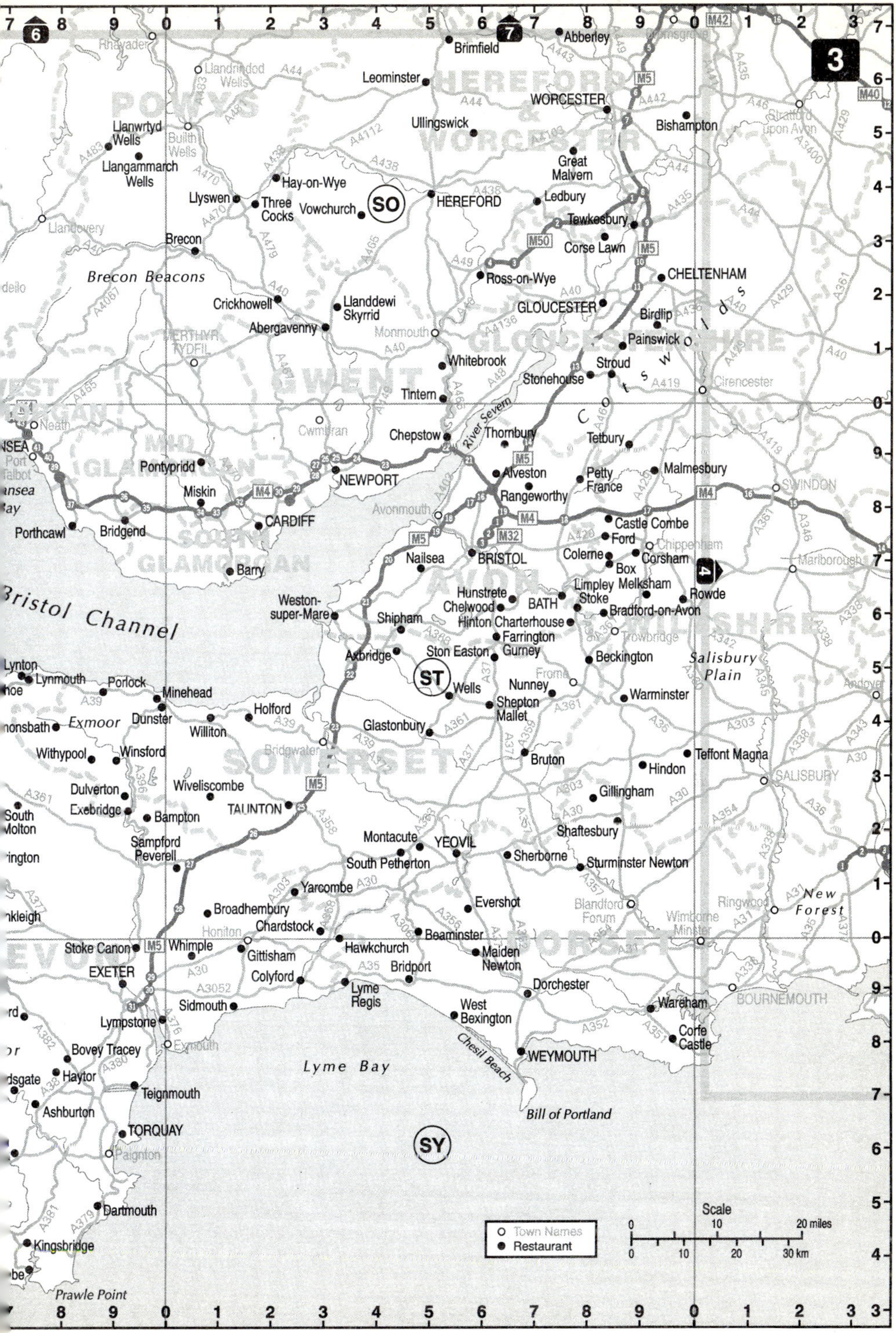
3
POWYS
HEREFORD & WORCESTER
GLOUCESTERSHIRE
GWENT
MID GLAMORGAN
SOUTH GLAMORGAN
AVON
WILTSHIRE
SOMERSET
DORSET
Cotswolds
Brecon Beacons
Bristol Channel
Exmoor
Salisbury Plain
New Forest
Lyme Bay
Chesil Beach
Bill of Portland
Prawle Point
River Severn
SO
ST
SY
Brimfield
Abberley
Leominster
WORCESTER
Bishampton
Stratford upon Avon
Llanwrtyd Wells
Llangammarch Wells
Builth Wells
Llandrindod Wells
Rhayader
Ullingswick
Great Malvern
Hay-on-Wye
Llyswen
Three Cocks
Vowchurch
HEREFORD
Ledbury
Tewkesbury
Corse Lawn
Llandovery
Brecon
Ross-on-Wye
CHELTENHAM
Crickhowell
Llanddewi Skyrrid
Abergavenny
GLOUCESTER
Birdlip
Painswick
Monmouth
Merthyr Tydfil
Whitebrook
Stroud
Stonehouse
Cirencester
Tintern
Neath
Cwmbran
Chepstow
Thornbury
Tetbury
Port Talbot
Pontypridd
NEWPORT
Alveston
Petty France
Malmesbury
Miskin
Rangeworthy
SWINDON
Porthcawl
Bridgend
CARDIFF
Avonmouth
Castle Combe
Ford
Chippenham
Nailsea
BRISTOL
Colerne
Corsham
Marlborough
Barry
Box
Melksham
Rowde
Weston-super-Mare
Hunstrete
Chelwood
BATH
Limpley Stoke
Bradford-on-Avon
Shipham
Hinton Charterhouse
Trowbridge
Farrington Gurney
Axbridge
Ston Easton
Beckington
Lynton
Lynmouth
Porlock
Minehead
Wells
Frome
Nunney
Shepton Mallet
Warminster
Andover
Dunster
Holford
Williton
Glastonbury
Withypool
Winsford
Bridgwater
Bruton
Teffont Magna
Hindon
Wiveliscombe
Dulverton
Exebridge
Bampton
TAUNTON
SALISBURY
Gillingham
South Molton
Sampford Peverell
Montacute
YEOVIL
South Petherton
Sherborne
Shaftesbury
Sturminster Newton
Yarcombe
Evershot
Blandford Forum
Ringwood
Wimborne Minster
Broadhembury
Honiton
Chardstock
Beaminster
Stoke Canon
Whimple
Gittisham
Hawkchurch
Maiden Newton
EXETER
Colyford
Bridport
Lyme Regis
Dorchester
Sidmouth
Lympstone
West Bexington
Wareham
BOURNEMOUTH
Exmouth
Corfe Castle
Bovey Tracey
WEYMOUTH
Haytor
Teignmouth
Ashburton
TORQUAY
Paignton
Dartmouth
Kingsbridge
Town Names
Restaurant
Scale
10
20 miles
0
10
20
30 km

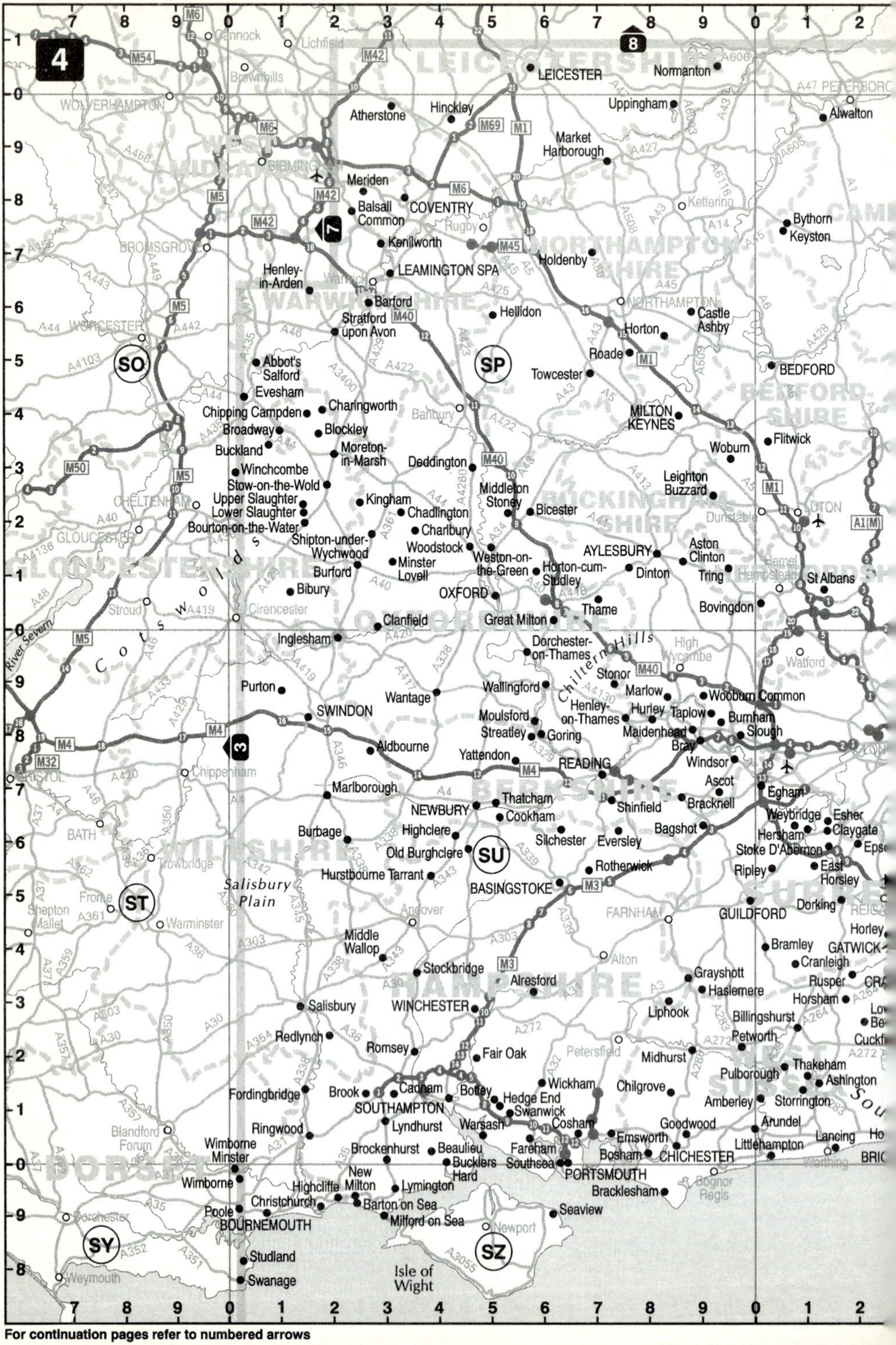

For continuation pages refer to numbered arrows

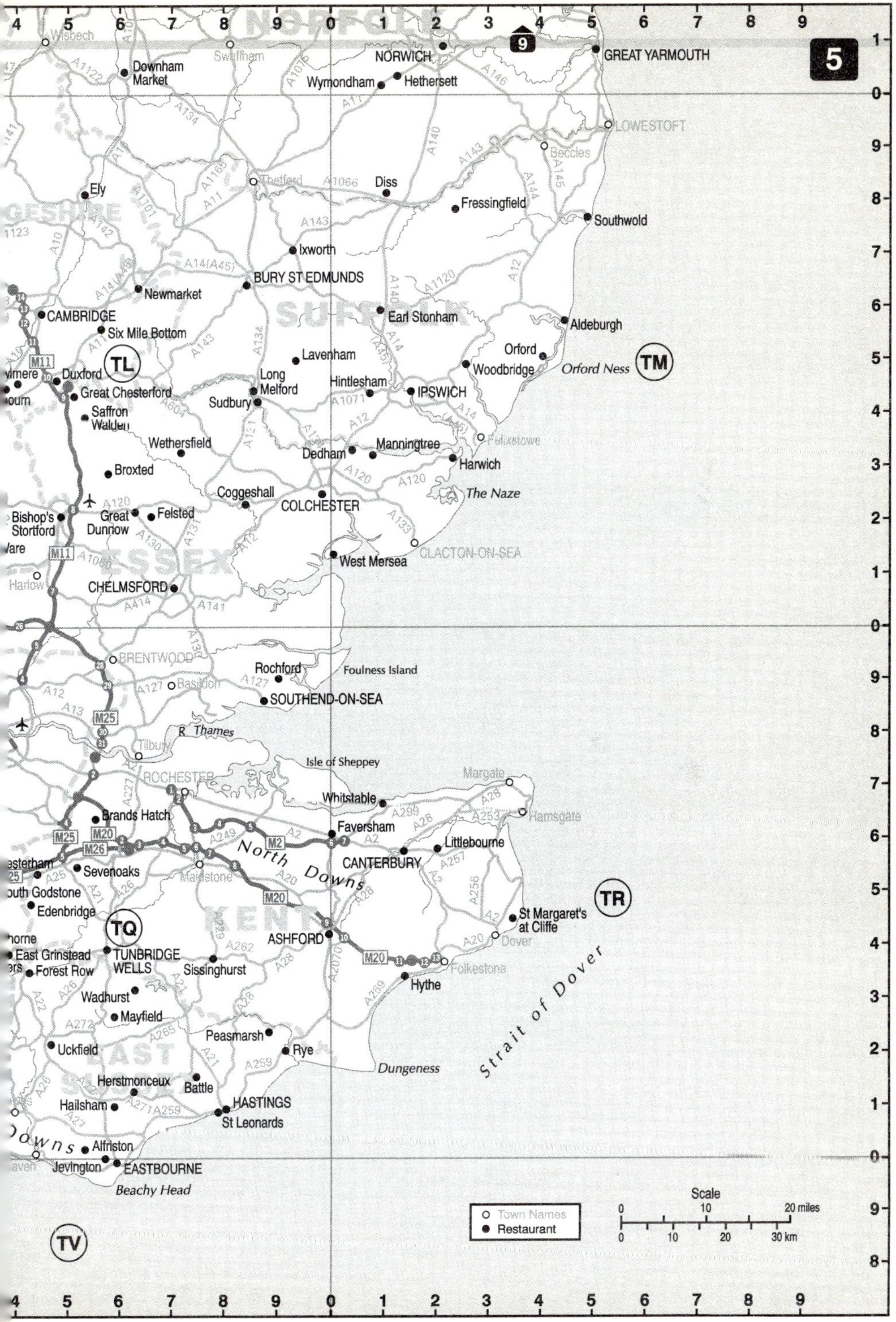
5
NORFOLK
9
Wisbech
Downham Market
Swaffham
NORWICH
Wymondham
Hethersett
GREAT YARMOUTH
LOWESTOFT
Beccles
Ely
Thetford
Diss
Fressingfield
Southwold
Ixworth
BURY ST EDMUNDS
Newmarket
CAMBRIDGE
Six Mile Bottom
SUFFOLK
Earl Stonham
Aldeburgh
Orford
Woodbridge
Orford Ness
TL
TM
Duxford
Great Chesterford
Saffron Walden
Lavenham
Long Melford
Sudbury
Hintlesham
IPSWICH
Felixstowe
Wethersfield
Dedham
Manningtree
Harwich
Broxted
The Naze
Coggeshall
COLCHESTER
Bishop's Stortford
Great Dunmow
Felsted
CLACTON-ON-SEA
ESSEX
West Mersea
Harlow
CHELMSFORD
BRENTWOOD
Basildon
Rochford
Foulness Island
SOUTHEND-ON-SEA
R. Thames
Tilbury
Isle of Sheppey
ROCHESTER
Margate
Whitstable
Ramsgate
Brands Hatch
Faversham
Littlebourne
CANTERBURY
North Downs
Sevenoaks
Maidstone
South Godstone
Edenbridge
TR
TQ
KENT
ASHFORD
St Margaret's at Cliffe
Dover
East Grinstead
TUNBRIDGE WELLS
Forest Row
Sissinghurst
Folkestone
Hythe
Wadhurst
Strait of Dover
Mayfield
Peasmarsh
Rye
Uckfield
EAST SUSSEX
Dungeness
Herstmonceux
Battle
Hailsham
HASTINGS
St Leonards
Alfriston
Jevington
EASTBOURNE
Beachy Head
TV
Town Names
Restaurant
Scale
0 10 20 miles
0 10 20 30 km

6

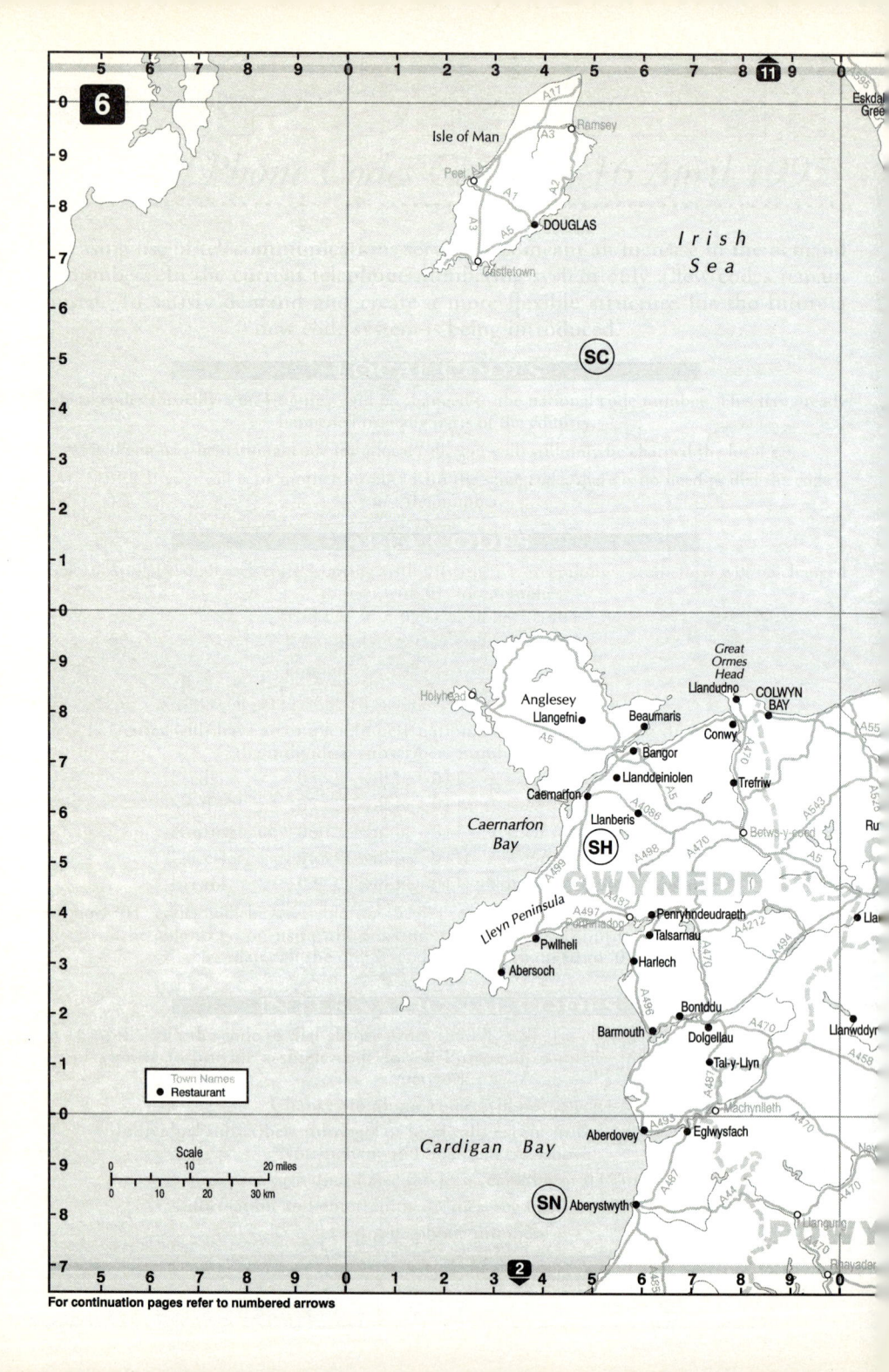

Isle of Man
- Ramsey
- Peel
- Castletown
- DOUGLAS

Irish Sea

SC

Great Ormes Head
Holyhead
Anglesey
Llangefni
Beaumaris
Llandudno
COLWYN BAY
Conwy
Bangor
Llanddeiniolen
Trefriw
Caernarfon
Caernarfon Bay
Llanberis
SH
Betws-y-coed
GWYNEDD
Lleyn Peninsula
Porthmadog
Penrhyndeudraeth
Pwllheli
Talsarnau
Abersoch
Harlech
Bontddu
Barmouth
Dolgellau
Llanwddyr
Tal-y-Llyn
Machynlleth
Aberdovey
Eglwysfach
Cardigan Bay
SN Aberystwyth

Eskdal
Gree

Ru
Lla

Llangurig
Rhayader

Town Names
● Restaurant

Scale
0 10 20 miles
0 10 20 30 km

For continuation pages refer to numbered arrows

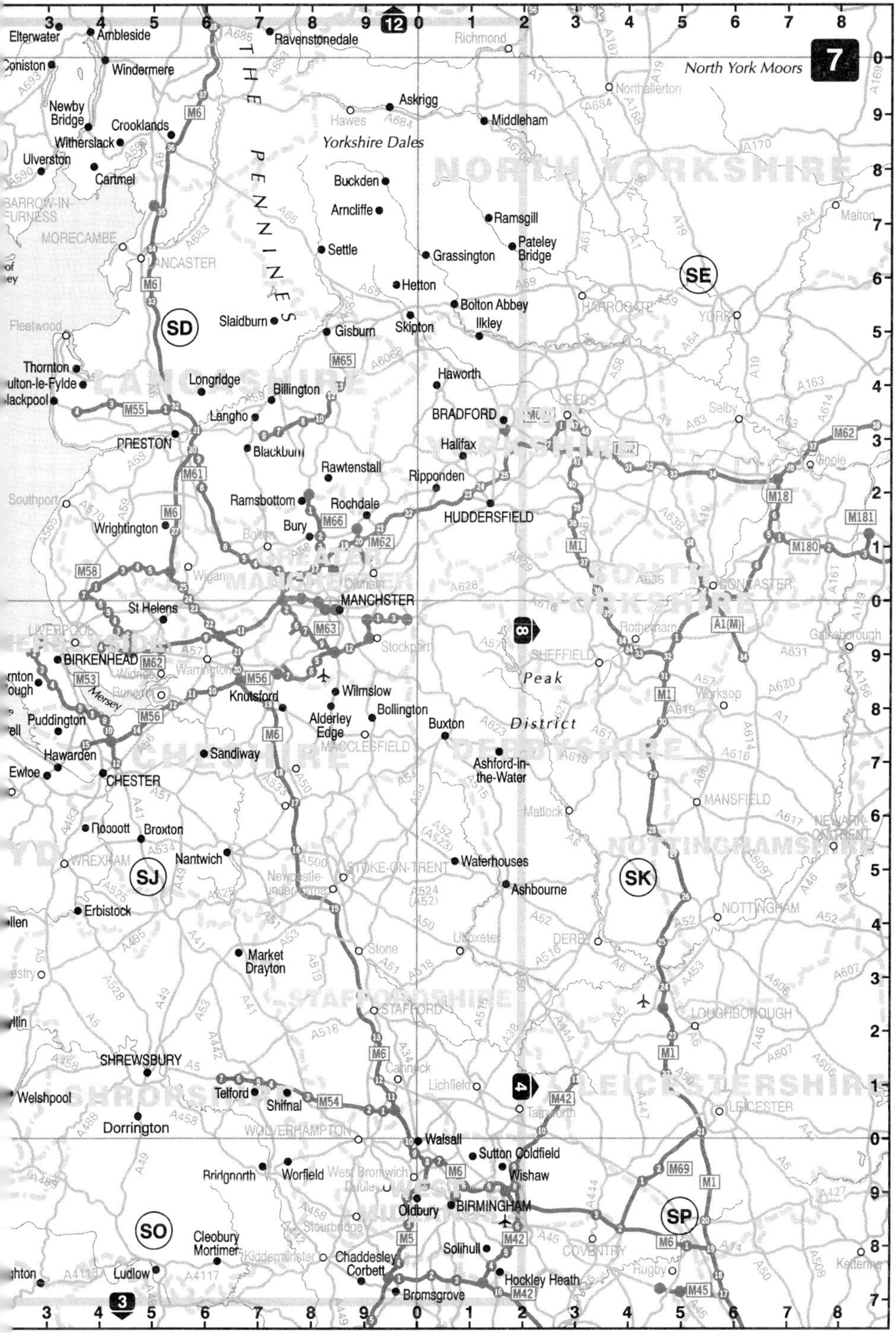
7
North York Moors
NORTH YORKSHIRE
Yorkshire Dales
THE PENNINES
LANCASHIRE
GREATER MANCHESTER
CHESHIRE
DERBYSHIRE
SOUTH YORKSHIRE
NOTTINGHAMSHIRE
STAFFORDSHIRE
SHROPSHIRE
LEICESTERSHIRE
Peak District
SD
SE
SJ
SK
SO
SP
12
8
4
3
Elterwater
Ambleside
Ravenstonedale
Richmond
Coniston
Windermere
Northallerton
Newby Bridge
Crooklands
Askrigg
Hawes
Middleham
Witherslack
Ulverston
Cartmel
Buckden
Arncliffe
Ramsgill
Malton
BARROW-IN-FURNESS
MORECAMBE
LANCASTER
Settle
Grassington
Pateley Bridge
Hetton
Bolton Abbey
HARROGATE
YORK
Fleetwood
Slaidburn
Gisburn
Skipton
Ilkley
Thornton
Blackpool
Longridge
Billington
Haworth
LEEDS
Selby
Langho
BRADFORD
PRESTON
Blackburn
Halifax
Goole
Rawtenstall
Ripponden
Southport
Ramsbottom
Rochdale
HUDDERSFIELD
Wrightington
Bury
Bolton
Wigan
Oldham
DONCASTER
St Helens
MANCHESTER
LIVERPOOL
Stockport
Rotherham
Gainsborough
BIRKENHEAD
Warrington
Widnes
SHEFFIELD
Mersey
Runcorn
Wilmslow
Worksop
Knutsford
Bollington
Puddington
Alderley Edge
MACCLESFIELD
Buxton
Hawarden
Sandiway
Ashford-in-the-Water
Ewloe
CHESTER
Matlock
MANSFIELD
NEWARK-ON-TRENT
Broxton
WREXHAM
Nantwich
STOKE-ON-TRENT
Waterhouses
Newcastle-under-Lyme
Ashbourne
NOTTINGHAM
Erbistock
Uttoxeter
DERBY
Market Drayton
Stone
STAFFORD
LOUGHBOROUGH
Cannock
SHREWSBURY
Lichfield
Welshpool
Telford
Shifnal
Tamworth
LEICESTER
Dorrington
WOLVERHAMPTON
Walsall
Sutton Coldfield
Bridgnorth
Worfield
West Bromwich
Dudley
Wishaw
Oldbury
BIRMINGHAM
Stourbridge
Cleobury Mortimer
Kidderminster
Chaddesley Corbett
Solihull
COVENTRY
Rugby
Kettering
Ludlow
Hockley Heath
Bromsgrove
M6
M55
M65
M61
M66
M62
M58
M63
M53
M56
M60
M1
M18
M180
M181
A1(M)
M54
M42
M69
M5
M45

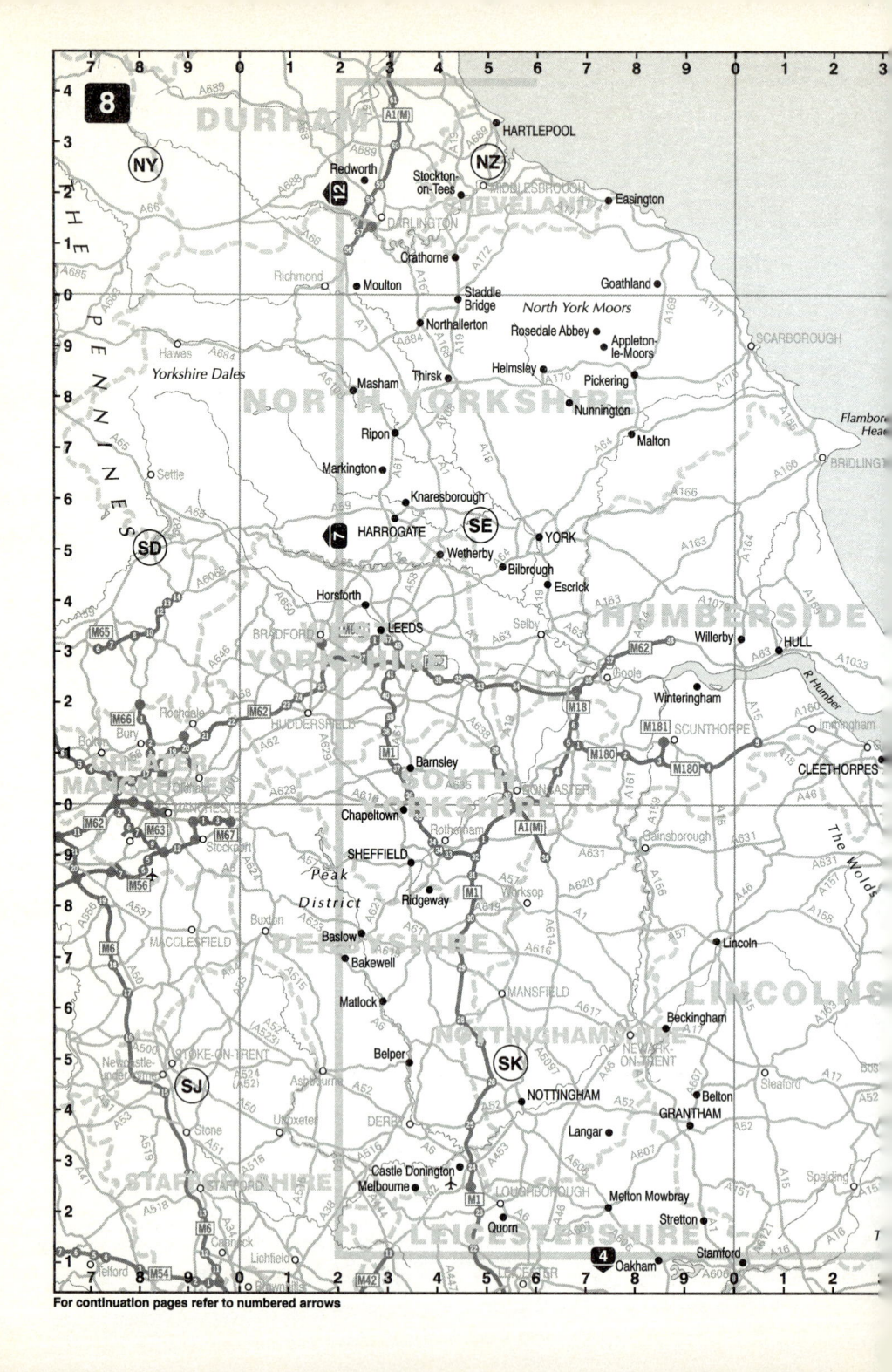

For continuation pages refer to numbered arrows

Scale
0 10 20 miles
0 10 20 30 km

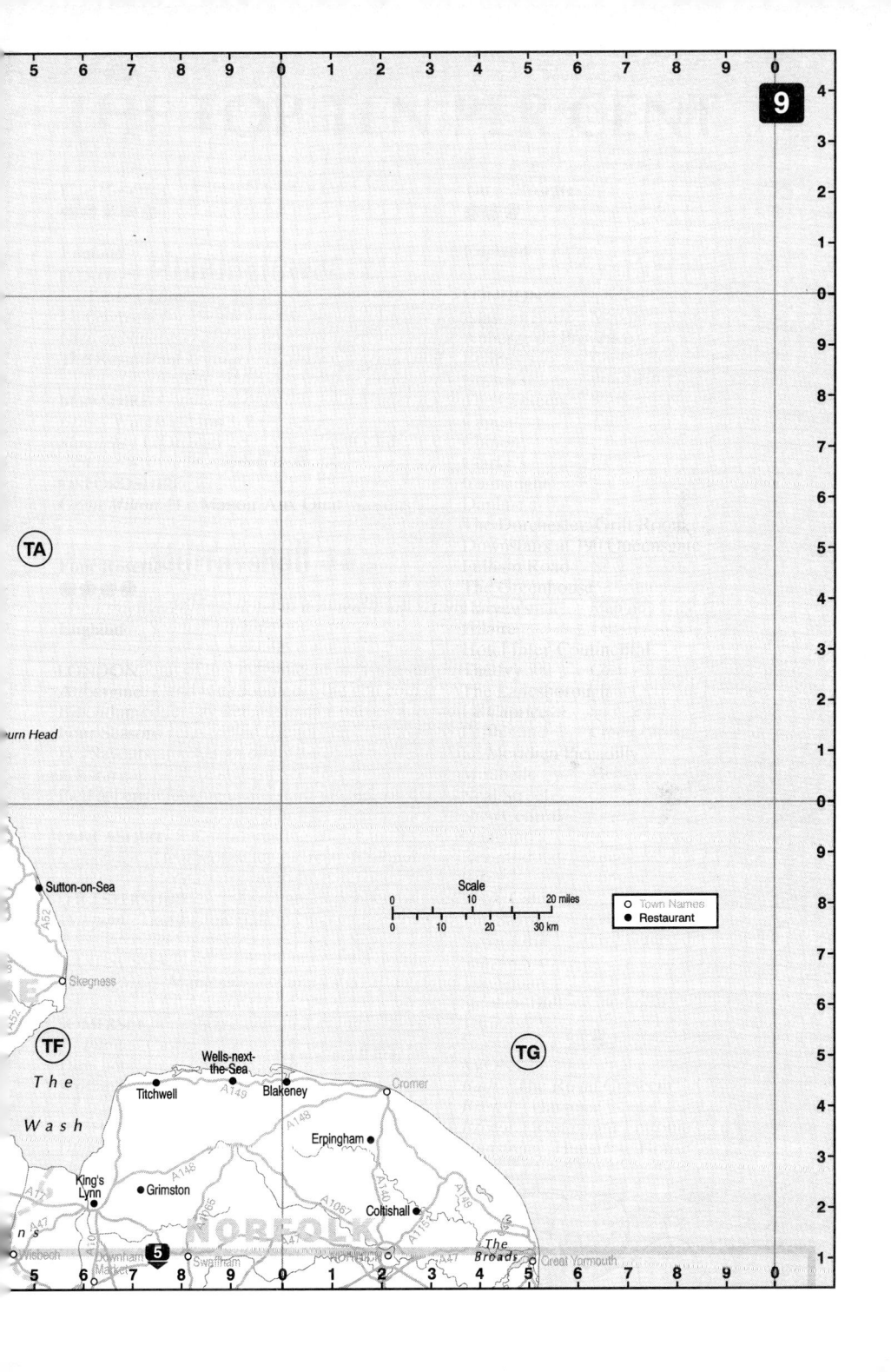

○ Town Names
● Restaurant

TA
TF
TG

● Sutton-on-Sea
○ Skegness

Wells-next-the-Sea
● Titchwell
● Blakeney
○ Cromer

The Wash

● Erpingham

King's Lynn
● Grimston
Coltishall

Wisbech
Downham Market
Swaffham
Norwich
The Broads
Great Yarmouth

NORFOLK

10

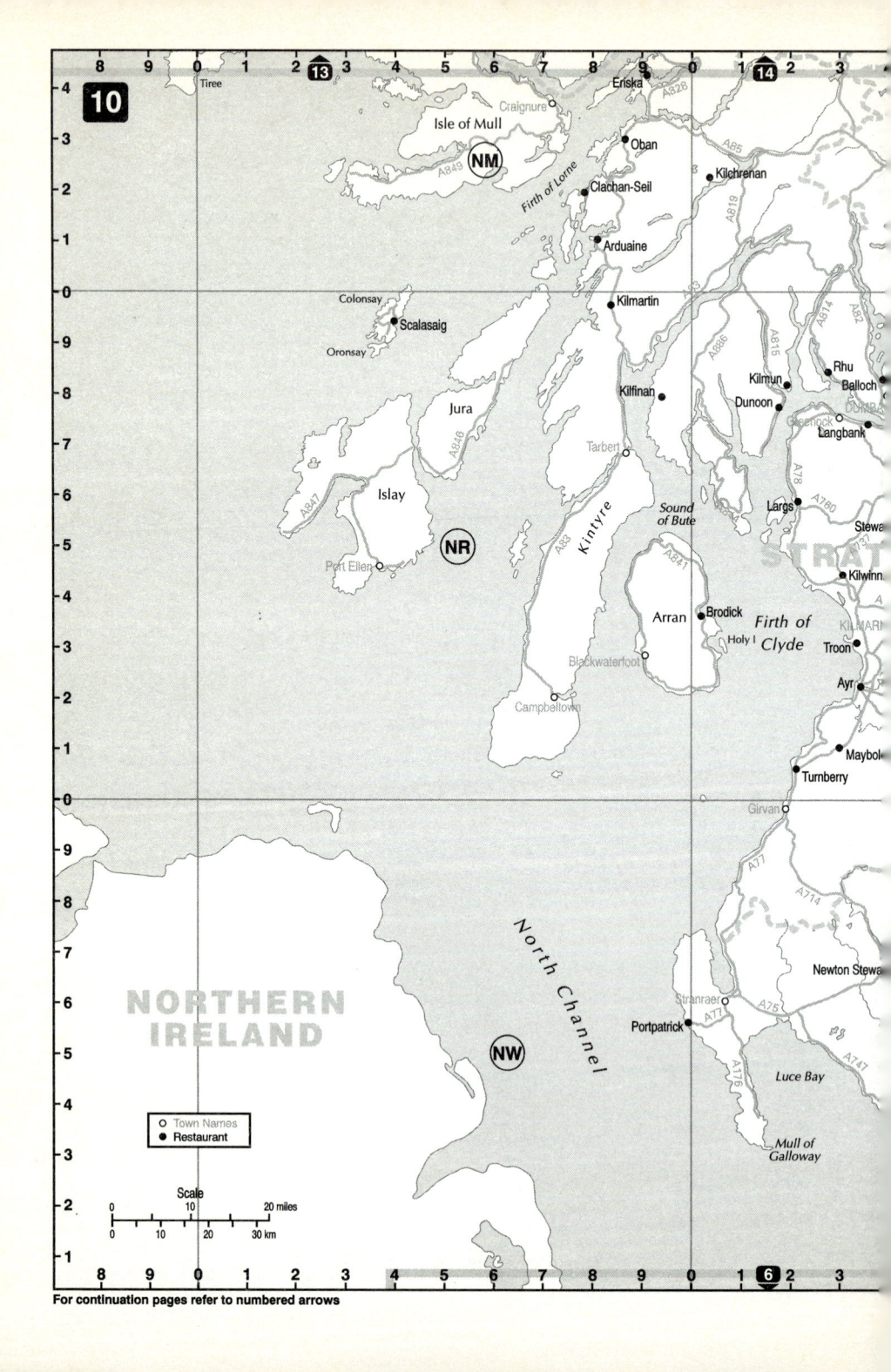

For continuation pages refer to numbered arrows

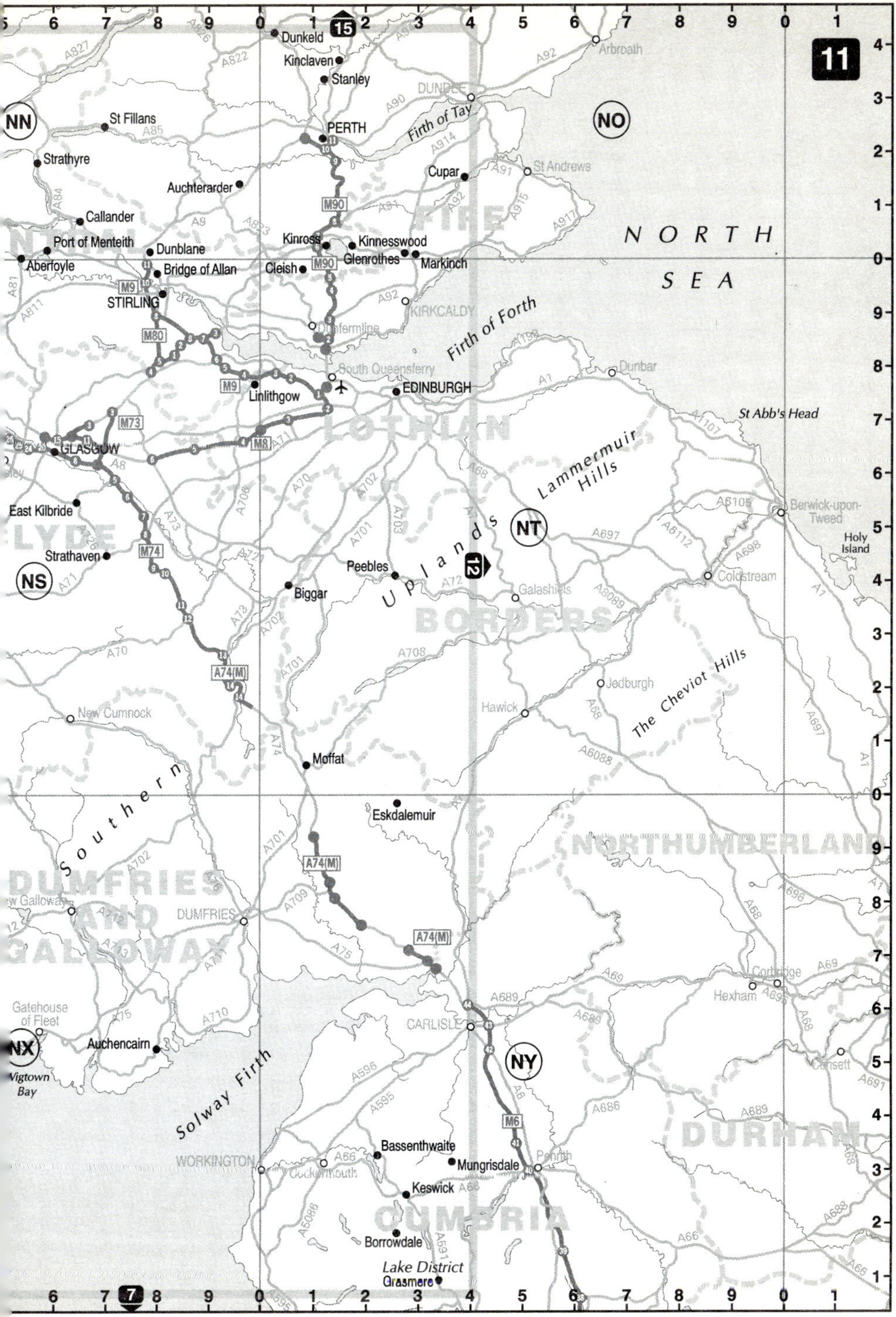
11
15
12
7
NN
NO
NT
NS
NX
NY
NORTH SEA
Dunkeld
Kinclaven
Stanley
Arbroath
Dundee
Firth of Tay
PERTH
St Fillans
Strathyre
Auchterarder
Cupar
St Andrews
Callander
FIFE
Port of Menteith
Dunblane
Kinross
Kinnesswood
Glenrothes
Markinch
Aberfoyle
Bridge of Allan
Cleish
STIRLING
Kirkcaldy
Dunfermline
Firth of Forth
South Queensferry
Dunbar
Linlithgow
EDINBURGH
St Abb's Head
GLASGOW
LOTHIAN
Lammermuir Hills
East Kilbride
Berwick-upon-Tweed
Holy Island
CLYDE
Strathaven
Peebles
Uplands
Coldstream
Biggar
Galashiels
BORDERS
Jedburgh
The Cheviot Hills
Hawick
New Cumnock
Moffat
Southern
Eskdalemuir
NORTHUMBERLAND
DUMFRIES AND GALLOWAY
Dumfries
Corbridge
Hexham
Gatehouse of Fleet
Carlisle
Auchencairn
Wigtown Bay
Solway Firth
Consett
DURHAM
Workington
Cockermouth
Bassenthwaite
Mungrisdale
Penrith
Keswick
CUMBRIA
Borrowdale
Lake District
Grasmere
M90
M9
M80
M73
M8
M74
A74(M)
M6
A9
A90
A92
A91
A914
A915
A917
A85
A84
A81
A811
A822
A827
A823
A8
A1
A70
A71
A73
A702
A703
A701
A708
A72
A68
A697
A6105
A6112
A698
A6088
A71
A76
A75
A709
A710
A711
A712
A713
A714
A69
A689
A686
A66
A595
A596
A591
A5086
A6
A688
A691
A696

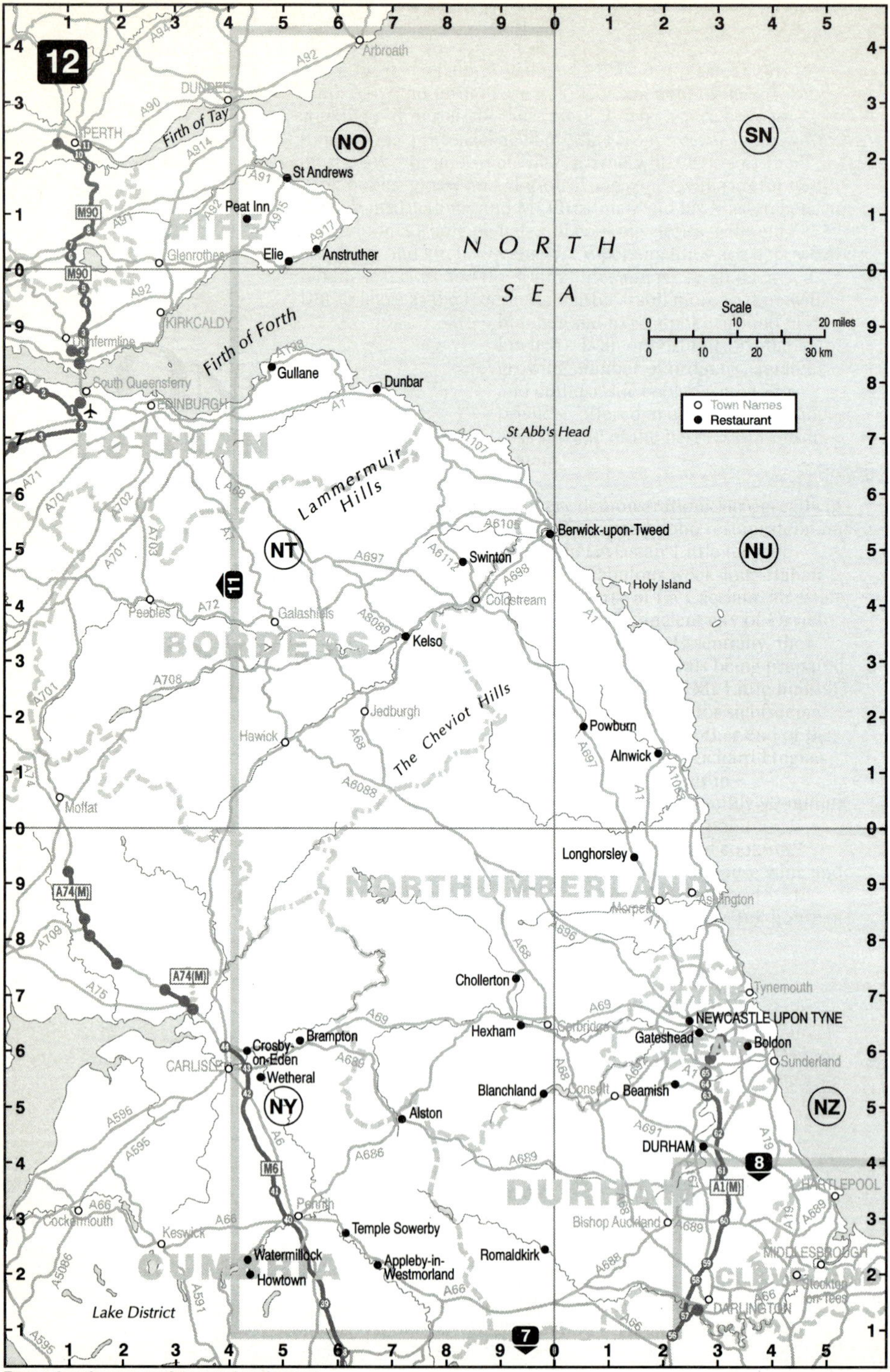

For continuation pages refer to numbered arrows

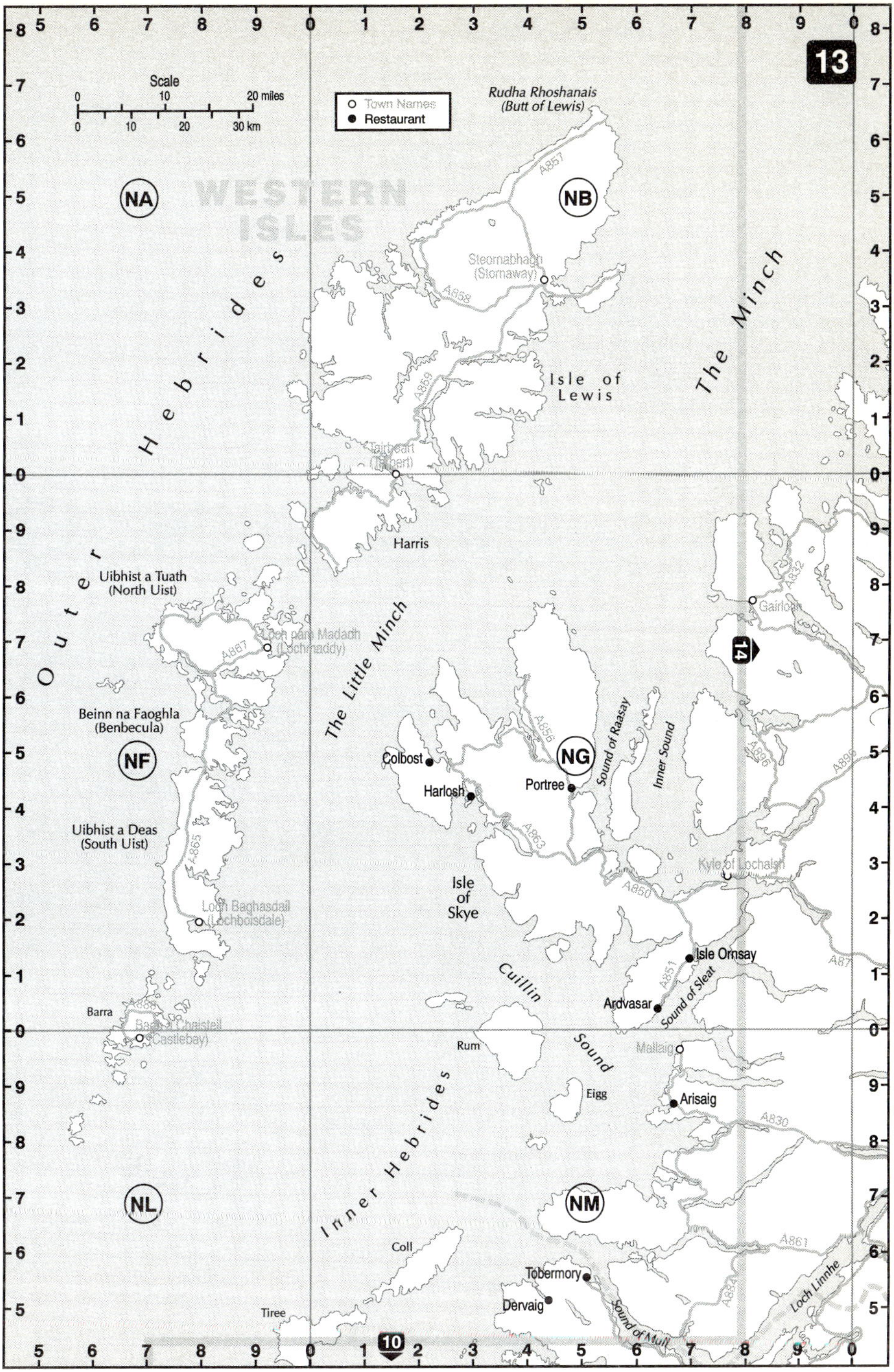
13
Scale
0 10 20 miles
0 10 20 30 km
Town Names
Restaurant
Rudha Rhoshanais
(Butt of Lewis)
WESTERN ISLES
NA
NB
NF
NG
NL
NM
Steornabhagh
(Stornaway)
Isle of Lewis
The Minch
Outer Hebrides
Tairbeart
(Tarbert)
Harris
Uibhist a Tuath
(North Uist)
Loch nam Madadh
(Lochmaddy)
The Little Minch
Beinn na Faoghla
(Benbecula)
Colbost
Harlosh
Portree
Sound of Raasay
Inner Sound
Gairloch
14
Uibhist a Deas
(South Uist)
Kyle of Lochalsh
Isle of Skye
Loch Baghasdail
(Lochboisdale)
Isle Ornsay
Cuillin Sound
Ardvasar
Sound of Sleat
Barra
Bagh a Chaisteil
(Castlebay)
Rum
Mallaig
Eigg
Arisaig
Inner Hebrides
Coll
Tobermory
Dervaig
Tiree
Sound of Mull
Loch Linnhe
10
A857
A858
A859
A867
A865
A856
A863
A850
A851
A832
A896
A87
A830
A861
A884

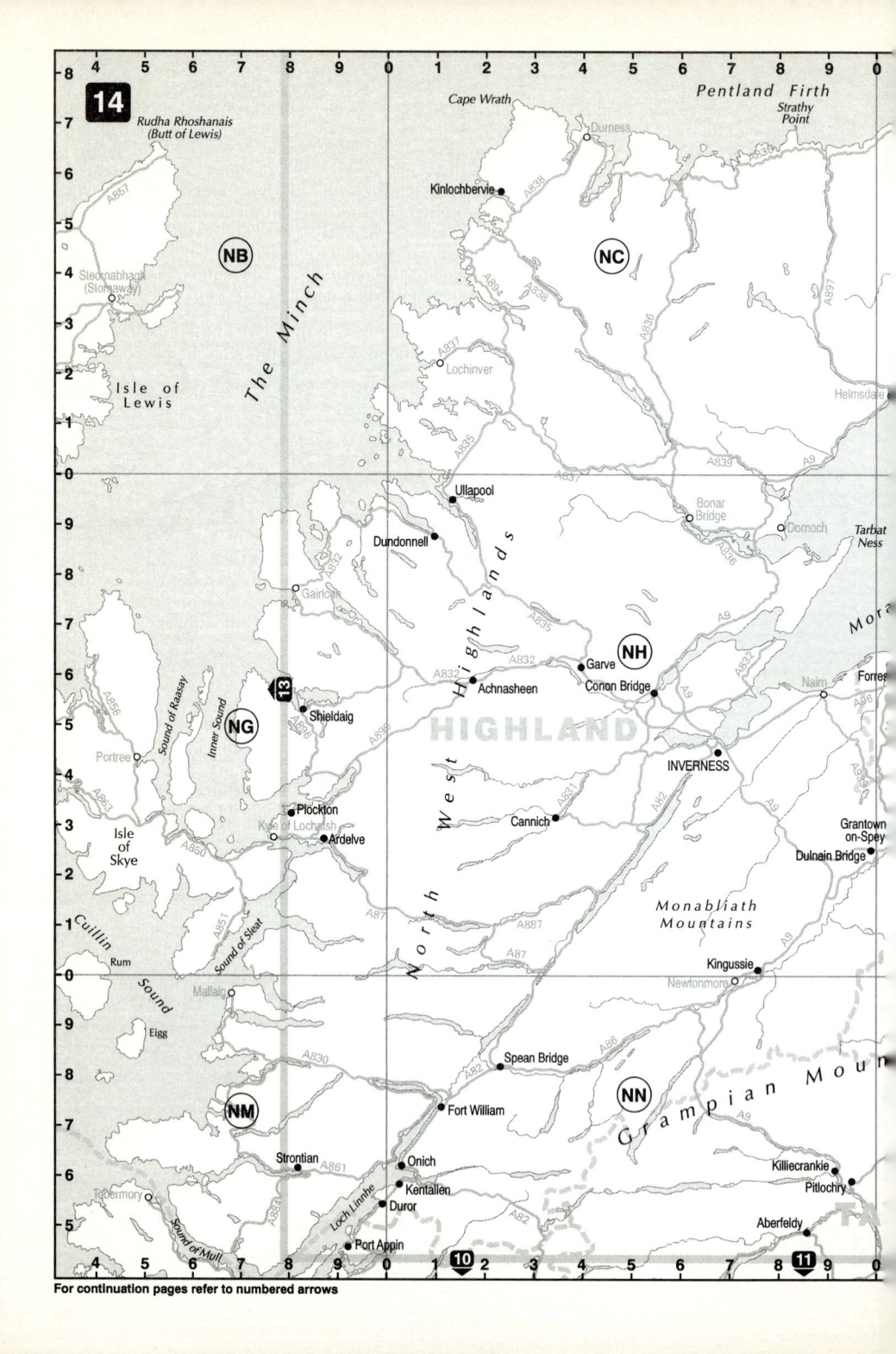

For continuation pages refer to numbered arrows

15

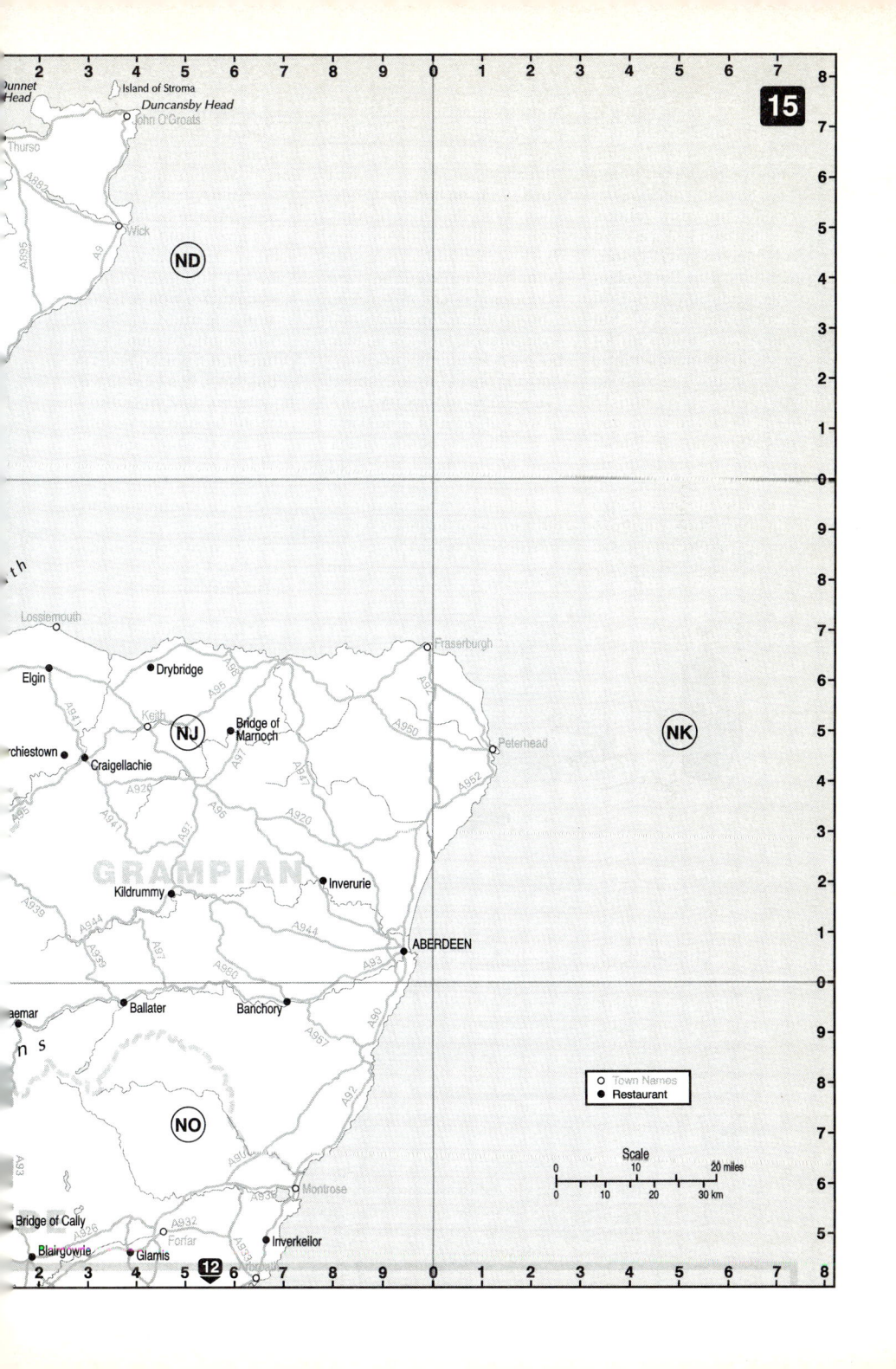

Dunnet Head · Thurso · Island of Stroma · Duncansby Head · John O'Groats · Wick

ND

Lossiemouth · Elgin · Drybridge · Fraserburgh · Craigellachie · Keith · Bridge of Marnoch · Peterhead

NJ **NK**

GRAMPIAN · Kildrummy · Inverurie · ABERDEEN · Ballater · Banchory · Braemar

NO

Bridge of Cally · Blairgowrie · Glamis · Forfar · Montrose · Inverkeilor

○ Town Names
● Restaurant

Scale
0 — 10 — 20 miles
0 — 10 — 20 — 30 km

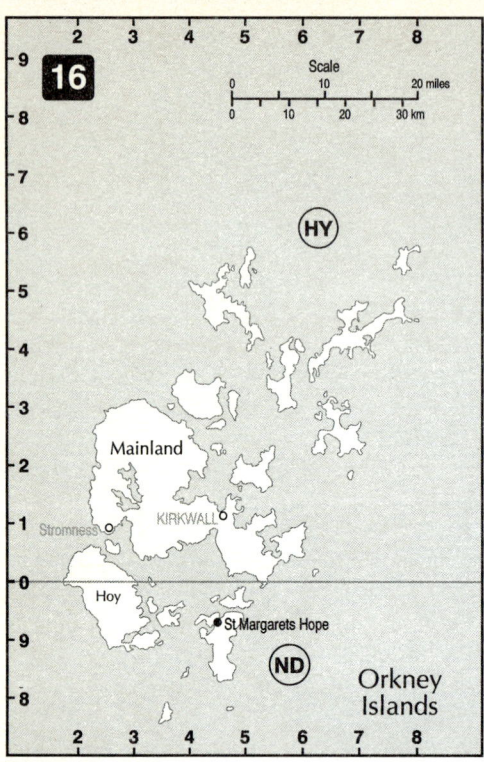

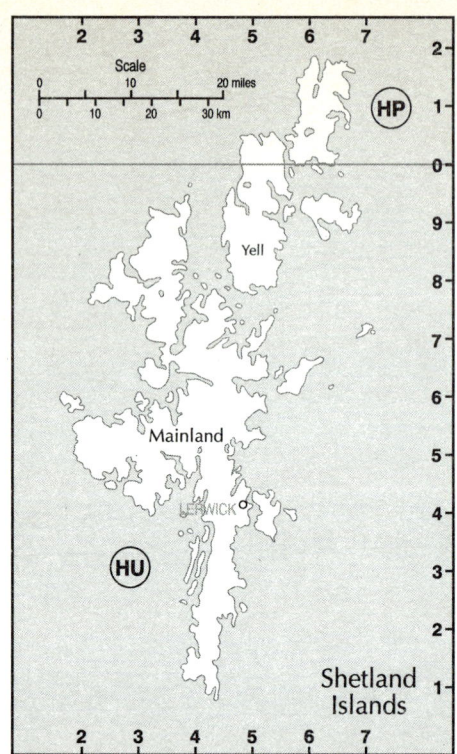

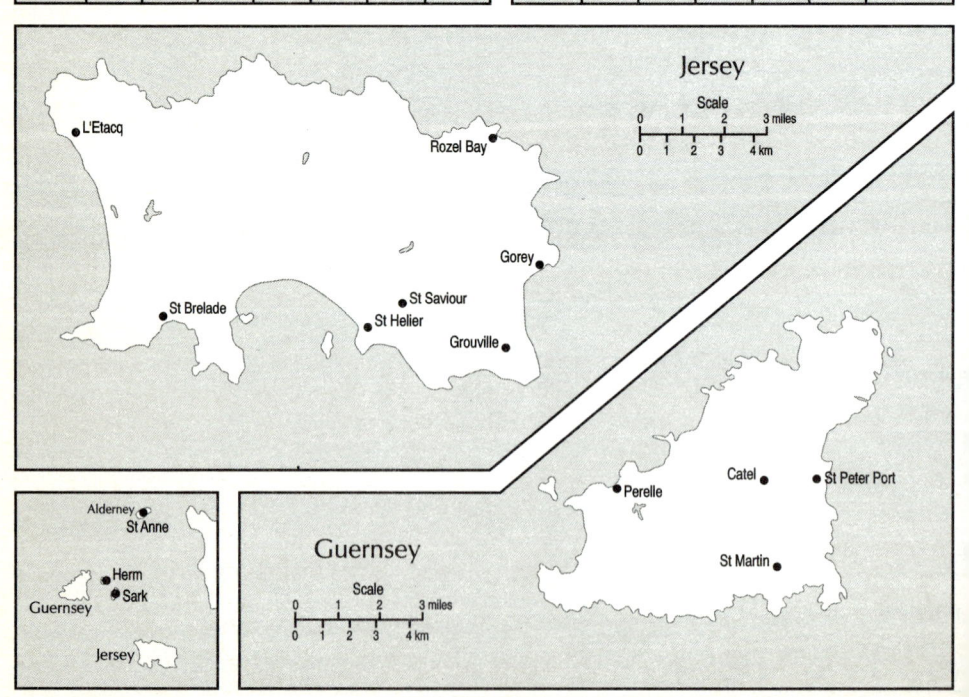

16

Orkney Islands

- Stromness
- KIRKWALL
- Mainland
- Hoy
- St Margarets Hope

(HY) (ND)

Shetland Islands

- Yell
- Mainland
- LERWICK

(HP) (HU)

Jersey

- L'Etacq
- Rozel Bay
- Gorey
- St Saviour
- St Brelade
- St Helier
- Grouville

Guernsey

- Alderney
- St Anne
- Herm
- Sark
- Guernsey
- Jersey
- Perelle
- Catel
- St Peter Port
- St Martin

Best Restaurants in Britain 1995

READERS' RECOMMENDATIONS

If you have recently eaten well at a restaurant that is not included in this guide we should be interested to hear about it.
Please send this form to HEAD OF GUIDEBOOKS, EDITORIAL DEPARTMENT, AA PUBLISHING, FANUM HOUSE, BASINGSTOKE RG21 2EA.

Recommendations, and/or any adverse comments will be carefully considered and passed on to our Hotel and Restaurant Inspectors, but the AA cannot guarantee to act on them nor to enter into correspondence about them. Complaints are best brought to the attention to the management of the restaurant at the time, so that they can be dealt with promptly and, it is hoped, to the satisfaction of both parties.

Your name and address

Name and address of the restaurant

Was the meal lunch or dinner?

Approximate cost for two £

Type of cuisine English/French/Italian/Indian/Chinese/Other

Comments

(continued over)

Best Restaurants in Britain 1995